# THE LAST TWO MILLION YEARS

Reader's Digest History of Man

# THE LAST TWO MILLION YEARS

Published by
THE READER'S DIGEST ASSOCIATION
London   New York   Montreal   Sydney   Cape Town

END-PAPERS *The illustration at the front of the book shows bowmen and cattle, in a rock-painting of c. 3000 BC from Jabbaren, on the Tassili plateau of the central Sahara. The illustration at the back of the book shows great buildings of the world, from the Pyramids to St Paul's Cathedral, as depicted in 1849 by C. R. Cockerell, a London professor of architecture, in a panorama entitled* The Professor's Dream

Printed in the United States of America.

# THE LAST TWO MILLION YEARS
## was edited and designed by The Reader's Digest Association, London

## MAJOR CONTRIBUTORS

**Anthony Atmore, BA**
Secretary, Centre of International and Area Studies,
University of London

**Peter W. Avery, BA(London), MA**
Lecturer in Persian, University of Cambridge,
Fellow of King's College, Cambridge

**Harold Blakemore, BA, PhD**
Secretary, Institute of Latin American Studies,
University of London

**Ernle Bradford**

**Warwick M. Bray, MA, PhD(Cantab), FSA**
Lecturer in Latin American Archaeology,
Institute of Archaeology and
Institute of Latin American Studies,
University of London

**Raymond Carr, MA**
Warden of St Antony's College, Oxford

**David Chandler, MA(Oxon), FRHistS, FRGS**
Deputy Head of Department of War Studies,
Royal Military Academy, Sandhurst

**Leonard Cottrell**

**Terence Dalley, ARCA**

**Raymond S. Dawson, MA**
Wadham College, Oxford

**Margaret S. Drower, MBE, BA**
Reader in Ancient History in the
University of London

**C. J. Dunn, BA, PhD**
Professor of Japanese, School of Oriental and
African Studies, University of London

**Michael Edwardes**

**Robert Erskine**

**Andrew M. Fleming, MA(Cantab)**
Lecturer in Prehistory and Archaeology,
University of Sheffield

**Nigel Hawkes, BA(Oxon)**

**Douglas Hill, BA**

**Ronald Hingley, PhD(London), MA**
Lecturer in Russian, St Antony's College, Oxford

**Douglas W. J. Johnson, BA, BLitt(Oxon)**
Professor of French History,
University College, London

**Geoffrey L. Lewis, MA, DPhil**
Fellow of St Antony's College and Senior Lecturer
in Turkish, University of Oxford

**Roger Morgan**
Deputy Director of Studies, The Royal Institute of
International Affairs

**F. N. L. Poynter, PhD, DLitt, HonMD(Kiel)**
Director, The Wellcome Institute of the
History of Medicine

**E. E. Rich, LittD**
Emeritus Professor of Imperial and Naval History,
Master of St Catherine's College, Cambridge

**Hugh Seton-Watson, MA(Oxon), FBA**
Professor of Russian History, School of Slavonic and
East European Studies, University of London

**Plantagenet Somerset Fry, FRSA**

**Richard Storry, MA**
Lecturer in Far Eastern Studies,
St Antony's College, Oxford

**D. E. Strong, MA, DPhil, FSA**
Professor of the Archaeology of the Roman
Provinces, Institute of Archaeology,
University of London

**Rev. R. Trueman, MA(Cantab), BD(Man)**
Lecturer in New Testament Studies,
King's College, London

**Geoffrey Trease**

**James Waldersee, BA, PhD, BSc**
Lecturer in History, University of Sydney

**Keith Ward**
Lecturer in Philosophy of Religion,
King's College, London

**David M. Wilson, MA, FSA**
Professor of Medieval Archaeology, University
College, London

**Maurice Wilson, RI, SWLA**

**Esmond Wright, MA(Durham and Virginia)**
Director, Institute of United States Studies,
University of London

# Contents: a four-part survey

# of the human adventure

# Part 1

# COUNTDOWN TO CIVILIZATION

*Man has lived on the earth for more than 2 million years, hardly more than the blinking of an eye in relation to the earth's total history, which stretches back for the almost inconceivable span of 4700 million years. If the age of the earth from its origin to the present time is imagined as equivalent to a single day, then man appeared less than a minute from midnight at the day's end. Yet the story of this great abyss of time before man's arrival is also part of his heritage.*

*Only for the last 5000 years has man left written records. For all but this tiny portion of man's total span, our only knowledge of what he looked like and how he lived is based on the rare traces of his existence that have survived—fossilised bones, stone tools, broken pottery, carvings on rocks and paintings in caves. The work of unearthing and interpreting these relics involves painstaking studies by experts. Their findings, though incomplete, give a glimpse of the evolutionary process which led to the emergence of our own species, Homo sapiens, which peoples the globe today.*

New land in the making: a volcanic eruption thrusts a new island, Surtsey, up from the ocean off Iceland

# From cloud of gas to inhabited planet

## FROM 4700 MILLION YEARS AGO

*Long before man emerged, continents and oceans
had been formed, mountains had been shaped,
and dinosaurs had roamed the land and disappeared*

Even the ever-broadening scientific knowledge of modern times has brought no unanimous agreement about the exact origin of the earth and the solar system. However, it is now generally believed that the solar system began as a finely dispersed mass of gas and dust, rotating and concentrating gently under gravitational forces. The heat generated by this process produced a dimly glowing infant sun at the centre, which threw off a flat disc of gas round it. Within this disc the gas condensed to form the planets, as the sun continued to shrink and become hotter and hotter. Near the sun, the heavier elements condensed to form the heavy inner planets, such as the earth; further out, lighter atoms condensed to create the outer planets.

The chances are, then, that the earth began its career as a mass of gas at a temperature of 4000°C, almost as hot as the sun. By about 4700 million years ago it cooled enough for the gases to become liquids, and then, at 1500°C, for the first solid particles of crust to appear, floating on the molten earth. At 700°C the crust was about 6 miles thick, and the cooling began to slow. Around the earth hung a dense veil of cloud, formed as the gases cooled to particles of liquid.

### Rain for 60,000 years

As the temperature dropped, spots of rain began to fall. Soon the drizzle became a downpour lasting for some 60,000 years as the high-banked clouds shed their rain, filling the oceans and scouring the land. Cooled by the water, the earth's temperature gradually fell to near its present 20–30°C. Finally, some 3000 million years ago, the rains stopped. But the earth at this early stage was not yet a habitable place. The atmosphere was made up of carbon dioxide, water vapour, methane and ammonia, which provided no protection against the ultra-violet radiation pouring down from the sun. The crust was still buckling and folding as volcanic lava escaped from the core. No plants decorated the bare rocks, and the oceans were simply salty water swilling about in the depressed regions of the crust.

Nevertheless, these unpromising circumstances did contain the seeds of life. When radiation and electrical discharges play on a mixture like the earth's primitive atmosphere, a startling range of complex chemicals may be produced. Amino-acids, formic acid and urea were probably produced by flashes of lightning and washed down into the sea, where they collected over millions of years and combined to produce a complex 'soup' of chemicals with almost all the essentials for life

### The beginning of life

Eventually, in this 'soup', an accidental combination of chemicals, including primitive nucleic acids and proteins, produced complex molecules which could reproduce themselves. The true beginning of life occurred when large numbers of these and simpler molecules combined to form different structures within a single, reproducible unit – the living cell. These first living cells, like all cells, were protected by a structure called the cell membrane, a skin-like layer. In another 500 million years, these single cells had divided into two types, algae and bacteria, and these are the origin of all life, plant and animal respectively, on earth.

Once living cells had reached a certain level of complexity, ultra-violet radiation from the sun then became harmful to life. Before evolution could proceed further, the earth's atmosphere had to be changed by the liberation of oxygen and the formation of its close relation ozone, which filters out most of the sun's harmful radiation.

The first 'oxygen factories' were a form of algae containing chlorophyll, a complex molecule which, by a process known as photosynthesis, uses sunlight as a source of energy. The energy so produced turns water and carbon dioxide from the atmosphere into sugars, which a plant uses for its own growth, and oxygen, which it releases into the atmosphere. It is by photosynthesis that nearly all plants obtain energy for growth – as distinct from animals, which live by consuming other forms of life. Gradually oxygen began to permeate the atmosphere. High up, normal oxygen became ozone, creating a shield beneath which life-forms multiplied and all life has since sheltered.

### Plants grip the dry land

By about 1500 million years ago, processes like these had begun to turn the earth into a habitable planet, able in its turn to support more complex forms of life. By 1200 million years ago, organisms with more than a single cell existed, and 450 million years ago the first sea-plants managed to get a grip on dry land. Some 100 million years later, animals began to invade the land. The invasion was led by amphibians, which began as scaly fish with fins which they used to scramble from pool to pool. They evolved lungs that breathed air, and legs that helped them to crawl; but they still needed to return to water to breed.

The amphibians were followed about 325 million years ago by the first reptiles – far better equipped, both in their build and in their method of breeding, to exploit the teeming resources of the virgin continents. For reptiles' eggs contain their own water supply, and so can be laid on land. In a great burst of evolution, different forms of reptiles filled the new niches available to them. At the same time, recognisable insects emerged – bugs and beetles among them. The climate at this period was hot and dry, and most of the land was a near-desert dotted with oases and swamps, conditions which drove the amphibians back to the sea and favoured the reptiles – among them the dino-

## HOW LIFE EMERGED FROM THE PRIMEVAL SEAS TO CONQUER THE LAND

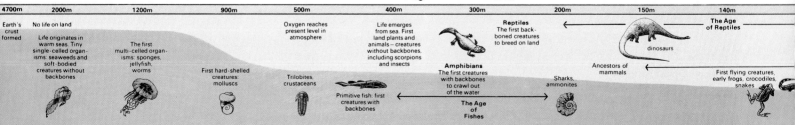

saurs. The sky 150 million years ago was the domain of leathery pterodactyls, ranging in wingspan from a few inches to 25 ft; and across the land roamed the great dinosaurs – Bronto- saurus, Stegosaurus, and Tyrannosaurus Rex.

These were the largest and perhaps the oddest land creatures that ever lived. The temptation is to think of these giants as failures, though they survived on the earth for 100 million years – 50 times as long as man's record so far.

## Continents on the move

While all this was going on, the earth itself had not been inactive. Although the total volume of water in the oceans has not changed very much, the extent of the oceans has varied with the comings and goings of the ice ages. The continents themselves have moved slowly about the earth like great boats floating on syrup, sometimes colliding to produce new mountain ranges. They still move, so slowly that even the most sensitive instruments can hardly detect the movement. But geology is more patient; even half an inch a year means a movement of 80 miles in 10 million years.

It is now believed that all the land masses on the earth once formed a single continent, given the name Pangaea. This continent first broke into two parts, Laurasia and Gondwanaland, and later broke up into the continental masses of today. A glance at a map shows how neatly the outline of South and Central America fits into the shape of Africa. The present shape of the continents can be explained by assuming that each of the continents was carried along on a huge plate floating on the earth's mantle. Where the edges of these plates met, they either collided head on (and mountains were formed) or they slid uneasily past each other in a jerky movement, producing earthquakes.

## The end of the dinosaurs

A hundred million years ago the great reptiles were lording it over the other inhabitants of the earth. Surviving, but only in a humble way, were another group of creatures called synap- sids, cold-blooded reptiles with mammal-like skulls and jaws, which had emerged long before the dinosaurs but were still waiting their chance for evolutionary success. Quite suddenly, about 70 million years ago, the dinosaurs disappeared and the synapsids, which by now had evolved into primitive mammals, took over. The reptiles survived in smaller numbers, and gave rise to

their very successful descendants, the birds. After their long wait, the mammals were well prepared for their period of evolutionary dominance. They were more versatile than the reptiles, and became adapted to most environ- ments. To enable them to respond to variable conditions they developed a larger brain, and had a long period of parental care; female mammals give birth to live young, which they suckle until they can begin feeding themselves.

A host of different mammals appeared quite quickly. Some did not last for long, but others were destined for much longer survival. The ancestor of the horse evolved in North America, the ancestor of the elephant in Africa, and early forms of rodents, primates and carnivores all emerged at the same period.

Many of these mammals have left such de- tailed fossil records that it is possible to trace their evolution in great detail. Not so the primates, which lived in the forests; here their remains were rarely covered up by sediment, and so left relatively few fossils. Apart from fragmentary evidence of a man-like mammal called *Ramapithecus*, dating from 14 million years ago, there is a gap in the record until the emergence of *Australopithecus* some 5 million years ago.

## In the steps of Darwin

Since Darwin shocked the world with his theory that men and apes have a common ancestor, experts have pieced together the likely pattern of the 70 million years which saw the first steps towards man. First, the group of mammals which took to the forests developed more versatile limbs for climbing tree trunks and swinging from branches. In particular, their front limbs became more flexible than the paws and claws of other animals, enabling them to grasp the fruit and insects which formed their main diet. These forest primates looked more like squirrels than men, and they have their modern descendants in tree-shrews, tarsiers and lemurs.

Another important development marked out these forest-living creatures from other mam- mals. On the ground, mammals could survive by using the senses of sight and smell alone; but life in the tree-tops required greater agility and alertness. As a result, the brains of these forest primates began to expand.

By about 40 million years ago there had developed a species of primates which could rank as Darwin's 'common ancestor' of the

great apes and of man. One group of these primates remained forest-dwellers, and from them descended the apes, monkeys and chimpanzees of today. But another group began, some 20 million years ago, to come down from the trees – perhaps at a time when the forests were thinning and ground food becoming more plentiful – and to live in the open country beyond the forest fringes. Over millions of years these creatures began to walk upright; their rear limbs became feet, while their front limbs became ever more sensitive organs of touch with which they learnt to mani- pulate objects like sticks and stones for their use.

## Africa as man's cradle

Because the earliest traces of these man-like creatures, dating back to 5 million years ago, have been found in Africa, it is generally assumed that it was in Africa that the human race originated. Certainly Africa offered favour- able conditions for man's evolution, being remote from the great earth movements and glaciations that were convulsing and moulding the northern land-masses.

Man first emerged before the beginning of a great ice age, the first for 100 million years. And throughout man's evolution there have been alternations between periods when ice crept southwards over the land and interglacial periods when the ice temporarily retreated. The violent fluctuations of the climate affected the distribution of plant species and mammals enormously, particularly in the Northern Hemisphere. When it was really cold, alpine flowers, reindeer and Arctic foxes flourished in Europe. But when the ice-sheets retreated, hippopotamuses swam in the Thames, and lions ranged as far north as Yorkshire.

To meet the challenge of inhospitable climatic conditions, some mammals developed special adaptations, like the woolly rhinoceros, or the mammoth, a kind of hairy elephant. Early man adapted himself in a different way – not by biological changes in his own body, but by learning to use fire for warmth and light and to wear the skins of animals for clothing. Even so, there must have been periods when survival, at least in the northerly regions, was difficult and migration to warmer climates occurred. Finally, 10,000 years ago, the ice-sheets re- treated for the last time. By then a far more advanced man, *Homo sapiens*, had emerged to take advantage of the favourable conditions. The long countdown to man was over.

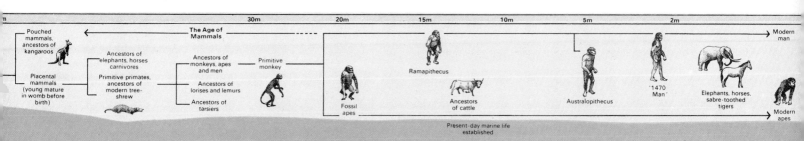

# Evolution's long path from 'missing link' to modern man

Until the mid-19th century it was generally believed in the West that all living creatures had been created separately at the Creation, and had remained unchanged ever since. This assumption was first challenged in 1859, when the English naturalist Charles Darwin published his *On the Origin of Species by Means of Natural Selection*. In this book Darwin showed that all species were related to each other, however distantly, and had evolved over a long period of time. Twelve years later, in *The Descent of*

*Man*, Darwin suggested that men and the higher apes had a common ancestor. In Darwin's own time there was little evidence to support his theory; but since then a whole chain of 'missing links' has been established by study of fossil bones found at prehistoric sites.

The chart below shows how, over 40 million years, descendants of the early primates gradually evolved to produce modern man. The drawings are based upon surviving fossil bones, where these exist; but the colour of

COMMON ANCESTOR *About 40 million years ago the primates, one of the many groups of mammals that had first emerged in the age of dinosaurs, were dividing into many forms. One of these is believed to have been a forest-dwelling primate moving on all fours, the ancestor from which modern apes and man both descend. But no traces of such a creature have yet been found*

RAMAPITHECUS *By 14 million years ago a more advanced primate had emerged. Its remains, found in the Siwalik Hills of India, are probably those of the earliest known creature on the direct line of descent to man. Remains of a similar creature have been found in Africa. Ramapithecus apparently stood upright, and had a jaw which did not jut far out*

AUSTRALOPITHECUS *This man-like ape lived in eastern and southern Africa from about 5 million years ago. His brain was no larger than that of a modern ape, but he walked upright and probably used tools. These earliest tools (below) were primitive instruments: bones remaining after meals, or naturally sharp pebbles, which were used for an immediate task and then abandoned*

'1470 MAN' *By about 2½ million years ago, '1470 Man', overlapping in time with Australopithecus, had emerged in East Africa. He walked erect and had a more advanced brain than any ape. He probably made the first true tools (below), striking a flake off a pebble to sharpen it and make a more effective cutting edge—the start of a culture that lasted for a million years*

*Life in the trees made the front limbs of the forest primate more flexible than those of other mammals, enabling it to swing from branches and grasp the fruit and insects on which it lived*

*With a developing brain and even more sensitive front limbs, Ramapithecus could pick up and manipulate sticks and stones for simple tasks such as frightening his enemies*

40 million years       14 million years       5 million years       2½ million years

skin, hair and eyes, and the distribution of hair are purely speculative.

The first breakthrough in man's evolution came when creatures became adapted to standing and walking in an upright position, enabling them to sight their animal prey further off, and freeing their hands for other uses. Most important, they were now able to make and use tools to supplement their hands and teeth when hunting and preparing food; it is this ability that is usually taken as distinguishing true man, the

genus *Homo*, from the man-like creatures that preceded him. As man's brain became bigger, responding to the demands of more complex hunting, he became taller, with more refined teeth and jaws.

As man's hands became capable of more precise manipulation, the implements he made became more sophisticated. By 2 million years ago tools were being made to a set pattern; and by the time of *Homo sapiens* tools were finished to a higher standard than their function required.

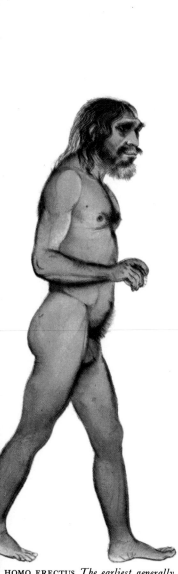
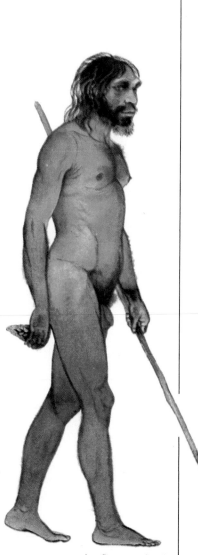
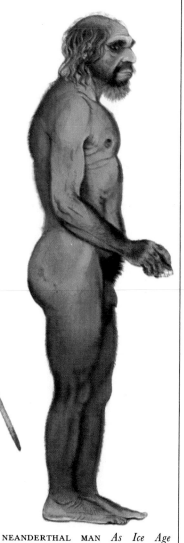
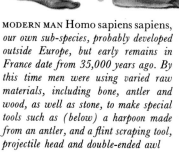

HOMO ERECTUS *The earliest generally accepted representative of the genus Homo was widespread in Asia, Africa and Europe 500,000 years ago. He used fire and hunted large animals. In Africa, 'Upright man' made simple hand-axes (below, left); but this skill did not reach south-east Asia, where much less sophisticated chopping tools (below, right) were still made*

HOMO SAPIENS *At Swanscombe in England and Steinheim in Germany have been found fossils which suggest that our own species may be up to 250,000 years old; their skulls look very like our own. Hand-axes of the period (below) produced in Europe, Africa and western Asia are more sophisticated and efficient than earlier tools, with flatter surfaces and straighter edges*

NEANDERTHAL MAN *As Ice Age glaciers advanced southwards for the last time, Europe was dominated by the Neanderthalers, a variant of Homo sapiens which did not survive. Neanderthal man made flint scrapers (below, left and centre) and spearheads (below, right) by using the struck-off flakes, rather than cores as before, and trimming small flakes from their edges*

MODERN MAN Homo sapiens sapiens, *our own sub-species, probably developed outside Europe, but early remains in France date from 35,000 years ago. By this time men were using varied raw materials, including bone, antler and wood, as well as stone, to make special tools such as (below) a harpoon made from an antler, and a flint scraping tool, projectile head and double-ended awl*

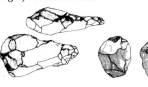

500,000 years      250,000 years      70,000 years      35,000 years

# Lakesides where the Stone Age began

## FROM 2 MILLION YEARS AGO

*Man's earliest ancestor was a creature, living
near water on the forest fringes, who could stand upright
and make simple tools from the stones around him*

**CRADLE OF MANKIND**

*The early dates of prehistoric sites in
Africa supports the belief that this
continent was the cradle of early man*

By 2 million years ago the earth's oceans and land areas had assumed roughly their present forms. Forests covered much of the land surface, thinned in places by forest fires started by lightning, and giving way to grassland on poorer soil. The loudest noises were the crash of thunder and the roar of waterfalls; there were no other sounds louder than the calls of birds, or the cries of small animals captured by larger creatures.

The age of the dinosaurs was long past, and mammals were the most successful class of animals on earth. Bearing live young, which the mother suckled and protected for months after birth, different species of mammals evolved to take advantage of the multitude of habitats on earth. The ancestors of the lion, elephant and rhinoceros were all represented, and among the smaller animals were the ancestors of the horse, wolf, cow, pig and deer.

Among these animals there had evolved a number of early forms of man, or 'hominids', whose descendants were one day to conquer the earth. Only a few bones of these hominids have

been found, in parts of Africa, and it is uncertain how far the remains that have been found are truly representative of the appearance of early man. But it seems that, by 2 million years ago or even earlier, ancestors of man were already walking upright, living on the edges of the forest, and eating plant food, fruit and small animals.

As well as an upright stance, these vulnerable-looking animals had one other unusual characteristic: they cut up meat not with their teeth and claws, as other animals did, but by using the edges of sharpened stones. Evolution had reached a significant stage; rather than take his place in the shifting and complex battle between the eaters and the eaten, at least one creature had begun to use natural objects as tools to extend the capabilities of his own body.

The oldest tools so far discovered come from an area near Lake Rudolf in northern Kenya, and date from as long as 2½ million years ago. In the same area, in 1972, Richard Leakey, director of the Kenya National Museums, discovered the skull and leg bones of the man-like creature who probably made the tools. He

THE FIRST TOOL-MAKER AND HIS AFRICAN HOME

*The hot, sandy shores of Lake Rudolf (left), in northern Kenya, have proved one of the world's richest prehistoric sites. Here, apparently, was the cradle of man the tool-maker; deliberately shaped flints found beside the lake have been dated as 2½ million years old. In 1972 a dramatic new discovery was made on the eastern shore of the lake: the skull and leg bones of one of the creatures who made the tools, and probably man's earliest known ancestor.*

*Known as '1470 Man', he was a hunter, and in the reconstruction (right) he is shown skinning one of the many varieties of small game which, together with plants, formed his diet. He is using a simple pebble-tool, a small natural stone from which flakes were chipped to leave a sharp cutting edge. The remains found at Lake Rudolf indicate that '1470 Man' could stand and walk upright, and had a brain more than half the size of modern man's—much larger than that of the man-like apes previously regarded as man's ancestors*

15

# 'Upright man', a skilled hunter with a fire to cook his prey

had a relatively large brain, of some 800 cc – double the size of a modern chimpanzee – and his leg bones clearly indicate that he was about 5 ft tall and could walk upright. This creature, almost certainly man's earliest known true ancestor, was given the provisional name of '1470 Man', after his catalogue reference in the Kenya National Museum.

Another early tool-making creature was *Homo habilis*, 'Handy man'. He was given this name by Dr Louis Leakey (1903–72), the father of Richard Leakey, who identified him from fragments of bone he had found at another important prehistoric East African site – Olduvai Gorge in Tanzania, once the shore of an ancient lake. *Homo habilis* lived about 1¾ million years ago. The few remains that have been found suggest that the brain size of *Homo habilis* was only 680 cc and that he was only about 4 ft tall – though, like '1470 Man', he could stand and walk upright.

Early man's upright posture was extremely important, for it left his hands free, enabling him to make and use tools. It also made it easier for him to see his enemies, and to catch small creatures such as shrews and lizards. Sometimes he fed on larger animals, usually by isolating and killing their young, or by driving the larger carnivores from their prey.

## The first stone tools

The hands of *Homo habilis*, and probably those of '1470 Man', were similar to our own, having stout, broad fingertips with flattish nails. But their grip might have been rather clumsy. A modern man has two types of grip – the power grip, used for grasping things firmly, and the precision grip, which is used when holding and manipulating objects between finger and thumb. Early man had a good power grip, but his precision grip was still primitive, because his thumb was much less flexible in relation to the fingers than the thumb of modern man.

Yet his grip was efficient enough to make man's first technological breakthrough – the making of simple stone tools, suitable for cutting up meat and shredding plant food. For the first time, a living creature was not limited

by physical attributes like teeth or claws, which had taken thousands of years to adapt to the environment, and which might prove unsuitable if that environment changed. Now man could design his own 'teeth' and 'claws'. He could choose their shape and material, and adapt them to prepare different sorts of food for eating. This new-found ability to make tools was the key which ultimately gave mankind mastery over all other species.

These early implements, known as pebble-tools, are so simple that it is sometimes difficult to distinguish them from naturally chipped stones. Usually early man used one stone to strike small flakes from the end of another, leaving a sharp cutting edge for skinning animals or cutting up meat. Sometimes flakes were struck off two sides of a stone to produce a more pointed tool.

Over thousands of years the tools produced from stone became more elaborate; but man continued to depend largely on tools of stone, supplemented only by wood, bone and other perishable materials, for a large proportion of his time on earth. This long period has become known as the Stone Age; and some primitive peoples, such as the natives of New Guinea, still depend largely on stone tools to the present day.

Both '1470 Man' and *Homo habilis* may have had a more primitive neighbour – a man-like ape whose origins go back at least 2½ million years, and perhaps much further. At Lake Rudolf in the same layers as the fragments of '1470 Man', and in Olduvai Gorge in the same layers as the remains of *Homo habilis*, there have also been found the remains of another creature, traces of which have been found in other parts of Africa too. This creature was given the name of *Australopithecus* (from the Latin *australis*, 'southern', and Greek *pithecus*, 'ape') by Professor Raymond Dart who in 1924 found the first skull of this species at Taung, in South Africa.

## Australopithecus – a side-branch

*Australopithecus*, like *Homo habilis*, had a small brain, and he could stand and walk erect. For a long time it was believed that he was part of

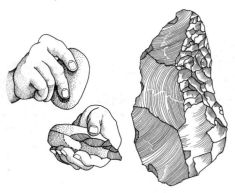
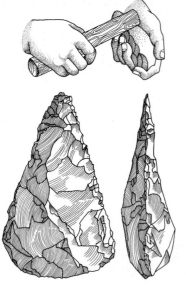
## LIVING IN THE ICE AGE

*Sites inhabited by* Homo erectus, *'Upright man', have been found as far apart as Africa, Java, France and China. The nearness of some sites to the ice sheets proves* Homo erectus *was a hardy creature, who could withstand extreme cold. The transition to* Homo sapiens *may have begun 250,000 years ago with men known from fragments of skulls found at Swanscombe and Steinheim*

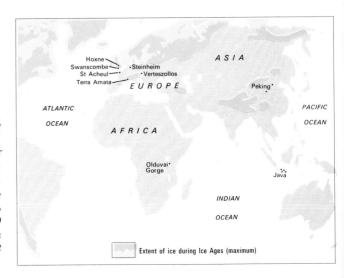

the trunk of the human family tree and a direct ancestor of man; but today it is thought more likely that he was only a side-branch. *Australopithecus* sometimes used split bones as 'tools' to extract the brains of baboons and other animals from their skulls. But this was very crude tool-making; a bone was casually used for an immediate task, and then abandoned. *Homo habilis*, by contrast, made his tools to a pre-conceived pattern; and the new finds from Lake Rudolf show that '1470 Man', a tool-making creature even more advanced than *Homo habilis*, at least in brain size, preceded him by nearly a million years.

Since *Australopithecus* co-existed both with '1470 Man' and with *Homo habilis*, changing little throughout this long period, clearly he cannot have been man's ancestor, but must instead have diverged from a common ancestor much earlier in time. It is still uncertain whether '1470 Man' and *Homo habilis* represent two different species, or two contrasting individuals from the same species. Perhaps *Homo habilis* was no more than an advanced form of *Australopithecus*, alike doomed to extinction, while '1470 Man' lies on the true line of evolution towards modern man.

## A hunter who learnt to speak

Evidence of the next known stage in the line of descent to modern man comes nearly 2 million years after '1470 Man'. This was *Homo erectus*, 'Upright man', a new species of Stone Age man who lived about half a million years ago. He was widely distributed in Asia, Europe and Africa, and for as long as 200,000 years his species replaced previous forms of man in various parts of the globe. To modern eyes *Homo erectus* would have appeared ugly; his jaw was heavy and chinless, with large teeth, and his low forehead swept back from heavy, over-hanging brows. But his brain capacity, about 1000 cc, is nearer a modern man's than an ape's.

Remains found in one of the best-known *Homo erectus* sites, at the Choukoutien cave near Peking in China, show that *Homo erectus* hunted and killed elephant, rhinoceros, horse, bison, water-buffalo, camel, wild boar, sheep, deer

and antelope. The pursuit of such large game required cunning and intelligence, which favoured an increase in the size of the brain. A man hunting on his own could stalk and over-whelm small game; but to catch larger animals, men had to learn to hunt in groups. This meant a degree of discipline, along with efficient ways of signalling and co-ordinating activities.

By this time *Homo erectus* had probably started to speak. Apes have a voice box capable of producing speech-like sounds, but they have never developed a speech centre in the brain. It was probably at this time in his history, too, that the male of the species developed his pre-ference for hunting while women probably stayed nearer home gathering plant foods, partly because the adult women were preoccupied with bearing and rearing children. Women, too, evolved to the stage at which they became sexually receptive most of the time, in contrast to female apes or monkeys; this may have been because such women could expect more atten-tion and protection and a steadier supply of meat for their children. They would pass on their greater receptivity to their daughters.

By half a million years ago, in places as far apart as Peking in China and Vérteszöllös in Hungary, *Homo erectus* was using fire for warmth, and probably also for cooking. For thousands of years men had probably watched bush fires, caused by lightning, raging across the land, before they grasped the idea of using a burning twig to create warmth and light where and when they wanted it. Alternatively they may have discovered fire accidentally by the effect of sparks struck while chipping flint tools.

Cooking, too, was probably an accidental discovery, after food dropped into a fire turned out to be improved and not spoilt by the heat. Early man probably used several cooking meth-ods. Food might be roasted directly over a fire, or cooked slowly in the embers. Again, heated stones could be dropped into a skinful of liquid to warm it, or combined with layers of leaves and clay to make a sort of oven.

Because cooking breaks down the tough, fibrous parts of meat and vegetables, the large, flat molar teeth which earlier forms of man had

developed were now unnecessary, and teeth and jaws could be reduced in size. Consequently man's whole face became lighter. The canine tooth of *Homo erectus* was smaller than that of his predecessors. Apes and monkeys have large canines, which they use for tearing up food and for fighting or threatening each other. The making of tools and weapons had made obsolete the use of teeth for these purposes.

## A new tool – the hand-axe

*Homo erectus* went on using chopping tools, made from pebbles and large flakes, but he also developed a more versatile tool, the hand-axe. Using first a stone hammer and later a wooden bar, he struck off flakes from all over a piece of flint or other stone to produce a beautiful flat, hand-held axe, neatly trimmed all over, which could be used for skinning and cutting up meat. These are often called Acheulian hand-axes, after a site in the suburbs of Amiens where many of them were found, and hundreds of others have been found elsewhere in Europe, Africa and western Asia. The earliest ones are about half a million years old, but such hand-axes were still made until about 50,000 years ago in parts of southern Africa. The flakes detached in trimming the axes were invaluable in their own right as knives.

The most exciting discoveries of the time of *Homo erectus* have come from a place called Terra Amata, not far from Nice in southern France. Here people lived in oval huts, up to 50 ft long and 19 ft wide, which were edged by rings of boulders. The floors were covered with skins or stone slabs, and the roofs were of tree branches. The inhabitants lit fires to keep warm.

Although early men came to Terra Amata on at least 21 occasions, it looks as though they stayed for only a few days on each occasion, because the flint chippings which they left show few signs of trampling or disturbance. Every time they returned to the site – always apparently in late spring or early summer – they rebuilt the huts in exactly the same positions, and replaced the little stone walls which pro-tected their hearths. These people had a diet which included deer, elephant, wild boar, ibex,

MAN MASTERS FIRE

*A more intelligent species than his pre-decessors,* Homo erectus *had learnt to hunt larger animals, pursuing them in groups and outwitting them by intelli-gent, co-ordinated action. He had also discovered fire, which played an impor-tant part in his development. Meat cooked over a fire was easier to chew than raw meat, and a massive jaw and large teeth were no longer necessary. Mastery of fire allowed* Homo erectus *to live in colder parts of the world*

# Neanderthal man, ugly genius of the last Ice Age

rhinoceros, ox, tortoise, rabbit and various birds and rodents. They also collected oysters and mussels, and fished. These huts are the oldest known houses in the world, and in one of them was found a human footprint.

## The first Homo sapiens

About a quarter of a million years ago, men much more like modern man than *Homo erectus* were appearing in Europe. Much of our knowledge of these newcomers is based on part of a skull found in the 1930's at Swanscombe, Kent, in England. The back and sides of the skull are thick, but rounded like a modern man's – though since the jaw and forehead have not survived we cannot know how advanced the face of 'Swanscombe man' was. A similar skull was found in 1933 at Steinheim, in Germany.

Many scientists suspect that Swanscombe and Steinheim man were early forms of *Homo sapiens*, 'Wise man', a more advanced species than *Homo erectus* and the one from which our own sub-species of *Homo sapiens sapiens* is descended. But before the first known appearance of fully modern man, an earlier very distinctive sub-species of *Homo sapiens* evolved. He is known as Neanderthal man, after the Neander Valley near Dusseldorf, in Germany, where his relics were first found in a cave in 1857. By modern standards Neanderthal man, who appeared some 70,000 years ago, looked

brutish. He surveyed the world from beneath overhanging brows; his upper jaw jutted forward, while the lower jaw was heavy and chinless, and contained large teeth. His limb bones suggest that he was rather heavily built.

Because his facial features were so crude, some early scientists believed that the first Neanderthal skull was that of a pathological idiot. This was a slander on a highly intelligent and sensitive being, whose brain was actually a little larger than modern man's on average, who developed the first religious ideas of which we know, and whose technology was a great advance on that of his predecessors.

## The spread of Neanderthal man

It is not known where Neanderthal man first developed, but he spread very widely; his bones have been discovered at several sites in western Asia and in almost all the countries of Europe, in an arc lying beyond the southernmost limit reached by the ice during the last glacial period, from 70,000 to 30,000 years ago. Neanderthals reached the Crimea and Uzbekistan, China and Java. A related form, Rhodesian Man, spread all over the African continent. So far as is known, Australasia, the Americas and the Pacific islands had not yet been populated.

The prey of Neanderthal man varied according to the climate; in the colder phases he followed the herds of reindeer, picking off the

young and the weak. In warmer phases, when the forests returned, cattle, bison and red deer formed the main part of his diet.

Tools made by Neanderthal man have been found as far north as the Ordos region of northern China and the southern end of Lake Baikal, near Irkutsk – both regions of extreme cold. Probably man by this time was wearing simple skin clothing of some sort, since Neanderthal remains are almost invariably accompanied by flint scrapers, which would have been suitable for scraping fat from skins. Although the hand-axe makers had made a few scrapers, it was Neanderthal man who first made extensive use of them.

The flint tools which were made by Neanderthal man are known as Mousterian, after the cave site of Le Moustier in the Dordogne area of France, where many of the best examples were discovered. Already *Homo erectus* had used as knives the waste flakes which were detached in trimming his axes; but Neanderthal man was the first to use the flakes systematically as the basis for all his tools, and to throw away the flint cores. From the detached flake he chipped further tiny flakes to sharpen it. Neanderthal man became adept at choosing flints from which he could strike off flakes of exactly the right shape and size for various purposes. He made small spearheads and hand-axes, and developed the knife – a long flint blade, with one side

### HOMES OF THE NEANDERTHAL

*The name of Neanderthal man is derived from the Neander Valley, near Dusseldorf in Germany, where his remains were first found. Other Neanderthal sites have been found over much of Europe and parts of Asia, while a related species, Rhodesian Man, lived in Africa. The Neanderthals began to appear about 70,000 years ago and survived for 40,000 years*

### BURYING THE DEAD

*The Neanderthals, far from being the brutish, insensitive creatures of legend, were the first of man's ancestors to bury their dead; and they did so in a ritual way which suggests that they had simple religious beliefs. Bodies were often accompanied by food and tools, possibly indicating a belief in an after-life. In many graves, bodies had been interred in a sleeping position and covered with stones (left), while at Shanidar in northern Iraq, where many graves were found in a cave, soil tests revealed that one body had been buried in a bier of pine boughs and wild flowers*

blunt, the other sharp. Some men made notches in the cutting edge of a flake to make an efficient 'saw' for shredding foods.

## The birth of religion

The period of Neanderthal man provides the first clear evidence for the growth of ritual practices, which suggests that he may have had some rudimentary religious ideas. Some of the higher apes, when bereaved, exhibit what is quite clearly profound grief; but only man tries to come to terms with his suffering by the positive actions involved in ceremonial burial.

One burial site, at La Ferrassie, in south-west France, contained the remains of two adults and four children. The adults were buried head to head, while two children were buried near their mother's feet and two others a little further away. One child's grave also contained a set of scraping tools; perhaps bereaved parents thought the child would need them in some sort of after-life.

Animals were so important to Neanderthal man's whole way of life that they prominently figured in his beliefs and ritual. At Drachenloch Cave in Switzerland, for instance, a stone box was filled with the skulls of numerous cave bears, while the limb bones of bears were placed along the cave walls. An apparent cult concerned with the cave bear was also practised in France, Germany and Yugoslavia. Possibly the bear was regarded as having a special relationship with man. Neanderthal man, seeking warmth and shelter in caves during the winter, must have learnt to dread the snores and grunts which told him that he was disturbing the hibernating tenants.

Neanderthal man may have practised ritual cannibalism at times, possibly in order to inherit the power and 'magic' of the victim. A skull found at Monte Circeo, in Italy, had a hole cut in its base through which the brain had probably been extracted; and human bones found at Krapina, Yugoslavia, had been cut, smashed and charred. Violence was an essential part of Neanderthal man's life; a high proportion of the skulls found had been damaged before death by blunt and pointed instruments.

## Neanderthal man disappears

Around 35,000 years ago Neanderthal man's Mousterian tools were succeeded both in western Europe and in the Middle East by the products of a totally different stone-working technique. Man was now able to strike long blades off a core by a wooden punch, and these were the basis for a new type of stone industry. These new tools are found alongside the bones of a new type of man – our own sub-species *Homo sapiens sapiens*. For a long time it was believed that the new form of man, with his more sophisticated tool-kit, had driven the Neanderthals out; but in fact their 'extinction' is more likely to have been caused by gradual interbreeding and absorption.

There were really two sorts of Neanderthal man – an early kind, whose features were not very different from those of modern man, and a later, uglier group. Probably the incoming modern men chose to mate with the more attractive Neanderthalers, so that gradually the cruder forms became rarer and rarer in the new, mixed population.

By observing the customs of primitive societies still surviving in the modern world, it is possible to judge that Stone Age man, by this time in his development, may already have had rigid rules governing social conduct and mating. Some relationships within a family were probably forbidden – but this was not because of genetic dangers or instinctive aversions. By insisting that their sisters married outside the family, a group of brothers could establish alliances with many other active males. In a society dependent on co-operative hunting, such bonds between different sets of brothers must sometimes have made the difference between starvation and survival.

## Peopling the globe

For the last 30,000 years or so, *Homo sapiens sapiens* has been the only form of man on the earth. One of the best known early types in Europe, called Cro-Magnon man, spread from south-west Asia about the middle of the last Ice Age glaciation. The name Cro-Magnon comes from a cave found at Les Eyzies in the Dordogne area of France in 1868; it means literally 'big hole' in the local dialect. Since then the discovery of hundreds more sites near by has shown that the Dordogne was a major centre of early occupation. There were similar forms of man living at an early date in Russia and western Asia, in China and Borneo, and all over the continent of Africa.

It was probably during the last 20,000 or 30,000 years that mankind became divided into the four separate racial groups recognisable today. The three main groups are the Caucasoids (roughly speaking, today's Europeans and their descendants in former colonies, and the Indians), the Mongoloids (Asians and American Indians) and the Negroids. But some of the world's peoples seem to descend from an even older stock than these, from people who lived before the three main groups became distinct. This is the case with the Australoid races (today's Aborigines) who probably reached Australia from Asia as long as 30,000 years ago. Some of the American Indians, too, may descend from these 'archaic white' stocks, as they are sometimes called. They probably moved across the Bering Strait, then a land bridge joining Asia to America, about 30,000 years ago, to be followed by later migrations of Mongoloid peoples across the same bridge.

Some races developed very distinctive characteristics as a result of living in isolation in areas with rather extreme climatic conditions. For instance, the Mongoloid races are well adapted to cold conditions, with relatively thick-set

---

### MAN'S EXPANDING BRAIN

As early man developed over hundreds of thousands of years his physical appearance slowly altered. The most important change was in the shape of his skull, which grew as the size of his brain increased. When man learnt to cook, and to use tools to cut up meat, he relied less on the strength of his teeth; these became smaller, and gradually the jaws became less prominent

THE FIRST MAN *This skull found near Lake Rudolf, Kenya, in 1972 is almost certainly that of man's earliest known ancestor. Known as '1470 Man', it lacks the protruding eyebrow ridges of other early skulls*

APE MAN *The brain size of* Australopithecus, *who lived in Africa some 5 million years ago, was about 480 cc – little larger than that of the apes he resembled, and only one-third the size of modern man's. His jaws were powerful, to chew raw meat*

'1470 MAN' *The most startling fact about the 2½-million-year-old skull found by Richard Leakey in Kenya in 1972 is that its brain capacity is about 800 cc – double that of a chimpanzee, and well on the way towards modern man's 1450 cc*

UPRIGHT MAN *The skull of* Homo erectus, *who lived half a million years ago, held a larger brain than that of his predecessors. Its capacity was about 1000 cc – more than twice that of an ape. His jaw was still prominent, but his teeth were getting smaller*

NEANDERTHAL MAN *The skull of the Neanderthaler, who emerged about 70,000 years ago, was large, and he had a brain slightly larger than modern man's. His jaws jutted out, but were becoming less prominent in proportion to the face. His brows were overhanging*

HOMO SAPIENS SAPIENS *The physical characteristics of modern man, with his well-proportioned face and fully developed chin, have finally evolved over the last 30,000 years. In this time our species has divided into three main racial groups – the Caucasoids, the Mongoloids and the Negroids*

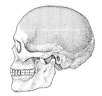

# Armed with new skills, modern man peoples the world

bodies to guard against heat loss, flattish noses and high cheekbones. In the tropics, darker skins and woolly hair protect Negroes against the sun's radiation.

Not all racial characteristics were transmitted because they helped their owners to survive; features like blue eyes or thick lips may have been selected because they were thought to make their possessors more sexually attractive. In small groups of people, features can either die out or become important characteristics, depending very much on who survives to breed, and how prolific he or she turns out to be.

## Spearheads like leaves

The new form of man was a master flintsmith, who created a new range of flint tools of increased complexity. He made long blades with the aid of a wooden or bone punch which he now struck with a hammer-stone – a technique known as 'indirect percussion'. Blades produced in this way were used for many different tools.

The Gravettians, named after the Dordogne site of La Gravette, produced knife blades with blunted backs. The Solutreans, named after a cave at Solutré, in central France, made beautiful spearheads shaped like laurel leaves, with tiny flakes taken off all over the surfaces; some of them were even adapted for use as arrowheads, with separate barbs and an extension for attachment to the shaft, so presumably the bow had by this time been invented. Man could also produce more homely tools; besides the traditional scrapers, there were awls for piercing skins, and gravers for cutting and engraving bone – one of the earliest art forms.

Other materials besides stones were widely used. Bone or ivory, for instance, was made into spearheads, fish-hooks, needles, and barbed,

vicious-looking points which may have been used in salmon fishing. The principle of leverage was discovered and used in the spear-thrower – a short bone baton, with a notch at one end to hold the spear-butt, which propelled a spear much further than the human arm alone could do. This invention was made by the Magdalenians, a group living between 15,000 and 10,000 BC in France and Spain and named after a rock shelter where they lived at La Madeleine in the Dordogne.

## The earliest jewellery

Men of these times also practised ceremonial burial of the dead. At Predmost, in Czechoslovakia, 20 people were interred in a mass burial, surrounded by a ring of stones. Usually, however, the dead were buried in ones and twos, in caves or among the tents of the hunters, in pits which were covered by heavy stones or the bones or tusks of mammoths. Often they were sprinkled with red ochre in powdered form; this substance must have had some magical or symbolic significance.

Because the dead were usually buried fully clothed, we know that the clothes of early modern man were quite elaborate. They were made of skins sewn together, using bone needles and threads made from animal sinews, and decorated at the base of the skirt or the wrists with fringes of shells or animal teeth. Sometimes the clothes were adorned with shells.

Men as well as women wore necklaces made from deer teeth, snail shells, discs of mother-of-pearl, and segments of the backbones of fish. Beads were carved from mammoth ivory, pendants were made from fired clay and other materials, and in southern Russia bracelets with beautiful incised patterns were made from

## A VERSATILE NEW TOOL-KIT

Many new ways of making stone tools were developed by the first known men belonging to our own sub-species, *Homo sapiens sapiens*, who had appeared by about 35,000 years ago and survived through the last Ice Age in Europe. They used a wooden or bone punch to pare blades from a flint; then, by a technique called pressure-flaking, they refined the blades by pressing pointed implements against them to detach slivers of flint

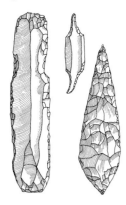

MAKING CLOTHES *Fat and ligament was cleaned off animal skins with a scraper (far left), made by chipping tiny flakes from the end of a flint blade. Then the skins were sewn together with sinews, after holes had been pierced in them with double-ended awls (centre) made from flakes of flint. Fine leaf-shaped spear-heads (left) were made from flint in southern France and Spain 20,000 years ago*

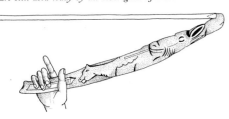

SPEAR-THROWER *To hurl their spears further and with more force, hunters devised the first 'machine' in history. This was the spear-thrower – a short, notched baton in which the butt of the spear was lodged before throwing. It worked on the lever principle and, in effect, increased the length of the hunter's throwing arm. Spear-throwers are still used today by the Aborigines of Australia*

## TENT-DWELLERS OF EAST EUROPE

*Groups of hunting people in eastern Europe 20,000 years ago lived in tents set in hollows in the ground. The tents were made from animal skins stretched over a frame of wood or mammoth tusks. The bones of the mammoths were used to keep the roof in place and to pin down the tent at its base. Other bones were ground down to provide fuel for warmth and cooking*

pieces of mammoth tusk. Love of display thus gave man the incentive to take an interest in a whole new range of materials.

## Death below the cliff

At this period, about 15,000 years ago, huge herds of grass-eating animals roamed the plains of central and western Europe. The reindeer and the mammoth migrated seasonally, so that it was possible for men to predict their movements, to follow them, and to decide where they might best be ambushed. Often, hunters stampeded herds of horses and other animals over cliffs or drove them into bogs.

A beast like the mammoth provided a variety of valuable materials in addition to its meat, which may have been smoked or dried to preserve it longer. Clothes and tent fabric were made out of the animal's hair, and in eastern Europe its tusks were used as tent-frames, while their heavy bones weighed down the tent-flaps or were ground up and burnt as fuel. Lamps were fuelled by the mammoth's fat.

Groups of people began to concentrate on hunting a particular species. In south Russia and Czechoslovakia the mammoth was the victim, while in western Europe and parts of northern Germany the reindeer herds were the favourite quarry. Near Paris, one hunting group established itself on the banks of the Seine, probably to intercept reindeer crossing the river. On some sites, man was exploiting rich salmon runs. In North America, too, man learnt to stampede bison over cliffs and finish them off with spears.

The abundance of the food supply at certain times of the year probably allowed men to congregate in groups of up to 50 or 60 at a time. In south Russia men lived in hollows in the

# HOW MAN SPREAD ACROSS THE GLOBE

Man's earliest true ancestor appeared on earth more than 2 million years ago, but it was not until 10,000 to 15,000 years ago that his descendants had peopled almost the entire globe. Man apparently evolved in the tropics, and not until he had mastered fire and learnt to protect himself from the elements did he venture north into colder latitudes. The first man known to have roamed beyond the continent of Africa was *Homo erectus*, who appeared about 500,000 years ago. During the 200,000 years of his existence he moved round the east Mediterranean coast to reach southern and western Europe; he also crossed into Asia, reaching as far as Java and Peking. By 70,000 years ago, Neanderthal man had appeared, and his remains have been discovered from south-west France to northern China. The differing climate of the regions in which men settled was one factor in the long process of evolutionary change by which, over many thousands of years, the peoples of the world became separated into the four distinct racial groups, with many sub-divisions, that exist today

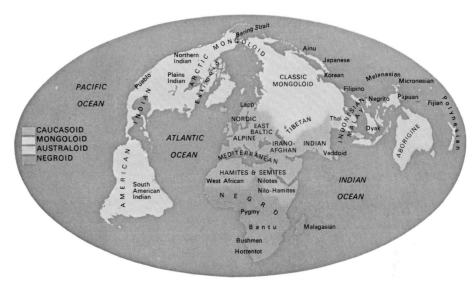

OUTWARDS FROM AFRICA *The greatest expansion of the populated areas of the globe has taken place during the time of our own sub-species,* Homo sapiens sapiens, *who had emerged by about 35,000 years ago and has been the only species of human being on earth for the last 30,000 years. The first* Homo sapiens sapiens *in Europe, known as Cro-Magnon man after the site in France where his first remains were found, arrived from south-west Asia, but similar forms existed in Russia, western Asia, China and Borneo, as well as all over* Africa. *Some 30,000 years ago men started to reach North America from Asia, across a great land bridge which joined the two continents where the Bering Strait now flows; in the last Ice Age so much water was locked up in the great ice caps that the level of the sea was 600 ft lower than it is today. From North America the newcomers worked their way down the western coast of North and South America. The first men probably reached Australia about 30,000 years ago, when the continent was still joined to the Asian mainland*

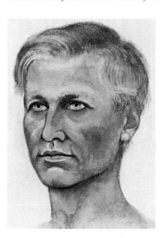

CAUCASOIDS *(left) These are native to Europe; they also include the Hamites and Semites of North Africa and Arabia and extend eastwards to India. They have light skin and eyes, narrow noses and thin lips. Their hair is usually straight or wavy*

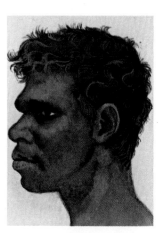

AUSTRALOIDS *(right) The Australian Aborigines are descendants of the earliest Caucasoids who arrived from Asia and developed in isolation. Other Australoids include the Ainus of northern Japan and the Veddoids of southern India. Their skins vary from brown to nearly black. They have black, frizzy hair, wide noses and thick lips*

MONGOLOIDS *(right) These live in central Asia and northern China; the American Indians and Eskimos are the descendants of Mongoloids who crossed the Bering Strait. All have flat, broad faces; their apparent 'slit eyes' are due to a fold of skin over the upper eyelid, protecting the eyes against snow glare*

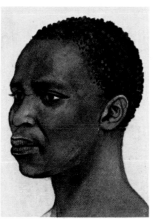

NEGROIDS *(left) The skins of Negroids range from light brown to almost black, an adaptation to tropical climates which helps to keep the body cool. Negroids are found mainly in Africa south of the Sahara. Negroids have broad noses, thick lips, brown or black eyes, and woolly hair*

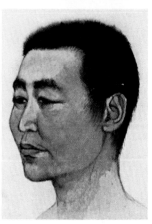

# Caves of the hunters where art began

One of the earliest and best-known prehistoric works of art is the 'Venus of Willendorf' (above), a 4 in. high limestone figure carved in Austria about 30,000 years ago. Its ample curves reflect early man's preoccupation with fertility

STYLISED CARVING *In the ivory carving (left), which was found in Czechoslovakia and is over 20,000 years old, the female figure has been reduced to a single sexual characteristic. Massive breasts and hips appear in the stone 'Venus of Laussel' (right), carved at the same period in the Dordogne area of south-west France*

ground, probably covering their homes with some form of tent. The size of some of these so-called 'tent-scoops', and the number of hearths within them, suggest that several related families lived under one roof. There were also large open-air 'scoops', which were used for flint-knapping, preparing skins, cooking and other domestic tasks. The tents and the area round them were strewn with the bones of prey and other refuse, for men were not yet fastidious about refuse disposal.

In Europe and North America, several animals, including the mammoth, became extinct or very rare at the end of the Ice Age 10,000 years ago. This may have been partly because the return of the forests diminished the grazing area. But man himself, with his wilful hunting methods, was probably also partly to blame.

## Artists – by accident

About 30,000 years ago man took a revolutionary step forward. On the walls of the caves of the time has been found the first evidence that has survived of men deliberately choosing to express strong feelings in pictorial form.

This great intellectual breakthrough may, perhaps, have come about by accident, when Stone Age man was exploring the darkest recesses of his winter cave. His nerves taut, his imagination heightened by the fear of the unknown, the flickering light of his lamp played strange tricks on him. Suddenly the cave must have seemed alive with the shadows of familiar creatures; the bumps on the ceiling became a herd of bison, the soft stalactite flows on the walls seemed like women's bodies, a natural cup in the rock became a malevolent eye.

As the cave became more familiar, the temptation to improve on nature – to add an eye here, a set of legs there, by scratching or painting the rock – must have become irresistible. Soon most men realised that large three-dimensional objects could be recognisably portrayed in miniature, or in two dimensions. They could be carved in the ivory of mammoth tusks or modelled in clay; they could be sculpted in low relief, engraved on bone or rock, or even painted on the walls of caves.

Once men had accepted this idea, the artist could capture for all time and for all the tribe his idea of an animal, a scene which had occurred in the past, or one of his fantasies. And what he created could be used for play, for teaching the young, for worship, or simply for looking at with pleasure. In effect, man could 'freeze' part of his environment long enough for his powerful intelligence to think about it, to manipulate it, to understand it fully. Soon he developed also symbols which were 'shorthand' representations of the real object. So were born not only art but also the diagram, the teaching aid, the scale model, the toy and the idol.

## Statuettes from La Gravette

One of the most exciting groups of these early artists were the Gravettians, named after the Dordogne site of La Gravette but living over a wide area extending as far as southern Russia. With uncanny insight into the nature of animals

and the properties of their available raw material, the Gravettians accurately reproduced the bulky mammoth and the lumbering cave bear. They also made little statuettes of women and animals. These figurines were carved in a wide range of materials, each one posing special problems for the artist – mammoth ivory, bone, limestone, sandstone and even coal. Sometimes they were moulded in clay and fired.

The women depicted in these figurines were obviously not intended to be flattering portraits of the contemporary Eve. Most of them have neither feet nor facial features, but the emphasis is on the sexual features. Large pendulous breasts droop towards an ample stomach supported on massive thighs; the buttocks are often large, and suggest that women of some races were storing fat there, as the Bushmen of the Kalahari Desert do today. The figures are largely naked, but there are sometimes tantalising details of dress – suggestions of hoods or hair-nets, and little aprons – and possibly elaborate hair styles.

Ancient man understood very simple, schematic art, just as we do today; sometimes a woman was represented simply by a pair of breasts on a stick. At the other end of the scale, however, is a delightful carving in ivory of a girl's head, found at Brassempouy in south-west France, which may be the first true human portrait. Man had to maintain a viable human community, with a balance between the dependent old and young and the active, productive adults, and perhaps he was led to think deeply about problems of reproduction. These figurines, with their emphasis on sexuality, pregnancy and lactation, may have helped him to focus his thoughts.

## Flowering of cave art

The finest cave art was that produced by the Solutreans and Magdalenians in south-west France and northern Spain between 18,000 and 10,000 years ago. The walls of caves at more than 100 sites are adorned with magnificent paintings, most of them showing the grass-eating animals of Stone Age times such as horses, reindeer, bison and aurochs (an extinct form of wild ox), which were man's main source of food. The artists also drew dangerous carnivores like the lion and bear, and sometimes fish and birds too. Occasionally the artists gave way to fantasy, depicting imaginary animals with spotted coats and unusual horns.

Many of the paintings of real animals are so accurate that they must have required long observation of the animals concerned, and exacting training in their portrayal. Engravings of animals have been found on pieces of bone and pebble; these may have been preliminary sketches produced by artists in training, or else the work of artists in the open. The attitude in which some animals have been painted on cave walls suggests, too, that the artists sometimes used dead animals as models. Man himself appears in few cave drawings, and when he does it is in the form of a caricature; it may have been thought that to paint a realistic likeness of a man's figure would bring him misfortune. Graphic representations of female sexual organs,

## A GALLERY OF PREHISTORIC ART

*Dramatic animal pictures on the walls and ceilings of the Lascaux cave in south-west France, painted over 15,000 years ago, are some of the richest examples of the art of prehistoric man. This painting of a bison captures the ferocity of the beast, even after a spear has delivered a death-blow to its entrails. By contrast the dead man lying on the ground is only a caricature; the bird on a pole is probably a totem, or emblem of the artist's tribe. The pebble (left), with many engravings on top of each other, may have been used by an artist practising his designs for the wall paintings*

the subjects of the earliest art of all, are a continuing theme; but the drawings gradually become less explicit and more diagrammatic.

### Colours from the earth
The paintings were done in one colour or several, applied sometimes to the entire figure, and sometimes in outline. The colours used were available in the local earth – different ochres for red, brown and yellow, and manganese oxide or charcoal for black. The paint was probably mixed with fat to make it waterproof, and then applied with a brush of animal hair, twigs or leaves, a stick with a chewed end, or a pad made of moss or fur. Often a picture was partly painted and partly engraved, and the artist would incorporate in his design natural features such as cracks or undulations in the surface of the cave wall. Outlines were sketched in the wet clay with fingers or sticks.

Sometimes the artist used a primitive stencilling technique, by placing a hand against the wall and blowing paint round it with some sort of blowpipe, such as a hollowed-out bone; these stencilled hands often appear in rows, and the short fingers on some of the hands suggest that

ritual mutilation was sometimes practised. Sometimes the artist cut his figures into the cave wall in relief, producing a sculptured frieze. Some of the paintings may have been made simply as a form of self-expression, or even as a deliberate adornment for bare cave walls. But some of them are so far from daylight, and so difficult to reach, that they cannot have been simply 'art for art's sake'. To reach them the artists used rudimentary ladders – perhaps small trees with the side-branches trimmed – and they painted by the light from moss wicks, floating in animal fat in cups of hollowed-out limestone.

### The meaning of the art
The secret placing of these paintings suggests that early man's 'art galleries' were in fact shrines, and that his art had a ritual purpose. This is confirmed by the fact that many of the paintings show animals with arrows stuck in them, or marked with savage blows. The purpose of this would be to ensure success in the chase, a form of sympathetic magic rather akin to witches sticking pins into the wax images of their intended victims. In some caves the artists have painted one animal on top of an earlier

### THE EARLIEST PORTRAIT

*The well-defined features of this tiny ivory head of a young girl, from Brassempouy in south-west France, make it perhaps the world's earliest known portrait. It was carved over 20,000 years ago*

# An existence that depended on dominance over the animals

**THE WORLD'S OLDEST MAGICIAN**

*Man the hunter was very dependent on luck in the chase, and the abundance of animals and his ability to catch them were his main worries. The creature above, painted 15,000 years ago on a cave wall at Les Trois Frères, in the French Pyrenees, may have been a sorcerer, who dressed in animal skins and conducted rituals which hunters believed would work magic on their prey*

**CAVE DWELLERS OF THE STONE AGE**

*Most of the known inhabited sites of the period during which* Homo sapiens *evolved are in Europe, particularly in France and Spain. In parts of the world where the climate was milder man did not need to shelter in caves, and as a result few remains have survived. The Dordogne region of south-west France, where hundreds of settlements have been found, was possibly the most densely populated area on earth 20,000 years ago*

painting – perhaps in an effort to repeat the success of the hunting party which had tracked down the first animal.

The representation of animals may sometimes have had a different motive. It may have been believed that the act of drawing an animal would ensure its increase, although often the animals drawn were not those most commonly eaten, and sometimes – as in the case of the mammoth depicted in south-west France – they were rare in the area.

Some experts believe that man thought of each cave as a temple or sanctuary, and that certain animals were painted regularly in certain positions to symbolise the relationship between male and female. Finally, it is possible that some of the art was used for teaching purposes at initiation ceremonies; in some caves, such as that at Le Tuc d'Audoubert in the French Pyrenees, footprints which are apparently those of children remain to this day.

This art is not only the oldest in the world. It lasted for at least 15,000 years, and is thus by far the longest artistic tradition ever known. Some of it may have had deep religious significance, some may represent pure self-expression. Art may well have served several different purposes at once, sacred and secular, and reflected many changing ideas about the world. The variety of motives which gave rise to it may be imagined by picturing what an archaeologist of the distant future, without the advantage of written records, would make of the inspiration behind a statue of Queen Victoria, a Toby jug, a Henry Moore sculpture or a garden gnome.

## The unending quest

Throughout the Old Stone Age, man's life was very much concerned with the everyday quest for food. Of course, conditions varied during this vast period. As the ice sheets retreated 10,000 years ago, the forests returned and man moved north or developed new methods of hunting in pursuit of different animals. He did not always live in caves, but at some periods and in some seasons he may well have preferred to do so, since caves are warm in winter and cool in summer.

For most people, the gathering of honey, fruits, nuts, tubers and berries was probably more important than hunting as a regular source of food. However, the further north man lived, the more important a supply of meat became; the protein was necessary to his diet in colder latitudes, while the season during which plant food could be gathered was shorter. Many hunting methods have left no trace, but sophisticated devices like nets or snares may well have been used.

Man's method of catching his prey changed gradually. At first, it was probably his intelligence and habit of co-operative hunting which established his dominance over the animals. He exploited the stupidity of larger, stronger animals by driving them over cliffs or into bogs. Speech, too, must have helped, not only in co-ordinating the hunt, but in advance planning and in passing on information about typical animal behaviour. Knowledge could thus be

accumulated and passed on from one generation to the next. Later in the Old Stone Age the emphasis shifted, and man learnt to save some of his energy by developing useful mechanical devices, such as the fish-hook, the bow and arrow, and the spear-thrower. He also learnt to draw his meat from one main source, such as the mammoth, the bison or the reindeer, and this too may have made his hunting techniques more efficient.

Stone Age men did not wander aimlessly from place to place, hoping that food would turn up; they exploited an area fairly logically, knowing that certain areas held abundant plant food at certain seasons of the year, that some animals have seasonal movements and periods when they congregate, and that one or two spots contained abundant raw materials, like flint for making tools. Thus the group would move in an annual cycle, developing a deep knowledge of its territory. It is uncertain to what extent man had a particular territory of his own which he defended against other groups; it may be that he simply roamed over a regular range, allowing others to exploit it sometimes.

## Leisure to talk and think

Man the hunter had more leisure than most of his descendants, including the earliest farmers. Hunting peoples do not spend every day or all day looking for food, and early man may well have 'worked' only some 15 hours a week, spending the rest of his time sleeping, playing games and telling stories. Because he had so much time to talk and think, early man's idea of the universe and the meaning of existence may have been very complicated. Simple material equipment does not necessarily mean simple ideas. Most of early man's art reflects his preoccupation with the search for food. The artists may have been the world's first occupational specialists. They may have been the same people as the 'Sorcerers', the mysterious human beings sometimes depicted in the caves, dressed in the skins of various animals, complete with horns and tails. Human communities from earliest times must have contained certain individuals who developed an interest in ritual and in religious ideas.

Although some people may have lived at times in groups of over 50 or even more, most early men lived in tiny groups of only two or three related families. This was usually the largest social unit that could support itself by hunting in one area, and groups became larger only when food supplies were unusually abundant. The average person would be unlikely to see more than a few hundred people in his lifetime, while his choice of a wife might have to be made from a dozen or so candidates.

The human group was held together by various needs – there had to be enough active men and women to gather food and rear the next generation. Almost certainly men and women had formed fairly stable unions, though not necessarily monogamous ones. Compared with other species, humans have an unusually long childhood and adolescence during which they have to be fed, protected and trained;

societies where marriage, or at any rate some prolonged partnership, was in force would naturally tend to survive more successfully.

It is likely, too, that each group had its leaders, who made decisions about movements and relations with other groups, and who directed hunting activities. Leadership would be informal, based on a combination of age, strength, intelligence and success in hunting.

## A short life in the Old Stone Age

For most of human life the Biblical lifespan of 'threescore years and ten' has been far beyond realistic expectation. Among Neanderthals and the earliest types of modern man, only one person in ten survived the age of 40. It would have been rare to meet a person of 50 who would speak from the experience of 40 seasons of hunting or gathering, 30 years of bearing, rearing and delivering children, or a lifetime of observing the use of medicinal herbs and attempts to alleviate human suffering. The individual possessing such knowledge would have commanded great respect.

Almost all women would be potential child-bearers, and the majority would be pregnant or nursing at any one time. A high proportion of each group would be children, many dying before adulthood. It is quite likely, again on the basis of more recent parallels, that infanticide was normal practice, since some infants, who were weak, or difficult to feed or carry, would have been simply redundant. Hunting accidents would have been a frequent cause of death, as would disease and starvation.

Man was not totally helpless against injury, disease or illness; most simple peoples have a wide knowledge of the medicinal properties of plants, and know something of anatomy, based upon their observations made while cutting up meat. Many diseases of historic times have spread because of such hazards as high population densities, polluted water supplies or an unsuitable diet, and ancient man would rarely have been affected in this way. Nonetheless, disease, injury and toothache must have been among his principal sources of pain and anxiety.

## Forests spread northwards

About 15,000 years ago, the climate started to improve. In the Northern Hemisphere the ice gradually melted, so that the edge of the ice-sheets retreated northwards; by about 8000 BC much of central and northern Europe was free of ice. As the climate became warmer, the almost treeless tundra zone flanking the ice-sheets moved northwards, and behind it advanced coniferous forests, followed by forests of broad-leaved trees.

Southern Scandinavia and Britain, for instance, had in 8000 BC the vegetation normally associated with tundra conditions – mostly moss and grasses, with some birch and willow trees. Gradually, as the climate became warmer, pine and hazel became the dominant trees. After about 5500 BC the climate became even warmer and wetter, so that the species of trees existing to the present day could flourish. The forests were dominated by very tall oak trees, which

## THE CREATURES THAT KEPT MAN ALIVE

Animals were vital to early man's survival; he needed their meat for food and their skins to clothe him. Wall paintings and carvings of animals, often vividly realistic, have been found at every major site settled by prehistoric man. He may have believed that depicting certain valued species of animals would ensure they remained plentiful, as well as giving him success in hunting them

PREHISTORIC COW *Most of the animals known to modern man were familiar in the Stone Age. This cow, delicately rendered and complete in every detail, was painted 20,000 years ago in a cave at Lascaux*

HORN MAMMOTH *This carving of a mammoth – the largest animal then on earth – follows the shape of the reindeer antler from which it was carved*

BIRD CARVING *Small creatures as well as large were shown. A bird decorates this pierced staff from southern France*

MIGRATORY HERDS *Early man's chief sources of meat were the great herds of migratory animals such as reindeer, which he hunted down as they crossed rivers or crowded into gorges. In this engraving on a reindeer's antler, found in the French Pyrenees, the artist has caught vividly the anxious backward glance of a frightened reindeer as it crosses a stream. The antlers and skin texture have been closely observed, and fish leap between the animal's legs*

STAPLE FOOD *Wild horses were a mainstay of early man's diet; they remained valued prey for 100,000 years, long after herds of other animals disappeared. This horse is one of many painted at Lascaux. Horses were often killed by being stampeded over cliffs, and at Solutré, in France, the remains of over 100,000 were found*

# New challenges for man as the ice recedes

strained upwards in competition for light; below these, depending on local soil conditions, were ash, elm, lime and alder, with smaller plants.

As the ice melted, the sea-level gradually rose. Eventually the land-masses, relieved of the weight of the ice, began to tilt upwards. Often the same regions were affected by both these changes, so that the outlines of coasts and the courses of rivers were drastically altered. The Thames, for instance, no longer flowed into the Rhine. Ancient beaches were drowned by the sea, or raised several feet above the contemporary sea-level. The southern part of the North Sea was land at this time, but it was gradually inundated by the sea. By about 8000 BC Britain became an island, and the land bridge joining Asia and America was submerged to form the Bering Strait.

## Problems for the hunter

The deciduous forests were not the natural habitat of large herd animals like the mammoth or the reindeer. These had retreated northwards, where a few men probably followed them. Man now had to adapt to the animals of the forest – red and roe deer, elk, wild ox and wild pig. The hunter faced new problems; there was less meat in the forests, since most forest animals were smaller than the reindeer or mammoth, and lived in smaller groups. The

deer liked to move into the hills in summer, but they did not migrate over long distances like many of the animals hunted during the Ice Age; man, too, had to adapt his movements.

To hunt deer, man had to understand many things; for instance, the composition of the herd varied from one part of the year to another. Sometimes the stags roamed by themselves, sometimes they joined the does. No longer could man simply follow the migrating animals and ambush them along their traditional routes; now his prey were thinner on the ground and less easily seen in the woods.

In North America, especially in the east, hunters faced similar problems; further west they were able to continue to hunt large herd animals. During a relatively cold spell, from about 9000 to 8000 BC, they hunted the mammoth; after about 8000 BC many of them specialised in living off the great herds of bison, a way of life which was to last for a very long time, until the arrival of the Europeans in modern times.

## Boats for the new fishermen

Some communities adapted to these changed conditions more successfully than others. Many groups learnt to use water resources more frequently than in the past. They discovered that if they lived on the banks of lakes and rivers, on

the seashore, or on islands, they could exploit the produce of land and water. Thus in northern and western Europe some groups lived on the beaches, among piles of shells and fishbones left from past meals.

Inland, others were taking freshwater fish and waterfowl, and the animals of the forest. Because some of the birds they killed migrate to northern Europe in winter, and others are summer visitors, it is possible to work out the seasons at which camps were occupied. At this period beavers were common in Europe, and man must have learnt to take advantage of the dams which they built, which would have been excellent sources of fish.

To catch fish and water birds, post-glacial man developed the world's first known boats; at Pesse in Holland a simple dug-out boat dating from 6200 BC has been found, and a paddle found in Yorkshire in England was used in 7500 BC. Fishing demanded special equipment; some peoples used a fish spear with several barbed bone prongs, lashed together at their bases. The first fish-hooks were carved from flint, shell or bone. Earlier still men used 'gorges', pieces of stone tied to a line and covered with bait; after a fish had swallowed one it would be hauled out of the water before it could spit out the gorge. Spears and arrowheads were made of wood, and small flint blade insets known as

FOWLERS AND FISHERMEN OF NORTHERN EUROPE

*After the end of the last Ice Age the peoples of northern Europe had to adjust to living in forested lands where animals were harder to track. Many of them turned to the seas, rivers and lakes for food. These hunters, who lived in the northern plains of Europe 10,000 years ago, made dug-out canoes and fished with spears whose* *barbed prongs were carved from the antlers of the red deer. As well as catching fish, they gathered shell-fish and speared or trapped water fowl; they also used domesticated dogs as retrievers. The forest trees were birch and pine, as the climate was still not warm enough for such deciduous trees as the oak, elm, ash and lime*

microliths were used to form the points and the rows of barbs along the sides of the weapon.

In some regions, deer were man's principal source of meat, and the habits of deer were therefore one of man's main concerns. He often made his camps at places with commanding views, from which he could study the movements of game. Trees were cut down – the hafted axe was developed for this purpose – and once a clearing had been created it was colonised by light-loving trees, such as the hazel, whose nuts have a high value as food. On poor soil, bracken and heather crept in.

Hunters after the Ice Age had new and invaluable hunting companions – the first dogs, a domesticated form of the wolf. For Stone Age man, grown wolves were cunning and ever-hungry competitors, circling round man's fires and even darting in to steal his kill. They were creatures to be killed without mercy, but sometimes the cubs may have been spared, to be kept as pets or used as decoys. Human contact would have made them less wild and, rejected by the wolf pack, they would have been forced to depend on man for food. The dog, like man, likes to hunt in a pack and subject himself to group discipline and the commands of a leader; it would not have been long before the scavenger became the trusted partner in the chase. Meanwhile, in the Middle East and in southern

Europe, a development of enormous significance was taking place: the settlement of groups of people in permanent villages for the first time.

## Success in larger groups
One of the earliest known settlements is at Lepenski Vir, on the banks of the River Danube in Yugoslavia. It dates from about 5000 BC, and had no fewer than 59 houses, built of wood and stone; they were shaped irregularly, partly to fit into the confined space available. The floors of the houses were carefully plastered and each house had a stone-lined hearth, set in a pit. Near the centre of each house stood a curious rounded sculpture; its primitive face, with staring eyes, thick lips and down-turned mouth, suggested a fish or frog god of some sort. It was partly by exploiting the local fishing resources that these people were able to live in such a large settlement.

Hunting groups survived in many regions not suitable for farming, such as cold regions, uplands and marshes, including southern Spain. These groups developed their own art, painting themselves and their activities on the walls of rock shelters, in a very different style from that of their predecessors. Man learnt to depict real-life scenes: a group of archers surrounding a wild boar, bows bent and dogs at the ready; or a woman halfway up a tree gathering honey,

menaced by enormous and terrifying-looking bees. In Israel a people known as the Natufians lived in villages of up to 150 inhabitants; at one village, Eynan, a chieftain was buried in a circular stone tomb covered by a stone pavement. The chief was propped up, and faced towards Mount Hermon. Among the Natufians, too, a most important new skill was developing – the harvesting of wild grasses for food, the first step on the road to farming.

## Lessons for the first farmers
For several hundred thousand years man had depended on what nature provided. In good times and places he had prospered. But hunting and gathering have their limitations. Man's numbers were kept low, partly because of years and seasons of scarcity, partly because his primitive means of exploiting his environment did not produce enough food to supply large populations.

Man, though by now he had spread throughout Europe, Asia and Africa, could not increase the size of his communities without altering the habits of the plants and animals which he ate. The success of the people of Lepenski Vir and Eynan was an indication of the skills developed by man the hunter. The next logical step was the domestication of plants and animals, and this was well on the way.

## NEW TOOLS FOR THE HUNTER

The hunters who lived in the well-watered forests of northern Europe between 8000 and 3000 BC developed intricate new tools and weapons to supplement their flint axes. Many of them were made from bone and the antlers of deer

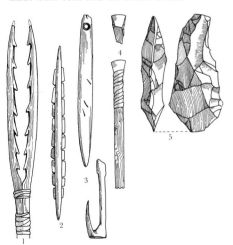

FITTING FLINT TO BONE *The heads of many of the new implements were intricately made, and flint was often combined with bone or wood to make a single tool. The tools drawn above are: 1. A barbed spearhead made from antler horn. 2. A wooden spearhead with flint insets. These insets, called microliths, were blunted on one side so that they would fit into a wooden or bone shaft without splitting it; the shafts have crumbled or rotted away over the centuries. 3. A needle and fish-hook made from bone. 4. A sharpened flint tip, fastened to a wooden shaft by a fibre rope to make an effective arrow. 5. A flint axe-head, chipped to a chisel edge (side and front view); flint axes, as made for thousands of years, were still used to fell trees and shape timber*

### FISH GODS OF THE DANUBE
*These stone heads, with fish-like features but no bodies, were carved in about 5000 BC by Stone Age men living in a settled community of 59 houses at Lepenski Vir, in what is now north-west Yugoslavia. The settlement* *was on the banks of the Danube, and the river probably provided the settlers with much of their food. The carvings, which were found at the centre of the houses, may represent fish gods revered by the settlers*

# Settlements of the first farmers

## 10,000–2500 BC

*As men learnt to herd animals and grow crops,
groups of hunters gave way to larger communities
supporting rulers and specialist craftsmen*

### WHEN FARMING BEGAN

*Nature was being tamed in south-west Asia by 10,000 BC. Knowledge of farming developed later in other areas*

By 12,000 years ago, bands of people who lived by hunting and gathering their food had spread to most regions of the earth, except for the bleak and inhospitable polar lands, and remote islands like New Zealand. Their way of life was much as it had been since the dawn of time, when their ancestors first learnt how to use stone tools. A few thousand years later, however, the world had been transformed by a new discovery: farming.

Of such paramount importance was this advance into the New Stone Age, or Neolithic period, that it has been given the name of the Neolithic Revolution; and no other revolution has been more far-reaching in its results. Farming produced more food, and as a result there was a rapid growth in the numbers of people. They began to crowd together and create the first city-states; and what had been occasional skirmishes between rival bands of hunters became full-scale wars. The immediate effects of the Neolithic Revolution were that much of

southern, western and eastern Asia, Europe, and extensive parts of Central America and Africa were opened up by farmers.

Wheat and barley, once rare species, now thronged the golden fields; and the domesticated descendants of animals which had wandered in the forests in small groups were now seen in larger herds, grazing in the meadows. Natural watercourses were reorganised and irrigation channels dug; huts were grouped into villages, and later into towns. Oxen pulled ploughs and carts; food was transported and stored in bulk. All this came about because man was able to create conditions in which certain species of animals and plants could spread far beyond their original homelands, increase their numbers, and even be changed physically in the service of mankind.

In the Old World, most of the critical steps in the farming revolution were taken between 10,000 and 5000 BC in a belt stretching from northern Greece to Iran and from Jordan to the

### WALLS TO DEFEND THE FIRST HARVESTERS

*Wheat and barley, reaped with flint sickles and gathered in baskets, were the main crops of the Old World's first farmers (right). They also kept sheep, goats, cattle, pigs and dogs. Good land was scarce and had to be protected. By 8000 BC – about 6000 years before its conquest by Joshua – the defences of Jericho, in the Jordan valley, included a stone wall dominated by a 30 ft tower (left) which has now been excavated. The entrance at the bottom led to an internal staircase*

# *Agriculture brings a new outlook*

Crimea. It was here that primitive forms of wheat and barley grew wild, and where the wild ancestors of goats and sheep lived.

On upland soils too thin to support trees, there grew isolated stands of wild grasses whose seeds were worth gathering because they were so packed with nourishment. These grasses stored a high quantity of food per plant, because they needed to survive through the dry summers, and then had to compete vigorously when the rainy season came.

Man soon learnt how to grind the grain to make flour. The grains that fell by chance around his camp found ideal growing conditions in the disturbed ground of the camp site, and were fertilised by the nitrogen content on refuse heaps. Some unknown genius – or perhaps there were a number at different times and different places – had an intellect keen enough to work out why the grasses grew so vigorously near his rubbish heaps, and an imagination powerful enough to exploit this new piece of knowledge. Finally men began deliberately to sow wheat and barley, preparing the ground carefully so that competition from other plants was lessened, and making sure that wild animals were kept away from the growing plants.

The intervention of man soon led to the breeding of new varieties of grain. Wild wheat scatters very easily from the ear as each grain ripens, to enable it to propagate. When men reaped, they cut those ears which still contained corn. By doing so, they were unconsciously selecting as seed corn those grains which were held tightly in the ear until all had ripened together. Gradually these characteristics were passed on, until all domestic wheat had grains which ripened simultaneously in the ear.

### Tools for the harvest
Once man had mastered the secret of raising crops, he needed a new range of tools to increase his output: axes to clear the forest and bring new land under cultivation; hoes to till the soil; sickles for reaping; baskets and, later, pottery to store the grain; and grindstones to process it. The earliest grain was not very suitable for bread – it was probably made into a sort of porridge or unleavened scone.

The harvest would have included what would now be regarded as weeds, but some of these had edible seeds, and were later to supplant the main crops in some areas. Oats and rye, weeds of the grain fields in south-eastern Europe, became staple crops in the poorer soils and colder climates of northern Europe, where wheat and barley grow less well.

The domestication of animals, too, was a gradual process. The more specialised hunters had probably already taken two essential steps in this direction. Some of them were killing male animals in preference to female ones, leaving females to bear and rear their young for later use. It was man the hunter, too, who first learnt to burn or fell the forests, opening up clearings which attracted animals and provided more food for them. Both these processes preceded the deliberate capturing and taming of animals. In fact the early domesticated animals

seldom wandered far from their own territories, so that it was unnecessary to capture them, and the 'taming' of animals probably only took place after years of breeding.

Soon man must have noticed that animals were passing on their distinctive characteristics to their descendants. This probably gave him the idea of trying to influence the character of the next generation by sparing the lives of those animals possessing characteristics he valued. After prolonged and calculated selection by man, cows started to give more milk than was necessary for their calves, pigs developed extra body fat, and sheep grew thick woolly coats. Man also bred for appearance and manageability – the shape of animals' horns changed, and piebald animals, very rare in nature, were selected for their appearance. And so distinctive breeds arose.

Probably the first farmers were originally hunters who happened to live in an area particularly suited to raising animals and growing cereals. Once having started farming they did not immediately abandon their hunting and plant-gathering; both types of economy existed side by side and an increasing diversity of foods became available, with the result that bad luck or misjudgment in one department did not threaten the survival of the group.

### Cotton, cucumbers and chicken
In the Old World, by about 5000 BC sheep, goats, cattle, pigs and dogs had been domesticated in many areas, while wheat, barley, oats, lentils and peas were cultivated in the fields. In other parts of the globe, many other plants and animals were domesticated. Mexico and Peru had pumpkins, squashes (a plant like a pumpkin), avocados and certain beans by 5000 BC. Maize, grown in central America by 5000 BC, reached Peru by 1400 BC. These crops were followed by cotton, chili peppers, sunflowers, and many other plants. The Peruvians domesticated the llama as a beast of burden and the alpaca for its wool.

In south-east Asia, the emphasis was first on roots, tubers and fruits; in Thailand by 6000 BC a wide variety of plant foods was eaten, some of them almost certainly domesticated species. They included almonds, broad beans, betel nuts, cucumbers, peas, water-chestnuts and some gourds. Rice was probably domesticated in south-east Asia, and reached eastern India by 2000 BC, but in China millet and wheat remained more important until 1600 BC.

Later, man started domesticating other fruits and vegetables, and barnyard fowls. Almost as interesting as the huge list of plants and animals pressed into the service of man are the species which might have been tamed but were ignored. There seems no reason, for instance, why animals like the giraffe and the hippopotamus should not have been domesticated, though this seems never to have been tried.

### An agricultural surplus
Agriculture for the first time allowed man to produce a surplus over and above his family's immediate needs. What he did with this surplus

## HONOURING THE HARVEST GODS

So much could go wrong between seed time and the harvest that the early farmers felt, perhaps as never before, the need to win the favour of the gods. Shrines in their honour were built in western Asia 6000 years ago. The most spectacular that have been found are at Çatal Hüyük, in southern Turkey, where some 5000 people lived. Their houses were built of mud-brick, clustered together for protection, and had no external doors. Farmers were as much concerned with performing the right rituals to make their crops grow as with the actual techniques of farming, and the numerous female statuettes discovered may have represented the earth-goddess, which the farmers worshipped as a fruitful mother. Examples of weaving have also been found

DEATH MASK *A rare portrait of one of the inhabitants of Çatal Hüyük 8000 years ago was found in this vivid wall-painting, believed to be of a dead man's face. The early farmers left the bodies of their dead in the open so that the vultures could pick them clean of flesh; then they buried the bones beneath their houses and shrines, often placing gifts in the graves*

was a matter of choice. He could store it up against future hardships; or he could exchange it for other types of food or for raw materials to make him more efficient around the farm; he could also use it to buy manufactured goods made by specialist craftsmen, such as new types of containers, tools, or trinkets for his wife.

When society became better organised, the surplus was spent as a tax, to pay for projects which no single household could provide from its own resources – such as defensive walls or the maintenance of an army, the building of temples and the digging of irrigation ditches. The taxes also supported specialists in government, such as kings, priests and civil servants.

Man's world was now much more complicated. He lived in bigger communities: true villages and towns, with specialists like leather-workers and metal-workers, and social divisions between rich and poor. Governments, too, had to take forms which gave the individual less contact with the people who made the decisions affecting the community. Trade, craftsmanship and a more settled existence allowed the family to accumulate more varied possessions.

In the Near East the first farmers lived in houses of stone, wood or sun-dried mud-brick, usually packed very closely together. The rooms of houses that have been excavated were square

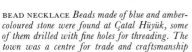

BEAD NECKLACE *Beads made of blue and amber-coloured stone were found at Çatal Hüyük, some of them drilled with fine holes for threading. The town was a centre for trade and craftsmanship*

CULT OF THE BULL *Heads and horns of animals abound on the 40 shrines uncovered among the huddled houses of Çatal Hüyük. In this reconstruction (right) of the Temple of the Bull God, based on the discoveries of the archaeologist James Mellaart, a huge bull's head is flanked by the heads of two rams, while a third is mounted high on an adjacent wall. The ladder leads down from an opening in the roof – the only access to the shrine. The heads are modelled in clay over the frontal skull bones of actual animals, and set with real horns. On the floor, three pillars and a low bench of mud-bricks bristle with cores from bull horns. Though heads were placed on any wall, paintings of bulls are found only on walls facing the Taurus ('Bull') Mountains*

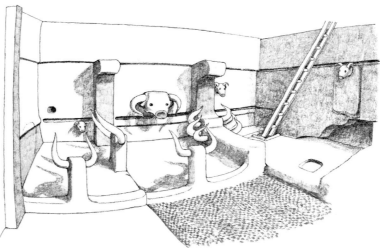

GODDESS'S SYMBOL *The earth-goddess worshipped by Çatal Hüyük's farmers was often represented in wall paintings and reliefs by leopards. These two leopards (above), modelled in plaster, are nearly life-size, and were repainted more than 40 times. Many of the pictures at Çatal Hüyük hint at strange and frightening beliefs. Headless men are attacked by vultures who have human legs, and massive bulls gallop across the walls pursued by men wearing the skins of the sacred leopards. Sometimes the hunters are shown touching the tongues or tails of the animals, symbolising mastery over them. Arranged in friezes are stencilled hands, and rows of plaster breasts – symbols of plenty. Some friezes incorporate symbols of death such as skulls of vultures, or jaws of boars*

or oval in shape, and their walls and floors were carefully plastered and sometimes painted. The inhabitants used woven mats, slept on raised clay benches, and had separate areas for cooking and preparing meals.

The roofs were often flat, since heavy rain was not common. When the mud-brick walls eventually decayed, or the buildings were destroyed by fire, houses were levelled and new ones built on the ruins. In this way high mounds, known as *tells*, were gradually built up on early village sites, from Bulgaria to Iraq. Some of these *tells* today have modern villages perched on top of them, and their successive levels, when excavated, reveal a fascinating record of hundreds of years of village life.

## Craftsmanship in pots

One of the first needs of a farming community was some means of storing grain and other foods until they were needed. Many enterprising craftsmen and artists emerged to meet the need. They learnt how to carve elaborate wooden tubs and platters, and to hollow out pieces of stone to make vessels of various shapes. Pestles and mortars were also made of stone. The early farmers also made containers of leather, and coiled grasses into basket work; the imprints of rush mats have been found at Jericho, though the mats have not survived. Soon, pottery was invented to store liquids to keep them cool. The early potters had no wheel, but instead built up their pots by coiling a continuous roll of clay round and round in a long spiral. The plasticity of the clay allowed them to make pots in a wide variety of shapes for the kitchen and the farmyard. Another important discovery of Neolithic times was the art of weaving. As long as 8000 years ago the women of western Asia spun threads of wool or flax by twirling a hand-held spindle, and then wove it into cloth on a simple horizontal loom.

Other craftsmen produced tools and ornaments, to make life more pleasant and efficient. At Beidha, in Jordan, each craftsman had his own workshop – the town had a butcher, a bead-maker, a man who made bone tools. At Çatal Hüyük, in southern Turkey, the absence of weaving equipment in most houses suggests that this, too, was left to specialists. Other skilled craftsmen polished mirrors of obsidian – a black glass-like volcanic substance – without leaving scratches on the surface. Some of them attached finely chipped obsidian knives to carved stone handles.

The activities of these craftsmen led to an intensive search for new raw materials, and villages often traded with each other. Obsidian, for instance, was taken all over western Asia from the mountains of Turkey and northern Iran, while farmers on the Greek mainland used tools made of obsidian from the Aegean island of Melos. To Çatal Hüyük, a town controlling important trade routes, were brought stalactite, marble, calcite, alabaster, lignite, shells and precious stones such as jasper, carnelian, rock crystal and chalcedony. The people of early Jericho obtained greenstones and obsidian from Anatolia, cowrie shells from the Red Sea, and turquoise from Sinai. Most of these substances were used in jewellery.

## In search of new lands

A more secure food supply and an improved diet led to the world's first population explosion, and the new communities expanded rapidly in search of new lands to till. By about 6000 BC most of the people between northern Persia and the Bosporus were farmers, and some had already begun to colonise Crete and the northern shore of the Aegean.

By 5000 BC farming communities had spread throughout the Balkans, as far north as Hungary, and into the mountains and islands of western Greece. A few groups crossed the Adriatic and settled in south-east Italy. In south-east Europe, especially in the broad river

# Farmers on the move in search of new lands

valleys of Bulgaria, the colonists carried on the traditions of their immediate ancestors. They still made very attractive painted pottery, with gay spiral designs and striking use of areas of red and white. This was probably intended as fine table ware, while there were also cruder vessels designed for the kitchen or the fields. These were unpainted grey pots, decorated by pressing the fingernails or fingertips into the clay before firing.

Like their ancestors, the Balkan peoples of about 5000 BC lived in fairly densely populated villages, with houses made of mud, sometimes with timber uprights, and possibly flat roofs. In time the decayed remains of these houses led to the formation of mounds of debris, or *tells*, like those further east. Each family now perhaps felt a little more independent of others, and houses were now set apart from each other, rather than grouped closely together.

## Jokes in potter's clay

If a farmer had to work hard, so did his wife. In Greece and the Balkans, most of the houses had special kitchen areas – raised clay platforms, sometimes partitioned off from the rest of the house, in which have been found ovens, hearths, clay bins for storing grain or flour, and the remains of household crockery.

Besides cooking and processing grain and other food, women probably made elaborate clothes of flax and wool, which would have been a good deal pleasanter to wear than skins or leather garments. The figurines of the period

wear complicated costumes, including tunics with V-necklines and long skirts, perhaps originally dyed in different colours.

The early Balkan peoples enjoyed the freedom of expression which was provided by the potter's clay. They turned drinking vessels into fat, hollow-bodied animals, or decorated the lids of jugs with solemn owl-faces with pointed ears. Some of their art had a more serious purpose. Inside many houses have been found little shrines containing pottery figurines – perhaps portraits of ancestors, or possibly the gods and spirits of the fields or the household.

Although some of the figurines were apparently used in rituals, others were probably made as toys. The Balkan peoples loved scale models and made the world's first dolls' houses – tiny square houses with roofs cut away, and complete with internal fittings like clay ovens and grindstones, and little figures seated on chairs or grinding grain.

The earliest farmers in central Europe were called the Danubians, after the river valley where they made their first settlements. From their homeland in Hungary they and the revolution they represented spread rapidly across Europe, reaching Holland before 4000 BC. The farming communities lived in villages of up to 300 people, accommodated in huge timber long-houses up to 150 ft long and about 18 ft broad.

The houses had steep ridged roofs of thatch to carry off the rain, and the walls were made of heavy oak timbers, between which were panels of interlaced twigs daubed with clay. Inside, the

houses were built to a complicated design. At one end was a raised floor, perhaps a granary, while the other end was strengthened to hold a few domestic animals. In the central portion lived a group of closely related families, including husbands, wives and children, together with unmarried relatives and surviving parents.

At the centre of each village was an extra-large long-house, sometimes with plank-built walls, which may have been the village meeting house. At one end was a cattle-pen for 40 or 50 head of cattle; possibly the villagers held their livestock communally. The people seem to have had no class divisions; at any rate, individuals were not distinguished by living in special types of hut or receiving abnormally rich burials. Certainly there would have been no point in private ownership of land at this time, for land was still plentiful. Farmers frequently moved on from plot to plot, and communal labour was needed for digging and harvesting.

## Farming in the virgin forests

The Danubians were able to take advantage of the accumulated fertility of centuries, stored in the humus on the floor of the great oak forests of central Europe. When they arrived they felled the smaller trees with stone axes and stripped enough bark off the larger ones to kill them. A few seasons later, when the piles of timber had dried properly, they were set on fire, and the farmers of the virgin lands planted their grain in the patches of ash left behind. They chose only the best drained and most

STONE AGE MINERS HACK OUT THE PRECIOUS FLINT

*Plentiful supplies of flint were vital to the early farmers of Europe who depended on flint axes to clear the dense forest land for their crops. This reconstruction shows miners at Grimes Graves, near Thetford in Norfolk. Shafts 30 ft deep were sunk into the earth to reach the best flint. Miners chipped out the flint with picks made from deer antlers, and lit their way with chalk lamps fuelled by animal fat*

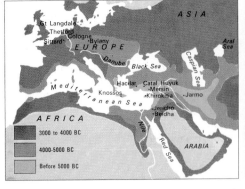

HOW FARMING SPREAD

*Farming began about 10,000 BC in south-west Asia, where the soil encouraged wild wheat and barley, and the forerunners of domestic sheep and goats lived. By 5000 BC farming communities existed in western Greece, the Balkans and Hungary, and reached Crete and south-east Italy. Sheep, goats, cattle, pigs and dogs had been domesticated, and in many areas wheat, barley, oats, lentils and peas were being grown. Over the next 1500 years, communities moved westward from the Danube Valley through northern Europe, reaching Holland before 4000 BC, and Scandinavia 500 years later. Southern and western Europe were settled by other pioneers, originating from the Balkans; by 4000 BC they had reached Italy, Sicily, Malta, North Africa, southern France, Spain and Portugal. Britain was colonised around 3500 BC, and by 3000 BC the process of expansion was complete*

fertile soil – the loess, which originated as wind-blown dust from the surface of north European ice-sheets. They must have had a keen eye for plants which indicated fertile sites.

Eventually, they found that they had exhausted the soil's reserves, and had to move on – normally after 10 to 15 years. They did not move on aimlessly, but used some half dozen sites in rotation, making the earth fit for cultivation with their slash-and-burn technique. After 50 or 60 years, they would move back to the first site, now covered afresh by oaks and undergrowth; the fertility would be partly restored, and the trees would be young enough to be felled more easily than the oaks in the primeval forest.

The farmers grew wheat, barley, peas and vetches for food, and flax for spinning and weaving. They also kept cattle, which were probably allowed to find their food in the woods. The forests would also have been full of acorns for pigs, and the early farmers still hunted woodland game and gathered wild plants and fruits. As they spread further westwards across central Europe, the Danubian farmers started to keep more stock; their later villages included large fenced enclosures.

Meanwhile, other groups of people ventured across the Mediterranean in primitive sailing vessels. By 4000 BC there were groups of farmers in Italy, Sicily, Malta and northern Africa, while others had reached southern France, eastern Spain and Portugal. By 3500 BC the first Neolithic colonists reached the North European Plain, and moved into Denmark and Sweden. Probably the numbers of these early farmers were swollen by groups of hunters, already living in the area, who eagerly adopted the new way of life. The newcomers halted in central Sweden and southern Norway, content to leave the northern region to the remaining hunters and gatherers, as its terrain and short growing season were unsuitable for farming.

## Farming reaches Britain

About this time, too, farmers from northern France crossed to the British Isles. The invaders arrived in simple boats, heavily laden with seed corn and terrified animals with feet hobbled. Once ashore, the colonists penetrated swiftly along chalk and limestone escarpments, where beech trees, with their dense foliage shutting out the sun, prevented undergrowth and so made progress easier. The first Britons were looking for well-drained land which was easy to clear, so they settled along the gravel terraces in the river valleys, or on the chalk and limestone upland country.

For felling trees, building houses and making tools, the farmers needed a regular supply of good stone axes. Suitable stone pebbles were to be found in most regions; these were chipped roughly into shape, then carefully ground down, keeping the centre of gravity towards the edge, which had to be as keen as possible. These axes would have been very effective, especially on smaller trees, though they needed frequent sharpening. They were fairly brittle, and their

### THE THINKER

*Balkan potters produced some of the finest sculptures in prehistoric Europe. This figure of a man sitting on a four-legged stool, his face propped on his hands, was made more than 5000 years ago in Romania*

## POTTERY FOR THE HOUSEHOLD IN AN EARLY FARMING COMMUNITY

One of the first needs of the early farmers was for a means of storing their produce. The invention of pottery gave them ideal storage vessels, particularly for liquids. The early potters of around 5000 BC were probably women. The potter's wheel had not been introduced, and a pot was made by coiling a roll of clay round and round in a spiral and then shaping it by hand. At first, the pots were hardened on an open fire, but soon it was discovered that they could be strengthened by firing them in closed kilns. The potters also learnt to coat pots with fine liquid clay to give a hard smooth finish, and to use ochre-based paints for decoration

DANISH POTS *These perfectly shaped pots from Denmark were made in about 2500 BC, without the use of the wheel. The shapes were based on those of earlier baskets and leather beakers, and the pots were decorated by making impressions in the clay while it was still soft*

MODEL HOUSE *Potters in central Europe made models of their houses, perhaps as toys. This one, found in Czechoslovakia, shows that farmers had abandoned the flat roofs and mud-brick walls of western Asia for sturdy timber houses with sloping roofs, more suitable for the European climate*

HUMAN-SHAPED JAR *The shape of the human body was often used not simply as a decoration but incorporated in the basic design of a vessel. The Balkan potter who made this jar based it on the form of a woman, her arms providing the handles. The jar still bears the traces of red and white paint*

# Engineering in wood and stone

users would have swung them only from the elbow, like a hammer. In some places, men took special trouble to obtain just the right stone or flint for their purpose. At Grimes Graves, not far from Thetford in eastern England, Neolithic miners in about 2500 BC sank more than 2000 shafts into the chalk, bypassing two seams of inferior flint until, 30 ft down, they came to the so-called bottom-stone, which was prized most highly of all. Galleries led out from the shafts into the flint seam.

The miners used picks made of deer antler and shovels made from the shoulder-blades of cattle, and worked by the light of small lamps made from hollowed-out pieces of chalk, containing animal fat and wicks of moss. All the flint and rubble had to be hoisted to the surface in baskets. The victim of one of the first known industrial accidents was a miner at Grimes Graves whose skeleton was found still buried under a pile of chalk which had fallen from the roof. On the European mainland, too, flint was mined in Belgium, southern France, Denmark and Poland, and to this day piles of debris and roughly shaped tools can still be found. Probably these flint axes were traded by specialists, who travelled many miles supplying roughed-out axes to the farmers, who then ground them smooth for use on their farms.

Many of these groups of early peasant farmers lived in well-organised communities. In about 2500 BC in Somerset, in south-west England, they even built wooden trackways across the swamps which lay between the Polden Hills and the Mendips. With great accuracy, the local people first picked out a course which made as much use as possible of natural 'stepping-stones'—dry areas of limestone or sand in the middle of the marshes. They then built wooden trackways, which wound through giant reeds, bypassing trees and pools of water. A wide variety of building styles was used to build the trackways; these included alder cross-supports, brushwood mattresses of birch, and bundles of hazel branches laid along the track. To stop the trackways from moving sideways, the bundles were often pegged in place with birch pegs, sharpened to a point and hammered into the peat with wooden mallets. The tracks extended for several miles, and must have required great quantities of timber; one of them needed no fewer than 50,000 birch pegs. Most of the trackways were about 3 ft wide, enough for one or two walkers.

## A plough to till the land

The growth of agriculture, and all the technology which went with it, proceeded at a different pace in different places. The first farmers in Europe used the digging-sticks which were appropriate in a forested environment. Later, when the land became more open, with fewer tree-stumps, and it was necessary to dig the ground more thoroughly, the farmers developed the 'ard', a very simple wooden plough drawn first by human beings and then by oxen.

At the time when northern Europe was being first colonised by farmers, cities were already flourishing in Mesopotamia, with populations

dependent on irrigation, skilled craftsmen using metal, and a complex system of government complete with tax-collectors, priests, and scribes who developed the art of writing.

By contrast, at the other end of the scale, many peoples in the world were still at the hunting and gathering stage. For a while some of them continued their old way of life, even after the first farmers arrived amongst them. In Denmark, people started making pottery under the influence of the newcomers, and they probably exchanged the products of the sea for meat and grain. In France, too, some hunter-gatherers may have started to domesticate animals, perhaps those which ran loose from the farmers' villages.

Where the two cultures met, the more primitive peoples were gradually absorbed, as some intermarried with or joined the incoming groups. But there was plenty of land for all, and no need for the newcomers to drive into the wilderness those already roaming the land and living a simpler life. Both hunters and farmers could use the same region peacefully together, since different stretches of its land would be suitable for different purposes.

## Builders of stone tombs

The first farmers of western Europe did not leave behind many traces of their homes, for wood soon perishes in the open. Instead, they left as their memorials the great stone-built tombs known as megaliths (from the Greek words *megas*, 'great' and *lithos*, 'stone'). The earliest of these tombs that have been found date from around 3500 BC, and for 2000 years they were erected over a wide area of Europe, from Portugal to Brittany, eastern Germany and the Shetland Isles.

The walls of the tombs were usually upright slabs of stone, with large flat stones set across them to make a roof—rather as children build houses from playing cards. The gaps between the slabs were filled in with drystone walling, and the whole tomb was then covered by a great mound of earth or small stones. Some tombs were built entirely of drystone walling, with corbelled roofs which made them look like old-fashioned beehives.

By this time society was probably organised into tribes, each tribe containing several clans whose members were related to one another, and all claiming common descent from a half-mythical ancestor. The building of the megalithic tombs must have absorbed a great deal of time and energy, indicating that there was close co-operation within a community over a long period, and it is likely that the early farming communities built them only for clan chiefs and their close relatives or associates.

Because resources of manpower had to be organised, a dead leader may have lain in state in a wooden mortuary until the tomb could be built. The tomb builders had to drag the stones from the fields or else quarry them from the rock face by heating the stone with fire and then throwing on cold water to split it. The only tools available to the builders were stone hammers. But before the mound was piled up,

Europe's first farmers had by 3500 BC banded themselves into tribes and clans which honoured their dead chieftains by burying them in enormous tombs. Massive slabs of stone were used to build the inner chambers of the tombs, which were then usually covered by a mound of earth or stones. Some of the stones used in the roofs weigh over 50 tons; yet the men who shifted them into place did so without the benefit of elaborate engineering devices, and laboriously shaped them without the aid of metal tools, sometimes even carving rain-water channels into the roof slabs. Many of the tombs are simple in shape; and some have such high mounds that they were probably also used as sites of worship

COLLECTIVE TOMB *In about 2500 BC farmers in north Wiltshire built the West Kennett long barrow, a huge tomb with separate chambers and covered by a mound 330 ft long. The tomb was built of large boulders and drystone walls. Inside were found the remains of over 45 people, buried at different times, as well as beads, pottery and arrowheads*

the ground plan had to be laid out. The architects had to consult the priests about the space needed to perform the correct last rites. In some regions an enclosed courtyard or forecourt was built; in others an impressive entrance was provided by a façade of tall upright stones, joined by panels of drystone walling. Different clans or communities had to be provided with their own burial chambers, which may explain tombs planned with side chambers, or a number of separate chambers.

## Raising the walls

The architects of the stone tombs must have had simple measuring implements, for they were often laid out on the basis of a neat triangular or rectangular design. At West Kennett, in southern England, the chambers fitted into a neat triangle, while designers of other tombs laid out rectangular mounds. After the outline of the mound had been marked out, often by removing a strip of turf, holes were dug for the stones and lined with wooden stakes to protect the sides of the holes and make it easier to slide the uprights into them. Then with ropes, sledges and rollers the stones were dragged

MALTESE TEMPLES *Some of the most impressive monuments of the early farming communities in Europe have been found on the islands of Malta. These are large stone temples which are often decorated with carvings. The temple at Mnajdra (above) was built about 2500 BC. Rollers were used to trundle into position the huge blocks of the local, easily worked sandstone, which were painstakingly pock-marked all over for decoration. The rooms were originally roofed with large wooden beams, and a 'speaking tube' allowed the disembodied voice of a priest to reach worshippers from a separate chamber hidden within the walls. It is believed that the prehistoric Maltese developed this way of life without any significant influence from outside*

SIDE CHAMBERS *A reconstruction of the West Kennett long barrow, with the roofing stones removed, shows the elaborate design of the tomb. Opening off the central corridor are four side chambers, constructed mainly of large stone slabs. In front, a forecourt has been blocked off by upright boulders joined by drystone walling*

IRISH TOMB *Ireland has more than 150 simple burial chambers of the type known as portal dolmens. This tomb at Kilclooney, Co. Donegal, is a single room formed of upright boulders capped by one flat stone; it dates from about 2500 BC. The earth mound which once covered it has been dug away*

SITES OF THE TOMB BUILDERS *The earliest stone tombs, or 'megaliths', found in Europe were built in Brittany about 3500 BC, and they continued to be built for 2000 years over a very wide area, stretching from Portugal to east Germany, and from southern Italy to the Shetland Isles. The effort needed to construct some of the tombs was colossal. To build one tomb in England, at Rodmarton in Gloucestershire, it has been calculated that 200 men would have had to work for a year to quarry and position the 5000 tons of stone used. At Bagneux, in the Loire valley of France, one roofing slab weighs 86 tons and was raised to a height of over 10 ft. Not all the tombs were built on the surface. In some regions, especially where the rock was soft, as in Sardinia, Portugal and around Paris, the tombs were built entirely underground, being cut out of the rock with the use of only stone tools*

to the edges of their holes, tipped in, and raised to a vertical position, perhaps with the help of simple wooden hoisting apparatus. The holes were then packed with smaller stones, and the roofing slabs were dragged on to the tops of the uprights, perhaps up an earthen ramp or with the aid of wooden cradles and levers.

While all this was going on there were great lateral stresses on the walls, which were supported by the half-built mound, and by wooden trusses which were afterwards burnt away. Sometimes arrangements were made to keep the tomb dry – at New Grange in Ireland rainwater channels were carved into the roof slabs.

After all the stones were in position the mound was piled up, often inside a kerb of heavy boulders or a neat drystone wall. The huge mounds of the Irish tombs – often as big as those on which, in later centuries, the Normans placed their castles – were carefully made with alternating layers of turf and river boulders to prevent subsidence. The shape of the final mound was elaborate, with vertical walls and flat platforms on top, or else low domes on the summits; sometimes the sides were stepped. At last all was ready for the burial. The dead

man or woman was laid in the tomb with pottery, beads, axes or weapons, possibly for use in an after-life. Often the long wait in the mortuary meant that only a bundle of bones, rather than a complete body, was finally interred in the tomb. Then the entrance was blocked with a pile of stones and earth, until the next burial took place. Sometimes elaborate arrangements of stones concealed the precise position of the entrance, perhaps because the builders feared that the bones might be moved for the performance of black magic – and at some tombs the absence of certain principal bones suggests that this did sometimes occur.

## Worship of sun or axe

Different areas in western Europe had different religious ideas: the early Irish worshipped the sun and carved simple sun symbols on their tombs, while the first Breton tomb builders had some form of axe cult. In France and Spain, gods and goddesses with special head-dresses, necklaces and religious emblems were sometimes carved or painted on tomb walls. The great concepts in architecture and engineering which inspired the megalithic tombs were

spread not by a wandering master race of colonists and missionaries as was first thought, but by traders, long-distance fishermen and those in search of land or raw materials.

Some groups went beyond simple tomb-building. In Malta, for example, prehistoric islanders had developed by about 2500 BC a complex of huge stone temples, which still stand. They contain semicircular rooms walled with stone slabs, beautifully dressed and cleverly fitted together. Inside the temples are carved stone benches, laid on cement floors; the temple walls were plastered and painted with flowing designs, and had secret chambers set into them.

These elaborate temples, built on the Maltese islands which were only intermittently in contact with other areas, show the heights of achievement which some prehistoric people of the Neolithic Age could reach with nothing more than stone tools to help them. The architectural principles and techniques embodied in these tombs formed a tradition which was to continue for 1000 years, and which reached its highest pinnacle of achievement in the stone circles and alignments erected in Britain and north-west France in the Bronze Age.

# Metal: a discovery that changed the world

## FROM 6000 BC

*Copper, bronze and iron, first used in western Asia,
provided new, stronger tools; and a skilled class of smiths
created the world's first industrial revolution*

A process which was to have far-reaching consequences for the whole of mankind began among a group of craftsmen in western Asia somewhere around 8000 years ago. This was the discovery of metal-working, which was finally to bring man out of his long Stone Age. And like many of the great discoveries in man's history it may have come about accidentally, rather than by deliberate experiment.

As the inhabitants of the early farming villages had become more skilled in making various kinds of pottery and clay figures, they began to use a kiln, or oven, to fire their products. This provided the high-temperature, airless atmosphere needed for making hard pots with a clear, non-absorbent surface against which painted decorations stood out well. The potters also ventured further and further afield in search of special types of earth which could now be used for making pottery. They also searched for materials to make cosmetics.

In their search the prospectors also discovered the first metals: lumps of gold or copper in almost pure form, not needing refining, which could be beaten into shape like clay but had the advantage of being much less fragile. It was only a matter of time before someone, perhaps searching for a new type of colouring matter, placed lumps of metal into a pottery kiln to see what would happen to them.

The result was startling. Here were some strange coloured stones which, instead of keeping their basic form, like flint or obsidian, became liquid at high temperatures. When the kiln cooled, this liquid became solid again and took on the shape of whatever it had been resting on. This new substance was soft enough, especially when slightly heated, to be hammered into a thin sheet with a stone, and its edge could be ground down. Soon the early metal-smiths discovered that the same intense heat could be used to extract copper from metal-bearing ores of rock, by the process known as smelting.

The use of metal was first discovered in Iran and Turkey about 6000 BC. Six centuries later, the inhabitants of Çatal Hüyük in southern Turkey, were smelting both copper and lead. They made small pendants, and also tubular

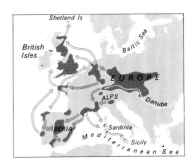

### THE MIGRANT SMITHS

*Knowledge of metal-working was carried across western Europe by the Beaker people, whose settled areas are shaded*

### AN EARLY FOUNDRY

*One of the earliest metal-workers pours molten bronze from a crucible into a mould, using tongs of peeled wood, while his assistant works a bellows with his feet to keep the furnace at a high temperature. The first axes and daggers were cast in open moulds; the required shape was carefully chipped out from the surface of a flat stone, and the heated metal poured into it. The mould was then covered with a clay cap to prevent it from cooling too rapidly. When the casting had cooled, the blade was then toughened by reheating and hammering it several times. Copper and gold, the first metals to be used, were discovered in Asia about 6000 BC. By 3000 BC smiths learnt how to make a harder metal, bronze, by adding tin to copper; and by about 1500 BC knowledge of mining and smelting had spread as far west as southern Ireland*

## A CHARIOT BUILT TO CARRY THE SUN ACROSS THE SKY

By about 1500 BC, European bronze-smiths had refined their art to make elaborate sculptures like this wagon of the sun, found in a bog at Trundholm, in Denmark, in 1902. The chassis of the wagon, the horse and the disc representing the sun are cast in bronze and decorated with gold leaf. The Danish smiths were among the most creative of the early metal-workers, even though their country had no deposits of copper or tin, the two ingredients of bronze, and both these metals had to be imported. By the time this chariot was made, knowledge of the wheel had spread to Europe from Asia, and bronze-wheeled vehicles began to play an important part in religious ceremonies; the wagon was seen as carrying the sun in its journey across the sky and down into the underworld at the end of the day

# Smiths and traders spread the secrets of metal-working

NEW WEAPONS FROM THE SMITHS

The dawn of the metal age gave smiths the opportunity to make stronger weapons, with sharper cutting edges. Wooden clubs, flint-tipped arrows and flint knives gradually gave way to more effective swords, spears and axes of bronze, which were in common use over a wide area of Europe and western Asia by about 1000 BC

FOR BATTLE AND DISPLAY *Metal-workers in Denmark were especially skilled in designing and producing bronze weapons. These swords (left) come from Stensgard and Torup-garde; the skill of the Danish smiths is shown in the casting of the hilts, rivets and ornamental ridges, or mid-ribs, down the blade. They were extremely effective in battle. But some shields, helmets and weapons were produced solely for ceremonial use. The processional axe (above) was found in a wood near Vejle, in Denmark. It dates from about 800 BC, and could never have been used in battle as it was cast with a clay core*

beads, from thin copper sheets which were beaten flat with a hammer and then rolled. The earliest smiths, however, were slow to realise what a valuable discovery they had made, and treated the new material as a curiosity rather than as a basis for progress. They went on using copper and gold for ornaments, but it was 2000 years before they used metal to make sophisticated tools or weapons. The breakthrough came about 4000 BC, when both in Iran and in south-eastern Europe smiths began to make copper axes, some of them having a central hole to take a wooden shaft. These new tools must have been invaluable for forestry and mining.

The craft of metal-working was flourishing about 3000 BC, in the early city-states of Mesopotamia. Better farming methods on the rich soil between the Tigris and Euphrates rivers provided the agricultural surplus to support craftsmen, and growing populations gave the craftsmen a larger market for their products. Soon the smiths experimented with mixing together different metals to produce alloys. By adding a small quantity of tin to copper they produced the first bronze – a harder metal than either, easier to cast than copper and giving knives and axes a sharper cutting edge. The smiths of Mesopotamia catered for several markets. They made personal ornaments, special ceremonial vessels, craftsmen's tools, and weapons for warfare or hunting.

## A search for rare metals

Knowledge of metal spread gradually through western Asia and Europe, but it was 2000 years before copper and bronze were in widespread use. Copper is fairly rare, and tin even more so; both would only be found by extensive searches. Probably the earliest metals were found where they were most accessible, on the beds of streams and rivers. Only after these resources were exhausted would man have worked out that the metal on the river beds must have been carried down by the river, and then sought out its source in remoter regions.

Mining was difficult and risky. The miners were in danger from roof falls and flooding, as well as from the foul atmosphere created by their method of mining: they lit fires to heat the metal-bearing rock, then threw on water to cool it suddenly, cracking the rock apart. The ore was broken into smaller pieces with crude stone hammers, and then shovelled on to wooden sledges to be taken for crushing, washing and smelting. The normal furnace was a large clay-lined hollow, packed with alternate layers of ore and charcoal, and raised to a temperature of over 1000°C by a forced draught created by a skin bellows or blowpipe. The pure metal collected in a crucible at the base of the hollow; from there it was poured into a mould, usually made of stone or clay.

Soon, complex three-dimensional objects were being cast in moulds, sometimes by the use of the *cire perdue*, or 'lost-wax' process. A wax model was encased in heat-resistant material, such as clay. The coated model was then heated, so that the wax ran out through small holes, after which metal was poured in to replace the wax. After the metal had cooled, the clay casing was removed, leaving a perfect metal replica of the original wax model. After casting, the object was re-heated, or 'annealed', to toughen it. Any roughness left by the mould was removed by grinding, and a whetstone was used to sharpen the edges of tools and weapons.

## New scope for the designer

The early metal-workers developed advanced techniques of fastening spear-heads, arrow-heads and dagger blades in position. These included rivets, special loops for binding, hollow sockets to take wooden shafts, and punched holes for the insertion of tiny pegs.

The fact that metal will take any shape imposed on it by man was the whole beauty of the new discovery. In the Stone Age, whatever the flint-worker dreamed of, his achievements as a craftsman had been limited by the nature of his material. All he could do was to knock chips, large or small, off lumps of stone. But metal-workers were free, right from the start, to develop their own designs. Their skills, and not the properties of their material, were the only limitations on what they could produce; and skills were improving all the time.

Metal proved to possess another important advantage over stone. An axe-head or arrow-head of stone might be resharpened when it was broken or damaged, but it was quite likely to be discarded. A broken metal tool, on the other hand, could be melted down and used to make a new one, sometimes more advanced than the old. Thus, although mining was a laborious business, the metal won remained in use for a long time, and was only lost to society when finished products were deposited in treasure hoards such as those that accompanied a chieftain's burial.

New designs gradually developed: the farmer had a slim axe instead of the clumsy, easily broken stone axe with its narrow cutting edge and sometimes ill-fitting haft. He could now cut corn and hay with a sickle made in one piece, instead of a series of easily blunted flint teeth stuck individually in their hafting. The huntsman now had a specially designed spear, with a more secure fastening; the craftsmen had copper-tipped drills, chisels, punches and awls.

## The dominance of bronze

By about 2500 BC copper was in use over a region stretching from present-day Portugal and Denmark in the west to Pakistan in the east; in the Asiatic part of this area bronze was used as well. A thousand years later, metal-workers in Europe had switched almost entirely to bronze, while in Asia Minor a revolutionary new metal, iron, was coming into use. Bronze, however, still remained the dominant metal in many regions, and it was the basis of the Aegean civilizations of the Minoans and the Mycenaeans. It was not until well after 500 BC that iron was in common use in north-west Europe.

In western Asia and around the eastern shores of the Aegean and the Mediterranean, the earliest smiths worked in towns and cities which had powerful centralised governments, commanding well-equipped armies and extensive civil service departments. Their leaders led worship in massive temples and palaces, and were laid to rest in monumental tombs.

In Europe, society was simpler; people were grouped in rural communities whose leaders were not remote, god-like figures glimpsed on the steps of a distant temple, but well-known individuals, often to be seen in the fields or round the farm. Nevertheless, they demanded symbols of their rank, like their counterparts in the east, if on a smaller scale. In life, they loved to display costly daggers in precision-made sheaths, and tunics decorated with sheet gold. It seemed only natural that the precious objects which had marked a man's rank in life should go with him beyond the grave. When a chieftain died, his grave was furnished with fine ornaments, and crowned by large round burial mounds of earth or stone. In some areas, such as southern Russia and China, the servants of a chief were slaughtered when their master died, so that they might accompany him in the next world. The new metal-workers were often called on to produce rank-symbols of various types, which in turn helped to consolidate the positions of their chieftains.

## Europe's earliest castles
Some of the earliest metal-using communities lived in fortified towns or fortresses. In about 2500 BC, in southern Spain and Portugal, for instance, some settlements were built on steep-sided spurs of rock, defended by one or even two high walls, with outlying fortresses to give warning of impending attack. The chieftain's stronghold, near the centre of the settlement, was a great keep, topped with turrets and fighting platforms, and the only entry was by a narrow passage.

The workshops of potters and coppersmiths were often clustered within the chieftain's courtyard for safety, but the ordinary townsmen lived in flimsy huts outside the high walls. These people fought primarily with bows and arrows – over 6000 arrowheads have been found in one castle keep, at Vila Nova de São Pedro, near Lisbon – and tall towers and bastions enabled them to fire down on enemies trying to scale the walls. To arm their defenders, the metal-smiths of the Spanish and Portuguese settlements made daggers and flat axe-heads.

These early metal-smiths also made tools such as chisels and saws. Using these tools, other craftsmen produced strange owl-eyed figurines in bone and stone, which were buried with the dead in stone tombs. Flint-smiths, who had for so long produced simple arrow-heads and knives, now had to pit their skills against those of the new craftsmen in metal. They responded by turning out beautifully worked flint daggers – not only in Spain but in Italy, France, Denmark and southern England.

## Beaker people on the move
Groups of people who knew how to work copper gradually moved into France, the Low Countries and the British Isles by 2000 BC, and took the secret of the new craft with them.

Many craftsmen of the early Bronze Age worked for one particular chief, making eye-catching ornaments as well as weapons for their rich and powerful patrons. The skills of European smiths extended to complicated work in gold, amber and jet. The luxury goods they produced probably changed hands frequently, as chiefs rewarded their followers for loyal and faithful service. But many of these treasures followed their owners into the elaborate burial mounds their people laboured to build for them. In Scandinavia, princes had their weapons laid beside them in their graves so that their rank would be recognised by the gods. Similarly, their wives were buried with the jewellery and ornaments they wore while alive

NECK ORNAMENT *This engraved gold collar which was found at Broighter, in north-west Ireland, dates from about 600 BC*

GOLD EAR-RINGS *Beaten gold was used to make these ear-rings found in southern England. They date from the 17th century BC*

DRINKING CUP *An amber drinking cup found in Sussex dates from 1500 BC. The cup's shape derives from the form of the single piece of amber from which it was made*

GOLDSMITH'S MASTERPIECE *The Rillaton gold cup is named after the burial mound in Cornwall in which it was found. The cup, dating from 1500 BC, was hammered from a single sheet of gold, and its handle attached by gold rivets and washers. Its design may derive from patterns used by the Mycenaeans and familiar in the Mediterranean world*

RURAL CHIEFTAIN *Bronze-workers in Sardinia often portrayed prominent local figures such as chiefs or clan elders in their sculptures. This 8 in. high statuette dates from between 1000 BC and 500 BC. It can be recognised as that of a chief by the round cap, cloak and raised right hand – all marks of dignity. Some figures held a long staff in the left hand, the symbol of their office*

GERMAN GOLD *The art of the earliest goldsmiths was very simple. A gold sheet was hammered out to the required shape, and then embossed or engraved in a variety of ways. Often gold ornaments were sewn on to clothing by the hoops at either side, like this 'solar disc' from Lower Saxony, in Germany. Gold discs with embossed crosses, sometimes within circles, have been found in many European regions and may indicate sun-worship. Gold was also used to coat and inlay buttons and beads. Later, gold wire was twisted to make neck-rings*

# Architecture inspired by priests

These migrants are known as the Beaker people, after the bell-shaped pottery cups they made. These were bright red or buff drinking vessels, with attractive horizontal decorations, often in white paste, arranged in bands around the pot. The beakers are the first known pottery vessels which appear to be designed specifically for drinking.

The Beaker people may have originated either in central Europe or in Spain. By 1800 BC they had spread all over Europe to areas ranging from Portugal to Hungary and from Sardinia to the Shetland Isles. Wherever they went, their smiths sought copper to make daggers, axe-heads and awls, while their womenfolk made neat woollen or linen clothes.

The newcomers had a dramatic impact on the peoples among whom they settled. They were skilled bowmen, able to fight for new territory; in Portugal they stormed the stone castles and took them over. In time they probably intermarried with subject populations. They crossed to Britain from the European mainland in several phases, and paved the way for the emergence of the well-organised rural kingdoms which were to erect monuments such as Stonehenge and attract skilled craftsmen from all over north-western Europe.

## Battle-axes and buttons

By about 1500 BC many skilled craftsmen were at the service of local rulers in the areas that were later to become southern England, Brittany, Ireland, Czechoslovakia and Germany. By then, the secret of bronze had spread from Asia Minor through central Europe to the west, and craftsmen made fine bronze daggers, which had wooden hilts studded with bronze rivets or tiny gold nails, and pommels of bone or amber. The daggers had sheaths of leather or basketwork, sometimes bound with metal strips and lined with cloth. The chiefs went into battle swinging bronze halberds.

Central Europeans fastened their cloaks by great bronze pins with elaborate ornamental heads. The British preferred buttons, and richer men could now afford to have these capped in gold. In southern England, clothing was sometimes decorated by sewing on to it a flat gold plate bearing a geometric pattern of fine lines. There were necklaces of amber, shale or faience beads. Amber is the fossilised resin of pine trees of long-submerged forests, washed ashore round the Baltic coast. Faience is a blue-green glassy paste which originated in western Asia, but by this time there were several European centres of manufacture.

Bronze-workers made axe-heads, useful both as tools and weapons, and bronze awls, which helped the leather-worker. But most of the products of the new metal technology seem to have been useful mainly as symbols of status, designed to impress subject peoples with the wealth and power of their owners. Goldsmiths in Ireland made *lunulae*, which were collars of sheet gold. Chiefs in southern England drank from cups of amber, shale or even pure gold. And the respect accorded to a barbarian ruler did not end with his death, for his subjects had

to labour to erect his burial mound. The rows of mounds within sight of Stonehenge are clear indications of the status of the chiefs buried beneath them. Probably society was rigidly stratified, each person's rank being determined by birth rather than by merit or achievement; not only rulers but rich, high-born women and children also were frequently given ceremonial burial.

## Craftsmen on the move

One person who could rise in this type of society was the independent craftsman, whose skill was so rare and valuable that he could move from one employer to another at will. Some craftsmen were content to stay within one chief's household, working with materials as diverse in origin and character as gold, bone, wood, leather, bronze, shale, amber and stone. But other smiths travelled to seek new markets; the early Irish metal-workers, for instance, brought their products to England and France, and crossed the Channel to reach the courts and markets of central Germany.

The itinerant metal-workers travelled along well-established routes, sometimes concealing their stock-in-trade in holes in the ground. Some were prevented from returning, and the hoards have survived to be ploughed up in modern times. In Germany, at the junction of the rivers Saale and Elster, no fewer than 750 bronze axe-heads have been discovered in different hoards. Some smiths crossed the Alps into northern Italy; and Hungarians sometimes worked in Denmark.

All this travelling helped to spread new techniques very quickly. Analysis of the copper halberds found in central Germany and in Ireland shows that smiths in both regions knew that it was better to use a hard copper, containing arsenic, for the blades, but that the rivets had to be made of a softer copper. Probably one group discovered this and spread the knowledge on to others.

The introduction of metal tools made possible a greatly improved form of one of man's earlier inventions – the wheel. The wheel was originally developed in western Asia, though it is uncertain how it was invented. Probably the germ of the idea came when some unknown genius, watching men hauling a laden sledge along the ground, first thought of placing segments of tree-trunk under the sledge to roll it over the ground. By about 3250 BC wheeled carts were being used in Mesopotamia and the Caucasus; they had solid wooden wheels made in three parts and strapped together.

## Making the wheel lighter

The wheel proved an ingenious work-saving device, and not only for vehicles; the potter's wheel, in particular, was an enormous advance on the old method of making pots by coiling a continuous roll of clay round and round in a spiral. But knowledge of the enormous advance that the wheel represented spread very unevenly. The early Egyptians, for instance, used the potter's wheel by 2500 BC but failed to see the advantage of the wheeled cart for nearly

AVEBURY RESTORED *Much of the stone circle at Avebury, 20 miles north of Stonehenge, was destroyed after 1300 as being a home of evil spirits. But some 100 stones have been replaced in recent times*

1000 years. In most of Europe, however, the sequence was reversed: wheeled carts appeared from 3000 BC, but wheel-made pottery not until after 1000 BC.

The great disadvantage of solid wooden wheels was their weight. The introduction of metal tools meant that for the first time spokes could be cut and shaped, so making wheels lighter. By 1500 BC some European chieftains had chariots with spoked wheels, and many farmers must have had wheeled carts. In central Europe there have been found little clay models of four-wheeled wagons with high sides and a tailboard, pulled by oxen and probably used to carry crops, animal fodder and manure.

## Advances in architecture

Besides craftsmen, another powerful class within Bronze Age society was that of the priests. It was probably the priests who, in north-western Europe, were responsible for new and more grandiose architectural schemes. In Brittany, round about 2000 BC, they ordered the erection of lines of great stones. In the main complex near Carnac nearly 3000 standing stones are

SOLAR OBSERVATORY *The stones at Stonehenge are arranged in such a way that on Midsummer Day a man standing at the centre of the monument and looking through the opening between two of the outer circle of sarsen uprights (left) will see the rising sun pass directly over the upright Heelstone, outside the monument. Midsummer Day was an important occasion in the lives of the people who built and used Stonehenge; they saw the full glory of the midsummer sun as symbolising re-birth after the darkness of winter. As late as the 1st century AD, when the Romans came to Britain, the Celts, under their priests, the Druids, were still using Stonehenge as a temple for sun-worship, and it was once believed that the builders of the monument nearly 2000 years earlier had the same purpose in mind.*

*The mathematical accuracy of the Heelstone's positioning, however, combined with other alignments indicating the exact position of midwinter sunset and two extreme positions of the midsummer moonrise during its cycle of $18\frac{1}{2}$ years, has led some scientists to suggest that Stonehenge and other stone monuments were designed as elaborate observatories. From them, Bronze Age priests might have been able to build up an accurate calendar of the seasons, for use in agriculture, and to predict eclipses of the sun and moon. The sightings could be taken along the sides and diagonal of an exact rectangle, marked out by the so-called 'Station Stones' on the banks of the monument. This rectangular layout would have been impossible as little as 30 miles further north or south*

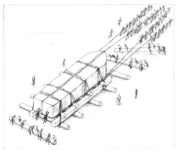

BRUTE STRENGTH *Some of the stones used in building Stonehenge were apparently hauled laboriously across Salisbury Plain on sledges and rollers by several hundred people*

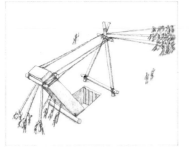

SINKING THE STONE *Sarsen stones from the Marlborough Downs were lowered into deep pits with one sloping side. Primitive hauling apparatus then raised them upright*

FINAL CHECKING *After the last adjustments had been made to the placing of the stones, boulders and rubble were tightly packed round their bases to stop them moving*

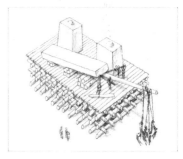

RAISING THE LINTEL *The lintel stone was raised on a cradle of timber scaffolding, and holes cut into it fitted projections on the waiting uprights – a mortise-and-tenon joint*

---

arranged in three sets of roughly parallel lines, running from east to west; each set extends for more than half a mile, and ends in a semicircular enclosure of upright stones. These alignments may have been designed simply for the performance of some sacred rituals; but some archaeologists believe they had a much more ambitious purpose, forming an astronomical observatory from which certain important positions of the sun and moon could be observed and possibly predicted.

In Britain, a remarkable series of earthworks were constructed between 2000 and 1600 BC, during the time that metal was gradually being introduced. Silbury Hill, in Wiltshire, dating from about 2000 BC, is a huge man-made hill, 130 ft high and containing over 12 million cubic feet of turf and chalk rubble – the biggest artificial mound in Europe. The purpose of Silbury Hill is unknown, but it was built with great insight into problems of soil engineering. The sides were carefully stepped, the interior contained radial chalk walls for added stability, and the whole structure was carefully built up in a series of layers. Soon after, four great

banked enclosures were built in Wiltshire and Dorset – the largest of a series of so-called 'henge' monuments, peculiar to Britain, which people had been building for at least 500 years. Each of the four was at least 1300 ft in diameter, and inside was a huge circular timber building, probably a temple. One of these monuments, at Avebury, contained a large stone circle – so large that a village now stands inside it – as well as two smaller circles, and various other stone settings. From two of its four entrances, stone avenues led off, in one case to another circular wooden temple. In other parts of Britain there were similar embanked circles, sometimes three or four together, and sometimes containing stone circles. They were accompanied by clusters of burial mounds – perhaps customary tribal meeting places.

### Monument on the plain

The most astonishing building achievement of all took place at Stonehenge, on Salisbury Plain. It began as an embanked 'henge' monument nearly 4000 years ago, in Stone Age times, and had a ring of pits, some of them used

for cremation burials. The second form of Stonehenge, which is not visible today, consisted of a double circle of 80 or more uprights, the so-called 'bluestones'; these originated from the Prescelly Hills, more than 200 miles away in South Wales, though recent research suggests that the stones were brought to southern England by glaciers during the Ice Age and not carried by man as was originally supposed. But before this second form of Stonehenge was completed it was replaced by a brilliant new design. Great sarsen stones from the surface of the nearby Marlborough Downs were loaded on to sledges and dragged to the site over rollers of logs. Then they were dressed to shape with heavy stone hammers.

The sides of the stones were made slightly convex, so that when they were stood upright, perspective would not create the illusion that they tapered. The uprights, forming a great circle and a horseshoe within it, were fitted with tenons, which exactly fitted the mortise holes on the lintels. The lintels were also locked together laterally, with tongue and groove joints. After some work on yet another new

# Skilled craftsmen at the courts of barbarian chiefs

DECORATED RAZOR *A bronze razor from Hvirring in Denmark, dating from between 900 and 500 BC, is decorated with a ship, sun symbols and a bird. It is not known for certain when men first began to shave; the practice may have begun as an indication of rank, and sometimes a man may have shaved as a sign of mourning*

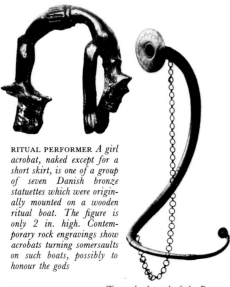

RITUAL PERFORMER *A girl acrobat, naked except for a short skirt, is one of a group of seven Danish bronze statuettes which were originally mounted on a wooden ritual boat. The figure is only 2 in. high. Contemporary rock engravings show acrobats turning somersaults on such boats, possibly to honour the gods*

MUSIC FOR CEREMONY *Towards the end of the Bronze Age in northern Europe, in about 900 BC, Danish smiths made bronze horns, known as* lurer. *The solemn bull-like notes they produced were ideally suited to religious ceremonies. The horns were made in three pieces, fastened together by a simple lock, and suspended by a chain*

design, the bluestones were finally placed in a circle and horseshoe to form the 'inner sanctum' of the Stonehenge that stands today.

The industry devoted to the building of Stonehenge in separate phases spread over several hundred years, and the number of burial mounds which surround it show that Salisbury Plain must have been the most important sacred place in Britain in Bronze Age times. Stonehenge itself, it is now believed, was much more than just a temple. The alignment of the stones on certain key positions of the sun and moon has led to suggestions here, as at Carnac, that Bronze Age man may have used the stones to build up, over the years, an accurate calendar of the seasons. Such a calendar would have been of great value to farmers in the north-west European climate, as a guide to the proper season for different agricultural tasks. Correct dates would also have to be agreed over a wide area for seasonal gatherings, such as rural fairs, which brought together people from different areas.

Subtle minds, as well as skilled hands, were at work in the Bronze Age. A chieftain could call on the skills of men who understood the complex problems of the calendar, and knew how to move heavy weights over long distances and raise them into position. These skills were not confined to the inhabitants of Salisbury Plain. In Scotland, too, priests became preoccupied with the movements of the heavenly bodies. Some Bronze Age specialists in geometry designed ellipses, egg-shaped rings, and enclosures with flattened sides, all laid out with meticulous accuracy. Some burial mounds were cleverly designed as oval forms, to make them look deceptively large from one side.

## Armies to defend the state

By 1500 BC knowledge of bronze had spread throughout Europe, south-west Asia, India and China. During the next 1000 years the implications of all the previous advances became apparent. The development of farming had made possible a steep rise in populations. Rivalries between the city-states of western Asia led to the formation of armies, and the coming of metal helped to speed up the development of more sophisticated weapons.

From time to time the city-states had to fight off powerful neighbours, as well as attacks by barbarians. To protect their property, many west Mediterranean communities built strong fortresses, often on fortified hill-tops. By 1500 BC the Sardinians were building towers several storeys high, with thick walls of closely fitting stone blocks. These *nuraghi*, as they are called, were probably chieftains' strongholds, often set on remote hill-tops dominating the countryside. They were later extended and became formidable castles, which their inhabitants defended against the Romans and Carthaginians. The *talayots* in the Balearic islands, the *torri* in Corsica, the *sesi* in Pantalleria – all these massive stone fortifications were an answer to the growth of violence between the peoples of the west Mediterranean. But even the well-established civilizations of the east Mediterranean

were not immune from the violence of the times. The Egyptians were frequently attacked by groups of raiders whom they knew as the Sea Peoples. These raiders included the Philistines, originally from Crete, who, by about 1180 had settled on the southern coast of Palestine. They went on to attack Egypt, but they were decisively defeated by Ramesses III (1182–1151 BC). The Mycenaeans of Greece, themselves a militaristic people who had taken over the flourishing Minoan Empire in Crete, had to make frantic defensive arrangements in the 13th century. Around 1200 BC the Mycenaean civilization collapsed, brought down by invaders from further north.

## Living on the hill-top

The unstable conditions of the times were not confined to the Mediterranean, but were general throughout the bronze-using world. In Europe, too, the barbarians were becoming numerous and better-armed. The dagger soon became a dirk, the dirk a thrusting sword, the thrusting sword a leaf-shaped slashing sword. By about 1000 BC, bronze swords and spears were common all over Europe, and peoples in the Alps used deadly bronze-tipped arrows. To defend themselves, men carried shields of wood or leather. Warfare was now an important instrument of policy; Europe had caught up with western Asia.

Many communities in Europe, like those in the Mediterranean, lived on hill-tops, which they carefully fortified with ramparts and ditches. The ramparts were usually solid walls of stone or turf, often strengthened by interlocking timbers and faced with timber or stone; parapets gave protection to the rampart walks. Some people in Ireland and southern Germany lived on fortified islands – called 'crannogs' in Ireland – strengthened by timber palisades and extended by timber platforms.

The violence of the times is reflected in rock engravings showing men in combat, found in the Camonica Valley of northern Italy, and dating from about 1000 BC. At the same time the changing nature of society seems to have led to gradual changes, too, in man's religious beliefs. Before 1000 BC, men had worshipped the unseen forces of nature, symbolised by the stag, the bull, or the sun's disc, and in their carvings they portrayed themselves in attitudes of prayer in front of these symbols. Around 1000 BC, however, there was a profound change, as the gods began to be seen as more like human beings, with their strengths and failings.

The rocks were now decorated with strange creatures, half-man, half-beast; the stag became a stag-god, a man with antlers upon his head. Gods were depicted as being drawn on four-wheeled carts, attended by worshippers; and the sun was seen as a chieftain riding across the sky in a chariot drawn by horses.

This new vision of the gods as having human attributes probably arose as man became increasingly aware that the course of his life could be affected by other men just as much as by the forces of nature. Societies had developed a clearly defined class structure, and each man

## A WAGON CARRIES A SACRIFICE TO THE GODS

*The high standard of craftsmanship reached by Bronze Age smiths is shown by this bronze wagon from Strettweg, in Austria, which was probably made in the 7th century BC. The tall figure holding a sacrificial bowl on a cushion on her head is only 8 in. high; she is thought to represent a fertility goddess or her priestess. She is guarded by mounted warriors with shields and helmets, and at each end of the wagon two attendants hold stags, perhaps brought for sacrifice*

had to behave exactly as befitted his social position. He had to serve others or make others serve him; he had to think about his hold on his land, which was now made more subject to confiscation by force or by law than before. Some rulers in Europe even strengthened their hold over the loyalties of their subjects by claiming direct descent from the gods, as the pharaohs of Egypt had done for centuries.

### Better tools for farming
Though bronze-smiths gave priority to better weapons, the new metal-working techniques also benefited the arts of peace. From about 1000 BC farmers had better axes, knives and sickles. Carpenters' tools, too, became common, making it possible to build better houses. At Wasserburg Buchau, in southern Germany, and at Crestaulta, in Switzerland, the peasants lived in well-built log cabins. By the 9th century BC,

the inhabitants of Wasserburg lived in substantial farmhouses of close-set timbers.

By this time the farmers had some domesticated fruits, such as the apple. They had also bred sheep, which originated in western Asia, to the point at which it was worth keeping them for wool as well as for meat. Farmyard manure was used to keep the land fertile, and simple crop rotation may have been practised.

Settlements in southern Britain were permanent enough to leave numerous traces on the chalk downlands to this day. Small fields, most of which could be ploughed by a simple scratch-plough in one day, were enclosed by fences or turf banks, and connected to small farmsteads by narrow sunken lanes. In the west and north, some people were forced to settle on high ground with poor soil. Usually these highland settlers built huts with stone foundations, stock enclosures, and walled fields small in size

and irregular in shape. Probably the stock herders often clashed with more settled peoples as they sought grazing land – continuing a theme at least as old as the story of Cain, the tiller of the ground, and Abel, the keeper of sheep. In southern England the land was crisscrossed by long boundary ditches, dug perhaps to establish title to land without having to fight for it. Eventually the original forests became open expanses of heather, bracken and grasses. The heaths and moors of present-day Denmark, Holland and highland Britain developed after the deforestation and overcropping of poor soil.

Feasts were now attended by men with tableknives as well as daggers to cut up the meat; and richer men drank from embossed bronze cups of sheet metal. Cauldrons and buckets, made of sheet bronze plates riveted together, were also used. Some men took considerable

# *Iron, the wonder-metal that gave the Celts supremacy*

care of their appearance, and by 1000 BC bronze tweezers and attractively decorated razors were in use. Pins and buttons were gradually being replaced by the safety pin for fastening clothes. Even music-making had new possibilities; the Irish had horns and rattles and the Danes had giant bronze horns called *lurer*.

Smiths became artists, as well as craftsmen; they could cast tiny birds and animals, as well as animated portraits of people. The dignity of bronze figures of priests and shepherds, cast in Sardinia, and the grace of little bronze acrobats, made in Denmark, show the heights of artistry these Bronze Age craftsmen could attain.

## Iron comes to Europe

By 800 BC the peoples of western Asia had already known 2000 years of civilization; empires had risen and fallen, and the pyramids of Egypt were already ancient monuments. But most of the continent of Europe, which was to become the centre of one of mankind's greatest civilizations, was still in the prehistoric stage, without organised city life, without writing. It was the ancient Greeks who were the first to bring civilization to the mainland of Europe,

and as the Greek city-states were rising to their peak of achievement in the 7th and 6th centuries BC, two developments took place among the barbarians further north in central Europe.

In the first place they began to use iron, a metal vastly superior to bronze for weapons, because it is harder and tougher. The technique of iron smelting had first been extensively used by the Hittites in Asia Minor from about 1700 BC. For a time it made them invincible but, after their empire fell, knowledge of the new wonder-metal spread rapidly; by 1200 BC western Asia had passed out of the Bronze Age and into the Iron Age. Iron-working spread to Greece with the Dorians, and shortly afterwards to central Europe, where for several centuries iron was used alongside bronze for both tools and weapons.

The second important development was that merchants in the central and western Mediterranean took an increasing interest in the regions north of the Alps, with which contact had already been established through trade in gold, bronze, axes and amber. In about 1500 BC the Mycenaeans of Greece founded a colony at Taranto, in south-east Italy, and their pottery

has been found in Sicily, Lipari and Rome. They were succeeded as colonists round the Mediterranean shores by the Phoenicians and their descendants, the Carthaginians of North Africa. Then came the Greeks, who settled all round the coasts of the central Mediterranean, pushing on to southern France and eastern Spain, and establishing colonies which became famous cities, such as Nice, Monaco, Naples and Syracuse. Marseilles, or Massilia as it was then known, was founded around 600 BC, and was superbly placed for trade with the European hinterland.

## Heritage of the Celts

Soon sophisticated bronze and pottery from the Mediterranean reached barbarians' tables in Germany and France. One huge bronze wine bowl more than 5 ft tall was shipped in pieces up the Rhone, its sections individually marked with Greek letters, to be reassembled and placed eventually in the burial chamber of a Celtic princess at Vix. It was through enterprising Greek merchants, too, that the literate, civilized world of the Mediterranean learnt in the 6th century BC of a hitherto unknown iron-using

### MAIDEN CASTLE — HILL-FORT HOME OF AN IRON AGE TRIBE

*One of the largest earthwork fortifications in Europe is Maiden Castle, built mainly after 300 BC on the downs south of Dorchester, in southern England. The hillside was terraced to make ramparts rising to a height of 80 ft, protecting the hill-fort on the summit. The Iron Age inhabitants lived in clusters of huts, which were usually circular and made of wood, with thatched roofs. The fort eventually fell in the 1st century AD to the Roman 2nd Legion under the command of Vespasian*

people further to the north, who sometimes referred to themselves as Celts.

The term 'Celtic' refers strictly speaking to the group of languages which survive today only in the north and west of the British Isles and in Brittany. But Celtic languages were once widely spoken in Britain, France, Spain, the Alps, northern Italy, parts of Yugoslavia and even in central Turkey (by the Galatians, referred to in the Bible). The arts, social customs and religious beliefs of the peoples of most of this area suggest that all of them, though divided into different tribes, shared a common cultural heritage which is generally referred to as Celtic. These peoples, skilled in iron-working, were to dominate much of Europe from 650 BC until they were confronted and conquered by the irresistible might of Rome's legions.

Celtic society was rigidly stratified. At the top of the social pyramid was the king, who controlled an aristocracy of numerous district chieftains. Most decisions were made by the king, but he took advice from his chieftains on political and military questions, and from the priests on the timing and religious implications of what he planned. Below the aristocracy

there was a class of free farmers, and these were helped in their work by landless men and slaves. Each man in the hierarchy had rights towards, and expectations from, those above and below him. In this way Celtic society foreshadowed the feudal framework of medieval Europe. The king was expected to be a generous and just ruler in peace-time, a decisive and successful leader in war. Sometimes, when pressure on land became intolerable, large groups of Celts would band together to migrate to new lands, as when the Helvetii poured out of Switzerland in Caesar's time. It was this kind of activity which the Romans dreaded – with good reason, for it ultimately helped to destroy their empire.

## Life in a hill-fort

Many Celts lived in villages and towns set on hill-tops and surrounded by one or more ramparts and ditches. The plans of these hill-forts were frequently changed as villages were enlarged and new lines of defence were added. Some planned hill-forts were so grandiose in design that they were never finished, probably because of shortage of manpower in a society which was almost constantly at war. The

### HEAD OF A GOD

*The Celts broke away from past tradition by modelling their gods on human figures. This head from Czechoslovakia dates from 200 BC; it may have been based on that of a local village chieftain*

---

### RICH TREASURE FROM CELTIC GRAVES

An iron-using people known as the Celts had by the 5th century BC become the most accomplished craftsmen that Europe had yet known. They worked in gold, bronze, enamel and coral as well as iron, and their work is marked by intricate yet rigidly disciplined patterns. The Celts probably learnt many of their skills from Mediterranean traders and from barbarian nomads from further east. They continued to dominate western Europe until the expansion of the Roman Empire

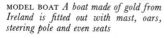

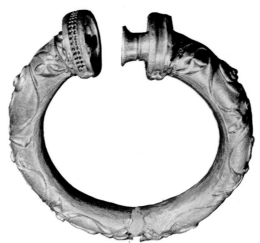

MODEL BOAT *A boat made of gold from Ireland is fitted out with mast, oars, steering pole and even seats*

DESBOROUGH MIRROR *Women appear to have held a high position in Celtic society, even rising to rule kingdoms. In Britain, one woman ruler, Boudicca (Boadicea), Queen of the Iceni tribe in East Anglia, in AD 61 led a revolt against the Romans which nearly succeeded. Such leading women had many treasures created for them, which were often interred with their owners in ritual burials. From the late 1st century BC until the Roman legions arrived in AD 43, British craftsmen made a series of bronze mirrors, with ornamental engraving on their backs and elaborate handles. This one was ploughed up at Desborough, in Northamptonshire. Celtic women wore necklaces and bracelets, and fastened their dresses with bronze safety pins*

NECKLET OF GOLD *The Celts often threw their most prized possessions into lakes, bogs and rivers as sacrifices to water gods, a tradition preserved in British folk-lore in the legend of King Arthur's sword Excalibur which, as he lay dying, was thrown into a lake by Sir Bedivere, one of his faithful knights. This neck-ring, dating from 200 BC and made out of sheet gold, was part of a hoard of gold objects, which also included the boat above, found at Broighter, in north-west Ireland. The ring is hollow and has a socket clasp. The decoration is typically Celtic*

WINE FLAGON *This bronze wine flagon, dating from the 4th century BC, is one of a pair found at Moselle, in eastern France. The sense of fun that Celtic craftsmen frequently displayed can be seen in the treatment of the duck on the spout of the flagon. It seems to be unaware of the menacing presence of the larger animal which forms the handle, or of the two animals on the lid*

# *Liveliness and savagery in the Celtic world*

THE FACE OF IRON AGE MAN

*Still perfectly preserved after being buried for 2000 years, the corpse of this Iron Age man was found in a peat bog at Tollund, in the Jutland area of Denmark, in 1950. He had either been put to death as a fertility sacrifice to the goddess of the earth, or executed as a criminal. Tannic acid in the bog had even preserved the leather thong with which he was strangled; the* *contents of his stomach, also preserved, showed that before his death 'Tollund man' had eaten a meal of gruel, made mainly of barley, linseed and sorrel, suggesting that he died in winter. Other men and women whose bodies were found in the same area had been put to death by hanging, by having their throats cut, or by being drowned or buried alive*

entrance to a typical hill-fort, such as that at Maiden Castle in southern England, built mainly in the last three centuries BC, was along a walled corridor. In front was an overhead wooden gantry controlling large gates, which swivelled on hinged posts and could be locked if necessary. The path was scarred by the ruts of cart and chariot wheels.

Inside the ramparts were clustered huts, usually circular, and made of wood with thatched roofs. Between the huts were square wooden granaries on stilts, and wooden racks on which hay or other fodder was hung to dry. Clay lids set into the ground concealed underground storage pits. There were also ovens, in which grain was dried and roasted, and carts for carrying produce and manure.

## A chariot for the chief

The interior of each hut was fairly dark, but its floor was swept clean, and smoke curled from a central hearth through a hole in the roof. Beside the wall was a great vertical loom, with a row of heavy weights dangling from a piece of unfinished work. At the door, a pair of spears or a bag of slingstones were let into a hole in the floor, ready for immediate use.

On the farmer's workbench lay a variety of useful iron tools – axes, billhooks, ploughshares, adzes, saws, scythes, files or harrows. Besides a smith, a village might have a wheelwright and a cooper. In the largest hut, which was sometimes set within its own palisade, lived the chief and his family. He usually owned a beautifully made war-chariot. The chief alone could afford to keep the ponies to draw a chariot, the trappings for the ponies, and the weapons and body armour needed to make an impressive showing in battle. The chief's prestige was the prestige of the village.

The hill-fort had only rarely to withstand a siege; warfare was more often a matter of rival bands of warriors meeting in open country. But the prelude to battle was extremely ceremonious. Sometimes champions from each side fought in single combat. In any case, psychological factors were very important. Before a battle naked warriors, bristling with weapons and blowing war trumpets, would shout insults to terrify the foe, while their leaders dashed about imposingly in their chariots, which had light chassis and wickerwork bodies.

The aftermath of war was even more terrifying for the losers. Many of the Celts were headhunters, and after a battle the skulls of enemies dangled from their belts, or were placed on wooden spikes at the gates, or in the local temple. Prisoners, including women and children, might also become slaves. For those sold to the Romans, this could mean a cross-Channel voyage in a Roman slave-trader.

## The Celtic arts of peace

Next to fighting, the Celts loved eating and drinking. Their hearths were embellished with wrought-iron spits, while food might be prepared in big cauldrons or stave-built tubs with iron hoops and bronze bindings. Richer men had bronze tankards and metal vessels in which wine was served, if Roman merchants had called recently. The Celts drank their wine neat, to the disgust of the Romans who were accustomed to mixing it with water. Beer and cider, too, were probably common.

Feasts were held to reward the chief's followers for their loyalty, and they involved elaborate rituals. Choice portions of roast boar were always reserved for leaders and heroes. Festivities lasted several days; the warriors feasted, drank, gambled, boasted, occasionally came to blows, and slept where they fell. Sometimes they had to listen to a bard chanting obsequious rhymes in praise of the chieftain's military exploits or his generosity.

Coinage was in occasional use in the Celtic world, though most transactions were by barter. The coiners chose semi-abstract designs, often re-interpreting the Greek patterns which they used as models and adding, in somewhat halting capitals, the name of the local king.

Iron was in common use – iron rivets were even used to mend pottery – and its cheapness helped craftsmen and farmers alike. A true plough, with an iron coulter to cut the furrow, enabled the Celts to exploit lands too badly drained for their predecessors. An industry new to central Europe, glass-making, turned out beads, arm-rings, gaming pieces and the occasional drinking vessel, though elaborate pieces were often imported from Roman workshops. Wheel-made pottery was common, in a variety of vigorous designs.

The Celts were skilled workers in beaten bronze and iron, in coral and enamel. They made great bronze shields and impressive horned helmets, long swords with ornate hilts and engraved bronze scabbards. There were decorated fittings for chariots, horse-gear and harness for the chariot ponies, and bronze war-horns. The craftsmen also made gold and bronze bracelets, armlets and torcs – neck-rings which symbolised great spiritual power.

## Artists with a sense of fun

Artists showed an enchanting liveliness in their approach. They drew closely observed bronze bulls, boars and horses, and were obsessed with foliage and tracery; patterns of leaves and stems flow all over the surfaces, with an appearance of disorder which is, however, carefully controlled. The artists had also a sense of fun. Strange little faces stare out from solid bronze; the hilt of a sword becomes a little man with arms outstretched; a bull's tail ends in a flower; the mouth of a trumpet becomes a dragon's head. Sometimes it is difficult to distinguish the abstract from the representational – a scroll from the face of a man, a tendril from the head of a bird.

Celtic art reflects Celtic religion. For the Celts believed that the gods and goddesses could change their shapes and take on the form of anything in the natural world. On a bronze cauldron discovered at Gundestrup in Denmark, and dating from the 1st century BC, are depicted gods who are half-animal, half-human, like Cernunnos, the horned god, who wears a torc around his neck as a token of his power.

The images of these gods and goddesses were placed in shrines, which varied in form from simple clearings in the forest to large wooden temples. In some parts of the Celtic world deep shafts were dug to try to reach the underworld.

Striking stone statues show the gods as dignified figures with large eyes and drooping moustaches. They were often double or triple-headed, like the Roman god Janus. The Celts sacrificed humans to their gods, and also deposited fine shields, cauldrons and swords in lakes, rivers and bogs. The story of King Arthur's sword, which had to be thrown into a lake when he died, must be a dim memory of these practices. The Celts had powerful priests, including the famous Druids, who were responsible for conducting human sacrifices and consulting the omens. They could recite the tribe's history, the correct religious rituals and legal procedures. But eventually Celtic civilization succumbed to the Roman military machine; one by one the tribes fell, in a process which started with the conquest of southern France in the late 2nd century BC and continued for another three centuries. In many places the Romans met fierce resistance, however, and in Germany, which they never fully conquered, they suffered heavy losses.

The lively, savage world of the Celts was tamed by the more sober virtues of the Romans. But the Celtic genius lived on in Wales, Scotland and Ireland, never conquered by the Romans. It passed into the art of the stone-masons, metal-workers and artists who served the early Christian Church in Ireland, and it was immortalised in the myths and legends written down by Christian monks.

The lasting contribution of Rome was to bring to the barbarians of northern Europe the rich heritage of the more ancient civilizations that had flourished around the shores of the Mediterranean. Europe's prehistory was at an end; with the Roman conquest it stepped into the pages of recorded history.

## CAULDRON OF THE GODS

One of the most prized pieces of Celtic art is a silver-plated bronze cauldron, 27 in. across, found at Gundestrup, in Denmark. It was discovered in 1891, in a peat bog where it had probably been deposited as a sacrifice to the gods. Such sacrifices were common in Celtic religion. The richly decorated cauldron, which probably dates from the 1st century BC, is a fine example of the Celts' skill in working metal. It is thought that it was the work of at least three artists. On the outside are carved various gods, and on the inside are scenes from Celtic mythology. The art of the cauldron reflects the Celtic belief that gods and goddesses could change their shapes to take the form of anything in the natural world – a belief shared with many other pagan religions, such as that of Greece, in which Zeus is supposed to have taken the form of a bull in his pursuit of the maiden Europa, whom he was determined to possess. Later she became a goddess

STAG BEARER *An unidentified god, with well-trimmed moustache and beard, engraved on the Gundestrup cauldron. He holds a stag in each hand*

HORNED GOD OF THE CELTS *The stag-god Cernunnos, the horned god, is depicted on the Gundestrup cauldron, with various animals, among them a stag, surrounding him. In his right hand the god holds a torc or ceremonial neck-ring, and in his left hand he grasps a serpent. Round his neck he wears another torc, as a symbol of his power*

# Part 2
## THE GREAT CIVILIZATIONS
### The achievements of man since the beginning of recorded history

*Most of the lasting achievements of mankind have been made within the framework of one of some 19 great civilizations, or groups of civilizations, which have existed during the last 5000 years. Civilization began among peoples living in the Middle East, on fertile lands particularly well-suited to farming. Because crops take time to grow, agriculture meant a more settled existence. The farmers built the first towns, and from these the first cities grew; the word 'civilization' meant originally 'living in cities'. While some of the new 'citizens' farmed, others specialised in craftsmanship, using newly gained skills in metal-working. Another class governed the state, and priests began to keep written records.*

*Permanent settlement based on city life within an organised state; division of labour, enabling people to develop specialised skills for the good of the community; some means of keeping records – these features of man's earliest civilized societies have been shared by all the great civilizations in man's history. But within this common framework, each civilization has developed its own distinctive character.*

# Dawn of civilization
# in a land of two rivers

3500—539 BC

*In Mesopotamia 5000 years ago men combined their skills
to set up an organised state, where writing
was invented and the world's first cities were built*

Between the rivers Tigris and Euphrates lies a broad, fertile valley that has a better claim than anywhere else on earth to be regarded as the birthplace of civilization. In the southern part of this long valley, an energetic and inventive people known as the Sumerians began to build the world's first cities more than 5000 years ago.

They invented a system of writing and discovered bronze; and they are the first people known to have used wheeled vehicles. With the new-found strength of large-scale organisation, and the precious waters of the two rivers to fight over, the Sumerians also waged the world's first wars, as distinct from tribal skirmishes.

The area settled by the Sumerians was known to the Greeks as Mesopotamia, 'the land between the two rivers'. This name came later to apply to the entire length of the valley which was in later centuries the home also of the Akkadians, the Babylonians and the Assyrians. Though these people came as conquerors, they absorbed much of the civilization of their predecessors and added to it their own architecture, their own sculpture, and their own skill in astronomy, mathematics and medicine. The

Mesopotamian peoples survived for more than 3000 years, until the conquest of Babylon by the Persians in 539 BC made Mesopotamia part of an even wider empire. Even today, the Marsh Arabs of the Euphrates delta live in reed houses little altered in style since ancient times.

The Tigris and the Euphrates pursue a meandering course from north-west to south-east across modern Iraq towards the Persian Gulf. The country on either side of their broad valley is today a vast desert. But before the glaciers retreated at the end of the last Ice Age, some 10,000 years ago, the valley was bordered by grasslands, supporting grazing animals and the nomadic hunters who followed the herds.

As the ice-caps retreated the climate gradually became drier, and the grasslands became desert. But the two rivers, flooding annually, brought down mud which they deposited along their banks, building a fertile green strip across the desert. Men moved with their animals towards the two rivers which, with a few desert oases, were the only remaining sources of water. Next the nomads learnt to sow cereals – wheat and barley developed from wild grasses – in the mud beside the river. Dams and irrigation

**BRONZE AGE MESOPOTAMIA**

*Civilization spread gradually northwards along the broad, fertile valleys of the Tigris and Euphrates*

### HOMAGE TO THE GODS

*The Sumerians of early Mesopotamia believed that their principal function in life was to serve the gods. When they were not actually praying in person, they left stone statuettes of themselves (right) before their altars to pray on their behalf. The huge eyes symbolise awed adoration, and the hands are clasped in endless worship. Each Sumerian city had a temple to honour its own patron god, and beside the temple was sometimes built a massive ziggurat, a stepped brick pyramid crowned by a sanctuary for the use of the god when he came down among his people.*

*The ziggurat at Ur (drawing, left) was built in about 2100 BC for Su'en, the moon-god. It measured 700 ft round the base, and a triple staircase climbed 80 ft to the summit. The core of the ziggurat, most of which still stands today, was a solid mound of mud-bricks*

# Among the Sumerians, civilized society takes shape

canals had to be dug to conserve and carry the water; this required co-operative effort. By about 5800 BC the nomads had begun to form settlements along the lower Tigris and Euphrates, building mud huts to protect themselves from the winter storms. Some wild animals, lingering near the settlements of men, were domesticated; their skins provided clothing, and they produced milk, and flesh for food. Although man still hunted, he was no longer dependent on wild game for food, and so he could settle for long periods in one place.

A people originating probably from central Asia had become the dominant settlers throughout Mesopotamia by 4000 BC. These early Sumerians, as well as being skilled farmers, used tools of stone and flint, built large temples and made pottery with black decoration. By about 3500 BC the foundations for civilized life had already been laid along the Mesopotamian river valleys.

## Waging the first wars
The separate settlements of those earliest times remained the basis of Sumerian civilization throughout its 1000-year history. Sumer never became a strong unified state ruled, like Egypt, by one king and his officials. Instead it remained a number of separate city-kingdoms. Sometimes they joined together in a loose form of federation; sometimes they fought each other for control over a stretch of the all-important water from the two rivers or from major canals.

After such a war, one king or governor would temporarily become overlord of subordinate rulers. Captives taken in battle created for the first time a class of slaves.

Over a long period the Sumerians prospered and multiplied. Agriculture and cattle-breeding remained the main sources of their prosperity; but in time the Sumerian farmers produced a surplus over and above their immediate needs, enabling them to support people who neither tilled the ground nor reared cattle. These new resources brought into being a new class of builders, craftsmen, priests and scribes, who gradually moulded the Sumerian cities into the first centres of civilized society.

Mesopotamia had no readily available building stone, but in the dry climate bricks of clay dried in the sun were a sufficiently durable material, and with them the Sumerian builders raised huge cities on the riverside plains. Later builders simply levelled off earlier debris and erected new buildings on top, and as a result the ground level of the cities was gradually raised, forming artificial mounds known as tells. The remains of many of these early cities have been discovered by 19th and 20th-century archaeologists. They include Ur, just west of the Euphrates, 200 miles upstream from the Persian Gulf; Uruk, 40 miles further north, mentioned in the Bible as Erech and on the site of the modern Warka; and Nippur, 100 miles south of Baghdad. The Sumerians believed that the gods ruled the earth and

that men were created to be their servants. Each city was regarded as belonging to a particular god or goddess–such as Anu, god of the Heavens, Enlil, god of the Atmosphere, or Enki, god of the Water. In this early civilization, when drought might wither the crops, or other natural calamities such as floods or locusts might destroy them, men feared the anger of their gods. To appease this anger a hierarchy of priests carried out elaborate rituals within each town's temple, the earthly home of its god. Alongside the temple was sometimes built a lofty temple-tower, called a ziggurat.

## Wheels of solid wood
Within the temple enclosure were workshops for the craftsmen whose products helped to make Sumer prosperous. They were accomplished metal-workers, who learnt to make bronze by adding tin to copper and made spears, axes, tools and ornamental figures out of copper, bronze, gold and silver. Though the potter's wheel had been invented in prehistoric times, it was the Sumerians who devised the first wheeled vehicles, for their farm carts and war chariots. The earliest known vehicle wheels, shown on Sumerian tablets, date from about 3250 BC. They were made from three sections of solid wood, bound together with wood battens and a leather tyre.

In Sumerian society the way to advancement was literacy, for it was in Sumer, about 3000 BC, that the art of writing as we know it first

developed. It arose with the growth of commerce, when the Sumerians had to find a way to record their business transactions. At first simple pictorial representations of actual objects – known as pictographs – were inscribed on clay tablets with a reed stylus. Important records were preserved by baking the tablets.

Within 500 years these primitive pictographs evolved for convenience into abstract signs representing either whole words or syllables. The impression made in clay by a square-ended stylus resulted in a wedge-shaped sign, and the combination of these signs formed what is now known as cuneiform writing, after the Latin *cuneus*, meaning 'wedge'. Cuneiform writing spread throughout the Near East, and was used to transcribe a large number of different languages, including Babylonian and Persian.

The Sumerians were expert mathematicians, too; they counted in tens, as the modern world does, but also in sixties – hence the division of the circle into 360 degrees, of hours into 60 minutes, and of minutes into 60 seconds.

### Death pits of Ur

The most remarkable surviving relic of Sumerian civilization is the Royal Cemetery of Ur, dating from about 2500 BC, but completely unknown to the modern world until it was discovered by an English archaeologist, Sir Leonard Woolley, during the 1920's.

Near the city wall of Ur, Woolley found a series of graves. Thousands of graves had been plundered; but digging deep down Woolley found untouched sepulchres, made of stone brought from 30 miles away. The graves lay at the foot of deep shafts, with ramps leading down into them. Within these stone chambers, or 'death pits', lay the intact skeletons of men and women, possibly kings, queens, princes and princesses, or members of the high priesthood. The skeletons were adorned with rich regalia of gold, and semi-precious stones of exquisite workmanship. Near them lay fine golden cups and decorated vases.

The people buried in these sepulchres were of such high importance in the land that they were accompanied at their burial by a mass sacrifice of their attendants. In one pit, Queen Shubad's grave, were the skeletons of 68 women of the court, wearing gold or silver headdresses. With them were soldiers armed with spears, and even two-ox wagons with their slain animals. The most extraordinary fact about this holocaust, in which the living went to their deaths beside the graves of their rulers, was that these men and women had evidently died voluntarily. There was no sign of violence. The bodies lay in orderly rows as if they had gone to sleep. They may have taken poison or a narcotic before the pits were refilled.

### Sargon the empire-builder

In about 2300 BC, nearly the whole of Mesopotamia, including Sumer, was conquered by a military leader named Sargon. He led the

### GILGAMESH AND THE FLOOD

Sumerian literature abounds in epic tales, which are among man's earliest inscriptions on clay tablets. The folk-hero Gilgamesh, king of the ancient city of Uruk, is depicted holding a forester's axe in this 8th-century BC alabaster relief from the palace of Sargon II at Khorsabad. In the *Epic of Gilgamesh*, the king meets the survivor of a great flood. One passage of the poem is so like the Old Testament description of the Flood as to leave no doubt that the writers of Genesis were drawing on very ancient sources. The passage reads:

'Mount Nisir held the ship fast, Allowing no motion . . . When the seventh day arrived, I sent forth and set free a dove. The dove went forth but came back; since no resting place was visible she turned round. Then I sent forth and set free a swallow. The swallow went forth but came back.'

A raven is sent forth when the flood recedes, '. . . and seeing that the waters had diminished, he eats, circles, caws, and turns not round'

### THE RULERS AND THE RULED

*Society in Sumer was complex enough to have several different social classes, some of which are represented on the mosaic panels of the Royal Standard of Ur. The 'standard', a wooden box, 18 in. long, was probably the sounding board of a musical instrument. A king (top left) drinks wine with his courtiers, while a musician plays a bull's-head lyre. Below are depicted the herdsmen and fishermen whose labour helped to support a leisured class. The figures are made from shell, lapis lazuli and red limestone*

# The first written records of man

Akkadians, a Semitic people who had for long been the northern neighbours of the Sumerians, sharing much of their culture. But while the Sumerians were divided into more or less independent city-states, Sargon wanted to create a unified kingdom. He made war on Lugalzaggesi, one of the principal rulers of Sumer, and imprisoned him in a cage in the city of Nippur, one of the Sumerians' chief religious centres. Then he conquered the rest of the country, becoming ruler of the combined kingdom of Sumer and Akkad.

Sargon did not stop even there. He added northern Mesopotamia to his conquests, campaigned as far north as Anatolia (modern Turkey), and probably reached the Mediterranean coast. Sargon reigned for 56 years and created the first empire known to history; but its administration was not secure enough to prevent it from collapsing after Sargon's death under the raids of the Gutians, a mountain people from the north-east.

After more than a century of Gutian domination, Sumerian power revived in about 2100 under a number of gifted leaders, of whom Ur-Nammu was the greatest. Among the enormous buildings created by Ur-Nammu was the great ziggurat to the moon-god Su'en at Ur. This ziggurat is impressive even in decay, but in its original glory it soared to a height of some 70 or 80 ft, with a steep flight of stairs rising to its topmost tower.

## Epics and epigrams

Sumerian writings preserved on tablets of baked clay range from trading and legal records to the so-called wisdom literature, which consists of philosophical reflections like the Proverbs. This wisdom literature is one of the most important legacies of ancient Mesopotamia, not only for what it tells us about life in Sumerian cities such as Ur, Nippur and Uruk, but as literature in its own right. Many of the homely, shrewd observations still have relevance today:

'A restless woman in the house adds ache to pain.'

'We are doomed to die; let us spend.
We shall live long; let us save.'

'He who possesses much silver may be happy.
He who possesses much barley may be happy.
But he who has nothing at all can sleep.'

'You can have a lord, you can have a king,
but the man to fear is the tax-collector.'

Sumerian literature also contains many epic tales centred round its early rulers. They include one of the great epic poems of the world – the *Epic of Gilgamesh*. Gilgamesh was said to be king of Uruk, though whether he was a real monarch or a mythical ruler cannot be certain. The epic shows him as a pioneer and man of action, venturing into the cedar forests with his companion Enkidu – representing the civilized nomad – to find and defeat Humbaba, the guardian of the forests. This story may symbolise the invasion of the distant cedar forests by plainsmen, who needed the wood for building. The epic goes on to describe how Gilgamesh,

in search of immortality, journeys to see the immortal Utnapishtim, survivor of a great flood. Lower Mesopotamia was subject to devastating floods when the rivers overflowed, and the story may commemorate one especially catastrophic deluge. In the poem, Utnapishtim helps Gilgamesh to discover the 'plant of youth' – but Gilgamesh loses it on his way home.

## Schooldays in Sumer

At a homelier level, there are records of the curriculum and punishments at Sumerian schools. One tablet describes a typical day at school 4000 years ago:

'Arriving at school in the morning I recited my tablet, ate my lunch, prepared my new tablet, wrote it, finished it, then they assigned me my oral work . . . When school was dismissed, I went home, entered the house, and found my father sitting there. I told my father of my written work, then recited my tablet to him, and my father was delighted . . .'

For scribes destined only for simple account-keeping, simple arithmetic was sufficient. But the gifted Sumerians knew algebra and geometry as well. They also studied medicine, had a rudimentary knowledge of anatomy and surgery, and understood the medicinal properties of such plants as myrtle and thyme.

The literature of the Sumerians was inherited by the Babylonians and the Assyrians, who succeeded them; copies of Sumerian and early Babylonian tablets were kept and stored in libraries, and provided a literary inheritance to which the later people added their contributions. In time, much of this knowledge was passed on to the Greeks and the Romans, and so to the Western world.

## Mari's 250-room palace

The power of the Sumerians was finally destroyed by a new Semitic invasion about 2000 BC, when Elamites from Persia and Amorites from the north-west established themselves in Mesopotamia and founded flourishing city-states, which were to struggle for supremacy in two centuries of civil war. The most remarkable of these city-states was Mari on the middle Euphrates, a city impressive for its size and regular plan. The remains of palaces, houses and workshops are laid out in orderly streets on a grid pattern like a modern city, and there are fine sculptures, coloured frescoes and cemeteries. The women who are depicted in statues and frescoes wear long, flounced skirts, similar to those worn by the high-born women of Minoan Crete at about the same time.

The main palace of Mari has 250 rooms, ranging from the residential quarters of the royal family to the school, still with its rows of mud-brick benches for the pupils. Writing implements were also found. In these rooms were trained the boys who were to become civil servants, administering the territory of god and king. Here also patient scribes and scholars copied poems, proverbs and palace accounts on tablets, of which some 20,000 have been

A glittering mass of treasure that had lain buried for 4500 years came to light when a royal tomb at Ur was excavated earlier this century. The Sumerians, who made the world's first bronze weapons and tools, were equally skilled in making rich and delicate ornaments which were often buried with the dead

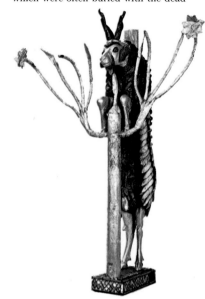

GILDED GOAT *The statuette of a goat rearing up on a tree has face and legs of gold leaf, and fleece of lapis lazuli and white shell. The tree is gold*

PRINCE'S HELMET *This helmet, shaped like a wig, was made from a single sheet of solid gold. The ears, the headband and the hair, knotted at the back, are faithfully reproduced. The helmet probably belonged to a prince. Laces through the holes round the edge held a padded lining. The gaming board, with counters (above, right), is inlaid with coloured stones*

preserved. The long period of warring among the Mesopotamian city-states was at last ended by the Amorite king Hammurabi, who ascended the throne of Babylon in 1792 BC. Babylon, on the middle Euphrates, had been a large and prosperous city for 300 years; but it was Hammurabi who made it the dominant power in Mesopotamia and the surrounding lands. In his 42-year reign he embarked on a programme of imperial conquest; he drove north into Assyria, westwards towards the Mediterranean and southwards to the Persian Gulf, overwhelming the Sumerians.

## Just and humane laws

Hammurabi was one of history's great law-givers. A stone pillar, or stele, found at Susa and now in the Louvre at Paris, is inscribed with the details of his legal decisions, showing evidence of a high standard of legal procedure which existed 15 centuries before the laws of

ADORNMENT FOR A LYRE *A magnificent bearded bull decorates the wooden framework of a lyre. It was found in one of the so-called 'death pits' of the Royal Cemetery at Ur, near the bodies of women who were probably court musicians. The bull's hair and the ringlets of its beard are of lapis lazuli, while the rest of the head is covered with gold leaf. Animal heads were often used as decorations on Sumerian harps, and their elaborate gilding preserved them under the earth long after the instruments themselves had perished. Experts have, however, been able to reconstruct some instruments by taking casts of impressions left in the soil by their wooden frames, long decayed*

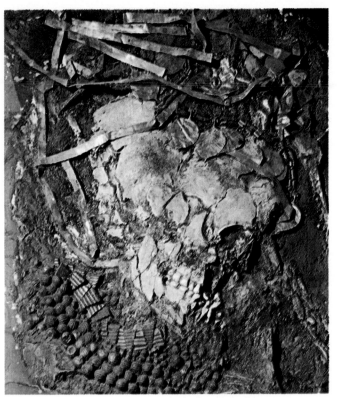

SACRIFICIAL VICTIM *The servants of Sumerian kings and queens were put to death when their rulers died, and buried in the same tombs. Many bodies and rich ornaments buried in the cemetery at Ur were crushed by the weight of the earth thrown on top of them. The shattered skull of a female attendant (above) lies exactly as it was found after 4500 years; her elaborate golden head-dress lies broken in pieces, but a jewelled necklace is still in place. Experts have pieced together a broken necklace (below); the pendants, some shaped like beech and willow leaves, are made of finely beaten gold*

the Romans. Many of the laws were based on earlier traditions dating from Sumerian times, but their scope was much more comprehensive. By the standards of the time, the laws were just, and reasonably humane:

'If a man has been made prisoner during a raid or an invasion, or if he has been carried off forcibly and stayed in a foreign country for a long time, and if another man has taken his wife and she has borne him a son – when he returns he shall have his wife back.'

Women's rights were protected also:

'If a man has turned his face away from his first wife . . . but she has not gone out of the house, the wife whom he married as his favourite is his second wife; he shall continue to support the first wife . . .'

Many crimes carried the death penalty; they included theft, adultery and making false accusations. There were stern provisions covering the responsibility of professional men towards their clients: one case recorded is that of a doctor who, through carelessness or inefficiency, caused a patient to lose the sight of an eye, and was penalised by the loss of his own hand. When a house fell on its owner, the builder was put to death, or at least heavily fined. This is the first record of the 'eye-for-an-eye' principle of retaliation which, through Moses, passed into the law of the Hebrews.

Hammurabi also made important religious reforms. The old Sumerian gods continued to be worshipped, but the Babylonian god, Marduk, was by now worshipped as head of the pantheon. Religion was centred upon the Esagila temple at Babylon, adjoining which was built an immense ziggurat, the original Tower of Babel, which was designed, according to the Book of Genesis, to reach heaven. Soon after Hammurabi's death the kingdom he founded fell into decay, to be conquered six centuries later by the Assyrians, another Semitic people who had established themselves further north, on the upper Tigris. Their principal city of Assur had formerly been ruled by Hammurabi from Babylon, but now it was the turn of the dark-haired, stocky Assyrians to build a great empire of their own.

## The rise of the Assyrians

The Assyrians were forced by their geographical location to fight many wars to keep their trade routes open. For a time their expansion was delayed by the powerful Hittites to the north, but with the collapse of the Hittite Empire in about 1200 BC the Assyrians took the offensive. Their superior iron weapons, skill in warfare and strong leadership made them more than a match for their relatively weak neighbours. One of their kings, Tiglath-pileser I, stormed and took Babylon, and by 1100 the Assyrians controlled territory which

# The Assyrian conqueror sweeps in, 'like the wolf on the fold'

The kings of ancient times were also the judges of their people. Hammurabi, the 18th-century BC King of Babylon whose stone effigy (above) was found at Susa, was one of history's earliest law-givers, and the record of his decisions in nearly 300 cases established precedents for his successors. Precise penalties were fixed for a wide range of offences, most of the punishments being based on the principle of 'an eye for an eye'

LAWS CUT IN STONE *The judgments of Hammurabi were inscribed in 3600 lines of cuneiform writing on an 8 ft high stone pillar. At its head, the king receives the symbols of justice from the Babylonian sun-god*

ROYAL LION-HUNT

*Assyrian kings enjoyed hunting, and it was one of their royal duties to destroy the marauding mountain lions which preyed on people and livestock. In this alabaster relief from Nimrud, King Assurnasirpal II draws his bow on a wounded lion as armed beaters drive it towards his chariot. Sometimes the king, armed only with a sword, challenged the king of beasts on foot*

stretched from the Mediterranean north to Lake Van in present-day eastern Turkey. There followed a period of decline, in the course of which the Assyrians, perhaps lacking forceful rulers, were apparently crowded out by their neighbours, losing Babylon and the western territories. Then, in the 9th century BC, Assurnasirpal II became king of the Assyrians. This aggressive military genius reorganised his country's army and opened a new age of Assyrian greatness, based on his capital of Calah, the modern Nimrud, on the Tigris. His son Shalmaneser III continued this expansionist policy, conquering city after city. The little kingdoms of Palestine and Syria allied against him, but still had to pay him tribute.

## Winged bulls of Nineveh

The conquests of the Assyrians, so hated by the Old Testament chroniclers, were as violent and brutal as they were numerous. The Assyrians used powerful siege engines and battering rams against enemy cities which broke the peace treaties they had signed. One of their rulers, who took the name of Sargon II, built his mighty capital at Khorsabad, where he adorned his palace walls with vigorous sculptures depicting the defeat of his foes and the sack of their towns.

Sargon's son, Sennacherib (705–681 BC), moved his capital to Nineveh, where some of the finest Assyrian sculptures have been found. They include winged bulls and carved reliefs of battle, showing how the Assyrians flayed the elders of rebel cities and hung their skins on the walls.

Sennacherib sacked and burnt Babylon. In his own words: 'The city and its houses, from its foundation to its top, I destroyed, I devastated, I burnt with fire . . . Through the midst of that city I dug canals. I flooded its site with water, and the very foundations thereof I destroyed.'

Jerusalem was also besieged, in 701 BC – the occasion on which, in the words of Byron's poem, 'the Assyrian came down like the wolf on the fold'. Sennacherib extorted tribute from Hezekiah; according to the Old Testament 'Hezekiah cut off the gold from the doors of the temple of the Lord and from the pillars, and gave it to the king of Assyria'. Inscriptions in Sennacherib's own palace boast of how he shut up Hezekiah 'like a caged bird'. But the Assyrians failed to take Jerusalem before plague forced them to withdraw.

For all their love of war, the Assyrians were far from being mere barbarians. Their cities were magnificently planned, and city life was highly organised by officials, who were members of the aristocracy, working under the direction of the king. Wealth came from the land and from foreign trade, plus the loot of conquest. To adorn the palace of Assurbanipal (669–627 BC), the last great Assyrian king,

gold and ivory were brought from Egypt, silver from Syria, lapis lazuli from Persia and cedarwood from the Lebanon. Merchants traded in manufactured goods, especially fabrics, and also in horses and camels. Gold, silver and copper were used as currency.

## The fall of an empire

Only 14 years after the death of Assurbanipal, this widespread empire collapsed entirely. The strength of his personality had drawn attention away from the forces that were undermining the empire: the over-extension of its boundaries and the drain on the exchequer of continual foreign wars; the rebellion of captive peoples; perhaps even a weakening of the morale of the army due to heavy losses in almost continuous campaigns. Whatever the reason, Assyria came to a bloody end and, in the Old Testament, the prophet Nahum exults over the fall of Nineveh.

'Woe to the bloody city! It is all full of lies and robbery: the prey departeth not, the noise of a whip, and the noise of the rattling of the wheels, and the prancing horses, and the jumping chariots. The horseman lifteth up both the bright sword and the glittering spear, and there is a multitude of slain, and a great number of carcasses . . .'

Nineveh fell in 612 BC after a joint attack by the Babylonians and the Medes. The Assyrian Empire was divided between the victors, and the Babylonians, under the leadership of

THE RULER'S REPRESENTATIVES AMONG THE PEOPLE

*As the Assyrians expanded their empire they created a large and efficient civil service to run it. The two officials in this wall-painting from the governor's palace at Til Barsip, Syria, have the characteristic* *Assyrian dark hair and wear the headbands, earrings and embroidered robes of formal court wear. A governor represented the king in each province, and his officials collected taxes in produce or in precious metals*

# Babylon, most splendid city of the ancient world

Reliefs in Assurnasirpal's palace at Nimrud show the skills which made the Assyrians an almost invincible fighting force. Archers (above) were the mainstay of the Assyrian infantry. They shot from behind tall wicker shields, and carried daggers and swords of iron – the new metal which made their weapons stronger than their opponents'

SIEGE WEAPON *After chasing their enemies from the field, the Assyrians used battering rams to breach the walls of their cities. The ram, as this drawing from a relief shows, was mounted on a six-wheeled vehicle. It was tipped with metal in the shape of an axe blade, and could be levered left and right from within the turret*

RUTHLESS VICTORS *The Assyrians were pitiless in battle. In this drawing from a relief, archers shoot at fugitives crossing a river on inflated goat-skins*

Nebuchadnezzar, took the region to the south and west. Under his rule, Babylon rose again, more than 1000 years after the age of Hammurabi, to become greater than ever. In the 5th century the Greek historian Herodotus described Nebuchadnezzar's Babylon as 'surpassing in splendour any city of the known world'. Even today its massive tumbled mounds of mud-brick have the power to awe.

At the beginning of the present century a German archaeologist, Robert Koldewey, conducted excavations at Babylon and found that its walls, 13 ft thick at the base, made a circuit of 11 miles. The city was divided into three districts, and near its centre stood the main palace of Nebuchadnezzar, near a sacred processional way.

The Babylonians had no stone, but they used glazed tiles to cover the mud-brick walls, and with this material Babylonian artists created sculptured patterns of great force and beauty. Koldewey and his successors were able to reconstruct many of these decorative motifs in glazed tiles or bricks, including the noble Avenue of Lions along the processional way – fierce beasts intended to intimidate the hearts of those approaching the monarch's palace.

'I laid the foundation of the new palace firmly,' Nebuchadnezzar wrote, 'and built it mountain high with bitumen and baked bricks. Huge cedars I caused to be laid for its roof, door leaves of cedar mounted with copper, thresholds and hinges made of bronze I fitted to its gates. Silver, gold, precious stones, all that is costly and glorious, wealth and goods, ornaments of my exaltedness I stored within it, and immense abundance of royal treasures I accumulated in it.'

## The 'hanging gardens'

During Nebuchadnezzar's reign also were built the Hanging Gardens of Babylon, accounted by the Greeks as one of the Seven Wonders of the World. Traces of these gardens have been found near the palace in the form of a massive arched substructure, with thick layers of earth on the roof. In chambers beneath this structure were three shafts, which may have accommodated pumps to raise water to the gardens above. These were probably on a huge stepped pyramid, its ledges covered with earth and planted with flowers and trees. There may have been footpaths winding up through the gardens.

The Babylonians were travellers and traders. Their ships, manned by Phoenician seamen, sailed down the Euphrates to the Persian Gulf to bring back produce from Arabia and India. Their caravan routes extended northwards into Asia Minor, westwards to Syria and eastwards to Persia. Their own exports included wool, woven fabrics and barley. Thousands of invoices, bills of lading and trading agreements have been found on cuneiform tablets. Minerals were imported from Armenia, floated down the river on rafts made of inflated skins.

The Babylonians also studied the heavens, made star maps, observed the movements of the planets, to which they gave names, and tried

to predict eclipses of the sun and moon. The city of Babylon fell in 539 BC to the Medes and Persians. Their joint attack came while the Babylonian king Belshazzar, last of his line, was giving a great feast, which is vividly described by the prophet Daniel.

'Belshazzar the king made a great feast to a thousand of his lords, and drank wine before the thousand. Belshazzar, while he tasted the wine, commanded to bring the gold and silver vessels which his father Nebuchadnezzar had taken out of the temple which was in Jerusalem, that the king and his princes, his wives and his concubines, might drink therein. They drank wine, and praised the gods of gold, and of silver, of brass, of iron . . . and stone.'

## After Belshazzar's feast

Belshazzar's command was a gesture of contempt towards the Jews, whom Nebuchadnezzar had brought in captivity to Babylon. But while all this festivity and splendour was taking place in the king's palace, outside in the darkness the forces of King Cyrus the Great of Persia had found a way to penetrate the city's apparently impregnable defences.

The Euphrates ran through Babylon, but it was too deep to be forded. Herodotus describes how Cyrus ordered his men to dig canals, so that the river was diverted into a marsh, and his troops could make their way along the river bed into the town.

'Owing to the great size of the city the outskirts were captured without the people in the centre knowing anything about it; there was a festival going on, and even while the city was falling they continued to dance and enjoy themselves . . .'

It was then, according to Daniel, that there 'came forth fingers of a man's hand, and wrote . . . upon the plaster of the wall of the king's palace; and the king saw the part of the hand that wrote. And this is the writing that was written, *Mene, mene, tekel, upharsin* . . . Thou art weighed in the balances, and art found wanting. Thy kingdom is divided, and given to the Medes and Persians.' Until Daniel interpreted the words, the Babylonians would have read them as a mathematical problem based on a series of weights – the *mana*, the *shekel* and the *pharsin*, or half-*shekel*.

## Centuries of plunder

The Persians did not destroy Babylon, but preserved it as part of their growing empire, for they in their turn were to become the dominant power in Mesopotamia. A century later still, Alexander the Great planned to revive the city as a jewel among his eastern dominions, but after his death and the division of his empire it fell into decay.

Its inhabitants abandoned it, and all that survives of Babylon today are the remains of 2000 years of plunder and neglect. Even so, its ruins stand as an awesome relic of one of the greatest cities of ancient Mesopotamia, a symbol of more than 3000 years of civilization in the 'land between the two rivers'.

## THE ISHTAR GATE, ENTRANCE TO NEBUCHADNEZZAR'S CAPITAL ON THE EUPHRATES

*Nebuchadnezzar, King of Babylonia from 605 to 562 BC, was a tireless builder who made Babylon the most splendid city of its time. Of eight gateways in the massive walls, each sacred to a different god, the most imposing was the huge Ishtar Gate, built in honour of the Babylonian goddess of love and battle, and rising 50 ft above a sacred processional way into Babylon. This reconstruction of the gate now stands in the Pergamon Museum in Berlin. The walls of the flanking towers were*
*clad from top to bottom in glazed blue bricks, which were decorated with yellow and white reliefs of dragons, symbols of the Babylonians' chief god Marduk, and bulls, symbols of the lightning-god Adad. Baked bricks cemented into bitumen formed a solid core for the wall, and the foundations went down as deep as the wall was high. Overlooking the Ishtar Gate rose the famous Hanging Gardens; underground chambers found this century probably housed mechanism for raising water to the gardens*

# A kingdom ruled by
# divine pharaohs

## 3200 BC–AD 300

*Along the fertile valley of the Nile, the Egyptians built
colossal tombs of stone for the kings
who for 3500 years reigned over them as gods*

### EGYPT IN 1450 BC

*From the 600-mile valley of the life-
giving Nile, Egypt expanded as far as
the Euphrates during the New Kingdom*

The most spectacular monuments left by
any people of the ancient world were
the work of a civilization which took root
in the narrow seed-bed of the Nile Valley, and
blossomed for the astonishing span of 3500
years. The legacy of Egypt includes the Pyramids of Giza, the Great Sphinx and the fabulous
treasures of the boy king Tutankhamun. But
perhaps the most remarkable remains of all lie
in a museum room in modern Cairo, where a
visitor may look on the actual faces of some of
the greatest rulers in Egyptian history, kings
who died 2500 years before Christopher
Columbus and his successors carried European
civilization to the Americas.

To the ancient Egyptian, the survival of his
mummified body was a guarantee of life beyond
death. The powerful religious belief of the
Egyptians was the mainspring of their civilization. It inspired the building of great temples
along the Nile which still stand today, such
as the pillared hall at Karnak and the great
monuments built by Ramesses II at Abu Simbel.

Religion provided the rules that guided all
Egyptian art. And despite popular belief, the
pyramids were not built by sweating foreign
slaves under the lash of brutal taskmasters, but
by the Egyptians themselves, who probably
saw their labour as an act of religious dedication to their pharaohs.

The other great influence in the history of
Egypt was the River Nile. Without it, Egypt
would be a lifeless desert. The Nile flows the
full length of the country – 600 miles from south
to north. It is Egypt's main highway and only
effective source of water – nowhere in the
country does the average annual rainfall exceed
$1\frac{1}{2}$ in. Rising at Lake Victoria in the heart of
Africa, the Nile at the southern border of Egypt
enters a long, narrow valley. Every August,
until the Aswan High Dam was completed in
1971, the river, swollen by rain and melting
snow in the far-off mountains of Abyssinia,
flooded much of this valley and spread a
blanket of silt as far as the edge of the desert.
When the flood receded, the mud remained,

### EMBLEM OF MAJESTY

*For 4500 years the Great Sphinx (left)
has guarded the pyramids of Giza. It is
240 ft long and 66 ft high, and was
carved from an outcrop of rock by order
of King Chephren. The statue represents
the king with the body of a lion, symbolising the awesome power of the ruler.
The pyramid of Chephren, to the left,
was the second of three pyramids built at
Giza as tombs to preserve the bodies
of Egyptian kings for eternity. Their
builders had neither iron tools nor
wheeled vehicles, yet they laid the huge
limestone blocks, some weighing as much
as 15 tons, within one-fiftieth of an
inch of each other.*

*The drawing on the right shows how
the blocks may have been pulled from
the quarries on sledges and then hauled
up the pyramid along ramps of mud.
When the pyramid was complete, workers
removed the mud from the top downwards,
polishing the stone as they went. The apex
of Chephren's pyramid still has some of
its polished limestone facing*

# God-kings who created the world's first nation

## WHERE RECORDS BEGAN

A 2 ft high palette found in the ruins of a temple at Nekhen dates from 3100 BC. It is the world's first historical record, and the earliest example of the Egyptians' hieroglyphic writing. In scenes and symbols it represents episodes in the struggles by King Narmer of Nekhen in Upper, or southern, Egypt to conquer the north and unite both parts of the country under his rule. Later tradition gave the king the name of Menes. He is shown clubbing an enemy, with naked fugitives beneath his feet. The picture symbols, upper right, are believed to read 'Horus (the king as a falcon-god) leads captive 6000 Northmen'. Symbols at the top of the tablet indicate the king's name – a cuttlefish, or *nar*, and a chisel, or *mer*

THREE CROWNS *As lords of two kingdoms, pharaohs after Narmer had a choice of crowns. The White Crown (left) symbolises rule over Upper Egypt, while the Red Crown (centre) represents Lower Egypt. Sometimes the two were combined in the Double Crown (right)*

and in this, every year for 6000 years, Egyptian farmers sowed their grain. Every year the crops sprang up under the warmth of the Egyptian sun. It was on this thin green strip along the Nile's edge that Egyptian civilization arose and flourished.

Beyond high-water level the Nile Valley is arid desert; the transition from rich cultivation to sterile wilderness is startling. The ancient Egyptians called the fertile strip the Black Land and the desert the Red Land. The Black Land held the fields and homes of the living; the low desert beyond was the realm of the dead, where the great pyramids and mortuary temples of the pharaohs were built, and the nobles had their tombs carved. Here too were the more modest cemeteries where countless generations of humbler Egyptians were buried.

The low desert extends to the cliffs which mark the limit of the Nile Valley – in some places only a few hundred yards away from fertile Black Land, in other places as much as 10 miles. These cliffs were the edge of the ancient Egyptian's world. Above them, the high desert stretches away into the distance, 100 miles to the Red Sea on the east and, on the west, 3000 miles across the trackless Sahara to the west coast of Africa.

## Controlling the waters

The first Egyptians were wandering hunters and herdsmen. By about 5000 BC they had begun to descend from the uplands into the Nile Valley. They learnt to sow grain in the silt following the summer flood. They bred sheep, goats and cattle, dogs for hunting and donkeys as their beasts of burden. These prehistoric Egyptians learnt to plant and weave flax, to fashion pots and to build shelters of mud and reeds. They began to live in settled and ordered agricultural communities.

The Nile, though bounteous and in the main predictable, would sometimes rise too high, in which case there would be disastrous floods; and sometimes not high enough, when famine might result. As a result the early farmers learnt to band together, building dykes to control the waters, and storing grain for the lean years when crops failed.

As time went on, villages grew into towns, and districts into kingdoms. Life became more complex, and crafts and techniques more specialised. Life became richer as men learnt to work copper and stone, to paint vases and weave baskets, to make beer and cultivate the vine. The potter's wheel was introduced, probably from western Asia.

The invention of a script soon followed. Though the idea of writing may have been introduced from Mesopotamia, the hieroglyphic system, which employs pictorial signs to represent ideas and sounds, is entirely different from the cuneiform script of the Sumerians and must have evolved on Egyptian soil. The earliest examples of hieroglyphic writing are not, as in Sumer, economic texts, but historical records. Though imperfectly understood, they tell us something of the activities and achievements of the earliest

pharaohs. By about 3400 BC there were two principal kingdoms in Egypt, one of them governed from the region of the Nile Delta, called Lower Egypt, and the other from Nekhen, a town 45 miles south of Luxor, in Upper Egypt. These two kingdoms co-existed until, about 3200 BC, a king of Nekhen whom tradition called Menes conquered the north and became the first King of Upper and Lower Egypt – a title which was preserved throughout ancient Egyptian history.

Menes was the first in a long line of pharaohs whose names were preserved in the temple records. 'Pharaoh' is a biblical word from the Egyptian for 'great house' or 'palace', and though it was used in later times to refer to the king it was never his proper title.

## The making of a nation

Menes and his successors welded the north and south together, and so the Egyptians became the first ancient people to achieve nationhood, in a world where small principalities and city-states were the normal pattern of society. During the four centuries of Egypt's so-called Archaic period (3200–2800 BC), Egyptian armies encountered Nubian tribesmen and desert Bedouin in the search for raw materials such as hard stone, copper and gold. Their ships sailed north along the Mediterranean coast as far as the Lebanon for the long timber that Egypt lacked.

Writing progressed from short sequences of picture signs towards a developed script with a large number of signs. The Egyptians discovered a new writing surface far superior to the clay tablets of Mesopotamia – papyrus. The pith of the papyrus plant was cut into strips of equal length, which were placed side by side and beaten flat to produce smooth sheets on which scribes wrote in ink. Papyrus is the origin of the English word 'paper'.

Stone cutters, using only copper chisels and bow-drills, shaped delicate vessels from hard stone like diorite and porphyry; they used alabaster for the beauty of its veining, and rock-crystal for cups with walls of eggshell thinness. Carpenters showed astonishing skill in making inlaid boxes and furniture. Gold-workers and jewellers fashioned ornaments of sophisticated design, and copper was cast or hammered into a variety of tools and weapons.

## A body for the after-life

In prehistoric times the Egyptians buried their dead in holes dug in the sand. The dry climate prevented bodies from decomposing entirely, and many retained their skin and hair. This may have suggested to the Egyptians the idea of preserving the bodies of their kings and other leaders by the long and costly process of mummification.

Kings and nobles of the Archaic period were buried in large rectangular tombs called *mastabas*, box-like structures made of mud-brick, elaborately decorated and painted and sometimes with wooden roofs and stone floors. These tombs contained the food, furniture, weapons and ornaments to equip and supply the dead in the after-life. They also had a 'false door' through which the dead could communicate with the living. Food and drink would be brought to the tomb by priests or members of the dead man's family.

Even at this early stage attempts were made to preserve the body, but they were not yet very successful. The deceased were represented in their tombs by statues carved to resemble them; these, though walled up for safety in a closed chapel, were believed to breathe the incense and taste the food through a hole in the wall. Even the poor had their most cherished possessions – a dagger, perhaps a string of beads – and a few jars of food and drink buried with them in their shallow graves.

The first great period of Egyptian civilization, the so-called Old Kingdom, was heralded by the first use of stone for an entire building. King Zoser, whose reign began in 2780 BC, built near his capital of Memphis the Step Pyramid, the oldest stone monument in the world. This pyramid at Saqqara was designed by Zoser's renowned architect Imhotep, and it is the first of the enormous pyramid-tombs which still proclaim the superhuman status of their builders. The Step Pyramid began as a traditional *mastaba*, but was enlarged by stages until it became a huge six-stepped structure, rising to a height of 200 ft and measuring 358 ft by 410 ft at the base.

Less than a hundred years later the true pyramid evolved, with the burial chamber no longer underground but in the heart of the pyramid. Smooth facing concealed the entrance, and the massive limestone blocks, which weigh an average of $2\frac{1}{2}$ tons each, made tunnelling a formidable problem for tomb robbers. Nevertheless, many of the pyramids, like the earlier *mastabas*, were eventually broken into and ransacked.

## Staircase to the sun

What the pyramid shape symbolised is uncertain; it may be that the Step Pyramid represented a gigantic staircase by which the king mounted to the sun, while the sloping sides of the later pyramids suggested the rays of the sun up which the king ascended. For in ancient Egypt the king was thought to be endowed with a divinity which set him apart from ordinary mortals. As in life he was thought to be the incarnation of the sky-god Horus, so in death he joined the sun-god, Re, and sailed the heavens in his celestial boat.

Of all the monuments of antiquity, none has captured the imagination more than the three great pyramids at Giza. Within these vast mounds of stone, a father, his son and his grandson were buried in the 26th century BC. The largest and first, the Great Pyramid, was built by King Cheops (or Khufu), who was entombed in a granite chamber at its heart. The pyramid covers more than 13 acres and contains nearly 6 million tons of stone; it is 480 ft high, and its only entrance is 55 ft above the ground on the north face. The four sides of the pyramid run almost due north–south and east–west. The Great Pyramid was originally

### A PHARAOH WALKS WITH GODDESSES

*A stone group found in a funeral temple at Giza shows King Mycerinus, who reigned in about 2520 BC, in the company of the gods. On his right hand the king is embraced by Hathor, the greatest of the goddesses.*

*On his left he is supported by the patron goddess of Assiut, one of the provinces into which Egypt was divided. Above her head is the emblem of the district, a recumbent jackal carried on a pole*

63

# Peasant labourers and pyramid builders

PULLING THE PLOUGH *Cattle served the Egyptian peasant in many different ways. A wooden model of 2000 BC shows them hauling a primitive plough to prepare the ground for the sowing of corn. Oxen were used at threshing time to tread the grain and separate the seed from the husk. They also drew the coffins of pharaohs and nobles to their burial places, and pulled sledges loaded with stones to building sites*

HARVEST TIME *Paintings in the tomb of Menna, a Scribe of Fields in the 15th century BC, show work in progress on the fields under his care. Above, winnowers scoop up the grain and let it fall, so that the wind carries away the chaff. Below, some of the corn has been reaped and the ears are being carried in nets to the threshing floor. The fact that his painting was intended for a tomb did not prevent the artist from including two humorous touches—a boy asleep under a tree and two little gleaners quarrelling. Wheat, barley and flax were Egypt's staple crops; vegetables and fruit were also grown*

faced with the finest quality limestone, but little of this facing now remains. The second pyramid at Giza was built by Cheops's son, Chephren (or Khafra). Though slightly smaller, it is in some ways more impressive, for here the whole pyramid complex has been preserved. This includes not only the pyramid tomb itself, but also the mortuary temple on the eastern side, where offerings were made for the use of the dead king in the next life; the long causeway leading up from the valley; and also the valley temple, built of huge granite pillars, where the king's body was embalmed before burial. A knoll of limestone beside the causeway was carved into the Great Sphinx, the likeness of King Chephren as a human-headed lion. The third pyramid at Giza, built by Chephren's son Mycerinus (Menkaura), covers less than half the area of the Great Pyramid built by his grandfather.

## Ropes, ramps and manpower

The pyramid builders had no elaborate mechanical devices; they had not discovered the use of the pulley or the winch, the windlass or the crane. Their only resources were ropes and levers, a plentiful supply of stone and mud – and unlimited labour.

But though the Egyptians' equipment was limited, their ingenuity and persistence were extraordinary. By the sheer manpower of hundreds of men, they hauled great blocks of stone up sloping ramps of mud-brick, wetting the surface of the mud to make it slippery. On hard ground, rollers made the blocks move more easily. The hauling teams used ropes of twisted papyrus. Blocks of stone were quarried by splitting the rock face with copper chisels or sometimes by a row of wooden wedges, soaked so that they swelled and split the stone; the surface of the blocks was dressed on the spot by pounding it with lumps of hard stone. Pools of water contained in little mud walls served as spirit levels when an even surface was required.

The blocks cut from the cliffs were hauled to the river's edge, and ferried by barge to their destination; the fine white limestone used for the facing of the Great Pyramid was probably floated to the desert edge immediately below the pyramid site at the time of the valley's annual flooding.

In building a stone temple, mud was used as interior scaffolding. The height of the mud was raised as the walls and the pillars grew, so that sometimes the whole interior of the building would be filled with mud by the time the roof was laid. Then, as the mud floor was gradually lowered, the carving and painting of the temple could be carried out by labourers working from the top downwards.

## Powers of the pharaoh

To take part in the building of the pyramids and temples was for the Egyptian an act of deep significance. For the whole land of Egypt and its people belonged to the gods, and in particular to Horus, whom the pharaoh was believed to represent on earth during his lifetime. The pharaoh's function was to maintain

the whole order of the universe, established at the moment of creation and embracing not only the social and political structure of Egypt but also the laws of nature, the movement of the heavenly bodies, the rotation of the seasons and the annual flood and fall of the Nile. The thousands of peasant labourers who took part in the huge effort of building a temple or a tomb for the pharaoh were sharing in a deed which it was thought would bring splendid consequences for the land and people of Egypt.

Throughout Egyptian history, the king was held to have absolute authority in every sphere of the administration, though his day-to-day responsibilities were by necessity delegated to his vizier and an ever-increasing number of officials. Since the king alone could reach the gods, he was the channel through which men made contact with the spiritual world. He must intercede with the gods on the people's behalf, performing the proper rites and making the required offerings, in order that the gods might look benevolently on Egypt. In theory, therefore, the king was the chief priest in every temple in the land, and it was he who appointed other priests to high office and endowed the temples with their lands and revenues.

## A religion of many gods

The Egyptians had hundreds of gods; some were worshipped in particular towns or districts, while others became more widely venerated. Some gods took the form of creatures such as cows, bulls, lionesses, monkeys or crocodiles; others were cosmic forces, the sun and moon, stars and sky. The reason for the number of these gods, and the conflicting and often contradictory beliefs held about them, lay in Egypt's past. When the country was unified, the state religion had to absorb numerous local cults, many of them perhaps originating in the worship of primitive totems or sacred objects. Some were combined, some remained as they had always been, and even later attempts to form 'families' of gods did not succeed in simplifying the pantheon.

There was, however, a tendency to unite in a single god the functions of different local divinities, and certain gods, patronised by the pharaohs and worshipped in the greatest cities and the largest temples, took on the character of national gods. Such were Horus, the personal god of the king, Ptah the god of Memphis, Re the sun-god of Heliopolis, Hathor the cow-goddess, the special patron of women, and Amun (or Amon-Re) who in the New Kingdom became the most wealthy and important of all the gods of Egypt.

Because the rituals of worship were so important to the Egyptians, their art was concerned primarily with religion, rather than with a deliberate search for beauty. Sculptures and paintings were created not for the houses of the living but for temples and tombs. Even the battle scenes on the walls of New Kingdom temples and the scenes of daily life in nobles' tombs had a religious purpose. Artists were therefore bound by a set of rigid conventions which were observed, with little variation, for

## SERVANTS FOR THE AFTER-LIFE

*Painted wooden models were sometimes placed in tombs; magic, it was believed, would bring them to life for the use of the dead. In the tomb of Meketre, a wealthy Theban nobleman living in about 2000 BC,* *models of servants and retainers were placed to serve their master in death as they had done in life. This model shows Meketre's cattle being inspected during a census of livestock, as Meketre looks on from his dais*

3000 years. Figures in the round had to be upright and symmetrical. In a standing figure, the left foot must be advanced, the hands clenched at the sides unless holding a staff or sceptre. The position of hands and arms, the hairstyle, dress and ornaments were all governed by strict rules, and the relationship in size between different parts of the body had to follow fixed proportions.

The rows of silent, majestic, striding or seated figures in Egyptian sculpture appear monotonous at first glance, but closer inspection reveals many subtle differences between the figures, introduced by skilful modelling, perceptive portraiture, fine detail, even a lightness of touch betraying a sense of humour in the artist. The static formality of royal figures often contrasts with the free and brilliantly observed portrayal of servants and labourers who are shown in an infinite variety of attitudes – running, leaping, hauling on ropes, reaping and winnowing, or dancing and playing musical instruments for their masters. The artists' portrayal of animals, too, is masterly and shows acute observation. One characteristic of Egyptian paintings and reliefs that appears strange to Western eyes is the fact that although the Egyptian artist could clearly have drawn exactly what he saw, he deliberately chose to

ignore perspective. The explanation lies in the practical function of Egyptian art. The artist's function was to set down not what he saw but what he knew to be there. So he drew in a way that displayed each essential part of the human figure – head, shoulders, arms, legs and feet – as clearly as possible and in its most familiar aspect, whether from the side or from the front. Some modern artists have drawn inspiration from this cubist treatment of natural forms by the Egyptians.

### Mathematics and medicine

To assist the administration of ancient Egypt a system of mathematics was evolved very early to deal with problems such as building, land survey and tax assessment. The system, though extremely limited, enabled scribes to work with fractions and square roots, and to calculate the area of a circle or the volume of a cylinder. Though the Egyptians made little progress in predicting the movement of heavenly bodies, they named and mapped the stars. The 365-day calendar still used today is probably a legacy from the ancient Egyptians; they dated their year from the appearance of the star Sirius just before the Nile's annual floods, and divided it into 12 months. The Egyptians learnt anatomy from the preparation

---

### A SCRIBE AND HIS SYMBOLS

The profession of scribe was held in great esteem in ancient Egypt, and knowledge of reading and writing was the first step to an official career. Education consisted of learning by heart and copying. Model letters were used as exercises

THE SCRIBE *A statue of 2500 BC shows a scribe waiting for dictation. He once held a reed pen. A scribe had to memorise 700 signs, each representing an object or an associated idea, or a word with a similar sound*

*life    eye, to do    old    with    ruler    night    a god*

# *Temples built to the gods of the Nile*

of human bodies for mummification, and Egyptian doctors and surgeons were famous throughout the ancient world. Imhotep, the architect of the Step Pyramid, was also later renowned as a physician, and was revered as the patron of doctors. Centuries of experiment with the healing properties of various substances and plants, including the opium poppy, had given Egyptian doctors a sound understanding of medicines.

Medical treatises that have survived from ancient Egypt deal with the diagnosis or treatment of a number of ailments. These treatments often involved the use of magic, and some maladies with no obvious cause had to be exorcised by spells or incantations. Nevertheless the treatment recommended for specific illnesses is in many cases endorsed by modern medical opinion, and one papyrus dealing with bone fractures shows remarkably advanced clinical knowledge.

## A century of civil war

The builders of the Giza pyramids left few records other than their portraits in stone and their huge monuments. But from these alone it is evident that the resources at their disposal must have been unlimited, and their power absolute. But after about 2500 BC dynastic feuds began to weaken the throne. Gifts of land

and tax exemptions granted to supporters drained the resources of the Crown, and the authority of the central government became less and less effective.

After the longest reign in history – that of Pepy II, who came to the throne as a small boy and lived to be 100 – unified rule collapsed and for the next 100 years Egypt was torn by civil war. Local governors claimed the right to wear the crown, but those who mounted the throne in Memphis, and then in Herakleiopolis in middle Egypt, were not recognised by the southern principalities. Insecurity and strife left the frontiers unguarded, and Nubians and Asiatic Bedouin raided the land.

In 2050 BC, the country was once more unified and order restored, by a family from the district of Thebes in Upper Egypt, led by Mentuhotep, 'Uniter of the Two Lands'. During his long reign Mentuhotep laid the foundations of a new prosperity. Quarries were reopened, temples and palaces built, and seaborne trade began again.

The Middle Kingdom, which lasted from 2050 to 1780 BC, was something of a feudal age for Egypt, during which the government was no longer centralised around the court of the god-king. Though the power of the pharaoh was still as absolute as ever, local rulers who had assisted the royal family to power were

permitted to live in almost vice-regal state in their own provinces, and some of them managed to extend their domains.

Royal pyramids of the Middle Kingdom were still massive structures, but they were now built of mud-brick rather than of stone, while the tombs of local rulers were large and elaborate. These wealthy nobles kept their own troops, and set up statues of themselves in the local temples. Nevertheless the king kept his own large standing army, and the frontiers were firmly held; a string of forts manned by strong garrisons protected the south from possible invasion by hostile African tribes, and another line of forts guarded the Nile Delta in the north against attack from Asia. Trading vessels sailed southwards down the Red Sea to the 'Land of Punt', probably Somaliland, for ebony and incense, and northwards to the city-states of Syria for timber, lapis lazuli and other luxury articles from western Asia.

## Warriors of the New Kingdom

The semi-feudal authority of local rulers was brought to an end by an energetic and forceful king, Senusret III, who reorganised the country under the direct control of his vizier and other ministers of the Crown. But the monarchy was soon to decline again, weakened by disputes between powerful rival families. The most successful of the power groups proved to be the Hyksos, or 'Shepherd Kings', immigrants from Palestine or Syria, who settled in the eastern part of the Nile Delta and gradually extended their sway over Memphis and southwards over part of the Nile Valley.

In 1560 BC, however, the Theban prince Ahmose drove the last Hyksos into Palestine and launched the New Kingdom, a new and glorious era of empire such as the Egyptians had not dreamt of before.

Contact with the Hyksos introduced new weapons into the Egyptian army. These included the composite bow, made of horn and sinew, bound together, which could shoot much further than the simple longbow; the scimitar; and the horse and light chariot, which gave speed of manoeuvre to a flying column. Egyptian warriors of the New Kingdom were no longer lightly clad, wielding lance and club; instead they were helmeted and clad in coat-of-mail, and they clattered into war accompanied by large troops of mercenaries – professional auxiliaries who changed the fortunes of Egypt.

## Spoils of conquest

The king himself, on his gilded chariot, led his forces into battle. From early youth, princes were given a rigorous military and athletic training, particularly in archery and horsemanship, to equip them for their warlike task. It was a new concept of monarchy, and it changed the destiny of Egypt.

The pharaohs and their armies, no longer content merely to trade with neighbouring lands, embarked on a career of conquest destined to bring them into conflict with one after another of the great powers of western Asia; success carried them to the banks of the

---

### GODS FROM THE ANCIENT PAST

The local gods worshipped in different parts of Egypt did not disappear when the country became united. Instead they were all absorbed into the state religion and still commanded respect, though some altered their attributes and others were joined together into 'families' of gods. Many of the most ancient gods, dating from prehistoric times, took the forms of animals or birds and continued to be worshipped until the end of Egyptian civilization. Often they were depicted as having human bodies and animal heads. A wooden tablet dating from 1400 BC (left) shows Re-Harakhte, a god who combines the characteristics of two other gods. He has the falcon's head of Horus, the king's personal god; and he wears as a crown the solar disc of Re, the sun-god worshipped in Heliopolis, 'Sun City'. The god is shown being worshipped by a woman who has heaped offerings of food and drink before him. The god's rays bless the woman as they touch her face; the artist has fancifully transformed the sun's rays into a stream of little flowers

HOLDING UP THE SKY *One Egyptian legend of the creation of the universe tells of a sky-goddess, Nut, who stretches above the earth on all fours, her body studded with stars. On this papyrus found in a tomb, Shu, the god of the air,* supports *Nut. Reclining below Shu is Nut's husband Geb, the earth-god. Ram-headed spirits help Shu to separate the earth from the sky. One version of the legend held that Nut swallowed the sun each evening*

## TRIBUTE TO AMUN AT THE HEART OF AN EMPIRE

The pillared hall of the temple of Karnak, on the eastern bank of the Nile near Luxor, is part of a huge edifice begun in about 2000 BC and added to by successive pharaohs of the New Kingdom. It was built to the glory of Amun, the patron god of the city of Thebes who, because of the city's importance as capital of the empire, became the most revered of all Egypt's state gods. The 134 great columns in the hall are decorated with hieroglyphic inscriptions and scenes of Ramesses II making offerings to Amun and other gods. Beyond the hall, the ruins of gateways, courts, obelisks and shrines stretch away into the distance for a quarter of a mile

# The king who rejected Egypt's ancient gods

Euphrates and far into the Sudan. They returned home laden with spoils and with large numbers of prisoners. Most of these were dedicated as slaves to serve the national gods, especially to Amun, the Theban deity whose temple became fabulously wealthy and whose priests enjoyed unprecedented power in the land.

Huge building projects were undertaken; Karnak, the vast temple to Amun on the east bank of the Nile at Thebes, was enriched by each pharaoh in turn with new shrines, halls, pylons and obelisks; opposite, on the western bank, large mortuary temples were erected in which funerary services for the king's *ka*, or spirit, might be performed by the priests as long as time should last.

## The Valley of the Kings
The kings of the New Kingdom were no longer buried in imposing pyramids for all to see; their tombs were sunk deep into the rock, and hidden away in the lonely valley, now called the Valley of the Tombs of the Kings, where it was hoped they would be protected from tomb robbers. But not even this precaution could save them, and by the end of the New Kingdom, nearly every royal tomb had been entered and rifled, the contents dispersed and the gold treasures melted down. One notable exception was the tomb of Tutankhamun, where the inner

chamber remained intact. By the time of the New Kingdom, Egypt's bureaucracy had become large and complex, even perhaps unwieldy, and it was the ambition of everybody to learn to read and write, to enter the civil service. Everything had to be noted, listed, docketed; every transaction recorded and every loaf of bread counted. In an age without coinage, when taxes were paid in barley and cattle and salaries in bread and beer, an elaborate system of accountancy was clearly necessary.

In theory the king appointed officials to high office; in practice, a son usually succeeded to his father's office, though promotion by merit was by no means unknown. As the fount of justice, the king's edicts were law, but there appears to have been a body of written law to which the vizier could refer, and most disputes were settled by magistrates in local courts.

Papyrus scrolls of the late New Kingdom record the trial of a number of conspirators accused of high treason, and also a trial of tomb robbers accused of plundering the Theban royal tombs. In both cases the judges appear to have conducted their enquiries with a careful regard for the principles of justice. The accused were allowed to plead in person, and though the ringleaders were condemned to death, others were acquitted. Wealthy Egyptians enjoyed a gracious and highly sophisticated style

of living – 1000 years before Greek civilization reached its peak. They lived in comfortable villas, ate delicately spiced foods, boasted of the vintage of the wine in their cellars, and discussed the merits of craftsmen and the accomplishments of musicians.

## Comfort in the home
The house of a well-to-do Egyptian was of mud-brick, plastered white, with one or two storeys. Shutters or blinds would keep sunlight from the windows, and the large inner room would be lit by a series of 'skylights'. The walls were often painted with designs in bright colours. Furniture was simple but well designed, and comfortable even by modern standards: stools and couches had cushions stuffed with goose-down, and chairs had sprung backs. Beds were of wickerwork on a wooden frame and, for coolness at night, people did not sleep on pillows but rested their necks on a wooden headrest made to their measure. Tables, stands and boxes were often decorated with inlay. Each household baked its own bread and made its own beer.

Although the Egyptian way of life differed from contemporary civilizations · in western Asia, Egypt was never isolated. There was constant trade with the Babylonians and Assyrians, the Phoenicians, the Hittites and the Israelites. Egypt was influenced by its neighbours, and profoundly influenced them in its turn.

Egypt had particularly close contact with the Aegean world. Envoys from Crete and Mycenae brought diplomatic presents to the Egyptian court from about 1450 BC, and when the Mycenaean Greeks settled in Cyprus and the western seaboard of the Levant, they became deeply influenced by the oriental world in which they found themselves. When Greek visitors first arrived in person in Egypt they marvelled at the ancient civilization they found, at the cities with their thronged streets and brightly painted temples, their festivals and their pageantry.

## Skills of the craftsmen
Egyptian craftsmen, working under royal patronage, achieved a very high standard in the manufacture of furniture, ornaments and objects of daily use and decoration. Some techniques, such as those of metal-working, originated in Mesopotamia, but they were perfected on Egyptian soil. Ample supplies of copper from Sinai and from Nubia were available, but bronze and iron-working were not fully developed until later, as the Egyptians had no direct access to ores of iron and tin.

Rich veins of gold in Nubia and the eastern desert of Egypt provided the pharaohs with a medium of exchange. Caravans shuttled to and fro between the Egyptian court at Thebes and the capital cities of the western Asiatic powers; each Asiatic king was anxious for gold to embellish his palaces and enhance his prestige, and he sent back inlaid furniture, metals and precious stones in exchange. The decorative material known as Egyptian faience was probably also an invention imported from western

## AKHENATON AND THE AGE OF HERESY

One of the strangest episodes in ancient history began in 1377 BC when Amenophis IV rejected the traditional Egyptian cult of many gods and set up the worship of a single deity, the sun-god Aton. The king changed his name to Akhenaton, 'pleasing to the Aton', and built a new capital city. But the revolution lasted less than 20 years, before Tutankhamun restored the worship of the ancient gods

KING AND QUEEN *The revolution in religion under Akhenaton was accompanied by a new style of art, during which the traditions of formal portraiture were abandoned in favour of an exaggerated realism. Colossal statues of the king (right), over 13 ft high, once stood against pillars in the temple he dedicated to Aton at Karnak. They emphasised his thick lips, long head and protuberant stomach. By contrast, the painted limestone head (left) found in a sculptor's workshop at El-Amarna is a model of womanly beauty for all time. It is thought to represent Nefertiti, the wife of Akhenaton*

Asia, but it was manufactured in Egypt from very early times, and the rich blue colour, in particular, was greatly in demand. It consists of a core of powdered quartz covered by a lustrous glaze. The manufacture of opaque glass, too, was perfected by Egyptian craftsmen, and was often used in inlay work on jewellery or furniture as a substitute for lapis lazuli, turquoise or jasper. Woven linen sometimes equalled in quality the finest modern cambric. Egyptian garments were nearly always white, but occasionally they were woven in colours or embroidered; they were draped and elaborately pleated.

## The queen who became a king

The great expansion of Egypt's empire during the New Kingdom was carried out by a single dynasty of pharaohs which lasted for nearly 250 years. Only twice during the success story of this remarkable Theban family was there tension and crisis. The first occasion was a result of the ambition of a redoubtable woman, the queen-dowager Hatshepsut. After the death of her husband in about 1504 BC, Hatshepsut became regent for her young stepson and nephew, Tuthmosis III. Seizing the throne, she assumed the functions, the insignia and even the dress of a male pharaoh and ruled for nearly 20 years.

One of the most notable events of Hatshepsut's peaceful reign was a naval expedition to the Land of Punt, to bring back myrrh and frankincense and also ivory, ebony, panther skins and gold, the exotic merchandise of inner Africa. The expedition is commemorated in carvings in Hatshepsut's mortuary temple in Thebes. After her death, Tuthmosis in revenge set about obliterating from the records all trace of Hatshepsut and the officials who had supported her.

## A new doctrine, a new capital

The second crisis of New Kingdom times came in the 14th century BC when the pharaoh Amenophis IV attempted a bold reformation of Egyptian state religion. He repudiated the traditional worship of many gods and replaced them by a single deity, Aton, the disc of the sun. Amenophis broke with many of the ritual practices of conventional religion and forbade the worship of other gods, especially that of the powerful Amun.

In his desire to make a clean break with the past, Amenophis removed the court from Thebes to a virgin site at El-Amarna, 250 miles down the Nile, where a new city, Akhetaton, the 'Horizon of Aton', was hastily built. Here the king, taking the new name of Akhenaton and with his friends as courtiers to flatter and encourage him, lived what appears to have been an idyllic existence with his beautiful wife Nefertiti and their six daughters. But his success was short-lived: after his death, which may have been violent, the court returned to Thebes, the worship of Amun and other ancient gods was restored, and the priests tried to obliterate every inscription referring to the sun-god Aton. The boy king Tutankhamun,

## PRESERVING THE BODY FOR A LIFE BEYOND THE TOMB

The ancient Egyptians believed that when men died they went to an after-life that was so similar to life on earth that they would continue to need their earthly bodies. It was for this reason that they studied and perfected the art of embalming: they believed that by preserving the body from decay, the various parts of the human personality – the soul, intelligence, heart and spirit – could be re-united in it for all eternity. Mummification – the word comes from an Arabic word meaning bitumen – was a long and costly process. Internal organs which would hasten decay were removed, after which the body was desiccated by soaking it in a solution of salt and then in natron, an embalming powder. It was treated with resin, and then wrapped in bandages soaked in oils. Finally the mummy was placed within a shaped and painted coffin. The funeral ceremonies were magical rites to ensure that the mummy would enjoy eternal life in the underworld and partake of the food and drink brought to the tomb. Frequently, rich Egyptians would set aside a portion of their wealth to maintain a priest, one of whose tasks was the regular re-stocking of the tomb

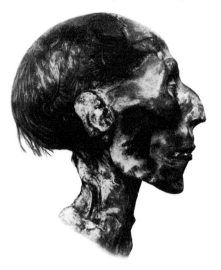

FACE OF A DEAD PHARAOH *The eagle-like head of Ramesses II, who died in 1237 BC when he was over 90, has been preserved for 3000 years. It was found in 1881. Ramesses was renowned as a warrior and builder during a reign of 67 years. He had four or five wives and more than 100 children*

MOURNERS AT THE FUNERAL *The knowledge that a dead man's spirit was destined for eternal life did not prevent his family and friends from bewailing him. A fresco from the tomb of Ramose, a vizier at Thebes in about 1400 BC, shows women mourners wailing and tearing their hair as the funeral cortège approaches on its way to the tomb*

THE JUDGMENT OF SOULS *In the after-life, every mortal had to face judgment. The ordeal is depicted on a 13th-century BC papyrus Book of the Dead from the tomb of Ani, a scribe. The jackal-headed god Anubis weighs Ani's heart against the feather of truth; if sins weighed down his heart, Ani would be devoured by the waiting monster*

INTO THE UNDERWORLD *The ancient Egyptians believed that after death every mortal became one with Osiris, the god of the underworld. Most tombs contained a model boat in which, it was believed, the soul would be able to make the pilgrimage to Abydos, the sacred city of Osiris, where his death and resurrection were yearly re-enacted. The mummy is tended by women mourners who play the parts of Isis and Nephthys, the goddesses who wailed for Osiris and brought him back to life*

# Legacy of a golden empire

the husband of one of Akhenaton's daughters, was a puppet in the hands of the priests and the army. He died at the age of only 19. When his widow Ankhesenamun found herself friendless she sent in despair to King Suppliluliumas of the Hittites asking for the hand of a Hittite prince in marriage. Her plan went astray, the prince was murdered on his way to Egypt, and the Hittites and the Egyptians became bitter enemies. After some 50 years of hostilities, the two armies met for the last time at Kadesh on the River Orontes in Syria. Ramesses II of Egypt, whose courage seems to have exceeded his prudence, was ambushed by the enemy and won the day only by a combination of luck and personal bravery.

The battle of Kadesh is commemorated in pictures and verse on the walls of several of his monuments, notably on the temple hewn into the rock face at Abu Simbel, on the orders of Ramesses. This majestic temple, fronted by four colossal stone figures, was cut out of the rock and reassembled at the top of a nearby cliff in 1968 to save it from being inundated by the waters of the lake formed behind the Aswan High Dam.

## A civilization in decline

By 1085 BC the Golden Age of the Egyptian Empire was past. No sooner had Ramesses II died than the Libyans from the western oases and sea raiders from the north began to press in upon the borders of Egypt. Ramesses's successors fought to protect the country from invasion, but corruption and inefficiency completed the ruin of Egypt, and for 200 years or more pharaohs had to struggle to keep their thrones in the face of civil strife and waning resources.

In the 8th century BC a family of energetic Sudanese kings from the region of Napata took control of Egypt and, emboldened by success, challenged the mighty Assyrian army in Palestine. The result was disaster. The Napatans were chased south, and Assyrian troops occupied Memphis. The Assyrian Empire, however, was nearing its overthrow and Egypt did not long pay tribute to Nineveh.

Under a new line of kings whose capital was Sais, a city in the delta, Egypt regained her independence and national unity. Saite rule brought about a brief but splendid revival of the arts and of the ancient cults, a reawakening of national pride and a vigorous though not always successful foreign policy. Prosperity returned, trade revived and new friendships were fostered with Lydia and the Greek city-states. It was the final grand flourish of the Egyptian civilization.

## Lessons in building and writing

In the 7th and 6th centuries BC, ties between Egypt and Greece were particularly close. Greek traders lived in the delta, and many Greek mercenaries served the pharaohs. Amasis II, one of the Saite kings of Egypt, sent gifts to the Delphic Oracle and other Greek shrines, and married a Greek princess. Statesmen and philosophers came from Athens to study in the university at Memphis, which had a renowned

medical school. Greek architects drew on the experiences of the Egyptians in achieving their own mastery in stone-working, and in their use of the column.

In the sphere of art, the influence of Egypt was far-reaching. A whole repertory of typically Egyptian motifs and symbols such as the 'Key of Life', the sphinx, the winged disc and the lotus were adopted by the Phoenicians and spread throughout the Mediterranean world. Some are still popular today. The Egyptian style of depicting human and animal figures was widely imitated, and it influenced early Greek sculpture and vase painting; the early statues of Greek gods and heroes have the same fixed stare and the advanced left foot that are typical of the classical tradition in Egypt.

The clumsy writing system of the Egyptians became an anachronism in a world in which the use of the alphabet had enormously simplified the task of scribe and reader. Yet the Egyptians may themselves have made a primitive alphabet when they used hieroglyphic characters representing a single sound to write the language of the Semitic-speaking Bedouin whom they met in the mining areas of Sinai. The Egyptians' use of the papyrus scroll was adopted by the Mediterranean world, and the Lebanese town of Byblos, the chief market from which papyrus was exported all over the Mediterranean, has given its name to the Bible.

## Stories and schoolbooks

The ancient Egyptians had a rich and varied literature. Though there are no great epics such as those which enriched Babylonian literature, a number of popular tales have survived—romances with a historical background, or stories based on mythology. Some of them have a familiar ring today, for they contain elements that were repeated in oriental folktales of later ages, and have been incorporated in nursery stories of our own times. There is the story of the shipwrecked sailor cast away, like Sindbad, on an enchanted island where he was befriended by an enormous snake: 'It was 30 cubits (45 ft) long and its beard was more than 2 cubits in length. Its body was plated with gold, and its eyebrows were of lapis lazuli.' There is the story of the doomed prince whose fate was predicted, like that of the Sleeping Beauty, at his birth, and whose success over rival suitors for the hand of a fair princess echoes other familiar fairy tales. An account of the capture of a city by the Egyptians says the attackers hid in baskets sent into the city on donkeys—heralding the tales of the Trojan Horse and of Ali Baba and the Forty Thieves.

Compilations of wise sayings were universally popular in the ancient Near East and are known as 'wisdom literature'. Such precepts of good behaviour and wise living, often attributed to some wise man of the past, were learnt by heart in the schools:

'Be not puffed up with thy knowledge, and be not proud because thou art wise. Take counsel with the ignorant as well as the wise . . .'

'If thou art a man of standing, found a

The most dramatic event in the history of archaeology was the finding in 1922 of the tomb of Tutankhamun, a king who died in about 1352 BC at the age of only 19. It was the first tomb of an Egyptian pharaoh to be found almost intact, and it was crammed with furnishings and ornaments that represent the finest craftsmanship of Egypt's imperial age. The archaeologist Howard Carter and his patron Lord Carnarvon had been searching the Valley of the Tombs of the Kings at Thebes for years when in November, 1922, Carter, who had been on the point of abandoning the search, came upon steps leading down to a sealed door. He wired Lord Carnarvon, who came quickly from England. As Carter broke down part of the mud sealing, Carnarvon asked him: 'Can you see anything?' Carter replied: 'Yes, wonderful things'

GOLDEN MASK *A mask of solid gold was placed over the head of the mummy of Tutankhamun. It shows the king in the guise of Osiris, the god of the underworld. His beard, and the vulture and snake on his forehead, are insignia of royalty*

family, and love thy wife at home as is fitting. Give her plenty to eat, and clothe her back; ointment is for her body. Make glad her heart as long as thou livest. She is a rich field for her lord . . .'

Moderation and sobriety are praised; so are humility towards elders, respect for parents and generosity towards people of lesser rank.

In the sphere of lyric poetry, there survive one or two tender love songs that must have been sung to the music of harp and flute. The blind harper at the funeral banquet would sing of the fleeting nature of life, or lament: 'Death greets me today as a remedy for sickness . . . like the perfume of balm.' Such a sombre note, however, is rare, and the Egyptians more often

DIVINE HUNTER *With harpoon poised, the young king Tutankhamun balances on a skiff made from papyrus stems, as he hunts hippopotamus in the marshes of the lower Nile. The statuette, 25 in. high, is carved from wood and gilded. It had a magical and protective significance, for it symbolised the victory of the god Horus, the king's personal god, over the forces of evil. Rulers were usually portrayed in formal poses, but the boy king is caught in a realistic moment of action*

PHARAOH AS WARRIOR *A painted casket shows Tutankhamun sweeping into battle to defeat his enemies, who are shown as a mass of dead and dying at the feet of his horses. Though Tutankhamun probably never went into battle himself, it was traditional for artists of the time to portray their rulers as warriors of more than human strength. The battle* is depicted as a hunting scene, with the king's dogs helping to bring down his enemies. Overhead the vulture-goddess protects the young king. The horse and the spoked wheel reached Egypt from Asia by about 1700 BC, and the Egyptian armies scored many victories with the help of their light two-wheeled chariot, usually holding a driver and an archer

LOTUS CUP *A goblet of translucent alabaster buried with Tutankhamun is in the shape of a white lotus flower. An inscription round the rim contains the wish that Tutankhamun 'may spend many millions of years sitting with his face to the cool breeze, his eyes beholding happiness'*

BOY PHARAOH *On the back of one of his thrones, King Tutankhamun is shown sitting at his ease, tended by his wife, a daughter of the former ruler Akhenaton. The rays of the sacred sun-disc, ending in little hands, bless the royal pair. The throne is made of wood, overlaid with gold*

GUARDIAN JEWEL *Elaborate jewels were placed within the wrappings of the king's mummy as amulets to ward off danger and invoke the gods' protection. This breast ornament of gold and semi-precious stones bears the winged scarab beetle, symbol of the sun-god and immortality*

appear in their tomb paintings and in their literature as a vigorous people with a sense of fun and a love of children, of bright colours, flowers, perfumes and simple amusements.

## The Greeks conquer Egypt

In 525 BC, Cambyses the Persian marched south from Palestine intent on conquest; resistance collapsed, he was crowned as pharaoh, and Egypt became a province of the Persian Empire. Two centuries later Alexander the Great, fresh from his triumphs in Asia Minor and Syria, entered Egypt and the last Persian governor surrendered. On Alexander's death Egypt was left under one of his generals, Ptolemy. For the next 300 years the Ptolemies,

Macedonian in their birth and Greek in their upbringing, were officially accepted in Egypt as 'the Horus, Lord of the Two Lands, King of Upper and Lower Egypt'. Though the ancient Egyptian language and religion persisted among the native population, the history of Egypt became that of her conquerors and of the Greek colonists who flocked to Alexandria and other new cities in the Nile Valley.

The Greeks were not untouched by the ancient civilization of their neighbours. Much of what the classical world termed the 'secret wisdom' of the Egyptians was based on an imperfect understanding of the ideas of a nation whose religious beliefs were totally alien to their own. Some of these ideas, however,

had a profound influence on Hellenistic thought, and the emotional cults of Egypt enjoyed great popularity in the world of Greece and Rome. The worship of Isis and her child Horus, in particular, spread widely.

It was the coming of Christianity that sounded the death-knell of the old Egyptian religion. The ancient temples crumbled, the gods were neglected and finally denounced, their very images on the temple walls defaced or obliterated. The tombs and their inhabitants were forgotten. After 3500 years the civilization of the Nile had finally succumbed. Only its language lives on to this day, preserved, by an irony of circumstance, in the form of worship of the Christian, or Coptic, Church in Egypt.

# Persia, enduring empire of the 'King of kings'

### FROM 546 BC

*The conquerors of Assyria, Babylon and Egypt gave
their wide realms a single rule of law and passed
a heritage of art and learning to the Arab world*

The Persian Empire rose like a freak tide in the 6th century BC, engulfing all the civilizations of western Asia and creating one gigantic dominion. It was the greatest empire the world had yet seen. The imperial armies of Persia even attempted to crush the brilliant civilization of Greece. Their invasions were repulsed; but when the Greek genius itself faded, Persian scholars preserved its scientific knowledge and added their own. The blend of cultures which they fashioned reached the West many centuries later and helped to lay the foundations of the 14th-century Renaissance of art and literature.

Persia lay across the ancient trade routes between Europe and Asia. It was a cross-roads through which, for centuries, the rich merchandise of the Orient flowed to the West: silks, embroidery, spices, gold, frankincense and myrrh. The Three Wise Men who brought their gifts to the infant Christ were in fact Magians, priests of the Persian religion of Zoroastrianism. These three kings of the East were also typical of the Persian merchants of the ancient world, who ventured as far eastwards as the shores of the Pacific and as far westwards as the coasts of Europe in quest of their goods and markets. They came from a hard land of great spaces, much of it inhospitable to man. One-third of the land is either desert or mountain, and other extensive areas can be cultivated only with the help of man-made irrigation works. But nearly all Persia is more than 1500 ft above sea level, giving the land a temperate climate; and in some regions the soil is very fertile.

These benefits made Persia attractive to invaders from the less temperate regions of the Asian steppes and the Arabian deserts. The country was often ravaged by marauding tribes, such as the Bedouin Arabs in the 7th century and the Mongols of Genghis Khan in the 13th century. Yet always the superior genius of the Persians enabled them, in the end, to absorb their invaders. Successive waves of invasion, although bringing destruction at first, introduced new stock and resulted in successive renewals of Persian civilization.

The first inhabitants of Persia, arriving probably from central Asia, began to settle on the land about 6000 BC, practising a primitive

### PERSIA IN 480 BC

*The early kings of Persia united most
of the Near and Middle East to create
the greatest empire the world had known*

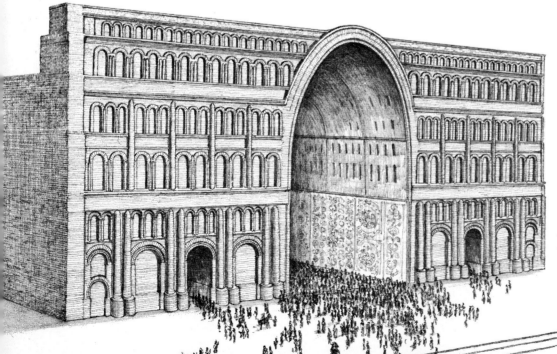

### 'IMMORTALS' ON GUARD

*Persian kings built great palaces
throughout their domains as symbols of
their power. A frieze of glazed bricks
at Susa (right) depicted the royal
bowmen, or 'Immortals', who helped
Darius to expand his empire and even
to challenge mighty Greece.*

*The palace at Ctesiphon (left) was
built by a later king, Shapur I, in about
AD 275. Its arch rose 120 ft to cover an
83-ft span – one of the widest arches ever
built in the ancient world. The arch
formed part of a vast throne room, open-
fronted like the tents of nomad chiefs.
The façade of the palace was decorated
by rows of smaller arches, diminishing
in height towards the top. The ruins still
rise like a cliff out of the Mesopotamian
Plain south of Baghdad*

# 'From antiquity those of our race have been kings'

form of agriculture. One of their early settlements was at Susa, later to become one of the capitals of the Persian Empire. These earliest Persian inhabitants were skilled potters. Working in black paint on a dark red ground, they at first depicted birds and animals in simple outline. But later the potters showed their ingenuity by developing abstract patterns based on the same subjects.

## Cyrus founds an empire

A great influx of Aryans from the region of the Caucasus Mountains occupied Persia about 1000 BC. (Iran, the Persians' own name for their country, means 'land of the Aryans'.) The Aryans established two rival kingdoms—the Kingdom of the Medes, just south of the Caspian Sea in the area of Ecbatana (the modern Hamadan), and the Kingdom of Parsa (or Persia) to the east of the Persian Gulf. Persia suddenly expanded in the 6th century BC when Cyrus II ('the Great') of Parsa defeated the Medes, and conquered Assyria, Asia Minor, Babylonia, the steppes of central Asia and lands as far east as India. In 546 BC he united his conquests into a single empire. It became known as the Achaemenid Empire, after Achaemenes, an earlier king of the Persians from whom Cyrus traced his descent.

When he conquered Babylon, Cyrus freed the 40,000 Jews who had been made captive there by Nebuchadnezzar, and allowed them to return to Jerusalem, where he helped them to rebuild the Temple of Solomon; the Old

### THE GREAT KING KEEPS VIGIL OVER HIS PEOPLE

*Throughout its history, Persia has been ruled by powerful kings. The greatest were the Achaemenids, who combined the lands of Media and Parsa into one kingdom and then swept on to conquer most of western Asia. This marble head of a bearded monarch represents one of the Achaemenid kings, probably either Cyrus the Great, who conquered Babylon in* *539 BC, or Darius the Great (521–485 BC), the first to style himself 'King of kings'. The Achaemenids were renowned for their tolerance to subject peoples and for the just but inflexible laws they imposed throughout their empire. Strong leaders enabled Persia to unite the different peoples of its empire and defend its extensive land borders against invaders*

### THE PARTHIAN SHOT

*Warlike Parthians, from the north-east, ruled Persia for 500 years after the collapse of Greek rule in 261 BC. This mounted Parthian king, depicted on a 4th-century silver plate found at Sari, is killing a lion by a technique which has given a phrase to the English language. Turning around in his saddle, he is delivering the so-called 'Parthian shot'—a final missile delivered while retreating at high speed. The representation of a king overcoming the king of beasts was a common feature of Persian art, probably derived from the Assyrians, whose kings also used it. The 'Parthian shot' was used as effectively in war*

Testament Book of Ezra opens with an account of how God stirred the spirit of Cyrus to show favour to the chosen people.

Cyrus adopted the best aspects of the laws and religions of conquered peoples for the benefit of his own empire. He earned a reputation as a tolerant ruler by leaving subject peoples free to practise their own faiths. Cyrus and his successor Darius have gone down in history as two of the world's greatest law-givers: the 'Laws of the Medes and the Persians' were respected throughout their lands.

In southern Persia, near Persepolis, Cyrus established his capital city, Pasargadae, 'The Camp of the Persians'. It was built of white limestone, and even today its terraces, floors and the remains of the columns of its audience halls are an impressive reminder of Cyrus's imperial achievement. Near by rises his tomb, its white limestone gleaming in the clear Persian atmosphere. This strong, simple building, 36 ft high, resting on a six-stepped platform, is more intimate in style than the great pyramids of Egypt or the ancient ziggurats of Babylonia, yet reminiscent of both. The guardian angel still visible on one of the doorways to the tomb is one of the earliest known portrayals in history of a mighty winged form.

### Tax in gold coins

In 525 BC, Cyrus's son Cambyses II added Egypt to the empire. Under Darius the Great (521–485 BC), the empire was divided into 20 provinces under administrators called satraps, and each of the satrapies paid tax to the empire according to its wealth. The richest province, Babylonia, paid 1000 talents a year (a talent was worth about $480 , and the total yearly income to the king's purse reached 14,500 talents. This taxation system was made possible by the introduction of coinage; the golden daric, named after Darius, became the world's first reliable international monetary unit of exchange.

In 520 BC Darius inscribed into a 300 ft high cliff face at Bisitun, near Kermanshah, an account of how he consolidated his empire. The inscription, which can still be read today, declares: 'I am Darius the king, the king of kings, the king of Persia, the great king of the provinces . . . from antiquity those of our race have been kings.'

Darius's emphasis on his royal ancestry is one of the earliest testimonies of Persian belief in the necessity of a monarchy. This belief was imposed on the Persians by three causes, all arising from the nature of the Persian landscape. Firstly, Persia's long land frontiers had to be guarded against invasion; this required a strong king capable of organising effective defence against potential invaders.

Secondly, scarcity of water meant that only part of Persia's population could farm the land. Another part had to remain nomadic, migrating with each change of the seasons in search of pasture for the cattle and sheep. But drought or pests could ravage a tribesman's flocks and turn him into a fierce marauder of prosperous areas. As a result there was often tension between the nomads and the settled farmers or town dwellers, and a strong king was needed to keep the peace. In a social situation as old as the conflict between Cain, the settled farmer, and Abel, the nomadic shepherd, the Great King protected the farmers against the warrior tribesmen – who, in their turn, provided the Great King with his fighters.

Thirdly, when the Persians conquered other lands, the Great King held the balance between their different peoples, as he did between farmer and herdsman at home.

### Cities for all seasons

As guardians of all their people, the Great Kings of Persia had to move to capitals in different parts of the country – Persepolis, Ecbatana, Susa, Ctesiphon – at different times of the year. All these capitals were, like Pasargadae, less like towns than royal camps built in stone. Their columns were adorned with carvings and their great halls festooned with richly patterned textiles. For the festival held to mark the Persian New Year in March, the kings would come to Persepolis. Cyrus adopted the New Year festival from the Babylonians, and made it an occasion for receiving tribute and homage from his peoples.

In summer the kings ascended to the cool heights of Ecbatana – the name means 'Place of Assembly' – 5000 ft above sea level. There they used a palace encircled by seven walls of different colours – white, black, scarlet, blue

## ANIMAL THEMES FOR ART IN POTTERY AND GOLD

STAG *A cup found at Susa is typical of the fine work of potters as early as 3500 BC*

Skill in depicting animals has been a feature of Persian art since the very earliest pottery of about 4000 BC. The first artists used simple outlines to depict animals realistically; but later they adapted the shapes of the animals to create decorative motifs, in the way the artist has exaggerated the stag's horns in the pot on the left. Sometimes the designs produced became entirely abstract. This artistic advance was to become important to Persia centuries later, when the coming of Islam prevented the representation of the human figure: symbolism in art was a Persian gift to mankind. As the early Persian Empire and its wealth grew, the intricate art of the goldsmith was added to the skills of the potter, but animals remained favourite subjects

LION *A 5th-century BC gold drinking cup found at Ecbatana*

CHARIOT *A 4th-century gold miniature depicts the vehicle used for transport throughout the empire*

# Marvels of intricate design in mosques and carpets

and orange for the five outer walls, and silver and gold for the two innermost walls. In winter the kings went to equally sumptuous palaces at Susa or Ctesiphon.

Under Darius the empire became famous for its gardens. These were originally called by the Old Persian word *pairidaeze*, which meant a walled-in enclosure, necessary for a garden in a land of strong winds and drifting desert sands. It is the origin of the English word 'paradise'. The beautifully ordered, flower-decked, tree-shaded Persian gardens, with their pools and canals, were indeed a paradise to a traveller from across the dusty plains.

The empire of Darius was crossed by a 'Royal Road' which ran from Sardes, near the Aegean coast, to the royal palace at Susa. This road, a precedent for the famous Roman roads, was about 1600 miles long and constantly patrolled by the army. Messengers of the king, changing their horses at the 111 post-stations strung out along the route, could complete the journey within a week. Persia also became famed for its seamen, and by 465 BC Persian sailors had sailed right round the coast of Africa.

## War with Greece

Darius was the first Persian monarch to style himself 'King of kings' (Shahanshah), and was considered by his subjects to be master of the world. But late in his reign the first warnings of impending disaster sounded on the outskirts of the empire, when the Greek cities in Asia Minor revolted against Persian rule. The Persians crushed the revolt and launched an attack on Athens itself in 490 BC, but they were defeated by the Greeks at Marathon.

In 480, Darius's son Xerxes led an immense army against Athens and Sparta. After an initial costly victory over the Spartans at Thermopylae, the Persians were defeated in a naval battle at Salamis near Athens and on land at Plataea and, after these defeats, rebellions broke out throughout the Persian Empire. Nearly 150 years later the Persians were no match for the military genius and well-trained cavalry of Alexander the Great who, in 334, led an army of 40,000 men across the Dardanelles and defeated the Persian army at Issus, on the Mediterranean coast. In 331 Alexander drove into the heartland of the Persian Empire, capturing Babylon, Susa and finally Persepolis, which he burnt in revenge for the destruction of Athens.

Like so many conquerors of Persia, Alexander quickly succumbed to the Persian way of life, and dismayed his generals by wanting to form a Greek-Persian empire on the Achaemenid

### A TEXT IN COLOURED TILES

*The walls of the Shah's Mosque at Isfahan are covered with multi-coloured tiles of blue, cream and gold. The gateway is framed by a text from the Koran, Islam's Holy Scripture, and at the sides rise tall minarets from either of which the muezzin makes the call to prayer five times a day. The mosque was begun in 1612 by Shah Abbas as the heart of his capital*

model, treating the Persians as equals of the conquering Greeks. In 327 he married a Persian noblewoman, Roxane, but four years later he died of a fever before realising his aim.

## Worship of the sun-god

For the next 500 years Persia came under the rule of the Parthians, a warlike people from the north-east. This was a period of almost ceaseless conflict with Rome, from which neither side emerged victor. Roman soldiers carried back to Europe the Persian worship of Mithras, the sun-god. If Mithraism had not been superseded in the Roman Empire by Christianity, Europe might have adopted the Persian religion.

After five centuries of Parthian rule, Persian imperial expansion and organisation were revived in AD 226 by another family from southern Persia, the Sasanids, who restored Persian prestige and created an empire comparable with that of the Achaemenids. The Sasanid king Chosroes II is shown in wall carvings in an ancient garden at Tak-i-Bustan, near Kermanshah. He is portrayed as a huntsman in a scene with wild boars, stags and other beasts and birds on different types of ground, marshy and mountainous. The detail of these superbly executed reliefs reveals the continuity, from the time of the unknown potters of 4000 BC, of the Persian skill in drawing animals and birds.

## The coming of Islam

The fall of the Sasanid Empire in the 7th century to bands of ill-equipped Bedouin Arabs, attacking out of the Arabian deserts across the Euphrates and the Tigris, was one of the most catastrophic destructions of a huge empire known to history. The Arabs lacked sophisticated weapons but more than made up for this by their zeal for their new faith of Islam. They were also hungry for the riches, luxuries and comparative plenty of the Persian Empire, on whose borders they lived their own sparse desert existence.

The result of the Arab conquest of Persia was a great blending of Arab and Persian religion and culture to form Islamic civilization. Baghdad became the capital of an Islamic Empire which took many of its institutions and most of its culture from the Sasanids. The Arab conquest was of vital importance to Persia, for Islam has been its state religion ever since. Before the coming of Islam most Persians had been followers of the Zoroastrian religion, which by then had largely replaced Mithraism. In Zoroastrianism, fire was worshipped as the

### A FLOWER GARDEN IN SILK

*The design of Persian carpets is based on flowers, birds, beasts and trees. This rosette, representing a tranquil pool at the heart of the ideal Persian garden, is part of a carpet woven in silk for the mosque at Ardabil, in northern Persia, in 1539; its pattern of leaves and petals also resembles the designs used for the mosaics inside the domes of many mosques*

# Omar Khayyam, poet and astronomer

symbol of power and cleanliness. The gods of this faith were Ahura Mazda, a force for light and good, and Ahriman, a force for darkness and evil. The Zoroastrian religion was conveyed to the west coast of India by a handful of Persian refugees whose descendants are the Parsees of today.

The Muslim Arabs recognised Zoroastrianism as one of the three faiths tolerated by Islam, the others being Christianity and Judaism. Nevertheless, the Persians soon began the time-honoured process of conquering their invaders. First of all they adopted the Islamic religion and the Arabic language. Then, from a position of strength, they were able to teach the Arabs how a country like Persia could be ruled. Persians were appointed as provincial governors for the Muslim Caliphs who ruled from Baghdad; they also became leaders among Islam's philosophers, poets and historians. Islamic culture could never have reached the peak it achieved without the initial conquest of Persia by the Arabs and their tuition by the Persians in the ways of civilization.

## Merchants and the muezzin

Since the 7th century, Persia has given the world a unique style in literature and in the arts, within the framework of Islamic civilization. In cities such as Isfahan, Shiraz, Mashad and Tabriz the heart of the medieval Muslim community can still be seen today in long, roofed bazaars, with their lanes of shops occupied by goldsmiths and brass hammerers, and sellers of fruit, fabrics and Turkish delight.

Adjoining the bazaar in medieval times was the walled courtyard, or caravanserai, where merchants' caravans arrived from all over the ancient trade routes of Asia. Dominating the city were the buildings which are among Islam's most enduring monuments – the mosque, from which the muezzin called the faithful to prayer five times a day; the *madrassa*, or college for religious instruction; and the palace of the shah or sultan.

Isfahan today is especially rich in beautiful mosques and colleges whose patterned brick-work satisfied the Persian artists' desire to fill space with decoration. In the 11th century, the traditional floral patterns of early Persian drawings were developed in the plasterwork of buildings. Later these same designs were carried out in mosaics of glazed tiles on domes and walls, an art which was to reach its perfection in the 16th and 17th centuries.

## Poetry and the potter

In the 11th century, the Seljuk Turks, one of the waves of nomads that swept across central Asia towards the west, conquered Persia, and by the 12th century a vast area stretching from the Mediterranean to the modern Chinese province of Sinkiang was under the rule of the Seljuk sultan. The Turks, however, like the Arabs before them, were fighters rather than administrators, and they appointed Persian governors to help them to run their empire. Under the Seljuks, Persian literature developed very rapidly. Philosophical and mathematical

treatises and historical chronicles were written, but it was in poetry that Persian writers achieved a special richness of ideas and imagery. One poetic form that was completely Persian was the *ruba'i*, a four-line stanza with three rhyming lines sealed by a final statement in a non-rhyming line. Certain stock images came repeatedly to be employed in poetry in successive ages. A striking example is the image of man as clay in the potter's hands, which suggests the transience of all mortal men and their worldly preoccupations.

The poet Omar Khayyam, who is believed to have died in 1123, was also famous for his work in algebra and astronomy; in 1079 he began to reform the calendar, and established astronomical tables that form the basis of those used in modern navigation. But it is for his *ruba'iyat* that Omar Khayyam is best known, since Edward Fitzgerald's translations into English stanzas in the 19th century. One stanza takes up the theme of the transience of man and his earthly treasures and power which must return to clay:

'Surely not in vain
  My substance from the common Earth
    was ta'en
That He who subtly wrought me
    into shape
Should stamp me back to common
    Earth again?'

More than two centuries later, Hafiz, whose skill in combining sensual appeal with a lofty spiritual significance make him one of the most remarkable poets of all time, took up the same theme when he said:

'Take the cup as etiquette decrees, for its
    clay is kneaded
From the skulls of Jamshid, Bahman and
    Kaykobad.'

The verse refers to three of Persia's greatest legendary heroic kings; they too, says Hafiz, had returned to their original clay, and one should treat with respect a cup made from clay containing the king's remains.

## Onslaught of the Mongols

The reign of the Seljuk Turks over Persia ended in 1200 under the crushing impact of the hordes of Genghis Khan which, in their quest for better grazing lands, swept across central Asia from their Mongolian homelands. The Mongols massacred the populations of whole cities in their path, and as many as two-thirds of the people of Persia died under their onslaught.

A Mongol dynasty set up by Genghis Khan's grandson, Hulagu Khan, ruled Persia for a century. It was overthrown by Timur the Lame, also known as Tamerlane, who marched his pigtailed Turkish troops down into Persia from the banks of the River Oxus in 1395 to ravage Persia, Syria and Asia Minor for the next five years. But on his death in 1405 Tamerlane, though he left a legend of conquest, left no empire, nor did his descendants succeed in reuniting Persia.

Reunification and the revival of a Persian state was the achievement of the Safavids, a great Persian dynasty established in 1502 by

Shah Isma'il I, who claimed descent from the Prophet Muhammad. The Safavids set up the first workshops for carpet weaving, an ancient Persian craft which began when early nomads produced wool from which their womenfolk wove furnishings for their camps. These later developed into rich hangings and floor coverings for rulers' palaces.

The Persian carpet weavers still continue, in wool, the art of the prehistoric potters. Their intricate designs are based on flowers, vases, birds, beasts and trees; they are vividly coloured in red, blue, green and even black, which is used to set off patches of white, representing pools and canals. Particularly high standards in carpet weaving were attained in the 17th

ILLUSTRATED EPIC *Illustrations sometimes occupied entire pages of the 'Shah-nama' manuscripts. Chinese influences combined with Persian naturalism*

ART IN LEATHER *Books were not only richly penned and illustrated, but had ornate leather bindings. This binding, made in 1522, is of tooled leather embossed in gold*

MOUNTED WARRIORS *Persian armies were renowned for their skilful use of cavalry. A 'Shah-nama' illustration shows Persian horsemen, armed with spears, confronting a force of Turks in a legendary conflict from Persia's past*

A LOVER AT THE GATES OF PARADISE *Persia's heroic love poetry gave the miniaturist inspiration for detailed and sensuous illustration. In this drawing of 1396, a prince, Humay, seeks admission to his beloved's castle, which is surrounded, like the typical Persian 'paradise' garden, by a walled garden of flowers and trees*

century, when Persian carpets were exported to Europe by way of Baghdad and Turkey. Under the Safavids, too, the great legends and poems of Persia were re-written in manuscripts decorated with delightful miniature illustrations.

The peak of the Safavid dynasty came under Shah Abbas the Great (1587-1629) who created new trade ties with Europe and transformed Isfahan from a provincial town into a magnificent city. After Abbas the Great, the dynasty declined and was gradually overrun by Afghans, Russians and Turks, until in 1729 a Persian military leader, Nadir Shah, drove out the invaders. Modern Persians, whose ruler is still called the Shah, call their country Iran, but for Europeans 'Persia' is too evocative a word

to be forgotten. From the 5th century BC, when the Greek historian Herodotus first wrote of Persia, the name has evoked an exotic land, ruled by a King of kings and with courts legendary for their magnificence.

## Legacy in law and science

Persia's contribution to the development of human society has included the idea of the rule of law under the custodianship of a Great King. But its contribution to civilization has not stopped there. Persian mathematicians laid the basis for much important scientific progress. The Greeks had admired theoretical mathematics; but the 11th-century Persians used mathematics to make accurate measurements

of the movements of heavenly bodies, to improve navigation and to perfect the calendar. Medieval scholars in Europe studied the Persian philosopher Avicenna (Ibn Sina) to discover the secrets of experimental science and reasoning from proved facts. The Persians respected doctors, whose profession was looked down on as ignoble in Greece and Rome, and built the world's first hospitals, the most famous of which was at Jundashapur, in south-west Persia, completed in AD 272.

The Persians have displayed throughout their history a concern with man's place and role in the universe. And they have given the world a lesson in art by singling out nature's beauties and making them a source of delight.

# Seafarers and prophets of Bible lands

## 3000 BC–AD 135

*Along the east Mediterranean coast, where the wandering 'sons of Noah' made their homes, trade flourished and men worshipped a new God*

**THE LEVANT IN 1500 BC**

*From their narrow coastal homelands, Levantine traders spread their influence throughout the east Mediterranean*

### THE WILDERNESS OF SINAI

*The sun rises to colour the mountains of Sinai, a scene of barren desolation which is etched deeply in Jewish history. Sinai is the triangular desert peninsula linking Africa to Asia; only in the brief rainy season do its streams swell and bring a fleeting fertility. It was in this wilderness that the Hebrews wandered for 40 years after Moses led them out of slavery in Egypt. The Book of Exodus tells how Moses went up Mount Sinai and received from God the Ten Commandments, which became the foundation of the Jewish faith. These rules not only held together the tribes of Israel during their wanderings in the wilderness, but became an enduring moral code for a large part of mankind*

Two of the world's great religions had their origins among a people of quick and lively intelligence, the groups of Semites who settled along the eastern shores of the Mediterranean some 5000 years ago. For among these settlers were the Hebrews, the first people in history to abandon the worship of many gods. They worshipped instead a single God, who was just and merciful but who demanded that his followers should keep the laws which he had given them. This fierce belief in a single God formed the cornerstone of the Jewish faith, and of the Christian faith which arose later among these same Hebrews.

The achievements of these Semites were not only in the religious field: another group of settlers, the Phoenicians, excelled as traders and sailors. Their commerce dominated a large part of the eastern Mediterranean. And their skills in shipbuilding and navigation enabled them to spread their influence as far as Spain, Sicily and North Africa – where they founded the colony of Carthage which was one day to challenge mighty Rome.

The Semites are named after Shem, described in the Old Testament as the eldest son of Noah and the ancestor of the Hebrews. But this name was not given to them until modern times. In ancient times they were simply a collection of tribes of various names, originating probably in Arabia. By 3000 BC, many of these tribes had moved north into the fertile lands of Mesopotamia and eastern Syria. The typical Semites, like most east Mediterranean peoples to this day, had dark hair and olive skins. They

were ruled by kings and princes, who were also their judges. Like many ancient societies the Semites were originally polygamous, and the wealthy families owned slaves; many tribal wars arose from the search for more slaves – the women for house and harem and the men for work in the fields.

Gradually, war and population pressures drove many Semites even further from their homelands, and one group of western Semites reached the Mediterranean and settled along its eastern shores. The territory they occupied, stretching nearly 500 miles along the coast from the Gulf of Iskenderun, in southern Turkey, to the Egyptian border, was not everywhere fertile; but the whole area was richer in ancient times than it is today.

The coastal lands settled by the western Semites are known as Canaan in the Bible, and much of the Old Testament is a record of the struggles between the earliest Canaanites and later immigrants, who fought them for occupation of the best lands. Among these later immigrants were the Hebrews who, led by Abraham, reached Canaan from Mesopotamia about 1950 BC. Eventually, by 1150, the Canaanites were pressed into the narrow coastal strip of present-day Lebanon, where they became known as the Phoenicians.

In about 1600 BC, a great famine drove the Hebrews to Egypt; but they returned in 1200. Canaan was the 'Promised Land' of the Hebrews, and their 12 tribes settled in the area known as Palestine. As the centuries passed, distinctions between the other Semitic tribes

**GIFTS FROM CANAAN FOR THE EGYPTIANS**

*The early peoples of the east Mediterranean coastlands had close contact with the Egyptians, their neighbours to the south. A wall-painting of about 1890 BC, from* *a royal tomb at Beni-Hassan in Egypt, shows Semitic nomads, in traditional dress, bringing gifts to the Egyptians. Two children ride the ass in the centre*

# The Phoenicians, skilled craftsmen and colonists

Phoenician craftsmen excelled in making fine decorations from the tusks of elephants killed in Syria and North Africa, and their work was prized throughout the ancient world. This open-work ivory panel of a lion in a lily grove was found at Nimrud on the River Tigris, where it was probably carved in the 9th century BC by a Phoenician artist working for an Assyrian king. The head-dress and breast-plate are Egyptian

HUMAN PREY *In this ivory panel from Nimrud, the Phoenician artist has depicted a lioness seizing a Negro boy by the throat. The naturalistic treatment contrasts with the more stylised lion of the top picture*

broke down through intermarriage and trading contacts. Only the Hebrews, because of their distinct religion, kept themselves apart from their neighbours.

## Where the alphabet began

From their origins as herdsmen and hunters, the earliest Semitic settlers along the Mediterranean coast soon became farmers. Before long they were to turn themselves into craftsmen, merchants, and sea-going traders. The Canaanite city of Byblos, a little north of modern Beirut, became the hub of trade within the Semitic world and between the Semites and the great civilization of Egypt to the south. Dating back to at least 2600 BC, it is among the oldest continuously inhabited towns in the world, and it remained the most important city in the eastern Mediterranean world for 500 years, until it was eclipsed by the Phoenician towns of Tyre and Sidon.

It was in Byblos that alphabetic writing was first practised. Earlier forms of writing had existed, such as the hieroglyphic picture-writing of Egypt, and the cuneiform or 'wedge-shaped' writing which originated in Mesopotamia and was common all over western Asia by 2000 BC. But it was among the Canaanites and Phoenicians that the alphabet seems to have first evolved.

The Phoenician letter *daleth*, for example, looked like the modern letter D and was sounded in the same way. The Phoenician letter *tau* was the same as T. Even where the letters have changed slightly over the centuries, through their transmutations in Greek and Latin to modern Roman script, the derivation of the modern Western alphabet from Phoenician is plain. The very word 'alphabet' derives from the names given by the Phoenicians to their first two letters – *aleph*, which meant 'ox' and *beth*, meaning 'house', which passed to the Greeks as *alpha* and *beta*.

Inscriptions in this alphabetic writing which may date back to about 1300 BC have been found in Byblos. At the same time the Phoenicians found a better way of keeping their written records than by inscribing them on tablets of baked clay. They began to use papyrus scrolls, made of reeds from the river split into strips and stuck together. Some scrolls were imported from Egypt, where they were already used for picture-writing, or hieroglyphs. Scribes wrote on these scrolls with reed-pens dipped into an 'ink' made from water mixed with gum and soot or vegetable dye.

Phoenician merchants also took papyrus to Greece, and the Greeks coined the word *biblia*, from the town of Byblos, to describe the books they made from it. The English word 'Bible' comes from this Greek original, while the papyrus itself provided the word 'paper'.

## Makers of textiles and jewellery

Fertile land in the Mediterranean coastlands inhabited by the western Semites was too scarce to support a growing population, and they soon had to import grain and livestock, and pay for them with the fine products of their craftsmen. In the early days Egypt and Mesopotamia were their main markets. Later, however, as colonies spread along the trade routes of the Mediterranean, islands such as Sicily provided grain in return for manufactured articles, while Sardinia supplied tin and iron.

The Phoenicians made textiles, using wool from their own land and from Mesopotamia, and flax and linen from Egypt. With imported ivory, metals and gems they established a large jewellery industry, and made richly embroidered garments, glass and decorated earthenware. From a shellfish called the murex the Phoenicians extracted a dye, the famous 'Tyrian purple'. The finest and most expensive shade of this dye became the traditional colour denoting royalty. It was from the Greek *phoinix*, meaning 'purple', that the Phoenicians derived their name.

The trees in the thickly forested mountains inland supplied resinous gums to make incense and perfumes, and also timber to build the ships which made the Phoenicians the outstanding explorers of the ancient world.

Large ports, such as Tyre, Sidon, Tripoli and Arvad, hummed with incessant activity as broad-beamed sailing vessels, or *gaulos*, brought in raw materials and took out the fine manufactured goods which became famous throughout the ancient world. The ports were defended against raiding neighbours by war-galleys, powered by 50 oarsmen sitting in two banks one above the other, and armed with a long ram mounted under water in the bow of the vessel. The task of defence was made easier by the siting of Tyre, Tripoli and Arvad on promontories or offshore islets; only Sidon was on the mainland proper.

## First voyage round Africa

Driven partly by increasing pressure from their Greek trading rivals, the Phoenicians looked further and further westwards for their trade, and established colonies at Cadiz in Spain, in Malta, in North Africa, in Sicily and in Sardinia. The Greek historian Herodotus wrote in the 5th century BC of Phoenician trading voyages to West Africa, and Phoenician ships regularly crossed the stormy Bay of Biscay to Britain to exchange their manufactured goods for the tin of Cornwall.

A major Phoenician achievement at sea was the first known voyage right round the coast of Africa. The Egyptian pharaoh Necho (609-593 BC) was curious to know what lay beyond the Red Sea, and as the Phoenicians were the finest sailors of the time he sent a squadron of their ships down the Red Sea with orders to follow the African coast as far as they could.

It was a long voyage; every autumn the Phoenician sailors went ashore, planted their grain and waited for the spring harvest before they moved on again. Three years after their departure they returned through the Strait of Gibraltar, and reported that Africa was washed on all sides by the sea, except where it joined Asia. Their feat was not to be accomplished by Europeans until the Portuguese explorer Vasco da Gama rounded the Cape of Good Hope in

## PROSPEROUS CANAAN

*The robe worn by a Canaanite on this 12th century BC glazed tile is typical of the decorated cloth produced in Canaan*

## CEDARS OF LEBANON FOR PALACE AND TEMPLE

*The Phoenicians were the outstanding seafarers, explorers and traders of the ancient world. They built their ships from the trees which once covered the hillsides near the Mediterranean coast. Among these trees were the famous cedars of Lebanon, used by Solomon in building his magnificent temple at Jerusalem in about 950 BC, and also by kings of Assyria in the 8th and 7th centuries for their palaces at Khorsabad and Nineveh. This stone relief from Sargon II's palace at Khorsabad shows Phoenicians loading huge logs of timber on to their curved galleys. The timber may have been bound for Egypt, where cedar was used to build the boats which carried the bodies of the pharaohs to their tombs. From their ports on the Lebanese coast the Phoenicians ventured abroad to found trading colonies in Malta, Sicily, Sardinia, North Africa and Spain. They were master navigators, steering by the stars at night, and Phoenician seamen manned the ships of Solomon and of Jerusalem's conquerors, the Babylonians*

# 'Chosen people' who worshipped a single God

AD 1497. The Phoenicians also earned a reputation as fine engineers. The Persians, when they were invading Greece in 480 BC, called in Phoenician experts to cut a canal across the isthmus of Mount Athos, so that they could tow their fleet through safely without having to risk a notoriously stormy sea passage.

## A spring from the sea-bed

Another example of Phoenician engineering flair was the water supply at their island city of Arvad. The inhabitants found that a fresh-water spring bubbled up under the sea halfway between the island and the mainland. They placed a hemisphere of lead over the spring and connected this with a leather pipe to a vessel anchored over the spot. The force of the water drove it up the pipe to a cistern in the boat, from which it was taken to the city. To bring water to Tyre, engineers tapped a source of water on the mainland and piped it under the sea to the islet on which the city was situated; today the site – now called Sur, in Lebanon – is joined to the mainland by a half-mile causeway. The Phoenicians acquired a good knowledge of astronomy, possibly from the Babylonians, and used the stars – particularly Polaris, the North Star – for night sailing. Even the Greeks conceded that the Phoenicians were the best navigators of their time; 'the men of Sidon steer the straightest course', said Strabo, the Greek geographer and historian.

In the evolution of the alphabet, in ship-building, navigation, commerce and the crafts, the Phoenicians were outstanding. Artistically they left little original work, borrowing most of their styles from the Egyptians, and later from the Persians and the Greeks. Their independent history in the Levant ended when Alexander the Great captured Tyre and the rest of their homeland in 332 BC. But long before that, in the 8th century BC, the Phoenicians had founded their great city of Carthage in North Africa. The Carthaginians were to establish a wide colonial empire in the central and west Mediterranean, which led to their ultimate conflict with Rome.

## Belief that made a nation

The Phoenicians, important though their achievements were as migrant traders and colonisers, seem to have developed little conception of nationhood. But the Hebrews, or Jews, relatively small in numbers though they were, saw themselves from the start as a distinct people because of their belief in *Yahweh*, or Jehovah, the only God. They despised the paganism and superstition of their neighbours along the Mediterranean coastal strip. The pagans' custom of sacrificing children to their gods was also abhorred by the Jews.

The Jews were particularly scornful of the Syrian religion, centred as it was around a fertility goddess whose worship demanded sacred temple prostitutes and orgiastic rites; devotees of Astarte were stimulated into wild sexual abandonment by music, wine and incense. However, there was often a good deal of licence among the Jews themselves, and many writings of the prophets reproach the people for imitating the pagan practices of their neighbours, and exhort them instead to hold fast to their God.

Abraham, the 'exalted father', traditional founder of the Jewish race, left Mesopotamia some time around 2000 BC as the leader of one of the groups then moving westwards towards the coastal area of the Mediterranean. Abraham, however, was more than a tribal chieftain. He was also a religious leader, proclaiming that there was only one God; a God to be worshipped

## JEWS AND PAGANS

The Old Testament tells of the struggles brought about by the fierce adherence of the Jews to the worship of one God, Jehovah. The neighbouring Semitic tribes bowed down to many gods, but the first of the Ten Commandments, handed down through Moses, declares: 'Thou shalt have no other gods before me.' The second forbids the making and worship of graven images; the prophets of the Old Testament inveighed against the idols worshipped by the pagans, and the licentious practices associated with them

GRAVEN IMAGE *Among many gods to whom the Semitic pagans paid homage, the principal male god was Baal, the subject of this 1900 BC bronze. Baal – the name means 'lord' in Hebrew – was honoured as the king of the heavens and lord of the pagans' fertility cult. Farming was the mainstay of the wandering Semites' lives; because of this, they looked on religion primarily as a means of ensuring that their lands remained fertile and that enough children should survive to defend and till them. The Jews denounced the cult of Baal, and also that of Astarte, pagan goddess of love and reproduction and the Eastern equivalent of the Greek Aphrodite. The ceremonies associated with Astarte were accompanied by sexual rites, and prostitutes serving at her shrines were honoured*

## EXILE FROM JUDAH

*This section of a stone relief from the palace of the Assyrian king Sennacherib at Nineveh shows Jewish women and children being deported from Judah, after the Assyrians captured the Judaean city of Lachish, south-west of Jerusalem, in 701 BC. Sennacherib, whose father Sargon II had subjugated Israel 20 years earlier, set out to conquer Judah, the Jews' second kingdom. He conquered more than 40 towns, drove out more than 200,000 Judaeans, and laid siege to Jerusalem, their capital. The city was saved when the Assyrian besiegers were struck by plague, but Sennacherib extorted massive tribute from King Hezekiah of Judah before he withdrew*

SERVANT OF A GODDESS *This 8th-century BC ivory found at Nimrud is believed to depict a sacred temple prostitute of the goddess Astarte, soliciting from her upper window*

SACRED LAWS *A curtained tabernacle to house the Torah, the written laws of Moses, is depicted in this 4th-century AD mosaic floor in a synagogue near Tiberias*

without images, a God of justice who would punish those who broke the laws given through his intermediaries, but who would protect those who obeyed them. Peculiar to the Hebrew religion, too, was the conception of a covenant between God and his chosen people. Other nations had their gods whom they called upon for help and protection, but the God of the Hebrews alone made pledges to his people. One of these concerned the Promised Land: according to the Book of Genesis, God 'made a covenant with Abraham, saying, Unto thy seed have I given this land, from the river of Egypt unto the great river Euphrates'.

## 'Land of milk and honey'

The land to which Abraham led his people, Canaan, or Palestine as it was later called, seemed to this people coming out of the desert to be 'flowing with milk and honey'. Some centuries later, however, there was a famine in Palestine, and the Jewish leader Jacob took most of his people southwards into Egypt, at the invitation of his son Joseph, chief minister of the ruling pharaoh. The Jews settled in Egypt and remained prosperous there for several centuries, until a new Egyptian dynasty with an

'anti-foreigner' policy reduced them to a condition of slavery. The cohesion of the Jews as a national unit stems from their sufferings in Egypt, from their subsequent wandering back home through the desert, and from their later enslavement in Babylon. Their faith in one God, whose people they were, was the only thing they had to keep them together.

The Jews were finally delivered from bondage in Egypt by their great leader, Moses, one of the most extraordinary figures in history. He, like Abraham, was a religious leader as well as a political and military leader; and he administered a unique set of laws – the Ten Commandments – which had been imposed upon the Jewish people in a covenant at Sinai.

The exodus from Egypt, the wandering in the wilderness, and the return to Canaan, the 'Land of Promise', under Joshua, the successor of Moses, are all chronicled in the Old Testament. In these Scriptures are enshrined the astonishing richness of the Jewish contribution to history, literature and poetry.

The Old Testament is the history of the Jewish people; but it is a great deal more. It embodies their ideas of how the world came into being and how, although God himself is

good, pain, death and sin also came to exist. It is a unique historical account of one of the peoples of the ancient world, and no later historians have ever equalled the vigorous story-telling of, for instance, the Books of Kings. There are moving love stories such as the Book of Ruth, and rich poetry such as the Song of Solomon. The Book of Job, telling of one man's determination never to forsake his God no matter how terrible his life, leads on to the magnificence of the Psalms and the profound wisdom of the Proverbs.

## A lesson from the Hittites

Throughout their history the Jews, while often at war with their neighbours, were also influenced by them. It was probably from the Hittites, for instance, that the Hebrews learnt the important technique of iron-working.

For centuries the Hittites were known only as an obscure tribe mentioned in the Old Testament as one of the many warlike enemies facing the Hebrews when Joshua brought them back to the Promised Land. But today they are known to have been a dominant power in the Middle East for nearly three centuries, from about 1500 to 1200 BC. The Hittites were an

# 'My kingdom is not of this world'

Indo-European people who came originally from the north and crossed the Caucasus Mountains to conquer the inhabitants of Anatolia (present-day Turkey). The Hittites' swift victory was made easier because they were the first people in the world to use iron on a large scale. Hitherto the extraction and working of iron had been a rare skill. The Hittites mastered the smelting of iron, probably by firing the metal-bearing ore with a mixture of charcoal and limestone, producing temperatures of up to 1300°C, the highest then known to man. Their superiority in iron technology gave the Hittites sharper blades on their swords and stronger edges on their ploughshares.

From their highly civilized capital of Hattusas, 50 miles east of modern Ankara, the Hittites spread southwards along the east Mediterranean coastline, clashing with the people who lived there and even challenging mighty Egypt for supremacy over the ancient world between the Mediterranean and the Persian Gulf.

The Hittite Empire finally crumbled before hordes of sea-raiders who arrived about 1200 BC. Among these raiders were another people often referred to in the Old Testament – the Philistines. Though the Philistines became the constant enemies of the Jews, they were not the uncultured boors suggested by contemporary Jewish propaganda against them.

## King David's new capital

The golden age of the Jews began about 1000 BC under King David, who inherited the throne from Saul, his father-in-law. David extended the boundaries of the Jewish kingdom to the Euphrates and the Red Sea. He made Jerusalem the capital of the Jewish people and the centre of their religious worship.

King Solomon, who succeeded David, was in many ways an oriental despot noted as much for his lavish expenditure and ostentatious style of living as for his wisdom. It was Solomon who, about 950 BC, gave his people the great temple of Jerusalem. Many of the craftsmen who worked to embellish this magnificent shrine to the God of the Jews were Syrians and Phoenicians. The building of the temple, and Solomon's great palace which was constructed at about the same time, marked the pinnacle of Jewish power and prestige.

## Solomon's temple falls

The decline of the nation began soon afterwards, and the 12 tribes of Israel became divided into two kingdoms. The majority formed the kingdom of Israel, with its capital at Samaria. But Judah, in the south, maintained the legacy of David and Solomon and kept Jerusalem as its capital and holy city.

The Jewish people were now caught between the great power blocs of Assyria and Babylonia. In 722 BC Samaria was captured by the Assyrian king Sargon II. He deported 28,000 Israelites, who became the 'ten lost tribes of Israel'. The Assyrians brought deportees from other countries to repopulate Samaria; these newcomers married Israelites who had escaped

deportation, and their descendants became the Samaritans referred to in the Bible.

Twenty years later the Assyrians turned their attention to Judah, the second Jewish kingdom; but though the invaders sacked many Judaean cities they failed to take the capital. Jerusalem survived for more than a century until it fell in 586 BC to the Babylonian ruler Nebuchadnezzar. The city and the great temple were razed to the ground, and there was a massive deportation of Jews into captivity in Babylon.

The Psalms, that Hebrew anthology of poetry, include one beginning: 'By the rivers of Babylon, there we sat down, yea, we wept, when we remembered Zion . . .' For 70 years a large proportion of the Jewish people lived in Babylonian lands and, although many of them probably settled happily enough in the more fertile country between the Tigris and the Euphrates, there were more who could never forget their homeland. Nor were they allowed to, for a succession of great prophets, from Amos to Isaiah and Jeremiah, never stopped reproaching them for accepting their situation and for tending to drift into the ways of their pagan neighbours.

The word 'prophet' did not then have its modern meaning of one who foretells the future, but implied a man who was a poet, orator and statesman, deeply involved with the social and political needs of his people. It was the prophets who, working upon the laws of Moses and their predecessors, helped to develop the whole Jewish way of life. Unlike other Semites who looked to their rulers for on-the-spot decisions, the Jews slowly evolved a book of laws, to which reference could be made for almost any conceivable human problem or situation which might arise.

## Under Rome's shadow

When the next dominant power, the Persians, overthrew Babylon in 539 BC the first Jews were allowed to return to their homeland around Jerusalem. Gradually the city was rebuilt, and by the time a new temple was completed in 516 BC the Jews were reunited as a nation. During the next century their fortunes revived, particularly under two distinguished leaders, Nehemiah and Ezra.

The fatal conflict that was to start the Jews' long and often terrible centuries of wandering and exile began in the 1st century BC when the Romans, having broken the power of Carthage and become masters of the Mediterranean, began to interest themselves in the affairs of the East. Large areas of Asia Minor fell under their control, and in 63 BC Pompey the Great took Jerusalem and made Judah part of the Roman Empire, under the name of Judaea.

Despite a relatively prosperous period under Herod the Great, the Romans' puppet king of Judaea, the kingdom gradually declined into anarchy. The Romans were largely responsible for this decline, for they refused to take into account the religious feelings of the Jews, whose Commandments forbade them to take part in the compulsory worship of the emperor. The idea of a 'Messiah', a descendant of David who

The Jews were sustained during centuries of oppression by the belief that a Messiah, or 'anointed one', would deliver them from foreign bondage. His followers' belief that Jesus was the Messiah, which he did not deny, was rejected by the priests, and the Romans crucified him. But Christ's teachings prevailed to found a faith which is shared today by a quarter of the world's population

PRICE OF BETRAYAL *A bronze vessel, or 'pyx', discovered at Jerusalem, contained 12 silver coins – nine shekels from Tyre and three from Judaea. The coins symbolise the 30 pieces of silver paid to the disciple Judas Iscariot for betraying Christ*

SACRED SYMBOL *This 4th-century church mosaic at Tabgha, Galilee, was inspired by the miracle in which Christ turned two fishes and five loaves into food for some five thousand people. The fish became a symbol to Christians. 'Icthus' is Greek for fish, and its initials are also the initials of Greek words meaning 'Jesus Christ, Son of God, Saviour'*

would return to free his country from foreign rule and restore it to its former greatness, had long been part of Jewish hope and belief. During their years under Roman rule numerous Jewish messiahs proclaiming an earthly kingdom led rebellions against their foreign masters.

## The first Christians

Many of the followers of Jesus of Nazareth, too, probably saw him as first and foremost a Jewish nationalist. It may well have been disappointment at hearing Jesus disavow any intention of being an earthly king – 'My kingdom is not of this world' – which drove Judas to betray him. It was the Romans who crucified Jesus; but they did so at the instigation of the Jewish leaders, who saw his teaching as undermining their authority and challenging traditional Judaism. In particular they resented

CHRIST ON THE CROSS *The Crucifixion has inspired some of the finest Christian art in history – yet it was 400 years after Christ was executed on the Cross before his Crucifixion was depicted in any art form at all. For 300 years the Christians remained a persecuted sect, their faith represented only in symbols; and even after Christianity had become the official faith of the Roman Empire artists rarely showed the Crucifixion – a painful and ignominious form of execution which the Romans reserved for the lowest criminals. This panel, carved on an ivory casket in about AD 420, is one of the earliest known representations of Christ on the Cross.*

*Above his head is the derisive Latin inscription meaning 'King of the Jews'; on the left Judas Iscariot, Christ's betrayer, has hanged himself from a tree. Crucifixions usually took place outside the walls of cities in the Roman provinces, and the bodies were left hanging as testimony to the price of crime. Christianity's holiest shrine, the Church of the Holy Sepulchre in Jerusalem, is said to stand on the site of Golgotha, 'the place of the skull', where Christ was executed. The church also includes the site of the tomb where Christ's body was laid after it was taken from the Cross, and from which the covering stone was later found rolled away*

his claim, in the Sermon on the Mount, that inner virtue is more important than conformity to mere rules of behaviour. Questioned by his followers, Jesus gave clear indications that they were right to believe he was the Messiah and Son of God, and the Jewish priests regarded this as blasphemous.

With the obscure teacher and reformer Jesus of Nazareth betrayed, judged guilty, and crucified, the Romans might have expected that history would hear no more of him, and that his disillusioned disciples would swiftly disband. But never has there been a more profound mistake, and it is upon the extraordinary event of the Resurrection that the whole of Christian belief hangs.

A number of his disciples were convinced that they had seen Jesus alive after his Crucifixion, and that he had spoken to them. Their belief in this was strong enough to enable them and their successors in the early Christian Church to endure persecution and death in the certainty that Jesus was the Messiah, or Christ, and that he had promised them and all believers that death was not the end of existence. But it was not until three centuries later that Christianity became the official religion of the Roman Empire, with a huge following.

## Faith survives the dispersion

The crucifixion of Jesus about AD 30 did not end Jewish resistance to the Roman occupation. In 70, when the country was again in a state of revolt, Jerusalem, the holy city, became the core of the resistance to the Romans. Titus, the son of Emperor Vespasian, proceeded to lay siege to Jerusalem. The city fell, and the inhabitants were enslaved in their thousands and dispersed throughout the Mediterranean world. This was the first dispersion, and worse was to follow.

Continual insurrections and revolts against Roman rule led to the total destruction of Jerusalem in 135. The city was renamed Aelia Capitolina and all Jews were prohibited from entering it. A second and more important dispersion now took place, and the whole of Judaea was renamed Palestine.

The later history of the Jews belongs in part to that of all the countries throughout the world into which Jewish communities spread. Yet despite their dispersion, or Diaspora, and despite their persecution, the strength of their religion and the hope that Jerusalem would one day become again the Jewish religious centre enabled the Jews to retain a national identity wherever they found themselves.

## THE FACE OF A MYCENAEAN KING REDISCOVERED AFTER 3000 YEARS

Artistry in gold was one of the principal skills of the wealthy Mycenaeans, the earliest civilized settlers in mainland Greece. The faces of their dead kings were often covered before burial with masks of beaten gold, like this one found in a tomb at Mycenae in 1876; the custom was probably adopted from Egypt. Though the Mycenaeans lived a thousand years before Greece's golden age, their exploits were kept alive in tales sung by wandering bards, and Homer later immortalised them in his epics. When the German archaeologist Heinrich Schliemann unearthed the graves at Mycenae he was convinced that he had found the very tombs of Homer's heroes: 'I have gazed upon the face of Agamemnon!', he exclaimed. In fact, this bearded king whose death mask was among Schliemann's discoveries lived about 1500 BC, near the beginning of the Mycenaean age and about three centuries before the war in which, according to Homer, Agamemnon led the Greeks against Troy

# Artists and warriors of the Aegean

3000–1100 BC

*In Crete and Greece, the wealthy settlements
of the Minoans and Mycenaeans
introduced Bronze Age civilization to Europe*

**THE AEGEAN IN 1500 BC**

*Skill in seamanship and trade across the
Mediterranean brought wealth to the
enterprising ancestors of the Greeks*

The narrow, mountainous island of Crete, at the southern end of the Aegean Sea, had become by 2500 BC the home of a peaceful people, endowed with a love of gaiety and beauty, and renowned as traders throughout the eastern Mediterranean. These Minoans –named after their legendary king Minos– were largely unknown to history until in 1900 the English archaeologist Sir Arthur Evans uncovered the ruins of a great palace at Knossos, near modern Heraklion in Crete. His discoveries revealed that an advanced European civilization was thriving in Crete nearly 4500 years ago, at a time which made it contemporary with the Old Kingdom period of Egypt's civilization and with the Sumerian age in Mesopotamia.

Further north, by about 1900 BC the first Greek-speaking peoples were moving into mainland Greece. These were Aryan warriors in search of new pastures, and with their superior bronze weapons and tools they took over the lands previously occupied only by Stone Age peasant farmers. By 1600 BC the fortresses of the new settlers–including Mycenae, after which they are named–rivalled Knossos in the splendour of their jewellery and their gold

ornaments. By the time Minoan civilization declined, about 1400 BC, Mycenaean traders and colonisers had absorbed much of the Minoans' culture into their own. In the mingling of these two civilizations can be traced the seeds of the classical age of Greece which was at its height 1000 years later.

The first settlers arrived in Crete about 3000 BC, probably from Anatolia or the eastern Mediterranean. They crossed the Mediterranean and the Aegean in primitive sailing boats, and sea-power became the basis of their civilization. The Minoans were skilled metalworkers, and they sailed to the coasts of Spain to buy tin. They bought gold and pearls from Egypt and ivory from North Africa. In exchange, the Minoans sold their wine and olive oil, and luxury products which were outstanding both for their craftsmanship and for their beauty. Minoan artists made extravagant jewellery of gold, beads from a type of glazed earthenware known as faience, and magnificent vases from stone quarried in Crete or imported.

Outstanding examples of Minoan craftsmanship found in Egypt, Greece and Italy are the products of a sophisticated way of life unique in

**HIGHWAY TO KNOSSOS**

*A stone viaduct, some traces of which still
stand, led across a broad ravine to the ornate
palace at Knossos, heart of the Minoan
civilization of ancient Crete. Beyond the palace
are the houses of a city which held 100,000
people – the biggest in Europe at the time*

# Decorated palaces of a lively and peaceful kingdom

the ancient world. The impression created by Minoan buildings, original wall-paintings and exquisite jewellery and gold work is of a gaiety, lightheartedness and a love of beauty that has rarely been equalled.

## Capital city of 100,000 people

For nearly 600 years, from 1950 to 1400 BC, Crete enjoyed a golden age. Homer was later to refer to the island in this period as 'a rich and pleasant land, densely peopled'. In the principal centres of Knossos, Phaistos and Mallia which have been excavated, the ruins of great palaces give evidence of the Minoans' architectural ability. Their buildings contained elaborate drainage and piped water systems unsurpassed until modern times.

Knossos, the capital city, was built a little inland from Crete's north-eastern coast – right across a fault in the earth's crust. Twice the city was destroyed by earthquakes, and twice it was rebuilt. At its peak Knossos, together with its nearby harbour town, may have housed as many as 100,000 people – an enormous population at that time, making it the largest European city of the day.

The great palace at Knossos was the centre of Minoan government and power. At its heart was a rectangular courtyard, more than 100 ft long. Round this was arranged a series of inter-connected rooms in two or more storeys, covering a total of six acres. The palace was the home of the king and queen and their court. It was also a religious centre, with homes for priests and priestesses, and the centre of the island's administration. There were offices and workshops, as well as storerooms for oil, grain and wine into which islanders paid the taxes levied on their farms.

The Cretan palaces abounded in brilliantly coloured wall-paintings, radiating the sense of a civilization in which war seems hardly to have intruded. The magnificent wall-paintings in the palaces were of birds, beasts and flowers, of young women and youths. The Minoans had an unrivalled feeling for nature, and their illustrations of a bull or a horse, an octopus or a fish, are as vivid today as when the artists painted them nearly 4000 years ago.

One subject which appears on several Minoan wall-paintings, as well as on numerous seals and vases, is the ritual 'bull-leaping', in which teams of young men and women somersaulted over a bull's horns. The bull had long been revered as a symbol of male potency: in Crete it may also have symbolised the terrifying power of the earthquakes to which the island was always subject. The bull in the Cretan ritual was not doomed to die. It was there as a symbol of the power of nature. The youths and maidens who somersaulted gracefully over its back were displaying not only their agility, but the power of man to trifle even with this most dangerous of the island's beasts. It was almost certainly

## DANCERS WHO DARED THE BULL

*A wall-painting from Knossos shows the famous Cretan bull-leaping, a ritual which may have originated in sacrifices to appease the 'Earth Bull' which periodically devastated the island by earthquakes. The girl on the left grasps the bull's horns, ready to somersault over its back when it flings her into the air. A youth is shown in mid-somersault, and the girl on the right steadies the acrobats as they land. The first bull-leapers were princes and princesses of the Minoan court; but later, slaves were trained to perform the ceremony*

the memory of this bull-leaping that gave rise, in later Greek tales, to the legend of the Minotaur or 'Bullman' – the monstrous offspring of Pasiphae, the wife of King Minos, and a bull. The monster was slain by Theseus in the labyrinth in which it was imprisoned.

The word 'labyrinth' was probably suggested by the maze-like palace at Knossos, the walls of which were decorated with the *labrys*, or double axe, the emblem of the Cretan Mother Goddess. Minoan religion centred around this Mother Goddess, regarded as the source of all life. She was depicted bare-breasted and slender-waisted, with a tall head-dress and an elaborate, full-length skirt – an embodiment of the ideal Cretan woman.

## Worship in caves

The Minoans are thought to have worshipped in sacred caves, and the fact that in some representations of the goddess she is wearing seed-pods of the poppy in her hair suggests that opium may have played a part in her rites. There is no trace in Crete of the obsession with religion which characterised the civilizations of Egypt and Mesopotamia. The Minoans, in their religion as in their art and palace architecture, appear to have been a more light-hearted and sophisticated people than their contemporaries.

The Cretans were also a literate people. Clay tablets found in excavated houses and palaces are inscribed with hieroglyphs – a form of picture writing derived from Egypt – and later with a non-pictorial script known as Linear A. This is the earliest known script in which the characters are arranged in horizontal lines; but it is also one of the few ancient scripts which have still not been deciphered.

## The rise of the Mycenaeans

The splendour of Minoan Crete was soon to be rivalled by an explosion of power and wealth on the mainland of Greece. The earliest known inhabitants of Greece were peasant farmers, still using stone tools. About 1900 BC, Greek-speaking warriors from the north, the Mycenaeans, took over the territory of these farmers. Their conquest was aided by their superior weapons and tools of bronze.

The Mycenaeans, however, were of a different stock from the Minoans. They were taller and wore beards, while the Minoans were clean-shaven. And they were a warrior race, worshipping Zeus, a sky god of lightning and violence. These Mycenaean warriors were the heroes whom Homer was later to immortalise as the ancestors of the Greeks of his own day.

While the culture of Crete was essentially peaceful and feminine, with Knossos acting as a kind of Paris of its time, the culture of the Mycenaeans was aggressively masculine. The city of Knossos, for instance, was unwalled, the Minoans basing their security on command of the sea. But the great Mycenaean cities – such

## A GODDESS IN COURTLY STYLE

*The Mother Goddess was the focus of religious worship in Minoan Crete. The Minoans made effigies of the goddess – like this one in faience, a form of glazed earthenware – and set them in shrines in their homes and palaces. The goddess is depicted brandishing two snakes; the snake was sacred to the Minoans, representing the renewal of life by the annual shedding of its skin. A seated leopard on the head of the goddess symbolises her command of the wild forces of nature. The goddess is dressed in the style of a fashionable woman of the Minoan court, as shown in many wall-paintings, with an elaborate flounced skirt, and ornamented stomacher below the bare breasts. Women had a high status in Minoan society, and were treated as men's equals. They wore their hair long and elaborately styled, and used paint on their lips and round their eyes. The freedom enjoyed by Minoan women was almost unknown elsewhere in the ancient world, where women were usually regarded as chattels*

# Heroic struggles immortalised by Homer

as Mycenae, Argos, Tiryns and Pylos – are fortresses dominating the surrounding country, rather like the castles which Norman barons were to build centuries later.

The splendours of Mycenaean art were first discovered in the late 19th century by the German archaeologist Heinrich Schliemann. In the royal tombs he excavated at Mycenae he found gold death-masks of kings, splendid tiaras of gold for their queens, and a host of wonderful bowls, daggers and wine cups. A people who could take such wealth to their graves must obviously have lived in splendour. Some of the gold jewellery – particularly the more delicate and elaborate items – show a resemblance to Cretan craftsmanship. It is probable that Minoans worked for these Mycenaean rulers, while the native craftsmen themselves imitated Cretan work.

### The real Atlantis?

Minoan civilization collapsed in about 1400 BC. Its fate was sealed by an immense volcanic eruption, when the Aegean island of Santorini, also called Thera, blew up in one of the greatest explosions in history. Crete, only 75 miles to the south, must have been devastated by the shock and by the tidal wave and hail of ash that followed. Rich frescoes in Minoan style have been found in Santorini, indicating that the island was a thriving part of the Minoan Empire. It may well have been the Santorini eruption that gave rise to the legend, known to the Egyptians and recorded by Plato, of the lost kingdom of Atlantis, overwhelmed by the sea because of the 'lawless ambition and power' of its inhabitants.

The Mycenaeans inevitably benefited by the fall of their Minoan trade rivals, and Mycenaean trade soon increased all over the Aegean and the Levant. Colonies and trading outposts that had formerly been Minoan were now taken over by the Mycenaeans. Cyprus, which had important deposits of copper, also came under the control of Mycenaean rulers.

A discovery made only in 1952 suggests that the Mycenaeans may even have ruled Crete for a short time before the Minoan world was engulfed. Clay tablets found at Mycenae and Pylos in Greece, and also at Knossos among ruins known to belong to the later stages of Minoan civilization, bear a similar linear script. This was given the name of Linear B, to distinguish it from the Linear A script used by the earlier Minoans. Despite innumerable efforts for half a century, nobody managed to decipher Linear B. Then, in 1952, a young English scholar named Michael Ventris 'broke the code' and discovered that the inscriptions were lists of stores and equipment in a form of Greek 500 years older than Homer.

### Halls of the warlords

On the islands they overran, as in their city-states in mainland Greece, the Mycenaean kings and nobles lived in great splendour – although never with the refinement of the Minoans. The life of a Mycenaean noble resembled that of a Viking chief. The heart of his palace was a great hall, with a central hearth and a smoke-hole above it. Near the main door there was a bathroom, so that the owner and his guests, dusty and hot from their riding, could wash on arrival. Around the hall, a number of out-buildings served as storehouses, living quarters for servants and followers, and stables for horses. There were also sheds for chariots, used by the Mycenaeans, like the Assyrians and Egyptians, for hunting and warfare.

Fighting, riding, hunting and looking after their estates, the Mycenaeans foreshadowed a long line of other warlords throughout the world. They drank deep from golden beakers in their great halls, and listened to the songs of the wandering minstrels, telling of the exploits of their ancestors, and of battle and travel in real or imaginary far-off lands.

The power of the Mycenaeans dwindled about 1200 BC as their trade routes were cut by sea raiders. According to Homer, the Trojan War (1194-1184 BC) was fought by the Mycenaean Greeks to avenge the abduction of Helen, wife of the Greek king Menelaus; she had been carried off by Paris, a Trojan prince. But the historical cause may well have been the stranglehold which Troy, at the western end of the Hellespont, exercised over the Mycenaeans' grain route from the Black Sea.

In the 'dark age' which followed, as Dorian invaders from the north destroyed Mycenae and pushed down through Greece, the stories of the Mycenaean heroes – Odysseus, Achilles, Nestor, Agamemnon – were kept alive in oral tradition, to be recorded by Homer four centuries later. His epic poems the *Iliad* and the *Odyssey*, written about 850 BC, were a Bible to the Greeks, and they remain one of the greatest achievements of the human genius. They are the culmination of all the centuries of unknown bards and saga-singers who had entertained the Mycenaeans in their palaces, but they bear the unique and individual imprint of one man.

### The siege of Troy

The *Iliad* concentrates on only a few days of the Greeks' ten-year-long siege of Troy. It ends with the death of Hector of Troy, killed in single combat by Achilles the Greek, before the city of Troy itself is captured. Yet the few episodes which Homer has chosen to describe enable him to compress the whole of war, human courage, ambition, cruelty and power into little more than 16,000 lines. Other poets, such as Virgil in the *Aeneid*, tried to emulate Homer; but throughout the history of European literature the sustained power of Homer's achievement has hardly been surpassed.

The *Odyssey*, about 13,000 lines long, is the greatest travel story of all time, describing the wanderings of the wily Odysseus as he tries to make his way back after the Trojan War to his island-home of Ithaca, and to his wife and son.

The events about which Homer was writing occurred several centuries before he was born. Living in the Iron Age, he often confuses the pattern of the world he himself knew with the Bronze Age of the Mycenaeans, whose story he was telling. Some of Homer's warriors, for

instance, carry the long, leather shields of the Mycenaean age, while others are described as using the smaller, round shields of the poet's own day. Some warriors use the long swords of the Bronze Age, while others do battle with the short sword, which was not perfected until the Iron Age. Again, Homer's heroes cremate their dead, in the fashion of the later Greeks, whereas the Mycenaeans buried their dead.

The Greeks themselves, who learnt Homer by heart, were never in any doubt that his stories were true. They saw them as the basis of all their history, and proudly claimed descent from the Homeric heroes. Many centuries later, European scholars dismissed the stories as pure fantasy. But these scholars were refuted in the 1870's when Heinrich Schliemann, excavating at Hissarlik, at the southern end of the Dardanelles, uncovered the site of the city of Troy – in the exact region where Homer had placed it, under the name of Ilium, in the *Iliad*.

## STONE LIONS ON GUARD AT THE MYCENAEANS' HILLTOP CITADEL

'A strong-founded citadel rich in gold' was how Homer described the fortress city of Mycenae, set on a hilltop above the Argive Plain in southern Greece. Its craggy massiveness contrasts with the delicacy of Minoan palace architecture; the warrior Mycenaeans had no sea to protect them against armed invaders. The Lion Gate, right foreground, built about 1350 BC, is the oldest monumental sculpture in Greece.

The carved decoration which gives the gate its name also serves an architectural purpose, saving the lintel of the gate from having to bear the weight of the giant stone blocks which form the ramparts on either side of it. The circle within the walls contains the six burial shafts which were discovered in 1876; inside were rich treasures of gold and bronze which dead heroes took with them to their graves

### LION HUNT ON A DAGGER

Hunting was a favourite relaxation of Mycenaean nobles. This bronze dagger found in one of the shaft graves at Mycenae shows huntsmen attacking three lions – animals which were then common in Greece. The design is inlaid with gold and silver

# The enduring miracle of ancient Greece

## 800–30 BC

*From a group of small city-states, isolated among high mountains, arose a surge of creative brilliance that laid the foundations of Western civilization*

**THE GREEK WORLD IN 750 BC**

*Emigrants sailed out from the city-states of mainland Greece to found colonies all round the Mediterranean*

The foundations of European civilization were laid by the Greeks. Their achievements in the arts, in building, in science and in philosophy were to mould the culture of the entire Western world, and 2000 years later a broad range of human activities, from sport to philosophy, still follow a pattern derived from the ancient Greeks.

The groups of eastern Europeans who migrated south and occupied one of the most beautiful countries in the world achieved an extraordinarily successful balance between the practicality of the north and the passionate vitality of the south. They were a violent people, ever prone to war. Yet at the same time they aspired to an ideal of moderation in all things, expressed in the words 'Nothing in excess' inscribed at their great shrine of Delphi. Balance and harmony, the classical ideals expounded by philosophers like Socrates and his pupil, Plato, were the guiding principles of the Greeks' architecture and painting, and of their statuary, with its restrained but vital form; the Venus de Milo is still regarded as the essence of womanhood. The Greek religion, with many gods and goddesses who intervened in the lives of mortals, inspired some of the

world's most poetic mythology. The strength of Hercules, the unrivalled beauty of Helen of Troy, the wrath of Zeus, the wiliness of Odysseus, the bravery of Achilles, the speed of Hermes, the loves of Aphrodite – all these have become part of the Western inheritance.

Greek myths abound in vitality and have something to say – wise, witty, bawdy or beautiful – about every conceivable human situation. The myths form a colourful framework underlying much of European literature; they show a profound understanding of human nature, and have provided themes for many of the greatest artists in painting, sculpture and music throughout the centuries.

The Greek conception of the importance of the individual was unique. At a time when most people were regarded by their rulers as no more than chattels, the Greeks asserted the dignity and rights of the individual human being – even though this did not prevent them from keeping slaves. Pessimistic regarding the future of the soul after death, they asserted the importance of life now; of courage, honour and love, and enjoyment of the beauties of the physical world. This joy in the sun, the earth, the sea, or in a perfectly proportioned human body, shines

### A CITY AND ITS GODDESS

*A 4th-century BC sculpture in bronze (left) depicts Pallas Athena, the Greek goddess of wisdom, after whom Athens was named. To the Greeks, the gods were very human in character: they joked, laughed, fell in love, grew jealous, and constantly interfered in the affairs of men. It was worth paying them homage.*

*The citizens of Athens built the Parthenon (right) in 438 BC as a temple to Athena, on the summit of the Acropolis. Originally the Acropolis, or 'high city', was a place of refuge in times of war; later it became the spiritual centre of the city*

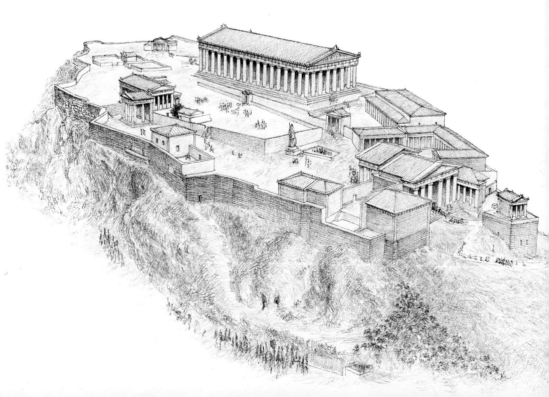

# Foreign shores beckon and from the mountains the gods look down

TRADE SPREADS GREEK CULTURE ACROSS THE SEAS

*As the population of their city-states grew, the Greeks sailed overseas to buy commodities, such as cereals and metals, which were scarce at home. On the cup above, King Arcesilas of Cyrene, a Greek colony in present-day Libya, checks the weighing of silphium, a plant whose juice was used as a medicine or condiment. A scribe beside the king records the weighing, and the*

*bales are stored in a vault beneath the king's feet. The vase below, made by the Athenian potter Nikosthenes in 520 BC, shows Greek merchant ships in full sail, with their loading ladders secured to their sterns. The Greeks sold oil, wine, pottery, jewellery and sculpture to pay for their imports, and colonies founded to foster trade spread Greek culture to distant lands*

through the Greeks' works of art. Th
their history the Greeks lived in sepa
munities, the so-called 'city-states', wh
united to form a single nation and we
war with each other. It was one of t
states, Athens, that by throwing o
powerful rulers and giving every free
citizen a voice in its government, fir
the world the concept of democracy.
itself is Greek—from *demos*, 'the pec
*krateo*, 'to rule' – as one word in every
in the Western world today is Greek.

### Into the Iron Age

Groups of Greek-speaking invaders, th
started pouring into mainland Greec
Balkans about 1100 BC. They probabl
with them the knowledge of iron wor
their iron swords proved more than a
the Bronze Age Mycenaeans, an earli
immigrants already established in G

The four centuries following the c
Mycenaean civilization were Greec
Age'. But during this period some c
out against the Dorian invaders, and
centres poured refugees from the ove
Mycenaean strongholds. As their pe
grew, boatloads of citizens sailed ou
new colonies in the Aegean islands a
west coast of Asia Minor, in p
Turkey. These settlements came to
Ionian; their inhabitants retained th
tional Greek way of life, and kept
epics of the Mycenaean heroes whi
was later to record.

As city life gradually revived afte
the first characteristically Greek c
began slowly to emerge. By now the
Hellas, originally a district in The
being used to describe the whole cou
both Dorians and Ionians saw them
and foremost as Hellenes – the wor
comes from *Graeci*, the Latin name
The Hellenes felt themselves united a
'barbarians' or non-Hellenes, but at
time the towns they set up reflected
start, the different character of their
settlers. This difference between the
branches of the Greek race was to l
numerable internal conflicts and, in
to the disastrous war between Sparta
çity, and Athens, whose history wer
pre-Dorian times.

### Farmers of a city-state

The Greek *polis*, or 'city', from whi
the English word 'politics', was both
an area of countryside around it.
population of Greece during the classi
was so small that only a few city-stat
Athens or Syracuse, had a populatio
than 20,000. The smallness of the
often separated from their neighbou
mountains, led to the innumerable
and shifting alliances of Greek his
number of separate states was also,
the core of the Greeks' cultural bril
in these small, self-contained co
every citizen could feel he had an

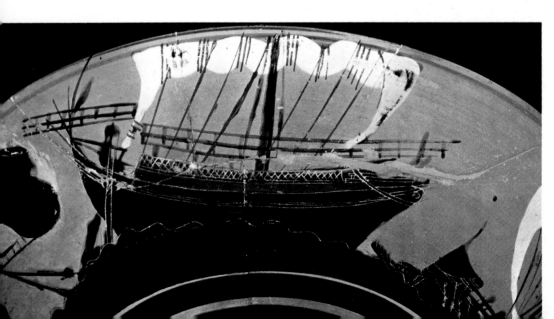

contribution to make to the life of the society around him. Everyday life was simple. Peasant farmers cultivated the fertile valleys and coastal strips. They lived on a diet of bread, olives and olive oil, wine and vegetables – very much as the Greek peasant does today. Meat was a luxury and goats provided most of the milk, for grazing was sparse. The long coastline, however, was excellent for fishing; Homer refers to the 'fish-infested sea'.

The olive, the tree sacred to the goddess Athena, was all important to the Greeks, not only for its fruit but also for its oil, which was the sole source of lighting for their houses. The yeoman farmer was the backbone of Greece. Frugal, hardy and industrious, he was the mainstay of the economy as well as providing the soldiery in time of war.

## Fortress of the 'high city'

In the three centuries from 800 to 500 BC, the so-called Archaic period, Greek towns were built to a standard pattern, whether they were on the Aegean islands, the Asian mainland, or in Greece itself. Most of the buildings were of timber and bricks of mud, dried in the sun. They clustered around a high and easily defensible point known as the Acropolis, the 'high city', which formed a fortress to which everyone could resort in times of war.

The ordinary houses were mostly cube-shaped and, like the temples and statues, brightly painted. The appearance was colourful and cheerful, but a far call from the grandeur of the Mycenaeans or the sophisticated elegance of Minoan Crete. The greatest achievements of the Greeks of the Archaic period were in their pottery, statues and poetry. By about 700 BC, ceramic artists in Athens were producing wonderful painted vases showing ships and warriors, lions, hunting dogs and battles, as well as peaceful scenes of domestic life. Their sculpture, at first influenced by Egyptian models, soon acquired its own qualities of grace and fine workmanship, which were to make sculpture the most representative of Greek art forms.

Greek sculptors excelled, in particular, in the portrayal of the human figure with realism and liveliness. The Greeks considered a healthy, well-proportioned body the most beautiful thing on earth. One reason why they despised the Persians and other 'barbarians' was for wearing so many clothes. Throughout Greece male athletes competed naked, and in Sparta the girls also ran and wrestled naked.

Most of the statues of gods or goddesses, youths or maidens, have their lips curved slightly upwards in what has been called 'the archaic smile'. They were carved from marble, which was usually painted – particularly the eyes and the hair, and in some cases the women's dresses.

## Poetry sung to the lyre

The Archaic period was also marked by the development of lyric poetry. Hymns to the gods, and epics such as Homer wrote about the history of the Greek race and its famous men,

The Greeks worshipped a colourful collection of gods and goddesses, each of whom had strongly defined human characteristics. These included human failings such as lust and deceitfulness – but this did not lessen the respect in which the gods were held. A vivid tapestry of myth was woven around the gods; other enduring legends grew up concerning mortal heroes, such as Achilles and Theseus, who claimed descent from the gods. The deeds of gods and heroes provided the basis for nearly all the works of Greek poets and dramatists, and shrines were built in their honour throughout the Greek world

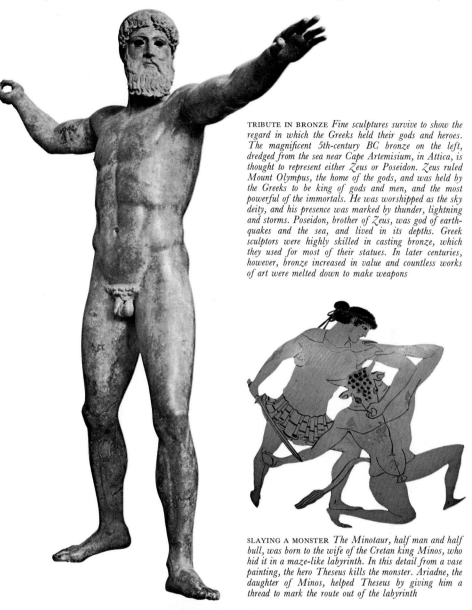

TRIBUTE IN BRONZE *Fine sculptures survive to show the regard in which the Greeks held their gods and heroes. The magnificent 5th-century BC bronze on the left, dredged from the sea near Cape Artemisium, in Attica, is thought to represent either Zeus or Poseidon. Zeus ruled Mount Olympus, the home of the gods, and was held by the Greeks to be king of gods and men, and the most powerful of the immortals. He was worshipped as the sky deity, and his presence was marked by thunder, lightning and storms. Poseidon, brother of Zeus, was god of earthquakes and the sea, and lived in its depths. Greek sculptors were highly skilled in casting bronze, which they used for most of their statues. In later centuries, however, bronze increased in value and countless works of art were melted down to make weapons*

SLAYING A MONSTER *The Minotaur, half man and half bull, was born to the wife of the Cretan king Minos, who hid it in a maze-like labyrinth. In this detail from a vase painting, the hero Theseus kills the monster. Ariadne, the daughter of Minos, helped Theseus by giving him a thread to mark the route out of the labyrinth*

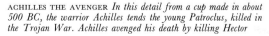

ACHILLES THE AVENGER *In this detail from a cup made in about 500 BC, the warrior Achilles tends the young Patroclus, killed in the Trojan War. Achilles avenged his death by killing Hector*

THE JUDGE *Hermes asks Paris of Troy to name the fairest of three goddesses. His choice, Aphrodite, helped him to seize Helen of Sparta*

# *A golden age dawns in the Athens of Pericles*

had already given the Greeks a sense of national identity. Lyric poets like Archilochus from the island of Paros, Alcman of Sparta, and Sappho, from the island of Lesbos, were doing something new. Their poetry was the product of small and cultured communities where, over the wine at a dinner party, a poet would recite – or more probably sing to the lyre – about personal affairs, loves and hates, to the friends around him.

In one typical lyric, Sappho wrote:
> On the black earth, say some, the thing
> most lovely
> Is a host of horsemen, or some, foot
> soldiers;
> Others say, of ships, but I – whatsoever
> Anyone loveth.

During the Archaic period there also began to emerge the beginnings of philosophy – the 'love of knowledge' which was to become one of Greece's enduring contributions to Western civilization. Contemporary peoples such as the Persians, the Syrians and the Phoenicians saw the world as being ruled by gods and goddesses, with ordinary men and women as servile creatures entirely in their thrall. The Greeks began to try to interpret rationally the secrets of the universe. In so doing, they gave man himself a new dignity and self-respect. For the first time in history, man was to some degree master of his own fate.

Nevertheless, for the majority of the people the old religion was rich and colourful enough to provide an answer to most of man's basic wants and fears. Religious processions and sacrifices played an immense part in Greek life, and it was to the gods sung of by Homer that the Greeks dedicated their superb temples. In time of trouble they still turned to prophets such as the oracle at the shrine of Apollo, god of the sun, at Delphi.

## Riches from the colonies

From 750 to 550 BC the Greeks spread outwards from their homelands round the Aegean shores. Colonisation began through the need to trade for metals that were unobtainable in Greece, or for cereals which could not be grown in the Greeks' mountainous homeland. In return they sold oil and wine and the products of their craftsmen – pottery, jewellery and statues.

After a time, emigration overseas was accelerated by population pressures within the small city-states. Soon, much of southern Italy and most of southern and eastern Sicily became planted with colonies, from which Greece was to draw much of its wealth. Cities such as Croton and Sybaris in Italy, and Syracuse and Agrigento in Sicily became immensely powerful, astonishing visiting Greek mainlanders with their wealth; it was from the luxury of Sybaris that the word 'sybaritic' was derived. Naples and Marseilles also handled a large volume of trade. To the east, a small Greek town called Byzantium grew up on the Bosporus; centuries later, it was to become capital of the Byzantine Empire, under the new name of Constantinople. In the 6th century the city-states of Sparta and Athens emerged as the two major powers

in Greece itself. Sparta was founded by the war-like Dorians in a plain on the banks of the River Eurotas in southern Greece. The city was unwalled, for its citizens boasted that their swords and their courage were walls enough.

The Spartans, an alien aristocracy, had subjugated the native peasants in the area called Laconia over which they ruled; but because of the continuing hostility of their subjects, as well as the constant enmity of their neighbours, the Spartans had always to be ready for war.

Their state was the most disciplined in Greece. When children were born they were inspected by the city elders and, if considered weakly, they were exposed on a hillside to die. At the age of seven, boys were taken from their parents, placed in military-style troops and trained to endure hardship and discomfort. The Spartan Code produced the finest soldiers in Greece – a 'master race' – but little culture.

Meanwhile, Athens, Sparta's old rival, was rising to the greatness of its classical age. The intellectual and artistic abilities of its citizens were encouraged by the growing political freedom introduced by the reforms of Solon (640–560 BC), the statesman who laid the foundations of Athenian democracy.

## Challenge from Persia

Despite the military reputation of Sparta, it was the naval skill of the seamen of Athens that saved Greece from falling a prey to the rising power of Persia, the greatest empire of its time. The threat from Persia first arose in 546 BC when Cyrus the Great, already ruler of much of Asia Minor, marched westwards and conquered the coastal lands of Greek Ionia. Mainland Greece was left alone for a time, although the threat to its independence was clear.

The first Persian invasion came in 490 BC under King Darius. The Athenians beat off this attack by a great victory at Marathon. A messenger ran 22 miles to Athens with news of the victory, the first 'marathon' run; he then collapsed and died. Ten years later the Persians came back, under Darius's son Xerxes. He bridged the Hellespont, the present-day Dardanelles, by lashing more than 300 boats together side by side, defeated the heroic but outnumbered Spartan army in the pass of Thermopylae and marched on Athens. Nothing, it seemed, could stop the victorious Xerxes from conquering Greece and making it part of his huge Persian Empire.

Xerxes captured Athens, but Themistocles, the Athenian commander, engaged the Persians in a great sea battle at Salamis, just off the coast near Athens, and routed their fleet. A further victory on land at Plataea in 479 BC – this time the Greeks were under the command of a Spartan general, Pausanias – completed the defeat of the Persians.

The main consequences of the defeat of Xerxes was to give the Greeks, and in particular the two major cities, Athens and Sparta, an enormous feeling of pride and liberation. They had challenged and defeated the greatest power on earth. Athens, whose navy had proved supreme, was left as the dominant

## ARENAS WHERE DRAMA BEGAN

Tragic drama in poetic form was one of the greatest Greek contributions to the world. Its finest flowering came in Athens in the 5th century BC. Every year a great open-air festival was held in honour of Dionysus, the god of revelry. There were dances and ceremonies, and finally a contest between dramatists who each wrote a series of three tragedies based on Greek legends. The audiences chose the winner. Later every major Greek city had its own theatre, where travelling companies played; and dramatists such as Aeschylus, Sophocles and Euripides set a pattern which much of Western drama was to follow

THE FIRST DRAMA *The idea of presenting epic or moral stories in an auditorium, out of which tragic drama was to develop, probably went back to primitive rituals honouring Dionysus, the god who was said to have taught the cultivation of the grape and winemaking. The Romans renamed him Bacchus. The rituals were often accompanied by frenzied dances; the 5th-century cup above shows a woman dancer, or maenad, wearing a snake as a head-dress and carrying a staff and a leopard cub. From these crude beginnings, drama developed. First poets began to compose lyric songs for the ceremonies, then gradually they came to deal with more profound themes, and the gods began to wear sterner faces than that of the perpetually revelling Dionysus. In the great tragedies, man often suffers through the inscrutable will of the gods. But Euripides, for the theme of his last great drama, The Bacchae, returned to the roots of Greek drama with a study of the wild followers of Dionysus*

naval power in the Aegean. Sparta was shown to possess the finest army in Greece, but the Spartans despised merchants and craftsmen and regarded trade with contempt. They thus cut themselves off from contact with other countries and the stimulus which such contact brings. Athens, however, was to build an empire of more than 200 associate city-states and islands – the so-called Delian League – from which flowed the wealth and inspiration which helped, for a brief 50 years, to support a period of culture without parallel in history.

## A city rebuilt with genius

The Athens that arose after the defeat of the Persians was the richest and most beautiful city in Greece. Nearly all the old city, including its walls, had been shattered during the brief Persian occupation, and the Athenians rebuilt it completely. The poet Pindar (518–438 BC) described the new city as 'shining, violet-crowned, and famous in song'. The Piraeus or

PERSONAL POETRY *Lyric poetry – first composed to be sung to the lyre – sprang from small, cultured communities and dealt with the affairs of individual people, in contrast to the epic themes of the tragic dramatists. Two lyric poets of genius who lived on the island of Lesbos about 610 BC, Alcaeus and Sappho, are depicted together on this wine-cooler. Sappho was the only outstanding woman poet of ancient Greece*

MASK DRAMA *The vast size of Greek theatres made it difficult for actors to convey emotion to distant spectators by facial expression alone. They therefore used masks that instantly identified the characters they were playing as happy or sad, young or old. This bronze tragic mask was found among ruins at Piraeus. The mask was called a 'persona' in Latin, and this is the origin of the English words 'person' and 'personality'*

OPEN-AIR THEATRE *Greek theatres were huge auditoriums where thousands could be seated in the open air. The greatest to survive the centuries is at Epidaurus in the Peloponnese. Fifty-five tiers of stone seats, accommodating 14,000 spectators, fan steeply like the sides of a bowl around the circular 'orchestra', where the chorus performed. The pillars on the right were part of the stage where the main action of the play took place. During drama festivals all business might be halted and the jails emptied as citizens sat through day-long programmes of tragedy and comedy. Plays by the great Greek dramatists are still performed in the auditorium at Epidaurus during the summer, and the acoustics are still so true that an actor speaking from the centre of the stage can be heard easily all over the auditorium*

harbour area was laid out to a geometric grid-plan, one of the first examples of town-planning in Europe. The Acropolis, which was originally a citadel and later became a religious centre, was adorned with the magnificent Parthenon, a marble temple to the goddess Athena.

Ictinus and Callicrates were the architects who achieved the Parthenon's harmonious proportions, while another genius, the sculptor Pheidias, gave it a gold and ivory statue of Athena 40 ft high. He also supervised work on the sculptured decoration round the exterior, much of which was taken to England by Lord Elgin. Meanwhile other sculptors, painters, potters and jewellers of Athens were creating unrivalled works of art.

## The birth of democracy

In the 5th century BC, Athens was at its peak under Pericles. He was an aristocrat and an Athenian imperialist, who had a dream of a city that would be worthy of its empire – a city which the allies of Athens would be proud to visit, and where they would see for themselves that the tribute they paid had been expended in creating the most gracious capital on earth. Pericles was also a democrat, at a time when the idea that every freeborn adult male citizen should have a say in the running of the state was a novel one. Most Greek city-states had hitherto been run by oligarchies – groups of powerful aristocratic families – or by single absolute rulers, or 'tyrants'. In 621 BC one Athenian law-giver, Draco, introduced a code of punishments which included the death penalty for stealing a cabbage – thus making 'Draconian' a byword for extreme severity.

One reason why a different form of government evolved in Athens was the fact that the city was primarily a naval power. Its war galleys were rowed by ordinary working men conscripted into the forces who, since they contributed so much to the state, felt they should have a share in determining how it was run. In aristocratic Sparta, where all manual labour was done by peasants and serfs, such an idea would have been unthinkable. At the same time the community of Athens was small enough for every citizen to make his voice heard. Fishermen, merchants, jewellers, potters and landowners met on equal terms in the governing assembly, and had an equal say in discussions on all important matters. This interchange of ideas between men from all walks of life made Athens a very human world, completely different from conservative Sparta. Not to show an interest in public affairs and matters of state was considered so stupid that our word 'idiot' derives from the Greek word meaning 'a private citizen' – someone who attended only to his own affairs and did not bother with those of the city.

One feature of Athenian democracy that distinguished it from modern democracy was that the Athenians owned slaves. These were either prisoners of war or, as in the case of the 'helots' of Sparta, peasants of an occupied

# A new respect for man and his exploits

PROUD WARRIORS OF SPARTA

*The Spartans were a sternly disciplined people whose code produced soldiers of unrivalled skill and courage. This bronze shows a warrior with locks of carefully dressed hair falling from his helmet. According to the historian Herodotus, Spartans combed their hair before battle 'that they might die with their heads tidy'*

region who were treated as serfs. Though most slaves were domestic servants and well treated, they did not qualify for a vote. Nor did women have a vote. Athenian society was largely masculine, and women were kept in almost as great seclusion as in the later Muslim world. Men even did the shopping, handing their purchases to slaves.

## Dramas of gods and man

In the field of human culture, one of the enduring legacies of Athens has been its achievement in poetic drama. The Athenian dramatists used themes from Greek mythology and history as a basis for examining man's fate and his duties in the world. Aeschylus, one of the greatest Athenian dramatists, fought at Marathon, and his drama *The Persians* dealing with the war is the oldest surviving Greek play. He and his two successors, Sophocles and Euripides, are known to have written more than 300 plays between them, though only 33 have survived in full, and the works of many other Greek dramatists have been lost entirely.

In the work of Aeschylus the moral element is all-important and man is seen as being dominated by his obligations to the gods. If he breaks their laws or becomes proud and boastful (the sin of *hubris*), then he will incur *nemesis* or the vengeance of the immortals. The powerful and austere world that Aeschylus created has moved men thoughout the centuries. In

*Prometheus* he portrayed the great rebel who stole fire from heaven to give to men; he was punished by Zeus by being chained to a mountain rock, where an eagle fed daily on his liver, but he remained defiant to the end. In the *Oresteia*, Aeschylus wrote a memorable drama of revenge and expiation, dealing with the murder of Agamemnon by his wife and her lover, and the vengeance taken upon them by her son and daughter.

Sophocles, too, presents the struggle in the world between right and wrong, but he is a greater master of the plot than Aeschylus, and he looks deeper into human psychology. Nevertheless, the plays of Sophocles convey an orthodox respect for the gods, through whose inscrutable wills the heroes and heroines of the dramas suffer. The hero of the famous *Oedipus Rex* unknowingly marries his own mother, then blinds himself when he learns the truth. Euripides, on the other hand, is more of a rebel. His tragedies anticipate modern realism, and he writes with a poetry and passion that few except Shakespeare have equalled.

The whole 5th-century Greek world, from Sicily to Asia Minor, was alive with brilliant talent. It was at Halicarnassus, a Greek city in Asia Minor, that Herodotus, 'the father of history', was born in about 480 BC. In his *Histories*, the central theme of which is the struggle between the Greeks and the Persians, Herodotus created not only a masterpiece of

### THE FIRST OLYMPIC GAMES

Even wars were halted for the great gymnastic and religious festival held at Olympia every four years from 776 BC in honour of Zeus, ruler of the gods. Athletes from all Greece competed in running, boxing, wrestling, jumping, javelin and discus throwing. The winners received only garlands of olive leaves, but to be crowned meant life-long fame. The revived Olympic Games of modern times date from 1896

GIRL RUNNER *The stern Spartan code trained girls as well as boys to be hardy athletes. In this bronze, a young girl lifts her frock to run*

prose but also a new way of looking at mankind. He analyses the peoples and the countries concerned, tells many fascinating tales and strives to be objective.

The continual rivalry between the two powerful states of Athens and Sparta made it inevitable that war should finally break out between them. For 27 years, from 431 to 404 BC – with only a few intervals of peace – war raged between the two powers. Since both sides had alliances, friendships and colonial attachments, there was hardly a city, an island or a territory throughout the Greek world that was not involved in the struggle.

## A victory for Sparta

Pericles, as leader of Athens, had a large share of responsibility for what became known as the Peloponnesian War. He dreamt of a united Greece, with Athens as its capital; but his aim was in advance of his time. Greece was not yet ready for unity, for the small city-states preferred to retain their individuality, even at the expense of prosperity. The war ended in the defeat of Athens, principally due to a disastrous expedition to Sicily in which the flower of the city's youth and the bulk of its fleet was lost.

The war was not accompanied by any cultural decline, however, for some of the greatest achievements of the Athenian genius occurred during these years. Sophocles and

TEN-YEAR WAR OVER A LOST QUEEN

*The Greeks were fired by the struggle of hero with hero in single combat. This famous late 7th-century terracotta plate, found at Kameiros in Rhodes, depicts King Menelaus of Sparta fighting with the Trojan hero Hector. On the ground lies the corpse of Euphorbus, a Trojan warrior whom Menelaus has already slain. According to legend, Greece fought the ten-year Trojan War to win back Helen, wife of Menelaus, who had* *been abducted by Paris and taken to Troy. The real cause, however, may have been a threat by Troy to the Mycenaeans' trade routes. The last days of the siege of Troy are immortalised in Homer's epic poem the Iliad. Its chief figure is the Greek warrior Achilles, who slew the Trojan Hector. According to a later legend, Achilles died after an arrow entered his heel—the one spot the gods had left vulnerable*

DISCUS THROWER *The Greeks valued all-round excellence in sport, and discus throwing was one of five events in which the same athletes competed in the Pentathlon; the other events were the foot race, the long jump, javelin throwing and wrestling. Discus throwing probably originated in the hurling of flat stones at an enemy. The Greeks exulted in physical fitness, and athletes competed naked*

THE WILL TO WIN *Greek athletes performed as individuals, and not in teams; this Athenian vase painting catches the sprinters' spirit of vigorous personal competition. The Olympic Games were the most famous of four regular athletic festivals in Greece*

THE PRIZE *Smaller games carried less honours than the major festivals, but the prizes were more valuable. At Athens the winner of the chariot race received 100 vases of olive oil. The prize was presented in urns like the one above, made about 530 BC, and bearing a picture of Athena, the city's patron goddess*

# Alexander the Great's campaigns expand the Greek world

Constant wars did not prevent the Greeks from cultivating the arts of leisure. In this vase painting, a citizen relaxes at the house of a hetaira, a woman trained in the art of entertaining by flute-playing and dancing. Athenian society was very much a man's world. A wife's role was simply to manage the household and look after the children. She took no part in public affairs, and was seldom seen in the street with her husband; men even did most of the shopping. When a man entertained friends to dinner, his wife, after preparing the meal, stayed out of sight in her own quarters

PLAYING TRUANT *Boys went to private schools at the age of six and were strictly educated until they were 18. But there were relaxations: a vase made in Athens about 480 BC shows one young boy taking time off to fish*

Euripides were at their peak; the *Bacchae* of Euripides was first performed in the very year that saw the collapse of Athens. Throughout these years, too, the citizens of Athens were laughing at the bawdy comedies of Aristophanes, such as *The Birds* and *The Frogs*.

In 404 BC the city of Athens surrendered unconditionally to the Spartans and their allies. Some of the victors were in favour of destroying the city and of selling all its men, women and children into slavery. During the discussion that followed, one Spartan stood up and chanted the opening chorus from Euripides's drama *Electra*. All those present were so moved that they decided it would be a crime without parallel to destroy a city that had produced such men of genius. The Athenian Empire was over, but the Athenian achievement was recognised as surpassing considerations of power or politics.

## In pursuit of knowledge

Spartan rule over Athens and its former empire proved ineffective. Many of the lands Sparta had won were quickly lost, and Athens itself had the chance to recover some of its earlier glory. The 4th-century Athenian revival was dominated by the spirit of inquiry springing from its philosophers, who were to add yet another distinctively Athenian contribution to Western civilization.

For many years Greek philosophers had been questioning the traditional view of the world. The most famous of them, Socrates, was born in Athens in about 470 BC. He left no writings of his own, and all that we know of him is contained in the records of his great pupil Plato, and of the historian Xenophon. The son of a stonemason, short and remarkably ugly, Socrates was the embodiment of the Greek genius at its best. He believed that it is the soul which distinguishes man from beasts, and that it is the duty of man to act in accordance with reason and not to allow his mind to be clouded by the animal nature of his body. He also stressed the fact that man lives in society, and that he has therefore an important responsibility towards his fellow men.

Plato, the brilliant pupil of Socrates, wrote the *Dialogues*, which represent Socrates talking with other citizens in Athens and striving to discover, through analytical discussion, what is really meant by friendship, justice, love and duty towards the gods. He attempted to be entirely truthful and to make his fellow Athenians equally honest with themselves.

Socrates, with his iron will and inflexible courage, could sustain such an investigation. Few other men could, and many Athenians disliked him intensely for his questioning of long-accepted standards and beliefs. Socrates was brought to trial at the age of 70, charged with not believing in the gods, and with corrupting the minds of the young. He was sentenced to death by drinking the poison hemlock. Although his accusers would gladly have let him free if he recanted, he chose to abide by their judgment, thus becoming one of history's first martyrs to conscience and

reason. Just before he died he commanded his friends: 'I owe a cockerel to Asclepius (the god of medicine); see that it is paid.' This was the customary ritual performed by patients on recovering from a long illness.

## The first 'Utopia'

Plato based his own system of thought largely on the fact that men are born unequal, both in their physique and in their spiritual and mental capacity, and that each has his own particular contribution to make to the state. His major work, the *Republic*, and his longer work the *Laws* describe the ideal state as Plato sees it, governed by philosopher-kings – the first vision in world literature of a 'Utopia'.

Plato founded an Academy in Athens, where men and women pupils dedicated themselves to study and the pursuit of knowledge. The Academy lasted for 900 years, until it was suppressed by the Byzantine emperor, Justinian.

Plato's equally famous successor Aristotle was born in Macedonia in northern Greece, but spent most of his life in Athens. He also gathered around him a group of pupils, and wrote on almost every aspect of human knowledge. He had an encyclopaedic mind, and his works have influenced the whole of European thought by the emphasis which they placed on the need for critical scientific inquiry as the starting point of all knowledge.

There was no distinction in ancient Greece between a philosopher and scientist. The self-imposed task of both was the study of man and the universe in which man lived. By the 6th century BC flourishing schools of philosophy and science had been set up all over the Greek world – many of them in Italy, including the school of the great mathematician Pythagoras at Croton. Added lustre was given to Greek philosophy in later years by men of such widely differing beliefs as Epicurus, who held that pleasure was the only goal of life, and Zeno, who founded the Stoic school which advocated the pursuit of virtue above all else.

## A pioneer in medicine

Greek achievements in science were not to be equalled in Europe for 1500 years, even though Greek science was inevitably more speculative and theoretical than practical. It was not until the 19th century that men had the equipment to put into practice many of the ideas that the Greeks had formulated centuries earlier. Hero of Alexandria, for instance, had by AD 100 given a written description of nine types of mechanical device that were powered by heat or steam, including a fountain and a steam engine. The Hippocratic school of medicine, called after its founder Hippocrates and established on the Aegean island of Cos, discovered the importance of listening to the heart and lungs in the diagnosis of disease. Many doctors today still take a form of the Hippocratic Oath, which embodies the code of medical ethics preserved in the writings of Hippocrates.

Archimedes discovered and gave his name to the principle of measuring the weight of an object by the amount of water it displaces. He is said to have discovered the principle when observing water overflowing from his bath, and to have leapt out shouting *Eureka!* ('I have found it'). Thales of Iona, as early as the 6th century BC, knew enough about astronomy to be able to predict an eclipse of the sun. Leucippus and Democritus propounded in the 5th century the theory that matter is composed of atoms. Anaximander made the first known map; he was also a geologist and, by a study of fossils, accurately deduced that there had been other forms of life millions of years before man.

## The rise of Macedonia

In about 350 BC divided Greece found an unexpected solution to its problems. Macedonia, a rugged and mountainous area in northern Greece, was the home of a Greek-speaking people who were much less civilized than their neighbours to the south. They were tough highlanders and great fighters, whom Philip of Macedon (382–336 BC) welded into the greatest military state in Greece. Philip was a great war-leader and a fine statesman, with a deep respect for Greek culture; he chose the philosopher Aristotle to be the tutor of his young son, Alexander.

Philip's aim, like that of Pericles before him, was a united Greece. After achieving this he intended to lead a united Greek army into Asia Minor and the Near East, seize the wealth of Persia, and secure vast tracts of land on which to settle Greek people. The Athenian orator Demosthenes, however, devoted his whole life to stirring up the Athenians and their allies to resist Philip's dream of building an empire. His so-called 'Philippics' had their effect, and in 338 BC Athens and its allies marched against Philip – only to be shattered at the battle of Chaeronea, largely through a brilliant cavalry charge led by the 17-year-old Alexander.

At the very moment when the victorious Philip was about to lead his army into Asia he was murdered. But his son, proclaiming 'Nothing has changed – except the name of the king', asserted his own hold over the country. Alexander was to achieve his father's dream; in doing so he spread Greek thought and culture over the whole of the Middle East, and inaugurated three centuries of Greek-inspired civilization which have become known as the Hellenistic Age.

## The legacy of Alexander

After freeing Ionia from Persian rule, Alexander and his army swept on to occupy Syria and Phoenicia. In 332 BC he captured the island city of Tyre, by building a dyke from the mainland; the dyke has survived through the centuries and, strengthened by accumulations of silt, now joins Tyre permanently to the coast. Egypt was the next country to fall to the young conqueror, and Alexander was proclaimed pharaoh. His astoundingly successful 11-year campaign brought the whole Persian Empire, including lands as far afield as India, into Greek hands. When Alexander died in 323 BC – at the age of only 32 – the immense territories he had conquered were divided among his

A PERSIAN BRIDE FOR ALL-CONQUERING ALEXANDER

*Alexander the Great united the Greeks to shatter the power of Persia, and in only 11 years of campaigning carved out an empire. He took a Persian wife, the Princess Roxane, who is depicted with him on this onyx cameo. Alexander realised that his domains could not be governed simply as colonies, and sought to bring* *Greeks and Persians together. Roxane bore him his only child, also called Alexander, but both mother and son were murdered in the struggle for power which followed Alexander's death at the age of 32. He had made no provision for the rule of his empire when he died, and it was divided among his commanders*

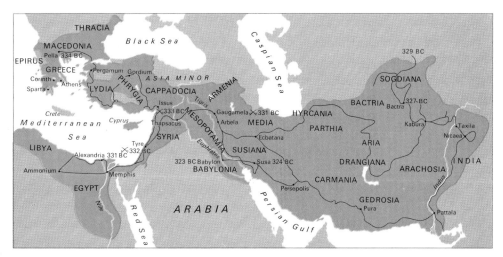

THE 11-YEAR MARCH THAT BUILT AN EMPIRE

*After uniting Greece, Alexander crossed into Asia with 35,000 troops in 334 BC and marched against the Persian Empire. In 333 he defeated King Darius at Issus, pushed south to capture Tyre and subjugate Egypt, and in 331 returned to break the main Persian resistance at Gaugamela. Babylon and Susa were taken, and the ancient capital of Persepolis sacked, before Alexander turned to subdue Persia's eastern* *provinces in an arduous three-year campaign. He then advanced deep into India, which he expected to prove to be the edge of the world, washed by the all-encircling ocean. But here his troops, perhaps apprehensive about advancing nearer to the world's end, refused to go further. Alexander turned back. He marched through the difficult terrain of Gedrosia (Baluchistan) to Susa, and in 323 BC reached Babylon, where he died*

# Monuments that gave the world a lasting style of architecture

generals. Ptolemy secured Egypt for himself and his successors, while Antigonus seized a large part of Asia Minor and founded a dynasty there.

For the next three centuries – until the death of Cleopatra in 30 BC – Greek culture spread throughout the East, altered and transmuted by its contact with countries like Persia, Egypt, Syria and Judaea. The old Greek world of city-states, each fiercely independent, was eclipsed by a wider world. Hellenism was a kind of 'universalism', and Greek became the dominant language in the Mediterranean area, from Marseilles to Persia and beyond.

## Cultural capital on the Nile

In his short life Alexander had established a number of cities to administer the vast lands he had conquered. Alexandria in Egypt, named after the conqueror, became the greatest port in the Mediterranean and the centre from which Greek culture spread throughout the Middle East.

The city was built on a narrow neck of land between Lake Mareotis and the sea. It faced the island of Pharos, to which it was joined by a dyke. On Pharos was an immense lighthouse over 400 ft high, which contained every known mechanical device for the protection of shipping, and even for weather forecasting. Its light was fuelled by wood, drawn up by hydraulic machinery, and it had mechanical devices that marked the passage of the sun, the wind direction and the hours of the day. There was even a giant periscope through which a watchman could see shipping beyond the apparent horizon. The lighthouse, one of the Seven Wonders of the Ancient World, was destroyed by an earthquake in the 14th century. Alexandria was laid out to a strict geometric plan, with public buildings of marble, a huge gymnasium, and even an artificial hill dedicated to the god Pan. The main street, the Canopic, was 100 ft wide and ran for over 3 miles through the city.

The papyrus-reed of the Nile delta provided the Hellenistic world, and later the Roman Empire, with a supply of 'paper' on which records and literature could be transcribed. A great library was founded in Alexandria, where the literature of the ancient world was recorded. It was here that writing was for the first time divided into 'books', these being determined by the length of a papyrus roll. Adjoining the

## THE THREE CLASSICAL 'ORDERS'

Working largely in marble, the Greeks in their temples and public buildings produced some of the world's finest architecture. There were three styles, or 'orders' – the austere Doric; the light and elegant Ionic; and the more elaborate Corinthian. The Greeks used neither the arch nor the vault, but topped columns or walls by flat beams

DORIC ORDER *The oldest and simplest style, used in mainland Greece from the 7th century BC, is the Doric. The magnificent Parthenon in Athens shows the massive strength and beauty to which the Doric style lends itself. Its plump, fluted columns stand directly on the pavement*

TWO CAPITALS *Doric and Ionic differ mainly in the capitals, or moulded decorations at the head of the columns. The Doric (left) is topped with a square slab, while the Ionic (right) has decorative spiral scrolls*

CORINTHIAN STYLE *This most elaborate and richly decorated type of Greek capital dates from the 4th century. Corinthian columns were more slender, and their deeper, basket-like capitals were carved with acanthus leaves. This style was extensively adopted by the Romans*

## SHRINE TO A CITY'S FOUNDERS

*The beautiful Erechtheum, built during the reconstruction of the Acropolis by Pericles after its devastation by the Persians, is unique among Greek buildings. While most temples are rectangular, symmetrical, and have a surrounding colonnade, the Erechtheum has porches on three sides, each quite different in size and rising from different levels. The roof of one porch is supported by pillars carved as female figures. The Erechtheum was constructed as a shrine enclosing the site where the city of Athens had its beginnings; under one corner is the tomb of Cecrops, mythical first king of Athens. The shrine also held the tokens given by two gods in their attempts to capture the citizens' devotion, the well of sea water opened by the sea-god Poseidon, and the first olive tree, with which Athena won the Athenians' hearts*

Royal Palace of the Ptolemies was the Mouseion, or 'museum', a studio for poets, scientists, librarians, craftsmen and artists.

It was in Alexandria in the reign of Ptolemy I (323–285 BC) that the great mathematician Euclid first evolved a system of geometry. It was here, too, that the astronomer Aristarchus of Samos came to the conclusion that the sun, not the earth, was the centre of our universe. In the 3rd century BC, another Alexandrian, Eratosthenes, managed with the simple tools at his disposal to calculate the circumference of the earth, with an error of only 10 per cent. Having discovered that in Aswan on midsummer day the noon sun was directly overhead, he then measured the angle of the shadow cast by a vertical pole at Alexandria, also on midsummer day. The angle of this shadow, $7\frac{1}{2}$ degrees, Eratosthenes concluded to be the proportion of the earth's circumference represented by the distance between Aswan and Alexandria.

## The shadow of Rome
The great struggle between Rome and Carthage which dominated the west Mediterranean during much of the Hellenistic Age came to an end in 146 BC with a total victory for the Romans. With the destruction of Carthage, Rome was free to turn her attention to the eastern Mediterranean. Mainland Greece soon became a Roman protectorate, and during the 1st century BC Rome gradually absorbed Asia Minor, Syria, Judaea and nearly all the remnants of Alexander's eastern empire. Culturally, however, it was the Romans who were absorbed. As the poet Horace wrote: 'Captive Greece made captive her rude conqueror.'

The influence of Greek art, science, literature and philosophy had already reached Italy through the Greek colonies in the south of the country, but the Roman conquest of the Hellenistic world had an even greater effect. Greece became a battleground during the Roman civil wars after Julius Caesar's assassination; the country was devastated and many of its major cities left in ruins. Yet even so, nearly every educated young Roman went to Athens to study art, philosophy and rhetoric, while Greek secretaries, slaves and tutors were found in Italy, and innumerable works of art from looted cities reached Rome. Greece itself produced little new after the Roman conquest, but the entire treasury of Greek thought was absorbed into the Roman world and diffused throughout the empire. In almost everything except the exercise of power Greece triumphed, and the new empire that came into being was a Greco-Roman world. The eastern half of the Roman Empire never lost its Hellenistic character, and 400 years later it survived the fall of the western Roman Empire to become the new empire of Byzantium.

The influence of Greek artists, architects and philosophers in subsequent centuries has been without parallel. Their architects bequeathed to the world an ordered, harmonious style of building which is still used and which is still known as classical. Their sculptors portrayed the human body with a vivacity that is at once characteristically Greek and also universal. It was the Greek alphabet, adopted by the Etruscans and later by the Romans, that became the basis of the modern Western alphabet. In their painstaking search for truth, Greek thinkers laid the foundations for nearly all subsequent inquiry and scientific research. Their principles still lie at the core of the culture of the entire Western world.

# The festive world of
# the Etruscans

800–200 BC

*The masters of central Italy before Rome rose to power
were rich traders and skilled craftsmen —
but their origin and language remain unsolved mysteries*

In the days when Rome was little more than a fortified township, the area that was to become the heartland of the Roman Empire was under the sway of a prosperous race who taught the Romans many of the arts of war and peace. At the height of their power about 600 BC, the rule of the Etruscans extended from their homeland in what is now Tuscany to cover most of Italy, from the Po Valley in the north to modern Salerno in the south.

Inhabiting an area well endowed with natural resources, including deposits of iron and copper, as well as fertile soil and rich forests, the Etruscans grew rich and powerful on the profits of trade and industry. They established city life in a region where the only form of settlement hitherto had been villages of simple huts. They were powerful at sea, too, and in alliance with Carthage their fleets dominated the western end of the Mediterranean.

Etruscan kings of the Tarquin dynasty ruled in Rome for a century and gave the city much of its political organisation. One Etruscan king, Servius Tullius, laid the foundations of the Roman army. In the end, however, the Romans threw off Etruscan rule and began their own

climb to power. The Romans' capture of Veii, one of the principal Etruscan cities, in 396 BC marked the beginning of Etruria's decline.

Etruscan civilization, swamped by the vigour of Rome, vanished. Its people left no history of their own. All that is known about them is based on the comments of Greek and Roman writers, and on the colourful paintings and everyday objects found in Etruscan tombs. Even the origins of the Etruscans are uncertain; the general belief in ancient times was that they came from the East, from Lydia in present-day Turkey, but modern scholars are more inclined to believe that they had always lived in central Italy.

Southern Etruria is a land of soft, volcanic rock, deeply indented by rivers. Before the Roman roads were driven through, this was difficult, isolating countryside which encouraged the development of independent communities. The places in which the Etruscans built their cities were usually natural strongholds, often surrounded by cliffs and ravines, suggesting that the sites were chosen at a time of conflict. The most impressive citadel of northern Etruria, Volterra, is described by

**ETRURIA IN 480 BC**

*From their homelands around Rome, the Etruscans expanded north and south to colonise much of the Italian peninsula*

**THE MONSTER WITH TWO HEADS**

*Etruscan craftsmen were famous for their bronzes, the main artistic inspiration for which came from the Greeks. This figure, 2 ft 7 in. high, is of the mythical chimaera, a lion which also has a goat's head and a serpent for a tail, which was slain by Bellerophon. It was probably made about 350 BC, and is among the finest animal sculptures of the ancient world*

## THE LIVING HONOUR THE DEAD IN ATHLETICS CONTESTS

The Etruscans decorated their elaborate tombs with colourful wall-paintings which tell a great deal about their everyday life and customs. In the Tomb of the Augurs at Tarquinia the walls are covered almost from floor to ceiling with a frieze of figures. They include these two wrestlers about to grapple for a prize of gold and silver bowls. The wrestlers are shown taking part in the funeral games which were held at the death of prominent Etruscans; these games also included boxing contests and a gladiatorial combat. The combatants are naked, following the custom of the Greeks, from whom the Etruscans inherited much of their style of recreation. But whereas Greek aristocrats and commoners alike took part in the sports, in Etruria the nobility left these activities to professional athletes. The Etruscans, in turn, passed on their sporting activities to the Romans. According to tradition it was Tarquin, one of the Etruscan kings of Rome, who introduced the Romans to horse-racing and boxing, while the gladiatorial contests to the death which became common in Rome originated in the Etruscan cities of the Campania region

# A race of warriors for whom death held no fears

**WARRIOR IN BRONZE**

*The Etruscans were formidable warriors, and many of their bronzes represent soldiers. The thin, elongated lance-bearer is typical of Etruscan sculpture*

## AN UNSOLVED MYSTERY

ETRUSCAN *A tablet of the 5th century BC*

One of the enduring mysteries of the Etruscans is their language, which is still largely untranslated. Inscriptions which survive show that the alphabet is Greek in origin, but the grammar and much of the vocabulary is still not understood. This gold tablet, inscribed in Etruscan script, is one of three found in 1964 at Pyrgi, near Rome. Two of the plaques are religious dedications in Etruscan; their meaning has been deduced with the aid of the third plaque, which bears a dedication in the Carthaginian language

Macaulay in his *Lays of Ancient Rome* as 'piled by the hands of giants for god-like kings of old'. Most of the Etruscan cities lay some distance inland; the only major city on the coast was Populonia, which imported iron from the island of Elba. But most of the other cities had direct road links to harbours along the coast, which provided anchorages for the ships on which so much of Etruria's prosperity depended.

The Etruscans modelled their cities on the Greek city-state, known to them through the Greek colonies in southern Italy with which they traded. Each city controlled the territory surrounding it, and sometimes made alliances with its neighbours. But the Etruscan states suffered the disease of all ancient city-states – the reluctance to combine against a common enemy. Twelve great Etruscan cities, including Veii, Tarquinia and Caere (the modern Cerveteri), were linked in a religious league, but the league never became a political alliance, and failed to provide strength in times of crisis.

### Town planners of skill

The cities of the Etruscans had streets of well-built rectangular houses, made of sun-baked mud bricks, on stone foundations. There were some impressive public buildings, including decorated temples made largely of timber, which was protected from the weather by gaily painted clay reliefs and sculpture.

Like the Romans after them, the Etruscans gave much thought to problems of drainage, and other city amenities. The drainage of the Forum in Rome was said to be the work of an Etruscan king, and road-cuttings and drainage tunnels in southern Etruria survive to this day.

In the Po Valley the Etruscans built a particularly successful and well-organised city at Marzabotto, near modern Bologna. It was planned with a series of broad, well-built and well-drained streets crossed by narrower streets, so creating a series of building plots which were occupied by well-constructed and spacious houses of mud bricks.

It was from the Etruscans that the Romans learnt the principles of town planning. They also inherited a series of rules for the founding and the layout of a city. First the Etruscan priests, by observing the flight of birds, had to determine that the right, or 'auspicious', time had been chosen for the founding of the city. Then the founder marked out the circuit of the walls by cutting a furrow with a plough drawn by a bull and a heifer; he raised the plough when he came to the places appointed for the city's gates. The Etruscans also bequeathed to the Romans many architectural forms, such as that of the characteristic Roman temple, standing on a high base and approached by steps from the front.

Though the Etruscans built their houses only of mud bricks and timber, which have not survived, their tombs were built of stone and built to last. Much of what is known of the enigmatic Etruscans today has been learnt from the huge cemeteries and elaborately decorated tombs which have been excavated. There are domed tombs covered by earth mounds at

Populonia, massive burial mounds covering many separate chambers at Caere, and at Tarquinia painted tombs which often look like banqueting pavilions inside. One cemetery at Orvieto even has a regular street plan, its separate tombs arranged like houses. Some of the tomb chambers at Caere appear to imitate the interiors of Etruscan houses, and one tomb, the Tomb of the Capitals, has elaborately carved architectural details.

The walls of many tombs were brightly painted with frescoes showing scenes of banqueting and merry-making, which recalled some of the pleasures of life on earth as well as expressing hopes for the life to come. These vivid wall-paintings are among the most attractive surviving examples of Etruscan art.

Jewellery and objects of ivory and precious metal found in the earlier tombs came from all over the Mediterranean world. Etruscans liked to have good craftsmanship around them both in life and in death, and their own workshops were particularly famous for the quality of their bronze candlesticks, mirrors and similar objects for use in the home.

In every branch of art, especially in the lively and colourful tomb paintings, the chief inspiration was Greek. The earliest Etruscan art was based on the Greek use of geometric patterns for decoration, and this early phase was followed – as it was in Greece itself – by one in which the arts and crafts of the Eastern world, of Anatolia, Mesopotamia and Egypt, played a major role.

Not only tomb paintings but pottery, gems and bronzework, too, all show strong Greek influence. But, despite this, Etruscan art had a distinctive element of its own. The art of modelling big terracotta sculptures for religious buildings flourished in Etruria as nowhere else, and the finest examples, such as the Apollo of Veii, are masterpieces of Etruscan art.

### Telling the future

The Etruscans worshipped many gods from many lands, but the chief interest of their religion lies not so much in their gods as in their way of worshipping. For the Etruscans had a set of ritual practices by which skilled priests claimed to be able to pull aside the curtain separating the present from the future, and to divine the will of the gods.

The priests based their predictions on thunderbolts, the flight of birds and the examination of animal entrails, especially the liver – a means of divination known as haruspicy. According to tradition, the knowledge of how to interpret these signs was revealed to the Etruscan kings of old by divine beings; and it was preserved in a series of ritual books. Every important event in Etruscan life came under the influence of religious rituals, on which the Etruscans became dependent to the point of abject subservience. Etruscan ritual practices were inherited by the Romans and became a part of Roman public life.

Another feature of the Etruscans' life which they passed on to the Romans was the custom of holding funeral games. These originated in

Greece, but to the vigorous athletic contests beloved by the Greeks the Etruscans added a more sinister spectacle: the fight to the death between trained gladiators, out of which were to develop the bloody combats frequently seen in the Roman amphitheatre.

Etruscan devotion to religious practices seems to be confirmed by what has survived of the Etruscan language. The longest surviving text is apparently a collection of religious formulas. Another long ritual text is inscribed on a tile from Capua, in south Italy, and there is a strange spiral inscription, presumably religious, on a lead plaque from Magliano. These inscriptions are among the very few lengthy Etruscan texts which survive. The rest are short inscriptions in tombs, or a few words cut on the characteristic Etruscan fine grey or black pottery known as bucchero.

The Etruscan alphabet is Greek in origin, adapted to suit sounds peculiar to the Etruscan language. But the origins of the language itself are unknown; to this day experts have been able to acquire only a smattering of Etruscan vocabulary and grammar, and still await the discovery of some lengthy bilingual inscription which will provide the key.

How far the written language was used in Etruria is not known precisely, though there was a large body of Etruscan religious literature and some Etruscan history, echoes of which occur in Roman traditions. The Etruscans had no poetry, as far as is known, and although music was popular, singing was apparently confined to religious utterances.

## Decline of the Etruscans

The power of the Etruscans rested on successful exploitation of their agricultural and mineral resources, and a flourishing trade supported by sea power which enabled Etruria to resist the advances of her rivals. Etruria's northward expansion enabled her to take advantage of Greek trade in the Adriatic, while in the south of Italy the Etruscans controlled the fertile lands of Campania.

From the 5th century BC onwards Etruria's enemies began to get the upper hand; Rome broke away early in the century, and in 474 BC the Etruscans suffered a disastrous defeat at sea off Cumae at the hands of the Syracusans. From then on, the Etruscans were at the mercy of Greek raiders, and their land empire began to collapse.

The scenes of festivity depicted in early Etruscan tomb paintings give place in the 4th century to much more specific references to death, with paintings of underworld demons or scenes of violent death and destruction. This change may reflect the increasing despair of the Etruscan people in the face of a series of military and political disasters.

After the fall of Veii, Rome began to annex Etruscan territory, and by 200 BC Etruscan independence was at an end. But the influence of the Etruscans lived on in the customs of the Romans who conquered them; and by spreading Greek thought and culture in Italy they left their mark on European civilization.

## JOY IN THE AFTER-LIFE

The Etruscans looked on death as simply a doorway to a new existence, in which they would continue to enjoy much the same pleasures as they had known in this world. Great artistry was devoted to the building and decoration of cemeteries. Statues depicted the dead engaged in everyday pursuits, and round them were placed the earthly possessions which it was expected the dead would continue to need in the after-life

TOGETHER IN DEATH *A clay sculpture found on the lid of a coffin at Caere (the modern Cerveteri) shows an affectionate husband and wife reclining together on a couch. Such scenes of men and women banqueting together – a practice which shocked the ancient Greeks – were common in Etruscan art. The outstretched hands may once have held a libation bowl, from which to pour an offering for the gods. The Etruscans, to judge from their tomb sculptures, were gentle and intelligent people; and their sculptors usually depicted their subjects smiling*

CREMATION URNS *Burial customs varied from place to place in ancient Etruria, and at Chiusi the older practice of cremating the dead persisted longer than in other cities. A common repository for the ashes was the canopic jar, a terracotta burial urn originating in Egypt. The earliest type of urn had simply a bronze mask on its lid, but later the lid itself was moulded to resemble a human head, and the urn was shaped like a body. Ashes were also deposited in small chests worked in local stone, carved with festive scenes expressing the idea of a joyous after-life; a warrior's urn might be capped with a replica of his helmet*

HOME FOR ASHES *Etruscans thought of the grave as the house of a dead person. Some cremation urns were shaped like the wattle-and-daub huts of the time, foundations of which have been found in Rome*

FORETELLING THE FUTURE *Etruscan priests, or augurs, claimed to be able to interpret the wishes of the gods by examining the entrails of certain animals. This bronze replica of a sheep's liver, found at Piacenza in north Italy, is thought to have been a 'text-book' for augurs. It is marked in sections, each bearing the name of a chief divinity and a number of lesser gods. Using the liver as a key, the augur could judge the will of a particular god from the condition of the appropriate part of the liver of a sacrificed animal. Priests also made forecasts from the flight of birds*

# How Rome shaped the modern world

## 753 BC–AD 476

*The empire won by the mighty legions 2000 years ago
has left its mark for ever on
the languages, laws and customs of the West*

The Romans dominated the ancient world for almost 500 years. In the heyday of their empire, they controlled an area that extended from the Atlantic coastline of Spain in the west to the shores of the Caspian Sea in the east; from the misty forests of Britain in the north to the sun-baked deserts of Egypt in the south. Today, 1600 years after the collapse of this empire, its marks on the landscape are widespread and include aqueducts, roads as straight as arrows, and the pillared ruins of once-mighty buildings.

When they conquered the world of ancient Greece, the Romans absorbed the best of Greek culture and passed on its legacy of art, architecture, science and philosophy to the Western world. They added to it a typically Roman sense of discipline and respect for the law which lies at the foundations of Western society to the present day.

What is so remarkable is that this spectacular world power grew out of the vigour and determination of the inhabitants of a single city. It was in 753 BC that, according to tradition,

Rome was founded on seven small hills by the banks of the River Tiber. But another 800 years were to pass before it became the centre of the largest empire the world had known, embracing, at its peak, 100 million people. Rome's imperial glory inevitably overshadows its achievements as a striving republic; yet it was the challenge of those early times that gave the Romans the drive and energy to win control of most of the civilized world.

The ancestors of the Romans were peasant farmers who moved southwards into Italy from central Europe about 1000 BC. One group, the Latins, settled on the south bank of the Tiber, on the plain to which these early settlers gave the name of Latium. At a good crossing point on the river, with an island in the middle, the Latins built a bridge and established a trading centre – the beginnings of Rome.

Romans of a later day looked back with pride on their origins, and saw themselves as a race descended from heroes. Legend told them that the city was founded by Romulus in fulfilment of a mission given by the gods to his

**ROMAN EMPIRE IN AD 117**

*A tiny settlement by the Tiber became the centre of an empire that, at its widest extent, covered 2 million square miles*

**CENTRE OF AN EMPIRE**

*From the Capitol Hill, on which Rome was founded in the 8th century BC, the Temple of Jupiter looks down on the Forum at the height of the city's power 800 years later. Around this open space, dotted with the statues of Roman heroes and arches celebrating their triumphs, the business of the state was carried out. Only one armed group, the Praetorian Guard (right), was allowed within the city. Its status as the emperor's personal bodyguard gave it the power to make and unmake emperors*

# Conquests that made the Mediterranean a Roman lake

ancestor Aeneas after the fall of Troy. But the real origins of Rome were humble rather than heroic. Houses clustered on the river bank beside the bridge across the Tiber, and others were dotted about on the slopes of nearby hills. On the rocky summit of the Capitol Hill – the steepest and highest of the seven hills – the Latin settlers built religious shrines, protected by rough fortifications, to which they could retire in times of danger.

## Rome's first pontiff
The early Romans were neither particularly warlike nor particularly prosperous; at first they were completely overshadowed by the wealthy Etruscan cities to the north. It was the bridge that provided Rome with its special advantage; for this bridge was an essential link in a valuable trade route, along which goods passed constantly between the Etruscans and the trading colonies, such as Tarentum and Syracuse, founded by the Greeks in southern Italy and Sicily. It was an enviable position, and the Romans soon learnt to be alert for dangerous alliances and groupings of rival towns. Today, nothing remains of this embryo Rome other than the traces of a few primitive huts. But the importance of its bridge in those earliest days gave the name of Pontifex Maximus – or 'Chief Bridge-builder' – to the high priest of Roman religion; and over 2500 years later, the pope in Rome is still styled 'pontiff'.

The story of the heroic defence of Rome's bridge by Horatius, commemorated in Lord Macaulay's *The Lays of Ancient Rome,* is one of the familiar legends of the earliest Roman state. For nearly a century Rome had been governed by a series of Etruscan chieftains who were called the 'kings' of Rome. But in 509 BC, the Romans revolted against the cruelty of their rulers, and expelled the Etruscans. The Etruscans supported a counter-attack on Rome under the leadership of Lars Porsena and, despite the bravery of Horatius, Lars Porsena conquered Rome. But the Etruscan monarchy was not restored; instead the Romans set up a republican system of government under which no man was allowed to become powerful enough to be a threat to the state.

Two consuls of equal status were elected by the citizens to serve for one year only. One consul went to war with Rome's citizen-army when danger threatened, while the other stayed to run the city. Other administrative offices were also held by two or more elected magistrates. As well as curbing excessive personal ambitions, the system encouraged more people to take a hand in the affairs of their city.

The free citizens of Rome were divided into two groups. The so-called patricians formed the city's aristocracy, and they alone were permitted to perform the all-important religious rituals. Boys born into patrician families could look forward to automatic public office, and

therefore grew up ready for its responsibilities. The republic was, in effect, governed by inspired amateurs who were dedicated from birth to the service of the state.

The plebeians, on the other hand, who formed the majority of the citizens, were debarred from holding public office until, in the 5th century BC, they fought for and won the right to elect their own representatives. These 'tribunes' could block any official measures by calling out *veto* ('I forbid') – the origin of the modern word 'veto'. Slaves, most of them prisoners captured in war, formed a third class and one that grew in numbers throughout the course of Roman history.

## The challenge from Carthage
Other Latin tribes in central Italy soon came to acknowledge Rome's leadership. By the 4th century BC the Romans had overcome the Etruscans and built up a series of vassal states and alliances with potential rivals which made them masters of Italy. Expanding trade in farm produce, leather goods and other products brought contacts with regions further afield, and these contacts led in turn to new rivalries for greater gains. In this way, Rome became an international power. Where once she had faced only local Italian rivals, such as the Etruscans, the Sabines and the Samnites, Rome now had to confront the other super-power of the day – the North African merchant state of Carthage, which had colonies of its own, great wealth and a large fleet.

From 264 BC onwards the Romans became involved in three Punic wars – Carthage was founded by the Phoenicians, in Latin *Poeni* – which lasted, on and off, for more than a century. At times the Romans seemed at last to have met their match. For 14 years the invader Hannibal roamed up and down Italy, after crossing over the Pyrenees and the Alps with his elephants. But the Romans carried the war into Africa and attacked Carthage. When the Carthaginians recalled Hannibal to defend their capital, the Roman general Scipio Africanus defeated him at Zama in 202 BC.

Even the Carthaginians, now, were vassals of Rome. But their city still stood, a potential danger to Rome, until in 146 BC the legions returned to destroy it. Carthage was burnt to the ground, the site of it ploughed over, and salt thrown into the furrows so that the land would remain forever infertile.

## Defeat for Alexander's heirs
The Punic wars taught the Romans how to build sea-going ships and how to use them in a naval engagement. With these skills, Rome became a power which sent new forces to Africa, Spain, Greece and the Middle East. They defeated the Macedonians of northern Greece – a people of immense prestige in the ancient world since the conquests of their leader, Alexander the Great, 150 years earlier.

One by one, other nations recognised Roman dominance and accepted treaties favourable to Rome. In 133 BC Attalus III, the last king of Pergamum in Asia Minor, bequeathed his

**IN THREE CENTURIES, ROME WINS MASTERY OF THE WESTERN WORLD**

*By 201 BC, after two wars with the Carthaginians, Sicily, Sardinia, Corsica and southern Spain had become part of the Roman Empire. The Romans then turned east across the Adriatic to win Illyria, and gained a foothold in Asia. Macedonia and parts of Greece were conquered next, and in 146 BC Carthage was finally crushed and its African territories annexed. At Julius Caesar's death in 44 BC, the empire had grown to include Gaul and nearly all the Iberian*

*peninsula in the west, and Greece, much of Asia Minor, and the coastlands of the Black Sea to the east. In the reign of Augustus, who died in AD 14, the imperial boundaries were pushed north to the Danube, while to the east Judaea and Egypt became provinces. The empire was at its largest when Trajan died in 117; Britain had been occupied and the European lands of the Dacians subjugated, and Rome's eastern frontiers stretched from the Caspian Sea to the Red Sea*

kingdom to Rome in his will. By 50 BC the Mediterranean was rapidly becoming a Roman lake, while further north Julius Caesar had conquered most of Gaul and made his first landing on the coast of Britain.

But success abroad brought troubles at home. The old Roman army that fought the early state's Italian neighbours had been an amateur army of farmer-citizens, who stopped fighting to return to their lands at harvest-time. The new armies that conquered Carthage and Macedon, however, were disciplined, energetic and led by talented commanders. They followed the man who led them to victory and plunder.

This change in the character of the Roman army meant that power in Rome lay no longer in the decisions of a Senate of experienced patricians, but in the control of armed troops. Ambition could now be backed by the sword, and when the interests of two rival military leaders clashed, the result was civil war.

Julius Caesar, Governor of Gaul, was ready to flout the constitution to seize supreme power for himself, while his opponent, Pompey the Great, remained loyal to the tradition of rule by the Senate. In 49 BC, Caesar marched against Pompey in Rome. In crossing the River Rubicon, the southern boundary of Gaul, he defied the law which restricted a Roman governor to his own province – a step so momentous that 'crossing the Rubicon' has become a byword for an irrevocable decision.

Both Caesar and Pompey enjoyed the fierce loyalty of their own troops, and the civil war which followed was fought out with terrible bitterness over a battlefield which included Spain, North Africa, Greece and Asia Minor. The first phase of the war ended in 48 BC, when Pompey was defeated at Pharsalus, in eastern Greece. He fled to Egypt, where he was betrayed and stabbed to death, leaving Caesar and his party in control.

## The fall of the republic

Rome's traditional system of government, developed to meet the needs of a small city, had proved too unwieldy to administer the large and complex state of which it was now the centre. Caesar, with his self-confidence and foresight, could not wait for the tedious machinery of government. He disregarded traditional republican methods in order to govern the cities and the provinces in his own way, as a dictator.

Caesar's one-man rule inevitably brought him enemies. Opposition hatched conspiracy, leading to Caesar's assassination by Brutus and his fellow plotters in 44 BC. The assassins, in their turn, were hunted down and killed by Mark Antony, who seized power after Caesar's murder. But Caesar had begun a process that nobody could stop; for the sake of efficient government, the Romans were to give up some of their political freedom for ever.

Further rivalries developed between Antony and the young Octavian, Caesar's great-nephew whom the dictator had named as his heir. The last battle of the civil wars ended in the defeat of Antony – who was ruling from Alexandria,

The Romans were masters of the art of war, and their well-equipped and well-disciplined fighting machine was more than a match for the armies of the barbarian outsiders. At the height of the empire the *Pax Romana* was defended by 30 legions; each legion was a self-supporting unit of between 3000 and 6000 men, every one of whom was as accustomed to building roads and digging ditches as to fighting. The legionaries were particularly skilled in building pontoon bridges (above) across rivers. Such devices, and an ability to maintain a pace of some 20 miles a day, enabled the legions to move very fast. Caesar won many victories by reaching his enemies days before they expected him; in Gaul, a force of only 25,000 Romans crushed a revolt by 250,000 Gauls under Vercingetorix

WAR AT SEA *The Romans were not a great maritime race, but their wars with Carthage taught them something of sea warfare. Their main tactic was to manoeuvre a heavily armed war galley, rowed by slaves below decks, alongside an enemy ship; a movable gang-plank, or 'corvus', would then be lowered on to the enemy vessel so that the Roman soldiers could swarm aboard for the hand-to-hand fighting in which they were rarely beaten. The sculptor of this relief has exaggerated the height of the soldiers in relation to the 'castellum', or deck fortification, near the prow. Pompey used the Roman navy against pirates off the Italian coast, and superior naval power decided the Battle of Actium in 31 BC, when Octavian defeated Antony to become the first Roman emperor, Augustus*

MESSAGE OF THE STANDARD *After each day's march through hostile territory, the Roman legion's 'aquilifer', or standard-bearer, would thrust his legion's standard into the ground at the site chosen for the night's camp. Then the legionaries had to build a fortified camp, putting aside their shields and swords and picking up picks and shovels to dig a broad square ditch; the earth was piled into a rampart. Even when a Roman army was beaten in battle, defeat rarely meant disaster; for the survivors could always make a stand from within their fortified camp. Each legion had its own standard, a wooden pole gilded and wreathed and bearing the legion's symbol. In battle it was raised or dipped to convey orders to the soldiers. The legions themselves did not have to fight in every battle; often the first men to go into action were the auxiliaries – bands of non-Roman conscript soldiers drafted from their homelands to other parts of the empire under the command of Roman officers. Only when the auxiliaries failed would the legion come up from the rear to hurl their javelins and then close in with their broad short swords for hand-to-hand combat*

# The benefits of 'Pax Romana'

with Cleopatra as his queen – at the sea-battle of Actium, on the west coast of Greece, in 31 BC. Octavian was left in undisputed control, and became the first Roman emperor, calling himself Augustus, 'the revered one'.

The difference between the closing days of the republic and the new age of Imperial Rome, which began with the triumph of Augustus, is mirrored in the works of two of Rome's greatest writers, Cicero and Virgil.

Cicero was a man of republican Rome – a senator and lawyer who was a consul in 63 BC and later a governor in Cilicia. His essays on philosophy, literature and every branch of public affairs perfected Latin prose as an instrument of lucid and dignified expression.

Cicero lived through the civil wars, and in his writings he tried to restore to his fellow Romans a respect for the traditional republican virtues of integrity, loyalty and service to the state. 'A man is finished when he makes pleasure, not duty, his main object,' Cicero wrote to a friend. He appealed for all sections of Roman society, from senators to plebeians, to form a common front, for the return of peace and for an end to dictatorship. But Cicero was too outspoken for the new Rome that was emerging: he publicly approved of Julius Caesar's assassination and this led to his own execution by Mark Antony a year later.

## Virgil, poet and patriot

Virgil, on the other hand, is a poet of Imperial Rome, the so-called Augustan Age. By the time of Augustus, the wealth flowing in from Rome's wide empire, and the influence of the wider world with which Rome was now in contact, were beginning to change the character of Rome itself and to alter its traditional ways of life and government. Augustus strove to counteract this by reminding the Romans of their traditions, and making people proud of all things Roman. Writers such as Virgil, Livy and Horace helped the emperor to fan the flame of Roman patriotism.

Virgil's *Aeneid,* the best known of all Latin poems, traces the founding of the Roman nation back to Aeneas and his followers, brought from Troy by divine guidance. It is a national epic, which makes the whole of Roman history seem destined by the gods.

The early emperors retained at least the appearances of republican rule: two consuls were still elected yearly (one of them usually being the emperor), and the Senate was still the legal source of power. But gradually, during the 1st century AD, the emperor and his staff took more and more of the government into their own hands, and paid less and less heed to the real interests of the governed.

Constant fear of treachery made emperors morbidly suspicious and increasingly autocratic, and their supreme power sometimes led to self-indulgent excesses. Emperor Tiberius, according to the Roman historian Suetonius, left Rome for a haven of debauchery on Capri, and his successor Caligula had his horse elected consul. Nero, as well as starting the persecution of Christians, was said to have started the great fire of Rome in AD 64 as a spectacular diversion for his own amusement. Such stories may well be exaggerations by writers of the day, but even so, the office of emperor was frequently the prize for murder in the palace or, at worst, civil war: and in the year 69, no fewer than three emperors – Galba, Otho and Vitellius – came and went in blood.

## Four great emperors

It was not until the 2nd century that the real benefits of imperial rule were felt, and the Roman Empire enjoyed its most settled and prosperous years under four great emperors. Trajan, emperor from 98 to 117, was a military commander born in Spain, and not an in-bred aristocrat from Rome. His successor, Hadrian (117–38), was also a Spaniard; under his rule, Roman architecture reached its peak. Antoninus (138–61) gave Rome a period of firm and kindly rule which earned him the name of 'Pius'; and Marcus Aurelius (161-80) was equally renowned as emperor, writer, and philosopher of the Stoic school.

The policies of these four emperors were designed to establish secure borders for the empire. They fought vigorous campaigns against tribes on the frontiers; they built permanent military installations, such as Hadrian's Wall across Britain – which Hadrian himself inspected, on a personal three-week visit which he made to Britain.

Although Rome was still the seat of power, it was now the heart of a huge empire that spread around the Mediterranean and over Europe, Africa and the Middle East. The peoples of this empire spoke many languages and worshipped many gods; but all, apart from the slaves, were Roman citizens and enjoyed the protection of Roman law. '*Civis Romanus sum*' was Cicero's proud boast; 'I am a Roman born' said St Paul to his accusers in Jerusalem, claiming the right to be taken to Rome for trial.

Inside this protective ring, most people were too contented to bother about revolt, and turned their energies to trade instead. Beyond the frontiers, however, danger always threatened from barbarian outsiders. Consequently, the 30 legions of the Roman army were stationed at strategic places near the perimeter. Besides the legions, the Roman army included auxiliary troops, recruited in the provinces and fighting with their traditional weapons. There were some defeats, but for the most part the Romans' enemies were too much of an unco-ordinated rabble to match the discipline and energy of the legions.

## Peace to farm and trade

Most of the people living within these well-guarded boundaries were country folk, tilling the land, gathering fruit or breeding stock by the methods their forefathers had used long before Rome existed. For them, Roman civilization meant a period of relative peace, the so-called *Pax Romana*, in which they could work their fields and carry on their business without interruption. For townspeople the 'Peace of

Bread and circuses were said by cynics of the time to be the major preoccupations of the Roman populace. The poor and the unemployed received bread from the public dole, while every large Roman town had an amphitheatre in which were staged huge and often brutal spectacles to keep people's minds off their discontents. In some cases, professional gladiators were matched against opponents of equal skill, and even the losing gladiator might be spared death if the crowd, judging that he had put up a courageous fight, made the gesture of the upturned thumb. But other so-called *ludi*, or games, were scenes of ritual carnage. Gladiators, criminals or members of persecuted sects such as the Christians were pitted against starved and maddened beasts; prisoners taken in war were brutally goaded to fight each other to the death

ARMED FOR BATTLE *Gladiators like the 'mirmillo' were heavily armed with helmet, sword and shield*

FIGHTING 'FISHER' *For variety, the Romans armed some gladiators with bizarre weapons. The 'retiarius' used the fork of the Mediterranean tunny fisherman*

Rome' meant that the goods they bought were better made and more varied; it was possible for a British landowner of moderate means to get drunk on wine from a Greek island, quaffed from a glass vessel made in Syria, as he ate Colchester oysters off his best dinner-service of silverware, which was manufactured in the south of France.

This network of trade was bound together by the towns the Romans created. Sometimes a town was founded as a colony for military veterans, and sometimes it was planned as the centre of the local civilian administration. It might be no more than humble brick and timber buildings grouped around cobbled streets, as at Verulamium (St Albans) in

SETTING FOR SLAUGHTER *The huge amphitheatre which still stands at Nîmes, in southern France, was built in about AD 50. It is 260 ft long, and it could hold 25,000 spectators. Amphitheatres were built in cities throughout the Roman Empire, to impress the people of the provinces with splendour and violent spectacle. All the arenas were modelled on the mighty Colosseum in Rome, which could hold 50,000 people. The games in the arena would last all day at festival time – and as the emperors proclaimed more and more festive occasions, more than half the days of the Roman year became public holidays*

TRAPPING THE VICTIMS *Wild beasts figured largely in the entertainments of the Roman arena. Lions, tigers and panthers would be let loose to face gladiators or archers; bulls and bears were chained together for a fight to the death. Immense slaughter took place – as many as 5000 animals were sometimes killed in a single day. To keep pace with the demand for fresh victims, governors in the Roman provinces had to arrange frequent animal hunts. This mosaic from North Africa shows beaters on foot and on horseback, armed with javelins, chasing the animals into an area enclosed by a huge net. They were then packed into crates for the long journey to Rome and other cities of the empire. The great round-up entirely eliminated lions from Mesopotamia and elephants from North Africa*

backward Britain: or it might be a city of marble colonnades and fine paved boulevards as at Timgad in Algeria. In either case, their designers aimed at a similar pattern, with streets arranged in a rectangular grid.

The town was guarded by high walls, which were pierced by four main gates. In the heart of the town was the forum – a large open area where citizens came in the morning to transact their business, and where the offices of the judges and the district council were to be found. Usually the chief temple of the town dominated the forum, and there were statues to distinguished citizens. The forum was a market-place, too, and nearby streets were lined by countless shops. People lived above their shops or, if they

were better off, behind them, away from the street. Some towns, such as Ostia, the seaport at the mouth of the Tiber, had brick-built tenement buildings rising as high as six storeys. Rich and poor did not live in separate areas, and it was quite usual to find the mansions of the wealthy next door to noisome, over-crowded tenements.

## Bath-house and circus

Public amenities in Roman towns were standard, as well. Most spectacular were the great bath-houses – one for each part of town in the larger cities. Just as the forum was the focus for morning activities, so the baths were the centre for the afternoon. In the elaborately

decorated *frigidarium*, or cooling-off room, citizens would stay for hours, talking business or just gossiping.

The leisured process of bathing in the Roman manner required several other rooms of increasing heat, to produce a sweat. The bather would then oil himself and then scrape off oil, sweat and dirt together with a *strigil* – a crook-shaped bronze instrument as personal in Roman times as a toothbrush is today. The bath-house was a complex building, showing skill in plumbing and heating.

The baths were one of the most civilized and attractive sides of Roman life. Completely different were the hideous 'games' in the amphitheatre where, for public amusement,

# Gods and heroes who guided the Romans' destiny

The Romans, used to worshipping many gods, saw Rome itself made a god in Virgil's *Aeneid*, the best known of all Latin poems. Virgil, depicted in a mosaic (above) seated between the muses of Epic and Tragedy and reading from his *Aeneid*, was a farmer's son who shunned city life. But he struck a chord in all Romans' hearts by making the whole of their history since the time of Romulus seem like the working out of a divine plan

'DIVINE' EMPEROR *Augustus, Virgil's friend and patron, seen in this 1st-century cameo, appears in the 'Aeneid' as the successor to a long line of heroes of Rome blessed by the gods – a portrayal which helped to give Augustus the authority he needed in rebuilding the Roman state after years of destructive civil war*

wild animals were hunted to death, or fights were staged between professional gladiators, or between dwarfs and women. Equally terrible were the occasions when the community combined public spectacle with 'justice', and set criminals to fight in groups, or goaded prisoners of war to destroy each other in vast set-piece battles.

The entertainments in the arena were developed from the funeral games that had marked the burials of wealthy Etruscans centuries before, and the amphitheatre was a standard feature of most Roman cities, particularly in the West. Many cities also had large, open sports grounds called *palaestrae* where city competed with city in athletic contests like those of the Greeks.

Common to nearly all cities, in East and West alike, was the circus, or race-course. This was a narrow, rectangular area, about a quarter of a mile long, surrounded by tiers of seats. Sturdy racing-chariots drawn by as many as four horses would contend over this course, hurtling round a hairpin bend at each end. Frenzied betting on the results took place among the spectators.

More intimate in character was the theatre, found in nearly every Roman town. The most popular forms of entertainment were stylised mime and ballet rather than plays: the Latin word for an actor in this sort of entertainment was *pantomimus* – hence our 'pantomime'. Straight plays, when they were performed, were seldom productions of the classical dramatists of ancient Greece. The Roman theatre was 'popular', avoiding serious issues in favour of cheerful bawdy, as in the verse plays of Plautus and of Terence – who coined maxims such as 'Where there's life, there's hope' and 'A word to the wise is sufficient'.

## From slave to freedman

Slavery was an accepted feature of Roman life, as it was throughout the ancient world; by about 100 BC more than one-third of the population of Rome were slaves. But the Romans' attitude to slavery was a practical one. In law, slaves had no real rights or status; but a master recognised that a well-fed, reasonably contented worker gave better value for money than an embittered one. As a result, most household slaves were well treated.

Well-educated slaves, such as Greek secretaries, and nurses and tutors for the children, became great family friends. Cicero wrote letters full of affection to Marcus Tullius Tiro, his secretary and former slave, who later wrote a life of his master. Less lucky were the gangs of slaves who worked in industry. Here, there was no contact between master and slave, and conditions could become wretched.

While industrial slaves had little chance of ever regaining their freedom, household slaves could look forward to being freed at the death of their master or mistress. In this case, they became *libertini*, or freedmen, and were allowed to enter professions hitherto closed to them. At the same time, the freedman owed the family of his former master or patron cer-

tain duties, just as the family was expected to take an interest in the continued wellbeing of the slaves it once owned.

## Respect for the patron

This relationship between 'patron' and 'client' ran right through Roman social organisation. Everybody had his patron – one social class above him all the way up the scale to the emperor himself. A client was expected to pay a courtesy visit most mornings to his patron's house, and would receive a gift of food or money if he were in need. This patron would himself have a patron to call upon, so that early morning in Rome saw the streets full of people hurrying backwards and forwards to pay their respects to their immediate superiors. A higher-class client naturally did not expect money from his patron; but he might ask for help in a business deal, or in obtaining an officer's commission in the army for a relative.

A common duty for a freedman who became well-to-do was to pay for his former master's tombstone, as a final and lasting tribute to their happy relationship. Such a memorial was important to Romans, who had a horror of being forgotten after death; they believed that the spirit of a dead man wandered in the underworld, to be nourished only on the good opinions that the living still held of him.

## Gods for all occasions

Roman religious practice was more an affair of state than a matter of personal conscience – a ritual performed on behalf of the people by their priests, in which the people themselves took no part. Most Roman towns had several temples dedicated to gods and goddesses representing different abstract concepts – Vesta for the hearth, Mars for military matters and warfare, and so on – and there was no difficulty in fitting new gods, representing new concepts, into the scheme of things, as the need arose.

The ceremony of blood sacrifice was a legacy from the Etruscans, who were regarded as the ancient experts in matters concerning religious ceremonial, divination and the occult. For a big public sacrifice the officiating priest, his head covered by a fold of his toga, ascended the tall altar in front of the temple steps, while the people looked on in silence. He had then to recite the ritual incantations designated for the occasion, word-perfect: if he slipped up in his diction, he had to start all over again.

A bull, a sow or a hen would then be killed, and its blood caught in a pan and offered to the god. The entrails were inspected, to make sure that there were no faults in the sacrificed animal's physique – for if there were, the sacrifice would be invalid and would have to be done again. If all went well, the god's attention would have been gained, and he could be expected to lend his influence to favour those who had made the sacrifice.

By the 2nd century many foreign religions were being practised as well, imported from the various regions of the empire by traders and soldiers. Most of these religions appealed because they contained an element of secret

## GOD OF THE HOUSEHOLD

*Every Roman house had its own household gods—the Lares, or spirits of the home, and Penates, or spirits of the larder. Little bronze figures of the gods, like this Lar, which once held a drinking vessel, stood in a special shrine just inside the front door of the house. Everybody going in or out of the house would make some gesture of respect to these gods*

## GODS OF THE STATE

*Abstract concepts that the Romans admired were represented by gods and goddesses in human form. Most Roman towns had several temples dedicated to various deities, and offerings were made at individual temples as circumstances demanded. Victoria (above), carved at the corner of a triumphal arch at Leptis Magna in Libya, personified military success; soldiers attended rites in her honour at a special temple on the Palatine Hill. Diana (right), painted on a wall at Stabiae, one of the three ports that served Rome, was the goddess of the open air and also of women and childbirth. The Romans adopted many of the Greek gods and goddesses; Diana was their version of the Greek Artemis, goddess of the hunt, and the Romans, too, portrayed her holding bow and arrow*

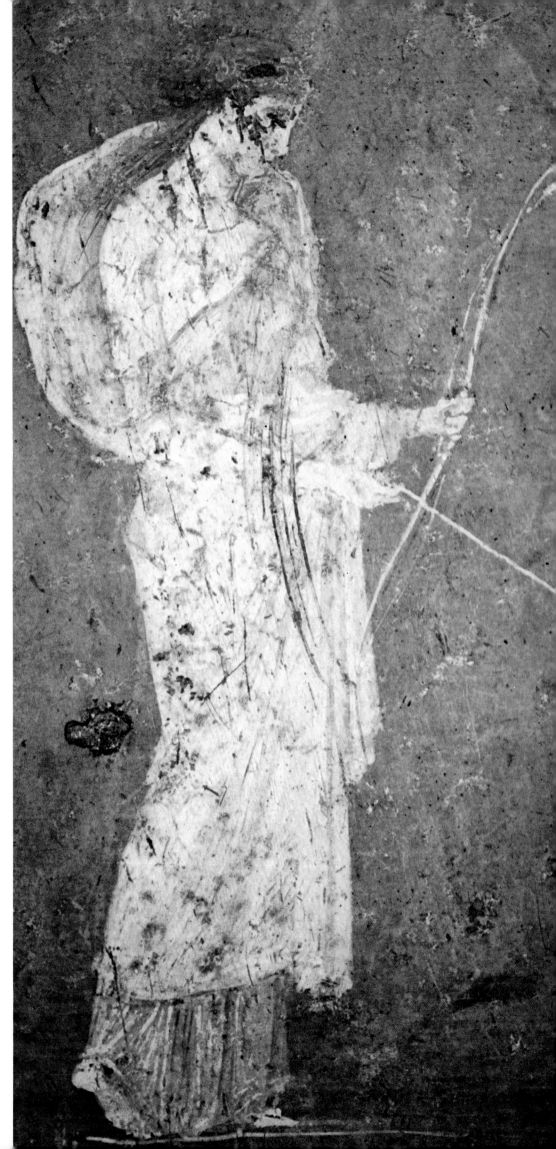

# *Builders in stone and concrete whose work has survived the centuries*

THE AQUEDUCT AT NIMES: MASTERPIECE WITH A PURPOSE

*The Pont du Gard, at Nîmes in southern France, is the finest surviving example of the Romans' skill in practical engineering. The great aqueduct, 885 ft long and made of unadorned stone blocks, was built in about AD 14 to bring water to Nîmes from higher ground to the north. The water ran in a concrete channel along the topmost tier of arches, 180 ft above the River Gard. The arch, first developed in Asia Minor, was given its important role in architecture by the Romans*

initiation and intense group-identity, which official Roman religion lacked. Thus the Persian cult of Mithras, which ennobled fighting as a manly virtue, attracted the soldiers, while Christianity offered a democratic after-life to the underprivileged, and made a particular appeal, in its early days, to slaves and women.

## Worship of the emperor

For those with a taste for Oriental mysticism there were the Egyptian cults of Isis, the mother goddess, and Serapis, her spouse; while for those who favoured hallucinogenic revelation through frenzy and trance there were the Bacchic rites from Greece.

Further off, in the more remote provinces, the weird local deities continued to flourish; all gods were tolerated, as long as everybody paid the proper respect on the appointed festival days to the official worship of the emperor, the focus of loyalty to Rome. It was the Christians' refusal to pay this homage that made Christianity the single faith that, for three centuries, Rome would not tolerate.

The fragmentation of religions was one of the causes which eventually weakened the political unity of the empire. Christianity was adopted as the official religion in the 4th century, but though this move was welcomed in the Greek East it failed to stop the decline in the greater part of the empire. Other causes of Rome's decline included the deterioration in the prestige of the emperor, as so few of the later emperors proved worthy of the office; and the fact that the legions were too often divided in support of rival emperors.

Pressures began to grow outside the empire from barbarian folk-movements from Central Asia, which drove displaced tribes towards the frontiers. The military system could not cope with infiltration at so many points at once, and the threatened localities were unable to organise an effective defence.

In this way, the barbarians dismembered the empire piecemeal, and by the end of the 4th century, Roman civilization in the West was virtually swamped. Rome itself was sacked by the Visigoths in 410, and the last emperor in

Rome was deposed in 476. In the East, however, Byzantium managed to resist the destructive tide, and carried on the Eastern aspects of the Roman imperial tradition into the Middle Ages.

## Roads among the ruins

Rome's first 1100 years beside the Tiber have left a vast legacy in the landscape, which has lasted to modern times. Many temples remain, but these are neither as frequent nor as representative of Roman energy as the great practical engineering works in which the Romans excelled. Suddenly in the countryside, a road abandons its meandering course and runs straight for a few miles: it is following its Roman predecessor. At Segovia in Spain, and at the Pont du Gard near Nimes, aqueducts that carried water to a city still span huge gorges with their rhythmic arches.

Shapeless ruins prove the indestructibility of the Romans' new building material, concrete; what still stands is the core of the structure, the stone facings having been quarried away in later times. The practical Roman style of civic architecture has not dated, and countless public buildings have been erected in later ages in the so-called Classical style perfected by the Romans.

At places like Timgad, in Algeria, and Volubilis, in Morocco, whole cities stand in ruins, unchanged since Roman times, still showing details of the teeming life so long ago – the olive-press, the brothel, the shop that sold hot drinks. Undulations in the ground show the course of vast drainage schemes to improve agriculture, while conduits below the streets show a concern for civic health and sanitation not paralleled until modern times.

Military campaigns have left their traces in the square camp-sites which can still be seen; while across northern Britain, and between the Rhône and the Danube, are the traces of the protective walls that for centuries kept the barbarians out.

## Rome's long shadow

Countless legal and political traditions and precedents have come down to us from Roman times. A citizen of Rome, from the earliest days, had great privileges. But the Romans recognised, too, that non-citizens, and even foreigners, should have legal rights, and to this end they developed a body of law called the *ius gentium* – the origin of international law. They appreciated that circumstances were constantly changing, so that law was left constantly open to interpretation by a body of *jurisprudents*, or jurists.

Throughout the years of the republic, an enormous body of laws and legal interpretations was thus built up, finally to be collected together in Byzantine times in the Code of Law of the Emperor Justinian. Every Roman man, woman or child – apart from slaves – had an established standing in the eyes of the law, so that the modern sense of political rights is Roman, too.

Hundreds of minor words and customs are derived from Rome: the Roman *libra*, 'pound', gave Britain her 'lb.'; and a husband still carries his bride across the threshold, as he did in Roman times. The modern calendar was devised by Julius Caesar, whose name is commemorated in the month of July.

It was through the expansion of the Roman Empire that the highest achievements of the ancient Greeks reached the West. Latin translations of Homer, Plato and Aristotle were familiar to Western Europe in the Middle Ages, long before Renaissance scholars began to study the original Greek texts. The Roman author Pliny's *Historia Naturalis* kept alive the scientific knowledge of the Greek world. The Latin alphabet, based on that of Greece, is used today throughout the Western world. Latin is the basis of the languages of modern Italy, France, Spain and Portugal, and supplies nearly one word in three of the English vocabulary.

Roman opinions and Roman tastes are remarkably similar to those of the modern world, for a blending of Roman and Greek culture survived the fall of Rome to form the very foundations of Western civilization.

## LIFE AND DEATH AT POMPEII

In AD 79 Vesuvius erupted and buried the nearby town of Pompeii. The volcanic ash which killed some 2000 of Pompeii's inhabitants also preserved the town's remains, and their rediscovery in modern times gives a clear picture of what life was like in a typical Roman community. Pompeii was a busy town, a centre of business and commerce. Its straight streets intersected each other on a grid pattern, and along the main street, lines of shops still stand today, looking as though their tenants had only just deserted them. Roman shops were simple square spaces, of identical size, with their goods stacked against the walls like an oriental bazaar. Inscriptions on the outer walls still show what each shop sold – oil, groceries, flour and so forth – and on some walls there are even inscriptions supporting a particular candidate in elections for a new consul. Here and there stands a *thermopolium*, which sold hot and cold drinks over a counter; and at several cross-roads there are drinking fountains for man and beast

VICTIM OF VESUVIUS *Choking gas from Vesuvius asphyxiated the inhabitants of Pompeii as they tried to flee the falling ash. The ash hardened round its victims, to form a mould, which in modern times has been filled with plaster and dug out of the ash*

VILLA LIFE *Rich merchants in Pompeii lived well, and decorated the walls of their villas with idealised paintings of town scenes. This 1st-century BC fresco in a bedroom shows the marble gates to a palatial town house. Above the gates a covered balcony juts outwards from the wall*

LADIES OF LEISURE *High-born Roman women, with slaves to do their housework, had plenty of time to cultivate the arts of leisure. They decorated their homes and painted their faces; some composed poems, or played musical instruments, like this lady with a cithara, or lute, painted on the wall of a Pompeii villa. The high-backed chair of bronze in which she sits was a sign of the lady's high status, like a modern throne; ordinary Romans sat on simple stools. Actual items of furniture in this style have been found in the ruins of Pompeii*

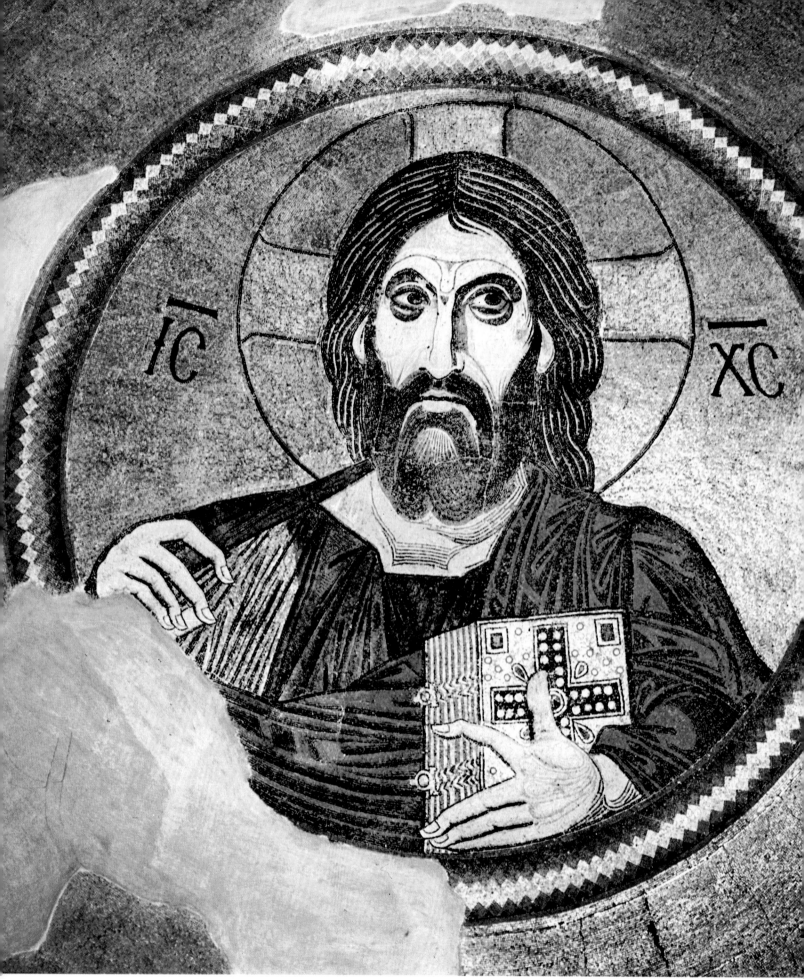

## THE BYZANTINE CHRIST: THE MAJESTIC FIGURE IN THE DOME OF THE CHURCH

*In every Byzantine church a huge and awesome figure of Christ as 'Pantocrator', or Ruler of the Universe, looked down from the centre of the main dome. Many of these glowing mosaics were destroyed during a wave of iconoclasm, or 'image-breaking', in the 8th century. This one in the monastery church at Daphni, near Athens, dates from about 1080. The Byzantines used art primarily as a means of* *expressing and heightening religious experience. They decorated the walls of their churches with religious mosaics and frescoes, in accordance with a pattern which was much the same in every church. Monks and martyrs had their appointed place on the lowest walls, mosaics of the apostles were set in the sanctuary, and events in Christ's life were depicted below the dome, which symbolised the canopy of Heaven*

# Byzantium: the world's first Christian empire

## AD 330–1453

*As Rome declined, its emperors moved east to make
Constantinople the heart of a glittering new civilization
built to the glory of God*

### BYZANTIUM IN AD 550

*Byzantium's power and wealth enabled
it to reconquer much of the former
Roman Empire round the Mediterranean*

Three centuries after the founder of Christianity died on the Cross in an outlying province of the Roman Empire, a new empire was created in his name. Christianity, the faith that Rome had persecuted, was the binding force that enabled Byzantium, the reorganised Roman Empire with its capital in the East, to survive for more than 1100 years, long after the Roman Empire in the West had perished. It was Christianity, too, and the urge to glorify God, that inspired Byzantine art and architecture, rich in wall-mosaics and domed churches.

Byzantium owed its wealth to its position astride trade routes from north to south and from east to west. It owed its traditions of law and government to Rome, and its language and learning to Greece. At its heart lay the fabulously rich city of Constantinople, dedicated by the Emperor Constantine in AD 330 as a new capital for the Roman Empire as it faced the threat of disintegration.

The idea of moving the imperial capital to the east was not new. As early as 45 BC Julius Caesar had considered transferring his capital to Alexandria or to Troy. The eastern regions were the most densely populated part of the Roman Empire, and the home of highly developed earlier civilizations like those of Greece and Egypt. Diocletian, when he became emperor in AD 284, tried to maintain control of the empire by dividing it into eastern and western halves, and himself administered the eastern half from Nicomedia, near the town which was to become Constantinople.

But Diocletian continued the persecution of Christians; his successor, Constantine, was the first emperor shrewd enough to see that Christianity, with its power to sway the minds of men and harness their loyalty, was the one force that could save the empire. In 313 he declared that Christianity was to be tolerated throughout its lands – though he was not baptised himself until 25 years later.

Constantine also saw that Rome, as well as being a centre of intrigues and feuds, was far too steeped in the older pagan beliefs to be suitable as the capital of a Christian empire. In 324, when he became undisputed master of the Roman world, its eastern and western halves now reunited, Constantine laid the foundation stone of a new city which was modelled on Rome but intended to be larger and richer than anything that had been built before. The site he

### WHERE EMPERORS WERE CROWNED

*The magnificent Hagia Sophia, the Church of Holy Wisdom, was completed by Emperor Justinian in 537 and became the focus of religious life in Constantinople. Processions filed in and out of its doors on the frequent saints' days, and most Byzantine emperors after Justinian were crowned in the church. More than 10,000 people worked on the building of Hagia Sophia; when it was finished, Justinian is said to have exclaimed, 'Solomon, I have outdone thee'. The huge central dome, 107 ft across and set on four sturdy piers over the square central area, is flanked by a number of smaller domes. This Byzantine style of church architecture was widely copied, especially in Italy and the Balkans. Hagia Sophia became a mosque after the fall of Constantinople, and is now a museum*

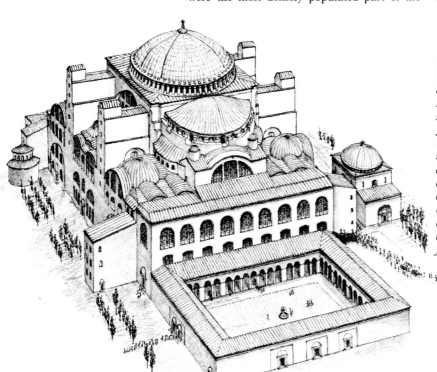

# East and West meet in Constantinople, the 'New Rome'

AN EMPIRE'S WALLED CAPITAL ON THE GOLDEN HORN

*The sumptuous fortress city of Constantinople was founded by Emperor Constantine in 324 on a natural harbour at the mouth of the Bosporus. In this impression by a 16th-century artist the centre of the city is dominated by the domed Hagia Sophia, the Church of Holy Wisdom (left). The Hippodrome (right), modelled on the Circus Maximus in Rome, had room for 60,000 spectators at the chariot races. The houses of the well-to-do were built of wood and had two storeys, with a balcony from which the inhabitants could watch processions passing through the streets below. Parts of the 13-mile wall (left) built round the city by Constantine survive in modern Istanbul*

chose was an old Greek trading town called Byzantium, founded 1000 years earlier by a Greek sailor named Byzas.

In six years Constantine's architects, engineers and builders completed the new city and decorated it with art treasures from every corner of the Roman Empire. To attract citizens to the new capital, the emperor tempted the upper classes with houses modelled on those of Rome and other important cities, and the lower classes with bread and circuses on a lavish scale. Constantine was going to call his city New Rome, but it quickly came to be known as Constantinople, the 'City of Constantine'.

Constantine chose his site well. His new capital stood on the Bosporus, between the Black Sea and the Sea of Marmara, at the crossing point of trade routes between Eastern Europe and Asia. The Byzantines became the busiest traders of the times. They bought, sold and exchanged an unparalleled variety of goods

– grain from Egypt and the northern Black Sea coast, silks from China, spices from the East Indies, gold and ivory from Africa, furs and wood from Russia.

By charging 10 per cent on all goods carried into and out of the city, the Byzantines earned money to pay for their buildings, their public services and their entertainments. The wealth that poured into Constantinople earned its fine natural harbour the title of the Golden Horn. The value of the Byzantine gold coinage was so consistent that it became the international trading currency, and merchants from as far as China preferred to use Byzantine money rather than their own.

## Christ's thirteenth Apostle

When Constantine became emperor he succeeded to a line of monarchs who had ruled with absolute power for many generations and who had been worshipped as gods. While the

absolute power continued, the divinity had to be dropped, for Christianity recognised only one God. A compromise was reached whereby the emperor was accepted as God's representative on earth, the thirteenth Apostle, with the title of 'equal to the Apostles'. It did not matter by what route an emperor came to the throne; his status was approved by God, even if sometimes the emperor was a monster of vice.

When Christianity was a persecuted faith, it was easy enough for Christians to make common cause without going into precise shades of meaning about what they believed. But when their faith became the official religion of the empire, the exact definition of its principles became an affair of state.

Church leaders and ordinary citizens alike began to dispute over shades of meaning, and the Byzantines, with their Greek-instilled passion for definition, gave fresh currency to two Greek words: 'orthodox', meaning a man who followed official belief, and 'heretic', meaning one who did not. Numerous councils of the whole Christian Church were summoned at which the emperor and his bishops tried to decide such difficult matters as whether God the Father was greater than God the Son.

With this obsessive interest in the state of a man's beliefs, the early years of the Byzantine Empire were the great years of the creed-makers. The bishops were set the task of producing for the use of all citizens a concise statement of basic beliefs. The first council called by the Emperor Constantine, at Nicaea in western Turkey in AD 325, produced the Nicene Creed, a resounding declaration of faith which is still used in many Christian churches today.

From the time of Constantine, the Roman Empire looked on Byzantine emperors as heads of the Christian Church. But disputes over doctrine weakened Byzantine authority, and in 800 Pope Leo III, head of the Church in Rome, crowned Charles, King of the Franks, as Emperor of the Holy Roman Empire. This was to lead to a rift between Western Christianity and Eastern ('Orthodox') Christianity which lasts to this day.

### God in everyday life

Religion was the mainspring of life in Byzantium. The festivals and carnivals, the gaiety in the streets, the splendour of the buildings, the riches of the markets, the games, the shows at the theatres – all were part of the Byzantine citizen's homage to God. Hardly a picture, mosaic, fresco or poem was produced that did not in some way speak of God's glory.

Ordinary people sought the Church's blessing on everyday activities. When a fishing fleet was about to set out it would be blessed, with long incantations, in the hope that the catch would be a good one. Every house that was built was dedicated to God. No event was celebrated

more fervently in a Byzantine city such as Constantinople than the arrival and display of a new relic of Christ or of one of the saints.

The Byzantines also worshipped icons – images of Christ, the Virgin Mary and the saints in painting, sculpture or ivory relief. A bitter controversy began in 726 when Emperor Leo III banned the worship of icons, which most churchmen regarded as idolatrous. For more than a century after this the iconoclasts, or 'image-smashers', whitewashed or defaced thousands of church paintings and sculptures.

### The golden age of Justinian

One of the greatest of the Byzantine emperors came to the throne in 527. He was Justinian I, whose 38-year reign was distinguished by three major achievements. He reconquered much of the old Western Empire; he modernised Roman law; and he built hundreds of churches, including the magnificent Hagia Sophia, the Church of Holy Wisdom, in Constantinople.

Justinian, though born like Constantine at Naissus (Nish), in what was then a Greek province and is now Serbia, part of Yugoslavia, was a Roman at heart. He devoted his long reign to trying to recreate the old Roman Empire as it was when it dominated the Mediterranean throughout the centuries before the barbarian invasions. He succeeded in driving the Vandals from Africa and the Ostrogoths from Italy.

Justinian was no general himself, but he knew how to pick good leaders of men. One of them, Belisarius, was the greatest military leader produced by Byzantium. In 534 he reconquered the North African states, in a campaign which culminated in the capture of Carthage. From Africa, Belisarius crossed to Italy, and after five years' fighting took Rome. By 555 all Italy and the southern part of Spain were in Byzantine hands. Justinian's conquests,

### PIETY ON PILLARS AND IN CAVES

*A 5th-century Syrian hermit, St Simeon, lived for 35 years on top of a pillar, hauling up his food by basket. Severe asceticism was greatly respected in Byzantium, and St Simeon had many imitators, called 'stylites' after the Greek for pillar. His reputation for sanctity was shared by a fellow Syrian, St Ephraeim, whose burial is shown in this contemporary painting. St Ephraeim played a large part in converting Syria to Christianity. Many Christian hermits of Byzantine times lived in mountain huts or in cells carved out of the rocks (top left), where they set up the first monasteries*

---

### RICH CASKETS FOR RELICS OF CHRIST'S CROSS

The worship of relics had an important place in Byzantine life, and objects connected with the Christian faith were brought to cities such as Constantinople from all corners of the empire. One expedition even claimed to have unearthed the actual Cross on which Christ was crucified

RELIC CASKET *This jewelled casket, or reliquary, made to hold a fragment of Christ's Cross, was paraded through the streets*

HOLY ART *Christ, with the Apostles, shown on a reliquary*

ENAMEL CROSS *This reliquary is in cloisonné enamel, made by pouring molten glass into a 'honeycomb' of gold or silver plates*

# A semi-divine emperor in an age of mosaics

**POWER BEHIND THE THRONE**

*Women had considerable power in Byzantine politics. Justinian had the law changed to enable him to marry Theodora, an actress and courtesan, who became his valued adviser for 20 years. Pearls hang from the empress's diadem in this 6th-century Ravenna mosaic. Some emperors chose their empresses from a parade of suitable candidates, presenting an apple to the chosen bride—the same gift by which, in the Greek myth, Paris selected the fairest of the goddesses*

however, did not last and by the end of the next century Spain, Africa and most of Italy were lost, never to be regained.

The most important and enduring of Justinian's achievements was the orderly system of law which he drew up, and which has been a major influence on the legal structure of most nations of the Western world.

## Severe but humane laws

The Code of Justinian was basically the Roman law, dating back to the days of the Republic and added to over the centuries by a huge collection of interpretations of the law by generations of jurists. Justinian set up a commission of ten experts who disentangled the essential principles from a mass of contradictions and irrelevancies; they then brought the laws up to date and published them, in 534, in a series of books, the *Corpus of Civil Law*. Justinian claimed that one volume of this series, the *Digest*, had reduced the original 3 million lines of law which he inherited down to only 150,000 lines.

In some ways the law remained severe. Laws relating to slavery were included, although slavery was in principle unacceptable to Christians. But the law was based, as Justinian claimed, on humanity and common sense. Emphasis was given to women's rights, which suggests something of the great influence on Justinian of his wife, Theodora. Mothers were given equal authority with fathers in the upbringing of children – a significant departure from Roman practice, which gave absolute power to the *pater familias*.

The administration of the law was tempered by humanity. The death penalty was the exception rather than the rule, imprisonment was regarded generally as a waste of a useful citizen's time and heavy fines resulting in impoverishment were regarded as unhelpful. A man might be sent to a monastery for the good of his soul, but even there he would make a contribution to the welfare of the state.

The usual punishment for serious crimes such as murder, robbery with violence or treason was mutilation, most often by chopping off a hand. Even in cases of treason, the state often showed mercy, though there were still public executions in the Hippodrome of some corrupt officials and rebellious citizens.

## New titles for the senators

Justinian wielded absolute power, ruling through a court and civil service administration in which many of the higher posts were occupied by eunuchs. Because they could not have children, they seldom had ambitions of seizing power themselves with a view to creating hereditary monarchies. Consequently they gave the state excellent service, and some parents would even go to the extreme of having their sons castrated to give them an opportunity of good appointments in government.

The Byzantine system of government included a senate which, like the senate of Imperial Rome, had little to do beyond endorsing the emperor's decisions. It was filled with members from an aristocracy created by Constantine,

and to compensate senators for their lack of power they were given new titles such as *nobilissimus* or *illustris*.

The ceremonial surrounding the emperor grew more complex with the centuries. Ritual, much of it inspired by the East, was an essential part of the apparatus of imperial rule. Justinian wore silk robes and a jewelled crown, and he made all men bow the knee on coming into his presence. Some had to prostrate themselves – as the emperor did himself before Christ – before he would speak to them.

An important role on state occasions was played by two separate *demes*, or citizens' societies, which recited acclamations and verses. These two factions, called the Greens and the Blues after the colours worn by their supporters, brought citizens' grievances to the emperor's attention and also managed many of the affairs of the city of Constantinople, including the staging of chariot races in the Hippodrome, the Byzantines' favourite sport.

Despite the emperor's semi-divine status and the ceremonies which protected him, the atmosphere of conspiracy that surrounded the court has made 'Byzantine' a byword for intrigue, and 29 of Byzantium's 88 emperors died violent deaths.

## The triumph of Greek over Latin

Because Constantine grafted a Roman society on to a Greek town, two languages were in common use in Byzantium. At first, Latin was the official tongue of the court, the government and the law courts. But more and more Greek-speaking people entered government and public service, while scholars, writers, poets and philosophers turned increasingly to the ancient Greek texts.

Justinian tried to keep Latin, the traditional language of the Roman Empire, as the language of the court, but he recognised that Greek was the tongue of the people, and he published his last great legal works, the *Novellae*, in Greek 'so that they may be more easily understood by all'. Soon after Justinian's death the Greek language became supreme.

The schools of philosophy in Athens, which had lasted for a thousand years since the time of Plato, were closed by Justinian, who saw them as relics of paganism. But scholars continued to study and copy the writings of the ancient Greeks. They also produced original works of value in history and theology. Their histories were much more than chronicles of events. Procopius, who was secretary to Belisarius, wrote a graphic account of Justinian's wars and also a *Secret History*, which was not published until after the author's death; this contained a wealth of gossip and scandal about Justinian, whom Procopius described as a 'demon incarnate . . . more savage than all the barbarians together'.

## The enemies of Byzantium

In more than 11 centuries of existence Byzantium rarely enjoyed one whole year of peace. Civil war broke out almost immediately after Constantine I's death in 337, and the empire

JUSTINIAN THE LAW-GIVER BRINGS TRIBUTE TO THE CHURCH

*A halo round the head of Justinian in a mosaic in the Church of St Vitale at Ravenna in Italy symbolises the semi-divine status of the Byzantine emperor as God's vice-regent on earth. The 6th-century artist, working with tiny cubes of stone and coloured glass pressed into wet plaster, has depicted Justinian bringing a gift of gold to the church. With him stand Archbishop Maximian, holding a jewelled cross,*
*and a retinue of churchmen and court officials. Justinian was born of a peasant family at Naissus in the Balkans, and became one of Byzantium's greatest rulers. He doubled the extent of the empire and left the world an enduring system of law. The emperor's purple cloak, decorated with embroidered gold cloth, shows how, in Byzantium, eastern splendour softened the severity of the Roman toga*

was assailed in turn by Goths, Huns, Persians, Avars, Bulgars, Slavs, Vikings, Arabs, Berbers, Turks, Crusaders and Normans. The boundaries of Byzantium expanded and contracted continually. Sometimes when Byzantium could not beat off attacks it bought peace. In 447 an earthquake outside Constantinople frightened Attila the Hun, poised with his hordes not far to the west, into accepting a bribe of nearly 3 tons of gold bars in return for moving off with his blood-hungry warriors.

The last years of Heraclius (610–41) co-incided with the beginnings of great Arab invasions of Byzantine territory in the Near East and round the Mediterranean. In 636 the Arabs won Syria, in 638 Palestine, in 641 Persia and Egypt. The Muslim invaders were unable to capture Constantinople either by land or by sea, especially after 650 when the Byzantines were armed with their invincible secret weapon, 'Greek fire'. But when Heraclius died the

Byzantine Empire had contracted to Asia Minor, Greece, parts of North Africa, Sicily and South Italy. Thus it remained for 200 years, smaller than ever before, continuously threatened by Arabs, Slavs, Bulgars and others.

## Conquest for loot and glory

The tide turned in the 9th century under a dynasty of emperors which included Michael III (842–67), known as Michael the Drunkard. He had gained a bad reputation in his youth for wild drinking and horse-racing parties, but settled down to become a good ruler, advised by his uncle, Bardas. Under the regency of his mother, Theodora, the icons had been restored in 843. Later Michael chose good generals who organised major campaigns to recover Byzantine land in the east of Asia Minor.

Michael was murdered by one of his grooms, who became Basil I (867–86). This humbly born man proved to be an outstanding military

commander and a skilful administrator. He began the successful Macedonian dynasty, which held the throne of Byzantium for the next two centuries. Basil's successors extended the empire's boundaries to the Euphrates, and made considerable inroads into Bulgaria. Two of the leading commanders during this time were the general-emperors Nicephorus II (963–9) and John I (969–76), who rank among Byzantium's greatest soldiers.

Byzantium had not only good leaders, but thousands of tough, enthusiastic men settled in the frontier areas with obligations to provide armies. For many years, as many as 100,000 men were serving at one time, stimulated largely by two incentives–the loot to be had from the riches of Muslim rulers and the glory to be had from recovering Christian lands.

John I was succeeded in 976 by Basil II, a man of strong will and courage, whose reign gave Byzantium a period of prosperity and

# Crusaders' greed paves the way for the collapse of an empire

expansion as great as that it enjoyed under Justinian. So successful was his campaign against the Bulgars in the Balkans that he became known as Basil the Bulgar-Slayer.

Military success led to a great upsurge in trade, and Constantinople established its supremacy as the principal market of the Mediterranean. When Basil died in 1025, the empire had reached a peak of success, though at the cost of overstraining its economy.

## An empire in decline

The next 200 years brought a steady decline in Byzantium's fortunes. In the east the empire was under constant attack by the Seljuk Turks from Central Asia, who in 1071 defeated the Byzantines at Manzikert in eastern Anatolia and overran the highlands of Asia Minor. At the same time, in the west, Byzantium lost territory in Italy and Sicily to Norman invaders, who also invaded Epirus, in the west Balkans. For help against Turks and Normans the Byzantines turned to Venice; in return for assistance, the Venetians demanded and got trading rights throughout the Byzantine Empire, so weakening Byzantium's long monopoly and her financial resources.

By the beginning of the 13th century the empire had shrunk to a little more than what is now Greece and the western half of Turkey. It was now to endure the supreme tragedy – the invasion of its capital in 1204 by Western European armies which had originally set out on the Fourth Crusade for the Holy Land. The predominant motive for this attack by Christians against Christians was greed. The

Crusaders, short of money, sought ships from Venice, Byzantium's long-standing trading rival. Despite its decline, Byzantium was still far richer than Palestine or Syria, the Crusaders' original goals. Consequently French and Venetian ships, having rounded the south of Greece, turned north-eastwards, sailed up the Dardanelles, and attacked Constantinople. With a mixture of skill, treachery and good fortune they broke into the city and took possession of it. The Emperor Alexius V fled and was later killed in Greece.

There followed one of the most systematic lootings in history. Countless treasures were stolen, and apportioned to the troops according to their rank. Nothing was spared – not precious relics of Christ, nor the mosaics of the Church of Holy Wisdom, nor the tombs of the emperors. The group of four sculptured bronze horses which now grace the front of St Mark's Cathedral in Venice once surrounded the emperor's seat at the Hippodrome in Constantinople, until the attacking Crusaders removed them and carried them off to Italy.

## Split in Christian ranks

The attack was a devastating blow to Byzantium, and one from which it did not recover. Successor states were set up by members of the ruling family, one of which, in Nicaea, eventually recaptured Constantinople. But the Crusaders' attack split the ranks of Christian Europe, and highlighted the growing indifference of the West to the civilization that had preserved the Christian faith and the ancient classical heritage. This indifference was to be

directly responsible for the final fall of Constantinople in 1453.

'A monstrous head without a body' is how the tough, ruthless, but cultured Ottoman Sultan, Mehmet II, described what was left of the Byzantine Empire in 1452. It was a fair comment. A huge city once containing over a million people had shrunk to only 60,000. It was governed by a top-heavy imperial court and a complex Church organisation, and it controlled only a few hundred square miles of land in Greece. Byzantium had become irrelevant, and Mehmet was determined to end it.

## The Turks triumphant

Mehmet, a young and brilliant ruler, formulated his plans with great care. He built a large fortified depot at Rumeli Hisar, not far from Constantinople, so that his troops engaged in a protracted siege would not be short of supplies. He had mines placed in tunnels under the walls of the city, which in places were 25 ft thick. Mehmet also ordered the construction of the largest cannon the world had seen. Its barrel was 26 ft long, and it could fire a 650 lb. ball of granite up to a mile. But the cannon was more a weapon of terror than of destructiveness, for the barrel grew so hot that it took an hour to cool before it could be fired again.

In April 1453 the order was given to attack, and 100,000 men moved into action. After six weeks of the most intensive siege operations of medieval history, little progress had been made. Mehmet then decided on a last assault, from across the harbour. The great wall was breached and Constantinople was then swiftly overrun.

THE FIRST 'FLAME-THROWER' MAKES BYZANTIUM MASTER OF THE SEA

*The rapid growth of the Muslim threat from about AD 630 inspired major naval improvements in Byzantium. By 675 Byzantine fleets had become almost invincible with the discovery of 'Greek fire' – an incendiary mixture which, as this illustration from a 14th-century manuscript shows, was fired through tubes mounted in the bows of ships. 'Greek fire' consisted of a mixture of sulphur, naphtha, quick-lime and* *salt-petre; the use of naphtha meant that the more water was thrown on to the flames, the fiercer they burnt – and they would continue burning even on the sea. By 800, Byzantium's 200 fast galleys had won supremacy at sea. But during the 9th century the Arabs discovered the secret of 'Greek fire' and began using it themselves against the Byzantines; they also used it against the Crusaders*

The last Byzantine emperor, Constantine XI, fell fighting with his troops at the St Romanus Gate. Mehmet entered the city on a white horse and rode straight to the Church of Holy Wisdom, which he had determined should be proclaimed a mosque for Islam. Unlike the Western Crusaders of 1204 the Turks left much of the city alone; indeed, the Sultan had a soldier flogged for trying to break up a mosaic in the Church of Holy Wisdom.

## Byzantium's lasting legacy

Islamic dominion over the Near East and the Mediterranean, for centuries the dream of Muslim rulers, had now become a reality. After 1100 years, the Byzantine Empire was at an end. But its influence was to live on. All-conquering Islam itself benefited by its contact with the Byzantine world and the attainments of Christians who lived in Muslim cities.

Byzantium had kept Christianity and civilization alive during the Dark Ages which in Western Europe followed the fall of the Roman Empire. The conversion of the barbarians, ensuring the eventual triumph of Christianity in Western Europe, was to be the work of missionaries sent by the popes in Rome and not by the emperors in Constantinople. Yet Western Christendom owes an important debt to Byzantium for its preservation of the ancient classical writings and art forms, so important to the revival of learning during the 15th-century Renaissance.

The Eastern European empires of Bulgaria, Serbia and above all Russia owed even more to Byzantine example. As early as the 9th century Bulgar chiefs, envious of the fabulous riches of Constantinople, commissioned Byzantine architects to build great palaces for them. The Bulgars became Christian and adopted the Byzantine, or Orthodox, version of the faith in preference to that of Rome.

The Serbian Empire, founded in the 12th century, also had close ties with Byzantium. Several Serbian nobles married Byzantine princesses, and a code of law adopted in the 14th century was based on the reforms of Justinian. Serbian artists copied Byzantine styles, and adorned their houses and public buildings with frescoes. Both the Bulgarian and Serbian empires were eventually to fall to the Ottoman Turks.

## Orthodoxy survives in Russia

Byzantine civilization began to spread in Russia when in 988 Vladimir, Grand Prince of Kiev, became a Christian and married the sister of the Byzantine emperor, Basil II. Vladimir's conversion inspired art and architecture in Kiev based on Byzantine models.

In 1439 an attempt was made to heal the rift between the Eastern and Roman Churches. But the Russians never supported reunion; in 1472 Ivan III married a niece of Constantine XI, the last Byzantine emperor, added the two-headed eagle of Byzantium to the Arms of Moscow, and proclaimed Russia as protector of the Orthodox Church. Ivan was taking to Moscow what was left of Byzantium.

# THE FALL OF CONSTANTINOPLE

The decline of the Byzantine Empire began after a disastrous defeat by the Turks at Manzikert, in eastern Anatolia, in 1071. Gradually more and more Byzantine territory fell to the growing power of Islam until, by the beginning of the 14th century, little more than the city of Constantinople itself and a small area north of it remained in Byzantine hands. By this time, the Ottoman Turks had begun the career of conquest which was eventually to make their empire the greatest of all the Muslim states. After conquering most of the Byzantine Empire by 1452, the Ottoman sultan, Mehmet II, determined to capture Constantinople – 'a monstrous head without a body', as he called it. Mehmet planned his assault on the Byzantine capital for more than a year before his troops laid siege to the city. The siege lasted for six weeks before Constantinople finally fell

CULTURED CONQUEROR *Mehmet II was a ruthless but cultured leader. When he captured Constantinople he turned many churches into mosques; but he allowed several to remain Christian*

CAPITAL UNDER SIEGE *Mehmet's siege of Constantinople is depicted in a painting by a contemporary French artist. The Turks encamped outside the city and bombarded the walls. But the entrance to the harbour of the Golden Horn was guarded by a floating boom. To get round this, the Turkish force, using oxen, dragged 70 of their ships overland from the Bosporus and made their final assault on the city from across the harbour*

# Church and tsar build the Russian nation

## FROM AD 988

*The Christian faith, brought from Byzantium, inspired
a flourishing culture whose legacy is preserved
even in the Communist Russia of today*

Russian civilization represents a remarkable blend of the old and the new, of the peasant's cart and the Sputnik. Old Russia began to emerge about AD 850, shaped by eastern European influences. Its culture, represented by Kiev and early Moscow, was primarily religious. It is the country of onion-domed churches and monasteries; of illuminated manuscripts and icons.

New Russia, on the other hand, stems from western European influences, the effect of which was accelerated by Peter the Great from 1700. Its culture, identified with St Petersburg and modern Moscow, has been more secular. New Russia is the country of stone-built palaces, academies and universities; of the lathe and the combine harvester.

Old Russia did not simply give way to the new from 1700 onwards. On the contrary, the older culture has persisted alongside the new ever since – increasingly submerged, but still vital. Russian civilization, old and new alike, has evolved against the background of the vast Russian plain, which is intersected by great river networks and seems to extend for ever, encircled by the *taiga*, or evergreen forest, of the north and the steppes, or prairies, of the

south. The country has a harsh climate, with long, dark, savage winters. During a history beset by major wars, invasions, famines, epidemics and revolutions, the Russians have expanded from tiny beginnings in a small area to occupy the entire Eurasian plain, and the Siberian and Central Asian mountains beyond it. For over four centuries the Russians have formed the core of an increasingly authoritarian state which has absorbed some 200 peoples and now has a population of about 250 million.

The ancestors of the modern Russians were a group of Slav tribes who by AD 400 had moved east, possibly from an original homeland north of the Carpathian Mountains, into territory which is now Russia. They made their settlements in clearings which they cut with their axes in the dense forests along the banks of the great rivers.

The Slavs remained a collection of scattered tribes until the 9th century, when Viking merchant princes, adventuring deep into Europe from Scandinavia, established their rule over the tribal areas. Under a measure of Viking guidance the first Russian state – still pagan, still illiterate – had emerged by 850, with its centre at Kiev. But the true beginning of

### RUSSIA IN 1462 AND 1725

*Ivan the Great made Moscow the centre of an empire which Peter the Great extended to cover most of modern Russia*

### RULER WHO MADE RUSSIA CHRISTIAN

*Vladimir, Grand Prince of Kiev from 980 to 1015, became a Christian in 988. He made his choice after sending envoys to watch the rituals of the Jewish, Muslim, Roman Catholic and Byzantine Orthodox Churches. The envoys were so impressed by the splendid rites they saw in Constantinople that Vladimir decreed that the infant Russian state should adopt the Byzantine form of Christianity. Byzantine culture also strongly influenced early Russian architecture and painting. Vladimir, shown in a 17th-century book illustration, fought many wars in extending the territory of Kiev, and became renowned as a hero of Russian folklore. Despite his conversion, Vladimir is reputed to have kept 800 concubines*

### A CHURCH OF WOOD

*The woodman's axe was the only implement used to shape the 22 silvery-scaled onion domes of the Church of the Transfiguration at Kizhi. The church was built in 1714 on an island in Lake Onega, between St Petersburg (later Leningrad) and the White Sea; the bell-tower on the left was added in 1894. The earliest Russians had to cut down thick forest to create their settlements, and they soon became adept at using the axe to fashion wood. The tradition of wood-carving has persisted in Russia to the present day*

# Christian zeal that united a people and inspired its art

Russian civilization dates from 988, when Grand Prince Vladimir of Kiev was converted to Christianity – the Orthodox version, as practised in Byzantium. According to legend, Vladimir sent envoys to study the religions practised by neighbouring states. They watched Jews, Muslims and Christians of the Roman Catholic Church at worship, but were not impressed. Then they visited the great Hagia Sophia, the Church of the Holy Wisdom, which the Emperor Justinian had built in Constantinople in the 6th century. There, the envoys said, they encountered such beauty 'that they knew not whether they were in heaven or upon earth'.

## A city of 200 churches

The sumptuous setting which the Orthodox Church provided for its congregations made an instant appeal to the Russians. Christianity quickly became the pivot of their lives and thoughts, and gave the art of Kiev a character which was to pervade Russian art until the 17th century. By choosing to adopt the Christianity of the Eastern Byzantine world rather than that of the Roman West, Vladimir also set Russia on a divergent path from that of western Europe. In doing so he helped to

forge a society which has never wholly belonged either to East or West, but has hovered, often uneasily, between the two. Byzantine Christianity also gave the Russians the basis of their present alphabet. Consisting today, after various reforms, of 32 letters, this alphabet still bears the name 'Cyrillic', after St Cyril, a Byzantine missionary.

The first great products of Russian civilization were its churches. Within 50 years of Vladimir's conversion, Kiev is said to have had 200 churches; many of these were wooden structures, which have long since perished. Vladimir's son, Yaroslav, set himself the task of making Kiev as beautiful as any town in Christendom. He commissioned Greek architects to design for the main square a Church of the Holy Wisdom to rival Justinian's mighty Hagia Sophia. It survives to this day, though in an 18th-century baroque restoration.

Originally Yaroslav's church at Kiev had 13 squat domes shaped like inverted saucers in the Byzantine manner. Inside, the mosaics and painted decorations still provide a superb example of the early blending of the Byzantine style with the more intimate native Russian style. Less influenced by Byzantine models, and

more characteristic of the developing Russian style, is another 11th-century cathedral, also named after St Sophia: that of Novgorod, completed in 1052. This has the typically Russian onion-domes, which soon established themselves as a feature of the national style.

These turban-shaped stone protuberances, often gilded and surmounted with crosses, sprout out of white masonry. They are admirably designed to prevent snow from settling on them, while beguiling the eye with their striking silhouettes and giving variety to the flat Russian landscape.

## Monks as historians

On the outskirts of Kiev was the Monastery of the Caves – Russia's first monastery and a stronghold of Russian Christianity. Its first church, built in the mid-11th century, survived until the Second World War. The monastery encouraged learning and the arts, and it was there that monks composed the first Russian historical chronicles and lives of saints. Translations were made from Greek, Latin and Hebrew; the Greek works included tales about Troy and Alexander the Great. Two literary monuments attributed to this period are the

### EASTER DAY IN MOSCOW 300 YEARS AGO

*The atmosphere of intense religious devotion in 17th-century Russia is captured in a drawing from the* Voyages, *written by a contemporary German visitor, Adam Olearius. It shows a huge procession celebrating Easter in front of the Moscow Kremlin, in what is*

*today Red Square. The Kremlin, with its turban-shaped and gilded domes, was the religious centre of the principality of Muscovy and the seat of the Russian Patriarch who, since the fall of Constantinople, had become head of the Russian Orthodox Church*

### THE SACRED ART OF THE ICON

When Russia adopted Christianity from Byzantium, it inherited also the Byzantine art of painting icons – sacred pictures on wood of Christ, the Madonna, saints and angels. The deep religious feelings of the Russian people were expressed in icons of brilliant artistry which were themselves regarded as sacred. Icons were an essential decoration for the walls of church and palace, and in every peasant's hut an icon – the family's most cherished possession – stood in a corner of the living-room, with a candle burning before it

DRAGON SLAYER *Various schools of icon-painting developed during the 16th century, the most important being at Novgorod. One particularly spirited 16th-century icon painted in Novgorod depicts a Russian St George slaying the dragon, the symbol of evil, in order to rescue the princess at the top of the tower. An angel sets a crown on St George's head, and God blesses him from a cloud (top right)*

*Lay of Igor's Raid,* a lament for warriors who died fighting Turkic tribesmen, and a travelogue, *Voyage of the Abbot Daniel to the Holy Land.*

Trade played a large part in the economy of early Kiev. Products of the forest lands such as furs, wax and honey were conveyed south by river and across the Black Sea to Constantinople. Slaves, too, were exported to the south in quantity, as well as playing an important role locally. Kiev's society was essentially agricultural. By no means all farm-workers were slaves or serfs, but the occupation of free peasant was held in little respect, as is illustrated by the Old Russian word by which he was known: *smerd* (stinker).

Russia in the Kiev period was not yet a centralised state, but rather a loose federation of princedoms presided over, often ineffectively, by the Grand Prince of Kiev, and exposed to the repeated attacks of marauding nomads who ravaged the southern steppes. Citizens of Kiev increasingly migrated to the densely forested north, the home of primitive Finnic tribes. In this northern area other early Russian cities – Rostov, Suzdal and Vladimir, 150 miles northeast of present-day Moscow, and finally Moscow itself – arose in rivalry to Kiev. In 1169

Prince Andrei Bogolubsky transferred Russia's capital from Kiev to Vladimir, and adorned it with beautifully proportioned churches constructed of scintillating white stone.

## Under the Tatar yoke

In 1237–40 the Tatars – heirs to the empire of Genghis Khan, and the most powerful scourge ever to emerge from the eastern steppes – conquered most of the Russian lands. These savage Mongol-ruled horsemen burnt many towns to the ground and massacred untold numbers of their inhabitants. But they did not keep the ruined country under permanent occupation, preferring instead to exploit it through heavy taxation levied under threat of a renewed terror. The Tatars also conscripted Russians into their armies, and removed skilled workers to their capital at Saray on the Volga.

Russian civilization survived during these brutal centuries largely because the Tatars were intent on plunder and blackmail, and had no interest in the spiritual beliefs of their victims. Since there was nothing to be gained by terrorising the Church, they tolerated it; and the Church became a haven for harassed Russians during the period of the Tatar yoke.

Russian monks, writing in their chronicles and in the lives of their saints, looked on Tatar domination as God's punishment for their sins. But they were able to found many new monasteries during this period, and to continue the colonisation of empty lands.

The Tatars bequeathed to the Russians a census, a postal system and a model of harsh autocratic government, together with the practices of kow-towing to superiors and keeping women in seclusion. Though the Russian native genius was not destroyed by the Tatars, their yoke deprived Russia of access to the most potentially fruitful contemporary European influence, that of the Italian Renaissance. By isolating Russian society for so long from its natural partners in western Europe, the Tatars held back Russia's development.

One Russian principality, Novgorod, was never conquered by the Tatars, though it was made to pay tribute. The Novgorodians were sturdy in spirit and independent in action. In the 11th century they banished their princes and developed a form of government on republican lines. All free men were entitled to voice their opinions at the *veche*, or assembly, which met at the summons of a bell in the

MIRACULOUS VICTORY *Historical events, as well as saints, were commemorated in icons, and formed an illustrated record of Russia's past for the benefit of the illiterate peasants. An icon from a church in the village of Kuretsa, near Lake Ilmen, Novgorod, painted in about 1460, tells the story of the victory of the Novgorodians over the people of Suzdal, a rival principality, in 1169. The Novgorodians attributed their victory to the Madonna, whose image is venerated in the top panel. Parish priests also carried icons round the fields to bless the crops*

GUARDIAN ANGEL *Russian icon artists portrayed their angels and saints with tender, expressive faces, like this* Head of an Archangel *painted in the late 12th century. Every Christian in Russia had a guardian angel who acted as a mediator on his behalf with the Almighty*

EARLIEST SAINTS *The first two Russian saints to be canonised, St Boris and St Gleb, are depicted in an early 14th-century icon. Boris and Gleb were both sons of Vladimir, Grand Prince of Kiev. After Vladimir's death in 1015 a civil war broke out among several of his 12 sons, but Boris and Gleb refused to take up arms; instead they allowed their elder brother Svyatopolk to murder them, without offering any resistance, regarding themselves as martyrs to Christian humility*

# *Peasants enslaved under the rule of all-powerful tsars*

### THE PAINTING THAT WORKED MIRACLES

*The most famous of all Russia's icons is the Virgin of Vladimir, painted in the early 12th century by an unknown Byzantine artist. Like many icons, the Virgin was believed to have the power to work miracles. It was credited with saving Moscow from foreign* *conquest on three occasions, including Napoleon's invasion of 1812. The icon was commissioned by an early prince of Kiev, then moved to the central Russian city of Vladimir. Later still it was placed in the Cathedral of the Assumption in the Kremlin in Moscow*

town's main square. By the 13th century many Novgorodians were literate. They used birch bark as a cheap writing material, reserving parchment for their books; the finest were adorned with splendid illuminations in the Byzantine style, and with ornate capital letters.

Few of the Novgorodians' personal possessions survived the fires which so often devastated Russia's wooden towns, and today their culture is chiefly represented by their religious arts. Church builders developed new variants of the onion-domed silhouettes, in buildings impressive for their height. But the finest achievements of the Novgorodians were in painting, especially the painting of icons.

While Novgorod was developing as the greatest centre of early medieval Russian painting, another town was beginning its rise to ascendancy. Moscow was only a small trading outpost when, in 1147, it was first mentioned in a Russian chronicle. But by the end of the 14th century it was a fast-growing city and capital of the leading Russian principality.

Ivan the Great, Grand Prince of Muscovy from 1462 to 1505, was the chief architect of Moscow's rise to power during the years when rivalry between Tatar khans sapped the strength of the Tatar Empire. He refused tribute to the Tatars and quadrupled the area under his rule by conquest, blackmail and intrigue. Ivan's chief gain came through the annexation of Novgorod with her far-flung colonies in the north. It was under his rule, too, that the Moscow Kremlin, administrative centre of Church and state, largely took the shape it retains to the present day.

## Moscow, the 'third Rome'

Even after throwing off Tatar thraldom, the Russians still could not call their land their own while their Church was controlled by the Patriarch of Constantinople. The break came at the Council of Florence in 1439, when the Byzantine emperor tried to unite the Orthodox Church to the Catholic Church in Rome and the Muscovites opposed this union. Soon afterwards, the sack of Constantinople by the Turks in 1453 left Moscow and its Church the sole representatives of Orthodoxy who remained independent.

Ivan the Great's marriage in 1472 to a niece of the last emperor of Byzantium seemed to carry with it the task of championing the Orthodox communities living in what had now become Muslim territory. Moscow undertook the task, and came to regard itself as Constantinople's successor, the 'third Rome'.

Ivan's attitude to serfdom was to have equally lasting effects. Although some peasants had been tied to the land from as early as the 12th century, their numbers had been small. Ivan's ambitions left him constantly in need of money and grain, to pay his armies and feed an ever-expanding population. He increased taxation and tightened the bonds of serfdom, condemning thousands of peasants and their children to a life of unremitting drudgery, in which they were not allowed to leave the land of their overlord. Some rebellious serfs fled to the wider frontiers of south and east, where they could live in comparative freedom. Here they became known as the Cossacks, a community of mounted desperadoes who were particularly dangerous to Moscow whenever they rallied in rebellion around some pretender to the tsar's throne. A tradition of insurrection grew up which was to culminate in the revolutions of 1917. By that time, however, the central power had succeeded in taming the Cossack freebooters of the steppes and turning them into defenders of the regime.

### The reign of Ivan the Terrible

Ivan the Great's grandson, Ivan IV (1544–84), was the first ruler to be crowned tsar, a title derived from the Latin *caesar* and chosen to stress the continuity with Rome by way of Byzantium. Grand Duke at the age of three, Ivan spent most of his boyhood under the sinister shadow of the boyars, powerful and self-seeking nobles of the Russian court. He emerged from this upbringing half-crazed with suspicion of almost everyone around him. In one neurotic rage, he struck his own son a blow that killed him, and when the head of his own Church, the Metropolitan Philip, dared to speak out against his cruelties, Ivan had him strangled. Even in an age hardened to the savagery of the Tatars, Ivan IV earned the title 'The Terrible'.

His terror, in the main, was directed against the enemies of Muscovy – against the Tatars who held the east, against the Poles and Swedes who barred his path to the Baltic, and against the boyars who opposed his will. Much of his reign was spent in warfare. Ivan failed in his ambition to win control of the Baltic, but he conquered the Tatar khanates of Kazan and Astrakhan, pushing Russia's boundaries as far as the Caspian Sea, and also won new lands in western Siberia. For the first time Russia was acquiring many non-Russian peoples as subjects, and beginning its long career as centre of a multi-national empire.

For all his cruelties, Ivan was always more than simply another Oriental despot. He helped scholars, encouraged the growth of literacy by installing a printing press in his capital, and sponsored commerce by inviting the merchant adventurers of Elizabethan England to trade in his domains.

Massacred, deported and ill-used by Ivan the Terrible, the Russians suffered yet more severe tribulations during the Time of Troubles (1605–13), a period of warfare and intense famine. Poland fought Sweden over which should have the pickings of Russian territory, and in 1610 Moscow itself fell to the Poles. The upheaval led to the rise of a patriotic party in Russia, whose leaders freed the city and in 1613 elected a new tsar – Michael Romanov, the first of a long-lasting dynasty.

Though the first three Romanov tsars varied from mild to feeble in character, the tsarist system became ever more powerful during their rule. Weary of bloodshed and still threatened by the power of Sweden and Poland, many Russians preferred the sway of

an absolute ruler to weakness and anarchy. By the middle of the 17th century the peasants' bonds had been tightened still further, tying them now to individual landlords who themselves owed absolute submission to the tsar. As well as commanding this system, the tsar was also its victim, a passive figure who often spent several hours of each day on his feet or knees, weighed down by his jewel-encrusted vestments as he attended the prolonged rituals of the Orthodox Church.

Though foreigners flocked to Muscovy during the 17th century, and though the country was gradually opening itself up to western European influences, Russia still clung tenaciously to her old-fashioned ways. Seventeenth-century Muscovites made an impression exotic in the extreme on foreigners newly arrived from western Europe. They practised the Christian religion in an unfamiliar, eastern form with flowing robes, elaborate headgear and full beards; with Oriental ceremonial; and with the clanging of innumerable church bells.

Felons were publicly tortured on a scale exceeding even that of contemporary western Europe. Wild drinking orgies, and self-flagellation with birch switches in steam baths, followed by a roll in the snow, did nothing to make the Muscovite less amusingly grotesque in visitor's eyes. Muscovites, for their part, found the foreign heretics no less quaint, and assigned them special quarters – the 'German suburb' – to prevent any intellectual and religious contamination from spreading among

true believers. Old-fashioned though 17th-century Muscovites might be, they were also adventurous, and the period also saw the extensive colonisation of Siberia.

### Reforms by Peter the Great

Towards the end of the 17th century the calm of traditional Muscovy was shattered by the impact of an aggressive new ruler, Peter the Great (1682–1725). A giant in physical stature, willpower and energy, Peter set himself to re-shape his realm on the western European pattern. Hating all that was backward in Russia, the young tsar made an 18-month tour of western Europe in 1697–8, recruiting foreign technicians and craftsmen for service in Russia. He spent most of his time in Holland and England, working with his own hands to get a true understanding of Western skills.

On his return to Moscow, Peter was welcomed by kow-towing boyars – the court officials who filled the highest offices in the army and the government. He hauled them to their feet and took scissors to snip off their beards and crop the voluminous folds of their old-fashioned sleeves. Peter later abolished the very rank of boyar, establishing a new elite of clean-shaven officials who wore western European dress and spoke western European languages.

He was also met by an attempted revolt by opponents of his reforms. Peter crushed the rebellion with awesome brutality, abolished the palace guard which had joined it, and set up instead a regular army, on Western lines.

### CREATOR OF A NEW RUSSIA

Peter the Great became sole master of imperial Russia in 1689 when his half-brother, Ivan, died. Previously he had overthrown the regency of his ambitious sister, Sophia. A restless and impatient moderniser, Peter was not only concerned with the internal reforms of the ramshackle country he had inherited, but determined also to make Russia the greatest military power in Europe.

Only one year of Peter's 43-year reign passed without war, and Russia's resources of men and money were stretched to their limits to provide him with a powerful army and navy. Nobles and peasants alike were drafted into the army 'for life'. Even Moscow's church bells were melted down to make cannon for Peter's army

IRON TSAR *Peter the Great, the tsar who modernised Russia, is portrayed in an iron bust by Rastrelli. The same Italian artist designed the Winter Palace in St Petersburg (now Leningrad)*

GIFT TO A PRINCE *The tsars filled the Kremlin with art treasures. Peter gave this jewelled cup to his son, the four-year-old Alexis, in 1694*

# A nation torn between West and East

As a climax of his policy of breaking abruptly with the past, Peter decided to found a new capital on the swamps of the lower River Neva, near the western boundary of his domain. But though this was the most daringly Europeanising of all projects in the history of Russia, it was, typically, accomplished by a method more Oriental than Western: the dragooning of thousands of enslaved peasants. Many of these serf-labourers perished while trying to pave the marshes and deck them with palaces. Peter transferred his capital from Moscow to his new city in 1712. He named it St Petersburg, but it was renamed Leningrad in 1924.

## From nation to empire

St Petersburg was conceived on the grand scale, with broad streets forming great rectangles, a layout largely devised by the French architect Le Blond. Peter chose for the capital's buildings a style which blended features drawn from contemporary Dutch and Italian architecture, adding to them to suit his personal taste. In 1721 Peter received the title of 'the Great' and also that of emperor, to add to the rank of tsar. Thus Muscovy became the Russian Empire.

Peter founded the Russian Academy of Sciences in St Petersburg. He sponsored the growth of literature and journalism; he founded schools, technical institutes and factories, and began to develop Siberia's mineral resources. Above all he began to transform Muscovy into modern Russia, and to bridge the gap separating his country's development from that of western Europe.

St Petersburg was further adorned in extravagant style under Peter's daughter, the Empress Elizabeth (1741–61), particularly by the Italian architect Rastrelli, who created the final version of the great Winter Palace. Other architectural monuments, such as the Hermitage

Museum, were added under Catherine the Great (1762–96). Her preference was for a simpler style of architecture. Many of the chief architects commissioned by Elizabeth and Catherine were foreigners, as was Catherine herself – a German princess who married the heir to the Russian throne, then connived at the murder of her weak-minded husband, Peter III, when he became tsar. It was under the Italian, Rossi, as architect-in-chief, that the characteristic classical Russian style attained its peak in the St Petersburg of Alexander I (1801–25). Through such a combination of talents St Petersburg became celebrated as Russia's 'Window on Europe', and 'Venice of the North'. The city is criss-crossed by canals, like its Italian counterpart.

Russia's first university, that of Moscow, was established under Elizabeth in 1755. Moscow University now bears the name of Michael Lomonosov, an 18th-century poet, scientist and scholar. His humble origins as a fisherman's son illustrate the fact that some Russians could rise to eminence from the most lowly origins, even in this autocratic age.

By comparison with western Europe, Russia was still politically and economically backward at the beginning of the 19th century. Its population was overwhelmingly rural and consisted largely of serfs who could be bought and sold at the whim of their owners, and whose living and working conditions were intolerably harsh.

Backward though it remained, the country possessed sufficient strength and patriotism to defeat Napoleon's invasion in 1812. The burning of French-occupied Moscow which, though probably accidental, forced Napoleon to retreat, is memorably described in Tolstoy's epic novel *War and Peace*, written over half a century later. But, though a wave of enthusiasm for the tsarist regime swept the country in 1812, Tsar Nicholas I (1825–55) became a byword

throughout Europe for reactionary policies both inside and outside his empire. And yet the harsh rule of this notorious tyrant coincided with the first major flowering of modern Russian intellectual and literary life.

## Literature from folklore

The poet Alexander Pushkin (1799–1837) is the Russian writer still most respected by fellow Russians. His lyric poems are among the finest in the language, and his works – many of them based on themes from Russian folklore and history – inspired such operas as Mussorgsky's *Boris Godunov*, Tchaikovsky's *Eugene Onegin* and Rimsky-Korsakov's *Le Coq d'Or* ('The Golden Cockerel'). No less original in his convoluted and eccentric manner was Nikolai Gogol (1809–52), author of the novel *Dead Souls*, in which he held up serfdom to ridicule. A third notable writer of the reign of Nicholas I was the romantic poet and novelist Yury Lermontov (1814–41), best known for his novel *A Hero of Our Time*.

Lively arguments took place during the reign of Nicholas I between two groups of intellectuals – Westernisers and Slavophils. Westernisers saw Russia chiefly as a European nation which should emulate France, Germany and Britain. Their Slavophil opponents emphasised the unique character of Old Russian civilization, stressing the value of early literature, painting and architecture – and above all of an elusive, uniquely valuable, Russian 'spirit' which foreigners were deemed incapable of appreciating.

Alexander II emancipated the serfs in 1861, but although this, in effect, abolished slavery throughout the empire, the peasants remained to some extent legally bonded to their village communes – the assembled heads of peasant households who were accustomed to take decisions unanimously. Alexander II's reign

## THE FANTASIES OF CARL FABERGÉ

Some of the most imaginative jewellery ever made came from the studios of Carl Fabergé, goldsmith and jeweller to the last two Russian emperors. Fabergé, a Russian of Huguenot descent, made flowers, animals and groups of figures prized by collectors everywhere

THE MUSICIAN *A variety of different materials were painstakingly carved and fitted together to create this 4½ in. high figure (left) of a peasant playing a balalaika. His hair is cornelian, his eyes sapphire, his blouse jasper, his breeches lapis lazuli and his balalaika silver-gilt*

EASTER EGG *The exchange of decorated eggs was a tradition of the Russian Easter, and among Fabergé's finest products were the jewelled and enamelled eggs which he made for the Imperial court. The egg (right) given by Nicholas II to his wife in 1898 opens to reveal miniatures of the emperor and his two children*

### FURS FOR AN EMPEROR

*Russian envoys, followed by merchants carrying furs for trade, visit the court of the Emperor Maximilian II at Rosenburg, in present-day Poland, in 1576. After nearly 250 years during which Moscow had been cut off from the West during Tatar rule, contact was renewed in the late 15th century. To their foreign hosts the visiting Russians, with their strange clothes and customs, had the fascination of the bizarre. The traffic was two-way: in the mid-16th century the English explorer Richard Chancellor obtained trading rights from Ivan the Terrible*

## A PALACE BUILT TO RIVAL VERSAILLES

When Peter the Great set out in 1700 to modernise Russia he marked the break with the past by abandoning Moscow and building a new capital at St Petersburg, now Leningrad, 400 miles to the north-west. Peter had toured western Europe, and in building St Petersburg he planned to rival the best that the West could do. Versailles was Peter's model for his new palace of Peterhof, on the Gulf of Finland, and he brought architects and artists from the West to build it and decorate it. A Grand Cascade descends from the palace to the sea, with numerous fountains decorated by nymphs and other sculptures in the classical style then in favour in the West. Peter was so determined that buildings of stone should be concentrated in the new capital that he forbade the use of masonry in any other part of Russia

# *Experiments in the arts that influenced the world*

also witnessed the rise of the first substantial Russian political terrorist movement, while at the same time Russian realist fiction was growing to full stature. The main works of Turgenev, Dostoyevsky, Leskov, Goncharov and Tolstoy are its crowning achievements. But nearly half a century was to pass before the great Russian novels, such as Tolstoy's *Anna Karenina* (1877) and Dostoyevsky's *The Brothers Karamazov* (1880), achieved widespread international renown and readership.

## The realist novel

Russian realist fiction appealed to readers in western Europe on several levels. There was the tantalisingly exotic flavour of a civilization sufficiently European to be recognised as familiar, yet sufficiently alien to appear ever fresh and unpredictable. Life in Russia seemed to drift by in a timeless world of dreamy country estates, a world of distant horizons beyond which lay the endless steppes – a concept of time and space vastly different from that of the business-minded West. Conversation in Russia appeared to be mainly about the soul and the purpose of life – subjects which rarely found their way into the brisker pages of, say, Dickens or Balzac.

The great Russian novelists were profoundly revolutionary, deeply committed to religious, social and political causes. Dostoyevsky was arrested by the tsarist police as an opponent of the regime, and told that he was to be shot. He was at the stake, in front of the firing squad, when the authorities told him the death sentence was only a joke, and that in fact he was to be sent to Siberia. Deeply religious and obsessed with salvation, Dostoyevsky tried to revive the centuries-old tradition of Russian Orthodoxy. He believed in a specifically 'Russian' Christ. Tolstoy, an aristocrat and landowner, also had his own version of Christianity. He freed his serfs and worked in the woods and fields alongside them. Towards the end of the 19th century, Russia embarked on an industrial revolution which rapidly developed her economy. But the empire still remained a largely peasant community and was still inferior in productivity and technology to the West.

In the last decade of the century a number of creative artists began to abandon the techniques of realism and the attempt to convey a 'message' through their works. Many were now embracing, instead, the opposite doctrine of 'Art for Art's Sake'. This was the start of 40 years of 'experimentation' in the arts – a movement that produced the theatrical reforms carried out by the Moscow Art Theatre, founded in 1898 by Constantine Stanislavsky and Vladimir Nemirovich-Danchenko. It was the aim of these pioneers to fuse drama, acting, scene-painting, incidental music and even programme design in a harmonious blend. Stanislavsky also evolved his 'method' technique of acting, based on emotionally involving the actor in his part, a technique which has had a profound influence on theatre and film acting.

In pioneering these techniques the Moscow Art Theatre did much to popularise the work of Russia's most original dramatist, Anton Chekhov (1860–1904), who is also one of the world's greatest short-story writers. Meanwhile Sergei Diaghilev reinvigorated the ballet.

## Culture of the Revolution

Revolutionary violence emerged in 1905 and culminated in the Bolshevik seizure of power under Lenin's leadership in 1917. The arts were left comparatively unmolested during the first dozen years of the new Soviet regime, and the 1920's were a continuing age of experiment. The art of the cinema acquired a Russian accent with Sergei Eisenstein's world-famous films such as *The Battleship Potemkin* and *October*, and became, like painting, sculpture, literature and architecture, a field for individual pioneering.

Josef Stalin, the Communist Party secretary, who had attained full totalitarian power by 1928, set in motion a reign of terror worse than that of any tsar because it was more efficient. He had no sympathy for abstract, experimental art, and creative artists had constantly to look over their shoulders for fear of offending the Party. Their position in Soviet Russia became difficult or impossible, and from 1932 onwards a new culture was evolved in accordance with the officially imposed 'Socialist Realism'.

The official Soviet view of this technique is that it harks back to the work of the great 'committed' novelists of the mid-19th century such as Tolstoy and Dostoyevsky. One important difference, however, is that the post-1932 artist has been denied all freedom in choosing his own brand of commitment. He has, instead, been conscripted as a political advertising copywriter, obliged to promote Soviet 'achievements' along propagandist lines.

Socialist Realism by no means killed the Russian novel. At least one masterpiece, Sholokhov's *Quiet Flows the Don*, a rumbustious

---

### ARTISTS WHO TAUGHT THE WORLD A NEW WAY OF DANCING

The 30 years before the Revolution were a period of brilliant creativity in the Russian theatre, and especially in ballet. The birth of modern ballet is generally dated from 1909, when the *Ballets Russes* under Sergei Diaghilev arrived in Paris and began to infuse new vitality into Western ballet, which had lost much of its original impetus and imagination. Diaghilev brought to the stage a brilliant combination of talents: outstanding choreographers and dancers such as Michel Fokine, Vaslav Nijinsky and Anna Pavlova, costume and scene designers such as Leon Bakst and Alexandre Benois, and the music of Borodin, Rimsky-Korsakov and many other composers, Russian and foreign. Diaghilev excelled in lavish, spectacular productions of startling originality, many of them based on Russian folklore. The three works which made Igor Stravinsky famous, *The Fire-Bird, Petrushka* and *The Rite of Spring* were all written for ballets presented by Diaghilev in Paris. At its first performance *The Rite of Spring* created one of the greatest musical scandals of the century, when a riot broke out in the theatre against the music. But it was ultimately recognised as a classic of 20th-century music. The *Ballets Russes* settled abroad in 1911

PAS DE DEUX *The two stars of Fokine's* Spectre de la Rose *were Nijinsky and Karsavina. Nijinsky was probably the greatest male dancer of all time; his awe-inspiring leaps seemed to defy gravity. He died insane*

THE SWAN *Ballerina Anna Pavlova was famed in her role of the Dying Swan, to music by Saint-Saëns. Pavlova appeared with the Ballets Russes in 1909, but later formed her own company to tour the world*

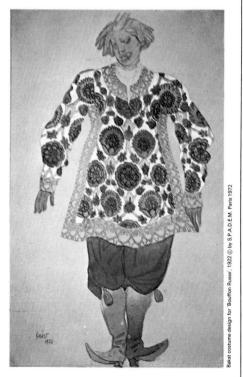

THE CLOWN *The painter Leon Bakst was among the leading artists who designed scenery and costumes for Diaghilev. His sketch for 'The Russian Clown' in 1921 shows the contribution of folk art to the Russian ballet*

Bakst costume design for Bouffon Russe', 1922 © by S.P.A.D.E.M. Paris 1972

saga of the Civil War of 1918–21 between Whites and Reds, is officially regarded by Soviet authority as written within the framework of Socialist Realism. More original studies of the human condition in a Russian context, however, such as Pasternak's novel *Doctor Zhivago* and the three long novels of Solzhenitsyn (*Cancer Ward, The First Circle* and *August 1914*) have not been published in the Soviet Union, but have appeared abroad from 1958 onwards. It is works such as these, rather than Soviet-published fiction, which have maintained the great Russian tradition of freely chosen literary commitment.

Many other features of Soviet Russian civilization seem to re-create – in distorted form – earlier Russian traditions. The tsarist concentration of power in the hands of one man was revived by Stalin between 1928 and his death in 1953. Stalin, himself a Georgian, became a fervent Russian nationalist by adoption, and was fond of having himself compared with such

forerunners as Ivan the Terrible and Peter the Great. During the Second World War many Russian soldiers fought to the death with the words 'for Stalin and country' on their lips just as their fathers had once laid down their lives 'for tsar and country'. Far from disappearing under Soviet conditions, the Russian tradition of authoritarian government has been greatly developed, and is reinforced by a new brand of 'Orthodoxy' – the cult of Marxism-Leninism.

## Survival of Christianity

In this totalitarian society, where all human activities are deemed to be the direct concern of the state, culture too has been taken under the wing of Soviet officialdom. The state supports in luxury those writers, painters and musicians whose work and record of behaviour remain politically acceptable, just as it subsidises those who excel in chess and other forms of sport. State support for science has helped to create a technology, an industrial and arma-

ments base and a record in space exploration second only to that of the USA. Persecuted over more than half a century, Orthodox Christianity has, however, by no means died out. Those churches which remain open are often crowded with worshippers. Although some secularised Russian churches have been converted to potato stores or bicycle factories, the Soviet government has an impressive record of restoring and preserving the glories of traditional Russian architecture.

It is partly due to such care that Russia still makes on foreign visitors a tantalisingly bizarre visual impact, just as did the Muscovy of the 15th century. In the days of austerely functional and often peeling apartment blocks, the Kremlin still rears its golden onion-domes over the Moscow River. Surrounded by the factories and motorised bustle of Leningrad, the sumptuous creations of Rastrelli and Rossi still delight visitors to the city which these, its chief architects, knew as St Petersburg.

### ART TO GLORIFY THE PEASANT AND HIS TRACTOR

*Popular decorative art since the Revolution has, like the other arts in Russia, had to celebrate Soviet achievements and to encourage increased productivity in field and factory. But the artists are still influenced by older traditions. This lacquered wooden box-lid combines modern motifs, such as the tractor, with more traditional peasant subjects. It comes from Palekh, a small town near Ivanovo, 200 miles east of Moscow, with a long tradition of icon-painting. After the Revolution the Palekh artists formed guilds to produce non-religious works of art. They make miniatures, illustrate books and produce and restore frescoes*

# A new Europe from the ruins of Rome's Empire

## AD 410–1100

*In four centuries of turmoil, hordes of
Germanic invaders founded a vigorous and lasting culture,
while Celts in Ireland kept Christianity alive*

**EUROPE IN AD 800**

*After the collapse of the Roman
Empire, its conquerors established new
areas of influence in Europe*

Although the four centuries which followed the sack of Rome by Alaric the Visigoth in 410 are often called the Dark Ages, it was during these years that western Europe was largely formed. The people who were to mould the shape of modern Europe arrived there during the last years of the Roman Empire. The Romans had for long depended for the security of their frontiers on alliances made with groups of barbarians, many of them Germanic-speaking, who lived on the other side of the frontier. But these barbarians were uneasy allies. By 400, Rome's hold on its distant provinces was growing weaker, while at the same time the tribes beyond the boundaries of the empire were themselves facing attack from peoples further afield.

From the easternmost edges of the great plains of Europe, hordes of nomads called Huns were sweeping into action, mopping up other peoples in their westward gallop and forcing tribes living on the boundaries of the Roman Empire to cross these frontiers in flight from the approaching menace. The Huns were formidable horsemen and great archers. Banded into a loose federation under a forceful chief such as Attila, they could move great distances very quickly. The authority of Rome seemed puny and ineffectual against the vigour of the invading barbarians.

To the people of the time, the Huns were bogeymen. One observer wrote: 'Those men whom they in no wise surpassed in war they put to flight by the terror of their looks . . . and horrible swarthy appearance. They have a sort of shapeless lump, not a face, and pinholes rather than eyes. These men live in the form of humans but with the savagery of beasts.' In the graves of the Huns have been found skulls purposely deformed by bandaging the heads of children from infancy.

From the east the Visigoths raided the Balkans, invaded and ravaged Italy and set up kingdoms in southern France and Spain. The Ostrogoths settled in Italy. The Vandals crossed the Rhine, the Pyrenees and Spain and founded a kingdom in North Africa from which in 455, like the Goths before them, they descended on Rome and sacked it.

The barbarians of the west and north also exploited the weakness of Rome. Germanic tribes crossed the frontiers and settled in richer,

## A BARBARIAN RULER AND HIS MOUNTED POWER

*A helmet of gilded copper (left) depicts Agilulf, pagan king of the Lombards
from 590 to 615, sitting enthroned between two of his warriors. The
Lombards, from eastern Europe, penetrated northern and central Italy about
600 in one of the last onslaughts by the hordes of Germanic-speaking
tribesmen who had swept in to overwhelm the Roman Empire.*

*The barbarians rode strong horses, which enabled them to cover thousands
of miles in their devastating invasions. The mounted warrior (right),
fashioned in gilt bronze, wears mail armour and carries a lance to impale
his victims. The figure is part of the ornamentation on a Lombard chief's
shield made about 700 and was found at Stabio, in Switzerland*

# *Laws and arts soften the barbaric Dark Ages*

The high standard of craftsmanship in Anglo-Saxon England is shown by the treasure hoard found at Sutton Hoo, near Woodbridge, Suffolk. One of its finest items is the belt buckle of solid gold (left), which weighs more than 14½ oz. and is decorated with a rich interlaced pattern. The treasures were found in 1939, concealed within an 80-ft ship buried in a mound to commemorate the death of an East Anglian king of the early 7th century. The treasures included gold and jewelled equipment, coins and tableware

GOLD CLASP *This hinged fastener of gold, inlaid with garnet and decorated with enamel, was used to join the front and back of a two-piece garment at the shoulder*

JEWELLED PURSE *This detail of a man spreadeagled between two beasts is one of the jewelled decorations from a purse lid. The purse contained 37 gold coins*

FIGHTING AS A WAY OF LIFE

*Egil the Archer, a legendary Germanic hero, defends his wife and home against armed attackers – a common incident in the violent Dark Ages. The skirmish is carved on the lid of a 7th-century whalebone box made in Northumbria; the round section in the centre probably held a knob to lift the lid*

more developed areas. The Franks crossed into Gaul and ultimately reunited it from the Rhine to the Pyrenees. The Angles, the Saxons and the Jutes crossed the North Sea from their homelands in north Germany and Denmark and settled in England. All over Europe during the 5th and 6th centuries nations rose, moved considerable distances, and fought great battles, only to disappear, swallowed by a stronger people or assimilated into the earlier population of the area they invaded.

History has judged the barbarians harshly, and their names have passed into legend as bywords for savagery and bloodshed. They were destroyers – they twice sacked Rome, and deposed its last Western emperor in 476. The very word 'barbarian' is an indication of the way the civilized world lumped the invaders together as being uncouth and outlandish. It is in origin a Greek word, describing the sound of what to the Greeks was the unintelligible speech of other peoples.

The way of life of the barbarians was different from that of the empire they had destroyed, but they had culture, law and traditions of their own. Their law was based on custom and precedent; it was not set down in a written code. At the centre of the law stood the family, which had an importance above any individual member: all legal penalties were aimed at the preservation of the family and its property. Damage to people or to goods was atoned for by a clearly defined system of fines or physical penalties. Every man's head had a price on it, and the penalties for killing or injuring a man varied according to the victim's social position.

The legal structure varied in detail from nation to nation, but there was a general unity which became clearer as Christianity spread among the pagan nations. This process was achieved at different times in different regions – in Gaul by the 6th century, for example, and in Denmark by the 10th century. Some idea of the artistic achievement of the so-called barbarians is provided by the objects which have been found in their graves; these include jewellery, brooches and buckles, many of them gilt or inlaid with semi-precious stones and glass, elaborately mounted weapons and coloured beads.

Little written history has survived from the first three centuries after the collapse of the Roman Empire. The sources used were not always reliable – 'I have made a heap of all that I have found', wrote one chronicler – though historians such as Gregory of Tours and the Venerable Bede were effective and critical chroniclers. Taken together, the chronicles that remain provide a picture of the era in which the modern western European nations – the English, French, Germans, Dutch, Irish and Scandinavians – emerged from anonymity.

## Drawing the language frontiers

The peoples who took part in the great European migrations mostly spoke Germanic languages. Only in the west and north of Britain and in Brittany was another group of languages

spoken – the Celtic tongue. The linguistic distinction between the two groups was as clear then as it is now, and the line drawn in the 8th century along the Welsh border by an English king, Offa, divided two distinct nations already speaking entirely different languages – Celtic in Wales and Germanic in England. Another language frontier of the present day – the boundary between French and Flemish speakers in Belgium – was drawn in the 5th century when Germanic invaders met the surviving remnants of Latin culture and settled down to an uneasy peace. By the 7th century the language map of western Europe had taken largely its present form.

During the 5th and 6th centuries, before they finally settled in the former Roman areas, the migrants were constantly on the move as they manoeuvred for position under pressure from the nomadic tribes of the east. Only in Scandinavia, the homeland from which many of the Germanic groups had originated centuries before, was life in any way stable.

In Scandinavia the centuries following the collapse of the Roman Empire were very rich; it was an age of extraordinary wealth. Goods of the sort which in earlier days had been traded to the Roman Empire – including food, furs, iron ore and jewellery in metal, amber or bone – continued to be carried southwards, probably along the rivers of central Europe. In return came silver and gold, silks and cloth.

Hoards of gold and other forms of portable goods which have been found reflect the wealth of the period. Some of these deposits were hidden by their owners in times of trouble and never reclaimed. A find at Timboholm, Västergötland, in Sweden, consisted of more than 14 lb. of gold bullion. Other rich finds represent sacrifices to pagan gods, some of which were almost certainly made after a successful battle. In some cases not only gold and jewellery were sacrificed, but also weapons, horse trappings and even the horses themselves. In 1959 the find of a single gold arm-ring led to the discovery of an enormous collection of weapons, jewellery and trappings of war in a bog at Skedemosse, on the Baltic island of Öland. With the objects were the bones of both men and horses, sacrifices offered to the gods by a victorious army.

## Artists inspired by nature

The Scandinavians added brilliant ornamentation even to articles in everyday use. They based their designs on nature, but they twisted and contorted the figures to fit the available space. The carved and gilded patterns on brooches and buckles, on swords and helmets, are sometimes recognisable as those of animals or birds only after careful study.

The vast majority of Scandinavians were farmers and herdsmen. Most lived on isolated farms; there were few villages or towns. Their houses were rectangular in shape and often very long – some in Norway are as long as 300 ft – for they not only housed the farmer and his family, but also provided shelter for animals and a storage place for food and grain. In times of trouble the people might flee to prepared defensive positions, fortress-refuges like the great circular construction at Gråborg in Öland, which would protect families, their cattle and their wealth until trouble passed. At all times violent death was near, and the warrior-farmer, his sword ever ready to defend his people, was the leading figure in society.

The most successful of the Germanic invaders of Europe were the Franks, who moved from the Rhineland into the well-developed lands of northern Gaul and, settling there, adapted a variety of the Latin tongue which ultimately became French. It was on the basis of the Frankish kingdom that Charlemagne established his empire, and France, Germany, Belgium and the Netherlands today occupy what was once Frankish territory.

One of the earliest Frankish chieftains was called Meroveus, or 'sea-warrior', and he gave his name to a dynasty of kings – the Merovingians – who grew to dominance in France. They were brutal by modern standards, renowned for their long fair hair and their prowess in battle, and much given to murdering their parents or their children, for wealth or political power. They were already wealthy when they first appeared on the stage of history, and Meroveus's son, Childeric, was buried in Tournai in about 481 with a vast display of wealth in the form of jewellery and rich weapons which were discovered in 1653. A seal ring bearing his portrait with an inscription

# A new literature and new skills from the Anglo-Saxons

**FATHER OF ENGLISH HISTORY**

*The Venerable Bede, a monk at Jarrow, left a vivid picture of life in Anglo-Saxon England in his* Ecclesiastical History. *Bede, seen sharpening his quill, was the first historian to date events from Christ's birth*

recording his name was found among the other treasures in the grave. Childeric and his son Clovis were heroic characters in the German tradition–successful if ruthless. Clovis was baptised in 496, after which the entire Frankish people quickly became Christians.

The Franks were attracted to Gaul by its richness, both in items such as silver and gold and in the fertility of its soil. Once they had settled France, they looked further afield for more wealth. They raided in Spain and Italy, and on a single raid into Spain, one Merovingian king, Dagobert, added 2 million gold coins to his treasury.

## Success in commerce and culture

The Franks were not simply farmers, as many other Germanic peoples were, nor were they simply mercenary raiders. They appreciated the economic value of towns as sources of revenue and were keen to trade with Mediterranean countries. They sold slaves, wine and swords, and nearly every town in France at one time or another in the 7th century minted its own coins. The Franks were also interested in trade with the Atlantic countries, and at Dorestad, at the mouth of the Rhine, they founded one of the greatest markets of Europe, which survived until the 9th century, when it was destroyed by Vikings.

To the Mediterranean peoples, the Germanic invaders were barbarians–simple, uncomplicated brigands who incidentally founded kingdoms on the territory of the former Roman Empire. But it was the empire that failed, while the barbarians succeeded, bringing to their new lands an independent and self-sufficient culture. They were not completely illiterate, for they had an alphabet–based on the Germanic runic alphabet–which they may have carved on sticks for everyday

communication and which they certainly used on more durable materials such as metal and bone. They had traditional stories and poetry, some of which have survived to be written down in later years, and which, even in translation, can express some of the brilliance of those pagan heroic times.

## The legend of Beowulf

The Franks preserved much that was Roman in Gaul–the language, the Church, the towns. The Angles and Saxons, however, who crossed the North Sea to settle in England, drove out Latin and in their poetry and prose produced the first major non-Mediterranean literature. Their greatest poem is undoubtedly *Beowulf*, one of the great heroic epics in the English language which, although surviving in a 10th-century manuscript, tells of legendary and actual happenings in 5th-century Scandinavia.

Literature reveals only a shadowy history of the first two centuries of Anglo-Saxon England. Leaders such as Hengist and Horsa, Vortigern and Arthur, have left behind legends but little actual history. Excavations, however, have produced graves, settlements and weapons which give some idea of the different social levels of the Anglo-Saxons.

The wealth of jewellery found in the memorial of an East Anglian king at Sutton Hoo, near Woodbridge, Suffolk, for example, demonstrates the high quality of workmanship executed in Anglo-Saxon England. It recalls the wealth of the furnishings for a funeral described by the poet of *Beowulf*:

> . . . They brought from afar
> Many great treasures and costly trappings,
> I have never heard of a ship so richly
> furnished
> With weapons of war, armour of battle
> Swords and corslets.

Despite the rich trappings uncovered at Sutton Hoo, no body was found: it was simply a cenotaph to a king who was buried elsewhere.

Further evidence of the way royalty lived in Anglo-Saxon England is given by the excavated buildings of the royal palace at Yeavering in Northumberland. This had great halls and out-buildings, a fort of refuge, an assembly place and a cemetery. It also contained a church, for the arrival of St Augustine in 597 had begun the conversion of England to Christianity. This was one of the palaces of the kings of Northumbria until it was destroyed in the 7th century. But like the kingdom, it fell into decay, for in England kingdoms rose and fell: Northumbria, Mercia, Kent and Wessex all had periods of greatness, and it was not until the 10th century that the Kingdom of England came into being.

## The world of the Celts

Beyond the lands of the English were the earlier inhabitants of the British Isles, the Celts, or Britons; they included the Picts of the north and the Irish, both of whom had often challenged the power of the Roman Empire. After the Romans left, the Scoti, from County Antrim, settled in present-day

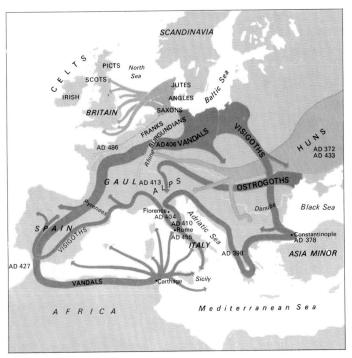

**THE GREAT MIGRATIONS**

*In a turmoil of peoples in the 5th century, barbarian hordes galloped westwards, before the advancing Huns, to engulf the former Roman Empire. The long route of the Visigoths took them through the Balkans to Italy, where they sacked Rome in 410, and on into southern France and Spain. The Vandals drove relentlessly through France and Spain before settling in North Africa, from where they also sailed to sack Rome. Further north, the Franks and Burgundians pushed into France, while England was settled by Angles, Saxons and Jutes from north Germany and Denmark*

Argyll and founded a rival Scottish kingdom to the Picts, with bases at a series of strongholds, such as Dunadd by the Crinan Canal, and Dunollie at Oban. Until the coming of the Vikings four centuries later, the Picts and western Scots dominated Scotland, fighting each other and people to the south. Finally the Scots of the west, with Scandinavian help, took over eastern Scotland and the Pictish nation disappeared.

Living in southern Scotland were Welsh-speaking tribes, some of whom were transferred to Wales to drive out Irish raiders. An ancient Welsh poem, the *Goddodin*, describes how some of these warriors made forays into English territory; it tells of a battle at Catraeth (Catterick in Yorkshire) in truly heroic terms:

> The men went to Catraeth, they were famous. Wine and mead from gilded vessels was their drink for a year, according to the honourable custom; three and three score men and three hundred more wearing golden bands. Of those that hastened forth after the choice drink only three escaped; the two battle hounds of Aeron and Cynon . . . and I with my blood streaming down, for the sake of my brilliant poetry.

The *Goddodin* typifies many attributes of the Celts: their love of fighting, drinking and gold adornment, and their conviction that a good poet was someone very special indeed.

The Celts were the heirs of the remarkable Iron Age people who spread from the Rhine as far as the British Isles and Asia Minor. In the 4th century BC they poured into Italy and sacked Rome. But the Celts never grasped the need for unity and by the 3rd century their power was on the ebb. They were harried by the Germans to the north, the Dacians to the east, and the Romans to the south. In the 1st century BC Julius Caesar conquered Gaul, which had by then become the heartland of the Celtic world. After initial resistance the Gauls settled down to enjoy the benefits of Roman rule. The first Celts to settle in Britain arrived in the 5th century BC, followed by another wave 200 years later and finally the Belgae in the 1st century BC. Though political unity always eluded the Celts, their culture and mythology were remarkably uniform.

The great hill forts of the Celts are still impressive after 2000 years, but their greatest contribution was in their deeply imaginative poetry and their well-developed art with its complex patterns and abstract forms. These traditions were to survive and reach dazzling heights in Ireland, which remained immune from outside aggression until the coming of the Vikings in the 9th century and the Anglo-Normans in the 12th.

## Ireland's early converts

The Irish are better known than any other Britons of the Dark Ages; they were the first people outside the Roman world to be converted to Christianity. Traditionally Ireland is said to have been converted in about 400 by a young Romano-Briton called Patrick, who is also said to have founded the church at Armagh.

## CULTURE IN GOLD AND JEWELS

The barbarian nations were virtually illiterate, but they left some record of the richness of their culture in metalwork of fine craftsmanship, which they buried in graves or hoards of treasure. The treasures were intended to equip a dead king in splendour for his time in the afterlife. The main motif of barbarian art was ornamentation based on animal designs, which they twisted and contorted almost out of recognition. To add interest to the drab life of the time, artists made rich use of colour in inlays of garnet and glass, and in the gilding and embellishment of precious metals. The barbarians' art, strengthened by absorbing styles from other countries, ultimately became a more powerful influence than that of Rome.

With the coming of Christianity, the styles and skills of barbarian art broke through into the manuscripts, sculptures and paintings of the Church. In Britain, northern Italy and Scandinavia the art of the jeweller came to predominate. Objects which have survived show examples of his skill; new techniques were introduced, style and taste changed, but the traditional love of glitter and complicated animal ornamentation still appeared. In western and northern parts of the British Isles, where the ancient traditions of pre-Roman art survived, the Celtic metalworker, already skilled in enamelling and spiral work, adopted also the crude vitality and love of colour of the Germanic jeweller. Art based on animal patterns flourished in Ireland and Scotland. Some figures were so contorted that they are hard to recognise as beasts

SYMBOLIC BIRD *The eagle was a popular motif among the Germanic peoples, and the cloak pin or brooch was a favoured ornament. This brooch, fashioned by an Ostrogothic jeweller in the late 5th century, is made of gold, and its surface was originally covered in precious stones. The filigreed metalwork is thought to have been influenced by Byzantine models. At the centre of the brooch, a circle encloses a Christian cross. The love of glitter and the flight from realistic representation of objects towards more stylised forms are typical of the Germanic craftsmen of the time*

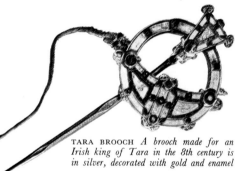

TARA BROOCH *A brooch made for an Irish king of Tara in the 8th century is in silver, decorated with gold and enamel*

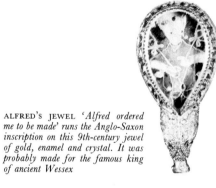

ALFRED'S JEWEL *'Alfred ordered me to be made' runs the Anglo-Saxon inscription on this 9th-century jewel of gold, enamel and crystal. It was probably made for the famous king of ancient Wessex*

BLEND OF CULTURES *The early 8th-century Ardagh chalice is the finest example of early Irish metalwork. Its silver body is decorated with mounts which combine Germanic animal ornamentation with Celtic spirals. Beneath the girdle are the names of the Apostles*

ROYAL GIFT *Pearls and sapphires encrust a gold circlet made for the 7th-century Visigothic king Recceswinth. The king gave the circlet to a church, possibly on his conversion, and the gift is commemorated in the letters spelling 'Reccesvinthus Rex offeret' which hang below*

# *When monks kept the light of Christianity burning*

### MESSAGE OF THE CROSS

*The Irish were the first converts to Christianity outside the Roman world. They carved great stone crosses, often decorated with biblical scenes, to illustrate preaching by monks. The Last Judgment is depicted at the head of this 9th-century Cross of Muiredach, at Monasterboice, Co. Louth, and other biblical scenes are carved below. The Irish brand of Christianity, which was distinctly independent, placed great emphasis on the value of the frugal life*

The first missionary known to history, however, was a bishop called Paladius, who was sent from Rome in 431 to minister to Irish Christians. For 500 years the Irish maintained their own fiercely independent brand of Christianity, notable for the zeal of their hermit-like monks and for the splendour of the carved stone crosses which still mark the sites of their isolated monasteries.

A typical monastery founded in the 6th century survives today on the island of Illauntannig, just off the coast of Kerry. Beaten by the Atlantic sea and winds, far from the comparative safety of the land, it stands a witness both to the beliefs of the early Irish hermits and to their skill as builders, for their tiny huts, clustered like bee-hives on the bare face of the rock, are still almost whole and completely roofed.

The most famous of Ireland's monks was Columba, who founded his monastery at Iona, off the west coast of Scotland, about 563. It was from Iona that Irish monasteries spread their influence into England and even to the Continent. The great monastery at Lindisfarne, off the coast of Northumberland, was founded from Iona, and the contact between Ireland and England resulted in one of the most magnificent schools of art ever known in the British Isles.

Under the patronage of kings and chieftains, bishops and abbots, 7th and 8th-century scholars produced such masterpieces as the Book of Durrow and the Lindisfarne Gospels, the Tara brooch and the Ardagh chalice. In these works, some produced in England and some in Ireland, there is an intricate blending of artistic motifs from three sources – the spiral motif of the Celtic world, animal ornamentation typical of the Anglo-Saxons, and ribbon designs from Mediterranean lands.

## Skill in portraits and poetry

In the Lindisfarne Gospels, painted on Lindisfarne island about 698, an English artist attempted for the first time since the Roman period to depict a man in a naturalistic fashion. The portraits of the Evangelists in the Lindisfarne Gospels are modelled on an Italian prototype inspired from a great book, the *Codex Grandior,* which no longer exists but which was brought to England and was used as a model for a number of Bibles.

The vigorous art of these books was common to both sides of the Irish Sea; it flourished until the Viking raids of the 9th century and continued to appear, especially in Ireland, until the Norman Conquest. The priceless 'Book of Kells' was begun by St Columba's followers on the island of Iona, early in the 9th century. When the Vikings raided Iona in 806 the fleeing monks took the manuscript across the sea to Kells, in Co. Meath, and completed it there.

The monasteries were centres of secular learning as well as art, and produced an impressive number of monk-scholars, particularly in the 9th century. Another feature of the Irish cultural tradition was poetry, handed down by word of mouth until scribes recorded it. The

poems still live – some poignant and beautiful, some deeply religious and some mocking:

> I have heard that he gives no
> horses in reward for poems:
> he gives according to his nature – a cow.

## The mission of St Augustine

Although the British Church was revitalised by the Irish arriving from the west, a Church based on remote monastic settlements could not cater for the spiritual needs of the ordinary people. To deal with this situation, Pope Gregory, at the end of the 6th century, sent St Augustine to England at the head of a band of missionaries. The Church they founded was closer in organisation to the continental model, with central bishoprics at Canterbury and York and subsidiary sees at places like Rochester and Dorchester. Their mission was largely successful, and by the middle of the 7th century paganism was dwindling in England. Worship of the old gods did not die out at once; Gregory himself advised his missionaries to leave the pagan shrines alone, and to try to introduce Christian worship only gradually alongside pagan practices. This mingling of Christianity and paganism is the reason why Christ's birthday is celebrated on December 25 – the date of the pagans' winter festival.

The English Church then turned its attention to its western and northern neighbours. In 663 a council of the old British Church and the new English Church was held at the monastery of Whitby. The English Church, which had been organised by Augustine and his successors, won the day, and the ancient customs of the British Church were brought into line with those of Rome. The date of Easter and the way in which monks' heads were shaved were to follow Roman practice; more important, the authority of bishops was recognised.

Much may have been lost in this reorganisation, but the cultural and spiritual life of the country was greatly enhanced. Monasteries of the continental type were founded, scholarship flourished, artists were encouraged and close contact was established with Rome and with the Christian monasteries in Gaul. The English as well as the Irish set out for the Continent in the 7th and 8th centuries to convert the Germanic nations to Christianity.

## The coming of the Vikings

Before the pagan gods were finally overthrown, the barbarian peoples were to launch one last savage onslaught against Christian Europe. From impregnable anchorages along the ragged coast of Scandinavia, and from the tree-fringed shores of Denmark, the Vikings set sail in their longships to terrorise Christendom. They attacked and looted monasteries, burnt villages, plundered towns, carried off slaves and blackmailed entire regions into paying protection money to be left in peace.

The pattern of destruction was set in the first of the great Viking raids – in 793, on the monastery founded by St Aidan at Lindisfarne. Monks and nuns were murdered or dragged off into slavery, cattle were killed and the monastery's treasures stolen. The Northumbrian scholar Alcuin described the effects of the raid in a letter: 'Never before has such terror appeared in Britain as we have now suffered from a pagan race... Behold the church, spattered with the blood of the priests of God.'

Their attacks on the monasteries of western Europe, rich storehouses of treasure, were largely responsible for history's hostile account of the Vikings. For the people who were most literate – the clerics – were the least able to combat their brutality and bore the brunt of their initial attacks.

The Vikings were active, too, in eastern Europe – but not as pirates. Scandinavian traders worked their way along the great rivers of Russia in search of markets in Asia and founded trading stations – Staraja Ladoga, Novgorod, Kiev – which were to become the great towns of the early Russian state.

In the West also, trade was probably the first motive of the raids of the Vikings. By the foundation of Dublin in the 9th century, they created a major Western market-place in which they could sell their slaves and furs in exchange for silver and continental luxuries.

## Settlements of the Danelaw

In England, by the end of the 9th century, the Danish Vikings had settled large areas north of a line from Essex to Herefordshire. This Danelaw, as it was called, was soon brought under English rule, but its people were to remain basically Scandinavian for centuries. The Vikings have left their trace throughout the north of England in a myriad of place-names of Scandinavian origin – such as Whitby ('white village'), Derby ('deer village') and Scunthorpe ('Skuma's farm'). Many basic words in the English language, such as 'law', 'bread', 'ugly' and 'husband', and many words connected with the sea such as 'ship' and 'mast', are also of Scandinavian origin.

Only in the far north and west of Scotland and in the Isle of Man did Scandinavian political settlement succeed for any length of time. There Scandinavian dynasties ruled, acknowledging the Norwegian crown, until the mid-13th century. Indeed, in Orkney a Scandinavian language – *norn* – was the common tongue until about 200 years ago.

The Scandinavians of the Viking Age have made their name as seamen. Even lands which had only sporadic contact with them retain traces of their intense activity on the sea. The names of some Channel Islands – Alderney and Guernsey, for example – and many landfalls on the Welsh coast and in the Bristol Channel – Swansea, Milford, Lundy, Orme's Head – are of Scandinavian origin. These were names given from the sea to prominent navigational points by people who extended the horizons of Europe beyond the main land mass. Norwegians discovered and settled Iceland, founded two major communities in Greenland, sailed to America and apparently even founded settlements there. They were the first people to realise that the Atlantic Ocean opened new opportunities and was not the end of the

## MONASTERIES FOSTER A NEW ART FORM

Tiny bands of monks in English and Irish monasteries helped to keep civilization alive during the Dark Ages. In their cells they created a unique art form, under the influence of illuminated books from Italy. Scribes copied the Latin text of the Gospels on parchment or vellum, and then artists painstakingly illuminated the initial capital letters and borders in complex spiral patterns typical of Celtic art. Figures of humans, animals and plants, often in a highly stylised form, are included in the designs, some of which are so elaborate that it must have taken the artist up to a fortnight to complete a square inch. Illuminating one book may have been a lifetime's work for a monk

INITIAL FLOURISH *This elaborate page introduces St Matthew in the 'Lindisfarne Gospels'. The miniatures in the book were painted about 698*

LION OF ST MARK *A fierce lion, symbol of St Mark, springs across a page of a 7th-century manuscript. The Anglo-Saxon St Willibrord used the book when he travelled to Europe to spread Christianity among the German pagans*

BOOK OF KELLS *One of the greatest art treasures of the Celtic world is the 'Book of Kells', a 680-page masterpiece containing an illuminated text of the four Gospels. This page shows St John the Evangelist. The pages are of calf-skin, and pigment for some of the colours came from the Mediterranean and central Asia. The book was begun by monks at Iona in about 800, and completed at Kells in eastern Ireland*

# Raiders who sailed for plunder and stayed as settlers

THE KEY TO MASTERY OF THE SEAS AND NEW LANDS

*The boat carved in the 8th century on a stone on the island of Gotland was a forerunner of the longship which gave the Vikings command of the seas. In the artist's impression below, the leading ship resembles a vessel found at Gokstad, in Norway. It was built of oak planks and measured over 76 ft long. At the broadest point it was 17½ ft across, giving room for a crew of 50 and space for extra warriors or prisoners; yet fully loaded the ship drew only 6 ft of water. The 32 oars passed through holes in the ship's sides*

world. The Scandinavians developed the art of sailing to an advanced level, and their ships spread northern goods and northern men through most of the known world. Some of their ships survive to this day; the most famous are those found in the royal burial mounds at Oseberg and Gokstad in southern Norway. All the movable equipment of a royal household was buried in the ships, which had a central mast, square sail, rising prow and stern and a multitude of oars. The clean-cut lines of these vessels, between 70 and 80 ft in length, demonstrate the skill of the shipwrights and sailing masters of this period. Other vessels of the Viking Age have been raised from the shallow beds of the fjords and harbours of the Baltic Sea. Five ships, one of them a war canoe, two others merchantmen, have been raised from Roskilde Fjord in Denmark.

With ships like these the Scandinavian traders ventured up the great rivers of Europe and by means of short overland journeys were able to reach the eastern end of the Mediterranean and the southern shores of the Caspian Sea. From these areas they brought back to Scandinavia vast quantities of silver – some in the form of Arab and Byzantine coins – which are still found in hoards in Scandinavia.

The sagas of the Icelanders, written down in the 13th century, tell of some of the great adventures of the Viking Age, but more immediately impressive are the contemporary accounts of voyages carved on the great series of 11th-century memorial stones of Scandinavia. In the runes (characters of the Scandinavian alphabet) are epitaphs to widely travelled men – sometimes in prose, often in verse.

A stone from Gripsholm, in central Sweden, tells of one Harald who had set out with others on a great journey:

> They fared like me
> far after gold
> and in the east
> gave the eagle food.
> They died southward
> in the Saracen's land.

## Scandinavia's first towns

The people left behind by the Scandinavian raiders lived a life little different from that of their forefathers, a life based on the land, on cattle-breeding and agriculture. But new elements were creeping in. For the first time, the need to provide places for selling and buying surplus goods led to the foundation of markets, which were later fortified. These formed the first towns in Scandinavia. The sites of three of these great markets have been identified at Birka, near Stockholm, Hedeby on the neck of the Jutland peninsula, and Kaupang in southern Norway. Several towns existing to this day, such as Trondheim and Ribe, were founded for trade during the Viking Age.

At the same time, the exploitation of mineral resources became more organised, and iron goods were exported to the rest of Europe. The towns were also the home of specialised industries, particularly for the manufacture of bone and antler objects, such as combs, and of glass beads and jewellery. Other industries were developed away from towns. Weaving, always an important occupation, became an important medium of trade, and in parts of northern Scandinavia a measure of cloth, called an 'ounce', was used as a unit of exchange.

The Viking Age was the final explosion of the Germanic peoples before the moulding of the countries now recognised in western Europe. One group of Vikings was destined to play a major role in Europe's later history. These were the 'Northmen' under Rollo, who in the 10th century settled in northern France, where they mingled with the earlier Frankish settlers and became Christians. Their descendants, the Normans, launched their conquest of Britain in 1066, and also established states in Italy and Sicily.

## Survival of the heroic ideal

The traditions of the Germanic invaders had mingled with the classical Mediterranean traditions of the Roman world into which they poured to produce a vital and original culture. As it survives it is best expressed in its contorted art, and in some of the finest European literature. Christianity was an important influence in this era of change, but the true Germanic heroic idea was never far from men's minds: the idea that a man should die for his lord, that he should never flee from battle, that his first duty was to the hand that, by rewarding him, placed him under obligation.

The lordless man was a lost man, without honour and friends, as the writer of the Anglo-Saxon poem *The Wanderer* writes:

> He knows who puts it to the test how
> cruel a comrade is sorrow for him who
> has few dear protectors. His is the
> path of exile, in no wise the twisted
> gold; a chill body, in no wise the
> riches of the earth. He thinks of
> retainers in hall and the receiving
> of treasure, of how in his youth
> his gold-friend was kind to him at the
> feast. The joy has all perished.

The warrior fought for his lord and expected rewards. Life was in many ways hard and brutal; men lived in hovels as well as palaces, some were very poor or slaves, murder was common, disease flourished. In the early 11th century, Archbishop Wulfstan, a thorough-going pessimist, listed England's burdens. The weather and taxation came at the top of the list, but 'devastation and famine, envy, hatred and rapine', joined the long list.

Suffering was the lot of man and was borne with fortitude; death was all around, but the spirit of man rose above the horror and barbarity of the times and broke barriers of ignorance to produce a lively culture which is the foundation of much that is good in European society. The fall of the Roman Empire was only partly a disaster. New life grew quickly out of its ashes. The people who were barbarians in the eyes of the Romans and historians of later centuries were also heirs to the Roman Empire and the founders of a great and lasting culture.

### A QUEEN'S GRAVE

Longships were so important a part of Viking life that chieftains were even buried with their ships. A magnificently carved 'grave ship' was unearthed at Oseberg, in southern Norway, early this century. Within an elaborately carved royal barge almost 70 ft long lay two bodies, probably that of a Viking queen named Asa and her servant. They were surrounded by costly treasures, a richly carved wagon and many objects probably intended for the queen's use in the afterlife, including kitchen utensils, chests, rich hangings and down quilts

FOOD FOR THE VOYAGE *A bronze bucket found in the Oseberg grave was almost certainly made in Britain. When found it contained wild apples – placed there to feed the voyagers on their way to the land of the dead*

BEARDED HEAD *This head, carved in oak on a ceremonial wagon at Oseberg, shows a typical seafarer of the time. Viking artists were skilled woodcarvers, who enjoyed decorating even the most everyday objects*

SNARL OF THE LION *A wooden post found in the Oseberg burial mound is capped by this intricately carved lion's head, its fierce eyes and snarling mouth expressing something of the violent character of its Viking creators. The post, which resembles the ornamental figureheads on Viking ships, may have been part of a piece of a chair or a bed; the Vikings, like other early peoples, believed that the dead should be buried among things that would be familiar and useful to them in the afterlife. The back of the lion's head is decorated with an interlaced animal ornament, a typical motif in the art of the Germanic peoples*

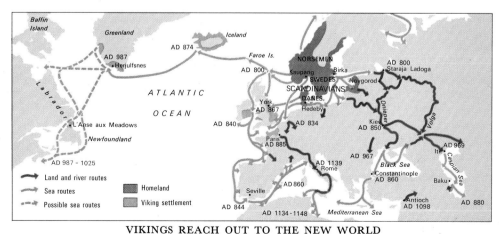

## VIKINGS REACH OUT TO THE NEW WORLD

*The Vikings sailed their longships from Scandinavia to reach much of western and southern Europe, and penetrate deep into Russia. Later they crossed the Atlantic to Iceland, Greenland and the New World*

# An empire built in the name of Allah

## FROM AD 622

*The rising tide of Islam engulfed the ancient world
and created a universal brotherhood
stretching from West Africa to the Far East*

At the beginning of the 7th century, the Arabian peninsula seemed doomed to a state of perpetual and exhausting small-scale warfare, as tribe clashed with tribe over grazing rights and water holes. Less than a century later, the Arabs had burst far beyond the desert wastes of their homeland, and by AD 732 they ruled an empire that stretched from the Pyrenees to the borders of India – larger than the Roman Empire at its height.

The force behind this explosion of Arab energies was a new faith – Islam, which means submission to the will of God. Its founder, Muhammad, was a man of political and religious genius whose message that there is only one God, Allah, united the warring Bedouin and was eagerly accepted by millions in the lands they conquered. According to tradition, Islam was spread by warriors holding the Koran in one hand and a sword in the other.

But the picture is false: though forced conversions did occur, they were the exception, not the rule. Islam had much to offer the faithful. It proclaimed that all men were equal before Allah; it promised Paradise to true believers; and it was tolerant enough to accept Moses and Jesus as prophets, along with Muhammad. Once the Islamic Empire was established there was another incentive: to become a Muslim conferred full membership in a vast and flourishing community.

The empire which had grown so rapidly was held together for nearly 200 years after Muhammad's death by two bonds: one was religion, and the other was the Arabic language, in which the Koran was written. Then it began to fall apart as a political unit, as one provincial governor after another threw off his allegiance to the central government. But Islam as a religion, and the civilization to which it gave

### OMAYYAD EMPIRE IN 732

*Under the Omayyads, the first Islamic Empire reached its height in 732. Arabia, Islam's homeland, is outlined*

### THE KAABA, SHRINE OF MUSLIM PILGRIMS

*The Kaaba, a granite cube in the centre of Mecca, was a centre of pagan worship among the wandering Bedouins of the Arabian desert long before Muhammad was born. It is said to have been built by Abraham; the name Kaaba means 'square house'. Muhammad and his followers, after conquering Mecca, gave the* *shrine an essential role in the new faith of Islam. This drawing shows the 50 ft high Kaaba as it appeared in 1800. The Koran decrees that every Muslim whose health and means permit should make the Hajj, or pilgrimage to the Kaaba, once in his lifetime, after which he can take the title 'Hajji'*

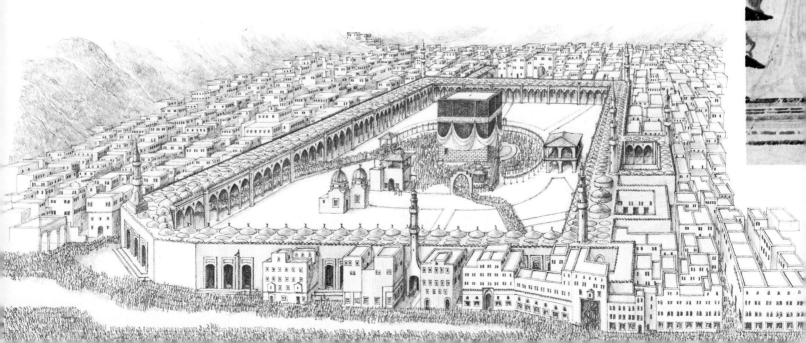

بقبون ان يصيب الوليد بآذر فلم يصبه شئ فاصبح الناس واخذوا المعاول وش عواني الق
الاساس على اساس ابرهيم واسمعيل علهما السلم   وقل انهم لما وصلوا الى الاساس ابرهم علهم عليه د
الانية  جرا فلم يزل يعالج فيه الى ان تخلخل فلما قلعه تزلزلت جميع مكه بتزلزل ذلك الجر فرف
وعرف الجر

## THE REPLACEMENT OF THE BLACK STONE

Embedded in one wall of the Kaaba at Mecca since earliest times has been a hallowed Black Stone, which non-Muslims are forbidden to approach. It is probably a meteorite, which is supposed to have fallen from Paradise with Adam and been given by the Angel Gabriel to Abraham when he was building the Kaaba. Legend says that the stone was white when it fell from the sky, but the kisses of millions of pilgrims have darkened it. A painting from a 14th-century manuscript shows the solution to the problem of replacing the Black Stone during a rebuilding of the Kaaba. A dispute had arisen as to which tribe should have the honour of putting the stone into place. According to one of the Hadith, or 'Traditions' of the prophet's deeds, it was Muhammad, before the start of his mission, who decreed that the sacred stone be raised on a cloth held by one member of each tribe, thus dividing the labor and the honour among them.

149

# *Converts who spread their new faith to distant lands*

**TRUMPETS SUMMON BELIEVERS TO THE FEAST**

*Trumpeters and standard-bearers of Mustansir, a caliph of the Abbasid dynasty, signal the end of the Muslim holy month of Ramadan and the start of the great feast that follows it, in a miniature painted in* *1237. It is the duty of every adult Muslim to fast during the daylight hours of Ramadan, the month in which Allah's will was revealed to Muhammad, and in which his followers won their first major victory*

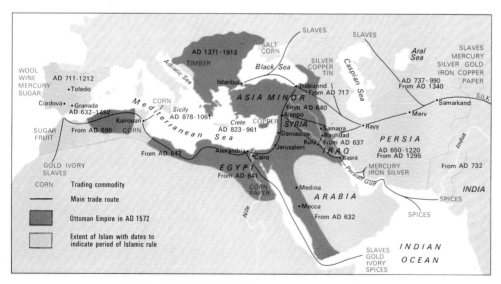

**THE OTTOMANS AND THE EXTENT OF ISLAM**

*At the height of their power, towards the end of the 16th century, the Ottoman Turks ruled from the Danube lands to the southern tip of the Red Sea, and trade routes criss-crossed this huge empire. Under earlier caliphates, the boundaries of Islam extended even beyond the Ottoman frontiers. Arabia, Persia,* *North Africa and Spain had come under Muslim rule as early as the mid-7th century; within another 100 years the Arabs had invaded the Indus Valley on the borders of India. They held Sicily for two centuries before losing it to the Normans, and the Muslim hold on Spain was finally broken in 1492*

rise, have proved enduring. More than 300 Muslim dynasties have ruled various portions of the Islamic world in the last 1300 years. Yet a Muslim could go into any of these sometimes isolated and sometimes warring states and find the same language, social order and laws.

## 'The messenger of God'

Muhammad, son of a merchant, Abdallah, was born in AD 570 at Mecca, a prosperous city on the caravan route between the Indian Ocean and the Mediterranean. Mecca had an unfailing water supply, and an ancient shrine, the Kaaba, which was a centre of pagan worship.

Muhammad was about 40 when he began to preach; he stressed that he was not divine, but only a man whom God had chosen to be his messenger. He said he had been sent to call men to God's worship, and to bid them put away evil before the end of the world and the Last Judgment, which would not be long delayed. This message was not to the taste of the ruling merchants, and in 622 the prophet and his followers were forced to flee. He eventually found sanctuary in Yathrib, an oasis some 300 miles to the north, which became known as 'The City of the Prophet' or simply 'The City' (Medina). The date of this migration, the 'Hegira', is the beginning of the Muslim era.

Apart from the attraction of his preaching, Muhammad had great talents as a strategist and diplomat, and recruits to his cause came in rapidly. In 630 he took Mecca, where two years later he died. After his death, the revelations he had delivered over a period of some 20 years were collected into a book, the Koran (in Arabic *Qur'an*, 'Recitation').

Islam teaches that the surest way to paradise is to die fighting in the cause of God, and the Arabs soon began their career of conquest. They erupted from the peninsula and, picking up recruits as they went, overran the neighbouring lands. As they advanced, they were joined by the discontented subjects of the older empires. The only formal requirement for the convert to Islam is to testify that there is no god but the one God, Allah, and that Muhammad is his prophet – a simpler faith to grasp than the tangled dogmas of Byzantine Christianity. Men of many races joined the Arabs in creating a new empire and a new civilization. The Arabs conquered Iraq (637), Syria (640), Egypt (641) and Persia (650). By 661 their empire stretched from Gabes in Tunisia to the River Oxus and the borderlands of India. It was run from Damascus by the Caliph Muawiya, founder of the Omayyad dynasty which ruled until 750.

## Art in the Holy Cities

Muawiya and his successors rapidly established an efficient government for the new empire. They continued to employ the civil servants they found in the conquered lands. St John of Damascus, one of the last great theologians of the Orthodox Church, was for a time the financial administrator of Damascus, like his father and grandfather before him. The Arab Empire had already become a melting-pot in which many peoples were fused together.

But one field in which the Arabs themselves predominated was poetry. Outstanding were the love-poems of Umar ibn Abi Râbia, regarded by the pious as the greatest sin ever committed against God. The Holy Cities, Mecca and Medina, because of the wealth that flowed into them and the number of visitors they attracted, soon became centres of the profane arts of music and dancing, despite the horror expressed by the devout. A cult of 'courtly love' arose; one governor of Mecca, Harith, himself a poet, kept a congregation waiting in the mosque for prayers to begin until his lady-love arrived. But this phase did not last long, for soon the caliphs adopted the harem from Byzantium, and women generally ceased to appear in public life.

The art of building was scarcely known in Arabia in the lifetime of Muhammad. The only substantial edifice at Mecca, the rebuilt Kaaba, was probably the work of an Abyssinian builder. In the former Byzantine provinces, the first Muslims converted churches into mosques. But soon the caliphs started to use local craftsmen to erect new buildings. Abd al-Malik built the Dome of the Rock at Jerusalem, with its ornate wooden cupola, and the deserts are still dotted with the remains of pleasure palaces and hunting lodges.

## Tales of the Arabian Nights

In 750 Marwan, the last caliph of the Omayyad dynasty, was defeated by armies under the leadership of the Abbasid family, descendants of an uncle of Muhammad. The years of the new Abbasid dynasty were the period of Islamic civilization which has passed into legend as the time of the Arabian Nights.

This collection of fairy-tales and popular romances forms the best-known of Arabic writings outside the Arab world. The stories were drawn from many sources, including India, but they were given an Islamic colouring and include much background detail of life in Baghdad and Cairo. The setting of the stories is, however, medieval; for though Harun al-Rashid, fifth caliph of the Abbasid dynasty, appears in many of the tales, they were not written down until long after what the poet Tennyson called 'the golden prime of good Haroun Alraschid'.

The Abbasids shifted their capital from Damascus to the more central location of Baghdad in Iraq; here in 762 Caliph Mansur laid the foundations of his Round City. Almost a mile and a half in diameter, walled and moated, it contained government offices, mosques, prisons, baths, houses for servants and officials, and shops. At the centre of its perfect circle was the Palace of the Golden Gate, surmounted by a great green dome, on top of which stood the statue of a mounted warrior. As the main building material was mud-brick, nothing of the palace has survived the centuries of battle and flood.

The three essential features of the Islamic city were the mosque, the public bath and the market. In Mansur's capital, the merchants, many of them foreigners, originally dwelt inside

The faith of Islam, which today has 466 million followers throughout the world, was founded by an obscure merchant's son called Muhammad, who was born in the Arabian city of Mecca in AD 570. He insisted that the religion he brought was not new, but the same belief in One God that had been preached by Abraham, by the Old Testament prophets, and by Jesus. The rulers of Mecca, keen to protect the pagan cult which brought lucrative pilgrim traffic to the city, in 622 forced Muhammad to flee. But within eight years the triumph of the new faith had been assured

FACING THE MOB *The citizens of Mecca tried to drive out Muhammad by stoning him. This 16th-century Turkish painting shows an angry mob being quietened by Abu Bakr, a merchant who was one of the prophet's earliest converts. Muhammad's head is surrounded by a halo of fire, a common device of artists to avoid sacrilege in depicting him. The dispirited prophet left Mecca in 622, on* *being invited to Yathrib (later Medina). Once established there, he and his followers attacked Meccan caravans, and a truce was agreed which allowed Muhammad to attend the pilgrimage to Mecca in 629. The dignified bearing and obvious devotion of the 2000 followers who accompanied Muhammad won so many converts that his conquest of the city the following year was virtually unopposed*

DIVINE WORD *The revelations delivered by Muhammad were collected after his death in the Koran, which is regarded by Muslims as God's word. One text of the opening chapter (left) is written in Naskh, the script generally used in Arab manuscripts, while a page from a 9th-century Koran (below) is written in Kufic, an early form of Arab script. The Koran is about the size of the Christian Bible's New Testament and consists of 114 chapters, called suras, each shorter than the one before it. They range from 60 pages to two lines*

# Merchant princes and students of science

the circle. But after they were expelled as a security measure great markets arose outside the Round City, with each street assigned to dealers in one commodity. Market inspectors kept an eye on quality, weights and prices, and stopped cruelty to animals. Baghdad and Basra thrived as centres of commerce. Most trade was in luxury goods, since every region was normally self-supporting in essentials, except for iron and salt. Baghdad was famous for its three-coloured fabrics; the weavers' district of Attabiya gave the 'tabby' cat its name.

From the Persian Gulf, ships sailed for China with camphor, ivory, copper, amber and rhinoceros horn, valued as an antidote to poisons and as an aphrodisiac. To the markets of Iraq came gold and ivory from Africa; furs and textiles from Constantinople and from Trebizond, on the Black Sea; carpets from Armenia; timber and iron from Europe; glass from Syria, and also the cloth which is still called damask, after Damascus.

## The perfect slave
Slaves came from all parts of the Arab Empire. Ibn Butlan, a Christian physician (d. 1066), quotes a dealer's recommendation: 'The ideal slave is a Berber girl who is exported from her country at the age of nine, who spends three years at Medina and three at Mecca, and at 16 comes to Iraq to be trained in elegant accomplishments. So, when sold at 25, she unites with her fine racial excellences the coquetry of the Medinan, the delicacy of the Meccan, and the culture of the Iraqi woman.'

The merchant princes were respected and envied. As one divine bitterly remarked, 'a poor man in Baghdad is like a Koran in the house

of an atheist'. The greatest prestige belonged to the dealers in cambric and spices, while the two basest occupations were weaving and street-sweeping. Merchants on their travels carried letters of credit or paid by cheque, and there was a bankers' clearing-house at Basra. With government support, farmers restored abandoned farmland; ruined irrigation canals were repaired and new ones dug. The Omayyads had set up a postal service for official correspondence; the Abbasids turned it into an intelligence service, with post-stations from 6 to 12 miles apart. Postmasters had orders to keep the capital informed about food prices in their districts, so that supplies could be sent where shortages threatened. In addition to the regular service by mounted courier, there was a pigeon-post, and pigeons were carried on merchant ships.

Harun al-Rashid's son, Mamun, set out to make the practical learning of the ancient world accessible to his people. He established a House of Wisdom in Baghdad, where under the direction of a gifted local Christian, Hunayn ibn Ishaq, Arabic translations were made of the works of Galen and Euclid, Ptolemy and Archimedes, Aristotle and Plato. Kindi, 'the philosopher of the Arabs', wrote over 250 works, on optics, music, alchemy, astrology and philosophy. Rhazes, a native of Rayy in Persia, wrote 141 works, including the first known clinical descriptions of smallpox and measles. His masterpiece, *The Compendium*, combined the medical knowledge of the Greeks, Arabs, Persians and Indians. The upsurge of scientific work was encouraged by the introduction of paper. It replaced parchment and papyrus after 751, when some Chinese, skilled

in its manufacture, who had been captured in a skirmish in central Asia, were set up in a factory at Samarkand. Within 40 years, factories had been opened at Baghdad and elsewhere throughout the Abbasid world, and the use of paper had become general.

## The coming of the Turks
Though the arts of civilization flourished under the Abbasids, politically and militarily the dynasty was never as strong as the Omayyads had been at their height. The Abbasid caliphs made the mistake of replacing the Omayyads' independent-minded but loyal Arab officers by a subservient and largely non-Arab bureaucracy. The most enterprising Arabs, crowded out of the administration, became scholars and merchants and lost their sense of allegiance to the dynasty. The rest, under-employed soldiers and city mobs, became a danger to the state. As a result the Abbasids called on non-Arabs for support, which angered the Arabs still further. Harun al-Rashid appointed a Turkish general to command an expedition in 806; his son enlisted a personal bodyguard of Turkish mercenaries; a later caliph brought Turks into the army.

So strained did relations grow between the mercenaries and the citizens of Baghdad, who were cruelly taxed to pay them, that in 836 the caliph and his guards moved to Samarra, 60 miles up the Tigris, which remained the caliphs' capital for 56 years. Its most spectacular monument must have been the Palace of Balkuwara, a rectangle almost two-thirds of a mile long, with three huge arches of brick at the western end. Its ruins still stand today.

From the mid-9th century, most of the caliphs were puppets of their Turkish generals, and one province after another broke away from their grasp. In 1055, when much of Asia was ruled by Turkish dynasties, an army of Turks led by the family of Seljuk entered and captured Baghdad itself.

## Cairo, the greatest Arab city
One of the foremost of the provinces to break away was Egypt in 868. A century later it was conquered by another Arab dynasty, the Fatimids, who had established themselves in North Africa 60 years before. It was the Fatimids who built Cairo proper; there had been earlier cities near its site, but the Fatimids gave the name Qahira to their capital because the ground-breaking for it began when Mars (Qahir) was in the ascendant. Within ten years it was already one-third the size of Baghdad, and it speedily became, and remained, the greatest Arab city of all.

The two centuries of Fatimid rule were a time of great economic and social well-being. Less than three years after the conquest they built the mosque of al-Azhar, later to be the main university in the Islamic world. The Fatimids ensured the maintenance of the mosque through a *waqf* – a form of endowment peculiar to Islam, whereby the revenues of a piece of property were assigned for ever to a charitable or pious purpose. Charity is one of

---

### A PEOPLE WITH A REVERENCE FOR TRADE

Muhammad approved of honest gain in trading; the hold that commerce had on the imagination of early Muslims is shown by the important role played by merchants in the tales of Baghdad and Cairo, later written down as the *Arabian Nights*. One 10th-century jeweller, Ibn-al-Jassas, is said to have remained rich even after the Caliph of Baghdad confiscated 16 million gold pieces from him

TRAVELLING SALESMEN *Mecca was at the cross-roads of profitable trade routes, and merchants banded together to cross the desert in vast caravans, which were heavily guarded against bandits. A miniature painted in 1237 shows a trader preparing to mount his camel before setting out on an expedition*

MOSQUE LAMP *Muslim glassware was prized for the elaborate designs enamelled or cut on the surface. The finest came from Syria; this 14th-century mosque lamp was probably made in Damascus. It was lit by oil and a wick, floating in water*

the obligations of Islam, and ordinary Muslims owed most of the amenities of their lives to the institution of the *waqf*.

A Persian traveller, Nasir-i-Khusraw, who visited Egypt in 1046, found it the only haven of peace and prosperity in eastern Islam. Cairo, he reported, had 20,000 brick-built houses, some of five or six storeys, and 20,000 shops, all the property of the caliph. The palace had 12,000 servants. Some of the streets were lit by lamps. Horses were for the military; citizens rode asses and donkeys, which could be hired at any street corner. Prices were fixed by the authorities. Following Muhammad's teachings, crime was punished so severely that it was only necessary for the shops of the jewellers and money-changers to be secured by a cord stretched across the doorway. A condemned pickpocket would have his hand cut off.

## Grandeur of the Mamelukes

The most splendid period of Egyptian architecture was in the 13th to 15th centuries, under the Mameluke sultans. Sultan Qalawun (1279–90) gave the city its most famous hospital, which consisted of three courtyards, two surrounded by cubicles for patients, the third by wards, lecture rooms, library, dispensary and treatment rooms. As in other medieval Islamic hospitals, the patients were entertained with music, and comforted by readings from the Koran. No fees were charged. Only the façade and entrance-hall survive today, but the founder's tomb next to it is still a place of pilgrimage for the sick.

Sultan Qaytbay (d. 1496) left two superb mosques, one of which contains his tomb, as well as a number of fortresses, palaces and caravanserais. The caravanserai was an essential feature of the landscape. It was a square or rectangular high-walled courtyard, lined on the inside with rooms for travellers, and storerooms where their goods were put for safe keeping by night. The baggage-camels and mules, with the camel-drivers' donkeys and the rich merchants' horses, were tethered inside the courtyard, in the centre of which was often a mosque, raised on pillars to prevent the animals from intruding.

The Mamelukes gave Egypt a new period of commercial and political importance. They maintained friendly relations with Byzantium. They ruled Syria as well as Egypt, and until the Portuguese discovered a route round the Cape of Good Hope in 1498, all trade between the East and Europe had to come through their territories, paying heavy customs duties at every stage. It was the extortionate rate of customs duty levied by Mameluke sultans – up to 160 per cent in some cases – that finally gave the Portuguese the incentive to find the alternative route to India.

## The 'Lands of the Sunset'

Islam had a strong foothold, too, further west on the African continent. By the beginning of the 8th century the Byzantine power in North Africa was broken, and this once-Christian province had become a province of the Omayyad

### THE MASTER CRAFTSMEN OF MOSUL

*The metalworkers of Mosul, a city on the River Tigris, were famed for their mastery of the difficult technique of inlaying silver on bronze and brass. The musicians, playing a harp and a flute, are delicately inlaid on a* *tiny section of a 12 in. brass ewer dating from 1232, which is signed 'Made by Shuja ibn Mana of Mosul'. The distinctive style of Mosul ware was copied throughout the Muslim world on jugs and candlesticks*

### STUDENTS OF THE SCIENCES

Arab philosophers and wise men obeyed the prophet's command to 'seek knowledge, even as far as China'. The knowledge they collected was passed on to Western Europe in the Middle Ages

LEADERS IN MEDICINE *Arabs led the ancient world in the study of medicine. A page from* The Book of Antidotes, *dated 1199, shows a physician (left) supervising gardeners at work on medicinal plants. The Arabs were particularly advanced in surgery, drugs and the treatment of eye diseases*

WATCHING THE SKIES *Astrology flourished alongside the more scientific study of astronomy, and buildings were commenced on days chosen by court astrologers. A 13th-century illustration shows Mars in the sign of the Ram, with Jupiter in conjunction*

# Culture and learning flourish in Muslim Spain

caliphate, with its local capital at Kairouan, in Tunisia. At first the native Berbers challenged the domination of the Arabs, but before long they joined the ranks of victorious Islam. In 711 a force of 7000 Berber and Arab Moors, under their leader Tariq ibn Ziyad (who gave his name to Gibraltar, called in Arabic *Jabal Tariq*, 'Tariq's Mountain'), invaded the south of Spain, defeated the last Visigoth king, and added a new province to the caliph's empire. They called it al-Andalus, after its earlier masters, the Vandals.

Although the south of Spain was ruled by Muslims until 1492, they were never in a majority there. There were no wholesale conversions as there had been in the previous conquests; the Spaniards, encouraged by the proximity of Christian Europe, held fiercely to their faith. In Sicily too, which was conquered by 878 and stayed in Muslim hands until 1061, the conquerors remained in a minority. In both countries there arose among the victors an unparalleled spirit of tolerance and an artistic and intellectual flowering. This survived the conquest of Sicily by the Normans, who used Arabic, as well as Greek and Latin, in their official documents. Cordoba and Toledo were the most brilliant centres of

civilization in the Western world of the 10th century. Their music and poetry, to which the themes and rhythms of local Christian singers contributed, influenced in its turn Christian poetry and song, which the troubadours carried northwards. The father of the Islamic music of the peninsula was Ziryab, a Persian singer from the court of Baghdad. After winning a musical contest before the Caliph Mahdi (775–85), Ziryab fled to Cordoba to escape the vengeance of the runner-up; there he founded an academy of music and became an arbiter of fashion. It was to Cordoba, not to Paris, that the ladies of the Christian kingdoms of Navarre and Barcelona sent for their new dresses.

At a time when London could not boast a single street-lamp, the streets of Andalusian cities were paved and lit. The houses had marble balconies for the summer and hot-air ducts under the mosaic floors for the winter. They were surrounded by gardens adorned with pools and artificial cascades, and by orchards of peaches and pomegranates.

## Heritage of Andalusia

The best-preserved of Andalusian palaces is the Alhambra in Granada, begun in 1230 but not completed until two centuries later. The

great mosque of Cordoba, now a cathedral, was founded in 785 and enlarged as the population grew; it has a forest of little columns bearing arches on which other arches rest. The magnificent royal pew, the *maqsura*, was joined to the palace by an underground passage.

Students from France and England came to sit at the feet of Muslim, Christian and Jewish scholars, to learn philosophy, science and medicine. What makes Andalusia so important in the history of civilization is not just that life was lived nobly there but that it passed on to the Christian West the learning of both the Islamic and the classical worlds. Toledo was reconquered by Alfonso VI of Leon and Castile in 1085. But the city remained a meeting-place for all creeds; and under the patronage of the Archbishop, Don Raymundo, many translations were made from Arabic into Latin. Most of the major works of Greek science and philosophy had already been turned into Arabic; now, through the translators of Spain, they reached Europe, along with many original Arab works of scholarship.

Gerard of Cremona (1114–87) came to Toledo to seek a copy of the *Almagest*, the treatise in which Ptolemy set forth his system of astronomy; he found it, and his translation

### ART IN SILK FROM ANDALUSIA

*By conquering southern Spain in 711 the Berbers of North Africa brought the culture of Islam into Europe. For seven centuries al-Andalus, as the Muslim's called their Spanish territory, was a centre of learning and the arts. Rich silk fabrics, like this peacock design woven in the 12th century, were exported all over the Mediterranean*

### SPLENDOUR OF A PALACE IN SPAIN

*The fairy-tale palace of the Alhambra, on a Granada hillside, was begun in 1230 but not completed for another two centuries. Above the arched window of the Queen's Room (left), stylised leaves in plaster are interwoven with Muslim script. In the Court of the Lions (right), slender columns frame a fountain guarded by lions*

remained the standard work on astronomy in Europe until Copernicus published his theory of the sun-centred universe in 1543. To Gerard and his contemporary the Spanish Rabbi ben Ezra belongs the credit for introducing to Europe the Indian system of arithmetical notation, using the zero, which had been known in Baghdad from 770. Its symbols, still used today, came to be called Arabic numerals.

Gradually Spanish knights drove the Muslims out of Spain in what became known as the 'Reconquest'. The vigorous intellectual life of Muslim North Africa survived; but somehow, when in 1492 Ferdinand and Isabella conquered Granada, the last Moorish stronghold in Spain, much of the colour and romance disappeared from Islamic history.

The 'Reconquest' of Spain was not the only Christian campaign against the Muslims. Between the 11th and the 14th centuries, the powers of Europe launched a series of Crusades to liberate the Holy Land from Islam, after Pope Urban II had demanded a 'Holy War' against the infidels. In 1099 the Crusaders captured Jerusalem from the Seljuk Turks, and went on to set up a chain of Christian kingdoms in Palestine. These kingdoms were soon menaced by a revival of Turkish power, and further Crusades had to be launched to relieve them. The most famous of these was the Third Crusade (1189–92), when Richard the Lionheart pitched his armies against the great Muslim general, Saladin. But such expeditions achieved little. In 1291 the port of Acre, the last Christian stronghold in Palestine, fell, and with the rise of the Ottoman Turks, Islam's position became impregnable throughout the Middle East.

### 'The Guarded Dominions'

The Ottoman Empire, which was to become the greatest of all Muslim states, in magnificence, territorial extent and duration, was founded at the end of the 13th century by Osman, son of Ertughrul, the leader of a band of Turks who had migrated into Asia Minor from central Asia. Most of them were only recently converted to Islam, and they displayed enormous energy in fighting the 'infidels' of the Byzantine Empire. The special contributions of the valiant, practical and hard-headed Turks to the multi-racial Community of Believers lay in administration and war. Islamic theory divided the world into *Dar al-Islam*, the abode of Islam, and *Dar al-harb*, the abode of war. The Turks were, in principle, in a state of permanent warfare with their Christian neighbours, and it was regarded as normal for the sultan every year to put himself at the head of his armies and march against Europe.

Before his death in 1481 Sultan Mehmet II had conquered the Byzantine Empire, sacked its capital of Constantinople and ruled all Asia Minor, Greece and the Balkans. A hundred years later the Turks had taken over the entire remaining Arab Empire, and ruled from the Adriatic Sea to the Persian Gulf, as well as over much of North Africa. This gigantic empire was known to the West as the Ottoman Empire, from a corruption of the name of its founder, Osman. But its own rulers called the empire 'The Guarded Dominions'.

The Ottoman Turks saw themselves as part of a universal Islamic empire. They had no racial prejudice; Christians and Jews were second-class citizens, but they were free to join the ruling class by adopting Islam. Towards the end of the 14th century, the dynasty enlarged its civil and military services by recruiting and compulsorily converting boys from the subject peoples. For 250 years most of the great officers of state were men of Christian birth; there were 20 Turkish grand viziers and 90 non-Turkish. As a result of this

# *Spreading the faith by force—and by trade*

**THE GREATEST ARMY IN THE WEST**

*When this miniature was painted in the mid-16th century, the war-loving Ottoman Turks under Suleiman the Magnificent were the most feared military power in the West, with 300,000 men under arms. Most of them were cavalry, who had no armour and* *carried only bows, lances and swords. But the Turks did not ignore modern advances in weaponry. They manufactured cannon as early as 1364, and could match the fire-power of their European enemies when Suleiman attacked the Hungarians along the Danube*

mixing of races in the ruling circles of the Ottoman Empire, Islamic civilization in the Ottoman period, which did not end until the 20th century, is a harmonious whole. A pre-Ottoman mosque can be identified as being, say, North African or Syrian, while an Ottoman mosque, generally speaking, is recognisable as such whether it is in Istanbul, Sofia or Aleppo. For this fact the genius of one man was largely responsible: Sinan (1490–1588), the architect of Sultan Suleiman the Magnificent, in whose reign the Ottoman Empire reached the height of its power. Early Ottoman mosques were roofed with as many as 20 small cupolas. In the early 14th century, the central area of the mosque began to be covered with one great dome, and this was the type which Sinan brought to perfection.

## Flowers instead of images

From the outside, Ottoman mosques are plain. Inside much use is made of tiles and mosaic and stained glass. The Islamic ban on the portrayal of living beings led to the decorative use of calligraphy, geometrical designs, and representations of flowers, both stylised and naturalistic. Another consequence of the ban was the perfection of the art of miniature painting; this was used to illustrate books for the libraries of the great, who in the main took the ban far less seriously than did the mass of Muslims, but did not wish to offend them by the public display of pictures. The Ottoman miniaturists learnt their art from Persia, but their work has an element of realism and greater boldness of colour which gave it a distinctive beauty.

The Turks have always been fond of flowers. The name 'Tulip Period' is given to the years 1718–30, when this taste was fostered by Sultan Ahmed III and his court as part of a deliberate effort to bring about an age of beauty and pageantry. The exuberantly fresh and natural lyrics of the poet Nedim, a baroque note in architecture, and a few indistinct traces of the pleasure gardens of Istanbul are all that remain of this brave but untimely experiment, which was ended by a mutiny of the army.

Though the Ottoman power began to decline towards the end of the 17th century, it took over 200 years more to die. For most of the people, for most of the time, life was reasonably secure, though it was less so for the men at the top, who when summoned to the sultan's presence would make their wills before complying. Grand viziers could come and go with terrifying frequency; one man, Zurnazen Mustafa Pasha, held office for only four hours on March 5, 1656. At least 25 grand viziers died by the executioner's hand. Some sultans had members of their own family put to death to prevent rebellion.

A highly organised bureaucracy kept the civil administration of the Ottoman Empire going, even when the armies were in retreat. Every man knew his place, whether it was in the ranks of the bureaucracy or the army, or in the *Ulema* (the hierarchy of teachers and judges) or in the organisation of a trade or profession. These organisations regulated entry to each craft or trade, and promotion in it. They punished bad workmanship or sharp practice with fines or expulsion, and gave loans or grants to members who needed capital to open a shop or who had fallen on hard times.

## The 'outer lands'

The Islamic Empire also finally embraced many 'outer lands' which the conquests did not reach. Here Islam was brought by the missionary activity of Muslim merchants who acted also as teachers and doctors. In West Africa the Berbers spread the faith, and Islam had reached the Negroes of upper Senegal by the early 11th century. Ibn Battuta, who spent 25 years journeying round the Islamic world, visited Timbuktu in about 1350 and wrote with approval of the low crime rate among the Muslim Negroes and of their scrupulous performance of their religious duties. For the congregational prayer on Fridays, he said 'anyone who does not go early to the mosque will not find room to pray, because of the crowd'. Slaves would go very early and spread prayer-mats, to reserve places for their masters. Great importance was attached to learning the Koran by heart; young men had heavy chains fastened to their feet until they had done so. But Islam was very much the religion of the rulers and merchants, while the mass of peasant farmers remained true to their pagan ways and beliefs. Even today, the Islam of the people is often a blend of two faiths; the ancient local cult of spirits is still active, though the demons may be given Muslim names and equated with the *jinn*, or evil spirits, of the Koran.

Since ancient times East Africa had supplied South Arabia with slaves, ivory, ambergris, ginger, timber, frankincense and gold. This traffic continued after the coming of Islam, and the Arab merchants and sailors made converts among the people of the coast. The missionaries, however, made no systematic effort to convert the tribes of the interior; this was the slavers' hunting-ground, and Islamic law would not have allowed Muslims to be enslaved.

## Expansion in the Far East

The Arabs had penetrated deep into the Indian sub-continent by 714, and by 1030 had extended their rule over the Indus Valley and the whole of the Punjab. Delhi became the capital of Muslim India in 1211. The founder of the 300-year Mughal Empire, Babur (1483–1530), was a descendant of the Mongol conqueror Genghis Khan; but he regarded himself as a Turk, and wrote in Turkish.

In south-east Asia, Arab trader-missionaries converted the local rulers and merchants with whom they had most contact. The new religion then spread slowly among the population. There was a settlement of Arabs at Palembang in eastern Sumatra within 50 years of the death of Muhammad, and northern Java was gradually converted from the end of the 13th century.

Malacca was the chief commercial centre of south-east Asia, and the principal centre from which Islam was spread. The people of this port were converted by merchants from Gujarat, in north-west India; among the goods they brought were ready-made tombstones, carved with all the necessary Arabic inscriptions except the name of the deceased. The Malays of Malacca were great conquerors, and they took their new religion with them to the rest of the peninsula. After the Portuguese conquest of Malacca in 1511, the missionary work went on from northern Sumatra.

## A self-sufficient world

Islamic civilization was a product of many minds, of many races. But their individual talents might easily have gone to waste had it not been for the genius of Muhammad. Every miniature, every mosque, every line of the poets is a tribute to him. The art and architecture of the Islamic world give ample evidence of the Muslim original creative genius; but one of Islam's greatest contributions lay in the encouragement which it gave to the spread of learning. The correspondence between learned men throughout the Arab-speaking world resulted in the extensive collection and analysis of facts, renewing a process begun by the Greeks. It also led to huge advances in mathematical, medical and physical science, which were passed on to Western Europe.

During the five centuries when Arabic was the international language of science, a man could live a full, useful, and rich life within the world of Islam, with no thought for the darkness outside. For Ibn Khaldun, a 14th-century Arab historian, civilization meant Islamic civilization. In his *Universal History* he says: 'It has recently come to my ears that sciences are flourishing in the country of the Franks, namely, in the land of Rome and adjoining portion of the northern coast of the Mediterranean, but God knows best what goes on there.'

But the Muslims were not allowed to go on for ever ignoring the West. Awareness of Europe and of the achievements of European science was forcefully brought home to them by successive military reverses. In 1798 their dreams of reviving past glories were brutally snapped by Napoleon's invasion of Egypt. The process of Westernisation began. Now the Muslims are a part of world civilization, a fabric to which Islam has contributed in full measure.

### MOSQUE BUILT ON A CHRISTIAN MODEL

*The splendid mosque overlooking the Golden Horn in Constantinople, now Istanbul, was built in the 16th century by Sinan, architect to the Turkish sultan Suleiman the Magnificent. It is still the city's chief mosque. Its central dome is modelled on that of Hagia Sophia, the Byzantine cathedral built in the same city 1000 years before. Earlier mosques had been built with as many as 20 smaller domes. The decorations inside Suleiman's mosque are restrained by contrast with the ostentation of earlier Turkish designs*

# India: a culture shaped by two religions

## FROM 2400 BC

*Hinduism and Buddhism produced a rich heritage of temples and sculptures, and a society which has kept its individual character during 4000 years of conquests*

The civilization of India is one of the most ancient in the world. Some aspects of this civilization stretch back for more than 4000 years – even though few countries have experienced so many invasions, endured so many periods of apparent anarchy, or seen so many great empires rise and fall.

The great majority of India's invaders came through the passes of the north-west, from Persia or central Asia. The armies of Cyrus and Darius of Persia passed this way; so did the forces of Alexander the Great, of the Bactrian Greeks, the Kushans and the Huns. From AD 700 there began a series of Muslim invasions, the last and most important being the coming of the Mughals in the 16th century.

Only the Europeans came from the sea – and, unlike the other invaders, were not absorbed. But the way in which Indian society has responded to the pressures of the modern world is testimony to the vigour of beliefs and institutions of great antiquity.

As long ago as 2400 BC, a civilization was growing in the valley of the River Indus, in present-day Pakistan. It had developed from farming communities settled in the valley since 4000 BC, and it was based upon a number of cities, the greatest of which were the wealthy capitals of Harappa and Mohenjo Daro. In about 1750 BC these cities were abandoned, apparently after floods caused by a change in the course of the Indus. They disappeared so completely under the mud of the Indus that men forgot they had ever existed. Modern discovery of the remains of the Indus Valley civilization began only in 1922.

But though these sophisticated people disappeared, they left legacies. Among them was a god who was later to become Shiva, one of the principal gods of the Hindus. They also invented many pieces of equipment, such as the bullock cart, which provided models for generations of Indian craftsmen.

The first people to inherit the legacies of the Indus Valley civilization were those who helped to destroy it – tribes of lighter-skinned nomads known as the Aryans, or 'noble ones', who migrated from Iran into north-west India in a series of waves from about 2000 BC. The names of India and its principal religion, Hinduism, had their origin in the Indus Valley: from *Sindhu*, the name given to the Indus in Sanskrit, the language of the Aryans, came the Persian *Hindu* and the Latin *India*. Modern knowledge of the Aryan conquerors comes mainly from their four great religious books, the

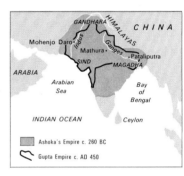

## TWO GREAT EMPIRES

*Ashoka, a Buddhist, ruled India's first empire. Under the Hindu Guptas, 700 years later, culture reached its peak*

## A TOMB FOR BUDDHA

*After Buddha's death in about 480 BC, parts of his body were buried under mounds called 'stupas' in various parts of India. This impression shows the Great Stupa at Sanchi as it looked in 150 BC, when the original simple mound had been enlarged into a brick building 50 ft high which still stands*

## A HINDU TEMPLE THAT REACHES LIKE A MOUNTAIN TOWARDS THE SKY

*The soaring tower of the Kandariya Mahadeo temple at Khajuraho, in northern India, is one of many richly ornate works of architecture which were built during centuries of competition between different sects of the Hindu religion. There were 85 temples at Khajuraho, but only 20 still stand. Since the gods were believed to dwell on a mountain high in the Himalayas, the temples were built like mountains reaching towards the heavens. The architects who built Khajuraho's holy places in the 10th and 11th centuries gave this notion of a symbolic 'sacred mountain' a refinement and luxury found nowhere else. Unlike the more sombre temples of south India, which were built under the shadow of the Muslim conquest, those at Khajuraho*
*are gay. The friezes sculptured on the beautifully symmetrical walls are peopled with hundreds of statues of male and voluptuous female gods as well as of human beings, and there are no demons or horrific scenes. Some of the carvings are extremely erotic, and variations of the sexual act are depicted in explicit detail. Despite its outward ornateness, the temple was built to a simple plan. On a very high plinth the entrance portico, topped by a low peaked roof, opened to an assembly hall with a higher roof, which in turn led to a sanctuary under the topmost tower. The interior, whose central shrine is sacred to the god Shiva, was also covered with carving, though this would have been only dimly seen as little light was allowed to penetrate*

# Four 'Noble Truths' that founded a new faith

Vedas, which are the holy books of Hinduism to the present day. The most important of the Vedic books, the *Rig-veda*, tells of barbarian tribes, glorying in their swift horses and light chariots, fighting battles and establishing themselves in small villages, grazing their flocks of sheep, goats and cattle, and cultivating crops. From these earliest farming days sprang the particularly high regard which Indians hold for cattle. The Hindu principle of non-violence, which forbids the killing of any animals, gave special protection to the cow, conferring on it almost the status of a sacred beast.

The conquered peoples of the Indus Valley and beyond were called Dasas or Dasyu, which at first meant 'dark skinned' and, later, 'slaves'. This distinction by colour was the basis of the Indian caste system. At first the only rigid division was between the light-skinned, blue-eyed conquerors and the dark-skinned dark-eyed conquered. But later, as the original Aryans inter-married with the local population, distinction by colour was superseded by a system which fixed not only a man's position in society, but that of his descendants as well.

## The making of Hindu India

Between 1000 and 500 BC the basic pattern of Hindu society became established. As towns grew up in the plain of the Ganges, the old tribal customs were abandoned. Chiefs took on the authority of kings and founded dynasties. Priests helped them by showing that the gods had ordained the division of society into castes. This was a far more rigid division than the Western class system, because while it was always possible for an outstanding or lucky Westerner to rise into a new class, a Hindu

could escape only by death from the caste into which he was born. The work a man did, the woman he married, even the people with whom he was permitted to eat a meal – all these depended on his caste.

With the settlement of towns and the growth of trade, those who were responsible for these changes came into conflict with the established privilege of the upper castes. Particularly resented were the privileges of the priests, their mysterious rituals, and their constant demands for cattle to be used in sacrifice. These demands fell most heavily on the cultivators, who were compelled to give up their draught animals without payment.

The misery of the people opened the way for reformers who attacked the priests and opposed the institution of caste. One such reformer was destined to have a profound effect not only on religion, but on society and civilization in the whole of eastern Asia.

The teachings of Gautama Buddha had all the elements of popular appeal. Born the son of a chief of the Shakya tribe, on the borders of Nepal, in about 560 BC, Buddha – 'Enlightened One' – became increasingly dissatisfied with aristocratic life. At about 29 he left home and joined a band of ascetics, seeking salvation through frugality. After six years he decided that asceticism was not the way, and turned instead to meditation, receiving enlightenment after sitting under a tree for 49 days.

The results of Buddha's meditation were first pronounced at a sermon given in the Deer Park at Sarnath, 4 miles from Banaras. This sermon, the 'Turning of the Wheel of the Law', is the foundation of Buddhist teaching. The world, said Buddha, was full of suffering. That

suffering was caused by human desires. Only by renouncing desire could suffering be eliminated. These three Noble Truths were followed by the fourth – that the way to salvation was through the Eightfold Path, eight principles of behaviour which included the practice of right belief, right thought, right speech and right action.

The Buddhist code was based, not upon acceptance of priestly powers or on the need for costly sacrifices to the gods, but upon the moral conduct of the individual. There was no discrimination by caste or class, occupation or wealth. Buddhism therefore appealed to the low-caste masses, and to the newly emerging merchant classes whose growing wealth was not reflected in the social status allotted to them. During the lifetime of Buddha, and for two centuries after his death in about 480 BC, his influence was mainly confined to a small area of north-east India. The full effect of his teachings – which amounted to a genuine humanitarian revolution – had to await the coming of a great king and a new empire.

## Emperor with a conscience

Early in the 3rd century BC most of northern and central India was united in a single empire, known as the Mauryan Empire after Chandragupta Maurya, who founded it in 322 BC, following the retreat from India of Alexander the Great. In 261 BC, Ashoka, the third emperor of the Maurya dynasty, set out on the conquest of what is today the Indian east-coast state of Orissa. In his own words, 'a hundred thousand people were deported, a hundred thousand killed, and many times that number perished'. So terrible was the cruelty that the emperor was struck with remorse. Within a year or two he was converted to Buddhism; he re-organised the state on humane lines, and renounced war as a means of conquest.

Ashoka's views on the right behaviour for both king and subject were engraved on pillars and rocks throughout the empire. One edict banned the killing of animals for sacrifice, another gave instructions for the digging of wells and the provision of medical services for man and beast. Yet another gave instructions on personal morality, insisting among other things that 'obedience to mother and father' was meritorious. Many referred to new standards of justice for all – in effect, a kind of Bill of Rights. There was also a new concept of the responsibilities of kingship. 'All men,' reads one inscription, 'are my children.'

The conflict between sects continued, however. The Buddhist-inspired revolution did not survive Ashoka's death, and failed to transform either the empire or its people. But the experiment, though short-lived, was one of the most remarkable in human history.

## The expansion of Buddhism

During the reign of Ashoka, the Buddhist Church, by then a sophisticated and wealthy organisation, began to expand. At a great council held at Pataliputra, near present-day Patna, in about 250 BC, it was decided to send

---

### A CIVILIZATION BURIED FOR 3500 YEARS

The relics of India's first civilized people lay buried for more than 3500 years beneath the soil of what is now Pakistan. Their civilization, as advanced as those of ancient Egypt and Mesopotamia, flourished from about 2100 to 1750 BC along the fertile valleys of the River Indus and its tributaries, and its ruins were discovered only this century. Excavations revealed settlements ranging from simple farming communities to seaports developed for foreign trade, and two thriving capitals at Harappa and Mohenjo Daro. The cities, dominated by fortified citadels, were carefully planned with their own water and sanitation systems, and streets of brick-built houses laid out in a grid pattern. Thousands of small inscribed seals show that the people had developed methods of writing and calculating, though their script has not yet been deciphered. They were also among the first ancient civilizations to have the wheel

INDUS HEAD *The style of this stone bust, possibly of a priest, dating from before 2000 BC, resembles figures found in Mesopotamia, where the people of the Indus Valley may have gone to trade*

TOY CART *Indus Valley potters excelled at small, delicately made objects and figurines. This terracotta toy cart, made about 1800 BC and found at Mohenjo Daro, is complete with ox team and driver. Similar bullock carts are used in India to the present day*

missionaries not only throughout the empire but across its borders, to the Hellenistic kingdoms to the north-west and, in the deep south, to the jungles of Ceylon.

The missionaries who went to the Hellenistic kingdoms found an area particularly receptive to the appeal of new gods. The Greek presence dated from Alexander the Great's entry into India in 327 BC. The kingdoms created after his death were easily brushed aside by new invaders from central Asia – Greeks from Bactria, Parthians from Iran, and finally the Kushans, from north of the Hindu Kush mountains, who were to rule north-west India for nearly two centuries until about AD 250. The new rulers took possession of a double heritage, in philosophy and in art, from Greece and from India. Buddhism had an immediate appeal for them, not least because it welcomed converts without discrimination – unlike Hinduism, which had only one place for foreigners, at the bottom of the social scale.

A revival of Hinduism after the death of Ashoka, however, threatened the hold of the Buddhist kings. If the masses were to return to the Hindu priests, a heretic ruler would be in grave danger. The answer, conceived by some unknown genius, was to increase the popularity of Buddhism by giving Buddha a face.

The Buddha had always denied that he was a god, and was long represented at places of worship not by his face, like the Hindu gods, but by symbols – such as footprints, the Wheel of the Law, an empty throne, or the tree under which he received enlightenment. Buddha was probably first depicted in human form some time in the 1st century BC, though the earliest dateable sculptures were made after AD 100. The sculptors took as their model the Greek Apollo, but soon Buddha's form became Indianised, and the face assumed the closed eyes and the smile of the Asian Buddha.

Buddhism was to fade in India, a casualty in the war between supporters of rival gods. But the long campaign produced some of the greatest monuments and most magnificent sculpture the world has known. Some of the finest examples are the Buddhist and Hindu cave temples at Ellura, near Aurangabad. Among these superb displays of sculptural virtuosity, the great Hindu temple of the Kailasanatha, a free-standing structure hewn out of the solid rock between AD 760 and 800, is outstanding.

### Rival gods and new epics

Trade with Rome helped to support the Buddhist religion and pay for its glories. Rome paid large sums in gold and silver for Indian luxuries, like pepper and other spices, pearls and ivory. Trade also developed with the Indonesian islands and with the mainland of south-east Asia. But there was no political stability, and kingdoms rose and fell. Meanwhile, the Hindu counter-reformation continued to gain ground. There developed at this time a concept of the Absolute or Universal Soul, and the idea of a trinity of gods – Brahma, Vishnu and Shiva. All were shown

### THE BUDDHIST IDEAL OF SPIRITUAL HARMONY

*When Buddha was transformed into a god, the first sculptors depicted him as a preacher, with his audience carved to the same scale. But by the time this magnificent sculpture was produced in the 5th century the figure of Buddha had been enormously enlarged, and the scene showing his first preaching in the Deer Park at Sarnath was confined to a frieze at the base. It was in this era that the noblest sculptures of Buddha were produced, embodying to perfection the Buddhist ideals of serenity and spiritual harmony*

# Prosperity and expansion under the Gupta rulers

as possessing several heads and arms, to symbolise their superhuman powers. Ancient epics were revised to supply the sacred literature of the new concepts. Works now considered among the greatest in Indian literature, the *Mahabharata* and the *Ramayana*, date from between AD 100 and 400.

The central belief of Hinduism as it evolved over the centuries is that actions in the present life dictate the level at which a man is reborn in the next. Though there is no heaven in the Hindu religion, it is conceived that the chain of re-birth may eventually end in a state of non-being from which there is no return. Good actions, naturally, produce the happiest modification of one's destiny, and good action is action which follows the sacred Law. Each man was required to do his duty without questioning the results of his action; even killing was not necessarily sinful if the cause was just.

There was also growing up the view, however, that it was possible to have a completely personal relationship with the gods, without the need for ritual or priest, and it was this which was to have the most tremendous appeal to the masses. But first another new empire was to rise and live out a golden age.

## Arts under the Guptas

The origin of the Gupta family is obscure, but by AD 319 they had established themselves in Magadha, the centre of what had been Ashoka's empire. The finest flowering of the new dynasty was reached during the reign of Chandragupta II (375–415), by which time the Gupta Empire covered much of northern India. The Gupta kings, though tolerant of all religions, were themselves Hindus.

One of the most influential developments of Gupta times was the establishment of new villages on virgin lands. The Hindu priest played an important role. His knowledge of the calendar was vital to an agricultural community, but he also knew about seeds, crops and cattle-breeding, and could work the necessary magic for protection against evils.

The growth of self-supporting villages, with their local Hindu priests, gave Hinduism a decisive advantage over Buddhism. For the Buddhist Church had become so wealthy that no village could afford to support a monastery; and in any case the Buddhist monks were not prepared to give up the comforts of urban living.

The daily life of well-off citizens during the Gupta period is described in the classic book of the period, the *Kamasutra*, or 'Pleasure Manual', as one of considerable luxury. The arts of painting and poetry were widely practised, as was the art of love – which is what the *Kamasutra* is principally about. It was at this period that what has come to be accepted as the Indian view of art was given its final form.

The world's oldest known manual on the arts, the *Vishnudharmottaram*, which dates from Gupta times, describes the types of painting and sculpture suitable for the decoration of palaces, temples and private houses. The most important statement in the work, however, is that sculpture and painting cannot be understood

### DECORATED TEMPLES CARVED IN THE HEARTS OF MOUNTAINS

*Wall-paintings in temple caves in the remote hills of Ajanta, in central India, give a colourful picture of the splendour of life at the court of the Gupta kings round about AD 400. The paintings show Buddha dressed in the trappings of an earthly prince, with kings, queens and holy men as his worshippers. Their richness also indicates the wealth which the Buddhist Church had accumulated, with the support of powerful rulers and merchants. The girl dancers and musicians shown in this detail formed only part of the retinue of* *entertainers who diverted kings and courtiers. The royal household also included troupes of actors, magicians, acrobats and wrestlers. Cave temples were excavated out of rock in many parts of India and are the oldest examples of religious architecture. They stem from an ancient tradition that natural caves were ideal retreats for holy men, and they also provided security in times of anarchy and violence. Many were extremely elaborate imitations of the interiors of free-standing buildings*

without a knowledge of dancing. The classical Indian dance style is essentially a mime, in which postures of the body, gestures of the hands and fingers, even the movements of neck and eyes, represent emotions such as fear and love and, together, narrate a sequence of events. During the Gupta period this body language was transferred to sculpture and painting, so that the poses of statues and of the figures in the wall-paintings which still adorn the caves of Ajanta are immensely theatrical, elements in a dance-drama. It is this sense of harmony, of rhythm and movement, which gives to the art of the Guptas its extraordinary vitality.

Figures of Buddha produced during the Gupta period are among the most impressive of the world's works of art. Expressing mildness, gentleness and great spirituality, they yet give a sense of vast energy lightly controlled. Buddha emerges from the hand of the sculptor as the god who is the origin of all things, half ascetic, half king and wholly noble. The face is majestic, sunk in deep meditation.

Another important and lasting element in Indian art is the erotic. In the 5th century new cults worshipping goddesses began to gain popularity, and both Hinduism and Buddhism were profoundly influenced by them. In both, female counterparts to the male gods appeared. In painting and sculpture, the female form reached a voluptuousness seen in the art of no other civilization.

## Gods on a mountain peak

The Gupta rulers helped to spread Hinduism in the new village settlements. Buddhism and Hinduism had always been antagonistic in philosophy and in action, but in their art and architecture there had been little difference. With royal patronage for Hinduism, things began to change.

The gods were assumed to live on Mount Meru in the Himalayas; the superstructure of the new style of temple was therefore designed to reach like a mountain towards the sky. And under it was the image of the god in a dark cell, the *garbhagriha,* or 'womb house', where the worshipper would be born again in contemplation of the deity. On this simple pattern were to be erected the great monuments of Hindu civilization.

During the Gupta period astronomical studies made great progress. Aryabhata, a 5th-century astronomer, believed that the earth was a sphere which rotated on its axis; this was at a time when in western Europe men were afraid to voyage too far out to sea in case they fell off the edge of the world. The same astronomer put forward the suggestion that the earth moved round the sun, an idea that was treated with scepticism by his contemporaries. Aryabhata also calculated the length of the solar year, using the Indian system of nine digits and the zero; this sequence later passed by way of the Arabs to Europe, where the figures became known as Arabic numerals.

A number of factors brought the golden age of the Guptas to an end. Trade with Rome declined, and in the 6th century the Huns,

# INDIA'S INFLUENCE SPREADS TO OTHER LANDS

Missionaries, traders and colonists spread the culture and religious beliefs of India throughout the mainland and islands of south-east Asia from the 5th century AD onwards. The laws, methods of government, court etiquette and royal regalia of many lands were at one time derived from Hindu India. The court and coronation ceremonial of Thailand still retain their Hindu forms today. Buddhism, and in particular Buddhist art, continued to provide a source of inspiration in other countries for centuries after their influence had waned in India itself. Large colonies of Indian traders, merchants and priests were commonly known as Brahma-desa, from which the word Burma is derived

JUNGLE TEMPLE *The great temple complex of the Khmer kings at Angkor Wat, in the jungle of Cambodia, which was built in the first half of the 12th century, shows the influence of southern Indian architecture in what is one of the outstanding architectural creations of the East. The vast pyramid-like structure, with its five towers reaching towards the sky, represents the sacred mountain of Hindu belief. The whole complex served as a temple for Vishnu and a palace sanctuary for the Khmer rulers, who were believed to be incarnations of the gods*

SHADOW PUPPET *The literature of south-east Asia contains the most lasting of Indian cultural influences. Versions of the great Hindu epics, the* Ramayana *and the* Mahabharata, *are still a source of popular legend. This puppet from Java, where shadow plays retell episodes from these works, represents a character in the Mahabharata. The epics, as well as being heroic tales, hold deep religious meaning. The* Ramayana *relates the experiences of Rama and his wife Sita, during 14 years of exile before he inherits his rightful kingdom. The phrase* Ramayana – *the 'reign of Rama' – is still a synonym for Utopia. The Mahabharata is the world's longest poem, with 100,000 verses*

MASK OF A KING *The kings of the Khmer dynasty of Cambodia were revered by their followers as god-kings – the earthly incarnations of either the Hindu deities Shiva and Vishnu, or the Buddhist Lokeshvara, the 'Lord of the World'. At the temple of the Bayon at Angkor Thom (above), built at the end of the 12th century, huge masks of King Jayavarman VII as Lokeshvara were placed on the four sides of every chapel tower, at the four corners of the city walls and over the gateways at the four points of the compass. They were intended to ensure the radiation of the king's magical powers*

# Rich temple-cities of the later Hindu kingdoms

followed by other nomadic tribes, broke through the passes of the north-west. They destroyed the flourishing Gupta towns, and left impoverished the merchant supporters of Buddhism. The priests came to play an increasingly political and economic role. Propaganda against other religions, particularly Buddhism, increased in viciousness. In the end, Buddha himself was absorbed back into the system he had rebelled against, taking his place in the ranks of the Hindu gods by becoming the ninth incarnation of the god Vishnu.

## The rigidness of caste

The alliance between priests and rulers led to a spate of temple-building, and as the sects of Hinduism became increasingly competitive, temples became more extravagant and their wealth greater. The temple became an immensely powerful institution. It invested some of its wealth in commercial enterprises. It controlled the education of the upper classes. Its patronage, and that of the rulers, produced great works of art and architecture, whose style was transmitted by traders and missionaries to the countries of south-east Asia. But the identification of Hinduism with the upper classes led to rigid caste discrimination.

Originally, each caste had a specific function. The highest, the *brahmin*, was made up of priests and scholars; the second, the *kshatriya*, of rulers and soldiers; the third, the *vaisya*, of herdsmen and, later, merchants; and the fourth, the *sudra*, of servants of the other three. Outside the four castes were the people whose occupations – the removal of dead bodies, or of human excrement, for example, were such that contact with them was considered polluting. These became known as the 'Untouchables'.

There were popular reactions to the caste consciousness of Hinduism. Northern cults of Vishnu or Shiva, emphasising personal worship and the irrelevance of ritual, were spread southwards by travelling preachers and poets. Unlike the priests, the popular preachers excluded no one from religious knowledge. A declaration of love for god was enough. The popularity of the devotional cults was finally recognised by rulers and priests, and a place was made for them in the temples. During the supremacy of rulers known as the Cholas in southern India (about 900–1150), temples ceased to be isolated buildings and became temple-cities; the main structure was surrounded by hundreds of shrines, and pavilions for religious dancing and the reading of sacred literature.

A number of thinkers suggested ways of clearing away the obscurities and inconsistencies of orthodox Hinduism and widening its appeal. The most important of these was a south Indian, Shankaracharya, and the system he taught is known as *Vedanta*. Shankaracharya accepted the Vedas as the fountain of knowledge, but rejected the meaningless ritual that had grown up over the centuries. He maintained that the world we see around us is an illusion, and that reality cannot be known through the human senses. Control of the senses through abstinence could, however, bring glimpses of reality. Another popular religious movement accepted

within the temple precincts also became the inspiration for exquisite sculpture. Known as Tantricism, it was open to all, including women. Tantric practices included magical rituals and the concentration of worship upon a particular deity, usually one of the female partners of the principal gods. Ritual culminated in the taking of the Five M's: *madya* (wine), *matsya* (fish), *mamsa* (meat), *mudra* (grain), and *maithuna* (sexual intercourse).

The appearance of erotic sculpture, usually of a very explicit sort, on such temples as those at Khajuraho (10th–11th centuries) and Konarak (12th century) was probably an attempt by individual rulers to identify their particular states with yet another expression of popular religion.

## Muslim challenge, Hindu response

Arab armies had reached India from the 8th century onwards, but it was not until the beginning of the 13th century that the Muslim invaders finally swept aside the Hindu rulers of the north and set up a new Muslim dominion in the old Hindu heartland. Then, at the beginning of the 14th century, the tide moved south. The Muslims captured the principal cities of south India, but were unable to hold their conquests. Out of the confusion new Hindu powers emerged. Most important was the kingdom of Vijayanagar, which survived until its destruction by the Muslims in 1565.

The style of Vijayanagar was rich and ornate, but around the temples were erected simple open pavilions where pilgrims could

---

### GODS WHO CREATE, PRESERVE AND DESTROY

The Hindu religion early developed a trinity of principal gods: Brahma the creator, Vishnu the preserver, and Shiva the destroyer. Brahma, though considered the greatest of the gods because he created the universe, declined in popularity after the Gupta era and is no longer worshipped; his attributes have largely been absorbed by Vishnu and Shiva

A GOD KNEELS *A painting shows Brahma kneeling humbly before Krishna, a hero-god who was one of the incarnations of Vishnu. Brahma's four heads symbolise his supernatural powers*

MAN'S HELPER *Vishnu is shown as a handsome youth in royal regalia in this bust of the 6th-century Gupta style. He is believed to appear on earth in a different form each time man needs help*

LOVELY CONSORT *The gods had wives who represented aspects of their power. A 10th-century bronze shows Shiva's voluptuous wife Parvati*

rest and buy souvenirs. This idea spread southwards, where the pavilions increased in size, losing their simplicity and becoming in the end one of the most typical and impressive forms of south Indian architecture – the 'Thousand Pillar Halls'.

But the defeat of the last Hindu kingdom in India was also a defeat for the Hindu spirit which, in its surviving strongholds in the extreme south, became more and more inward-looking. The walls of temples were built even higher to deter attackers, and the open courts were roofed over. Interiors were dark and gloomy, and statues were made of dark materials, their grotesque shapes emphasised by the light from flickering oil lamps. The common view of Indians as a god-ridden, pessimistic people springs largely from the image of this style of architecture.

In northern India, the Muslim rulers allowed the Hindu aristocracy to keep their lands, as long as they paid tribute, and the priests to attend to the Hindu rituals. In time, however, there emerged a number of new faiths influenced by both Islam and Hinduism. The most significant was that taught by Nanak (1469–1530), the founder of the Sikh community. His call – 'There is no Hindu, there is no Muslim' – met with an instant response from the artisans of the towns, who were despised and discriminated against by both high-caste Hindus and upper-class Muslims.

Within the framework of Muslim rule, Hinduism took on a new strength. In the 15th and 16th centuries, a wave of popular mysticism

LORD OF THE DANCE *Shiva, as Lord of the Dance, performs the ritual which symbolises the act of creation. In one of his four hands is a small drum, the sound of which signifies creation, and in another hand he holds a flame, the symbol of destruction. They are held at the same level to illustrate the balance between the two. Beneath Shiva's foot lies a dwarf, personifying evil, which is crushed in the dance*

## GIANT HORSEMEN OF A SPLENDID KINGDOM

*The enormous 17th-century temple dedicated to Vishnu at Srirangam, in southern India, is one of the richly ornamented 'Thousand Pillar Halls' which were typical of the sumptuous and ostentatious style of the Hindu kingdom of Vijayanagar. The façade of the main shrine at Srirangam is decorated with huge prancing horsemen, each nearly 9 ft high and carved from single blocks of granite. The figures have no religious significance, and are simply idealised battle scenes. The conquering Muslims left the temples untouched, and later they were fortified to become places of physical as well as mental refuge*

# A new nation forged by the Mughal conquerors

### THE GOD WHO FELL IN LOVE WITH A MILKMAID

*A popular cult based on the god Vishnu, in his incarnation as the cowherd Krishna, swept northern India in the 15th and 16th centuries. This 18th-century painting from Rajputana shows Krishna lingering in a grove with his beloved, the milkmaid Radha – a love*

*which symbolised for Hindus the soul's union with god. The theme is celebrated in thousands of pictures, stories and songs, and was also the subject of plays with which young princes and their concubines whiled away the tedium of days at court*

swept across India. Like earlier devotional cults it was the creation, at least in part, of poets and preachers. The object of devotion was Vishnu in his incarnation as Krishna or Rama, the god of all-embracing love.

The origins of the Krishna cult went back to about the 6th century, when a story described the appearance of Vishnu on earth in order to destroy a tyrant. He was born into a princely family in the city of Mathura in northern India. So that he should not be killed by the tyrant, the child Krishna was handed over to the care of a wealthy cattle owner and spent his boyhood as a cowherd, playing the flute and making love to the milkmaids.

In the early stories Krishna leaves the milkmaids, kills the tyrant, and takes up his rightful position as a prince. But this part of the tale was soon eclipsed by the story of Krishna as the divine lover; his love-making with Radha, his favourite among the milkmaids, was declared to be a symbol of the soul's union with god. Salvation was believed to come through love and praise of Krishna. Paintings by artists inspired by the cult of Krishna are among the masterpieces of Indian art.

### An artificial paradise

In the middle of the 17th century, Shah Jahan, the 5th emperor of the Mughal dynasty, ordered to be inscribed in letters of gold on the marble wall of his palace at Delhi:

'If there is a paradise on earth,
Then this is it, this is it, this is it.'

It was an arrogant claim, but the Mughals – a further wave of Islamic conquerors who established themselves in northern India in the early 16th century – created out of a mixed inheritance of Hindu-Muslim culture not only an imperial art and architecture of great magnificence but a rich and satisfying life style.

Shah Jahan's grandfather, Akbar (1556–1605), was a conqueror who deliberately set out to identify his regime with the conquered, and to create an empire which was neither Muslim not Hindu, but Indian. The Mughal Empire did, in fact, become a national state in the minds of both the Indian aristocracy and the ordinary people. Akbar encouraged the creation of an Indo-Islamic style in architecture and art. In 1571 there began the construction of a new imperial capital at Fatehpur Sikri, 24 miles west of the old capital, Agra. The grandiose conception brought together craftsmen from all parts of his dominions, each contributing local forms and motifs. From the architectural experiments of Fatehpur Sikri, the Mughal style slowly emerged, to reach its highest form in the buildings of Shah Jahan.

The supreme monument of Shah Jahan's reign is the Taj Mahal. It is the symbol of the emperor's love for his wife, Mumtaz Mahal, who died at the age of 39 in giving birth to her fourteenth child. An element of remorse may also have been involved, as Shah Jahan had always insisted that she accompany him on his travels, whatever her condition or state of health. But standing across the river from the fort of Agra, the white-marble Taj is a lasting tribute to the taste of the emperor and the genius of its designers. The building, probably the work of two Persian architects, is subdued and feminine, with a dreamlike purity.

The Mughals were the last great contributors to traditional Indian civilization. The British, spreading inland in the 18th century from a series of coastal trading posts, became successors to the Mughals as the rulers of all India; but they offered British ideas of politics and government, of science and technology. They saw aspects of Hindu society which revolted them, and set about reforming India. The burning of widows, or *suttee*, was stopped; so too was the killing of unwanted female children. The Thugs – bandits who murdered their victims in the name of their religion – were hunted down and suppressed.

Western ideas were absorbed on some levels, as new and alien ways had been absorbed and transformed in the past. But Hindu society on the whole remained as firmly based on tradition as it had been before. The gods remained and continued to be worshipped. But without the patronage of powerful rulers, the arts produced no more golden ages. Indians even forgot that they once had a glorious past.

Ironically it was the British who rediscovered the past for them. At the end of the 18th century, the British – searching for information on traditional law and custom – stumbled upon fragments of India's great literature, and the 19th century saw the translation of many of the great works of sacred Hindu literature – the Vedas, the *Mahabharata* and the *Ramayana*. Archaeology, too, began to reveal the wonders of Indian architecture.

## Unity through Hinduism

In the second half of the 19th century, new Indian political leaders sought to mobilise mass support through an appeal to tradition and history. Many of the new leaders were forward-looking, but to create mass movements they had to support conservative Hindu practices, setting Hindu against Muslim even if this resulted in violence.

It was left to Mahatma Gandhi (1869–1948) to seek a way to ally traditional symbolism with reformist and progressive ideas. He did not fully succeed, but he did demonstrate that such traditional Hindu values as asceticism and non-violence could be related to a modern mass movement and the building of a nation.

Since independence in 1947, the emphasis of government has been upon introducing into Indian society the essential elements of modern technological civilization. Yet traditional India still goes on striving, in many ways successfully, to absorb new ideas. For example, independence has brought an increase in the creation of caste organisations deliberately set up to influence politics to the advantage of their members. Their activities have undoubtedly helped a peasant society to make a success of representative democracy. Once again the institutions of Indian civilization have demonstrated their remarkable capacity for proving relevant to the needs of the times.

### MONUMENT TO AN EMPEROR'S GRIEF

*The superb white marble mausoleum of the Taj Mahal was built on the banks of the River Jumna, near Agra, by the grief-stricken Mughal emperor Shah Jahan (1628–58), in memory of his wife Mumtaz Mahal who died in childbirth at the age of 39. Both their tombs lie inside. Twenty thousand men laboured for 18 years to create the monument, which was completed in 1648. The subdued dignity with which Muslim and Hindu styles are blended in the Taj Mahal make it one of the world's masterpieces of architecture*

# The ageless mystery of China

## FROM 1500 BC

*A civilization founded on the Yellow River more than 3000 years ago has often led the world in arts, science, philosophy, and the skills of government*

To the Chinese, their country has always been the 'Middle Kingdom', the centre of the world and the home of civilization, with only barbarians to the north, west and south. To Westerners, on the other hand, China has traditionally been a land of mystery, far away, little known and often misunderstood. The increasing study in the West of Chinese history, inspired by the modern resurgence of Chinese political power, has made it easier to understand the Chinese people's proud view of the central importance of their own civilization.

In literature and the arts, in science and technology, in philosophy and in the skills of wise and peaceful government, China has, at different times, been far in advance of the rest of the world. Four inventions that were to change the history of the world came from China—paper, printing, gunpowder and the magnetic compass. China's civilization has demonstrated great powers of survival, emerging time after time from periods of foreign domination and displaying a remarkable degree of continuity over more than 3000 years.

The roots of Chinese civilization go back a thousand years earlier still. At a time when the Sumerian city-states were flourishing in Mesopotamia, and Egypt was ruled by the pyramid-building pharaohs, people living along the Hwang-Ho, or Yellow River, and its tributaries were developing agriculture and a settled existence in small villages. They were probably descendants of the prehistoric men whose bones have been found near Peking. They built huts of sticks and mud, and made utensils of painted pottery. As farming techniques improved, food became more plentiful and the population began to increase and spread to other areas of central China.

By about 2000 BC, some of the distinctive features of later Chinese civilization had begun to develop. The silk-worm was domesticated, and jade, China's principal precious stone, was

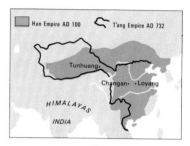

### HAN AND T'ANG CHINA

*Two great peaks of expansion were reached six centuries apart under the powerful Han and T'ang dynasties*

### WALL TO REPEL INVADERS

*The size of the Great Wall of China makes it the only man-made structure which, it is said, can be seen from the moon. The Great Wall was constructed in the 3rd century BC by the Ch'in emperor Shih Huang Ti to repel barbarian tribesmen raiding his northern provinces. Forced labour was used to join together a series of earlier walls to reach a total length of 1500 miles. This artist's reconstruction shows the wall in AD 1368, when it was extensively repaired. It is 25 ft thick at the base, tapering to 15 ft at the top, and its height varies between 20 ft and 30 ft as it follows the contours of the country across mountains, gorges and plains. The wall was patrolled by watchmen who could summon troops by lighting beacons from numerous towers along it*

## SKILL OF THE CHINESE CRAFTSMEN IN JADE AND SILK

Two skills in which craftsmen in China excelled come together in this 300-year-old jade screen showing women weaving silk yarn into cloth. Silk-worms were domesticated in China 4000 years ago, and silk-weaving machinery was in use by 100 BC—some 1200 years before it reached Europe. At one time the Chinese used bolts of silk instead of money, and the prized fabrics passed to the Western world along the famous 'silk route' across Asia. Jade was treasured in China as a symbol of supreme excellence, similar to gold in the Western world. Artists were carving jade before 2000 BC; at first they made only small, ritual objects, but in later centuries craftsmen mastered the technique of carving large pieces. Jade was also used increasingly for everyday articles such as screens and chopsticks

169

# Confucius, the philosopher who put ability before rank

carved into rings and miniature axes, which were placed in graves for the use of the dead. There is evidence, too, of ancestor-worship, the oldest and most deep-rooted of all Chinese religious practices. Soothsayers divined the future by 'oracle-bones'. These were animal bones in which cracks were produced by applying a heated bronze point; the soothsayers then studied the cracks to interpret the will of the gods and to foretell future events.

## Bronze vessels of the Shang

Chinese history begins to emerge from the shadows in about 1500 BC, under a dynasty of rulers known as the Shang. Some settlements of this period were sizeable towns, in which the simple peasant culture had given way to a more complex society, with people specialising in various trades and crafts. The Shang capital of Anyang, on the north China plain, was excavated between 1927 and 1936. Evidence was found of human sacrifice, and among the artistic finds were a number of bronze ritual vessels used by the king and the aristocrats for offering food and wine to the spirits of their ancestors. Powerfully shaped, and decorated with vigorous animal motifs, they suggest an age of strong religious feeling.

Inscriptions on ritual bronzes and oracle-bones show that the Chinese had a distinctive script as early as the Shang period. This script was once thought to have been derived from ancient Sumerian or Egyptian writing, but it is now believed to have originated independently in China. The characters of the Chinese script originated as pictures, and these show the genius for vivid and economical line-drawing that later distinguished Chinese painting.

A language expressed only in pictures is a clumsy means of recording speech, especially to communicate abstract ideas, but the Chinese showed considerable ingenuity in developing devices to represent such concepts. 'Bright' is represented by a picture of sun and moon, 'east' by the sun behind a tree, 'to have dealings with' by a picture of a man sitting down cross-legged on the ground.

Even in ancient times the great majority of characters already contained elements used to indicate the pronunciation rather than the meaning of the character—as though, in English, pictures of an eye and a saw were to be used to form a character indicating the statement 'I saw'. In ancient times books and documents were generally written on slips of wood or bamboo, which were tied together. Silk was also sometimes used to write on.

Around 1100 BC the Shang dynasty was overthrown. Its conquerors came from the valley of the River Wei, a tributary of the Yellow River, and they founded the Chou dynasty which lasted for about eight centuries. The Chou period made a lasting contribution to Chinese history by its particularly brilliant flowering in philosophy—the study of the meaning of life and the right way to live. So many rival theories flourished that they became known as the 'hundred schools'. Many philosophers were wandering teachers who earned their livelihood travelling from one feudal court to another, advising the warring rulers on moral questions and on the prudent handling of political affairs.

## Tutors in paternal rule

The most influential of these philosophers was K'ung Fu-tzu, or Confucius, who lived from 551 to 479 BC. His teaching was developed by his most famous follower Meng-tzu, or Mencius (390–305 BC). The familiar Latinised versions of the philosophers' names were introduced some 2000 years after their deaths by the Jesuit missionaries to China, who often wrote in Latin. Confucius and Mencius both stressed the advantages of humane government over rule by force, and founded a lasting Chinese tradition that a ruler and his officials should regard themselves as 'father and mother' of the people entrusted to their care.

The Confucians also maintained that all human beings had unlimited potential, and that men should be promoted on grounds of ability rather than birth. This established the principle of the career open to talent, which soon inspired the appointment of civil servants through competitive examinations—another

ADVICE FOR THE EMPEROR *The Han emperor Wu calls on a scholar to seek his views on the government, in this painting by an unknown Chinese artist. High offices of state were filled by learned men who had won honours in competitive examinations, and it was a part of Confucian belief that they should not be at the beck and call of their rulers*

## AN AGE OF PROSPERITY

The four centuries of the Han dynasty, from 206 BC to AD 220, included long periods of stability and prosperity on which later generations of Chinese looked back as a 'golden age'. China's armies added vast new territories to the empire, which was unified under one ruler. Trade routes to the West were opened up, and the export of Chinese silk brought rich profits. Confucianism became the dominant philosophy; its teachings stressed the advantages of humane government over rule by force, and founded a lasting tradition that rulers and officials should act in a paternal way towards their subjects.

The Han empire was administered by a huge but efficient civil service, drawn from an elite schooled in Confucianism. Scholarship flourished: histories were compiled, while the Confucian classics were deeply studied and commentaries written to explain them. It was a time, too, of invention: the Han Chinese used a compass to select auspicious sites for building, and astronomical instruments to predict eclipses. They also learnt how to make paper from tree bark, hemp and old rags, to supplement the strips of bamboo or silk cloth on which messages had been written

HOME FOR THE DEAD *The pagoda has an ancient history in China, as this painted pottery model of a Han manor house shows. Model houses were buried with the dead to give them homes in the after-life*

enduring feature of Chinese government through the ages. Another important element in Confucian tradition was the theory that the basic justification of the ruler's power was the Mandate of Heaven, which he forfeited if he were guilty of unkingly behaviour. Rebellion against an evil sovereign and the overthrow of a corrupt dynasty could therefore be justified.

Confucian writings laid great emphasis on such virtues as loyalty, good faith, and respect for parents, particularly for the father. Moral principles were taught primarily for their value in maintaining good order, not because they were God's command; even the Confucian insistence on the importance of ritual and ceremony, which has left a deep mark on Chinese civilization, was concerned above all with the ordinary politeness of social and family life, and with proper conduct in public.

## Religion of 'the Way'

A second development in Chinese thought was the philosophy of the Tao, 'the Way', usually attributed to Lao-tse. Taoists maintained that there was no such thing as absolute right or wrong; they rebelled against the artificiality of society, and sought a return to the Way of Nature. From the viewpoint of the Tao, everything in the world has its own natural role, and so people should 'embrace the myriad things' and not judge between them. To the Taoist, the craftsman who naturally and

BURIAL GARB *These jade and gold funeral vestments were made for Liu Sheng, a prince of the Han dynasty who died in 113 BC. His tomb lay undiscovered for 2000 years until Chinese soldiers found it in 1968*

### BUDDHISM TRANSFORMS CHINESE CULTURE

*The expansion which took place under the Han dynasty brought the Buddhist regions of central Asia into the Chinese Empire, and when the religion took root in China itself it gave sculptors and metal-workers new subjects to portray. This gilded bronze shrine depicts Gautama Buddha (left), the founder of Buddhism, conversing with Prabhutaratna, one of the mystical Buddhas of the past. Buddhism developed in China alongside Confucianism and Taoism. It was particularly encouraged by the non-Chinese rulers who occupied the northern half of the country in the 4th and 5th centuries; by adopting an imported religion they hoped to avoid being submerged by traditional Chinese culture. Buddhist shrines and temples dotted the country, and artists honoured Buddha both in miniatures and in colossal statues*

# An epoch of invention and a new faith

unthinkingly exercises his skill is nearer to the truth than the intellectual who spoils primitive simplicity by making judgments.

All Taoist arguments led ultimately to the goal of a mystical experience which would bring a person into harmony with nature. Taoist ideals stimulated a love of nature in painters and poets, and inspired many Chinese to withdraw from society in search of philosophical insight, wisdom, or simply peace of mind. Taoist ideals were in direct contrast to the teachings of Confucianism, which was the creed of authority and of the established order of society.

## A Chinese empire

The feudal states which acknowledged Chou leadership gradually assumed independence and fought amongst each other, especially in the 'Warring States' period from 403 to 221 BC. Finally China was reunited by the powerful state of Ch'in which, like the Chou, came from the Wei River valley, a natural stronghold surrounded by mountains. The Ch'in state was dominated by a so-called 'Legalist' school of hard-headed thinkers who rejected Confucian morality in favour of a stern system of rewards and punishments. The ruler, they held, must not rely on moral exhortation but must reward behaviour that helped to sustain the state and punish whatever did not.

The Ch'in state had control of an area approaching that of China today, and the founder of the new dynasty took the title of Ch'in Shih Huang Ti ('first emperor of the Ch'in'). But his empire was menaced from beyond its borders by barbarian tribes, such as the Hsiungnu, ancestors of the Huns. For these nomadic horsemen, plunder and warfare were a way of life. Erupting from the heartlands of central

Asia, they set off mass movements of refugee peoples that were eventually to topple the Roman Empire. China's response to the barbarian threat was to try to keep the nomads out, by building a massive wall across its mountainous northern frontier.

Shih Huang Ti linked and strengthened various lengths of wall which the northern states had already built, and eventually the Great Wall stretched for 1500 miles. In later centuries it was much altered and rebuilt, and in its present form it is largely the work of the Ming dynasty (1368–1644).

The Ch'in dynasty survived the death of its founder by only a few years, and in 206 BC a new dynasty, the Han, seized power. The triumph of Confucianism was completed when the huge and prosperous empire of Han China was governed by means of an elite schooled in the Confucian literature and selected through examination. The great prestige of the Han dynasty, and the chaos that followed it, made the Confucian system a model of lost excellence to which future generations would look back with nostalgia. Until modern times the Chinese often referred to themselves as 'men of Han', and Confucius himself became a kind of patron saint, revered by the scholar class throughout Chinese imperial history.

The Chinese have always been deeply interested in their past, and have regarded historical writing as a guide to present conduct. As early as the Chou period, the feudal states had kept records of the main events in their history, but the first great historian was Ssu-ma Ch'ien, who lived during a great period of expansion under Emperor Wu (141-87 BC) and compiled a complete history down to his own times. In this enormous work he demonstrated a con-

scientious regard for accuracy and soundness. Ssu-ma's arrangement of his material shows an appreciation of the many aspects of history: he included a biographical section, and accounts of various government matters such as ritual, the calendar and economic affairs. This arrangement became a permanent feature of the dynastic histories, the first of which was *The History of the Former Han Dynasty*, compiled by Pan Ku, who lived in the 1st century AD. In later times the dynastic histories were composed by teams of scholars under official auspices, using material collected in the course of the previous dynasty.

Chinese history writing was subject to some distortion, since the doctrine of the Mandate of Heaven meant that dynastic founders were invariably praised and the characters of those who had lost the imperial throne were blackened. Nevertheless, no other people has made throughout its history such a sustained and systematic attempt to record its past.

## Makers of the first paper

One of China's great gifts to the world was the invention of paper, originally made from tree bark, hemp, old rags and fishing nets. It was traditionally said to have been invented in AD 105; but not until 751, when some Chinese papermakers were captured by Arabs at a battle in central Asia, did the secret come to western Asia and thence to Europe.

Magnetism was also known to the Chinese long before it was understood by anyone else, and the compass was in use 2000 years ago. At that time, though, it was used to select auspicious sites for buildings and tombs; another thousand years were to pass before it became a navigational aid. Many other Chinese inventions were to have far-reaching

**PLEASURES AT COURT**

*Music was a popular feature of life at the royal palace in Changan during the golden age of T'ang China. A convivial party is vividly portrayed in this 10th-century painting. The artist has an eye for the detail of contemporary musical instruments, the delicate robes, and the furniture – including the chairs, which were developed in China during the T'ang period. Even the pug-dog under the table is painted with an individuality of its own*

effects. In warfare an important early invention was the stirrup, seen on tomb-figurines of about AD 300. By giving the rider more control over his steed, stirrups guaranteed the military supremacy of cavalry for centuries to come. The Chinese mastered the technique of making cast iron 1800 years before the process was known in Europe, and the first weapons and tools of cast iron, dating from the 4th century BC, have been found in China. After breeding silk-worms since earliest times, the Chinese also pioneered textile machinery. The wheelbarrow appeared in China in the 1st century AD, 1200 years before it was used in Europe.

## Buddhism, the 'third doctrine'

A third distinctive development in Chinese thought, in addition to Confucianism and Taoism, was Buddhism, which originated in India with the teaching of Gautama Buddha (560–480 BC). Buddha taught that the suffering and pain of this world can be overcome by renouncing all worldly desires, because such desires are the cause of suffering; eventually the devout Buddhist may hope to reach Nirvana, a final state of bliss or non-existence reached only by the most devout, and after many lifetimes. Reincarnation is a crucial Buddhist belief, and each life is seen as part of the constant struggle towards perfection.

Buddhism spread through south and east Asia at about the same time that Christianity was spreading through Europe. Both were alien faiths from distant countries, and both were to transform the regions into which they spread. But in China Buddhism did not supplant existing beliefs; Confucianism, Taoism, and Buddhism became known as the 'Three Doctrines', and they were to intermingle and co-exist in China for the next 2000 years.

## THE SISTER ARTS OF WRITING AND PAINTING

Writing and painting were regarded as sister arts in ancient China, and the same brush and ink were used for both. Writing was held to be the superior art, however, since the Chinese have a deep respect for the written word, and a man's writing is thought to give unique evidence of his learning and moral worth. Consequently artists often used poems as part of their paintings. The brush strokes used to write the characters of the verses are in perfect harmony with the lines used in painting the pictures which accompany them

BAMBOO PAINTINGS *The similarity between painting and writing is most evident in the economical brush strokes used to depict the bamboo plant, a favourite subject among Chinese artists. This painting and its accompanying poem are from a hand-scroll by the 16th-century artist Hsu Wei*

The Museum of Fine Arts, Boston

FATHER OF WRITING *The invention of Chinese writing is traditionally attributed to Fu Hsi, a legendary emperor who is said to have ruled nearly 5000 years ago. He is seen in this 13th-century painting as the inventor of the eight symbols (bottom left) used in foretelling the future. These symbols, based on the markings of a tortoise shell, were thought to be the basis of Chinese writing*

WRITER AT WORK *The writer in this 11th-century portrait (far left) works with his hand clear of the paper and holds the brush with a distinctive grip at right angles to it. Many of the tools of his trade, such as the brush with a porcelain handle (left) were works of art in themselves*

## TRADERS FROM FAR-OFF LANDS

*The alien clothing and features of the traders with a bullock cart on this glazed T'ang pottery figure show that foreign merchants were a familiar sight in the cities of ancient China. As early as 100 BC, in Han times, trade routes had been established westwards across central Asia, and Chinese silks were prized as far afield as ancient Rome. The T'ang rulers further extended Chinese influence and their capital, Changan, situated at the end of a great transcontinental trade route, grew to become the largest city in the world. Thousands of foreign merchants lived in Changan and in other Chinese cities; Canton had a large colony of Persian and Arab merchants who traded with their own lands*

# Arts flourish as the empire expands

People did not follow one doctrine exclusively; their religious beliefs and practices generally owed something to all three. But as a religion of compassion which held out hope of reward in a future life, Buddhism had a wide effect among the mass of the people.

## The great age of T'ang

After a long period of decline, the Han dynasty collapsed in AD 220, and for most of the next 400 years China was split up between a number of short-lived regimes. But in 618 the T'ang dynasty was founded, and there began one of the greatest periods in all Chinese history. Trade grew and developed, prosperity returned, and the arts of civilized life began to flourish as never before.

The capital, Changan (present-day Sian), was a square-walled city criss-crossed by imposing tree-lined streets. The blocks into which it was divided were separately walled, with gates closed at night. The city contained over a million people, making it the largest in the world at the time. Many inhabitants came from distant parts of Asia, bringing their own religions and customs and the exotic products of their own countries.

Art and music were influenced by foreign styles and motifs, and the result was a truly cosmopolitan culture. Pilgrims who travelled to India in search of Buddhist texts brought back valuable accounts of remote regions, which stimulated the Chinese imagination. Exotic imports from the tropical lands to the south—fine woods for furniture, gems and scents and spices, strange new foods—enriched the everyday lives of the well-to-do families. Tea became a popular alternative to the traditional wine made from rice or millet.

People began to sit on chairs instead of mats, the Chinese being the only Far Eastern people to use chairs before modern times. When chairs came into use, other furniture had to be designed to match. Dress also changed, since it was no longer necessary to wear what was seemly or comfortable for sitting on the floor, like the *kimono* still worn by the Japanese.

## Poet of the mountains

The T'ang dynasty was the golden age of lyric verse, and the fame of such poets as Li Po and Po Chü-i has spread to the English-speaking world, especially through translations into English by the late Arthur Waley. Li Po (701–62) was a Taoist who lived much among the mountains. His poems reflect his love of the wilderness and his sadness at the fleeting nature of human joys. Too fond of drink, however, to be entrusted with responsibility, he had no public career and never took the civil service examinations.

Po Chü-i (772–846), on the other hand, was a prominent civil servant who composed important official correspondence. A devout Buddhist, whose poetry was full of compassion and concern for the poor, he thought it was the poet's duty to influence public affairs. By this time literary ability was the chief route to a distinguished career in the public service,

and skill in writing poetry was an essential accomplishment of the civilized man. Po's poems were easy to understand, and his ballads were learnt and repeated by ordinary people.

Most Chinese verse is very difficult to translate, because it is full of allusions which cannot be understood without a deep knowledge of Chinese history and literature. Furthermore, no other language can convey without extreme artificiality the complicated rhyme-schemes and skilful parallelisms between couplets, which are a feature of the original Chinese. Yet the writing of poetry was such a natural occupation that much of it was written to celebrate trivial social occasions, with no epic or dramatic themes. The dominant moods of the verses are gentle nostalgia, love of nature and the joys of friendship.

## Buddhas in rock

In China, unlike Greece and Rome, there are no architectural remains surviving from antiquity, since wood rather than stone was generally used for building. But monuments to Buddha still exist in the form of colossal figures hewn out of the rock-face at such sites as Yunkang and Lungmen. The statues at Yunkang, in the extreme north, were carved in the late 5th century to show repentance for a recent persecution of the Buddhist faith, and at the same time to provide a splendid example of imperial patronage.

The oasis city of Tunhuang on the central Asian trade-routes was an important Buddhist centre. Near by there are hundreds of cave-chapels decorated with wall-paintings dating from the 5th to 8th centuries. Some illustrate Buddhist legends, and others show scenes of paradise. In 1900 a great Buddhist library was found, unopened since it was sealed up in 1035 to save it from raiding Tibetans. The dry climate had preserved thousands of manuscripts, including Buddhist texts and works of popular literature, and many painted silk banners.

In the T'ang period the great tradition of Chinese landscape painting was beginning. In his landscapes the artist sought a perfect understanding and representation of the forces of nature. Human beings were often depicted as tiny figures by contrast with the majesty of mountain and lake; this reflected the Taoist conception of the insignificance of man by contrast with the universal Tao. Painting and writing were closely related, and the same brush that had long been used for painting pictures had also by now become the instrument for writing.

Artists normally painted on silk, on vertical or horizontal scrolls. Some horizontal scrolls were very long, and this gave an added dimension to the appreciation of a picture: as it was slowly unrolled, the spectator felt the sensation of movement through the landscape.

The early T'ang rulers expanded their empire by force of arms; but this meant giving considerable power to military leaders, and after a rebellion by a military governor in 755 the state began to disintegrate into a number of small kingdoms. A new dynasty, the Sung,

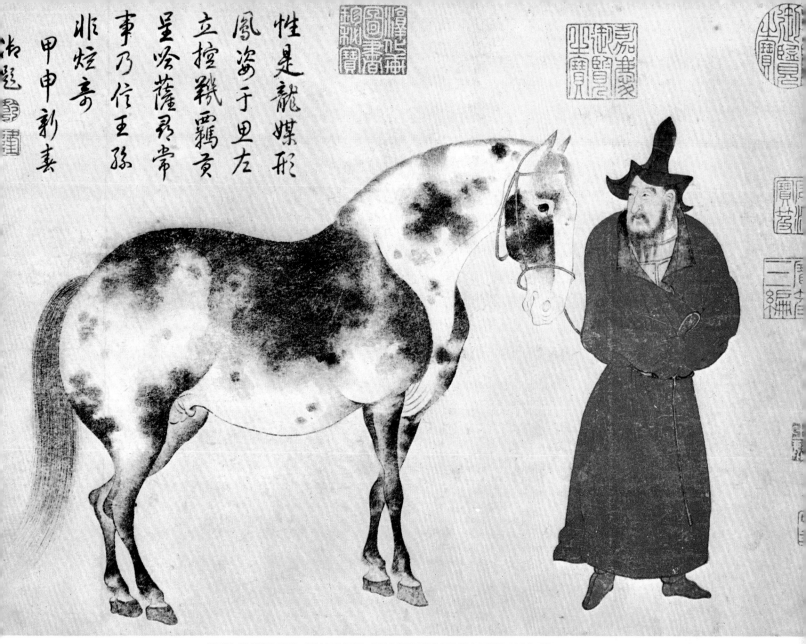

性是龍媒形
鳳姿于里左
立控鞚靈貢
呈咬薩羅常
事乃信王孫
非烷奇
甲申新春
治題書

THE MONGOLS, WARRIOR HORSEMEN FROM THE NORTH

*Fierce Mongol horsemen swept through China to occupy the whole country by 1279, and ruled for nearly a century. The new masters were fond of horse paintings, and this picture, painted in 1347, shows a Mongol groom leading a dappled mount.*

*In spite of the Great Wall built across China's northern frontier, the Chinese were always vulnerable to attack from the nomadic horsemen who lived in the steppes beyond it, and for long periods northern China was under foreign domination*

became established in 960 and set out to re-unify the country. The Sung rulers renounced the military virtues and bought peace by paying tribute to the northern barbarians. To make their administration more efficient, the Sung placed it firmly in the hands of bureaucrats who had entered government through the civil service examinations.

The idea behind the examinations was that a thorough grounding in the Confucian classics would produce men of virtue who were well fitted to govern. Consequently, practical topics played little part in the Chinese examination system. Soon the country became so used to the bureaucratic system that men even began to consider the gods as forming a civil service of their own. Indeed, minor deities were thought of as being subordinate to the emperor, who could promote or demote them, and worthy human beings, after their deaths, were selected to fill celestial appointments.

The great increase in learning during the Sung period was made easier by the use of printing, which for the first time became widespread. Its origin lay in the Chinese skill in carving jade and other hard stones, from which had

developed the practice of carving characters on seals for use in stamping documents. By the time of the Han dynasty, in the 2nd century AD, an official edition of the Confucian classics was engraved on stone tablets under the direction of the government. Copies of these tablets were taken by ink squeezes, a laborious process resembling brass-rubbing.

It was soon realised that carvings could be reproduced many times if ink were applied to them and paper pressed against the wet ink. The carvings had simply to be inked afresh for each copy. Writing and drawing is, of course, reversed when printed in this way, so everything had to be specially cut back-to-front before it could be printed.

## The first printed book

The art of printing from wooden blocks carved with the characters in reverse developed first in Buddhist monasteries, and the oldest surviving printed book that can be reliably dated is a Buddhist text, the *Diamond Sutra*, made in China in AD 868. Buddhist proficiency in this craft arose from the belief that the mere repetition of prayers had great religious value,

so that a device for reproducing large numbers of small charms and spells would be a means of acquiring a great store of merit.

In the 10th century, wood blocks were first used for printing the Confucian classics, a much easier and more productive process than the old ink squeezes. But although one of China's greatest and most revolutionary inventions was by now well established, its value was not universally recognised. On the contrary, printing was regarded as a cheap and makeshift expedient, very inferior to the dignified engraving on stone of Confucian tradition.

However, the development of printing continued. The next step was the invention of movable type—a mass of small wooden blocks, one for each character, arranged in position and clamped together. With this refinement, a new set of blocks did not need to be carved for each new book: the characters on the blocks could be re-arranged in new combinations, and so used over and over again. The invention turned out to be less useful for printing Chinese characters than it was to prove for the alphabetical languages of the West. There are thousands of Chinese characters for the printer

# Mongol rule opens a way to the West

to file, not just 26, so that re-use of individual blocks is hindered by the difficulty of finding the right one. Even so, movable type was developed in China in the 11th century, 400 years before it reached the West. The first time it was extensively used anywhere in the world was in Korea, soon after 1400.

The first capital of the Sung dynasty in 960 was Kaifeng, which owed its importance to its key position on the canal which linked the Yellow River with the east-coast city of Hangchow. An administrative and commercial city and a military stronghold, Kaifeng also developed into a great manufacturing centre. Textiles, metalwork and porcelain were among its most important products, while the coal and iron industries reached a peak of production which was not to be surpassed anywhere until modern times. Coal had been in use since the 4th century, soon after the founding of the city, and by the time of the Sung it had begun to replace charcoal as a means of domestic heating and cooking. Iron was used for agricultural implements, bridges, gates, pagodas, Buddhist images, weapons and ships.

## City of a million people

When in 1126 barbarian invaders known as the Jurched drove the Sung court to take refuge in the south, it eventually settled at Hangchow. This city flourished so vigorously under the Sung that within a century it was the richest and most populous city in the world, with a population in 1275 of over a million. Chinese houses were generally single-storey structures built round courtyards, but in Hangchow dwellings several storeys high were constructed to accommodate the crowded population. Canals formed the main thoroughfares. Shops sold luxury goods from all over the known world, while outside the city the people could stroll in the gardens beside a famous beauty spot called the West Lake.

Within the city there were taverns, restaurants, tea-houses, and singing-girl establishments. There were all kinds of theatrical and musical entertainments, together with acrobats, story-tellers, jugglers and wrestlers. Chinese culture was changing, now that its focal point had moved from the cold, windswept north to the milder south, where people could spend much more of their lives in the open air. The old aristocratic and exclusive style was being replaced by a more varied society, which the new prominence of commerce and the pleasures of the city crowds did much to shape.

Among the finest products of the Sung period were its superb pottery and porcelain, some of the finest ever made in its perfection of form, beauty of glaze, and taste and simplicity of decoration. The spread of printing and literacy, and the elevation of civilian rather than military virtues, led to an increased interest in scholarly pursuits. The typical Sung man of letters was an all-rounder like Ou Yang-hsiu, who played a part in literature, philosophy and archaeology, and also won distinction as historian, poet and statesman. He had wine, music and a form of chess called *wei-ch'i* to

amuse him during his leisure hours. The refinement of the Sung period lasted for 300 years before it was shattered by the brutality of Mongol invaders. Their career of conquest was started by Genghis Khan, and after supplanting the Jurched in northern China they completed the occupation of the whole country by 1279.

At first the Mongols abolished the well-tried Chinese methods of administration and tried to rule according to their own traditions. Gradually they learnt to accept the methods of the superior civilization, although they continued to place themselves and their foreign allies in the higher ranks of government. The famous Kublai Khan (1216–94) ruler of the Mongols in Marco Polo's time, moved the capital from Karakorum to Peking. In 1315 the Mongols restored the Confucian civil service examinations, and some of the later Mongol emperors were deeply imbued with Chinese culture.

The journeys of the Venetian Marco Polo and the various European missionaries who reached the Mongol court from the late 13th century onwards were remarkable events in the history of human exploration; but China's contacts with the Arab world were much closer, with a flourishing trade both by land and by sea. It was during this period that many Chinese technological achievements, including printing and gunpowder, made their way westwards. As early as the 9th century the Chinese had first made an explosive by mixing potassium nitrate, charcoal and sulphur. At first gunpowder was used only in firework displays; but later the Chinese used it for a wide range of weapons, including bombs, grenades, flame-throwers, rockets and guns.

The heavily outnumbered Mongols finally succumbed to a rebel force, which inaugurated a native dynasty, the Ming, in 1368. Many of the Mongols stayed in China, mainly serving in the army, and the Ming followed the Mongol practice of making the military career and other important occupations hereditary.

## Skill in seamanship

The use of waterborne transport had been important to the Chinese since earliest times, and under the T'ang the canal system had helped to secure the unity and prosperity of the country. Later, when the loss of the north to the barbarians put an end to commerce with central Asia, the Sung with their capital at Hangchow had to develop overseas commerce as a means to prosperity, and the government organised a coastguard and convoy system to protect merchantmen from pirates.

Some important developments in naval technology were due to the Chinese. They invented the stern-post rudder, which appears on a pottery model of a boat dating from the 1st century AD; they introduced the principle of watertight compartments, which made a vessel's hull less vulnerable; and they pioneered paddle-wheel propulsion, descriptions of which date from the 5th century AD. In the early Ming period naval power was built up, and fleets voyaged to the East Indies, southern India, the Persian Gulf, the Red Sea, and the

coast of East Africa, as far south as Kenya. The fleets were composed of huge junks, sometimes over 400 ft long and having four decks. The leading Chinese admiral was Cheng Ho, a eunuch. The imperial palace was generally staffed with eunuchs, and they were often chosen to lead important expeditions to emphasise that the missions came from the emperor personally. These missions served to demonstrate China's wealth and strength throughout the known world, and to reassert its position as the greatest power in the East.

In 1421 the Ming emperor Yung-lo moved his capital from Nanking to Peking, where he greatly expanded the city that had been used as the seat of government by Kublai Khan and his Mongol successors. Modern Peking is Ming in origin, and many of its important buildings have since been rebuilt or restored to the original designs. The city is built on a chess-board pattern, with its roads running due north-south and east-west. The old houses are grey, single-storey structures built round courtyards, which often contain trees and shrubs, while the centre of Peking is occupied by the old imperial palace, with its three great halls of state, within an oblong of vermilion

THE LOVERS *Polo blamed the subjection of the southern Chinese to Mongol rule on the fact that they were 'anything rather than warriors; all their delight was in women, and nought but women'. A detail from a 17th-century painting shows Ts'ui Ying-ying, heroine of a famous romantic drama, with her lover, while her maid acts as chaperone. Each city had large numbers of courtesans—'a multitude of sinful women', according to Polo, who was shocked by the licentiousness he found. Wealthy men kept concubines, and although they did not have the status of a principal wife, their children had the same rights as legitimate offspring*

BEAUTY SPOT *Outside the great city of Hangchow was a famous beauty spot, the West Lake. The boats in this 13th-century picture appear just as Polo describes them: 'Roofed over with decks on which men stand with poles, which they thrust into the bottom of the lake and thus propel the barges where they are bidden.' He recounts the feasts and entertainments held in the boats and the palatial restaurants on the islands in the lake, and found what he saw even more delightful than his native Venice. A voyage on the lake 'offers more refreshment and delectation than any other experience on earth', he declared*

THE GREAT KHAN *Marco Polo served in the administration of Kublai Khan, seen here in a 13th-century portrait. The Mongol rulers preferred to employ foreigners rather than Chinese in government posts, but they were segregated so completely from the local population that, even after 17 years in China, Polo still knew little of the language. Polo was deeply impressed by Kublai Khan—the 'greatest lord that is now in the world, or ever has been'—and by the magnificence of his great palaces at Peking and Shang-tu*

walls. Other notable buildings that survive from the Ming period are the three-tiered marble Altar of Heaven and the so-called Temple of Heaven near by. Here the emperor, the Son of Heaven, made his annual sacrifice to Heaven at the winter solstice, an important part of traditional state ritual. To the north-west of the capital are the tombs of the 13 Ming emperors who reigned at Peking. Each has its own enormous burial mound, set in a spacious walled compound. One tomb was excavated in 1958, and the stone-lined vaults were found to contain priceless treasures of gold, jade, silk and porcelain.

## Advice from the Jesuits

The Portuguese, who had trading settlements in India, had taken back to Lisbon samples of Chinese porcelain and silks. After the capture of Malacca in 1511, they explored routes to south China. Commercial and missionary contacts gradually developed, but it was not until the end of the century that a Jesuit mission was established by Matteo Ricci.

The Jesuits advised the emperors on astronomy, mathematics and other technical matters. But they made relatively few converts, and at this stage the impact of the West on China was much less than the influence of Jesuit accounts of China on European intellectual history. From these accounts the West learnt how Chinese society was 'governed by philosophers', and how Chinese emperors lived in huge palaces and had thousands of eunuchs and concubines to minister to their needs. The elegance of court life stimulated a demand for luxury goods, so that the palace workshops and imperial factories turned out large quantities of fine porcelain, jades, ivories, lacquerware, silk robes and furniture. Rich families competed to lavish their wealth on their houses, libraries and gardens.

The ancient crafts continued to flourish. Jade-carving, for example, had developed through the centuries, and craftsmen could now carve large vessels and realistic human and animal forms. Although in antiquity jade had been much used for ritual objects, in later times it was increasingly used for everyday articles such as jewellery, dress accessories, tableware and chopsticks. In his study the Confucian gentleman would use brush-pots, brush-rests, and seals made of jade, which he prized not only for its beauty but also because it had been revered in antiquity. In China, jade has always been a symbol, or standard, of supreme excellence, much as gold has been in the West. Chinese jade, furniture, lacquerware and ivories have all been admired in Europe, but porcelain has been especially associated with the name of China (hence the word *china* as a name for the material). In the late Ming and Ch'ing periods huge quantities were exported to Europe and other parts of the world. Ming blue and white wares were copied in Japan, Indo-China and Persia, and inspired European potters at Delft and elsewhere, although it was not until 1708 that Europeans understood how to make porcelain themselves. The cult of *chinoiserie* greatly influenced European taste in the 17th and 18th centuries, culminating in the popularity of the famous 'willow pattern' design—which is English in origin, not Chinese, and dates from 1780.

## Novels for the people

Literature in China had been traditionally confined to classics, history, philosophy, poetry, essays and similar works. These were written in a classical language which, though no longer spoken, was regarded as the only proper medium for literature. Some novels and short stories were, however, written in the language of everyday speech. Their origin lay in an

# *Ancient tradition and Cultural Revolution*

**A FATHER AND HIS FAMILY**

*Blood ties have traditionally been strong in China, with the family playing a major role; ancestor-worship is the oldest of all Chinese religious practices. This portrait on silk shows a prosperous family of 15th-century Ming times. A father held his sons in total subjection, and his daughters married early, after which they came under the absolute rule of their mother-in-law. The Chinese were the first to use surnames and hand them down, chiefly to symbolise continuance of a family line through sons*

ancient story-telling tradition, which played an important part in a society with a low level of literacy. Many of the stories were written to spread Buddhist teachings. In Mongol times some intellectuals began to compose written works based on these traditional story-cycles, and from the 16th century they also began to write original novels in Chinese for readers who were not interested in the 'highbrow' literature of the scholars. The most famous such novel is *Hung-lou Meng (Red Chamber Dream)*, the story of a great house in decline after it loses the emperor's favour. It is perhaps the only Chinese novel that approaches the finest fiction writing of the West.

## Arts under the Manchus

Following an apparently inevitable pattern, the Ming provoked unrest and internal rebellion before succumbing in 1644 to foreign invasion. This time, the conquerors were the Manchus on China's north-east frontier, descendants of the Jurched who had conquered northern China in the 12th century. Once the Manchus had established their Ch'ing dynasty, China enjoyed a period of high prosperity.

The individual scholar-aesthete was concerned to define and preserve whatever was best in the artistic and literary tradition. As a spare-time painter he followed the old masters, and as a connoisseur he collected ancient bronzes, or rubbings of famous inscriptions and reliefs. Just as his non-practical and non-specialist education in the Confucian classics was intended to make him morally fit to govern, so the same amateurism prevailed in his leisure activities. The Manchu emperor Ch'ien-lung was an admirer of Chinese culture, and a supreme example of the scholar-aesthete.

The wealthy families could enjoy these aesthetic pleasures and also secure the education that enabled them to become officials – or mandarins, as they were later known. But they seldom maintained their status for more than a few generations. For social pressures forced them to spend a fortune on their libraries and art collections, in accordance with their position in society, and many families were impoverished in the process.

## 'Devils from the ocean'

Until the early 19th century the Chinese could not compare their culture with that of other major civilizations, since they knew very little about the outside world. The European nations were referred to as 'devils from the ocean' and classed with the pirates who harassed the coasts. The Chinese felt themselves to be self-sufficient both in their ideals and in material things. The Confucian philosophy was regarded as a system of universal truth, and their vast domains provided for all their worldly needs. Other peoples, such as the Japanese, Koreans and Manchus, had absorbed Chinese culture, and other countries depended on Chinese products; it was even thought that Europeans would die of constipation if deprived of Chinese rhubarb.

When Europe suddenly soared above China

on the springboard of modern science and technology, this old and proud people suffered a shattering blow to its self-confidence. At first, the Chinese attempted to absorb Western technical knowledge for its practical value, while retaining Chinese traditional culture as the basis of society; but young men who went to study abroad could not be inoculated against European political ideas. In the last decades of the 19th century the resistance to wholesale change began to crumble. In 1905 one of the last bastions of traditional culture vanished when the Confucian examinations were abolished.

China's sufferings increased when the revolution of 1911 failed to produce a solution to its problems, and the long war with Japan meant another period of foreign occupation. But the Communist revolution, completed in 1949, brought a sense of national resurgence after more than a century of humiliation.

## Red China's roots in the past

In the early years of the People's Republic, China's past cultural achievements were emphasised, at the same time as efforts were made to change the pattern of society. Famous poets and painters of the past were celebrated, and the inventiveness and craftsmanship of the ordinary people were stressed in museums and exhibitions, and at national monuments such as the Lungmen cliff-sculptures. The government refurbished the imperial palace and placed its priceless treasures on view for all to see, while in the arts and crafts much traditional work continued to be done.

Later the mood changed, and there was less time for pride in the past as energies were harnessed to the task of transforming society. As this movement gathered momentum with the Cultural Revolution of the late 1960's, art and literature were completely subordinated to revolutionary purposes, the educational system was transformed to wipe out the old-fashioned elitist attitudes that still persisted, and the 'Thoughts of Chairman Mao' became the final criteria by which every achievement in the nation was to be judged.

It is often assumed that the Communist regime has changed China utterly, and killed the old Chinese way of life for ever. But much in present-day China does have deep roots in Chinese tradition. Mao himself has achieved distinction as a poet of a very old-fashioned kind. His uprising can be seen as part of the tradition of peasant rebellions, and tactically he learnt much from an ancient Chinese military strategist called Sun-tzu.

The present regime does not mean that the Chinese have had to abandon long-cherished concepts of individual liberty, for these never existed in China. Communist cells replace Confucian scholar-bureaucrats, and Maoism fills the place of the rigid Confucianism of Ming and Ch'ing times. Under Ch'ien-lung, those who wrote books considered harmful to the state were punished far more severely than those writers who have fallen foul of the present regime. The harsher side of Mao's China has its precedents in Chinese history.

DRAGON VASE *Vast quantities of pottery and porcelain were made for use in the palace of the Ming emperors, and the imperial dragon was a common motif*

GARDEN SCENE *A plate of the type known as* famille verte *('green family'), after its predominant colour, shows women musicians in a garden. This dates from the Ch'ing period (1644–1911), when potters made porcelain for Europe*

## THE MAJESTY OF NATURE

*The Chinese landscape painters' view of nature is typified in this 16th-century silk hanging scroll by Ch'iu Ying, showing the Han emperor Kuang Wu fording a stream. The artist has exaggerated the height of the mist-shrouded mountains to emphasise the insignificance of the tiny human figures in the foreground*

## THE FIRST BUDDHISTS MOURN THEIR DEAD MASTER

The face of Gautama, the original Buddha or 'Enlightened One', is serene in death, while grieving saints and disciples surround him. The scene is part of a silken banner painted in AD 1086, during a brilliant flowering of Japanese art under the Fujiwara rulers. The banner is still brought out each year for a ceremony in the central temple of the esoteric sect of Buddhism on Mount Koya, near Osaka.

The Japanese adopted their Buddhist religion, like many other features of their civilization, from China; it originated, however, in India with the teachings of Gautama (560–480 BC). Today Gautama is one of many Buddhas who are worshipped throughout the world: some of these are believed to have lived in the past, some are to come in the future, and others dwell in paradise

# Artistry amid violence: the enigma of Japan

## FROM AD 300

*Looking to ancient China for their model,
the Japanese created a vigorous and distinctive
culture which survives into the modern world*

### JAPAN IN 1615

*The 17th-century Tokugawa shoguns of
Japan began a policy of isolation which
lasted more than 200 years*

**M**ore than once in its history, Japan has turned its back on the world. One 17th-century ruler, Iemitsu, was so suspicious of foreign contacts that he made it a crime punishable by death for any Japanese to go abroad. Yet at other times no country has been more ready than Japan to borrow and adapt foreign ideas.

Contacts in the 6th century with the brilliant civilization flourishing in China had a far-reaching effect on Japanese art and religion. When the Japanese needed a script in which to write down their language, it was to Chinese that they turned, though it proved less than ideal for the purpose. The Chinese were to the rest of eastern Asia what the Greeks and Romans were to the West: they set a pattern which others followed. But the Japanese were always more than mere imitators. They adapted Chinese philosophy and religion, Chinese art and the Chinese approach to life to produce a unique culture, and one which touched great heights.

The feudal society which grew up in Japan was abruptly brought face to face with the modern world on July 8, 1853, when Commodore Matthew Perry of the United States navy arrived off the coast with four warships and a mission to open the door which Japan had closed on the West. Accepting the inevitable, the leaders of Japan embarked on a wholehearted programme of modernisation on Western lines, which in less than a century was to make the country one of the world's leading industrial and military powers.

The earliest inhabitants of Japan came mainly from Korea and China, but others may have come from as far north as Siberia, and from the islands of south-east Asia. Among the early peoples from the north were the Ainu, a white-skinned race who spread through Japan's northern island of Hokkaido and into the north of the main island. Until about 300 BC – centuries after civilization had reached a high point in China – these ancient peoples were still using stone tools and making crude pottery.

In the next two centuries, Mongoloid immigrants from the mainland brought new skills. The newcomers knew how to weave cloth and make bronze. Soon the use of iron enabled them to make even stronger tools and weapons, and they learnt also how to grow rice.

The mountains that cover much of Japan, as well as being ruggedly beautiful, had an important effect on the political life of the country. This kind of terrain was ideal for the development of independent communities, but unfavourable for the spread of national unity.

### A TEMPLE IN WOOD

*The Horyuji Buddhist temple near Nara contains the oldest surviving wooden buildings in the world. The main hall, pagoda and middle gate, and part of the cloisters, date from the early 7th century AD, when the temple appeared as shown in this artist's impression. Horyuji was a combination of temple and college; it had a library and lecture-hall and places for worship and meditation. It was built by Prince Shotoku, who brought artists and craftsmen from the Asian mainland to work in Japan. The pagoda was derived from Indian 'stupas', and like them it housed a Buddhist relic in a hollow in the stone on which the central pillar stood*

# Rulers who set up a government department for poetry

For centuries, Japan was made up of small independent tribes, sometimes with female chieftains. It was not until about AD 300 that one group, under a chieftain called Jimmu, was able to conquer most of the country.

The fierce strength of local tribal feeling made it necessary to emphasise the importance of Jimmu and his descendants. And so was born the myth that the Japanese emperor was different from other men, that he was descended in a direct line from the sun-goddess.

The religion of the early Japanese was based on the beliefs that came later to be known as Shinto, the way of the gods. It was a religion of nature-worship in which spirits were believed to reside in rocks or trees, or to be protectors of families or of the whole country. At the head was the sun-goddess.

By the beginning of the 6th century, Buddhism had begun to reach Japan from China and Korea. It carried with it the glamour of the civilization of China, and was soon making converts. In the Shinto religion, the gods were not given physical form, but were thought of as invisible spirits. The Buddhist universe, on the other hand, was inhabited by Buddhas of the past and future, and by beings who attended them. These were all thought of as having physical shape, and so there began the building of temples in which to worship them.

## The first constitution

In 593 a prince named Shotoku was appointed regent to a ruling empress. Shotoku was strongly influenced by Chinese systems of government, and made the first attempt at a constitution for Japan. He also encouraged artists and craftsmen from the mainland of Asia to settle in Japan, and reproduced Chinese and Korean styles of sculpture and architecture.

Two great temples built by Shotoku still stand. One, in Osaka, has altered in style over the centuries; but the other, Horyuji, has remained relatively isolated until recent times, and many parts have preserved their old appearance. Buddhism flourished throughout the 7th century in Asuka, today a small village 15 miles south of modern Nara. In the temples of the period were placed statues showing a tall and slender Buddha, his face displaying a brooding tenderness and concern for humanity. In 710 a new imperial capital was carefully laid out at Nara in imitation of a Chinese city.

## Literature in a foreign script

So dazzling were the cultural achievements of China that the Japanese at first used the Chinese language for all their official documents. When the Japanese began to write down their own language, they did so in Chinese script without adapting it in any way. A history of Japan entitled *Kojiki*, 'Records of Ancient Matters', published in 712, was the first time that the Japanese language had been used in an important document. It had a political purpose: to give the ruling family the support of history by stressing its descent from the gods.

The *Kojiki* included a number of poems, and by the middle of the 8th century there appeared a collection of over 4000 poems in Japanese called *Manyoshu*, 'A Collection for a Myriad of Ages'. The poems were written in alternate lines of seven and five syllables – a technique which was to become characteristic of Japanese poetry. They are mainly concerned with the relationship of the poet to the gods and to the emperor, to his beloved, to humanity and to the world of nature. The authors were mainly members of the official class, though some of the poems were by ordinary people.

The country's wealth stemmed from the land, which belonged to the state and was worked by peasants who were heavily taxed, paying partly in crops and partly in labour or military service. In theory, all land holders were equally taxed, but in practice, many powerful families were exempt from taxation. Ordinary peasants thus had to bear more than their share of the tax burden, and life was so hard that many abandoned their fields. Much of the vacant land fell into the hands of great lords or of Buddhist temples. In 794 the capital was shifted to modern Kyoto and given the name of Heian-kyo, the 'Capital of Peace and Content'. The principal reason for the move was that the Buddhist priests of Nara were thought to be growing too powerful, and the emperor wanted to move away from their influence.

During the first 150 years after the capital moved to Kyoto, Chinese influence remained very strong; the written language of officialdom was Chinese, and some members of the court were composing passable Chinese poems. The Japanese were not able to develop a real literature of their own until the 9th century, when they adapted the Chinese script to make it more suitable for writing down their own language. In the Chinese script, separate characters, some formed by more than a score of individual brush strokes, were needed to represent each object or abstract idea. A Chinese had to study for years, and learn thousands of separate characters and their meanings, before he could call himself literate. But by simplifying the Chinese script for their own language, the Japanese were now able to use its characters for their sound, and not solely for their pictorial meaning. Since the ancient Japanese language had only 47 syllables, only 47 characters of the Chinese type were needed to write it. As the language became more complicated, however, and adapted more Chinese words, additional Chinese characters had to be used to avoid ambiguity. Even today, there are still 1800 essential characters in Japanese writing.

## A new Buddhist sect

The 9th-century genius credited with devising the new syllabic script was a scholar called Kukai, also known as Kobodaishi. He also introduced into Japan one of the two sects which make up what is known as esoteric Buddhism – a form of the Buddhist religion characterised by symbolic rituals, handpositions and diagrams understood only by the initiated. The new form of Buddhism affected sculpture, and the simple, humane

### AN INTIMATE PICTURE OF COURTLY LIFE

When the Fujiwara clan became unquestioned rulers of Japan in about AD 900, they passed most of the work of running the country to regents, while the emperor and his vast retinue of courtiers passed their time in religious rituals and refined games and entertainments. The world's first great novel, *The Tale of Genji*, relates in about 630,000 words the adventures of Prince Genji and his descendants, and at the same time gives an intimate picture of love, personal conflicts and tensions at the imperial court. It was written by Murasaki, a lady-in-waiting, to be read out in instalments to the 11th-century empress she served. Women of the time were prominent as novelists, diarists and poets, and love affairs were conducted through sophisticated poetical letters. Women also enjoyed a high status in society and had remarkable freedom; they were allowed to own property, and many had powerful positions as absentee landlords, with peasants working their distant estates

LOVE LETTER *A picture from a 12th-century illustrated version of* The Tale of Genji *shows a jealous wife watching her husband read a letter from another woman. Before him is his writing box, with brushes ready for his elegant reply. Writers devoted as much care to the choice of the paper they wrote on as to the actual contents of the letter. Great importance was attached to the colour of writing paper and the way it was folded. A form of polygamy was common at the Japanese court. Men sometimes had several 'wives', temporary or permanent, whom they visited in their own homes*

figures of earlier times were often replaced by monstrous forms, sometimes many-headed or many-handed. Buddhism became difficult to understand and the layman, however educated he was, could not become an expert.

To run a complex central government called for an efficient civil service on the pattern developed in China, where high office and the powers that went with it could be won only through success in examinations. The Japanese, recognising the need for skilled bureaucrats, created a central university and held examinations; but they ignored the spirit of the Chinese idea. Only rarely did anyone rise to a position of responsibility on merit alone, without family backing and the invoking of hereditary rights. The result was that court posts passed to nobles, and in the country at large authority stayed with local aristocrats in their new guise of civil servants.

## Imperial power diminishes

The number of courtiers and aristocratic families grew steadily, but by the end of the 9th century one family had acquired virtual control over the court. This was the Fujiwara clan who, by an astute process of marrying their womenfolk to the emperors, came to monopolise the ministries and eventually exercised a sort of regency. The emperors lost true governing power and even began to abdicate as soon as they had a crown prince mature enough to replace them. But their hereditary authority, however worthless in practice, and their role in Shinto ritual, made an outright takeover of power out of the question.

At the beginning of the 11th century, the various elements of this aristocratic society had come together to form one of the most remarkable closed societies of all time. The emperor had no duties to distract him, so he concentrated on religious observances and the many ritualistic entertainments which had developed from old folk practices and games. The palaces and mansions were full of women who were easily reached by questing males,

and short-lived affairs were not difficult to conduct. It was a world of sentiment, in which men and women fell in and out of love for all sorts of reasons which would today seem trivial, such as the fact that a girl lived in a romantically deserted place, or that she wrote a good poem. The intimate details of courtiers' lives were recorded in superb novels and diaries written by women of the times.

Poetry acquired great social significance. Not only was it the vehicle for carrying on personal relationships, but it also attained public importance with the creation of an official government department to deal with poetical affairs. Professional critics were appointed to arrange and judge poetry competitions, and to compile collections. As a result, verse lost much of the lyrical spontaneity of earlier times, and became an intellectual pastime in which poets expressed fictional emotions.

While the courtiers lived in their mansions in Kyoto, surrounded by exquisite furnishings, the lower classes still dwelt in squalid huts. The running of the country was not particularly efficient. Members of the court went off reluctantly to the provinces from time to time to represent the central government, but they always pined for the cultured life of the capital. Gradually Shinto became absorbed into the world of Buddhism, and its gods and goddesses were treated as equivalent to Buddhist deities. Nevertheless Shinto continued to exist, and its periodical festivals flourished in both town and country. It became the custom to rebuild some Shinto shrines at fixed intervals, so that, however ancient, they should always be new and undefiled by time; the shrine at Ise, which dates back to the 1st century BC, is still rebuilt to the same design every 20 years.

## Samurai and priests

By the mid-12th century, families other than the Fujiwara were becoming more powerful, so ending the former dominance of Kyoto. Two families in particular, the Taira and Minamoto, rose to prominence. After a series

### FIGHTING THE DEMONS

*A painted clay figure nearly 6 ft high, made in the mid-8th century during the Nara period, depicts a ferocious god who protected the sacred buildings from the demons of the Buddhist underworld*

### EXILE OF A MINISTER

*At the end of the 9th century the members of one family, the Fujiwaras, eliminated rivals ruthlessly to win power in Japan and keep it. This 13th-century painting shows the banishment of Sugawara Michizane, an important minister who was the victim of Fujiwara intrigues; armed men guard the shore as he and his attendants are rowed away. The painting is from a picture scroll, a typical Japanese art form in which a story is related as the manuscript is unrolled. Michizane died in exile, and there were so many calamities after his death that it was feared his spirit was taking revenge*

# *Zen, and 'the sound of a handclap made with one hand'*

of campaigns between 1156 and 1185, the Minamoto crushed their rivals and set up a military government in Kamakura, hundreds of miles to the east of the corrupting decadence of the imperial court. The result was the beginning of a period in which the warrior families, the samurai, were to dominate Japan. It did not end until the mid-19th century.

The wars between the Taira and Minamoto families brought into being a new sort of literature – a series of military romances written in a style which was much more comprehensible to ordinary people than the earlier poetry had been. The new romances were circulated not in written manuscripts but by blind wandering musicians, who chanted to their own accompaniment on the *biwa*, a stringed instrument like a lute. These minstrels became immensely popular, and even had access to the imperial court; the tradition survived long enough for the last of them to record their voices on gramophone records.

The land was now dominated by the samurai – the name means 'one who serves' – tough, professional fighters who gave their allegiance to chieftains and fought with fanatical ferocity. The samurai's main weapon was a massive two-handed sabre, and an accomplished swordsman could slice a man in half with one blow.

The wars that continued to rage, and the decline of the glamour of the old court, aroused in some the desire to get away from the world and to take refuge in nature. Men started living for long periods in remote cells or huts, with only the murmur of brooks and the passing of the seasons to occupy their interest. They were encouraged in this by the rise in importance of the Zen sect of Buddhism. This was a step towards making Buddhism more popular, for it taught not only priests, but also laymen who could show themselves worthy, how to achieve a state of enlightenment, in which the world was shown to be of only superficial importance. This enlightenment might come in a single flash, as a result of severe and intense mental and physical discipline. Zen believers sought this enlightenment by meditating upon problems which were incapable of solution by rational means, such as the sound of a handclap made with one hand.

## Rigorous training of Zen

Zen and the arts exercised a considerable influence upon each other. For example, sculptures of priests and other figures in the temples at Kamakura give an impression of complete realism, and of grim and intelligent self-denial. Warriors found satisfaction in the similarity between military discipline and the rigours of Zen training, and even today a Zen training monastery is run on ruthless and stark lines that make it very like an old-style military training depot. At the same time many soldiers sought in Zen an escape from violence. They travelled the country and wrote poems expressing their emotion at natural sights, finding

particular satisfaction at the sad scenes of autumn. In the middle of the 13th century the Mongol hordes which had swept through Asia stood poised for an invasion of Japan, and in 1274 Kublai Khan, grandson of Genghis Khan, sent an invasion fleet from Korea. The invaders were repulsed, but in 1281 they returned, this time 150,000 strong and sailing in 4500 ships.

For seven weeks the samurai were locked in battle with the ferocious Mongols, and the outcome seemed in doubt until a hurricane blew up and raged for two days. The invasion fleet was scattered and wrecked, and the marooned invaders were slaughtered on the shore. The Japanese called the hurricane *kamikaze*, the 'divine wind', a name that was given centuries later to the Japanese suicide pilots of the Second World War who flew aircraft loaded with explosives into American warships.

The defeat of the Mongols did not, however, mean peace for Japan. For now there was violent conflict at home, as powerful lords fought each other for domination, emperors tried to re-establish their power, and rival emperors clashed with each other. Buddhist priests became warriors, and many of the great temples had their own troops.

The sons of farmers went off to fight for their lords and returned, if lucky, with experience and perhaps some reward, especially if they had managed to take the head of an important enemy. Craftsmen produced exquisitely wrought swords, lacquerware, and delicately

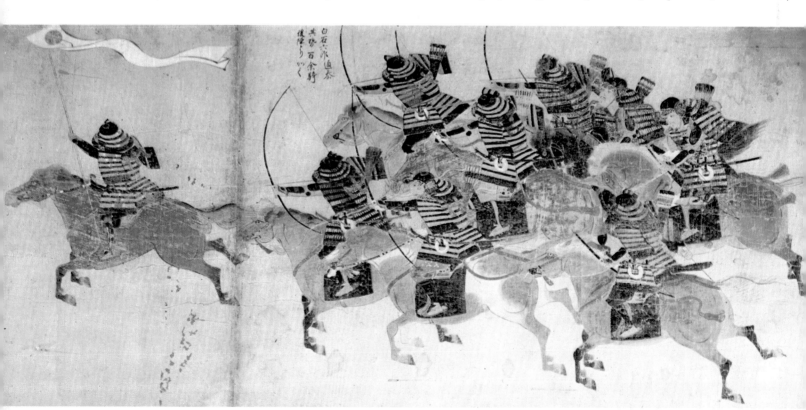

### THE 'DIVINE WIND' THAT SAVED JAPAN

*The Mongol hordes of Kublai Khan twice tried to conquer Japan. In 1274 the invaders were repulsed by samurai warriors, seen charging into battle in this 13th-century picture scroll. The soldiers carry bows developed for cavalry, with the* *upper portion longer than the lower. In 1281, seven weeks of fighting ended dramatically when a hurricane wrecked the Mongol fleet, and the stranded invaders were massacred. The Japanese named the hurricane* kamikaze, *the 'divine wind'*

decorated screens and fans and standards of living and culture gradually rose. Some temples flourished, particularly those of the Zen sect, which kept up relations with China and grew rich through commerce.

## Tea drinking as an art

Kyoto was once again the seat of government and the main centre of civilization. One influential group of Buddhists, not liking the outside world, turned inwards and developed new ways of elegant entertainment. One of these was the tea ceremony, at which people of like minds indulged in cultured conversation while enjoying green powdered tea. The ceremony was one example of a general trend towards setting up a tradition to which only the initiated were admitted. Similar cults began in flower arrangement and incense appreciation.

Perhaps the greatest of the art forms developed at this period was the *nō* play. This originated partly in the songs and dances performed at Shinto shrines, and partly in other ancient songs and dances which sprang from such country rites as the planting out of young rice seedlings, a monotonous task requiring rhythm for efficiency.

By the 14th century, annual *nō* performances were being held at temples in and around Nara. One man associated with these, Zeami, established a repertoire of plays which still provides the majority of pieces performed in Japan's *nō* theatre. *Nō* plays are performed on an almost bare stage, with the minimum of symbolic scenery but elaborate costumes. The actors, who are all men, wear masks of delicate colouring and design to portray gods, ghosts, women, or people from the past. A chorus on stage sets the scene and sometimes takes over the main actor's words, and emotion is expressed by dancing, to flute and drums.

Many plays have a religious element appropriate to their performance in temples. Older popular entertainments were preserved as interludes, and they either parodied the serious plays or were comic masterpieces in their own right. These too have survived. When they originated, *nō* plays were not the aristocratic entertainment which they were later to become, but were attended by all classes.

## Jesuits bring Christianity

The Portuguese came to Japan in the middle of the 16th century, when the civil wars were coming to an end. Among the early Portuguese arrivals were Jesuit missionaries, who settled in Nagasaki. The missionaries used Japanese drama to help spread their doctrine, and they also introduced European painting and printing. The newcomers also brought Western costumes and food, which were eagerly seized upon by a population to which peace was bringing some prosperity. The whole population of a town sometimes indulged in communal dancing in the streets, when rice-wine flowed and fantastic European-style clothing was worn.

The older Buddhism, with its warrior-priests, suffered a setback when one ruler, Oda Nobunaga, brutally suppressed one of the greatest

## FEROCIOUS FIGHTERS WITH A STRICT CODE OF HONOUR

The samurai were a class of ferocious warrior-noblemen who arose in the 12th century and dominated Japanese society for 700 years. They were bound by a strict unwritten code of courage and loyalty which came to be known as *bushido*, 'the way of the warrior'. The most valued possession of the samurai was his huge two-handed sabre, a razor-sharp weapon which was often passed down from father to son for generations. Famous swords were coveted by other families, and feuds were fought over them. The most treasured blades were those which had been proved in battle, but new ones might be tested on human corpses or criminals condemned to death. The samurai also carried a shorter sword which he used to cut off an enemy's head or, when even death by suicide came to be thought more worthy than dishonour, to commit *hara-kiri*

A DRESSING RITUAL *Putting on the elaborate samurai armour was a lengthy business. These illustrations made in 1853 by the artist Go-un Sadahide, show a warrior strapping on his shin-guards and sandals. By the 19th century, samurai were no longer called on to fight and there was time to follow a formal, ritual sequence. In time of war, however, warriors used stands or hangers on which their armour was already assembled. Special undergarments went beneath the armour. On top of a breechclout which reached up over the chest the samurai wore a short-sleeved robe, often richly embroidered. Loose pantaloons were worn over the robe, and on his head the warrior tied a skull cap to cushion the weight of his iron helmet*

BATTLE ARRAY *Samurai armour was light and flexible despite its complexity. The body of this armour, made in the style of the 14th century, was formed from hundreds of lacquered iron scales linked with braided silk cords, which allowed the wearer to move easily. The samurai's head and neck were protected by a visored iron helmet, shoulder guards, and a metal collar. He wore a mask of iron, elaborately bearded, to add to the impression of fierceness*

MASTER CRAFTSMEN *The swordsmiths of ancient Japan worked in a religious atmosphere and wore priest-like clothing. In this early 16th-century illustration, a sword-maker polishes a blade whose sharp cutting edge has been made by folding together and hammering out as many as 20 paper-thin layers of steel of varying hardness*

# *Two centuries of isolation from the outside world*

temple complexes at Mount Hiei, near Kyoto, and when support increased for new sects which allowed ordinary believers hope of gaining access to Paradise at once, without gradually rising through a series of incarnations. One group, the Pure Land sect, merely asked that their followers repeat formulae which praised the Buddha Amida.

In 1603 Tokugawa Ieyasu became shogun, the shortened form of an ancient title which meant 'supreme commander for the conquering of the barbarians', by which the emperor conferred upon him the right to govern the country. Tokugawa Ieyasu set up a complex organisation chiefly directed to maintaining power for himself and his successors. The country was divided into great estates under the control of feudal lords, who lived in magnificent castles built to demonstrate their supremacy and to protect themselves against revolt. These castles are still to be seen all over Japan, their interconnecting moats and massive fortifications enclosing buildings with thick walls, which rise to several elegantly roofed storeys before culminating in a lofty viewpoint. Roads were developed, because the provincial

lords were compelled to visit the shogun in the new capital at Edo (later to become Tokyo), and had to leave their wives and families there as hostages when they returned to their own lands. Movement on the roads was closely controlled by a system of barriers, and they were not allowed to become large enough to take wheeled traffic. The same routes were followed when the railways were built in the late 19th and early 20th centuries, and later still by the motor highways.

## Expulsion of the foreigners

Patronage for the arts increased enormously. Superb screens and wooden decorations were carved to separate the halls in the great temples and palaces. In the great mausoleum at Nikko, in the mountains north of Edo, erected for Ieyasu after his death, there is a wealth of highly coloured and intricate carving, which contrasts sharply with the simplicity of much of the art of the earlier period.

As the Tokugawa family increased its grip on the country, much of the exuberance disappeared. Iemitsu, shogun from 1622 to 1651, virtually closed the door on the outside world.

Fearful that Christianity was breeding a spirit of independence, and that foreign trade would lead to foreign domination, he expelled all the Portuguese and Spanish missionaries and traders. Only the Dutch were allowed to stay, and they were confined to a tiny island off Nagasaki. To enforce his policy, Iemitsu ruled that no ship should be more than 75 ft long, and that all vessels should have open sterns so that they dare not venture on the ocean.

The samurai ran the government, the great estates, and industries like the gold mines of the Isle of Sado. When not occupied with those duties they spent their time in refined pursuits or military training, which became formalised through lack of warfare. The farmers had to produce enough rice to pay the salaries of all the samurai officials, as well as feeding the rest of the population.

Traditionally the samurai occupied the highest position in the Japanese class system, followed by the farmers, the craftsmen and then the merchants. But in the 17th century the merchants grew in power; in particular they gained control of the country's rice, buying the excess from the samurai and making fortunes by selling it to the people. The growth of great merchant houses with multiple interests, such as textile weaving and dyeing, drapery shops, finance, transport and warehousing, meant that when the country was opened to world trade in the mid-19th century, the foundations on which to build were already there. The *zaibatsu*, the great families which were dominant in Japanese trade and industry until the Second World War, had their origins in these early days, and even today industry is to a large extent in the same hands, though the old giant corporations have been broken up.

## New styles of entertainment

New entertainments began in Kyoto in the 17th century. A river runs to the east of the city, and except during the rainy summer season there was space to spare on its banks. Booths and temporary stages were set up, and these were used by the first performers of the live and puppet theatres which were to spread to Osaka and Edo. The live theatre was from the start closely connected with the areas which housed brothels, and consequently high-grade courtesans and female entertainers became the ideals of culture for much of the population.

The courtesans were given an extensive training in many of the arts, as are the geisha, or entertainers, of the present day. They could sing, dance, play musical instruments and perform the tea ceremony, and in the idealised portrayal given on the stage they even became paragons of virtue. More often than not they were a product of the cruel conditions in which the farmers lived, for they were nearly always daughters of poor men who had sold them to keep the family solvent.

This system went on unchanged until after the Second World War, when the brothels were finally abolished. The distinction between geisha and courtesans, who combined prostitution with entertainment, had in the mean-

---

### TEA MAKING — ART AND RITUAL

An elaborate cult surrounding the drinking of tea spread throughout Japan in the 15th century. The tea ceremony, as it became known, began as a Zen activity, but it soon developed a form of ritual all its own

FLOWER RITUAL *Formalised flower arrangements, too, originated in Zen and became part of the Japanese way of life*

ELABORATE PREPARATION *A Japanese girl makes tea, as her lover stands watching, in this 18th-century print by Koryusai. In front of her a kettle boils on a charcoal fire, and beside it are a water pot and a tea caddy with ladle. A code of rules was laid down for the handling of these tea-making utensils. Powdered green tea was placed in a bowl, then hot water was poured over it, and the resultant mixture lightly whisked. The ceremony was often very formal. Tea masters presided at elegant gatherings where cultured conversation was carried on over bowls of tea*

TEA BOWL *Special vessels like this 17th-century Shino tea bowl were designed for use in the tea ceremony. These, too, had to be held in accordance with rules. Different shapes of bowl were used according to the season of the year; the bowls for winter were deep and narrow so that the liquid in them would remain hot for a long time*

time become clear. Every major town in Japan still has a diminishing number of geishas who can be hired to help at parties, and to sing, dance and play music. Their training is still similar to that of the old days, but in modern times they are no longer sold by their parents.

The merchants had a code of conduct under which they acquired wealth for passing on to their descendants. But they also made a habit of great display in their costume, residences, furnishings and pleasure. So glamorous did the merchant culture become that many samurai indulged in secret in the same pleasures, and by the 19th century the division between the warrior and commercial classes began to blur. Samurai were not above adopting merchants and their families in return for financial reward, and many found it profitable to become merchants themselves.

Early in the 19th century the Japanese repeatedly refused to open their ports to foreign ships. But in July 1853, America forced the issue. Four warships dropped anchor in what is now Tokyo Bay, and their commander, Commodore Matthew Perry, demanded the opening of a supply port and regular trade between the two countries. When Perry returned the next year with a bigger flotilla, the request was met. By 1858 commercial treaties had been signed with America, Britain, France and Russia.

## Legacies from the past

Japan henceforth was to be in close touch with the wider world. But many features of the way of life the Europeans found in Japan in the mid-19th century still flourish vigorously today. One is the live traditional theatre, *kabuki*, played by male actors, with complicated sets and stage machinery, and everything larger than life. Another is the puppet drama, *bunraku*, with life-like dolls worked by three manipulators, and words declaimed by a virtuoso chanter, a descendant of the old blind musicians of the military romances. The *bunraku* theatre still plays pieces that reflect the great dilemma of traditional Japan: how to reconcile duty to one's lord or one's parents with love for one's wife or children.

Yet another survival, and perhaps the greatest influence on the world at large, is the art of the colour print, which fascinated artists in France and elsewhere at the end of the 19th century. Colour prints began as pin-up pictures of girls and actors. They advertised the brothel districts and theatres, and later became illustrated guides to the great highways.

Much of Japan's traditional culture, such as drama, art and costume, survives from the past, but there are other, less tangible legacies. The whole range of personal relationships within families and other institutions, including the mutual loyalty and obligation between superior and subordinate, were developed during the traditional period. The importance of the head of the family, the subservience of women, national solidarity, respect for learning, admiration of military prowess – all these features of modern Japan had their roots in earlier times, and survive despite new ways of living.

## ZEN GARDEN OF TRANQUILLITY

*Buddhist priests of the Zen sect liked to meditate while gazing at gardens which were laid out with infinite care to mirror the world of nature in miniature. The Saihoji garden at Kyoto, which appears to be merely a shadowy grove, is in fact painstakingly designed not so much for aesthetic beauty as to in-* *duce reflective calm. The pond is shaped to form the Japanese character meaning 'heart' or 'soul', and the sunlight is filtered through elegant maple trees. Over 50 different varieties of moss carpet the earth. As the cult of Zen spread throughout Japan, wealthy enthusiasts copied the Zen gardens*

---

## TRADITIONAL THEATRE WHICH STILL SURVIVES

The 14th-century *nō* plays and the *kabuki* dramas of the 17th century are still staged in Japan. *Nō* plays are enacted with the minimum of scenery but magnificent costumes, and the actors, who are all men, wear masks. Emotion is expressed by dancing. The *kabuki* melodramas also include music and dance, and are performed on huge stages with movable scenery and special effects

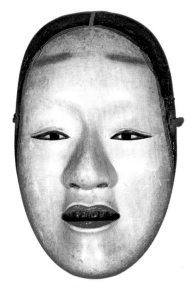

ACTOR'S MASK *The masks used by the* nō *actors – like this one representing a young woman – were often artistic masterpieces in their own right. By moving their heads to change the shadow pattern of their masks,* nō *players can express the full range of human emotions. The formal simplicity of the classical* nō *plays strongly appealed to Japan's aristocracy, and contrasted sharply with the flamboyance of the* kabuki *drama, supported by the merchants*

FEMALE IMPERSONATOR *A colour print, produced about 1800 for sale to admirers, shows Nakayama Tozaburo, an 'onnagata' or female impersonator of the* kabuki *theatre, in one of the roles for which he was famed. Actresses were banned from the* kabuki *stage in 1629, when the government found that many of them were also earning a living as prostitutes. The* kabuki *audience was mainly drawn from the merchant class, which found an escape from the official regimentation of their everyday lives in the extravagant spectacle of the theatre. Their favourite plays were stylised melodramas in which commoners outwitted the aristocracy in love or combat*

## A MASSIVE PYRAMID RAISED TO THE MAYA GODS

The pyramids built by the people of Middle America, unlike those built in Egypt more than 3000 years earlier, were raised as temples and not as tombs. The Pyramid of the Soothsayer, at Uxmal in Mexico, was built and rebuilt by the Maya five times, the final version dating from the 8th century. The sanctuary on top, reached by wide, steep steps, was for priests and initiates only; other worshippers had to watch from ground level, 100 ft below. The pyramid had an earth core, and was faced with stone blocks, joined by mud mortar and painted with white plaster; the only tools the Maya used in building it were primitive stone chisels

# Bloodthirsty cultures of ancient America

## AD 300–1540

*The Maya and Aztecs of Mexico created civilizations
of a wealth and splendour which dazzled
the Spaniards who came to conquer*

**MIDDLE AMERICA, AD 1520**

*Spanish explorers found two powerful
civilizations in the lands that now form
Mexico, Guatemala and Honduras*

From the moment when Columbus's fleet dropped anchor off the Bahamas in 1492, the Americas became a part of European history. Columbus himself, in four voyages of exploration, never reached the mainland of Mexico, and it was left to his successors to make contact with the civilizations of Middle America. The Maya, living in the peninsula of Yucatan, were discovered by Hernandez de Cordoba in 1517, and the next year Juan de Grijalva explored Mexico's east coast, bringing back hundreds of gold trinkets and stories of rich and civilized tribes.

His success inspired other fortune-hunters. The governor of Cuba financed another expedition to the mainland, and chose as his commander Hernando Cortez, a tough and ambitious colonist who had come to the Indies as a young man to escape the poverty of his home town in Spain. In 1519 Cortez and 600 Spanish adventurers landed at San Juan de Ulua, on the Gulf Coast of Mexico, and for the first time heard tales of a powerful Aztec lord called Montezuma who ruled most of Mexico from his island capital of Tenochtitlan,

high in the mountains and several days' march from the coast. The arrival of Cortez was reported to Montezuma by Indian spies. Uncertain how to meet this threat, he first tried to awe the Spaniards with costly gifts.

It was a fatal mistake, for Montezuma's gifts only fanned the Spaniards' greed. Spread before them, for the taking, were foodstuffs, cotton cloth and an enormous quantity of treasure: gold trinkets in the shape of dogs, jaguars, ducks, monkeys and other creatures, a snake-head of gold with the eyes inlaid with precious stones, a gold helmet with a crest made from green feathers, objects of crystal and turquoise mosaic, dishes, necklaces, and even bows and arrows made of gold. The most magnificent presents were two discs, one of gold, the other of silver, as big as cartwheels, and covered with figures and designs, symbolising the sun and the moon.

From San Juan de Ulua the Spanish force marched inland to Cempoala, a city of nearly 80,000 inhabitants with paved streets and squares, busy market-places, and palaces whose walls were covered with shining white plaster.

## SCENE OF SACRIFICE

*The religious centre of the Aztec Empire was a great walled precinct inside the capital city of Tenochtitlan. Crowds assembled to watch high priests sacrifice human victims on platforms in front of the temples. On top of the large pyramid in this artist's reconstruction are the twin shrines of Tlaloc, the rain god, and Huitzilopochtli, a fierce warrior god who was only appeased by blood and hearts torn from human victims. In front stands a rounded temple sacred to Quetzalcoatl, the feathered serpent creator god, and in the foreground is the court where the Aztecs played their sacred ball-game. On the right is a rack upon which the skulls of sacrificed victims were stored*

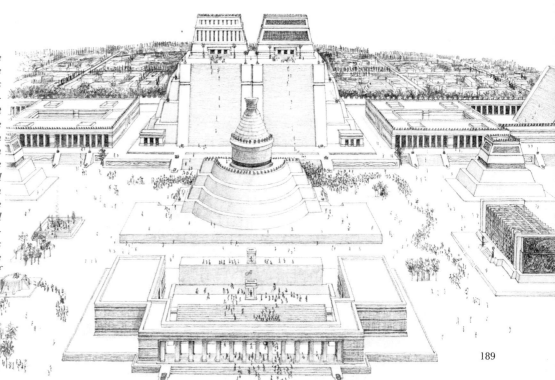

# Life in the New World without iron, horses or ploughs

Raised high on a pyramid platform stood the main temple, in whose blood-spattered interior Cortez found several large idols and all the paraphernalia of human sacrifice – the block on which victims were spreadeagled, flint knives with which their hearts were cut out, and piles of offerings to the gods consisting of sheets of bark paper soaked in human blood.

The Spaniards had discovered not just a new world, but also a new type of civilization of a kind which no European had seen before, or could have imagined.

## Volcanoes and forests

Beyond the northern frontier of civilized Middle America stretched the Mexican desert, where settled life was impossible. The southern boundary cut across the isthmus of Panama, beyond which lay more primitive peoples. The Aztecs were the most powerful and successful of the different tribes and nations inhabiting this area of high culture.

The countryside of Middle America ranges from the snow-capped volcanic peaks of the interior, to the tropical rain forest of the lowlands and the arid valleys of central Mexico. Each of these areas had its own way of life, but underlying this variety was a cultural heritage shared by all Middle American peoples from earliest times.

Their ancestors had crossed the Bering Strait, then a land bridge joining Siberia to Alaska, some time before 25,000 BC and made their way southwards to Mexico. Cut off from the rest of the world by the Atlantic and Pacific oceans, Middle America remained isolated from the technological and intellectual discoveries of the Old World and developed a unique form of civilization.

The Middle American peoples lacked many of the things which are today taken for granted. Iron and steel were unknown, and even bronze was not in general use for tools and weapons. Spears were tipped with flint or obsidian, a black volcanic glass, and swords were made of wood, edged with obsidian blades so sharp that a man could shave his head with one.

All trade was carried on by barter, without the use of coined money. Architects were ignorant of the keystone arch and the dome, though builders had discovered how to make concrete. The principle of the wheel was understood, but was not applied to anything more functional than children's pull-along toys. There were no wheeled vehicles – and indeed no animals big enough to pull a cart – no wheels for pottery-making, and none of the mechanical devices which depend on wheels, gears or rotary motion.

Farmers tilled the land with simple digging sticks, for the plough was unknown. Even the plants and animals were unlike those of Europe. There were no horses, cattle, sheep, pigs or goats in the New World until they were introduced by Europeans; and the only domesticated animals in Middle America were the turkey, the edible dog, a species of duck, and a kind of stingless bee. In compensa-tion for the lack of animals, the region was rich in useful plants. Maize, amaranth, and other seed plants grew abundantly.

Squashes, belonging to the pumpkin family, were an important food, as were beans, a source of protein, and chilli peppers, which were used as a flavouring. Thread was spun from cotton and from the fibres of a variety of cactus, whose juice was fermented into an alcoholic drink. Tobacco was smoked or ground into a snuff, and herbalists had discovered the hallucinatory properties of peyote, the source of the drug mescalin, and of the bitter black mushroom which the Aztec people called *teonanacatl*, 'sacred fungus' or 'flesh of the gods'.

## Art in altars and temples

In spite of these great differences, the Spaniards recognised that the culture of Middle America had all the elements of civilization: powerful rulers, an efficient civil service, written records, a state religion, and an honest and well-organised legal system.

What the conquerors did not realise was that this civilization had roots as ancient as their own. Between 1300 and 500 BC an early civilization grew up in the swamps and rain forests of the Gulf Coast. Its builders, known as the Olmecs, were already master sculptors and architects. As always in Middle America, their greatest efforts were devoted to religion: the round, fluted temple-pyramid at the island site of La Venta is over 100 ft high, and more than

---

## MEN AS JAGUARS IN THE CARVINGS OF THE OLMECS

The first civilized people of Middle America were the Olmecs, who lived near the Gulf Coast of Mexico from about 1300 BC. They were accomplished artists, working almost entirely in materials which had to be brought to the craft centres across miles of wild country. Sculptors made huge altars and carved reliefs on slabs of stone; by contrast, they also produced delicate jade ornaments only inches high. Many Olmec carvings are in the shape of baby-faced, sexless human beings with snarling animal features and fang-like teeth. These creatures, which also appear on ceremonial jade axes, may have been rain gods, and jaguars also became important cult figures in many of the later American Indian religions. Wherever the gifted Olmecs travelled their distinctive art style is found

RITUAL FACES *The features on these jade carvings are characteristic of Olmec craftsmanship. The thick lips, down-turned mouths and brooding eyes are associated with the cult of a jaguar-being, a mystical creature worshipped by the Olmecs, who believed it was the offspring of a woman who mated with a jaguar. They made offerings to it of food and fruit*

COLOSSAL HEADS *The monumental side of Olmec art is represented by colossal sculptures of helmeted heads. This 8 ft head from La Venta weighs almost 40 tons, and was carved from a single block of basalt, using only stone tools. The nearest source of the stone is 80 miles away, and as the Olmecs had no wheel they must have floated it along rivers on rafts*

2 million man-days of labour must have been needed for its construction. Scattered throughout La Venta were massive stone altars and huge sculptures, and buried beneath many of the structures were offerings to the gods: axes, jewellery and figurines of jade and serpentine.

The most spectacular offerings were pavements made of stone blocks laid out in the form of a stylised jaguar mask. These, too, belonged to the gods rather than to man, for they were buried under several feet of clay immediately after they were made.

In the highlands, civilization reached its first climax in the period AD 300–600 at Teotihuacan, 25 miles north-east of present-day Mexico City. Teotihuacan was a city of more than 100,000 people, and was laid out to a precise grid plan. Close to the centre were rich houses with walls covered by paintings and frescoes, and alongside the main avenue of the city were two pyramids which legend says were dedicated to the sun and moon. Another temple-pyramid was adorned with stone heads of the rain god, Tlaloc, and of the feathered serpent god, Quetzalcoatl, so named because he had the feathers of the quetzal bird instead of scales. Both these gods were still being worshipped in Mexico nearly a thousand years later when the Spaniards arrived, even though Teotihuacan itself was sacked and burnt in about AD 750.

## A scattered civilization

Two regional civilizations in Middle America stand out above the rest: the culture of the Maya, between AD 300 and 900, and that of the Aztecs which flourished from 1350 to 1521. Maya culture represents Middle American life at its finest. The Maya people lived in the Yucatan peninsula of Mexico, occupying also most of what is now Guatemala, Belize and the neighbouring parts of Honduras and El Salvador. The southern part of this territory is mountainous, but the remainder of the Maya zone is lowland forest, ranging from thorny scrub in Yucatan to semi-tropical forest in the central region, where more than 10 ft of rain may fall in a year.

In these unpromising conditions, the Maya created a strange, diffuse civilization. The peasants lived in scattered communities throughout the jungle, moving their maize fields every few years when the fertility of the soil became exhausted. The great Maya sites were ceremonial centres, inhabited only by rulers, nobles, priests, officials and their servants. The farmers lived in pole-and-thatch huts in the forests, and came into the centres only when it was necessary – to visit the markets, carry out official business, or to attend religious festivals.

Dominating the ceremonial centres were temples and shrines, placed high on pyramid platforms and approached by steep staircases. The temple interiors were reserved for priests and initiates, and the ordinary worshipper had to watch the ceremonies from the square below. Religious festivals were frequent and often spectacular, with processions, dances

MAYA BOOKS WHICH STILL KEEP THEIR SECRETS

*Though the art of printing was unknown in Middle America, the Maya were the first civilized people of the region to devise their own script, and they possessed books. This detail is from the finest of the three surviving Maya books, which dates from about 1200 and is thought to have been copied from an even earlier manuscript. In it a young maize god stands before the god of death, who is seated naked on a throne, and their confrontation symbolises the conflict between the creative and destructive forces. Both gods are painted like warriors, and wear jade beads around their arms, legs and necks. The book is constructed as a continuous strip 11 ft long, made by beating out the inner bark of a wild fig tree and coating it with smooth plaster. It is folded, like a concertina, into 78 pages. Hieroglyphic inscriptions at the foot are accompanied by illustrations of gods associated with different ceremonies and periods of time. The contents remain largely undeciphered, but the book apparently deals with astronomy and foretelling the future*

# The Maya, experts in arithmetic and the calendar

### THE MAYA IDEAL OF BEAUTY

*The Maya enjoyed wearing flamboyant clothing; this sculpture is of a seated Maya aristocrat wearing an elaborate hat shaped like a flower. The figure, dating from about AD 800, was found at Jaina, an island just off the coast of Yucatan in Mexico. It is made of hollow pottery, shaped partly with a mould and partly with the fingers, and then painted after firing. The sculptor has exaggerated the prominent nose and sloping forehead which represented the Maya ideal of beauty. Some Maya aristocrats bound their infants' heads between boards to make their skulls grow long and narrow*

and offerings to the gods. A fresco from a Maya building at Bonampak in southern Mexico depicts musicians carrying long trumpets, rattles and drums, accompanied by dancers with huge crab-like claws covering their arms and hands, and wearing masks of the long-nosed water god.

Other scenes, painted on pottery, illustrate dancers with jaguar masks, or with wings attached to their shoulders. Many of these figures were god-impersonators, who wore the costume and regalia of the god and who represented him in the ceremonies. Several of the dances were to ensure good harvests or success in hunting, though there were others which the Spaniards condemned as obscene and erotic.

### Blood for the gods

Religion entered into every activity. Success for the Maya depended on the goodwill of the gods, and had to be earned by prayers and offerings. The most common gifts were animals or birds, maize gruel, beans, squash seeds, flowers, or incense made from the gum of trees. But from time to time the gods demanded blood offerings. Human sacrifice was less frequent among the Maya than in highland Mexico, but artists illustrated scenes showing human hearts being removed, and others showing a victim tied to a wooden frame as a target for warriors armed with throwing spears. Before an important festival, worshippers fasted, abstained from sexual intercourse, and mortified the flesh by drawing blood from their own arms, legs, noses, ear lobes and tongues.

Although the size of Maya temples is impressive, their architectural principles are simple, and the rooms are small and window-less. However, buildings were decorated inside and out with carved panels, coloured frescoes, and plaster reliefs. Artists excelled at painting and sculpture, which they used to glorify rulers and gods. Figures of men and gods are grouped in dignified and formal postures, and the insignia of their rank are shown in elaborate detail. Every item of clothing and every part of the body is decorated: crests made of coloured feathers curve gracefully away from sloping foreheads, and feather banners wave over the heads of important personages; belts, cuffs, wrists and ankles are covered with ornaments of jade, semi-precious stone or pearl shell.

### Mystery of the Maya language

The figures and decorative patterns painted on Maya walls are often accompanied by inscriptions in hieroglyphics, or picture-writing. A number of the signs have now been deciphered, in particular those dealing with dates and astronomy, but scholars are still unable to read the longer and more complicated passages.

It is clear that the signs do not represent either letters or syllables. Each symbol normally stands for a single word or idea, though individual units are sometimes combined. Thus, the signs for earth and seed together

indicate a maize field. The signs themselves usually consist of stylised pictures, and many of them, especially those for the different units or periods of time, have alternative forms. The full version of a symbol indicating time consists of the head of the deity which ruled over that segment of time, but there is also an abbreviated form consisting of an item taken from the mythology surrounding the god – just as in Christian symbolism a pair of crossed keys indicates St Peter.

It was a Maya custom to erect carved and inscribed stone slabs to commemorate great events, both on earth and in the heavens. The Maya were obsessed with the passage of time, and this is recorded on several of their monuments. At Tikal, upright stone slabs, or *stelae,* were put up to mark the end of each *katun* (a period of 20 years, each of 360 days) from AD 629 to 790, and on each stela were carved the date, the age of the moon, and the symbols for the gods who were ruling at that time.

Most of the deciphered Maya texts deal with religion, ritual, divination and astrology, or with astronomical matters. Optical instruments, and glass itself, were unknown in America but, by sighting through a pair of crossed sticks and noting the way in which the position of the sun and planets changed in relation to natural features on the horizon, Maya priests had made important astronomical discoveries. Although they did not realise that the earth revolves round the sun, their calculation of the length of the year was more accurate than the system of leap years used in the Christian calendar. They also studied the cycles of the moon and of the planet Venus, and composed tables to predict eclipses.

### Mastery in mathematics

Maya arithmetic and the Maya calendar represent the high point of intellectual achievement in the Americas, and owe nothing to contacts with the Old World. At a time when the Romans were still using a clumsy, cumulative system, some unknown genius in Middle America invented a system of numbering which has all the features of present-day arithmetical systems.

Only three symbols were used: a bar for 5, a dot for each unit up to 4, and a stylised shell for zero. Any number could be written as a combination of bars and dots, while the existence of a zero symbol allowed value to be indicated by position. The modern system counts in 10's and increases in value from right to left. The Maya counted in 20's, and the value increased from bottom to top in a vertical column; the lowest group of bars and dots gave the number of units, the one immediately above it the number of 20's, and the one above that the number of 400's (or 20 × 20). The only thing lacking was a notation for dealing with fractions.

Dates were expressed in the so-called 'long count', a system which records how many days have elapsed since a fixed point in the past. The modern calendar counts onwards from the birth of Christ: the Maya calendar, for some reason still unknown, took as its mythical starting point a day in the year 3113 BC, and dates were expressed as the number of days which had passed since that moment. Instead of the weeks, months and years of the Christian calendar, the Maya employed the *kin* (day), the *uinal* (20 days), the *tun* (18 uinals, or 360 days), the *katun* (20 tuns, or 7200 days) and the *baktun* (20 katuns, or 144,000 days).

## Decline of the Maya

After nearly six centuries of uninterrupted development, Maya civilization collapsed throughout the central lowlands. Between AD 800 and 900, one centre after another ceased to erect sculptured stones. The rulers, priests and nobles disappeared from their homes; palaces and temples crumbled, jungle invaded the ruins, and the centres became almost deserted. The cause of this downfall is still an unsolved mystery.

Whatever the reason, by the end of the 10th century many sites were abandoned, and the central lowlands suffered a fall in population from which they have never recovered. Further north, in Yucatan, the damage was less severe, but even here there were great and violent changes. From this time onwards, Yucatan occupied the centre of the stage, and a new episode of Maya history began.

One legend of this period tells of the arrival in about AD 987 of non-Maya invaders from the west, led by a chief called Kukulkan— 'feathered serpent' in the local Maya dialect. Kukulkan, it is said, conquered all Yucatan and chose as his capital the site of Uucil-abnal (better known under its later name of Chichén Itzá). The newcomers brought with them new forms of art, with stiffly carved warrior figures, reliefs showing eagles and jaguars holding human hearts, and stone columns in the form of feathered serpents. One of the more gruesome carvings depicts human skulls skewered on a framework of poles, and is a copy in stone of the wooden rack on which the heads of sacrificed victims were placed. It was at this time, too, that metal tools and ornaments first became common in Yucatan.

The Mexican invasion did not lead to the disappearance of Maya culture. The newcomers were absorbed by the older population and the foreign elements were grafted on to the existing way of life. Long-nosed Maya rain gods are found side by side with feathered serpents and other Mexican gods, carved in relief on the main temples. New halls roofed by beams resting on pillars were built alongside rooms built in the old Maya style of corbel-vaulting, in which each course of masonry slightly overlaps the one below, until the gap at the top can be bridged with a single slab. Maya remained the language spoken in Yucatan, and the native system of recording dates continued to be used, though in an abbreviated form.

Maya chronicles mention a second group of invaders called the Itza, a Mexicanised tribe from the western fringe of the Maya zone.

Maya sculptors and potters presented a vivid picture of life at all levels of society. They also used their art to glorify gods and rulers, portraying them in dignified and formal postures. Panels and carved slabs showed the high and the mighty carrying out their appointed duties, while potters, with greater freedom of expression, decorated their vessels with scenes from everyday life

BLOOD OFFERING *Maya worshippers had sometimes to sacrifice their own blood. This carving over a doorway at Yaxchilan, on the Mexico-Guatemala border, shows a richly dressed woman kneeling before the Yaxchilan ruler and drawing a cord set with thorns through a hole in her tongue. The blood drips on to bark paper in a basket in front of her. The carving, which is 3 ft 7 in. high, was made in about AD 700, when Yaxchilan was ruled by a lord called Shield Jaguar. He is depicted with the typical sloping forehead of the Maya aristocracy, and above his head-dress are the elaborate hieroglyphic symbols of the Maya script*

TRADING CARAVANS *A miniature scene painted on a Maya pot of the 8th or 9th century shows a deputation of travelling merchants being received by a chief holding a spear. Long-distance trade was in the hands of specialists who were organised into rich and powerful guilds. They dealt in a wide range of luxury goods and regional products, such as salt, cotton cloth, rubber, turquoise, chocolate beans and stones of volcanic lava used for grinding maize. Travel was slow, and a trading caravan might be away from home for months or even years. All merchandise was carried on the backs of porters, and the caravan marched like a military expedition, guarded by armed men*

# The rise of the Aztecs, from vassals to rulers

Coloured plumes as decorations were popular among the Aztecs; this wooden shield is covered with a mosaic of blue and pink feathers. The design, in gold leaf, represents a mythical animal which was the symbol of an Aztec emperor

SKULL MASK *The front of a human skull was encrusted with turquoise, lignite and sea-shell to make this mask. The skull was neatly lined inside with red leather*

GOD AS SNAKE *A double-headed snake, made of wood covered with turquoise and sea-shell, forms an Aztec breast ornament probably representing the Aztecs' god Huitzilopochtli, 'humming bird of the south'*

Their migrations took them all over the Maya lowlands, and between 1224 and 1244 they reached the former Maya capital, which they found abandoned. They set up their own capital on the same spot, renaming it Chichén Itzá (Mouth of the Well of the Itza). These new invaders took control of Yucatan, but were hated and despised by their subjects for the uncouth way in which they spoke Maya, for their bloodthirsty habits, and for their indulgence in unnatural vices.

Because of this unstable political situation, some communities moved to defended sites. For the first time true cities were built in the Maya lowlands and these were walled in stone or protected by ditches and wooden palisades. The later history of the Maya is one of shifting political alliances, cultural degeneration, and a decline in the quality of craftsmanship. By the time the Europeans came, Yucatan was divided into 16 rival and warring states. The Spanish conquest began in earnest in 1528, and by 1540 most of Maya territory was in Spanish hands.

## Coming of the Aztecs

By the time the Spaniards arrived in Middle America, Maya civilization was already past its best. Further west, however, in the highlands of Mexico, the Aztecs were relative newcomers at the moment of conquest.

After a period of chaos which followed the destruction of Teotihuacan by barbarian invaders in about 750, a warlike people called the Toltecs created a new empire in the highlands of Mexico. Tula, their capital city, was founded in the 10th century by a leader called Topiltzin. He worshipped the god Quetzalcoatl ('feathered serpent') and as a sign of respect he added the god's name to his own. Native myths record that Topiltzin-Quetzalcoatl's reign was troubled by religious and political strife, and that he was driven out of Tula. He fled with his followers to the east coast, and there, one of the legends says, he sailed away on a raft of serpents, promising to return to his people at some future time. At about this time, a group of invaders, who may have included Toltec refugees, suddenly appeared in the Maya country, led by a chief named Feathered Serpent and bringing with them Toltec forms of architecture and sculpture.

Topiltzin-Quetzalcoatl's promise to return was kept alive, the legend blending man and god together. The power of this legend caused Montezuma, the last Aztec ruler, to believe for a while that the Spaniards were the god Quetzalcoatl and his followers returning after six centuries to regain their inheritance.

The city of Tula was destroyed by barbarian tribes in 1168, and with the collapse of the Toltec Empire central Mexico entered yet another period of troubles. Semi-civilized tribes poured into the area from outside, and founded petty kingdoms which were perpetually at war with each other. The last of these tribes to arrive was the group which became known to history as the Aztecs, although they referred to themselves as the Mexica or

Tenochca. Their origins are still shrouded in mystery. Their own legends say that in the 12th century they left an island home (whose site has never been located) and spent about 100 years wandering all over Mexico, following the instructions of Huitzilopochtli, their tribal god—his name means 'humming bird of the south'.

When they eventually reached the central Valley of Mexico they found that all the best land had been taken by earlier arrivals. The Aztecs were regarded as intruders, and for many years they lived a miserable existence as vassals of the more powerful tribes.

In 1345 they were allowed to settle in a permanent home, and as the site of their future capital the priests chose an unoccupied island in the great lake which then filled the Valley of Mexico. They called the site Tenochtitlan, 'the Place of the Prickly Pear Cactus'. In 1428 Tenochtitlan gained its independence and, in alliance with the neighbouring cities of Texcoco and Tlacopan, it soon became the dominant power in Mexico. By 1519, some 489 city-states were subject to the alliance the Aztec rulers had formed.

During their period of wandering, the Aztecs had a fairly simple, tribal form of society, but by the 16th century they had become much less democratic. Class distinctions were rigidly enforced, and a man could be executed if he were caught wearing the insignia of a rank higher than his own. At the top of the social pyramid was the ruler, and below him came the main officials, counsellors, judges, military leaders, and governors of conquered provinces. These men were granted private estates, and were the only people allowed to wear cotton cloth, sandals, patterned garments, and ornaments of gold or precious stones. The common people had to make do with plain cloth made of cactus fibre, and with cheap ornaments of wood, semi-precious stones and shell.

All free-born commoners were grouped into *calpullis* (clans). Each *calpulli* owned the land which was tilled by its members, and was also responsible for the upkeep of local temples and the schools which every child was compelled to attend. Below the freemen, and outside the *calpulli* system altogether, were the landless peasants of non-Aztec origin, and the slaves. The priests, who numbered several thousand in Tenochtitlan alone, also constituted a class apart.

## Tribute for the capital

Tenochtitlan had by this time grown into an imperial city, living on the tribute and taxes of subject provinces. Every year the city received more than 9000 tons of food in the form of maize, beans and edible seeds. The rich lowland provinces sent jaguar skins, jade, gold dust and metal articles, sea-shells, feathers of tropical birds and loads of cocoa beans; the beans were made into a drink, and were also used as currency in the market-places.

Most of the expensive materials produced by the subject peoples were either offered to the gods or consumed by the ruler and the nobility.

With the raw materials came the craftsmen, many of them foreigners, so that Tenochtitlan became the most important trade and craft centre in Mexico. Palaces and temples were filled with carved statues and friezes; feather-workers made sumptuous capes, head-dresses, fans and banners. Other specialists worked with precious stones brought from all over the country, and developed the art of covering objects with a mosaic made of turquoise, lignite and coloured shell. Mexican jewellers were famous for the pendants, lip plugs, ear spools, necklaces and nose ornaments which they cast from gold and its alloys. They could also make objects half of gold and half of silver, and were able to manufacture items with movable parts.

## Canals of a capital city

Very little of the Aztec capital is visible today, and the picture of Aztec Tenochtitlan has to be reconstructed from eyewitness accounts by Spanish soldiers and from material found underneath present-day Mexico City, which was founded on the former Aztec site after the conquest.

Tenochtitlan was a great metropolis, between 4 and 5 square miles in extent and with 150,000 to 200,000 inhabitants. It was an island city connected to the lake shore by three causeways and surrounded by irrigated gardens made from reclaimed swamp. Aqueducts carried fresh water from mainland springs. Like a Mexican Venice, Tenochtitlan was a city of canals, and all parts of it could be reached by water. A regular grid of canals and streets divided the city into blocks, and at its heart was a great walled precinct. Outside the wall were the palaces of successive rulers, and within the precinct were the principal temples, priests' quarters, the wooden rack on which were displayed the heads of sacrificed victims, and the stone to which war captives armed with dummy weapons were tethered to be slain by Aztec warriors in a sort of one-sided gladiatorial combat.

Also in the precinct were long I-shaped courts used for a sacred ball-game. Players propelled a rubber ball back and forth over a line drawn across the centre of the court, and were allowed to use only their hips, knees and elbows. At the mid point of each side wall, high above the ground, was a projecting stone ring with a hole just big enough to allow the ball to pass through. If any player managed to drive the ball through a ring, his team won outright and he was allowed to confiscate the clothes and possessions of any spectators he and his friends could catch. The ball-game was a favourite spectator sport, and people wagered all kinds of goods on the result. But at the same time the game was a very important ritual activity. The court symbolised the universe, and the movement of the ball represented the path of the sun, moon or one of the planets.

The ball-game was an ancient custom in the whole of Middle America. The Olmecs and all later peoples played it, and it formed part of several religious ceremonies. The Aztecs also

## A TREASURE WHICH ESCAPED THE CONQUISTADORES

*A breast ornament fashioned in an alloy of gold and copper was among nearly 150 gold and silver objects discovered in 1932 in a tomb at Monte Alban, in territory occupied in the 15th century by peoples known as the Mixtecs. The ornament, which is $4\frac{1}{4}$ in. high, takes the form of a man wearing a crown and a hideous mask with a fleshless mouth, and it is believed to represent the Mixtec Lord of Death and Darkness. The panels on the base include signs representing dates in the Mixtec calendar*

# *When slaughter was a sacred rite*

used the game for divination – as when Montezuma played against the lord of Texcoco to test the truth of a prophecy that strangers would come to rule in Tenochtitlan. The legend records that Montezuma won the first few games but was finally defeated, and it was not long afterwards that Cortez landed and began his conquest of Mexico.

## Sacrifice at the temple

It was human sacrifice more than anything else which appalled the few Europeans who visited Tenochtitlan before its destruction. Human sacrifice has a long history in Mexico, and was practised by most of the tribes of Middle America, but the Aztecs carried it to new heights. It is reported that in 1487, when the temple of Huitzilopochtli was dedicated, as many as 20,000 captives were sacrificed; one of Cortez's companions counted 136,000 skulls on the rack which stood beside that same temple in 1519.

Some of the victims were slaves or criminals, but most of them were war captives. During the rare interludes of peace, when the supply of victims was in danger of drying up, the Aztecs and their allies arranged a kind of tournament with the warriors of neighbouring states. Each side tried to take captives, and once enough sacrificial victims had been obtained the rival armies ended the 'war' and returned home.

To the Spaniards this slaughter, naturally enough, appeared brutal and blasphemous, but to the Aztecs the shedding of blood was a holy act and an essential part of their religion. The gods watched over everything, and were all-powerful. It was they who had created the universe and who controlled man's fate, who sent or withheld rain and sunshine, guarded every hour of the day and night, and influenced even the most trivial aspects of daily life.

Like all Middle American peoples, the Aztecs worshipped a multitude of gods and goddesses, some of whom were already known in the Valley of Mexico during the Teotihuacan period, while others were taken over from the conquered tribes. The national god of the Aztecs, Huitzilopochtli, was a son of the earth goddess and a warrior god, identified with the sun. Every night he battled against the forces of darkness so that the sun would be reborn the next morning. If ever Huitzilopochtli grew weak and feeble, darkness would triumph, the sun would not rise, and the universe itself would come to an end. It was vital that Huitzilopochtli should remain strong and vigorous, and man's duty was to help him by providing nourishment. The most precious food that man could offer was life itself, human hearts and blood, and in this belief lay one of the justifications for the wholesale sacrifice of human beings.

The Mexicans believed that the world would come to an end, for this was foretold in their creation myths. The two original deities were said to have been a divine couple remote from earthly affairs. Their sons were the four powerful creator gods: Huitzilopochtli, the war god; Xipe Totec, the god of springtime and new crops; Quetzalcoatl, the feathered serpent god, and his enemy Tezcatlipoca – 'Smoking Mirror' – warrior of the north, god of the night sky, giver and taker of all life on earth.

According to Aztec legends, the universe had been created on four separate occasions, and each time had been destroyed with all its inhabitants. The Aztecs believed that they were living in the fifth era, the age of Tonatiuh, the sun god, and that their present existence had been made possible only by the self-sacrifice of the gods. To create the sun once again, and to give it strength to move across the heavens, the gods had offered themselves as sacrifices in a mass ceremony. The task of creating mankind had been entrusted to Quetzalcoatl, who journeyed to the underworld to collect the bones of previous generations, which he sprinkled with his own blood in order to give them life. Human sacrifice repeated in a symbolic way the original self-sacrifice of the gods. The myths also prophesied that the fifth era would come to a violent end. The only question was 'When?'

## Two calendars used at once

The Aztecs used two calendars simultaneously. The first was a calendar of 365 days, based on the apparent movement of the sun round the earth. This was the calendar which determined the seasons and the times for planting and harvesting, and it is known to have been more accurate than the solar calendar used in 16th-century Europe. The second calendar, used only for religious and ritual purposes, was based on a 260-day cycle. Each day of the year was thus fixed in terms of two independent calendar cycles and, since the solar and ritual years were of different lengths, it was 52 years before any particular combination could come round again. These 52-year periods had great significance, for at the end of one of them the universe was due to be destroyed by earthquakes. Nobody could foretell which epoch would be the last.

The final day of a 52-year period was therefore a time of crisis and fear, for no one could be sure that the sun would ever rise again. In the evening, the priests went to a mountain top near Tenochtitlan to watch the stars. When the constellation of the Pleiades had slowly climbed to its zenith, they knew the world was safe for another 52 years. A prisoner was quickly stretched over the altar, his chest was opened, and the astronomer priest kindled a fire in the victim's body cavity. Messengers lit their torches from this flame, and ran to carry the New Fire to every temple and every home in the Valley of Mexico. Life would continue – but the next crisis was only 52 years away.

## Torture for the rain god

Aztec philosophy is full of symbolism, and the taste for the symbolic shows itself in the ceremonies and festivals held at regular intervals throughout the year. At the feast in

### GODS HUNGRY FOR BLOOD

The ancient peoples of Middle America believed that their destiny lay in the hands of the gods, each of whom demanded his offering – often in human blood. At ceremonies in honour of the Aztec rain god priests poled a canoe containing human hearts out into a lake, and let it sink beneath the waters. When Emperor Ahuitzotl consecrated the temple of Huitzilopochtli it took four days to slaughter the 20,000 prisoners of war offered to win the god's favour. Warriors often sacrificed captives taken in battle, and the victims went joyfully to the block, believing that after death they would go to a special paradise which they shared with those who had died in battle. To try to avoid this fate was to disobey the will of the gods, and legends praise prisoners who rejected all opportunities to escape and submitted to the priests' knives

FEARSOME GOD *Aztec religious art abounds in macabre themes and representations, doubtless intended to instil fear and awe in the worshippers. In this stone figure of Xolotl, the god has the body of a skeleton and his head is a hideously snarling dog-mask*

honour of the maize goddess, young women were beheaded as they danced, to symbolise the harvesting of the maize cobs. And at one of the ceremonies for the rain god, little children were tortured until their tears fell like the raindrops which gave life to the crops. But not all the gods were warriors and shedders of blood. There were gods of feasting, games, and even of drunkenness, and their festivals were like carnivals, with sports, buffoonery, and offerings of flowers and foodstuffs.

The same kind of symbolism is reflected in Aztec sculpture and painting. Artists were capable of realism, and produced some naturalistic carvings of men, animals, and even insects and plants, but when depicting the gods it was important to include as much information and symbolic detail as possible. In the painted books Tezcatlipoca is shown as a warrior carrying a shield and a bundle of throwing spears. His face is painted black to show that he is a night god, and horizontal stripes on his

TEMPLE GUARD *The warlike Toltecs, who succeeded the Maya as rulers of Yucatan, brought bloodthirsty gods. Before a ruined temple of Chichén Itzá is a reclining figure on which victims may have been sacrificed*

FLAYED ALIVE *Xipe Totec was the Aztec god of spring, and every March the priests flayed living victims and paraded in their skins. Sculptors showed the gaping mouth and the flayed hand dangling at the wrist*

TEMPLE VICTIMS *An Indian artist living shortly after the Spanish conquest of the 16th century has left a picture of human sacrifice as he watched it in his youth. The victim lies on his back over a stone block in front of the temple. One priest holds the man down while another cuts through the ribs and breastbone to tear out the heart, which was offered to the gods or rubbed on the faces of the temple idols. The operation took only a few seconds. The body of a previous victim is being dragged away by assistants. The Spanish conquistador Bernal Diaz explored the temple quarter of Tenochtitlan, the Aztec capital, where he was shown baskets of human flesh which had been prepared for the ceremonial cannibalism which played a part in certain festivals. The temple walls were crusted with blood, as were the clothes and the long hair of the officiating priests. Diaz said, with great disgust, that the place stank like a Spanish slaughterhouse. A great rack was filled with the skulls of thousands whose hearts and blood had been offered to the insatiable gods*

SACRIFICIAL WEAPON *Metals were not uncommon in Mexico, but for rituals the Aztecs preferred traditional materials. This sacrificial knife has a blade of chalcedony and a wooden handle encrusted with turquoise, shell and lignite. The figure is dressed as an eagle warrior, a member of an order dedicated to the sun god*

cheeks show that he is one of the four creator gods. On his head, or in place of one of his feet, is the mirror of black volcanic glass in which he can see everything that is happening in the world.

## The Spanish conquest

The Aztecs saw themselves as a chosen people especially favoured by the gods, but in return for these benefits the gods expected their reward. War had given the Aztecs land and riches, but it was equally important as a source of captives for sacrifice. Because of this, war was a religious as well as a military and political activity. All men had been trained to handle weapons during their school years, and physical bravery was taken for granted. Songs and poems were written in praise of war and of bravery in combat; promotion and high office were given to successful warriors; and it was the wish of every man to shed his quota of blood in honour of the gods. This was very

different from the 16th-century European concept of war, and the story of the conquest shows how little the two sides had in common.

The Aztecs, once the greed and treachery of the Spaniards had made their human origins all too clear, fought as if the war was just another tribal conflict, in which the defeated nation lost its political freedom but was allowed to keep its gods and customs. The Spaniards were fighting a more total kind of war in which there was no room for religious toleration.

The struggle was not just between two armies, or even two technologies, but between two completely different types of civilization. The eventual outcome was never in doubt; even if Cortez had not succeeded, others would have followed in greater strength. The confrontation between Europe and America was inevitable, and the Spanish triumph established 16th-century European ways in the place of native Indian culture. At first glance, Middle American civiliza-

tion seems the greatest blind alley in the whole of human history. Apart from certain food crops and medicinal plants, Middle America has contributed little to the industrial and technological civilization of the modern world. But a closer look shows that Indian culture is not extinct. Half the population of present-day Guatemala is Indian, mostly Maya-speaking, and the old languages can still be heard in villages only a short bus ride from the factories of Mexico City. On Sundays the people of the capital pour out to Teotihuacan to see the pyramids built by their ancestors.

In the folk culture of these villages many of the native customs have survived. There are still people who understand the ancient calendars, keep the old social traditions alive, and burn incense to pre-Spanish gods who are only thinly disguised as Roman Catholic saints. After more than four centuries of European influence, the gap between the two civilizations has not yet closed.

# A golden empire put to the sword in Peru

## AD 1440–1532

*In the mountains of the Andes, the Incas built cities where civilized life flourished for nearly a century before the Spanish conquerors arrived*

No other empire in history had a more dramatic rise and fall than the empire of the Incas. In only 90 years, between 1440 and 1530, it expanded from a small kingdom based on the city of Cuzco to a huge empire including much of present-day Ecuador and stretching southwards through Peru to central Chile. Within a few years of reaching its peak, the Inca Empire was torn apart by a small and ruthless army of European invaders. But while it lasted it was a remarkably well-organised society, ruled by an emperor, the Sapa Inca, who was regarded as a god, and administered by a state civil service.

The Inca capacity for social and economic planning was matched by engineering skill. No matter how forbidding the landscape, the Incas overcame it. Across the desert coast in the west and between the snow-swept heights of the Andes in the east ran the roads which knit the empire together, spanning deep gorges and ravines on suspension bridges, and crossing broad rivers on pontoons made of rafts lashed together. Strongly built forts of well-cut stone perched on highland ridges; and everywhere in the high Andes, land for farming was extended by terraces constructed at dizzy angles. A single

king ruled, and the same gods were worshipped, throughout an empire of extraordinary diversity in climate and landscape – ranging from the rainless, hot desert of northern Chile to the tropical wet lowlands of coastal Ecuador, from the fertile basins of Peru to the barren highlands of Bolivia.

It was the Inca achievement to create a political unity in defiance of geography, and even in defiance of history, for the tribes they conquered were forced into the Inca pattern. But earlier peoples living in the Andean area before the Incas prepared the ground for them.

The first Peruvians migrated from the north, where their ancestors had arrived from Asia some 30,000 years ago over the land bridge which then connected Alaska and Siberia. They were hunters and fishers with primitive weapons of wood, stone and bone. But about 2000 BC agricultural settlements began to spring up, based on the cultivation of beans and squashes – a vegetable like the pumpkin.

Between 300 BC and AD 800, the northern coast of Peru was dominated by a people called the Moche, who built enormous platforms of sun-dried clay and huge aqueducts and canals up to 75 miles long. They made thousands of

**INCA EMPIRE IN 1532**

*At the time of the Spanish invasion the Inca Empire stretched 2500 miles along the coast of South America*

## PRIZED ANIMALS

*Two silver figurines fashioned by Inca craftsmen depict two animals that, for different reasons, were both essential to the nation's economy. The alpaca (far left) was prized for the silky wool of its long coat, which was woven into cloth. The llama (left), while producing a coarse wool, was valued chiefly as a pack animal. The Incas did not have the wheel or the horse, and the llama was their sole means of transport; it could only carry loads of 100 lb., however, and was not strong enough for a man to ride. The government owned large herds of both animals. The Inca army relied on caravans of llamas for its baggage transport, and for supplying the forts and storehouses along the roads which crossed rivers and gorges to link the empire together*

## THE INCA CITY THAT WAS LOST FOR FOUR CENTURIES

Machu Picchu, the 'lost city' of the Incas, stands on a mountain ridge high in the Peruvian Andes. On three sides rock walls plunge 1000 ft into a gorge. More than 100 stairways link the city's temples, palaces and houses, which were built of white granite blocks fitted precisely together without mortar. On the high rock to the left was the Temple of the Sun, worshipped by the Incas as the life-giving force. Reservoirs were built, and the slopes were terraced so that maize and beans could be grown. The Spaniards did not find the city, but the Incas abandoned it some time after the conquest and it remained unknown to the outside world until 1911

# *Religion and ritual in the kingdom of the sun*

**WARRIOR ARMED FOR BATTLE**

*A baked clay statuette depicts a kneeling warrior, looking rather like a knight of medieval Europe with his heavy mace and shield, conical helmet, and tunic with colourful heraldic devices. The figure was modelled before AD 600 by a potter of the Moche people, who dominated the northern coastal regions of Peru for several hundred years. The highly realistic treatment which Moche potters gave to their subjects was copied by the Incas. Maces of bronze and stone were standard weapons in the powerful Inca army, too; but such Bronze Age weapons were to prove no match for the steel weapons of the Spanish invaders*

pots with modelled and painted scenes showing trees, animals and birds, the weapons they used in hunting, and realistic human faces.

The designs on the pottery and textiles of the early Peruvian peoples were affected between AD 500 and 1000 by an important religious influence originating from the bleak plateau near Lake Titicaca, 13,000 ft above sea level, and spreading widely over highland and coast. Artists began to depict a winged god with weeping eyes, carrying a staff in either hand, and attended by figures which represent pumas and condors. This was the creator-god Viracocha, later venerated by the Incas, and at Tiahuanaco in north-west Bolivia stands what was probably his major shrine. Huge stone figures, granite pillars, terraced courts and stone-lined enclosures cover the site today, and a gateway is embossed with a frieze of a weeping god; his tears may symbolise rain.

The final pre-Inca stage of Peruvian history was between 1000 and 1400, when powerful kingdoms emerged on the coast and in the highlands, and true cities were built. On the north coast, the kingdom of the Chimu, successors to the Moche, had a capital, Chanchan, covering some 8 square miles and made of dried mud-brick. The Chimu built roads and fortresses and had a well-organised state, as did similar kingdoms further south. When the Incas came to power, they learnt much from the peoples they conquered.

## Building an empire

The Incas began as just one of many tribes in highland Peru. What transformed them into an aggressive empire-building military force will never be known precisely. But individual genius probably played a large part. In 1438, Pachacuti Inca Yupanqui became Sapa Inca, and it was he who began the deliberate expansion of the Inca state, and the policy of absorbing defeated foes into Inca civilization. He was brilliantly successful, not only in warfare and diplomacy, but also in government and administration, and his heir, his son Topa Inca, had the same kind of organising ability. Between 1438 and the death of Topa in 1493, the Inca Empire was largely established.

The arms which helped the well-trained Inca soldiers to conquer wide territories were the same as those used by other tribes in the area of the Andes. The long-range weapon was the sling, and there were spears, axes of bronze, and vicious-looking star-shaped maces of bronze or stone for hand-to-hand combat.

All boys had organised physical training from an early age, and they acquired practice with the sling as they kept wild animals and birds away from flocks and crops. For the sons of officials there was more rigorous training in the form of an annual competition when teams of boys were turned out on to the mountains, without weapons or sandals, for a survival test lasting nine days.

After defeating an enemy, the Incas brought in their engineers to construct impressive forts and to extend the communications system. The excellence of the Inca roads gave the armies great mobility, and storehouses of food, clothing and weapons were placed along them at regular intervals – roughly a day's journey apart for a marching man, for the Incas had no wheeled vehicles or horses.

But the Incas preferred to extend their empire by diplomacy rather than by conflict. Enemy chiefs and their lords would be offered posts in the imperial administration, and the local gods would be respected and given a place among the Inca gods, provided that the sun-god, chief god of the Incas, was recognised as supreme. The Incas also spread their own language, Quechua, as the common tongue.

## Rule of a 'living god'

The emperor, the Sapa Inca, was surrounded by veneration and ritual. He was the son of the sun, a living god, and mere mortals entering his presence bowed their heads, went barefoot and carried a small parcel on their backs to symbolise their lowly status in comparison with his divine power. For most people he was a remote figure, a living god dwelling in semi-isolated grandeur in his great capital of Cuzco, in the south of modern Peru; the name Cuzco means 'navel' or centre, for the Inca world revolved around it.

By the middle of the 15th century the emperor had become so exalted that only his sister could become his consort – a remarkable parallel with the incestuous customs of some of the pharaohs of ancient Egypt. The Inca's sister was his *ccoya*, or principal wife, though he had the right, since he was the law, to take large numbers of secondary wives. The god-king ruled in splendour. He dined off gold dishes, eating food carefully prepared by young women chosen for their beauty and skill. These maidens also spun the silk-like wool of the vicuña, an animal like the llama, to make the emperor's richly embroidered clothes, which were so sacred that when he had finished with them they were ceremonially burnt.

The Sapa Inca also wore large gold plugs attached to the lobes of his ears, and a royal band, hung with gold beads, around his head. When the emperor died, his body was mummified and wrapped in gorgeous textiles, to be kept in his palace, still attended by retainers and available for the festivals where its presence was essential. The emperor's close wives and servants, however, would accompany him in death, to serve him in the next world; after great festivities, during which they became intoxicated, they were strangled.

## A garden made of gold

The royal palace was built by master-craftsmen whose bronze tools cut stone into rectangular blocks of varying size, fitting each block so perfectly to the next that no mortar was needed between them. On the walls hung rich tapestries and massive ornaments of gold, for this precious metal was sacred to the sun-god. The royal palace at Cuzco even had a garden of gold, with life-sized stalks of maize and corn-cobs, animals and birds. Gold was purely ornamental, for the Incas used no money.

The Incas absorbed many earlier Indian cultures which had been established in western South America for over 1000 years. In southern Peru, as early as 300 BC, bodies buried in the dry sand of Paracas were wrapped in brilliant, multi-coloured textiles. Another southern people, the Nazcas, made fine pottery. The Moche of northern Peru were skilled potters, too; while their successors, the Chimu, survived until the emergence of the Incas

PREY OF THE JAGUAR GOD *The jaguar was sacred to many of the peoples of early Peru, and was often depicted in clay models and carvings on temples. This pot, made by a Moche potter about AD 500, shows a jaguar attacking his victim*

AN ART RICH IN COLOUR *Bright colours were used by the potters of the Nazca people, one of the forerunners of the Incas, who flourished in fertile valleys in southern Peru from 300 BC to AD 800. They moulded their jars into imaginative shapes, like this effigy of a woman holding fruits*

GOURD BOWL *Fine inlay work in stones and shells is typical of the work of the Moche, early settlers in northern Peru, and their successors, the Chimu. This bowl, made by a Chimu craftsman and dating from the 12th century, is made from a gourd elaborately inlaid with mother-of-pearl*

SHROUDS FOR THE DEAD *Mummies of chieftains of the Paracas people, who lived in an arid peninsula of southern Peru, were wrapped in richly coloured and intricately woven fabrics which were preserved for over 2000 years by the dry sand. In this fragment from one shroud, three demon figures wear head-dresses ending in snakes' heads, and carry ceremonial axes and staffs*

# Strangers, mistaken for gods, who sacked an empire

Seldom have the lives of the mass of the people been so highly organised, from birth to death, as they were under the Incas. This was the society of the ant hill, with thousands of civil servants collecting tribute and administering justice. Trained officials kept the accounts but, since writing was unknown in Inca Peru, they used a system of coloured and knotted cords, *quipus*, the colours and knots representing commodities and quantities.

All land belonged to the state, and was divided on a three-fold basis: the product of one part supported the court and administration; another part paid for the state religion, temples and priesthood; and the third part was divided locally among the people. Taxes were paid in the form of labour, the able-bodied being required to till the lands owned by the state in their own areas before turning to their individual plots.

The economy of the Inca Empire was based on farming. In the highlands, where herding of llamas and alpacas was important, the common fibre was wool, but on the warmer coast it was cotton. Maize was the staple grain, but in the higher altitudes grains peculiar to Peru – quiñoa, oca, olluco – were grown instead.

Most of the Inca Empire had a uniform and rigid social organisation. Above the immediate family was the *ayllu*, a group of families living as a community in the same place, and considering themselves as related to each other, working as a unit and owning their lands collectively. The *ayllus* were grouped into provinces, each of which had its own capital,

and all members of that province wore a distinctive badge in their head-dresses. The provinces were grouped into the four quarters of the empire, the heads of which, together with the emperor, formed an imperial council. Thus a net of authority, from Cuzco, the capital, to the smallest *ayllu*, was thrown over the whole empire, and commands were passed down through a chain.

The word of the divine emperor was law. No one could challenge the orders of the living god, but the council which advised him could clearly influence his decisions, and the system was no mere tyranny. The Inca emperors accepted that they also had a job to do – to keep their people content, and to govern wisely.

## Privileges and penalties

The rapid expansion of the empire created a large governing class. The Inca nobility, together with chiefs of conquered tribes who had accepted Inca rule, formed the high administration. Their way of life was a less brilliant image of the Sapa Inca's. They lived well at the state's expense, did no manual labour, and had servants and secondary wives.

Nevertheless, status meant responsibility, and Inca laws brought swift and severe punishment on any member of the governing class who failed to do his duty. A noble who committed adultery was sentenced to death, since he had demeaned his class, while a commoner committing the same offence was tortured, but not killed. On the other hand, crimes committed by commoners against the state or against the

aristocracy often carried the death penalty. The offender might have his brains beaten out with a club, or be hanged upside-down until dead, thrown from a cliff or stoned to death.

The horizons of the common man were limited, though he might travel if serving in the army for a period or recruited for special work such as road-building, panning for gold in the river beds, and other public work. Potters, metal-workers and builders were craftsmen, and so exempt from labour service, and they were supported by the state in return for their skill, producing luxury goods for use by the court and the nobility. The working of gold and silver had reached a high level of skill. Craftsmen made necklaces, bracelets, ear-rings and other ornaments by casting them in moulds, or by beating the soft metal to paper-thin sheets on which designs were embossed. Gold and silver inlay work on wood and shell was another outstanding craft.

Most women married commoners and shared their routine lives, but the most beautiful girls were picked out at the age of ten and sent to special schools in the capitals of the provinces. Here, after learning how to cook, weave and so on, a further selection was made. Some went to court to wait on the living god, or to be given by him to favoured nobles. Others, known as the Virgins of the Sun, were sent for temple service and were sworn to chastity.

Ordinary people led a well-ordered, hard-working and very modest existence. They lived in simple one-roomed dwellings, made either of mud-brick on the rainless coast, or else of

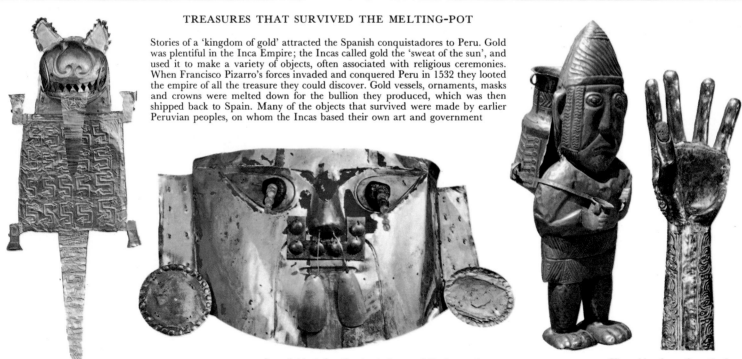

### TREASURES THAT SURVIVED THE MELTING-POT

Stories of a 'kingdom of gold' attracted the Spanish conquistadores to Peru. Gold was plentiful in the Inca Empire; the Incas called gold the 'sweat of the sun', and used it to make a variety of objects, often associated with religious ceremonies. When Francisco Pizarro's forces invaded and conquered Peru in 1532 they looted the empire of all the treasure they could discover. Gold vessels, ornaments, masks and crowns were melted down for the bullion they produced, which was then shipped back to Spain. Many of the objects that survived were made by earlier Peruvian peoples, on whom the Incas based their own art and government

DRUG POUCH *A gold pouch in the form of a puma skin held the leaves of a plant known as coca, used as a narcotic*

MASTER METAL-WORKERS *Immediately before the rise to power of the Incas, the most powerful people along Peru's northern coastlands were the Chimu, a nation whose richness and splendour were reflected in the work of their goldsmiths. This gold funeral mask for a chieftain, complete with nose and ear ornaments, bears traces of red and green paint and has eyes of stone. Many Chimu craftsmen were pressed into service by the conquering Incas, and continued to produce fine metal-work for their new overlords*

LIFE AND CUSTOMS *The golden figure from the Inca period (left) depicts a man carrying an aryballus, a jar used for transporting liquids. The hollow hand made in gold (right) is from a Chimu tomb, and may have been used to hold incense. The arm is elaborately tattooed, a frequent practice among the Chimu*

uncut stone plastered with mud in the high-lands. Their roofs were thatched and gabled, and smoke from the fire simply drifted through the thatch. Glass, like the wheel was unknown; the houses had no windows, and only one low door. Furniture was rare. Cooking was done over a stone-and-mud stove, and the diet was monotonous, consisting largely of soups and stews, with maize, beans, squashes and potatoes as staple foods. Meat was scarce.

In this status-obsessed society, clothes were status symbols. The nobility adorned them-selves with gold ear-plugs and other ornaments, and dressed in fine woollen clothing rich in design and brilliant in colour. The common man, on the other hand, had a rather meagre wardrobe, consisting usually of a breech-clout and cloak of coarse cloth, a simple poncho and blanket, a head-band, and sandals of llama hide. His wife's basic garment was a one-piece dress, descending to the ankles and gathered at the waist by a long, wide sash.

## Worship in the 'House of Gold'

Faith and worship were woven into the daily lives of the Incas. The higher classes believed in Viracocha, the shadowy creator-god who had made all things, including the heavenly bodies. Viracocha was so great a force, in-habiting the whole universe, that only one temple, near the capital, was dedicated to his name, and only the court and the high nobility were allowed to worship him. For most people, the sun-god, Inti, was supreme; he was represented in temples by huge golden discs with a human face, while his consort was the moon-goddess, Quilla.

The Sapa Inca, as the son of the sun, played a leading part in many festivals. When the time came for planting the crops, it was he who broke the first sod with a golden hoe, in the presence not only of the court and the people but also of the mummified bodies of his ances-tors. Then all the living celebrated with music and singing, followed by feasting and drinking.

The empire had imposing temples in many places, particularly in provincial capitals, but none matched the great sun temple at Cuzco, called Coricancha, or the 'House of Gold'. This temple, made of perfectly shaped rec-tangular blocks of stone, contained a huge disc of solid gold representing the sun. It was the religious centre of the Inca Empire, and in charge of it was the Villac Umu, or high priest of the sun. He was the second most important man in the empire, and invariably a close blood-relative of the emperor.

Human sacrifice was rare in the Inca Empire, though it was practised at times of great national crisis, such as the illness of the emperor, plague or famine. The victims were usually children, ten-year-old boys and girls chosen for their perfect physique and appear-ance; they were killed by strangulation or by cutting their throats.

This confident, expanding empire of 12 million people was about to suffer a shock before which it was utterly defenceless, like a human body attacked by some strange and irresistible virus. Late in December 1530, a Spanish force of 180 men sailed southwards from Panama. Their commander, Francisco Pizarro, an illiterate but experienced soldier, knew precisely what he was after, for in 1528 he had voyaged along the Inca coastline and seen something of the empire's riches.

His task appeared a hard one. The Inca Empire had been created by the best military machine in ancient America, and its com-munications were good. But the Spaniards arrived in the wake of a civil war which split the empire. The Sapa Inca, Huayna Capac, died about 1525 and the succession was dis-puted between his sons Atahuallpa and Huascar. Atahuallpa, with the aid of the best Inca generals, defeated Huascar in battle and became emperor. But the realm had suffered an enormous shock and had not yet settled down when Pizarro reached Tumbez in 1532.

Other factors favoured the Spaniards. Being so few, they had nothing to lose and everything to gain, and they fought with a savage ruth-lessness. Moreover, while the Inca armies were superb at their own technological level, firearms and weapons of steel were a different matter. The Spanish horses were an unknown terror: the first Indians to see an unhorsed Spaniard fled, believing that a strange animal had come apart to form two separate beings.

Finally, Inca lore had long forecast that the god Viracocha would return one day to his kingdom; some legends said that the god was light-skinned. When white strangers arrived, with weapons that made thunder and lightning like a god, the psychological impact was immense. Pizarro murdered Atahuallpa and captured Cuzco. The Inca Empire dis-appeared, and its people became subjects of a new Sapa Inca across the seas.

## Land of pineapples and cocaine

The visible legacy of the Inca Empire is seen most clearly in the Indian races of Andean America and in the physical remains of a glorious past which still lie on the landscape – the myriads of cultivation terraces found everywhere in the mountains, and the still impressive fortresses such as Sacsahuamán, Machu Picchu and Ollontaytambo.

There is something to be learnt from the advanced social structure of the Inca state, which looked after the material needs of its people in return for certain clearly understood duties. But the intellectual legacy is not all. The discovery of America doubled the range of food plants known to Europe, and the Andean contribution to this process was considerable. The potato, in many varieties, the pumpkin and the pineapple were three of the plants known to the Incas and their pre-decessors which have spread throughout the world. Other plants and trees with medicinal properties, such as coca, the source of cocaine, and cinchona, from which quinine is obtained, are gifts of Peruvian civilization to the progress of mankind. The humble Indian farmer, no less than the Inca emperor, contributed to the achievements of the land of the living god.

**WINGED GOD OF THE CHIMU**

*This Chimu gold knife or* tumi *was meant for religious ceremonial use rather than sacrifices. It is 18 in. long and weighs over 2 lb. The elaborately wrought hilt, inlaid with turquoise, depicts a winged god. He wears the ear-plugs popular among the Inca nobility, and humming birds hang from his head-dress. When the Incas conquered a nation they absorbed its deities into their religion, which recognised many minor gods beneath Viracocha, the creator-god. The Incas also venerated their emperors as living gods*

# Early kingdoms of tropical Africa

## FROM 1000 BC

*The continent where man began was the scene of
civilizations that prospered centuries before the
Europeans came, and whose values still endure today*

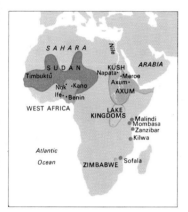

### AFRICAN STATES

*From the forests of West Africa to the
open bush of Rhodesia, early peoples
made their mark on tropical Africa*

Africa has a history of settlement by man
and his remote ancestors spanning the
whole of the last 2 million years. Yet
little of Africa's early history was known to the
world until 150 years ago; and when the first
European explorers of the so-called 'Dark
Continent' began to discover the traces of early
civilizations they often refused to believe, from
their limited knowledge of the continent, that
the tribes they encountered could have created
these civilizations.

Stone tools and fragments of bone from prehistoric times have been found in the Olduvai
Gorge of northern Tanzania. These suggest that
Africa may have been the nursery in which the
first man-like creatures began to learn those
skills in hunting and in shaping primitive stone
axes which were to set mankind on the long
path towards civilization.

Just as Africa has provided this important
evidence of man's most primitive ancestors, so
too has the continent preserved some of the
earliest known examples of the creative skills
which distinguish modern man from his predecessors. Some 8000 years ago the Sahara,

today the largest desert in the world, was a
fertile region of wooded hills, lush valleys and
great rolling plains. For centuries, Stone Age
men lived there, and on the walls of their rock
shelters they left thousands of paintings.

Between 4000 and 2000 BC, however, the
Sahara gradually dried up, and its inhabitants
moved north, east and south. To the north they
founded the earliest dynasties of Egypt. To the
east and south they mixed with people long
settled in the vastness of tropical Africa; their
descendants built cities and founded empires
which were to reach the level of high civilizations. The earliest of these was contemporary
with Ancient Egypt; the latest were still
flourishing when European traders arrived off
Africa's coasts in the 15th century. Some
survived even after European power became
predominant in the late 1800's, and have
influenced modern independent Africa.

The earlier settlers whom the migrants from
the Sahara found in tropical Africa included
primitive peoples who had lived in scattered
bands all over the continent since earliest
times; their descendants today are the pygmies

### THE MAJESTY OF KINGSHIP

*Throughout Africa, great monarchs have
left evidence of their power. The magnificent bronze plaque (left) which
decorated a palace wall in Benin
(modern Nigeria), in the 16th century
shows the oba, or king, protected by a
heavily armed bodyguard. The sculptor
has exaggerated the size of the oba's
necklace and war hammer, to emphasise
his semi-divine authority. Two thousand miles away, the Rozvi monarchs
who built the walled fortress at Zimbabwe (right) in the 16th and 17th
centuries did so as much to hide their
divine rulers from the sight of commoners as for the sake of defence. The
conical tower and parts of the 31 ft
high wall still stand*

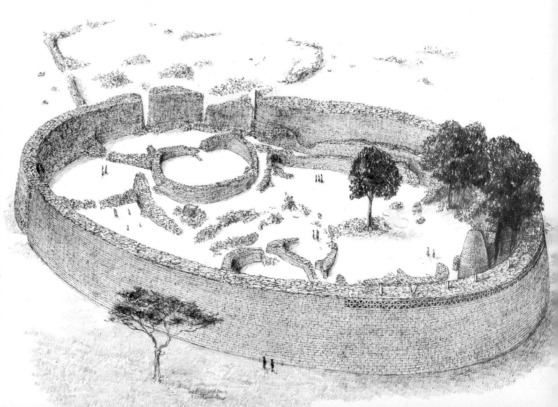

# *An early Christian empire in the Ethiopian highlands*

**CHURCH IN THE ROCK**

*Some of the most unusual Christian churches in the world are those built out of solid rock at Lalibela, high in the mountains of Ethiopia, in the 13th century. To construct this Church of St George, the builders had to sink a 40 ft deep trench into the rock, leaving in its centre a huge block of stone which was then hollowed out to form the church. Its cross-shaped roof is at ground level*

of the Zaïre forests and the bushmen of the Kalahari Desert. The Negroes, who were eventually to people much of the continent south of the Sahara, emerged later; the first Negroes probably lived as fishermen along the banks of the Niger and the Nile about 6000 years ago.

By about 500 BC the early Negroes had learnt how to mine and work metals, especially iron. Their population increased and they began to spread into eastern and southern Africa. They took with them the knowledge of iron-working, and their language, Bantu, became the ancestor of most of the languages which are spoken today in Africa south of the Equator.

Meanwhile cattle, sheep, horses and camels had been introduced into northern and north-eastern Africa, possibly by lighter-skinned peoples from Asia. The rearing of cattle soon spread southwards and became a central feature of the life of many African peoples.

Nearly all the peoples of tropical Africa were illiterate; written records began only after contact with Arab and European traders and missionaries. African societies never invented the wheel; and because of lack of suitable stone they have left few buildings. They have, however, left some monuments; particularly impressive are small figures made of stone, metal and wood, often used in rituals to mark birth, marriage and death and for the fertility of humans, animals and crops.

The principal African characteristic, however, has been the way in which the people of the continent conquered harsh environments to develop societies which proved balanced and stable. African states were ruled by chiefs or kings who in many cases were believed to be

## LIFE IN A GREEN SAHARA

For thousands of years up to about 2000 BC, much of the Sahara was fertile enough to support groups of farmers and their herds, as well as many wild animals. Artists of the time left graphic paintings on the rocks among which they lived. During the last 20 years thousands of these paintings have been discovered in the Tassili region of the central Saharan uplands, now surrounded by scorching desert. They are vivid reminders of the great changes which have affected the earth even within the short time of man's existence.

The Saharan paintings give the impression of a generally peaceful and comfortable way of life. Cattle-keeping played a major role, as it has done in many African communities, and the Saharan artists showed an exact and loving memory of the physical characteristics of their livestock. They also portrayed wild animals such as elephants, giraffes, rhinoceroses, gazelles and ostriches. The paintings show that music and dancing, too, were as important to the Saharan peoples as they have been to later generations of Africans. Ritual dances linked the living with the spirits of their ancestors, giving them a sense of continuity

BIG GAME *The elephants shown in delicate outline in this painting are recognisable as the ancestors of the herds that roam parts of Africa today; but elephants had left the drying Sahara by about 1000 BC*

GRAZING HERD *The Saharan artist has even recorded the colouring of individual cows. Mature animals graze in pastures; the calves are tethered to a rope, and women and children work by the huts*

gods; but even the king was subject to the rules which governed the smooth running of the entire community. This spanned the whole range of human existence. Each individual – man, woman and child – had an appointed place in society, and the dead and those still to be born were regarded as being just as important as the living.

## Golden cities on the Nile

The earliest of the major civilizations of tropical Africa arose about 1000 BC among the peoples of the Nile Valley in Nubia, part of modern Sudan, and flourished for more than 1000 years. The northern Nubians were dark-skinned people, whose ancestors probably originated in Asia. Further south – around modern Khartoum – there were Negroes. The Egyptians knew this whole area as the land of Kush, and it was the source of much of the gold of the ancient world.

The first capital of Kush was Napata, set in a great bend of the Nile. On either side of the fertile valley now lies barren desert, but 3000 years ago the whole area was fertile grassland. In the 8th century BC the rulers of Kush were strong enough to conquer and rule Egypt; but between 676 and 666 BC the mighty Assyrians swept into Egypt, driving the Kushite pharaohs back into Kush.

From their contacts with the Assyrians, the Kushites learnt to use iron for weapons and for tools. There was iron ore around Napata, but by the 6th century wood for burning to smelt the ore was becoming scarcer and the land was becoming spoilt by over-grazing. The Kushite rulers therefore moved to a new capital at Meroe, 300 miles further up the Nile. Meroe

was situated on rich deposits of iron ore, which the Kushites mined in large quantities. To this day, huge slag heaps still stand amid the barren landscape.

The ruins of Napata and Meroe, and of other sites, still stand. There are the remains of pyramids like those of Egypt, but there are influences from other sources too – pillars that are Hellenistic in origin, arches that resemble those of southern Arabia, hieroglyphs with Hindu-like symbols.

At its height, Kush was immensely rich. As well as having its own gold and iron, it controlled extensive trade routes. But by AD 300 much of the kingdom had fallen prey to desert nomads, and it was finally overthrown by the emperor of Axum, the rising power on the Ethiopian plateau to the south.

## Empire of the Queen of Sheba's son

The early inhabitants of Axum, who were probably of mixed Asian and Negro origin, were joined about 500 BC by settlers from southern Arabia who increased the area's agricultural production and trade. In turn they were influenced by Judaism – there is an Ethiopian Jewish community to this day – and by Christianity. From these contacts arose the legend that the Queen of Sheba (Sabaea, an ancient kingdom of southern Arabia whose people migrated across the Red Sea to Ethiopia) visited King Solomon, and on her return to Sabaea bore his son, who became emperor of Ethiopia and founded the Solomaic dynasty. This is the royal line of the Lion of Judah, from whom all Ethiopian emperors claim direct descent. By AD 100 a strong empire emerged, based on the highland city of Axum and the

port of Adulis (the modern Massawa), and drawing its strength from a flourishing Red Sea trade. As the wealth of Kush had been founded on gold, so that of Axum was founded on ivory; the regions to the south and west of Axum were the world's chief source of ivory in the early Christian era. Axum was a city of palaces and temples, the most impressive remnants of which are tall needles or obelisks, probably built for some religious purpose.

In the 4th century AD, King Ezana of Axum, the emperor who overthrew Kush, was converted to Christianity by a Syrian Christian called Frumentius. The culture, religion and written language of the Axumites spread to most of the people of highland Ethiopia, and still survives today.

Ethiopia – the name comes from the Greek *aithiops*, 'dark skinned' – is thus one of the oldest Christian empires in the world. It owes its survival largely to its isolation; while Egypt and the coastal Red Sea lands fell to Islam, Christian Ethiopia remained cut off from the outside world until the arrival of the Portuguese around 1500. It was not until the 19th century that Europeans regularly visited Ethiopia, to find there a unique mixture of Byzantine and African Christianity, represented at its finest in the 13th-century churches of Lalibela.

## Trade across the Sahara

The drying up of the Sahara by 2000 BC had made the desert a formidable obstacle between north and south. But so important were the trans-Saharan trade and cultural links that men continued to brave the terrors of the desert crossing. A succession of powerful states emerged in the Sudanic belt – named after the

## PRESTER JOHN'S LAND

*The dim interiors of the rock churches at Lalibela glow with brightly coloured frescoes and other paintings. One fresco shows a light-skinned Christ entering Jerusalem in triumph, to the welcome of darker-skinned believers who pour libations in his path. Ethiopia became a Christian kingdom in AD 333, and after Egypt fell to Islam in 640 it was entirely cut off from the main centres of Christianity for 800 years. This remote kingdom gave rise in the Middle Ages to the legend of Prester John, who was said to rule over a Christian empire in Africa. Ethiopia remains Christian to the present day*

# In East and West Africa, Arab traders bring a new faith

Arabic word for 'black' – with a prosperity based on their control of the southern markets of the trans-Saharan trade routes. The ancient kingdom of Ghana (well to the north-west of modern Ghana) arose in the 8th century and flourished for 300 years. In the 13th century the empire of Mali absorbed Ghana and spread westwards to the Atlantic coast. Mali's famed capital was Timbuktu, on the Niger River. When the Arab explorer Leo Africanus visited Mali in the 16th century he described its people as 'superior to all other Negroes in wit, civility and industry'. Timbuktu was then a town of 6000 houses with a splendid royal court, and markets where European cloth was sold.

After 1350 the expanding empire of Songhai began to take over the territory of Mali, maintaining the reputation of Timbuktu and also creating a prosperous new capital at nearby Gao. To the east, around Lake Chad, the separate empire of Kanem-Bornu survived for 1000 years, from 800 to 1800. Between Songhai and Kanem-Bornu were the Hausa city-states. Hausa never became a unified empire, but the Hausa cities – Kano, Katsina and others – were rich and industrious. The best-known Hausa products were its leather goods, which were traded across the desert to North Africa; they were bought by European merchants, and taken as far as England where they became known as 'Moroccan' leather.

The Sudanic kingdoms and city-states were visited from earliest times by Arab explorers and traders, who gradually converted their inhabitants to Islam. The civilizations of the Sudanic belt thus became a blend of Islamic and Negro African. Although the trading prosperity of cities such as Timbuktu has vanished, enough still remains to recall their former days of glory.

## Trading states of the east coast

On the east coast, too, Africa had a flourishing network of trade, both internally and with Europe, India and the East, long before European explorers set foot in the continent. As early as the 9th century AD a great wave of trading activity swept the countries bordering the Indian Ocean. It gave rise to a string of city-states along the east coast of Africa, to handle commerce in ivory, gold and tropical goods. These east coast states are believed to have been founded by Muslims from the Persian Gulf, while later immigrants came from southern Arabia.

Attracted by this commercial prosperity, Bantu-speaking Africans spread to the east coast, and mingled with the Arabs to produce a distinct culture and language – Swahili, now the common language of East Africa. By the 13th century, the trading states were on the threshold of a golden age. Muslim rulers were extending their sway over India and into Malaysia and Indonesia; the Indian Ocean was becoming a vast Muslim lake, and the Muslim cities on the East African coast were caught up in this great commercial venture. From Somalia in the north to Mozambique in the south, dozens of little coastal states

### ISLAM LEAVES ITS MARK IN AFRICA

*A mosque has stood at Jenne, on a tributary of the Niger in Mali, since the 14th century. The present building is made of clay and earth rammed together, and timber supports bristle from its walls. Jenne was one of the rich Saharan market centres whose inhabitants were converted to Islam by Arab traders*

flourished. Some of these, such as Malindi, Mombasa, Zanzibar and Kilwa, became powerful in their own right. The island of Kilwa was the greatest medieval East African city; in its Portuguese form of Quiloa, the name appears in Milton's *Paradise Lost*.

The wealth of Kilwa depended partly on ivory and other tropical produce, but chiefly on its monopoly of the trade in gold, which was mined inland and exported from Kilwa all over the Arab world, to form the basis of much of the commerce of medieval Islam.

When the great Muslim traveller Ibn Battuta visited Kilwa in 1332, he described it as one of the most beautiful and best conducted towns he had seen. Little of the medieval city now remains, though the stones of the ancient buildings have been used for the later city, which dates from the 16th century. The mosques, however, have survived, because the stones used in building them could not be used for secular purposes.

## Dhows sail with the monsoons

The Great Mosque of Kilwa was the largest mosque on the East African coast; its ruins still stand, surrounded by dense tropical vegetation. Also remaining today are the ruins of a palace fort covering about 2 acres. From the lofty, cool rooms of this clifftop palace, the rulers of Kilwa witnessed the arrival of gold from the south, probably in small coastal dhows, and of caravans carrying ivory from the interior, around Lake Malawi. The sultans also watched the great ocean-going dhows setting out for southern Arabia, India and China on the monsoon winds. Here at Kilwa, black Africa had united with the world of Islam to produce an impressive and prosperous civilization, which was disrupted only by the arrival of the Portuguese around 1500.

Much of the gold which made the eastern coastal states rich came from the region of Zimbabwe, in present-day Rhodesia. The granite ruins which still stand at Zimbabwe, of a palace on a hilltop and a temple in the valley below, are some of the most impressive remains of a great African civilization.

The first Europeans who saw the Zimbabwe ruins were Portuguese explorers seeking the legendary King Solomon's Mines, and they jumped to wild conclusions, attributing the building of Zimbabwe to the south Arabians of the Queen of Sheba's time, or to Phoenicians. Later studies have shown that Zimbabwe – the name means 'Great Place' in the Shona language – was the achievement of a succession of Bantu-speaking African peoples. It is the descendants of these peoples who form the majority of Rhodesian Africans of today.

## Gold from Zimbabwe

Stone buildings were first erected at Zimbabwe between the 11th and 14th centuries. By the 15th century Zimbabwe was an established and prosperous centre, perhaps the capital, of a great empire called Monomatapa. The Swahilis and Arabs of the East African coast established trading links with this empire, and

## MERCHANTS WHO BRAVED THE SAHARA CROSSING

The most important physical change to take place in Africa in historical times was the drying up of the Sahara between 4000 and 2000 BC, when changing wind patterns apparently brought in drier air from southern Europe. The inhabitants were driven out – but trade between north and south continued. A network of caravan routes brought European goods into the heart of Africa centuries before Europeans themselves set foot in the continent. Cloth and luxury goods travelled southwards across the Sahara; so did salt, an essential element in human diet which is found in the desert but is scarce in the tropical belt to the south. From south to north passed gold, kola nuts – a mild narcotic valued in Muslim countries where alcohol was forbidden – and leather goods. Negro slaves also crossed the Sahara northwards in considerable numbers, and were prized as domestics in the countries of the Mediterranean and Middle East. Cities grew up as the bases of this trans-Sahara trade; they were large and impressive, though stone was rare and most buildings were made of sun-dried mud

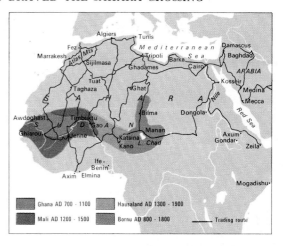

TRADE NETWORK *European cloth and manufactured goods reached the North African coast by boat and were carried inland by donkeys to desert 'ports' such as Sijilmasa and Ghadames. Here the goods were loaded on to camels for a journey of nearly 1000 miles southwards across the Sahara. From towns such as Timbuktu and Gao, on the southern fringe of the desert, porters carried the goods further southwards into the Sudanic kingdoms, while the camel caravans returned northwards with gold, hides and kola nuts*

ACROSS THE DESERT *A 13th-century illustration shows one of the Arab merchants who in medieval times braved the dangers of the Sahara to lead caravans of laden camels from the Mediterranean lands to the kingdoms of West Africa and back. As a barrier, the desert was like a wild and unpredictable ocean. Desert caravans were the ships that sailed this ocean; the market towns of North Africa and the Sudanic belt in the south were the ports; and the dreaded black-veiled Tuareg tribesmen were the pirates. The hazards of the crossing were extreme. Caravans could cover 200 miles in a week, but if the wells and oases failed, men and beasts could perish*

# *Ivory and bronze sculptors of the forest kingdoms*

Monomatapa gold reached the Muslim world after being taken down the Zambezi valley to Sofala and Kilwa.

Later the king of Monomatapa left Zimbabwe and established a new capital on the northern edge of the Rhodesian plateau. Zimbabwe rapidly declined in importance. It revived, however, under a new dynasty of kings, the Rozvis, in the 16th century, and it was during this period that some of its largest buildings were constructed. The end of the Rozvi state came dramatically in the 1830's, when war bands from Zululand – the far-off kingdom founded 20 years earlier by Shaka – delivered a death blow.

The Monomatapa ruler was a divine king, like so many African monarchs. His subjects approached him prone on their stomachs; the ordinary people, although they could hear him, were never allowed to see him. The king's every action was imitated by his courtiers; if he coughed or hiccoughed, they did likewise. The empire depended upon the king's health and virility. When he became seriously ill, or very old, he had to take poison. The commoners had to pay dearly for the pomp and circumstance of the Monomatapan kings.

## Kingdoms of the great lakes

Throughout history, Africans have been attracted to the fertile lands around and between the great lakes of eastern Africa. One of the earliest of the lake kingdoms was that of

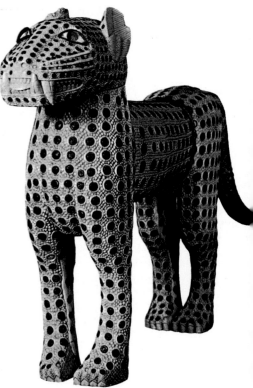

### BENIN'S KING REIGNS SUPREME OVER HIS EUROPEAN VISITORS

*An ivory mask representing the king of Benin, and hung from his waist on ceremonial occasions, has a tiara of small heads depicting the Portuguese who first visited Benin about 1470. The mask symbolises the intention of the rulers of Benin to take over the newcomers' magic without being dominated by them*

### THE ROYAL LEOPARD

*Figures of lions and leopards symbolise royal power in many African civilizations. This leopard from Benin is made of ivory inlaid with brass*

the Buchwezi, who by the 15th century had established an extensive kingdom in what is now central Uganda. Later, Buchwezi was succeeded by Buganda, the state to which European explorers came in the 19th century.

Towards the end of the 18th century, the lake kingdoms had made contact with the outside world, especially with Arab and Swahili merchants on the east coast. In the middle of the 19th century several European explorers, including Burton, Speke, Grant and Stanley, reached Buganda along the merchants' caravan routes. They came from the south, through dry and difficult bush country, rather than by the more direct approaches over the highlands of Kenya, which were inhabited by hostile Masai herdsmen. The explorers had to walk for months over barren lands, plagued with tropical diseases; all their goods had to be carried on the heads of African porters, because the tsetse fly made the use of pack animals impossible.

The kings or *kabakas* of Buganda kept law and order, and provided a generally peaceful existence for their subjects. The lake peoples carved wooden sculptures, and made fine pots, but their most notable artistic achievement was the architecture of their palaces, shrines and ordinary houses. In an area almost devoid of good building stone, or even of suitable clays, the inhabitants used reeds, grasses and the fronds of banana plants to build remarkable dwellings, spacious, cool and clean. Small houses were linked by passages open to the sky, and surrounded by a high fence. The palaces included huge audience chambers made entirely of grasses.

The most important symbols of kingship in the lake states were the royal drums. Through the rhythm of the drums a king communicated with his ancestors; and the larger drums a king had, the more powerful it was believed to make him. Some drums that have survived are 12 ft across. They were housed in shrines, where a special class of people looked after them and played them at the appropriate times. Smaller drums were used by the ordinary people for dancing and other rituals.

### Heads in clay and bronze
A collection of sculptured heads and figures in terracotta, discovered in the 1940's near Nok, in central Nigeria, were found to date from 500 BC to AD 200 – making them the oldest sculpture known in tropical Africa, outside Egypt and Kush. These sculptures were the inspiration, a thousand years later, for the art of Ife, a kingdom south of Nok, on the edge of the great forest belt of West Africa, which flourished between AD 1100 and 1500.

The sculptures of Ife, in terracotta and bronze, are perhaps the greatest artistic creations produced in tropical Africa. As in the case of Zimbabwe, the first men to find these Ife sculptures believed they were the work of non-African artists who had reached the area. The Ife bronzes were cast by the process known as cire-perdue, or 'lost wax', probably the oldest method of metal casting in the world. The

sculptor builds a wax model, which is covered with coats of fine clay. The model is heated, causing the wax to melt and escape through small holes, after which molten metal is poured in to replace the wax. After the metal has cooled, the clay mould is broken off, leaving an exact reproduction in metal of the artist's original wax model.

### Sculptors of Ashanti and Benin
West of Ife, around the lower reaches of the White and Black Volta Rivers, the state of Ashanti was founded in the middle of the 17th century and rapidly expanded to absorb neighbouring kingdoms. Its king, the *asantehene*, lived in Kumasi, where a golden stool was his sacred symbol of kingship.

The territorial expansion of Ashanti co-incided with the rapid growth in the European trans-Atlantic trade, the chief commodity of which was slaves. Europeans – first the Portuguese, followed by Dutch, English and French – established themselves on the coast from the 15th century, and slaves captured by the Ashanti were sold to European slavers by African dealers. Britain conquered Ashanti at the end of the 19th century, long after the abolition of the slave trade; it is now part of modern Ghana. Like other West African kingdoms, Ashanti is famous for its wood carvings, which are still often used in fertility ceremonies. These ceremonies were the occasion for ritual singing and dancing, and for the declamation of the history of the state, in the form of stories or parables.

Another people who colonised the forest areas of West Africa were the Edo, who developed bronze sculpture as a great art in their kingdom of Benin, which was at its height from the 15th to the 17th centuries. Benin was near the coast of Nigeria, and long before the inland states of West Africa were known to Europeans it had contacts with Portuguese, Dutch and British traders.

Benin was then a walled city 25 miles in circumference, with wide, straight streets. Its spacious houses, mostly built of wood, were circled by verandas, with courtyards or galleries inside and rooms leading off them. The palace of the *oba* (king) was extremely elaborate; the galleries were covered with remarkable bronze sculptured plaques which recorded the great events of Benin's past.

### Independence lost and regained
Three centuries of slave trading began a process of change, and led some Africans to adopt European habits and beliefs, a process which was ultimately to affect people living in even the most isolated parts of the continent. After the European slave trade ended, Europeans came to Africa with new motives – to open up the continent for trade, to free the tribes from Arab slavers, and to bring Christianity to the 'Dark Continent'. The first glimpse of the continent's vast commercial opportunities started a 'scramble for Africa' in the 1870's, and within 30 years the whole continent, except Ethiopia and Liberia, was under European

control. By 1960, most of Africa was back in African hands – but the newly independent states were states on the Western pattern, in which the growth of towns and the spread of education and technology had changed many aspects of the tribal way of life for ever.

Since the 1920's, the Africans have shown an increasing awareness of the value of their own traditional culture, and have made a conscious effort to establish, or restore, an African 'identity'. Some of the old traditional African ways of doing things survive. Away from the towns in particular, there is still a clearly understood relationship between each individual and his kinsman, and a belief in a continuity between the ancestors, the living, and those not yet born. Even Christianity has taken specifically African forms, with an emphasis on singing and dancing, which have always accompanied every important African ceremony or occasion.

Meanwhile African art and music have, in their turn, profoundly affected the outside world. African art forms have become established in modern European painting through the genius of Picasso and Matisse. The varied and subtle rhythms of African music, transported by millions of slaves to the New World, have emerged in the 20th century as jazz, blues and the music of Latin America. The process of change, since Africa ended its isolation and became part of a wider world, has not been entirely one way.

### IFE ARTISTRY IN BRONZE
*The bronze head of a 14th-century king of Ife, in what is now Nigeria, is one of the finest surviving African sculptures. He wears the headgear of a sea-god*

# WESTERN CIVILIZATION

*Many strands from the distant past join the peoples of the Western world in their complex civilization. From Greece sprang belief in democracy and respect for beauty, truth and moderation. From Rome came practical lessons in administration, architecture and the law. From the Hebrew world emerged Christianity, which became for a thousand years the sole unifying force in Europe.*

*Throughout its long history, European civilization has been characterised by its strong sense of purpose and destiny. The creative and dynamic spirit of Western man has acted as a continual driving force, resulting in a society that has gradually spread its influence throughout the globe. The process of change and evolution has been continuous; but five major phases stand out, each marked by its own distinctive values and achievements.*

The essence of Christendom: a 14th-century painting of the Crucifixion on an altar screen at Dorchester Abbey in Oxfordshire

## MEDIEVAL EUROPE, A SOCIETY IN WHICH EVERYONE HAD HIS APPOINTED PLACE

*The might of the state and the authority of the pope came together in the Middle Ages in alliances that were sometimes close, but at other times uneasy. A rigid pattern of society emerged, in which every man knew and kept his appointed place. This hierarchy of the times is vividly portrayed in a fresco painted in 1355 by the Italian artist Andrea da Firenze in the Church of Santa Maria Novella in Florence. Against the backcloth of the church itself stand Christ's representatives*

*on earth – the pope and, at his left hand, the Holy Roman Emperor. Before them lie sheep, representing the Christian flock, guarded by black and white dogs representing the Order of Dominicans (from* Domini canes, *Latin for 'hounds of the Lord'). At the pope's right are a cardinal, a bishop and an abbot, and with them are monks, nuns, friars and hermits. Beside the emperor are men of all ranks of society – a king and count, supported by noblemen, merchants, peasants and beggars*

214

# The Middle Ages:
# an era of faith

## AD 500–1500

*In the wake of the barbarian invasions, the
authority of the Christian Church brought
a thousand years of unity to Europe*

**EUROPE TAKES SHAPE**

*Charlemagne unified much of Europe
by 800, but by the end of the Middle
Ages separate nation states had emerged*

For 400 years the Roman Empire gave unity and security to the Mediterranean world and to Europe up to, and at times beyond, the Rhine. After the final collapse of Rome in 476, when its last emperor, Romulus Augustulus, was deposed by the Goths under the leadership of Odoacer, the Christian Church gave Europe a similar measure of unity for the next 1000 years. The pope was more powerful than the barbarian kings who tried to recreate the Roman Empire; for the pope claimed his authority descended from St Peter, to whom Christ had said: 'Thou art Peter and upon this rock I will build my Church.'

The pope's armies were bishops and clergy and Crusaders. His Master and his creed were supernatural. The core of Christian belief defied reason. The believer held that Christ was both God and Man, that he bore the sins of the world, that he had risen from the dead, and that all who believed this would inherit eternal life. The notion of the Trinity of God as Father, Son and Holy Ghost may have been difficult to grasp, but the Christian ideal of the brotherhood of man was revolutionary. The persecution of Christians ended in 313, when Emperor Constantine granted religious freedom to all faiths, and in 380 Christianity was proclaimed as the empire's official religion.

In earlier times, Christianity had been only one of several competing religions, the most important of which was the Persian cult of Mithras, the sun-god, which had been brought to Rome by legionaries serving in the East. But the early Christians were ready, in some cases even eager, to die for their faith. Constantine was impressed by the strength of a religion which could produce so many martyrs, and whose missionaries could hold out to converts the promise of a future life. So Christianity, which had once been a threat to the power of Rome, now became its ally.

At the beginning of the 4th century the imperial government moved to Constantinople, and as the western branch of the empire declined, the Christian Church filled the power vacuum in Rome. It was Leo I – a pope, not an emperor – who persuaded Attila the Hun not to

## THE POWER OF CLUNY

*Many monastic orders sprang up in the
Middle Ages and acted as powerful instruments of the pope's authority. None
was more important than the Cluniac
order, based on the Abbey of Cluny, in
France. This reconstruction shows the
abbey's great complex of buildings in
the mid-12th century, when the Cluniac
order was at its most powerful. Its
abbot ruled over 1500 monasteries and
priories, and ranked second only to the
pope; several Cluniac monks even
became popes themselves. The Cluniacs
were renowned for their reforming zeal
and devotion, at a time when corruption
and laxity were bringing some orders
into disrepute. The Cluniacs spent
nearly all their time in prayer, leaving
manual work to servants – a way of life
which brought increasing criticism*

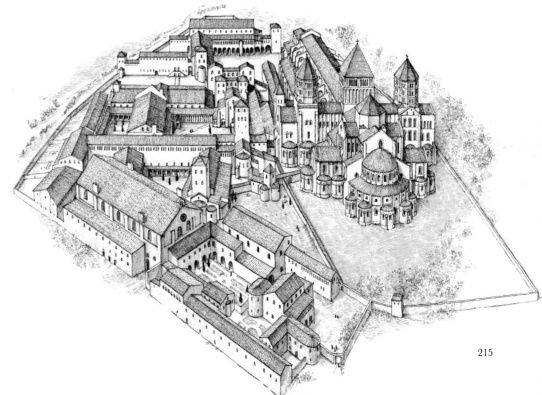

# *Monasteries secure the Faith and keep learning alive*

### THE FIRST OF EUROPE'S GREAT RULERS

*Charlemagne was crowned King of the Franks in 768, and in his 46 years' reign he welded the barbarian kingdoms into a Christian empire stretching from the Baltic to the Mediterranean. He saved Pope Leo III from being deposed, and in gratitude the Pope made* *him Emperor of the Roman Empire in the West in 800. Charlemagne administered his empire successfully and encouraged the spread of learning throughout his realms. This jewelled bust at Aachen was made about 1350 to hold parts of Charlemagne's skull*

march into Rome when the city appeared to lie at his mercy in 452, and who halted some of the savagery of Genseric the Vandal in 455. Indeed, when the Goths finally conquered Rome in 476 they did not attempt to set up a barbarian empire. They were content to adopt Roman methods of government and to use Roman titles. They even accepted the authority of the emperor in Constantinople. And for guidance in ruling their newly acquired territories they looked to the Christian Church, with its long administrative experience.

The organization of the Church was itself imperial, with parishes grouped into dioceses. It had its own system of law, its own courts, its own taxes and tithes (a 10 per cent levy on the produce of all land). Its clergy claimed exemption from paying taxes to kings or emperors and from being tried by secular courts. Their churches could even offer sanctuary to the king's enemies. Clergy could punish the disobedient, fine a man for absence from church, whip a woman for doing her washing on a Sunday and hand over heretics to the state for burning. Their ultimate weapon was the power to excommunicate – to cut a man off from the mercy of Christ, and so condemn his soul to eternal torment.

Archbishops and bishops were the pope's lieutenants. They decided what was heresy, what was lawful marriage, and who could appeal to the pope against a decision of the king. Pope Gregory the Great (590–604) sent out missions to heathen lands, to England, Spain and France. One of these missions was led by St Augustine who, at the head of 40 monks, reached Kent and became the first Archbishop of Canterbury. As Christian missionaries and then royal converts grew in numbers and in territory, so did the spiritual authority of the Bishop of Rome.

### Pagan rites absorbed

By a stroke of tactical genius the Church, while intolerant of pagan beliefs, was able to harness the powerful emotions generated by pagan worship. Often, churches were sited where temples had stood before, and many heathen festivals were added to the Christian calendar. Easter, for instance, a time of sacrifice and rebirth in the Christian year, takes its name from the Norse goddess Eostre, in whose honour rites were held every spring. She in turn was simply a Northern version of the Phoenician earth-mother Astarte, goddess of fertility. Easter eggs continue an age-old tradition in which the egg is a symbol of birth; and cakes which were eaten to mark the festivals of Astarte and Eostre were the direct ancestors of our hot-cross buns.

Since bishops were educated men at a time when education was a rarity, they became civil servants, chancellors and secretaries to rulers. Much of the history of medieval England, for instance, revolves around its bishops and archbishops, such as Augustine, Stephen Langton and Thomas Becket. Many such men had a first loyalty to the pope; some, like Cardinal Wolsey, Henry VIII's chief minister for nearly 20 years, even had ambitions to be pope themselves. Meanwhile at the centre, in Rome itself, the popes had an efficient organisation, the *curia*, patterned on that of the Roman Empire. Papal legates abroad reported back to the pope on shifts of policy and political power, and held a powerful diplomatic weapon in their right to refer disputes to Rome. The pope claimed the sole power to grant absolution for sin. Through the bishops and the parish priests, his authority reached into almost every corner of Europe.

## Growth of the monasteries

In every country the popes had another powerful and dedicated instrument: the monasteries. The notion of withdrawal from the world to escape from its vices and seek salvation through self denial and even physical agony was very old. St Simeon Stylites (390–459) set a standard for victory over the flesh when he spent 35 years on top of a pillar 60 ft high at Telanessa, near Antioch in Turkey. But the monks, as well as withdrawing from the world, also returned to it, their energies renewed by prayer and meditation, to carry out the work of Christ.

Monasticism in the West owed its shape largely to one man of vigour and command, Benedict (480–543) of Nursia – the modern Norcia in Umbria, north-east of Rome. He had been so outraged by what he saw as the vice and corruption of Rome that he spent three years as a hermit in a cave at Subiaco in the wild hill country of Latium to the east of Rome. The fame of his piety brought him disciples and he moved to Monte Cassino. There he set up a monastery on the site of an ancient temple of Apollo – a monastery which still survives, despite having been destroyed on five occasions, the last by Allied bombers in 1944.

In 529 Benedict drew up his rule or *regula*, which was gradually adopted by most monasteries in the West. The *regula* required the monks to take vows of poverty, chastity and obedience, and their monastery was organised as a family, under the abbot – the word comes from the Greek *abbas*, meaning father. Life in 6th and 7th-century monasteries was severe but not harsh, being divided between sleeping, working and praying. The monks had a pound of bread, two cooked dishes and a measure of wine each day, though eating meat was forbidden.

The Benedictine fashion spread. The monasteries became workshops for craftsmen and refuges from anarchy. They were welfare centres and hospitals for the poor, inns for travellers and schools for local children. Monastic farms and fields became the testing grounds of new agricultural techniques, such as a three-field rotation of crops. The monasteries were centres of scholarship. Monks copied the writings of the great Christian teachers in superb illuminated manuscripts, and also reproduced the works of Caesar, Cicero and Ovid.

The Benedictines, known as the 'black monks' from the colour of their garments, produced great scholars, such as the Venerable Bede in 8th-century England who produced treatises on history, theology and astronomy. They built

some of the greatest abbeys – Monte Cassino in Italy, Cluny in France, Westminster and Glastonbury in England. But as their wealth grew, especially in land, discipline relaxed, and secular rulers looked at them with a greedy and jealous eye. Land-holding abbots rivalled bishops and the nobility in wealth and power, and by the 14th century the great abbots were automatically summoned to the English Parliament, to sit in the House of Lords.

Papal authority grew steadily in the early Middle Ages. For a time Irish monks and British clergy were cut off from Rome, and northern Britain was converted not from Canterbury but by monks of the Celtic Church from Lindisfarne and Iona. But by 800 the authority of the pope prevailed throughout western Europe between the Pyrenees and the North Sea. Spain was still Muslim, but the papal missionary St Boniface had completed the conversion of German tribes east of the Rhine.

In 496 Clovis, King of the Franks, was baptised a Christian. So earnestly did the Franks, both German-speaking and French-speaking, embrace the new faith that they became the foremost defenders of Christendom. In 732, under Charles Martel, they halted the great Muslim invasion of Europe in a battle at Tours

in central France. And Martel's grandson Charlemagne – 'Charles the Great' – became one of the great Christian rulers of European history. He became King of the Franks in 768, and by the time of his death in 814 he had extended his empire to include nearly the whole of western Europe.

## An empire created by the pope

In 800, in return for Charlemagne's intervention to protect him against his rival, Adrian, Pope Leo III revived an old title and crowned him Emperor of the Roman Empire in the West. Charlemagne had no wish to appear to owe his title to Leo, and would have preferred to crown himself; but the pope took him by surprise in St Peter's on Christmas Day, 800, and placed the crown on his head before Charlemagne could prevent it. So originated the idea of the Holy Roman Empire, a creation of the papacy which was to rival the popes and which survived until the 19th century.

Charlemagne led no fewer than 53 military expeditions. He campaigned against the Moors in Spain. By 785 he had defeated and converted the pagan Saxons in Germany. In 796 he destroyed the Asiatic Avars on the middle Danube. His empire stretched from the Baltic

---

## PRAYER — AND WORK

The monasteries of the Middle Ages were not only centres of worship and teaching; they were also proving grounds for new farming techniques, and many crafts were taught and fostered in the workshops where monks spent much of their day when not in prayer. The monasteries also served as hospitals and welfare centres where the local poor were cared for, and as resting places for travellers on the road

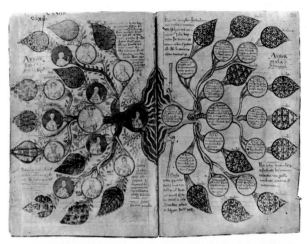

MASTER COPYISTS *The production of books was for centuries the painstaking handiwork of monks. Many volumes were richly decorated, like these pages, showing the Trees of Good and Evil, from an early 12th-century manuscript*

STRICT RULES *An 11th-century manuscript shows St Benedict drawing up his 'rule', or regula, a set of regulations for the running of a monastery which were widely adopted. Monks had to take vows of poverty, chastity and obedience*

A JOB FOR EVERYONE *Each monastery had to be self-sustaining, according to the 73 chapters of St Benedict's regula, and monks were allotted productive tasks as part of their daily routine. Some laboured in the gardens and grain fields (left) while others, like the cellarer (right), had important jobs in the household. Monks also wove cloth and made their own simple garments and footwear, and each monastery had stone masons and carpenters*

# *Feudalism: a network of loyalties rooted in the land*

to the Mediterranean. He united France, Germany, northern Spain and northern Italy. And even the Eastern Roman Empire acknowledged his imperial title.

Charlemagne, like all great men in history, is as much a figure of legend as of reality. He was at once the last of the great barbarian conquerors and the first of the European Christian emperors. His empire, though Roman in title, was centred on the Rhine, and Charlemagne was of German ancestry. He could speak Latin and German and understood Greek; he could ride, hunt and swim, and had many children by many mistresses. Though he never learnt to read or write, he was highly cultured and interested in the arts. He took over what he could of Roman law and administration, used priests for his civil service, and sent out counts and bishops across his dominions to act as his lieutenants. He was as successful in governing a vast and unwieldy empire as he had been ruthless in creating it by war. His emissaries saw that the laws were obeyed, taxes collected and Church rules enforced. And by calling inquests of good men and true to tell judges what they knew of local crimes, Charlemagne foreshadowed the jury system. He also established parish schools, and higher schools were attached to abbeys and cathedrals.

It took a man of Charlemagne's calibre to hold his empire together, and it did not long survive his death in 814. But though the empire broke into its French, German and Italian kingdoms, the memory of Charlemagne's skill as administrator, and of the way he used clerics as statesmen, never died. The kingdoms that followed had his standards of unity and good government to match.

## Centuries of strife

The Holy Roman Empire which originated in Charlemagne's conquests was to be racked for centuries after his death by a series of conflicts between pope and emperor. These stemmed from the inevitable conflict which developed between the two rival authorities. There were clashes over appointments to bishoprics, with their huge estates; over the claims of the Church to be free of tax; over the Church's right to offer sanctuary; and over the exemption of churchmen from obligations to the state.

After Charlemagne, the Holy Roman Emperors were chosen for life from among the rulers of central Europe. From 1273 they were chosen by seven electors, three of them archbishops; but though the form of 'election' was observed, the office became in practice hereditary in one family – the Hapsburgs of Austria. Popes were chosen by a College of Cardinals, and were usually old by the time of their election. Nevertheless there were two outstanding reformers among them – Gregory VII and Innocent III.

Gregory VII (1073–85) commanded that all clerics were to be respected and obeyed as servants of God. He sought to prevent emperors and kings from appointing their own candidates as bishops – largely to annex Church revenues. When Gregory declared that the pope could depose emperors and princes, Emperor Henry IV called a synod, or church meeting, at Worms in January 1076, which declared the pope deposed. The pope in turn did what no pope had done before him: in the following month, he excommunicated the emperor.

### 'Vicar of Christ'

The test of strength between emperor and pope ended when Henry IV found his German vassals siding with the pope, and realised that he was beaten. As the pope travelled to Augsburg in Germany to confer with Henry's rebels, Henry hurried south to meet Gregory at Canossa in Tuscany. Gregory forced him to stand barefoot in the snow before his castle gates for three days before pardoning him. Even though Henry later drove Gregory out of Rome and into exile, the principles of Canossa inspired a compromise reached at Worms in 1122, long after both men were dead. It laid down that a bishop paid homage to the king or emperor for the lands he owned, but was chosen and consecrated by the Church. By the time of Pope Innocent III (1198–1216) the authority of the pope was all but supreme. Innocent III kept an iron discipline over his clergy, and summoned his bishops regularly to Rome. He was a patron of two new monastic orders, the Franciscans and Dominicans, and he was the first to use the title 'Vicar of Christ' when he said: 'No king can reign rightly unless he devoutly serves Christ's Vicar.'

Innocent III exerted enormous influence in affairs of state. He forced King John of England to accept Stephen Langton as Archbishop of Canterbury and to become a 'vassal' of the pope. He arbitrated between the rival claimants to the Holy Roman Empire. He even prevented for a time the coronation of his own ward, Frederick II, who was later to become the most brilliant of the Holy Roman Emperors – an accomplished artist and scientist, who encouraged trade, reformed the legal systems of Italy and Sicily, founded Naples University, and earned himself the title of *stupor mundi*, 'wonder of the world'.

The time of Innocent III represents the high peak of papal power. It was also during his papacy that the Church adopted the doctrine of transubstantiation – the belief that in the Mass the bread and wine are converted into Christ's actual body and blood. In thousands of churches, cathedrals and monasteries, at least once a week, often daily, and for some even more regularly, the faithful throughout Europe worshipped in an atmosphere of reverence. They were surrounded by images of the saints, sharply aware of the crucifix and of the Passion of Christ, and of the gentleness and mediating power of Mary. For 1000 years the Church brought what art and aspiration and colour there was into drab lives.

### The castle as haven

The conflict between pope and emperor was not the only struggle which convulsed Europe during the centuries after Charlemagne. Another threat came from the north, as the coastal regions of Europe collapsed before the Viking invaders. 'From the fury of the Norsemen, good Lord deliver us,' was the prayer of a Northumbrian abbot. One group of Vikings settled in Normandy, where they became Christians, and from there they swept as far south as southern Italy and Sicily. Both of these lands became Norman kingdoms – Emperor Frederick II was of Norman Sicilian descent – and so, eventually, did England.

In these turbulent times, monasteries offered one means of escape from both civil war and outside marauders. Walled towns offered another. But only one refuge seemed really secure – the castle, with its thick, high battlemented walls, wide defensive moat, narrow slits for archers, and winding stairs that only one man could use at a time. Such castles were best defended outside the moat by horsemen, in chain mail and with lance.

At the Battle of Tours in 732, Charles Martel had been impressed by the skill of the Muslim horsemen, and especially by their use of the

**HORSEMEN REVOLUTIONISE WARFARE**

*Mounted nobles and knights dominated the battlefields of Europe for most of the Middle Ages. The Norman victory over King Harold at the Battle of Hastings in 1066 was due largely to the fact that William of Normandy had a large force of mounted men – seen on* *the left in this section from the Bayeux Tapestry – while Harold had only foot-soldiers to support him. The English were finally routed when the Norman knights made a cavalry charge combined with a volley of arrows shot into the air*

stirrup, which enabled them to fight on horseback with sword or lance. He recruited a class of armed horsemen and gave them land, in return for which they took an oath to serve him when called upon. Such grants of land were known as fiefs, and from the Latin word for fief, *feudum*, the system of feudalism got its name. It represented in essence the obligation of service in return for land, and the grant of land in return for service. Service was in origin military, and usually for a period of 40 to 60 days. But feudalism developed into a system of government and society which was to dominate Europe for four centuries.

Feudalism was a recognition that the only security lay in land. Land was immovable property; it could be tilled and improved; its value could be clearly assessed and taxed; and it could be passed on to the next generation after suitable payment of tribute. 'No land without a lord; no lord without a land' was the watchword of the time. Those who served a lord got his protection and subsistence, and shared in his honours. Everyone was, in theory, a vassal of someone else. The lord himself was the tenant of a king; kings were vassals of emperors; and even an emperor, an absolute ruler, was the vassal of God. William of Normandy was a vassal of the King of France, and had 1400 tenants-in-chief on whom he could call. The Count of Champagne had 2017. But the count had also ten overlords, all of whom could call on him, sometimes with contradictory claims, since they included the Emperor, the King of France, the Duke of Burgundy, two archbishops, four bishops and an abbot. If more than one called for his help, he faced a problem of conflicting loyalties.

The interlocking system of obligation and indebtedness on which feudalism depended was symbolised by the homage paid by a vassal to his superior. That homage was a physical act, in which the vassal would kneel before his superior, placing his hand in that of his lord and promising to be his man and serve him in war. As with any political system, it called for mutual trust. For centuries it gave some stability to Europe, and it continued in central and eastern Europe well into the 19th century.

The feudal system bred a code of chivalry, placing loyalty and physical courage at the head of the list of virtues. It produced a nobility accustomed to arms and horses, knowing how to ride and to use lance, battle-axe and sword. At first a knight could be almost any man who owned a horse and a sword. In return for military service he was given his fief, on which he built some fairly primitive form of stronghold. But gradually knighthood took on an elaborate code of chivalry which called on every knight to honour Christ as well as his lord.

## The burden of serfdom

For centuries the economy of western Europe was based on the manor, the big house or castle, with its surrounding farmland. It was a fairly primitive and static economy. Glass was rare; the draughty interior of manor house or castle was lit by tallow candles and torches; and with

### FAIRY-TALE FORTRESS OF A POWERFUL DUKE

*By the late Middle Ages the simple castles of earlier centuries had given way to vast, elaborate fortresses. An early 15th-century calendar illustration shows the castle of the Duc de Berry at Saumur, in France. It provided a gracious home in time of peace, its soaring* *towers and gilded weather-vanes giving it a fairy-tale appearance. In time of war the castle was a secure base; after crossing the drawbridge, attackers would still face a hail of stones and boiling lead dropped through 'murder holes' beneath the battlements of the towers*

# Crusades to rescue the Holy Land from Islam

only an open but distant fireplace to heat a vast hall it was forbiddingly cold. There might be roast ox or boar to eat, but even in the 15th century forks were still rare, and eating habits unrefined. When a nobleman drank himself under the table with wine or mead, he would find the dogs there, gnawing at the bones, and fall asleep among them on the straw and rushes that served as carpet. Even in a castle, it was neither a hygienic nor a civilized age.

The hardships of feudal society were borne by the serfs who had to work on roads and bridges and in the fields. They lived in cottages, with thatched roofs and earth floors. Their lives were harsh and their diet poor. Vegetables, barley, oats and beer were the staple diet in northern Europe, wheat and wine in the south. Meat, game and fish were rare treats away from the lord's table – and, in winter, the meat was often salted. Sugar was rare, and made from honey; coffee and tea were unknown. Illness was widespread and privileges few. Clothing was made of animal skins tanned into leather, of wool, or of linen, worked by womenfolk. Nearly all food was home-produced, and almost every village was self-supporting, with its own miller, its blacksmith and its carpenter.

A serf did enjoy some security: he could not be uprooted or dismissed. But on the other hand he could not move or even marry without his lord's consent. In return for working on his master's fields, each peasant was allotted 3–4 acres to farm for himself. But this land was divided into separate strips, often some distance apart, so that the peasant would have a share of good and bad land alike. This was subsistence farming. There was little incentive to work hard or to introduce improvements, since holdings were periodically changed.

The serf was at the lord's mercy, and could not escape. His own holding could be ravaged by passing armies, by wild animals or by local hunts, while the penalties for poaching on his lord's land were maiming, blinding and death. He rarely moved more than a mile or two from home. He was deeply religious but profoundly ignorant, without any chance of controlling his own destiny.

## Marching under the cross

The high point of militant Christianity in the Middle Ages was the zeal that inspired 200 years of Crusades to the Holy Land between the 11th and the 13th centuries. Under the red cross of the Crusades, the noblemen of feudal Christendom – and on occasion the peasants and children as well – marched to rescue the holy places of the Christian faith from the Muslim Turks. The Crusades began as a feudal enterprise, but they ended by supplanting feudalism in Europe with a new era of commerce. Merchant princes replaced warrior barons, and trading cities took the place of walled fortresses. However, this process was gradual. The immediate cause of the Crusades was a threat to Constantinople, the eastern stronghold of Christendom, at the end of the 11th century. The city had for long taken the brunt of Muslim invaders from Asia, known as Saracens. The latest threat came from the Seljuk Turks, who at the end of the 11th century had only the Straits of Bosporus between them and Constantinople. The Turks were already in possession of Jerusalem, and the Byzantine emperor, Alexius Comnenus, sought the pope's help to drive the infidels from the Holy Land and recapture it for Christendom – and at the same time drive the enemy from his own gates.

In 1095 Urban II called the warriors of Christendom to the First Crusade. Before the armies could set out, popular preachers, like Peter the Hermit, of Amiens, stirred up the common people with tales of Christian sufferings at Muslim hands. A vast undisciplined horde, the so-called People's Crusade, set off for Palestine. This great host numbered possibly 50,000, and included entire families with small children. Many were lost or killed on their way through Hungary. The remnants who reached Constantinople were shipped across the Bosporus by Emperor Alexius, but were massacred by the Muslims.

The first organised military columns were led by French, German, Norman and Italian knights. They started moving east in 1096 and, after many squabbles among themselves and

---

### GALLANT KNIGHTS WHO FOLLOWED THE CODE OF CHIVALRY

The Middle Ages saw the rise to glory of the mounted knight in shining armour, whose entire life was ruled by an elaborate code of chivalry. This code bound any man who won his spurs to defend to the death his feudal master, his belief in God, and the honour of his lady. Medieval knights set great store by personal bravery, and death was preferable to dishonour. The qualifications for knighthood were exacting. A boy of well-born parents started his apprenticeship at the age of seven, serving as a page in the household of a lord and learning horsemanship and the use of weapons. At 14 he would become a squire to a knight, and spend as long as seven years in his service, dressing his master and caring for his horse and weapons while learning from him the arts of combat. If thought worthy, he was given his spurs at a ceremony in which another knight struck him a severe blow – the last his honour would allow him to suffer without striking back. From this ceremony arose the practice of dubbing a knight with a gentle touch of a sword on his shoulder

ROYAL BANQUET *Castle life was comfortable for the richer lords and knights of the Middle Ages. They ate and drank well, usually of local fare and game from the hunt. This 15th-century Flemish picture shows the King of Portugal (centre) dining with John of Gaunt, England's Duke of Lancaster, on the king's right, at a castle on the Portuguese border. Heraldic shields decorate the walls, and the wealth of the castle is indicated by the fact that its walls are tiled and its windows glazed, instead of being left open as they were in simpler homes*

MOCK BATTLE *Many knights were killed not in action against the enemy but in tournaments, which often included fights to the death. Later, these were succeeded by the type of joust shown in this 15th-century French manuscript, when two knights tried to unhorse each other with their lances*

READY FOR BATTLE *The medieval knight rode into battle or jousted in tournaments wearing a rich and splendid array. His horse was decked in an extravagant livery. The knight wore heavy armour of chain mail and plate and carried a broad shield, and his head was protected with a visored helm. He was armed with a lance, and also with a broadsword or mace which he wielded when he was dismounted*

much loss of life from dysentery and disease, captured Jerusalem in 1099 after a 40-day siege. An appalling massacre of Muslims and Jews followed. From this and other incidents it became clear that the motives of the Crusaders were by no means simple. Many were sincere and dedicated Christians, seeking salvation or the remission of penance for sins by devoting themselves to war, and if necessary death, in Christ's service, on the very land that he had trodden. But mixed with religious zeal was hope of new lands and the spoils of war. The Christian impulse was soon submerged in waves of private quarrelling and personal greed.

## The founding of Outremer

Even in the First Crusade the liberated lands were not returned to the pope or the emperor but instead carved up into four feudal states – the kingdom of Jerusalem, the principality of Antioch, and the earldoms of Edessa and Tripoli. The four states were known as Outremer, the land 'beyond the seas'. Many Crusaders, having liberated Jerusalem, returned home, but some stayed to hold Outremer for Christianity.

Crusader Palestine became an extension of feudal Europe, with churches, monasteries and castles – some of which, like Krak des Chevaliers in Syria, still stand as magnificent evidence of the 200 years of Crusader rule. Krak des Chevaliers withstood 12 sieges before it fell in

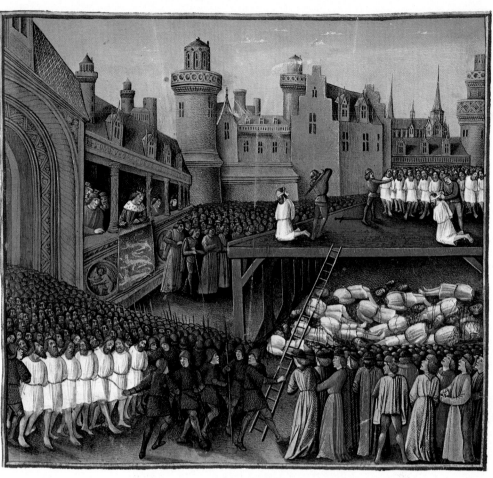

SAVAGERY IN THE NAME OF CHRIST

*Both sides fought with great ferocity in the Crusades, and the banner of Christ did not deter the Crusaders from acts of fearful savagery. A French manuscript of 1490 shows Richard I of England looking on as* *hundreds of Saracen prisoners wait to be led to slaughter. An executioner swings his sword, while another blindfolds his next victim. Underneath the bloodstained platform the headless corpses pile up*

A NEW STYLE OF CASTLE

*The design of European castles changed dramatically after Crusaders returned from the Middle East, where they had been impressed by the massive and almost impregnable fortresses of the Byzantine Empire. Bold new concepts were incorporated in the construction of castles such as Harlech, one of a chain built by Edward I to secure Wales, and shown in this reconstruction as it appeared when completed in 1290. The simple stone keep, walls and moat of earlier centuries were replaced by double rows of thick walls guarded by tall, rounded towers, arranged so that their lines of fire covered all approaches. The keep, in which the lord of the castle lived, had formerly been built well inside the walls so that his forces could make a last stand within it. Now, however, this defensive thinking was abandoned. The keep became a formidable gatehouse where an attacking force, if it crossed the moat, could be trapped between two portcullises. When it was built, Harlech Castle stood at the top of cliffs which were washed by the waves of Tremadoc Bay 200 ft below, but the sea has since receded. Its strength was such that in 1294 a garrison of only 37 men successfully resisted a siege by a Welsh prince, Madog*

# *An influx of wealth and wisdom from the East*

1271. The castle was built by the Knights Hospitallers of St John. This order, formed originally to maintain a hospital for sick pilgrims on their way to Jerusalem, later became a military organisation whose members, mainly recruited from well-born families, took monastic vows and dedicated themselves to the defence of the Christian lands. They were soldier-monks, their uniform carrying a white cross on a black background; and gradually they built a number of centres scattered around Europe. Alongside the Hospitallers were the Knights Templars, founded in 1118 to protect pilgrims travelling along the road from the Palestine coast to Jerusalem. They wore a red cross on a white background.

Without the knights, the Christian kingdoms would not have survived. Even despite their

help, Edessa fell in 1144. As a result, the Second Crusade was called by Bernard, Abbot of Clairvaux, a powerful prelate renowned for piety. Although it was led by two rulers, Conrad III, the Holy Roman Emperor, and Louis VII, King of France, it proved a disaster. The two monarchs quarrelled bitterly. They failed to take Damascus, and even Bernard admitted that their Crusaders were now a motley army of followers, among whom thieves and murderers outnumbered the men of God.

The Third Crusade was made necessary by the conquests of Saladin, who recaptured for Islam every Christian city of Outremer except Tyre. The Crusade was led by the three most powerful figures in Christian Europe: Philip II (Augustus) of France, Richard I of England and the Holy Roman Emperor, Frederick I

(Barbarossa). But the emperor died on the way of a heart attack caused by the cold water of a mountain stream in which he bathed, and the two kings quarrelled. Philip abandoned the Crusade, and on returning home took advantage of Richard's absence to invade English territories in Normandy and other parts of France.

Meanwhile Richard, left in sole charge of the Crusade, earned the name of Coeur de Lion, 'Lion Heart', by his bravery, captured Acre and got within sight of Jerusalem's walls. He established chivalrous and even cordial relations with Saladin, and a truce secured the coast for the Crusaders and gave them right of access to Jerusalem. On his return, however, Richard was shipwrecked and made a prisoner by the Duke of Austria. He was released only after the payment of an enormous ransom, partly collected from taxation in England.

Bitter rivalries blighted each successive Crusade in turn. The real gains went to the trading cities of Italy, especially Venice, which profited from transporting the Crusaders and obtained trading privileges in the Levant ports from which the brocades and silks of the East reached the western Mediterranean.

## Route of the 'Pied Piper'

The mercenary motives of the Crusaders were most evident in the Fourth Crusade in 1204. They had to pay Venice 85,000 silver marks in advance for ships and provisions, and Venice demanded also a share in the direction of the Crusade and half of any conquests. The Crusaders were then invited by a Byzantine prince to Constantinople, in order to replace his deposed father on the throne. In the end the Crusaders and the Venetians captured and sacked Constantinople, which the Venetians saw as a trade rival.

Treasures were removed and manuscripts and paintings destroyed. The four bronze horses now above the portico of St Mark's Cathedral in Venice were seized from Constantinople. Venice took control of one area of Constantinople, and a 'Latin Emperor of the East' was proclaimed. Not a single Crusader reached Palestine. With this episode the Crusades began to lose prestige, and the numbers of those taking part in them dwindled. The Crusaders' rule in Byzantium lasted only 50 years.

The saddest Crusade of all came in 1212 – the Children's Crusade. Thirty thousand children were persuaded by a French farm boy, Stephen of Cloyes, to set out for Palestine from France, and few ever returned. When they reached Marseilles, expecting the waters to part for them as had the Red Sea for Moses, they were lured on to ships and sold into slavery in North Africa. Twenty thousand German children who set out in the same year did not get beyond Italy. Of those who began the return journey, some were captured and made servants, and some girls ended up as prostitutes. The fable of the Pied Piper of Hamelin may have originated in this miserable episode.

There were still more Crusades to follow, but in 1271 Krak des Chevaliers had to surrender,

## HERO IN AN AGE OF CHIVALRY

*The hero of one of the world's great epic poems, The Song of Roland, is depicted, to the left of Emperor Charlemagne and the Archbishop of Rheims, in the famous 13th-century 'Window of Charlemagne' in*

*Chartres Cathedral. Roland, fearless and chivalrous in battle, was idealised in a heroic legend which grew out of the ambush and defeat of Charlemagne's rearguard at Roncesvalles, a mountain pass in the Pyrenees, in 778*

and 20 years later Acre, the last Christian stronghold, fell after a six-week siege, its inhabitants being massacred or enslaved. The Muslims held Jerusalem until British troops arrived in 1917, during the First World War.

What should have been a great Christian adventure proved to be a story of greed and ambition, and ended in disillusion. 'The Crusaders forsook God,' said a chronicler, 'before God forsook them.' The stirring of missionary zeal in Europe led to ugly anti-Semitic outbreaks. The war against the heretics enlisted many younger sons keen not for the glory of God but for land and gold. The East was not liberated but looted; and by the time of the Eighth Crusade in 1270 the notion of a papal 'Army of Salvation' had got lost in the squabbles and rivalries of the orders of the Knights Templars and Knights Hospitallers.

## Heritage of the Crusades

The Crusades were not entirely futile. In one sense the crusading energy moved elsewhere. Venice and the Italian ports profited from the Crusades, and Prince Henry of Portugal sought to follow their example by looking to the sea and to a merchant fleet for prosperity. His ships sailed to Madeira and the Azores. In 1487 Bartholomew Diaz, a Portuguese mariner, reached the Cape of Good Hope. The voyages of discovery flowed out of the spirit and wealth of the Italian merchant adventurers.

Another result of the Crusades was that their failures revealed the military feebleness of feudalism, with its rivalries and vendettas. It was the cities that prospered, and not only in Italy. To finance his expeditions, Richard the Lion Heart had to sell municipal charters which gave boroughs rights of self-government.

Europe acquired new standards of comfort from the East. The Crusaders brought back spices such as ginger and pepper, cinnamon and cloves; fruits like figs, dates and raisins; and rice, almonds and sugar. Rugs and carpets came to replace straw and rushes on the floor. Silk and brocade made for changes in fashion; so did henna and rouge. Glass mirrors on the pattern of those used in Constantinople replaced the polished metal discs of the earlier Middle Ages. And the military orders learnt the art of building massive concentric castles, with rounded turrets, to replace the earlier single square stone towers.

There was wisdom to be learnt, too. The West learnt much of Greek philosophy from the Arabs, who brought from India the numerals we use today, created algebra and studied astronomy. The Arabs used opium as an anaesthetic in surgery; they were aware of fertilisers; and they had learnt from the Chinese the secret of manufacturing paper, which now began to be used in the West to supplement the traditional parchment or papyrus.

## The first Renaissance

By the 12th century the anarchy and disarray in Europe following the barbarian invasions had been overcome. Strong central governments were being created in England, France

# CHURCHES TO GOD'S GLORY

Thousands of cathedrals and churches were built in Europe in the 11th and 12th centuries, more than 1500 of them in France alone. The era saw the flowering of two classic styles of building – Romanesque and Gothic. Romanesque churches were solid and heavy, with thick walls and rounded arches to support the massive weight of the superstructure. Small windows let in little sunlight. In contrast, Gothic churches were taller and more graceful, with high pointed arches, slender columns and huge stained glass windows

FRESH APPROACH *Sculptors added to the Gothic splendour by introducing a new realism. In this carving of The Three Kings in Autun Cathedral in France, the master-mason Giselbertus portrayed recognisable figures in his Bible illustration*

ROUNDED ROOF *The 12th-century abbey church of La Madeleine, at Vézelay, in France, shows a gradual change in styles. The roof of the nave is rounded in the Romanesque manner, though higher than usual, and strengthened with cross vaults. The choir's pointed Gothic arches were added later*

ROMANESQUE STYLE *When the church of Notre-Dame-la-Grande was built at Poitiers in the first half of the 12th century, the solid and rigid style of Romanesque architecture was at its peak. The façade is broad and squat, with rounded arches and thick, windowless walls. The Romanesque style became known in Britain as Norman, after the Norman conquerors who brought it to England with them from the Continent in the late 11th century*

*Thick walls (above) bore the weight of rounded Romanesque arches. Flying buttresses (below) supported pointed Gothic arches and the higher walls and vaults they made possible. The Gothic style gave buildings a lighter, more airy appearance*

GOTHIC STYLE *The pointed arches, vertical lines, and lofty twin towers of the cathedral of Notre-Dame, in Paris, give a soaring elegance to its western façade, despite its massive size. Completed in 1245, it is a perfect example of classic Gothic architecture*

ARCHITECTURAL TRIUMPH *Only a small part of the support for the wide vaulted ceiling at the 13th-century cathedral of Notre-Dame-la-Grande, at Chartres, designed in the High Gothic style, comes from the pillars, which are seen rising 123 ft from the floor of the nave. Most of the stress is borne by huge flying buttresses and arches which line the aisles on either side. As a result the walls were left clear for a gallery and rows of stained glass windows*

# *Love songs at the court and inquiry at the universities*

A code of courtly love which spread through Europe in the 12th century idealised the relationship between a knight and his chosen lady, who was often not his wife. The code arose in Provence, in southern France, where troubadours composed love songs and poems and performed them as they wandered from castle to castle. Some were accompanied by musicians, and employed professional entertainers, called *jongleurs*, to sing for them. Among the nobility, marriages were made for political and domestic reasons, so love was often sought outside marriage. Even children were betrothed. The troubadours idealised such illicit liaisons and, although the code revered love that was spiritual, many of the words of the poems and songs were blatantly sensual

OBJECT OF WORSHIP *A courtly lady is flanked by a lion and a unicorn, emblems of chivalry, in a tapestry which symbolises reverence for women of noble birth*

QUEEN OF LOVE *Eleanor of Aquitaine, whose tomb (above) is at Fontevrault Abbey, in France, was a leading patroness of the troubadours; at Poitiers she presided over a Court of Love whose members ruled on matters of courtship and drew up a code for lovers. Eleanor was the wife of Louis VII of France. After his death, she married Henry II of England*

and Sicily, even if they were rooted in feudalism. In northern Italy and across France and Germany there were walled cities, giving protection to merchants, traders and townsfolk. Men could turn to the arts of peace, and the Crusaders brought back new ideas and a new sophistication. From this new intellectual freedom there arose a rebirth of art and learning which was to be a precursor of the true Renaissance 300 years later.

Europe was still dominated by the Church. Peter Abelard, the renowned philosopher of the University of Paris, lived at the same time as one of the greatest of the popes, Innocent III. Even though Abelard questioned the dogma of the Church, he never sought to set his judgment against the Scriptures. In his last letter to the nun Heloise, his pupil, with whom he had fallen in love, he wrote: 'I will never be a philosopher, if that is to speak against St Paul; I would not be an Aristotle, if that were to separate me from Christ.'

But the new spirit of inquiry penetrated the monastic orders and aroused in them an interest in the outside world. The notion gradually grew of turning away from preparation for the next world towards humanitarian action in the present. The supreme example of this was St Francis of Assisi (1182–1226) and his order of friars. After a spell in trade and as a soldier, St Francis gave away his wealth to work with the poor and the unfortunate. His interest was not in theology or in the politics of power, but in the world of man and of nature around him.

This was the great age of European church building; each city strove to outdo its neighbour by expressing in architecture its religious zeal. Over 1000 cathedrals and churches were built in France in the 11th century, and at least

another 500 in the 12th; and to them townspeople gave their money and the labour of their hands over many generations. It was in the churches that medieval art also flourished, for art, too, was almost totally concerned with religion. Stained glass was possibly its most perfect form. To stand in the Sainte Chapelle of St Louis built by Louis IX ('The Saint') in Paris, with its sunset-red stained glass, has been compared to standing inside a ruby, and to stand in Chartres Cathedral, with its cool blue light, to standing inside a sapphire.

Artistry was lavished on polyphonic music, (in which two or more melodies were united), on frescoes and tapestries, on woodcarving on church pews, on carvings in stone on churches, on the patient decoration by monks of Bibles or other religious books. For the cathedrals were more than centres of worship; they were at once theatre and stage, library and art gallery and school. And those cathedrals that could claim they were closely connected with a saint became centres of pilgrimage and trade–like Durham, burial place of Cuthbert; or Canterbury, where Thomas Becket was murdered in 1170; or Santiago de Compostela in Spain, the reputed burial place of St James the Apostle.

## Legends of the heroes

Although the themes of the art and architecture were still clearly religious, there was a new spirit. Part of it was evident in the troubadours who flourished in Provence, in the trouvères of northern France, in the trovatori of Italy and the minnesingers of Germany. They went from castle to castle, reciting poetry and singing songs of their own composition accompanied by musicians with viols and flutes. Their lyrics were of love, adventure and heroism, and the

love was as often sensual as spiritual in nature.

In France one of the favourite legends told by the troubadours was the *Song of Roland*, based on the great national hero Charlemagne. The facts are mostly lost in history, but the story goes that Roland, Earl of the Breton March, was in command of Charlemagne's rearguard after a campaign in Spain, when his party was ambushed in the mountain gorge of Roncesvalles and annihilated. Roland had been given a horn with which he could summon help, but his courage made him scorn to use it until it was too late. With his dying breath, he blew a great blast on the horn, and Charlemagne, hearing it on the evening wind, returned to find him slain.

In England, a mythical king, Arthur – who may or may not have been a 6th-century Romano-British leader – and his Knights of the Round Table became similar subjects of legend, fighting with a magic sword and with a knightly code of honour. In later centuries, Siegfried in Germany and William Tell in Switzerland represent the same chivalric ideal.

Singers and poets used local dialects, and helped to create distinct national languages and cultures. Their songs and fables were endlessly repeated – for their magic was in their familiarity rather than in their novelty.

But the most important factor in the 12th-century renaissance was a new spirit of Socratic inquiry. This was accompanied by a rediscovery of Aristotle, and by the rise of universities. Peter Abelard established the fame of the University of Paris by endless questioning of religious dogmas. His treatise *Sic et Non (Yes and No)* showed how contradictory these could be. Questioning, said Abelard, was the key to wisdom: 'By doubting we come to inquiry, and by inquiry we arrive at the truth.' In 1140 he

was condemned as a heretic, and compelled to spend his last years a virtual prisoner at Cluny. But his method of inquiry became the fashion in the medieval universities. These universities originated as collections of students gathered at the feet of an individual teacher. As a teacher moved, so his students might go with him. Cambridge came into being in this way, when a group of discontented teachers moved from Oxford.

The method of teaching was by lectures and by the questioning of accepted dogmas. The student was trained to think in a systematic manner. A university course might last six years, a student's goal being the ability to defend a controversial thesis. Almost all debates were religious in origin; scholars even disputed how many angels could stand on a pinhead. The subjects were the basic seven that are still the core of traditional university teaching: philosophy, mental and moral and natural; the liberal arts; rhetoric; and civil and canon law.

Universities were organised in one of two ways. Those modelled on Paris consisted of a guild of teachers, who laid down rules and whose students were usually young, sometimes as young as 12 or 14. Those modelled on Bologna, however, were guilds of students, usually much older and studying advanced law or medicine; they themselves paid the teachers, shaped the courses of study and elected their senior university administrator, the rector – a practice that still survives in the older universities of Scotland.

## Reason and faith reconciled

The effect of this ferment of learning was an intellectual challenge to the Christian creed. Abbot Bernard of Clairvaux, the powerful

prelate who had launched the Second Crusade, opposed Abelard. He maintained that 'the faith of the righteous believes; it does not dispute'. Successive theologians struggled to reconcile reason and faith until St Thomas Aquinas, professor of theology at the University of Paris, showed, in his *Summa Theologica*, completed in 1273, that the two are not incompatible. He emphasised that reason as well as faith was a road to truth. Reason established that everything must have a cause – until, following back the chain of cause and effect to its ultimate source, the inquirer came to God, the original cause of all things. The teachings of St Thomas are officially accepted by the Roman Catholic Church to this day.

The tension between the two worlds of Church and state is most clearly shown in the work of Dante Alighieri (1265–1321). The son of a poor but noble Florentine, he never forgot his youthful longings for the wealthier and distant Beatrice. He was a member of the Florentine governing council, but was expelled in 1302 because he supported the emperor's party against the pope's. Dante was thus an exile, and lived a wandering life. His poem *The Divine Comedy* is the story of his imaginary journey through Hell and Purgatory and into Heaven, but in it he talks of philosophy and earthly love, of popes and politicians.

In England, Chaucer's *Canterbury Tales*, completed in about 1387, are in form a series of tales told by a procession of pilgrims going to the shrine of 'the holy blissful martyr' St Thomas Becket; but the men and women Chaucer describes vividly and boisterously include the miller, the prior, the doctor, and men of many crafts; and the language, part Anglo-Saxon, part 'modern' English, has in it

### PRIDE IN THE NEW CITIES

*New towns appeared and older cities grew bigger from the 12th century onwards, and proper municipal organisation became essential. A painting by Ambrogio Lorenzetti, called* Good Government in the City, *gives a vivid picture of contemporary life in the painter's native city of Siena and reflects the pride felt by citizens everywhere in the orderliness and stability of their societies. Girls dance in the streets; peasants and merchants with laden asses, sheep and baskets of produce pass before open-fronted shops; and masons work on the roof of one of the high-towered buildings. Siena was one of several bustling Italian city-republics which, during the Middle Ages, eventually grew rich and powerful enough to wage war to protect their own interests*

### TAKING CHRISTIANITY TO THE PEOPLE

New religious orders founded in the late Middle Ages sent their monks to preach among the people instead of staying cloistered in monasteries. One of the most important orders was the brotherhood of Friars formed by St Francis of Assisi, the son of a well-to-do family who forsook his wealth to work among the poor and sick, and took a vow of poverty. The Franciscans preached of a Christ who was gentle, and of a merciful God who cared for all creatures, birds and animals as well as men and women. The Friars were not allowed to possess money, and lived by begging or working to meet their needs. Francis died in 1226 at the age of 43; two years later he was canonised. But the cult of poverty did not long survive him. The Church, because of its own financial interests, rejected the doctrine, and those who clung to it were burnt as heretics

FIGHTING EVIL *Famous Italian painters decorated the great basilica built by the citizens of Assisi to honour St Francis shortly after he died. This painting of the saint banishing demons from the town of Arezzo was one of a series of rich frescoes depicting incidents in the saint's life painted by the Florentine artist Giotto di Bondone (1266–1337)*

# *A rival for the Church as cities grow strong*

in places the gusto and imagery of Shakespeare. The pungency, the humour, the sharp focus on the follies and vanities of men and women in the real world, are indications of a new spirit.

The Middle Ages in Europe ended as powerful new monarchs arose, ruling entire nation states, and supported by the wealth of expanding commercial cities. The rise of royal power at the expense of the nobles was caused partly by a change in the art of war. The strength of the feudal knight had depended on castles, horses and armour. When gunpowder was introduced, castle walls were no longer impregnable. Furthermore, it was possible for disciplined pikemen and bowmen on foot to repel a cavalry charge. Edward III's victory at Crécy in 1346, over a French army that outnumbered his own by as many as three to one, was due to the speed, accuracy and range of the English archers using the long-bow. And kings could now hire professional soldiers who would be permanently in their service, instead of the feudal levies who were prompt to go back to their farms after the 40 or 60-day duty that was all that feudalism required.

Kings stood for unity, for the enforcement of written laws and for trade and peace. And the business groups and middle classes in the towns were tired of war and anarchy. They needed food from the countryside, and a new class of merchant landlords came into being, farming for profit. Kings came to rely less on the nobility than on businessmen or educated clergy as their advisers and men of affairs. Since kings needed cash, they turned increasingly to the merchants for it. All this was part of a determined drive to concentrate power in royal hands. The king's judges moved around the country on circuit, trying cases on the spot. Every offence was seen as a breach of the king's peace, which it was the task of the king's judges to maintain. It became the custom to call on a jury of local men to establish the true facts concerning crimes, and gradually royal justice replaced the primitive methods of medieval justice such as trial by combat.

It was in the towns that the effects of the forces of change were most marked. The contrast between two words illustrate the change clearly. The German word *burg* – as in Edinburgh or Freiburg – indicates a fortified place, usually a city on a rock. But *borough* indicates a town with a charter, and with some powers of self-government.

## The first trades unions

Merchants and traders – such as tailors, carpenters, weavers, goldsmiths, glovers and furriers – were organised in guilds, in part trades unions defending their rights as workmen, in part associations of employers and shop-owners. The guilds in some towns dominated city government, and their members built churches and guild halls that are still, in such cities as Florence and London, superb examples of late medieval craftsmanship.

But town life was neither healthy nor safe. Towns were crowded and filthy places, at intervals swept by fire and plague. There was no distinction between street, pavement and gutter; refuse was everywhere. From 1335 an epidemic of bubonic plague, the Black Death, carried by rat-borne fleas, swept across Europe. Its effects were particularly severe in the towns, where one in three people died in agony.

Alongside cathedral and castle as powers in the land there now stood the city. The Hanseatic League of north European cities had trading posts in Norway and England, maintained a fleet, and had a power that rivalled that of some kings. From the cities came inventions such as glass, clocks and cannon. Bruges and Antwerp in Flanders, Cologne and Augsburg in Germany, Florence and Venice, Milan and Genoa, Pisa and Bologna in Italy were important for invention, trade and culture. In the towns, modern capitalism was born; it was the money power of the towns that destroyed the feudal world. The Medici in Florence were bankers for half of Europe, while even the Holy Roman Emperor Charles V depended on the Fugger banking house of Augsburg.

The Church suffered most from these new forces. It too needed money, but could get it only by devices that angered the new breed of kings. Internal disagreements weakened the papacy: between 1378 and 1417 there were two popes, one in Rome, one in Avignon. Church corruption led to the first movements that foreshadowed the Reformation. John Wycliffe (1320–84), in England, and Jan Hus (1373–1413), in Bohemia, attacked the worldly ways of the clergy and claimed that the Bible was the supreme authority. And voices like that of Roger Bacon in England were heard saying that observation and experiment were the keys to knowledge. The past was losing its grip on the present, A new spirit had appeared.

DYERS AND SPINNERS *The cloth industry had dozens of different trades, each with its own guild. In this miniature, painted in 1482 in Flanders, the most important cloth centre in Europe, dyers are dipping fabrics in heated vats of red dye. Women were employed in the textile crafts – a 'spinster' was originally a single woman who earned a living by spinning*

## POWER FOR GUILDS

Trade increased with the growth of towns and cities, and merchants and craftsmen became prosperous. For mutual protection and advancement they formed themselves into guilds, which often grew powerful enough to dominate city governments. The guilds were 'closed shops', and only guild members could trade within a town or engage in a craft. Entry to a guild was governed by strict rules. A would-be member had first to serve a lengthy apprenticeship under a master craftsman, but before he could set up in business on his own he had to spend a further spell as a journeyman under a master, then pass an examination. This often entailed the production of a 'masterpiece', the original meaning of which was an example of work that proved a journeyman's mastery of his craft. The guilds also fixed prices

FINAL TEST *Under the critical eye of a guild warden, a stonemason and a carpenter work on their 'masterpieces', in a 15th-century Flemish book illustration*

Alexander Rex Scotor

lewellin princeps wallie

## THE RISE OF PARLIAMENT: A CHALLENGE TO SOVEREIGN POWER

*By the end of the Middle Ages, a new force was challenging for a share in the government of European states. In England, this process started as early as the mid-13th century, when a rebel baron, Simon de Montfort, called together the first parliament, but nearly 400 years were to pass before the authority of the Crown*
*was successfully challenged. In this 16th-century illustration, Parliament sits before Edward I. The king is flanked by the rulers of Wales and Scotland; in front are his bishops and red-robed barons; between them the judges sit on wool-sacks. The barons had already won a share in the king's power through Magna Carta*

# A new role for man and the Church

## AD 1350–1600

*A spirit of adventure seized Europe, as Renaissance men
took a new pride in worldly achievement,
discovered new lands and challenged the authority of the pope*

Revolutions apart, there are few abrupt breaks in history. But when Europe turned its back on the Middle Ages and stepped into the modern world, the sense of newness was so intense and the results of the change so far-reaching that a special name has been given to the period – the Renaissance, or 'rebirth' of Europe.

It began in Italy, about the middle of the 14th century, with a re-awakened interest in the Greek roots of European culture. It spread over the rest of Europe as scholars crossed the Alps, bringing with them the fruits of the new learning. And it ended in Germany nearly two centuries later, with Martin Luther leading the first successful challenge to the Roman Catholic Church, which had for so long dominated Europe's life and thought.

In all fields – philosophy, science, theology, painting, sculpture, architecture, poetry, fashion, exploration – the men of the Renaissance challenged accepted ideas. It is this that marks them out as modern men, no longer content to accept ideas handed down by authority, even when those ideas seemed to be the plainest truth.

Common sense told men that the earth was flat, and that anybody venturing too far from land would sail over the edge. But Columbus questioned this belief, and discovered a New World. The teachings of the Church and the evidence of their own eyes told men that the earth was the centre of the universe, and that the sun and stars moved across the sky. But Copernicus questioned this belief, and discovered for the world a new and lesser place in the universe.

Meanwhile, men were discovering for themselves a new and more exciting way of life. Tired of the cloistered world of medieval scholarship, they rediscovered the joy to be found in this world, as distinct from the anticipated delights of the next.

The Renaissance had been heralded as early as the 12th century by the curiosity and rational outlook of Peter Abelard in Paris. The move-

**RENAISSANCE CRADLE**

*New ideals were born and fostered in the
14th century among the multitude of city-
states in central and northern Italy*

**MEDICI SPLENDOUR**

*Florence was the leading city of the
Renaissance, and its leading family, the
Medici, lavished the profits they made
from banking on making the city renowned throughout Europe. Their Pitti
Palace (left, foreground) was the
largest in Florence, with landscaped
gardens stretching up to the Belvedere
Fortress; it is now an art gallery.*

*The most famous of the Medici,
Lorenzo the Magnificent (1449–92),
is shown on horseback (right) in a
detail from a painting by Benozzo
Gozzoli called* Journey of the Magi.
*The artist has represented Lorenzo as
one of the three biblical kings, riding
out in a hunting party of the Florentine
court – an example of artistic licence
which would have been regarded as
blasphemous a few years earlier*

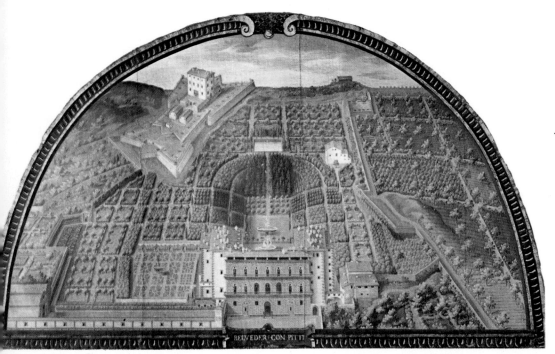

# *All knowledge was their province*

ment was carried forward in the 13th century by the enlightened Holy Roman Emperor Frederick II in Germany and Sicily; by the experimental science of Roger Bacon in England; and, in Italy, by the vision and language of Dante and the paintings of Giotto, the first artist to burst free from ceremonial stiffness and medieval mysticism and to paint in a naturalistic style.

The Italian poet Petrarch (1304–74) admired Cicero and Livy as stylists and was interested in the roads, the ruins and the law of ancient Rome. Petrarch, like Dante, wrote in Italian as well as in Latin. People in Italy were becoming more and more interested in the ancient world. They began to hunt for statues and long-lost manuscripts, and to look on Rome not only as the seat of the popes but also as the capital of what had been the world's greatest empire – the city of Augustus and of Virgil, rich in its pagan past.

### The gift of the Greeks

When the Byzantine Empire began to collapse before the Turks in the mid-14th century, the wealthy cities of Italy offered a welcome to Greek scholars fleeing from Turkish rule. The Greeks brought with them an enthusiasm for the classical world, and a tradition of learning that stretched back a thousand years. They added discipline to classical studies by setting up academies in Italy on the lines of Plato's original Academy in Athens. The men of the Renaissance soon began to regard those who separated them from their great past as 'barbarians', and the years since the fall of Rome in 476 as the 'Dark Ages'. Later the introduction of printing vastly multiplied the number of minds that could be reached by the wisdom of the scholars.

Though the Renaissance began as a return to Europe's roots in the classical past, it soon took on aspects that were entirely modern. Franciscan friars began to dwell on the human side of the Christian story rather than on the dogmatic beliefs required of the faithful, and they preached in the language of the market-place. The freshness in the wall-paintings of Masaccio (1401–28), with their strong realism and contrasts of light and shadow, owed little to ancient models. Artists such as Benozzo Gozzoli (1420–97) and Fra Lippo Lippi introduced the contemporary world into their paintings; they depicted the houses and gardens of Florence and the lovely valley of the Arno, peopled by the richly clad families of their patrons, the Medici or the Tornabuoni.

### Growth of the merchant bankers

During the century after Constantinople at last fell to the Turks in 1453, the character of Europe changed dramatically, and some of the underlying forces that worked the change were economic. The Crusades had stimulated trade and the growth of towns; and in cities like Pisa, Milan, Genoa, Venice, Florence and Siena a merchant class had grown rich and influential. These merchants acted as investors and tax collectors for the popes. They backed trading

expeditions to distant lands, and were specialists in finance and insurance. Powerful families emerged, their wealth based less on the ownership of feudal estates than on the proceeds of investing money at risk. The bank owned by the Medici family in Florence, for instance, had branches at Milan, Naples, Pisa, Venice, Geneva, Lyons and Avignon, Bruges and London. Special branches were opened for papal councils at Constance and Basle.

Such banks as these could transfer credit over the whole of Europe, and they became essential to popes and kings. Increased wealth meant that many people had more leisure; as a result there was increasing demand for the products of craftsmen to beautify the great palaces and villas of the leading families.

There were other causes of change. The papacy, for centuries a commanding voice in the affairs of Europe, had been gravely weakened by what came to be known as its 'Babylonish Captivity'. This began in 1309, when Clement V put himself under the protection of France and left Rome for Avignon; for the next 70 years a succession of French popes ruled the Church – an exile likened to that of the Jews in Babylon. No sooner had the popes returned to Rome than the Church was further weakened by the 'Great Schism' between the pope in Rome and a rival 'antipope', in Avignon, which lasted until 1417.

### A new pride in man

New ideas led to a challenging of medieval conceptions in all fields. Man might still be a sinner, as the Church taught – but he was capable of greatness, and interesting for his own sake. Men ceased to be anonymous, and instead became proud of themselves and their achievements. The architects who built the fine cathedrals of the Middle Ages are seldom remembered even by name; but the personalities of Renaissance artists and sculptors have been recorded in sharp detail.

Artists of the Renaissance were not ashamed to express delight in the physical beauty of men and women, and in the sights of the natural world. Though their settings and their subjects were often still religious, the feeling behind their paintings or sculptures was increasingly humanist and secular. Artists still portrayed the Madonna and Child; but gradually they came to emphasise the beauty and grace of the woman, rather than the pride of the Mother, or the holiness of the Madonna.

Portraits were no longer flat and stylised, with stiff postures, elongated hands and almond-shaped eyes. There was a new and bold interest in anatomy, in gesture and position, and a knowledge of perspective. The rich costumes shown in the paintings were contemporary, and the scenery was Italian. There was a new interest in people in movement, and in depicting human character – as in Donatello's statue of Erasmo da Narni, the *condottiere*, on horseback, and the work of Michelangelo in Florence and Rome. Florence was the outstanding city of the Renaissance – the city of the Medici, a family which rose from obscure

The revolutionary new approach to life which was to spark off the Renaissance, or 'rebirth', of Europe first emerged in Italy in the mid-14th century. In the Middle Ages, men's idea of a virtuous life had been a life lived apart from the world, often in the cloistered seclusion of a monastery. But the painters, sculptors, poets and scholars of 14th-century Italy began to rediscover the joys and rewards of a life lived in the larger world – and to believe that this life could be equally virtuous. So exciting was this discovery that the leading spirits of the Italian Renaissance refused to limit themselves to one sphere of knowledge. The typical 'man of the Renaissance' was an all-rounder, equally versed in public life and in many different branches of the arts. Schools saw it as part of their task to train men for public life, and professional and humanistic studies flourished in universities. Artists were no longer humble and anonymous servants of the Church, but individuals proud of their achievements and reputation

ENGINEERING FEAT *The dome of Florence Cathedral, built by Filippo Brunelleschi in the early 15th century, was the largest dome built since the Pantheon of ancient Rome. By using bands of stone, Brunelleschi avoided the need for the vast internal framework of scaffolding which usually held the masonry in place. Brunelleschi had to argue with the Florentines to get his controversial plan accepted*

origins to found a bank in 1397. The Medici made their money out of money itself, and with their resources acted as patrons for gifted artists. They ruled the city from the 15th century until 1737. Florence was a city distinguished by skilled work in wool, leather, gold and silver, and also by craftsmanship in stone and brick which survives today in such buildings as Giotto's marble Campanile, the cathedral with Brunelleschi's great dome, and the Ponte Vecchio, with its jewellers' shops straddling the water.

### The Renaissance art of war

Florence had its rivals. Lucca was famous for the quality of its silk, and Prato for its wool. Milan was a great arsenal; two of its armouries in the early 15th century could equip a force of 4000 cavalry and 200 infantry at a few days' notice. In Venice, the state-owned shipyard

FAMILIES OF POWER *The artists of Renaissance Italy had a valuable patroness in Isabella d'Este (above, left), the wife of the ruler of Mantua, Francesco II. Isabella, seen in a sketch by Leonardo, held salons which attracted artists and writers from all over Italy. Cesare Borgia (above, right) was the most infamous member of a powerful family. His father became pope, as Alexander VI, and made his son a cardinal. But Cesare resigned this office for a political career which made his name a byword for murder and treachery*

CITY'S SYMBOL *The citizens of Florence were fiercely proud of its power and prosperity, and of its role as a centre of the Renaissance. The heraldic lion carved by Donatello to symbolise the power of Florence guards a shield bearing the city's emblem, the* fleur-de-lis

DEATH AT THE STAKE *A Dominican friar, Girolamo Savonarola, in 1494 started a one-man crusade against the worldliness of Florence and the tyranny of its rulers. In 1498 he was burnt as a heretic, as shown in this contemporary painting. But for three years, after the expulsion of the Medicis, Savonarola had been virtual ruler of Florence. He won vast popular support by his religious zeal, political skill, and knack of prophecy. Savonarola's popularity flagged when the pleasure-loving Florentines tired of his exhortations, and when the pope brought pressure to bear against him*

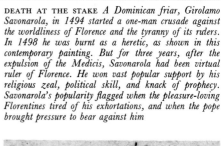

ASSASSIN'S VICTIM *Intrigue and murder in the constant struggle for power and fame were the uglier side of Renaissance Italy. Giuliano de Medici, seen in a painting by Botticelli, was stabbed to death by the Pazzi family in 1478 during mass at the Cathedral of Santa Maria del Fiore. His brother, Lorenzo, fought his way to safety*

HEAD OF STATE *The head of state of the Venetian Republic was the doge, and this portrait by Giovanni Bellini is of Leonardo Loredano, doge from 1501 to 1521. Real power lay in the hands of the inner cabinet of the Great Council, whose members were drawn from the leading families of the city*

SOLDIER-DUKE *Francesco Sforza was one of the most successful of the new class of* condottieri, *or professional soldiers. In 1450 he became Duke of Milan, and he and his successors dominated the state for nearly a century. Milan eventually fell to Spain in 1535*

FIRST TANK *As an engineer the versatile Leonardo da Vinci turned his prodigious talents to the needs of war, and in the sketch above outlined his design for 'covered cars, safe and unassailable, which will enter among the enemy with their artillery'. These were, in effect, tanks – envisaged over four centuries before they first appeared on any battlefield. Leonardo also drew up plans for a flying machine, but, like his tank, it was never built*

covered 60 acres, and produced as many as eight fighting galleys a year. For centuries, Venice dominated the Mediterranean. The power and style of its head of state, the doge, was demonstrated each year at a ceremony symbolising the marriage of the city to the sea.

Inter-city warfare was a feature of 15th-century Italy; it was also good business. It bred the *condottieri*, the professional soldiers, one of whom, Francesco Sforza, usurped the duchy of Milan in 1450. War and trade, as well as Church and state, now offered careers and opportunity to men of enterprise. The Italian city-states, rivals in all these fields, took as much pride in their engineers, diplomats and *condottieri* as in their artists and scholars.

The city-states were constantly at war, against each other or within their own walls. The Pitti Palace in Florence was a fortress even more than a home. This was an age of open prostitution, of rioting, of guerrilla war and endless intrigue, of torture and violence. War, with all its plumed and glittering accoutrements, was itself a Renaissance art.

## Men of many skills

The men and women of the Renaissance were bursting with a confidence that encouraged them to take all knowledge for their province. The typical man of the time was hungry for new experiences and new worlds. Leonardo da Vinci (1452–1519) straddled many worlds and was dazzlingly original in each. He was scientist, painter, sculptor, engineer, anatomist, botanist, mathematician and philosopher. His projects ranged from plans for irrigating the plains of Lombardy to designing a bronze monument of Francesco Sforza (which was never cast) and painting the *Mona Lisa* and *The Last Supper*. Benvenuto Cellini (1500–71) was

musician, architect, goldsmith, soldier, poet and painter; and he too was outstanding in all his roles, as he proudly records in his lengthy and vainglorious autobiography.

All the leading Renaissance personalities were versatile, and many were active in state affairs. Niccolo Machiavelli (1469–1527), a writer on history and statecraft, was also a practical politician who served in the Florentine civil service for 14 years. In 1512, however, he was dismissed by the Medici, and wrote his most famous work, *The Prince*, in an attempt to win back his lost position.

The tactics described in *The Prince* have made Machiavelli's name a byword for cynicism and devious cunning. To survive and prosper in the jungle of statecraft, he writes, the successful ruler must be both lion and fox. He is justified in using any means to preserve his power: 'A prince . . . must have a mind disposed to adapt

# From Italy, the ferment of ideas spreads north

itself . . . and must if necessary be prepared to do evil.' But Machiavelli was not entirely the unscrupulous schemer of legend. He was inspired by a burning patriotism and a desire to make Italy strong enough to throw out the French, German and Spanish invaders who were destroying his country. The treachery of Florence's mercenary armies led him to call for a citizens' militia, as had existed in republican Rome. For Italy to be strong, he claimed, any methods of statecraft could be justified; he modelled his ideal 'prince' on the infamous Cesare Borgia. In many respects, Machiavelli was the first Italian nationalist.

Michelangelo (1475–1564) was another all-round man: a poet and philosopher, the architect of St Peter's, the painter of the Old Testament story and the Last Judgment in the Sistine Chapel, and sculptor of the figures on the family tombs of the Medici. He was also one of nine citizens who were in charge of the defence of Florence under the Medici in 1529.

Preachers turned their attention from the medieval goals of poverty and celibacy to exploring the expanding and exciting world around them. Universities flourished. Books of instruction in manners and behaviour appeared,

notably Castiglione's *The Courtier*, which gives a picture of the man of taste and wit, gracious to women and loyal to his patrons. But at the same time Castiglione carefully defines his attitude to the lower orders. A courtier should never wrestle with a peasant 'unless he is sure of getting the upper hand'.

## The power of the printed word

The Renaissance was marked also by a series of innovations which helped to make men masters of their world. One of the most important of these was printing, known in China 600 years earlier but unknown in Europe until now. The first use in Europe of movable type made of metal is attributed to the inventor Johann Gutenberg of Mainz (1398–1468) and his partner, the goldsmith and financier Johann Fust; their first great work was the Latin Bible of about 1456. They used paper made from cloth rags, a process introduced into Europe in 1150 by the Moors of Spain.

By 1500 there were printing presses in 183 European towns. Printing made new ideas in politics and religion available to thousands of thinking men all over Europe. Latin and the Bible were no longer the monopoly of churches,

universities and abbeys. Through the use of the printed word, thinkers like Erasmus, a Dutch scholar famed for his wit and intelligence, could reach a far wider audience. Erasmus's *In Praise of Folly*, an attack on abuses within the Roman Catholic Church, was one of the first books to influence the thinking of the whole of Europe. The printer became a key figure in society, and was often himself a man of learning and scholarship, like Aldus Manutius in Venice, who printed Greek and Roman classics, and Johannes Froben in Basle, for whom Erasmus edited the New Testament.

It was in Italy that this new learning had its sharpest impact, and not only in cities like Florence, Mantua and Milan, but also in Rome. Nicholas V, pope from 1447 to 1455, was a collector of books who founded the Vatican Library. Julius II (1443–1513) built the Vatican Palace and made it his home. In the 16th century, 53 new churches were built in Rome, which became the city of the golden age of the Renaissance, the home of Michelangelo and of the artists Raphael and Bernini.

The artistic creative force of the Renaissance period has perhaps never been equalled; and its ferment soon spread northwards from Italy

## A NEW JOY IN THE NATURAL WORLD

Renaissance painters and sculptors delighted in the world around them, and their work became increasingly lifelike. They studied living models, enabling them to depict figures accurate in anatomy, gesture and expression, instead of the stylised portraits of medieval times. They also learnt the technique of perspective, so adding depth to their pictures

PALACE MADONNA *Heaven itself becomes part of the everyday world in this painting by the Flemish artist Jan van Eyck showing Chancellor Rolin of Burgundy talking directly to the Madonna. The features of the subjects are realistically painted, and faultless perspective leads the eye to the idealised landscape beyond the palace*

CLASSICAL MASTERS *In* The School of Athens, *a fresco in the Vatican, the artist Raphael painted the philosophers and scholars of ancient Greece, a reflection of the revived interest in the classical world which led to the Renaissance. Raphael included portraits of some of his contemporaries: the white-bearded Plato, who stands in the centre with Aristotle, is given the features of Leonardo da Vinci, and the figure in the foreground, leaning on his elbow, is Michelangelo*

HERO IN BRONZE *Donatello's statue of the Venetian condottiere Erasmo da Narni, known as the* Gattamelata, *'honeyed cat' – da Narni's nickname. It was the first bronze statue of a man on horseback to be cast since Roman times*

through France and Germany. Its influence was felt soonest in areas where capital was available and where merchants and princes were ready to be patrons and protectors. Northern artists, such as Albrecht Dürer in Germany and Hans Holbein and the Brueghels in Holland, rivalled those of Italy.

Scientific experiment flourished in Europe north of the Alps. Paracelsus (1493–1541), a Swiss, saw the importance of minerals as medical drugs, investigated the diseases of miners, and wrote not in Latin but in a Swiss-German dialect. Nicholas Copernicus (1473–1543), the Polish astronomer who had been a canon, undermined the teaching of the Church in his conviction that the earth and the other planets move round the sun – though he dedicated his *De Revolutionibus orbium coelestium* ('Concerning the movement of heavenly bodies') to Pope Paul III and his publisher claimed that his theory was merely a mathematical contrivance.

## The age of exploration

At the same time that scientists were beginning to probe the workings of the universe, an age of exploration was beginning to reveal to man more of the secrets of his own planet. Until the 15th century most Europeans believed that the earth was a flat plain, with the Holy Places of Jerusalem at its centre. There were only vague notions about Africa south of the Sahara. Arab traders had brought back some knowledge of India; and in the 13th century Marco Polo, the Venetian, had visited China and returned with tales that many people found hard to believe about great cities and the splendour of the court of the Great Khan. Beginning in 1492, when Columbus discovered the New World, a total revolution in European knowledge of the world took place. Within 100 years, explorers had found an ocean larger than the Atlantic, and a continent larger than their own.

The incentive for exploration came from many sources. Europeans needed the spices and silks of the East, yet the land route to the East had been closed by the expansion of Ottoman Turkish power. Some missionaries were anxious to find and help the Christian kingdoms of the Copts and of Prester John, which were rumoured to lie somewhere in Africa or Asia.

Christopher Columbus (1451–1506), born in Genoa, was convinced that the world was round and that he could reach China by sailing west. He toured the courts of Europe looking for financial backing, but was refused by ruler after ruler, including Henry VII of England. Finally he obtained the money to fit out three ships, partly from Isabella of Castile and partly also from private capitalists. Columbus's flagship, the *Santa Maria*, was only of 100 tons. Its crew of 52, drawn largely from prisons, was superstitious, violent, and threatened mutiny. But on October 12, 1492, two months after leaving Spain, Columbus landed in the Bahama Islands, the first land to be sighted in the New World. He went on to discover and set up a colony on Hispaniola.

The success of this first voyage, enhanced by the Indian captives whom Columbus brought back and the tall tales told by his crew, ensured support for three more voyages. But it was not until 1498 that Columbus discovered the mainland of South America, and even then he held to his belief that he had reached the Indies.

## Rewards of the New World

Spaniards led many of the early voyages of exploration, but people of other countries took part in the discoveries too. John Cabot, who discovered Labrador in 1497, was a Venetian in the English service. Amerigo Vespucci, after

STONE PIETA *Michelangelo's unfinished* Rondanini Pietà *conveys the anguish of the Virgin mourning over the dead Christ*

### THE LURE OF MONEY

*Europe's merchant class grew rapidly in the 15th and 16th centuries as new trade routes to the East were opened, and the Spaniards brought back enormous wealth from their new territories in Central America. The major cities of Europe became money markets. Foremost among them was Antwerp, where Quentin Massys in about 1500 painted this telling picture of* The Moneychanger and his Wife; *the wife has been distracted from her study of a religious book by the gleam of gold and silver coins.*

*Banking houses arose to deal in money and bills of exchange. In time these banks became so wealthy that they could lend money to governments and to monarchs. Henry VIII borrowed about £1 million from the bankers of Antwerp. With the new prosperity came inflation, and the situation was worsened by a population explosion. Production could not keep pace with the rising population, and prices rose by as much as 400 per cent in 90 years*

# A quest for wealth, fame and new continents

whom America was named, was a Florentine working for Spain. Magellan, whose expedition became the first to sail right round the world (1519–22), though he himself was killed by Filipinos in 1521, was a Portuguese sailing under the Spanish flag. Giovanni da Verrazano, who explored the North American coast, was a Florentine in the service of Francis I of France. And Henry Hudson, who gave his name to New York's river and to Hudson's Bay, was an Englishman employed by the Dutch.

But it was Spain that drew the richest dividend. Spaniards explored the coasts of both North and South America, and sent expeditions inland. Hernando Cortez, with 500 men, took Mexico from the Aztecs by 1521; ten years later Pizarro, with only 180 men, took Peru

from the mighty Incas. Coronado in 1540 set off on a voyage to the interior of North America and found the *pueblos* (villages) of the Zuni Indians, and the great canyon of the Colorado.

Portugal was equally active. Vasco da Gama sailed from Lisbon to Calicut, in south-west India, returning with spices and gems, and thus destroyed Venice's grip on trade with the East. Portuguese sailors like Francisco de Almeida and Afonso de Albuquerque fought the Arabs to win command of the Indian Ocean, and reached the Moluccas and Spice Islands.

## Treasure and the pirates

The new discoveries did not merely give the European countries the prestige of having an overseas empire; they also had important eco-

nomic effects within Europe. New wealth was tapped. Portuguese routes to the Spice Islands threatened the monopoly of Italian merchants. Spanish gold and silver from Mexico and Peru was carried home to Seville in great treasure fleets which sailed twice a year, in April and August. They were threatened by Dutch and English pirates, but they usually got through. However, this was not always the case. In the course of his voyage round the world in the *Golden Hind*, Sir Francis Drake captured Spanish treasure worth over $2 million.

The steady increase in the amount of money in circulation in Europe led to a rapid rise in prices, by as much as 400 per cent in 90 years. The familiar economic problems of the modern world – inflation, speculation and boom, followed by deflation and unemployment – which had first been felt in the 1300's, revived in the 16th century. Along with this went a steady rise in the population of Europe's towns. In 1500 there were only five European cities with 100,000 inhabitants or more, while in 1600 there were 12 and London's population had increased from 50,000 to 200,000.

The voyages also introduced to Europe potatoes, maize, tobacco, sugar, tomatoes, turkeys and the furs of previously unknown animals. Novelty, rarity and human credulity combined to give some of the new foodstuffs a value far beyond their merit as sources of nourishment; at one time in England potatoes were sold as aphrodisiacs for more than $600 a lb. The voyages also made Europeans aware of exotic civilizations flourishing in hitherto unknown parts of the world – such as those of the Aztecs and Incas which the Spaniards found in the Americas.

## An era of individualism

The discoverers, driven by the lust for glory as much as for gold, embodied what was most novel in the age of the Renaissance – the determination to win personal fame. It was an age of rampant individualism, and in this it strikes an aggressively modern note.

One typical figure of the age was Francis I of France, who led his troops into Italy in the 1490's and waged long, but unsuccessful, war with the rival House of Hapsburg for the mastery of Europe. Francis was also a great patron of the arts. He established the College de France and brought painters from Italy to his court.

It was in literature, however, that 16th-century France excelled. The masterly use of wit and satire by François Rabelais (*c.* 1490–1553) in such works as *Gargantua* and *Pantagruel* has probably never been surpassed. Poets like Pierre de Ronsard and Joachim du Bellay – the leaders of a group of writers known as *La Pléiade* – created a French national literature. They also tried to broaden the French language by adopting new words from Greek and Latin, as well as copying the style of classical authors.

The high adventure of the age also gave rise to a great upsurge of literature in England, which enjoyed the glories of its Elizabethan age, led by poets such as Edmund Spenser and play-

### INSTRUMENTS WHICH BROADENED MAN'S HORIZONS

*During the Renaissance the frontiers of the known world were extended by adventurous explorers at a faster rate than ever before – or since. The obsession of the age with discovery is shown by this detail from the work of a Flemish artist depicting maps, illustrated travel books, a globe, a compass and an astrolabe – a* *device known since ancient Greek times which helped navigators to determine their latitude. Craftsmen took pride in the design of aids to navigation, and by the time this picture was painted, in the early 1600's, such objects were already being treasured as works of art and had found places in galleries*

wrights such as William Shakespeare and Christopher Marlowe. Shakespeare was the chief glory of the Elizabethan cultural revival, and his work summed up that age's spirit.

## Rebellion in the Church

Inevitably, the spirit of questioning that marked the Renaissance was directed finally against what had been the highest authority in medieval Europe – the Universal Church. By the end of the 15th century, it was far from being the same Church that had spread the gospel to the pagan lands of Europe. Rome lost much of its spiritual authority when it became just another Italian state, and the pope another Italian ruler, intent on extending his lands and filling his purse. There could be no respect for a man like the Borgia Alexander VI, pope from 1492 to 1503, who kept mistresses, fathered illegitimate children, had his enemies murdered and said, after he had bribed his way to the papal throne: 'God has given us the papacy; let us enjoy it.'

Unscrupulous priests squeezed money out of gullible people by exhibiting what were supposed to be the miracle-working relics of saints, but in some cases at least were simply collections of animal bones. Ordinary people could not help but notice the contrast between their own poverty and the wealth of the clergy.

Neither the abuses of Church power nor the criticism they caused were novel. In 14th-century England, the reformer John Wycliffe attacked the very foundations of the Church, declaring that the pope had no special authority, and certainly no right to drain money from England. In Bohemia, Jan Hus, a follower of Wycliffe, first had his writings burnt, then was burnt himself, as a heretic. In Italy, the monk Savonarola attacked the luxury and scandals of both the Church and state; and he too ended his life at the stake. The Dutch scholar Erasmus mocked the superstitions that had crept into the Church. But a new power and a new savagery soon came into the attack. Its chief voice was Martin Luther.

## The challenge of Luther

Luther (1483–1546) did not come quickly to revolution. He was a poor boy, the son of a miner in Saxony. He became an Augustinian friar and a professor of biblical theology at Wittenberg, where he won a reputation as a lecturer and authority on the Bible. He had an intense religious zeal and a strong personal sense of sin. He went on a pilgrimage to Rome, and returned shocked by its depravity.

Like Wycliffe before him, Luther attacked the sale of Indulgences – pardons for sin, based on the idea that the Church, through the merits of Christ and the saints, possessed a store of grace which outweighed the sins of the world. A sinner who bought an Indulgence was dipping into the surplus of grace, and so cancelling some of his punishment in the next world. Pope Leo X, desperately in need of money to build St Peter's in Rome, turned to the sale of Indulgences as a quick and certain way of raising it.

Luther set out his protest and his beliefs about salvation in the form of 95 theses, or written

statements of belief, which he nailed to the door of Wittenberg Castle's chapel in 1517. Dramatic as the gesture was, it was meant as an academic exercise, not as a war on Rome. But Luther had moved far beyond mere criticism of Church abuses. He now believed that man's only path to salvation lay through faith, rather than through pilgrimages, prayers to saints, and the purchase of Indulgences. He set the authority of the Bible above the authority of the pope.

The pope recognised the danger and brought into play his most powerful spiritual weapon. In 1520 he published a bull threatening to excommunicate Luther, cutting him off from the mercy of Christ, if he did not recant his views. Luther's answer was to burn the bull in public. Formal excommunication followed the

next year, and Charles V, the Holy Roman Emperor, summoned the rebellious priest before him at Worms. There Luther stated his views and held to them. 'Here I stand,' he said, 'I can do no other.'

Luther's protests had strong support. They appealed particularly to the German princes, who wanted to block the flow of money to Rome. When the emperor declared Luther an outlaw of the land, by the Edict of Worms in 1521, Frederick of Saxony gave him shelter in his castle at Wartburg. There Luther began his translation of the Bible into German – a task which was to take him more than ten years to complete. Though Luther was not a 'Lutheran' in the modern sense of the term – he never saw himself as anything but a good

### A GOLDEN AGE FOR ENGLAND

In 45 years on the throne, from 1558 to 1603, Elizabeth I ruled over a united and fervently loyal England. The Elizabethan Age was a time of high adventure for the English, led at sea in action against the Spanish and in search of new lands by such admirals as Sir Francis Drake and Sir John Hawkins. England had no painters or sculptors to match those of Italy and Spain; but a cultural Renaissance which was to prove equally enduring came from poets and playwrights such as Edmund Spenser and William Shakespeare. A portrait of Shakespeare appears on the title page of the First Folio edition of his plays in 1623 (right), prefaced by a tribute by Ben Jonson. In this book Shakespeare's mighty plays were brought together for the first time

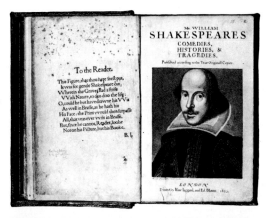

DEFEAT OF THE ARMADA *England's greatest military triumphs during the reign of Elizabeth I were at sea, crowned by the event commemorated in this portrait of the* queen – *the defeat of Philip II's Armada which was to be the vanguard of a Spanish invasion of England in 1588. The ships not sunk in battle were wrecked by storms*

# Reformation, and a new Church

Reformed Catholic – he was now at the head of the Reformation. His pamphlets, vigorous and vulgar in style, were printed by the thousand, and reached an international public. He was in no sense a liberal. His advice to his supporters among the princes, during the bloody Peasants' Revolt of 1524–6, was summed up in a pamphlet – *Against the Thieving and Murderous Gangs of Peasants*. In this he advised the German princes that 'this is a time for anger and the sword, it is not a time for mercy'. His one concern was with the salvation of a man's soul.

## Man without free will

The logic of Luther's views was pushed still further by John Calvin (1509–64), a wealthy lawyer from Picardy who came under the influence of Luther's ideas and was forced by the local authorities to leave Paris in 1533. He settled in the little city-state of Geneva, which he dominated until his death, and which became a hothouse for Protestant ideas. The Scottish Protestant reformer John Knox called it 'the most perfect school of Christ that ever was on earth since the days of the apostles'.

In his *Institutes of the Christian Religion* (1536) Calvin argued that man's destiny is in God's hands. Whether or not a man will reach salvation is not something in his control, but has already been decided by God. In this doctrine of predestination, those marked out for salvation are known as the Elect and they need no priest to intervene between themselves and God. Some of Calvin's followers took his doctrines to even greater extremes, proclaiming that the identity of the Elect and of the damned had been determined even before the Creation.

Calvinism was a strong and militant faith. It bred the Huguenots in France, the Dutch Reformed Church, the Presbyterians in Scotland and the Puritans in England and America. Denying the importance of sacraments and priests, downgrading the altar and the ceremonies of Catholicism, Calvinism put high value on education, as it was essential for followers to read the Word. It was deeply concerned with morality, and had a long list of forbidden activities. Worldly enjoyments, from maypoles to Christmas festivities, were the Devil's work. Death was the penalty for adultery in Geneva, and in this climate of fierce intolerance it was even forbidden to ring church bells to summon people to services.

In the Scottish and Dutch forms, Calvinism was to prove a faith useful for reformers in political as well as Church affairs. It reinforced the Dutch in their struggle against Spain and the Scots in their struggle against their own rulers, the Stuarts, as well as the English. But it came close to destroying the Swiss Confederation, which split between Catholic and Calvinist factions, and it added a further religious division to the vexed political map of Germany.

## A new English Church

In England, Henry VIII, who saw himself to the end as a good Catholic, wanted an annulment of his first marriage to Catherine of Aragon, who seemed unable to give him a male heir. When the pope refused, Henry broke with Rome, married Anne Boleyn, mother of the future Elizabeth, and set up the Church of England, with himself at its head. As a Catholic he put Protestants to death for heresy; as head of the Church he also put Catholics who stayed loyal to the pope to death for treason. The monasteries were dissolved and their lands sold to bring wealth to the Crown and its supporters.

Under Elizabeth I, however, there emerged a Church of England which, though its services were conducted in English and not in Latin, had a more elaborate ritual than the Protestant churches of Europe. Its services were graced by the superb literary style of Archbishop Cranmer's Prayer Book of 1552, and by the Authorised Version of the Bible of 1611, two of the finest sustained pieces of English writing.

A Bible in the language of the country was a stimulus to education. The Reformation produced distinguished scholars in Holland and England, Germany and Switzerland, France and Scotland. In the fiery John Knox (1505–72), a savage critic of both Elizabeth of England and Mary, Queen of Scots, it produced a preacher whose sermons were likened to 'five hundred trumpets and a thousand drums'. Learning, leadership and statecraft were no longer monopolies of Court and Catholic Church. But for the next 150 years Europe was torn by warfare that was as much religious as political in its origin.

## Inquisition and 'Index'

Bitter conflicts between pope and emperor had already weakened the Church. In 1527 Rome itself was sacked – not, this time, by the barbarians but by the forces of the Holy Roman Emperor, Charles V, waging war in Italy against the French. For many years after that, Italy was the stage for dynastic wars between France and Spain. Against this political background, the Roman Catholic Church struggled to combat the advance of Protestantism by introducing its own Counter-Reformation.

A number of reforms, mainly the work of the Council of Trent (1545–63), gave more independence to the bishops, and sought to strengthen the devotion of parish clergy. But in doctrine the Church stood hard by the old Faith. The Inquisition, begun as early as 1233 by Gregory IX to root out a heretical sect, the Albigensians, in south-west France, was strengthened; heretics were burnt at the stake.

A campaign was launched against printing itself as a vehicle through which heresy spread. The first Index of forbidden books was published under Pius IV in 1559. More and more pictures and statues of the Virgin Mary, of saints, angels and martyrs, were produced in an effort to stir the emotions of the true believers. This thinking introduced a style of art which came to be called the baroque. It is marked by a new sense of the involvement of the worshipper, and by an emphasis on movement and on the contrast between light and shade. The baroque style is represented at its finest in the ornate decoration of Il Gesu Church

The Roman Catholic Church, which had dominated Europe's life and thought for 1000 years, was inevitably affected by the ferment in the Renaissance world around it. There was growing criticism of practices such as the sale of Indulgences remitting punishment in the next life, the veneration of holy relics and the worship of the saints. A spirit of rebellion which began in Germany about 1500 spread across Europe to bring about a permanent Reformation, which destroyed for ever the unity of western Christendom dominated by Rome. The name Protestant originated when, in 1539, a group of princes in southern Germany 'protested' to the pope that they were not allowed to handle religion in their own way. By contrast with the splendour of the Catholic churches, the 'reformed' church was unadorned in style and its services simple

REFORMING DUTCHMAN *A strong challenge to the authority of the Church came from Erasmus (1466–1536), a Dutch priest, scholar and teacher who exposed, in his 'In Praise of Folly', the abuses he found in the Church. Erasmus taught that men should think for themselves in spiritual matters*

in Rome; by the ecstatic expressions in the portraits of El Greco; and by the work of Lorenzo Bernini, who decorated the canopy of St Peter's.

## Wars of religion

The Counter-Reformation also produced a religious reformer of its own. Ignatius Loyola was a soldier who was lamed for life fighting for the Emperor Charles V against the French at Pampeluna in 1520. During a long and painful convalescence he decided to devote his life to Christ and the Roman Catholic Church. In 1540 Pope Paul III gave Loyola consent to set up an order known as the Society of Jesus. The members of this order, the Jesuits, were organised with a strict discipline, loyal to their general who in turn owed loyalty only to the pope. They proved outstanding as educators and as advisers to kings, and they were extremely successful as missionaries in America and Asia. Perhaps more than any other force the Jesuits halted the drift to Protestantism. But they were unable to recapture the lost flocks of the Roman Catholic Church. Despite bitter religious wars in the 17th century, the religious settlement agreed between the religious factions at Augsburg in 1555 survived.

FRIAR WHO REBELLED *Martin Luther (1483–1546), an Augustinian friar and Bible scholar, became the leading figure of the Protestant Reformation in Germany. His attacks on the pope's authority and practices such as the sale of pardons to sinners led to his being excommunicated as a heretic. But the invention of printing spread Luther's writings, including a translation of the Bible into German, to a wide and eager public. Luther's belief in the Scriptures as the only source of revealed truth, and in faith, not well-intentioned deeds, as the only path to salvation, became the principles of the Protestant Church. Outside religion, however, Luther was an extreme conservative*

CRANMER'S PRAYERS *Henry VIII's breach with Rome in 1534 brought the Reformation to Britain. Henry was supported by his Archbishop of Canterbury, Thomas Cranmer, who helped set up the Anglican Church and in 1549 supervised the production of the First Book of Common Prayer (left), writing many of the prayers himself. Three years later Cranmer published a revised version, which remains the basis of the Church of England's prayers today*

WORSHIP IN SIMPLICITY *The austere style of worship of the followers of the French reformer John Calvin is shown in this 16th-century painting of a Calvinist service held in a converted house at Lyons, in France. There is no altar, the decorations are simple, and the congregation wear subdued dress. The men, who all wear hats, sit separately from the women. The seats vary in comfort from simple benches to upholstered pews, indicating further segregation by rank, although Calvin's followers believed in equality, and their churches were administered by elected bodies which included laymen as well as churchmen. Beside the pulpit hangs an hour-glass to time the preacher's address*

The Treaty of Augsburg declared that the religion of the ruler should determine the religion of his people, so that every Protestant prince in Europe became his own 'pope'.

For Germany, with its 340 duchies and principalities, this was a form of political, as well as religious, anarchy, and the Thirty Years' War (1618–48) was the inevitable result. The Treaty of Westphalia in 1648 confirmed the religious settlement of Augsburg but left Germany a ravaged land, weakened by the long wars, and also by banditry, famine, and plague. Some 5 million Germans – one-sixth of the population – were said to have died.

One exception to the weakness of the German states was Brandenburg-Prussia which, through the ability of its rulers, had prospered as a result of the wars. It was Protestant and enterprising, well administered and defended by a formidable army; it became the centre from which its Hohenzollern rulers were to create the Germany of the future.

The early 17th century was a time of civil war over religion in England and Scotland. In Italy, the cities of the north – Milan, Genoa, Venice, Florence – were rich and flourishing. But the papal states, sprawling across the Apennines from Tuscany to Naples, divided

the country and blocked its unity. During this century, too, Roman Catholic Spain lost its leadership in Atlantic trade to the Dutch and to the English. By 1700 the Spanish state was bankrupt, with taxes at ruinous levels and offices shamelessly bought and sold. Yet despite its gloomy ceremonial, its sense of sin and doom, and the tight grip of priests and favourites, the Spanish Court was also the centre of a flourishing school of painting. The rich, intense paintings of El Greco, Velasquez, Zurbaran and Murillo make the Prado Museum in Madrid one of the major art centres of Europe. Intolerance, like tyranny, proved no necessary enemy of art or of civilization.

## Anarchy and achievement

The two centuries of the Renaissance and the Reformation were turbulent, contentious and immensely creative times. There was a new internationalism among scholars, artists and craftsmen. It was made possible by new money as well as by 'new men', for the Renaissance arose partly from the exercise of patronage by rival artistic patrons – bankers, princes and sometimes popes. The artist was ready to go where his patron bade; the age, indeed, was noticeable for the ease with which scholars and

artists crossed boundaries. But the consequences were not all favourable. Critics of the popes, who saw them as arrogant and greedy emperors, became themselves city despots, enmeshed in politics and war. The Reformation produced over a century of international religious wars; and in France, the Netherlands, England and Scotland it produced civil wars of savage cruelty, in which Catholic rulers burnt Protestants as heretics, and Protestant rulers executed Catholics as traitors. It was accompanied by economic and social disruption. Monasteries were seized not for doctrinal reasons but for greed, and their stones used to build the homes of the new commercial aristocracy.

Beginning as a call not to reason but to faith, the Reformation never lost this character; it was marked by witchhunting, bookburning, bigotry and dogmatism, and the persecution of scientists and freethinkers on a scale rarely paralleled. Wars became struggles not just for territory and for 'glory', but for control of the human mind. It was nearly two centuries before the passions cooled and the divided nations agreed to regard their religious disputes as being in a state of permanent truce. The map of Europe today is still the legacy of these two centuries of contention and conflict.

## ART TREASURES TO INCREASE THE GLORY OF FRANCE'S 'SUN KING'

*A plumed and red-brocaded Louis XIV watches craftsmen at the Gobelins factory in Paris displaying their silver, furniture, carpets and tapestry. The scene is itself one of a series of 14 great tapestries made by the state-controlled Gobelins factory and depicting France's 'Sun King' in a variety of roles – as warrior, patron of the arts, family man, lover of hunting and international statesman. Louis XIV was the most illustrious of all the rulers of Europe in an age when the absolute power of kings was hardly challenged. During his 72-year reign, French art, literature and architecture reached great heights. It was Louis himself who bought the Gobelins factory in 1662 and made it a centre for royal craftsmen. He also paid an annual allowance to writers such as the dramatists Racine and Molière, and built a lavish palace at Versailles. The French style of living set a standard for the whole of Europe*

# New learning in an age of kings

AD 1600-1762

*As monarchs wielded absolute power, philosophers*
*and scientists used reason and experiment*
*to unravel the laws of the universe*

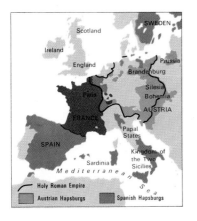

**EUROPE IN 1648**

*After 30 years of religious wars, large*
*areas of the Holy Roman Empire were*
*divided among new secular states*

For more than a thousand years after the fall of Rome, Europe was held together by a concept of order based on a largely feudal society united by the bonds of religion. During the 200 years after the Reformation, however, all this was to change. The traditional power structure of Europe was challenged from all sides and gradually collapsed, finally to expire in the bloodbath of the French Revolution.

The first challenge came from a spate of scientific discoveries at the start of the 17th century. New philosopher-scientists demonstrated that the universe could be understood by the gathering of information and the application of reason. Their theories challenged the teachings of the Christian Church, which had been the basis of European civilization for a thousand years, and placed in doubt the very existence of God. Men were urged to think for themselves, and to have the courage to reject established authority. The educated middle class, which was increasing as commerce grew, adopted the spirit of scepticism from the philosophers and turned it into a movement that was to culminate in revolution.

The year 1609 saw two events which marked the birth of modern science and introduced a source of disruption to the social fabric of Europe. Johannes Kepler, a German astronomer, formulated the theory that the planets move round the sun in ellipses rather than in perfect circles, and that the time taken to complete their revolutions varies according to their average distance from the sun. The new 'Laws of Planetary Motion' which Kepler drew up destroyed the old belief that the universe was made up of heavenly bodies moving in perfect circles and at uniform speeds.

In the same year, Galileo Galilei, in Padua, made the first astronomical telescope, which enabled him to study the movement of the planets. By his observations Galileo confirmed

**AFTER THE GREAT FIRE**

*The example of glitter and elegance set by the court of Louis XIV was followed in England after the Restoration in 1660 of Charles II, who had spent much of his exile in France. The effect of the new king's influence was all the more striking by contrast with 11 years of Puritan rule by Oliver Cromwell which had preceded it. Even the physical appearance of London was transformed, after the Great Fire in 1666 had destroyed two-thirds of the city and Sir Christopher Wren was chosen to supervise its rebuilding. One of Wren's finest achievements was St Paul's Cathedral; the design for the south side of St Paul's (right), little altered in its final form, was drawn by Wren himself*

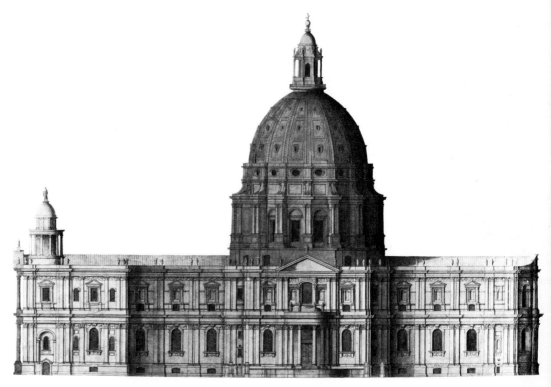

# A king who claimed: 'I am the state'

the theory of Copernicus that the earth and the planets move round the sun, formulated the laws governing the speed of falling bodies and concluded that the whole universe obeyed the same physical laws.

In England at this time Francis Bacon, Lord Chancellor to James I, was advocating the 'scientific method', by which theories based on observation are tested by experiment. Bacon also proposed that scientists should join together in academies and pool their work, a suggestion that led eventually to the foundation of many European academies, including the Royal Society in London.

## Knowledge through reason

A group of 17th-century European philosophers, the Rationalists, claimed that basic truths about the universe could be discovered by reason alone, unaided by experience. Possibly the greatest of these was the French philosopher René Descartes (1596–1650). In his *Discours de la Méthode*, 'Discourse on Method', published in 1637, Descartes rejected all established authority and decided to begin at the beginning. Was there anything, he asked, that was indisputable? There was just one fact that he could not doubt: that his mind was doing the thinking, and that he therefore existed. '*Cogito ergo sum* (I think, therefore I am)', he said.

On this simple cornerstone Descartes built a new system of philosophy which saw the universe as governed by mathematical laws. His philosophy accepted God – but the existence of Descartes's God was proved by reason, and not dependent on faith alone. The influence of Descartes can hardly be exaggerated. By relying exclusively on reason, and following wherever reason led, he helped to free philosophy from the straitjacket of medieval thought.

The climax of the new scientific era came in 1687 in England when Isaac Newton, professor of astronomy at Cambridge University, published his 'Law of Universal Gravitation'. This stated that all bodies in the universe, however large or small, have a mutual attraction for one another. Newton called this attraction gravity. Newton's teaching provided powerful mathematical support for Descartes's contention that the great truths of the universe might be discovered by the application of reason. And just as Newton showed that there was a universal law in astronomy and physics, so the English philosopher John Locke set out to prove that society, too, was governed by a simple, all-embracing 'law of nature'; this taught that as all men were equal and independent, 'no one ought to harm another in his life, health, liberty or possessions'.

## An empire in ruins

At the dawn of the 17th century, however, the new scientific thought was still a century away from exerting any real influence on the common man. Europe was still suffering the aftermath of the Reformation. Religious wars were sweeping the Continent. The Thirty Years' War (1618-48), fought mainly in Germany, brought terrible privations to the people

and left the Holy Roman Empire in tatters. As a Puritan preacher proclaimed in a sermon to the English House of Commons in 1643: 'These days are days of shaking . . . and this shaking is universal.'

France, too, suffered greatly from wars of religion, which had reached a peak of savagery in the Massacre of St Bartholomew in 1572, when many of the Huguenot population of Paris were shot down. Henry of Navarre, one of the Huguenot leaders who survived the massacre, accepted the Roman Catholic faith and in 1589 became Henry IV, first of the Bourbon dynasty of French kings. Nine years later he signed the Edict of Nantes, extending freedom of worship to the Huguenots, and even allowing them their own fortresses. But Cardinal Richelieu, chief minister of France after Henry's death, crushed the Huguenot strongholds and ended their political power. The Huguenots, however, were still allowed freedom of religion.

Despite the power of three French cardinals – Richelieu himself, Mazarin and Fleury – the influence of the Church over the rulers of nations was coming to an end. The old feudal forms of government were proving unable to deal with a new aggressive commercial society which lacked the cement of one common religion. Instead, rulers all over Europe tried to concentrate all power in their own hands – a concept which became known as absolutism. The absolute king did not depend on feudal vassals, but ruled through a complex civil service responsible entirely to him.

## Louis XIV, 'Grand Monarque'

The most brilliant example of the absolute monarch was Louis XIV of France (1643-1715), the 'Grand Monarque' who became a model for imitation in other countries. His object was unfettered power at home, expansion abroad: he wanted the French frontier to reach the Rhine, and he wanted to put Bourbon princes on the thrones of Spain and Italy. Louis believed that he was God's Lieutenant, called to rule, and he spent at least a nine-hour day at affairs of state. All other institutions – the Church, the nobility, the courts – became obviously subordinate. Louis depended on a large army for foreign wars, and efficient royal servants at home, but the initiative and the energy came from him. A remark attributed to Louis typifies his attitude: '*L'Etat c'est moi* (I am the state)'.

Architecture was designed to glorify the monarch who became known as the 'Sun King'. His palace of Versailles took 47 years to complete, a Vatican for the secular pope. The new grandeur was evident also in the replacing of the old fortifications of Paris by a ring of boulevards and the laying out of the Champs Elysées, the Place Vendôme and the Place de l'Etoile.

At Versailles, Louis practised extravagantly the trade of king, with high-heeled shoes to exaggerate his height. He saw himself as being on a stage, and acted the part. His whole retinue of 5000 courtiers, drawn from the nobility, lived at the palace, proud to be his servants, and another 5000 servants lived near

## THE GREAT PATRONS

Just as Italian thought and culture had dominated the years of the Renaissance, so France became the cultural capital of Europe throughout much of the 17th and 18th centuries. The vast palace of Versailles which Louis XIV built for himself south of Paris became the centre of a glittering court over which the Sun King and his successors ruled in splendour. Other absolute monarchs followed their example; when Peter the Great set out to Westernise Russia he modelled his own palace at St Petersburg on Versailles and commissioned a French architect, Le Blond, to build it for him. The self-confidence of the French court was matched by a huge upsurge in the arts. Writers and makers of fine jewellery, furniture and textiles found ready patrons, and in the salons of Paris the French language was perfected to become the language of the upper classes throughout Europe

GREAT MONARCH *Louis XIV rides out to crush France's foes, while Victory holds a laurel wreath over his head. The king's classical garb in this portrait by Pierre Mignard expresses Louis's self-conscious view of himself as acting the role of supreme monarch on the stage of history. Even his rising in the morning and going to bed at night were attended by elaborate ceremonies, called the 'levée' and 'couchée'; each nobleman had his own duty at these rituals, and strict etiquette governed who should hand the king his shirt and his shoes*

by. Every aspect of life at court was minutely regulated and hierarchical; every man had his immediate superior, to whom he paid all deference and loyalty. The king himself was supreme – under God alone.

In matters of religion Louis was an absolute ruler. He reversed the tolerant policy set by Henry IV, revoked the Edict of Nantes and drove many Huguenots from France. Louis also dominated the national economy. He sought to build up France's wealth and power by encouraging agriculture and industry; by developing the French Navy, shipping fleets and trading companies; and by winning markets and colonies overseas. The high priest of this policy was Jean Colbert, the king's controller of finance. Colbert paved the streets of Paris, policed them, and lit them with oil-burning lanterns –

SITE OF THE SUN KING'S PALACE *Louis XIV's principal memorial is the home he built for his court at Versailles, a palace of such size and grandeur that it cost more than $360 million and took 47 years to complete. This painting by Pierre Patel shows the original chateau on the site, built by Louis's father, which Louis turned into a palace with a façade 1361 ft long and surrounded by vast formal gardens designed by André le Nôtre*

BOY KING *Louis XV, great grandson of Louis XIV, came to the throne at the age of only five. This anonymous painting shows him learning the lessons of kingship from his ministers and tutors. Louis XV maintained the same recklessly extravagant court at Versailles as his grandfather, but for much of his reign the real power at Versailles was wielded by Mme de Pompadour, the king's mistress. The classical grandeur of the decorations that surrounded the infant king in his schoolroom gradually gave way to a more flamboyant style of ornamentation known as rococo, which made elaborate use of such motifs as shells and scrolls. But as well as redecorating their palace, the king and Mme de Pompadour built a new simply designed country house, the Petit Trianon, in a corner of the grounds*

KING'S MISTRESS *Mme de Pompadour rose from humble origins to become mistress of Louis XV and a power at his court for nearly 20 years. This portrait is by François Boucher*

STARS OF THE SALONS *Intellectual life in 18th-century France centred around the salons, or meetings for cultural conversation, held in the homes of influential women. One of the leading salons was that of Mme Geoffrin, third from the right in the front row. Under a bust of Voltaire, the actor Le Kain gives a reading; his audience includes Rousseau and Diderot*

a fashion that spread. He built and subsidised textile, tin and glass works, roads, shipyards and canals. The Languedoc Canal, still in use, is 160 miles long and has 75 locks. The Gobelins tapestry works in Paris was bought by the king. Colbert saw to it that taxes were systematically collected, and he tried to curb luxuries, such as the use of gilt on the coaches of the nobility, and the excessive number of annual public holidays, 17 of which he banned.

Colbert sought colonies, notably in Canada, as providers of raw materials not easily available at home, and as markets for home manufactures. He was especially jealous of Spain's wealth of gold and silver from the New World, since bullion and a favourable balance of trade were his key objectives. Colbertism meant state monopoly, state bureaucracy and

state protection. The economy of the country was to serve the state. 'Trade,' he said, 'is a source of public finance; and public finance is the vital nerve of War.'

## The great dramatists

Ironically, the real French triumph was in the arts of peace. By the middle of the 17th century, France had taken over cultural and intellectual leadership of Europe from Italy. Literature reflected the glory of Louis XIV. The great dramatists, Corneille, Racine and Molière, not only entertained the Court and enjoyed its patronage, but established new theatrical traditions, with permanent theatres and travelling companies as well as strongly defined styles of acting. The themes of Corneille and Racine were tragic and severely classical, set in Greece

or Rome, like Racine's *Phèdre*. Directly inspired by the great playwrights of Greece and Rome, they were to the France of Louis XIV what Virgil was to the Rome of Augustus.

The French Academy was given the role of dictating literary style and the form of the French language. A French Royal Academy of Sciences was founded, and members were named to it only by the king's consent. Active members were paid by the king and had to live in Paris, and their research costs were met from the royal exchequer. Learned periodicals came into existence, notably the *Journal des Savants*, 'The Scholars' Journal', the oldest of them all, founded in 1665 and still published today.

The opulent style of living at Versailles encouraged the production of luxuries such as fine silks and brocades, exquisite leather gloves

# *Travellers on the 'Grand Tour' rediscover Italy's rich heritage*

and shoes, ribbons and laces, embroidery and jewellery. This was a time, too, of fine furniture, often decorated with inlay and the gilded bronze known as ormolu, of musical instruments, porcelain, silver and gilded tableware, fine linen, handsome mirrors, tapestries and carpets. French porcelain and tapestry were famed throughout Europe. All these products became even more exquisite and delicate as the taste for classical and baroque grandeur gave way to the light-hearted and expansive style known as rococo, favoured in the 18th-century courts of Louis XV and the German princes.

## Italy in decline

Meanwhile Italy, which had played a leading part in Roman and Renaissance Europe, was by 1713 prostrated and divided after generations of wars fought upon her soil. Few of her states were still ruled by Italians, and nearly all her once-proud rival cities had lost their independence. Even Venice and Genoa, still free republics, were entering upon a long decline, for commerce was passing from the Mediterranean to the Atlantic, the Cape of Good Hope, the North Sea and the Baltic.

Yet Italy was still an enormously creative force in Europe. Her influence was spread in two ways. Firstly, as travel became safer and more comfortable, more leaders of taste and fashion visited Italy during their 'Grand Tour' of Europe, and returned stunned and excited by its beauty, by the richness of its heritage and by the virtuosity of its craftsmen. Secondly, division and conquest had scattered Italy's craftsmen all over Europe, in the service of French, Spanish or Austrian masters. The great sculptor and architect Giovanni Bernini went to Paris to serve Louis XIV. Italians created splendid floors, handsome plaster or painted ceilings, elaborate furniture and gardens for palaces, churches and country houses in France, England, Spain, Russia and Austria.

It was perhaps in the worlds of music, the dance, musical drama and mime that 17th and 18th-century Italy excelled. Instrumental music took on new forms as instruments such as the violin, flute and oboe were developed and improved, to supplement the traditional lute, viola and harpsichord. Italian musicians had many traditions to draw upon – sacred music, madrigals and opera, suites of dances, miracle plays, pageants and masques for great occasions. These were combined with ancient myths and traditional folk plays to produce, in the new age of wealthy secular patrons, bawdy comedy and farce for the masses on one hand and elaborate opera and ballet on the other. In the theatre,

Italian comedy foreshadowed the work of playwrights such as Congreve in England and Molière in France, and Italian opera was performed at the French, Russian and Prussian Courts. Although French was now the language of politics and fashion, the language of painting, architecture and music was still Italian and remains Italian to the present day.

Italian craftsmen even followed Spanish and Portuguese administrators and Jesuit teaching-missionaries to the New World, to India, China and the islands of the China seas. They excelled in silver filigree, ivory carving and mechanical conceits such as cages of singing birds and exquisite clocks; and their skill in this field had effects that can still be seen today in Indian bazaars and Hong Kong shops. The travellers' own excitement at what they saw and learnt in the East helped to create the passion for the Chinese style of decoration, or *chinoiserie*, in 18th and 19th-century Europe, shown in buildings ranging from La Favorita in Sicily to Walpole's Strawberry Hill and the Royal Pavilion at Brighton.

## 'Dare to know'

While the absolute rule of Louis XIV prevented any criticism of established authority in France, the new science and philosophy of Newton and

### CANALETTO'S VENICE: A SOUVENIR OF THE 'GRAND TOUR'

*Though France, and not Italy, was the intellectual pacemaker for 18th-century Europe, the city-states where the Renaissance began still kept their hold on men's imaginations. The painter Canaletto captured the colour and light of his native* *Venice; the view above is of the Church of Santa Maria della Salute seen across the Grand Canal. Canaletto's paintings were especially popular among wealthy travellers making the 'Grand Tour' round the main cities of Europe*

Locke flourished in England, where two kings – Charles I and James II – were overthrown during the 17th century. From England the new theories, and a new questioning of all authority, spread across Europe, and became known as the Enlightenment. It drew together scholars who opposed the established Church and who were hostile to despotic government. The German philosopher Immanuel Kant was to summarise the movement when he urged men: 'Dare to know! Have the courage to use your own intelligence!'

The advocates of Enlightenment became known as the *philosophes*, a French word that was used far beyond the borders of France. The early *philosophes* were largely people who believed that God was a master planner, 'the Eternal Geometer', who had created an intricate mechanism and left it to run by itself. Politically, the *philosophes* agreed that men should obey the law, but they also advocated the right of dissent and of free speech.

One of the most renowned *philosophes* was the French scholar Denis Diderot, who edited the 28-volume *Encyclopédie* between 1747 and 1772. This was an attempt to classify all man's knowledge alphabetically, and to spread the beliefs of the *philosophes*. Some of the greatest French scholars of the day contributed articles on a multitude of subjects to the *Encyclopédie*, though not always on the most scholarly subjects; Voltaire, for instance, wrote the article on hem-stitching.

## The enlightened despots

Even in the authoritarian states east of the Rhine – Prussia, Austria and Russia – the effects of the Enlightenment were felt. This time it was not through the scholars but through the rulers themselves. Frederick the Great of Prussia, who reigned from 1740 to 1786, the Hapsburg Empress Maria Theresa of Austria (1740-80) and Catherine the Great of Russia (1762-96) all modelled themselves on Louis XIV, who had died in 1715 after a 72-year reign. But whereas Louis had said 'I am the state', Frederick called himself more modestly the 'first servant' of the state.

These three rulers, whose reigns coincided so closely, were all autocrats who, like Louis, built extravagant additions to their palaces and kept attendant but largely powerless noblemen as courtiers and servants. But despite their despotic trappings they made genuine efforts to improve the quality of administration in their kingdoms.

Frederick, an admirer of Voltaire, improved farming methods in Prussia; he reorganised and filled the Prussian treasury, introduced new industries, and built roads and canals. Foreigners – French Huguenots expelled by Louis XIV, Jews, even Jesuits – were welcomed in Prussia when they were driven out of their Catholic homelands for political activities. If Turks came to his country, Frederick said, he would build mosques for them. In the 46 years of his reign, more than 250,000 immigrants settled in Prussia.

Frederick was a gifted musician, and in his youth had written in French a book, *Anti-Machiavel*, which argued that a ruler must be

It was in the 18th century that many arts, including that of music, assumed roughly their present form. Many of the innovations came from Italy. Orchestras were enriched by new instruments such as the piano, violin, flute and oboe; the new variety of stringed instruments available led in particular to the development of chamber music, which was written to be performed in a room rather than a hall or theatre. Italian composers such as Scarlatti, Vivaldi, Boccherini and Cimarosa developed the forms of the modern opera, oratorio, quartet, concerto and symphony. Haydn, Mozart and Beethoven were their direct heirs. From Italy, too, came a lowlier form of entertainment – the improvised comedy known as the *commedia dell 'arte*, with characters such as Harlequin and Pantaloon. This type of comedy, performed by travelling bands of players, was the origin of the traditional characters of English pantomime

PORCELAIN *The art of making porcelain, long familiar to China, was introduced to Europe in 1710 by J. F. Böttger at Meissen in Saxony. Böttger became famous for his delicate figurines, often called Dresden china, such as this Harlequin*

PIERROT *The Italian commedia dell 'arte gave rise to a variety of harlequinade entertainments in Europe. One of its characters was the pierrot, a white-faced unhappy lover, seen in this 1721 painting by the Frenchman Antoine Watteau*

CHILD PRODIGY *At the age of seven, Wolfgang Amadeus Mozart plays the harpsichord to guests at a tea party given by the Princess Conti in Paris in 1763. In the 35 years of his life Mozart produced a continued flow of brilliant compositions; and it was his preference for the piano that eventually ended the dominance of the harpsichord*

NEW SOUNDS *Instruments introduced in the 17th century widened the range of the orchestra, which was now built around an enlarged string section comprising instruments of the violin group. Italians like Antonio Stradivarius of Cremona produced instruments which were beautiful as well as functional; his Messi violin (above left) was made in 1716, and the form of the violin has changed little since his day. Another newcomer was the oboe, a middle-toned woodwind with a plaintive incisive tone; the instrument shown (above right) was made in Germany in the 18th century*

STAGING THE OPERA *The increasing popularity of musical performances gave rise to a spate of theatre building. The sumptuous Teatro Regio in Turin (above) opened in 1740 with an elaborately staged opera*

# Commerce and culture survive in an age of continual war

### THE TRANQUILLITY OF A DUTCH HOUSEHOLD

*The life of ordinary men and women came into its own as a subject for great art in the paintings of the 17th-century Dutch masters. Jan Vermeer (1632–75) lived all his life in Delft, and brought the little town and its people to life on canvases remarkable for the brilliance of their light effects. Most of his paintings were* *interiors, such as* The Letter *(above). Light pours in through an unseen window to illuminate a domestic scene glimpsed through an open door. The atmosphere of peace and harmony, typical of all Vermeer's work, reflects the contentment and prosperity of the Dutch after their success in throwing off Spanish rule*

liberal and benevolent. Like Louis, Frederick worked hard at his job, delegating little and trusting no one completely. But even as he preached liberalism, his interests lay in aggressive expansion. Frederick was a master strategist, as he proved by defeating the armies of France, Austria and Russia, so gaining new territories and establishing Prussia as one of Europe's great powers. His army, the best in Europe and the most cruelly disciplined, was doubled in size to more than 150,000 men, and four-fifths of the national income was devoted to it. Enlightenment marched with war, greed and cynicism.

### Women of empire

Empress Maria Theresa of Austria was equally progressive and equally warlike. During the first partition of Poland in 1772, in which Russia, Prussia and Austria all grabbed territory, Frederick said of Maria Theresa, 'As she wept, she also took'. However, Maria Theresa modernised state administration, eased the oppression of serfdom and introduced some legal reforms. Her son, Joseph II, followed in her footsteps. In 1781 and 1787 he issued a penal code, which abolished torture and the death penalty. Austria's example in legal reform was to be followed in Prussia and, most notably of all, in France by Napoleon.

Catherine of Russia, who added 200,000 square miles and 7 million people to her empire, was in intention equally enlightened. She read Diderot's *Encyclopédie*, and described herself as a pupil of Voltaire. In her *Instructions* (1767) she proposed to abolish torture and capital punishment; she was tolerant of all religions; she planned a constitution and a code of laws. She commissioned the English naval architect, Sir Samuel Bentham, to build Sebastopol; his brother Jeremy, the philosopher, also visited Russia. The epitaph Catherine composed for herself in the middle of her reign expressed her intentions, if not her achievements: 'She wished to do good and strove to introduce happiness, freedom and prosperity.'

Despite the good intentions of these rulers, their legacy of reforms was small. Many of the peasants of Prussia and Russia remained serfs, and the despots did not intend it otherwise. Even where a monarch himself proposed fundamental changes, he encountered obstacles and near failure. Joseph II tried to reorganise the Austrian Empire, for the sake of administrative uniformity. But he faced intractable problems, including a population of 24 million people spread over distant provinces, from Transylvania to northern Italy; sharp religious and linguistic divisions; and century-old conflicts of race and history. On his death bed, Joseph annulled most of his reforms, and bitterly proposed as an epitaph, 'Here lies a prince whose intentions were pure, but who had the misfortune to see all his plans fail'.

### Cruel and confused laws

Almost the whole of Europe suffered from an inadequate supply of trained and loyal administrators. Offices of state were sold as deliberate policy, even in efficiency-minded Prussia. The criminal law was savagely cruel, and the civil law was confused. Many of the administrative and judicial tasks, especially in provinces and villages remote from the central government, had to be done in feudal courts and by private landowners.

Most serious barriers of all to administrative reform were the hosts of regional, local and class privileges, internal customs posts and tax exemptions. Throughout Catholic Europe, the Church paid little in taxes. It had its own courts and taxation systems, and controlled education. The nobility and guilds were equally privileged, and townsmen had privileges that countrymen were denied. Even in populous and advanced France most taxes were 'farmed' – a system by which a local collector, in return for the payment of a fixed sum to the state, was entitled to keep all the taxes he could collect. The unfairness of the tax system on the lower classes was soon to prove a major contributory cause of the French Revolution.

All these factors were obstacles to economic growth and irritants to the rising professional class, including merchants, lawyers and small traders, who lived by commerce and movement of goods. The legacy of a thousand years of regional variation and feudalism was to defy even the most zealous of reformers – until one came armed not only with the dream of reason but also with the energy released by a total revolution, like that which was to convulse France in 1789. Napoleon Bonaparte, like Louis XIV, dreamt of one King, one Law, one Faith. But he was not merely an Enlightened Despot. He was also, in his own words, 'the child of Revolution', and carried its ideas across Europe.

## Holland's age of greatness
Two states were exceptions to the pattern of autocracy in 17th-century Europe. In the Dutch Republic and in Britain, progress and enlightenment took a different, and more recognisably modern form.

Holland was a tiny country, open to the North Sea and its tides, and open also to the invader. Throughout the 17th century it was at war on and off with France and with its trading rivals – England and Portugal. Yet this was also the great age of Holland. The Dutch, even as they struggled against their enemies, became the leading shipping and trading nation of the world. Amsterdam by the 1650's had a population of 150,000, and was the centre of the Baltic trade and of the East and West Indian trade. Northern grain, naval stores and English cloth were exchanged for oil, fruits and silks from the Mediterranean, and for sugar from America and spices from the East.

From this base, a financial empire followed: Amsterdam replaced Antwerp and Venice as the money market for Europe. It was not a democratic society, being run by its wealthy merchants and bankers, but it was free from persecution on grounds of religious or political opinion. Holland produced its own characteristic schools of painting – the quiet Dutch interiors and family groups, the still-lifes,

landscapes and portraits of Rembrandt, Pieter de Hooch, Jan Vermeer and Frans Hals.

Neither its wealth nor its greatness in painting, however, could make Holland a great power. It was a small country, unwarlike and geographically at risk. England was another story. It too was small, but, being an island, it was much less vulnerable. It was threatened by the Spanish, by the Dutch, and constantly by the French – yet it survived by the skill of its captains, generals and diplomats.

## Civil war in England
In 17th-century England and Scotland, the new science and philosophy were at their most active; and in many ways the philosophies that evolved were the seed-bed of much that is still seen as revolutionary today. The Stuart kings believed as devoutly in Divine Right as Louis XIV did, but they did not have his resources of population and money, or his army, or his skill. They encountered a formidable opposition: a strong parliament, a rich merchant class and a thorough-going Presbyterian Reformation in Scotland. The Civil War of 1642-9 ended in the beheading of Charles I, followed by a Puritan Commonwealth under Cromwell which was too austere to be popular. Charles's son was restored to the throne in 1660 and had the sense, during his 25-year reign,

not to press the claims of absolute monarchy as his father had done. But Charles II's brother, the Roman Catholic James II, was of a different temper. The nobility of Protestant England combined to depose him in the Bloodless Revolution of 1688, offering the throne to the Dutchman William of Orange.

In spite of their political failures, the Stuart monarchs were discriminating and cultivated patrons of art and learning, and leaders of fashion. Charles I, small and dandified, amassed a superb collection of paintings and employed Lely and Van Dyck, Inigo Jones and Rubens. The Banqueting House in London's Whitehall still gives a glimpse of the Whitehall Palace of Charles I's day. Charles II and James II both enjoyed court masques and music, and both kings did all they could to encourage Christopher Wren, who rebuilt London after the Great Fire of 1666. The men who worked with Wren, such as Grinling Gibbons and Jean Tijou, were miracle-workers in delicate wood and iron, with their motifs of flowers and fruit, birds, insects and cherubs. This was also the age of poets and playwrights such as Marvell, Milton, Congreve and Dryden.

Charles II was also a patron of the sciences, and gave his encouragement to scientific academies and learned societies, paving the way for the great improvement in technical

### PORTRAIT OF AN ARTIST'S PATRONS

*The role of patrons of art, which in other European countries was played by kings, princes and cardinals, was filled in the 17th-century Dutch Republic by wealthy merchants and city elders. In* The Syndics of the Cloth Drapers' Guild *by the greatest of the Dutch painters, Rembrandt van Rijn (1606-69),* *these burghers of Amsterdam stand out as down-to-earth human beings with a solid middle-class composure and independence. Rembrandt excelled in conveying character through the expression on the faces of his sitters; he also left a series of vivid self-portraits painted at various stages of his life*

245

# *A society of squires and serfs in which old age began at 35*

## CHANGES ON THE FARM

Until the 18th century, farming practices had changed little since the Middle Ages. Fields lay fallow every third year, and cattle were slaughtered in the autumn for lack of winter food. But now farmers learnt how to rotate crops scientifically and began experimenting in stock-breeding

BETTER SHEEP *The new gentlemen farmers commissioned flattering portraits of the livestock they bred, like this sheep bred in Leicestershire by Robert Bakewell*

LAND ENCLOSURE *Surveyors measure a field. To make new farming methods economical, landlords enclosed large areas of what had formerly been communal land*

HAY-MAKING *Work for the hired labour on the new farms meant long hours of unremittingly hard work*

and medical knowledge that would produce the farming and industrial revolutions of the 18th century. In architecture the period that began with Inigo Jones reached its peak with Wren and Hawksmoor, and culminated in the ostentatious genius of Vanbrugh and his great palace of Blenheim. This was the expression of a nation's gratitude to the Duke of Marlborough who, as conqueror of Louis XIV's armies, opened a way to sea-power and world-wide empire for Britain.

The Stuarts' Hanoverian successors collected excellent pictures, and employed the composer Handel. In 18th-century England science was applied to the land, and farming became profitable for the great landowners. The profits produced the aristocratic culture of the English country house, with its music room and library, galleries and statues, parks, cascades, ornamental lakes and fountains, all owing as much to the Grand Tour as to the long English rural tradition. This country house society re-created the life of the ancient Roman villa in a new form, and pioneered improvements in stock and seed that would enable the countries of Europe to support much larger populations.

## Conflict and class

The dominant characteristic of 18th-century Europe was not, however, enlightenment or reason, but war. For the first 14 years of the century, after the death of Charles II, the last Hapsburg king of Spain, the European powers fought over his vast possessions in Europe and the New World, in the War of the Spanish Succession. In 1733 came the War of the Polish Succession; from 1740 to 1748 the War of the Austrian Succession, in which Maria Theresa defended her territories against a coalition of Prussia, France, Spain, Saxony and Bavaria.

In 1756 the Seven Years' War found Maria Theresa in alliance with France against a renewed Prussian threat; in 1736 and 1768 Russia was at open war with the Ottoman Empire – a war resumed, with Austria as an ally, in 1787.

Armies were large and professional but men were too costly to risk too often in pitched battles, and most wars were fought by siegecraft. The limitations of musketry meant that battles were short in duration, and they were usually governed by gentlemanly rules and close seasons. Perhaps the real reason why Louis XIV was admired and imitated was that he had been able to put 200,000 men in the field, and this involved great skill in organisation, recruitment, training and medical supplies. New weapons were developed – the bayonet replaced the pike, and hand grenades were invented. Crack regiments of musketeers and grenadiers were trained; the Frenchman Colonel Martinet has left his name as a byword for ruthless discipline. Until Britain organised a vast coalition against him, Louis had Europe at his mercy.

Yet in social terms this was a stable, even a static, society. Movement up the social scale was possible but rare. Officers' commissions were for gentlemen, and were bought. It was possible in Britain and France and northern Italy to move from 'trade' into the gentleman class, but this was usually by way of the purchase of a country estate, and it usually took a generation or two.

## The all-important harvest

It was rare for a peasant to escape his origins. In eastern Germany, Hungary, Russia and Poland there stretched vast estates owned by rich families who dominated court and army. Few of these were merchants or traders: land

was held by the great nobility and by them alone. In Hungary after 1731 they paid no taxes at all. In Russia after 1762 they were exempt from service in the government or the army, and they owned thousands of serfs.

Rural life for the masses in the 17th and 18th centuries was grim, with a subsistence economy, poor food, primitive hygiene and hardly any knowledge of the cause of disease. Life was restricted and local, different regions varying widely and ignorant of each other – as, for instance, the Highlands of Scotland were distinct from and feared by the Lowlands, and by England. Life was largely dependent on the harvest. Practically all work on the land was done by human hand, or by horses and oxen. Capital was scarce, roads were poor, and communication by coach difficult and costly. Robbery was common in town and country.

Yet by the middle of the 18th century, there were signs of great change in western Europe. Famine on a large scale was now rare, and Europe's population was growing fast. From about 120 million in 1700 it reached 140 million in 1750 and 185 million by 1800. Towns such as Paris, London, Hamburg, Amsterdam, Bremen, Frankfurt, Marseilles and Vienna were growing rapidly, and becoming great merchant and banking centres. In them there was developing also a wealthy class of craftsmen and traders who were critical and envious of the aristocracy. Trade and travel spread ideas of street lighting, drainage and police.

Meanwhile in the countryside there were the first signs of an agricultural revolution. Waste lands were brought under cultivation and fens drained. New tools were introduced, such as the seed-drill and more efficient ploughs. Crops were rotated and scientifically selected, and lands manured artificially. Canals were dug and experiments in stock-breeding begun. In Britain, this was largely the work of enterprising landowners like Thomas Coke of Holkham, who insisted on attending at court in his country clothes; Charles ('Turnip') Townshend of Raynham, with his 'Norfolk Four' rotation of crops (wheat, turnips, barley and clover); and Sir John Sinclair of Thurso in northern Scotland, who corresponded on farm problems with George Washington.

Lands which had hitherto been farmed communally were now enclosed, to create large estates on which the new techniques could be applied. Such changes hurt the small farmers and others who had not the knowledge or resources to use new experimental methods. But these changes were mainly confined to southern England and some parts of France. They were still rare in Germany, Spain, Italy and eastern Europe.

## Sophistication and squalor

The Age of Enlightenment was also an age in which manners and morals ranged from sophistication to coarseness; an age in which baths were rare luxuries, in which the needs of nature were satisfied in public, and scents were essential to kill the smells of poor drains and dirty linen. Even Louis XIV was addicted to aniseed lozenges to 'sweeten his breath'. Water was rarely pure or safely drinkable, so beer and cheap gin were less luxuries than necessities. Raw spirit was the only anaesthetic available: if a man had to endure an operation, he was lucky if he could afford to be drunk. It was an age of serfdom and slavery, of impressment in the navy and flogging in the army.

Fewer than one farmer in 5000 was literate, and death was an early and regular visitor to every household: to reach 35 was to reach old age. This was especially so for that half of the human race little mentioned before 1900: women. Life for them was harsh, with constant childbirths and frequent loss, husbands whom they did not choose to marry, and life a series of heavy chores. Catherine of Braganza, the wife of Charles II of England, had nine miscarriages, no children and a husband openly faithless who fathered many bastards; yet she adored him. Queen Anne, who ruled in Britain as the last of the Stuarts, had 17 children, none of whom survived her.

Yet this was also the world of Bach, Handel and Mozart; of the British Museum, founded in 1753; of Benjamin Franklin's experiment with electricity in Philadelphia; and of the Frenchman Antoine Lavoisier's discovery of the true nature of combustion, which transformed chemistry. And progress, even if it did not greatly improve the conditions of life for women or for ordinary folk, was visible. The pace-making countries were not the despotisms, nor the land powers, but those bourgeois states that lived by trade and by the sea. The days when kings and aristocrats could monopolise all political power were numbered. Wars were fought for economic as well as military reasons.

Religious differences mattered less, and traditional religion was losing its hold. The privileges of the clergy, like those of the aristocracy, belonged to the feudal age and had outlived their usefulness. On the surface the Age of Enlightenment, with its polished manners, its steady progress in the arts, science and agriculture, and its enlightened monarchs backed by well-drilled armies, seemed set to last for ever. But it denied power, and in some cases freedom, to the emerging classes. The Century of Reason was about to end in bloody Revolution, and Europe was to be transformed.

### THE COUNTRY SQUIRE

*A new class of landowning gentry in 18th-century England became the patrons of great artists. Thomas Gainsborough painted this portrait of Mr and Mrs Robert Andrews in 1748. He placed them not indoors, as in the portraiture of earlier centuries, but out in the open on their East Anglian estates*

### 'DRUNK FOR A PENNY'

*Farm workers dispossessed by land enclosure poured into the cities; the consequent urban squalor was brilliantly portrayed by William Hogarth. In* Gin Lane *he attacked the evils of addiction to alcohol: 'Drunk for a penny, dead drunk for twopence'*

# Revolutions that changed the world

## AD 1763–1870

*Inspired by the teachings of the Enlightenment,*
*peoples on both sides of the Atlantic raised the cry of liberty*
*and overthrew their royal masters*

The pressures that had been developing in Western society exploded in the late 18th century with a force that shattered the foundations of Europe. That explosion was the French Revolution, and the detonator for it was the American War of Independence, inspired by the revolutionary ideal that all men were created equal.

With that example before them, and with 'Liberty, Equality and Fraternity' as the prize, the common people of France, for long the main centre of the Age of Enlightenment, rose against their rulers in 1789. In the terror that followed, French aristocrats and others regarded as enemies of the revolution died by the hundred on an instrument designed for the execution of criminals – the guillotine. The French Revolution spawned numerous revolts against the rule of king and aristocracy. It led to the rise of nation states governed by the people. And it has come down to the modern world as the great precedent for violent change.

Europe had been moving towards revolution for two centuries. The feudal system had long outlived its usefulness; yet almost all kings still held absolute power over their subjects, while the clergy and nobles still retained many of their feudal privileges, such as exemption from taxes. An increasing number of voices began to ask two questions that have remained fundamental questions in democratic political argument: by what right does one man govern another? And where should the line be drawn between the power of governments and the liberty of the governed?

The answer of the 17th century – except in England, which beheaded one king and deposed another – was that kings were appointed by God, ruled by Divine Right, and had absolute power. The answer of the 18th century, however, was that men have natural rights, and that rulers attacked these rights at their peril, for if they did so they could be legitimately overthrown.

It was in England, already building up a tradition of political tolerance, that these ideas first took form. The philosopher John Locke (1632–1704), writing to defend the Protestant 'Glorious Revolution' of 1688 which deposed James II, argued in his *Two Treatises on Civil Government* that there was a natural law that all men were equal and independent and that no

**EUROPE IN REVOLUTION**

*Revolution spread from America to reach France in 1789. During the next 60 years it spread widely through Europe*

## VOLTAIRE, PHILOSOPHER AND WIT

*The brilliant wit and cynicism of the French philosopher Voltaire (left), dominated the intellectual life of Europe for over a quarter of a century and played a large part in undermining its existing social order. Voltaire first came to fame in 1718, when he published a tragedy, Oedipe, containing violent anti-clerical sentiments. Four years later, in his poem 'Le Pour et Le Contre', 'For and Against', Voltaire proclaimed himself a non-Christian. As a result of his attacks on the Church and a quarrel with a powerful nobleman, Voltaire was exiled to England from 1726 to 1729. There he gathered material for his* Lettres Philosophiques, *a classic analysis of English society. But his real fame in his lifetime rested on his savage satires on 18th-century society and morality, such as* Candide

## A·NATION IN ARMS

*French patriots leave for the Belgian frontier with 'Liberty or Death' as their slogan. In 1792 the people of France rallied to defend their infant republic against the invading armies of Austria and Prussia, showing the same fervour with which they had swept their king and aristocrats from power in 1789. The revolutionary government took advantage of this to mobilise the whole of France's society and economy for war. Later, under the leadership of brilliant generals like Napoleon, the soldiers of the revolution were to drive the invaders out of France and carry revolutionary ideals across the breadth of Europe*

# First victory for a new concept of man

man should harm another; that the authority of the government comes from the consent of the governed; and that this consent forms the basis of a social contract between the rulers and the ruled. If the rulers broke their side of the contract, Locke claimed, then their subjects were entitled to rebel.

Fifty years later, the French Baron de Montesquieu (1689–1755), in his *De l'esprit des Lois* ('On the spirit of Laws'), claimed to have discovered the secret of Britain's success in maintaining stable government. He considered that power in any state could be separated into three main parts: a legislative power to make laws, an executive power to enforce them, and a judicial power to judge when the laws had been broken. If all these powers were concentrated in one body, the result was tyranny. If they were separated – as Montesquieu believed was the case in Britain – then freedom was protected, because the misuse of power by one branch of government would be cancelled by the other two branches.

Montesquieu was mistaken about Britain, for there the government both made and enforced laws, and an entire section of English law had been created by the decisions of judges. Nevertheless, his conclusions about the separation of power had an immense appeal, for here, it seemed, was a scientific law of politics as clear as Newton's law of gravity. The teachings of Montesquieu and Locke were absorbed eagerly by the men who were to lead the American Revolution against Britain and to frame the American Constitution.

## Critic of the Church
Another French thinker who helped to undermine the existing order was François Marie Arouet (1694–1778), better known as Voltaire. He admired the liberty of speech and religious tolerance that he found when he lived in exile in Britain from 1726 to 1729; he praised Locke, and had the good fortune to have the book he wrote on his return to Paris burnt by the hangman. This gave it great publicity.

Voltaire was a savage critic of the Church, because of the intolerance of the clergy. He was no revolutionary, but in his essays and plays he was a critic and a mocker of accepted ways. The Papacy – that 'infamous thing', as he called it – and the Church were favourite targets. He was twice exiled, and twice imprisoned in the Bastille, a fortress jail in the middle of Paris. But he lived a full life and died, aged 84, from exhaustion after a boisterous party to celebrate the first performance of his tragedy *Irène*. Characteristically, he gave a different explanation: 'I am dying,' he said, 'of 250,000 cups of coffee.'

The most original thinker of this Age of Enlightenment, the French philosopher Jean-Jacques Rousseau (1712–78), began his book *Le Contrat Social* ('The Social Contract') with one of the most resounding sentences in the history of political thought: 'Man is born free, but everywhere he is in chains.' Rousseau believed that men were by their nature good. If a child was given freedom, he stated, he would grow up free and virtuous. It was institutions that corrupted, and civilization that enslaved. Men should be set free, Rousseau argued, and return to a state of nature to live simple lives in small communities, where everyone would have equal rights. In his work, Rousseau added to Locke's ideas of a social contract between government and people by defining the concept of the 'general will'. It meant, he said, the will of the community as a whole, acting in its own best interests; but this was not always the same thing as the will of all the citizens on any particular issue. Rousseau's explanation was confusing, but fruitful. The idea of the 'general will' is the basis of the modern conceptions of democracy and majority rule; but at the same time, it is a concept which can justify any unpopular action taken by a dictator or a determined minority claiming to act in the highest interests of their people.

There is no evidence that Rousseau or any of the other philosophers of the age inspired or 'caused' the revolutions that were to come. They had, in fact, few proposals for political reform; they were merely publicists for the idea of change. But they set in being, not only in Paris but in all the capitals of Europe, a fashion of satire, scepticism and questioning which loosened the ties of order and tradition.

## The American Revolution
On another continent, the ideas of the Enlightenment were influencing another group of intellectuals who were not content merely to talk about change. The thinkers of America were about to put their ideas into practice, and to make America the scene of the first revolution fought for the sake of the new ideals.

In 1763 the British dominated North America. That year saw the addition of Canada, won from France, to Britain's American possessions. The 13 original colonies already stretched 1500 miles down the Atlantic coastline, from the foggy shores of Massachusetts Bay to the steamy Georgia coast. The colonists were British subjects and proud of it; they sent tobacco, sugar and timber to Britain, and in return they received linen, books and finery.

But once the threat from French Canada was removed, the colonists objected to paying to keep a British army on colonial soil – especially since the taxes for that army were imposed by a government 3000 miles away. The first sign of revolt appeared in 1765, in response to the imposition of a new tax to raise money for defence. The colonists claimed 'No taxation without representation'. If they were to pay taxes, they said, these must be levied by their own elected representatives. So successful were they that by 1770 only one direct tax – on tea – remained. But Britain insisted that this tax must be paid.

The tea tax was enough, however. When in 1773 large cargoes of cheap tea, on which tax would have to be paid, were about to be landed at Boston, a crowd of colonists half-disguised as Mohawk Indians marched aboard the merchant ship *Dartmouth* and threw its cargo of 342 chests of Indian tea into the harbour. The

The War of Independence, by which the North American colonies threw off British rule, was inspired by dedicated men, influenced by new ideas about the rights of man which had reached them from Europe. But the majority of Americans had more practical grievances.

After Britain had won Canada from France in 1763, the Americans saw no reason why they should pay taxes to keep a British army on their soil, especially as they had no say in the government which imposed the taxes. They refused to buy British goods, and by 1770 most of the taxes were abolished. But Britain insisted on maintaining the tax on tea, and this was to prove the spark that lit the revolution.

A succession of armed clashes between British troops and colonists led to open war in 1775, and a year later the Americans formally proclaimed their independence. In the eight years of war that followed, the British won every pitched battle, but always the Americans managed to withdraw steadily and in good order. In the end it was the land – with its vast forests, its wide rivers and its untenable mountains – that won, together with the skill and patience of George Washington, the American commander-in-chief. Defeat for Britain became inevitable when Louis XVI of France sent a fleet and troops to help the American revolutionaries – only 11 years before the outbreak of the Revolution in France which was to overthrow Louis

KING WHO LOST AN EMPIRE *In a contemporary print George III of England is seen with James Wolfe (right) and the elder Pitt – the general and the minister who won Canada for Britain from the French in the Seven Years' War. But George's obstinacy soon drove his American subjects into rebellion, while Pitt, now in opposition, became a sympathiser with their cause*

British Government saw the so-called 'Boston Tea Party' as inflammatory, closed the port of Boston and stepped up the number of troops stationed there. Further clashes with the British government led to a demand for independence, voiced at a Continental Congress of delegates from all the colonies, except Georgia, in Philadelphia in 1774; another was held in 1775.

Not all the colonists were in favour of independence, but from the second congress came a call to arms, and the appointment of George Washington, a Virginia planter, as commander-in-chief. In April 1775 British troops seized military stores at Lexington and Concord, near Boston, and war began.

In the American decision to resort to force, the writings of Tom Paine, a discontented Norfolk farmer who had emigrated to the colonies in 1774, played a vital part. In 1776 his pamphlet *Common Sense* was decisive in turning American opinion against George III. In the same year, a committee of five, with

BLOODY BATTLE *The fierce American resistance at Bunker Hill (above), near Boston, made the British realise that a long war with the American colonists was inevitable*

Yale University Art Gallery

FIRST PRESIDENT *Commander-in-chief of the American armies during the War of Independence, George Washington (1732–99) became his country's first president in 1789*

HONOURED DIPLOMAT *Benjamin Franklin (right) is portrayed on a snuffbox lid with the two French philosophers Voltaire (left) and Rousseau. As war-time American Ambassador in Paris, Franklin was respected by the French as a symbol of republican simplicity. The fur cap which Franklin wore to hide his eczema came to be regarded as a badge of the frontier*

MAN OF IDEALS *Thomas Jefferson (1743–1826) was one of the driving forces behind the American Revolution. At first, he argued simply that the British Parliament had no authority in America, but that the colonists should remain loyal to the Crown. But he went on to call for full independence*

FIRST PATRIOTS *Thomas Jefferson and Benjamin Franklin lead the delegation presenting the draft of the Declaration of Independence to the Continental Congress for debate in 1776, in a painting by John Trumbull. The Declaration, largely the work of Jefferson, summed up the ideas of the Age of Enlightenment in words that have become an immortal statement of the principles of democratic government. It states: 'We hold these truths to be self-evident, that all men are created equal, that they are endowed by their Creator with certain unalienable rights, that among these are Life, Liberty and the Pursuit of Happiness.' Jefferson based his ideas partly on his reading of the philosophers Locke and Rousseau*

Thomas Jefferson as writer, drew up the Declaration of Independence. In the final draft of the Declaration, Jefferson listed 'Life, Liberty and the Pursuit of Happiness' as among the rights of man; but it is significant that in his first draft he used the phrase 'Life, Liberty and *Property*' – for, as much as any English land-owning politician, he believed that a positive stake in the community was the only sure basis for political responsibility.

## Franklin, the 'new man'

Among the men who helped Jefferson to draw up the Declaration of Independence was Benjamin Franklin (1706–90), a representative of the middle-class civilization of 18th-century America. Born in Boston, he rose from poverty to wealth by his own efforts. By the age of 42, thanks to his printing press and his skill as journalist, pamphleteer and tradesman, he had made enough money to retire, and to devote his remaining 42 years to public service, as postmaster, diplomat and ambassador. Franklin transformed Philadelphia, giving it a police force, and paving and lighting the streets. He created the American Philosophical Society, the University of Pennsylvania, and the first circulating library in America. He set up an efficient postal service for the new republic, even before it became independent.

Franklin left his mark on the American character. He was an experimenter with electricity; he loved company and conversation; he was a plain man who liked the comforts and graces of life, at once an idealist and a sceptic. He was at home in France. In England, he was thought of as too much of an American, and in America was deemed too much of an Englishman. He was rightly thought of as a citizen of the world, and this, too, is part of his legacy to Americans. As American Ambassador to Paris during the War of Independence, Franklin was largely responsible for the alliance with France, signed in 1778, which helped to win the war.

By the terms of the Treaty of Paris in 1783, Britain recognised the independence of the United States and accepted the Mississippi River as its western boundary. A new, independent federal republic came into being.

Four years later, a congress of the independent states, with Washington presiding, drew up a constitution. Underlying it were ideas drawn from Locke and Montesquieu. The power to make laws was vested in Congress, which comprised two separate bodies: the House of Representatives, elected by the nation as a whole, and the Senate, elected by the individual states. The power to enforce laws and the command of the armed forces were given to a President, to be elected every four years. And the independence of the third arm of government was ensured by setting up a Supreme Court, with judges appointed for life. The Constitution devised in 1787 for 4 million farmers is still in effect today, changed only in inessentials, for a vast nation of more than 200

# *Popular rising that became a reign of terror*

million people, stretching from the Atlantic to the Pacific. It has also been a model for constitutions in other independent countries round the world.

## The French Revolution

In contrast to the new frontier nation of America, France in 1789 was a populous, unified and powerful state. Its language and culture dominated Europe. But socially the country was divided into four groups, the nobles, the clergy, the peasants, and – potentially the most powerful of all – the new middle class, composed of traders and other professional people in the towns. The nobles owned nearly all France's land; but they spent most of their time away from their estates, many of them at court, and were exempt from paying taxes. The clergy shared many of the privileges of the nobles. The peasants lived in poverty and misery, paying heavy taxes to the Crown, to the Church and to their local lords. The middle class, now becoming as wealthy as the nobles, resented their lack of the social privileges that depended on ownership of land. And in 18th-century France there was no parliament through which the people could express their grievances. The previous parliament, the Estates General, had last been called in 1614.

The right to collect government taxes was 'farmed out' to agents, who made sure of collecting more than they were required to pay to the government. As these tax 'farmers' worked through other agents, who sometimes had sub-agents, all taking a cut, the demands imposed on the peasant at the end of the chain were exorbitant. But despite the heavy taxes, which included the notorious *gabelle*, or salt tax, and the *corvée*, which conscripted peasants to work on the roads, the French Government was labouring under a huge national debt. In the 50 years before 1789, France had lost the War of the Austrian Succession and the Seven Years' War; defeat in war had lost it Canada and its fortresses in India. Its solitary success, in the American War of Independence, had been won at enormous financial cost.

To add to France's problems, Louis XVI soon proved incapable of running the despotic administration he had inherited. Louis was a modest and moral man, happy in his domestic setting and tinkering with clocks and watches, but he was totally incompetent to control the government of France. His queen, Marie Antoinette, was the daughter of the Empress Maria Theresa of Austria, but had none of her mother's skill and resolution. She was extravagant, frivolous and vain.

By 1789 the French Government was bankrupt and Louis was forced to call the Estates General together, after the 175 years during which the French monarchs had got along without it. He expected this feudal survival of Church, nobles and the 'Third Estate', or middle class, to meet in separate sections, as in the past, and dutifully vote taxes to the Crown without question. When the Estates met, however, they insisted on meeting as a single National Assembly. They were dominated by the delegates of the 'Third Estate', who spoke the language of reform and drew on American examples. They were determined above all to limit the power of the monarchy.

As in America, the most outspoken delegates in the Estates General were the representatives less of the ordinary people than of the new middle class tasting power for the first time; two-thirds of the Assembly were minor government officials or lawyers who resented the fact that they could never rise high in their professions, as all major appointments went to the nobles. But the members of the Assembly, supported by the more liberal clergy and nobles, saw themselves as the true voice of France. Their president, Jean Bailly, summed up their feelings in his reply to the king's demands and orders: 'The assembled nation', he said, 'cannot receive orders.'

## The power of the mob

At this point a new force moved on to the stage of history and remained there: the people of Paris. The harvest of 1788 had failed, and famine threatened. The streets of Paris were crowded with hungry people who looked to the Assembly for help. But they grew tired of the long debates, and in July 1789 the Paris mob rose. They marched on the prison and fortress of the Bastille, which they saw as a symbol of royal authority. It immediately surrendered – July 14, Bastille Day, has been celebrated ever since as France's Day of Liberation – but the

### PARIS IN REVOLUTION: THE MOB TAKES COMMAND

The city of Paris, capital of France, was also the capital of the Revolution. In July 1789 the Paris mob, tired of the long and inconclusive debates of the National Assembly, rose and stormed the fortress of the Bastille, symbol of royal oppression. Three months later, the women of Paris marched on Louis XVI's palace at Versailles and forced the king and his family to return to the city. Henceforth, the Paris mob had the power to make and unmake governments – a fact soon realised by the orators of the Left, such as Robespierre and Danton, who used the mob as a weapon to sweep to power. But the mob was fickle in its affections: having demanded the mass execution of aristocrats and so begun a reign of terror, the mob then turned on the leaders it had supported, who themselves perished on the guillotine

VICTIMS OF THEIR OWN RIVALRY *Four leaders of the Revolution were (left to right) Jacques Brissot, Madame Roland, Maximilien Robespierre and Georges Danton. The first two were members of the moderate republican party, the Gironde, the others leaders of the rival Jacobin party. All were eventually guillotined themselves, Robespierre being the last to perish, in July 1794*

THE BASTILLE FALLS *The fortress of the Bastille, dominating the centre of Paris, under attack by the Revolutionary mob on July 14, 1789. Although the fortress surrendered almost without resistance, 'Bastille Day' has been celebrated ever since as France's Day of Liberation. The Revolutionaries believed that the Bastille contained thousands of political prisoners, imprisoned without trial. But when they broke down the doors they found only seven men inside – four forgers, two lunatics and one dissipated nobleman, the Marquis de Sade. All were released, but the prison's governor, de Launay, here seen surrounded by guardsmen, was killed*

king remained popular and there was a proposal to erect a statue to him on the site of the fallen Bastille.

But one rising provoked others: at the news of the fall of the Bastille the peasants in country areas rose, and refused to pay taxes or feudal dues. The National Assembly decreed the ending of serfdom and began steadily to destroy the privileges of the nobles and the Church. King, court and clergy became totally opposed to such reforms. Many nobles fled the country and stirred up support abroad for the king.

Caught between the two extremes – the mob and the reactionary aristocrats – were the hapless moderates who now served as the king's ministers. Chief among their number were Honoré de Mirabeau and Marie Joseph de La Fayette, commander of the National Guard. La Fayette had fought with George Washington in the American War of Independence, and so won a reputation as a friend of liberty. But he, too, eventually lost the support of the Paris mob.

Matters came to a head in June 1791. Louis himself tried to escape from France with his queen. But they were recaptured at Varennes, near the Luxembourg border, and this attempted flight destroyed what was left of the king's reputation. He was now seen as a traitor.

As the revolution gathered momentum, and foreign governments began to show their uneasiness, new and more radical leaders came into power. In August 1792, Louis was thrown into prison. Austrian and Prussian armies crossed the frontier and moved remorselessly on

Paris, while some provinces, like the Vendée, loyal to the throne, rose in civil war. In the National Convention, as the National Assembly had been renamed, the orator Georges Danton thundered for courage – 'De l'audace, encore de l'audace et toujours de l'audace, et la France est sauvée!' ('Boldness, more boldness and yet more boldness, and France will be saved!') When revolutionary troops from the south marched to Paris to offer support, a young revolutionary poet, Rouget de l'Isle, welcomed them with what became the marching song of the revolutionary cause and the national anthem of France, *La Marseillaise*.

### 'The king must die'

In September 1792 the Austrian and Prussian advance was halted at Valmy, and in the same month a republic was formally proclaimed. The National Convention which met in September 1792 and remained in session until 1795 was the grand climax of the revolution. It was called to make a republican constitution, but found itself at war with practically all Europe and with parts of France itself, such as the Vendée, Lyon and Toulon. It set up a revolutionary executive of 12 men, the Committee of Public Safety, which governed Paris and France by the deliberate application of terror. The king was tried and executed in January 1793. 'The king must die,' said the lawyer Maximilien Robespierre, 'so that the state may live.' The queen was executed in September. Robespierre, young, intensely radical and

visionary, was wildly popular with the mob. He sent to the guillotine in a frenzy of zeal all whom he saw as less dedicated than himself. But in the end Paris turned against him and in July 1794 he was himself arrested and, after trying to kill himself, guillotined.

The revolution, a dramatic event in itself, became the great symbol and prototype of violent change. It was greeted by many European liberals at its outbreak with a chorus of approval. 'How much the greatest event it is that ever happened in the world; and how much the best!' said the English politician, Charles James Fox, on the fall of the Bastille. But the hopes of most liberals were soon disillusioned, for the revolution had a blacker side. It was bloodthirsty and led to a generation of European war. It destroyed much that was gracious in the old order, and the nobility disappeared almost totally. It began a long discord between Church and state in France. It brought on to the political stage those unpredictable and erratic factors that remain permanently there – the mob, the psychology of intimidation, rumour producing terror and terror feeding on rumour, and the carrying of ideological struggles across frontiers.

But the embattled citizens of France now had something to value. Their rights and liberties included not only a share in government – for which many of them might not care – but a stake in the soil. They owned their land as free farmers. About this they could be, in their way, as possessive and as conservative as

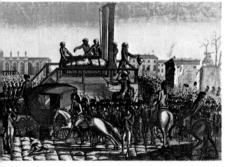

ROYAL VICTIM *Protected by troops, the executioner holds up the head of Louis XVI, guillotined for treason in January 1793. The sentence of death 'without respite or reprieve' was passed by a majority of only one vote. Louis's queen, Marie Antoinette, was guillotined nine months later*

PARISIAN GARB *The long trousers worn by the ordinary Parisian working man came to be regarded in revolutionary Paris as the uniform of the model patriot. And so the revolutionaries became known as sans culottes, meaning 'without the knee-breeches' worn by aristocrats*

MURDER OF MARAT

*The murder of the revolutionary extremist Jean Paul Marat was portrayed by Jacques Louis David, who became known as 'the artist of the Revolution'. Marat was one of the leaders of the left-wing Jacobin party; calling himself l'ami du peuple, 'the friend of the people', he not only demanded the extermination of all Royalists, but also attacked the rival republican party, the Gironde. In July 1793 a young woman named Charlotte Corday stabbed Marat to death as he lay in the bath he took for the treatment of a skin disease. Marat's death was used as an excuse for an even more intensive purge of suspected aristocrats. But in fact Charlotte Corday was a member of the Gironde, who killed Marat in revenge for the attacks he had made on the leaders of her party*

À MARAT
DAVID

# Napoleon, master of Europe who crowned himself emperor

any noble or despot. For this they would fight hard and long, for they had now a lot to lose. Moreover the French were determined to spread the freedom they had won to the rest of Europe. Their armies threw back the invading forces of Austria and Prussia, then went on to carry the message of 'Liberty, Equality, Fraternity' across the whole of Europe. But what was originally designed to be a war of liberation against the tyranny of despotic monarchs soon turned into a war of conquest by France. In such a war, new and untried commanders rose from the ranks by sheer brilliance. Chief among them was a young Corsican lieutenant, Napoleon Bonaparte.

## The Napoleonic Empire

Napoleon's energy and military genius brought him swift promotion; his victories brought popularity; and he used that popularity to climb to supreme power, not as a mere king, but as emperor. At the height of his power, in 1807, Bonaparte was the master of Europe, from the borders of Russia to the Channel ports, from the northern boundaries of Germany to Naples. What he did not control directly he controlled through satellite states, with his brothers and marshals of France as his agents.

At the centre of power was the pomp and pageantry of an imperial court. Napoleon

created 31 dukes, 388 counts, 1090 barons and 1500 knights. He formed an Imperial Guard and in 1810 married an Austrian princess. But in ordering his empire Napoleon acted without illusion. He said of the Legion of Honour, which he set up in 1802: 'It is with toys that mankind is governed.' He appointed Jacques Louis David as court painter to catch the colour and pageantry of the Napoleonic Empire. Another artist, Jean Ingres, saw and painted Napoleon as a Charlemagne. The likeness was not too far-fetched – Napoleon showed all the skill and administrative genius of a Charlemagne or a Julius Caesar.

Napoleon's ambitions embraced the whole world. In 1798 his march on India was halted when his fleet was destroyed by Nelson at the Battle of the Nile; and by 1804 Napoleon had also to abandon his dream of a Caribbean Empire, after his army in Santo Domingo had been ravaged by war and yellow fever. Napoleon now planned the conquest of Britain, with 2000 ships and 90,000 men assembled and ready at a host of camps from Ostend to Etaples. 'The Channel is a mere ditch,' he said. 'Six hours' control of it would do the job.' But in 1805, after his navy was defeated at Trafalgar, Napoleon had also to abandon all thoughts of invading England. Napoleon's land empire still remained vast and formidable. But though

France mastered the Continent, Britain had command of the sea; it was a struggle of the elephant against the whale. Britain held on grimly in Sicily, Malta and Sardinia, and British goods continued to reach Europe in defiance of Napoleon's blockade.

A British army, supplied by sea, tied down 250,000 French troops in Spain. This was the 'running sore' which weakened Napoleon, but it was the invasion of Russia in 1812 which led him to disaster. The emperor put 675,000 men into action, but the Russians countered with a 'scorched earth' policy. They fell back, avoiding set battles when they could, and destroying as they went, so stretching the French supply lines to breaking point. Napoleon marched his Grand Army to Moscow in the heat of summer and brought it back in the snows of winter; only 30,000 survived.

The retreat from Moscow acted as a signal to the Europe that Napoleon had conquered. At Leipzig in October 1813 he was defeated by an Austrian, Prussian and Russian alliance. Six months later Paris saw its first foreign conquerors for 400 years – Germans, Austrians, Russians and British. Napoleon abdicated and was exiled to the island of Elba, off the west coast of Italy. Louis XVIII, brother of Louis XVI, was restored. When Napoleon escaped from Elba in March 1815, many of his veterans rallied to him, but he was defeated by British and Prussian forces at Waterloo in June 1815 and exiled, finally, to St Helena.

## A new system of laws

Napoleon's empire was too grandiose for one man to master – even a man of his superhuman ability, superlative military skill and frightening ruthlessness. In the end Napoleon was seen outside France as a supreme egotist and a supreme destroyer. It was no longer possible in a world of intense nationalism to play the role of Charlemagne: language and national loyalties were now too strong.

But Napoleon's work was not all negative. He took justifiable pride in his Civil Code, which, with other laws he devised, was exported in the train of the French armies. The revolution had given land to the peasants and had given opportunities to men of lowly birth; the codes confirmed the paramount value of private property, and the idea that careers should depend on talent not on birth.

Under Napoleon the monopolistic powers of the guilds, and state regulation of industry, were abolished. In the same spirit the secondary schools were replaced by *lycées*, in which courses in military drill were allied to a strenuous classical education. These were the breeding grounds of the next generation of officials and civil servants. Higher education became a department of state, tightly controlled from Paris. Its concern was education not for the masses but for a governing class of officers, engineers and officials – a Napoleonic élite. Nevertheless it gave France for the next two generations the best educational system in Europe. Though no profound believer in religion, Napoleon was aware of the influence of

### GOYA: A PAINTER WHO CAPTURED THE HORROR OF WAR

*The armies of Napoleonic France carried destruction to every corner of Europe. The execution of Spanish patriots by a French firing squad in Madrid was recorded by the Spanish artist Francisco de Goya* *(1754–1828) in his painting,* The Third of May 1808. *The brutal realism of the many paintings which Goya made during the French occupation of Spain helped to dispel the romantic concept of war*

the Roman Catholic faith. In 1801 he made a *Concordat* (agreement) with the pope. This recognised Roman Catholicism as the religion of the majority of Frenchmen, but accorded equal rights to other religious faiths.

Napoleon built a great network of roads and canals – often by the forced labour of prisoners of war – and curbed food prices. He gave France not only glory, but prosperity – but only for a time. For his wars were phenomenally costly, and brought no long-term economic gains. For a generation French industry was sheltered from British competition, but denied raw materials and overseas markets. Those with money to invest put it into land, not industry. After 1815 landowners remained the dominant class, and the Industrial Revolution was as a result a late arrival in France. The grip of the soil has remained strong in France to the present day.

Napoleon's basic interest was not in liberty but in social order and authority, in rules and regulations; he even devoted part of his time in Moscow in 1812 to drawing up new rules for the Comedie Française theatre company in Paris. He gave autocratic power to his prefects, whom he chose himself and who were always strangers to their departments. 'Abroad and at home,' he said, 'I reign only through the fear I inspire.' Napoleon's regime was a blend of ruthless but efficient despotism and appeals to the people. His memory was, and still in a measure is, cherished as a symbol of the revolution. Napoleon blazed across Europe like a meteor, and after him the Continent was never the same again.

## The Romantic legacy

When Louis XVIII was finally restored to the French throne in 1815 it seemed that an ugly and violent chapter in European history had been closed. Such at least was the hope of all the major powers of Europe, who united under the guidance of the Austrian statesman Metternich to form an alliance to crush revolution wherever it arose. But despite the apparent political inactivity of Europe after the Napoleonic age, it was to prove impossible to turn the clock back to before 1789. When Charles X, who came to the French throne in 1824 on the death of Louis XVIII, set out to re-establish royal power in 1829, the response was rapid. In July 1830, barricades were erected in the streets of Paris, Charles fled, and the vacant throne was offered to Louis Philippe, Duke of Orleans. He accepted it, like the good businessman he was, and ruled as a constitutional monarch.

The ideals of the French revolutionaries had provided the impetus for two closely linked forces which no political alliance could crush. One of these was the Romantic movement in music, art and literature which flourished after 1815. The other was nationalism itself, the search of each country for political freedom, the end product of the revolutionary ferment in politics, ideas and culture.

The Romantic movement was a reaction against the orderly and polite style of the 18th century. It set a high value on the emotions and

## SUCCESSOR TO THE CAESARS

The rise of a young Corsican officer, Napoleon Bonaparte, to become Emperor of the French and master of Europe is one of the great adventure stories of modern history. Born in 1769 on the island of Corsica, Napoleon was commissioned a sublieutenant of artillery in the French army in 1785. The outbreak of the Revolution gave him his great opportunity. By sheer military genius, Napoleon became a brigadier-general before he was 25. In 1797 he took command of the French army in Italy, and three years later overthrew the government in France itself by a military coup. In 1804 he crowned himself emperor, seeing his domains as the re-creation of Imperial Rome.

At its greatest extent, Napoleon's empire stretched from Seville to Warsaw and from Naples to the Baltic. He had defeated all the major powers of the European continent and tied them to France as allies. But the disastrous failure of Napoleon's invasion of Russia in 1812 at last broke his stranglehold on Europe. He was defeated at Leipzig in 1813 and exiled, returning only to further defeat at Waterloo. Finally exiled from power at the age of 45, never to return, Napoleon died a prisoner on the lonely island of St Helena, held captive by the British, the 'nation of shop-keepers' he had despised. His dream of empire was now reduced to a few bleak storm-ridden square miles, deep in the South Atlantic, where Napoleon died of cancer at the age of 51

IMPERIAL SPLENDOUR *Napoleon seated in glory on the imperial throne, painted in 1806 by Jean Auguste Dominique Ingres (1780–1867). Ingres was one of a group of artists commissioned by Napoleon to produce paintings exalting his imperial status in classical style. Napoleon's rule brought considerable long-term benefits to France; the Code Napoleon is still the basis of French law. But his wars ruined the prosperity he tried to create*

SCENE OF FAREWELL *In this study at Malmaison, near Paris, designed by the architects Percier and Fontaine, Napoleon said farewell to his family after Waterloo*

SPHINX PLATE *This plate from Napoleon's dinner service commemorates the excavation of the Sphinx in Egypt by his troops during his invasion of 1798*

CORONATION CEREMONY *Napoleon, at the age of 35, crowns himself Emperor of the French, using the crown worn 1000 years earlier by Charlemagne, the first Holy Roman Emperor. Pope Pius VII (centre) was summoned to Notre Dame Cathedral in Paris for the ceremony, which was painted by Jacques David*

# *A new society built on the Industrial Revolution*

the imagination. This new spirit was caught in France by the artist Eugene Delacroix (1798–1863), and later by the writer Victor Hugo (1802–85). In his poetry, drama and historical novels, written in a prodigal wave of words for over 50 years, Hugo dominated the age. His novel *Les Misérables* appeared in 1862 simultaneously in ten European languages. Hugo combined his Romanticism with an acute awareness of social habits and customs. In Germany, the master spirits of the Romantic movement were the writers Goethe and Schiller.

Britain was rich in Romantic poets—Shelley and Keats, with their love of pagan Greece; William Blake, the mystic; the talented if egocentric Lord Byron, who died helping Greece to win its freedom from the Turks; and especially Coleridge and Wordsworth, who loved both nature and the past. With their *Lyrical Ballads*, published in 1798, Coleridge and Wordsworth showed that poetry could be written in simple English, without searching for especially 'poetic' words and phrases.

Britain produced a Romantic novelist to match its poets in Sir Walter Scott (1771–1832).

In his historical novels, such as *Ivanhoe* and *Quentin Durward*, Scott's loving re-creation of the past won him a European reputation. But other British writers, notably Jane Austen and Thomas Love Peacock, reacted against Romanticism's exaggerations, and the British novelist of the age was undoubtedly Charles Dickens (1812–70), who wrote novels rich in personalities drawn from everyday life.

Musicians, too, were gripped by the Romantic fever; by the 1850's composers such as Mendelssohn, Schumann, Liszt and Berlioz had thrown off the formal restraints of the Classical period and made the expression of emotion the first concern of their music. Frédéric Chopin captured the longing of his Polish countrymen for freedom and unity. In Italy, the operas of Giuseppe Verdi came to epitomise the fervour of Italian nationalism.

Even earlier, Ludwig van Beethoven (1770–1827), while firmly adhering to the Classical forms of composition, was a supremely Romantic figure, triumphing over deafness to express his faith in freedom and in mankind in immortal music. He thought he recognised a

kindred soul in Napoleon, and intended to dedicate his third symphony, the *Eroica*, to him. But when Napoleon made himself emperor, Beethoven dramatically struck out the dedication. Napoleon himself was a Romantic, in his belief in his own destiny. And the recurrent theme of all the Romantic works of art was the Napoleonic striving of ordinary people for freedom and for expression; the new struggle by irrational and sometimes titanic forces to break through the restraints and disciplines of government and society. It was these forces that kept revolution alive in 19th-century Europe.

### The force of nationalism

In the first half of the 19th century, nationalism was a creative and emancipating force. It was still under the spell of the revolutionary ideas of liberty, equality and fraternity. It was world-wide and shaped the politics of Latin America, and the sentiments of Abraham Lincoln. It produced distinguished statesmen, such as Cavour in Italy and Bismarck in Germany, who became the founder-fathers of their countries. The emotional appeal of nationalism was stronger than any political force yet known. Loyalty was no longer to king or lord, to class or creed or Church, but to the nation, to territory on maps. Nationalism stood for the rights of men and the career open to talent; the nation would be defended not by a professional class of warriors but by all its citizens. All these concepts were the legacy of 1789 and the 25 years of revolution which followed.

But the liberal nationalism which triumphed in 1789 suffered an almost mortal blow in 1848. This momentous year saw a wave of liberal revolutions throughout Europe which were all equally unsuccessful. The German nationalists met at Frankfurt and offered the crown of a united Germany to the King of Prussia. But he refused to, as he put it, 'pick up a crown from the gutter' and sent his troops to crush the revolutionaries and their working-class allies. Similar scenes took place all over Europe. In France, the Second Republic which dethroned Louis Philippe itself lasted only three years before its President, Louis Napoleon, nephew of the great Bonaparte, became Emperor as Napoleon III in a *coup d'état*.

The strength of nationalism was not quelled. But in future national unity was brought about by intrigue from above rather than by pressure from the people below. This was especially true of German nationalism, which, born out of defeat by Napoleon I at Jena in 1806, and blooded in 1848, reached its maturity in 1870, when Napoleon III was defeated by Bismarck's diplomacy and Prussian troops. France had ceased to be the dominant Western power and Bismarck's Germany, forged in blood and iron, had taken its place.

Nationalism had triumphed again; but at a cost. The German constitution, based though it was on a vote for every adult male, left effective control in the hands of Prussia; and inside Prussia the monarch's power was virtually unchecked. Bismarck's ambitions were limited: he did not attempt, as Hitler was to

### THE COMING OF THE RAILWAYS

*Railways followed canals as the backbone of the Industrial Revolution, and in them, as in other inventions which made the revolution possible, Britain led the way. The romantic aspects of the new age inspired many 19th-century artists, such as J. M. W. Turner in his* Rain, Steam and Speed *(above). The first British passenger line was opened in 1825, and 50 years later railways criss-crossed the country*

attempt later, to unite all German-speaking areas into his empire, or *Reich*. But he had humiliated France, and part of the price of his success was a legacy of hate between France, with its desire for revenge, and Germany.

## Investing in machines

The political upheaval was not the only revolution in 19th-century Europe. Another revolution which was to have equally far-reaching effects took place in industry.

Up to 1789 life for the ordinary people of Europe had changed little since Roman times. They lived in small, isolated rural communities; their food and clothing were home-made; and their beer was home-brewed. There was little possibility of change as long as roads were bad and markets limited. The same limitations prevented the growth of trade in the towns themselves, where the guilds were still powerful and machinery primitive. Industry still depended on water power, on muscle power and on horses. But by the early 1800's, merchants were ready to invest in speedier methods of production. The machine age was at hand.

Historians argue over the 'causes' of the Industrial Revolution. But one underlying cause was undoubtedly Europe's rapidly expanding population, which nearly doubled in the century between 1750 and 1850, from 140 million to 275 million. The population of London alone grew from 875,000 to 2 million.

The rise in population was not due, initially at least, to a surge in the birth rate. It was the result, rather, of a dramatic fall in the death rate. Better food and better hygiene meant that more and more children were surviving the crisis period of the first few years of life. The improvement in diet was due notably to increased cultivation of the potato, and the use of the turnip as winter fodder for cattle, making fresh milk and meat available throughout the year. It was helped by the use and development of artificial fertilisers, the specialisation of crops and by the cross-breeding of cattle.

Many more people lived in the country than could find work there; they moved to factory work in the towns, and the availability of jobs stimulated earlier marriages. The increasing population began to demand political changes and to bring pressure on governments. Towns became restless places, full of change and plans for improvement.

## Britain sets the pace

New machines, using first water power then steam power, ushered in the modern industrial age. The first of these machines were almost all British. Britain was the pioneering industrial society, blessed at the outset by rich supplies of coal and iron ore, and for two generations, until challenged by Germany and the USA, the British were the industrial pace-setters of the world.

One result of the Industrial Revolution was to bring the factory system into being. It made for the concentration of people in towns, since factories, other than textile mills, no longer had to be near streams. And it produced competi-

tion for markets and a wage economy, in which employers looked for 'hands'. It unleashed a transport revolution in canals, in roads and railways, and it stimulated what seemed an endless demand for coal and iron, and later for steel. Goods, people and ideas now travelled fast. In Russia the tsars were at first afraid of railways, which they saw as causes of basic change and a threat to the established order.

The Industrial Revolution was uneven in its impact. Europe as a whole was still rural in 1789. Serfdom was not abolished in France until the revolution, and in Prussia it lasted until 1807. East of the Elbe a large, landless, agricultural labouring class still remained; in Russia in 1815 the tsar alone still owned 16 million serfs. But Hamburg and the Ruhr, Ghent and Brussels, Liege and Lille – towns all over Europe – soon became industrial centres for textiles, metal working, coal and steel. Behind all these developments lay money, especially in London, Paris and Amsterdam.

The effect of new inventions was most dramatic in Germany, where a web-like spread of railway lines enabled rich supplies of coal and

iron to be exploited, and factories boomed through the use of steam engines. The story of Alfred Krupp of Essen was typical of one aspect of German – and European – industrial growth. What in 1826 was a near-bankrupt household business had become by 1870 a vast private, paternalist empire of steel and bronze and guns, with pension schemes, hotels and stores. In the 60 years between 1850 and 1910 iron production rose 26-fold in Germany – and only trebled in Britain. Germany was now the dominant industrial force in Europe.

In less than a century a new Europe had been built on the ashes of the old. The triumphs of industrialisation had changed the economic face of the European continent, just as nationalism had transformed the political map. But in both these forces were the seeds of ultimate conflict. Rapid industrialisation had given birth to social problems which the *laissez-faire* ('leave alone') philosophy adopted by almost all businessmen and politicians made it impossible to solve, while out of the clash of rival nationalisms was to come the most destructive of all forces – that of war.

## A NEW AGE

Within only 50 years Europe was transformed from an agricultural society into an industrial society. Great trading exhibitions in many countries reflected national pride in this achievement. Britain, aided by its rich supplies of coal and the inventiveness of its engineers, was the pioneer in this Industrial Revolution

THE FIRST MINERS *A painting of 1800 gives a romantic picture of coal mining's first scars on the peace of the British countryside*

GERMAN CHALLENGE *A monster gun, forged by Krupp, on show at the international exhibition in Paris in 1867*

SHOW-PIECE OF THE WORLD *A linen handkerchief shows the Crystal Palace, built in Hyde Park by Sir Joseph Paxton to house the Great Exhibition of 1851. The exhibition was designed to show Britain's industrial leadership. The palace was later moved to Sydenham, south of London, where it burnt down in 1936*

# The making of
# the modern world

## FROM AD 1870

*A mass civilization, based on the growth of science and technology, has built great new cities and taken man into space*

**THE WORLD IN 1914**

*Early in the 20th century, European powers straddled the world. But after 1945 most of them lost their empires*

| | |
|---|---|
| Britain | Germany |
| France | Portugal |

The rise of a mass urban civilization, based on the products of science, technology and industry, and marked by vast complexity and rapid change, has been the major social development of modern times. Originating in western Europe, and especially in the Britain of the mid-19th century, it took its most comprehensive and typical form in the United States from the early 20th century, and has now spread throughout the world.

This new civilization of the West has concentrated millions of people into cities. It has changed the village craftsman into the factory worker with a vote. It has bred businessmen and captains of industry, scientific researchers and bureaucrats. It has replaced the horse with the tractor and motor-car, the scrubbing-board with the washing-machine, the candle with electric light, and in countless other ways improved the material quality of life. It has brought universal education, popular journalism, mass entertainment, annual holidays with pay, and social security designed to protect families from 'the cradle to the grave'. It has led the mass of the people to expect an ever-

rising standard of living, and has in the long run lived up to this expectation, though there have been setbacks.

In its most recent phase Western civilization has turned the world into what the Canadian social scientist Marshall McLuhan has called a 'global village', thanks to the instant communication across space made possible by radio and television. And this world-wide social transformation continues, at an ever-accelerating rate. But overshadowing the life of Western man in the 20th century is a fateful paradox. Through science and technology, he has not only found the means to master his environment – he has also developed the capacity to destroy it.

Man has set foot on the moon. He has split the atom, created new elements, and begun to unlock the secrets of the living cell. He has conquered distance, and wiped out or brought under control most of the diseases which afflicted his ancestors. Automation and the computer have given him the key to infinite material riches, and the promise of boundless leisure in which to enjoy them. Yet the spectacular advance of modern science has also

**STEPS TO THE MOON**

*Two dramatic expressions of the technological prowess of modern man. The clustering skyscrapers of steel and concrete, which dominate New York's Manhattan Island (left), symbolise the dynamic energy and aspiration of the 20th century – an age which has been described as one of 'heroic materialism'. The great height of these buildings, including the Empire State, at top right, which at 1250 ft was for long the world's highest, was made possible by revolutionary new engineering techniques dating from the 1880's. It was engineering genius, too, that enabled man in 1969 to reach out into space and walk on the moon (right)*

# *A way of life transformed by the coming of machines*

enabled man – in the cause of patriotism or ideology – to wage the two most destructive wars in history, engulfing almost the entire world. The use of the atomic bomb in the second of these global wars opened up for mankind the appalling possibility of his self-destruction as a species. It is this development, more than any other, which marks out the 20th century from all previous ages.

## The dawn of a new age
On the night of December 31, 1900, vast crowds gathered in London's Trafalgar Square, in the Place de la Concorde in Paris, and the other traditional centres of the world's capitals, to celebrate the arrival of the new century. The bells ringing in 1901 at midnight seemed to sound a note of renewed confidence for the nations of Europe, which by the close of the last century had secured an unquestioned dominance in the world. It was the heyday of

imperialism, especially in Britain, whose queen, Victoria, had celebrated 'sixty glorious years' at her diamond jubilee in 1897. London was the pivot of the world's trade, and the heart of an empire which covered a quarter of the earth. The Boer War was still being fought; despite some humiliating setbacks suffered by British forces, there was little doubt who would win.

On the Continent, a newly unified Germany had emerged as the dominant economic and military power, at the expense of France, which was still bitter with memories of its defeat in the Franco-Prussian War of 1870–1. Both Germany and France were busy carving out empires overseas, under the suspicious gaze of the British.

Germany owed its strength not only to its army – the largest and most efficient in the world – but also to its driving economy. It pioneered the development of two vital modern industries, electrical and chemical engineering. Even in traditional industries, in which Britain

had hitherto been dominant, Germany was taking the lead. Education, concentrating on science and technology, was the basis of German technological progress.

## Pleasure, progress and poverty
For the rich and privileged, the first decade of the 20th century was a time of gaiety and elegant living. Queen Victoria outlived the century by only a few months. Then came for Britain the Edwardian 'long week-end'; for France, with Paris the sparkling centre of international fashion, it was *la belle epoque*. The whole European pageant – complacently moving against a setting of ornate opera-houses, fashionable race courses, and military parades – was dominated by emperors, kings and princes, most of whom were related. Britain's king-emperor, Edward VII, was known as the 'uncle of Europe'. But it was a quarrelsome family: the bellicose Kaiser Wilhelm II, one of Edward's nephews, loathed him, and was convinced that he was plotting with France and Russia to encircle Germany.

Behind the glitter, men were developing ideas and inventions which were to have profound consequences for 20th-century man. Scientists were beginning to question the picture of an orderly universe, operating by rigidly mechanical laws, which the 19th century had unquestioningly accepted. A German-born physicist, Albert Einstein, an obscure official in a Swiss patents office, published his revolutionary paper on relativity in 1905. His intensely complex mathematical ideas, challenging Newton's system of physics, won speedy recognition among scientists. American and British scientists applied his theories, with devastating results, in the creation of the atomic bomb in the Second World War.

Five years before, another epoch-making work had been published – *The Interpretation of Dreams*, by the Viennese physician, Sigmund Freud, the founder of psycho-analysis. Freud's discovery of the unconscious mind and the importance of sexuality in the formation of character was to have a radical influence on Western thought and behaviour. Freud's emphasis on sex outraged even many of his scientific colleagues, and it was only in the 1920's that his theories were widely accepted.

The arts of this period were also in a state of ferment. Accepted conventions in music, painting and literature were all being broken down. The Viennese composer Arnold Schoenberg was forging a new musical system, based on a scale of 12 notes instead of 8; to audiences reared on the melodies of the Romantic composers, the intensely abstract music of Schoenberg and his school seemed meaningless. Picasso and Braque were experimenting with Cubism in Paris, while the American-born poet T. S. Eliot, also in Paris, was developing a technique known as *vers libre* (free verse) for expressing the moods and rhythms of contemporary urban life.

Such developments in science and the arts left the great mass of people untouched, as did the world of wealth and fashion. City slums

### CITIES, SLUMS AND SQUALOR

*By the 1850's many of Europe's towns were bursting at the seams as people flocked into them to work in the new industries. Slums like these in the north of England came into existence. In an age whose economic philosophy was* laissez-faire *('leave alone'), little provision was made for working-class needs .*

were a grim reminder of the gulf between rich and poor. Many people lived below what is called today the poverty line. In these conditions, international socialism, with Marx and Engels as its father figures, was spreading its roots. Strikes were becoming more common, as the trade union movement, strengthened by the widening of the vote, asserted its demands for radical reform. In late 19th-century Germany, Bismarck had shrewdly realised the danger of disaffection among the growing working class, and had introduced measures of 'state socialism' to improve their living and working conditions. In the early 20th century, many Western governments began to copy Bismarck's policies.

## Prelude to war

On the eve of the greatest war mankind had yet seen, Europe was in the grip of two rival military alliances, each with elaborate plans for dealing with attack. France and Russia were linked in opposition to Germany and Austria-Hungary, while Britain had established an understanding with France known as the *Entente Cordiale*. Intense nationalist rivalries and suspicions had built up over the long years of peace. Britain, for over a century the unchallenged mistress of the seas, was alarmed by Germany's growing naval power. Germany for its part feared a concerted attack by France and Russia.

Many other complex factors played a part in driving Europe to war. The Balkans seethed with rebellion against the once-mighty empire of the Hapsburgs, now regarded as the 'jailer of the Slavs'. On June 28, 1914, in the Bosnian town of Sarajevo, a Serbian nationalist, Gavrilo Princip, assassinated the Archduke Franz Ferdinand, heir to the Austro-Hungarian throne. This was the spark which exploded the powder-keg of Europe. Austria made the assassination the pretext to declare war on Serbia, and within weeks the demands of military plans and timetables were imposing their grim logic on events. With Austria mobilising, Russia also mobilised, to protect Serbia. Germany stood by Austria, and France mobilised to stand by Russia and to protect itself. Britain declared war, too, when Germany refused to respect the neutrality of Belgium. Britain's foreign secretary, Sir Edward Grey, remarked prophetically: 'The lamps are going out all over Europe. We shall not see them lit again in our lifetime.'

## World war and its aftermath

Few people imagined the war would last more than a few months. All over Europe, millions of men were cheered on their way to the fronts. But by the autumn of 1914 the pattern for the war had emerged – two great armies on the Western Front faced each other, in a condition

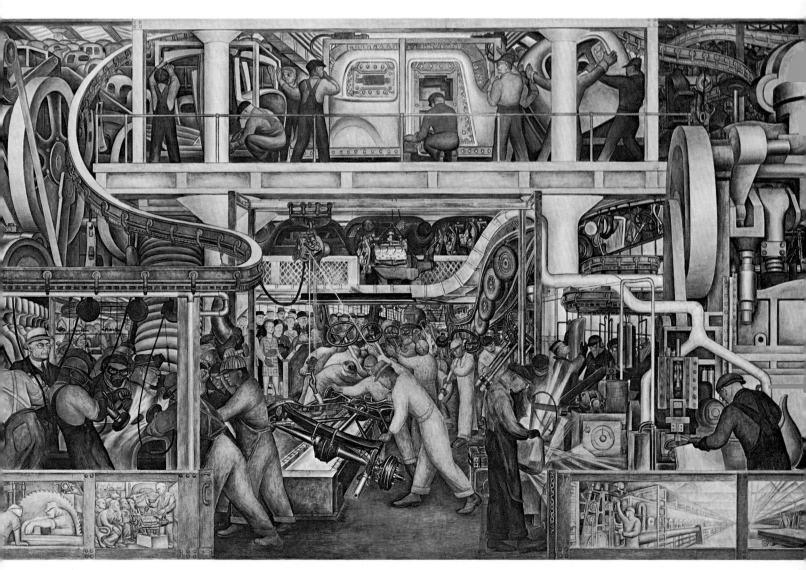

### THE ASSEMBLY LINE: MAN'S COLLABORATION WITH THE MACHINE

*The achievements of industrialism depended on minutely detailed planning, with each worker carrying out precisely defined tasks. This fresco of the Ford motor-car works at Detroit, painted in about 1933 by the Mexican artist Diego Rivera, shows the assembly line in smooth operation. But with mechanisation of labour came an inescapable monotony, and some feared that man would become the servant, not the master, of the machines he had created*

# *Democracy survives the battle with dictatorship*

CROSSES OF WAR *French dead at Verdun, the First World War's most costly battle. In ten months the combined dead and wounded of both sides reached over 700,000*

MASS MILITARISM *Men believed that the First World War was 'the war to end wars'. But Hitler shattered this dream by reviving German military ambitions*

GRIM INHERITANCE *The ruins of Berlin in 1945, part of Hitler's legacy to Germany. The Nazi dream of a 1000 year Reich brought Europe close to destruction*

of stalemate. Confidence in a speedy end to the war melted away. Attempts to break the stalemate failed with immense casualties. The horror of trenches, barbed wire and machine guns burnt itself into the minds of a generation.

The First World War became the first total war in history, involving civilians as well as soldiers, and the full mobilisation of national resources. With so much manpower at the front, women gained a new status in society, taking over essential tasks in offices and factories. In 1918, most women over 30 in Britain were given the vote, and this was the prelude to a much wider emancipation of their sex in the peace that followed.

An exhausted Germany, together with its allies, surrendered in November 1918. An important factor in Germany's final defeat was the entry of the USA into the war in 1917. This event signalled the emergence, for the first time, of the world's richest country as a world power. Europe had lost more than 10 million men, and both victors and vanquished alike were weary and impoverished as a result of the titanic struggle. With its vast economic resources intact, the United States was able to aid Europe's recovery. Huge loans from the financiers of Wall Street emphasised Europe's dependence on the New World.

## An uncertain decade

One thought united the Western world in the immediate post-war period – that the war of 1914–18 had been the 'war to end wars'. International institutions based on good will, such as the League of Nations, would ensure that no generation would ever have to fight again. But this spirit of hope for the future soon gave place to nervous uncertainty. It proved impossible to return to the stability which had existed before 1914. Inflation, unemployment and acute social unrest dominated much of Europe during the 1920's. Germany, partly as a result of the burden of war reparations, was gripped by an inflation which reduced its currency, the mark, to worthlessness, and destroyed its middle class. In Britain, workers' discontent led to a General Strike in 1926; the government defeated the strike, but bitterness remained. The spectre of Communist revolution haunted statesmen; and in several countries there was an ominous trend towards militaristic dictatorship.

In these uncertain times, most people hungered for the 'normalcy' of the pre-war world, which appeared to them as a 'golden age' of order and prosperity. But there were some who, blaming the war on what they regarded as the criminal blunders of statesmen and generals, condemned the society which had allowed such men to hold power. They looked to a new future, built on ideas of socialism and equality. A minority saw the solution for mankind's problems in Soviet Russia, where the Bolshevik Revolution of 1917 appeared to them to have swept away all social injustice. But this was to prove another great illusion.

Several best-selling books captured the embittered and disillusioned spirit of this period. One of the most famous was a war novel, *All*

*Quiet on the Western Front* (1929), written by Erich Maria Remarque, a German who had served in the trenches. The English writer Robert Graves voiced a passionate protest against the futility of the war, and turned his back on the old Europe, in his autobiographical work *Goodbye to All That* (1929).

## The Jazz Age in America

American society, riding on a wave of prosperity, offered a vigorous contrast to the troubled Europe of the 1920's. The standard of living of the nation aroused the admiration and envy of the world. There seemed no limits to what American dynamism could achieve. A typical figure was Henry Ford, whose mass-production methods brought the motor-car within the ordinary citizen's reach.

American vigour in the 1920's was also reflected in the culture and entertainment which it exported to the world. Jazz – which became the label for the age – and the cinema were its main contributions. Novelists such as F. Scott Fitzgerald, Sinclair Lewis and Ernest Hemingway brilliantly mirrored aspects of the jazz age – its tensions and glamour, as well as its brashness – and gave American literature a new status at home and abroad.

In 1929, with the Wall Street crash, the bubble of this unparalleled prosperity burst, and the collapse of America's economy brought Europe's down with it. The worst hit country was Germany, with 6 million out of work in the early 1930's. Out of the disaster of world economic depression grew forces which were to threaten Western civilization.

## Crisis in Europe

In the 1930's there emerged what has been called the 'Revolution of Destruction' – the creed of Nazism. Adolf Hitler, a failed artist, was ill-educated and temperamentally unbalanced. But he had the gift of mesmeric oratory, intense devotion to his vision of the German people's destiny as a 'master race', and ruthless skill in mastering men and moods. Profiting by the massive slump in Germany, he came to power in 1933. The brutal excesses of his dictatorship – such as the persecution of the Jews – revealed the depths of barbarism that 'civilized' man could still plumb.

The most persistent feature of the Nazi outlook was its brutish irrationality. Democracy was at bottom based on reason – on compromise, tolerance and agreeing to differ – but this was language that was foreign to Hitler. Only by 'thinking with the blood', he argued, is there national strength. The ties of race played a crucial part in Hitler's philosophy, one of his goals being to unite all peoples of German origin in his *Reich* (empire). This *Reich*, he believed, would have to be given, or fight for, *lebensraum* ('room to live'), either by expansion in Europe or by recovering the colonies Germany had lost after the First World War.

Scorning the democracies for their 'decadence', Hitler played on their fears to achieve his ends. In 1933 Germany was disarmed and helpless. A few years later, it had built up a huge army and the greatest air force in the world. Most statesmen in Britain and France, together with their peoples, still remembered the agony of 1914–18. They refused to accept that Germany was prepared to plunge the world into another war. Afraid of the risks involved in challenging Hitler's aggressive demands, they embarked on a policy of appeasement.

Appeasement reached a climax in the Munich agreement of 1938 when, at the behest of Britain and France, democratic Czechoslovakia was forced to give up the German-speaking Sudetenland to Germany. But when even this did not satisfy Hitler, more and more people came to realise the threat that Nazism posed to all the values of Western civilization. This threat seemed to be made even more menacing by Hitler's involvement in the Spanish Civil War (1936–9). The war was fought between the Republican government, supported by Soviet Russia, and a military junta, led by General Franco, with the backing of Germany and Italy. The intervention of outside powers inflamed what would otherwise have been a local conflict into an ideological battlefield of world significance. 'Arms for Spain' and the demand for a Popular Front – an alliance of Socialists and Communists – against the dictators became popular rallying cries. By the time the war ended with Franco's victory in 1939, new menacing developments in central Europe were claiming the world's attention. In September, Hitler attacked Poland and the Second World War began.

## Disaster and recovery

The Second World War brought Europe the profoundest crisis in its history. From 1939 to 1945 the war cost Europe 30 million lives, and a financial and social loss beyond calculation. Though Nazism was ultimately defeated, the unspeakable record of its concentration camps and 'death factories', which came to light at the end of the war, left a deep scar on the conscience of the civilized world. Mingled with admiration for the wartime heroism of the Russian people there was, too, a growing realisation of the evils of Stalin's totalitarian regime. In his satirical novel *Animal Farm* (1945), the English writer George Orwell attacked the belief held by many leading intellectuals that Soviet Russia was a model state.

Despite what seemed a spiritual and physical bankruptcy in 1945, the vitality of Europe was not extinguished. Massively aided by the United States, post-war Europe soon rose from the ashes. The problem of 'displaced' persons – the millions of refugees who had been uprooted from their countries in the war – was largely solved. Europe had lost much of its political power in the world, but still possessed its

### A FRENCH ARTIST'S VIEW OF THE WORKING MAN AT LEISURE

*In a democratic age, the kind of leisure formerly enjoyed by a privileged few came increasingly to be regarded as the right of ordinary people. The spirit of a typical Sunday outing was captured by the French artist Georges Seurat in his* Baignade *(The Bathers), a study of Parisians on the banks of the Seine at Asnières, an industrial suburb, painted in 1883. Factory chimneys in the background symbolise the era's prosperity. Seurat was influenced by the French Impressionist painters, especially in his use of open-air subjects. His technique of using small dots of colour to build up his pictures is known as Pointillism*

# Progress and peril in the age of technology

economic potential. Its rapid growth in population more than replaced the numbers lost in the war. The speed of its economic and human recovery was astounding.

## Dissolution of empires

In the new age, however, none of the European powers alone had the strength to maintain a world role. The United States took on the burden of guarding the Western world's security against the Communist threat, which had increased with the expansion of Soviet Russia over central and eastern Europe.

The Second World War brought about many far-reaching changes in Europe's relations with the world. None was more dramatic than that resulting from the upsurge of nationalism among the subject-peoples of the surviving European empires. This nationalism was encouraged by the astonishingly rapid conquests by the Japanese during the war, which had shown Asians that their European masters were not invincible. The fall of the supposedly impregnable fortress of Singapore in 1942 dealt Western prestige in Asia a blow from which it never fully recovered.

The hand-over of power by Britain to India in 1947 was the first recognition that the era of colonialism was drawing to a close. But in other areas, notably in Dutch Indonesia and French Indo-China, the transition to independence

was not achieved without bitter struggle against the ruling powers. By the early 1950's, Europe's empires in Africa were also feeling the effects of what the British Prime Minister Harold Macmillan was later to call 'the wind of change'. By the end of the decade, most of Africa was being governed by its own peoples. Yet in the newly independent countries, the influence of Europe remained, in its technology, its institutions, its languages and its culture.

## America sets the pace

The United States emerged from the Second World War as the unquestioned leader of the Western world. Even though it gave vast financial and material aid to Europe in the postwar years, it was rich and powerful enough to maintain and extend its prosperity at home. Like Soviet Russia, the United States had become a 'super-power', possessing a strength without precedent in history.

Europe in earlier ages had given America its culture and technology; now the process was dramatically reversed, with new American living styles and 'know-how' dominating Europe. As Europe rebuilt its cities, skylines reminiscent of New York and Chicago began to emerge. On the factory floor and in the board room, American techniques, methods of management, and values increasingly prevailed. In the arts too, Americans set the pace.

The 'action painting' of Jackson Pollock and others, with its uninhibited, explosive use of colour, was the first-ever American art form to capture Europe. Later, 'pop art' became a dominant fashion. Artists such as Andy Warhol tried to relate art to contemporary life, by the free use of everyday objects and images drawn from comics and advertising. These developments helped to make New York the capital of the art world. In the theatre and cinema, the works of Arthur Miller and Tennessee Williams, exploring social tensions, won international acclaim in the post-war years. And successes such as *Oklahoma!* and *West Side Story* injected new vitality into the musical.

The emphasis placed on youth and enterprise in American society, together with the comparative absence of social barriers to advancement, had an immense appeal for the new generation of Europeans rising on the ruins of an old order. Under the spreading influence of American manners, language, clothes and tastes, the young people of the West came closer together in outlook than ever before.

New material expectations were developed by the spread of affluence and the impact of American-style advertising. More and more people came to regard as necessities of life objects which before the war had been thought of as luxuries. To the motor-car, refrigerator, vacuum-cleaner and washing-machine were added the products of a new technology – such as tape-recorders and transistor radios. By the mid-1950's, television was no longer a novelty. And increasing exposure to American television programmes brought the American way of life even closer into Europe's homes. Many of the gadgets which so quickly became part of everyday life were by-products of the giant strides made in new fields of technology during the Second World War.

American dominance in modern technology was spectacularly demonstrated in the 1940's by the creation of the atomic bomb in the Manhattan Project, in which thousands of scientists and engineers were given unlimited backing by the American government. This set the pattern for the technological developments which followed after the war – leading to the conquest of space in the 1960's.

## Problems of the new age

In spite of two devastating world wars, and the disruption caused by the Great Depression of the 1930's – the biggest economic upheaval in history – Western man in the 1970's was, on the whole, more prosperous than ever before. He was also healthier and had a much longer expectation of life, thanks to better living conditions, greatly improved nutrition and the development of such 'wonder drugs' as penicillin. In most Western countries, the new wealth created by technology was widely distributed, as were opportunities for education and advancement. In Europe, material expansion went hand-in-hand with the development of comprehensive social services, and the Welfare State, with all its benefits, was born. But this progress brought its own problems.

POLLUTION – A THREAT TO THE QUALITY OF LIFE

*The developments in technology which have raised man's standard of living have brought with them the menace of pollution, epitomised by these factory chimneys belching* *smoke near Cologne, in Germany. Governments everywhere are today seeking to reconcile the claims of industry with the need to protect the environment*

Pollution of the environment, resulting from the ruthless exploitation of resources by industry and the uncontrolled use of industrial products such as the motor-car, was seen as a long-term threat to human survival. And paradoxically, the affluence and security which men had struggled to achieve did not bring them the satisfaction they had expected. This feeling was especially strong amongst young people, who felt alienated from modern materialistic society, and as a reaction sought to assert their individuality. Much of their protest was expressed through 'pop' music, but more extreme protest was expressed in the wave of student riots which swept many cities in the late 1960's.

The right to vote had become almost universal in the West. But many people were increasingly concerned about their remoteness from the 'decision-makers' in government and industry, and the demand for 'participation' was a popular one. At the same time, from 'Black Power' to 'Women's Lib', minorities clamoured for greater freedom and equality.

Two urgent social problems of the new age are the continuing increase in drug-taking and in crimes of violence – problems sometimes related to each other. In cities such as New York, where extremes of wealth and poverty meet, 'muggings' and other crimes involving violence have become features of daily life.

Violence has also increased in politics. In many parts of the world, extremists resort to the hijacking of aircraft, the murder of statesmen, and indiscriminate bomb attacks in pursuit of political ends. The 'urban guerrilla' has become a grim fact of contemporary life.

## Westernisation of the world

The 20th century has seen the conquest of the world by Western ideas and methods, which were first born in the European Renaissance almost 500 years ago. European values, culture and science were planted throughout the world by missionaries, traders and empire builders. Even though the great empires of the 19th century have vanished, the material legacy they left behind survives. Today the whole globe is Westernised.

Throughout its long history, Western civilization has almost always shown a deeply purposeful character, although the ends to which it has been directed – from the medieval Age of Faith to the modern Age of Democracy – have changed continuously. Its achievements have been immense and they are continuing.

Yet for all his progress, Western man has entered the 1970's in a mood of sombre doubt about what the future holds for him. He has lost much of the faith in the inevitability of progress which he held for centuries. But to a large extent the future lies in his own hands. He is confronted by a stark choice. The atomic mushroom cloud symbolises one road. The other road is that of peaceful co-operation between nations, however difficult, and a willingness to emphasise the interests which the family of man has in common rather than those which divide it.

COMMUNICATIONS THAT HAVE CREATED A GLOBAL CULTURE

The media of mass communication used in journalism, advertising and entertainment have created a world-wide culture which cuts across classes and frontiers. With increased prosperity and more sophisticated tastes, more and more people have come to regard as necessities objects which before the Second World War were thought of as luxuries. Radio, films and records have given rise to a new pattern of entertainment and education, while television, in the 1930's a novelty for the rich, has become an integral part of ordinary life, turning the whole world into 'a global village'

TELLING THE PEOPLE *The coming of radio provided not only a new medium of entertainment, but also a new means for statesmen to address the people. One of the first to do so was Franklin D. Roosevelt, elected president of the USA in 1932. His 'fireside chats' helped to promote the policies of the 'New Deal'*

SCREEN IDOL *The rise of the cinema produced a new type of star whose reputation was based not on live appearances, but on being seen on cinema screens all over the world. Charlie Chaplin's down-trodden tramp, who preserves his humanity through courage and cunning, became a hero for generations of filmgoers. Originally an English music-hall comedian, Chaplin sprang to prominence when he made his first films in Hollywood during the First World War*

TELEVISED HISTORY *Television brought historic events, such as the assassination of US president, John Kennedy, into the home*

ATTRACTING CONSUMERS *New techniques in design, packaging and promotion have greatly increased the persuasive power of advertising in the 20th century. Vast sums of money are spent every year in launching new products. Some, like Coca-Cola, have become symbols of the modern age*

'POP' CULTURE *In the 1960's, many young people turned away from what they saw as the unthinking materialism of contemporary society. Much of their revolt was expressed in 'pop' music, and 'superstars' such as the Beatles (above) became cult heroes*

THE PRINTED WORD *Almost universal literacy in the West and an ever-rising standard of education have encouraged the growth of books, magazines and newspapers catering for varied tastes and interests. Popular newspapers and magazines originated at the turn of the century. With the development of paper-back books, the works of leading novelists and thinkers became available to a wide audience*

| **MESOPOTAMIA** 3500–539 BC | | **3500–2500** Sumerian city-states founded *c.* 2500 Royal cemetery at Ur | **2371–2316** Unity under Sargon of Akkad **2113–200** Sumerian revival |

| **EGYPT** 3200 BC–AD 200 | | **3200** Unity under Menes *c.* 2800 Old Kingdom founded *c.* 2700–2500 Giza pyramids | **2160** Old Kingdom falls 2050–1780 Middle Kingdom |

| **PHOENICIANS AND HEBREWS** 3000 BC–AD 135 | | *c.* 3000–2600 Canaanites settle Syria-Palestine. Byblos founded | *c.* 2400–1800 Rise of Byblos under Amorite princes | *c.* 2000 Hebrews led by Abraham settle in Canaan |

| **MINOANS AND MYCENAEANS** 3000–1100 BC | | *c.* 3000–2500 Minoans, sailors and traders from the east, establish a civilization in Crete |

# Calendar of the great civilizations

## FROM 2500 BC

*As empires created by man rose, flourished and declined, the civilized world gradually spread to embrace almost the entire inhabited land area of the globe*

Few civilizations in mankind's history have existed in total isolation. From earliest times, people of different societies were in contact with one another. Traders travelled by land, river and sea to exchange the surplus products of their own society for those of another, so enriching the quality of life among both peoples. Explorers risked life and limb to satisfy their craving for knowledge of distant countries. Missionaries, in the zeal of their faith, took ideas of gods and creation to distant lands. Warriors conquered alien civilizations in the quest for new lands or for glory.

The chart on these two pages sets the major civilizations of the world in perspective. It shows at a glance when each civilization arose, and the most important milestones in its history; it shows also how, while one civilization was at its height, another people on the other side of the world were just starting their own climb to great achievement. On pages 268–81 a calendar of events traces in more detail the course of each civilization's history; accompanying maps show the steadily increasing extent of the civilized world at certain key dates in history.

### Steps to civilization
True civilization, marked by the development of life in cities, was established by 2500 BC; but men took their first steps towards a civilized way of life much earlier. Modern man, who first appeared about 35,000 BC, had by 10,000 BC peopled almost the entire globe, apart from polar lands and remote islands like New Zealand. Throughout this long period men lived by collecting honey, fruits, nuts, tubers and berries, by hunting wild animals and later by fishing. They were directly dependent on what nature gave them, and until men found ways of altering the lives and yields of the plants and animals they ate, communities could not grow beyond a certain size.

This stage in the journey to civilization, the Old Stone Age, ended in much of Europe, Asia, and North Africa about 8000 BC, after hunters tamed wolves as hunting dogs and villagers in Israel began collecting wild grasses for food. But some communities continued their traditional way of life. And even today, when 20th-century civilization has spread to nearly every corner of the globe, there are isolated peoples

such as Australian Aborigines, Indians of the Amazon Basin and tribes of highland New Guinea who still remain in the Old Stone Age, using stone tools, spears, bows and arrows, and primitive containers made of woven leaves.

### Farmers and smiths
For most of the world, however, an entirely new stage in the advance towards civilization began with the introduction of true farming, when men learnt to herd animals and to cultivate grasses for grain. They still depended on stone tools, but the coming of farming was so important that this stage in man's history has been called the New Stone Age. It began in the fertile crescent of the Middle East about 9000 years ago, and spread to south-east Asia and south-east Europe by 6000 BC. Farming began in central America about 6500 BC and in Peru about 2000 BC: but it did not reach Australasia until Polynesian islanders from the Pacific settled New Zealand about AD 1000.

Another new stage in man's history began before 6400 BC in Turkey and Iran, where men began working copper. By 3000 BC, the Sumerians in Mesopotamia were producing bronze, an alloy of copper and tin. The Bronze Age made possible a whole new range of tools and weapons. Metal blades replaced blunter ones of stone, and objects were made in cast metal. By 1500 BC bronze was widespread from Portugal to China and India; it first appeared in the New World by about 900 BC.

### Into the Iron Age
The latest stage in man's technology, the Iron Age, had its beginnings with the Hittites of Turkey around 1700 BC. Sharper and more durable iron blades for tools and weapons were now possible, and were known throughout the Middle East and Greece by 1200 BC. Iron did not reach the Bronze Age civilizations of the Americas until the first Europeans arrived around AD 1500. Australians, still in the Stone Age, were thrust directly into the Iron Age after the arrival of European colonists in 1788.

Modern technology has taken men to the moon. The questing spirit that made this possible is seeking new materials with which to conquer new worlds. In the 1970's, men may be on the threshold of yet another 'Age'.

| **INDIA** From 2400 BC | | *c.* 2400 Indus Valley civilization founded | *c.* 2000 First Aryan invasions |

| **CHINA** From 1500 BC | |

**HOW TO READ THIS TIME CHART**
On the white bands of this time chart are shown key events in the history of each major civilization. The grey panels indicate a period during which a civilization was becoming established, or declining in importance.

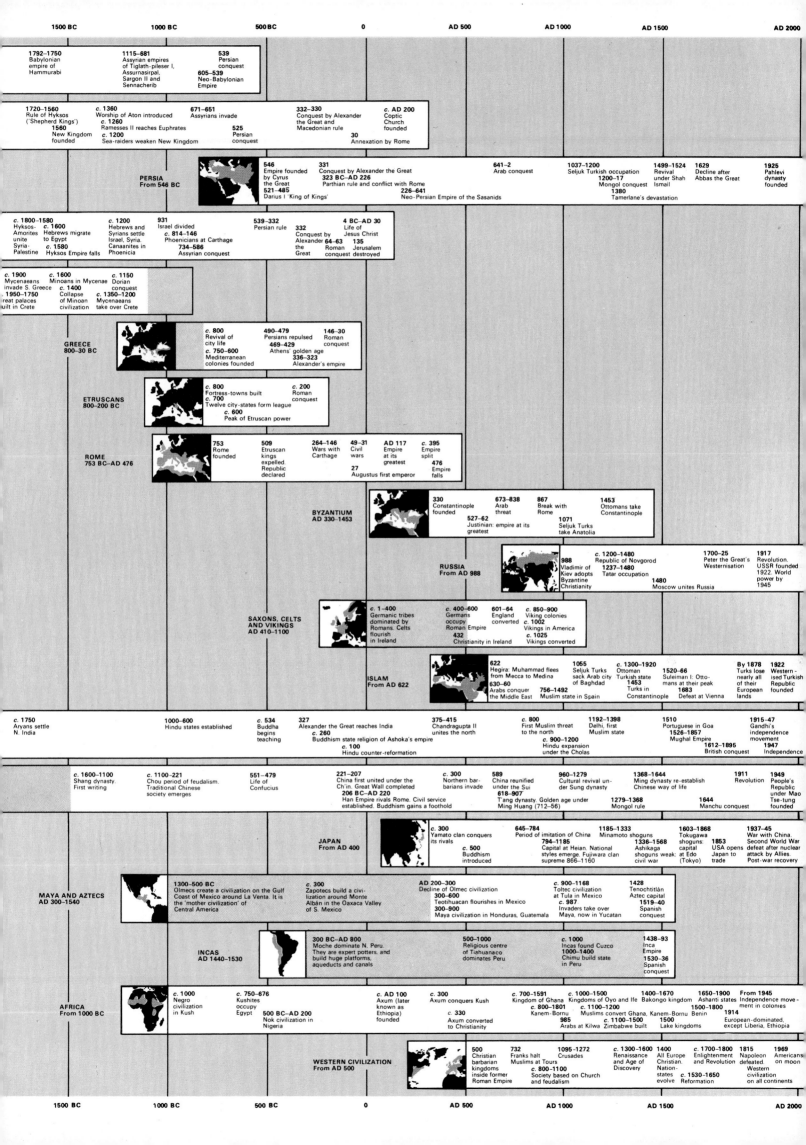

**Timeline: 1500 BC – AD 2000**

Top scale: 1500 BC | 1000 BC | 500 BC | 0 | AD 500 | AD 1000 | AD 1500 | AD 2000

---

**Mesopotamia**

- 1792–1750 Babylonian empire of Hammurabi
- 1115–681 Assyrian empires of Tiglath-pileser I, Assurnasirpal, Sargon II and Sennacherib
- 539 Persian conquest
- 605–539 Neo-Babylonian Empire

**Egypt**

- 1720–1560 Rule of Hyksos ('Shepherd Kings')
- 1560 New Kingdom founded
- c. 1360 Worship of Aton introduced
- c. 1260 Ramesses II reaches Euphrates
- c. 1200 Sea-raiders weaken New Kingdom
- 671–651 Assyrians invade
- 525 Persian conquest
- 332–330 Conquest by Alexander the Great and Macedonian rule
- 30 Annexation by Rome
- c. AD 200 Coptic Church founded

**PERSIA From 546 BC**

- 546 Empire founded by Cyrus the Great
- 521–485 Darius I 'King of Kings'
- 331 Conquest by Alexander the Great
- 323 BC–AD 226 Parthian rule and conflict with Rome
- 226–641 Neo-Persian Empire of the Sasanids
- 641–2 Arab conquest
- 1037–1200 Seljuk Turkish occupation
- 1200–17 Mongol conquest
- 1380 Tamerlane's devastation
- 1499–1524 Revival under Shah Ismail
- 1629 Decline after Abbas the Great
- 1925 Pahlevi dynasty founded

**Israel / Hebrews**

- c. 1800–1580 Hyksos-Amorites unite Syria-Palestine
- c. 1600 Hebrews migrate to Egypt
- c. 1580 Hyksos Empire falls
- c. 1200 Hebrews and Syrians settle Israel, Syria. Canaanites in Phoenicia
- 931 Israel divided
- c. 814–146 Phoenicians at Carthage
- 734–586 Assyrian conquest
- 539–332 Persian rule
- 332 Conquest by Alexander the Great
- 64–63 Roman conquest
- 4 BC–AD 30 Life of Jesus Christ
- 135 Jerusalem destroyed

**Minoans / Mycenaeans**

- c. 1900 Mycenaeans invade S. Greece
- c. 1950–1750 Great palaces built in Crete
- c. 1600 Minoans in Mycenae
- c. 1400 Collapse of Minoan civilization
- c. 1350–1200 Mycenaeans take over Crete
- c. 1150 Dorian conquest

**GREECE 800–30 BC**

- c. 800 Revival of city life
- c. 750–600 Mediterranean colonies founded
- 490–479 Persians repulsed
- 469–429 Athens' golden age
- 336–323 Alexander's empire
- 146–30 Roman conquest

**ETRUSCANS 800–200 BC**

- c. 800 Fortress-towns built
- c. 700 Twelve city-states form league
- c. 600 Peak of Etruscan power
- c. 200 Roman conquest

**ROME 753 BC–AD 476**

- 753 Rome founded
- 509 Etruscan kings expelled. Republic declared.
- 264–146 Wars with Carthage
- 49–31 Civil wars
- 27 Augustus first emperor
- AD 117 Empire at its greatest
- c. 395 Empire split
- 476 Empire falls

**BYZANTIUM AD 330–1453**

- 330 Constantinople founded
- 527–62 Justinian: empire at its greatest
- 673–838 Arab threat
- 867 Break with Rome
- 1071 Seljuk Turks take Anatolia
- 1453 Ottomans take Constantinople

**RUSSIA From AD 988**

- 988 Vladimir of Kiev adopts Byzantine Christianity
- c. 1200–1480 Republic of Novgorod
- 1237–1480 Tatar occupation
- 1480 Moscow unites Russia
- 1700–25 Peter the Great's Westernisation
- 1917 Revolution. USSR founded 1922. World power by 1945

**SAXONS, CELTS AND VIKINGS AD 410–1100**

- c. 1–400 Germanic tribes dominated by Romans. Celts flourish in Ireland
- 432 Christianity in Ireland
- c. 400–600 Germans occupy Roman Empire
- 601–64 England converted
- c. 850–900 Viking colonies
- c. 1002 Vikings in America
- c. 1025 Vikings converted

**ISLAM From AD 622**

- 622 Hegira: Muhammad flees from Mecca to Medina
- 630–60 Arabs conquer the Middle East
- 756–1492 Muslim state in Spain
- 1055 Seljuk Turks sack Arab city of Baghdad
- c. 1300–1920 Ottoman Turkish state
- 1453 Turks in Constantinople
- 1520–66 Suleiman I: Ottomans at their peak
- 1683 Defeat at Vienna
- By 1878 Turks lose nearly all of their European lands
- 1922 Western-ised Turkish Republic founded

**India**

- c. 1750 Aryans settle N. India
- 1000–600 Hindu states established
- c. 534 Buddha begins teaching
- 327 Alexander the Great reaches India
- c. 260 Buddhism state religion of Ashoka's empire
- c. 100 Hindu counter-reformation
- 375–415 Chandragupta II unites the north
- c. 800 First Muslim threat to the north
- c. 900–1200 Hindu expansion under the Cholas
- 1192–1398 Delhi, first Muslim state
- 1510 Portuguese in Goa
- 1526–1857 Mughal Empire
- 1612–1895 British conquest
- 1915–47 Gandhi's independence movement
- 1947 Independence

**China**

- c. 1600–1100 Shang dynasty. First writing
- c. 1100–221 Chou period of feudalism. Traditional Chinese society emerges
- 551–479 Life of Confucius
- 221–207 China first united under the Ch'in. Great Wall completed
- 206 BC–AD 220 Han Empire rivals Rome. Civil service established. Buddhism gains a foothold
- c. 300 Northern barbarians invade
- 589 China reunified under the Sui
- 618–907 T'ang dynasty. Golden age under Ming Huang (712–56)
- 960–1279 Cultural revival under the Sung dynasty
- 1279–1368 Mongol rule
- 1368–1644 Ming dynasty re-establish Chinese way of life
- 1644 Manchu conquest
- 1911 Revolution
- 1949 People's Republic under Mao Tse-tung founded

**JAPAN From AD 400**

- c. 300 Yamato clan conquers its rivals
- c. 500 Buddhism introduced
- 645–784 Period of imitation of China
- 794–1185 Capital at Heian. National styles emerge. Fujiwara clan supreme 866–1160
- 1185–1333 Minamoto shoguns
- 1336–1568 Ashikaga shoguns weak: civil war
- 1603–1868 Tokugawa shoguns: capital at Edo (Tokyo)
- 1853 USA opens Japan to trade
- 1937–45 War with China. Second World War defeat after nuclear attack by Allies. Post-war recovery

**MAYA AND AZTECS AD 300–1540**

- 1300–500 BC Olmecs create a civilization on the Gulf Coast of Mexico around La Venta. It is the 'mother civilization' of Central America
- c. 300 Zapotecs build a civilization around Monte Albán in the Oaxaca Valley of S. Mexico
- AD 200–300 Decline of Olmec civilization
- 300–600 Teotihuacan flourishes in Mexico
- 300–900 Maya civilization in Honduras, Guatemala
- c. 900–1168 Toltec civilization at Tula in Mexico
- c. 987 Invaders take over Maya, now in Yucatan
- 1428 Tenochtitlán Aztec capital
- 1519–40 Spanish conquest

**INCAS AD 1440–1530**

- 300 BC–AD 800 Moche dominate N. Peru. They are expert potters, and build huge platforms, aqueducts and canals
- 500–1000 Religious centre of Tiahuanaco dominates Peru
- c. 1000 Incas found Cuzco
- 1000–1400 Chimu build state in Peru
- 1438–93 Inca Empire
- 1530–36 Spanish conquest

**AFRICA From 1000 BC**

- c. 1000 Negro civilization in Kush
- c. 750–676 Kushites occupy Egypt
- 500 BC–AD 200 Nok civilization in Nigeria
- c. AD 100 Axum (later known as Ethiopia) founded
- c. 300 Axum conquers Kush
- c. 330 Axum converted to Christianity
- c. 700–1591 Kingdom of Ghana
- c. 800–1801 Kanem-Bornu
- 985 Arabs at Kilwa
- c. 1000–1500 Kingdoms of Oyo and Ife
- c. 1100–1200 Muslims convert Ghana, Kanem-Bornu
- c. 1100–1500 Zimbabwe built
- 1400–1670 Bakongo kingdom
- 1500 Lake kingdoms
- 1650–1900 Ashanti states
- 1500–1800 Benin
- 1914 European-dominated, except Liberia, Ethiopia
- From 1945 Independence movement in colonies

**WESTERN CIVILIZATION From AD 500**

- 500 Christian barbarian kingdoms inside former Roman Empire
- 732 Franks halt Muslims at Tours
- c. 800–1100 Society based on Church and feudalism
- 1095–1272 Crusades
- c. 1300–1600 Renaissance and Age of Discovery
- 1400 All Europe Christian. Nation-states evolve
- c. 1530–1650 Reformation
- c. 1700–1800 Enlightenment and Revolution
- 1815 Napoleon defeated. Western civilization on all continents
- 1969 Americans on moon

Bottom scale: 1500 BC | 1000 BC | 500 BC | 0 | AD 500 | AD 1000 | AD 1500 | AD 2000

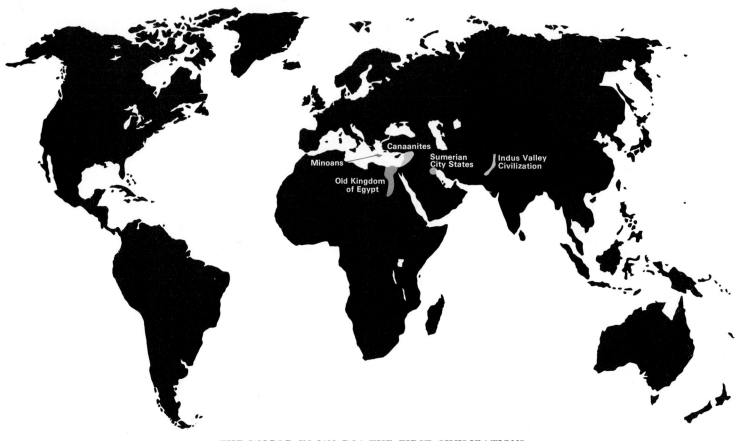

THE WORLD IN 2400 BC: THE FIRST CIVILIZATIONS

The earliest experiments in civilization are over. Cities with literate priests flourish in Sumer beside the Tigris and Euphrates, and in Egypt along the Nile.

The Egyptian cities are united under a god-king or 'pharaoh'. Civilization is beginning in the newly founded cities of the Indus Valley. The Canaanites –

Semites from Arabia – have settled the farmlands of Syria-Palestine and built wealthy cities based on trade with Sumer and Egypt, whose ways they are

copying. Other sailors and traders have sailed westwards to Crete, where they are developing the Minoan version of civilized life.

## 2500-2100

**Mesopotamia** Sumerian cities of clay-brick have stood in the irrigated Tigris and Euphrates valleys since *c.* 3000, each with a temple or ziggurat (temple-tower). Fine jewellery, wheel-made pots and the first wooden-wheeled carts and chariots have been made. Cuneiform writing and the decimal and sexagesimal systems have been invented.

The *Epic of Gilgamesh*, one of the world's oldest poems, is written down. It tells of Gilgamesh, king of one of the first Sumerian cities. Semitic Amorites from Arabia found Akkad, whose ruler Sargon the Great (2371–2316) unites the city-states to control irrigation, and builds the world's first empire.

**Egypt** Cities have stood by the Nile since *c.* 3300. Hieroglyphic writing has been invented. Menes has united Upper and Lower Egypt (*c.* 3200) for irrigation control. Since *c.* 2800 copper has been in use and records have been written on papyrus reed. Vessels of stone have been exported to Syria. The embalmed bodies of pharaohs have been buried in mud-brick mastabas. During the Old Kingdom (*c.* 2780–2300) the Step Pyramid of Zoser at Saqqara, the earliest known building entirely of stone, has been erected by the first application of mathematics to large-scale building.

The 24-hour day and 365-day year are introduced. Medicine advances. Art glorifies a host of gods. Provincial rulers revolt *c.* 2300 and

Semites from the north and Nubians from the south pour in. A prince of Lower Egypt founds the united Middle Kingdom *c.* 2100.

**East Mediterranean** Canaanites, Semitic nomads from Arabia, have taken over the rich farmlands of Syria-Palestine. The ports of Byblos and Ugarit have grown rich through trade with Sumer and Egypt.

From *c.* 2380 Amorites from Arabia infiltrate Syria, Palestine and Mesopotamia.

**Crete** Minoan traders have established a civilization; they use copper tools and make fine jewellery and stone vases.

By *c.* 2200 the Minoans are the first people in Europe to use bronze.

**India** Dravidians build a civilization in the Indus Valley. Wealthy, well-laid out capital cities made of mud-brick, Harappa and Mohenjo Daro, stand beside irrigated land; bullock carts are used. The Dravidians are the first people to grow cotton, which they export to Sumer. They use bronze for tools, statuettes, and cylinder-seals like those of Sumer.

**Europe** Wheeled carts are used, and Somerset peasants build some of Europe's earliest roads. Simple ploughs replace digging sticks. From the Shetland Isles to Malta, peasants build great stone (megalithic) tombs covered by earth-mounds (barrows). Wealthy copper-users build Europe's first forts and, in Malta, Europe's first stone temples.

## 2100-1700

**Mesopotamia** The Sumerians throw off Akkadian rule and rebuild their cities (2113–2006). Civilization revives until Elamites from Persia and Amorites from Arabia conquer Sumer. The Amorites found Mari, where *c.* 1900–1760 a library is amassed of 20,000 cuneiform tablets in Sumerian and Akkadian, now the international language of the Middle East. Amorites found Babylon *c.* 2100 and Assur *c.* 2000. Hammurabi, King of Babylon 1792–1750, imposes a great law code, based on earlier Mesopotamian laws. By 1760 he conquers all Mesopotamia but Assyria.

**Egypt** A new dynasty is founded at Thebes in 2050, and Middle Kingdom civilization begins. City life returns, and pyramids of mud-brick are built. By *c.* 1720 Hyksos warriors from Palestine, the 'Shepherd Kings', conquer most of Egypt. They introduce bronze weapons and tools, an improved bow and light horse-chariots.

**East Mediterranean** Amorites settle as peasants in Syria and Palestine (Canaan) *c.* 2000. The Hebrews, led by Abraham, leave Mesopotamia and settle in Canaan, the land covenanted to Abraham by his sole God. Amorite princes annex wealthy Byblos and Ugarit *c.* 1900. Byblos exports cedar as far as Crete, and fine jewellery all over the Middle East. Aryan Hyksos warriors sweep in from the north and introduce horse-chariots, bronze weapons and feudalism. By *c.* 1750 Amorite-

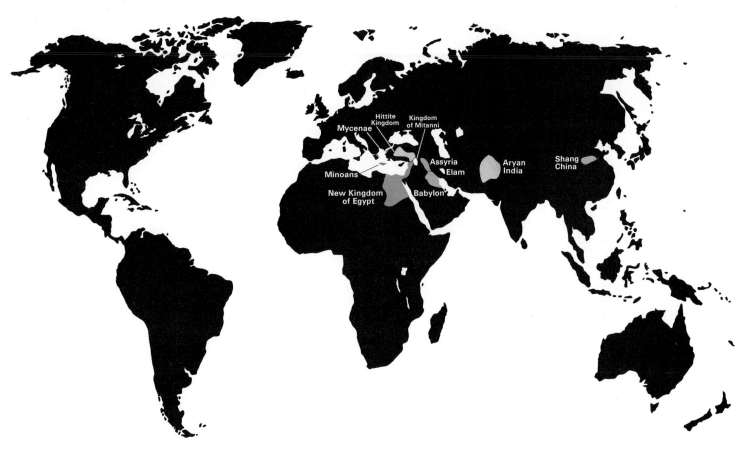

THE WORLD IN 1500 BC: ARYAN WARRIORS ON THE MOVE

Since *c.* 2000 waves of Aryan warriors have gushed from the Caucasian steppes. They have conquered the Indus Valley and set up the kingdoms of the Hittites and of Mitanni; by 1000 BC they will found five more kingdoms in the Middle East. Greek-speakers have built Mycenaean civilization. Descendants of other Aryans, the Hyksos, have ruled Egypt (*c.* 1710–1580) and inspired Egyptian military ambitions. Semites have founded Babylon and Assyria; Babylon has achieved greatness under Hammurabi. In the Yellow River Valley of China, farmers are creating a civilization.

## *1700–1300*

Hyksos princes unite Syria-Palestine for the first time. In *c.* 1900, Aryans with superior bronze weapons impose an aristocracy on the peasant-farmers of Anatolia, and set up the Hittite city-states.

**The Aegean** The Minoan golden age begins *c.* 1950. Great palaces are built at Knossos, Phaistos and Mallia, with piped water schemes. Around the palaces grow Europe's first cities, which are undefended. Accounts are kept in hieroglyphic script. The palaces are destroyed *c.* 1750, probably by earthquakes. About 1900, Mycenaeans, Greek-speaking warriors from the north, take over the farmers of S. Greece and build great stone fortresses.

**India** In *c.* 2000 the first wave of Aryan warriors from Persia arrives, and by 1750 the Indus Valley cities are abandoned. The Aryans impose a caste system with Aryan priests (Brahmins) and nobles at the top, and dark-skinned Dravidians as their serfs. The Aryans adopt Dravidian gods, and settle in villages as farmers and herders. Brahmins tell the earliest Hindu scriptures, the Vedas (hymns and epics).

**China** Millet-farmers in the Yellow River Valley keep silk-worms, place carved jade objects for the use of the dead in graves, worship their ancestors and divine the future from 'oracle-bones' by 2000.

**Peru** Farmers domesticate the alpaca for its wool, grow cotton, and begin to weave.

**Mesopotamia** Babylonians and Assyrians collect Sumerian literature on science, which later passes to the Greeks. The week of seven days and a 28-day month are introduced.

**Egypt** Theban princes expel the Hyksos, and Ahmose founds the New Kingdom in 1560. Karnak is founded as a religious centre with temples of stone, and in the nearby Valley of the Tombs of the Kings, pharaohs are buried in rock-cut tombs. Amenophis I begins the age of imperialism, and Tuthmosis I (1528–1510) reaches the Euphrates and the Sudan. A large, complex bureaucracy keeps records of taxes paid in kind. Trade flourishes. Amenophis IV (*c.* 1367–1350) takes the name Akhenaton, and with his wife Nefertiti introduces worship of a single god, the Sun (Aton), at El-Amarna, his new capital. Theban priests force Akhenaton's son-in-law, Tutankhamun (1347–1339), to reinstate the old gods.

**East Mediterranean** The Hebrews migrate from Canaan to Egypt *c.* 1600 during a famine. By 1550 they are captives of the pharaohs, but survive as a nation, united by their faith. Labarnas I unites the Hittite city-states *c.* 1680 and Hattusilis I founds the capital of Hattusas *c.* 1650. The Hurrians of Mitanni bring down the Hyksos Empire and Telepinus (1525–1500) founds the Hittite Empire. The Hittites dominate the Middle East and are the first people to use iron on a large scale.

**The Aegean** The Minoan palaces are rebuilt *c.* 1700–1570, with fine frescoes. A script with characters written in straight lines, Linear A, is developed. Minoan traders reach Mycenae *c.* 1600, where the great fortress-palace is built *c.* 1570–1500. Minoan and Mycenaean influences blend to produce exquisite gold-work at Mycenae. The labyrinth-like palace at Knossos is built *c.* 1500, and by 1400 the city of Knossos, with its nearby harbour town, is the largest European city. Another script, Linear B, is used for palace records at Knossos and Mycenae. In *c.* 1400 the island of Thera (Santorini) erupts and Minoan civilization collapses. Mycenaeans take over Minoan trade and colonies.

**China** Towns develop in the Yellow River Valley, and *c.* 1600 they are united by the Shang dynasty of Anyang. Craftsmen produce fine bronze vessels in which the king and lords offer libations to the spirits of their ancestors. A picture-script, which already contains elements that indicate pronunciation, is inscribed on bronzes, oracle-bones, bamboo and silk.

**Europe** Priests order the erection (*c.* 2000–1500) of standing stones at Carnac and at Stonehenge, for use in rituals or as observatories. Silbury Hill (Wiltshire), the largest man-made mound in Europe, is built and, soon after, the stone circles and temple at Avebury, probably as a tribal meeting place. By 1500 bronze is used throughout Europe.

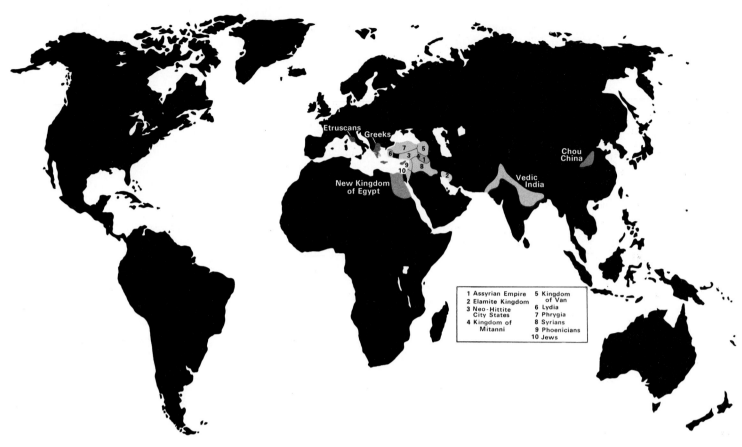

**THE WORLD IN 1000 BC: A NEW WORLD IN THE MEDITERRANEAN**

West Mediterranean raiders, the Sea Peoples, rampaging eastwards since *c.* 1200, have brought down the Hittite Empire, devastated Syria-Palestine and weakened Egypt. In their wake, the Assyrians have built an empire, and Aramaeans from Arabia and Hittite survivors have established city-states in Syria. The Canaanites have been pushed into Phoenicia; the Hebrews have entered Canaan and their golden age. The kingdoms of Mitanni, Van, Lydia and Phrygia have grown to power. The Dorians have swept away Mycenaean civilization, heir of Crete, and Greece enters its Dark Ages.

## 1300–900

**Mesopotamia** The Assyrians, with their superior iron weapons and strong leaders, throw off Babylonian rule. Tiglath-pileser I (1115–1077) takes Babylon and by 1100 rules from the Mediterranean to Lake Van. But the empire declines after 1000.

**Egypt** The empire of Ramesses II (*d.* 1237) extends from Syria into Nubia. Ramesses defeats the Hittites at Kadesh on the Orontes, and completes the temples at Abu Simbel and Karnak. Ramesses III (*d.* 1151) repels invading Libyans and raiding Sea Peoples, but by 1085 the empire collapses.

**Persia** Aryans from the Caucasus establish, *c.* 1000, the rival kingdoms of the Medes and of Parsa beside the Elamites.

**East Mediterranean** Canaanite civilization reaches its height in wealthy Byblos, where the alphabet is used and papyrus replaces clay tablets for writing. Invading Sea Peoples and Phrygians topple the Hittite Empire and push the Canaanites into Phoenicia, *c.* 1200–1180. The sea-going Canaanite-Phoenicians found colonies and take over Mycenaean trade. Aramaeans and Hittite survivors establish city-states in Syria, which Damascus, with its trade, comes to dominate. The Hebrews, led from slavery in Egypt by Moses, settle Canaan and establish the kingdom of Israel under Saul, then David. Under Solomon the Temple at Jerusalem is built and the Jewish scriptures are begun. In 931 oppressive rule by Solomon's son, Rehoboam, leads to division of the kingdom into Israel, under Jeroboam, and Judah.

**Greece and the Aegean** Mycenaean trade is disrupted by the Sea Peoples *c.* 1200, and Mycenaean civilization declines. The Trojan War (1194–1184) is fought over Troy's hold on the Hellespont. Aryan Dorians from the north, with iron weapons, destroy Mycenaean fortress-cities. During the Dark Ages (*c.* 1100–700) Mycenaean refugees found Ionian colonies in the Aegean and Asia Minor, and preserve the tales which Homer writes down.

**Italy** The Latins from central Europe settle on the Tiber, on the site of present-day Rome, *c.* 1000. They later build a bridge and foster trade between the newly founded Etruscan cities and the Greek cities to the south.

**China** The Chou dynasty of the Wei Valley overthrow the Shang *c.* 1100. A brilliant flowering of philosophy produces many theories, the 'hundred schools'.

**Mexico** The Olmecs create a civilization in the highlands of the Gulf coast. They build the religious ceremonial centre of La Venta.

**Africa** Negroes build the civilization of Kush in Nubia, around Napata on the Nile, where Egyptian-inspired pyramids are built.

**North Europe** By 1000 bronze weapons are common, and constant warfare leads to hilltop farming communities and forts.

## 900–500

**Mesopotamia** The Assyrian Empire revives under Assurnasirpal II (883–859) and Sargon II, and under Sennacherib, who makes Nineveh his capital. Nebuchadnezzar II (605–562) builds a new Babylonian Empire which includes Assyria. The 'Hanging Gardens' are built at Babylon, which the Persians take in 539.

**Egypt** A dynasty at Sais unites Egypt (663) after Kushite and Assyrian occupations. Culture, Greek contacts and trade revive. But Egypt falls to Persia in 525.

**Persia** After Assyrian rule (705–625) and a Median Empire (625–559), Cyrus of Parsa creates the dual nation of Medes and Persians. He founds the Achaemenid Empire and is a tolerant law-giver. Zoroaster (628–551) teaches salvation by faith in one God of Light, who triumphs over evil. Darius the Great (521–485) extends the empire, creates 20 satrapies (administrative provinces) and four capital cities. He becomes 'King of kings'.

**East Mediterranean** Assyrians take Damascus in 734. In the Jewish kingdoms, Israel and Judah, the age of prophets opens with Elijah. Israel falls to Sargon II (722). Judah resists until Nebuchadnezzar of Babylon takes Jerusalem in 586. The Phoenicians prosper and found colonies such as Carthage, until Tyre falls to Nebuchadnezzar. Under Cyrus the Great, Syria-Palestine revives within the Persian Empire. Jewish exiles return home from

## THE WORLD IN 500 BC: THE FIRST CIVILIZATIONS IN TROPICAL AFRICA AND THE AMERICAS

Inspired by their Egyptian neighbours, Negroes have since 1000 built the civilization of Kush. By 500, the Olmecs have established in Mexico the mother civilization of Central America. The Aryans have consolidated Hindu society all over N. India and in Ceylon. Cyrus the Great of Persia has founded an empire, the greatest the world has yet known. But even greater empires are germinating. The Greeks have built city-states where a golden age is beginning, while in Italy the Etruscans are flourishing and to the south of them the Romans, their successors, have just declared their republic.

## 500–100

Babylon and complete a new Temple in 516.
**Greece** Cities revive after 800. Each city-state clusters round a fortress, or acropolis. Pottery, sculpture, lyric poetry, astronomy and philosophy develop, and colonies are founded throughout the Mediterranean. Nearby Lydia issues the first coinage in the West, c. 700. Militarist Sparta, and Athens where Solon's reforms (c. 594) establish democracy, emerge as the major powers. Ionians in Asia Minor surrender to Persia in 546.
**Italy** Twelve Etruscan cities attain great wealth and sea power by 600. The arts, including music, flourish, and fine temples and stone tombs are built. In 509 Rome expels its Etruscan 'kings' and sets up a republic.
**India** Hindu society is established as Aryan chiefs found dynasties and towns. The Vedas, Hindu hymns, are written down; but priests and their ritual arouse hostility and the Jains try to abolish both. Buddha (c. 560–480) teaches salvation by moral conduct alone, based on the Eightfold Path which leads to the elimination of desire, the cause of suffering.
**Africa** Napatans learn to work iron. Wood for smelting grows scarce, and Meroe is founded c. 600 near forests and iron deposits.
**North Europe** Farmers live in timber houses and use scratch ploughs in enclosed fields. Iron weapons appear in central Europe c. 700, and spread with the Celts from the Rhineland.

**Egypt** Alexander the Great conquers Egypt in 332. Ptolemy, his general, founds a dynasty.
**Persia** The empire falls to Alexander the Great (331). During wars between his successors, Seleucus conquers Syria and Babylonia. Arsaces of Parthia (248–212) founds an empire which by 138 includes Seleucia and Persia.
**East Mediterranean** The Jews, led by Nehemiah and Ezra, and the Phoenicians flourish under Persia. But Alexander the Great conquers Syria-Palestine in 332. Carthage takes over Phoenicians' Mediterranean dominance.
**Greece** After Persian invasions (490–479) Athens is rebuilt. The Parthenon, with sculpture by Pheidias, adorns the Acropolis. Pericles (c. 490–429), leader of the Athenian democratic party, starts a golden age, with dramatists Aeschylus, Sophocles and Euripides, historian Herodotus, and philosophers Socrates, Plato and Aristotle. Science flourishes in the Greek world under Hippocrates, Archimedes and Hero of Alexandria. In the Peloponnesian War (432–404) Sparta defeats Athens, but its rule is ineffective. Philip of Macedon (382–356) unites Greece, and his son Alexander builds an empire which reaches India. During the following Hellenistic Age, Greek culture pervades the Middle East. Alexandria is a centre of learning. By 300 the three-field crop rotation is used.
**Italy** Romans end Etruscan power to become by 300 the masters of all Italy. Three Punic

Wars (264–146) end with the razing of Carthage. Rome annexes Greece in 146.
**India** Chandragupta Maurya unites N. and central India after the retreat of Alexander the Great in 332. Ashoka builds a greater empire c. 261. He becomes a Buddhist and sends missionaries to the Hellenistic lands and to Ceylon. After his death Hinduism revives.
**China** Confucius (551–479) and Mencius (390–305) advocate a moral code to maintain order, humane government and promotion by merit. But the Taoists seek peace of mind by withdrawal from society. Feudal states gain independence and 403–221 is a period of 'Warring States'. The Ch'in of the Wei Valley reunite China c. 220 and reject the Confucian code. Shih Huang Ti joins up the Great Wall. In 206 the Han family seizes power, restores Confucianism and institutes civil service examinations based on Confucian classics.
**Mexico** Zapotec tribes build a civilization in the Oaxaca valley, around Monte Alban c. 300.
**Africa** The Negro kingdom of Nok flourishes, producing fine terracotta sculptures. Negroes from the Nile and Niger, with knowledge of iron working, cattle rearing and the Bantu language, expand south-eastwards.
**North Europe** Celts settle from Italy to Ireland, and trade iron goods with the Germanic tribes to the north. The Celts are head-hunters, fond of feasting and music, and fine craftsmen.

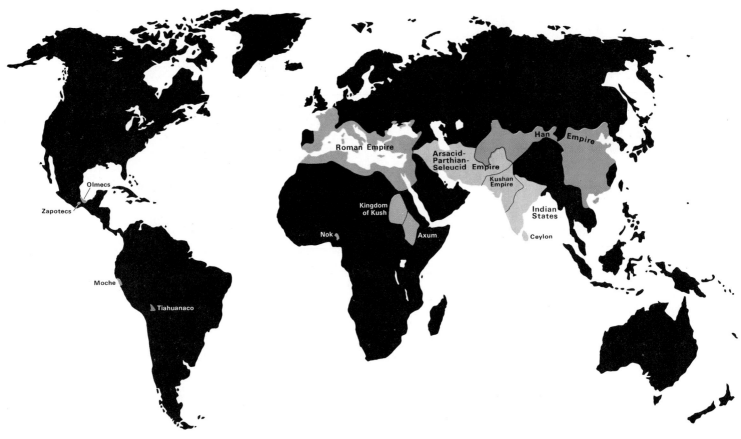

THE WORLD IN 25 BC: THE DAWN OF THE GREAT ROMAN PEACE

The vast territories of Rome and China dominate the map. Rome is ruled by its first emperor, Augustus, and China flourishes under the Han dynasty. Alexander the Great's empire has come and gone. After his death his generals fought for its territories among themselves; now the western lands belong to Rome, and the eastern lands are part of the powerful Parthian and Kushan Empires. In Africa the Greek-speaking empire of Axum is emerging. The Olmec and Zapotec civilizations are flourishing in Mexico, and S. America's first ordered society has been established by Moche warriors.

## 100 BC — AD 100

**Egypt** Queen Cleopatra (69–30 BC) attempts to manipulate the Romans by becoming the mistress of Julius Caesar, then the mistress of Mark Antony. But she and Antony are crushingly defeated by Octavian in a sea battle off Actium (W. Greece) in 31 BC, and Egypt is absorbed into the Roman Empire.

**Rome** Republican government declines. Rome expands as Pompey annexes Syria-Palestine in 64 and Julius Caesar conquers Gaul in 58. He visits England in 55 and 54. In 49 Caesar, one of three joint rulers, tries to seize supreme power. He is assassinated in 44, and the republic falls in 31 BC. Octavian becomes the first Roman Emperor as Augustus. A golden age of literature, with the poets Virgil and Horace and the historian Livy, follows. Augustus reorganises the army and civil service. The ensuing peace lasts for 200 years, despite the unbalanced emperors Caligula, Claudius and Nero.

In the Jewish province of Judaea, Jesus of Nazareth is executed in AD 30, and Christianity gains a foothold in the empire despite persecution. A revolt is savagely crushed in 70, when the Temple is destroyed and Jews flee Palestine – the prelude to the great Diaspora.

**Persia** The Parthian Empire reaches the height of its power in the 1st century BC when it threatens Roman provinces in Syria and Asia Minor. But after *c.* 30 BC decline sets in.

**India** Scythians, Parthians, Afghans and Kushans invade the north. The Kushan Empire prospers under Kaniska (AD 78–96), a Buddhist convert. The first representations of Buddha in human form are made in Greek style by the Gandhara school in 100 BC–AD 50.

**China** The Han dynasty expands the empire and encourages arts and science. The first maps are drawn and the first history of China written. Fine naturalistic sculpture and pottery are produced. Buddhism arrives from central Asia and India *c.* AD 10. When the Han dynasty is restored in AD 22 after 100 years of unrest, the capital is moved to Loyang. The silk route to Rome is opened in AD 74–94. Woven cloth is sold for its own weight in gold. In exchange the Chinese import glass and wool.

**Africa** The Greek-speaking empire of Axum emerges in N. Ethiopia.

**Americas** In Mexico, Tres Zapotes supersedes La Venta *c.* 31 BC as the main centre of the Olmecs, who devise an accurate system of recording time. The Zapotecs at Monte Alban produce fine jewellery with elaborate religious symbolism connected with their worship of the rain god and their cult of the dead. The great urban centre of Teotihuacan in the Valley of Mexico is founded. The Maya build a civilization in the highlands of Guatemala and Honduras. An embryo civilization emerges in S. America: Moche warriors establish a highly organised society on the north coast of Peru.

## 100 — 300

**Rome** The 2nd century AD is a settled and prosperous period, and under the emperors Trajan and Hadrian the empire reaches its greatest extent. A high value is placed on Roman citizenship, and trade flourishes. Antoninus Pius and Marcus Aurelius introduce discipline and order. Aurelius (161–80) is a Stoic – the follower of a rational philosophy with a strict moral code which has a tremendous hold over the Roman world in the 1st and 2nd centuries AD, inspiring the great Roman lawmakers. But more popular appeal lies in the more mystical religions that have sprung up in outposts of the empire – the cults of Cybele, Mithras and Isis, and Christianity, which is illegal and constantly persecuted. The eastern part of the empire builds on its Greek culture – Galen of Pergamum (130–200) writes his treatise, which is to dominate medicine in Europe until the Renaissance, and Ptolemy of Alexandria (85–165) publishes his astronomical theories. Diocletian accords the eastern half of the empire separate administration in 284.

**Persia** The Parthian Empire finally breaks up. In 226 the Sasanids come to power and establish a magnificent capital at Ctesiphon, where art and literature flourish and the ancient religion of Zoroastrianism is revived.

**India** A satrapy (province) founded *c.* 120 at Ujain in N.W. India becomes a centre for Sanskrit learning, and the six schools of Hindu

THE WORLD IN AD 400: BARBARIAN HORDES SWEEP ACROSS THE OLD WORLD

The hard-pressed western Roman Empire is under attack from the barbarian hordes now beginning to sweep across Europe, ravaging as far afield as the Balkans, Italy and Britain. But Christianity is well established – it has become the state religion of the prosperous eastern (Byzantine) empire. The Sasanid Empire has grown in strength until it rivals Rome. In India, reunited by the Guptas, Hindu culture is flourishing. In America, Mexico's golden age is dominated by the ritual centre of Teotihuacan. The Maya are expanding into Yucatan from their highland homeland to the south.

## 300–500

philosophy are formulated. Buddhism divides into two sects, the Lesser Vehicle (Hinayana Buddhism) which adheres to the original simplicity of the faith; and the Greater Vehicle (Mahayana Buddhism), a less pessimistic cult, closer to Hinduism. The Mathura school of sculpture imitates the Gandhara work of the Kushan Empire which collapsed *c.* AD 98.

**China** Paper, made from vegetable fibres, is invented, and the dawn of printing occurs when in 175 ink-rubbings are taken of Confucian texts carved on stone tablets. The manufacture of porcelain begins. The Han dynasty collapses in 220 and the ensuing political insecurity contributes to the revival of Taoism, whose followers withdraw from society and claim oneness with nature.

**Japan** Tribal structure is consolidated and the animistic religion, Shintoism, becomes more defined. The Yamato clan gradually establishes supremacy over its neighbours. Iron is developed and rice grown.

**Americas** The Olmecs at La Venta sculpture huge and mysterious heads of basalt, and the Zapotecs at Monte Alban build their capital city on a rocky promontory. At Teotihuacan, the largest ceremonial site in Mexico, huge pyramid temples are built. The Maya develop hieroglyphic writing and a complex calendar. In Peru the Moche build platforms of sun-dried clay, and aqueducts.

**Rome** Although administered as separate halves, the empire proves too large to defend. Waves of nomads sweep in from eastern Europe. Visigoths raid the Balkans and Italy, sack Rome in 410 and set up kingdoms in S. France and Spain; Ostrogoths ravage Italy; Vandals establish a kingdom in N. Africa; Rhineland Franks enter Gaul. The last western emperor is deposed in 476: the Roman Empire in the west is ended and the Dark Ages begin. But the barbarians adopt Roman law, language and Christianity. The Visigoths are converted *c.* 360 and the Frankish king in 496. The Latin Fathers of the Church are writing: Jerome (340–420) in the east and, in the west, Ambrose (340–97) and Augustine of Hippo (354–430), the founder of Western theology.

**Northern Europe** Angles and Saxons settle England after the Romans withdraw in 407. The Romano-Celtic peoples are pushed into Cornwall, Cumberland and Wales, and St Palladius and St Patrick take Christianity to Celtic Ireland *c.* 400. Tribes north of the Rhine and in Scandinavia begin to trade with the new barbarian kingdoms to the south.

**Byzantium** Constantine reunites the eastern and western Roman Empires in 324. He founds a sumptuous new capital at Constantinople, which becomes the pivot of Old World trade. The first Church council to formulate Christian dogma is held at Nicaea in 325. In 380 Theo-

dosius makes Christianity the state religion. Goths constantly attack the empire.

**Persia** The Sasanid Empire rivals Rome. Zoroastrians become more fervent. In the 6th century they persecute Christians, and produce their major scripture.

**India** The Guptas, Hindu rulers, unite the north. They encourage Sanskrit scholarship and Vedantic philosophy. Buddhist learning also flourishes, in richly endowed monasteries, and the Ajanta cave-temples are adorned with fine paintings and sculpture. Under Chandragupta II (375–415) there is peace and a single law-code in most of India. But by 465, barbarian Huns from the north-west destroy the empire.

**China** Invading barbarians introduce Western influences and educated Chinese flee south.

**Japan** The Yamato clan campaigns in Korea. Rulers begin to absorb Chinese language and culture, and develop a myth of the dynasty's divine origin to ensure their authority.

**Africa** Axum expands and conquers Kush. Axum's ruling classes are converted to Christianity by Byzantine missionaries *c.* 330.

**Americas** Mexico enters its golden age at Teotihuacan; literacy is widespread, although the people still use Stone Age tools. The Maya, who live in rural communities based on maize, which they worship, expand into Yucatan. In Peru, the Moche produce fine ceramics decorated with scenes from everyday life.

273

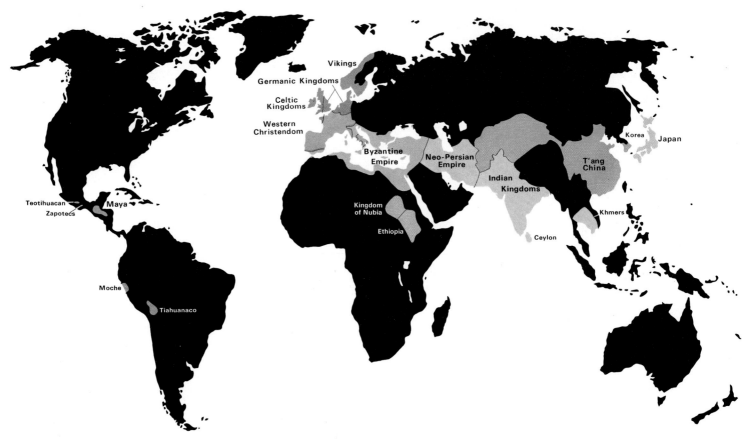

## THE WORLD IN 610 : ON THE EVE OF THE ARAB ERUPTION

The barbarians, heirs of the Roman Empire in the west, are successfully resisting further invasions from central Asia. But in Arabia a faith is founded which is soon to become a major world force: in the name of Islam the converts of the prophet Muhammad sweep out of Arabia and conquer the Middle East and N. Africa. Islam soon threatens Europe, too, until the Franks save western Europe for Christianity in 732. In India, Hinduism revives, and the north is briefly united by Harsha. China, too, is united by the brilliant T'ang dynasty, and Chinese civilization is being copied in Japan.

## *500–700*

**Western Europe** Barbarian kingdoms flourish throughout most of the former Roman Empire. The barbarians, however, soon accept Christianity; the Church, under the pope, provides the new rulers with civil servants, and its organisation and law give Europe a measure of unity. In 529, Benedict of Nursia draws up his 'rule' for monastic life, and Benedictine monasteries provide hospitals, schools, inns and economic centres. Pope Gregory the Great (590–604) sends missions to England, Spain and France. St Augustine becomes the first Archbishop of Canterbury (601) after converting the Saxon King of Kent.

**Northern Europe** Wealthy warrior-farmers are settled throughout Scandinavia. Saxons conquer Romano-Celtic England, while Celts flourish in Brittany, Cornwall, Wales and Ireland. The Scots of Ireland, settled in Scotland since the 5th century, are converted to Celtic Christianity, with the Picts, by St Columba *c.* 570. St Aidan takes Christianity from Scotland to Saxon Northumbria *c.* 635.

**Byzantium** Justinian (527–65) reconquers much of the former western Roman Empire and rebuilds Constantinople, including St Sophia. But the soldier-emperor Heraclius (610–41) fails to stem the Arab threat, and Africa, Spain and N. Italy are lost.

**Islam** Muhammad, born in 570, founds Islam; after his death (632) his teachings are collected into the Koran. The Arabs erupt from Arabia, and by 661 their empire reaches from Gabes in N. Africa to the borders of India.

**Persia** The Sasanid Empire reaches its greatest extent under Chosroes II (589–628), but in 641 it falls to the Arabs, who absorb Sasanid institutions and culture. Islam becomes the state religion, and Arabic is adopted, but Persian literature and arts still flourish.

**India** Huns destroy the flourishing Gupta towns. Hinduism revives, absorbing Buddhism, and Hindu priests gain political and economic power. The Tantric sect of Hinduism, which emphasises magical rituals, develops in N.E. India. Harsha briefly unites the north (606–47). A Hindu civilization is established by the Khmer people of Cambodia.

**China** The T'ang dynasty unites the country (618), and one of the greatest periods of Chinese history begins: trade grows, prosperity returns and the arts and scholarship flourish. Changan, the capital, is the largest city in the world with over a million people.

**Japan** Buddhism reaches Japan from Korea. Japanese imitation of Chinese culture extends to the use of Chinese in official documents.

**Mexico** The city of Teotihuacan in Mexico, with more than 100,000 people, flourishes until *c.* 600. The Maya devise a calendar, calculating the solar year more accurately than Europeans of the time.

## *700–900*

**Western Europe** Viking raids cause havoc throughout the Atlantic coastlands, but in Northumbria scholarship flourishes under the historian Bede and the *Lindisfarne Gospels* are produced (*c.* 700). The Franks under Charles Martel halt the Moorish invasion of Europe at Tours (732) and adopt feudalism. Charlemagne is crowned King of the Franks (768), and Holy Roman Emperor (800). His empire includes most of western Europe, but after his death it soon breaks up. Alfred the Great, Saxon King of Wessex (871–99), unites S. England.

**Northern Europe** The Vikings, with their sturdy ships, colonise Iceland, northern Scotland, Orkney and Shetland, and settle in N.E. England. In Scandinavia, towns grow from fortified markets into centres producing cloth and jewellery. The golden age of Celtic Ireland is ended *c.* 900 by Viking raids.

**Byzantium** Religious controversy divides the empire when Leo III bans icons in 726; their use is restored in 843. In 867 Basil I founds a new dynasty and revives Byzantine power.

**Russia** Slav tribes are united under Viking merchant-princes, and by 850 the first Russian states are founded at Kiev and Novgorod.

**Islam** The Arab Empire reaches its greatest extent in the 750's, and in 762 the Abbasids found a capital at Baghdad, where Mamun the Great (813–33) establishes the House of Wisdom. But from mid-9th century Abbasid

THE WORLD IN 800: A 'GOLDEN AGE' FOR SIX CIVILIZATIONS

The energy of the Arabs produces a brilliant civilization centred on Baghdad, a trading centre and 'clearing house' for knowledge. China, too, enjoys a period of growing trade, prosperity, and achievement in the arts and sciences. Hindu civilization has expanded into 'Greater India'. In western Europe, Charlemagne is crowned Holy Roman Emperor, and his authority encourages a revival in trade and learning. This is soon to be threatened by the Vikings, now at their height, who are also colonising Russia. In the central American highlands, Maya civilization is at its peak.

# 900–1100

caliphs become puppets of the Seljuk Turks.
**India** From the 8th century onwards, Islamic invaders threaten northern India. But in the south the Chola dynasty survives and takes Hinduism to Burma and N. Sumatra.
**China** Under the T'ang emperors Chinese landscape painting begins, and calligraphy develops. Buddhist monks print the first books, and Li Po (701–62) opens the golden age of lyric verse. After 755 the empire breaks up.
**Japan** Nara, a new capital on the Chinese model, is built c. 710. Society is divided, like that in China, between the peasants and the powerful aristocrats; the aristocrats are supported by ritualistic Buddhist priests. The Chinese system of civil service examinations is introduced. Japanese is written for the first time, in an adaptation of the Chinese script.
**Mexico** About 750 the Toltecs create an empire in the Valley of Mexico. The highlands of Guatemala and Honduras settled by the Maya become depopulated in the 9th century.
**Peru** About 800 the culture of Tiahuanaco spreads widely; its dominant art motif is the Creator Lord, later worshipped by the Incas.
**Africa** The Kingdom of Ghana is founded in the 8th century, its wealth based on trans-Saharan trade. Prosperous Hausa city-states such as Kano produce fine leather goods, and the empire of Kanem-Bornu is founded. Muslims set up trading ports on the Indian Ocean.

**Western Europe** Unity is maintained by feudalism and the Church, and the population is kept static by plagues and famines. Otto I of Germany revives the Holy Roman Empire when he is crowned in 962. But fears of strife between pope and emperor begin when Gregory VII (1073–85) tries to prevent rulers from appointing bishops. Pope Urban II initiates the Crusades in 1095, and the Crusaders capture Jerusalem in 1099.
**Northern Europe** Viking expansion continues. Greenland is discovered and colonised (c. 982), and Leif Ericson discovers America c. 1002. A Celtic revival begins in Ireland after Brian Boru defeats the Vikings at Clontarf (1020).
**Byzantium** The empire's revival continues under Basil II (976–1025). But pursuit of military success overstrains the economy; in 1071 Anatolia falls to the Seljuk Turks, and S. Italy and Sicily fall to the Normans.
**Russia** Vladimir I of Kiev is converted to Byzantine Christianity in 988. The Cyrillic alphabet is adopted when books are translated into Russian, a newly evolved language based on Slav. In Novgorod, independent since 997, St Sophia is completed in 1052. It sets the style of Russian church architecture.
**Islam** Egypt, conquered by the Fatimids in 969, becomes the bastion of eastern Islam against the Seljuk Turks and foreign mercenaries. In 1055 the Seljuks capture Baghdad.

**India** Tantric Hinduism, with its emphasis on female deities, leads to exquisite erotic sculpture. Angkor Thom becomes the permanent Khmer capital c. 1000. Burma is united c. 1050 under the kingdom of Pagan, where Buddhism supersedes Hinduism.
**China** The Sung dynasty, established in 960, unifies the country, and buys peace by paying tribute to the northern barbarians. Printing increases the spread of learning. Kaifeng, the capital, is a manufacturing centre for textiles and porcelain. Its iron and steel industries are not surpassed until the Industrial Revolution in the West 700 years later.
**Japan** The emperor is deprived of power by the Fujiwaras, and the rift between rich and poor widens. Buddhism absorbs Shintoism.
**Mexico** Maya civilization revives in the lowlands of the north Yucatan peninsula. Invaders introduce human sacrifice and the cults of the feathered serpent and jaguar. The Toltecs learn metal-smelting c. 950.
**Peru** Incas, warrior tribes living in caves in the highlands of S. Peru, found their capital of Cuzco c. 1000.
**Africa** By the 10th century the kingdom of Ghana reaches from the Atlantic nearly to Timbuktu. In 1075 it is conquered by the Almoravids, Saharan warriors, who Muslimise its culture. Arab trade in East Africa expands: Kilwa and Zanzibar are founded.

THE WORLD IN 1230 : MONGOLS THREATEN THE GREAT CIVILIZATIONS

Mongol herdsmen under Genghis Khan, savagely erupting from their Asian homeland, now rule all Persia and lands from the Black Sea to the Yellow Sea. In the next 30 years the combined hordes will subjugate China, Russia and the Seljuk Turks, penetrate central Europe and topple the caliph in Baghdad; the Mongol scourge is destined to last for another 300 years. Western civilization has extended eastwards and northwards to new lands. A Western emperor, a Crusader, temporarily rules Byzantium; but the Crusades are nearly over, and medieval society is beginning to break down.

## *1100–1200*

**Western Europe** New land is cultivated, and urban life revives with the rise of trade. The merchant class is born, and trading towns in N. Germany and Flanders become free cities. Wars between Emperor Frederick I and successive popes enable N. Italian cities to seize independence, and the first companies to share risk and profit are formed. A money economy evolves, and feudalism weakens. Strong central governments grow in the England of Henry I, the Sicily of Roger II and the France of Philip II (Philip Augustus).

Man's outlook is still spiritual rather than material: the Church is guardian of culture. Chartres (1194) is the first great Gothic cathedral. But Peter Abelard of Paris shows Church dogma to be contradictory, and scholars seeking to reconcile reason and faith found Bologna, Paris and Oxford universities. Minstrels idealise romantic love.

By 1155 only Prussia and Lithuania are still pagan. Crusades to wrest the Holy Land from the Muslims, campaigns against the Moors and trade by the Normans bring Europe into touch with Islam's more material outlook.

**Byzantium** Revolts in Bulgaria and Serbia, and attacks by Seljuks and Normans, reduce the empire to Greece and half of Turkey. Trade is lost to Venice, and Byzantine money ceases to be an international currency. Frescoes replace the more expensive mosaics.

**Islam** Saladin, sultan of Egypt and Syria, nearly succeeds in driving the Crusaders from Palestine, and makes Damascus a centre of Muslim culture. Moors such as Averroes and Rabbi ben Ezra are brilliant scholars. In the most important geographical work of the time, Idrisi describes the earth as a sphere.

**Persia** Literature, philosophy and mathematics advance under the Seljuks. The poet Omar Khayyam (*d.* 1123) reforms the calendar and originates modern navigational tables.

**India** Hindu civilization reaches new magnificence. Under the Chola dynasty, temples at Tanjore become temple-cities, and exquisite bronzes are produced. Hinduism is taken to Buddhist Ceylon. The Khmers of Cambodia expand into Thailand, Burma and Vietnam (1128). They build the temple complex at Angkor Wat. Afghans implant Islam in India, founding the sultanate of Delhi in 1192.

**Japan** The Minamoto clan sets up military rule at Kamakura, away from the court. Domination by samurai warriors begins, and minstrels popularise military romances.

**Mexico** Semi-civilized tribes including the Aztecs pour into the Valley of Mexico and destroy the Toltec capital of Tula (1168).

**Africa** Muslims take over Kanem-Bornu, which gains control of the Hausa states; Kano becomes a centre of Muslim learning. The Negro Yoruba found a civilization at Oyo.

## *1200–1300*

**Western Europe** The Crusades fail to win the Holy Land because of Crusader rivalry and greed; men begin to question medieval concern with the future life. Francis of Assisi advocates joyful love of man and nature, and the individual quest for spiritual revival. Thomas Aquinas reconciles reason and faith, and justifies a life active in the affairs of both men and state. Roger Bacon advocates observation and experiment, the basis of modern science. Giotto paints from life. Naples, Prague and Cambridge universities are founded. The great Gothic cathedrals at Rheims, Amiens and Cologne are begun.

In the growing towns, guilds of craftsmen and merchants gain power. The Hansa, a league of trading cities, pushes into Slav lands. Marco Polo returns from China (1292) with the first accurate accounts of the Orient. A Mongol threat is stemmed (1237–43), and Moorish Spain is reduced to Granada. After Innocent III (*d.* 1216), papal power declines and Emperor Frederick II, a man of learning and the arts, attacks the papal lands.

**Byzantium** Crusaders sack Constantinople and set up an empire (1204–61); East-West relations never recover. Michael VIII (*d.* 1282) recovers the capital and revives the empire.

**Russia** The Tatars, heirs of Genghis Khan, pillage the south (1237–40). They extort tribute but tolerate the Church. But in the free Repub-

THE WORLD IN 1400: VICTORIOUS TURKS EXPAND THE MUSLIM WORLD

One of the most brilliant Muslim civilizations, the empire of the Ottoman Turks founded in 1290, has driven the Byzantines from Asia. Arab traders dominate the Indian Ocean, and Islam has reached the East Indies. Byzantium, reduced in size, has lost its trade to Sicily and the N. Italian cities, where the Renaissance is beginning. Europe's last pagan strongholds have been conquered. The Chinese have expelled the Mongols and are expanding their own civilization. New Hindu powers have arisen in India against the Muslims, and Hindu society and arts are being revitalised.

## *1300–1400*

lic of Novgorod, the citizens, many of them literate, produce great architecture and fine Byzantine-style manuscripts and icons.

**Islam** Mongols subjugate the Seljuk Turks, and sack Baghdad, ending its Arab civilization. Mamelukes, freed slaves, take over Saladin's empire and the last Crusader stronghold in Palestine. Osman founds the embryo Ottoman Turkish Empire.

**Persia** Genghis Khan's hordes kill two-thirds of the people; but his Muslim descendants, rulers until 1335, encourage the arts.

**India** Mongols raid N. India. Tamils take Hindu civilization to Java. The Thais rise to dominate the Khmers and Burmese.

**China** The Sung capital of Hangchow, the world's richest and largest city with over a million people, exports fine porcelain. The Mongols take the north (1225) and Korea. Kublai Khan conquers the Sung in 1272, but invasions of Japan and Java fail.

**Mexico** The first Maya cities are begun and the religious centre of Chichén Itzá revives after an influx of Itzá tribes from the west.

**Peru** The Chimu build pyramid temples, fortresses and roads, and a well-organised state.

**Africa** At Lalibela, the Ethiopians build unique rock-cut churches. The Yoruba of Ife produce fine bronze portrait busts, and found Benin. The state of Mali around Timbuktu, a centre of Muslim learning, conquers Ghana.

**Western Europe** By 1400 all Europe is Christian. Feudalism is dying. With the introduction of gunpowder, lords can no longer defend their castles and their power; architecture is revolutionised. After the Black Death (1347–50) kills three-quarters of Europe's population, wages replace labourers' payment in protection and kind; inflation is rife.

An intellectual revolution, the Renaissance, is sparked off by the rediscovery of Classical authors, and humanism – concern for human affairs – grows. The free cities of Italy are the scene of increasing private enterprise, interest in local government and education, and civil patronage of the arts. Latin, the Church's language, is challenged. Dante establishes Tuscan as Italy's literary tongue. Boccaccio writes stories about ordinary people, which inspire Chaucer. Under Wycliffe the Bible is translated into English. William of Occam introduces the revolutionary idea that nature should be interpreted by reason not faith. Hus of Bohemia and Wycliffe attack Church abuses.

**Byzantium** The Black Death ravages the Balkans (1334–6). Stephen Dusan of Serbia takes Byzantine territory. He bases a law code on Justinian's, and Serbian and Bulgarian arts copy Byzantine styles. The Ottoman Turks take the last Byzantine possession in Asia.

**Russia** The Tatars impose an autocratic government and conservative aristocracy, and cut Russia off from the Renaissance. Moscow becomes the capital of a leading principality.

**Islam** The Indian Ocean becomes an Arab trading lake. The accounts of the traveller Ibn Battuta stimulate the study of geography, while Ibn Khaldun writes a *Universal History*.

**Persia** Hafiz writes some of the most remarkable poetry of all time. Tamerlane's Mongols ravage Persia and Syria (1395–1400).

**India** Kashmir falls to Delhi: Buddhism is wiped out in India but survives in Ceylon, Burma, Thailand and Cambodia. Muhammad Tughluk briefly holds S. India, where Hindu powers arise: Vijayanagar, a centre of trade and art, develops the 'thousand pillar hall' temple. Tamerlane sacks Delhi (1398–9).

**China** The Mongols adopt Chinese ways and restore the Confucian civil service (1315). The Black Death breaks out in 1330. The Ming dynasty expels the Mongols (1368), promotes all things Chinese and repairs the Great Wall.

**Japan** Zen Buddhism becomes popular; realistic sculpture is produced, and tea drinking is introduced as a stimulant during meditation. Civil wars come to a head, and fine swords are made. *Nō* drama takes its present form.

**Mexico** The Aztecs settle in the Valley of Mexico and found Tenochtitlan (Mexico City).

**Africa** The last Christian kingdom in Nubia falls to Islam; only Ethiopia remains Christian. The Songhai take over Mali-Ghana.

# The world AD 1400-1700

## THE WORLD IN 1500 : THE AGE OF EXPLORATION AT ITS HEIGHT

The Renaissance is revolutionising life in western Europe. It has also inspired great explorers: Europeans have discovered America, but they have not yet found the Aztec and Inca civilizations, now near their height. Europeans have contacted the African civilization of Benin, and reached India by sea. Christianity is fighting Islam: the Spaniards have absorbed the Moors, and the Russians, united under the Byzantine-inspired Princes of Moscow, have pushed back the Mongols. But the Ottoman Turks have seized Constantinople, the centre of Byzantine civilization, and are in central Europe.

## 1400–1500

**Western Europe** The introduction of printing in 1456 hastens the Renaissance. In Italy, Massaccio achieves realism in painting; Uccello scientifically portrays perspective; Brunelleschi and Donatello, in architecture and sculpture, reflect classical buildings; Botticelli paints classical subjects. Villon writes France's greatest lyric poetry, and Jan van Eyck of Flanders achieves strikingly realistic portraits. Private enterprise increases; Florence, Ulm and Augsburg are centres of international banking and trade. Venice controls Mediterranean trade, and introduces modern diplomacy by posting ambassadors permanently abroad.

The Hundred Years' War between France and England (1337–1453) stimulates nationalism. Poland becomes the largest and most tolerant country of Europe, but Hungary remains dominant in central Europe. Ferdinand and Isabella unite Spain in 1479, and take Granada, its last Muslim state, in 1492.

The Portuguese settle Guinea, and sail to India (1498) and Brazil (1500). Columbus discovers the West Indies (1492) and Venezuela (1498). Cabot lands in Canada (1497).

**Byzantium** The fall of Constantinople in 1453 brings the Byzantine Empire to an end after 1100 years, but its culture lives on in Russia.

**Russia** Ivan the Great of Moscow (1462–1505) unites the states and stops paying tribute to the Tatars. The Moscow Kremlin, centre of Church and state, takes largely its present shape. Moscow is the 'third Rome' – heir to Byzantine civilization. Serfs are tied to their lords' lands.

**Islam** The Ottoman Turks capture Constantinople and make it their capital (1453). In Egypt a great period of architecture ends with Mameluke Sultan Qaytbay (d. 1496). In southeast Asia, 20 states adopt Islam.

**Persia** The Mongol cities of Samarkand and Herat become centres of Persian civilization. Northern nomads bring chaos in 1449.

**China** Ming emperors revive scholarship, trade and painting. Settlers take the Chinese way of life to the East Indies and Malaya. In 1421 the capital is moved to Peking; modern Peking dates from this time. Multi-coloured glazes for porcelain are introduced after the art of painting it with cobalt blue is perfected.

**Mexico** After 1428 the city of Tenochtitlan leads an Aztec alliance to dominance. Its temple of the sun god is dedicated in 1487 with the sacrifice of 20,000 war captives.

**Peru** The Incas expand from Cuzco c. 1440. They weld differing tribes into an organised society with a prosperous, state-run economy.

**Africa** The Buchwezi from Nubia set up a powerful kingdom in Uganda c. 1450, and build fine palaces and shrines of reeds and grasses. In 1482 the Portuguese find the highly organised Bakongo kingdom. In 1483 they reach Benin and later export slaves.

## 1500–1600

**Western Europe** The Renaissance continues. The N. Italian city-states – Florence, Venice, Genoa – are at their peak, producing all-round geniuses such as Leonardo da Vinci and Michelangelo. Copernicus of Poland shocks the Church when he suggests that the earth is not the centre of the universe (1543). One of Magellan's Portuguese ships sails round the world (1517–22).

Conflict between pope and Holy Roman emperor leads to the sacking of Rome by Charles V's troops in 1527. In Germany, Luther attacks Church corruption and preaches salvation by faith. This Reformation spreads to Switzerland, Scandinavia, Holland (which proclaims independence from Spain in 1579), France under Calvin, and Scotland. The Inquisition crushes Protestantism in Spain, Portugal and Italy in the Counter-Reformation.

In England, Henry VIII proclaims himself head of the Church. Holbein paints portraits, and drama reaches a peak with Shakespeare. Renaissance architecture reaches France and Francis I begins the Loire châteaux. Writers such as Ronsard and Rabelais flourish.

**Russia** Ivan the Terrible (1544–84) doubles the empire's size, encourages scholarship and trade and brutally crushes the boyars (nobles). Cossacks, rebel serfs, settle in the Ukraine.

**Islam** Sinan, architect to Suleiman the Magnificent (1520–66), embellishes Constantinople.

THE WORLD IN 1600: THE DAWN OF EUROPE'S FIRST COLONIAL AGE

The Spaniards, in their search for riches, have swept away the native New World civilizations. The Portuguese have settled in Brazil, and set up trad-ing posts around Africa and India. English and Dutch traders are chal-lenging the Spaniards and Portuguese. The Reformation is sweeping western Europe, bringing strife between Catho-lics and Protestants. A glittering Mongol, or Mughal, civilization is established in N. India. But the Chinese world has expanded into Inner Mon-golia, and the Russians are settling Siberia. Ottoman Turkish civilization is nearing its greatest extent.

# 1600–1700

The Turks menace Europe: in 1529 they are at the gates of Vienna, but at Lepanto in 1571 a Christian alliance breaks Turkish sea-power.

**Persia** In 1502 Shah Isma'il founds the Safavid dynasty and unites Persia. Workshops are set up to weave carpets, and elaborate illustrated manuscripts are produced.

**India** Nanak founds the Sikh sect (*c.* 1500) to foster Hindu-Muslim reconciliation. In 1526, a descendant of Tamerlane the Mongol estab-lishes the Mughal Empire. Akbar (1556–1605) builds a new capital at Fatehpur Sikri, where he promotes the arts and religious tolerance.

**China** Under the Ming dynasty, great libraries and art collections are amassed, and novels based on early story-cycles are written.

**Japan** In 1542 the Portuguese give Japan, torn by civil war, its first contact with the West.

**Americas** The Aztec Empire, at its peak under Montezuma, is plundered by Spaniards under Cortez. In 1528 another Spanish force defeats the Maya, and the Incas fall to Pizarro in 1533. In 1565 the Spaniards colonise Florida. The Portuguese have an empire in Brazil by 1549.

**Africa** The Portuguese set up trading posts in Arab East Africa. Early Zimbabwe, capital of the Bantu Monomotapa Empire, is completed with walls, 'temple' and fortress of stone. It trades via Kilwa. The Portuguese, English and Dutch ship 900,000 Negro slaves from West Africa to the Americas.

**Western Europe** The intellectual centre of Europe has moved from Italy to the France of Louis XIV, the last great Renaissance despot, who reigns 1643–1715. Classical drama reaches a peak with Racine and Moliere, and in 1682 the court moves to sumptuous Versailles. The great Rationalists, Descartes and Leibniz in France and Spinoza in Holland, devise philoso-phical systems. In England, Francis Bacon formulates modern scientific method, and Locke advocates government by the people's consent. From 1608 Kepler and Galileo use telescopes in astronomy. Harvey publishes a description of the circulation of the blood (1628), and Newton discovers gravity (1665).

But the Church condemns Copernican astronomy. In central Europe the religious Thirty Years' War (1618–48) reduces the population by one-third, except in Prussia. Spain is weakened by war and by its expulsion of the Moors (1609), but at the near-bankrupt court Velasquez paints fine portraits.

The Dutch Republic leads the world in trade, finance, art and science. Its merchants create unprecedented prosperity and commission paintings from Rubens, Rembrandt and Vermeer. Civil war in England in 1642–9 culminates in the execution of Charles I and a republic (1649–60).

**Russia** After warfare, famine and the fall of Moscow to the Poles, Michael Romanov is elected tsar in 1613. Serfs are tied to individual landlords. Peter the Great (1682–1725) tours western Europe and Westernises Russia.

**Persia** The Safavid dynasty reaches its height with Abbas the Great (1587–1629), when trade flourishes. Isfahan, the capital since 1599, is replanned. But Afghan, Russian and Turkish encroachments weaken the empire.

**India** Shah Jahan, Mughal emperor from 1628 to 1658, holds magnificent court at Delhi and builds the Taj Mahal as a tomb for his wife. Persian-influenced literature and painting flourish. The English and French found trading ports as Portuguese sea-power declines.

**China** The declining Ming dynasty is ousted by the Manchu people (1644). Their system of social segregation and adoption of Chinese culture results in stability and expansion.

**Japan** Under the Tokugawa clan, a period of strict feudalism begins. Travel abroad and Christianity are banned in 1640. Merchant power grows with the transition from a rice economy to a money economy.

**Americas** The French, English and Dutch found colonies in North America: the Pilgrim Fathers reach New England in 1620. The New World imports nearly 3 million Negro slaves.

**Africa** Zimbabwe revives under the Rozvi kings. Bakongo breaks up *c.* 1670 after slave wars. Buganda unites the Great Lakes states. In 1652 the first Dutch settlers reach the Cape.

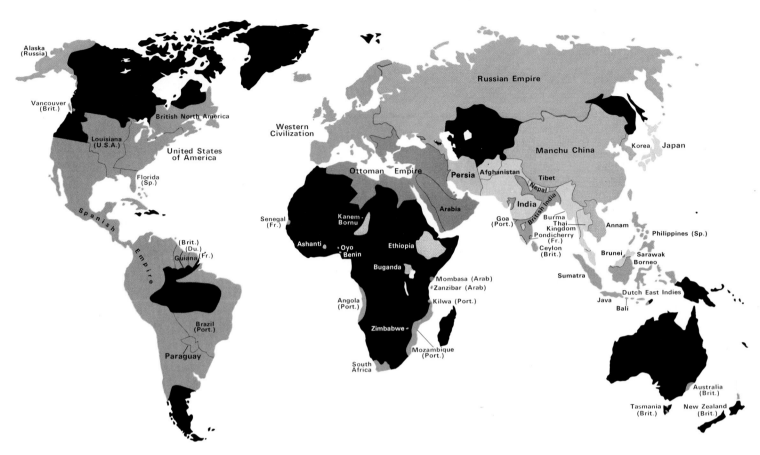

THE WORLD IN 1815: THE MODERN INDUSTRIAL AGE BEGINS

Western civilization is established on every continent, while in Europe itself the Industrial Revolution, with its attendant social problems, has spread from Britain to the Continent. Napoleon's brief empire has vanished, leaving the map much as it was before. Russia and China have expanded to a common frontier. China, Japan and Korea are 'hermit kingdoms', cut off from the world, but the European powers and the newly formed United States of America seek to open them up to trade. The European powers are on the threshold of their scramble for African lands.

## 1700–1800

**Western Europe** In a century dominated by warfare, the European countries jostle for supremacy and territory. Rulers such as Maria Theresa of Austria and Frederick the Great of Prussia also use their power to promote the well-being of their people. Inspired by such thinkers as Rousseau and Voltaire, these enlightened despots allow religious freedom and reform the law. But in France bad harvests and oppression lead to the Revolution of 1789, and the monarchy is overthrown in 1791.

The population of Europe rises from 120 million to 185 million, and the populations of London and Paris double. In England, writers such as Defoe and Fielding describe the changing scene, and Hogarth paints the urban squalor. The French artist Watteau and the English artist Gainsborough paint in rococo style. Scientists initiate a spirit of international collaboration in chemistry, physics and medicine.

**Russia** Peter the Great in 1712 transfers his capital to St Petersburg, a magnificent new city designed by the French architect Le Blond. Peter's grandson, Peter III, tries to model Russia on Prussia. His widow, Catherine the Great, is influenced by the French Enlightenment, but during her reign serfdom is extended and vast areas of Turkey and Poland conquered.

**Islam** The Ottoman Empire is weakened by wars with Russia, Austria, Poland, Venice, Persia and France.

**India** Anarchy follows the death in 1707 of Aurangzeb, the last great Mughal emperor. In 1739 the Persians sack Delhi. The British East India Company increases its political power; in 1759 it defeats its French rivals.

**China** Under the great Manchu emperor, Kang-hsi, historical chronicles, encyclopaedias, anthologies and literary criticisms are written. China's population doubles to over 200 million as agriculture expands.

**Japan** The popular culture of the merchant class, with its puppet and *kabuki* theatres, is at its height. In 1720, the ban on European culture is removed, and the study of Western science is introduced.

**Americas** In 1763, French Canada is conquered by Britain. Liberal ideas filtering in from Europe increase resentment against British rule. George Washington becomes leader of the N. American colonists in 1775, and in 1776 Thomas Jefferson drafts the Declaration of Independence. The War of Independence ends in 1783, with British recognition of the USA. The slave trade is at its height – 140,000 Negroes a year are shipped to the New World.

**Australia** William Dampier explores the west coast in 1699–1701, and between 1768 and 1780 Captain Cook charts the east coast. In 1788 some 1000 British convicts arrive at Port Jackson (Sydney).

## 1800–1900

**Western Europe** In 1815, Napoleon's empire falls and the Congress of Vienna attempts to restore the old order. Revolutions in 1848 fail. But nationalism increases and by 1871 Bismarck of Prussia unites Germany. Idealism inspires the writers of the Romantic movement.

England is the first country to be gripped by the Industrial Revolution, and Greater London's population rises from 875,000 to 5 million. Later, France and Germany also industrialise. Schopenhauer publishes his pessimistic philosophy. The Communism of Marx and Engels sees history as the story of class struggle. Great strides are made in medicine, astronomy and physics; Darwin publishes *On the Origin of Species* (1859) and Mendel conducts researches into heredity.

**Russia** Napoleon's invasion of 1812 is repulsed. The repressive rule of Nicholas I (1825–55) is criticised by Gogol. In 1861 the serfs are emancipated, but unrest increases. Dostoevsky and Tolstoy probe Russian society, in novels that achieve world fame.

**Islam** The Ottoman Empire is in decline. In 1829 Britain, France and Russia help the Greeks to free themselves from Turkish rule. Britain occupies Egypt (1882) and the Sudan (1896–8).

**India** Native troops rise against the British in the Indian Mutiny (1857–8). After its suppression, government is transferred from the East India Company to the British Crown.

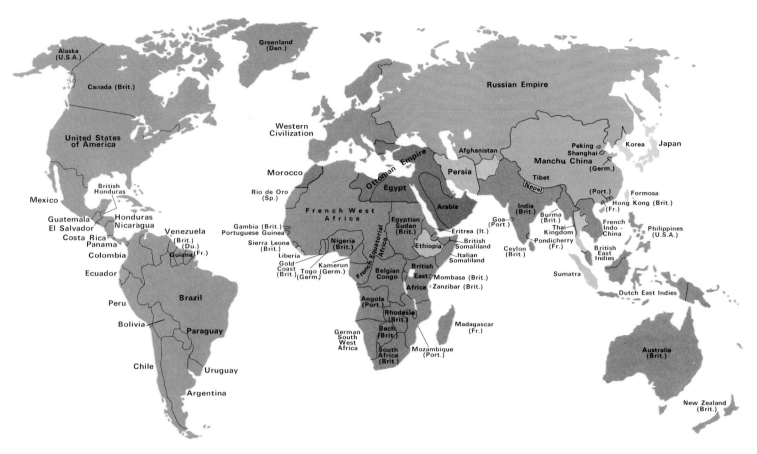

THE WORLD IN 1900 : FROM COLONISATION TO SELF-GOVERNMENT

The Spanish and Portuguese colonies in mainland Latin America have gained independence. But now the European powers have divided Africa between them, and India is firmly part of the British Empire. However, a new concept of colonialism has arisen; Canada has become a self-governing dominion within the British Empire (1867). The Ottoman Empire, 'sick man of Europe', has lost most of its possessions in North Africa and Europe. Japan has been opened up to Western influence and is involved in world trade. In America the West has been won, after railmen and farmers reach the Pacific.

## Since 1900

**China** The USA and the European powers vie for a commercial foothold. By 1900, China is dominated by foreign powers and nationalist resentment erupts in the Boxer Rebellion.

**Japan** An American mission forces Japan to abandon its isolation, and by 1858 it has made commercial treaties with the USA, Britain, France and Russia.

**Americas** New areas of the USA and Canada are settled, and the West is opened up by railmen and immigrants. In the American Civil War (1861–5) the slave-owning Southern states fight for the right to secede from the Union, and lose. The Spanish and Portuguese colonies of South America achieve independence.

**Africa** The European nations 'scramble' for African territory, and by 1900 the whole of the continent south of the Sahara (except for Liberia and Ethiopia) is in their hands. The British capture Capetown from the Dutch in 1814, and Dutch Boers make the 'Great Trek' in 1836 to found the Orange Free State, Natal and Transvaal. Discovery of diamonds (1867) and gold (1886) leads to Britain annexing Boer territory, and the Boer War (1899–1902).

**Australasia** Convict settlement in Australia ends in 1868, and British colonisation increases. The discovery of gold in Victoria (1851) attracts adventurers from all over the world. In 1897 the colonies join in a confederation. British settlers reach New Zealand (1815).

**Western Europe** Successive diplomatic crises lead to world war (1914–18). Germany is defeated and, by the Treaty of Versailles (1919), disarmed and stripped of its colonies. The world's economy is disrupted by a severe economic depression (1929–33). In Germany resentment against the Treaty of Versailles wins support for Adolf Hitler, who embarks on a savage persecution of the Jews. In 1939 Hitler invades Poland, and Britain and France declare war. By the end of 1941 Germany controls almost all Europe, and the war involves Russia, Japan and the USA. Germany surrenders to the Western Allies in 1945, and the war with Japan ends when the USA drops atomic bombs on Hiroshima and Nagasaki. New philosophies emerge, among them Sartre's Existentialism. Experiments in art, music and literature are carried out by Picasso, Stravinsky and Joyce.

**Russia** Unrest and defeat by Germany lead to the Revolution of 1917, led by Lenin and Trotsky. Stalin, Lenin's successor, conducts a series of savage purges of intellectual and military leaders in the 1930's. As a result of the Second World War, Russia dominates central Europe, and invades its satellites Hungary (1956) and Czechoslovakia (1968).

**Islam** The dwindling Ottoman Empire loses most of its territory to the European powers in 1920. A republic is declared in 1923 with Kemal Ataturk, a great Westerniser, as president.

Proclamation of the Jewish state of Israel in 1948 leads to Arab-Israeli conflict.

**India** The pacifist leader Gandhi seeks independence from Britain for a united Hindu-Muslim state. When independence as India and the Muslim state of Pakistan is achieved in 1947, bloodshed results. In 1972, East Pakistan secedes from Pakistan as Bangladesh.

**China** Unrest leads to declaration of a republic under Sun Yat-sen (1911). From 1927 civil war rages between Nationalists led by Chiang Kaishek, Sun's successor, and Communists under Mao Tse-tung. Japanese invasions are resisted. By 1945, most of China is controlled by Communists, who take over in 1949.

**Japan** Military and economic expansion is halted only by defeat in the Second World War. Afterwards, a spectacular economic recovery results from the intensive development of technology and overseas trade.

**North America** The USA emerges from isolation, fighting in two world wars. Its prosperity is checked by the depression of the 1930's, but it recovers to develop one of the world's highest living standards. Involvement in Vietnam from 1960 leads to increasing social unrest. In 1969 an American is the first man to land on the moon.

**Africa** From the mid-1950's, the black African nations achieve independence. Attempts are made to establish pan-African unity.

# Part 3

# MAN AND
# HIS WORLD

Ideas and discoveries that
have changed the course of history

*Throughout history, enlightened men and women have looked beyond the everyday routine of existence to investigate the mysteries of the world around them, to master it and to exploit its resources. Explorers, prophets and inventors in all lands have opened up new continents, sought meanings for man's existence on this planet, and developed the technical skills which have given man an increasing measure of control over his environment.*

*The lessons so learnt and the theories so formed have seldom been confined to the countries in which they originated. More often they have passed from one civilization to another in the wake of conquest or exploration. Creeds developing among a single people have become faiths with a world-wide following, and secrets unlocked by the experimenters of one nation have become instruments in the hands of scientists on the other side of the world.*

*The names of the pioneers belong to the national legend of many countries; their achievements are milestones in the history of all mankind.*

# The quest for truth

*Through religion and philosophy, man has sought to determine the ultimate meaning of his existence*

*In many different times and places, man has looked to his gods to protect him from the real or even imaginary dangers of the world. A bronze ritual vessel of the Shang period in China (16th–11th centuries BC) shows a person in the benevolent grip of a guardian spirit, represented by a tiger*

Religion has been one of the great shaping forces of human history, transforming the way of life of entire peoples. The collision of rival faiths, or of different versions of the same faith, has split empires and destroyed nations; and religious intolerance has sparked off some of the cruellest wars and persecutions in history. Yet religion, and its offshoot, philosophy, have helped man to attain his highest ideals of justice and morality, and inspired many of his noblest achievements in the realms of thought, art, architecture, music and literature.

## Beginnings of religion

Man's religious urge through the ages has found expression in a bewildering variety of beliefs, ideas and practices. But one factor seems permanent and universal in religious experience: the sense of a supernatural 'other world' which, though invisible, is believed to have power over men's lives. Even in the few religions which do not recognise a God, or are indifferent to the idea of one, such as early Buddhism or Jainism, this supernatural world is assumed to exist.

Since the dawn of human consciousness men and women have regarded the supernatural world with a mixture of awe, fear and hope, and sought to bring their lives into harmony with it. Early religion – in ancient Egypt, for instance – had a strongly practical basis. Life was a struggle for survival, and a preparation for death. And so men offered up sacrifices and prayers to the mysterious forces or spirits which they believed to control the workings of nature, hoping to ward off catastrophe, to ensure good hunting, to obtain better harvests, and to live again beyond the grave.

Even prehistoric man seems to have shared in this most powerful of all religious ideas: the belief that in some way a person lives on after the death of his body. The evidence of ceremonial burials, and the provision of food, utensils and weapons for the use of the dead on their journey into the next

*These Melanesian chalk figures from New Ireland in the Pacific were designed as abodes for ancestral spirits*

*The Phoenicians, like other ancient peoples, worshipped several gods. This 3rd-century BC slab depicts a sacrifice to their gods Baal and Tanit*

life, goes back to the Neanderthal men who lived in Europe more than 50,000 years ago.

## Gods of the ancient world

With the rise of civilization in the lands of the Mediterranean and the Middle East – in Egypt, Mesopotamia, Greece and Rome – the 'other world' came to be filled with innumerable gods and goddesses, most of them depicted in recognisable human or animal shape. Each culture had its own cluster of divinities, usually ruled by a supreme god. And this multiplicity of gods, called polytheism, after

*The Greek sun-god Apollo, in a Roman mosaic of the 2nd century AD*

two Greek words meaning 'many gods', is typical of religious ideas in the ancient world.

Polytheism's roots probably lay in primitive man's attempts to understand the elements of nature – storms, floods, rivers, fires, rain, drought, the sun and so on – by regarding them as powers to be worshipped because they affected his life so directly. It developed as different peoples with their own gods were brought under one rule. The various gods were grouped together in a unified system, and each god was recognised as having his special interests.

A striking example of such growth was the pantheon (assembly of gods) which emerged in ancient Egypt as a result of the fusion, about 3200 BC, of the kingdoms of Lower Egypt, or the Delta, and Upper Egypt to the south. One of the major gods of the two kingdoms was Osiris, the god of the Nile and the ruler of the land of the dead. He personified goodness, in opposition to his evil brother Set, who killed him. The story was probably a mythical version of the conflict between Upper Egypt, where Osiris was worshipped, and the Nile Delta, where the religion was one of worshipping the sky and the sun.

A similar growth underlies Greek mythology. As the early Greeks migrated southwards towards the Aegean, from about 2000 BC, they intermingled with peoples who paid homage to earth-mother goddesses. From the Greek point of view, Zeus, their supreme god, had to dominate the lesser female deities of separate tribes and cities. Thus arose the myths telling how Zeus seduced or in some cases married them.

*A papyrus of c.1250 BC depicts the Egyptian Nile-god Osiris, holding a crook and a whip, with his wife Isis. Their worship spread to many countries*

### The idea of one God
A remarkable religious experiment was carried out in Egypt 1400 years before the birth of Christ. The pharaoh Akhenaton turned his back on the traditional gods, the greatest of whom was Amun, and established the worship of one god, the sun-god Aton. But after Akhenaton's death, Egyptian religion reverted to the worship of many separate gods.

This brief phase of monotheism, the worship of one God, came in the century before the Jewish leader Moses lived in Egypt, and it is possible that he was influenced by it. Moses set out to convince the Hebrews that the god Jahweh had chosen them; they were uniquely his people, and should serve him only; and it was their duty to live by his Ten Commandments. According to the Bible, God revealed the Commandments to Moses on Mount Sinai during the Hebrews' journey out of Egypt to Palestine, the Promised Land.

This uncompromising set of rules, with its prohibition of crimes which set man against man, such as adultery, covetousness and theft, and its insistence on the duties

*A relief from the temple at El-Amarna in Egypt shows Akhenaton and his queen sacrificing to the sun-god Aton, who sheds his rays over their household*

owed to God, to parents and to other people, was originally framed for an obscure tribe when it was wandering in the desert; it has become one of the most potent and enduring moral codes of all time.

### Hebrew prophets
After establishing itself in Palestine the national religion of the Jews made remarkable progress, giving birth to ideas which were to have a revolutionary impact on world religion, especially Christianity and Islam. From about the 8th century BC, prophets such as Amos and Hosea tried to make sense of the apparent injustice in human life. Prosperity must be God's reward for goodness, and adversity must be seen as punishment. Most of the Jewish scriptures reveal this view of man's moral destiny.

A more difficult concept appears in the 4th-century BC Book of Job, which states the paradox of the ideally virtuous man who suffers intolerably. The lesson to be drawn from Job's suffering is that a man should worship God because he is

*Fragments of the Dead Sea scrolls from the 2nd century BC, found in 1947. The scrolls include passages from the Bible*

God, not because he dispenses favours. The idea of an impartial God – indeed a God for all mankind – had been movingly expressed in the 6th century BC by an Old Testament prophet called the 'Second Isaiah'. At this time Judah, the southern kingdom of the Jews, was wiped out by the Babylonians, and all the leaders of the nation were taken into exile. There they realised that Jahweh was not the god of one territory only, and that they could still sing the Lord's songs, even in a strange land. The 'Second Isaiah' draws the conclusion that the gods of Babylon are no more than images of wood and stone; there can be only one God for all men.

### Ferment of ideas in Greece
From the 6th century BC onwards, there was a stir of questioning in the Greek world about the nature of reality. The men engaged in such speculation, notably the Athenian philosophers Socrates, Plato and Aristotle, were among the most remarkable intellects in the history of mankind. Socrates annoyed the citizens of Athens by continually questioning them about their beliefs. Because of his relentless concern to establish the meaning of concepts such as truth, beauty and justice, he was accused of corrupting the youth of Athens, and sentenced to death by drinking hemlock. His work, however, went on. Plato, his pupil, held that there are two worlds, the world of appearance and the world of

reality. The world of appearance is known by means of the five senses, and is full of illusion, change and decay.

But the real world is one of eternal, changeless 'Ideas', which can be known only by the intellect. This 'two-worlds' theory greatly influenced early Christian thinkers, notably St Augustine (354–430). But far earlier, Aristotle had rejected the 'two-worlds' theory, holding that the 'Ideas' described by Plato

*The Athenian philosopher Socrates, portrayed in a mural of the 1st century AD, died for the sake of his beliefs*

exist only in material things, not in another world. Yet he believed that there must exist a perfect, non-material and changeless being from which all 'Ideas' ultimately derive; and this being is God.

Numerous philosophical 'sects' flourished at this time, the most influential being the Stoics, who tried to rise above both pleasure

---

### RELIGION OF THE JEWS

Judaism is the religion of a single people, the Jews, who have suffered more persecution on account of their faith than any other nation in history. The essence of Judaism is its strict belief in one God, and obedience to his moral law. Orthodox Jews believe that God's law was revealed to Moses as the Torah, in the first five books of the Hebrew Bible, more than 3000 years ago. The Torah, and the teachings of later Hebrew prophets, in time gave rise to the Talmud, a vast body of writings interpreting the Scriptures. The Talmud is the authority for all orthodox Jews

*The Old Testament book of Exodus tells how Moses, with God's help, led the Hebrews out of bondage in Egypt towards the Promised Land. A picture in a 15th-century Jewish prayer book depicts him guiding his people across the Red Sea*

*Jewish ritual objects, including two seven-branched candlesticks, are shown on the base of a gold goblet of the 2nd century AD found in a Jewish catacomb in Rome, where it was hidden from the Romans. The objects shown on the goblet are believed to have been taken from the Jews' Temple in Jerusalem when it was desecrated by Antiochus IV of Syria in about 170 BC*

*An 18th-century scroll relates the biblical story of Esther, the Jewish wife of a Persian king. She pleaded for the Jews in his empire, who had been condemned to death. The Jewish festival of Purim commemorates the event*

# Faith in a universal God

In a 12th-century French miniature, the Hebrew patriarch Abraham gathers Jews, Christians and Muslims to his bosom. Historically, the three great faiths are closely related. Christianity arose out of Judaism, seeing itself as 'the new Israel'; Islam grew out of both religions, claiming to complete the process, which was started by Judaism, of revealing God's Word to man

and pain. But Greek philosophy, with its rigorous use of reason to explore the essential nature of things, appealed only to an intellectual elite. There was nothing in it for ordinary men and women; the way was open for any religion that had an emotional appeal, that carried the promise of fertility and power. So there developed the mystery religions (so called because of their secretive nature). Foreign cults, such as Persian Mithraism, were imported into the Greek and Roman worlds during the three or four centuries before Christ.

A Persian relief shows a 4th-century king (centre) with Ahura Mazda, chief god of the official Zoroastrian religion (right), and the god Mithras (left)

## Teachings of Jesus

About the year 27 or 28, a young Jewish carpenter called Jesus left his home at Nazareth in Galilee, and moved about the country ministering to the sick and preaching that 'the Kingdom of God is at hand'. Some Jews saw him as the expected Messiah, or Anointed King, who would lead them to prosperity. But to most Jews this idea was blasphemous.

The preaching mission of Jesus lasted less than three years, and ended with his Crucifixion in about AD 30. His few followers were convinced that they had seen him alive after his death, and from their preaching the Christian Church began. The four Gospels of the New Testament, written between AD 65 and AD 100, tell of his teaching and his life, and

death and resurrection. Throughout his career, Jesus challenged all formal and legalistic religion, calling men to acknowledge in everything the Kingship of God. He held out the promise of eternal life. In the Sermon on the Mount he proclaimed that it was more blessed to give than to receive, that a man should love even his enemies, and that inner virtue mattered more than outward conformity to mere rules of behaviour.

Such teachings brought Jesus into conflict with the religious authorities, but he continued to preach, despite the growing danger to himself. He was crucified by the

## RELIGION OF THE CROSS

From being a small and despised religious sect in a remote province of the Roman Empire, Christianity arose to conquer that empire, and even to outlast it. Today Christianity is the most widely established of the world's religions, with the greatest number of adherents – approximately 925,000,000, almost a quarter of the world's total population. It is unique among the religions of the world in claiming that its founder was the incarnation of God, through whom God revealed his purpose to mankind. After almost 2000 years, Christians still accept the message of the Gospel, as preached by the apostles, that it was Christ's mission in the world to redeem man from sin and to restore him to God

A medieval French manuscript shows the three Magi – 'the wise men of the East' – visiting the newly born Jesus

A medieval artist's version of a miracle related in the Bible. The Holy Ghost inspires the apostles to speak 'with other tongues', during the feast of Pentecost

Architects of faith: Peter and Paul, portrayed on a medal. Peter became established as the first head of the Catholic Church. Paul's teachings gave it a universal outlook

Roman occupying power, but at the instigation of the Jewish leaders. Later, mainly through the teachings of St Paul, Christ's death was represented as an act of sacrifice, undertaken to redeem man.

## Foundation of Christianity

The arrival of the first Christians (the word 'Christian' was at first a term of abuse) made little impact on the world of Rome. They were looked on as merely another foreign sect, like the cults and mystery religions from Egypt and Persia. Slowly, however, their discipline and missionary zeal brought them to official notice. At last, when they had become powerful, official attempts were made to suppress them.

Persecution was intermittent, and never widespread. In Rome itself, Christians were imprisoned and tortured, or thrown into the arena to be devoured by lions. But persecution simply gave the sect even greater cohesion and powers of resistance – a fact not lost on Emperor Constantine. In 313 Constantine granted freedom of worship to all religions, and Christianity later became the state religion.

Constantine made an immense contribution to the spread of Christianity, but he failed in one of his primary aims. He wanted to unite all Christians in one Church, but in fact he succeeded in splitting them. The Christians of the West claimed

that the Pope in Rome was the leader of Christendom. Those in the East recognised the Patriarch of Constantinople as their leader. These two forms became the Roman Catholic Church and the Eastern Orthodox Church.

The Byzantine emperors maintained a large Christian empire covering much of Asia and North Africa until a new dynamic religious force appeared in the East. This was the religious faith of Islam.

*Eastern Orthodox Christians have always shown special reverence towards the Virgin Mary, the mother of Jesus Christ. This 7th-century mosaic of the Virgin and Child is from Cyprus*

## Spread of Islam

The new religion had a remarkable early success. It was simple, uncompromising, and attractively easy to grasp. It drew on the austere strength of the Old Testament, honouring the Jewish patri-

archs such as Abraham. Like Judaism and Christianity, Islam believed in one universal God. It proclaimed Muhammad, its founder, to be the greatest of the prophets, and asserted that the book recording God's revelations to him, the Koran, was the most complete expression of God's commandments.

Muhammad was born in Mecca in Arabia in AD 570. The Muhammadan, or Muslim, era is reckoned from the *Hegira*, or emigration, of 622, when Muhammad fled to Medina from the persecution of Mecca. At Medina he built up his new religion, and after his death, in 632, his fanatical followers, to whom conquest in the name of Allah was a duty, had one remarkable triumph after another in their military onrush.

By 640, Syria had fallen to Muslim forces. Egypt fell in 641, Spain in 711. These conquests were helped by the weakness of some of the victims, and also by the tolerance shown to Christians and Jews, among others, who were left to their own religious observances. But those classed as pagans had only one choice: conversion to Islam or death.

In the West, the onrush of the Muslims was stopped at Tours by the Franks under Charles Martel in 732. However, Spain was not completely reconquered by Christianity until the end of the

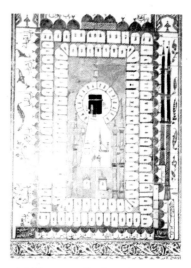

*A 16th-century tile shows Mecca's holy building, the Kaaba, seen as a dark cubic shape in a circular setting. All Muslims face towards it when praying*

Middle Ages. But in the East – where the remnants of the once-mighty Persian Empire had fallen in 641, only nine years after the death of Muhammad – the advance went on, only coming to a temporary stop at the gateway of India. It was several centuries before the Muslims successfully invaded and conquered India. When they did, it was to create one of history's most brilliant empires, that of the Mughals. But powerful

---

*An ivory carving of the 12th century depicts the Deposition, or taking down of Christ's body from the Cross*

*A 5th-century bronze cross in the form of the 'chi-rho', the first two letters of Christ's name in Greek. The hanging letters alpha and omega symbolise God as 'the beginning and the end'. The idea of an all-knowing God soon became an established part of Christianity*

## RELIGION OF THE PROPHET

Islam, the religious faith of an estimated 466,000,000 people, is established in Arab countries, parts of Africa, and in the East. It is based on the Koran, a book containing revelations of the divine will which Islam's founder, the Prophet Muhammad, claimed to have received direct from Allah. Islam's roots lie partly in Judaism and Christianity, and Muhammad saw himself as the last in a line of prophets which included Abraham, Moses and even Jesus Christ

*A 16th-century Turkish miniature shows the infant Muhammad being attended by angels. His mother, wearing a veil in accordance with custom, is seen kneeling on the right*

*Muhammad declares his cousin and son-in-law, Ali, to be his successor, in a Persian illustration. Ali carries the 'Sword of Islam'*

*A 16th-century Turkish artist painted this miniature (left), which depicts a miraculous event supposed to have taken place during a battle at Uhud, north-west of Medina, fought by Muhammad against an army from Mecca. During the battle, there was no water, so the prophet held out his hand, and water issued from his five finger-tips. Muhammad himself never claimed to be divine, and such popular legends about his miraculous powers were frowned on by the strictly orthodox. Although his forces were defeated at Uhud, Muhammad later went on to conquer the whole of Arabia. Muslim armies later carried the faith as far afield as Spain, India and China*

*Title-page from a 14th-century Egyptian copy of the Koran, the sacred book of Islam which tells of the mercy of God and man's ingratitude, as revealed to Muhammad, his prophet*

# Wisdom and teaching of the East

*A 13th-century painting of Lhasa, capital of Tibet. In the centre is the Potala, traditionally the palace of the Dalai-Lama, ruler of the country. For many centuries Tibet was the home of Lamaism, a form of Buddhism developed by the Tibetan lamas, or monks. The religion was repressed by the Chinese Communists after their annexation of Tibet in 1950*

though that empire became, it never swamped the great civilization of India, with its ancient, deeply conservative religion of Hinduism.

## Origins of Hinduism

About 2000 BC, fair-skinned invaders had entered India from the north-west. They were Aryans, related in language and culture to the ancestors of the Greeks and Romans, and to the earliest Germanic tribes. Their religion was similar to that of Homeric Greece, with gods who in character were like the human heroes of the Greek epics or the Norse sagas.

These gods were believed to influence human life, so it was advisable to ask for their help, or to placate them by prayer and sacrifice if they seemed angry. The religion of these early Aryans or Indo-Europeans can be seen in the hymns of the Sanskrit Rig-veda, part of the sacred literature of Hinduism. It was written down many centuries later, but the religious ideas of the invaders had been kept alive over these centuries by word of mouth, from generation to generation. Besides the Rig-veda there are two more important works – the Sama-veda and the Yajur-veda.

## Indian beliefs

Hinduism, the world's oldest living faith, has many different sects and

*A seal from the Indus Valley, about 4500 years old, shows a horned god of animals. The Hindu religion is thought to have derived in part from the civilization which flourished in the Indus Valley*

schools of thought. Underlying all its forms is the caste system, which ties people to the social class into which they are born. What seems an unjust system to outsiders is made acceptable to Hindus by the idea that they are placed in their social positions by their Creator, and are graded according to their good or bad behaviour in a previous existence. No power on earth can change this, and so they must be content. This is the law of *karma*. For those Hindus who are placed in the lower levels of society, the hope of advancement lies not in this life, but the next.

For most Hindus, Hinduism is

## RELIGION OF INDIA

Hinduism, the world's oldest living faith, is practised by the great majority of the people of India. It has many different sects. Unlike Christianity and Islam, or its own great offshoot, Buddhism, it does not look back to a single founder. Central to the religion is the belief that every creature, human and animal, has an immortal soul. Although the creature itself dies, the soul is constantly reborn in different types of body. This chain of rebirth, or reincarnation, is ended only when the soul attains union with the Absolute. India's complex caste system, tying people to the social class into which they are born, is also a basic feature of Hinduism; Hindus believe their place in life is pre-ordained. Each caste has its own customs and rituals

*Hinduism has a large variety of gods, corresponding to those of other polytheistic religions. They range from the great gods such as Vishnu, the preserver (above, left), to obscure local deities worshipped in villages. The god Shiva (right) is often regarded as a destroyer*

*This Hindu temple at Mamallapuram, south of Madras on the east coast of India, was built in the 8th century AD. Known as the Shore Temple, because it stands by the sea, it was intended to express the Hindu idea of a 'World Mountain'. With its seven steps, rising to heaven, it recalls the ancient step pyramid at Sakkara in Egypt*

as much a way of life as a religion. The faith can accommodate a remarkable diversity of beliefs and practices, whatever contradictions may result. It has many gods, the most popular of whom are the great gods of the Hindu classical tradition, Vishnu, the preserver, and Shiva, the destroyer.

Jainism, an offshoot of Hinduism, arose about the 6th century BC, and is today a small but well-established religion, with about 2 million adherents. Unlike Budd-

*A Jain monk is shown seated, in a 14th-century Indian miniature. The most important feature of the Jain religion is its emphasis on non-violence, which applies even towards insects*

hism, a much greater development out of Hinduism, it has mainly remained in India. Jains carry the Hindu principle of respect for life to its extreme. Since man is only a part of the whole scheme of living things, he has no right to exploit even the lowliest form of life. In any case he himself may have to endure, in some of his incarnations, the life of an animal or an insect. Jainism might have been taken up into Hinduism, had not its adherents rejected caste.

## Growth of Buddhism
Buddhism, which arose in India at about the same time as Jainism, also abandoned entirely the concept of caste. But, again like Jainism, it kept Hinduism's belief in reincarnation of souls. Its main teaching was that all life is suffering, and suffering is due to unsatisfied desires, so the only solution is to eliminate desire.

Buddhism spread from India into central Asia and China about the time of Christ. In its new settings it underwent considerable changes, and in the form known as Mahayana ('The Great Vehicle') it is so different from the mental and moral self-discipline of Gautama – Buddhism's founder, born in about 560 BC in northern India – as to be virtually a new religion.

Mahayana Buddhists encourage prayer and devotion to Gautama as a means of attaining salvation

*A portrait of the Chinese sage Confucius. His philosophic teachings emphasised duty and respect for others*

for oneself and others. Instead of facing an interminable series of rebirths, all worshippers might now hope that by faith they would be welcomed after death into a wonderful existence called the Western Paradise, or Pure Land. In southern Asia another form of Buddhism took root; it is known as Hinayana or Southern Buddhism, and has stayed nearer to the teaching of Gautama, with its pessimism and stress on individual effort.

By the time Buddhism arrived in China, two main systems of belief

were already established there: Confucianism and Taoism. They originated in the teachings of two philosophers, Confucius and Laotse, in the 6th century BC.

### Chinese wisdom
Confucius, born about 551 BC, was concerned to help man to live in society, and since he took an optimistic view of human nature he hoped that by education men could be improved. But he did not wish to be thought an innovator; he was a traditionalist. He hoped that by influencing the ruler of one Chinese state he might do something for justice and peace. But he was disappointed.

The movement known as Taoism is usually traced back to Lao-

*An 18th-century Chinese porcelain dish pictures an island paradise where the immortals dwell in bliss – an idea typical of Taoism in its popular form*

*This 18th-century Sanskrit scroll depicts legends about the kind and good Lord Vishnu, one of the three supreme gods of Hinduism; the others are Brahma and Shiva*

*The god Shiva, his wife Parvati and their children – the 'Holy Family' of Hinduism – are shown seated in a cave on Mount Kailasa, in this 19th-century painting. Shiva has been worshipped for thousands of years. To some Hindu sects he is the Supreme Being*

### BUDDHA'S MESSAGE
The founder of Buddhism, Gautama, was born in about 560 BC. At 35, as a result of long meditations on the meaning and problems of existence, Gautama underwent 'enlightenment' (Buddha, as he came to be called, means 'the enlightened one'). He began preaching a new message to his fellow men: all life is suffering, and suffering is due to unsatisfied desire, so the only solution is to quench desire. By reducing his attachment to this world, the wise man may hope to obtain release from the endless wheel of rebirth. This release is called *nirvana* – the cessation of all desire.

Buddhism spread from India into central Asia and China, where it went through considerable changes, about the time of Christ. Today its adherents number about 300,000,000

*This sculpture of the Gandhara school, which flourished between the 1st and 6th centuries AD, is one of many depicting legends about Buddha. He is seen as a young prince, travelling to his lessons in a carriage drawn by two rams, accompanied by his schoolfellows who carry ink-pots and writing boards*

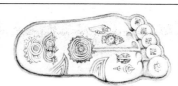

*During the early spread of Buddhism, the footprint of Buddha was often represented in places which he was believed to have visited. This depiction of his footprint is covered with Buddhist symbols, including, on the toes, the lotus and swastika*

*A carved stone relief in the Gandhara style portrays Queen Maya's dream of the white elephant, by which she conceived Buddha. There are many legends about Buddha's miraculous birth and later life, but little is known with certainty about him*

*A 19th-century bronze sculpture from Thailand, of the death of Buddha. According to tradition, Buddha achieved enlightenment under a bo-tree at the age of 35, and then he preached until his death at 80. Since he had overcome all attachment to existence, there was nothing left which could require another birth. He had achieved nirvana*

*The elaborate temple of Wat Phra Keo, or Chapel of the Emerald Buddha, in Bangkok, Thailand, was built in the 18th century. Thailand is a centre of the orthodox branch of Buddhism known as Hinayana ('Lesser Vehicle')*

# Spreading the Word to the world

The Triumph of St Thomas, *by a 14th-century Italian artist, honours medieval Christendom's greatest thinker, Thomas Aquinas (c. 1225–74). Standing to his right is the Greek philosopher Aristotle, whose philosophy was reconciled with Christian faith in Aquinas's work, notably his* Summa Theologica. *Below Aquinas lies the Muslim philosopher Averroes, whose commentaries on Aristotle, written a century earlier, influenced Aquinas's thought*

tse, 'the Old One', who may have lived at about the same time as Confucius. He composed the work called the *Tao-Te-Ching* (the Way and its Power).

The message of this is that there should be no deliberate attempt to lead a virtuous life, still less to save men from the consequence of sin and evil. A follower of Taoism does not want to change the world, but to find his proper place in it.

## The spread of world religions

The two most dynamic faiths in history have been Christianity and Islam, both of which believe in a universal God. In the past they expanded by military conquest as much as by missionary endeavour, and they also grew by the formation of many new sects, adapted to local needs. Islam partly lost its

*A statue of a Bodhisattva, a Buddhist saint who postponed the bliss of* nirvana *to stay and help mankind*

unity with the formation of two main sects, the Sunni and the Shia. However, it continued to spread, until its cultural and religious community reached from the Atlantic right across central Asia to the Pacific.

In the 9th and 10th centuries Christendom was outshone by the brilliance of Arab culture. The Crusades, from 1096 to 1270, led to greater contact between the two civilizations and indirectly to

*A 14th-century Italian bronze statue of a Crusader, who campaigned to recover the Holy Land from Islam*

a revival of missionary work by Christians; St Francis of Assisi in AD 1220 preached before the Sultan of Egypt. Knowledge of Greek philosophy was revived in Europe because of Arabic versions and commentaries, translated in many cases by Jewish scholars into Latin.

During the 14th and 15th centuries Islam spread down the east coast of Africa to Zanzibar, into central Asia by way of Samarkand and reached, by sea, as far as Malacca and modern Indonesia. But the expansion of European influence began in the 15th century, and Islam's frontier with Christianity, from Spain to the Black Sea, was outflanked by Portuguese traders and settlers, who rounded Africa and reached India in 1498. The new explorers took Christian clergy with them to preach the Gospel. One of the declared motives of Columbus was the conversion of peoples he might discover when he sailed westwards in 1492.

## Control of religious ideas

For centuries the Christian Church was as much concerned to preserve orthodoxy within its own ranks as to convert heathens to the faith. With its triumphant emergence as the official religion of the Roman Empire in the 4th

*A print of the 1800's shows a Christian preacher in India. The 19th century was the great age of Protestant missionary effort throughout the world. Some converts were made in India, especially among the lowest social castes*

century, the Catholic Church in Rome claimed to be the sole guardian of Christian truth. Christ had said to St Peter: 'Thou art Peter and upon this rock I will build my Church'; and the popes were regarded as the direct successors of Peter.

Dogma developed through the ages as the result of debate within the Church on such matters as the nature of God and Christ. Any new ideas which seemed to contradict established teaching in these matters were denounced as dangerous heresy, and punished with varying degrees of severity. Excommunication (cutting a man off from the Church and so from the mercy of Christ), torture and sometimes burning at the stake were methods used to root out heresy. The most notorious device for maintaining orthodoxy, the Inquisition, was

*One of the 150 mosques in Kairouan, in Tunisia, a sacred city of Islam founded by Arab conquerors in the 7th century*

set up by Pope Innocent III, in the 13th century. It continued its work of investigating and punishing heresy for centuries – often with the support of the state.

### Medieval philosophy
Within the limits of faith, the leading intellects in the Church were often given the widest freedom to speculate on fundamental questions, such as the nature of God and the immortality of the soul. During the Middle Ages, the time of the Church's greatest power and confidence in the West, there was a remarkable flowering of religious philosophy.

At the summit of medieval thought stand the monumental works of St Thomas Aquinas, an Italian, who was deeply influenced

*Jesuits (left) visit the Indian Mughal Emperor Akbar, famed for his tolerance*

by the ideas of the ancient Greek philosopher Aristotle. In his *Summa Theologica* Aquinas sought to close the gap between reason and faith, holding that reason can prove the existence of God, and that nothing in Christian teaching is contrary to reason. His ideas were intensely debated by other contemporary thinkers, and vehemently opposed by some; but in time his vast system of thought came to be accepted as the official philosophy of the Catholic Church.

### Reformation leads to war
The most momentous and far-reaching conflict of ideas within the Church occurred with the Reformation, which began in Germany in the 16th century. Previously, reformers had merely questioned aspects of Church teaching and policy. But now a monk, Martin Luther, challenged the authority of the pope and replaced it by the authority of the Bible. All a man needed to enter the Kingdom of Heaven, said Luther, was to have faith. The Reformation, which upheld the right of the individual conscience to seek its own relationship with God, without the intervention of priests and saints, spread like wildfire throughout Germany.

Soon reformers in other countries, notably Jean Calvin and Ulrich Zwingli in Switzerland and John Knox in Scotland, took up the challenge against the Church. Impassioned disputes over doctrine

*The 16th-century Protestant leader Jean Calvin saw thrift, sobriety and hard work as the true Christian virtues*

quickly led to armed conflict. In both the 16th and 17th centuries, Europe was engulfed by religious warfare, climaxed by the Thirty Years' War, mainly fought in Germany (1618–48), when 10 million Germans are estimated to have met their deaths. The war was ended with the Peace of Westphalia in 1648. By the time men turned away from the horrors of this conflict, vast bodies of Christians had permanently broken away from the Catholic Church. An era of religious toleration followed, which saw the emergence of numerous new Protestant sects and the establishment of national Churches.

### The search for a new certainty
The spirit of humanism, born in Italy towards the end of the 15th

---

## REWARD AND PUNISHMENT

Most religions have the idea of a heaven and hell – places or states of supreme bliss or unrelieved misery, where human souls dwell after death. Heaven, the place where the virtuous are rewarded, has usually been identified with the sky; and sometimes it has been located on a mountain which soars far above the clouds, such as Mount Olympus, abode of the Greek gods. Some Chinese Taoists thought of heaven as an island, off the coast of China. Hell, the place where sinners are punished, has usually been thought of as subterranean, but not always as a place to roast in – pagan Scandinavians pictured it as freezing with ice and snow. In literature, the most harrowing vision of hell is Dante's *Inferno*. The modern world tends to reject, as naïve and man-made, the traditional conceptions and imagery of heaven and hell, in favour of more abstract notions of divine reward and punishment

*A Tibetan painting of the 'Western Paradise' of Amitabha (centre), who was regarded as an incarnation of Buddha*

*In Christian theology, heaven is not so much a place as a state of bliss; here is a more popular idea of heaven as a luxuriant garden*

*The use of imagination to convey the horrors of hell is taken to an extreme in this painting by the Flemish painter Hieronymus Bosch (c. 1450–1516), part of his work* The Garden of Earthly Delights. *Its macabre imagery and obscure symbolism give it a quality of nightmare intensity, which seems to anticipate modern surrealist art*

*A Japanese scroll painting shows a Buddhist hell scene. The King of the Underworld presides over his fiery domain, where sinners are tormented and punished. In the top left, the bad deeds of a sinner are reflected in a mirror; on the right, a sinner is being weighed in the scales. In the centre, the tongue of a liar is being torn out*

# The challenge posed by reason

The 17th-century French philosopher, mathematician and scientist René Descartes (above) is known as the father of modern philosophy. He was educated by Jesuits, and remained a faithful Catholic all his life. Yet as a thinker he completely rejected the Catholic tradition of philosophy, whose greatest authority was St Thomas Aquinas. Descartes began his system with universal doubt, arriving at a single certainty: doubt itself cannot be doubted. Hence his famous formulation, Cogito, ergo sum (I think, therefore I am). Descartes's great endeavour was to extend the mathematical method to all fields of human knowledge. Out of his system of thought developed the great European tradition of philosophy called Rationalism

century, placed a new emphasis on man, and turned many of the best minds away from the preoccupation with God and the afterlife which had dominated medieval thought. The Reformation of the 16th century shattered the unity of Christendom, and the Church could no longer convince all men that it was the sole transmitter and guardian of universal truth.

The powerful challenge of science, too, made by such men as the astronomers Copernicus and Galileo, further weakened the Church's intellectual authority. But it was with the French philosopher René Descartes (1596–1650) that a systematic new rationalist philosophy arose, in keeping with the restless, inquiring spirit of the time, yet offering to satisfy men's

Benedict Spinoza, a 17th-century Dutch-Jewish philosopher, adopted the rational method of Descartes. He held that God and Nature are identical

hunger for certainty. Though himself a Catholic, and deeply influenced by the structure and methods of St Thomas Aquinas's thought, Descartes rejected entirely the authority and tradition which Aquinas represented.

**'I think, therefore I am'**

Descartes believed that a man should try to doubt everything, until he arrived at first principles which could not be doubted. His argument was on these lines: 'My senses may deceive me. Perhaps

The liberal ideas of the English philosopher John Locke dominated 18th-century political thought

For the 18th-century Scottish thinker David Hume, an extreme sceptic, there could be no certain truth about things

my life is only a dream; even my knowledge of mathematics may be perverted by a malignant demon. But there is one thing I cannot doubt: "I think, therefore I am" (cogito ergo sum); if I think at all, there must be something which is thinking.' On the basis of this and other 'clear and distinct' ideas, Descartes then built up a picture of reality as a whole. He saw the material world as being a machine, wholly separated from the mind. This approach is known as Dualism. Only by God's intervention, Descartes believed, were the material and mental worlds connected. Descartes's teachings influenced

Jean-Jacques Rousseau (1712–78) asserted that man, to be virtuous, should obey his heart rather than his reason

two later 17th-century philosophers, the Dutchman Benedict Spinoza (1632–77) and the German Gottfried Leibniz (1646–1716).

All three of these philosophers are known as Rationalists, for they based much of their thinking on the new science of mathematics, and had an unbounded faith in the power of reason to deduce, from self-evident principles, the whole nature of reality.

**The Empiricists**

But a new philosophy opposing that of the Rationalists became established in Britain; it was called Empiricism. The founder of the Empirical school of philosophy was John Locke (1632–1704) who set out to show the origin, nature and limits of human knowledge.

Locke took as his starting-point the concept that all knowledge must derive from sensations of smell, sight, taste or touch, or from reflection on the act of thinking about such sensations. (Hence the term 'empiricism', after the sect of physicians called Empirici, who drew their rules of practice only from experience.) Influenced by the work of Isaac Newton, Locke

*The 18th-century German philosopher Immanuel Kant is best known for his notion of the 'categorical imperative', an inborn sense of moral duty*

held that some sensations accurately reflect the external world (those of shape, size and so on), whereas others ('ideas' of colour, smell and taste) do not. So the external world consists of colourless, odourless atoms; all the rest of our knowledge is contributed by our senses.

Bishop Berkeley (1685–1753) took Locke's view further by pointing out that, if all our knowledge is of sensations, we have no way of knowing whether any of

them truly resemble external objects. So, he said, there is no need to believe in any external world at all. Objects are just collections of 'ideas', and matter does not exist. However, all 'ideas' are always in the mind of God; so the world still exists, even when we are not perceiving it. Dr Johnson dealt with Bishop Berkeley's argument that matter does not exist in typical down-to-earth fashion. He kicked a stone, as solid a lump of matter as anything on earth, and said: 'I refute it thus.'

The Scottish philosopher David Hume (1711–76) took Empiricism to its most extreme point, holding that nothing exists but sensations – there is no God to underlie them, and not even a mind to perceive them. He argued that there is nothing permanent in the world, just sequences of sensations; and even the individual person is nothing but one such sequence.

**The German school**

The Empiricists were concerned to emphasise the importance of sense-observation, and the limits of reason, in opposition to the extreme claims for reason made by the Rationalists. The German philosopher Immanuel Kant (1724–1804) set out to mediate between the two schools by showing that reason can give true knowledge of reality, but only of things experienced by the senses. His view was that space and time do not exist independently, but are imposed by the mind on the world. For Kant, the mind largely creates what it knows.

Georg Hegel (1770–1831), one of the most difficult of all philosophers to understand, developed a view known as Absolute Idealism. On this view, matter is only an appearance or illusion; the only reality is 'Absolute Spirit', which expresses its nature in an historical

process of struggle and conflict. Out of this process emerges the true expression of Spirit – a perfect society where all conflicts are resolved in a higher synthesis.

Hegel's idea of the clash of opposites was taken over and adapted by Karl Marx (1818–83). But Marx turned Hegel's ideas upside-down. He made 'matter' the basis of his system, instead of 'Absolute Spirit'. In Marx's philosophical system, a series of class struggles will produce the lasting synthesis of Communism.

**Modern philosophy**

Today, philosophers are divided into two main schools, both of which have reacted against Ger-

*Hegel, a 19th-century German philosopher, has had a vast influence on modern thought. He viewed history as a rational process, always taking man forward*

man philosophy. In Europe, the Frenchman Jean-Paul Sartre, born in 1905, developed the philosophy of Existentialism, originated by the Dane Sören Kierkegaard (1813–55). This starts from concrete

*The 19th-century Christian thinker Kierkegaard developed the intensely subjective philosophy of Existentialism*

individual experience, instead of abstract theories. It analyses such features of experience as anxiety and death, and stresses man's freedom to determine his own future.

In contrast, philosophy in the English-speaking world has seen its main role as helping to analyse and clarify the nature of language and its relation to the world. It has tended to draw back from making pronouncements about the meaning of human existence. The works of the Austrian-born Ludwig Wittgenstein (1889–1951) are the dominant influence in this branch of 20th-century philosophy. Wittgenstein started his career under Bertrand Russell at Cambridge,

*The Englishman Bertrand Russell, pioneer of a revolutionary new method of logical analysis based on mathematics, saw philosophy as the 'handmaiden of science'. He won international fame as a pacifist in later life*

which was a leading centre of philosophy under Russell and his colleague A. N. Whitehead. But later he reacted against Russell.

**Religion today**

The strongest challenge to organised religion comes from Communism – an openly atheistic ideology which nonetheless has much of the appeal of a religion. The spread of materialistic values in many parts of the world, and the accompanying decline in religious belief, especially among educated people, are further challenges. Yet religion holds powerful sway over the minds of millions. The major religions claim more than 2000 million adherents in all. Religion still appeals to a deep-felt need in man, and in church, synagogue, mosque and temple the quest for spiritual truth continues.

---

**MAKERS OF IDEOLOGY**

*The Englishman John Stuart Mill was a leader of liberal democratic thought in the 19th century. He passionately defended the importance of the individual*

The 19th century saw a revolution in man's way of looking at his world. In the quiet back-rooms of philosophy were forged new ideologies which, in the hands of ruthless men, threw

*Friedrich Nietzsche attacked Christianity as decadent, saying 'God is dead'. He looked to the 'superman' to bring about a heroic new way of life for mankind*

nations and classes into violent conflict in the 20th century. Nietzsche's 'superman' influenced the Nazis, and Marx's 'scientific socialism' took distorted form in the tyranny of Stalinism

*Marx, founder of modern Communism, saw history as a class struggle. He believed the philosopher's role was not only to understand history, but to change it*

# The secrets of the universe

*By observation and experiment,
man has probed the workings of nature
and the origin of life itself*

*God the Father plans the architecture of his universe with a pair of dividers: an illustration from a 13th-century French Bible sets the instruments of mathematical inquiry against the background of medieval faith*

Man is a thinking animal. And the most intriguing set of questions he has ever set himself to think about are those concerned with the nature of life. How was the universe created? When did life begin? What is the difference between living and non-living? Between mind and matter?

For long ages, mankind's first preoccupation was with the struggle for survival. Men sought no explanation for the working of natural forces which affected their lives, but accepted that they were controlled by gods who ruled every aspect of their destiny. If a volcano erupted, the gods were angry; if a man prospered in love or war, the gods had favoured him.

Even man's earliest deliberate observations of the heavens had a severely practical purpose – that of building up a calendar of the seasons to help him tell when to plant and harvest his crops; there was still no attempt to draw conclusions from his study of nature.

*Adam awakening into life at God's touch, as depicted by Michaelangelo*

*Islam, like Christianity, is based partly on the Old Testament. A 13th-century manuscript depicts Adam and Eve*

It was not until the time of the ancient Greeks that some men began to turn away from myth and to question the nature of their universe. As early as the 5th century BC the Greek philosopher Democritus put forward the theory that matter is composed of atoms. But such theories could not be proved until relatively recent times. Instead of explaining 'Why', the early thinkers could merely theorise about 'How'.

**Myths of creation**
There is a striking similarity about the creation myths of many lands which probably embody man's earliest thinking about the origin of his world. In most myths, the earth and the sky are gods. The universe is an egg, or a vast, formless ocean without light. A supreme

## THE MYSTERY OF CREATION

*Tangaroa Upao Vahu is revered by the Polynesians of the Pacific as their creator god*

The question of how man and his world began has been a theme of compelling interest to the mind of man for thousands of years. From earliest times, when primitive tribes invented gods to explain the unknown, almost all peoples unquestioningly accepted that creation was the work of some supernatural force. Even a sophisticated civilization like that of the Aztecs of central America, capable of building mighty temples and cities, believed that the sun would not rise unless the gods were paid a regular tribute of human blood. The most widespread and enduring creation story is the Old Testament account of how God brought order out of the chaos of a dark and formless world, and finally created man. It was not until the 19th century, when Charles Darwin produced his theory of evolution, that the Biblical account of the creation was challenged

*An Aboriginal myth: the east wind pushes up the morning star to make daylight, which in turn creates the earth and man*

*An Egyptian papyrus of 1000 BC shows Nun, god of the waters, supporting a boat containing a disc and sacred scarab, representing the sun-god. Reaching for the disc are Nut, the sky-goddess, and her son, Osiris*

being emerges, to bring order out of chaos, and to create light and life, including man.

So powerful were these early myths that they remained for nearly all mankind the main basis of belief about the creation of the universe and the origins of life until little more than a century ago. The people who built up these imaginative legends to account for their everyday world were also capable of impressive mathematical and astronomical achievements. Clay tablets made 4000 years ago in Mesopotamia, one of the seed-beds of religious speculation, show a sophisticated knowledge of mathematics; and in Egypt the need to predict the rise and fall of the life-giving Nile led to the development of an accurate calendar, with a year of 365 days.

## Putting reason first

The greatest flowering of man's early speculation came in ancient Greece, from about 500 BC. The Greek philosophers regarded reasoning as the highest attribute of man. According to Plato (427-347 BC): 'every soul possesses an organ, the intellect, better worth saving than a thousand eyes, because it is our only means of seeing the truth'. The Greeks were mainly concerned with how men should live – with the nature of abstract qualities such as beauty and truth, justice and virtue. But they were also much concerned with the nature

*On this Yoruba bowl from Nigeria, the snake, to the Yoruba a symbol of eternity, wisdom and knowledge, teaches man and woman how to reproduce themselves*

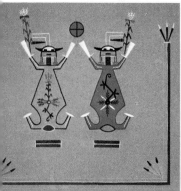

*The Navajo Indians of North America believed in two creator gods, Mother Earth (left) and Father Sky (right). Both combined to create the world and man*

*Noah (right) builds his ark: a medieval view of the story of the flood by which God punished man's disobedience*

of matter. Thales, known as one of the seven wise men of ancient Greece, had put forward as early as the 7th century BC theories that were halfway between the mythologies of the past and the scientific approach that was yet to come. He thought the earth might be a disc that floated on the seas, like wood on water, or perhaps a plant-like organism that grew out of the water. Thales believed that water was the basic stuff from which all things were derived.

Another Greek thinker, Anaxagoras (500–428 BC) proceeded more like the scientists of today. He gave laboratory demonstrations to his pupils, and prepared a written account of his theories. He tried out his ideas by experiment. He recognised that gases tend to rise

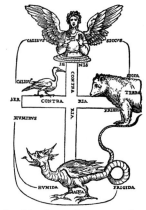

*Aristotle's theory that matter is composed of earth, air, fire and water was accepted for 2000 years. In this 1546 drawing creatures represent the elements*

above solid matter, in the same way as steam rises from a cauldron or smoke from a fire, and he identified air as a gas. He saw in wind the power of air to exert pressure, and therefore to move objects.

Like the Babylonians before him, Anaxagoras thought of the earth as a flat solid, which he believed was suspended in space on a mattress of air. He demonstrated his idea by filling a wineskin with air and twisting its neck, like a child with a balloon, until the compressed air made the skin so firm that it would bear heavy weights.

From his observations, Anaxagoras could see how matter changed its form, but remained indestructible. A tree extracts matter from the soil, and is nourished by rain from the clouds. When cut down and burnt, part of the tree goes up in smoke into the clouds

to be returned in the form of rain. Part of the tree remains as ashes, which crumble into the soil to nourish plants. To Anaxagoras, it seemed that in these transformations the matter of the log would eventually pass through every state of every substance in the world, and indeed in the universe.

## The first atomic theory

Another Greek, Democritus, argued that there must be an ultimate, unsplittable particle, to which he gave the name *atom*, meaning indivisible. He thought the basic matter of the universe consisted of two substances: space, and an infinite number of atoms. Everything was made of atoms, and objects differed from each other according to the shape, size, arrangement and position of their atoms. All these atoms, said Democritus, were in motion, like specks dancing in a sunbeam. This motion brought atoms into contact, so that they combined to form larger units. Heavier atoms formed the earth and lighter ones the sky. Vast numbers of atoms came together to form countless worlds, and after a time the atoms scattered, and the worlds disappeared into the void.

These theories, which were not based on scientific evidence but rather on intuition, bear an uncanny resemblance to modern theories about the structure and origin of things. But they got little support at the time.

### THE ASTRONOMERS

After the break-up of the Roman Empire, the study of the heavens languished in Europe. Even after learning revived, scientific inquiries were inhibited by the dogmatic teachings of the Catholic Church. But in the Middle East, Muslim astronomers continued their researches in great observatories at Damascus, Alexandria and especially at Baghdad. Arab knowledge of the sciences ultimately flowed westwards back to Europe, and east to India and China

*Astronomers at work in an Islamic observatory. The scientist at upper right is holding and pointing to an astrolabe, used to measure the altitude of stars*

## Aristotle's four elements

In the rich ferment of ideas in the ancient Greek world, the names of great men are like stars in a galaxy. And most of them lived and taught in Athens, a city-state with a population of free citizens of some 68,000 – no larger than present-day Eastbourne. One Athenian who was to assume a dominant influence well into medieval times was Aristotle (384–322 BC), the teacher of Alexander the Great and the

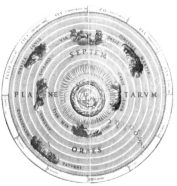

*The universe as seen by the 2nd-century Greek astronomer Ptolemy: the earth is at the centre, and the sun, moon, stars and planets revolve around it*

philosopher who drew together all the most important findings of ancient knowledge.

Building on the work of his predecessors, Aristotle described four basic substances – earth, air, fire and water – from which all matter on earth was made up. The sun, stars and the other planets were not, however, composed of any of these, but of a fifth element. They shone, said Aristotle, because their motion through the heavens caused friction, producing light and heat.

Aristotle's intellect influenced man's thought for nearly 2000 years. However, his teachings contained errors which were also perpetuated. He said that everything on earth contained the four elements in varying proportions, and that if the proportions were changed they could be transformed into other substances. This belief laid the basis for the experimental work of the medieval alchemists, who tried to change base metals such as lead into gold.

Another error of Aristotle which was to have far-reaching effects was summed up in his confident statement: 'Every dry body that turns moist, or every moist body that turns dry, produces animals, provided only that it can give them nourishment.' This theory of the spontaneous generation of life was to be unquestioningly accepted for nearly 2000 years.

## Man the centre of all things

About 500 years later another Greek, living in Alexandria, put forward theories that were also to be influential for centuries. Claudius Ptolemaeus, better known as Ptolemy, declared that the earth was a sphere, placed motionless at

295

# *From superstition to science*

*A fantastic creature from a 16th-century Italian manuscript represents the 'essence of mercury', which alchemists believed was an essential ingredient of all matter. Although alchemy was deeply tinged with such superstitions, its practitioners made some important scientific advances*

the centre of the universe, and that the sun, moon and planets revolved around it. This theory, which seemed to place man at the centre of all things, became a keystone of Christian thought, until in the Middle Ages a few thinking men finally risked life and liberty to disprove it.

Soon the Dark Ages were to descend on Europe, and the ingenious speculations of the Greeks were cut short. The Arabs, however, translated Greek scientific works and tested and developed their theories. They not only kept Greek thought alive, but made discoveries of their own and thus accumulated knowledge which was passed to Renaissance Europe.

## A friar's experiments
In the Middle Ages, although the Catholic Church suppressed any questioning of the traditional teaching about the workings of nature, some men dared to question and to experiment. Notable among them was a Franciscan friar in England, Roger Bacon (1214–94).

Despite the command of St Augustine, one of the great early Fathers of the Roman Church, to 'go not out of doors. Return into

*The English friar Roger Bacon was imprisoned by the Church in 1277 for refusing to stop his scientific experiments. He was released just before his death*

thyself . . . In the inner man dwells truth', Bacon experimented in mathematics, optics, chemistry and astronomy, but this brought on him the displeasure of his religious superiors. He had, however, a secret arrangement with Pope Clement IV, who was interested in Bacon's scientific projects, and in his idea of setting up an institute to produce and maintain an encyclopaedia of all the known sciences. Bacon accordingly began to produce results and dispatch

## THE SEARCH FOR THE PHILOSOPHER'S STONE

The science of alchemy spread from the Arab world to Europe in the Middle Ages. The medieval alchemist was a mixture of chemist, philosopher and charlatan. His science was dominated by two quests – one for the so-called philosopher's stone, which would turn base metals into gold, and the other for the elixir of life. The 13th-century alchemist Arnald of Villanova said this elixir would 'turn an old man into a youth, dispel poison from the heart, fortify the lungs, regenerate the blood and heal wounds'. Atomic physics has produced a 'philosopher's stone' – a nuclear accelerator which can make new elements

*An allegorical picture shows the three stages by which it was believed that base metal might be transmuted into gold. As the metal is heated in the first flask, its spirit, represented by a dove, is separated from its body. This body, represented by the toad in the second flask, is then put into solution. The two are re-united in the third flask to produce gold*

*An alchemist at work with a still. In their search for the philosopher's stone, the alchemists set up the first laboratories, where they developed many basic techniques, such as distillation, which are still used in the chemical laboratories of today. They are also credited with the discovery of five elements – antimony, arsenic, bismuth, phosphorus and zinc*

them to the pope. Clement's death in 1268 removed all hope of Bacon's projects gaining recognition. But he went on with his researches and teaching until the Franciscans imprisoned him in 1277, and just before his death he was writing as defiantly as ever.

Bacon had great imaginative vision, and his highest ambition was to have a planetarium, in which the heavenly bodies would move automatically and accurately across a man-made sky. This goal invited opposition from the Church; for the heavens were still regarded as the exclusive territory of the theologians, who accepted the theory of Ptolemy that the earth was at the centre of the universe.

## The Renaissance

In his refusal to be overawed by authority, and in his respect for scientific truth, Bacon stood out as a man nearly two centuries ahead of his time. In his struggles for the right to keep on asking awkward questions he was like a John the Baptist, preparing the way in the wilderness for the Renaissance – the intellectual rebirth of western Europe. At last, artists and men of science discarded the blinkers that had stultified scientific inquiry. Adventurous minds, with wide-open eyes, looked outwards and upwards and saw things as they really were, and not as Aristotle, the theologians or some other authority ordained that they should be. They saw all nature waiting to be explored and questioned. And the new printing presses were producing books to spread knowledge and generate disturbing ideas in the minds of the new scholars.

## The 'Universal Genius'

The men of the Renaissance were astonishing in what they attempted. The talents and interests of Leonardo da Vinci (1452-1519) were so various that he has been called the 'Universal Genius'. He was an artist, mathematician, physicist, chemist, botanist, geolo-

*Isaac Newton's reflector telescope of 1672 (above) was the first to use a system of mirrors instead of lenses to focus the light it received*

gist, anatomist, astronomer, musician, engineer and town-planner. Leonardo called himself a 'man without letters', by which he meant that he had not been academically educated. He knew no Latin or Greek, and his classroom education ended at 15 when his father apprenticed him to the artist Verrocchio.

Verrocchio was an enlightened master. He interested Leonardo in perspective, and this led Leonardo to astonishing discoveries

about the working of the human eye. He watched glassmakers grinding the lenses for spectacles, and soon he was grinding his own lenses, the better to study the heavens. Leonardo's astronomical studies produced the idea, more than a century before Galileo, that the sun does not move. Leonardo had begun to displace man from the centre of the universe.

Another typical man of the Renaissance was Nicholas Copernicus (1473–1543), a Polish scholar learned in all the sciences of the time, who reached the conclusion that the earth revolved around the sun once a year, and that it and the other planets move in uniformly circular orbits. Copernicus had found the essential key to understanding the universe. There was

*Two moon phases drawn by Galileo; he wrongly assumed the darker areas on the lighted portion to be seas*

*The observations by which Galileo (above) proved that the earth moved round the sun made him a heretic in the eyes of the Roman Catholic Church*

to be no going back now. A Dane, Tycho Brahe (1546–1601), produced systematic star-maps, and his colleague Johannes Kepler (1571–1630) went on to define the laws that are the foundation of modern astronomy.

## Discovery by telescope

The influence which the Church still exerted over the study of the workings of the universe was soon to be demonstrated in the case of Galileo Galilei (1564–1642), a

---

*The Danish astronomer Tycho Brahe (1546–1601) is framed by a giant quadrant in his observatory on the island of Hven. Sponsored by his king, Brahe spent 21 years in drawing up the first catalogues of stars by naked-eye observations*

*One of the two observatories, or 'Castles of the Stars', which Brahe built for his work. It had a library, laboratory and living apartments, as well as rooms for his instruments. From these observatories Brahe established the position of 777 stars*

### THE EARTH MOVES

It was not until the 16th century that man first began seriously to question the theory of Ptolemy, unchallenged for more than 1000 years, that the earth was the centre of the universe. The Polish astronomer Nicholas Copernicus was the first man to work out, in 1533, that the earth must move round the sun. His work was followed up by a Danish astronomer, Tycho Brahe, who, although he did not accept Copernicus's theory, produced the first systematic star-maps. Brahe's observations were used by his German colleague, Johannes Kepler, who went on to work out laws governing planetary motion, and so supplied the 'missing links' in the findings of Copernicus

*Nicholas Copernicus (1473–1543) was a canon of the Catholic Church as well as a successful astronomer. He studied in Italy under Domenico Navarra of Ferrara, whose measurements and observations made Copernicus question the whole system of Ptolemaic astronomy. In his De Revolutionibus Orbium Coelestium, 'Concerning the Movements of the Heavenly Bodies', Copernicus attacked Ptolemy's theory because it could not satisfactorily account for the movements of the planets; instead he concluded that the earth revolves round the sun. Because of the opposition of the Church, which held that the earth must be the centre of all things, Copernicus did not publish his work until he lay dying – and even then his publisher insisted that the theory was nothing more than a 'mathematical fiction' to help in calculating the movements of the planets*

*Figures of earlier astronomers, Hipparchus, Copernicus, Tycho Brahe and Ptolemy decorate the frontispiece of the* Tabulae Rudolphinae, *dedicated by the German astronomer Johannes Kepler (1571-1630) to the Holy Roman Emperor Rudolf II, whom he served as court mathematician. Kepler worked with Brahe after the Danish astronomer resigned from his post at Hven, and continued his observations after his death. Kepler began by attempting to prove Brahe's theory that while other planets revolve round the sun, the sun and moon revolve round the earth; but he ended by proving instead the accuracy of Copernicus's theory that all the planets, including the earth and the moon, revolve round the sun. In his 'Laws of Planetary Motion', Kepler showed that the planets move in ellipses and not in perfect circles, as Copernicus stated. Kepler also proved that the speeds of planets are proportional to their mean distance from the sun. In the* Tabulae, *published in 1627, Kepler used his laws as a basis for tables of planetary positions. There were so accurate that they were used by astronomers for a century*

---

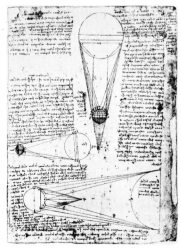

*A page from Leonardo da Vinci's notebooks shows his unsuccessful attempts to devise a method of calculating the distance between the earth and sun*

# By trial and error to the truth

*The chemists of the 18th century, shown at work in a typical laboratory of the period, were obsessed with experiment; no theory was accepted unless it could be backed by practical tests. In 1789 the Frenchman Antoine Lavoisier produced a treatise which marked the foundation of chemistry as a science*

professor of mathematics at Pisa in Italy. After hearing of the invention of the telescope by a Dutch optician called Hans Lippershey in 1608, Galileo built himself several of the instruments, and he was the first man to use them in astronomy. By observation, he found that the moon did not shine by its own light, as Aristotle had believed, but by reflected light from the sun. He discovered that the Milky Way was composed of distant stars, that Jupiter had satellites, and that the sun had spots. These sun-spots convinced him that Copernicus was right; their apparent movement across the face of the sun confirmed that the earth was really moving around the sun.

This was no longer a matter which the Church was prepared to tolerate as a mental exercise. In the 1630's the Catholic Church was fighting for survival against the forces of the Protestant Reformation, and Catholics and Protestants were destroying central Europe in the Thirty Years' War. The Copernican theory that the

*Early scientists explained reproduction by fantastic theories. A drawing of 1605 shows a lamb growing on a plant*

earth moved round the sun was heresy, for it denied what the Church officially taught. Galileo was denounced to the Inquisition, imprisoned, and forced to recant. But legend has it that even as he publicly denied that the earth moved, he muttered to himself: 'And yet it moves.'

## Beginnings of science

The Inquisition thus managed to silence the voice of inquiry in Italy, the birthplace of the Renaissance, for some centuries. But at this very time the torch was being taken up elsewhere. Francis Bacon (1561-1626), Lord Chancellor of England, though himself scarcely a laboratory scientist, is usually re-

*The frontispiece of William Harvey's 17th-century* De Generatione Animalium. *Harvey concluded that almost all animals are produced from eggs*

garded as having founded modern scientific method by insisting that every theory should be tested and proved by experiments.

In a series of books, Bacon established the modern procedure for science. First the scientist, by observation, forms a theory, or hypothesis, that links certain facts together and provides a reasonable explanation for them; from this hypothesis he deduces further facts, which he then constantly subjects to checks or experiments. If these facts prove to be true, and his deductive reasoning is correct, then the original hypothesis is also deemed to be accurate. Bacon had been trained as a lawyer, and he applied to science the laws of evidence and the burden of proof.

The advantage of recorded scientific theories or laws is that the new student does not have to rediscover or check each fact. He has a reliable framework in which to operate until new facts emerge which the theory does not seem to fit. So it was with the work of the man who put the finishing touches to the new astronomy, Isaac Newton (1642-1727).

Newton stated that each body in the universe exerted a gravitational pull on the other bodies. The same force that pulled an apple earthwards from a tree also kept the planets in their orbits. The strength of the force of gravity depended on the mass of the bodies, and the

*An engine propelled by a jet of steam was built to explain Newton's third law of motion – that for every action there is an equal and opposite reaction*

distance between them. The attraction between the earth and an object, explained Newton, accounted for the object's weight.

Newton's laws of gravity and mechanics remained undisputed until the behaviour of the planet Mercury was found not to conform to them. This discrepancy was not explained until Einstein's Theory of Relativity in the 20th century.

### Discovering how life began

While some men were reaching out to grasp the secrets of the universe, others looked inwards, for the secrets of life itself. Few people before Galileo's time had bothered much about the origins of life. Most people either believed explanations such as those of the Old Testament, or else accepted the assumption that life developed from non-living matter, as stated by Aristotle.

It was not until the 17th century that William Harvey, physician to Charles I of England, came to the conclusion that 'almost all animals . . . and man, himself, are produced from eggs'. Shortly after Harvey's death, the Italian naturalist Francesco Redi demonstrated conclusively that maggots in rotting

*Voyaging on the survey ship* Beagle, *here seen beached for cleaning, Charles Darwin made the observations on which he was to base his theory of evolution*

meat hatched from eggs deposited by flies. But belief in the idea that life generated itself spontaneously continued into the mid-1800's.

Dutch scientists led the search for the secrets of reproduction, helped by the development of the compound microscope in Holland, beginning about 1590. Regnier de Graff, a Dutch anatomist, took Harvey's egg theory a stage further. Finding that eggs were present in all female animals, he stated in 1672 that the function of the female ovaries was to produce eggs and bring them to maturity. A major breakthrough came in 1677, when the Dutch microscopist Antonius von Leeuwenhoek (1632-1723)

discovered spermatozoa in the semen of men, animals and fish. He concluded that foetuses developed from sperms that were nourished inside the female eggs. Then, in the 1700's, Lazzaro Spallanzani (1729–99), an Italian physiologist, succeeded in artificial fertilisation by moistening virgin frog eggs with frog semen.

In the 1850's the Frenchman Louis Pasteur (1822-95), a professor of chemistry and physics, finally swept away the idea of the spontaneous generation of life by showing that fermentation in beer and wine results from the presence of minute organisms called bacteria. Later, even smaller microorganisms, called viruses, were discovered. These seem to be in a state between living and non-living things; they are so minute that they are beyond detection by the most powerful optical microscopes.

While Pasteur was quietly demolishing some of the pillars of established belief, an Englishman, Charles Darwin (1809–82), was shaking another pillar with his work on the evolution of the human species. His work was carried a stage further by the researches of Gregor Mendel into heredity.

### Understanding the atom

One of the most dramatic stories of the 19th century is that of the discovery of the nature of the atom. The British meteorologist John Dalton (1766–1844) came to think that all matter consists of atoms that cannot be artificially created, destroyed or split; that the atoms of one element differ from those of another, particularly in weight; that chemical reactions result from a rearrangement of atoms; and that compounds come about from the formation of what he called 'compound atoms'.

Dalton's greatest contribution was to state his atomic theory in precise, if not altogether accurate, terms, and to assign atomic weights to the known elements. Later, the Russian chemist Dmitri Mendeleev (1834–1907) cleared up many errors with his Periodic Table.

The discovery by Becquerel that some substances gave off rays led Marie and Pierre Curie in France to prove that, entirely contrary to the classical notion, some atoms were not indivisible: the radiation, Marie demonstrated, came from inside the atom and, therefore, the atom was dividing. Using primitive equipment, she and André de

---

## DARWIN AND THE DESCENT OF MAN

In 1859, the English biologist Charles Darwin, in his book *On the Origin of Species by Means of Natural Selection*, cast doubt on the creation of man as described in the Old Testament. Man, Darwin argued, was not created by a single act of God, but was the result of millions of years of evolution and natural selection.

Darwin's theories arose from his observations of differences between living things. For instance, finches of the Galapagos Islands had different types of beak according to their diet. From this he concluded that either God must have created each type of finch separately, or else they had developed over thousands of years, during which time unsuitable bills were bred out of the species in the struggle for survival.

Darwin based this concept of struggle on the observed fact that every living creature produces far more offspring than can survive, and that only those best suited to life survive and breed. After 20 years of research, Darwin applied his theory to man

*Charles Darwin (1809–82) was 50 when he published his findings on evolution, later summed up as 'the survival of the fittest'. But he based his theories largely on the observations he had made as a young man when sailing round South America as ship's naturalist on a scientific expedition*

*A bewildered ape puzzles over his place on the evolutionary 'ladder', in a* Punch *cartoon of 1861. Darwin's theory of evolution sparked off a furious controversy between science and religion. The majority of Victorian clergymen felt that Darwinism was a blasphemous attack on the Bible and swept away the basis of the Christian religion. But today many Christians accept that the truths of the Bible and the theory of evolution can exist side by side.*
*Many of those who attacked Darwin did so from ignorance. They accused him of saying that man was descended from the apes. In fact, what Darwin suggested was that both man and apes might have shared a common ancestor. Many eminent figures were drawn into the controversy. When asked his opinion of Darwinism, the British Prime Minister, Benjamin Disraeli, replied that if man was either an ape or an angel, he was 'on the side of the angels'. But the researches of Darwin's fellow biologists, such as Thomas Huxley, all tended to confirm his theories*

---

## HEREDITY FROM A PEA

Darwin's theory of natural selection had left unanswered the question of how characteristics were passed on from generation to generation, and how variations of species therefore occurred. The answer to this mystery was supplied by an Austrian monk, Gregor Mendel, when he discovered that inherited characteristics are passed from parent to offspring in a predictable way by means of what are now called genes. Mendel established this by cross-fertilising a strain of tall garden pea with a dwarf variety and studying the ratio of tall plants to dwarf plants in the resulting hybrid plants. Mendel's findings were to lay the foundations of modern genetics

*Gregor Mendel (1822-84) was born in an obscure Austrian peasant family and entered the Church to escape the poverty of his background. He was ordained at 25 and became a teacher. In 1858, as abbot of a monastery at Brno, in what is now Czechoslovakia, Mendel began his famous experiments. He worked for eight years before publishing his reports. Mendel's work remained ignored in his life-time, and its importance was not recognised until 1900*

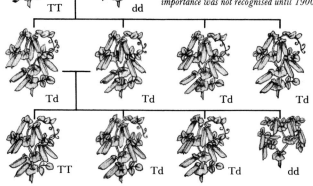

*When Mendel crossed a tall pea with a dwarf pea, all the first generation of plants were tall because the gene of tallness was dominant, and the gene of shortness recessive. Cross-breeding among this second generation produced, in the third generation, one short plant to every three tall plants. This happened because, out of the four different combinations of genes possible, only the pairing of the recessive 'short' genes from both parents produces a dwarf plant; in the other three, the gene of tallness remains dominant*

# Discoveries in outer space

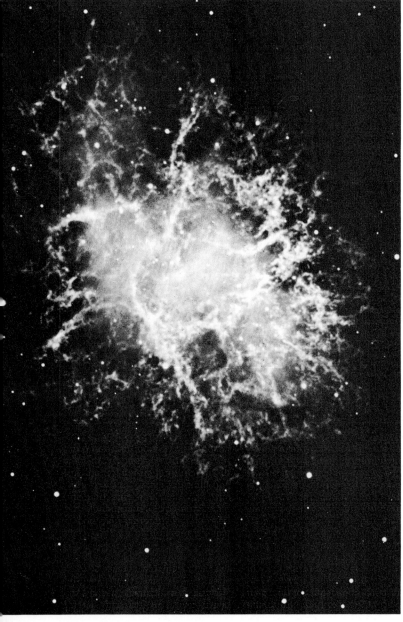

Light from outer space takes thousands of years to reach the earth. This cloud of dust and debris known as the Crab Nebula was formed when a star exploded and expanded in flaming gases. The explosion took place 4000 years before Chinese astronomers saw it in AD 1054 – and a continuing outburst of expanding gases produced radio signals which are still reaching the earth today

Bierne toiled for years until she had separated a new element – radium. Later, radium was found beneficial in the treatment of cancer, because its rays destroy tissue, and so can check the growth of cancer cells.

## The path to atomic power

Ernest Rutherford (1871–1937), a young New Zealander working at the Cavendish Laboratory at Cambridge in the 1890's, was also interested in what happened outside the atom. Why, he asked, did radium give off rays? By persisting with the question, Rutherford became the first man to split the atom, and so established the new

John Dalton (1766–1844) is caricatured holding a rain gauge. Dalton's fame rests on his atomic theory

science of nuclear physics. He gathered around him a group of brilliant nuclear physicists, whose work led to the release of nuclear energy and eventually to the atomic bomb. Among his pupils were 14 future Nobel Prizewinners.

Rutherford and his followers built up a picture of the atom. At the centre was the nucleus. Revolving around it, at fantastically high speeds, were electrons. These, said

This simple apparatus was used by Ernest Rutherford in 1919 to split the nucleus of the nitrogen atom. The split atomic particles were tracked on a screen

Rutherford, have fixed orbits around the nucleus, like the orbits of planets in their journeys around the sun. The main secrets of atoms had been discovered. They were not solid building blocks, but like tiny solar systems, composed almost entirely of space. Research continued until, on the eve of the Second World War, German and

In his Theory of Relativity, Albert Einstein revolutionised men's concept of the nature of time and energy

Austrian scientists found that nuclear fission – splitting the atom and so liberating particles called neutrons – released vast stores of energy. This discovery made the construction of an atom bomb a possibility.

The warning that Nazi Germany would try to produce such a bomb was given in a letter to President Roosevelt by the physicist Albert Einstein (1879–1955), a German Jew who had fled to the United States to avoid Nazi persecution. Einstein's work had been one of the factors that made the atomic bomb possible. For his Theory of Relativity shattered the traditional concepts of time and space, motion, mass and gravitation.

## Big Bang or Steady State?

In the 1940's, atomic research held the centre of the scientific stage. But in the 1950's attention centred on the so-called New Cosmology – new ideas about the origins and evolution of the universe.

It had long been known that the universe is expanding and that the great star clusters, called galaxies, are moving away from each other at almost incredible speeds. In 1927, the Belgian astronomer, Georges Lemaître, had put forward the 'Big Bang' theory to account for this expansion. He suggested that the universe began with a huge mass of matter exploding as a 'primeval fireball' and breaking up to form separate galaxies. This would explain the way in which the galaxies are still moving apart from each other.

But in 1949, the outside world heard for the first time about the ideas of a group of Cambridge scientists on the origins of the universe. Their leader, Fred Hoyle, put forward a theory which ap-

The interior of the nuclear accelerator at Berkeley, California. The accelerator can be used to make new elements – the medieval alchemists' dream realised

peared to account for the expanding universe in a different way. In place of the Big Bang, Hoyle and his collaborators offered the 'Steady State'. According to this theory, the universe has no beginning and no end. It has always been, and will always remain. So how can the expansion be explained? The Steady State scientists suggested that matter, in the form of hydrogen atoms, is being perpetually created throughout the universe. The hydrogen gradually accumulates into vast clouds that form new galaxies. As the old galaxies move further apart, new ones form in the spaces which open up between them.

The simplicity of the Steady State theory was strongly challenged in the mid-1960's, especially by radio astronomers, who preferred the evolutionary theory of the universe. These radio astronomers, using instruments like the giant radio telescope at Jodrell Bank in Cheshire, had been studying the radio waves from distant stars, and they detected a much greater number of weak radio sources than of strong ones. This suggested that the number of stars increases further out in space.

This conclusion contradicts one of the principles of the Steady State theory, which is that the universe is uniform throughout. Most astronomers, including Hoyle, have now begun to abandon the Steady State theory in favour of an idea on the lines of the original Big Bang of a primeval fireball.

### The blueprint of life
While radio astronomers were using their new scientific equipment to reach into the depths of space, scientists were using other new ultra-powerful instruments, such as electron and proton microscopes and X-ray crystallography, to penetrate deeper and more inquisitively into the recesses of living things. Molecular biology was revealing how the living cell itself was built up.

Scientists began to study the chemistry of the genes, which dictate not only how the cells in the body are formed and replaced, but also the characteristics of unborn generations. The significance of deoxyribonucleic acid – DNA – as the basic stuff of life, was first discovered at the Rockefeller Institute, New York, in 1944. In the following nine years, the study of viruses disclosed that they possessed genes. It was found that these genes consisted entirely of DNA, and it was therefore concluded that DNA must be the vehicle for passing on genetic information.

A brilliant discovery followed in 1953 – the so-called 'double helix' structure of the DNA molecule, shaped like a spiralling ladder. In this ladder, the spirals contain sugars and phosphates, whereas the rungs are composed of chemicals called bases. The discovery was made by James D. Watson, an

*Niels Bohr, a Nobel Prizewinner in 1922 for his work in atomic physics, escaped from Nazi-occupied Denmark to the United States in 1943 and helped build the first atomic bomb*

American biologist, and Francis Crick, a British physical chemist, working together at Cambridge University. Their work was based on X-ray observations made by Maurice Wilkins, of King's College, London: all three men were awarded a Nobel Prize in 1962.

Watson and Crick succeeded in constructing a model of the DNA molecule. They showed that according to the arrangement along its twisted ladder of four groups of chemicals, called nucleotides, a code is spelt out. This chemical

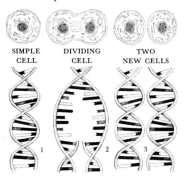

*When a cell divides, each of the DNA molecules (1) in its nucleus also divides, producing two half-molecules (2). Fragments join on to these to form two complete new DNA molecules (3), each an exact replica of the original. In this way genetic codes are passed on*

SIMPLE CELL    DIVIDING CELL    TWO NEW CELLS

code is a genetic blueprint that controls the formation of body cells, and transmits characteristics from one generation to the next by reproducing itself exactly every time a cell splits in two. The implications are profound. It means that man now has the potential power, by tampering with the code, to change the very nature of living things.

### The earth's moving plates
It is almost certain that many of the theories now cherished by scientists will be swept away in the course of time, to be replaced by others as more exact information becomes available. For example, in the late 1960's, doubts grew

about the real nature of the earth's crust. As a result, the science of plate tectonics – the study of the movements of the plates of the earth's crust – has developed. It is now generally accepted that the crust is broken into plates, much like a cracked eggshell, and that one plate can slide against another. In this way whole continents have 'drifted' about the earth's surface, to form the world map we know today. Collisions between plates have thrown up mountain ranges, and earthquakes are caused where plates are still in gradual motion, sliding jerkily past or towards one another.

Discoveries like these are giving man new knowledge of his own world, while space travel gives scientists new opportunities of probing the secrets of the universe. Space exploration has already provided one key to man's further understanding of the universe. Astronauts on the moon have found samples of the so-called 'genesis rock', dating back to the period when the earth's crust was formed, more than 4700 million years ago. Today, the sum of know-

*The earth's crust is formed from separate plates, which are constantly moving. Adjacent plates sliding against each other have produced this fault-line through a Californian orange grove*

ledge is increasing at a rate which makes it easy to forget that modern science, based on experiment, began only 400 years ago – and that only 30 lifetimes have passed since man's comprehension of life and the universe began to progress beyond the stage of myth-making.

### STUDYING THE HEAVENS
Ever since civilization began, man has been fascinated by the heavens above him. Astronomers in ancient Egypt, Babylon and China could predict eclipses, and the Egyptians mapped the stars. All such observations were made with the naked eye, however, and it was not until the invention of the telescope in Europe in the 17th century that precise observations could be made.

Even the largest optical telescopes are limited in their capabilities by the earth's atmosphere, which distorts light reaching the earth from stars and planets. The development of radio telescopes has enabled astronomers to penetrate this barrier.

Just as the mirror or lens of an optical telescope focuses light waves reaching the earth, so the dish of a radio telescope focuses radio waves emitted by the sun, stars and other heavenly bodies, which pass unhindered through the earth's atmosphere. Most of the radio waves reaching the earth began their journeys long before telescopes were invented – and the stars from which they originate may long ago have ceased to shine. Radio astronomers are journeying through time as well as space, and can 'listen in' to events that took place in the heavens thousands of years ago.

*The world's largest optical telescope, at Mount Palomar, California, has a mirror 200 in. across. The astronomer sits inside the telescope itself to make his observations*

*The 250 ft telescope at Jodrell Bank in Cheshire was a pioneer in radio astronomy. It tracks artificial satellites as well as probing the mysteries of outer space*

*In India, the study of astronomy reached a peak in the 18th century. Structures of the Yantra Observatory provided fixed angles for checking the positions of the stars*

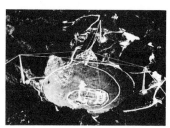

*The world's largest radio and radar telescope 1000 ft across, is suspended in a natural depression in the ground at the Arecibo Observatory, Puerto Rico*

# Writing and counting

*From crude marks on slabs of stone, symbols were refined to make them an accurate method of record*

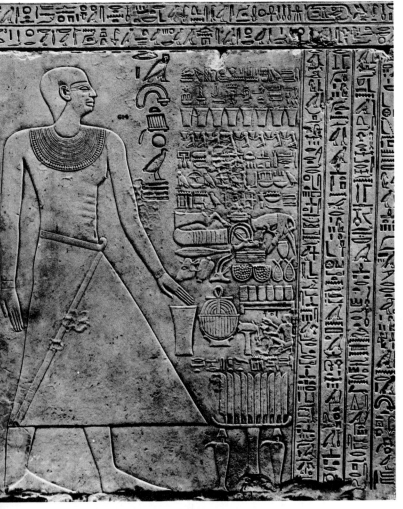

The monuments of ancient Egypt, like this 2000 BC tomb of the courtier Thethi, were inscribed with hieroglyphics, a form of picture-writing in which the Egyptians honoured their gods and extolled the achievements of the departed

The oldest known writing in the world is on a tablet of solid limestone found in the ancient Sumerian city of Kish in Mesopotamia, the 'Land between the Two Rivers'. It is probably a tax account. Some 5500 years ago, a scribe carved into it the outline of a foot, a hand and a sledge, with other marks beside them probably representing numbers.

The exact meaning of the message on the slab is not clear, but beyond doubt it is a form of picture-writing, mankind's first momentous step in the invention of writing. History begins with writing, and with this invention man was able to advance at a rate that would have been unthinkable in prehistoric times. Without writing, the sum total of knowledge of each isolated tribe or clan was limited by the memories of its oldest men and by what each generation could discover anew for itself. With writing, each succeeding generation could learn from the experience of the one before.

At first, though, writing was probably in the main a convenient memory aid for tax collectors – made necessary by the increasing complexity of life once men had begun to live together in cities. It is no surprise that the earliest known writing comes from Sumer, the world's earliest civilization.

**Pictures to represent ideas**

Carving inscriptions on solid stone slabs such as the one found at Kish was a laborious business, and it was not long before the early Sumerian scribes began to write instead on tablets of soft clay, which were afterwards baked in the sun to harden them and preserve the inscription. The first clay tablets, dating from about 3100 BC, were inscribed with symbols denoting various objects and parts of the body.

The main shortcoming of this early form of picture-writing was the difficulty of conveying ideas, feelings and actions. Scribes gradually introduced symbols called ideographs, which represented more than the object drawn. A circle might mean not only the sun but light or warmth as well, or a sun-god, or even a day.

So far, all the symbols used by the scribes were crude pictures of recognisable objects. But soon there came a new development – the first writing in a non-pictorial style. The wedge-ended pieces of reed which the scribes used made it easier to build up each picture by a

*In ancient Mesopotamia documents were fastened with small seals inscribed with pictures and cuneiform writing*

*The Assyrian king Assurbanipal (above) gathered together thousands of inscribed tablets in a library he built at Nineveh during the 7th century BC*

combination of wedge-shaped symbols drawn with single strokes; and as time went on these symbols became more abstract. This writing is known as cuneiform, from the Latin *cuneus*, 'wedge'.

As cuneiform writing developed, scribes began to use symbols to indicate sounds as well as objects or ideas. For instance, in the language of the Sumerians the word for 'arrow', pronounced 'ti', was the same as their word for 'life', so the symbol for an arrow came to be used for both words.

## THE EARLIEST WRITING

Writing began among the Sumerians of ancient Mesopotamia, who kept records by drawing simple pictures in soft clay. The reeds used as pens were awkward devices for drawing accurate pictures, and scribes began to use wedge-shaped symbols instead. The symbols were simplified until they bore little resemblance to the original objects

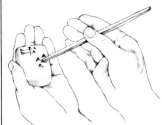

*The wedge-shaped strokes of cuneiform script were pressed into clay, which was baked to give a permanent record*

*The signs for 'ox' and 'grain' began as stylised pictures. Scribes soon found it easier to draw them sideways, and over the centuries they were simplified and reduced to a series of strokes*

## Understanding syllables

Each symbol still stood for a single word or idea. But having mastered the principle of using symbols to represent sounds, it was a relatively easy step for scribes to make up longer words by combining the signs for each of their separate sounds, or syllables. If, for example, a scribe writing present-day English in this syllabic system wanted to write the word 'betray', he might draw the picture of a 'bee' to denote the first syllable and a picture of a 'tray' for the second.

This reduced the number of symbols to be learnt to the number of syllables in the spoken language; but the Sumerian scribe still had to learn about 600 different signs, and most people were illiterate.

Despite its shortcomings, cuneiform writing was adopted by many other peoples, including the Babylonians, the Assyrians and the Persians, and it remained in use for more than 3000 years, until the 1st century AD. Cuneiform was not deciphered until 1834. A German, Georg Grotefend, and an Englishman, Henry Rawlinson, solved its secret.

## A separate script in Egypt

While cuneiform spread widely in the Near East, the ancient Egyptians developed another type of picture-writing which remained confined to Egypt. This was the hieroglyphic script, which was in use by about 3000 BC and survived until Roman times. *Hieroglyph* comes from the Greek words *hieros*,

*The Minoans of ancient Crete used pictorial characters as well as a linear script. The symbols on this disc of about 1700 BC are still undeciphered*

meaning 'sacred', and *glyphe* meaning 'carving': hieroglyphs were used primarily for sacred inscriptions on buildings and monuments. The characters, of which there were some 700, were simplified pictures of men, animals or objects in everyday use, and could be used in two ways. They were either used as ideographs, representing the idea of the actual object shown, or else as sound-pictures, spelling out the sound of a word by symbols representing its consonants.

A simplified form of hieroglyphs – the so-called hieratic, or 'priestly' script – was developed for speedier writing on papyrus, and was used mainly for religious texts. It was difficult to learn and write, and therefore cumbersome for use in everyday affairs. By the 7th century BC another style of hieroglyphs had developed from the hieratic

script, and was being used side by side with it. This was the demotic or 'popular' script, in which the pictorial quality of the hieroglyphs was sacrificed for faster writing. It was used up to the 5th century AD.

## First linear scripts

Egyptian hieroglyphs, like all the early picture scripts, could be written in any direction, though the separate pictures in a sequence of hieroglyphs were drawn facing the direction from which the script was to be read. Two forms of syllabic script used by the Minoans on the island of Crete, however, were the first scripts to be written consistently in horizontal lines, and because of this they are known as Linear A and Linear B.

Linear A has 90 syllables. It dates from about 1600 BC and it has not been clearly deciphered. Linear B has 89 characters, 48 of which can be traced back to Linear A. Many jars and tablets inscribed with the latter script have also been found in Greece, and when the language was translated in 1952 it proved to be early Greek. Its use was limited mainly to receipts, accounts and inventories.

Another important early syllabic script was that used in the Phoenician city of Byblos – from which comes the world Bible, meaning book. Examples of the Byblos script are written on stone and bronze objects, found in the 1920's, and contain 114 different symbols, nearly half of which are similar to Egyptian hieroglyphs.

*The Maya of central America devised a system of writing in sound-pictures. Many examples have survived, but so far they have largely defied translation*

## Symbols of early America

Two early civilizations of central America both developed sound-picture writing systems of their own in total isolation from the developments in the Old World. The Maya, who flourished in the Yucatan peninsula from AD 300 to 900, left many examples of their script carved on huge pillars, engraved on metal, or painted on pottery. The meaning of the stylised pictures, which are grouped in frames, has largely baffled scholars to the present day; only the signs dealing with dates and astronomy have been deciphered with certainty.

The writing of the Aztecs of Mexico, too, is almost entirely in the form of crude pictures. It is probably based on the Maya script, though the Aztec version has proved easier to decipher.

The only sound-picture form of writing still used in the modern world is Chinese, which has a history going back nearly 3500 years. The earliest examples of Chinese script are found on 14th-century BC 'oracle bones' – flat, polished animal bones used in foretelling the future – though the script is thought to have existed some centuries earlier. More than 2000 characters have been found on these bones, and more than 1000 of

**UNRAVELLING THE RIDDLE OF THE ROSETTA STONE**

Egyptian hieroglyphs were not deciphered until 1822, when a young Frenchman, Jean François Champollion, finally solved the riddle of the Rosetta Stone (below), a broken slab of black basalt unearthed by French soldiers digging trenches in Egypt in 1799. The slab is inscribed

with a decree drawn up in about 197 BC and honouring Ptolemy V. Its Egyptian inscriptions, which are in both the hieroglyphic and demotic, or 'popular' script, are repeated in ancient Greek – a language known to scholars, and the key which made it possible to 'break the code'

P T O L M Y S

K L E O P A T R A

*Jean François Champollion (below) worked for 14 years before the Rosetta Stone yielded up its secrets. The first vital step had already been taken by earlier scholars. This was the recognition of a single word – the name Ptolemy – enclosed in a cartouche, or oval-ended frame (above), reserved in Egyptian writing for royal names. The name appears as 'Ptolemaios' in the stone's Greek text. Champollion's achievement was to interpret correctly the hieroglyphs making up the word, and to match them to their Greek equivalents. His interpretation of the hieroglyphs corresponding to p, o and l was confirmed when they appeared also in a cartouche of Cleopatra found on an obelisk at Philae. Armed with these three symbols, he deduced the meaning of the rest from their positions, then worked out further symbols from other cartouches of the period*

*The Chinese character 'li' (top) began as a stylised drawing (above, centre) of a three-legged pottery jar (above, left). This altered in 1000 BC to a character (above, right) resembling the bronze vessel which replaced the jar. By 200 BC the character had its present form*

## *The coming of the alphabet*

*A scribe laboriously copies out the Gospels by hand, a knife at the ready to scratch out mistakes. The practice of linking characters to produce the small letters used today originated in the monasteries of the Middle Ages. Scribes found it easier to write whole words without lifting their pens from the paper*

*Arabic is the language and script of the Koran (above), the holy book of Islam, and it spread with the expansion of the religion. It is written from right to left*

them have been interpreted. They include references to ancestor worship, birth, death, war – and the weather.

### A survival in China
The Chinese script has remained based on word signs for so long, largely because of the nature of the spoken Chinese language. Other scripts developed into systems taking a syllable or a letter as their smallest unit rather than a complete word; but the simplicity of the Chinese language, in which words have only one syllable, made this refinement unnecessary. Only in 1972, faced with the necessity to compete in technological advance with the other super-powers, did China decide to bring its script into line with that of the rest of the modern world.

### Japan's '50 sounds'
Japan adopted the Chinese system of writing from the 3rd century AD, but 500 years later the Japanese developed a syllabic system known as *kana*, which was better suited to their own language and reduced drastically the number of characters that had to be learnt.

There are two types of Japanese writing, one used mainly for learned works and official documents, and the other for popular literature and word endings. Today both

contain the 47 symbols of the traditional *kana* and three others, making up the *goju-on* ('50 sounds') of modern Japanese dictionaries.

### Symbols for basic sounds
The main drawback of syllabic writing, in which a different sign was used for every one of the hundreds of different syllables in a language, was the large number of signs which had to be memorised. The most important advance in the history of writing came when it was realised that syllables themselves are made up of a relatively small number of elementary sounds. There are three such sounds in the one-syllable word 'dog', for instance, while exactly the same three

### WRITING MADE EASY: HOW THE ALPHABET BEGAN

Alphabets – writing systems in which a symbol represents a basic sound in the spoken language – are the most convenient forms of writing. Most languages have only 20-30 basic sounds, so the number of symbols to be learnt is small

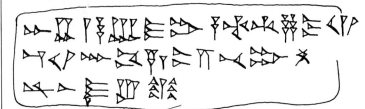

*Clay tablets found at Ras Shamra, once the ancient Canaanite city of Ugarit, show that scribes were writing in a cuneiform alphabet 3400 years ago. It had 30 different symbols*

*Above: A Greek schoolmaster of 480 BC uses a stylus to write on wax tablets. Right: The Romans evolved a distinctive type of capital letter for use on their monuments*

sounds, arranged in the reverse order, make up a different word, 'god'. Most languages have no more than 20 or 30 of these elementary sounds, and the simplest form of writing that man has invented – the alphabetic system – is based on the use of one symbol for each sound.

Like the invention of writing itself, the alphabet came from the Middle East. All the world's important alphabets come from one parent alphabet, which is thought to have been invented about 1600 BC among the Canaanites, early Hebrews and Phoenicians who lived on the eastern shores of the Mediterranean.

This first North Semitic alphabet, which remained almost unchanged for centuries, consisted of 22 characters which were placed in a set order and given names to make them easier to remember.

Learning the alphabet is literally child's play compared with the years of grinding study needed to master thousands of characters for individual words, or scores of symbols for different syllables. Its invention meant that the ability to read and write was no longer confined to scribes and priests.

Two main offshoots developed from the first alphabet – the Canaanite and Aramaic systems. Nearly all the alphabetic scripts west of

*A runic inscription on a casket made in Northumbria in the 7th century. Runes were the earliest form of writing among the Germanic peoples*

Syria have sprung from the Canaanite system, while the alphabetic writings of the East derive from the Aramaic system.

The Aramaic alphabet was probably developed in the 10th century BC. Though the Aramaeans were never politically important, their language and writing were too convenient to ignore, and both spread widely to become the most important in western Asia from the 7th century BC. The Aramaic language and script were adopted by the Persian Empire, and writings and inscriptions in this script have been found in Egypt, Palestine, Syria, Arabia, Asia Minor, Mesopotamia and India.

### Scripts of two faiths
Two particular alphabets which descended from the Aramaic were linked closely to religion. Square Hebrew, a distinctive Palestinian Jewish script, became standardised just before the Christian era, and is the ancestor of the modern Hebrew alphabet.

The Hebrew alphabet has changed only slightly in the last

*This 15th-century Russian manuscript is written in the Cyrillic alphabet, which is an adaptation of the Greek alphabet*

2000 years, because of the rules laid down by the Talmud, the book of Jewish civil and religious law. Arabic, the language and script of the Koran, evolved from another descendant of the Aramaic alphabet and spread rapidly with the new religion of Islam to many parts of Asia and Africa. The modern Arabic alphabet has 28 letters – six

more than the first alphabet – and is written from right to left.

### Adding the vowel signs
In the earliest alphabets only the consonants were written; as in shorthand or in some newspaper small advertisements, the vowels were understood by the reader. Modern Arabic has letters only for consonants to this day. But when the Greeks introduced the Canaanite system into Europe for the first time, in about 1000 BC, they added characters for vowels as well as consonants. The Greeks also standardised the direction in which lines were written; first they used lines reading alternately from right to left and then from left to right, but from about 500 BC they adopted what has become the modern Western practice of reading from left to right throughout.

The Greek alphabet passed to the Romans by way of the Etruscans, rulers in central Italy before the rise of the Romans. Over 10,000 Etruscan inscriptions survive, the earliest dating from the 8th century BC, but the language has not been fully translated. The Romans adopted 21 letters of the Etruscan alphabet in the 7th century BC, and six centuries later, after the conquest of Greece, the letters Y and Z were added to represent Greek sounds. To this 23-letter alphabet the letters J, U and W were added in the Middle Ages, to give the 26-letter alphabet used in the West today.

Another quite different adaptation of the Greek alphabet travelled to eastern Europe. This is the Cyrillic alphabet, attributed to the 9th-century Greek St Cyril, who used an adaptation of the Greek alphabet to represent more closely the many sounds of Slavonic languages. In time this developed into the scripts of those Slavonic peoples who adopted the Christian religion from the Byzantine Empire – including Russians, Bulgarians, Macedonians and Serbs.

### Styles of writing
The characters used in writing today were evolved by the Romans, who had several styles of writing, the best known being the 'monumental' capitals used on classical monuments such as Trajan's Column in Rome.

The Carolingian script, which appeared in France at the end of the 8th century AD, spread widely under the patronage of Emperor Charlemagne to become for two centuries the leading literary style of western Europe. Small letters, derived from the capitals, came into use when medieval scribes, in order to write more quickly, ceased to lift their pens from the paper between characters.

The Carolingian script in turn gave rise over the centuries to various styles, including the 'black letter' or Gothic script developed in Germany; and the rounder, more easily read *littera antiqua* of

*The invention of printing led to greater standardisation of alphabetic characters. This page is from a Bible printed in 1454-5 by Johann Gutenberg*

the Italian Renaissance. *Littera antiqua* itself produced two main styles, one of which was the ancestor of modern 'roman' lettering and the other a Venetian script from which the sloping letters known as italics are descended.

Handwriting only became general in Britain in the 18th and 19th centuries, with the spread of literacy and the increase in the writing of letters that followed the introduction of a postal service. Styles became informal, and penmanship degenerated as characters were run together.

---

### INITIAL FLOURISH

In early manuscripts, initial letters were elaborately drawn and decorated by painstaking scribes, who were usually monks. Such illustrations often occupied most of the page and a whole book took years to produce

*St Augustine is depicted in an initial letter from an 11th-century* City of God

*A dragon is attacked in an initial 'R' from a 12th-century French manuscript*

---

NORTH SEMITIC

PHOENICIAN

EARLY GREEK

CLASSICAL GREEK ABΓ

MONUMENTAL ROMAN ABC

GOTHIC

*All the world's main alphabets have developed from an alphabet invented 3600 years ago in the Middle East, and known as the North Semitic. The names given to its symbols were the same as those of the objects on which they were based. The first symbol was the head of an ox, or 'aleph'; the second a house, or 'beth', and from these came the word 'alphabet'. The North Semitic alphabet had two main offshoots, the Canaanite and Aramaic systems. The Phoenicians developed the Canaanite method and about 1000 BC the Greeks adopted it from the Phoenicians and added vowels. It reached the Romans about the 7th century BC, and the Latin alphabet, with modifications such as the 'black letter' or Gothic style, is still in use today. Two important alphabets derived from the Aramaic system are Hebrew and Arabic*

# Keeping count through the ages

*A calendar used by the Maya of central America is based on a method of counting devised without any knowledge of systems used in the Old World. The Maya used only three symbols – a dot, a dash and two curved lines*

## Counting by fingers

Man's first adding machine was his own body. As he bartered the spoils of a successful hunting expedition for crude weapons or drinking vessels, he reckoned their worth on his fingers and thumbs. At first such calculations were probably a dumb show, but as societies advanced, numbers were given names which sprang directly from the practice of finger-counting.

Some names survived into modern times among primitive societies. In the language of an American Indian tribe who counted by bending down the fingers of an upraised hand, starting with the little finger, the word for 'one' was literally 'the end is bent'. For 'two' they said 'it is bent once more' (the second finger); 'three' was 'the middle is bent', and 'four' was 'only one remains'. Their word for 'five' meant 'my hand is finished'.

The Zulus traditionally counted on their hands in this way. For the number 'six' they spoke of 'taking the thumb', which meant they had finished the fingers of one hand and started on the second. For 'seven' they said 'he pointed'; that is, they had reached the index finger, which is used for pointing.

## The decimal system

Finger-counting probably gave rise to the now universal practice of counting in tens and parts of tens – the decimal system, from the Latin *decem*, meaning 'ten' –

*The Incas of ancient Peru counted and kept records on quipus – devices made of cords whose length, thickness, colour and knots denoted different values*

which arose independently among many peoples who had no contact with each other. This system made it easy to count up to numbers big enough for everyday use. When a shepherd had used up his fingers and thumbs in counting his sheep, a second shepherd could record the tens by raising one finger, and so take the count up to a hundred. A third shepherd, using his fingers and thumbs to count the hundreds, could take it up to one thousand.

This simplicity and convenience made the number ten an attractive scale to count in. But the Maya of central America counted in a scale of 20, a system probably derived from counting on fingers, thumbs and toes; and the Sumerians and Babylonians used a scale of 60, the smallest number which can be divided by two, three, four, five and six. This scale of 60 survives in the divisions of hours and minutes, and in the division of the circle into 360 degrees.

## Records on clay tablets

As civilizations developed, the need grew for a system of recording transactions. The earliest accounts were kept by cutting notches in tally sticks or wax tablets, a practice followed by the ancient Egyptians, Greeks and Romans, and even into late medieval times in western Europe. As numerical systems evolved, clay tablets and papyri replaced the tally stick, and symbols were devised to represent numbers. Thousands of inscribed tablets surviving from many different early civilizations contain details of receipts, accounts and inventories for goods such as grain, cloth and cattle.

As late as the 16th century AD, the Incas of Peru counted on the quipu, a device using knotted cords of varying length, thickness and colour. Knots of natural-coloured cord represented numbers: single knots for tens, double for hundreds, and triple for thousands. Quipus were also used to transmit messages, which were coded into numbers.

Counting by knots was not confined to the New World. The Greek historian Herodotus refers to a

---

### THE FIRST CALCULATOR

Before the introduction of simple Arabic numerals, man's systems of counting were so cumbersome that calculation was slow and awkward. Multiplication could only be done by a series of repeated additions. To overcome this problem counting aids like the abacus (below) were developed. In its most primitive form in Egypt and Sumer, pebbles representing 'ones', 'tens', 'hundreds' and 'thousands' were moved from one groove of sand to another

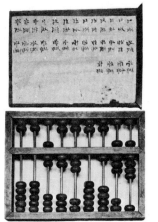

*In this Chinese abacus, known as* suan pan *(counting board), the beads in the smaller part of the frame each have a value of five. Those in the larger part represent one. Beads are moved towards the central bar to record the numbers*

Persian king who gave the Ionian Greeks a two-month calendar in the form of a thong with 60 knots; and in parts of India knotted cords were used by census-takers up to the 19th century.

## Counting in Egypt

In the earliest examples of written numbers, which were found in Egypt and Mesopotamia and date from about 3000 BC, numbers were represented by simple strokes. Later, the Egyptians, still using strokes for numbers from one to nine, developed symbols for tens, hundreds and thousands.

The Babylonians used numbers which were variations of the same wedge-shaped symbols used for their cuneiform writing. They also developed a system of place notation serving the same purpose as the modern use of separate columns to denote units, tens, hundreds and thousands. This enabled the Babylonians, working in their chosen scale of 60, to use the same symbol for 1 as for 60, since its position indicated which of the two figures it stood for.

The Greeks at first used a system of counting similar to that of the Egyptians. But later they adopted a different method, using the first nine letters of the alphabet for numbers up to 9, the next nine letters for numbers from 10 to 90, and the last nine for 100 to 900. Any number could be increased a thousandfold by placing a stroke in front of it. The Romans, also,

*The Egyptians made practical use of their knowledge of mathematics. In this tomb painting an official (left) is surveying a cornfield to assess it for taxes*

used letters of the alphabet to denote certain fixed numbers. 'V' (5) and 'X' (10) were chosen because they were easy to write; the letter 'C' stood for *centum* ('hundred') and 'M' meant *mille* ('thousand'). Unlike the Greeks, the Romans used vertical strokes to denote values which fell between their lettered numbers. But calculating was awkward in both Greek and Roman systems.

Between AD 300 and 900 the Maya of central America had a highly developed number system which arose completely independently of outside influences. The Maya could write any number with the help of only three symbols – a dot, a dash and two curved lines. The dots and dashes were used to build up numbers from one to 19. The curved lines multiplied a number by 20; a second pair of curved lines multiplied the original

number by 20 again. The Maya, in fact, were using the curved lines in a way similar to the modern zero – 1000 years before the zero, an Indian innovation, became generally accepted in Europe.

## The first ready-reckoners

The early numerical systems were adequate for counting and recording the results of calculations, but they did not permit written arithmetic. The Babylonians devised tables for multiplication and addition, but most calculations had to be done with aids such as abacuses.

In the earliest Sumerian and Egyptian abacuses, pebbles were moved from one groove in sand to another (the name 'abacus' may have come from the Semitic word *abac*, meaning dust). In the Roman version, additions and subtractions were done by moving pebbles or beads along slots in a metal plate;

the Latin word for the markers was *calculus*, from which comes the word 'calculate'. In later times the abacus took the form of counters moved from square to square on a 'chequer board' – the origin of the word 'exchequer'. Variations of the abacus continued to be the main means of calculating in commerce for centuries.

Bone reckoning rods were used in Korea until recent times; modern abacuses, in which beads are moved along parallel wires, are still used in some Asian countries and in Russia.

## The coming of the zero

Two major steps were necessary before arithmetical sums could be worked out without the use of an abacus. One was the refinement of place notation – a system of setting figures on paper to correspond to the respective grooves or rods of an abacus. The other was the introduction of the concept of zero. The Babylonians were familiar with both devices, and the Maya had their oval 'zero', but the systems now used throughout the world originated in the Hindu temples of India some 1500 years ago.

The Indians adopted a system of place notation whereby the symbol on the extreme right indicated the 'ones', the symbol immediately to its left the 'tens', and the next 'hundreds'. Where there was no number to be registered they wrote a dot, as a zero is now used. In this way there could be no confusion between 73, 703 and 7003.

The actual numerical symbols now in use also originated in India, though they are known as Arabic numerals since they were brought from India by Arab scribes and merchants. They reached southern Europe by AD 1200, but in northern Europe the use of zero caused great controversy and the system was not fully accepted until another 300 years had passed.

The decimal point, which simplified the system of fractions, first appeared in the 15th century, and its use was perfected by a Belgian mathematician, Simon Stevin, in 1585. Fractions were now counted in a scale of ten, just like whole

## FROM CUNEIFORM TO COMPUTER: THE GROWTH OF MODERN NUMERALS

Many methods of counting and recording numbers have been devised since men first cut notches in sticks, but even those employed by such advanced civilizations as the ancient Greeks and Chinese were cumbersome for all but the most simple calculations. The breakthrough which led to the practice now in universal use originated in India 1500 years ago; this involved the concept of the zero, and the introduction of a system of writing numbers in which

an individual symbol's position in any number indicates whether it refers to 'hundreds', to 'tens', or to 'ones' – as in 607 the 6 refers to 'hundreds', the 0 to 'tens', and the 7 to 'ones'. Indian mathematicians also simplified the writing of numbers so that only ten different symbols – 0, and 1 to 9 – were needed to represent any number. All these concepts reached Europe through the Arabs by AD 1200, but were not accepted for another 300 years

**BABYLONIAN**
*The same wedge-shaped cuneiform symbols were used for writing and counting*

**ROMAN**
I  II  III  IV  V  VI  VII  VIII  IX  X
*Simple vertical strokes and letters of the alphabet were used to build up numbers*

**CHINESE**
一 二 三 四 五 六 七 八 九 十
*Horizontal strokes were used up to 3 and signs for higher numbers up to 10*

**MAYA**
*Numbers were written with dashes and dots: curves multiplied them 20 times*

**HINDU**
*Early Indian symbols, including a zero, were the forerunners of today's numerals*

**MODERN ARABIC/EUROPEAN**
1 2 3 4 5 6 7 8 9 10 0
*'Arabic' numerals have developed from the symbols brought from India by the Arabs*

**COMPUTER DIGITS**
1 2 3 4 5 6 7 8 9 10 0
*Special symbols, based on Arabic numerals, have been designed for computer use*

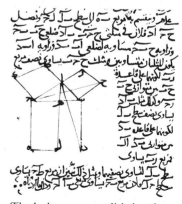

*The Arabs were accomplished mathematicians and translated the Greek texts into Arabic. This 13th-century illustration explains Pythagoras's theorem about the right-angled triangle*

## Measuring the passage of time

*Throughout the centuries scholars like these astronomers in a 13th-century French manuscript have tried to reconcile the difference between the lunar year of 354 days, and the 365¼ days which it takes for the earth to circle the sun*

numbers – 1·1 meant $1\frac{1}{10}$, 1·11 meant $1\frac{11}{100}$ and so on. Each symbol in the chain indicates tenths of the one to the left.

### Man's first clock – the sun

Man's earliest concept of time was based on the day, and was directly linked to movements of the sun. Observant people must have noticed that a tall straight object, such as a pole, cast a shadow that moved in a regular pattern each day. By noting the position of the shadow, they could tell roughly what fraction of the day had passed, and the pole thus acted as a simple sundial.

Early Egyptians and Greeks used a pole with a crossbar, and measured the shadow it threw. The Egyptians split the period between sunrise and sunset into 12 equal parts, and from this division came the hour, at first very inexact.

In Europe, primitive sundials were made to record the passing of the hours, but they were not very efficient, as the period of time between sunrise and sunset was not constant; winter days, with little daylight, would therefore have shorter hours than summer days. Furthermore, sundials functioned only when the sun shone, and were of little use to people such as sailors who needed to know the time during the night. This was done by

*This tablet from Babylon records the intervals between new moons. Babylonians also divided a month into weeks*

watching for the appearance of particular stars on the eastern horizon, and dividing the night into 12 'watches'.

### Telling the time by the candle

Neither sun nor stars could be used to divide time indoors, and to do this several kinds of clocks were invented. One of the earliest forms of clock was a candle, marked with notches corresponding to hours, which were counted off as the candle burnt. King Alfred in England is said to have used such a clock. The hour glass was in use at least 2000 years ago.

Simple water clocks were used in Egypt, Greece and Rome before 150 BC. A cylinder was slowly filled at a constant rate with water upon which a floating base supported a vertical notched stick. As the stick

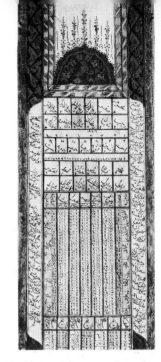

*The times of dawn, sunrise, afternoon prayer hour and sunset are given on this 19th-century Muslim calendar*

rose in the water it turned a gearwheel, moving a clock hand round a 24-hour clock. More complex forms of water clocks were developed by the Chinese. One, designed by Su Sung nearly 900 years ago, had an 11-ft waterwheel replenished by buckets; in addition to showing the time of the day, it also indicated the movement of the stars. The forerunner of the mechanical clocks now in use had evolved in Europe by about 1300.

Aboard ship, the duty 'watches' were recorded by bells, for which the French word is *cloches*, and from ships' time come the modern words 'clock' and 'watch'. Early clocks had only one hand, denoting the hour, but later the hour was divided into 60 small or 'minute' parts. Eventually, even greater accuracy was needed and another hand was fitted to the clock to divide minutes into 60 equal parts; these were called 'seconds', because they were the second division of the hour.

The Romans wanted to establish a definite and consistent system of time for their cities. To do this, they took the moment when the sun was at its highest point in the sky above Rome. This moment was called the meridian (noon),

*The Aztecs' calendar year contained 18 months of 20 days each. At the end of this period five extra days were added*

and each day was reckoned to stretch exactly 12 hours before and after noon. This is the origin of the abbreviations a.m. and p.m. – derived from the Latin *ante* and *post meridiem*, before and after noon.

After the sun, the most impressive body in the sky is the moon, and early men noticed that the moon appeared to grow from the 'new' or crescent moon to the full moon in a regular pattern. Ancient peoples dated their events by months rather than years, and the Muslim year is still 354 days long, because it is equivalent to the period of 12 moons (12 periods of 29½ days each).

### Seven-day weeks

It was the Babylonians who first divided the month into four seven-day periods, or weeks, and carried the remaining days and hours on to the next week, but for a long time few peoples followed their example. The Romans, for instance, used a cumbersome system that counted days back from the *ides*, a day near the middle of the month, or from the *nones*, a day that came nine days before the ides.

One people who did adopt the Babylonian seven-day week were the Jews, to whom the seventh day

*In the Middle Ages patrons of the arts commissioned 'Books of Hours' which included richly decorated calendars*

was the *sabbath*, a holy day. The concept of the week spread from Judaism into Europe through Christianity. In Latin countries, the days of the week are still named after Roman gods, but four English days – Tuesday, Wednesday, Thursday and Friday – are named after old Norse gods. English months still have Roman names – October because it was once the eighth month; January after the

god Janus; July after Julius Caesar; and August after Augustus.

### Measuring the year

The concept of a year as representing the complete cycle of the seasons developed wherever communities practised agriculture, but the exact length of a year took a long time to establish. Before 4000 BC the Egyptians knew that the year had about 365 days – but the Babylonians and Chinese kept a 360-day year.

The incompatibility of the moon's year of 354 days and the sun's year of 365¼ days troubled people for centuries. The ancient Chinese divided their 360-day year into 12 months, normally of 30 days each. About 1300 BC, an extra month was added at the end of a year when required; later it was added at the end of any month as soon as it became necessary.

The Babylonians inserted three extra months every eight years, to adjust their 360-day calendar almost exactly to solar time – the period taken for the earth to complete an orbit around the sun. In Egypt, where life depended entirely upon the Nile, priests discovered that the annual flood came shortly after the star Sirius reappeared in

the sky following a long absence. From this phenomenon they devised a 365-day calendar, leaving an error of about one day every four years. Their year had eleven months of 30 days each, and a twelfth month of 35 days.

Central America produced several remarkable calendars. To the Maya, time was a holy concept looked after by the priests. They had a sacred year of 260 days, a state year of 360 days and an astronomical year of 365 days. Though they did not realise the earth revolves round the sun, the Maya priests calculated the length of the sun's year. They also had a remarkably accurate lunar calendar based on 405 lunar revolutions, taking 11,960 days; in fact these revolutions take exactly 11,959·888 days.

### A sacred calendar

The Aztecs of Mexico also had a sacred calendar in addition to their solar calendar, both with 20 name days dedicated to gods. The sacred calendar had a 13-day 'week' which was repeated to give the Aztecs a 260-day sacred year.

The solar calendar of 365 days was divided into 18 months of 20 days, at the end of which were five 'unlucky' days. Aztec years were grouped in 52-year cycles, after any one of which the world might come to an end. Each cycle closed with the five unlucky days – a period of mounting fear. Possessions were destroyed, fires put out, and children were forcibly kept awake to prevent them from being changed into rats. Pregnant women were locked up in case they were transformed into wild beasts.

At sunset on the final day, priests climbed an extinct volcano to search the night sky for certain stars. At the exact moment when the cycle of time ended they lit a fire in the open breast of a newly killed human victim, whose sacrifice helped to ensure that the world would continue to exist. As the key star passed the centre of the sky, the whole nation rejoiced that a new cycle of time had been allotted to it by the gods.

### Atomic accuracy

Number systems, simple measurements of time, distance, weight and volume, were implements devised by man to serve him, but the sciences and technologies they helped to build have now outstripped the tools. They are no longer fast and accurate enough to measure the concepts which they themselves made possible.

Modern electronic calculating machines count in a way of their own, going up in two's on the 'binary system'. A metre is now the wavelength of light from a gas. And since the beginning of 1972 a second, as a fraction of a minute, is defined by an atomic clock, which uses not mainsprings but gas molecules, and is accurate to one second in billions.

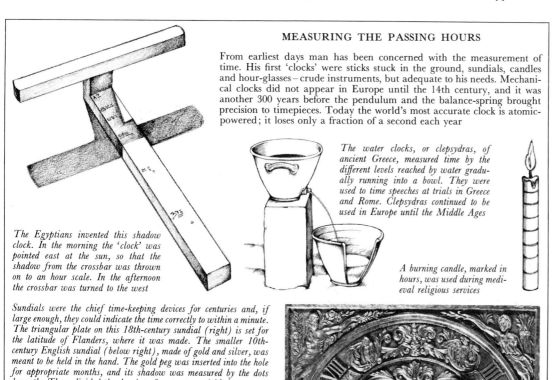

## MEASURING THE PASSING HOURS

From earliest days man has been concerned with the measurement of time. His first 'clocks' were sticks stuck in the ground, sundials, candles and hour-glasses – crude instruments, but adequate to his needs. Mechanical clocks did not appear in Europe until the 14th century, and it was another 300 years before the pendulum and the balance-spring brought precision to timepieces. Today the world's most accurate clock is atomic-powered; it loses only a fraction of a second each year

*The Egyptians invented this shadow clock. In the morning the 'clock' was pointed east at the sun, so that the shadow from the crossbar was thrown on to an hour scale. In the afternoon the crossbar was turned to the west*

*The water clocks, or clepsydras, of ancient Greece, measured time by the different levels reached by water gradually running into a bowl. They were used to time speeches at trials in Greece and Rome. Clepsydras continued to be used in Europe until the Middle Ages*

*A burning candle, marked in hours, was used during medieval religious services*

*Sundials were the chief time-keeping devices for centuries and, if large enough, they could indicate the time correctly to within a minute. The triangular plate on this 18th-century sundial (right) is set for the latitude of Flanders, where it was made. The smaller 10th-century English sundial (below right), made of gold and silver, was meant to be held in the hand. The gold peg was inserted into the hole for appropriate months, and its shadow was measured by the dots beneath. These divided the day into four parts, or 'tides'*

*A set of sand-glasses (below), which were made in England in 1720, measured the quarter of an hour, half hour, three quarters, and one hour*

# Man the inventor

*Out of the primitive skills of early man developed technical advances which transformed his way of life*

*The shadoof, a primitive irrigation machine, is still in use in some parts of Egypt, 3250 years after it was depicted in this wall-painting from a tomb at Thebes. The weight of the water is balanced by a counterweight at the end of a long pole. Using a shadoof, one man can raise 600 gallons of water in a day*

Man's first inventions hardly seem to qualify for the name. Sharp fragments of rock, pointed sticks, clubs made of branches torn straight from the trees – these must have been man's first tools, hardly more sophisticated than the implements used by apes or some birds. Roughly 2 million years ago came the first signs of an awakening technical skill in man, with the first deliberately fashioned tools.

From a stone such as a flint, of a size which fitted into the palm of his hand, primitive man chipped away splinters with another stone until he had formed a sharp edge which he could use for cutting, scraping or hacking.

**Hammer and hand-axe**

Simple pebble-tools like this were all man used for at least his first million years; then he learnt to use a stone hammer to produce a more effective blade, hammering off flakes from all over his flint to trim it into a flat and pointed hand-axe. At first the chipped-off flakes were thrown away, but later they were found to have a usefulness of their own, and were turned into arrowheads or blades.

It is thought that man first started using fire for warmth and cooking about 500,000 years ago. Evidence for this has been found in China and Hungary. The first fire to be used was probably of natural origin, but man soon learnt the art of making fire.

Early man had only natural materials to work with – stone, wood, bone, antlers and mud. His houses were made from boulders or mud-bricks dried in the sun, his cooking vessels and lamps from stone, and his weapons from wood, antlers and flint fragments.

**The first pottery**

The development of pottery was a distinct advance because it is the first known example of man altering the nature of the material he used, as distinct from merely changing its shape. Soft, wet clay, moulded with the fingers into the shape of a basket, was modified by fire into a hard substance, making a pot in which grain could be stored and food cooked. Clay was augmented when man's inventiveness began to accelerate as the first

*This prehistoric clay beaker from Britain was made by coiling a roll of damp clay and then moulding it with the hands*

*Copper and bronze were the first metals worked by man to make useful or beautiful objects. This bronze horse's bit, with a cheekpiece shaped like a winged animal, was made in Iran c. 800 BC*

metals came into use. Gold, silver and copper were all found and used by about 6000 BC. Supplies of copper in its pure form were limited, and the real breakthrough came when it was discovered that copper could be smelted from its plentiful ores, cast into ingots and hammered into shape. Tougher and more plentiful than gold or silver, it could be used for weapons or tools.

By about 3000 BC, man had discovered that smelting copper with tin produced an even better product – bronze. It melted at a lower temperature than pure copper, so it was easier to cast, and it was harder and more durable.

With the development of agriculture came the wheel and the

## HOW THE WHEEL BEGAN

Few inventions have been more important, or have origins more obscure, than the wheel. The first recorded wheel, made of solid wood, appears on a Sumerian tablet of about 3250 BC. A thousand years passed before copper rims were added, and the first spoked wheels did not appear until around 2000 BC, in eastern Iran

*An early three-piece wheel from Ur (left) and an Egyptian spoked wheel of 1500 BC*

*A Greek wheel of about 400 BC (left) and a Roman spoked wheel of AD 100*

*Leonardo da Vinci designed the 'flared' wheel (left) in the 15th century; the pneumatic treaded tyre dates from 1907*

plough. The first ploughs were pulled by oxen yoked by their horns, but it was soon discovered that a shoulder-yoke allowed the animals to pull far more efficiently.

The massive achievements of the Egyptian dynasties did not require sophisticated tools. The building of temples and pyramids owed more to organisation than to technology: huge numbers of workers had to be housed, fed and kept working, but the tools used were simple.

Blocks of stone were dragged from the quarries to the Nile on sledges, floated on barges to where they were required, then once again dragged along by sheer brute strength. Far more advanced in a technical sense were the objects left inside the pyramids with the bodies of the dead kings—glass vessels, fine bronze castings, stylish wooden furniture and delicate ornaments of gold and silver.

## A work force of slaves
The story of invention is a history of fits and starts. The success of an invention depends on the right social environment as much as it does upon the genius of the inventor, and the climate for invention has not always been favourable. The ancient civilizations made many labour-saving inventions but put few of them into practical use, because they had armies of slaves.

By 500 BC the Greeks had at their disposal the components of a

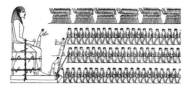

*An army of Egyptian slaves moves a colossus. Plentiful manpower made labour-saving devices unnecessary*

machine. They called them the 'Simple Five' – the lever, the wheel and its axle, the pulley, the inclined plane and the screw. But inventions which might have transformed history were treated as little more than toys.

Human labour in the Greek world was preferred to that of animals, largely because of an ignorance of animal anatomy. Oxen had been used for ploughing, and so the ox-harness was unquestioningly transferred to asses, horses and mules, even though the different anatomy of these animals made the throat and girth harness of an ox unsuitable. Thus, instead of pulling 15 times as much as a man could, horses pulled barely four times as much. Since 'sense' could be whipped into a slave, human labour was much more economical. It was left to the barbarians of central Europe to devise a proper harness, and also to provide horses with metal shoes. Even a great mathematician and

inventor such as Archimedes of Syracuse (287–212 BC) was contemptuous of the idea of using his inventions for practical purposes.

## A pump for irrigation
Archimedes realised, however, the potential of mechanisms like the lever: 'Give me but a place to stand,' he said, 'and I can move the world.' Archimedes impressed King Hiero of Syracuse by rigging up a system of pulleys and ropes, and hauling single-handed along the shore a fully loaded, three-masted merchantman. Hiero responded by hiring Archimedes to design him weapons of war.

One of the inventions of Archimedes, the Archimedean Screw, did come into use for pumping

*Archimedes invented a device to raise water by rotating a spiral-shaped screw*

water in irrigation schemes, and such pumps can still be seen in Egypt. They consist of a spiralling screw operating inside an inclined watertight cylinder; when the lower end is placed in water, and the screw rotated by hand, water 'climbs' up the cylinder and out at the top. The Archimedean Screw still fascinated men during the Renaissance 1700 years later.

Archimedes died when Syracuse was sacked by the Romans. Intent on a drawing, he was not aware that the city had fallen, and when a Roman soldier ordered him to go to the Roman commander Archimedes refused, saying that he had to solve his problem first. The soldier stabbed him to death.

Much of Greek engineering ingenuity was devoted to improving weapons. The Greeks knew of the crossbow and the catapult, which may have originated with the Carthaginians. According to tradition, Archimedes' weapons enabled Syracuse to withstand a three-year siege before it fell.

## Homes with hot water
The Romans took over and perfected Greek technology, though they were not great inventors themselves. Their magnificent engineering schemes depended on massive supplies of slave labour, and their roads and drainage were often no better than the Greek and Persian models of earlier times. Their talent lay in freely borrowing other people's technology and applying it. One way in which the Romans were innovators, however, was in the scale of their operations. Their buildings, in particular, were more splendid in construction than

*A Roman double-acting water pump, made of bronze, has two cylinders operating alternately to produce a continuous flow of water from the central tap*

any which had gone before. From a local volcanic earth called *pozzolana* the Romans made a cement which resisted fire and water, and helped them to build domes like that over the Pantheon, built about AD 120, with an internal diameter of 142 ft.

Using lead, they devised plumbing systems of great efficiency, which could even provide hot water on tap, and they also used the hypocaust, a form of under-floor central heating. The Romans also devised an airbed made of inflated leather bags.

Roman technology was a mass of contradictions, for they did not find a use for all the skills they knew. Only towards the end of the Roman period, for example, did the use of water-mills become common, when the supply of

*The chariots on the Royal Standard of Ur, which was found in Mesopotamia and dates from about 3000 BC, show that the Sumerians of the time pegged together separate pieces of wood to make their wheels. This was an improvement on earlier wheels, which were merely slices cut from a single tree trunk. It meant that wheels could now be made from planks cut from the hard core of a log, while the softer wood on the outside, which would quickly wear out, was discarded. The chariots were drawn by onagers, or wild asses*

*The military might of the Hittites owed much to the wheel. Their light war chariots made them the most formidable warriors of their day*

*Wheels were known to the Aztecs of Mexico, but as they had no draught animals they used them only for toys*

### INVENTIONS OF HERO
One of the foremost inventors of ancient times was Hero of Alexandria, who in the 1st century AD compiled a textbook of engineering. Using only devices like the lever, the pulley, the wheel and the screw, he designed a clock operated by dripping water, a fire pump – and a machine for opening temple doors when an altar flame was lit

*Hero's turbine, or 'whirling aeoliphile', first demonstrated the power of steam. Water in the lower vessel is boiled, and the steam passes through pipes into the spherical turbine above. It escapes under pressure through the two nozzles on the circumference, producing a force which turns the turbine. Despite its potential Hero never saw his idea as anything more than a clever toy; another 1700 years were to pass before a British inventor produced the first successful steam engine*

311

*In the Middle Ages the monasteries kept technology alive. This plough decorates the 1340 Luttrell Psalter*

# *When water gave the only power*

*Renaissance inventors persisted in a vain quest for a perpetual-motion machine. The idea behind this 1580 design was that water from the trough at the top would power a grindstone and also an Archimedean Screw to raise the water back to the trough. But it failed to take into account the energy used in overcoming the friction of the machine's various cogs*

slaves from military conquest began to run out. In China, however, where a golden age of civilization began under the Chou emperors in 1100 BC, water-driven rice-mills and water-powered bellows for furnaces and forges were being used as early as 100 BC.

The Chinese also led the way in many other fields of invention. They had silk-weaving machinery by 100 BC; a rotary winnowing machine by 40 BC; paper by AD 105 and gunpowder by AD 800. None of these inventions reached Europe before the 12th century. And in some cases they were re-invented in the West, so little contact was there between China and the rest of the world.

## Lessons from the monks

In Europe, inventiveness went into decline after the fall of the Roman Empire. The monasteries,

however, did much to keep alive technical skill and craftsmanship. It was probably the monks who substituted a three-field rotation of crops for the two-field system practised by the Romans.

The rapidly expanding populations of the early Middle Ages and the growth of towns once more made invention a profitable activity, and medieval Europe was a scene of intense and sustained development. During the 12th, 13th and early 14th centuries the skills of farming, metal-working,

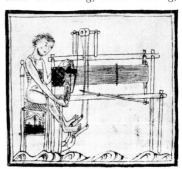

*Looms had been used since Egyptian times, but it was not until the 13th century that foot pedals were introduced*

## PIONEERS OF PRINTING

*Johann Gutenberg (1397–1468), a Strasbourg goldsmith, introduced movable type to Europe between 1446 and 1448. His first book was a Bible*

Of all the inventions of the Middle Ages, the one which did most to bring them to an end was printing. Before the 15th century, books in Europe had been printed by the laborious process of carving each page as a separate woodcut. Johann Gutenberg, with his colleague Johann Fust, produced movable metal type – in which each letter is a separate block which fits perfectly together with other letters to form a line of type. The process had been developed in China four centuries earlier, but was hitherto unknown in the West. Gutenberg's books were set in Gothic type, the nearest he could devise to the handwriting of the day. By 1470 Roman type had been invented, and Italic followed in 1495. The development of printed books was rapid; by 1500 more than 16,000 different works had been printed in 40,000 recorded editions

*William Caxton set up the first English printing press in Westminster in 1476, after learning the trade in Cologne. He printed about 80 books, many of them his own translations*

*The first printed edition of 'Aesop's Fables' in English was produced by William Caxton. A page (right) from the book shows the fox failing to reach the grapes – after which he decided that they were sour*

*Four mounted horsemen appear at each hour in one of the first mechanical clocks, built for Glastonbury Abbey in 1392 and moved to Wells Cathedral during Henry VIII's reign. The clock also records the phases of the moon*

paper-making, glass-blowing, silk manufacture and architecture all made massive strides, to be halted only temporarily by the Black Death which killed millions all over Europe in 1335–50.

## Inventors of the Middle Ages

The most important invention of the Middle Ages was printing. Following this, anybody with a cause to argue could influence a far greater number of minds by his message. Works like Erasmus's *In Praise of Folly*, an attack on some of the practices of the Roman Catholic Church, helped to prepare the ground for the upheavals of the Reformation.

Medieval inventors also perfected gunpowder for use in battle, 500 years after its first use in China. Alcohol was first distilled from wine to make spirits in Italy in the 11th century, and sulphuric and nitric acids were discovered by the alchemists in the 12th century. The Middle Ages also produced a number of visionaries. Villard de Honnecourt, of Picardy, completed in 1235 a series of plans of mechanical apparatus, including a design for a perpetual-motion machine – since recognised to be a technical impossibility.

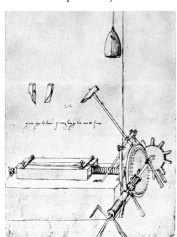

*Leonardo da Vinci's engineering skill made his design for an automatic file-cutting machine perfectly feasible. But like most of his designs it was never built*

## From Bacon to Leonardo

Even more remarkable was the 13th-century English writer Roger Bacon. 'Vessels can be made which row without the force of men,' he wrote, 'so that they can sail onward like the greatest river or sea-going craft, steered by a single man; and their speed is greater than if they were filled with oarsmen. Likewise carriages can be built which are drawn by no animal but travel with incredible power . . . flying machines can be constructed, so that a man, sitting in the middle of the machine, guides it by a skilful mechanism and traverses the air like a bird.'

It seems likely that these predictions of Roger Bacon, foreshadowing the ocean liner, the motor car and the aeroplane, were known to Leonardo da Vinci (1452–1519), the Italian genius who combined an astonishing skill in draughtsmanship with a close knowledge of engineering design. Whereas Bacon was content to talk of flying machines, Leonardo drew them, recognising that muscle-power alone would not be sufficient to turn man into a bird. He also designed a parachute – 'if a man

*The Middle Ages brought the first spectacles to aid those with defective sight; a woodcut of 1493 shows a salesman offering his wares*

has a tent 12 ells wide and 12 high covered with cloth he can throw himself down from any great height without hurting himself', he wrote. In the course of his experiments, Leonardo devised a lathe worked by a treadle, boring machines, automatic file-cutting machines, rolling mills with conical rollers, and a military tank.

Another important mechanical principle which emerged in the Middle Ages was the crankshaft, which made it possible to transform motion in a circle, as from a water-wheel, into motion in a straight line. Thus pumps could be designed and driven, and the books of technical drawings published in the 16th century are full of such devices. The camshaft was common, often being used in workshops to lift heavy hammers.

*Water was the main source of power until the 18th century. Here a German water-wheel operates a bellows to heat iron, and swings a trip hammer*

## The scientific method

It was in the centuries following the Renaissance that science, as opposed to simple invention, came into its own. Though medieval inventors had made startling advances, they had done so almost accidentally, and without understanding the scientific principles underlying them. This was demonstrated at the time of the Black Death, to which prayer seemed the only answer. Man's knowledge of biology was so scanty that he never realised the plague was spread by flea-infested rats.

But in the 17th century it was at last recognised that an understanding of scientific principles provided a more methodical way of making inventions. There were still many examples of inventions which preceded the scientific knowledge necessary to understand them; the steam engine, for instance, was to be invented more than a century before scientists understood the laws of thermodynamics which made its workings comprehensible. Nonetheless, the growth of scientific knowledge changed the nature of invention; and in the 20th century, whole new industries, like aeronautics and electronics, have depended entirely on scientific knowledge. The 17th century saw the very beginning of this development, and many of its inventions arose from the need to equip the scientist with better tools for his researches. The microscope,

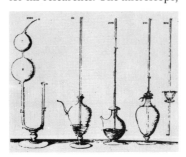

*Barometers were among the inventions of the 17th century. They used columns of mercury, like modern barometers*

the telescope, the barometer and the thermometer all made their appearance for the first time.

## New sources of power

The end of the 17th century found an abundance of engineering ideas waiting only for a new source of power. Water power, which had met industry's needs for four centuries, reached a peak in 1681, when engineers of the French king, Louis XIV, began to build a vast pumping system designed to raise water from the Seine to a reservoir at Marly-la-Machine to supply the fountains of Versailles. The system was in use up to 1804. But 14 large water-wheels, each nearly 40 ft in diameter, and ingenious arrangements for driving more than 200 pumps, were able to produce the trifling output of only 80 horsepower. The limitations of water power were obvious, though the development of the turbine was later to enable water power to be harnessed as a source of hydro-electricity.

In 1698, Thomas Savery, an English military engineer, devised an 'atmospheric' engine to pump

---

### THE FIRST PAPER

Paper originated in China in the 1st century AD, but did not reach the West for 700 years. It was cheaper than parchment, and made possible the spread of learning

*A page from a manual of papermaking by Kamisuki Chohoki, published in Osaka in 1798, shows the mixing of a paste of mulberry and bamboo fibres. The mixture was then pressed and dried*

*Papermaking changed little between the Middle Ages and the early 19th century, when this illustration was drawn. The man on the left holds a tray of pulped rags. A sieve at the bottom of the tray allowed the water to drain away. When dry, the rags were squeezed in the press on the right, and then hung up on a line*

# Steam heralds the industrial age

water from deep mines. Savery's engine used the force of atmospheric pressure to drive water into an airless vessel. The vacuum was achieved by first filling the vessel with steam, then cooling it rapidly by playing water on its surface. The steam condensed to a few drops of water, reducing the pressure in the vessel and sucking water up the mine shaft.

The engine was inefficient and dangerously liable to explode, so a few years later Thomas Newcomen, an English blacksmith, designed an improved version which he installed at Dudley Castle, Worcestershire, in 1712. It was a huge success. The last Newcomen engine in use was dismantled at Parkgate in Yorkshire in 1934, after more than a century of trouble-free operation.

### Watt's steam engine: 1765

Newcomen's engine was evidence of the first stirrings of the Industrial Revolution. By 1760 the process was well under way, and new inventions were appearing ten times as fast as at the beginning of the century. The new men who produced them came from the middle classes – men with a little capital, just sufficient education and boundless ambition. It was these men who turned invention from an occasional happy accident

*Thomas Newcomen's steam engine of 1712, heavy and ponderous as it was, could pump coal and tin mines clear of water efficiently and quickly*

into a routine of scientific progress.

Such a man was James Watt, a Scottish instrument maker, who converted Newcomen's atmospheric engine into a steam engine.

In 1765 Watt realised that it was unnecessary to cool the cylinder each time to condense the steam inside. Watt's steam cylinder was kept hot all the time, and the steam sucked into a separate cold condenser to be cooled. Watt also made his engine double-acting, admitting steam alternately to each side of the piston so as to drive it up as well as down. The development of Watt's engine was at first limited by technical difficulties. At one stage he even contemplated giving up, after his partner, John Roebuck, had come

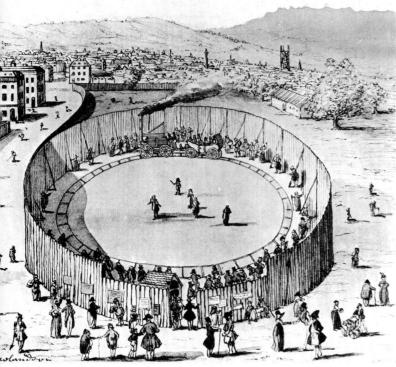

*The first steam coaches on rails, forerunners of the railway locomotive, were built by a Cornishman, Richard Trevithick. In 1808 he ran one on this track in London, and charged passengers a shilling a ride. It was 17 years before George Stephenson built the first permanent passenger railway*

## FROM IRON TO STEEL

The Industrial Revolution created a demand for reliable metals, and this was met by rapid advances in the process of refining iron. Blast furnaces smelted the iron ore to produce pig iron; this could be re-smelted to turn it into cast iron, and further purified to make wrought iron. Finally the invention of the Bessemer converter in 1856 enabled pig iron to be made directly into steel, a tough yet malleable alloy of iron and carbon

*For centuries the blacksmith was the only manufacturer of iron. This woodcut showing a smith at work is from a book published by Caxton in 1483*

*An illustration of 1802 shows the making of cannon balls from cast iron, a heat-resisting but brittle metal. The seated worker is trimming the castings with a chisel*

*Until the 18th century, the only means of smelting iron was with charcoal – the black residue of partially burnt wood. In a 17th-century blast furnace (above) iron ore and charcoal were mixed and a blast of hot air blown through, heating the charcoal. Once the iron was molten, a small clay dam at the bottom of the furnace was broken, allowing the iron to flow out. The furnace on the left of this picture is being cleaned and repaired before being recharged. Because large amounts of charcoal were needed, the iron-masters built their furnaces in wooded areas.*

*During the 17th century, however, a new fuel, coke, came into use. Its discovery came about when the brewers of Derbyshire found that the drying of malts over fires of pure coal gave the beer a sulphurous taste; so they charred the coal first and used the resultant coke to dry the malt. In 1709, Abraham Darby made the first successful attempt to use coke for smelting at his foundry in Coalbrookdale, Shropshire. As supplies of charcoal dwindled and became more costly, other iron-masters saw the advantages of coke, and by 1790 more than three-quarters of Britain's blast furnaces were fuelled by it*

to the end of his resources. Watt moved to London to take up a safer career as a civil engineer, and fortunately met the brilliant engineer Matthew Boulton. Together Boulton and Watt made nearly 500 engines which were used to drive pumps, machinery and blast furnaces throughout the Industrial Revolution.

## The textile industry is born
The beginnings of steam power coincided with the birth of the textile industry. Mechanical spinning machines for turning cotton into thread date from the 1760's, with Richard Arkwright's new spinning machine and the 'Spinning Jenny' of James Hargreaves. The mechanical spinning machines greatly increased the rate at which yarn could be spun, and enabled one man to do the work of many – a

*Hargreaves's 'Spinning Jenny' of 1770 revolutionised the cotton industry*

*A 19th-century picture shows a typical blast furnace. Air is blasted upwards, through a melted 'charge' of coke, iron ore and limestone. At first, cold air was used, but it was later found that hot air was more efficient. The chemical reaction releases molten iron, and impurities float on top of it as slag*

*The world's first iron bridge, built at Coalbrookdale, Shropshire, in 1782, was the product of three generations of Darbys. Abraham Darby I developed the use of coke; his son manufactured cast iron; and his grandson built the bridge*

*Henry Bessemer (left), the engineer, patented his tilting converter for making steel in 1860. Hot air is blown through molten iron, oxidising its impurities; carbon is then added, in quantities which vary according to the steel required*

*George Stephenson designed* Rocket, *the most famous locomotive of all time, in 1829, with the help of his son Robert. It won a competition against all comers in trials organised by the Liverpool and Manchester Railway*

process opposed by many workers on the ground that it took away their livelihood.

By the end of the 18th century, spinning and weaving machines had been successfully married to the steam engine of James Watt. The balance tipped in favour of steam in 1785, when a Boulton and Watt steam engine was installed in a spinning factory in Papplewick, Nottinghamshire. From then on, the use of steam power increased while the use of water power stood still. Costs fell dramatically, as steam was more economical. By 1812 the cost of spun yarn was only one-tenth of what it had been 30 years before, and by the 1830's the cotton of Lancashire accounted for half of all British exports.

## Steam for transport
The success of steam power in the mills suggested that it might find applications elsewhere. The first steam coach was devised by a Frenchman, N. J. Cugnot, in 1769, and a Cornishman, Richard Trevithick, tried out his own independent design on Christmas Eve 1801. In the next ten years Trevithick produced a series of steam locomotives capable of running over rails. He took one to London in 1808 and charged a shilling for a ride around a circular track. These early experiments were often thwarted by the breaking of the cast-iron rails, an obstacle not really surmounted until wrought-iron rails were introduced in 1820.

Nobody seems to have seen the possibilities of the early steam cars. Although Trevithick's 'London Carriage' of 1802 proved its effectiveness by trundling along Oxford Street at 10 mph, the inventor was unable to persuade anybody to invest money to develop it.

## The coming of the railways
It was left to locomotives pulling trains of coaches to take advantage of the power of steam. And to George Stephenson, born in Newcastle in 1781, goes the honour of building the first successful passenger steam railway, between Stockton and Darlington in 1825. Once the railways were under way, investors flocked to support them, setting off a boom to rival the canal-building boom of 50 years before. In an orgy of speculation in the 1840's, railways were built everywhere across Britain; the Great Western Railway, broad gauge from London to Bristol, was built in only seven years. The gauge, however, had later to be changed to conform with other lines. The Great Western and other

railways were much advanced by improvements in materials. The production of iron from its ores by means of a blast furnace, in which air is blown through a mixed charge of ore, limestone and charcoal, so forcing out impurities, had been known for some time.

In 1709 the Englishman Abraham Darby discovered a way of substituting coke for the costly charcoal. A further major step forward came in 1856, when Sir Henry Bessemer discovered a technique for converting iron into steel.

*The early steamer* Charlotte Dundas *was built in Scotland in 1801. It had a steam cylinder linked to a paddle wheel*

## 'Leviathans' at sea
The first experiments in marine steam propulsion took place in France and the United States, but one of the most successful of the early steamboats was the *Charlotte Dundas*, designed by William Symington, and built in a Grangemouth dockyard in 1801. Built to operate along the canals, she was banned by the canal owners, who believed that she would wash away the banks. The first commercially successful steamship was the *Comet*, built in Glasgow in 1812, and designed to run between Glasgow and Helensburgh.

It was not long before massive ocean-going 'leviathans' were being built. Gradually, the screw replaced the paddle. Then in 1884 came another improvement, when Charles A. Parsons of Newcastle patented his steam turbine – ideal for marine propulsion. He demonstrated this in 1897 at the Jubilee Naval Review when his little *Turbinia*, capable of the amazing speed of $34\frac{1}{2}$ knots, outpaced the navy's stately battleships.

## Academies of science
The word 'scientist' did not appear in English or any other language until 1840. The '-ist' signified that professionalism and specialisation were at last being recognised. Many of the first scientists were

### THE VERSATILE BRUNEL
One of the most versatile engineers of the 19th century was the Englishman Isambard Kingdom Brunel. He helped his father, Sir Marc Brunel, to construct a tunnel beneath the Thames, and also designed bridges, railways and steamships

*Brunel at the launching in 1838 of his* Great Western, *the first transatlantic steam vessel. It silenced critics who said ships could not carry enough coal for the crossing*

*Brunel was engineer to the Great Western Railway for 26 years. In pushing the line westwards he built a series of fine bridges which still stand. The Royal Albert Bridge over the River Tamar was opened in 1859 by the Prince Consort*

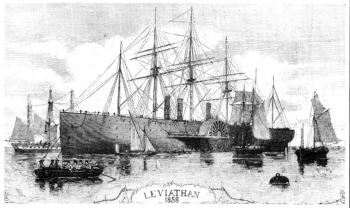

*The* Great Eastern, *nicknamed* Leviathan, *was designed to carry 4000 passengers to Australia and back without refuelling. Launched in 1858, she was a technical success but a commercial failure, and never operated on the long run for which she was designed. Many years later, however, she laid the first telegraph cable across the Atlantic*

# *Electricity lights up the world*

The first experiments with electric lamps were made by the Englishman Joseph Swan in 1848, but he did not produce a satisfactory bulb until 30 years later. This photograph of 1884 shows a Swan bulb fitted to a traditional gas bracket. In 1883 Swan and the American electrical engineer Thomas Alva Edison set up a joint company to manufacture bulbs

gifted amateurs, such as Henry Cavendish of the ducal family of Devonshire who, by exploding a mixture of hydrogen and oxygen with an electric spark, established the composition of water. Antoine Lavoisier, a French nobleman, founded quantitative chemistry and was later guillotined during the French Revolution; Benjamin Franklin, the Philadelphia printer and one of the founders of the United States, was also the first man to recognise the existence of two types of static electricity, positive and negative.

A milestone in the development of scientific technology was the founding in London in 1799 of the Royal Institution, by the American-born Count Rumford. The idea soon spread. In 1816 France established the *Académie des Sciences*, which grew out of the famous 18th-century academy of the same name. On the other side of the Atlantic, James Smithson, illegitimate son of the Duke of Northumberland, left his fortune to the United States to found another seat of scientific endeavour, the Smithsonian Institute, in 1846.

Michael Faraday discovered in 1831 the principles of the electric motor and the dynamo. Within a year the first small generators had been built

The Royal Institution provided research facilities for the chemist Sir Humphry Davy (1778–1829), inventor of a safety lamp for miners, and for Davy's protegé, Michael Faraday (1791–1867), famous for his work on electricity.

## Understanding electricity
Electricity was not a new discovery. Thales, the Greek philosopher, had noticed that amber decorations on spinning wheels attracted threads, feathers and light objects through what is now known to be static electricity. The Greek word for amber is *elektron*, from which William Gilbert, physician to Elizabeth I, coined the word electricity. In 1672, Otto von Guericke set sparks jumping between metal balls. Seventy years later, Pieter van Musschenbroak invented the Leyden jar, which stored static electricity, and released it when touched. Then in 1752, Franklin successfully drew

down an electric charge from a thunder cloud. By this experiment he proved that lightning consists of a gigantic electric spark.

Thirty years later, the Italian Luigi Galvani thought he had discovered 'animal electricity' when he observed the twitching of dead frogs' legs on a zinc plate when touched by a steel scalpel. But another scientist, the Italian Alessandro Volta, recognised that the effect was due to the two different metals, and went on to

Faraday's scientific relics show the simplicity of his apparatus. He used these items in his experiments with electro-magnetic induction

make his 'voltaic pile', composed of copper and zinc discs separated by brine-soaked paper. This was the first electric battery.

Hans Christian Oersted, a Danish scientist, was giving a lecture at the University of Copenhagen in 1819, and unintentionally placed a wire carrying an electric current near a simple mariner's compass, causing the needle to swing. He did not even draw his class's attention to it, but went to

### EDISON THE WIZARD

The most prolific inventor of the 19th century was an American, Thomas Alva Edison, who took out 1093 patents for his various inventions and earned the nickname of 'the wizard'. He promoted his inventions by parties to which scientists and journalists were invited. One party illuminated by Edison's electric lights was described as 'a heavenly spectacle'

Edison sits in his study at Menlo Park, New Jersey, with a phonograph operated by a foot pedal, perhaps intended to be used as a dictaphone. Edison invented the phonograph in 1877, and with one of the first models marched into the office of the journal 'Scientific American'. After a brief description, Edison turned the handle, and the machine said: 'Good morning. How do you do? How do you like the phonograph?' Despite the amazement which greeted the invention, ten years passed before it was perfected, using wax cylinders instead of tinfoil, and an electric motor instead of a hand crank. In 1887 Emile Berliner replaced the wax cylinders by flat discs

his laboratory and conducted further tests, with the same result. He had discovered the relationship between magnetism and electricity, the starting point for Faraday.

## Dynamo and generator

In 1831 Michael Faraday, at the Royal Institution, discovered that by combining any two of the three factors, magnetism, electricity and motion, he could produce the third, so discovering, simultaneously, the principles of the dynamo and the electric motor. Within a year the first mechanical generator using Faraday's principles had been demonstrated in Paris by Hippolyte Pixii. From then on, larger generators were built to cope with the increasing demands for electricity.

Electricity became the vogue. Humphry Davy used a voltaic battery to produce an incandescent spark between two pieces of carbon. This discovery, the carbon arc lamp, was later used to light factories and railway stations, and continued much later as the carbon arc in floodlights and cinema projectors. But Davy's arc light had the great disadvantage that, in air, the carbon was rapidly consumed, and the rods had to be renewed frequently. What was needed was a surrounding vacuum, and in 1848 the English inventor Joseph Swan, using strips of carbonised paper in a bulb from which the air had been extracted, produced the first incandescent filament

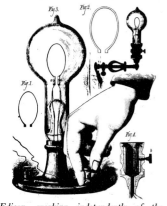

*Edison, working independently of the English inventor, Joseph Swan, produced his first successful incandescent lamp in October 1879. This drawing shows the bulb, methods of fitting it to wall brackets and the details of its holder*

*Edison's first phonograph was cranked by hand, which required some care if voices were not to be distorted. The playing time of the cylinders was also very short*

lamp. It was short-lived, because the vacuum was imperfect, but he eventually produced a successful version.

In 1877 Thomas Alva Edison announced that he was going to work on the incandescent lamp. Six years later Edison and Swan agreed to form the Edison and Swan United Electric Light Company, and in 1886 the first house-to-house installation of electric light was established in Kensington, London. At the same time, a

*The Central Telegraph Office in London at the height of its activity in 1873, before the coming of the telephone*

successful electric motor was at last devised. Nicola Tesla, an expatriate Hungarian working for the Westinghouse Company in the United States, invented a motor operated by alternating current in 1888, and the use of electric motors increased rapidly. Electric railways, which had been first demonstrated on a small scale in Berlin in 1879, and tramways in towns were two large consumers of electricity.

## Messages by wire

Meanwhile a new body of science was building up. Men in Europe and America were investigating the electro-magnetic phenomena, first noted by Oersted in 1819. Eventually their discoveries were to result in the telegraph, telephone, radio, television and the complex electronic devices that allowed men to investigate outer space.

*Alexander Graham Bell's first telephone was the main attraction at an exhibition held at Philadelphia in 1876*

But the first reference to the possibility of passing messages by electric currents along wires occurs in a detailed but anonymous letter in a 1753 issue of the *Scots Magazine*.

The letter proposed using 26 separate wires, each representing a letter of the alphabet, along which messages could be passed letter by

*Isaac M. Singer produced the first practical sewing machine in 1851, and sold thousands of models. It was among the first articles sold by hire purchase*

letter. More economical schemes, using only a single wire, were proposed in the 1770's, and a successful electrostatic telegraph was demonstrated by Francis Ronalds in England in 1816.

Electric telegraphs began to catch on in the 1840's, helped in Britain by publicity after a telegraph developed by the Englishmen Cooke and Wheatstone was used to capture a suspected murderer seen getting on to a train at Slough. The message, telegraphed to London ahead of the train, enabled the police to make a dramatic arrest.

With similarly good timing, the American Samuel Morse, inventor of Morse Code, managed to complete the Washington–Baltimore link the day before the American Democratic Party met in Baltimore to pick its presidential candi-

*The early Remington typewriter, designed by C. S. Sholes, was an elaborate machine. The single keyboard enabled capital letters only to be typed*

date. In 1876 the Scottish-born American Alexander Graham Bell developed the first successful telephone, in which the human voice is translated into electric impulses, passed along a wire, then re-translated back into sounds. By the end of the 19th century the telephone was in everyday use in many countries.

In 1877 Thomas Edison invented the phonograph. The first records were made by scratching grooves in a sheet of tinfoil wound round a cylinder, but Charles Tainter, another American inventor, substituted wax in 1885, and Emile Berliner, a German-American, introduced wax-coated discs in 1887. Tape-recording of sound followed,

in principle at least, in 1898. It was the invention of the Danish engineer Valdemar Poulsen, but it did not become a practical technique for another half century. The potential of early records was also limited because they had to be made without microphones.

In America in 1851 Isaac Singer built the first sewing machine, and in 1873 the Remington Company began to manufacture the first successful typewriter. The first typewriter had been designed 40 years earlier by a Marseilles printer, but it was an American typographer, C. S. Sholes, who overcame the principal problem – the clashing together of type bars during rapid touch typing. He did this by devising a keyboard in which the letters most often used are set far apart; the same keyboard is in use today.

## From bicycle to motor car

The last years of the 19th century were those of the 'bicycle revolution', enabling great masses of people for the first time to travel cheaply to the country. The advances which made this possible were the Rover safety bicycle of 1885, which replaced the alarming 'ordinary' bicycle, or penny farthing, and the pneumatic tyre, devised in 1888 by J. B. Dunlop. The safety bicycle used a geared-up chain driving the rear wheel, instead of the enormous front driving wheel of the penny-farthing. Better balance, steering and braking were all made possible by this innovation.

The most important invention of the last quarter of the 19th century was the internal combustion engine. Attempts in the 17th century to use the explosion of gunpowder inside a cylinder to push a piston anticipated the invention, but were not successful. Early in the 19th century internal combustion engines burning turpentine or hydrogen had been tried, but did not become a practical possibility.

*Oil spouts from the ground at Maidan-i-Naftun, Persia, in 1917 – one of many Middle Eastern wells exploited to provide fuel for the internal combustion engine during the First World War*

*An ungainly beast, with front wheels up to 5 ft across, the penny-farthing bicycle flourished between 1872 and 1885*

# The engine that changed society

*Within 30 years of the invention of the internal combustion engine, the motor car made its presence felt in the streets of Europe's big cities. Traffic jams had become a familiar part of the London scene by 1914, when buses and motor cars mingled with the occasional horse-drawn vehicle in Oxford Street*

However, the discovery of petroleum in Pennsylvania in 1859 by Edwin L. Drake meant that now there was a seemingly inexhaustible source of power to drive the new engines.

## The first motor engines

In the same year the French engineer Etienne Lenoir built a gas engine. It worked, though less efficiently than contemporary steam engines. In 1876 a German, Nikolaus Otto, devised the four-stroke cycle for use in his gas engine. This uses the force of gas expanding in a closed cylinder to drive a piston and so power an engine. Otto's engine was a great success; 50,000 were sold in the first 17 years of production, and by 1917 gas engines of up to 5000 hp were in use.

An Austrian engineer, Siegfried

Markus, is said to have built several petrol-driven vehicles between 1864 and 1874, but the first major development came from the German engineer Gottlieb Daimler in 1885. He devised a single cylinder, air-cooled petrol engine using the Otto four-stroke cycle, and the next year attached it to a bicycle. At the same time he made a four-wheeled vehicle. The work of Daimler and his fellow-German Karl Benz made the motor car a practical possibility.

Where Daimler and Benz had led, other engineers followed. Henry Ford in the United States made his first car in 1896, and

*The gas-powered internal combustion engine invented by Nikolaus Otto was the petrol engine's forerunner*

followed it with the Model T in 1908. Possibly the most influential car ever, it sold for 19 years, and 15 million were made. Ford's

## A CENTURY OF THE MOTOR CAR

The motor car evolved as a combination of the engineering ideas of a host of designers, initially in Germany and France and, later, in many other countries. The German Karl Benz made one of the first practical, petrol-burning cars in 1885. The French firm of Panhard and Levassor was the first to design a 'modern' motor car, with the engine at the front, a sliding-pinion gearbox, a friction clutch, and drive through the rear wheels. Panhard and Levassor was also among the earliest companies to put the motor car into serious commercial production. Many ideas, such as the multi-cylinder engine, had to await the coming of better materials and manufacturing methods before they could develop their full potential

*Gottlieb Daimler, one of the fathers of the motor car, in 1886 installed a 1½ hp single-cylinder engine in a carriage*

*The Benz patent motor car of 1885 was really a motorised tricycle. Its single-cylinder engine was placed at the rear and drove the rear wheels through a belt; this could be shifted from a fixed to a movable pulley, thereby acting as a simple clutch. The car was steered by a tiller, and could reach 8 mph*

*The first engines of Rudolf Diesel, such as this 1909 model, provided a power source for lathes and other machines*

major contribution towards putting the world on wheels was to adopt the principle of mass production using standard interchangeable parts, a system first applied commercially by the American gunsmith Samuel Colt.

The years before the First World War were the age of the massive Edwardian motor car, with its solid and slow-revving engine. Successful military use encouraged development of motor vehicles, and the 1920's were the period of what is now the 'Vintage' model. Many hundreds of manufacturers tried to break into the market,

though most went bankrupt at the end of the 1920's when economic collapse set in. Those who survived, like Herbert Austin and William Morris, flourished, producing family cars throughout the 1930's.

Throughout the entire history of the motor car, the petrol-driven internal combustion engine has reigned supreme. Another form of internal combustion engine using a cheaper oil fuel, the diesel engine, named after its German inventor Rudolf Diesel, has been widely adopted for lorries and buses. An innovation of the 1970's has been the Wankel engine, still operating by internal combustion but based on a new rotary principle.

### Radio waves detected

A host of new technologies were developed during the late 19th and early 20th centuries. In 1888 a German physicist, Heinrich Hertz, first detected the presence of radio waves, predicted theoretically 20 years earlier by the Scottish physicist James Clerk Maxwell. By the 1890's, Edouard Branly and Oliver Lodge had shown that it was possible to send and detect 'Hertzian waves' over short distances, and in 1896 the Italian Guglielmo Marconi extended the range to 9 miles. In 1901 he broadcast the first message in Morse Code across the Atlantic. By the end of 1906, it was possible to

*Guglielmo Marconi pioneered long-distance wireless telegraphy by sending a Morse signal across the Atlantic from Cornwall to Newfoundland in 1901*

broadcast music and speech as well. The development of the triode valve, by the American Lee de Forest in 1907, enabled the feeble signals to be amplified, and in 1921 the first radio programmes were transmitted by Frank Conrad from a station in Pittsburgh.

In the first form of television, produced by the Scotsman John Logie Baird in 1926, a rotating perforated disc 'scanned' a scene, enabling information to be transmitted piecemeal and picked up by the receivers. Baird's invention, however, was to be superseded in 1928 by the invention in America by Vladimir Zworykin of the iconoscope, an electronic means of achieving the same result.

The first television transmissions by the BBC used Baird's system, but when television broadcasting

was resumed after the Second World War, the electronic system was preferred. Because the waves carrying a television signal can travel only in straight lines, the necessary range for the signals could be achieved at first only by broadcasting them from the top of tall towers.

In 1945, the British science writer Arthur C. Clarke suggested the idea of communications satellites orbiting the earth, which could in effect act as masts thousands of miles high, picking up the signals and re-transmitting them to earth stations. The idea was first realised

*In 1926 a form of television was invented by John Logie Baird, standing here in front of its disc 'camera'*

in 1962 with the satellite Telstar, and greatly improved with the introduction of satellites, which remain above a single point on the earth's surface.

---

*The Model T Ford was the first motor car designed to be cheaply mass-produced. In 1911 this Ford T Tourer, known universally as a 'Tin Lizzie', cost $322 Other manufacturers followed Henry Ford's example; one of the most successful was William Morris, an Oxford bicycle maker*

*The 4½-litre Bentley of 1928 won the 24-hour race at Le Mans that year. 'The world's fastest lorry', jibed Ettore Bugatti*

*A rocket was used in 1970 to power the American 'Blue Flame' automobile at over 500 mph. Air friction at high speeds presents a new problem – the so-called 'heat barrier'*

### THE FIRST PHOTOGRAPHS

The principles on which photography is based were known to Archimedes; if a small hole is made in a wall around a darkened space, images of outside objects appear upside-down and reversed on the wall opposite the opening. But it was more than 2000 years later that the first camera was produced. In the early 1800's attempts were made to record the images with a sheet of paper impregnated with silver nitrate, which darkened on exposure to light. But the image soon faded. In 1839 two Frenchmen, Louis Daguerre and Joseph Niepce, using a copper plate coated with silver iodide, found a way of developing the images by treating them with mercury vapour and 'fixing' them with cyanide

*Louis Daguerre (1789–1851) invented the first practical process of photography, which was called the daguerreotype after him. He photographed Napoleon III*

*The earliest daguerreotype still in existence, showing a wall and its decorations, was taken by Daguerre in 1837. Later inventors, including the Englishman William Henry Fox Talbot, succeeded in producing photographic negatives from which any number of positives could be made by contact. They used paper or glass plates, sensitised with a solution of silver salts in collodion, which dried rapidly in the air. But this 'wet plate' process was an unwieldy system. It was the introduction between 1868 and 1871 of dry plates made of celluloid or gelatine, providing a transparent, flexible backing, which enabled films to be made commercially*

*In 1888 George Eastman made photography available to everybody by introducing the portable Kodak camera, mass-produced, simple, and using film wound on a spool*

*Many inventors attempted to produce moving pictures, but the Lumière brothers in France were the first to achieve any success. One of the brothers is shown operating their combined camera and projector at Lyons in 1895. The first photographs of moving objects had been taken by Eadweard Muybridge in America in 1877, when he managed for the first time to record how a horse gallops. Muybridge visited Europe in 1882 with his 'zoopraxiscope', a device for animating his series of pictures to give the impression of movement. Inspired by these, and by a 'kinetoscope' invented by Thomas Edison, the Lumière brothers devised their combined camera and projector and filmed delegates arriving at a French photographic congress. Forty-eight hours later they projected the developed film. Unlike Edison's kinetoscope, the Lumières' invention could be shown to a large number of people at once, and by the end of 1895 they had opened their first cinema in Paris. Others soon followed. The early films were simple affairs, but they soon became more sophisticated. Sound followed in the United States in 1927, and colour in 1932*

# Man's conquest of the air

*Otto Lilienthal, a German flying pioneer, made more than 1000 flights in the 1890's in his elegant 'hanging gliders'. They were designed on principles worked out by Sir George Cayley, an English scientist who flew unmanned gliders from hilltops as early as 1804, and may have even flown a manned glider, too. Lilienthal was killed in a crash in 1896*

## Man takes to the air

The 19th century came to a close in a fever of activity over flying in heavier-than-air-machines. The

*The Montgolfier brothers, the first men to fly in a hot-air balloon, take off from Versailles in 1783. The English Channel was crossed by balloon a year later*

balloon had been known for many years (the first balloons were flown in France by the Montgolfier brothers) and had been used by the French to take messages out of Paris during the German siege in 1870. Sir George Cayley had devised a glider in 1853 which could carry a boy aloft, and the German, Otto Lilienthal, brought gliding to a fine art before his death in an accident in 1896.

In 1902 Samuel Pierpoint Langley, the American physicist, almost managed to get off the ground in a powered glider. The feat was finally achieved in a series of flights on December 17, 1903 at Kitty Hawk, North Carolina, by the brothers Orville and Wilbur Wright. The first flight lasted 12 seconds, covering 120 ft; but not until the Wrights managed flights of 25 miles did people become really aware of the new invention. In 1909 the Frenchman Louis Blériot, using a monoplane of his own design, flew the English Channel for the first time.

## War as the spur

During the 20th century, the main stimulus for invention has been provided by war. The process began when the First World War

*The first powered flight was made by Orville Wright at Kitty Hawk, North Carolina, on December 17, 1903. His brother Wilbur watched*

*The English inventor Frank Whittle (right) demonstrates one of his own jet aircraft engines in June 1945*

turned the aeroplane from a curiosity into a highly efficient means of reconnaissance or of delivering freight, people or bombs. All such early aeroplanes used internal combustion engines driving propellers. The idea of jet propulsion, however, occurred to many people, and a French engineer, René Lorin, took out a patent as early as 1913. In the 1930's the first successful jet engines emerged almost at the same time in Germany and Britain, and the two men who did most to make them a reality were Professor Ernst Heinkel and Frank Whittle. Jet aircraft, in which a powerful backwards thrust of ignited fuel and air pushes the plane forwards, were

## THE LURE OF FLIGHT

Man dreamt of flight for many centuries, but the dreamers tried to copy the action of the birds. Only in 1800 did an Englishman, Sir George Cayley, realise that fixed wings would be needed. The internal combustion engine eventually provided the motive force

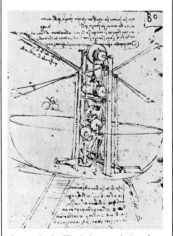

*Icarus, of Greek legend, falls from the sky after flying too near the sun; the heat melted his wax and goose-feather wings*

*Leonardo da Vinci drew a design for a flying machine with flapping wings. The man in the middle was intended to crank away, making the wings flap like a bird*

being used by the end of the Second World War. In the Korean War in the early 1950's they predominated.

## Discovering nuclear power

The pressures of the Second World War gave rise to two major new technologies, nuclear power and electronics. The major development in electronics was radar, used by the Germans initially to aim the guns of battleships but by the British to detect approaching hostile aircraft.

In 1939 the German physicists Otto Hahn and Lise Meitner split the uranium atom, thus discovering the secret of nuclear fission, the disruption of a heavy atomic nucleus into two lighter ones. It was quickly realised that this process would produce vast amounts of energy which could be used in a bomb of unprecedented destructive power.

The Allies were determined that Nazi Germany should not produce the bomb first. A massive scientific team was marshalled in the United States, under the code-name of the Manhattan Project, to produce

*The hovercraft, invented in 1959 by Sir Christopher Cockerell, is supported by a cushion of air and can travel over any surface. Hovercraft services now travel across the English Channel*

the first atom bomb. The bomb was to have enormous political and military consequences; in addition, it altered the time-scale of change. It was the first of the great 'crash programmes', and it reduced the interval between a scientific idea and its full-scale fulfilment from centuries to months. The project mobilised the most brilliant scientists on the Allied side and gave them a single purpose. It recruited physicists, chemists and every kind of technologist. It had absolute priority in building construction and first claim on all kinds of components and materials, some of which, like uranium and beryllium, had never been used on an industrial scale before.

Huge research laboratories and bomb-assembly workshops were built in the desert of New Mexico, and there the American J. Robert Oppenheimer and his team produced the device which they first successfully exploded at Alamogordo at 5.30 a.m. on Monday July 16, 1945.

The nuclear age began with the explosion of a bomb equivalent to 20,000 tons of TNT. The physicist Isidor Rabi, who witnessed the

explosion, was asked later what he had seen. 'I can't tell you,' he said. 'But don't expect to die a natural death.' However, scientists were also working on ways of using the power of nuclear fission for peaceful purposes. The first controlled nuclear pile, or reactor, became effective in December 1942 in a squash court in Chicago under the control of the Italian Enrico Fermi. A telegram was sent to Washington, bearing the cryptic message: 'The Italian navigator has entered the New World.' Within 15 years the first experimental nuclear reactors producing electricity were operating in Britain and the United States.

In 1952 the Americans first exploded the even more destructive H-bomb, using the new principle of nuclear fusion. In this, light atoms of hydrogen are made to combine with each other to form heavy atoms, so releasing energy.

## Rockets in war and peace

Man's conquest of space was also given its impetus by the demands of war for even more effective weapons. During the Second World War the first long-range rockets were developed by Werner von Braun and a team of German scientists at Pennemünde. Rocket power, like jet power, uses the backwards thrust of burning gases to push the engine forwards. But unlike a jet engine, a rocket motor carries its own supply of oxygen for combustion, and so can work in outer space.

Hitler's second 'vengeance weapon', the V2, used to bombard London in the winter of 1944, was rocket-powered, and the experience the Germans gained was later used in both the Russian and American space programmes. The first successful earth satellite, the Russian Sputnik I, was launched in October 1957, to be followed on April 12, 1961 by the first manned flight into space, carried out by the Russian cosmonaut, Yuri Gagarin.

The first American orbital flight, by John Glenn, took place in

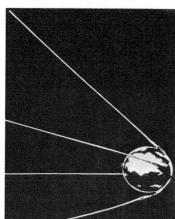

*Sputnik 1, the first man-made earth satellite, was launched on October 4, 1957. The long aerials sent its 'bleep-bleep' signals back to earth*

*A Saturn I rocket. A later development of the rocket was used to launch the first moon mission flown by the Americans*

February 1962, and the United States became the first nation to land men on the moon when Neil Armstrong and Buzz Aldrin stepped from the Apollo 11 lunar capsule in July 1969 on to the moon's surface. A three-year series of moon missions followed.

## Into the future

Technology in the 20th century is no longer the product of the inspired amateur, like Benjamin Franklin with his kite. The expensive research involved in perfecting a new technique today requires the backing of huge international firms, or even governments.

Yet the pace of progress continues to accelerate. Much of the technology that we take for granted was developed during living memory, and the detailed application of such discoveries as electronics and nuclear power is still very much in its infancy. In particular, the application of electronic devices to industry may usher in a new Industrial Revolution.

In the factories of today, automation has already reduced the number of workers needed. In the near future scientists believe that it will be possible to link all a factory's machines directly to a central controlling computer. This may bring greater efficiency, but raise new social problems by making human labour redundant.

---

## MACHINES THAT COUNT

Computers, already able to calculate at breathtaking speed, may prove the most influential invention of the 20th century. The idea of a device to make addition easier goes back to the abacus; but the first successful machine for the task was designed by a French philosopher, Blaise Pascal, in 1642. In the 19th century, an Englishman, Charles Babbage, designed a machine for more complicated calculations. Since the 1950's, progress has been rapid. Valves gave way to transistors, and then in 1958 to the first tiny 'integrated' circuits

*Blaise Pascal's calculating machine of 1642 enabled a clerk to add eight-figure numbers by turning a series of wheels*

*Charles Babbage (1792–1871), an eccentric and irascible English inventor, was the first man to plan a machine that would perform long and complex calculations. But although he spent a large part of his personal fortune and received a substantial grant from the Treasury, Babbage never fully achieved his aim. The technical knowledge of his time was too limited to enable Babbage's 'computers' – which were purely mechanical – to perform all the complex tasks he envisaged for them. Electronic computers which could perform these tasks came into being only during the Second World War, when both German and American scientists developed them to help in the radar-controlled interception of enemy bombers. Since then, computers have become part of everyday life in industry*

*A fragment of Charles Babbage's first design shows the tiers of wheels representing the digits in a five-figure number. The machine was operated by turning a handle*

*At the heart of modern computers are thousands of integrated circuits. A triumph of miniaturisation, each contains all its necessary components in a tiny panel less than a millimetre across*

# Man under the microscope

*Disease is as old as life, and experiments in medicine have helped to reveal the workings of the human body*

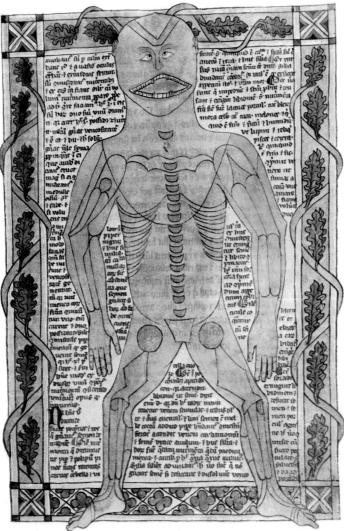

*Man's knowledge of human anatomy remained primitive as late as the Middle Ages, as this 13th-century diagram of bone structure shows. Until the 14th century, religious taboos prevented the dissection of bodies to increase knowledge*

Over the ages, man has evolved successfully by adapting himself to meet most of the hazards of his natural environment. He has learnt to use the plant and animal life around him to provide food, clothing, shelter and labour. But disease is one enemy he has been able to fight only on very unequal terms. Parasitic organisms, too small to be seen without a microscope, may infest the body, living and feeding on its very substance until they weaken and finally kill it. Deficiencies in any of man's basic needs, such as food or warmth, may reduce the body's natural defences against attack. Even when the basic necessities are available, disease may arise through ignorance or neglect of simple hygiene.

But man is not helpless against the onslaught of disease. Nature has its own defence mechanism, by which a species gradually adapts itself to its environment by developing immunity to diseases which might threaten its survival. This form of unconscious biological adaptation is a slow process, but man has been able to add conscious and deliberate adaptation by treatment and surgery.

The many techniques of modern medicine could never have been devised without a profound understanding of the structure and function of the human body, and of the forces that can cut short its normal life span. The history of medicine shows how gradual has been the growth of this understanding; and even today some of the mysteries that confronted the earliest physicians remain mysteries still.

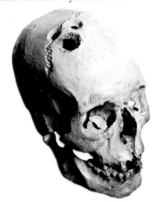

*A prehistoric 'cure' was to drill a hole in a patient's skull to let out the 'spirits' which were thought to carry disease*

### The dawn of medicine

Ignorant of the physical causes of disease, people in primitive societies to this day see illness as being caused entirely by evil spirits. They seek cures in worship and sacrifices, and the functions of doctor and priest are inseparable. But some progress towards a more practical approach was made even in earliest times. The lore of the medicine-man was based on a study of nature, and plants were probably used in the treatment of disease. Surgery, too, had early

beginnings, for prehistoric skulls have been found in various parts of the world with holes bored in them, probably with a pointed flint tool. This process, known as trepanning, was generally intended to allow the escape of the evil spirit which was thought to be causing sickness whose symptoms were mental. Surprisingly, patients survived the 'operation', for in many skulls the rims of the perforations have been blunted by healing processes in the bone tissue.

*A man with a withered leg, depicted in a 4000-year-old Egyptian carving, was probably suffering from poliomyelitis*

### Egypt's health service

Medicine grew somewhat more sophisticated in the great civilizations of the ancient world. In Egypt, there were doctors for different parts of the body. For really important people, the degree of specialisation was taken to extremes: the Egyptian pharaoh, for example, had a different doctor for each of his eyes. Egypt also had an early national health service, with doctors paid by the state and free treatment for the sick while they were travelling and in war.

Medical papyri of about 1500 BC show that although Egyptian doctors recognised and treated many diseases affecting various parts of the body, their medicine remained primarily a religious practice, and their knowledge of anatomy was extremely limited.

The ancient civilizations of India and China also had well-established systems of medicine. The Indians had little knowledge of anatomy, but their surgeons could remove tonsils and limbs, using a range of instruments which included scalpels, saws and forceps.

### Plastic surgery

Physicians in India were skilled in plastic surgery, and could create new noses for people whose noses had been mutilated – the standard punishment for some social offences such as adultery.

Indian doctors also developed a formidable knowledge of plant drugs and their effects. The tranquilliser drugs used in the modern treatment of mental illness date back to American research in the 1940's on a plant called rauwolfia – which had been used in India for the same purpose for over a thousand years. The Hindu religion from earliest times had many rules that helped to maintain personal and public hygiene, especially in tropical climates.

## Yang and Yin

The origins of medicine in China were attributed to a legendary ruler, Shen Nung, under the inspiration of the great Taoist god P'an Ku. In Taoist philosophy, order depends on the balance between two opposing principles, *yang* and *yin*. *Yang* is associated with light, the sun, the south, masculinity and dryness; *yin* with darkness, the moon, the north, femininity and moisture. These two opposing principles were thought to combine with the blood and pass around the body. Illness was held to be caused by imbalance between the two principles, and death occurred when their flow stopped.

Chinese medicine still relies heavily on the ancient practice of acupuncture – the painless insertion of needles at various points of the body in order to secure the correct balance of *yang* and *yin*. The needles, 1 in. to 10 in. long, are left in position for periods varying from one to several hours. The points of insertion are precisely charted along lines which are thought to control the actions of the chief organs. To the present day, Chinese surgeons still prefer to use acupuncture, instead of conventional Western anaesthetics, in performing even the most elaborate hospital operations.

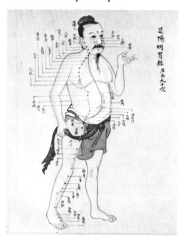

*Special charts showed ancient Chinese physicians some of the many points where acupuncture needles could be inserted*

## Lessons of Hippocrates

The ancient Greeks, who showed how man's powers of reasoning could be applied in so many fields of philosophic and scientific inquiry, were also the fathers of rational medicine, divorced from religious belief and mere speculation. The breakthrough came with

*The teachings of the 2nd-century AD Greek physician Galen, though in many cases misleading, were not seriously challenged for 1400 years*

the realisation that certain common symptoms always appeared together, and that certain drugs brought relief.

The founder of this new type of medicine was Hippocrates, who lived on the Aegean island of Cos in the 5th century BC. He was hampered by an inadequate knowledge of anatomy and physiology, and believed that disease was caused by an imbalance among four basic 'humours' in the body; but his method of diagnosis, based on reason and on careful observation, became the basis of medical practice for centuries.

Of great importance for the future was the emphasis Hippocrates placed on a doctor's duties to his patient – now enshrined in

### THE FOUR 'HUMOURS'

For centuries physicians accepted the teachings of the ancient Greek doctor-philosophers, who believed that four elements – fire, air, water and earth – made up the universe and had their counterparts in the human body. These counterparts were the four 'humours' – blood, bile, phlegm and black bile. Depending on which of these humours was uppermost, a man was either sanguine, choleric, phlegmatic or melancholy. Illness was treated by balancing the properties of the elements: fire was hot and dry, air hot and wet, water cold and wet, and earth cold and dry. So if a man was suffering from a raging fever his temperature needed to be lowered

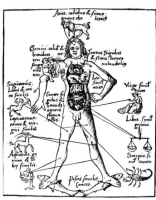

*The body was thought to be influenced by the heavens as well as 'humours'. A 16th-century illustration shows parts affected by the planets and the signs of the zodiac*

the 'Hippocratic oath', which is still the basis of medical ethics. He also emphasised the healing powers of nature and the value of personal hygiene and correct diet. 'One man's meat,' he said, 'is another man's poison.' For Hippocrates, the physician's task was to assist nature in the fight against disease – not by dangerous remedies for minor ills but by waiting for the moment when medical intervention would be most effective.

But the new scientific school of medicine founded by Hippocrates did not at once sweep away the earlier type of treatment based on religious belief. A system of temple medicine dominated by the cult of Aesculapius, the god of medicine, survived throughout Greek history. Thousands of people flocked for cures to vast sanctuaries in Athens,

*Dogs were used to dig up the root of the mandrake plant, a medieval pain-reliever. The roots, shaped like a human body, were believed to shriek when uprooted with a cry that drove humans mad*

Epidaurus, and even Cos, the homeland of Hippocrates. The treatment at these sanctuaries began with a ritual purification, followed by the use of drugs or hypnosis to induce sleep. The patient was then licked by snakes, after which the temple gods were thought to appear to him and diagnose his sickness. On awakening, the patient related his dreams to the temple attendants, who interpreted them to suggest a cure. Offerings bearing representations of afflicted parts of the body were left at the temples, presumably in gratitude for successful cures.

## Fact and fiction in Galen

The Greek tradition of inquiry was extended several centuries later by Galen, who was born at Pergamum, in Asia Minor, in about AD 130. From experience gained during his first job, as doctor to the gladiators at Pergamum, he became the first man to recognise that the muscles are controlled by the brain. Later Galen became the personal physician of five Roman emperors.

In his writings Galen summarised the results of five centuries of medical inquiry. But he added findings of his own, too. One of the most important of his own teachings was the principle that everything in nature has its function, and that injury brings about a change in this function. But un-

*The Arab physician Avicenna is shown treating a patient, in a 17th-century edition of his Canon. The work was a standard reference book for 600 years*

fortunately Galen's usual method of argument – by analogy from animals rather than by clinical observation of human patients – led him to make many serious errors. He thought, for instance, that blood passed direct from one side of the heart to the other, and had no idea that it circulated right round the body. Instead he thought

### A GREEK DR SPOCK

The ancient world's foremost expert on female complaints, childbirth and childcare was Soranus of Ephesus, who practised medicine in Alexandria and Rome in the 1st century AD. Breast-feeding, said Soranus, was not to begin until the third day; a baby should first be fed on diluted and boiled honey. He also showed how a baby should be bathed and dressed, and advised on weaning, teething and teaching

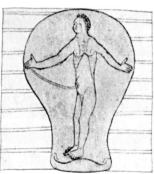

*Soranus made a careful study of the female anatomy and described the various positions of a foetus in the womb; this illustration of one position of the unborn baby, attached by its umbilical cord, is from a 13th-century edition of one of his works on gynaecology. Soranus described causes of difficult childbirth, and demonstrated procedures for correcting abnormal positions of the foetus. He also urged the use of forceps and hooks in cases of awkward deliveries. Some of his recommendations are still in accord with modern practice*

# Lessons from the anatomists

*Treatment was simple in 16th-century hospitals set up by the religious orders*

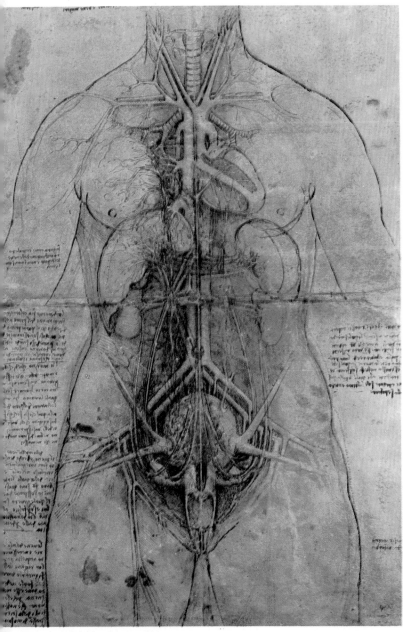
*Leonardo da Vinci (1452–1519) was an anatomist far in advance of his time, but his remarkably detailed drawings and copious notes were not discovered until two centuries after his death. Leonardo learnt by dissecting over 30 bodies*

that 'natural, vital and animal spirits' were distributed by a kind of ebb and flow through veins and arteries. The skill with which Galen presented his arguments caused his errors to go unchallenged in Europe until the Renaissance, more than 1400 years later.

## Legacy of the Arabs

With the fall of Rome in the 5th century AD, medical teaching ceased to exist in Europe. But the Arabs collected, studied and translated numerous Greek manuscripts on science and medicine, not only preserving them for later generations but also making useful comments and additions.

Rhazes (865–925), chief physician at the hospital of Baghdad, was the first writer to distinguish between smallpox and measles, and Avicenna (980–1037) compiled a *Canon* of medicine which became compulsory reading for medical students in European universities until the 17th century.

## Schools of medieval Europe

Interest in the medical knowledge of the ancient Greeks began to revive in western Europe in the 10th century. Latin translations of the medical classics were made from

the Arabic versions, and a school of medicine was founded at Salerno, in Italy. Students learnt their lessons in verse form, as an aid to memory, and the school specialised in surgery and in diagnosing ailments from the examination of a patient's urine. From Salerno, the revival in medical teaching spread to the new universities of medieval Europe – Bologna, Padua, Montpellier, Paris and Oxford. But medicine was studied as a mental discipline rather than for its healing value, and the practical effects of the revival were strictly limited. Medical research was still discouraged by the widely held belief that sickness was God's punishment for sin; in the words of the Bible, the sins of the fathers were visited on the children.

There was still an unquestioning acceptance of the work of earlier medical authorities such as Galen. Practical medicine throughout the Middle Ages remained largely confined to the charity of the religious hospitals, where emphasis was laid on day-to-day care rather than on medical investigation.

*Lepers and cripples were social outcasts and objects of pity. Lepers had to carry clappers to warn of their approach*

### THE PLAGUE THAT SWEPT THROUGH EUROPE

The Black Death – bubonic plague – which killed 25 million people in Europe, began in China in 1333. It was carried along trading routes to the West by fleas on black rats, and reached the Crimea in 1346. By the following year the disease was brought to western Europe by people who were fleeing from its advance

*Citizens of Tournai, in France, carry the coffins of plague victims; often the dead were shifted in cartloads and buried in mass graves. Every town and village in Europe came to know and dread the signs of the plague – blotches, boils, swellings and hardening glands*

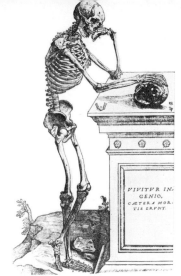

*An illustration from Vesalius's* De humani corporis fabrica, *published in 1543, shows the accuracy of his investigations into human anatomy*

### The first anatomists

The questioning spirit of the Renaissance and the Reformation – both twin aspects of the revolt against accepted authority – had important results for medicine. Just as the teachings of Luther challenged the powerful hold of the Roman Catholic Church, so the work of Renaissance anatomists shook the hold of the ancient medical authorities. In 1527 Paracelsus, Professor of Medicine in the University of Basle, publicly burnt the books of Galen and Avicenna and demanded that a doctor should see with his own eyes rather than accept the teachings of men dead for centuries.

This meant that doctors must be able to dissect human bodies to find out how they worked, rather than argue by analogy from researches on apes, pigs and other animals as Galen had done. Human corpses had been dissected in Alexandria as early as the 3rd century;

*Bubonic plague is spread by the bite of a flea carried by the common black rat*

*Doctors covered themselves with protective clothing from head to foot when treating victims of the plague, since it was thought that the disease was carried by impure vapours in the air which could enter the body through the pores of the skin. The beaks on the masks were filled with spices, which were believed to purify the air the doctors breathed. Contact with a patient was avoided, and doctors carried wands with which they felt pulses*

but such experiments ceased during Roman rule, and in the early days of Christianity people regarded the human body as too sacred to allow it to be cut up even after death. Not until the 14th century, in Italy, did doctors begin to conduct post-mortems on the bodies of leading citizens to determine how they had died. From these post-mortems it was a short step to dissecting bodies simply to find out how the human machine worked, and the bodies of executed criminals were made available to doctors for anatomical researches.

A young Belgian named Vesalius, who became Professor of Anatomy at Padua at the age of 23, earned the title of 'father of human anatomy' by his work *De humani corporis fabrica*, published in 1543. This was the first systematic presentation of human anatomy by illustration and careful description based on personal observation of a dissected human body. Vesalius inspired intense loyalty among his followers; a group of his students once walked 14 miles at night to bring him a body from a distant gallows. Yet in his own lifetime the work of Vesalius was far from generally accepted; the teachings of Galen remained well entrenched for years to come. Vesalius's teachings were so unpopular that after defending them for only a few years he resigned his professorship, burnt all his unpublished work, and took up an important and influential post as personal physician to Emperor Charles V.

### An artificial limb

Surgery was stimulated both by the reforming spirit of the Renaissance and by the series of wars which broke out when the French, hungry for glory and for plunder, invaded Italy in 1494. The greatest surgeon of the time was the Frenchman Ambroise Paré (1517–90), surgeon-general to three French kings and their armies, who learnt his trade from bodies rather than from books.

Paré introduced new surgical instruments and new operation techniques; to prevent loss of blood after the amputation of a limb he tied the patient's arteries, rather than relying on the old method of sealing the stump with a red-hot iron or boiling pitch. Paré also designed useful aids for crippled soldiers, including an ingenious artificial hand with fingers that moved by springs and cog-wheels and even enabled a cavalryman to grasp the reins of a horse.

The 16th century brought another major advance towards man's mastery over disease. In 1546, Fracastoro, an Italian poet-physician, published his *De Contagione*, the first comprehensive explanation of how infectious diseases spread: by direct contact, by indirect contact – for example through clothing – and through the air. Fracastoro went as far as to claim that each disease had its

*Amputation was the most common operation in the 16th century; the inside of the human body was little understood*

own specific 'germ', a concept that was not to be confirmed until the late 19th century.

Fracastoro also wrote a long poem about syphilis, a disease which reached epidemic proportions in Europe after spreading through the French army which had invaded Italy; it is from the shepherd-hero of Fracastoro's poem, Syphilus, that the name of the disease is derived.

### Circulation of the blood

One of the major misunderstandings of 16th-century medicine concerned the way blood is supplied to every part of the body – and it sprang from the erroneous account given by Galen 1400 years earlier. In 1628 the Englishman William Harvey published his account of the circulation of the blood. Harvey was not the first to challenge Galen's account, but he was the first man to prove that the blood circulates through the body

continuously and always in one direction – out from the heart through the arteries and back to the heart through the veins.

Harvey's pioneer work on the circulation of the blood was one of the most striking discoveries of the so-called Age of Enlightenment in the 17th century, when philosophers such as Descartes taught that the human body was a machine governed by natural laws and that it was therefore capable of being finally understood.

New instruments such as the thermometer and the microscope were developed to measure the performance of this marvellously complex machine. The thermometer was invented by Galileo in 1590. In the same year, in Holland, the microscope was invented by Johannes and Zacharias Jansen; but it was an Italian, Marcello Malpighi (1628–94) who first showed its value.

Malpighi was the first man to observe the red corpuscles in the blood and, in 1661, he added the final piece of evidence to Harvey's work by direct observation of blood in the capillaries. He also

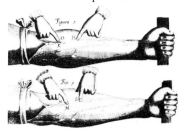

*William Harvey was the first man to show that blood flows around the body in one direction only. He pressed the blood out of a section of vein; when he unblocked the end nearer the wrist the blood flowed in, but no blood entered when he unblocked the other end*

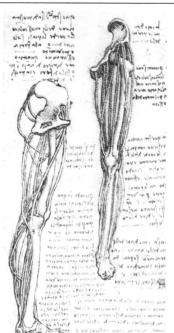

*The workings of leg and arm muscles are illustrated in painstaking diagrams*

### MAPPING THE MUSCLES

Leonardo's curiosity at the workings of the human body grew from his interest in mechanics. The way in which he used physics, mechanical principles and mathematics to explain the action of human joints and muscles was unique for his time. Leonardo injected molten wax into body cavities such as the heart, lungs and womb to take moulds of them

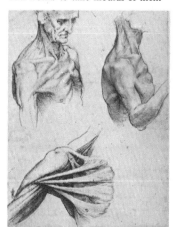

# The making of modern medicine

*The English doctor Thomas Sydenham was a brilliant observer who believed in studying disease at the bedside of sufferers*

discovered the intestinal glands, and made detailed studies of the microscopic structure of the skin, tongue, kidneys, spleen and lungs.

## Remedies that failed

A better understanding of the workings of the human body did not immediately lead to better methods of treatment. Bleeding and purging on a heroic scale were the only answers of most doctors for most diseases. What drugs were available were used quite indiscriminately, regardless of the disease being treated. The poor, who could not afford doctors, were often less at risk than the rich, who could. Some of the revolting remedies prescribed by doctors in the 17th and 18th centuries were more likely to impress the relatives than to improve the condition of the patient: folk medicine, involving the use of animal dung and urine, was frequently practised, and the six doctors tending Charles II on his deathbed could suggest no better treatment than cutting open a live pigeon and applying it to the king's feet to draw out the disease.

An important but lonely figure in bringing about an improvement in medical treatment at this time was Thomas Sydenham (1624–89), whose patients included the philosopher John Locke and the chemist Robert Boyle. Sydenham is often called the English Hippocrates because, like the Greek doctor, he advocated simple remedies, the use of the appropriate drug, and sympathetic care.

## Clinics at the bedside

The education of doctors was revolutionised in the 18th century, largely because of the efforts of one man – the Dutchman Hermann Boerhaave (1665–1738). A pioneer in medical chemistry, Boerhaave introduced teaching at the bedside as a regular part of the university course for medical students at Leyden. This practice rapidly spread throughout Europe as Boerhaave's pupils dispersed; one of Leyden's successors, the Edinburgh Medical School, in turn exerted a strong and lasting influence on the development of medical education in the United States.

The move away from the authority of books and towards the clinical examination of actual patients was given added impetus by the French Revolution. For the first time the poor were regarded as having as much right to medical

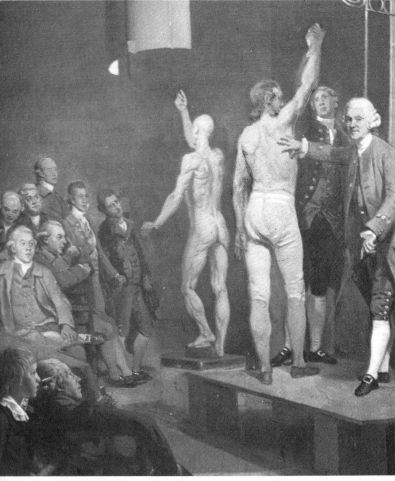

*Two Scottish brothers, William and John Hunter, pioneered many advances in anatomy and surgery in the 18th century. Above, William Hunter lectures to his students. Men like the Hunters led medicine away from the realms of theory, insisting that experiment alone could establish the nature of disease*

## THE COUNTRY DOCTOR WHO CONQUERED SMALLPOX

Vaccination against smallpox, one of the great breakthroughs in preventive medicine, was first performed by an English country doctor named Edward Jenner, at the end of the 18th century. Jenner was intrigued by the belief in his native Gloucestershire that dairymaids who had contracted the mild disease of cowpox never caught smallpox, one of the most dreaded diseases then known. He deduced that the immunity came from the cowpox, and proved it true

*Jenner's discovery was not immediately acclaimed, and in 1802 the British Anti-Vaccination Society issued this cartoon which played on public fears of the dangers of being vaccinated. Some of those who had taken the serum are shown as turning into cows, while others sprout cows from their heads and bodies. Despite the sceptical attacks, the use of vaccination spread rapidly throughout the world, and Jenner received a grant from the government*

treatment as the rich. In organised hospitals, doctors could compare the progress of different patients suffering from the same disease and so compile the first case-histories – an invaluable step forwards in deciding which type of treatment was most effective.

At about the same time an entirely new means of diagnosing ailments was discovered – almost by accident – by an Austrian doctor, Leopold Auenbrugger. His father was a vintner, and Auenbrugger used to watch him tapping a cask to discover the level of wine inside it. This gave Auenbrugger the idea of tapping a patient's chest with the fingers and listening to the sound produced as a guide to the internal condition of the patient. His findings were published in 1761, but remained almost

*Physicians of 19th-century England gathered in pharmacies to examine their patients and to meet colleagues*

*Quack doctors and medicine peddlers, seen on a china figure, were a feature of every market-place. They offered single potions claimed to cure all ills*

unnoticed until they were translated into French in 1808. The invention of the stethoscope made the doctor's task easier still, because it picked up and magnified the sounds of breathing.

## Pathology, a new science

Another important development in the 18th century was the new science of pathology. The key figure was Giovanni Battista Morgagni (1682–1771), a successor to Vesalius as Professor of Anatomy at Padua. Morgagni carried out a series of post-mortem examinations to compare the internal effects of the disease with the case-history of a patient during the progress of the disease. This enabled him to build up for the first time a rational account of the relationship between

diseases and changes in various organs of the body, and for this he is generally regarded as being the founder of modern pathology.

Morgagni's work was followed up by important clinical studies of the effects of disease on individual organs. The young Scottish surgeon John Hunter (1728–93) was a brilliant experimenter who is regarded by surgeons everywhere as the chief founder of modern surgery. He studied under his brother, William, and later set up a menagerie at Earls Court, in London, where he studied the results of disease in animals. Among Hunter's pupils was Edward Jenner (1749–1823), who founded the science of immunology in 1798 through his work in the prevention of smallpox by vaccination.

Jenner's first great step forward in preventive medicine led in advanced countries to the compulsory vaccination of children against smallpox, and to a mounting attack on other infections which were bred and propagated in the insanitary slums of the rapidly growing industrial centres. Gradually the efforts of reformers led to improved water supplies, more efficient sewage disposal systems, improved housing, and compulsory notification of infectious diseases such as tuberculosis.

## Lessons from the microscope

A system of medical care was created which, despite its low standards, made the first half of the 19th century a period of progress in clinical medicine. The develop-

*Giovanni Battista Morgagni's studies of the effect on health of diseased organs laid the foundations of modern pathology*

ment of better microscopes made further progress possible. Using an improved microscope the German, Theodor Schwann (1810–82), discovered that cells are the basis of both plant and animal life.

Schwann's work was extended by another German, Rudolf Virchow (1821–1902), a versatile genius who, as well as being an anatomist and pathologist, was a social reformer and great liberal politician. Virchow's greatest book, *Die Cellularpathologie* (1858), introduced a new way of looking at the body and its disorders. He described it as 'a cell state in which every cell is a citizen, diseases being merely a conflict of citizens in that state, brought about by the action of external forces'. His doctrine

---

*Jenner's first success in proving his theory came when he inoculated an eight-year-old boy with infected matter from a dairymaid with cowpox. The boy contracted cowpox, but when he was later injected with smallpox, he was found to be immune*

*The pustules which erupted on a cowpox victim, although unsightly, did not leave unpleasant scars like smallpox. Milkmaids were often called 'pretty maids' because they escaped the disfigurement left by smallpox*

## INVENTIONS COME TO THE AID OF THE DOCTOR

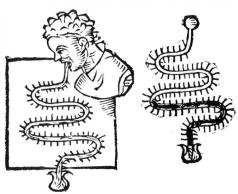

*Early attempts to measure temperature were made by Sanctorius (1561–1636), a professor at Padua. In this 'thermoscope', a patient's body-heat drove liquid down a zigzag tube. Fahrenheit's first mercury thermometer appeared in the 18th century. In 1866 a Briton, Clifford Allbutt, produced the short clinical thermometer*

Until the 19th century the diagnosis of disease was often largely a matter of guesswork. But in the 1800's diagnosis became much more accurate with the introduction of a whole range of new scientific instruments. These enabled doctors to examine internal organs and to measure the functions of the body with greater precision than ever before. Thermometers were perfected; in 1868, in Germany, Karl August Wunderlich published records of body temperatures in health and disease and established their value as an aid to diagnosis. Stethoscopes came into general use, and new instruments allowed physicians to see inside a living body

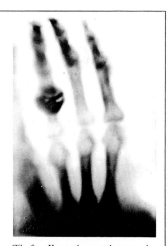

*The first X-ray photographs were taken by Wilhelm Röntgen, a German, in 1895. The photograph of his wife's hand (above) shows a ring on one finger. Below is one of the first X-ray tubes*

*The first stethoscope (above), a hollow wooden cylinder, was invented in 1816 by René Laennec, a Frenchman. The microscope (far left) made by Edmund Culpeper in 1735 improved on a device invented in 1590 by Johannes and Zacharias Jansen. The ophthalmoscope of 1869 (left), for examining the eye, was the first with a light*

# Compassion for the suffering

finally demolished the ancient Greek theory of the body's four ruling 'humours'.

An understanding of one of the most important causes of disease – germs, or bacteria – was arrived at during Virchow's lifetime. The theory of germs was not a new one; three centuries earlier Fracastoro, in Italy, had said that disease could spread from the sick to the healthy by contact, or 'contagion'. But despite Fracastoro's theories, no practical advance in understanding germs was made until 1795, when a Scottish doctor, Alexander Gordon, demonstrated the effect of germs during an epidemic of the dreaded 'child-bed fever' in his home town of Aberdeen. Gordon recommended disinfecting the hands and clothing of doctor and midwife, and this simple precaution resulted in 49 out of 77 cases recovering – a remarkable record for the time.

Gordon's pioneer work attracted little notice until the American essayist and doctor Oliver Wendell Holmes drew attention to it in an essay published in Boston in 1843. The first man to prove conclusively the connection between bacteria and disease was the French physician Casimir Davaine, who in 1864 succeeded in transferring anthrax germs from one rabbit to another.

*Louis Pasteur showed that germs were always present in the atmosphere, but that heat would kill them. Liquids could be made safe by heating them to 60°C, a process now known as 'pasteurisation'*

### Pasteur's discovery

It was with Louis Pasteur (1822–85), a French chemist, that the real breakthrough came in the war against germs. Before Pasteur, it was generally thought that germs grew spontaneously in decaying organic matter. Pasteur's experiments on the problems of fermentation in the wine industry gave scientific proof that this was not the case. Germs, he showed, were present in the atmosphere and reproduced themselves if the conditions were right. Pasteur went on

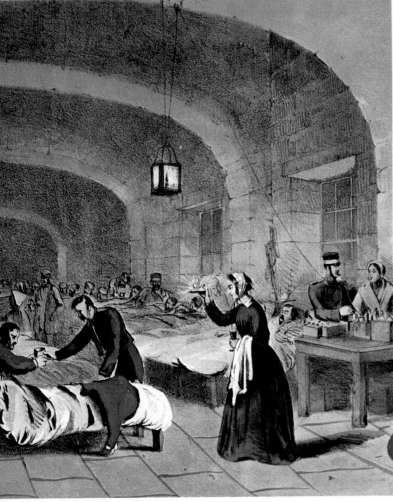

*The nursing service was revolutionised by the reforms of Florence Nightingale, who devoted her life to nursing and became known as the 'Lady with the Lamp' during her tireless work among the sick and wounded of the Crimean War. Later she founded a nurses' school and helped to form the International Red Cross*

## THE TREATMENT OF MENTAL ILLNESS

Mental disorder was the last type of illness to be treated rationally. For thousands of years its victims had been outcasts, thought to be possessed by demons and often locked away and treated with great harshness. Only in the 1790's did Philippe Pinel, in France, and William Tuke, who set up a retreat at York, show that nervous illnesses were merely aggravated by forced confinement and restraints such as chains and fetters. During the 19th century such treatment was discarded, and doctors began to understand the central nervous system. Some nervous illnesses were shown to be the result of disease or injury, such as brain tumours or damage to the spinal cord, and they were treated with surgery or drugs

*The most infamous mental institution of its time was the hospital of St Mary of Bethlehem in London, commonly called Bedlam. There, as in most asylums in every country, conditions were appalling; the sick were thrown in together with criminals, and all were restrained with manacles and chains. The little medical treatment that was administered was misguided and frequently barbarous. Violent patients were beaten into insensibility, and others were often bled or purged to the point of collapse. Some spent several years under close restraint, like William Norris (left), whose harness of chains allowed him to move only up and down. There was little compassion from the outside world. The public were allowed to visit the asylums, and it became a popular pastime to goad and jeer at the inmates*

to show that germs could be filtered out of the impure air by passing the air through cotton wool, mineral granules or a simple 'S-bend' pipe. The germs could also be destroyed by heating.

Pasteur's method for preventing wine or milk from turning sour by heating the liquid for a few seconds to a temperature of 60°C (140°F) is still employed. This principle, now known as 'pasteurisation', is used today to destroy tuberculosis germs carried in milk.

Still more valuable was Pasteur's discovery that germs that had been weakened by heating could be safely used for inoculation. Sheep that he had inoculated with weakened anthrax bacillus did not contract the disease when later injected with virulent bacteria. Pasteur had the opportunity to show that inoculation worked on humans, too. A small boy was brought to him whose life was despaired of after he had been bitten by a dog with rabies. Pasteur inoculated the boy with weakened rabies virus – and the boy lived.

The science of bacteriology owes its origin to Pasteur, but its rapid development stemmed from the work of the German bacteriologist Robert Koch (1843–1910). Koch first discovered many of the organisms that cause specific

*Pierre and Marie Curie, seen in a contemporary caricature, discovered radium in 1898. Radium's power to destroy animal tissue makes it effective in treating certain forms of cancer*

diseases – among them cholera and tuberculosis – and many of his laboratory methods for studying bacteria are still in use.

### Making surgery safe

Surgery remained at a primitive level until the middle of the 19th century. Operations were carried out very much as a last resort, and mortality was high. Amputations accounted for a large proportion of all operations, and speed was the prime consideration for the surgeon – since if an operation lasted too long, the patient would bleed to death. A fine exponent of the art of surgery by the standards of his day was Baron Larrey, surgeon to Napoleon's army, who is said to have performed over 200 operations in 24 hours during one of Bonaparte's campaigns.

The first great advance in operating techniques came with anaesthesia. In 1800 Sir Humphrey Davy suggested that nitrous oxide, or laughing gas, might be used as an anaesthetic in surgical operations, but the idea was not taken up.

The 1840's saw the real breakthrough in anaesthetics, with the introduction of two alternative substances. In 1846 the use of ether was demonstrated by William Morton at the Massachusetts General Hospital, and in 1847 the Scottish obstetrician Sir James Simpson demonstrated the value of chloroform as an anaesthetic and began to advocate its use in childbirth. Simpson's work was strongly attacked by the Scottish Church, but Queen Victoria's decision to allow the use of chloroform in two of her confinements did much to popularise the use of anaesthetics.

Anaesthesia alone would not, however, have revolutionised surgery. Before the work of Joseph Lister on antisepsis, many patients whose lives had been technically saved by the surgeon died after the operation, from infection, or sepsis,

ever-present in the dirty hospitals of the day. In 1867 Lister published his findings and revealed that the risk of infection could be reduced by using a chemical antiseptic – carbolic acid – on wounds and in the operating theatre.

Further research showed that neither ether nor chloroform was a completely safe form of anaesthetic, and the 20th century has seen the introduction of new anaesthetics and the development of anaesthesia as a science practised by specialists. Carbolic acid has been superseded by more effective chemical antiseptics, and the risk of infection has been further reduced by the sterilisation of surgical instruments by steam heat, the wearing of sterile gowns, masks and rubber gloves, and the development of machinery which can sterilise all the air in an operating theatre.

Having tackled the problems of anaesthesia and infection, two other major problems needed attention – severe bleeding and surgical shock. Bleeding is now lessened by the use of delicate arterial clamps, and a form of electric treatment, known as diathermy, which coagulates the blood. The risk of surgical shock is reduced by careful preparation, dedicated nursing and aftercare.

*Colourful advertising helped to sell patent medicines in the 19th century*

### Age of specialisation

When Charles Darwin in 1859 put man into place as a part of the animal kingdom, most of the religious and social taboos which had previously limited the scope of research were removed. Since then the growth of medical knowledge has been so phenomenal that many doctors today have to become specialists in the treatment of a specific part of the body, a certain type of illness, or a particular problem, such as old age. Research, too, has changed in character. In the past, many of the

*The value of hypnosis in healing was demonstrated by Dr Jean-Martin Charcot, an eminent French neurologist who specialised in the treatment of hysteria. Here he shows colleagues how a woman who had been paralysed by hysteria was able to get up from her bed after she had been hypnotised. Charcot carried out a number of similar experiments during the late 19th century, and attracted students from all over the world. As well as being able to convince a patient who was in a trance that his symptoms would disappear after he awoke, Charcot could also induce symptoms of illness in a healthy person. Charcot's pupils included Sigmund Freud*

*Scientific knowledge of the workings of the mind was changed profoundly in the early 1900's by Sigmund Freud, a Viennese psychiatrist. By stressing the importance of unconscious factors, especially the sexual drive, he changed attitudes towards mental illness*

### NEW WEAPONS FOR THE SURGEON

The perils of surgery decreased rapidly after two major advances in the mid-19th century – a breakthrough in the development of anaesthetics, and the use of antiseptics. Since ancient times doctors had used simple anaesthetics such as mandrake, Indian hemp and alcohol, or else knocked their patients out by force. These methods were replaced in the 1840's by the introduction of ether and chloroform. Deaths from infections caught during operations were cut dramatically by using carbolic acid as an antiseptic

*Chloroform, first used in 1847 as an anaesthetic by Sir James Simpson, was administered through a special inhaler*

*An anaesthetic is being used in this operation in 1870, but there is no protection against infection. The surgeon and his helpers wear everyday clothes and operate in an ordinary ward. Later, doctors aimed to exclude all germs from operating theatres*

*Joseph Lister, who was the first man to use antiseptics in surgery, employed a spray (left) to spread a fine mist of carbolic acid throughout the operating theatre, and then directed it on to the site of the operation while he worked. Few of his patients died from post-operative infection*

# Discovering the nature of life

greatest discoveries were made by individuals working independently. This century most discoveries have been made in the laboratories of teaching hospitals, and world-wide research organisations are backed by international as well as national authorities.

## The work of hormones

One of the major advances in medical science in the 20th century has been the building up of a more accurate understanding of the chemistry of the body – an understanding which has led to many new treatments. The century was only two years old when two London physiologists, Sir William Bayliss and Ernest Starling, discovered the existence in the bloodstream of a chemical which controlled the production of digestive juices by the pancreas. They gave this chemical the name 'hormone', from the Greek word for 'messenger'. Since then, it has been discovered that hormones, produced by various internal glands, are responsible for the way the body uses energy, for regulating growth and sexual development, and for enabling the body to adapt to changes in its internal and external environment.

The lack of a hormone, normally supplied by cells in the pancreas, was suspected to be the cause of the disease of diabetes. In 1921, two Canadians, Frederick Banting and

*Penicillin was discovered accidentally by Alexander Fleming in 1928, when he observed that a specimen of bacteria was destroyed by a mould which had drifted in through his laboratory window*

Charles Best, demonstrated that this hormone, insulin, could be extracted from the pancreas of animals in a form pure enough to be used in treating diabetes.

## Discovering vitamins

In the early years of this century other serious diseases were also shown to be caused by the lack of chemical substances which are generally found in a normal diet. The diseases, which include rickets, scurvy and beri-beri, came to be known as 'deficiency diseases', and these vital chemical substances were given the name 'vitamins' by

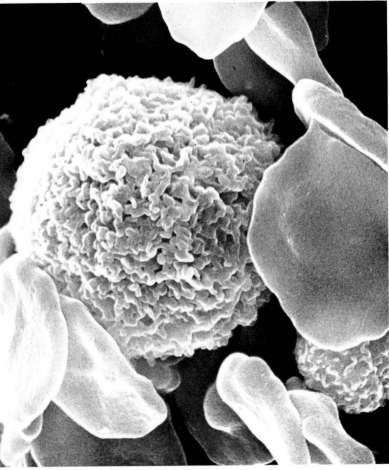

*Advances in technology have enabled scientists to study the living cell in action, so bringing to light many of the hitherto unseen organisms that cause disease. A Stereoscan electron microscope was used in photographing the cancer cell (centre) among the blood corpuscles of a leukaemia sufferer*

## NEW LIMBS AND ORGANS TO REPLACE THE OLD

Man has been a tireless experimenter in replacing defective parts of the human body. The replacements may be either artificial devices, or healthy organs from other human beings. Blood transfusions were first carried out in the 17th century, though it was not until 1900 that they became an accepted part of medical science. In 1954 a kidney was the first internal organ to be successfully transplanted from one human to another. Many kidney transplant operations have been performed since then, and even hearts have been transplanted by an operation pioneered by Dr Christiaan Barnard in South Africa in 1967. Such operations are remarkable achievements, but two serious problems are the scarcity of suitable donors and the body's tendency to reject transplanted tissues

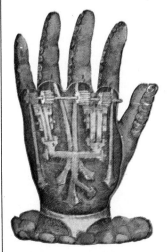

*An artificial hand, with fingers moved by cog-wheels and levers, was designed in 1551 by a Frenchman, Ambroise Paré*

*Doctors in ancient India replaced noses with triangular pieces of skin (right) cut from the patient's forehead and sewn in place. The patient breathed through reeds placed in his nostrils*

the American bio-chemist Casimir Funk in 1912. Research was led by the Dutchman Christian Eijkman and the English biochemist Frederick Gowland Hopkins, who discovered vitamins A and D.

Research into the chemistry of the human body has brought a number of discoveries about the nature of life itself. These include the highly complex manner in which nervous impulses are chemically transmitted, and the way characteristics are handed down from generation to generation by a system of chemical substances called genes which are found in the sperm and female ovum.

*The invention of the 'iron lung' kept alive many polio victims who could not breathe normally. Less cumbersome machines now perform the same function*

### 'Wonder drugs'

Drugs have been used to combat disease from earliest times, but only in this century have synthetic chemical compounds been deliberately produced to counteract particular diseases. The first such drug to be developed was salvarsan, produced by the German scientist Paul Ehrlich in 1910; it was found to be of some value in the treatment of syphilis, replacing earlier treatment by mercury, a highly dangerous poison.

A revolutionary step forward in the chemical treatment of disease came when it was found that drugs derived from living organisms could be used to combat bacteria. The first of these drugs, or antibiotics, was discovered in 1928 when the Scottish scientist Sir Alexander Fleming found that a culture of bacteria he had been examining was being destroyed by the spore of a fungus, *Penicillium notatum*, which had accidentally blown through the window of Fleming's laboratory in Paddington, London. The produce of this fungus, which was called penicillin, was purified and isolated by Sir Howard Florey and Ernst Chain at Oxford in 1940. Production on an industrial scale was begun in the United States, and the new drug greatly reduced the number of Allied soldiers who died from infected wounds in the later years of the Second World War. Since the war a whole range of antibiotics has been discovered, such as streptomycin, used to combat tuberculosis, and improved varieties of penicillin.

### The war on viruses

Today, effective drugs are available for the treatment of nearly all bacterial diseases. But not all diseases are caused by bacteria. Pasteur, who revealed to the world the harmful effects of bacteria, had

*Medicinal drugs, in the shape of pills, capsules and ampoules, are prescribed and taken by the million each day; and millions of pounds are spent each year on researching new drugs*

a theory that some diseases were caused by a different form of organism, so small that it could not be seen even with a microscope.

Pasteur's theory was proved in the 1890's both by the Dutchman Martin Beijerinck and by the Russian Dmitri Ivanovski. Beijerinck gave the name 'virus' to this newly discovered single-celled organism, so mysterious that scientists to this day cannot decide whether it is an animal or a plant.

Finding satisfactory ways of fighting diseases caused by viruses has proved very difficult. They have been responsible for a series of devastating epidemics in this century; the worst was the worldwide influenza epidemic which followed the First World War and killed some 21 million people – a heavier toll than the war itself.

It was not until this century that the way in which viruses take control of living cells came to be understood. And although many viruses have now been studied with

*The pattern of echoes produced by an ultra-sonic scanner makes it possible to build up a clear 'photograph of the unborn child in the mother's womb*

the aid of the electron microscope, and have even been photographed and classified, research on this smallest form of life is still in its early stages. Some forms of cancer are now associated with the presence of certain viruses. Successful vaccines have been produced against some virus-borne diseases, such as the Salk vaccine against the previously deadly poliomyelitis, which was produced in 1954.

### Making new life

Scientists still disagree about the nature of viruses; some believe they are chemical molecules, while others hold that they represent the simplest forms of life on this earth. If viruses indeed are forms of life they may well make it possible to produce from inorganic material a living organism which is capable of reproducing itself.

Over thousands of years, man has gradually built up a detailed knowledge of the structure and functions of his own body and the diseases which ravage it. The study of viruses may one day enable scientists to unfold one of the most puzzling secrets of nature: the way life itself began.

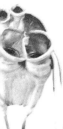

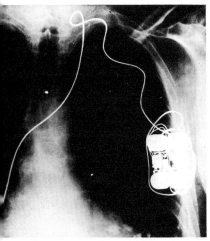

*American surgeons have attempted to devise an artificial heart, but the research problems are immense. Dr Willem Kolff has produced an experimental model made of silicone (left), which has four chambers and valves, and two main arteries. The chief difficulties are finding materials that will not cause blood clots or damage blood cells, and perfecting a pumping system with a reliable source of power*

*Artificial heart pacemakers make use of minute electric shocks to regulate the heart muscles' contractions. The X-ray photograph above shows a pacemaker with four batteries, giving out electric shocks 72 times a minute, embedded in the flesh under a patient's arm. A plastic-coated wire runs through a vein to the heart, and carries four-volt shocks into the muscle where it is anchored. A periodic operation is necessary to renew the batteries*

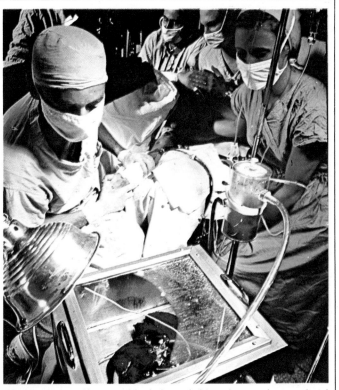

*To side-step the problems caused by the human body's tendency to reject transplanted organs, surgeons have carried out operations in which organs have been kept functioning outside the body to which they were connected. In the glass box above is a pig's liver, which has been linked to a patient's blood supply through tubes in her arm. The blood flowing from the tubes first passes through a substance which prevents it from clotting, and then through the pig's liver, which carries out the cleansing functions normally performed by the patient's own liver. A succession of pig's livers kept this patient alive for 18 days while surgeons waited for her own liver to regenerate. Meanwhile, efforts continue to overcome the difficulties of liver transplants*

# Exploring the wide world

*Trade, war and simple curiosity drove adventurers across uncharted seas to open up new continents*

*Among the earliest European explorers were the Vikings, seen invading Britain in their sturdy longboats. The Vikings sailed westwards from Scandinavia in the late 8th century and, after raiding Britain, passed on to discover Iceland in 870 and colonise Greenland. They even crossed the Atlantic and became, in 1002, the first Europeans known to have landed in North America*

The world's first explorers left no record of their names, and there are no monuments to mark their exploits. They were explorers by necessity, moving where hunger took them. Before them stretched entire continents, and the explorers who came after them were in most cases not discovering the world, but re-discovering it.

For the explorers of antiquity, voyaging into the unknown required considerable courage. It was not until about 2500 BC that men first took to the seas with the deliberate intention of seeking unknown lands, when the Egyptians sailed down the Red Sea to the mysterious Land of Punt – probably the coast of Somalia. By 1500

*In ships built of cedar from Lebanon, the Egyptians ventured across the Arabian Sea to Socotra by 1500 BC*

BC they had reached out eastwards across the Arabian Sea as far as the island of Socotra, and begun to understand the cycle of the monsoon winds.

The Egyptians, living in an almost treeless land, used papyrus reeds from the Nile for their river craft; but for many of their sea-going vessels they brought timber from the cedar forests of Lebanon, in the eastern Mediterranean.

## Phoenicians reach Britain

After 2000 BC the Minoan civilization of Crete dominated the seaways of the eastern Mediterranean. But the Minoans were not explorers; they felt no urge to push out the boundaries of their prosperous little world. Another Mediterranean people, the Phoenicians, were far more ambitious. In the 12th century BC this great seafaring and trading people set up colonies throughout the Mediterranean to buy raw materials in exchange for luxury goods. They even passed beyond the 'Pillars of Hercules' – the Straits of Gibraltar – into the Atlantic to reach the Canary Islands and West Africa,

*Oarsmen made Phoenician ships independent of sail. The ram in the bows shows that the vessel was a warship*

and crossed the stormy Bay of Biscay to barter for tin in Cornwall. The ships of the Phoenicians, like those of the Egyptians, were built from the cedar trees of Lebanon, and banks of oarsmen made them independent of their sails when becalmed or close to shore.

Two main types of vessel were used on long voyages: the biremes had two sets of oars on each side, one above the other, while the larger and deeper triremes had a third deck of rowers.

The Phoenicians were master navigators. They discovered the importance of the Pole Star and sailed by it; to this day, Greek sailors still call it the 'Phoenician star'. Because of their skill, their services were much in demand by other countries as helmsmen. The Greeks and the Persians used Phoenician navigators, and it was under the orders of the Egyptian pharaoh Necho in about 600 BC that Phoenician mariners undertook the greatest mission of navigation the world had yet seen – a voyage round Africa. Three years later, they returned to report that the continent was surrounded by sea except at the point in Egypt where it joins Asia.

## Carthage's African voyages

In the 7th century BC, the Phoenician homelands along the eastern Mediterranean coastal strip fell to the Assyrians. But this was far from being the ultimate disaster for this enterprising sea-going people. They became established in Carthage, the colony they had created about 800 BC near where Tunis stands today. The city and its hinterland grew to become the leading Mediterranean power.

The Carthaginians launched a series of voyages along the coasts of Europe and Africa. In 470 BC their senate ordered an expedition, under the navigator Hanno, to sail west, founding new trading colonies along the West African coast. With 30,000 men and women colonists crowded into 60 galleys of 50 oars apiece, the expedition rowed west through the Straits of Gibraltar. They built settlements down the coast of what is now Morocco, then rounded the huge 'hump' of Africa to reach the delta of the Senegal River.

Hanno is believed to have continued down the coast of Africa, past the mouth of the River Niger, until he reached an active volcano, possibly Mount Cameroon. The flames of the volcano so frightened the voyagers that they turned for home, to report that the earth ended in a sea of fire.

## Travels by a Greek historian

The Greeks were renowned sailors and colonisers, but they acquired little fresh knowledge about the shape of the world and what it held. Throughout the classical period in the West the centre of interest remained the Mediterranean – the 'middle of the earth'

*A 16th-century Icelandic map of the North Atlantic shows sites where Leif Ericson, the Viking, landed in North America 500 years earlier. Winlandiae, or Vinland, may be Newfoundland*

*Alexander the Great (right) took sailors on his expeditions, and planned to explore the ocean which he believed was all that lay beyond India*

in Latin. But one man, the Greek historian Herodotus, was a renowned traveller. He wrote an account of his travels in 443 BC, by which time he had visited the shores of the Black Sea, Persia, Arabia and Egypt. He also knew North Africa – though his theory that the Nile rose in the Atlas Mountains on the north-west coast caused considerable confusion among later geographers.

A century later Pytheas, a Greek navigator living in Marseilles, made one of the longest sea voyages of ancient times. He sailed out into the Atlantic, then turned northwards and appears to have sailed right round Britain. Six days' sailing north of Britain he reported the existence of Thule – an island, possibly Iceland, which he supposed to be the most northerly point in the world; its Latin description *ultima Thule* was to become a byword for remoteness.

## Alexander reaches India
Alexander the Great (356–323 BC) added realistic detail and understanding to contemporary knowledge of the world when he led his troops to the invasion of India. Alexander was educated by the philosopher Aristotle, and throughout the course of his great military expeditions he shipped home to his old teacher specimens of animals, flowers and minerals from the new areas he invaded.

Alexander left Macedonia in 334 BC and subdued Syria, Palestine and Egypt. He founded at Alexandria the first of a chain of cities that were to bear his name, then turned to conquer the Persian Empire to its eastern limits. Next he crossed the mountains into Afghanistan, marched down into northern India to invade the Punjab and then pressed southwards down the Indus to a point near Hyderabad.

Alexander believed, like most men of his time, that India was the edge of the world, and he had brought with him skilled seamen – many of them Phoenicians – to explore the all-encircling ocean that he believed lay beyond it. But his troops, wearied by years of endless marches and fighting, refused to go further. The great

marches of Alexander and the voyage of his admiral, Nearchus, from India to the Persian Gulf brought new knowledge and understanding of the world, and stimulated further voyages in the Persian Gulf and the Red Sea.

In the next generation, Greek explorers reached the valley of the Ganges and tried to reach India by way of the Caspian Sea. Around 150 BC, navigation at sea became less haphazard with the invention of the astrolabe, possibly by the Greek astronomer Hipparchus. The instrument helped sailors to determine their latitude – their exact distance from the equator.

In 146 BC the defeat of Carthage by Rome marked the arrival of a new dominant power in the Mediterranean. Through their relentless empire-building, the Romans gained an unparalleled geographical knowledge. In Afghanistan they reached the 'silk route' from China, along which caravans brought silk and metalware from the Orient to the Mediterranean.

## Writings of Strabo
Strabo, a Greek who died about AD 19, wrote a 17-volume *Geographia* (from the Greek words *ge*, 'earth', and *graphia* 'writing'), in which he described most of the lands of the Roman Empire. Some of Strabo's information came from men who had marched over and lived in the Roman provinces; but he relied entirely on the epics of

Homer for his description of Greece, and he ignored the first-hand researches of the Greek historian Herodotus, whom he dismissed as a 'marvel-monger'.

Strabo was particularly inaccurate in his accounts of northern Europe. This area was better known by AD 150 when Ptolemy, a dedicated scholar at the great Library at Alexandria, published his *Geographia*. Though often inaccurate, Ptolemy handed to his medieval successors a knowledge of the main features of the known world from China to the Scillies.

## The Arab world expands
The next initiative in exploration was taken by the Arabs. After Muhammad's flight from Mecca in AD 622 the new faith of Islam burst like a torrent through Arabia, north-eastwards to Bukhara, the Indus and China, and north-west to Africa, Spain and into France. As their civilization developed, the Arabs became the outstanding geographers of the world.

Arab and Persian ships sailed the Indian Ocean to China. For their journeys, Arab and Persian seamen developed the lateen or 'Latin' sail, so-called because it was common in the Mediterranean. This is a triangular sail set on a long yard at an angle of 45 degrees to the mast.

On their voyages in the Indian Ocean and the Pacific the Arabs met Chinese junks 200 ft long,

trading along routes familiar to Asian seamen long before the great voyages of the Europeans. One noted Arab traveller, Al-Masudi, a Baghdad scholar, visited Arabia, Persia, India, Ceylon, China, Madagascar and Zanzibar. He drew upon his experiences to compile the *Muruj al-Dhahab* ('Meadows of Gold'), a social history of the world from the Creation until 947.

## Voyages of the Vikings
In western Europe from the late 8th century a daring breed of sea-borne adventurers, the Vikings, sailed from the inlets or *viks* of Scandinavian fiords on voyages of pillage and plunder. The storm-tossed waters of the North Sea called for stronger and sturdier vessels than those of the Mediter-

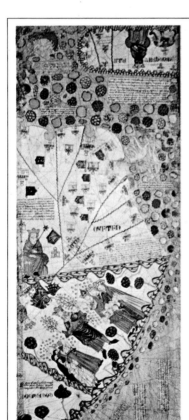

*Many maps were based on Marco Polo's travels. The section above is from the Catalan Atlas of 1375. It shows China, with Kublai Khan's Grand Canal from Peking to Hangchow in the centre*

## MARCO IN CHINA

A young Venetian, Marco Polo, was only 17 when he set out on a journey to the Far East which was to prove one of the classic explorations of all time. The journey overland to Peking through Persia, Afghanistan, Tibet and Mongolia took Marco and his father and uncle three-and-a-half years. They remained in China for about 20 years before returning by sea around the coast of south-east Asia, visiting Siam, Malacca and India

*The first printed edition of Polo's accounts appeared in 1477, and remained the main source of information about the East for five centuries*

*An illustration from a late 14th-century manuscript shows the Polos setting out from Venice in 1271. Marco's father and uncle, both Venetian merchants, had visited China before and had been received by its ruler, Kublai Khan. They now returned bearing him gifts, including sacred oil from the sepulchre at Jerusalem. On arrival in China, Marco was introduced to the Khan by his father as 'my son and your servant'; he was taken into the Khan's service, and his official travels were to take him all over the Chinese Empire. Eventually, the Polos persuaded the Khan to let them return to Venice, where they arrived in 1295. Three years later, Marco was captured in a sea-battle by the Genoese. During his imprisonment he dictated to a fellow-prisoner, a writer named Rustichello, an account of his travels which was later published as The Adventures of Marco Polo. Marco's book is a rich blend of fact and fancy. He wrote that China had safe, tree-lined roads, with good inns to welcome travellers; but less credible to modern readers are his tales of unicorns, wizards, dog-headed men and headless men with their faces buried in their chests. The Venetians, however, found it easier to believe even such fantastic stories as these, rather than Marco Polo's description of coal fires, which they had never seen*

# *Quest for a route to the East*

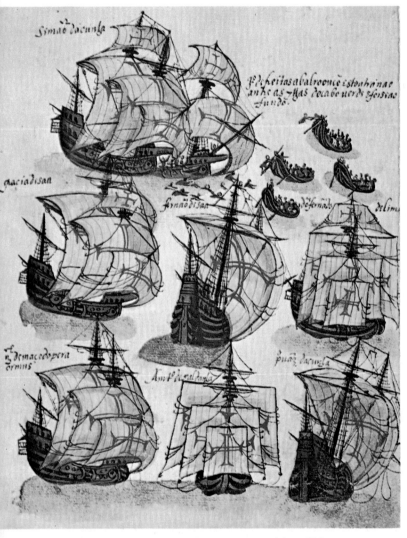

*The pride of Portuguese shipping, commemorated in a 16th-century watercolour. The Portuguese were the foremost explorers of Renaissance times. Their mariners slowly voyaged down the coast of Africa, rounded its southern tip and eventually found a route to India and beyond. From the 'spice islands' of the East Indies, Portugal created the first European empire*

*The first slaves were shipped from Africa by the Portuguese in 1446. This collar, designed to prevent slaves from escaping, also stopped them from lying down*

ranean, and the Vikings developed shallow longships, over 70 ft in length and carrying oars as well as a large square sail. The Vikings opened up trade routes from the Baltic to the Black Sea along the Vistula and Dnieper rivers. They sailed west to England, and even crossed the Atlantic. It is generally believed that a party of Vikings under Leif Ericson who landed near Cape Cod in 1002 were the first Europeans to land in America; in recent years, however, it has been suggested that a few Minoan and Phoenician ships may have reached the New World and set up settlements there during Bronze Age times, more than 2500 years earlier.

## Marco Polo in China

In 1055 the Seljuk Turks from central Asia overwhelmed the Abbasid caliphate at Baghdad. The menace of the Turks, as well as provoking the Western Christian nations to launch the Crusades to recapture the Holy Land, also affected the prosperity of Italian cities, particularly Venice. The heavy taxes imposed by the Turks on luxuries passing through their territories from the east drove the Venetians to re-open trade routes used by the Romans. Among the travellers who used the re-opened 'silk route' to China was the Venetian, Marco Polo.

## Life in 14th-century Timbuktu

The conquests of Islam during the Middle Ages established a unified pattern of culture and trade throughout most of the Middle East. Within this area, Muslims were able to travel freely.

In 1325 Ibn Battuta, a scholar in Morocco, left on a pilgrimage to Mecca and felt the lure of travel so strongly that he wandered on for 24 years, visiting Persia, eastern Africa, central Asia, Siberia, India, Ceylon, Sumatra and China. He also crossed the Sahara to visit Timbuktu, capital of the ancient African kingdom of Mali.

Ibn Battuta's account of his travels, re-discovered in Algeria in the 19th century, throws a fascinating light on the life, customs and manners of the non-European world of the late 14th century. In Mali, for example, Ibn Battuta deplored many local customs. 'The women,' he wrote, 'have "friends" and "companions" among the men outside their own families, and the men in the same way have "companions" among the women of other families.' He also complained that the Sultan was a niggardly man, who instead of giving him rich presents, handed him 'three

cakes of bread, a piece of beef fried in native oil, and a calabash of sour curds'.

## Chinese expand trade

In 1405 a Ming dynasty emperor of China despatched Admiral Cheng Ho with a fleet of 60 ships loaded with gold, porcelain, silks and spices, to open up trade with countries regarded as vassal states in the East and South China seas.

For more than 30 years Cheng Ho plied across regular routes from the East Indies to eastern Africa. The Chinese eventually abandoned these costly expeditions because Arab, Persian and Indian ships brought dyes, perfume, incense, opium, pearls and tapestries to Malacca, in Malaya, to exchange for the wares taken there by the Chinese junks. By 1500 Malacca had developed into one of the world's great trading centres.

## Age of European discovery

The world known to the Europeans 500 years ago was a tiny place. The Middle East was partly known from the expeditions of the Crusaders and from Bible accounts, while travellers' tales had described Africa north of the Sahara, Arabia, India, central and south-eastern Asia and China. Few knew of the Vikings' voyages beyond Iceland. The Americas, Australasia, Africa south of the Sahara, and Russia were almost totally unknown.

European explorers began in about 1420 to venture out into the open sea. Most of them did so because they wanted to find gold, new commodities or new trading routes. Merchants helped to finance the exploration of new routes, and were quick to exploit them when

---

### AIDS FOR THE NAVIGATOR

Improved navigational aids made 15th- and 16th-century explorers' tasks easier; but sightings of sun and stars were the only means of calculating positions until the 20th century

*An astrolabe (left) helped to determine time and latitude. The nocturnal (right) was used to tell the time by the stars*

*The most important navigational aid was the compass. This compass dates from the late 16th century, though the instrument had been known in China 700 years before*

*Henry the Navigator, a Portuguese prince, set up a school at Sagres, near Cape St Vincent, where map-makers and mathematicians practised*

they had been found. Especially important in the days when the scarcity of winter fodder brought a desperate shortage of fresh meat every winter were spices, to preserve food or at least hide its taste if it had gone beyond preserving. The home of spices was in the East, in India and the islands of south-east Asia; this accounts for the East India companies set up by merchants of such comparatively cold northern lands as England, Holland and France.

### Prince Henry the Navigator

In the early 15th century Prince Henry of Portugal, called 'the Navigator', became fascinated by the idea of finding a sea route to India. He set up a school for geographers at Sagres, where everyone who could further the Prince's purpose was made welcome – shipbuilders, instrument makers, as-

tronomers, mathematicians, mapmakers and travellers.

By 1446 the Portuguese had colonised Madeira and the Azores, reached Cape Verde, the most westerly point of the African continent, and were probing the Guinea coast, setting up trading posts. Negro slaves and gold were in particular demand.

### Southwards to the Cape

Prince Henry died in 1460, but the pioneering spirit survived him. The Portuguese reached Sierra Leone in 1461, and ten years later pushed on past the equator to reach Fernando Po. There they were disappointed to find that they had not yet opened the sea route to India, since the coast turned south again. The epic voyage of the Phoenicians who had sailed right around Africa 2000 years earlier had long been obliterated from human memory.

The Congo was reached in 1483 by Diego Cam, who, in the following year, sailed on to Walfisch Bay and added some 1500 miles to the known coast of Africa. He had almost reached the Indian Ocean

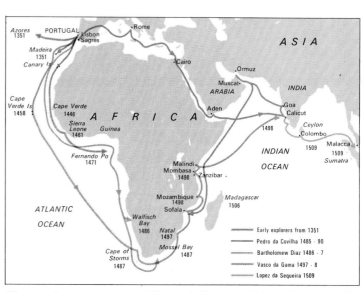

*The quest for sea routes round Africa to the East was led by the Portuguese. Explorers such as Pedro da Covilha, Bartholomew Diaz, Vasco da Gama and Lopez da Sequeira pushed the limits of the known world further with each voyage*

*Vasco da Gama was the first European to reach India by sea. But his efforts to open up trade there for Portugal were resisted by Arab and Persian rivals*

when he was superseded as expedition leader in 1487 by Bartholomew Diaz. Passing the limits of Cam's voyage, Diaz's ships were driven south-west by trade winds for almost a fortnight until westerly winds took them east again. Failing to strike the African coast, Diaz steered north and made land in Mossel Bay, some 200 miles to the east of present-day Cape Town.

### Portuguese reach India

Without seeing it, Diaz had rounded the Cape, and as he explored further and found the coast running east, he knew that he had sailed into the Indian Ocean. Soon afterwards, Diaz's crew forced him to turn back. On his return voyage he defined the position of the Cape, naming it the Cape of Storms. John II of Portugal renamed it the Cape of Good Hope, to boost the morale of future crews.

In 1497, another Portuguese, Vasco da Gama, rounded the Cape and named his landfall Natal, as he reached it on Christmas Day.

Sailing north, he met opposition from Arab traders at Mozambique. But a friendly Persian ruler at Malindi, in modern Kenya, provided a pilot to guide him to Calicut, in south-western India.

Da Gama's efforts to trade in India were resisted by the Arabs and Persians. He returned to Portugal in 1499, by which time his ships had travelled more than 24,000 miles and spent 630 days on their journey, half of them on the open sea. During the outward journey they sailed for over 5000 miles out of sight of land.

The cost of Da Gama's expedition was recouped 60 times over from the sale of spices and precious stones which he brought back. But

as usual on long exploratory voyages, the crews suffered terribly. Da Gama lost more than three-quarters of his 170 men, most of them victims of scurvy, a disease caused by lack of vitamins.

While the Portuguese were opening up a route to the East, Spain was exploring the golden New World that lay to the West. The discovery was accidental, for in the first place the Spanish, like the Portuguese, were looking for a sea route to China and India.

### Westwards to the East

Towards the end of the 15th century explorers had become increasingly attracted by the theory – first advanced by Aristotle – that

*John Harrison won a prize of £45,000 in 1735 for inventing a time-keeper enabling sailors to determine longitude accurately*

*A quadrant (left) and its later development, the sextant (right). Both enabled latitude to be calculated more accurately than was possible with the astrolabe*

### SHIPS FOR ALL TASKS

As the Portuguese sent their expeditions further and further into the unknown, they needed more powerful and better designed ships to brave the stormy South Atlantic and reach the riches of the Indies. Under the inspiration of Prince Henry the Navigator, the shipyards of Lisbon became the most advanced in Europe. The ships they built also included the speedy caravel, whose shallow draught made it ideal for inshore exploration. The caravel's small size made it less useful for long voyages of exploration, however, and it was later replaced by the nau and the galleon which could carry more men and provisions

*The three-masted nau, seen on an Arabian bowl, was developed by the Portuguese from a design by Bartholomew Diaz, the first European to reach South Africa*

*The caravel had two or three masts and was 'lateen-rigged', with triangular sails*

*English galleons like this Tudor man-of-war were noted for their manoeuvrability*

## Empire builders set forth

*The fascination of Europeans with the New World is shown by this map of the west coast of South America drawn by a 16th-century French cartographer, Le Testu. The coastline is accurately defined, though the land and sea animals are imaginary. In the tradition of the time Le Testu reversed south and north, placing the Strait of Magellan at the top and Peru at the bottom*

the quickest way to the East might be to sail west. Christopher Columbus (*c.* 1451–1506), a Genoese navigator, canvassed for years seeking support for his plan to sail direct to China and India across the Atlantic. Eventually, envy of the maritime success of the Portu-

*Christopher Columbus (above) was so convinced that he would reach the East by sailing westwards that he failed to identify America as a new continent*

guese spurred Queen Isabella of Spain into backing him.

In August 1492 Columbus set sail for the Canary Isles with three vessels, the *Santa Maria*, the *Pinta* and the *Nina*. In October, 33 days after leaving the Canaries, Columbus landed at San Salvador in the Bahamas. He sailed on for Cuba – mistaken for Japan – and Haiti.

In three more voyages Columbus visited Puerto Rico, Trinidad and Jamaica; he landed on the South American mainland in Venezuela, and in Central America on the Isthmus of Panama. But the discoverer of the Americas never knew that the great continent existed. While searching for a sea passage west of Panama, Columbus thought he was approaching China, and when he heard that another great sea lay only nine days' march from the Atlantic, he assumed it was the Indian Ocean. It was because of this mistaken belief that the Carib-

*Roman Catholic missionaries, determined to win souls for God, followed the early explorers to South America*

bean islands came to be called the West Indies, and the natives of the New World to be called Indians.

Dropped from favour and cheated of his agreed rewards, Columbus died a poor and unhappy man in 1506. The continent he had found did not even bear his name, but that of another Italian sailor, Amerigo Vespucci.

Vespucci equipped the ships for Columbus's third expedition, was appointed 'Chief Pilot' of Spain, and claimed to have made four voyages to the New World. He certainly crossed the Atlantic in 1499 and again in 1501, striking the coast of South America and exploring southwards in search of a passage through the land-mass.

In none of his voyages was Vespucci the commander. But he was a lively writer and his letters describing the new land prompted a German scholar to name the continent Amerigo after him in 1507.

Vespucci did make at least one major contribution to exploration; he readily accepted South America as a new continent while others still thought it was part of the East Indies. With his primitive mathematical instruments he also calculated the earth's circumference at the equator to a figure only 50 miles short of the correct measurement of 24,902 miles.

### THE CONQUISTADORES

The Spanish *conquistadores* who crossed to the New World from 1500 discovered two civilizations which had been flourishing in total isolation from the rest of the world. They destroyed them to build an empire for Spain

*Montezuma, emperor of the Aztecs, discusses with the Spanish adventurer Hernando Cortez terms for his release from captivity. When Cortez and his 500 followers landed in Mexico in 1519, they were at first peacefully received. This may have been partly because Montezuma and his priests believed Cortez was the reincarnation of the Aztec god Quetzalcoatl, whose reappearance had been predicted for the year in which Cortez landed.*

*Soon, however, the Spanish and the Aztecs fell out, and Cortez took Montezuma prisoner. His aim was to establish the Aztec leader as a puppet-emperor through whom the Spanish could control Mexico. However, the demands by Cortez for gold and for the abandonment of human sacrifice – an essential part of Aztec religion – sparked off an Aztec rising. Montezuma desperately tried to preserve peace, but he was stoned to death by his own people. Cortez withdrew from the Aztec capital of Tenochtitlan, but later returned with reinforcements and, after a 75-day siege, totally destroyed the city*

*A 16th-century drawing of the* Victoria, *the only one of Magellan's five ships to complete its voyage round the world*

## 'Sharing out' the New World

At a meeting in the Spanish town of Tordesillas in 1494, the Portuguese and Spanish kings signed a treaty dividing the non-Christian world between them by a line passing through the mid-Atlantic from north to south, to the exclusion of other nations. Nearly all the New World except the easternmost part of South America fell to Spain, while Portugal took India and Africa. Rising nations such as England rejected the claim, however, and in 1497 John Cabot, a Genoese who adopted British nationality, took possession of Newfoundland for England.

In 1500 a fleet of 13 ships left Portugal under the command of Pedro Alvares Cabral, bound for India. Making a wide sweep into the Atlantic to pick up a favourable wind, Cabral was swept by winds and currents westward to the coast of Brazil, which he

claimed for Portugal. Cabral then rounded the Cape of Good Hope and reached India. From the early 16th century a steady stream of gold-hungry Spaniards crossed the Atlantic. These were the celebrated *conquistadores* – 'the conquerors'. It was one of their number, Vasco Nunez de Balboa, who set out across the Isthmus of Panama in 1513 with 160 men.

After struggling through some of the most difficult terrain in the Americas, Balboa saw the Pacific, the first white man to do so. Four days later he stepped into the sea – in full armour – and claimed it for Spain. Balboa was followed by other *conquistadores* – two of whom, Cortez and Pizarro, won Mexico and Peru for Spain.

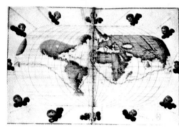

*A 16th-century view of Magellan's voyage round the world. The major landmasses were beginning to be accurately charted, but the Moluccas, Magellan's goal, were still placed east of Asia*

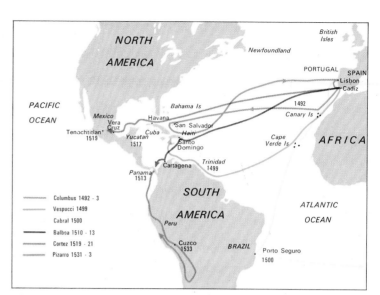

*The New World was discovered and opened up by Portugal and Spain. The Portuguese claimed Brazil, but otherwise they concentrated on their empire in the East, and left it to the Spaniards to stake out a full-scale American empire*

*Hernando Cortez (1485–1547) conquered the Aztec civilization of Mexico by 1521. He also set up colonies as far north as California*

*Mexico at the time of its conquest by Cortez. The Aztec capital, Tenochtitlan, lies in the middle of a lake, surrounded by causeways*

*Before the Spaniards came, Peru was the home of the highly civilized American Indian empire of the Incas, ruled by the Sapa Inca, Atahuallpa, seen in a portrait by a Spanish priest. The Incas were conquered by Francisco Pizarro, who had spent years serving at a Spanish base in Panama before he left for Peru in 1531, with only 180 men and 37 horses. Pizarro's methods of conquest were as brutal as those used by Cortez in Mexico. In a pitched battle at Cajamarca, he wiped out the entire leadership of the Inca Empire and took Atahuallpa prisoner. Although Atahuallpa's people raised the huge ransom the Spanish demanded for his release, Pizarro eventually ordered him to be strangled; he had promised not to spill a drop of Atahuallpa's blood. Pizarro, too, died by treachery. After conquering the whole of Peru, he was disowned by the Spanish government, after which some of his followers rebelled against him and assassinated him in his palace in 1541*

## Voyage round the globe

Columbus's dream of a western route to the East Indies still lived on, and in September 1519 the Spanish court sent five ships westwards to find the Moluccas and their spices. They were commanded by Ferdinand Magellan, a Portuguese, in the *Trinidad*.

Discipline was stern on the ships of the early explorers: when a mutiny broke out during a five-month stay in Patagonia, Magellan had one of his captains beheaded in front of 40 chained mutineers. One vessel was wrecked but with his four surviving ships Magellan entered the narrow channel at the southern tip of the South American mainland that is now called the Strait of Magellan. After 38 days of perilous navigation, Magellan's fleet reached the Pacific. On the way the mariners saw fires, probably volcanoes, burning on land to the south and named it Tierra del Fuego, 'Land of Fire'.

The expedition sailed on northwest across the unknown sea, which Magellan called the Pacific Ocean because of its general calmness compared with the turbulent Atlantic. One of the ships deserted and, when the rest of the expedition reached the Philippines, Magellan was killed by natives on the island of Mactan. The Spanish navigator Sebastian del Cano took the three remaining ships on after Magellan's death but when they reached the Moluccas only one of them, the *Victoria*, was fit to sail for Spain, which it eventually reached in September 1522 – three years after the expedition had set out.

## Europeans reach Japan

At about the same time that the Spanish expedition sailed round the world, Portuguese traders first visited the southern ports of China. But in 1577 the Chinese confined them to Macao, which has remained Portuguese to the present day. In about 1542 a party of

Portuguese became the first Europeans to land in Japan. Seven years later a Jesuit missionary from Spain, Francis Xavier, known as the 'Apostle to the Indians', took Christianity to Japan, while other Portuguese took a product the Japanese rulers valued more highly – the smooth-bore musket.

Priests accompanied most of the voyages of discovery, and also made many lone journeys to spread their faith. Pedro Paez, a Spanish Jesuit sent to Goa in 1588, was later enslaved by the Turks. He escaped to Ethiopia and became, in about 1613, the first European known to have visited the source of the Blue Nile.

## The English adventurers

England came relatively late to world exploration, but was soon to make its mark in extending the frontiers of the known world. John Cabot claimed Newfoundland in 1497, and his son, Sebastian, organised the opening-up of a trade route to Russia. Others tried to find a north-west passage round the American continent. But the greatest of these adventurers was the Elizabethan sailor Sir Francis

*Sir Francis Drake, the English explorer, was nicknamed 'El Draco' ('the dragon') by the Spanish because of his raids on their American empire*

## Across the open Pacific

*The* Resolution *heads out to sea at the start of Captain Cook's second voyage to the Pacific in 1772. Cook's instructions were explicit: with a sister-ship, the* Adventure, *he was to round the Cape of Good Hope and then circumnavigate the world from west to east – sailing as far south as possible so that he would find the unknown southern continent,* Terra Australis

Drake, who completed the second circumnavigation of the world. Drake did not set out with the intention of sailing round the world. His voyage began as one of plunder against the Spanish possessions along the Pacific coast of South America, a task which he successfully completed.

The only part of Drake's voyage that was purely exploratory was his progress up the west coast of America as far as modern Vancouver. He was seeking the strait which Sir Humphrey Gilbert had believed lay at the Pacific end of a north-west passage that curved southwards from Labrador.

Since the coast continued north instead of north-east, as Gilbert's theory indicated it should, Drake turned back and refitted his vessel in the region of present-day San Francisco. From there, he sailed across to the Moluccas, then rounded the Cape of Good Hope to return to England in 1580, laden with $28 million worth of gold, silver and jewels from Spanish treasure ships.

### The Dutch in North America

The rigours of navigating in the icy waters of the far north did not deter explorers in their quest for a shorter route to the East. Henry Hudson reached Greenland and Spitsbergen in 1607 and 1608 in vain attempts to discover a north-east passage for the English Muscovy Company. While sailing for the Dutch East India Company in 1609 he sought a north-western route instead. He explored the bays and rivers of Long Island Sound, so giving the Dutch the basis of their claim to the area around New York; and in 1610 he explored the huge land-locked opening that is called Hudson Bay

*The variety of plants found in Australia made Cook call his landfall Botany Bay. His artist drew this red honeysuckle*

after him. The freezing wastelands proved too much for his crew, however, and they mutinied and cast Hudson and his young son adrift in a small boat to die.

The entrance to the elusive north-west passage was eventually found by William Baffin in 1615. It lies to the west of Greenland, through Davis Strait. But because it passes through the largely ice-bound seas within the Arctic Circle, a passage through it was not completed until the 1903–6 expedition under the Norwegian Amundsen. In 1670 the Hudson's Bay Company was set up to trade in furs with the Indians.

### Pioneers move west

By 1650, man had at least an outline knowledge of most of the world except for three large areas: the polar regions, the interior of Africa and the huge expanse that stretches southwards from the East Indies. But even within the 'known' world much exploration remained to be done in huge

---

### THE SEARCH FOR A NORTH-WEST PASSAGE

After proving that America was separate from Asia, explorers searched for a north-west passage round it. The search began in the 16th century, but it was not until the 20th century that the first ship passed through the passage

*The Tudor explorer, Sir Martin Frobisher (1535–94), went on three Arctic voyages. In 1576 he discovered southern Greenland and explored the coast of Labrador*

— John Cabot 1497
— Willoughby & Chancellor 1553 - 4
— Frobisher 1576
— Barents 1596 - 7
— Hudson 1607 - 10
— Bering 1725 - 41

*English explorers searched for a north-west passage to the east, but their only success was to establish a north-easterly link with Russia. It was through the north-east route, too, that Vitus Bering, a Dane working for Russia, finally reached the Pacific*

*James Cook, scientist and seaman, led three Pacific voyages of exploration*

*A decorated Maori war canoe 100 ft long, hollowed out of a single tree trunk, was drawn by Sydney Parkinson, the official artist on James Cook's first voyage*

continental interiors where no European had so far set foot. Large areas of central and southern America were discovered by the Spanish, and the interior of Brazil was explored by the *mestizos*, descendants of Portuguese sailors and native women.

A good deal of detailed exploration arose incidentally as the result of military conquest by European powers – as in India under the British. It was the interest of Britain and France in the North American continent which brought the first westward migrations of pioneer settlers.

Russia, having thrown off Tatar domination in 1480, expanded south and eastwards to the Pacific. Much of the exploration and colonisation of Siberia was spearheaded by Cossack adventurers. The Cossacks, skilled sailors as well as horsemen, explored the waterways of Siberia north to the Arctic; and in 1648 Semyon Dezhnev, with 90 men in six open boats, sailed round the eastern-most part of Asia.

The area was explored scientifically by Vitus Bering, a Danish navigator, between 1725 and 1741, on the orders of Peter the Great.

The strait between Russia and Alaska and the sea to the south were named the Bering Strait and Bering Sea after the explorer. From 1799, Russian hunters and traders penetrated the coast of North America as far south as San Francisco, where they founded a colony. But in 1867 Tsar Alexander II, tiring of the burden of so remote a territory, sold all of Russian North America, which included Alaska, to the United States for 7¼ million dollars, or 12 dollars a square mile.

### The southern continent
The lure of a legendary southern continent, *Terra Australis Incognita*, had long fired the imagination of explorers and adventurers. Pedro Fernandez de Quiros, a Portuguese explorer sailing for Spain, thought he had found Australia when he anchored in the New Hebrides in 1606 and claimed all land southwards to the Pole for his masters.

A Dutchman, Willem Janszoon, was the first European to discover the real continent. After leaving Java in 1605 to survey the New

*A map of New Zealand drawn up by Cook in 1769 rightly concluded that it was not part of a continent*

Guinea coast Janszoon ventured into the Gulf of Carpentaria, in northern Australia, and named the land he found there New Holland. But it was not until 1642 that the Dutch navigator Abel Tasman made the first attempt to discover the nature of Holland's newest acquisition.

Tasman made landfall on an island which he named Van Diemen's Land (present-day Tasmania) in honour of the governor of the Dutch East Indies. He found more new land six weeks later when his eastward course brought him to New Zealand, and on his way back to Java across the uncharted Pacific he discovered Tonga and Fiji. Although he rounded Australia, Tasman never saw it, and as a result maps of the southern land-mass remained sketchy and incomplete.

### Captain Cook in the Pacific
An English pirate of intellectual disposition, William Dampier, plundered his way round the world and published an account of his voyages, including accurate charts and coast surveys. In 1699–1701 he surveyed the coasts of northern New Guinea and western Australia for the British Government; but it was not until 1768 that a detailed survey of the Pacific was attempted.

It was the prevailing interest in astronomy that took a British

scientific expedition under Captain James Cook to Tahiti in 1768, to report on the passing of the planet Venus in front of the sun. After leaving Tahiti, where he witnessed human sacrifice, Cook searched for the elusive southern continent. He sailed round New Zealand, revealing that it consisted of two islands, and landed on the unexplored eastern coast of Australia, which he named New South Wales. The voyage took four years, and much scientific knowledge was acquired, though Cook did not realise he had found

*Vitus Bering (1681–1741), a Danish explorer, discovered a north-east passage into the Pacific in 1728 through the Strait that bears his name*

*In 1577 an English artist, John White, painted this watercolour of Eskimos attacking English sailors. But Eskimo hostility was only one of the dangers that explorers had to face in their search for northern routes around America to Asia. In 1554, Sir Hugh Willoughby and his crew died of scurvy and were found frozen in their bunks, while in the 1840's Sir John Franklin's entire expedition of 129 men perished after being forced to abandon their ships when they became frozen in the ice. It was not until the 1903–6 expedition by the Norwegian Roald Amundsen that a successful journey through the north-west passage was made. By then the passage had been proved commercially worthless*

### PACIFIC WANDERERS
Centuries before Europeans began to explore the oceans, Polynesian islanders were voyaging thousands of miles across the Pacific. They had no navigational instruments, and were dependent on generations-old techniques and instincts. They guided their canoes by the stars, and could tell if they were nearing land by interpreting the pattern of the waves

*A Polynesian double-hulled canoe, sketched by the Dutch explorer Abel Tasman in 1643. Powered by a sail made from coconut fibre, it could sail more than 1000 miles in all kinds of weather. The wooden hulls – as long as 80 ft – were lashed together, with a deck-house between them*

*Stone statues up to 30 ft high dot the slopes of Rano-Raraku volcano on Easter Island in the South Pacific, nearly 1500 miles from the nearest habitable land. The statues were probably erected by Polynesian migrants, who reached the island by AD 1400. The significance of these massive monuments is unknown, but they may have been connected with burial rites. The statue shown was demolished soon after Captain Cook visited the island, and re-erected in 1956*

*Among the Polynesian peoples of the Pacific discovered by Captain Cook were the Maoris (above), who were unfriendly to his party. They had settled in New Zealand by AD 1100, and by the 18th century had established a settled society, becoming experts in agriculture, fishing and canoe-building. Soon, however, they were conquered by the white man*

# Into the uncharted interiors

From the middle of the 19th century, European interest turned increasingly to Africa, the last unexplored continent. This contemporary painting shows the journalist Henry Morton Stanley's 1000 mile march into the African interior in search of David Livingstone, the Scots missionary-explorer

the great southern continent he was seeking. Cook continued his exploration in a second voyage from 1772 to 1775, when he sailed south of the Antarctic Circle and discovered South Georgia.

In 1776 he embarked on a third voyage, which took him again to New Zealand and then north on an unsuccessful search for the northwest passage from the west side, near the Bering Strait. After turning south again, Cook was killed in Hawaii in 1780, when he tried to settle a dispute between his crew and the islanders.

No other explorer had charted so much of the surface of the globe or worked with such precision as Cook. He found that the Pacific islands had a long tradition of seafaring all the way from Hawaii to New Zealand. Polynesian Maoris, for example, had gone 'island-hopping' southwards to colonise New Zealand between 900 and 1350. The Tongans, who knew 156 islands, mainly in the Tonga, Samoa and Fiji groups, told Cook that they navigated by the sun and stars when they could. When these were obscured, they steered by observing the direction from which the wind and waves beat upon their boats, working out the positions of unknown islands from the way that these areas of land disturbed the wave patterns. Many voyagers missed their way and were lost, but others made journeys of 1000 miles and more.

In 1947 Thor Heyerdahl, the Norwegian author of *Kon-Tiki*, sailed with five companions in a balsa-wood raft from Peru to Polynesia, in support of his theory

In 1803–6 the American explorers Meriwether Lewis (left) and William Clark found an overland route to the Pacific

that the islands were originally discovered and settled by South American Indians who made the crossing in similar craft.

## The crossing of Australia

Britain's interest in Australia increased after the loss of the American colonies, and in 1787, 13 years after Cook's discovery of New South Wales, nearly 1000 convicts were shipped there and the building of Sydney began. During the 1800's the interior was gradually explored, in the face both of hostile Aborigines and of the harsh land itself, much of it waterless desert.

Hamilton Hume and Charles Sturt, in separate expeditions,

Vast buffalo herds which roamed the American interior and provided the Indians with food and clothing were almost wiped out by the white man

---

## THE FIRST AMERICANS

The first explorers to reach North America called its native inhabitants 'Indians', because they thought they had reached India and did not know they had discovered a new continent. The American Indians were the descendants of peoples who had crossed the land bridge from Asia – now the Bering Strait – more than 20,000 years ago. They were divided into numerous tribal groups, each with its own language and way of life, and these divisions made it easier for the invading white men to defeat the Indians group by group

A Comanche village in Texas, drawn by George Catlin, a lawyer turned artist, in 1834. According to Catlin's account, the village consisted of at least 600 tepees, or tents

John White painted this ritual dance in North Carolina in the 1580's, for Sir Walter Raleigh. The central dancers are virgins, and the poles marking the circle are carved with human heads

The pineapple, found in the Caribbean, was popular in Europe

charted the Murray-Darling river system, and in 1841 Edward John Eyre crossed southern Australia from east to west, proving from his own bitter experience that no river from the interior flowed into the Great Australian Bight. Eyre set off from Fowlers Bay on horseback with John Baxter and three Aborigines, and at one period they struggled on for 135 miles, kept alive only by dew and moisture from roots. Baxter was murdered by two of the Aborigines, who made off with the supplies, but Eyre, lying almost insensible across his horse, was led to safety by his loyal remaining guide.

The first south to north crossing of the continent was made in 1862 at the third try by John McDouall Stuart, after earlier attempts by him had been thwarted by hostile Aborigines and a belt of scrub.

## Westwards across America

When it was realised that no north-west passage to China could be of commercial value, attention turned to the search for a route across the North American continent, either by land or by water.

Louis Jolliet, a fur trapper, left Quebec in 1672 and was joined by Jacques Marquette, a French Jesuit. They went down the Wisconsin River to the Mississippi, reaching it at about the site of present-day St Paul, and then paddled down to within ten days' journey of the Gulf of Mexico. The lower Mississippi valley was explored in 1699–1720 and the city of New Orleans was founded.

The Pacific was finally reached in 1792–3 when a Canadian fur

trader, Alexander Mackenzie, succeeded in crossing the Rockies from the Saskatchewan and Peace Rivers to the fast-flowing Fraser, and then down the Bellacoola River to the Pacific, north of Vancouver. In an earlier expedition, Mackenzie had

*The lure of gold was one incentive which spurred the American drive westwards. This detailed plan of a mine was made in Nevada in 1876*

journeyed from Lake Athabasca into the Great Slave Lake and down the Mackenzie River, which took him not west to the Pacific as he had expected, but northwards into the Arctic Ocean. Between 1789 and 1812 David Thompson, a Canadian fur trader and explorer, accurately surveyed 50,000 square miles of territory between Lake Superior and the Pacific.

In 1803 the United States was almost doubled in size by the Louisiana Purchase, under which Napoleon I of France sold to the Americans all the French territory west of the Mississippi, including what is now Louisiana and a vast area to the north and north-west. America paid 16 million dollars –

20 dollars a square mile. Immediately, the Americans began a systematic exploration of the west. In 1804 President Jefferson sent an expedition under the command of Meriwether Lewis and William Clark to find a way to the Pacific. Their report proved that the Atlantic and Pacific were not connected by a river system.

In 1806, Zebulon Pike, a lieutenant in the American army, left Louisiana to explore the headwaters of the Arkansas River and gather information about the Spaniards in New Mexico. He found the Rio Grande, but was arrested as a spy. Later he returned to the United States with information about the vast territories which the Americans were to annexe in the 1840's.

In the American west, the Great Salt Lake was discovered in 1824 by James Bridger, and during the next seven years Jedediah Smith explored the huge area between the lake and the Pacific. Relations between explorers and the Indians were often difficult, and Smith was ambushed and killed in 1831.

John Fremont, called 'the Pathfinder', explored the land between the Rocky Mountains and the Pacific in 1842–8, and the following year the California gold rush finally opened up the Pacific coast. By 1869 a railroad spanned the continent.

## The Dark Continent

There were good reasons why Africa was the last of the inhabited continents to be explored. The climate, and the diseases which thrived in it, were often fatal to

Europeans; for years, the steamy jungle of West Africa was known as 'the white man's grave'. The tribes of the interior were often hostile, for Europeans had made slaves of their fathers and grandfathers. There were few bays and natural harbours, and the rivers offered no easy highway to the interior. Finally, apart from the coastal areas, the continent was thought to be poor in natural resources.

In 1794, Mungo Park, a Scottish doctor and explorer, was commissioned by the Africa Association to gather information about the Niger. Four explorers had already perished in searching for its source, the direction it flowed, and where it emptied its waters. Park abandoned his first attempt through exhaustion. He returned in 1805 and followed the river as it wound north-east and then southeast, but he and his companions were drowned 300 miles upstream from the river mouth.

### First white man in Timbuktu

A Frenchman, René Caillié, became the first European to return

*Mungo Park's encounter with a lion is shown on the title page of his account in 1799 of his African travels*

---

## EXPLORERS OF THE DARK CONTINENT

Its hostile climate and difficult terrain made Africa late on the list of continents explored by Europeans. A century of exploration which began in 1794 charted its coasts and rivers and showed its value to the expanding European powers

*The most famous scene in exploration history: the journalist Henry Morton Stanley meets the explorer David Livingstone at Ujiji, on Lake Tanganyika, in 1871. Livingstone had not been heard of for four years when a newspaper commissioned Stanley to search for him. After eight months Stanley found the lost explorer and greeted him with the words: 'Dr Livingstone, I presume'*

*Stanley journeying in search of Livingstone. Stanley later returned to Africa, and conducted important explorations for the Belgian Government in the Congo*

For 24 years, from 1849 until his death, the Scots doctor and missionary David Livingstone (left) made a series of epic journeys into the heart of central Africa, healing and converting natives and fighting Arab slavers. Among his many achievements, he discovered the Victoria Falls and made the first crossing of the African continent. Livingstone died in Africa in 1873. So revered was he by the Africans that bearers carried his body 700 miles to the coast, from where it was brought back to England to be buried in Westminster Abbey. Livingstone's work was continued by Stanley, who explored Lake Tanganyika, Lake Victoria and the Congo River

Members of Livingstone's expedition of 1859, on board the steam-launch Ma Robert travelling up the River Zambezi, open fire on a bull elephant, which trumpets in anger. The scene was recorded by Thomas Baines, Livingstone's official artist. The explorer believed that the Zambezi, on which four years earlier he had discovered the Victoria Falls, could form a useful trading route into the African interior, and he planned to take the launch up the river from its mouth on the East African coast. But its fierce currents proved too powerful for the vessel's engines, and he was forced to turn back

## First steps into space

One of the latest challenges accepted by exploring man is the weightlessness of outer space. In June 1965 the American astronaut Edward White (above) became the second man to leave his spacecraft and 'walk' in space. The first was the Russian, Alexei Leonov. White's 'walk' lasted 21 minutes; he was linked to his craft by gold-coated tubing

alive from Timbuktu, which he reached disguised as an Arab in 1828; and in 1850 the German explorer Heinrich Barth visited it on his journeys through the Sahara to Kano and Lake Chad. His five-volume *Travels and Discoveries in North and Central Africa* became the standard reference book for future explorers of the continent.

The major discoveries of central Africa in the 19th century were set afoot either by the quest for precise geographical knowledge or else by missionary zeal. Britain's Royal Geographical Society took a special interest in seeking the sources of the Nile. Richard Burton and John Hanning Speke set off into the heart of Africa with the Society's backing. Speke discovered Lake Victoria, surmising correctly that it was the prime source of the Nile – though his conclusion was hotly disputed. Three years later, in 1861, Samuel Baker and his wife sailed up the river to discover that Lakes Nyanza and Albert (now Mobutu Sese Seku) were secondary sources. But most

Members of John Ross's expedition to the Arctic in 1818 try to establish contact with the native Eskimos

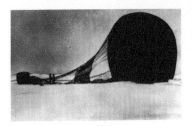

Saloman Andrée's attempt to reach the North Pole by balloon in 1897 ended in a disastrous crash-landing

important of the African explorers were the Scot, David Livingstone, and the Welsh-American, Henry Morton Stanley. Between them they explored much of east and central Africa.

### The last frontiers

The Arctic and Antarctic were the last areas of the globe to be explored. Commercially, the Arctic was the more promising prospect because it was thought there was a possibility of finding trading routes across it between the continents.

John Ross probed the coasts of Canada and Greenland from 1818, and in 1850 James Clark Ross searched unsuccessfully for Sir John Franklin, who had perished with 128 men in 1847 while looking for a north-west passage. It was not until 1906 that a Norwegian, Roald Amundsen, finally sailed through the north-west passage after a three-year expedition.

Nils Nordenskjold, a Swede, sailed north of Europe and Asia

### THE RACE TO THE NORTH AND SOUTH POLES

The hazards of polar exploration were such that it was not until 1909 that an American explorer, Robert Peary, reached the North Pole at his third attempt – an expedition which he had been planning for 23 years. Two years later, a Norwegian, Roald Amundsen, reached the South Pole, beating his British rival, Captain Robert Scott, by a month. The Arctic and the Antarctic are still the only two major areas of the globe not to have been settled by man

The *Terra Nova* was Captain Robert Scott's supply ship in his quest for the South Pole. Scott set sail from England in June 1910, and six months later arrived in the Antarctic, where he moored his ship in McMurdo Sound. This photograph was taken in January 1911. On his way south, Scott received the news that Amundsen, too, was on his way to Antarctica

Roald Amundsen of Norway (above) was the first man to reach the South Pole, on December 14, 1911; two years earlier he had been beaten by his American rival, Commodore Peary, in a race to the North Pole

*This painting of an Eskimo was made during Frobisher's second Arctic voyage*

into the Pacific in 1878–9 to find the north-east passage. Later he explored Greenland, which was crossed on skis by Fridtjof Nansen's Norwegian expedition in 1888.

Five years later, Nansen and 12 others aboard the *Fram*, a sailing ship specially built to withstand ice pressure, left the New Siberian Islands, hoping an ocean current would carry them over the North Pole. After drifting for 16 months, Nansen and one companion left the *Fram* to escape the tedium, and went on with sledges, dogs and kayaks to 86°14′ N – further north than anyone had previously ventured – before turning back. Their efforts led to more attempts.

Saloman Andrée, another Swede, and two companions attempted to pass over the North Pole in a balloon in 1897; their bodies were discovered 33 years later on White Island, north of Russia. Even today, the cause of their death remains a mystery, as Andrée's party still had plenty of

food as well as warm clothing and sleeping bags. Finally, in 1909, at his third attempt, Robert Peary, an American, became the first man to reach the North Pole, after his expedition had travelled by sea to Ellesmere Island, and then by sledge across the polar ice cap.

**Tragedy at the South Pole**
In Antarctica a British seal-hunting expedition was led by James Weddell in 1821–4, and James Ross discovered the sea and ice shelf that bear his name in 1841. But interest in the continent then waned until the 1890's.

A party led by Roald Amundsen finally planted the Norwegian flag at the Pole in December, 1911, and Robert Falcon Scott's British expedition reached it a month later. On their return journey from the Pole, Scott and his last two companions perished only 11 miles from their supply depot.

In 1957–8 a well-equipped British party, led by Dr Vivian Fuchs, became the first to cross Antarctica, covering 2200 miles in 99 days. The expedition was part of the International Geophysical Year, during which the still unknown continent was extensively surveyed and researched.

At various times territorial claims have been made in Antarctica's 5,100,000 square miles by Argentina, Australia, Britain, Chile, France, New Zealand and Norway. In 1961 these nations, together with Belgium, Japan, South Africa, America and Russia,

*Earth rises above the moon's horizon. The first men to see this sight were the American astronauts Neil Armstrong and 'Buzz' Aldrin, who touched down in the moon's Sea of Tranquillity on July 20, 1969. Six-and-a-half hours after landing, Armstrong took mankind's first step on the surface of another planet*

ratified the Antarctic Treaty; this permitted free use of the continent for scientific purposes but banned activities of a warlike nature.

**The conquest of space**
By the 1960's the globe's land surface held few secrets. But new challenges presented themselves. Oceanographers now began systematically to explore the seas, which occupy seven-tenths of the globe's surface In 1934, the Americans William Beebe and Otis Barton made the first bathysphere descent half a mile into the sea off Bermuda. Since that time, man's knowledge of the ocean depths has increased enormously. Modern technology led to the development of deeper-diving bathyspheres; in 1960 a world record was set by the *Trieste*, which descended 35,800 ft (nearly 7

miles) into the Marianas Trench in the Pacific off Guam Island. Scientists now probe the depths in mini-submarines, which enable them to range much more freely over the ocean floor than they could do in bathyspheres with their restricting cables.

The space age began in 1957 when the USSR launched its first earth satellite, the Sputnik. In 1961 the Russian, Yuri Gagarin, was the first man to orbit the earth, and in 1969 Neil Armstrong, an American astronaut, became the first man to step on to the surface of the moon.

Despite their almost complete reliance on the achievements of modern technology, the astronauts who have explored the moon's surface share two qualities with explorers of the past – courage and dedication to their missions.

*On January 18, 1912, Scott, on the left, and his companions reached the South Pole, only to discover a tent and a Norwegian flag left there by Amundsen a month earlier. The photograph was developed from film found with the bodies of the expedition. Scott's expedition was fatally weakened by his decision to rely on ponies rather than dogs to haul his sledges, for by the time he was ready to begin his dash to the Pole all the ponies were dead and the party were forced to haul their sledges by hand. Exhaustion slowed the return journey from the Pole. One member of the expedition, Captain Oates, whose feet were so severely frost-bitten that he could no longer walk, stumbled out into the snow to give his companions a chance to continue without him. But Scott and his two remaining companions also perished, after struggling to within only 11 miles of a supply base. Their bodies were discovered the following November. Among the objects recovered was Scott's diary. Its last two sentences read: 'It seems a pity but I do not think I can write more. For God's sake look after our people.' Scott and his companions were buried where they lay*

**CONQUERING THE PEAKS**

After the conquest of the North and the South Poles, the greatest challenges left to exploring man were the mountain peaks, the highest 40 of which are in the Himalayan ranges. Attempts on these peaks began as early as the 1890's, but it was not until 1953 that Mount Everest, the highest of them all, was finally conquered. Assaults on these towering summits have to be timed with great care, because, in the monsoon season, blizzards can last for weeks without ceasing

*Mount Everest (29,028 ft), the highest peak in the world, was discovered in 1852 and named after Sir George Everest, a former Surveyor-General of India. It was conquered by a British Commonwealth expedition, led by Sir John Hunt, in 1953. Hunt's expedition was the eighth all-out attempt on the summit, and followed the newly discovered southern route up the South Col from Nepal*

*The New Zealander Edmund Hillary and a Nepalese Sherpa, Tensing Norkay, approach the last camp before the final assault on the summit of Everest. Both men had taken part in previous reconnaissance expeditions to Everest – Hillary in 1951 and Tensing as early as 1935, when he was only 19. The lightweight oxygen equipment they carried was a major factor in their success*

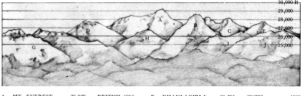

| | | | | | | | |
|---|---|---|---|---|---|---|---|
| A | MT. EVEREST | 29,028 | BRITISH 1953 | F | DHAULAGIRI I | 26,795 | SWISS 1960 |
| B | K2 (CHOGORI) | 28,741 | ITALIAN 1954 | G | MANASLU | 26,760 | JAPANESE 1956 |
| C | KANGCHENJUNGA | 28,208 | BRITISH 1955 | H | CHO OYU | 26,750 | AUSTRIAN 1954 |
| D | LHOTSE | 27,923 | SWISS 1956 | I | NANGA PARBAT | 26,660 | AUSTRO-GER 1953 |
| E | MAKALU | 27,825 | FRENCH 1955 | J | ANNAPURNA I | 26,545 | FRENCH 1950 |

*Between 1950 and 1960, a spate of mountain climbing conquered the world's ten highest peaks – all of them in the Himalayas. This chart shows the height of each peak, the date it was scaled, and the nationality of the successful expedition. Having conquered the big peaks, mountaineers in recent years have concentrated on climbing lower peaks, many of them as challenging as the world's highest, and on pioneering new routes up already-climbed mountains. Five attempts have been made on the South Face of Everest alone*

# Man the warrior

*The instinct for aggression and the demands of defence led nations to master the techniques of war*

In their ceaseless quest for booty, the Assyrians, early rulers of an empire between the Tigris and Euphrates, made themselves masters of siegecraft, as this relief from the palace of the Assyrian King Tiglath-pileser III (745–727 BC) at Nimrud shows. A wheeled battering ram assaults the fortifications, while its operators, hidden behind armour, are given covering fire by two archers. The Assyrians were also among the first people to use iron weapons in their campaigns

Warfare was one of the first fruits of civilization. As soon as men gathered in settled communities along river valleys they created wealth that others coveted: to protect it, or to seize the territory of their neighbours, they had to arm and band together. Where once there had been tribal skirmishes, there were now campaigns.

The first armies in history were formed by the Sumerians, who began 5000 years ago to build the first cities, in the land between the Tigris and Euphrates rivers. Sumerian foot-soldiers, armed with bows and spears and protected by leather helmets and simple body armour, fought in dense, close-order formations protected by leather shields. They also had cumbersome two and four-wheeled chariots drawn by four asses and

*Leather-armoured Sumerian infantry in action. Sumer formed the first regular army in history in about 3000 BC*

manned by a driver and soldier. The chariots were driven close enough to the enemy for the soldier to hurl a javelin. Then the asses were whipped to move in closer still, so that the soldier could use his spear in the savage hand-to-hand combat which followed.

## Weapons of bronze
Weapons improved as knowledge of metals and metal-working increased. Copper was used to fashion maces and the heads of arrows and spears in Mesopotamia and Egypt, but in Mesopotamia it was replaced about 2000 BC by bronze, a harder alloy of copper and tin, which gave a more lasting cutting edge to swords, daggers and axes.

Most of the armies of earliest times had similar weapons, and victory usually went to the side which could muster most troops. Only a new weapon or a skilful general could tip the scales against superior numbers. The Akkadians, a people of central Mesopotamia who conquered the Sumerians about 2300 BC, were lucky enough to have both.

Led by their king, Sargon the Great, the Akkadians defeated armies of 15,000 although outnumbered three to one. They were armed only with javelins and bows, but the bows were made to a new design – a composite of wood, sinews and animal horn glued together in a way that produced extreme tension in the string. The result was a weapon that could far

outshoot any other bow in existence, and bring the enemy under fire from long range.

## Egypt's 'shock troops'
The early Egyptians fought ponderous hand-to-hand battles with lance and club. But in about 1600 BC the introduction of the horse by Aryan invaders, the Hyksos, revolutionised the Egyptian battle line. Light two-wheeled chariots, drawn by horses and each carrying a driver and an archer, formed the first 'shock troops' in history.

The speed and mobility of these chariots enabled them to race from place to place on the battleground, and they played a major part in the expansion of the Egyptian Empire during the New Kingdom, founded in 1560 BC. The armies of the pharaohs included more than 20,000 professional soldiers, drilled and organised in regiments.

## The earliest cavalry
Iron weapons were first brought into use by the Hittites, but it was the fierce Assyrians who used them to build an empire centred on the Tigris and Euphrates from about 1300 BC. Armed with iron weapons, and protected by shields, breastplates and pointed helmets, the ruthless Assyrians were the scourge of all who crossed their path. In about 1000 BC they were the first to use cavalry, when archers and spearmen went into action on horseback. Two centuries later, under Shalmaneser III, the Assyrians could field an army of

---

### WITH AXE AND SWORD

The stone axe was one of man's first weapons. Stone eventually gave place to copper – and copper to bronze in about 2000 BC, when the sword originated. Bronze itself was superseded by iron; this gave weapons an even harder cutting edge

Four examples show the development of hand weapons. The Egyptian bronze axe (1) was made about 1450 BC, but its softer cutting edge made it inferior to iron weapons. Despite its cumbersome appearance, the German two-handed sword (2), dating from the late 16th century AD, was lethal in the hands of a skilled warrior. The halberd (3) combined the dual functions of axe and spear, while the use of steel gave flexibility as well as strength to the German rapier (4)

*Chariots were used in war by the ancient Greeks as a mobile striking force to prepare the way for their infantry*

20,000 infantry, 12,000 light cavalry armed with bows and spears, and 1200 two-horse chariots.

In open battle the main weight of the Assyrian onslaughts came from chariots charging the enemy masses. Under Assurbanipal (669–627 BC), when the Assyrian Empire reached from the Nile to the Caucasus, the chariot was enlarged, and four horses were needed to haul it and its crew.

## Persia, the first super-power
Great empires were carved only with great armies, and by 480 BC the empire of Persia had become the world's first super-power.

The Persian army, impressively trained and disciplined, was made up of conscripts, who were paid in coin, for the first time in history. Their battle array included heavy and light infantry, chariots with scythe blades on the wheels, and archers mounted on camels. The Persians also used elephants in war. These had an immense psychological impact. But because of the menace of stampeding animals trampling their own troops, each elephant driver was armed with a spike to drive into his animal's brain – the first 'self-destruct' device in history.

## Victory of the phalanx
The formidable armies of Persia suffered their first major setback at Marathon, in Greece, in 490 BC. The Greeks owed their victory to their heavy infantry, called hoplites, who carried swords and 21 ft long pikes, and were protected by crested helmets, breastplates, shin armour and large round shields. All Greek citizens were expected to serve in the infantry whenever the need arose. The hoplites fought in dense formations called phalanxes, which faced the enemy in closely packed lines of interlocking shields, bristling with pikes. The phalanxes were supported by screens of light infantry wielding slings, bows and javelins. Victory was won by weight of numbers. Discipline was vital, since a break in the ranks could lead to a rout. Moreover, the cumbersome nature of the phalanx meant that it could only fight effectively on flat ground.

## Power in the Far East
Military might in the ancient world was not confined to the Middle East. The civilizations of China and India also had large numbers of men under arms. It was in China, in about 500 BC,

that the first known manual on the art of war appeared, written by a military genius called Sun-Tzu. By about 200 BC, under the Chin dynasty, China had become the greatest military power in Asia. The peasant-emperor Shih Huang Ti completed the 1500 mile Great Wall to hold back the barbarians.

India's first armies were composed of foot soldiers who used bows, swords and spears, with the support of a few chariots. The Indians were skilled at siege warfare, but cavalry was not widely used, and iron weapons did not replace bronze in the Indian subcontinent until the 5th century.

## The birth of sea power
At first warfare was confined to the land; only in the 6th century BC did the Greeks and the Persians

*A Greek phalanx fights off a cavalry attack. This fighting formation was perfected by Alexander the Great*

begin to use specially built war galleys, often with Phoenician crews. Manoeuvrability was more important in a warship than a merchant vessel, so oars were preferred to sail for propulsion.

The first Greek vessels were penteconters, with 25 oars on each side. Later, rowers were arranged in banks to increase oar-power without lengthening the ships, and during the 5th century BC the first triremes put to sea. These had 170 oarsmen in three banks, and were 100 ft long and 20 ft wide. The bows were shaped to form a ram.

The first great sea battle in history was at Salamis, in 480 BC, when 366 triremes and seven penteconters of the Greek navy defeated the 500 ships of the Egyptian, Phoenician and Ionian fleets mustered by Persia. This Persian defeat, and later battles at Plataea on land and Mycale at sea secured the Greek homeland; Greek supremacy at sea meant Persia could not transport its armies and secure its communications.

## Alexander the Great
The army with which Alexander the Great of Macedon forged his empire between 336 and 323 BC was the most sophisticated fighting machine yet created, and won him a place among history's greatest generals. He had 35,000 men under arms, and the key formation was still the phalanx, now trained to be highly manoeuvrable. Supporting this were light troops and the 'Royal Army' of two crack corps –

*Carthage's general, Hannibal, one of the greatest soldiers of the ancient world*

one the 'Companion Cavalry', usually led by Alexander himself, the other an elite band of 3000 infantry called hypaspists.

Mercenaries swelled the ranks; these included archers from Crete, lancers from Thrace and heavy cavalry from Thessaly. Other warriors were enlisted in conquered lands to guard Alexander's ever-stretching lines of communication.

Catapults that could hurl rocks or large spears were part of the armoury, and Alexander mastered siege tactics. His engineers developed the 'crow', which operated on the principle of a huge ball and chain to batter down walls, and the telemon, a kind of crane, which allowed a small force of men to be lowered into a fortress from outside. Persia fell to Alexander's genius, but his empire, which eventually stretched to India, did not long survive his death in 323 BC.

## Wars with Carthage
After the death of Alexander and the disintegration of Macedonia's empire, the two most powerful

---

### THE LEGENDARY LEGIONS OF ROME

Rome's chief weapon in its struggle for mastery of western Europe was the legion. This fighting force, about 5000 strong, was organised into 30 maniples, which fought in three lines, the veterans backing up the less-experienced soldiers. The first Roman armies were composed of citizen soldiers, who were conscripted for the duration of a campaign, and went back to their peace-time jobs afterwards. But the long wars with Carthage made the creation of a regular army essential, and Caius Marius carried out this reform towards the end of the 2nd century BC. Marius also altered the size and composition of the legion, abandoning the maniple in favour of ten cohorts, each containing 600 men, separated into centuries under the command of centurions. Eagle standards were given to the legions, and the loss of a standard in battle meant disgrace

*A series of brilliant generals led Rome's armies in their drive to conquer an empire. Among them were Pompey (above left), who conquered much of the Middle East, and Julius Caesar (above right), who won Gaul. Eventually they fought for the mastery of the Roman state. Pompey was defeated, and Caesar triumphed. But many saw his ambitions as a threat to the republic, and he too was assassinated by a group of conspirators in Rome. The soldier-politicians of Rome found it easy to gain the personal allegiance of their armies, as Roman soldiers were equipped and paid, not by the state, but by the generals who recruited them into their legions*

*The Roman fighting formation known as the testudo (tortoise), in which legionaries protected themselves by interlocking their shields, was devised for use in sieges*

*A Roman triarius in full equipment. The triarii were veteran soldiers who were spared the first onslaught of heavy fighting in battle, and held in reserve to strike the decisive blow. They were protected by bronze helmets and breastplates, and carried deep rectangular shields, made from leather-coated wood and trimmed with iron. As armament, the triarius carried a long thrusting spear and the 2 ft stabbing sword, the principal Roman weapon in hand-to-hand combat. The soldier's normal marching load weighed 88 lb.*

*This 15th-century Italian horse-drawn war chariot, though ingenious, proved of little practical use in action*

# *Warriors on sea and land*

*Boarding parties storm aboard warships in this medieval French illustration of the Battle of Sluys, fought in 1340 between an English fleet under Edward III, which numbered about 250 ships, and a French squadron of 190 preparing to invade England. This sea action, in which the English were victorious, was the first major battle of the Hundred Years' War; its tactics in close-quarter fighting scarcely differed from those in use on land*

Mediterranean nations were Rome and Carthage, a former Phoenician colony which had grown to dominate much of the western Mediterranean from its capital in what is now Tunisia. A clash between the two was inevitable, and between 218 and 201 BC the Romans were almost brought to their knees by the brilliant generalship of the Carthaginian leader Hannibal, whose greatest victory was at Cannae in Italy in 216 BC. He drew up his army in a crescent bulging towards the enemy, then allowed the Romans to press forward, forcing his centre back until the crescent became concave. Then he swung his infantry and cavalry in on the Roman flanks, surrounding and destroying the entire army of 70,000 men.

Hannibal was an inspired battlefield general but a poor strategist, for he did not capitalise on his devastating victories by laying siege to Rome. By 207 BC Rome was strong enough to carry the war to Carthage and in 203 BC Hannibal himself was recalled from Italy to deal with the menace. At Zama, in 202 BC, Scipio Africanus defeated him in a decisive battle. Rome's legions went on to conquer much of western Europe and the Middle East, and penetrate into Asia. Their leadership, fighting skill and superior weapons made them masters of the known world for over 500 years.

## The Dark Ages
The Roman Empire in the West collapsed before the onslaughts of barbarian invaders – swift-riding

---

### KNIGHTS IN AN AGE OF CHIVALRY

The mounted knight, heavily armoured and securely based in a fortress-castle, was the key figure of the medieval age of chivalry. The castle reached a high point of development between 1096 and 1270, when the Crusaders in the Holy Land perfected its design along Byzantine lines. Their designs were soon copied in western Europe, but with the introduction of cannon in the 14th century the castle became virtually useless against a determined foe. Few could withstand a persistent bombardment from even the crudest forms of artillery. Armour, too, declined in importance with the introduction of fire-arms

*A 12th-century illustration of a Visigoth foot soldier, armed with sword and lance. He wears a conical helmet with a nose guard, and is clad in a knee-length tunic of overlapping steel scales. The tunic was flexible, but not proof against an opponent's arrows*

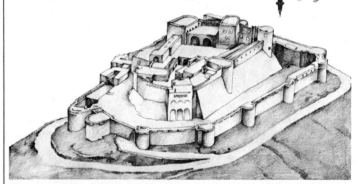

*Krak des Chevaliers, built in the Holy Land, marks the triumph of Crusader architecture. The main walls were enclosed by lower walls, so that attackers could be pinned down*

*A Crusader knight watched over by a saint, in a medieval manuscript. The early Crusaders secured much of Palestine, but they were soon driven on to the defensive by the armies of Islam*

*By the 16th century, armourers were producing elaborate armours for both man and horse. This armour belonged to Henry VIII of England*

*Charlemagne (left), seen with his son Pepin, safeguarded his empire by building a chain of frontier fortresses. But his main tactics were to harry his enemies on their own territories*

*A Mongol horseman from the steppes, armed with a bow and quiver of arrows. Warriors such as this conquered a quarter of the globe in the Middle Ages*

horsemen who made up for lack of military finesse by sheer weight of numbers and fearful savagery. In the 'Dark Ages' that followed the fall of Rome in AD 476, the development of tactics and weapons slowed down. The sole exception was in Byzantium, the eastern half of the empire, whose military success was based largely on the cataphracts, armoured horse archers given firm seats on their mounts with the widespread introduction of stirrups and saddles. Mounted archers made up half Byzantium's forces, and on occasion completely mounted armies went into battle under great generals such as Belisarius and Narses, both commanders for Emperor Justinian. Belisarius led Byzantium's fight against the Vandals in Africa and then campaigned against the Ostrogoths in Italy itself. His work was continued by Narses, who took Rome and ended the Goths' power in Italy.

Officers were trained in tactics, in how to seize the initiative and use it to mount a crescendo of co-ordinated blows. They also chose suitable tactics for particular enemies, attacking the Huns in winter or the Arabs in wet weather, when they knew the morale of the other side was low. By AD 1000, the Byzantine forces totalled 150,000 men. With the rapid growth of the Muslim threat from AD 600 onwards, Byzantium improved its fleet too. The discovery of the incendiary mixture known as 'Greek fire' which was fired from ballistae, or through tubes mounted in the bows of galleys, aided this process. By 800 Byzantium had won supremacy at sea.

## The Arab tide
The first Muslim armies, which began to sweep out of Arabia in an explosion of religious zeal even before Muhammad's death in 632, were more noted for fanaticism than for military ability. But their skill at warfare grew as they adopted Byzantine weaponry, and when their leaders became the redoubtable Seljuk Turks.

Armed with lances and bows, the light cavalry of Islam became the most formidable attacking force in the world, driving east into Asia and west through the Middle East and North Africa and into southern Europe. They were halted only at Tours, in France, where in 732 the Frankish leader Charles Martel fought in a tight infantry phalanx before counter-attacking the exhausted Muslims. The victory established the Carolingian dynasty in France, and by 771 Charles Martel's grandson, Charlemagne, had begun to create his empire.

## Charlemagne's feudal system
The military system created by Charlemagne, though crude compared to those of Rome and Byzantium, represented an enormous advance for western Europe at that time. Between 808 and 813 Charlemagne issued five Ordinances, model military regulations in their clarity and comprehensiveness. He also encouraged the use of heavy cavalry, a policy that was to lead to the growth of the feudal system and to put great power into the hands of rich noblemen.

It was impossible for the state to bear the cost of mounting and equipping a large standing army of heavily armed and armoured horsemen, so the Crown granted an allotment of land, known as a fief, to a nobleman. In exchange, he and his retainers performed a period of military service each year and looked after the organisation of the defence of their own locality. The local peasantry performed services for the lord in return for the protection afforded by his arms and his castle. So the nobleman and his castle, with a feudal array backed by the peasant masses, became the standard form of military organisation in the West. But the system had its drawbacks; for a rebellious nobleman, secure in his castle, could easily defy his own ruler's authority. Feudalism lasted until the introduction of fire-arms and cannon brought the supremacy of the mounted knight to an end in the 15th century.

## Mongols and Tatars
By 1200 a new military force was erupting in the East. Under the leadership of Genghis Khan, a vast invasion of Mongols and Tatars swept through Asia. A Mongol horde was far from being a disorganised mass of men, horses and baggage, chaotic though it may have appeared. It consisted of three *toumans* of cavalry, each 10,000 strong. One-third of them were heavy cavalry and the rest light cavalry, and they combined to give superb mobility, flexibility and hitting power.

Each Mongol owned at least two horses, usually mares, whose blood and milk formed an important part of his diet; he was armed with two bows – firing different types of arrows – a scimitar and a lance. The Mongols' ferocity and their excellent intelligence system and skill at siege warfare – which they learnt from the Chinese – made them masters of vast areas. By 1241 they had conquered a huge expanse of territory stretching from the Yellow Sea to Poland and the Danube. Byzantium and the West were saved from their depredations only by the death of Ogotai, son of Genghis Khan, which caused the recall of the *toumans* in 1242. In the East, the Mongols remained supreme for another two centuries; their Khanate of the Golden Horde, which included much of present-day Russia, lasted from 1243 to 1405.

## Bowmen and pikemen
By 1300, the mounted knight was facing a new challenge in the West. The archers of England, armed with longbows and 'clothyard' arrows 3 ft long, had adopted these weapons from the Welsh. Later at Crécy (1346) and Poitiers (1356),

*The heraldic markings on the shields of medieval Spanish warriors enabled them to be easily identified in battle*

---

### FROM BOW AND ARROW TO CANNON

Two types of weapon, the steel-tipped arrow and the cannon, spelt the doom of the mounted knights, who dominated the medieval battlefield. English longbowmen wrought havoc among the knights of France in the Hundred Years' War, while the cross-bow, though slower in rate of firing, was as deadly. Cannon battered the knights' strongholds into submission

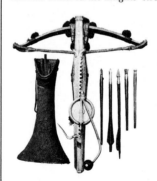

*English longbowmen at practice. The longbow, introduced by Edward I, was the foundation of English success in the Hundred Years' War*

*A German cross-bow, with quiver and bolts, made in about 1570. Bows of this type had been banned by the pope from being used against Christians. But this prohibition was short-lived*

*The proudly walled castle of the Middle Ages was doomed by the introduction of artillery. In this painting of the siege of Ribodane in France in about 1480, old siege methods are shown combined with the new; siege towers and ladders are still in use, but it is the cumbersome bombards (left) which are battering down the walls for the attackers*

# The gunpowder revolution

when they were supported by dismounted men-at-arms and protected by hedges of stakes, they were more than a match for the mounted knights of France. Swiss pikemen, reverting to phalanx-type formations bristling with long pikes, crushed the Hapsburg knights at Sempach in 1386.

Suits of plate armour and horse armour became increasingly complex in a vain attempt to counter the arrow and the pike, but the gallant knight, galloping into battle on his charger, was doomed. His end finally came with the introduction of fire-arms.

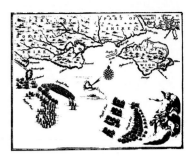

*The defeat of the Spanish Armada in 1588 demonstrated the superiority of English naval design and the superb leadership of the country's admirals*

## Guns and gunpowder

Guns were first fired in action at the siege of Metz in 1324, and were increasingly used during the Hundred Years' War between

*The Battle of Lepanto in 1571 saw the eclipse of Turkish naval power by the combined fleets of Spain and Venice*

England and France. They were bombards, crude wrought-iron cannon which could shoot large stones or iron balls.

The Chinese had used gunpowder as a noise-maker on the battlefield, and may even have used rockets in the early 1200's, but gunpowder was not introduced in the West until over a century later. The new weapons made traditional castles virtually useless against a determined attacker; few walls could withstand a persistent cannonade from even the crudest of artillery. Hand-guns soon appeared, and with them came a new

*An engraving of the Battle of Nieuport between the Dutch and the Spanish in Flanders in 1600, gives an impression of the 17th-century battlefield. Rival regiments of cavalry advance, while in the centre, tercios (brigades) of infantrymen are drawn up. Each tercio was made up of musketeers and pikemen; the artist has stylised the pikes as haystack shapes*

---

### SHIPS BUILT TO MASTER THE OCEANS

The earliest-known fighting ship was the oar-powered galley; this, however, was only suitable for use in sheltered waters, and sailing ships eventually replaced it. In late medieval times, single-masted converted merchantmen were used to carry troops in time of war, and out of these, men-of-war evolved. The first sailing ships designed specifically for fighting were built by the Portuguese, who were also the first nation to fit their fleets out with cannon. Both innovations were soon copied by other maritime powers

*The* Peter, *a four-masted warship built for Henry VIII. English designers were the first to pierce the sides of vessels for cannon, making possible several decks of guns, which together formed a broadside*

*The Dutch were skilled in designing and constructing warships, particularly in the 17th century. During three wars against Britain from 1652 onwards, they came close to winning mastery of the Channel*

*HMS* Victory, *launched in 1765 at a cost of $161,694 was reputed to be the fastest-sailing 'three decker' of her day. She was used as a flagship by many admirals, and won fame at Trafalgar in 1805, when Nelson was fatally wounded on her flag-deck*

type of army based on contract instead of feudal duty. Though soldiers needed far less training to use guns, only the state could afford the cost of making muskets and cannon on a large scale. So armies became larger, long-term forces, whose allegiance was to the state rather than to feudal lords. Ambitious nobles could now be easily crushed.

## The rise of Spain

France and Spain were the chief military rivals of the 16th century, but the Spanish soon outstripped the French in military skill. Spain's close-packed *tercios*, or brigades, of pikemen and musketeers were the terror of Europe. A *tercio* was made up of three columns, or *colonellos*, each commanded by a colonel. Each consisted of 1250 men. Cavalry kept some armour, but wielded swords rather than lances, and were soon being equipped with horse arquebuses, ancestors of the pistol.

Spanish artillery was the most efficient in Europe, and an important result of the growing power of cannon was a revolution in fortifications. Towers and walls gave way to squat, deeply entrenched fortresses. Following the

*A handbook by Marshal Vauban illustrates siege techniques. Vauban built forts for Louis XIV of France*

and tactical skill of the English defeated the Spanish Armada in 1588.

## Land warfare transformed

Armies grew as nations became wealthier in the 17th century. The new tactics that fire-arms demanded required longer training; it was cheaper, too, and more efficient to have regular forces which could campaign all the year round, and garrison long frontiers. Gustavus Adolphus, King of Sweden, led the way, forming the first truly

modern army, and reforming his cavalry and artillery. But it was France which became mistress of Europe, for by 1691 Louis XIV had over 400,000 men under arms. Only a rich monarchy and an able central administration could produce and control forces of this order, and Louis was well served by Louvois and Colbert, ministers who reformed the army and navy and raised the taxes to support them. As a result Bourbon France enjoyed 50 years of almost continuous military success on land in pursuit of *la gloire* and its 'natural frontiers' – the only one which was unattained was the Rhine.

Governments grew wary of major battles; casualties had soared dramatically when the improved flintlock muskets and socket bayonets replaced the slower matchlock and the pike. Louis encouraged his marshals to wage wars of manoeuvres and sieges, and his military engineer Vauban perfected the design of fortifications.

Vauban's bastions, supplemented by numerous outworks, were copied, as was his method of attacking a stronghold by sapping and mining. Great chains of fortresses were built; France's frontiers were ringed by more than 300. But

in the end French ambitions were defeated by a coalition organised by England; the coalition's armies were led by John Churchill, 1st Duke of Marlborough.

Mobility and firepower were the order of the day. Infantry, formed into platoons 40 strong, produced withering small-arms fire, and when under attack by cavalry formed into hollow squares. Every regiment had grenadiers, and artillery was integrated more closely with the infantry. The cavalry, armed only with swords, were sent into battle at a manageable trot instead of racing at a headlong gallop.

## Russia, Prussia and France

The first half of the 18th century

*Marlborough at the Battle of Blenheim. His tactical flair defeated Louis XIV's attempt to win mastery of Europe*

*Gustavus Adolphus, King of Sweden from 1611 to 1632, made his country a great power. His revolutionary military ideas were widely copied.*

defeat of the Moors in Spain in 1492, Spanish adventurers sought action further afield, and it was largely the possession of fire-arms and horses that enabled Cortez to conquer Aztec Mexico and Pizarro to subjugate Inca Peru at the head of only a few score of men. Spain's new overseas empire led to the development of towering galleons to ply the Atlantic in *flotas*, or treasure fleets, escorted by warships. Naval warfare, however, was revolutionised by the English in war against Spain, and later the Dutch in the 17th century.

Henry VIII introduced threemasted warships with sides pierced to take cannon, and by Elizabeth I's reign naval architects had produced smaller, more manoeuvrable vessels, whose tactics were based on evasion and long-range gunnery. The superior seamanship

## FIRE-ARMS REVOLUTIONISE WAR

Fire-arms were first introduced into European armies in the 14th century. Their main advantage over the bow was that it took far less time to train a soldier to use them; early fire-arms were less accurate than bows, however, and had a slower rate of fire. The first nation to exploit the potential of fire-arms was France, which used them in the 15th century to gain final victory in the Hundred Years' War against England. The English clung to the longbow as their main infantry weapon until well into the 16th century. The Swiss, the leading mercenaries in Europe, also affected to despise firearms, relying instead on the pikes with which they had crushed the Hapsburg knights at the Battle of Sempach in 1386. The introduction of fire-arms meant that only kings could afford the cost of equipping armies, and so they became stronger at the expense of their nobles

*This double-barrelled wheel-lock pistol was made in about 1542 for Emperor Charles V, ruler of Spain and Germany. A spring mechanism set in motion a wheel, which rubbed against a metal arm coated with iron pyrites, and the resultant spark lit the charge in the flash pan. Less accurate than the musket and firing a shorter distance, pistols were mainly used by cavalry*

*A Flemish matchlock, dating from the early 17th century. It took its name from the slow-burning match held in a metal arm on the side of the gun. When the trigger was pulled, the arm descended to plunge the match into the touch-hole*

*Flintlock muskets, like this double-barrelled piece made for Louis XIV of France, were at first mainly used for hunting. But by the late 17th century they were being widely used in battle. The musket was fired when a revolving flint held in the cocking mechanism struck the metal firing pan to create a spark*

*For over a century, from 1720 onwards, the 'Brown Bess' musket – probably so-called because its barrel was coated with iron oxide to turn it brown – was the standard British fire-arm and became the favourite weapon of the British infantry in many battles. Weighing 12 lb. and with a 42 in. barrel, it could be fired at least twice in a minute. The ball it used weighed an ounce*

*A 17th-century matchlock musketeer in his firing position. Because of its weight, the gun had to be supported on a forked rest. The weapon had an effective range of under 100 yds, and its rate of fire was only one shot every two minutes*

*This carbine, its barrel 'rifled' with seven spiral grooves to give greater accuracy, was issued to British cavalry from 1792 to 1839. It was fitted with a fixed bayonet which a rider used for fighting at close quarters when dismounted*

# Moving towards total war

The 1863 Battle of Gettysburg was one of the key clashes between North and South in the American Civil War. In this painting, a column of Southern prisoners is led away into captivity while battle still rages. The war was the first great struggle between conscript armies, and the North's victory was a triumph for industrial methods applied to war

saw the rise of Russia and Prussia as military powers. By 1716 the 'westernising' policies of Peter the Great had created a Russian army of 300,000 men and a fleet of almost 40 vessels. In this work he was helped by French, Scottish and German advisers, and by the time of his death, after wars with Sweden and Turkey, tsarist Russia reached from the Baltic to the Urals and the Black Sea.

The Prussian army grew from 30,000 men in 1713 to 130,000 in 1740, and Frederick the Great improved its weapons, training and discipline and created an aristocratic officer caste. Prussian bravery became a byword. Frederick's generalship was based on a mastery of tactics and his methods and reforms were widely copied, especially in France.

British redcoats clash with American colonists in the American War of Independence. The colonists surprised Europe by defeating Britain's regulars

Military reforms in the France of Louis XVI bore full fruit after the explosion of the French Revolution in 1789. But there was a difference. For the first time, an entire nation rallied to arms in defence of its ideals. The cry of la patrie en danger, 'the country in danger', swept through the towns and villages of France. Men rallied to the colours in the first-ever 'people's war'. Lazare Carnot, Minister of War, introduced mass conscription. Promotion was awarded solely on merit. The whole of France's society and economy were geared to the concept of a 'nation in arms'.

## Genius of Napoleon

Eventually, the superiority of the new Republican armies began to tell, and new leaders began to emerge – pre-eminent among them Napoleon Bonaparte, who began his rise to prominence at the siege of Toulon in 1793.

Time and again Napoleon defeated every European opponent. In 1804 he became emperor, and years of success followed. Austria was crushed at Austerlitz in 1805; Prussia was humbled at Jena and Auerstadt the next year, and in 1807 Russia came to terms after defeats at Eylau and Friedland. Only in Spain, where Napoleon delegated command to his marshals, did his Grande Armée taste

Napoleon crossing the Alps in 1800, portrayed by the painter Jacques Louis David. At its peak, Napoleon's empire dominated Europe, Britain alone holding out

### THE CORSICAN AND THE DUKE

The onset of the age of total war was accompanied by the emergence of one of the greatest generals of modern history – Napoleon Bonaparte. Napoleon, born in Corsica, was not an innovator, but primarily an executive genius, who gained his great victories by enveloping his opponents, or by driving a wedge between his foes before defeating them one by one. He reorganised his artillery into a potent weapon of war. More important still, he gave the French such confidence in themselves that he was able to win many battles against numerically superior forces. Speed and the ruthless exploitation of success were further ingredients of Napoleon's strategy. But in 1812 he lost the flower of his army in Russia, and three years later he met his final defeat at Waterloo

Arthur Wellesley, Duke of Wellington, leads his troops forward at Waterloo. Wellington's defeat of Napoleon on June 18, 1815, with the aid of the Prussians under Blücher, ended the French emperor's career. Earlier, Wellington had fought in India, and during the Peninsular War in Spain from 1808 to 1814 he had shown his qualities of generalship by defeating many French armies; but Waterloo was his only clash with Napoleon in person

*A group of officers and soldiers of Frederick the Great's army. Prussia's troops were renowned for their strict drill and their savage discipline*

defeat. Napoleon's 'Spanish ulcer' was to prove a fatal drain on French military strength; while the Royal Navy, led by great sailors such as Nelson, became supreme at sea after the Battle of Trafalgar in 1805 and kept Britain's shores safe from French invasion.

The disastrous invasion of Russia in 1812 was the turning-point in Napoleon's career. Driven back into Germany, Napoleon's unwilling Prussian and Austrian allies turned against him. Defeat at Leipzig (1813) was followed by abdication in 1814. Napoleon returned the next year, but suffered

## FASTER FIRING

Fire-arms developed rapidly in the 19th century. The main purpose was to increase their rate of fire

*The mechanism of the Dreyse needle gun, standard weapon of the Prussian infantry*

*The American arms firm founded by Samuel Colt produced this rifle in 1836. Its rate of fire was improved by the use of a rotating chamber*

*The Maxim 'cartridge magazine rifle' of the late 19th century. This weapon was the first real machine gun, and its future development ended the dominance of cavalry on the battlefield*

his final defeat at Waterloo at the hands of Wellington and Blücher.

The time of Napoleon saw the perfection of the divisional system in the French army, which was imitated by others. Armies could now move in a number of separate units and not just as one lumbering mass. Light infantry, fighting as skirmishers, preceded advancing columns bristling with bayonets, though the British fought in line with telling effect. All armies adopted lighter artillery. Britain was in the forefront of the field. Congreve developed rockets, first used in an attack on Boulogne in 1806, and Henry Shrapnel, a British officer, invented the shell, packed with explosive and projectiles, to which he gave his name.

### Technology advances
The 19th century saw great technological advances in the wake of the Industrial Revolution. The American Civil War, waged from 1861 to 1865, was the first great struggle between armies made up largely of conscripts. The war saw the introduction of cannon whose barrels were rifled to give greater accuracy, and the replacement of muzzle-loading smooth-bore muskets by faster-firing breech-loading rifles, some of which were magazine-fed. These new weapons greatly increased the power of defensive and field fortifications, and entrenchments took on a new importance. Attacking troops had to modify their tactics to avoid high casualties. Cavalry became increasingly regarded as mounted infantrymen, and large-scale cavalry actions became rare. Railways had a profound influence on strategy, making possible the rapid transfer of forces.

In Europe, the Franco-Prussian War of 1870–1 was similarly affected by railways and technology. Prussia was able to mobilise over 400,000 men in the first three weeks of the war, compared to France, with less than 250,000. Equipment continued to improve; important advances included breech-loading artillery which could fire longer, streamlined shells, smokeless powder which made it difficult to pinpoint artillery positions, machine guns, and metal cartridges with pointed noses.

As the 19th century ended, most nations hastened to copy the German General Staff system for administering large armies, based

*The multiple-barrelled French mitrailleuse, used in the Franco-Prussian War, was an ancestor of the machine gun*

*The Anglo-Boer War in South Africa (1899–1902) saw British regulars hard put to defeat Boer farmers, seen here with a captured mountain gun*

on special training colleges. But it took the defeats meted out by Boer farmers in the Anglo-Boer War to shake British complacency and inspire similar changes – though some reforms had been introduced after the Crimean War, 50 years earlier. Khaki uniforms finally replaced red coats on active service, and in 1904 the war's lessons led to the adoption of a British General Staff, a modernisation of training and the creation of a new force, the Territorial Army.

Great advances were being made, meanwhile, in naval design, particularly by Britain. Gunnery was transformed by new recoil mechanisms which made the most of the discovery of TNT to fire huge shells over great distances.

### CIVIL WAR IN AMERICA

From 1861 to 1865 the armies of the North and South fought a bloody civil war in America. The war saw great improvements in armaments and defensive and offensive tactics. The North's numerical superiority, its naval blockade and its industrial strength brought it victory

*In 1862 a new era of naval warfare dawned, when two steamships, the Confederate* Merrimac *and the Northern* Monitor *clashed in Hampton Roads in the first battle between two iron-clads*

*Appeals to Northern patriotism by 'Uncle Sam' were widely used in the opening period of the war. But conscription was soon introduced to swell the ranks of the volunteer Union Army*

Improved torpedoes, propelled by compressed air, brought into being the destroyer and torpedo boat, while the development of diesel and electric engines led to the first fully effective submarines.

### Modern warfare
The major wars of the 20th century have been fought on a scale larger than any others in history. The costs have been far higher, both in casualties and materials. The economic output needed to wage modern war on a world scale has drawn whole populations into the war effort, and since the advent of bomber aircraft even civilians at home have been in the front line. Technology has advanced so rapidly that weapons have often been made ineffective or obsolete soon after being brought into use. Because of its global scale, the Second World War cost an estimated 1,150 billion dollars, more than five times as much as the First.

The First World War of 1914–18 was confidently expected to be over in a few months. But it soon settled into a massive stalemate on the Western Front, a struggle in which armies laid siege to each other's trench systems across a no-man's-land strung with barbed wire and dominated by machine guns and heavy artillery. It was not until after the invention of the tank by the British that the stalemate of trench warfare was eventually broken in 1918.

Air warfare was a major development. Aircraft were used first as artillery spotters, but soon fighters were introduced, and then aircraft specially designed to carry bombs. Strategic bombing was originally a German idea. Lighter-than-air Zeppelins and long-range bombers were used in raids on London and other cities, but the threat was more to civilian morale than to industrial potential. At sea, the inconclusive Battle of Jutland in 1916 proved to be the last old-style fleet action; but far more significant, and potentially more deadly, was the war waged by German submarines against British shipping. Submarine warfare reached a peak in 1917, when Britain was almost starved into defeat. Only the adoption of the convoy system saved the situation.

### War on a global scale
Out of 65 million men mobilised

*The battleship* Dreadnought, *launched in 1904, made all others obsolete and began a naval race between Britain and imperial Germany*

# BRITONS

"WANTS"

## YOU

### JOIN YOUR COUNTRY'S ARMY!

#### GOD SAVE THE KING

*Britain's Minister of War in 1914, Lord Kitchener of Khartoum, urges his countrymen to enlist to fight in France*

Warfare became truly global in the Second World War, during which the theatre of battle was wider-ranging than ever before and only a handful of nations could remain uncommitted to the struggle. Civilian populations were totally involved. In Nazi Germany, long before war broke out, the whole economy was planned for war. But this was to be a war of a new type – the blitzkrieg, or 'lightning war', in which fast-moving armies, led by tanks and backed by the overwhelming air power of the Luftwaffe, would smash the enemy armies. Only after Hitler's invasion of Russia in 1941 did his panzers become bogged down.

The most important single factor of the Second World War proved to be air power; without control of the skies no commander could win victory on the land. At sea, the battleship became obsolete, its place being taken by the aircraft carrier. A new and decisive factor in war was the massive 'combined

operation' – the co-ordination of land, sea and air units into a single, cohesive force for assaults such as the invasion of North Africa. Such an operation as this would have been impossible without a protective umbrella of air power. Similarly at sea, carrier-borne air power became decisive, as the Japanese success in crippling the American fleet at Pearl Harbour in 1941 amply demonstrated.

Since the Second World War, which was ended by the dropping of atomic bombs on the Japanese cities of Hiroshima and Nagasaki, the pattern of warfare has changed again. The great powers have developed sophisticated weapons systems, based on nuclear warheads, which are capable of wiping out entire cities from thousands of miles away. Russia and the United States, armed with huge nuclear arsenals, now hold a delicate balance of power, based on the knowledge of the devastation their weapons could wreak on a global

*An American Atlas missile rises. The dawn of the age of rockets armed with nuclear warheads revolutionised war*

scale. In this situation, the great powers have steered clear of head-on collisions with one another. Wars have been confined to limited areas of the globe, and the typical form of warfare has become that of subversive and guerrilla-type operations, with few pitched battles.

to fight in the First World War, 36 million were killed or wounded. But out of the carnage of war came rapid technological progress. As each nation mobilised its industry, new inventions were seized on. Many of these were later to be applied to civilian uses.

---

## FIRST WORLD WAR

The main protagonists of the First World War of 1914–18 were Germany, Austria and Turkey, who fought against the British Empire, France, Italy, Russia and, from 1917, the United States. The war was expected to be over within a few months but, on the Western Front in France, it soon developed into a stalemate, dominated by vast trench systems. Offensive after offensive launched to break through these defences failed. In 1918, the Germans pushed back the Allied line in the west; but their exhausted army was defeated by Allied counterblows

*The Battle of Jutland in 1916 was the biggest clash of the war between the British and German fleets. It ended without a decision, but the German High Seas Fleet, having returned to port, sailed again only to surrender to the Allies in November 1918*

*Troops in their trenches. Trench warfare lasted from late 1914 until virtually the end of the war, despite many offensives such as those of the Somme and Verdun*

*The invention of the tank resolved the stalemate of trenches, barbed wire and machine guns. The tanks' first major success was the British attack at Cambrai on 1917*

*Germany's U-boat fleet almost succeeded in starving Britain into surrender in 1917*

*In an attempt to break the deadlock of trench warfare, the German army used chlorine gas in its attacks during the second Battle of Ypres in 1915. Though unprepared at first, the Allies soon developed gas-masks and gas precautions, and it was found that the cumbersome equipment that the attacking troops had to wear made them still more vulnerable to the defenders' machine gun fire. The Germans used an even more destructive and deadly gas – Phosgene – against the French at Verdun in 1916, but still failed to break through*

---

## SECOND WORLD WAR

The most important single factor of the Second World War proved to be air power. Without control of the skies, no commander could win victory on land or sea. Thus the Battle of Britain thwarted Hitler's planned invasion

*The Messerschmitt 109 was the main weapon of the German fighter squadrons in the Battle of Britain. It had already been battle-tested in the Spanish Civil War and, in various versions, remained the mainstay of the Luftwaffe until 1945*

*The Hurricane, together with the Spitfire, won the decisive victory of the Battle of Britain. But, despite the bravery of the 'Few', the battle could not have been won without the British invention of radar*

*From 1942 onwards Lancasters of Bomber Command struck at the towns and cities of Germany with ever-increasing force. However, the effect of the RAF's indiscriminate blanket-bombing of urban centres to destroy German industry is still disputed*

*The long-range American B29 – nicknamed 'Superfortress' – was the most formidable bomber to be developed in the war. An earlier Boeing, the B17, or 'Flying Fortress', had been used against Germany; the B29 struck at Japan*

*Hitler's second 'vengeance weapon' – the V2 rocket – stands on its launching pad. The V2 was the first long-range rocket to be used in warfare, and is the ancestor of the intercontinental missiles of today*

*On August 9, 1945, an awesome mushroom cloud over Nagasaki signalled the explosion of the second atomic bomb to be used in war. Most of the city was destroyed. The first bomb was dropped on Hiroshima three days earlier; 78,150 Japanese died*

# Part 4

# THE NATIONS OF THE WORLD

## An A–Z historical gazetteer

*The explosion of nationalist and democratic sentiment that began with the American and French Revolutions has led today to a complex and fragmented world of more than 150 distinct states. Long-established European dynasties and modern colonial empires have alike fallen apart under the fierce blast of the people's will to govern themselves. New nations have been forged on the basis of common attachments to language, race, religion, territory or way of life.*

*In the tumult of change that has resulted from the drive towards national 'self-determination', frontiers have been revised, names of countries altered, new forms of government adopted. But even the newest states are heirs to the past, through the histories of the individual peoples who inhabit them. These histories stretch back through successive civilizations to the beginnings of human society.*

# Tiny island-states and gigantic 'super-powers'

Since 1945 the map of the world has largely been redrawn, as four centuries of European dominance have come to an end. But as the great European empires have split up into dozens of successor states, so the powerful embrace of Western industrial civilization has drawn the peoples of the globe closer together. And despite the triumph of nationalism today, which has given statehood even to some of the smallest of the world's communities, the idea of larger groupings of people has not vanished. Various international organisations have been set up, many of them on a continental basis, in which countries are relinquishing some part of their sovereignty for the sake of common political, cultural or economic interests.

## North America: powerhouse of modern technology

It has taken 400 years for settlers of mainly European stock to tame North America, to harness its resources and to create the powerhouse and prototype of 20th-century technological civilization. Of the continent's two giant territories, the United States has grown during the present century into the world's richest and most powerful nation. America's wealth is a magnet to the world, much of which remains poor and backward. Emergent countries wish to learn the secret of American 'knowhow'; yet they are often reluctant to accept the system of capitalist democracy which, Americans affirm, is the basis of their prosperity.

Canada is bigger than the United States, but its population is barely more than a tenth. Canada cannot yet match the power of its neighbour; but its international trade, natural resources and highly developed industries make it one of the world's most advanced countries.

## Emergence of a new Europe

Political ideologies originating in Europe have, since 1945, split the continent and the world. The liberal and democratic countries of western Europe, weakened by two great wars and the loss of their colonial empires, have looked to the United States for support against the Soviet Union, far and away the strongest power on the European continent and 'bastion' of revolutionary Communism. The Soviet Union,

inheritor of the old Russian Empire of the tsars, extending across northern Asia to the Pacific, rivals the United States as a 'super-power' on account of its size, its population and its economic and military strength. The powers of western Europe, with the loss of empire, have fallen back on their long-established role as international traders and manufacturers. At the same time, an increasing amount of trade is carried on amongst the European nations themselves, within the powerful economic bloc of the Common Market.

## Instability and growth in Latin America

The Spanish and Portuguese empires in the New World once stretched from California to Cape Horn. These Catholic European cultures left as deep an imprint on their successor states as did Protestant England on North America. Latin America's 150 years of independence have brought little prosperity to the mass of its peoples, whose meagre living standards are now further threatened by a population explosion which rivals that of parts of Asia. Political instability has been the curse of the area, with

coups, dictatorships, assassinations, revolutions and bitter factionalism. In recent years Latin America's giant, Brazil, has entered the first stage of an industrial revolution which, together with Mexico's impressive record of growth, points the way to a more hopeful future for the region.

## Africa's road to independence

Of all the world's continents Africa has seen the most dramatic political changes since the end of the Second World War. Many of the new states of Africa, although maintaining the often arbitrary boundaries of the colonial era, have departed from the systems of parliamentary government that they inherited from their former rulers. Older traditions have been more powerful in shaping the political structures of the new nations. In the Muslim north, the pull towards the sister Arab nations of the Middle East has been strong; while in Black Africa south of the Sahara, tribalism has threatened the unity of the states and often made democratic forms of government unworkable. In spite of this, a strong African consciousness has emerged, finding political expression in the Organisation of African Unity, and strengthened by hostility to the European-dominated states of southern Africa, which remain the most highly developed territories of the continent.

## Population explosion in Asia

The largest and most populous of all the continents is also the centre of two major world problems. There is the pressure of an exploding population upon inadequate resources, particularly in India. And there is the clash between Communism and Western interests, highlighted by the Vietnam war and the emergence of the world's most populous country, China, as a leading Communist power.

But while hundreds of millions of peasant cultivators struggle for survival in conditions not greatly changed for many centuries, the east Asian islands of Japan have made rapid and spectacular progress. Adopting Western techniques but retaining the mould of a traditional society, the Japanese have achieved world status as an industrial and trading power.

Across the north of the continent stretches the Asiatic part of the Soviet Union, its 3000 mile border with China a potential friction-point between these two great rival claimants to leadership of world Communism. South-west Asia, where the continent joins Muslim Africa and Mediterranean Europe, is another area of international tension: here Arab faces Israeli in seemingly endless hostility. The world's need for the region's oil gives it a vital importance.

## Australasia: prosperity based on agriculture

The largely barren island-continent of Australia, discovered late in history, is today the home of a prosperous and sophisticated Western culture, concentrated largely on the south-eastern fringe of the continent. Australia's wealth, like that of New Zealand, 1200 miles to the south-east across the Tasman Sea, is based largely on the efficient large-scale export of agricultural products to the rest of the world, and in particular to Britain, whose peoples were largely responsible for settling the region.

## The search for world unity

The United Nations was founded in 1945 to provide a forum for the nations of the world and to uphold international peace and security. But great-power rivalries, lack of funds, and the proliferation in the General Assembly of new nations speaking with many conflicting voices, have weakened the organisation's effectiveness and caused it to fall short of the world's hopes at the time of its foundation. In the field of welfare, however, UN agencies such as the World Health Organisation (WHO) and the United Nations Educational and Scientific Organisation (UNESCO) have substantial achievements to their credit.

*The world's 3800 million people occupy about 57,510,000 square miles of land. The largest country is the USSR, with over 8,640,000 square miles; in industrial and military strength it ranks as a 'super power'. The smallest country is Vatican City, a mere 0.17 square miles. Of over 150 sovereign states, more than half have gained their independence since 1945. These new states include countries as tiny as the island of Nauru in the south-western Pacific—only 8.25 square miles, with a population of 8000*

AFGHANISTAN    ANDORRA
ALBANIA        ANGOLA
ALGERIA       ARGENTINA

# Afghanistan

The mountainous, land-locked country of Afghanistan did not develop a national identity until the 18th century. Before that time, its lands served as little more than a cross-roads for conquerors and empire builders. They were part of the Persian Empire until *c.* 500 BC, and then eventually became part of Alexander the Great's vast conquests. After his death the country was ruled by other foreign overlords such as the Persians and Mughals until 1747, when the native-born Ahmad Shah established Afghanistan as an independent kingdom.

**Wars and reforms** Russia's advance into central Asia led Britain to secure the north-western frontier of its Indian empire by invading Afghanistan. In the First Afghan War (1838–42) a British army occupied Kabul, but it was forced to retreat; only 20 survivors reached India. Fear of Russian penetration again led Britain to make war on Afghanistan in 1878–9, and in 1881 a new ruler, Abdurrahman Shah, came to power with British financial backing. He carried out reforms, and brought the country's rebellious tribes under firm government control.

Abdurrahman's successor, Habibullah, aroused the hostility of his Muslim subjects by remaining neutral in the First World War, instead of fighting on the side of the Muslim Turks, and he was assassinated in 1919. The new ruler, Amanullah, attacked the Indian frontier in order to arouse Afghan patriotism, but was speedily defeated by the British. At home, his reforms made him so unpopular that in 1929 civil war broke out and he was forced to flee the country.

Zahir Shah came to the throne in 1933. During the 1960's he introduced reforms to give the people of Afghanistan more voice in government, and settled an old dispute with Pakistan. But discontent grew, and in 1973 the king was deposed. A republic was formed, with General Sardar Mohammed Daud as president.

250,000 sq. miles
18,714,000 people
Capital: Kabul

*Abdurrahman came to the throne of Afghanistan with British support in 1881. He established a firm central government for the first time in Afghan history*

# Albania

In recent years this tiny Communist republic has achieved an importance out of proportion to its size, as a result of its role in the ideological quarrel between the USSR and China, in which Albania – though part of the Russian bloc – has openly sided with China.

Subjected throughout their history to foreign conquest and interference, the Albanian people have somehow always managed to preserve a distinct identity. Once part of the Roman and Byzantine empires, the country was later invaded by Slavic tribes and was absorbed in the 9th century by Bulgaria. The Turks conquered it in the early 15th century and ruled it until 1912, when the Albanians rebelled and proclaimed their independence.

**Dictatorial rule** After the revolt of 1912, the great powers – Britain, France, Russia, Austria, Hungary, Germany and Italy – intervened and placed a German prince, William of Wied, on the throne. William arrived in the country in March 1914, but in September he was forced to flee.

After renewed internal struggle, Ahmed Zogu became Albania's first president in 1925 and its first king in 1928, taking the title of Zog I and ruling with dictatorial powers. Zog made trade agreements with Italy and encouraged Italian investment, but in 1939 Mussolini ordered the invasion of Albania and Zog was forced into exile. Italian and later German occupation lasted until the winter of 1944.

After the Germans withdrew, Communist partisans, under the leadership of Enver Hoxha, established the Albanian People's Republic. After Stalin's death, Albania – still led by Hoxha – refused to follow the new Soviet leaders in denouncing his policies. Albanian support for China in its ideological quarrel with the USSR led to the breaking off of diplomatic relations between Albania and the USSR in 1961.

11,100 sq. miles
2,432,400 people
Capital: Tirana

*The Albanian Communist leader, Enver Hoxha, greets the Chinese premier, Chou En-lai. The Chinese gave Albania economic aid after its break with the USSR*

*A mid-19th century view of Trajan's triumphal arch in the Roman city of Timgad in Algeria. Founded by Emperor Trajan in AD 100, Timgad was destroyed by Berbers in the 7th century*

# Algeria

After more than a century of French rule, the oil-rich country of Algeria became an independent republic in 1962. First came a long and bloody colonial war which shook France itself to its foundations. Afterwards, once the political power struggle had been resolved, the government was faced with the problems of widespread poverty, an expanding population and an economy damaged by the mass exodus of French settlers.

**Early history** The country's turbulent past goes back to pre-Roman times, when it was inhabited by light-skinned nomadic tribesmen called Berbers. Though it later became part of the Carthaginian and Roman empires – the Romans conquered it in the 2nd century BC – the Berbers still clung fiercely to their independence. Roman and then Byzantine rule lasted until the end of the 7th century AD.

In the mid-7th century AD, Arab followers of Muhammad began to penetrate north-west Africa from the east, but it was not until the 11th century that full Arab rule began. The country's new Muslim rulers united Algeria with their other conquests, Morocco and southern Spain, to form a great Moorish empire.

**Home of pirates: 1500–1800** The Moors' African empire fell into decline in the 16th century when its rulers – fearing Christian Spain – called in Turkish mercenaries to protect them. Algiers and Oran became the haunt of the notorious Barbary pirates, who terrorised traders in the western Mediterranean until the end of the 18th century.

**Rule by France** France invaded Algeria in 1830. In a protracted conquest, the French Foreign Legion, founded in 1831 for service in Algeria, played a large part. French *colons* (settlers) followed and gained control of Algeria's best land.

After the Second World War, the nationalist leader Ferhat Abbas campaigned for an Algerian republic which would be federated with France. Although they made some concessions, the French firmly upheld the status of Algeria as an integral part of France.

In 1954, a group of nationalists, the FLN (Front de Libération Nationale), organised a rising against the French. Over half a million troops were moved into Algeria to crush the revolt, but in 1958 a moderate French government decided to negotiate. French military leaders in Algeria then seized power. Their coup caused the downfall of the Fourth Republic and General de Gaulle's return to power.

The colons, with their slogan *Algérie Française,* counted on de Gaulle's support, but he negotiated a cease-fire and finally granted Algeria independence in 1962. In France and Algeria, a secret army (the OAS) led by anti-Gaullist officers conducted a terrorist campaign against the Muslims. Over 900,000 of the 1 million colons emigrated to France, where, mostly settled in the south, they made up a powerful dissident minority.

919,685 sq. miles
16,374,000 people
Capital: Algiers

*The port of Algiers in an 18th-century print. For centuries Algiers was the base from which the Barbary pirates terrorised the Mediterranean. In the 1830's the French intervened to stop piracy, and went on to stake out an Algerian empire*

*A corporal of the French Foreign Legion, in full marching order. Founded in 1831, the Legion soon became a fertile source of romantic tales of adventure*

**Independent Algeria** Ben Bella, a leader of the FLN, was elected the country's first president. In 1965 Ben Bella was overthrown by a military revolt, led by Col. Houari Boumedienne. Opposition to the regime was suppressed. Relations with France temporarily worsened when the two countries failed to agree on the development of the Saharan oil and natural gas fields.

*Ben Bella won independence for Algeria in 1962, after years of war with France*

# Andorra

Picturesque scenery and duty-free goods attract thousands of tourists every year to Andorra, a tiny principality of gorges and valleys nestling in the eastern Pyrenees on the French and Spanish borders.

According to tradition, Charlemagne (AD 742–814) granted the Andorrans a charter of independence in return for their help in his wars against the pagan Moors. Andorra's present political system dates from 1278, when the Spanish Bishop of Urgel and the French Count of Foix were made co-princes of Andorra. The count's rights later passed to the kings and then the presidents of France.

As the price of its independence, Andorra pays a nominal tribute every two years of 960 francs to France and 460 pesetas to the Bishop of Urgel. Since 1868, administration has been carried on by the 'General Council of the Valleys'; the Council's 24 representatives are elected for four-year terms by residents of the country's six villages. Women won the right to vote in 1970.

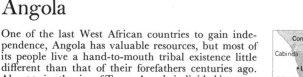

180 sq. miles
23,000 people
Capital: Andorra
la Vella

# Angola

One of the last West African countries to gain independence, Angola has valuable resources, but most of its people live a hand-to-mouth tribal existence little different than that of their forefathers centuries ago. About twice the size of Texas, Angola is divided into two separate parts. A small area of Angola called Cabinda lies north of the Congo River, squeezed between Congo to the north and Zaïre to the south. The larger part of Angola lies south of the Congo River. Tropical rain forests cover most of northern Angola, while the dry Moçámedes Desert is in the south.

The first European explorer to discover the area, Diogo Cão, claimed the region for Portugal when he landed at the mouth of the Congo River in 1483. During the next four centuries some 3 million Angolan Africans were sent as slaves to work for Portuguese colonists in Brazil. In 1951 Angola was made an overseas province of Portugal and given seven representatives in the Portuguese national assembly. Beginning in 1961 an independence movement sparked guerrilla warfare that engaged 50,000 Portuguese troops over the next 13 years. After Portugal's government was overthrown by a revolt in 1974, Angola was granted independence.

481,351 sq. miles
5,900,000 people
Capital: Luanda

# Argentina

Rich pastures and agricultural lands have helped to make Argentina wealthy. Yet for long after the Spanish navigator Juan Diaz de Solis discovered the country in 1516, while he was searching for a south-west passage to the Orient, Spain considered Argentina the least promising of its South American territories. Argentina's capital of Buenos Aires – today the third largest city in South America and one of the world's wealthiest ports – remained a muddy and inconspicuous town for many years after it was first founded by Pedro de Mendoza, a Spanish conquistador, in 1536.

**Declaration of independence: 1816** Buenos Aires had to defend itself against numerous attacks by the French, Portuguese and Dutch. The city rebelled against its Spanish rulers in 1810; the viceroy was deposed and a *Cabildo* (city council) set up. After armed struggle, independence was won from Spain in 1816.

1,073,700 sq. miles
24,766,000 people
Capital: Buenos
Aires

**Struggles for power** Civil war and anarchy followed independence. On one side were the merchants, the intellectuals and the townspeople of Buenos Aires, who wanted a centralised government dominated by Buenos Aires; on the other were the provincials, backed by the *gauchos*, wild, lawless cowboys of mixed Spanish and Indian blood, who roamed the country's *pampas* (plains). The provincials wanted the provinces to retain a large share of power within a federal form of government.

Gaucho support helped the provincials to overthrow the early 19th-century government of Juan Martin de Pueyrredon, and brought to power such *caudillos* (military strong men) as the gaucho chieftain Juan Quiroga, nicknamed 'the tiger of the plains', and Juan Manuel de Rosas. Rosas, twice dictator, was an army officer and a powerful landowner. The gauchos normally despised representatives of law and order and wealth, but they respected Rosas for his skill as a horseman.

**National constitution: 1853** General Justo José de Urquiza (1800–70) led an army revolt which overthrew Rosas in 1852, and the following year a national constitution was drawn up which united all the Argentine provinces. This constitution was accepted by Buenos Aires province in 1861.

For the first time the country was known as Argentina. Under General Bartolomé Mitre, who became president in 1862, and Domingo Sarmiento, president from 1868–74, Argentina flourished, attracting thousands of European immigrants.

**Political reforms: 1912** Backed by massive British investment, railways and roads were laid, telegraph and postal systems introduced, schools and libraries built. Foreign trade and investments grew and Argentina's trade expanded. But although the country was prospering at the turn of the century, it was still shackled by a small governing group of wealthy landowners which monopolised all political power.

The power of this group was eventually broken in 1912 by Roque Sáenz Péna, who pushed electoral reforms through the Argentinian Congress, making voting secret and compulsory for all men over 18. This brought to power the radical administrations of Hipolito Irigoyen from 1916–22 and 1928–30.

**Perón becomes dictator: 1946** A military coup that overthrew Irigoyen in 1930 marked a turning-point in Argentina's history. The military again became embroiled in politics, bringing to power in 1946 the dictator Juan Perón, an admirer of the fascist movements which had flourished in Germany and Italy. Perón introduced to South America a new type of popular dictatorship, based on the support of trade unions.

Perón seized newspapers, suppressed free speech and jailed his opponents. But at the same time he raised wages and reinforced the labour movement.

**Exile and return** Plans by Perón to legalise divorce and prostitution antagonised the Roman Catholic Church, and in 1955 church leaders, along with the navy and a part of the army, revolted. Perón resigned and fled to Spain. A series of military-dominated governments succeeded each other until the armed forces again took control in 1966, making Juan Carlos Onganía president. Political parties were abolished and labour demands for wage increases were rejected.

The commanders of the armed forces again moved in, ousting Onganía in June 1970, and appointing another of its generals, Roberto Marcelo Levingston, in his place. In 1971, Levingston was in turn removed in favour of another general, Alejandro Lanusse. But in 1972 Lanusse finally allowed Perón to return from exile, and in the 1973 elections the Perónist party candidate, Héctor Cámpora, was elected president. Cámpora later resigned, enabling Perón himself to become president.

Perón's dramatic return to power lasted only a short time. He died in 1974 and his widow, Isabel Martinez de Perón became president, the first woman chief of state in the Western Hemisphere.

*A gaucho in pursuit of a rhea, a type of ostrich. Above his head, the gaucho whirls a bolas, which, when released, tangles itself round the bird's feet and fells it*

*Under Bartolomé Mitre, president from 1862 to 1868, Argentina prospered, attracting European immigration and investment*

*The dictator Juan Perón, with his former wife, Eva (d. 1952). Perón was overthrown and exiled in 1955. But he retained a large following, and in 1973 he returned home in a successful bid to regain power*

# Australia

Opening up the Pacific in the 17th and 18th centuries was one of the last stages in the history of European exploration, and a direct consequence of it was the settling and development of the vast island-continent of Australia. Much of the western and northern coast had been mapped by Dutch explorers such as Janszoon and Tasman between 1606 and 1644, and the island came to be known as New Holland. It was not until 1770, however, that the east coast was charted by the Englishman James Cook. He formally took possession of the eastern half of the island, calling it New South Wales. The harsh, barren aspect of the land, which every explorer noted, had discouraged settlement for nearly 200 years, and the first Europeans did not establish a colony there until 1788.

2,967,909 sq. miles
13,467,400 people
Capital: Canberra

*Aborigines perform a ritual dance. A primitive people leading a simple material existence, the Aborigines were unable to withstand European domination*

**The Aborigines** The first Australians had, however, preceded these settlers by thousands of years; a unique, dark-skinned Stone Age people, the Australian Aborigines, had arrived from the Asiatic mainland via the islands of Indonesia about 30,000 years before. They were not numerous; when the white men arrived, there were probably fewer than a quarter of a million on the entire continent. The spread of white settlement and the resultant clashes between white and black took a heavy toll among the tribes; in Tasmania, the whole aboriginal population was wiped out by the middle of the 19th century. Today there are about 50,000 'full-bloods' (Aborigines of unmixed blood) in Australia, and there are signs that their numbers are at last increasing.

**Arrival of British settlers** Before the American War of Independence, Britain had disposed of many of its convicts by transporting them to the American colonies. But loss of the American colonies, together with the rise in crime that followed the Industrial Revolution, made Britain's convict problem a serious one. The government finally decided to send convicts to Botany Bay on the east coast of New South Wales.

The 'First Fleet' of eleven ships carried in all about a thousand settlers, of whom 736 were convicts. It arrived at Botany Bay in January 1788, but the first governor, Arthur Phillip, decided that the location was unsuitable. Within a few days, he fixed the new settlement at Port Jackson, a fine harbour a few miles to the north (the site of the future city of Sydney), where he established the colony of New South Wales.

*Convicts under guard break new land at Hobart in 1831. The convict system was not fully abolished until 1868*

**Early years** For the pioneers, the first years were marked by difficulties and privations. A tortuous and rugged range known as the Blue Mountains restricted settlement to the Cumberland Plain, a flattish, rather infertile region extending about 40 miles around Sydney. Barren soil, unsuitable seeds and farm implements, ignorance of agriculture and convict apathy made survival doubtful, and for many years the colonists had to rely on supplies from England. Later fleets brought food, but also more mouths to feed, and by 1810 there were about 12,000 people in the colony.

Phillip and his three successors also had to face the problem of the New South Wales Corps, a military unit specially recruited in England for service in the colony. Many of its officers, together with some of the colony's civil servants, had secured a virtual monopoly of trade, particularly in rum, from which they profited personally while the colony as a whole languished. Governor Bligh, of *Bounty* mutiny fame, attempted to put down this trafficking once and for all, but his firmness led to a revolt in 1808 – the 'Rum Rebellion'. On the twentieth anniversary of the colony's foundation, officers of the Corps arrested the governor and took over the administration. They remained in power until the arrival of Governor Lachlan Macquarie at the end of 1809.

*William Bligh was deposed as governor of New South Wales by the 'Rum Rebellion' of 1808*

**The Macquarie era** Macquarie's long rule was a turning-point for the colony. More free settlers arrived; the governor's ambitious building programme began to change Sydney from a frontier town into a city; the Blue Mountains were crossed in 1813, opening up the vast interior. Macquarie gave many convicts free pardons and grants of land. This policy led to social tension between the *emancipists* who had been transported and the *exclusives* who had never known bondage. Between 1810 and 1820, the population doubled, and in the newly opened-up territory Australia's most important primary industry, wool-growing, was established. The pioneer in this field had been John Macarthur, who introduced some of the first fine-wool merino sheep into New South Wales in 1797.

The growth of the wool industry produced problems. The need for shepherds and stockmen led to a stepping-up in the transportation of convicts, so that in the years before transportation to New South Wales was ended in 1840, the convict system was actually intensified. (The convict system was not finally abolished until 1868, in Western Australia.) There was also the new problem of 'squatting' – the unauthorised use of Crown lands by settlers for pasture. Not until 1847 did the squatters win recognition of their rights of occupation.

*In 1813 Gregory Blaxland became the first man to find a way across the Blue Mountains, which until then had barred exploration of Australia's interior*

**The outer settlements** Meanwhile the continent was developing in other directions. Penal outposts had been established in Van Diemen's Land (now known as Tasmania) in 1804 and at Moreton Bay (now the city of Brisbane) in 1824. Explorers such as Hume, Oxley and Sturt attacked the unknown interior and solved the riddle of the river network; the myth of a Great Inland Sea was disproved. Settlements of free colonists were established in Western Australia (at Perth in 1829), Victoria (at Melbourne in 1835) and South Australia (at Adelaide in 1836).

**Self-government** As settlement grew, demands arose that the form of government in New South Wales should be changed from what had been virtually autocratic control of an open-air jail to representative and finally fully responsible institutions. In 1823, a nominated Legislative Council was established and the Supreme Court was reformed. New South Wales was the only colony and included all the settlements until 1825, when Van Diemen's Land became a separate colony. New South Wales was granted limited self-government in 1842, and full self-government followed in 1854 and 1855 for all the colonies except Western Australia.

Matters stood thus for nearly another half-century; there was considerable rivalry and distrust between the colonies, and British proposals for federating them met with little support in Australia.

*Large numbers of merino sheep were introduced into New South Wales by John Macarthur in 1797. By 1850, there were 16 million sheep in Australia*

*The discovery of gold at Bathurst in New South Wales in 1851 sparked off the first Australian gold rush. Miners such as those shown left won the nickname 'diggers'*

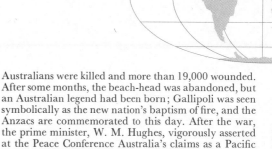

**Gold and wool** The rate of colonial development was dramatically accelerated with the discovery of gold by Edward Hargraves at Bathurst (New South Wales) in 1851, followed by further 'strikes' at Ballarat (Victoria) and other places in both colonies. Between 1851 and 1861, the total population trebled to over a million. The 'gold-rush' period is best remembered for the so-called Eureka incident. Many miners (or 'diggers') resented having to pay for licences, and they intensely disliked the methods of licence inspection and the way the goldfields were run. In December 1854, a mass burning of licences took place at the Eureka lode near Ballarat, and when troops were sent to restore order some miners barricaded themselves into a stockade under their own blue and white Southern Cross flag. In the brief siege that followed, about 30 miners were killed. After a public outcry, the arrested rebels were acquitted and the licence fee was reduced to a nominal sum. The Eureka incident later became an Australian folk legend.

The years that followed the gold rushes saw agitation for 'unlocking the lands', which it was widely believed were unfairly tied up for grazing while ex-miners were in need of farms. Land Acts were passed making purchase easier, but much of the country was simply not suitable for small farming. Wool still dominated the rural scene, and by 1890, over 100 million sheep were yielding 600 million pounds of wool for export; in addition, about 3 million acres were under crops. With the development of refrigeration, frozen meat could be exported, and by 1895 this amounted to nearly 4 million sheep and cattle carcasses.

**Australia comes of age** The 1880's and 1890's were in many ways a watershed in Australian history. They saw the first real beginnings of a national self-awareness in literature and art, in politics and social thought. The fame of Australians as a sporting nation dates from 1877, when the country played its first cricket Test with England. Agitation for the rights of organised labour resulted in the formation of the Australian Labor Party; parallel with this ran agitation against coloured immigration, especially by Chinese – a fear that had persisted since the gold-rush days. An anxiety to protect working and living standards underlay both movements. A unified Australia could clearly do more in this direction than six mutually suspicious colonial governments, and the social climate of the 1890's made federation a possibility at long last. A Federal Constitution was drawn up and accepted by the people in nation-wide referenda; it became law, symbolically, on the first day of the new century. The two-chamber Commonwealth Parliament met in Melbourne from 1901 to 1927, when it transferred to the new national capital, Canberra.

One of the first measures of the new legislature was the 1901 Immigration Restriction Act, which virtually banned coloured immigration. Perhaps equally important was the creation of the Commonwealth Arbitration Court in 1904. In a famous judgment three years later the court defined 'fair and reasonable wages' as those adequate for an average man 'regarded as a human being in a civilized community'. This concept of a 'basic wage' is one which governments, industry and organised labour have continued to accept.

**World War and after** The implications of the 'White Australia policy' had led to considerable friction concerning Australia's place within the British Empire, but when war broke out in Europe in 1914, differences were soon forgotten, and many thousands of young Australians volunteered for overseas service. They took part in operations on the Western Front and in the Middle East, but the best-remembered was the Gallipoli campaign of 1915. Here, units of the Australian and New Zealand Army Corps – the 'Anzacs' – landed with other Allied troops on April 25, with the objective of storming the Dardanelles and opening up a supply route to Russia. The campaign was disastrous; over 8000

*The outlaw-hero Ned Kelly wears home-made armour as protection against police bullets in this painting by Sidney Nolan, Australia's most famous artist*

Australians were killed and more than 19,000 wounded. After some months, the beach-head was abandoned, but an Australian legend had been born; Gallipoli was seen symbolically as the new nation's baptism of fire, and the Anzacs are commemorated to this day. After the war, the prime minister, W. M. Hughes, vigorously asserted at the Peace Conference Australia's claims as a Pacific power, and it received a League of Nations mandate over north-eastern New Guinea (now part of Papua New Guinea, which became semi-independent in 1973).

Between the two world wars Australia suffered economic difficulties; by 1933, one-third of the nation's work-force was unemployed. By the inter-war period a two-party system of government was fairly well established. The Labor Party has preserved its original name, with its American spelling, but non-Labor has been known by various names – Nationalist, United Australia Party and now the Liberal Party. During the 1920's, there developed a third group, the Country Party, whose objective was the protection of rural interests.

**Second World War** Australia went to war in 1939 as a small nation (7 million), yet with the sixth highest living standard in the world. It was now a dominion under the Statute of Westminster (1931), but the realities of the war in the Pacific soon showed that it could no longer rely exclusively on Britain for its own defence. The Second World War was therefore another turning-point, as Australian foreign policy and commercial interests now came to focus more on America than on Europe. Battles in New Guinea and the Coral Sea brought the war to Australia's doorstep; there was a brief shelling of Sydney, and Darwin was bombed.

**Post-war period** A Labor government was in power for most of the war, but post-war foreign policy was to a great extent shaped by the Liberal Party, which came to power under Robert Menzies in 1949 and remained in office for 23 years. The American alliance, the Cold War in Europe, the 1949 Communist take-over in China, Australia's insecure position in the Pacific, and the Liberal Party's own ideology, meant that there was preoccupation with halting the spread of Communism. From 1965 to 1971 Australian troops fought in South Vietnam in support of the Americans.

Only with the return of a Labor Government in December 1972, under Gough Whitlam, was the way paved for diplomatic recognition of Communist China, although there had long been lively trading between Australia and China. Whitlam's policies seemed to herald a vigorous new spirit of national self-awareness. Among his first acts were the ending of Australian participation in the British honours' lists, and of the reference to the Queen in the oath of allegiance. A new national anthem was adopted: 'Advance Australia Fair.'

**Growth and change** Since the war, European immigration has been encouraged in an effort to stimulate national development, and between 1951 and 1970 some 3 million 'New Australians' arrived. Many were from Mediterranean countries. This influx introduced Australians to new cultures and ideas, but also placed a strain on housing and education.

Australia can no longer be considered in rural terms alone; in 1970–1, agricultural products made up only a quarter of exports. Industry has made enormous progress since 1945, and the pattern has been further diversified by a boom in mineral exports and by strikes of oil and natural gas. The population of over 13 million has become largely concentrated in a narrow belt along the south-east coast, over a third of it in the huge urban complexes of Sydney and Melbourne. After 200 years, most of the continent remains as sparsely inhabited as it was when the white man first arrived.

*A recruiting poster urges young Australians to rally to Britain's aid in 1914. Australian troops won a formidable reputation in two world wars*

*Australia's prime minister for a total of 16 years, Sir Robert Menzies won fame as an elder statesman of the Commonwealth*

*Two Australian landmarks – Sydney Harbour bridge and the city's new opera house, which was opened in 1973*

# Austria

The republic of Austria was formed in 1918, out of the wreckage of the vast, sprawling, multi-national Austrian Empire which the Hapsburg family had ruled for over six centuries. Vienna, its capital, still reflects the country's past as one of the great powers of Europe in the ornate grandeur of its palaces, churches and museums.

Austrian influence owed as much to the country's intellectual and cultural achievements as to its imperial power. In the 18th, 19th and early 20th centuries, Vienna was the home of such composers as Mozart, Beethoven, Schubert, Brahms, Mahler, Schoenberg and, in a lighter vein, the 'waltz king' Johann Strauss; and it was there that Sigmund Freud developed his system of psycho-analysis.

32,374 sq. miles
7,568,400 people
Capital: Vienna

**Before the Hapsburgs** Man first settled in Austria in the Stone Age. By *c.* 500 BC this area was the centre of a flourishing Iron Age civilization.

Conquered by Rome in a campaign lasting from 15 BC to AD 10, it became part of the province of Noricum. But, as Roman power crumbled, the Romano-Celtic people who lived there were absorbed between the 4th to the 6th centuries by barbarian invaders, such as the Vandals, Visigoths and Huns.

In the 8th century, Austria became part of Charlemagne's realms. After his death it was again conquered – this time by the Magyars, who ruled it until their defeat by Otto the Great, ruler of Germany. In 976 Otto III made Leopold of Babenberg Austria's new ruler. Babenberg rule lasted until 1246. The kings of Bohemia tried to seize power in Austria, but they were thwarted by the arrival of a new force, the House of Hapsburg.

*The primitive tribes of Austria had become highly skilled in decorative art by c. 700 BC when this bronze statuette of a woman was made*

**The first Hapsburgs** By origin the Hapsburgs were a Swiss-Alsatian noble family, who held some land in Austria. In 1282, Rudolf of Hapsburg, a German king, defeated the Bohemians, and gave the provinces of Austria and Styria to his sons. From this base, the Hapsburgs gradually expanded their power by marriages with the Spanish and other royal families. By the end of the 15th century they were usually elected Holy Roman Emperors, and their own hereditary domains stretched over much of Europe.

Such an empire was not easy to hold together. Charles V concentrated on ruling Spain, the Netherlands and his Italian domains, and handed over control of Austria, Bohemia and Hungary to his brother, Ferdinand. In his will, he legalised this division of the empire. The threat of the Turks made the Austrian Hapsburgs the more determined to secure their territories in central Europe.

**Turkish menace: 1529–1683** The Turks first besieged Vienna in 1529 and the menace to central Europe that they represented was not removed until 1683, when a second major siege of Vienna was lifted by the Polish king, John Sobieski, who came to the aid of the emperor Leopold I. Because of their concern with the Turkish menace, the Hapsburgs abandoned their attempts to control the whole of Germany. Though they continued to be elected Holy Roman Emperors, their power was to a large extent confined to their hereditary lands. Even here the emperors were forced to make concessions to demands for autonomy by the Magyars in Hungary.

*Maximilian I (1493–1519) greatly expanded Hapsburg dominions through his marriage to Mary of Burgundy*

*Vienna besieged by the Turks in 1529. Though this attack was repulsed, the Hapsburg Empire was constantly threatened by the Turks in the 16th century*

**War of the Austrian succession: 1740–8** Charles VI (1711–40) had no male heir and, by the law of the empire, his daughter, Maria Theresa, could not succeed to the Hapsburg lands. Determined that she should, Charles drew up the 'Pragmatic Sanction' establishing her rights, which he persuaded all the European powers to sign. But after Charles's death the empire was invaded by Frederick the Great, ruler of Prussia, who conquered Silesia. France then intervened in support of a rival claimant to the imperial throne, Charles Albert of Bavaria. It was only after stubborn resistance, in alliance with Britain and Holland, that Maria Theresa won recognition of her title. Maria Theresa was an able ruler who, aided by her chief minister, Kaunitz, carried out many administrative reforms in the Austrian part of her empire. But, in order to gain support from the Magyars of Hungary in the war, she had to promise not to extend the reforms into Hungary.

**Enlightened despotism** When Maria Theresa died in 1780 she was succeeded by her son, Joseph II. Like her, he was an 'enlightened despot', but his impatient temperament led him to initiate far more sweeping reforms. He abolished serfdom and gave the liberated peasants security of tenure on the land they occupied, an act which won him the nickname of the *Volkskaiser* (people's emperor). But this and Joseph's other reforms – especially a move to limit the autonomy of Hungary – aroused great hostility, and just before his death in 1790 he was forced to revoke most of them.

**The great composers** During the reigns of Joseph II and his successors the arts flourished in Austria. The emperors patronised the *Burgtheater* (court theatre) and the opera in Vienna. There was also considerable support for composers from aristocrats throughout Austria. For most of his adult life the Austrian composer Mozart lived and worked in Vienna, while Count Esterhazy employed Mozart's compatriot Haydn as his court composer.

A later generation of musicians also benefited from aristocratic patronage. These included the German composer Beethoven, who worked in Vienna for the greater part of his life, and the Austrian Franz Schubert, whose melodic genius drew strength from the folk music of rural Austria and the street music of Vienna.

*Austria's enlightened queen, Maria Theresa, in a patriotic pose. Disputes over her right to the throne resulted in eight years of war*

*The young Mozart (1756–91) accompanies his father and sister. He wrote his first symphony at the age of eight; when he was 17, he had completed 25*

**War with Napoleon** Austria, like the rest of Europe, was profoundly affected by the French Revolution, especially since Marie Antoinette, the executed queen of France, was the emperor's sister. War between the two countries broke out in 1792. As a result of the long years of war that followed, the Hapsburgs were expelled from northern Italy and the Rhineland. Vienna was twice occupied by the armies of Napoleon, who overwhelmingly defeated Hapsburg forces at Austerlitz (1805) and Wagram (1809). Francis II was forced to give up the title of Holy Roman Emperor in 1806.

By the end of 1809, the Hapsburg Empire was weakened and humiliated. Its most positive asset in the years from 1809 to 1815 was the gifted diplomacy of Prince Metternich (1773–1859).

*Linked by marriage to the Bourbons of France, Austria's rulers were determined to crush the French Revolution. But in battles such as Austerlitz (left), their armies were totally defeated by Napoleon*

*Statesmen at the Congress of Vienna in 1815. Their aim was to restore stability to Europe after the upheaval caused by the Napoleonic Wars*

**Metternich's Europe: 1815–48** As a non-Austrian – he was born at Coblenz, on the Rhine – Metternich was not allowed to control Austria's internal affairs, but as its foreign minister he established a European system which provided a considerable degree of stability in international affairs. The prime mover of the Congress of Vienna (1815), he took the lead in establishing, with Prussia and Russia, the 'Holy Alliance', which was mainly directed against any revival of French militarism. He also persuaded the European powers to co-operate in suppressing any liberal or democratic movements on the Continent which threatened the principles of absolute monarchy.

**Revolution of 1848** The European system established by Metternich was outwardly stable, but in the 1840's its survival was threatened by the developing forces of nationalism, liberalism and socialism. The Hapsburg emperor, Ferdinand I (1835–48), refused to compromise with these new forces. In March 1848 revolution broke out in Vienna.

The challenge to the Hapsburgs came mainly from the empire's subject peoples – Slavs, Hungarians, Italians and others. The most successful were the Hungarians who, under Lajos Kossuth, succeeded in breaking away completely. But they were eventually crushed, with the aid of Russian forces, in 1849.

Ferdinand had been forced by the revolutionaries to proclaim a liberal constitution and to send Metternich into exile. But his new chief minister, Prince Schwarzenberg, ordered the army against the revolutionaries. Ferdinand abdicated, and his nephew, Franz Joseph, succeeded him in 1849, and restored imperial power.

**Decline of Austria: 1849–67** The early years of Franz Joseph's reign saw a dramatic decline in Austria's power. The 1850's ended with a shattering military defeat in Italy, when France and the rising north Italian kingdom of Piedmont combined to destroy Austria's rule over its Italian province of Lombardy – though it held Venetia (Venice) until 1866. But in that year Austria was again defeated, this time by Prussia, in a lightning campaign culminating in the Battle of Sadowa. This defeat ended Austria's right to a say in the future of Germany, which was now well on the way to unity under Prussia.

**Foundation of the dual monarchy: 1867** These defeats gravely weakened the power of the empire, and Franz Joseph was no longer able to resist the demands of his Hungarian subjects for complete autonomy in their part of the empire. By the *Ausgleich* (compromise) of 1867, Austria became Austria-Hungary and the power of the imperial government in Vienna was shared with one in Budapest – hence the dual monarchy.

**Imperial decadence: 1867–1914** In the course of the 1870's, faced with a succession of crises in the Balkans, Austria became an ally of the rising German Empire. But its role was that of junior partner. Franz Joseph maintained an uneasy alliance with Russia as well as with Germany, in the so-called *Dreikaiserbund* (League of the Three Emperors). But by the turn of the century the incompatibility of Austrian and Russian interests in the Balkans was strongly evident. Russia's stirring up of Slav nationalism against the Ottoman Empire menaced the Austrian Empire as well. In the meantime, the atmosphere of conflict between the many various nationalities living within the Austro-Hungarian Empire became increasingly bitter.

In Vienna itself, the unpopularity of the Jews, many of whom were leaders of commercial and social life, was exploited by the city's mayor, Karl Lueger. His anti-semitic propaganda was to influence deeply a young Austrian, Adolf Hitler, a failed artist who was born at Braunau, Upper Austria, in 1889 and lived in poverty in Vienna before 1914.

**World war leads to collapse: 1914–18** Mounting tension in the Balkans came to a head in the summer of 1914, when the heir to the imperial throne, the Arch-

*Metternich, the Hapsburgs' chief minister from 1809 to 1848, helped to re-shape Europe after Napoleon's fall. His rigid conservatism was the chief cause of his eventual overthrow*

*Franz Joseph succeeded his uncle, Ferdinand, in 1849. In his 67 year reign, Austria's prestige as a great power declined*

duke Franz Ferdinand, was murdered by a fanatical Slav nationalist, Gavrilo Princip, at Sarajevo. The resulting conflict between Austria-Hungary and Serbia – whom the Austrians accused of plotting the crime – led to the First World War, which ended with the fall of the Hapsburgs and the dismemberment of their empire. Austria – reduced in size to its German-speaking areas – became a republic in 1918.

**Division in the republic: 1918–34** The infant republic faced desperate problems. It was unable to support itself economically, and it was surrounded by hostile neighbours – with the exception of Germany with whom it was forbidden to unite by the victorious Allies.

Although the republic was at first ruled by the Social Democrats of Vienna, most people in the rural areas, strongly influenced by the Roman Catholic Church, were deeply conservative. Bitter animosity developed between 'red' Vienna and the 'black' Roman Catholic rural areas. Civil war threatened in the late 1920's. It finally broke out in 1934 between the Socialists of Vienna, and the ruling Roman Catholic Party, led by Engelbert Dollfuss.

**End of the republic: 1934–8** Dollfuss swiftly crushed the Socialists and established a dictatorship. But his triumph was short-lived. In July 1934 he was murdered by Nazi extremists supported by Hitler's Third Reich. Austria's incorporation into the Reich – the 'Anschluss' – seemed imminent, but the Italian dictator Mussolini, at that time Hitler's rival for influence in central Europe, mobilised troops to warn Germany off.

**Anschluss and war: 1938–45** Hitler, an Austrian by origin who was now Chancellor in Berlin, had failed to bring Austria into his Third Reich in 1934. He saw another opportunity early in 1938, having come to an agreement with Mussolini, Austria's former protector. By now the Austrian government included several Nazis, who helped Hitler to overcome resistance. In March 1938 Austria became part of the 'Greater German Reich'.

**Occupation of Austria: 1945–55** The Allies considered Austria to have been a victim of Hitler's aggression rather than a willing ally of the Third Reich. In 1945, Austria was liberated by Western forces and the Red Army, and the Austrian people were allowed to set up their own form of government.

The first president of the new republic was Karl Renner, one of the Social Democratic leaders of 1918. Unlike the first republic, the second encouraged political and religious toleration. For 20 years, power was shared in coalition governments between the Social Democrats and the Catholic Austrian People's Party. In 1955 the USSR agreed to withdraw from Austria and to respect its neutrality; a peace treaty was signed and the occupation of the country came to an end.

**Between East and West: 1955–73** By the peace treaty of 1955 Austria promised to remain strictly neutral. The treaty gave advantages to the USSR. As its terms did not permit Austria to join NATO, the West's direct lines of communication between Bavaria and northern Italy were broken; as a result, everything had to pass to the west of Switzerland. Austria developed a policy of neutrality and non-alignment, seeking to become a mediator in the Cold War. Vienna became the headquarters of the European Atomic Energy Authority and the centre for the first stage of the Strategic Arms Limitation Talks (SALT). Austria joined the European Free Trade Association (EFTA) in the late 1950's and played an active part in the deliberations of the Council of Europe at Strasbourg.

Austria's policy of encouraging an understanding between East and West was strengthened by Bruno Kreisky, a Socialist who became chancellor in 1970. In May 1971 he established diplomatic relations with Communist China, and in October of the same year he was reappointed chancellor.

*Flats in the workers' quarter of Vienna in the 1920's. They were the centre of Socialist resistance to Dollfuss's regime in the rising of 1934*

*Austria's conciliatory role in international affairs was highlighted by the appointment in 1972 of Kurt Waldheim as the Secretary-General of the United Nations*

*Weavers shown at work in a medieval manuscript. Wool, largely imported from England, was the foundation of Flemish prosperity in the Middle Ages*

BAHAMAS    BELGIUM
BAHRAIN    BHUTAN
BANGLADESH   BOLIVIA
BARBADOS

# Bahamas

Some 700 islands off the coast of Florida – only about 40 of which are inhabited – make up the Bahamas, the first land sighted by Christopher Columbus when he reached the New World in 1492. Settlement did not take place there until the 17th century, when the Bahamas were reached by British colonisers from Bermuda. Pirates used the islands as a base to attack the Spanish, but they were expelled after 1717. Today, the islands are rapidly becoming a major tourist centre. Internal self-government was granted by Britain in 1964, and independence followed in 1973.

5386 sq. miles
211,700 people
Capital: Nassau

# Bahrain

Oil, discovered in 1932, has brought prosperity to Bahrain, which has one of the largest oil refineries in the Middle East. Like many states in the Persian Gulf, the country has been under British influence for much of its modern history. In 1882 Bahrain's ruler agreed to British control of his country's defence and foreign policies. This arrangement lasted until 1968, when Britain announced plans to withdraw from the area. Confronted with this situation, the smaller Arab principalities of the Gulf tried to form a political union. But negotiations to include Bahrain ended in deadlock and the country's ruler, Sheikh Isa bin Sulman al Khalifa, opted for complete independence in 1971.

231 sq. miles
239,700 people
Capital: Manama

# Bangladesh

Pakistan was dismembered in 1971 when East Pakistan broke away to form the republic of Bangladesh ('Bengal Nation') under Sheikh Mujibur Rahman. The Bengali peoples of East Pakistan, bitterly resenting what they regarded as exploitation by West Pakistan, began their attempt to break away early in 1971, and months of bloodshed and destruction followed. The attempt was crushed by government forces, but 6 million refugees fled from East Pakistan into India. India accused Pakistan of brutality, while Pakistan alleged Indian interference in its internal affairs. War broke out between the two countries. Indian forces took East Pakistan, and its independence as Bangladesh was quickly established. The new state was troubled by acute inflation and faced possible famine. In 1974, the country was devastated by floods, which killed thousands and made millions homeless.

55,126 sq. miles
69,087,000 people
Capital: Dacca

# Barbados

The most densely populated island in the West Indies, Barbados depends largely on tourism and the export of sugar for its survival. Sugar plantations cover much of the island, and for centuries their owners had a monopoly of political power.

The island was uninhabited when it was claimed for Britain by Captain John Powell in 1625, though there was evidence that it had been previously inhabited by Arawak Indians. Nobody knows, however, what made them leave Barbados. The first settlers arrived there in 1627, importing slaves from Africa to work their plantations. These slaves were finally freed in 1834, when slavery was abolished throughout the British Empire. Today, 77 per cent of the islanders are of African origin.

The plantation owners' political power was broken in 1937 by a Negro lawyer, Sir Grantley Adams, who took up the cause of the voteless descendants of the former slaves. Universal suffrage was won in 1950. In 1966 the island became an independent state within the British Commonwealth, after the break-up of the Federation of the West Indies.

With an economy so dependent on the export of sugar to Britain, Barbados was alarmed by Britain's move to join the Common Market; but safeguards to protect its economy were agreed.

166 sq. miles
239,700 people
Capital:
Bridgetown

*Barbados-born Gary Sobers became the greatest all-rounder in cricketing history*

# Belgium

Because of its strategic position in Europe, Belgium has often been an arena for battles between warring powers. It is the land of Waterloo, Ypres and the Battle of the Bulge. Its people have suffered centuries of conquest and foreign domination, and won their independence only in 1830 when they threw out the last of their foreign rulers, the Dutch. Since then Belgium has been an independent kingdom – although occupied by the Germans in both world wars. Today the country is a leading nation in the drive towards a united Europe; the headquarters of both the Common Market and of NATO are in Brussels.

Belgium has two main languages – Flemish and French. The Flemings (56 per cent of the population) are concentrated in the north, while the French-speaking Walloons (33 per cent) dominate the south. Differences in language and culture have been a frequent source of friction between them.

11,781 sq. miles
9,818,800 people
Capital: Brussels

**From Caesar to Charlemagne: 58 BC–AD 814** The Belgae, an Iron Age Celtic tribe, arrived from the east in the 4th century BC to settle in the area corresponding to present-day Belgium. Julius Caesar conquered them in a series of campaigns from 58 to 50 BC, after which the country became part of the Roman province of Belgica. By AD 300 Belgica had been overrun by a Germanic tribe, the Franks.

In the 9th century Belgium became part of the Holy Roman Empire of Charlemagne, whose family had its ancestral lands in eastern Belgium. Charlemagne's rule greatly contributed to Belgium's economic prosperity, and the wool-mills of Flanders, the first of which were founded during his reign, remained the mainstay of the country's economy for centuries. After Charlemagne's death in 814, however, Belgium was divided into semi-independent principalities.

**Prosperity and unity** The prosperity of these independent states suffered in the years immediately after Charlemagne's death, but by *c.* 1000 they had recovered to become one of the richest areas in Europe. This affluence aroused the envy of France.

The Hundred Years' War, which broke out in 1337 between England and France, weakened Belgian prosperity. Trade declined, rival factions in the cities fought for power, and the nobles tried to overthrow the princes. Order was brought out of chaos by the French dukes of Burgundy, who united the principalities in the late 14th century.

**Foreign rule: 1477–1797** With the marriage in 1477 of Mary of Burgundy to Maximilian, the Hapsburg ruler of Austria, Belgium came under Hapsburg rule. In 1555, when the Hapsburg lands were divided, Philip II of Spain, a fervent Catholic, became its ruler. He refused to grant religious toleration to his Protestant subjects in the Low Countries – modern Belgium, Holland and Luxembourg – and a revolt broke out in 1568. During the harsh repression which followed, the Spanish general, the Duke of Alva, became feared for his ruthlessness and cruelty. The revolt ended in 1598, with what is now Belgium remaining under Spain. The rest won its independence as the Netherlands.

In the 17th century, with the rise of France under Louis XIV, Belgium – now known as the Spanish Netherlands – became a battleground between France and Spain. The French occupied it in 1700, but in 1713, as part of the Peace of Utrecht, it passed into the hands of Austria, which ruled it until 1789. Under Austria, Belgium was allowed considerable autonomy and its prosperity greatly increased.

In 1789, the Belgians, spurred on by the example of the French Revolution, rose against their Austrian rulers and drove them out. France annexed Belgium in 1797. Despite the introduction of some reforms, most Belgians resented their lack of political freedom and the forced conscription of their men of military age into Napoleon's armies.

*This gold torque, now in the British Museum, shows the skills of Belgium's Iron Age tribes in making elaborate jewellery*

*A Protestant caricature of the Duke of Alva, Spanish viceroy of the Low Countries from 1567 to 1573. A fanatical Catholic, Alva was determined to crush what he thought was heresy*

## United Netherlands: 1815–30

After the final defeat of Napoleon on Belgian soil – at Waterloo – the victorious Allies united Belgium with Holland and Luxembourg to form a buffer state against France. This union, under the Dutch king, William I, was unpopular with the Belgians, as the two countries differed over religion – Holland being a Protestant state, and Belgium largely Roman Catholic.

In 1830 the Belgians rose and drove out the Dutch and proclaimed their independence. William I appealed for help to the Allied powers, but they recognised Belgian independence. The following year, a German prince, Leopold of Saxe-Coburg, was elected the country's new ruler.

Because so many wars had been fought over Belgium in the past, all the great European powers agreed to recognise Belgium as 'an independent and perpetually neutral state'. Even when the Franco-Prussian War broke out in 1870, this guarantee was zealously observed.

## Reform under the Leopolds: 1831–1909

Under Leopold I, Belgium became a democratic constitutional monarchy. His son, Leopold II, encouraged industrialisation, which transformed the face of Belgium. Aided by the journalist-explorer Henry Morton Stanley, he set up the Congo Free State as a private African colony in 1884. Profits from rubber in the Congo made the Belgian monarchy rich, but the colony was transferred to the state in 1908, after reports of corruption and cruelty there had led to agitation in Belgium.

By the beginning of the 20th century, the development of industry had created a large working class, who soon realised their political strength and demanded the right to vote. Demands were also made for the use of Flemish as an official language, together with French.

*Leopold I was elected king of newly independent Belgium in 1831. Under his rule were laid the foundations of the country's material prosperity*

*Leopold II gave Belgium a colonial empire by annexing the Congo*

## Conquered in both world wars

Belgium refused to allow the German armies to pass through it to invade France in 1914, and Germany's violation of Belgian neutrality brought Britain into the war. All but a tiny part of Flanders was occupied by the Germans, but the Belgian army fought on under the leadership of Albert I (1909–34). Belgium was the scene of some of the most devastating fighting of the war, especially at Ypres.

Belgium remained neutral at the start of the Second World War but Germany launched a blitzkrieg on May 10, 1940, without warning. After 18 days of fierce fighting, the Belgian king, Leopold III (1934–51), without consulting his French and British allies, surrendered. The government fled to London, but Leopold gave himself up to the Germans and was interned for the rest of the war. Many Belgians fiercely denounced the king's actions.

Leopold's unpopularity caused a prolonged political crisis after the country's liberation in 1944. He did not return to Belgium until 1950, when a referendum showed 57 per cent of the population in favour of his resuming the throne. But continued hostility to his rule led Leopold to abdicate in 1951 and his son, Baudouin, came to the throne.

## Union in Europe

One of the first European countries to recover its prosperity after the Second World War, Belgium led the way towards European political union and economic co-operation. Its chief politician, Paul Henri Spaak, was leader of the Council of Europe. In

*The 13th-century Cloth Hall and cathedral at Ypres in 1916, devastated by German guns. Some of the most destructive battles of the First World War were fought on Belgian soil*

1948 Belgium formed the Benelux economic union with the Netherlands and Luxembourg, and in 1952 joined the European Coal and Steel Community. In 1957 Belgium became a founder member of the Common Market.

## Congo crisis

In 1960, Belgium gave the Congo independence – a decision forced by international pressures. Within a few days the Congolese army, the Force Publique, mutinied against its European officers and Belgian paratroops were sent to restore order. The decision to intervene split public opinion in Belgium itself. The Congolese believed that the Belgians were trying to regain control and appealed to the United Nations, which ordered the withdrawal of the paratroops.

## North versus south

A constitutional crisis arose in 1968 when riots broke out between Belgium's two main groups, the Flemish-speaking people of the north and the French-speaking Walloons of the south. In 1972 a coalition government representing both groups was formed under the Fleming Gaston Eyskens. After new elections in 1974, Leo Tindemans, head of the Social Christian party, became premier.

*The Atomium was built for the 1958 World's Fair in Brussels. It symbolises man's achievement in harnessing the atom*

# Bhutan

Eight fertile valleys make up the small kingdom of Bhutan, whose terrain varies from the 24,000 ft Himalayas to the steamy jungle of the south. The country came under the influence of the British Raj in India in the 19th century; in 1907 a British-supported potentate became king and established a dynasty which still rules today. After Britain withdrew from India in 1947, the Indian government took over Britain's role, aiding Bhutan in a dispute with China in 1950. King Jigme Dorji Wangchuk, who ascended the throne in 1952, gave up his absolute powers in 1969. He died in 1972 and was succeeded by his son, Jigme Singhi Wangchuk.

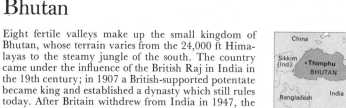

18,147 sq. miles
911,600 people
Capital: Thimphu

# Bolivia

The remote and mountainous republic of Bolivia has had its full share of the violent upheavals that have marked the history of South America. During the past 450 years its lands have been plundered for minerals. Its boundaries have been eroded by a succession of disastrous wars, its people crushed by poverty and social inequalities; and military coups have wrecked attempts to create a stable government, frequently bringing the country to the brink of bankruptcy.

## Incas and Spain

A pre-Inca culture was established c. AD 900 in Bolivia – known as Upper Peru until the 19th century – by the Aymaras, a farming race descended from peoples who crossed the Bering Strait from Asia to North America more than 30,000 years ago. The Aymaras were subjugated by the Incas from Peru in AD 1200. The Incas were overthrown in 1538 when two conquistadores, Gonzalo and Hernando Pizarro, led the Spanish conquest.

Spanish explorers followed, searching for minerals. They found in the mountains of the Andes wealth far in excess of their dreams. The huge silver deposits discovered in 1546 at Potosi were the richest the world had ever known, and by 1650 Potosi was the largest city in

424,165 sq. miles
5,468,300 people
Capital: Sucre

*Potosi in the 18th century. The town was once famous for its rich silver mines*

## BOLIVIA *continued*

the New World, with a population of 160,000. The Indian peasants were forced to work the silver mines, under conditions of extreme hardship.

**Shrinking boundaries: 1879–1935** Independence was won from Spain after a war which lasted from 1809 to 1824. When independence was declared in 1825, the country named itself after its liberator, General Simon Bolívar (1783–1830). It then covered an area more than two-and-a-half times its present size, with a sea coast on the western side of the continent. This coastal region, which included the rich nitrate and copper deposits of the Atacama desert, was seized by Chile in the War of the Pacific, which was fought from 1879 to 1883.

Bolivia's riches tempted other neighbours, too. The Bolivian army was made up of Indian peasants who, though strong in numbers, were weak in patriotism. Brazil took over the rubber-tree state of the Amazonas in the south-west in 1903, and Paraguay claimed further lands in the Chaco War (1932–5). This war created a new generation of young and educated revolutionaries in Bolivia. Internal strife increased. Coup followed coup, each one further weakening the country's economy.

In 1952 there emerged a powerful new regime led by Victor Paz Estenssoro, a lawyer and economics professor. Under Estenssoro, drastic reforms were introduced. A new army was organised, land was shared, foreign-controlled mines nationalised and industries modernised with massive financial aid from the United States. But Bolivia lacked the skilled technicians and the up-to-date equipment to complete the industrial reforms; and attempts to develop roads and social services failed. Strikes plagued the economy and financial chaos followed.

**Bolivia today** Estenssoro was overthrown in 1964 by General René Barrientos, the vice-president. A guerrilla campaign against the government started in 1967 with guidance from Che Guevara, an Argentine-born revolutionary who was a chief lieutenant in the 1956 invasion of Cuba that put Castro in power.

Guerrilla activities waned after Che Guevara was killed in Bolivia in 1967. Barrientos was killed in a plane crash in 1969. His successor, Luis Siles Salinas, was ousted by General Juan José Torres in 1970, and in 1971 Torres in turn was overthrown by a right-wing coup led by Colonel Hugo Banzer Suárez.

Mining is still Bolivia's most important industry, and its tin output is the second highest in the world. Bolivia's backward peasants, who make up more than two-thirds of the population, are still isolated in the mountain mining regions. Almost 70 per cent of them are uneducated, and almost all are wretchedly poor.

*Bolivians named their country after their liberator, General Simon Bolívar*

*Che Guevara tried to spread revolution from Cuba to the mainland. He was killed in Bolivia in 1967*

## Botswana

The land-locked republic of Botswana is largely dependent on South Africa for its economic survival. Most goods exported by Botswana have to pass along trade routes controlled by South Africa, which also gives work to many of Botswana's people.

Little is known of the history of Botswana before the 19th century when, under Khama the Great and other chiefs, the Botswana people fought off their rivals, the Matabele. Threatened with annexation by the Boers of the Transvaal Republic, they asked for protection from Britain, which was granted when the Bechuanaland Protectorate was established in 1885.

Between 1910 and 1955 Bechuanaland was repeatedly threatened with incorporation into South Africa, but its leaders staved off such demands by appeals to Britain. In 1961, the year South Africa left the British Commonwealth, the protectorate was given its own multi-racial constitution. In 1966 it achieved full independence from Britain, taking the name of Botswana, with Sir Seretse Khama as its first president.

231,828 sq. miles
705,900 people
Capital: Gaborone

## Brazil

When the Portuguese admiral Pedro Alvares Cabral landed in Brazil in 1500, the country was populated by primitive Indians who had hardly progressed beyond the Stone Age. Today it is a fast-growing modern state – the largest country in South America, occupying almost half the continent. In the past, much of Brazil's economic development has been tied to four staple products: sugar, gold, coffee and rubber. The country has now entered a phase of spectacular industrial expansion.

As Brazil's vast natural resources are exploited and the dense forests opened up, the Indian tribes, such as the Mundurucus, Guaranis and Carajas, are declining in numbers. They are threatened with extinction by land-hungry developers following in the wake of two giant highways being ploughed through the jungle. The roads will link the resources of the Amazon basin with the industrial south, and carry surplus people from the dry north-east to more fertile territories.

**Early history: 1494–1700** The country – named after the brazilwood trees found there – was claimed by Portugal under the 1494 Treaty of Tordesillas, which divided the New World between Portugal and Spain.

Sugar cultivation was begun in the eastern coastal region in 1532. Thousands of Negro slaves were brought from West Africa to work the plantations. Intermarriage between them and the Indians, and other groups, accounts for the richly mixed character of Brazil's population today – a source of pride to most Brazilians.

Excessive soil cultivation, coupled in the late 17th century with competition from Caribbean sugar-cane planters, damaged the nation's economy.

**Gold found: c. 1690** Brazil entered a period of prosperity in the 1690's with the discovery of gold in the central region of Minas Gerais – today one of the richest states in Brazil. The discovery was made by bandeirantes, armed slave-raiders who roamed the interior and extended the western boundaries of Brazil deep into Spanish territory. It led to a gold rush in which many of the sugar-cane planters joined, taking their slaves with them. A few years later diamonds also were found in Minas Gerais, and for a century Brazil flourished as the major supplier of gold and diamonds to the world.

In 1763, Rio de Janeiro, which had become the leading port for shipment of this wealth, replaced Salvador as the colony's capital; and in 1808, when the Portuguese royal family fled to Brazil after Napoleon's troops reached Lisbon, Rio became the seat of the Portuguese Empire.

The king, John VI, returned to Portugal in 1821 and left his son Pedro as regent. This was to start a vigorous new era in Brazil's development.

**Pedro proclaims independence: 1822** Within a year, Pedro proclaimed Brazil an independent country, with himself as emperor, and this independence was officially recognised by Portugal in 1825.

Pedro abdicated in 1831 and his son, Pedro II, became emperor in 1840 at the age of 15. Under his leadership the country made steady economic progress which laid the foundations of modern Brazil. The first railways and roads were built, rivers were opened up for

3,286,490 sq. miles
103,648,800 people
Capital: Brasilia

*The hostility of Indian tribes was one of the hazards facing early explorers of the Amazon River*

*In this early print, Brazilian Indians pan for gold found near a waterfall*

*Pedro I proclaimed himself Emperor of Brazil in 1822 after being appointed regent by the King of Portugal*

navigation (26,000 miles of waterways are now in use in Brazil), and towns were linked by telegraph systems.

*A well-to-do Rio family of the early 19th century on their way to church*

**Republic declared: 1889** In 1888, an Act abolishing slavery led to unrest. Faced with the threat of civil war, Pedro II abdicated. On November 15, 1889, Brazil was declared a republic, with Manuel Deodoro da Fonseca (1827–92) as its first president.

By the end of the 19th century, the best gold and diamond deposits had been exhausted, but in the meantime exploitation had begun of Brazil's two other staple products – coffee on plantations in the south-east, and rubber from the Amazon forests.

The coffee plantations, employing thousands of Italian immigrants who flooded into Brazil towards the end of the 19th century, were soon supplying 75 per cent of the world's needs. The rubber industry boomed with the overseas demand for tyres for the motor industry, and also with the need for insulation in the electrical industry.

Landowners and employers made fortunes which helped to stimulate in the jungle regions the growth of cities such as Belem and Manaus – cities where money was so plentiful in the early 1900's that the wealthy were said to light their cigars with banknotes.

In 1912, however, Brazil's rubber monopoly ended when the rubber plantations of the Far East began to flourish. These had been started in 1876 by an Englishman, Henry Wickham, who smuggled rubber seeds out of Belem. In the Far East, plantations were properly supervised, but in Brazil most rubber was collected from the virgin forests, and many trees were destroyed in the rush to make fortunes.

*The coffee plant has been a mainstay of Brazil's economy. Thousands of Italians emigrated to work on the plantations*

**Vargas becomes president: 1930** The slump that followed was disastrous to Brazil's economy. Another equally disastrous slump came 18 years later, when over-production of coffee led to a fall in prices in 1930 during the world-wide economic crisis. A revolution brought Getúlio Vargas to the presidency in 1930. His regime degenerated into a dictatorship, and was overthrown in 1945. Vargas again became president in 1950, but, disheartened by the incompetence displayed around him, he committed suicide in 1954.

**Brasilia, the new capital: 1960** A vast gulf still separates rich and poor, despite rapid strides made in recent years. Agricultural workers – more than half the country's labour force – continue to live in shanty towns and earn low wages. Meanwhile the capital city of Brasilia, designed by a Brazilian, Oscar Niemeyer, is a beautiful and spectacular achievement of modern architecture. It was created out of the virgin forests by President Juscelino Kubitschek to encourage the development of the interior.

Kubitschek's successors struggled in vain to stem rampant inflation, and strikes and riots by hungry workers, until in 1964 a military coup forced leftward-leaning President Joao Goulart into exile. There followed a succession of political upheavals. President Emilio Garrastazú Medici was elected by a triumvirate of military leaders in 1969, and he was followed by Gen. Ernesto Geisel in 1974. The nation is ruled by a strict, sometimes ruthlessly authoritarian regime, which gives full scope to the planners and technocrats who are bent on furthering Brazil's 'economic miracle'.

Iron, tin and copper are mined; cotton weaving, chemicals, steel, paper and petroleum production are being expanded. There are more than 20 television and 700 radio stations and 1200 airport terminals.

*'King' Pele, a legend of football. He played for Brazil 110 times*

*Work in progress at Brasilia, which became Brazil's new capital in 1960. The city is laid out in the shape of an aeroplane*

# Bulgaria

The Slav country of Bulgaria, in the eastern Balkans, sprang into international prominence in the late 19th century, when the ruthless slaughter of Bulgarians by Turkish forces stirred the conscience of liberal Europe. Bulgaria was rescued by Russia, and the Bulgarians have been closely linked with Russia ever since.

42,823 sq. miles
8,720,600 people
Capital: Sofia

**Slavs in Bulgaria** Slavic tribes first settled in Bulgaria *c.* AD 500, but a century later these Slavs were conquered by the Bulgars, a Turkic-speaking race from beyond the Danube, who gradually adopted the Slavs' language and culture. Bulgar independence – apart from a short period of Byzantine rule – lasted until the Ottoman conquest in 1396. The Bulgarians were the most oppressed subject people of the Ottoman Empire. Their suffering reached an extreme point in the 19th-century suppression of Bulgarian nationalist movements, in which thousands were massacred.

**Congress of Berlin: 1878** Russia intervened in 1878 in support of the Bulgarians, whom they regarded as brother Slavs, and independence followed. But other powers became involved. Britain's prime minister, Benjamin Disraeli, did not want to see Russia grow too powerful, so he opposed the formation of a 'big Bulgaria', which he thought would become a natural ally of Russia. The south remained part of the Ottoman Empire, while the north, though still owing nominal allegiance to Turkey, was placed under the rule of a German prince, Alexander of Battenberg. In 1908, however, Ferdinand of Saxe-Coburg-Gotha, who had succeeded Alexander in 1887, took advantage of revolt in Constantinople to proclaim himself tsar of independent Bulgaria.

*This gold pitcher in the shape of a female head, dating from the 3rd century BC, was excavated in the south of Bulgaria*

**Wars and dictatorships 1911–36** Under Ferdinand, Bulgaria became involved in war against Turkey, and against its Balkan neighbours in 1911 and 1912. In the First World War it took the side of Germany. But the result was defeat for Bulgaria and, in 1918, Ferdinand abdicated in favour of his son, Boris III.

After a few years of stability under the new tsar, there followed a decade of political confusion, during which Macedonian terrorists tried to overthrow the Bulgarian regime. In 1936 a military dictatorship was established, and a year later Boris assumed supreme power.

*Byzantine influence is seen in the domes and arches of Sofia's Orthodox cathedral*

**Modern Bulgaria** Bulgaria again backed Germany in the Second World War, thereby gaining Greek and Romanian territory in 1940 and 1941. But Boris refused to declare war on the USSR, in view of the long ties of friendship between the two countries.

In 1944 the Bulgarians abandoned Germany and tried to make a separate peace with Britain and the USA – but the USSR took over the country. The monarchy was abolished; in 1946 a Communist 'people's republic' was set up, under Georgi Dimitrov.

Since the Second World War, Bulgaria has co-operated very closely with the USSR. A friendship pact was signed in 1948 and renewed in 1967. Since Todor Zhivkov became president in 1971, Bulgaria has begun to prosper. Zhivkov encouraged this by introducing increased competition into Bulgarian life.

*Allies in war: Kaiser William II visits Ferdinand of Bulgaria (right) in 1917. The two monarchs have exchanged uniforms*

# Burma

An independent republic since 1948, when it left the British Commonwealth, Burma has in recent years tried to follow a policy of strict neutrality. In the 1960's many foreigners working in the country were expelled in a drive to exclude foreign influence, although aid was accepted from China and the USA.

The original homeland of the Burmese was the present upper Burma, centred on Mandalay. The Burmese gradually expanded, conquering and absorbing the Mon peoples of lower Burma, and subduing, but not assimilating, various people of the hill areas, such as the Shans, Karens, and the coastal Arakanese. Since independence, there has been a good deal of friction between these hill peoples and the ruling Burmese.

261,789 sq. miles
30,100,000 people
Capital: Rangoon

**Early kingdoms** The earliest state in Burma flourished in the 7th and 8th centuries AD around its capital city of Srikshetra, about 200 miles north of where Rangoon now stands. Its people, called the Pyu, were Hindus and used the Sanskrit language. In the 11th century the people from whom the modern Burmese are descended conquered their non-Burmese neighbours and established a kingdom that lasted 200 years. A Burmese king, Anawratha, introduced Buddhism, which is still the main religion of the country. He and his successors ruled from a capital in Upper Burma called Pagan, 'the city of a thousand temples'.

*The Ananda temple was one of thousands of Buddhist shrines and temples which adorned the city of Pagan from c. 1050 to 1299. Their ruins today are among the most impressive in south-east Asia*

**The drive to unity: 1301–1824** Several independent states emerged in the 14th century. The Burmese established the city of Ava, in the north, while the Mons built Pegu in the south. A third people, the Shans, captured Ava in 1527: but further south, at Toungoo, a new Burmese state had been evolving, and it seized control of Pegu in 1539 and conquered many of the Shan territories. The Burmese thenceforward dominated the country, despite a Mon revolt against them in 1740.

*A whoongee, or first minister's wife, with female slaves in early 19th-century Burma*

**Anglo-Burmese wars: 1824–85** Frontier tension between Burma and British India led to a war in 1824–6, ending with the British annexation of the provinces of Tenasserim and Arakan. British trading ambitions, which caused bitterness between the Burmese and British merchants in the country, led to a second war in 1852–4. As a result, lower Burma, including Rangoon, became a British province. Finally, in 1885, after a third war, the British took over the rest of Burma.

**Growth of nationalism: 1906–42** Burmese nationalism in its modern form began with the organisation from 1906 onwards of Young Men's Buddhist Associations. Buddhist monks played a leading part in the political activity of the 1920's, but in the 1930's the initiative passed to English-educated students, who organised a major strike in 1936. The British permitted some measure of constitutional development and in 1937 a Burmese cabinet with limited powers was formed. But by then nationalists were calling for independence.

**Japanese occupation: 1942–5** The Japanese invaded Burma in 1942, forcing British withdrawal by May. In 1943, the Japanese proclaimed Burma's independence and set up a puppet government. But during 1945 Allied troops, mainly British, defeated the invaders in a hard-fought campaign, climaxed by the battle of the Irrawaddy River. The Allies were assisted by the Burma National Army led by Aung San, which had previously supported the Japanese. Aung San formed an Anti-Fascist People's Freedom League (AFPFL) whose aim was to achieve independence from Britain.

**Independence: 1947–8** In July 1947 Aung San was assassinated, and it was another member of the Freedom League, U Nu, who became prime minister of the independent Union of Burma in 1948. Independence was followed almost immediately by a series of revolts, two led by different groups of Communists and a third by nationalists among the Karens, one of the minority hill peoples. Order was not restored for more than three years, and revolts continued through the 1950's. Nevertheless, a constitutional system was established in Rangoon, and U Nu won two successive elections.

**Military rule: 1962** U Nu's regime was overthrown in 1962 by an army leader, General Ne Win. The new military government pursued a policy of the 'Burmese way to Socialism', and nationalised most industries and businesses. The military regime, which laid great stress on its determination to follow a neutralist foreign policy, faced serious economic problems. In 1974, the regime adopted a new one-party constitution that renamed the country as the Socialist Republic of the Union of Burma. Burma's most pressing problem, that of its minority peoples, remained unresolved, however, and fighting continued between the rebels and government forces.

*U Thant, a Burmese diplomat, was Secretary-General of the United Nations from 1961 to 1971*

# Burundi

A struggle between two tribal groups, the Batutsi and the Bahutu, has dominated the political life of the small neighbouring African states of Burundi and Rwanda. In each country, the Batutsi minority, a tall warrior people, were for long the masters of the Bahutu majority. In the late 1950's, the Bahutu overthrew the Batutsi in Rwanda, while in Burundi the Batutsi have clung to power despite fierce Bahutu opposition to them.

The Batutsi, believed to have come from Ethiopia, invaded the area formed by present-day Burundi and Rwanda in the 15th century, and subjugated the native Bahutu. The whole region was absorbed into German East Africa in 1894. After Germany's defeat in the First World War it was administered by Belgium as Ruanda-Urundi, under a League of Nations mandate. The United Nations took up the mandate in 1945.

The mandate lasted until 1962, when Rwanda and Burundi became independent as separate states. In Burundi, the Batutsi – one-sixth of the population – set up governments which were largely hostile to the Bahutu majority in parliament. In 1966, the Mwami (king) Ntare V was ousted by the former police chief Colonel Michel Micombero, a Batutsi, who declared himself president, and ruled through a National Revolutionary Committee. In 1972, the Bahutu rose against their rulers and slaughtered Batutsi by the thousands. An estimated 100,000 Bahutu were killed in reprisals. Violent fighting broke out again in 1973, and thousands of Bahutu fled the country.

10,747 sq. miles
3,836,300 people
Capital: Bujumbura

Although caught in the toils of modern war, Cambodia still largely retains its traditional way of life. Elephants are the transport used by herbalists on a rural 'sales trip'

# Cambodia

The people of Cambodia – officially the Khmer Republic – trace their origins to a Hindu people, the Khmers, whose empire extended in medieval times from Cambodia into present-day Thailand and Vietnam. This ancient empire has left magnificent temple ruins and works of sculpture, especially at its former capital of Angkor. After the 15th century, however, the power of Cambodia declined, and it lost territory to its two immediate neighbours, Thailand and Vietnam. In the 19th century it became a French protectorate. Following the Second World War, Cambodia – after achieving independence and maintaining a period of shaky neutrality – was caught up by external conflict, becoming a battleground in the Vietnam war.

**Engineers of Funan** The earliest known state in Cambodia was Funan, an empire that flourished from *c.* AD 200 in the southern region of what is now Cambodia and in the Mekong Delta of South Vietnam. The people of Funan were skilled engineers who built a complex network of canals. Chinese travellers reported that ships could penetrate far inland on Funan's canal system. Funan derived its wealth from trade, some of which was carried on with Rome and India.

Funan was replaced in the 6th century by a Khmer state which the Chinese called Chenla. Hindu temples and inscriptions, identified with Chenla's culture, have been found scattered over a wide area of Cambodia.

**Age of Angkor: 800–1300** In the 800's a Khmer king, Jayavarman II, laid the foundations of the state that later developed around the impressive city of Angkor in central Cambodia. This strong ruler founded a royal cult called *devaraja*, which identified the king with the Hindu god, Shiva. Angkor itself became the centre of the Khmer Empire by the late 9th century.

The Khmer Empire left behind a series of temples dating from the 9th to the 13th centuries; the finest is Angkor Wat. Angkor reached the height of its wealth and power under Jayavarman VII (1181–*c.* 1219). His conquests extended to the Menam River (in present-day Thailand) on the west, and to Champa (now central Vietnam) on the east. But both these areas had become independent by the later 13th century, and Angkor began to decline.

Sculpted figures in the great 12th-century temple of Angkor Wat show poses like those used by Cambodian dancers today

**Fall of an empire: 1300–1800** During the 14th century, the Thais to the north and west began to threaten the Khmer state. Angkor itself fell to Thai forces at least twice, probably in 1369 and 1389, and by the mid-15th century the Khmer kings had abandoned it as a capital, retreating to the Mekong.

From the middle of the 17th century until the mid-19th century, the lands that were once ruled by powerful Khmer kings began to be eaten away by Thailand and Vietnam. From 1659, Vietnamese armies, taking advantage of internal conflicts, penetrated Cambodian territory, and between 1700 and 1760 Cambodia lost the area which now forms the Mekong Delta region of South Vietnam. After 1775, the Vietnamese suffered internal disruption, but this simply gave the Thais another opportunity to interfere in Cambodia. Another partial occupation by the Vietnamese after 1834 was ended by a Cambodian revolt in 1845.

**Arrival of the French: 1861** In 1861 a revolt forced King Norodom (1859–1904) to seek outside help. The French, already influential in Indo-China, imposed a French protectorate over Cambodia. Uprisings in 1865–7 and 1884–6 failed to shake French authority, which was strengthened by a new treaty in 1884.

**Independence and interference** Japan occupied much of Cambodia during the Second World War. Under Japanese pressure, Cambodia declared its 'independence' in 1944, but the following year, when Japan was defeated, the French returned. Cambodia's king, Sihanouk, negotiated a degree of self-government in 1949; full independence was granted to Cambodia at the Geneva Conference (1954) which followed France's defeat in Indo-China by the Viet Minh nationalists.

In 1955 Sihanouk abdicated the throne, but he kept effective power. His policy was one of neutrality, but following a break with the United States in 1965, after his refusal to accept further US aid, he moved closer to China and North Vietnam. In March 1970 he was overthrown by a pro-American coup, which was followed by a South Vietnamese advance into Cambodia against the North Vietnamese troops who were also in the country. Later in 1970, while a royal 'government-in-exile' formed around Sihanouk in Peking, Cambodia was declared a republic. Under a new constitution, President Lon Nol assumed greatly increased powers in 1972. Cambodia remained torn by armed conflict, with Sihanouk's predominantly Communist forces in control of most of the country outside the towns, and threatening to take the capital, Phnom-Penh. Intensive American bombing of territory held by the Sihanoukists aroused strong opposition in the US Congress, and the bombing was halted in August 1973.

69,898 sq. miles
7,435,000 people
Capital:
Phnom-Penh

Prince Sihanouk (right), ruler of Cambodia from 1941, first as king and then as prime minister, set up a government-in-exile in Peking after being ousted by a military coup in 1970

# Cameroun

One of Black Africa's economically more advanced countries, which has grown prosperous on the exports of coffee and cocoa, present-day Cameroun was created in 1961 by linking the former French Camerouns with the southern part of the British Cameroons. The interior of Cameroun was probably the original homeland of Africa's Bantu-speaking peoples, who spread from there to the rest of the continent south of the Equator.

Portuguese explorers discovered the coastline in the 15th century. Between the 16th and 19th centuries the Cameroun coast was a regular source of supply for countries engaged in the transatlantic slave trade. In the mid-19th century the British and Germans competed for the trade of the region, and in 1884 the Germans proclaimed a protectorate. They pushed into the interior, building railways and establishing plantations. During the First World War Britain and France occupied the colony, and in 1918 it was divided between them under a League of Nations mandate.

Political agitation in the French Camerouns mounted after the Second World War and led to the granting of independence by France and the UN in 1960. In the following year, after a referendum was held in the British Cameroons, the northern part opted to join Nigeria while the southern part voted to join the former French territory. Ahmadou Ahidjo, leader of the French section, became the new country's first president.

183,568 sq. miles
5,840,000 people
Capital: Yaoundé

British Nigerian troops marching in Cameroun in 1916. The First World War put an end to German colonial rule there

By 1758, when this drawing was made, Quebec was the centre of France's North American empire. When the city fell to the British a year later, French Canada fell with it

# Canada

The world's second largest country (only the USSR is larger), Canada is also one of the youngest established powers. Its people celebrated the 100th anniversary of their confederation as recently as 1967. The opening-up of Canada's vast hinterland owed much to the courage and resourcefulness of explorers in the face of such awesome natural obstacles as the Rocky Mountains. Even today, aerial surveys are mapping hitherto uncharted areas of Canada's Arctic wilderness.

Canada shares an undefended frontier almost 4000 miles long with the United States. Almost two-thirds of its total foreign trade is with its neighbour. The two countries have many similarities in their styles of living, yet Canada retains a distinct and still developing individuality, combining the traditions and experience of its British and French communities.

Canadian forces made a significant contribution to the Allied cause in both world wars, but Canada has only once had to fight a war in direct defence of its freedom. The history of the country has been largely peaceful – a steady process of discovery, territorial expansion and economic growth. Yet the country's vast resources – including timber, oil, natural gas and uranium – are still relatively untapped.

In recent years, Canada's stability and progress have been overshadowed by the revival of old antagonisms between English-speaking and French-speaking Canada. English-speaking Canada itself suffers from divided loyalties – with British traditions pulling one way and the country's close economic and social ties with the United States pulling the other.

**First Canadians** Canada's first immigrants probably crossed the land bridge over the Bering Strait from northern Asia into Alaska some 20,000 to 30,000 years ago. From them descended Eskimo and Indian tribes – eastern crop-raisers, far-western fishermen, the hunters of the forests and the nomads of the plains. By the 1490's, numbering only about 200,000, these Indians had spread over much of Canada.

In the 11th century Norsemen sailed across the north Atlantic from Iceland to Greenland and then probably on to Labrador. One of their leaders, Leif Ericson, is thought to have visited the Canadian coast. Nearly 400 years later, John Cabot sailed west from Bristol in 1497 and found an island which he named Newfoundland. He was followed in 1534 by the French explorer Jacques Cartier, who made two subsequent voyages, during which he explored the St Lawrence River as far as the site of Montreal.

**New France** Nearly a century passed before the French began to realise the potential riches of Canada. In 1602 Henry IV granted a monopoly of the Canadian fur trade to a group of merchants in Rouen, whose agent, Samuel de Champlain, arrived in Canada in the following year, determined to create a French empire in the New World. In 1608 Champlain founded the fort of Quebec, which was to become the centre of French power in Canada.

Champlain explored the St Lawrence valley and discovered the Great Lakes. His empire nearly foundered in fierce wars with the Iroquois Indians, but the French slowly gained the upper hand. The fur trade flourished and in 1663 Louis XIV declared the colony an official province of France.

**English challenge** At the same time, the English and the Dutch were pushing up from the south, while the English-controlled Hudson's Bay Company, formed in

An ivory doll used as a charm in Eskimo religious ceremonies. Eskimo shamans (priests) hold seances in an attempt to communicate with the spirit world

Samuel de Champlain (1567–1635), explorer, coloniser and trader, was the true father of French Canada – 'New France'. He strove to create an American empire despite little support from Paris

1670, was setting up posts on the coast of the bay that the explorer Henry Hudson had discovered in 1610. The English soon clashed with the French coureurs-de-bois (fur traders) who were penetrating deep into the western wilderness, finding routes up to Hudson Bay and down to the Mississippi.

A series of wars in Europe were reflected in the New World. English and French fur traders burnt each other's forts. Both sides used the Indians as allies in the fighting. Colonial armies clashed in the east, while the British navy raided the coasts. The decisive conflict came with the Seven Years' War (1756–63). The French leader, General Montcalm, beat off British attacks until 1759, when General James Wolfe led his men up an undefended cliff to the Plains of Abraham. From there he attacked and took Quebec; both he and Montcalm were killed. Wolfe's success ended French imperial hopes in Canada, and in 1763 the Peace of Paris made Canada a British colony.

**British North America** Britain divided its new colony into two parts, Quebec and Nova Scotia. In Quebec the Indians, under their chief, Pontiac, rose against their new overlords, only to be crushed. But French fears of change were not so easily dealt with. Then in 1774 the Quebec Act set up a system of colonial governors and councils; it also eased French minds by conceding rights to Catholics as well as appeasing the English settlers of Quebec by extending its boundaries to include the wilds of Ohio south of the Great Lakes. This gave the English control of much of the former French empire and allowed them to compete with French-Canadian fur traders.

When the American War of Independence broke out the Canadian colonies remained loyal to the British Crown. In 1775 the Americans attacked British settlements in Canada and took Montreal, though the city of Quebec and Nova Scotian centres such as Halifax remained safe under the wing of the British Navy. When the War of Independence ended, Britain and America agreed on an international boundary that gave Ohio to the new republic. As an unexpected recompense to Canada, some 40,000 settlers left the United States to swell Canada's population. These immigrants became known as the United Empire Loyalists.

Many of the Loyalists settled in different parts of Nova Scotia. Britain later divided it into three separate areas, corresponding to the areas in which Loyalists had established settlements – a smaller Nova Scotia, New Brunswick, and Cape Breton Island (re-absorbed into Nova Scotia in 1820). Many Loyalists also settled on the upper St Lawrence and Lake Ontario, and the Canada Act of 1791 divided Quebec province into two parts – Lower and Upper Canada. The division recognised that Lower Canada (today Quebec) was dominated by the French, and that Upper Canada (today Ontario) was predominantly British.

**Expansion to the west** The end of French dominance of the fur trade at first left the Hudson's Bay Company a clear field in the north-west. But then rival groups, backed by businessmen in Montreal, appeared. By 1783 they had come together to form the giant North West Company. Explorers, travelling by canoe, pushed deeper into unknown territory. Alexander Mackenzie, from a far northern post on Lake Athabaska, found his way to the Arctic Ocean in 1789. Four years later, with a party of French Canadians and Indians, he overcame the natural barrier of the Rocky Mountains to make the first northern continental crossing to the Pacific coast in 1793. Such feats established Canada's presence throughout the far west.

**War of 1812** Just 29 years after the American colonies had won independence from Britain, war broke out between the two powers in 1812. The clash was mainly caused by Britain's determination to preserve its blockade of Napoleon's France, which involved stopping and searching neutral American shipping when it reached the area under blockade. In the war, though

A Canadian pioneer, armed with musket and equipped with warm winter clothing and snow shoes, travels into the interior

The arms of the Hudson's Bay Company – founded in 1670 to secure the wealth of Canada's furs for England

A late 18th-century view of York (now Toronto), capital of Upper Canada. The British government created Upper Canada in 1791 when they divided the old province of Quebec into two parts

greatly outnumbered, British and Canadian troops fought off American attacks, and a Canadian contingent under General Isaac Brock took Detroit. The Americans burnt the town of York (later Toronto); the British countered by burning Washington. A negotiated peace in 1814 left things as they had been before the war.

**Change and unrest** Increased immigration helped the growth of industries such as lumber and fisheries. The Hudson's Bay Company established the first colony in the west on the Red River. Violence between settlers there led to the take-over of the entire fur trade by the Hudson's Bay Company. In the east, the Welland Canal, opened in 1829, by-passed the mighty Niagara Falls, and thus funnelled Upper Canada's produce to booming Montreal.

But a shadow was cast over this prosperity by social unrest. Upper Canada was controlled by a group of privileged families known as the 'Family Compact'. In French Lower Canada, too, power was in the hands of a small group, operating an outmoded social and governmental system. Resentment against these powerful groups was stirred up by such men as the newspaper editor William Lyon Mackenzie. In 1837 the Upper Canada protest movement led to rioting and then to an ill-organised rebellion, bloodily put down by British troops. Mackenzie escaped to the United States.

The outcry which followed led the British Government to set up an official inquiry under Lord Durham in 1838. His report contributed to reducing the powers of the privileged groups, to the union of the two Canadas, and eventually to the granting of 'responsible government' in 1847. This last measure made the governors of the colonies responsible to elected parliaments.

**Taste of nationalism** In the 1840's America threatened war over the issue of the Pacific boundary. It acquired the rich Columbia valley from Britain but still coveted the remainder of the west. Relations between the two powers were somewhat improved by the so-called Reciprocity Treaty of 1854. Both powers agreed that there should be no tariff barriers between Canada and the United States. This helped Canadian trade and industry to develop, but American expansionism remained a threat until the end of the century.

On the basis of the decisions of the Quebec Conference (1864), the British North America Act was hammered out in London in 1866. The following year a Confederation called the Dominion of Canada came into being, though Prince Edward Island and Newfoundland remained outside.

The dominion consisted of four provinces: Ontario, Quebec, New Brunswick and Nova Scotia. The Act established an elected and responsible national government and fixed its powers in relation to the provincial governments. It gave the new dominion mastery of its own house – except, to a certain extent, for foreign policy and defence, in which Britain still had a voice.

**Building a nation** Federal Canada's first prime minister, John A. Macdonald, then turned to Canada's continental expansion. By a massive cash payment he persuaded the Hudson's Bay Company to give up its title to the west. This move was briefly resisted by Louis Riel with the support of the métis (people of mixed white and Indian blood), but after some concessions had been made to them, the first western province, Manitoba, joined the confederation. A year later the Pacific province, British Columbia, also joined. British Columbia had expanded in population and wealth during the Cariboo gold rush of the 1860's and it had to

The Hudson's Bay Company played a vital part in the opening up of the Canadian west. An 1824 drawing shows the governor of the company's Red River colony travelling by official canoe

be tempted into union by the grandiose promise of a trans-continental railway. But in 1873 Macdonald's government fell after a scandal about the financing of the railway, in which it was revealed that railway funds had subsidised Macdonald's re-election.

The new prime minister, Alexander Mackenzie, brought caution and delay to Canadian affairs, especially in railway building. Stagnation and recession followed. In the east, old racial and religious conflicts flared up again, while in the west 300 North-West Mounted Police tried to keep the peace among Indians, métis and settlers over thousands of square miles. It was not until 1878, when Macdonald regained office, that Canada's economy began to expand once more.

**From coast to coast** Through the efforts of the financier George Stephen of the Bank of Montreal and the engineer William van Horne, the Canadian Pacific Railway gradually thrust its way from east to west – across the swamps of northern Ontario, the open plains and the towering Rocky Mountains. By 1883 enough of the line had been built to carry ever-growing numbers of settlers into the west.

In 1885 Louis Riel and the métis, alarmed by the flood of Anglo-Saxon settlers into what had been their traditional territories, rose in rebellion. They were joined by many Plains Indians, in the first and only Indian war of the Canadian west. A force of 8000 troops crushed the rising within weeks. The métis went north where settlers would not follow, while the Indians were forced on to reserves. The old west of legend, like the buffalo that supported its way of life, was finished.

In the same year Louis Riel was hanged – an act which inflamed French-Canadian tempers. Macdonald had created a nation 'from sea to sea', but the old animosities between the British and French communities in Canada persisted.

**Boom times** In the early 1890's Canada was torn by disunity. The provinces of the west and the Atlantic coast resented the domination of national affairs by Ontario and Quebec. French-English antagonism also continued. But in 1896 Wilfrid Laurier led the Liberals to power, and his political tact – along with economic improvement – soothed heated emotions. Immigrants poured into the west to turn its plains into wheatfields, and others mined for gold, discovered in the Klondike in 1897. In 1905 the increase in population led to the formation of two new provinces, Alberta and Saskatchewan. At the same time, traffic east and west led to the building of two more trans-continental railways. But both were to end in bankruptcy.

**Out into the world** At the turn of the century, Canada was seeking more independence in foreign affairs, but still responded when Britain called for aid. Canadian volunteers fought for Britain in the Anglo-Boer War, while in the First World War more than 600,000 men out of a total population of fewer than 8 million fought on the Western Front. But, despite this display of unity, disagreements emerged in the years after the war. Pro-British fervour had angered French Canada; rising

A Canadian 'Mountie'. The Royal Canadian Mounted Police was originally formed in 1873 to bring law and order to Canada's western frontier. The Mounties' determination to 'get their man' became a part of Canadian legend

Immigrants travelling west on the Canadian Pacific Railway. Linking Montreal with the Pacific coast, the line was started in 1880 and completed five years later

The first issue of a Klondike newspaper celebrates gold production figures for the opening months of 1898

## CANADA *continued*

prices and eastern profiteering led western farmers to form pressure groups to demand just treatment; and an increasing wave of strikes indicated the rise of a militant industrial working class.

In 1921 the Liberal leader, William Lyon Mackenzie King, became prime minister. His caution calmed some of the growing unrest. He was helped by a 'spill-over' of American economic growth but in 1929 America's speculative bubble of prosperity burst, and the 'dirty thirties' brought massive unemployment and poverty to Canada. The Depression cost Mackenzie King the election of 1932; he was re-elected in 1935, but with a less secure power basis. The slump had given birth to a socialist party in the west, and a 'Social Credit' party, whose political philosophy was based on a curious form of right-wing economic radicalism.

But beyond domestic concerns, Canada maintained its ties with Britain, and in 1939 rallied to its side by declaring war on Germany. Canadian troops again went to Europe, and again they enhanced their country's reputation throughout the world.

*The Liberal leader William Lyon Mackenzie King dominated Canadian politics between the two world wars*

**Post-war development** Mackenzie King retired in 1948, but his successor, Louis St Laurent, carried on the cautious style of his Liberal government. In 1949 Newfoundland, 82 years after confederation, agreed to join Canada. The nation's prosperity grew apace.

Internationally Canada took part in the formation of the United Nations and of NATO. Canadians fought in Korea. In 1954 Canada joined India and Poland on the International Control Commission in Indo-China, and in 1956 played a central role in the settlement of the Suez crisis. At home, the autocratic regime of Maurice Duplessis in Quebec kept a tight check on nationalist ferment in that province. But throughout Canada, more and more voices were raised against the disproportionate American control of Canadian business and industry, which some saw as a threat to Canadian independence.

**Unity disturbed** In 1957 the Conservative party, under John Diefenbaker, gained power. Expansion continued, though there were several brief recessions. With the death of Duplessis in 1959, unrest in Quebec boiled over. Militant demands for French-Canadian control over Quebec intensified after 1963 when the Liberals, led by Lester Pearson, came to power. Wrangles over a new national flag and national medical insurance were overshadowed by deeper rifts, when some Quebec *séparatiste* groups resorted to terrorism.

**Entering a new era** In 1968, Pierre Trudeau, after only three years in politics, succeeded Lester Pearson both as Liberal leader and as prime minister. Projecting the popular image of an intellectual playboy, Trudeau nonetheless brought a vigorous new style to government and underlined Canada's growing sense of maturity. Among many reforming actions, Trudeau inaugurated a series of federal-provincial conferences to revise the constitution. But old sectarian rivalries between Canada's communities thwarted his plans.

Under Trudeau, Quebec separatism remained near boiling point. In late 1970 extremists of the *Front de Libération du Québec* kidnapped a Quebec politician, Pierre Laporte, and a British diplomat, James Cross. Laporte was murdered; Cross was released. Canada was one of the few western industrial nations that benefited from the 1973–74 worldwide fuel crisis, because unlike most other major powers Canada produces more petroleum than it uses. As fuel prices soared its government collected a windfall in oil export taxes.

*Pierre Trudeau became prime minister in 1968. The seriousness with which he approached Canada's problems contrasted with his 'intellectual playboy' image. In the 1974 general election his government was endorsed with a landslide victory*

*This revolutionary housing complex was a prominent feature of the world fair, Expo '67, held in Montreal in 1967*

# Central African Republic

Because of its remoteness, the Central African Republic was one of the last areas in Africa to be opened up by Europeans. It is one of the continent's least-developed regions. The French became established there in the late 19th century, and the country was united with Chad in 1906 to form the French colony of Ubangi-Shari-Chad. It was made part of French Equatorial Africa in 1910. Because of the harshness of French rule, there were rebellions in 1928, 1936 and 1946. Chad was separated from the country in 1920.

As part of their plan to grant independence to their African colonies, the French gave the territory internal self-rule in 1958. In 1960 the country became fully independent, with David Dacko as its first president.

Dacko soon outlawed all opposition, and established close ties with Communist China. But in 1966 he was ousted by General Jean Bedel Bokassa, who ordered the Chinese embassy out of the country. Bokassa promised to re-establish democracy in the republic, but instead set up his own repressive dictatorship.

240,534 sq. miles
1,747,400 people
Capital: Bangui

# Ceylon

An island off the sub-continent of India, Ceylon – now officially Sri Lanka ('Holy Ceylon') – has long been affected by the proximity of its giant neighbour. The present population of Ceylon is descended mainly from Indian invaders; its principal religions are Buddhism and Hinduism, both carried south from India.

In the 16th century, Ceylon's abundance of spices began to attract traders from Europe. The island passed from Portuguese to Dutch and then to British control. It gained independence in 1948, and in 1960 became the world's first country to have a woman as prime minister – Mrs Bandaranaike.

25,332 sq. miles
13,663,000 people
Capital: Colombo

**Conquerors from India** The first inhabitants in Ceylon were the Veddas, who emerged there *c.* 3000 BC. They were conquered in the 6th century BC by invaders originating from northern India, and survive today only as a small group living in the remote interior. The invaders, the Sinhalese, at first inhabited northern Ceylon, where they laid out a complex irrigation system. They founded their capital at Anuradhapura, which became one of the major Buddhist centres of the Eastern world. Buddhism was the inspiration which brought about Ceylon's classical period of fine arts, between the 4th and 6th centuries AD.

Because Ceylon lay so close to India it was easily invaded, and the Sinhalese were followed in the 11th century by another wave of invaders from India, the Hindu Tamils. By the 12th century, a Tamil kingdom had spread across the north of Ceylon and the Sinhalese had been driven into the south – a wet, forested region. The irrigation works in the north fell into decay.

**European control: 1505–1948** Ceylon's spices attracted Arab traders during the 12th and 13th centuries, and a prosperous trade developed. Descendants of the Arabs – the Muslim Moors – still live on the island.

The outward-looking Europeans of the 16th century were also lured by the profits to be made from spices. The first to arrive were the Portuguese, who from 1505 to 1597 controlled the whole island except the mountainous kingdom of Kandy.

The Dutch East India Company gained control from the Portuguese in 1658, but the Dutch were forced out by the British in 1796. Throughout this time, Kandy remained a free kingdom, but in 1815 it, too, was overcome. The British introduced coffee, tea and rubber cultivation. Self-government was achieved gradually in the 20th century. In 1948 Ceylon gained full independence, but remained a member of the Commonwealth.

*Large-scale tea cultivation was introduced into Ceylon by British planters in the 19th century. The country quickly became one of the leading tea producers of the world*

**Independent Ceylon** In 1956 the United National Party (UNP), the ruling party since independence, was beaten in elections; and the leader of the Sri Lanka

A Ceylonese temple
dancer. The island's
two main religions,
Buddhism and Hindu-
ism, were both intro-
duced from India

Freedom Party (SLFP), Solomon Bandaranaike, became prime minister – replacing Dudley Senanayake,
the son of Ceylon's first prime minister. After this, the
government's policies became increasingly socialist.

Ceylon was shaken by bloody rioting in 1958 between
Sinhalese and the Tamil minority – who make up 22 per
cent of the population. The Tamils demanded recognition of their language as the alternative official tongue,
and a separate Tamil state in a federal government. The
prime minister was assassinated in 1959 by a Buddhist
monk, and in 1960 his widow, Sirimavo Bandaranaike,
became prime minister after an election victory.

Under the Bandaranaikes, Ceylon moved closer to
the USSR and Communist China, and nationalisation
of some Western business groups caused strained
relations with the United States and Britain. The pro-
Western Senanayake returned to power in 1965, but
in 1970 Mrs Bandaranaike again became prime minister
and formed a leftist coalition government. The following
year, driven on by economic crisis and acute unemployment, an extreme left-wing group – the People's
Liberation Front, mostly made up of young students –
tried to seize power. But they were crushed by the army.
In 1972, a new constitution changed the name of the
country to the Republic of Sri Lanka. Food shortages in
1973 and 1974 brought riots.

In 1960 Ceylon's Mrs
Sirimavo Bandara-
naike became the first
woman prime minister
in the world

# Chad

This landlocked country in the remote region of north-
central Africa was once part of a series of Islamic states.
Walled cities lined the eastern shore of the broad,
marshy Lake Chad. Modern Chad is torn by a struggle
between the Arab and Muslim majority in the north and
the Negro and partly Christian minority in the south.

In 1970, Chad began to suffer from severe drought, in
common with other states bordering the southern
Sahara; by 1973 it was in the grip of famine.

**Islamic empire** About AD 700, it is believed, peoples
from the upper Nile moved into Chad and built a string
of cities. Some 200 years later, pressure from the
Berbers of the Sahara made these city-states unite into
a kingdom which was given the name Kanem-Bornu.
Over the course of centuries it was converted to Islam.

**French rule: 1900** The French entered Chad in the
1890's and created the Military Territory of Chad in
1900. Six years later Chad was united with Ubangi-
Shari (now the Central African Republic), and in 1910
it became part of French Equatorial Africa. Chad was
detached from Ubangi-Shari in 1920 and placed under
its own administration. In 1958 it became self-governing
within the French community; and in 1960 the country
gained complete independence.

495,752 sq. miles
4,068,300 people
Capital: Ndjamena

**Guerrilla fighting** Independent Chad, under its first
president, François Tombalbaye, faced internal problems caused by differences between the pastoral,
Arab-oriented and Muslim north, and the wealthier
south. Tombalbaye, a Christian, imprisoned several
leading Muslim officials in 1963 on charges of subver-
sion. Most were later freed.

In 1965, fighting broke out between Muslim guerrillas
in northern Chad and the central government. A bloody
struggle followed, in which thousands died. After Chad
broke relations with Israel, Arab nations stopped
supplying and training the guerrillas.

Two tribesmen hunt
big game on the
shores of Lake Chad,
in this 19th-century
print. Chad came
under French influence
in the 1890's

# Chile

Before 1973, Chile was noted for its tradition of peaceful
democratic change, which made it a rarity in a continent where change usually spells violent revolution. In
1970 it became the only Western state with a democratically elected Marxist government. But the radical
measures speedily imposed by the new leader President
Allende in his 'Socialist experiment' antagonised many
Chileans. In September 1973, after months of worsening political conflict and economic crisis, Allende's
regime was ended by a violent military coup.

**Early history** Spanish conquistadores occupied
northern Chile in 1533 after conquering the Incas.
An attempt in 1536 to extend Spanish territory southwards met with fierce resistance from the region's
Araucanian Indians, a warring and cannibalistic race
who were not completely subdued until 1880.

In 1541 Pedro de Valdivia (c. 1500–54) founded
Santiago, the capital of Chile. It was a further 200 years
before Spain completed its occupation of present-day
Chile down the 1200 mile coastal strip south of the River
Bio-Bio. Finding little mineral wealth there, the
Spanish developed an agricultural society.

292,256 sq. miles
9,375,000 people
Capital: Santiago

**An Irishman's son becomes president: 1818** With
the decline of Spanish power throughout South
America, Chilean patriots rose against their Spanish
overlords in the early 19th century. They were led by
Bernardo O'Higgins, the Chilean-born son of an
Irishman, and José de San Martin. Chile proclaimed
its independence in 1818, and O'Higgins became the
country's first president.

The constitution of 1833, which paved the way for
parliamentary government, remained virtually unchanged until 1925. With internal stability, Chile
prospered, though agriculture remained backward. In
1884 the country emerged from the five-year 'War of the
Pacific' against Bolivia and Peru with vast new riches –
the mineral deposits of the northern Atacama lands won
from its defeated enemies. The most important minerals
in this rain-free desert region of white sands were
nitrates and copper. The value of nitrates to Europe as a
fertiliser transformed Chile's economy at the turn of the
century. When this boom came to an end after the First
World War, a second period of prosperity for Chile
followed with the development of copper mining.

Bernardo O'Higgins
in a heroic pose. The
Chilean-born son of
an Irishman, he led
the revolt which threw
off Spanish rule

**A Marxist experiment that failed** Unemployment
and political unrest brought Chile to the verge of
revolution in the 1920's, but this was avoided when
President Arturo Alessandri Palma (1868–1950), who
had the support of the working and middle classes,
introduced labour reforms and a new constitution in
1925. From then until 1970, despite a period of severe
inflation in the 1950's, the economy remained stable.
The country suffered a major set-back in 1960 when a
disastrous earthquake razed entire cities.

In 1970, Dr Salvador Allende Gossens became
president. His Marxist coalition government – the
Popular Union – soon ran into difficulties. Its nationalisation programme led to tension with the United
States – controller of much of Chile's copper interests. It
also alienated middle-class Chileans, who in 1972
combined in an employers' 'strike' against the government. Inflation, pressure from left-wing extremists, and
peasant opposition to state planning added to Allende's
difficulties. In September 1973, the army under General
Pinochet took power. Its measures against Allende's
supporters were marked by extreme severity. Allende
himself died in the coup, allegedly by his own hand.

Chileans play football
in the shadow of one
of the country's copper
mines. Chile is the
third-largest producer
of copper in the world

Dr Allende, elected president of Chile in 1970, was
the first Marxist leader in the West to win power
through the ballot box. His regime – and his life –
came to a violent end in 1973

371

# China

The People's Republic of China is the world's third largest country after the USSR and Canada, and the most populous: about a fifth of the world's population is Chinese. Chinese civilization, which has had a major influence on the development of mankind, has lasted continuously for over 3500 years.

The Chinese traditionally regarded their country as the sole centre of civilization, and called it the Middle Kingdom. Yet China suffered long periods of chaos and division, and was constantly harassed by northern nomadic peoples, who sometimes succeeded in occupying large parts of its territory.

Among China's contributions to world civilization were inventions such as paper, printing, gunpowder and the magnetic compass. By the 19th century, after having once led the world in science and culture, it had become a relatively backward country, deeply humiliated by maltreatment at the hands of the West.

China survived the impact of Western imperialism, and is the only large area of the world which has never been under European rule. But it was not until after the Communist revolution of 1949 that China regained its confidence and began to challenge for a place among the world's great powers. By the mid-1960's it had become a nuclear power, and rivalled the Soviet Union for leadership of the Communist world. It joined the space race by launching a satellite in 1970. With the country's long-delayed admission into the United Nations in 1971, China won formal recognition as a leading power.

**Beginnings of Chinese history** An ancestor of modern man, Peking Man *(Homo erectus pekinensis)*, lived in China half a million years ago. The Chinese people first emerged into history with the Shang dynasty in the 16th century BC. Bronze sacrificial vessels surviving from this age point to the existence of an aristocratic class, with a developed religious and ceremonial life. Ancestor-worship, which remained an important ingredient in Chinese religion, was already practised. Servants were sacrificed and buried with the dead kings to attend them in the afterlife.

**Chou rule: c. 1027 BC** The Shang were conquered in the 11th century BC by the Chou people, who came from the Wei River valley. Little is known about the early Chou period, but later generations regarded it as a 'golden age'. The founders of the dynasty, King Wen, King Wu and the Duke of Chou, were revered as sages.

By the 8th century BC, Chinese civilization was centred on a loose confederation of states in the central and lower reaches of the Yellow River. These states owed nominal allegiance to the Chou sovereign, whose own dominions lay in the region of present-day Loyang. They were linked by close ties of kinship between their ruling families – and by the belief that their ancestors had received their lands in return for their help in overthrowing the Shang.

3,691,502 sq. miles
830,453,000 people
Capital: Peking

*A Shang dynasty bronze axe, dating from the 12th century BC. It was used to behead human sacrifices at funerals*

*Bronze vessels of this type were used in ritual ceremonies during China's classical Chou period (from c. 1027 BC)*

**'Warring states' period** Although the Chou king was still officially supreme, large states, whose rulers had usurped the title of 'king', contended with each other. Small states were swallowed up by these kingdoms, which extended from the River Yangtze to the area of present-day Peking.

Social changes brought opportunities to men of merit in place of the high-born. These upheavals raised important questions about the nature of government and the duties of men in society. As a result, the period became famous for philosophical disputes. The most famous of the so-called 'hundred schools' of philosophy which flourished at the time was that of Confucius (551–479 BC). The humane teachings of this school later formed the basis of traditional Chinese education, and inspired high ideals in social and political life.

*The Great Wall of China runs for 1500 miles along the country's northern frontier. It was built by Emperor Ch'in Shih Huang Ti to keep nomadic invaders out of his empire*

**Ch'in unification: 221–206 BC** Having wiped out the Chou royal domain in 256, the Ch'in who, like the Chou, came from the Wei valley, defeated the other Chinese states and unified the country in 221 BC. The Ch'in victory was an important milestone in Chinese history; it marked the start of the imperial period, since the Ch'in held sway over most of north China as we know it today – and penetrated into parts of the extreme south, including the region of Canton. It is from Ch'in that the name China is probably derived.

The founder of the Ch'in dynasty, Ch'in Shih Huang Ti, governed by means of a centralised civil service. Hoping China would stay united, he standardised weights and measures and introduced a simpler form of writing, which was to be used throughout the country. But he was also reviled for his harshness. The common people suffered greatly in the building of the Great Wall, designed to keep out nomads from the north. Intellectuals were alienated by the 'Burning of the Books', an attempt to stamp out rival ideologies by destroying all literature in private hands except the records of the Ch'in state, and certain practical works.

**Expansion under the Han: 206 BC–AD 220** Ch'in harshness provoked rebellion and they were replaced by the Han. Under Han rule, the Chinese Empire was further expanded to incorporate most of present-day south China, much land beyond the Great Wall, part of Vietnam, and the Tarim Basin in central Asia. This opened up trade routes which carried silk to Rome.

A large bureaucracy was needed to administer this great empire. An imperial university was founded and examinations were introduced for entry into the civil service, nearly 1600 years before this practice was started in Europe. Once the dynasty had become firmly established, scholars sought to restore the literature destroyed under the Ch'in, both from memory and through the recovery of hidden manuscripts. The books associated with the teachings of Confucius came to be regarded as the ideal writings for every student to follow. The Chinese revered scholarship: the men who filled high posts in the civil service – the so-called mandarin class – were selected for their knowledge of literature.

But the Han had expanded too rapidly to hold their territories securely. The Hsiung-nu (Huns) to the north were a powerful menace and had to be appeased by the payment of tribute. The dynasty was also weakened by economic decline: great estates employed a growing proportion of the peasantry as tenants, which reduced the number of taxpayers and thereby lessened the revenue for the government.

*A model of a pleasure palace – probably a prototype of the pagoda – found in a tomb of the Han dynasty (206 BC–AD 220)*

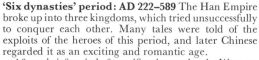

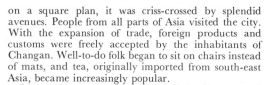

## 'Six dynasties' period: AD 222–589

The Han Empire broke up into three kingdoms, which tried unsuccessfully to conquer each other. Many tales were told of the exploits of the heroes of this period, and later Chinese regarded it as an exciting and romantic age.

After a brief period of reunification under the Western Chin (Tsin) dynasty (265–316), civil war in north China early in the 4th century opened the way for barbarian invasion. Until 439, when north China was reunited under the barbarian Northern Wei dynasty, this area was a battleground of non-Chinese regimes.

Only the south remained in Chinese hands. But the government based on Nanking was weak and for three centuries six short-lived dynasties in turn held power. Despite these setbacks, China suffered no cultural decline into a Dark Age. Indeed, the spread of Buddhism, which had reached China during the Han period, was a great enrichment of Chinese life.

## Sui reunification: 589

Having ruled north China since 581, the Sui dynasty reunited the country in 589. Its emperors reintroduced the paraphernalia of imperial government, including the civil service examinations which had long been in abeyance.

The second Sui emperor, Yang, caused the death of untold numbers of his subjects, who were forced to work on rebuilding the Great Wall and on canal digging. But Yang's canals, linking the Yellow River with the northeast and Hangchow, were a vital means of securing unity and collecting the grain paid as tax.

The end of the Sui was hastened by unsuccessful campaigns against the vassal state of Koguryo in north Korea and Liaotung, an area which had been colonised during the Han dynasty. Widespread revolts put an end to the dynasty which, like the Ch'in, succeeded in unifying China but tried to do too much too quickly.

## Golden age of T'ang: 618–906

The T'ang dynasty was founded by a prominent Sui official. The early T'ang period was dominated by three famous sovereigns. Under the second emperor, T'ai-tsung, China reconquered large areas of central Asia which had been lost since Han rule. His successor, Kao-tsung, was a sickly man, whose illnesses allowed his wife to gain much influence. After his death in 684 she usurped the throne, ruling for the next 20 years as the Empress Wu, China's only female sovereign.

The third outstanding T'ang ruler was Hsuan-tsung. Under his rule, from 713 to 756, China reached a peak of cultural achievement; art and literature flourished, and Buddhism inspired magnificent temples and sculptures. His capital, Changan, was the greatest city in the world, with a population of more than a million. Built

*Magnetic compasses were used in China at least 1700 years ago. The figure in this sketch of an early Chinese compass is mounted on a magnetic stone; its extended finger always points south*

*A page of the Diamond Sutra of AD 868 – the oldest printed book in existence. Buddha is shown in the centre*

on a square plan, it was criss-crossed by splendid avenues. People from all parts of Asia visited the city. With the expansion of trade, foreign products and customs were freely accepted by the inhabitants of Changan. Well-to-do folk began to sit on chairs instead of mats, and tea, originally imported from south-east Asia, became increasingly popular.

But a series of rebellions weakened the dynasty, and in 906 the T'ang were overthrown and China was again divided. Five short-lived dynasties reigned in the north, while the south broke up into several kingdoms.

## Success of the Sung: 960–1126

In 960 a new dynasty, the Sung, founded by a prominent general, seized power in the north. By 978 it had brought the independent southern kingdoms under its sway. The early Sung government developed highly sophisticated procedures for recruitment and promotion in the civil service. Kaifeng, its capital, which had become important because of its key position on the canal linking the Yellow River with Hangchow, was a thriving industrial city.

Militarily, the Sung never restored the early T'ang position and were willing to pay tribute to the Liao dynasty, which had held territory around Peking since 947. After 1044 they also paid it to the Tibetan Tangut tribes, who had founded the strong state of Hsi Hsia in what is now Kansu. But in 1126, another barbarian people, the Jurched from Manchuria, having overthrown the Liao, conquered north China and set up their own Chin Empire. The Sung fled to the south, setting up a new capital at Hangchow, from which they ruled China south of the Hwai River. Stability was achieved through the payment of tribute to the Chin, and the country soon prospered through a great expansion of overseas trade.

## Mongol conquest: 1280–1368

Mongol invaders wiped out the Chin in the north in 1234 as part of an astonishing series of world-wide conquests initiated by Genghis Khan. However, these nomads needed another 45 years to subdue the rest of China, largely because they were not used to fighting in a populous country with walled cities. But eventually the Sung were driven further and further into the south, and they were finally defeated in a sea-battle off Hong Kong in 1279.

With the whole of China now in foreign hands there was an abrupt break with tradition; the civil service examinations were suspended and the government run by Mongols and their foreign allies. China's conqueror, Kublai Khan, not only dissipated his energies in attempts to conquer Japan and spread Mongol influence throughout south-east Asia, but also became involved in civil war with a rebel member of the imperial clan. With so many calls on its strength, the huge Mongol Empire, which covered most of the Euro-Asian land mass, began to disintegrate and Kublai became increasingly dependent on the wealth of China.

## Ming resurgence: 1368–1644

China was once again united under a native dynasty, the Ming, in 1368. Its founder, Chu Yuan-chang (who became Emperor Hung-wu), was of peasant origin – the only man of humble stock apart from the Han founder to become emperor, or 'Son of Heaven'. The capital was now at Nanking, but in 1421 the emperor Yung-lo moved to Peking, where a fine new city was built. The Mongols continued to be troublesome and large armies had to be maintained on the line of the Great Wall, which was extensively rebuilt. Hung-wu had re-established suzerainty over China's neighbouring peoples, and in Yung-lo's reign great fleets under the eunuch admiral Cheng Ho voyaged as far afield as India, the Persian Gulf and East Africa. Partly as a result of the Mongol influence, government

*Emperor T'ang T'ai-tsung's horse – a stone detail from his tomb. The stirrup was one of many Chinese inventions whose use eventually spread to Europe; there it helped to revolutionise warfare*

*Genghis Khan and his marauding hordes swept from central Asia into the Chin Empire in 1234. On this occasion the Great Wall failed to act as an effective barrier*

*The art of painting on silk scrolls was highly regarded in Sung China. This picture of women preparing silk was painted by Emperor Hui-tsung*

The port of Maçao, on the south-east coast of China, in an early print. A Portuguese-held trade port since 1557, it is the oldest European settlement in the Far East

*The Dowager Empress Tz'u-hsi backed the Chinese Boxer uprising against foreign influence*

## CHINA *continued*

had become increasingly despotic. Intellectual life was more stereotyped, and essays for the civil service examinations had to conform to a strict pattern, abiding by the orthodox interpretation of the Confucian classics which had been established under the Sung.

During the 16th century, Europeans began to arrive in the Far East by sea. Portuguese traders reached the Chinese coast soon after the capture of Malacca in 1511. Missionaries followed, but it was not until 1601 that Matteo Ricci established a Jesuit mission in Peking.

**Manchu conquest: 1644** Early in the 17th century serious rebellions broke out against Ming corruption. The Manchus on the north-east frontier had built up a strong state, whose administration owed much to Chinese example. With the aid of Chinese sympathisers, the Manchus reached Peking, expelled the Ming and set up their own dynasty, which ruled China until 1912.

The Manchus interfered as little as possible with the existing Chinese bureaucracy, though they made sure that senior Chinese officials had Manchu counterparts. They were, however, determined to resist assimilation with the Chinese, forbidding intermarriage and keeping their homeland as a separate region with its own government. They forced the Chinese to wear the pigtail, the Manchus' own traditional form of head-dress.

**K'ang-hsi – a great Manchu emperor** K'ang-hsi, the second emperor of the Ch'ing dynasty of the Manchus, was one of China's greatest rulers. Skilful in domestic administration, he also had to fight several wars. A serious revolt in 1673 attempted to restore a native Chinese dynasty, and only after this had been stamped out was he free to complete the conquest of Taiwan, where a regime had been established by the Ming partisan Koxinga. Meanwhile Russian expansion had caused trouble in the north.

**Prosperity under Ch'ien-lung: 1736–95** In the early part of Ch'ien-lung's reign China reached a peak of prosperity. Agricultural production had been rising speedily since the late 16th century with the development of early ripening strains of rice and the introduction of maize and sweet potatoes. The population rose from 150 million to 300 million in the 18th century.

Under Ch'ien-lung, China regained its central Asian empire, which it had lost since the days of the T'ang. The emperor's image was that of a great poet and patron of letters, though he was also responsible for a literary inquisition that suppressed works critical of the Manchus.

**The 'Opium War': 1839–42** In the late 18th century, Europeans were allowed to trade only at Canton – except for the Portuguese who had been established in Maçao since the mid-16th century. The Chinese, who regarded their country as self-sufficient, showed little interest in importing foreign goods in return for their own large exports of porcelain, silk and tea.

Britain tried to expand its trade by selling to China opium produced in Bengal. As addiction spread, imports increased alarmingly, and the Chinese – for economic as well as moral reasons – tried to stop the traffic. In retaliation the British fleet took control of several Chinese coastal cities in what became known as the 'Opium War'. Peace was made at Nanking in 1842. Hong Kong was ceded to Britain, whose traders were allowed to live in the ports of Amoy, Foochow, Ningpo and Shanghai.

*K'ang-hsi, painted by an unknown artist, sits firmly on the 'Celestial Throne'. A skilful administrator, he did much to bring China under Manchu control*

**Treaty of Tientsin: 1858** After renewed fighting, in which France took part on Britain's side, a treaty was signed at Tientsin in 1858. It provided for more open 'treaty' ports, established formal diplomatic relations, and gave foreign missionaries the right to travel and work freely throughout China. But the Chinese refused to ratify the treaty, war broke out again, and in 1860 an Anglo-French force reached Peking and compelled the government to accept its demands. Members of the force also sacked the Summer Palace, outside the city. Central China was thrown into turmoil by the Taiping rebellion led by Hung Hsiu-ch'uan, who established a regime at Nanking. It was suppressed in 1864.

**Decline of the Ch'ing** In spite of desperate Chinese attempts to modernise their technology so that they could resist European aggression, the late 19th century saw great areas of the Chinese Empire hacked away. European powers, such as Russia, even gained territory in China itself. Finally, in 1895, China was heavily defeated by Japan. Afterwards the Treaty of Shimonoseki gave Taiwan to Japan and declared Korea independent – a prelude to its annexation by Japan in 1910. Part of the reason for these defeats was that modernisation in China was resisted by the older generation of officials who refused to accept that the Celestial Empire could learn anything from the 'barbarians'.

The anti-foreign feelings of the Chinese people came to a head with an uprising, instigated by a secret society known as the Boxers. Their first targets were the foreign missionaries and their Chinese converts. In 1900 they gained the support of the sinister Dowager Empress Tz'u-hsi and laid siege to the foreign legations in Peking. An international expeditionary force was sent to liberate the diplomats and harsh peace terms were imposed.

**Revolution: 1911** Discontent among young Chinese, who had adopted Western political ideas, led to revolution in 1911. The chief promoter of republican ideas was Sun Yat-sen, but in 1912, when the Manchus had been deposed, he yielded the presidency of the new republic to a leading general, Yuan Shih-k'ai. Yuan died four years later, having failed to establish himself as emperor.

After Yuan's death, China fell into chaos: the internationally recognised government at Peking was a military clique; local warlords ruled the provinces, while a government of the Kuomintang nationalist party was established in Canton by Sun Yat-sen.

**Japanese aggression: 1914–20** When world war broke out in 1914 Japan seized German-leased territories in China. In 1915 the Japanese presented the 'Twenty-one demands' to Peking, which were designed to make China a Japanese satellite. Though the Chinese resisted these demands, the Versailles Treaty at the end of the war legalised Japanese occupation of Shantung province. In protest the Chinese refused to sign the treaty.

Anti-Japanese agitation, started by Peking students in 1919 in the Fourth of May movement, developed into a wholesale demand for change, which was further inspired by the success of the Russian Revolution. In 1920 the Soviet regime gave up all the concessions which the tsarist government had won in China, and in 1921 the Chinese Communist Party was formed, with Mao Tse-tung as one of its founder members.

**Rise of Chiang Kai-shek** In 1925 Sun Yat-sen died, his dream of a united republican China unfulfilled, and the leadership of the Kuomintang passed to Chiang Kai-shek, the head of the Whampoa military academy. In 1926 Chiang led his army against the warlords and the Peking regime. In alliance with the Communists, his forces took Nanking, Shanghai and other cities.

But by 1927 Chiang had come to the conclusion that the Communists were becoming too powerful and turned on them, ordering the execution of their leaders in Shanghai and other cities. In 1928 he established a government at Nanking, but could not control the whole country. Meanwhile, Mao Tse-tung was building up peasant support for the Communists.

*British diplomats meet their Chinese counterparts in negotiations at Nanking in 1842 to end the 'Opium War'. The concessions which the reluctant Chinese were forced to make meant that European influence was firmly established in China*

*Sun Yat-sen, a leading Chinese nationalist, fled his country in 1895 after an abortive revolt. He returned in 1911 to become provisional president of the Chinese republic*

**The Long March: 1934** In 1931 Manchuria, China's most industrialised area, was occupied by the Japanese, who, in the following year, made it into a puppet state, Manchukuo, under the rule of the last surviving Manchu emperor, P'u-yi. But Chiang was unwilling to come to grips with the Japanese until he had settled with the Communists, who were winning increasing support in the rural areas. After repeated Nationalist attacks, the Communists decided to evacuate their main base in Kiangsi. They embarked on the famous 6000 mile Long March to the northern province of Shensi, where they settled at Yenan. Out of the force of 100,000 less than one-third reached their destination. During the course of the march Mao became undisputed leader of the Chinese Communist Party.

*China invaded Tibet in 1950. The Tibetan leader, the Dalai Lama (on the white pony), fled across the Himalayas to India*

**War with Japan: 1937–45** All-out war broke out between China and Japan in 1937. The Chinese suffered heavy casualties and lost much territory. The capital had to be removed to Chungking and by 1939 the Japanese had occupied the entire coast and captured six of China's seven major cities.

In a drive for national unity, the Communists called for collaboration with Chiang's Nationalist forces against the Japanese. Chiang at first refused, but his generals forced him to consent. But relations between the two soon deteriorated. The ineffectiveness of the Nationalists contrasted with the Communists' success in organising peasant resistance.

Japan's attack on Pearl Harbour made China the ally of the USA and Britain in the Second World War, and Chiang pinned his hopes on Allied victory. After the Japanese defeat in 1945, US mediators failed to secure agreement between Nationalists and Communists and in 1946 civil war broke out again.

**People's Republic: 1949** The civil war ended in Communist victory in 1949 with the establishment of the People's Republic of China under the leadership of Mao Tse-tung. The Nationalists under Chiang retreated to the island of Taiwan (Formosa).

US support for Chiang was seen by the Chinese as interference in their internal affairs and the threat of foreign intervention made the regime fearful of counter-revolution. Many landlords were executed and their property handed over to the peasants. The new regime's appeal was partly nationalistic, for it aimed to restore pride in traditional Chinese culture, which had been denigrated in the mood of humiliation of the early years of the 20th century.

Much was also done to improve hygiene, welfare and literacy, and enormous efforts were made to turn China into a major industrial power as quickly as possible. The cost was severe regimentation of people's lives.

*Sculpture used as propaganda for a new society: soldier and peasant stand together in a rising against the tyrannical landlords*

**Foreign relations: 1950–70** Chinese 'volunteers' were sent to the aid of the North Koreans in the Korean War in 1950, when UN forces looked like reaching the Chinese border. In the same year China forcibly occupied Tibet, over which it had long claimed territorial rights. In the early 1960's, China asserted its claims to other disputed territories on its border with India. After a short but successful campaign, the Chinese army withdrew to the positions it had originally occupied.

**Relations with Russia** In the early years of the People's Republic, the USSR and other Communist countries gave China much financial and technical aid. But relations between the two main Communist powers deteriorated after Stalin's death in 1953. Russian Communism had been based on success in the cities; the Chinese experience was that the peasants in the country were the most important element. By the mid-1950's the two powers had little in common. In 1956, the Soviet leader, Nikita Khrushchev, denounced the previous Stalinist regime in Russia and proclaimed a new policy of 'peaceful co-existence' with the West.

Mao regarded this as a betrayal of international Communism and accused the Russians of being 'revisionists' who had betrayed the spirit of Marxist-Leninism. He started a campaign to increase Chinese influence among the emergent states of Asia, Africa and South America. Russian aid to China was stopped in 1960 and Russian technicians left. Despite this, China tested an atomic bomb in 1963. Its first H-bomb was tested in 1967.

**Internal developments** In 1956, the Communist leadership let it be known that it would welcome criticism, after Mao's plea, 'Let a hundred flowers bloom, let a hundred schools of thought contend'. But comments were so harsh that the 'Hundred Flowers' movement was abandoned in 1957, and many critics of the regime were severely disciplined.

Mao now urged the Chinese into an economic revolution, called the 'Great Leap Forward'. Peasant farms had been combined to form collectives in 1954. In 1958 they were further combined to form communes, in which no specialisation was allowed; peasants were to produce steel and students were to become farmers. This was heralded as a move towards true Communism, but after bad harvests the project had to be modified. This failure caused a rift between those, like Mao, who gave priority to ideological considerations, and those who preferred technological progress.

**The 'Cultural Revolution'** The same fundamental difference of attitude was the cause of the Cultural Revolution which convulsed China in the late 1960's. Mao launched it because he feared that the Chinese revolution had lost its impetus and that the country was becoming 'bourgeois' in outlook. 'Red Guards' – many of them students from the now-closed universities – marched through the country, reciting from the 'little red book', *Quotations from Chairman Mao Tse-tung*.

The main aim of the revolution was to get rid of the 'three great differences' between town and country, industry and agriculture, and mental and manual labour. But its excesses led to strain within the country's leadership. Order was restored and the universities were reopened in 1967.

A 'New Cultural Revolution' under Mao's leadership began in 1974. It was directed against Confucius and 'reactionaries' who continued to cling to his beliefs.

**World recognition: 1971** Chinese hostility towards its Soviet neighbour continued into the 1970's.

In 1971 China's status as a potential super-power was confirmed by its admission to the United Nations, where it took the place of Taiwan, which since 1949 had held the Chinese seat on the Security Council and in the General Assembly. Taiwan was expelled from the UN despite US protests.

*China's enormous manpower is its greatest asset. Here student volunteers help to build a road on a people's commune*

*The 'Thoughts of Chairman Mao' inspire Chinese people in all walks of life, according to this official poster*

*Bitter enemies ever since the establishment of the People's Republic in 1949, China and the United States took a step towards friendship when President Nixon visited Mao in 1972*

# Colombia

The growth of Colombia has been marked by some of the most bitter struggles of any country in South America. In the 70 years up to 1903 the country was ravaged by 27 civil wars, while in the first half of the present century hundreds of thousands were killed in strife between political factions.

Colombia is a land of snow-capped peaks, vast low-land pastures and torrid jungles, still inhabited in some regions along the Venezuelan border by primitive tribes. Similar tribes occupied much of Colombia when Spanish explorers arrived in 1499.

The explorers found valuable gold deposits, and between 1525 and 1533 they established the first settlements at Santa Marta and Cartagena. Bogotá, founded in 1538, became a lively cultural centre and was known as 'the Athens of South America'.

439,735 sq. miles
23,929,700 people
Capital: Bogotá

*A 17th-century print showing the port of Cartagena which, with Santa Marta, was the earliest Spanish settlement in Colombia*

**New Granada becomes independent: 1819** Spain ruled the territory around Bogotá. It was known as New Granada, and included parts of present-day Panama, Venezuela and Ecuador, as well as most of Colombia. New Granada won independence from Spain in 1819. Simon Bolívar, the South American revolutionary and victor of the decisive Battle of Boyacá, became the first president of the new republic. Venezuela and Ecuador later broke away to become separate states.

By the end of the 1800's two strongly opposed political parties had developed – the Conservatives who wanted a strong, centralised government and close ties with the Roman Catholic Church; and the Liberals who wanted less government control and a separation of the state from the Church. The strength of these parties was almost equal, and no caudillo, or strong man, emerged.

Political strife and civil unrest followed. One civil war was followed almost immediately by another. Guerrilla and bandit groups flourished and the economy was disrupted. In 1903 Colombia lost Panama, which proclaimed itself an independent republic.

**Coffee the economic mainstay** Helped by an increased world demand for its coffee, Colombia was able to progress towards stability in the 30 years up to 1948. Coffee-processing industries were expanded, and steel and textile mills started. But the assassination of the Liberal leader Jorge Eliecer Gaitán in 1948 plunged the country back into chaos. Riots and crime were met with violent rule, under such men as Gustavo Rojas Pinilla. Some semblance of order was restored in 1958 with the election of a moderate Liberal leader, Alberto Lleras Camargo, and an agreement that the Conservatives and Liberals would take the presidency in alternate four-year terms until 1974. A new political movement, however, emerged in the late 1960's, backed by the former head of the armed forces, Rojas Pinilla. Rojas was defeated for the presidency in 1970 by the Conservative Misael Pastrana Borrero.

The first free elections in more than two decades were held in 1974. A Liberal, Alfonso López Michelsen, was elected president. López was the son of Alfonso López-Pumarejo, honoured as a reformer when he served as Colombia's president in the 1930's and 1940's.

**Congo, Democratic Republic of,** *see Zaïre*

*Rojas Pinilla, who seized power in 1953, subjected Colombia to four years of corrupt and violent rule before being ousted in 1957*

# Congo, People's Republic of

This republic on the north bank of the River Congo achieved independence from France in 1960 – the same year in which its southern neighbour Zaïre (formerly the Democratic Republic of the Congo, and before that the Belgian Congo) became independent. There has been frequent tension between the two 'Congos'.

**Explorers and traders** The region around the River Congo was first visited by the Portuguese in the 15th century, and later by French explorers and traders. Beginning in the 17th century the French set up outposts for the profitable trade in slaves and ivory. French explorers pushed into the interior in the 1870's, and a conference in Berlin in 1885 recognised French claims to the area.

The territory was first called French Congo, and later Middle Congo. It was merged with other areas into French Equatorial Africa in 1910, but by 1956 it had been granted local autonomy.

**Independence** In 1958 the colony voted to become a self-governing republic within the French Community, to be known as the Congo Republic. The country became fully independent in 1960.

The first president, Fulbert Youlou, was toppled by a popular revolt in 1963. Alphonse Massamba-Débat became president under a new constitution, but when he dissolved the National Assembly in 1968 the army seized power and he was forced to co-operate with army leaders in a new government. A new constitution went into effect in 1970 under which the president of the newly created Congolese Labour Party was automatically to be president of the country. Major Marien Ngouabi, leader of the 1968 army coup, was chosen president. The country became officially known as the People's Republic of the Congo.

132,046 sq. miles
1,022,600 people
Capital Brazzaville

*The Franco-Italian explorer Pierre Savorgnan de Brazza founded the city of Brazzaville in 1880*

# Costa Rica

In contrast to many other Latin American countries, Costa Rica, with the highest standard of living in Central America, has enjoyed a large measure of stable and democratic government, as well as a tradition of friendly relations with its neighbours.

Columbus discovered and named Costa Rica – the 'rich coast' – in 1502. But Spain had little use for the colony. There was no gold or silver and not enough Indian labour to work large estates. As a result, Costa Rica was settled largely by poor peasants.

**Dictatorship and democracy** Costa Rica threw off Spanish rule in a bloodless revolution in 1821. In 1824 it joined the Federal Republic of Central America and became formally independent in 1838. During the 19th century, Costa Rica began to prosper with the development of coffee plantations.

Costa Rica has seen four attempts at dictatorship since it became an independent democracy. In 1856 an American adventurer, William Walker, tried to take over the country, but he was soon driven out. In 1870 a Costa Rican, General Tomás Garcia, seized power, which he held until 1882. A military dictatorship was established by General Federico Tinoco from 1917 to 1919. When Otilio Ulate was elected president in 1948, he was prevented by an allegedly Communist group from taking up office. The revolt was put down by José Figuéres Ferrer, who installed Ulate in power. Figuéres himself became president in 1953.

**Peace and prosperity** For the next two decades Costa Rica was peaceful and prosperous. In 1970 Figuéres again became president. The United States opposed him when he established diplomatic relations with the Soviet Union. In 1971 he claimed there was a 'US plot' to overthrow him and his regime, and relations between the two countries deteriorated. Figuéres was succeeded by Daniel Oduber Quirós in 1974.

19,575 sq. miles
1,963,000 people
Capital: San José

*William Walker (1824–60), an American adventurer, tried to take over Costa Rica in 1856. His later exploits in Central America led to his execution*

Christopher Columbus, who discovered Cuba on his first voyage to America in 1492, is welcomed on the shore by the native Indians

# Cuba

Christopher Columbus discovered Cuba, the largest and most westerly island in the Caribbean, on his first voyage to the New World in 1492. The island came under Spanish rule in the early 16th century and remained part of the Spanish colonial empire until 1898.

Modern Cuba was created by the struggle to achieve independence from Spain, and then to preserve that independence from economic and political domination by the United States. The revolution led by Fidel Castro in 1959 not only transformed Cuban society; it also made Cuba an ally of the Soviet Union, and the threat that this alliance posed to the United States brought the world to the brink of war in October 1962.

44,218 sq. miles
9,268,200 people
Capital: Havana

Tobacco processing in the 19th century by imported slave labour. The tobacco crop is Cuba's second largest export after sugar

**Colonial rule: 1500–1800** After Cuba's discovery by Columbus it became a Spanish base, first for exploration of the Americas, and then for military expeditions against anti-Spanish rebels on the mainland. During the 17th and 18th centuries Havana was the last port visited by Spanish ships carrying treasure back to Spain. As a result it was often attacked by British and French buccaneers. In 1762 Havana was captured by the British, who were at war with Spain, but their occupation only lasted a year.

Cuba started to prosper in the late 18th century with the cultivation of sugar cane in large plantations, which were worked by Negro slaves imported from Africa. Direct descendants of these slaves, as well as mulattos – people of mixed Negro and European blood – form about 30 per cent of the island's present-day population. Because of its prosperity, Cuba became known as the 'Pearl of the Antilles' (West Indies).

**Independence: 1901** At the beginning of the 19th century, Spain's empire in the Americas began to break up, as the peoples of such countries as Mexico and Uruguay fought for and won their independence. Cuba achieved independence late, because its wealthy slave owners, though disliking Spanish rule, needed the protection of Spanish forces against a possible slave revolt. They were haunted by the example of neighbouring Haiti, where slaves had overthrown their masters to found a black republic.

Cubans who wanted freedom from Spain at first looked for help from the United States. When this did not arrive they rose on their own against Spain in 1868 and 1895. In 1898 the United States declared war on Spain and sent an expeditionary force to Cuba. The Cubans declared themselves independent in 1898 and adopted a republican constitution in 1901. Tomas Estrada Palma became president in 1902.

**Domination by USA** From its beginnings the Cuban republic was bedevilled by the problems of creating a stable government and of escaping the domination of the United States. An article of the Cuban constitution, known as the Platt Amendment, gave the United States the right to intervene in Cuban affairs. American businessmen invested heavily in the sugar industry, and this had the effect of tying Cuba to the American economy. Many Cubans resented this, raising the cry of 'Yankee imperialism'. Soon the country's politics became corrupt and chaotic. Democratic government was

discredited. These conditions favoured the rise of military 'strong men' such as Gerardo Machado, who ruled as a dictator from 1925 to 1931.

**Radicalism and Castro's rise** Radical, left-wing politics in Cuba date from the revolution of September 1931 which overthrew Machado. After a short period of rule by student revolutionaries, radicalism was halted by the rise to power of Fulgencio Batista, who ruled through 'puppet' presidents, but in 1952 took control in a military coup.

A socialist student leader named Fidel Castro, deeply influenced by the radicals of the 1930's, denounced Batista as a tyrant. In December 1956 he and a group of supporters, including the Argentinian Ernesto Che Guevara, returned to Cuba from exile in Mexico, went into hiding in the Sierra Maestra mountains and launched an uprising. The rebellion spread. Although an attempt in 1957 by the 'Student Revolutionary Directorate' to take over the presidential palace and a General Strike in 1958 both failed, Castro's guerrillas were aided by anti-Batista movements in the cities.

Castro rejected formal alliances with other opposition parties, relying for popular support on his own programme of social reform, the nationalisation of the sugar estates and a return to democratic government. The army deserted Batista, who fled the country, and in January 1959 Castro entered Havana in triumph.

After a brief period of co-operation with the democratic parties, Castro took over complete control of government in February 1959, and silenced opposition in the Press and the trades unions. Many of his early sympathisers went into exile, feeling that Castro had betrayed them by becoming another dictator.

The beginnings of what was to become a socialist economy were made with the Agrarian Reform Law of May 1959. The 'democratic' phase of the Cuban Revolution finally ended with Castro's declaration of December 2, 1961: 'I am a Marxist-Leninist and shall be until I die.'

**Breach with the United States** Castro was determined to end Cuban reliance on the United States. Most US-owned property was nationalised, and in reprisal the USA broke off diplomatic relations with Cuba. But these policies left Castro dependent on the USSR, which took increasing quantities of Cuban sugar in return for Russian oil and industrial equipment. The signing of a trade agreement with Russia in 1960 led to a boycott of Cuban goods by the USA and by many of its allies in Central and South America.

**Bay of Pigs invasion: 1961** President Kennedy backed an invasion of Cuba by exiles in April, 1961. But a landing at Playa Giron – the 'Bay of Pigs' – was a fiasco. The invaders were quickly overwhelmed and many were captured. Castro's position in Cuba was strengthened and he became the hero of the Left throughout South America. But he was now further committed to the USSR for support.

**Missile crisis: 1962** An international crisis developed when the United States discovered that the USSR was setting up missile bases in Cuba. The crisis, which raised the spectre of nuclear war, was eventually settled by a dramatic 'eyeball to eyeball' confrontation between President Kennedy and the Soviet leader Khrushchev without reference to Castro. This embittered Castro's relations with the Russians.

Without actually criticising the Soviet Union, Castro emphasised the uniqueness of 'his' technique for revolution, of which violent guerrilla action formed an essential part. The Russians, however, believed that Communists could take over power legally in some South American countries by allying themselves with other Left-wing parties in elections. The failure and death of Castro's former comrade, Che Guevara, in Bolivia in October 1967, together with the continuing weakness of the Cuban economy, did much to lessen Castro's influence in other countries.

The regime of Fulgencio Batista (centre) was swept away by Fidel Castro's guerrilla forces in 1958

Cuba's economy has always relied heavily on sugar. Under Castro, an intensive drive to increase production was begun

Fidel Castro, whose achievement of power through guerrilla action became known as the 'Cuban model' for revolution

There were skilled sculptors among the early inhabitants of Czechoslovakia, as this figure from Brno shows. It was carved between 15,000 and 30,000 years ago

# Cyprus

Throughout most of its history, Cyprus has been exploited by foreign countries as a strategic base for trade or war. In modern times, the island has been bedevilled by strife between its two communities – Greek Cypriots (about 80 per cent of the population) and Turkish Cypriots (about 18 per cent). The Greek group includes supporters of enosis, union with mainland Greece, while many of the Turkish Cypriots want permanent partition between the two communities. This conflict led to the Turkish invasion of the island in 1974.

3572 sq. miles
658,400 people
Capital: Nicosia

**Pawn of ancient empires: 1500 BC–AD 1489** The island of Cyprus was inhabited as long ago as 4000 BC, and by *c.* 2200 BC it was the ancient world's largest source of copper; the name of the mineral comes from Kypros, the Greek name for the island. Greeks colonised the island from *c.* 1500 BC, and Phoenicians settled there from *c.* 800 BC. Cyprus later passed through periods of Assyrian, Egyptian, Persian, Greek, Roman and Byzantine rule.

In the early Middle Ages the island was won from the Byzantine Empire by the crusading Richard I of England, who in 1192 presented it to a French nobleman, Guy of Lusignan. Lusignan's descendants reigned there until 1489, when Cyprus was annexed by Venice, then the leading Mediterranean power.

**Roots of modern strife** The Turks conquered Cyprus in 1571, and a separate Turkish community began to develop on the island. In 1878 Cyprus passed from Turkish to British hands as part of the agreement reached at the Congress of Berlin. In the 20th century a movement for enosis – union with Greece – developed among the Greek community, flaring into violence against both Turks and Britons in 1954 under a former Greek army officer, Colonel George Grivas, who led a guerrilla group known as EOKA.

The head of the Cypriot Greek Orthodox Church, Archbishop Makarios, was deported by the British in 1956, accused of complicity in terrorism. But in 1959, when an independence settlement was reached, he returned to be elected as president. Britain then withdrew. It was written into the constitution of the new state that there should be a Greek Cypriot president and a Turkish vice-president. But civil war broke out in 1963 after a move to give the Greek community control of the central government. A United Nations peace-keeping force went to Cyprus in 1964, but inter-communal tension increased again in 1967, and Turkey threatened to invade the island to protect the Turkish minority. War between Greece and Turkey was averted by UN and United States diplomacy, and it was agreed, in 1967 and 1971, to prolong the stay of the UN force.

Led by Greek Army officers the Cypriot armed forces overthrew Makarios in 1974, triggering a Turkish invasion of the island. Fierce fighting was halted by a UN imposed cease-fire, and negotiations were undertaken to work out a more permanent settlement of conflicting Greek and Turkish interests.

Archbishop Makarios, arrested and deported by Britain in 1956, returned to Cyprus in 1959. He led the island to independence, and was elected its first president. He was deposed in 1974 in the coup which prompted the Turkish invasion of the island

# Czechoslovakia

The name Czechoslovakia reflects the fact that the country is made up of two major nationalities – the Czechs and Slovaks. The republic came into existence only after the First World War, but its people trace their history back to the kingdom of Bohemia.

Throughout its modern history, the country has been sandwiched between powerful neighbours. From 1620 to 1918 it was part of the Austrian Empire; in the 1930's it was overrun by the might of Nazi Germany; and since 1948 it has been a satellite of the USSR.

49,370 sq. miles
14,674,700 people
Capital: Prague

**Early conquerors** In the 1st century BC the Celtic settlers of the Czech lands were conquered by Germanic tribes. By AD 500 these tribes had been displaced in their turn by nomadic Slavs, among whom were the Czechs, moving from the east. By the 7th century these Slavs had set up a group of states, which were absorbed into Charlemagne's empire *c.* 800. After the break-up of the empire the Slavs formed the kingdom of Greater Moravia. But at the end of the 9th century this was destroyed by Magyar invasion. The region of Slovakia, in the east, came under Magyar rule.

**Under the sway of Austria** By the late Middle Ages the Czechs had established the kingdom of Bohemia as a prosperous and well-run monarchy, thanks to the efficient rule of several monarchs, including Charles IV, who was also Holy Roman Emperor.

The Czechs' strong nationalist feelings were fostered by the religious teachings of Jan Hus (1369–1415), a teacher at the University of Prague. Foreshadowing Luther, he put forward the idea of a national church for Bohemia, independent of the dictates of the pope in Rome. Though Hus was burnt at the stake for heresy by order of the Council of Constance, his teachings continued to inspire Bohemian patriotism. But in 1526 Bohemia fell under the sway of the Hapsburg dynasty when Ferdinand of Austria succeeded to the Bohemian throne. In 1618 the Protestant Bohemian nobility, invoking the name of Jan Hus, broke away from the Catholic Hapsburgs. After the 'defenestration of Prague', in which the emperor's envoys were thrown out of a window, they elected the German Protestant Prince Frederick, son-in-law of James I of England, as king.

Czech independence was short-lived. At the Battle of the White Mountain, outside Prague, in 1620, the Czech armies were totally defeated by those of Austria and its Roman Catholic allies; Bohemia was reduced to the status of a province of the Austrian Empire.

For almost three centuries, Bohemia remained under Austrian rule. In 1848 the intellectuals of Prague, in the first stirrings of Czech revolt, organised a congress to demand independence for Bohemia. But the revolutionaries were weak and divided; they were speedily crushed by the Austrian army under Windischgrätz.

Despite the failure of the 1848 revolution, the nationalist movement continued to grow, aided by the slow disintegration of the Austrian Empire, as its subject peoples began to agitate against Hapsburg rule. The achievements of composers such as Smetana and Dvořák, and of writers such as Franz Kafka, showed the vitality of Czech culture over this long period.

The religious teachings of Jan Hus in many ways foreshadowed those of Martin Luther. Hus was convicted of heresy and burnt at the stake in 1415

Wenceslas IV ruled Bohemia from 1378 to 1419. For part of that period he was ruler of the Holy Roman Empire, too, but his neglect of German affairs led to his downfall in 1400

**Independence: 1918** Independence only came with the final collapse of the Hapsburg Empire in 1918. Under the leadership of Thomas Masaryk and Edvard Benes, Czechoslovakia developed into a liberal democracy, with higher standards of political tolerance and economic prosperity than many of its neighbours.

But the new country had serious racial problems. It contained a $3\frac{1}{2}$-million-strong German minority, as well as Hungarians and Ukrainian Ruthenes. Racial tensions were aggravated by the Depression of the 1930's, which also worsened the plight of the peasants

**Munich: 1938** The Germans, concentrated in the Sudetenland just inside Czechoslovakia's western border, formed the most active racial minority. The

Antonin Dvořák, Czechoslovakia's best-known composer, used his country's folk-melodies in many of his works

*Thomas Masaryk, founder of modern Czechoslovakia, began his career as a lecturer in philosophy. He turned from academic life to politics, and worked for Czech independence*

Sudeten German Party, led by Konrad Henlein and actively supported by Nazi Germany, demanded the right to join the Reich. German pressure increased after 1935, when the Czechs made a defence agreement with the USSR to strengthen the pact they had with France.

In 1938 Hitler threatened war if the Sudeten Germans were not given the right of 'self-determination'. France and Britain refused to protect the Czechs, and by the Munich agreement of September 1938 they persuaded Czechoslovakia to give the Sudeten territory, which included all the Czech frontier defences, to Germany.

The Munich agreement further weakened Czechoslovakia by dividing it into a federal state, with a Czech government in Prague and a Slovak government in Slovakia. In March 1939, the Prague government determined to re-assert its authority and dismissed the Slovak government, under its Catholic leader, Monsignor Tiso, who then appealed to Hitler for support. German troops were ordered to invade Prague.

**From liberation to Communism: 1945–8** With the outbreak of the Second World War in September 1939, the Allies recognised a Czech government-in-exile under Benes. Mindful of Munich, he took especial care to keep on good terms with the USSR, signing a treaty of friendship with the Russians in 1943. In 1945 Soviet troops liberated the country and Benes returned to power.

Elections were held in 1946 in which the Communists, with 38 per cent of the vote, emerged as the strongest single party. Their leader, Klement Gottwald, formed a government – which still included 12 non-Communist ministers. But in February 1948 these ministers resigned in protest at Communist infiltration of the police.

In new elections, the Communists, backed by the Soviet Union, which threatened to send the Red Army into Czechoslovakia, were virtually unopposed. After the Communist take-over in 1948, the Czech patriot leader, Jan Masaryk (son of Thomas), met a violent death, perhaps by suicide; the official explanation was that he threw himself from a window. Benes died later in the year and Gottwald took over the presidency.

The new Communist regime was one of the harshest in the Soviet bloc. A series of purges and 'show trials' culminated in the trial and execution in 1952 of the party's secretary-general, Rudolf Slansky. In the same year, Gottwald was succeeded as president by Antonin Zapotocky, who was replaced in 1957 by Antonin Novotny. None of these leaders deviated from a 'hardline' Stalinist policy, even after Nikita Khrushchev's denunciation of Stalin's rule in 1956.

**Soviet invasion: 1968** Hard-line leadership came to an end in 1968, when Alexander Dubcek became the country's new leader. He set in motion an ambitious programme of 'Socialism with a human face', designed to liberalise the regime and give the Czech people more economic and political freedom. The USSR viewed these reforms with alarm. Dubcek was summoned to Moscow and told to halt his programme. On his refusal to do so, Soviet troops and tanks invaded Czechoslovakia in August 1968.

The invasion led to the drastic curtailment of Czechoslovakia's short-lived freedom. In April 1969, Dubcek was forced to resign and was replaced by the Russian-backed Gustav Husak. The reform programme was abandoned and Dubcek's supporters were purged from the party. A series of long drawn-out political trials, marked by heavy sentences, began in 1971.

Czechoslovakia and West Germany ratified a treaty in 1974 normalizing relations between the two nations for the first time since World War II.

*Edvard Benes broadcasts to his people. He resigned as president of Czechoslovakia after the 1938 Munich agreement. Later, he headed a government-in-exile in England*

*Alexander Dubcek's reforming policies won him massive support from the Czech people. But he was driven from power after the 1968 Soviet invasion and given an obscure post*

*A Czech student defies a tank in a Prague street during the Soviet invasion of Czechoslovakia in 1968*

# Dahomey

Since the former French colony of Dahomey gained independence in 1960, the country has been divided by continual power struggles between politicians representing different tribes and regions in the north and south of the country.

The earliest known settlers of southern Dahomey are thought to have been Fou-speaking peoples, who set up a kingdom in the 12th century. By the early 17th century, four distinct kingdoms existed of which Abomey was the most powerful.

Though traders from Portugal and other countries had profited by the slave trade in Dahomey, it was not until the 19th century that the European powers showed any great interest in the area. In 1851, France signed a treaty with Abomey; but after Abomey broke the treaty by attacking French trading posts on the coast in the late 19th century the French government proclaimed a protectorate.

Dahomey was given autonomy in the French Community in 1958 and passed peacefully to independence in 1960. But the country was torn by rivalry between north and south – each region seeking to make its own nominee president. Hubert Maga, a northerner, was overthrown in 1963 by Colonel Christophe Soglo, a southerner. Soglo relinquished authority to a civilian government. But in 1965 he again seized power and held it until December 1967, when he was in turn overthrown by a military coup.

The new leaders called for elections to be held, but these were boycotted by many of the population. The military regime gave place to a civilian government, but this was overthrown in 1969 by a three-man military junta. In 1970 this junta was replaced by a presidential commission, which was to serve for six years, the presidency rotating among its members. But in 1972 another military coup, led by Major Mathieu Kerekou, ended this system and set up an army regime.

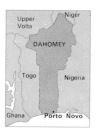

43,483 sq. miles
2,972,200 people
Capital: Porto Novo

*A potter at work in Dahomey, where pottery is exclusively a female occupation*

# Denmark

In medieval times Denmark was the centre of a vast Scandinavian empire. Today it is a small but highly developed country, famous for its farming products, particularly its butter and bacon. Its prosperity, based on farming, is of fairly recent growth; it was not until the mid-19th century that an agricultural revolution transformed Denmark from being a relatively poor country into one of the richest for its size in the world.

**First Danes** In prehistoric times, mainland Denmark and the islands guarding the approaches to the Baltic were settled by Lapps and Finns, hunters and fishermen. By AD 250 these people had been replaced by Germanic tribes, including the Danes; the newcomers soon formed a loose confederation of states. The name 'Denmark' was first used in the 9th century.

**Viking age** In the late 8th century, Scandinavian warriors known as the Vikings launched a series of searaids along the coast of western Europe. Danes played a leading part in the raids.

At first the Viking raids were simply acts of piracy. But when a Danish state was formed *c.* 950 the raids became attempts at conquest. In 982, Greenland was colonised by the Viking chief Eric the Red. Other raiders under Sweyn Forkbeard had conquered much of northern Britain by 1013. Forkbeard's son, Canute the Great, added Norway to his father's conquests in 1028 and established a Scandinavian empire, which by that time had largely been converted to Christianity. This process started in the mid-10th century, when St Ansgar brought Christianity to Denmark. The empire broke up soon after Canute's death in 1035.

**Disunity and recovery** During the 11th and early 12th centuries, Denmark was weakened by internal feuding among its rulers and people. The country's

16,629 sq. miles
5,068,000 people
Capital: Copenhagen

*Picture stones were carved by the Vikings between the 5th and 11th centuries. The top of this stone shows a battle scene*

Columbus discovered Hispaniola for Spain in 1492. Its native Indians, seen in this early print, were soon to be enslaved by the colonists who followed him

## DENMARK *continued*

rulers, who were chosen by election, depended for their power on the support of the nobility. At times the nobles combined with the peasants to resist the attempts of rulers to strengthen their power.

With the election of a strong king, Valdemar the Great (1157–82), Denmark recovered its strength. Valdemar and a successor, Valdemar the Victorious, built up a new Danish empire, centred on the Baltic Sea. At its height, this empire included much of northern Germany. But the rise of the Hanseatic League – a group of powerful Baltic trading cities – led to the loss of Denmark's German territories.

**Union and war** In 1397 Denmark formed a union with Norway (which ruled Iceland) and Sweden under the Danish Queen Margaret. The union lasted until 1523, when Sweden broke away, but Norway remained united with Denmark until 1814.

There were frequent wars with Sweden during the 16th and 17th centuries. The Danes fought to re-establish the unity of the three kingdoms, while the Swedes wanted access to the Atlantic and control of the Baltic. Between 1649 and 1660 Denmark lost all its remaining territory on the Swedish mainland. Finally, after Denmark had sided with France in the Napoleonic Wars, Norway (but not the colony of Iceland) was lost to Sweden as part of the peace settlement of 1815.

**Royal power** Denmark adopted Lutheranism from Germany in 1536. The Swedish wars of the 16th and 17th centuries, together with Protestant Denmark's brief and disastrous involvement in the Thirty Years' War (1618–48), lowered the prestige of the monarchy. But when the aristocracy proved itself to be no better at managing the country's affairs, Frederick III, with the support of Denmark's rising middle classes, was able to establish a hereditary monarchy in 1660.

Under this system, Denmark made some economic and social progress. The peasants were formally emancipated from serfdom in 1788. Commerce and the arts flourished, while scientists such as Ole Römer and Niels Stenson followed a tradition established by the great Danish astronomer Tycho Brahe.

Royal supremacy lasted until 1849, when Frederick VII introduced a liberal constitution. From 1864, Denmark developed into a modern industrial nation and became one of the first countries in Europe to introduce a social welfare system.

**War with Prussia: 1864** Unrest in the Duchies of Schleswig-Holstein, which had large German minorities, led to war with the rising power of Prussia in 1864. Denmark looked to Britain for help, but none came and Prussia annexed the Duchies.

It was not until after the First World War, in which it remained neutral, that Denmark recovered northern Schleswig after a plebiscite in 1920. In the same year Denmark recognised the independence of Iceland, but the Danish king remained king of Iceland until 1944. Denmark, however, still controls Greenland and the Faroe Islands.

**Invasion and peace** In April 1940, Nazi Germany attacked Denmark and brought it under total foreign occupation for the first time in its history. At first the German military government let the Danes manage their own affairs, but in 1943 the Danish king, Christian X, was placed under house arrest and martial law was imposed in an attempt to halt the activities of the resistance. The country was liberated with Germany's surrender in 1945. After the Second World War, Denmark became a member of the UN, NATO and EFTA (European Free Trade Association). Queen Margaretha II ascended the throne in 1972, the first woman to rule Denmark in more than 500 years. In 1973 Denmark, together with Britain and Ireland, joined the Common Market – a decision which was backed by a national referendum.

Queen Margaret of Denmark united her country with Norway and Sweden in 1397

The Danish writer Hans Christian Andersen (1805–75) won lasting fame as a story-teller with such tales as 'The Ugly Duckling' and 'The Snow Queen'

At work in a bacon factory. Denmark's world-famous agricultural products are the foundation of its prosperity

# Dominican Republic

This small republic, a mainly agricultural country whose chief export is sugar, occupies the eastern two-thirds of the Caribbean island of Hispaniola. Its people, Spanish in culture, are largely mulattoes (of mixed white and Negro race). The west of the island is occupied by the more densely populated Negro state of Haiti.

Christopher Columbus discovered Hispaniola in 1492 and claimed it for Spain. Santo Domingo became the first European city to be built in the Western Hemisphere. The French gained control under the Treaty of Basle in 1795, but in 1801 the region was conquered by a Negro Haitian, Toussaint L'Ouverture, leader of a slave rebellion. French rule was restored by force, but was again overthrown by an uprising in 1808.

The republic which emerged suffered constant revolts, changes of rule, and attacks by Haiti during the 19th century. Its rulers sought protection first by re-entering the Spanish Empire (1861–5), a move which was abandoned after opposition from many Dominicans, and then by proposing annexation by the United States, an offer which the USA declined. From 1905 to 1941, however, the USA controlled the finances of the republic, which had become bankrupt, and US troops were stationed there from 1916 to 1934.

The republic experienced harsh oppression under Rafael Leonidas Trujillo Molina from 1930 until his assassination in 1961. In 1962 Juan Bosch, a reform-minded writer of the democratic left, was elected. But he was overthrown by the military in 1963. Fighting broke out again in 1965 between Bosch supporters and their opponents, and US troops arrived to back the anti-Bosch junta. In 1966, however, elections were held. Joaquin Balaguer, a moderate conservative, overcame Bosch, and was re-elected in 1970 and 1974.

18,818 sq. miles
4,556,500 people
Capital:
Santo Domingo

The dictator Trujillo ruled the Dominican Republic ruthlessly from 1930 until 1961, when a rival assassinated him

# Ecuador

Crossed by the Equator, from which it takes its name, Ecuador was one of the poorest states of South America until development of its petroleum industry in the 1970's. The country's life is dominated by a small aristocracy and by the Roman Catholic Church.

**Inca and Spanish rule** The original Indian inhabitants of Ecuador had reached a high level of culture before they were conquered at the end of the 15th century by the Inca Empire, to the south. But Inca rule was overthrown in less than a century by Spanish conquistadores. Ecuador became part of Spain's vast South American empire, and the native Indians became slaves on tobacco and sugar plantations.

**Independence and dictatorship** Ecuador revolted against Spain in 1822, winning its independence after the Battle of Pichincha. It joined Simon Bolívar's Gran Colombia, but when this state broke up in 1830 Ecuador became fully independent.

After 1830 the country suffered from nearly 30 years of civil war. Two factions fought for power – the Conservatives, led by Juan José Flores until his exile in 1845, and the Liberals. In 1860, after a disastrous war with Peru, the Conservative leader, Gabriel García Moreno, a religious fanatic, seized power. His dictatorial rule lasted until his assassination in 1876.

After two more decades of unrest and disorder, another revolution brought the Liberal leader Eloy Alfaro to power in 1895. Successive Liberal presidents held office until 1944. They curbed the power of the Church and established a measure of civil liberty. But after 1944 political rivalries and army intervention brought about frequent changes in the government.

Ecuador's longest period of political stability was under Galo Plaza Lasso from 1948 to 1955. Plaza, the

109,483 sq. miles
6,961,400 people
Capital: Quito

Statues of Simon Bolívar (left) and José de San Martin, fighters for independence, stand beside Ecuador's River Guayas

first of Ecuador's presidents to survive for a full term of office, was succeeded by José Maria Velasco Ibarra, who within a year brought Ecuador to the brink of war with neighbouring Peru.

Velasco, who had been driven from office in 1956, returned to power in 1960. But a year later a coup forced him into exile and his vice-president took over office. Continuing instability led to army rule in 1963. In 1966 a Constitutional Assembly chose Otto Arosemena Gomez as provisional president, but when this was put to the popular vote in 1968, Velasco, who had returned from exile, was again elected. In 1970 he set up a dictatorship but later announced that elections would be held in 1972. This led to his overthrow by a military junta under General Guillermo Rodriguez Lara.

*José Maria Velasco Ibarra, several times president of Ecuador, was driven from power in 1972 by a military coup*

# Egypt

For thousands of years the life of Egypt has depended on the Nile. Until recently its annual flood deposited fertile silt along the banks, enabling the *fellahin* (peasants) to grow the crops, mainly cotton, on which the economy is based. The river's flow is now regulated by the High Dam at Aswan, providing irrigation all the year round.

The classical Greek historian Herodotus described Egypt as 'the gift of the Nile'. Agriculture formed the basis of the great civilization which flourished in the Nile valley, under a succession of 'divine' pharaohs (kings), from *c.* 3200 BC to 332 BC. The surviving monuments of that civilization, such as the sphinx and pyramids at Giza, are among the most impressive man-made spectacles in the world.

Since the 7th century Egypt has been an Arab country, a main centre of Islamic life and religion. In the 1960's, under President Gamal Abdul Nasser, it embarked on a programme of socialism, attempting through industrialisation to lessen its dependence on agriculture. But farming remains the livelihood of more than 90 per cent of its people, and Islamic conservatism has proved strongly resistant to attempts to revolutionise Egyptian society along socialist lines. Overshadowing Egypt's struggle to modernise itself is its long conflict with Israel, its neighbour and enemy since 1948.

386,700 sq. miles
36,754,300 people
Capital: Cairo

**Ancient glory: 3200–1200 BC** Egypt was united into one country under King Menes *c.* 3200 BC. By 2600, the pyramids were being built, to preserve the embalmed bodies of the pharaohs in the afterlife. This early era, during which the capital was at Memphis, is known as the Old Kingdom. It ended about 2420 when local rule seems to have replaced central government.

By 2050, the pharaohs had re-established unity, with a central capital at Thebes, and Egypt moved into a new period of stability known as the Middle Kingdom, during which a uniform system of writing was adopted. Aryan invaders, the Hyksos, dominated Egypt between 1700 and 1600, but native dynasties re-emerged in 1560 to herald the era of the New Kingdom. In this phase, under such determined leaders as Ramesses II, Egyptian rule reached the River Euphrates.

**Loss of independence: 1200 BC–AD 600** From *c.* 1200 BC, Egypt, hard-pressed by the rise of rival empires, went into a decline, a process started by the attacks of raiders known as the 'sea peoples'. The country came under the control of Assyria, then Persia, and in 332 BC fell to the Greek armies of Alexander the Great. After the death of Alexander, one of his generals, Ptolemy, ruled Egypt as king and founded a dynasty

*A detail from an Egyptian tomb of c. 1300 BC shows its occupant drinking the Nile's waters in the afterlife. Then as now, the Nile was vital to the country's well-being*

*For 1500 years the great Pharos (lighthouse), built by Ptolemy II, guided ships into Alexandria. One of the seven wonders of the ancient world, it was destroyed by an earthquake in the 14th century AD*

which reigned for 200 years. During this period, the Egyptian city of Alexandria developed into the intellectual hub of Mediterranean civilization.

In the last century BC, the Ptolemaic Empire was threatened by the increasing power of Rome. Cleopatra, daughter of Ptolemy XI, tried to preserve Egyptian independence by winning over Roman leaders such as Julius Caesar and Mark Antony. But following her death Egypt was annexed by Rome.

The country became a granary for the Roman Empire. Egypt's irrigation system was improved, and ships took wheat to all parts of the Mediterranean world. Later, the country went through a period of Byzantine rule, under which the Coptic Church was founded.

**Islamic rule: 639–1798** During the rise of the great Islamic Arab Empire, Egypt was speedily conquered by the Arabs between AD 639 and 642.

By 1200, the Arab rulers of Egypt had come under the influence of their soldiers and advisers, the Mamelukes, originally slaves. The Mamelukes seized power in 1250 and maintained their rule until 1517, when Egypt fell victim to another emerging and expanding empire and was conquered by the Ottoman Turks. Yet even under Turkish rule, the Mameluke beys (princes) continued to control the provinces of Egypt.

*A Mameluke on horseback, with an Arab slave. Originally a warrior caste of slaves, the Mamelukes overthrew their Arab masters during the 13th century AD*

**Birth of modern Egypt** Napoleon in July 1798 defeated the Mamelukes at the Battle of the Pyramids. He hoped to march on and conquer British India, but his defeat at the Battle of the Nile prevented him.

The French, under the pressures of the Napoleonic wars, withdrew in the early 1800's, and in the disorders that followed, Muhammad Ali, an Albanian mercenary in the Turkish service, seized power in 1805 and massacred the last of the Mamelukes in 1811. Under Muhammad Ali, Egypt began industrialisation, and gained a technical lead over the Arab countries of the old Ottoman Empire. But the improvements later strained the country's financial system.

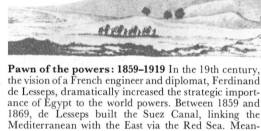

**Pawn of the powers: 1859–1919** In the 19th century, the vision of a French engineer and diplomat, Ferdinand de Lesseps, dramatically increased the strategic importance of Egypt to the world powers. Between 1859 and 1869, de Lesseps built the Suez Canal, linking the Mediterranean with the East via the Red Sea. Meanwhile, economic problems and extravagance had brought Egypt to bankruptcy, and the British government was able in 1875 to take advantage of Egypt's desperate financial situation to buy the controlling shares in the canal.

In 1882 a nationalist revolt against foreign interference led to the bombardment of Alexandria by British ships on July 11, and the landing of British troops. By the Convention of Constantinople (1888), Britain became the guarantor of a neutral Suez Canal through which ships of all nations would be allowed passage. The modernisation of Egyptian government and society went ahead. A nationalistic middle class began to develop.

While the British were consolidating their control of Egypt between 1883 and 1907 – when Lord Cromer was consul-general and virtual ruler – the neighbouring Sudan was being conquered and pacified by an Anglo-Egyptian army. From 1899, the Sudan was administered by a governor-general appointed by Egypt with the assent of Britain, and the territory became known as the Anglo-Egyptian Sudan.

**Uneasy independence: 1922–45** As a result of increasing nationalist demands, Egypt was declared independent in 1922. A Western-type constitution was proclaimed, with a parliament, and the country became

*Science and conquest went hand-in-hand in Napoleon's invasion of Egypt. Here, French archaeologists measure the dimensions of the Sphinx. Napoleon's plans to conquer India through Egypt collapsed after his defeat by Nelson at the Battle of the Nile, in August 1798*

*Home without a roof: one of many families in El Salvador who are forced by poverty and overcrowding to live on the streets*

## EGYPT *continued*

a kingdom under Fuad I. But British troops still occupied the country, and Britain refused to consider Egyptian claims to the Anglo-Egyptian Sudan. An agreement in 1936 ended the military occupation but gave Britain the right to garrison the canal zone.

The British faced growing nationalist opposition. In the Second World War, Britain, defending its empire, was confronted with crisis in Egypt. When Axis forces were seriously threatening Egypt in 1942, the British had to surround the royal palace with troops to ensure co-operation from the king, Farouk. Egypt became the base from which the British eventually won their decisive victory in North Africa at El Alamein in 1942.

In talks after the war, Egypt and Britain failed to come to terms on the future of the country. Egypt wanted the Sudan, but Britain, backed by a United Nations Security Council decision, would not agree.

**Nasser and Suez: 1948–56** After the creation of the Israeli state in Palestine, Egypt bitterly opposed Palestine's partition by the United Nations in 1948, and became the major power in the Arab League against Israel. In the Arab-Israeli war of 1948, the Egyptians were unsuccessful and the conflict was regarded as a humiliating defeat for the Arabs, revealing corruption in the Egyptian government. King Farouk lost control as political unrest shook the country, and he was exiled in 1952 after a coup staged by an army movement called the Free Officers, led by Colonel Gamal Abdul Nasser. Farouk's son, Ahmed Fuad II, became monarch for a few months, but the monarchy was abolished in 1953 and General Muhammad Naguib was declared president of the new republic.

In 1954 Naguib was ousted after a quarrel with Nasser, who was the real power in the country. Under Nasser's leadership, the long Sudan dispute ended in 1956 when the Sudan became an independent republic with the consent of Egypt and Britain. The same year, British troops evacuated the Canal Zone. But in July 1956 the United States and Britain – concerned about Nasser's purchase of arms from Communist Czechoslovakia – withdrew their pledges of financial aid for the building of the Aswan High Dam. Nasser retaliated by nationalising the Suez Canal.

Meanwhile, relations between Egypt and Israel had become tense because of a dispute over the borderland of Gaza. Israel, now barred by Egypt from using the canal, invaded Gaza and the Sinai Peninsula in October 1956. The canal's nationalisation also led to intervention in Egypt by Britain and France. But an international outcry forced the three nations to withdraw.

**Arab-Israeli wars: 1967, 1973** In 1958 Nasser set up the United Arab Republic with Syria, but Syria reverted to independence in 1961. Involved in border skirmishes with Israel, Syria appealed to Egypt for aid in 1967 and Egyptian troops moved to the Israeli border. Nasser demanded and obtained removal of the United Nations peace-keeping force from the area between Egypt and Israel which he had lost in 1956. He blockaded the Gulf of Aqaba, Israel's only access to the Red Sea. The result, on June 5, 1967, was another Arab-Israeli war; Israel was victorious after a six-day blitz that brought its forces to the east bank of the Suez Canal.

Yet Nasser himself survived this defeat. He was persuaded not to resign and he maintained his strong position as Egyptian leader. Egypt rebuilt its forces with Soviet aid. Nasser died from a heart attack in September 1970 and Anwar Sadat became the new chief of state.

Sadat continued the confrontation with Israel, and in 1973 Egypt and Syria launched a full-scale war on the Israelis, with the declared aim of recovering territory lost in 1967. A peace settlement of the 18-day war negotiated by US Secretary of State Henry Kissinger resulted in withdrawal of Israeli troops from the east east banks of the Suez Canal in 1974 and Egyptian cooperation with western powers in reopening that important waterway.

*King Farouk became world-famous for his 'playboy' extravagance. This, combined with incompetence, led to his overthrow by a coup in 1952*

*Gamal Abdul Nasser was undisputed leader of Egypt from 1954 until his death in 1970. He was a passionate believer in a united Arab world*

## El Salvador

The smallest country in Central America is also its most thickly populated. Overcrowding is El Salvador's main problem, and has resulted in continuous emigration to neighbouring countries such as Honduras. Over 92 per cent of the population are mestizos (of mixed Indian and white race).

**'Land of Jewels'** Before the Spanish conquest, El Salvador was known to its Indian inhabitants, a tribe related to the Aztecs, as Cuscatlan, the 'land of jewels'. But when the Spanish conquistador Pedro de Alvarado conquered the country in 1525 he found few jewels or precious metals. Spain therefore neglected this part of its empire in favour of wealthier territories, and the settlers there concentrated on farming.

**Independence** El Salvador threw off Spanish rule in 1821, when it became part of a short-lived Mexican empire ruled by Agustin de Iturbide. When that empire collapsed in 1823, El Salvador joined the Federal Republic of Central America, finally becoming independent in 1838 when that federation, too, broke up. During the rest of the 19th century, El Salvador was plagued by internal unrest and by conflicts with its neighbours, especially Guatemala and Nicaragua. From the 1850's onwards, however, with the introduction of coffee, the country began to prosper – and its population began to expand rapidly. In 1931 a catastrophic drop in world coffee prices led to widespread unrest. General Maximiliano Hernandez Martinez seized power and ruled as dictator until he was overthrown by a coup in 1944.

A succession of short-lived military dictatorships held power until 1961, when a government of three civilians and three army officers was set up. Its leader, José Julio Rivera, became president in 1962, holding office until 1967. Under him, land, tax and social reforms were introduced, as well as a huge hydro-electric power scheme on the River Lempa.

Honduras, which for years had absorbed the bulk of El Salvador's emigrants, tried to halt the flow in 1969, expelling thousands of Salvadorans. War broke out with Honduras in July 1969, sparked off by riots at a football match between the two countries. After five days of fighting, a cease-fire was arranged by the Organisation of American States. About 2000 people lost their lives in the war, and thousands were made homeless.

In August 1969, Fidel Sanchez Hernandez, who had succeeded Rivera, introduced further economic reforms. His party won the congressional elections of 1970. In 1972, however, the presidential election was bitterly disputed. The right-wing candidate, Arturo Armando Molina, was elected, but his opponents claimed that the votes had been unfairly counted.

## Equatorial Guinea

About the size of Maryland, the West African republic of Equatorial Guinea consists of two provinces – Macias Nguema Island and other islands in the Gulf of Guinea, and the territory of Rio Muni on the West African mainland. Most of its people are Fang, descendants of Africans whom the Spanish enslaved. The country's chief exports are cacao, coffee and timber.

Macias Nguema Island, formerly called Fernando Po, was discovered by the Portuguese in 1471 on their voyages of exploration down the African coast. In 1778 the island was ceded to Spain which, in 1885, also acquired the mainland region. The whole area then became known as Spanish Guinea.

In 1963 the colony was granted internal self-government. It gained independence in 1968, when it took its present name and President Francisco Macias Nguema became its leader. In 1969 Macias assumed dictatorial powers and began to adopt anti-Spanish policies, which led Spain to evacuate almost all of its 7000 citizens, and break off diplomatic relations. These were restored in 1971, when Spain resumed aid to the country.

8261 sq. miles
4,067,000 people
Capital: San Salvador

*Fidel Sanchez Hernandez became El Salvador's president in 1969. He introduced much-needed economic reforms*

10,830 sq. miles
301,300 people
Capital: Malabo

# Ethiopia

In late medieval times, the mountainous, remote land of Ethiopia, known to Europeans as Abyssinia, was thought to be the home of the legendary Christian king, Prester John, and tales of his fabulous wealth lured Portuguese explorers to the country. The legend had some factual basis – Ethiopia became a Christian country in the 4th century, and it remains one today.

Ethiopia was unique in surviving the 'scramble for Africa' of the 19th century, when European powers divided the continent among themselves. But it was conquered by Italy in 1936. The country's emperor, Haile Selassie, won the world's admiration by his dignified plea to the League of Nations for support, but Italian rule continued until 1941.

**Earliest Ethiopians** According to Ethiopian legend, the country was founded by Menelik, the eldest son of Solomon and the Queen of Sheba, c. 1000 BC. This belief has led Ethiopia's kings to claim descent from Solomon, and accounts for their titles 'King of kings' and 'Lion of Judah'. By c. AD 100 – when historical records began – a pagan state, Axum, was founded by Sabaeans from southern Arabia. It extended over northern Ethiopia and part of the Sudan and took its name from Axum, its capital, in Ethiopia.

**Conversion to Christianity: c. AD 300** Axum became Christian in the 4th century and the Ethiopian Orthodox Church, a branch of the Egyptian Coptic Church, spread over the highlands in the north.

With the rise of Islam in the 7th century, Axum was threatened by hostile Muslim neighbours. It lost its Red Sea ports, and its Christian inhabitants retreated to the highlands, where they remained in isolation until the 16th century. In 1270 a new dynasty, claiming to be a restoration of the line of Solomon, was founded there. Under it Ethiopian culture flowered.

**Portuguese intervention: c. 1500** In the early 16th century the Ethiopian state faced complete conquest by the Muslims. The pope sent Portuguese soldiers to the country who helped to bring about the final defeat of the Muslims in 1542. This intervention brought Ethiopia under Catholic influence for the first time. As the doctrines of the Coptic Church had been declared heretical in AD 451, Jesuit missionaries tried to convert the Ethiopians to Catholicism. Emperor Fasilidas, who took over power in 1632, expelled the Jesuits and closed the country to foreigners.

**Centuries of conflict** A series of weak and incompetent rulers brought Ethiopia two centuries of almost constant civil war. There were also frequent wars against the Muslims and the Galla, a pastoral people settled in central and south Ethiopia. In 1855 a bandit turned courtier, Ras Kassa, seized power and was crowned as Emperor Theodorus. In 1864 Theodorus arrested members of a British mission and imprisoned them at Magdala. After three years of fruitless negotiation for their release, a British expedition rescued them and took Magdala. The emperor shot himself.

Theodorus was succeeded by Johannes IV who tried to assert his supremacy over the tribes by war. But Italy,

471,776 sq. miles
26,636,000 people
Capital: Addis Ababa

*Effigy of a saint in an Ethiopian rock-carved church. Though cut off from Christendom by their Muslim enemies for many centuries, the Ethiopians managed to preserve their Christian faith*

which saw Ethiopia as a potential protectorate, supported Menelik, the most powerful of the provincial leaders, against him. Johannes was also threatened by the Mahdist forces of the Sudan, and he was defeated and killed while fighting them in 1889.

**Modernisation under Menelik** After Johannes's death, Menelik took over power. He chose the title of Menelik II to stress the supposed continuity of Ethiopia's royal line since biblical times. Menelik soon broke with Italy and in 1896 defeated an invading Italian army at Adowa, capturing 3000 Italians. After this Italy was forced to recognise Ethiopia's independence.

Menelik tried to modernise his country, building its first railways, establishing schools and creating a new capital, Addis Ababa. But his successors proved incompetent and in 1916 Haile Selassie was appointed regent. In 1930 he became emperor.

**Italian invasion: 1935** In October 1935, Mussolini, the Italian dictator, revived Italy's claim to Ethiopia. Haile Selassie's ill-armed troops were soon defeated by the Italians, who used all the weapons of modern war against them. The emperor appealed to the League of Nations, which imposed sanctions against Italy. But these did not halt the Italian armies, and Haile Selassie was forced into exile in Britain in 1936.

The Italians ruled the country until 1941, when a British army re-established Haile Selassie on the throne.

**Modern Ethiopia** A land-locked country for centuries, Ethiopia won access to the Red Sea in 1952, when Eritrea formed a federation with it, with United Nations approval. Internally, Haile Selassie continued Menelik's reforms, though trying to reconcile modernisation with Ethiopia's age-old customs. In 1955 he established Ethiopia's first-ever constitution.

In foreign affairs, Haile Selassie won himself the role of independent Africa's elder statesman. Ethiopia's importance in the new Africa was shown in 1963 when leaders of 30 African nations met in Addis Ababa to found the Organisation of African Unity.

After a severe drought in 1973, Ethiopia's armed forces revolted in what they called a 'war on feudalism.' The Emperor and his closest advisers were arrested. The military leaders dissolved parliament but promised a quick return to democracy, with free elections. Haile Selassie's son, Crown Prince Asfa Wossen, was offered the throne as a 'figurehead.'

*Haile Selassie – 'Lion of Judah' – with his wife and children. Driven off his throne by Fascist Italy in 1936, he was restored by Britain in 1941. He was deposed in 1974, and his son, Prince Asfa Wossen, offered the throne*

# Fiji

More than 320 islands in the South Pacific make up Fiji. Native Fijians, people of Melanesian origin, whose ancestors are thought to have sailed from Asia to reach Fiji, make up only 41 per cent of the population. They are outnumbered by Indians, whose ancestors were brought into the islands in the 19th century to work sugar plantations. Today, the Indians still work the plantations. Chinese settlers also arrived in the islands during the 19th century: most are employed in trade and market gardening, while native Fijians concentrate mainly on traditional crafts.

The first European to set foot in the Fiji islands was the Dutch explorer Abel Tasman in 1643, and the British explorer Captain James Cook visited them in 1774. In the 19th century, European traders in search of sandalwood – out of which large profits were being made – arrived at the islands. They set up their first settlement at Levuka in 1804.

The Fijians, who had lived in isolation for centuries, were drastically affected by European influence. Many died from newly introduced infections such as the common cold, because their bodies had never built up any immunity. The firearms the Europeans sold to the Fijians intensified tribal warfare. In 1874, after repeated requests by tribal chiefs, the British annexed the islands. They remained under British rule until 1970, when they became independent.

7055 sq. miles
571,800 people
Capital: Suva

*Emperor Theodorus, with two lions at his feet, painted c. 1856. The emperor took his own life after a British expedition had captured his capital*

# Finland

Situated in the far north of Europe, Finland has two great natural assets – water and timber. Thousands of lakes are scattered throughout the country, many of them joined by rivers and canals into a vast waterways system. Two-thirds of Finland is covered by forest, and the timber industry, served by the waterways, is the mainstay of the prosperous Finnish economy.

For many centuries Finland was ruled by foreign powers – first by Sweden and then by Russia. It won independence from Russia in 1919. The intense patriotism of the Finnish people was celebrated by its leading composer, Jean Sibelius, in such works as 'Finlandia'. The strength of this feeling was shown in the 'winter war' of 1939–40, when the Finns stood up to an attack by their giant Russian neighbour.

**Early history** The first Finns were migrants, who thousands of years ago moved from their original homes in the Urals to the Baltic, and then in about the 1st century AD to Finland. They displaced a sparse Lapp population, who had themselves emigrated to the country from the Baltic shores.

In 1157, Eric IX of Sweden led a crusade to Finland – ostensibly to convert the Finns to Christianity, though his main purpose was to get control of the country. Finland officially became part of Sweden in 1540, Finns having equal rights with Swedes in the union.

**Russian rule: 1809–1917** Swedish domination lasted until 1809, when Russia, which had already occupied part of south-eastern Finland in the 18th century, annexed the entire country. Finland was made a Grand Duchy of the Russian Empire but the Finns were allowed a degree of self-government.

Towards the end of the 19th century, however, Tsar Alexander III initiated a policy of 'Russification', which was bitterly resented by much of the population. Unrest led to the suspension of the Finnish constitution in 1901, but it was restored after 1905.

With the outbreak of revolution in Russia in 1917, Finland declared itself independent. Finnish nationalists, led by Marshal Mannerheim and helped by Germany, thwarted Soviet attempts to reconquer the country. The Finnish republic was set up in 1919.

**'Winter war': 1939–40** A secret clause of the Russo-German non-aggression pact of 1939 gave Russia a free hand in Finland. The Russians demanded that the Finns should give up the Karelia isthmus and some islands in the Gulf of Finland, and allow Russia to build military bases to secure the approaches to Leningrad. But the Finns refused to give in, and the Russians declared war in November 1939. The heroic resistance of the Finnish troops under Marshal Mannerheim won the admiration of the world. But overwhelming Soviet force compelled the Finns to yield. The USSR occupied the Karelia isthmus, and the war ended in March 1940.

The Finns allied themselves to Germany when Hitler attacked Russia in 1941. They re-occupied their lost territories, but in 1944 they were driven back by a Russian counter-offensive and forced to make peace.

**Post-war Finland** In the final peace treaty of 1947, Finland gave Russia the Karelia isthmus, Petsamo and right of access to the Arctic Sea. The Finns also granted the USSR a 50 year lease of the Porkkala military base, as well as having to pay enormous reparations. In 1948 Finland signed a 10-year friendship treaty with the USSR. This was renewed for 20 years in 1955 (at the same time the Russians gave up their base at Porkkala), and renewed again in 1970. The Finns had completed their payment of reparations by 1952.

Finland became an associate member of the European Free Trade Association (EFTA) in 1961. Britain is the country's most important trading partner followed by West Germany and Sweden.

**FORMOSA,** *see Taiwan*

130,119 sq. miles
4,740,000 people
Capital: Helsinki

*The Finnish composer Jean Sibelius (1865–1957) is best known for his many orchestral works inspired by national themes*

*Marshal Mannerheim (1867–1951) led the Finns' heroic resistance to Russia in the 'winter war' of 1939–40*

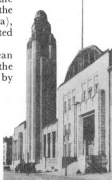

*Helsinki's impressive railway station was designed in the early 1900's by the Finnish architect Eliel Saarinen*

# France

France's rise to greatness has been a major theme in the history of Western civilization, and the language, culture and ideas of its people have left their mark throughout the world. In peace and war the country has often played a dominant role in Europe. It has appeared at its strongest under the rule of determined and able individuals, and usually after periods of great confusion and instability. Some of its rulers, such as Louis XIV and Napoleon, have wielded almost absolute power.

France has often been torn by conflict between people who advocated strong central government and those who championed regional interests. The revolutionary leaders of 1789 made a determined effort to impose uniformity, laying the foundations of modern French government. But even today, regionalism is a potentially disruptive factor in French politics – as well as giving France its rich variety of life and customs.

**Prehistoric man** The first evidence of modern man in Europe comes from south-west France, where he settled some 35,000 years ago, living by hunting and fishing. About 6000 years ago his descendants began to develop a culture based upon farming and the use of polished and sharpened tools. They erected large stone monuments called megaliths; those still standing in Brittany were built between 2500 and 1500 BC.

Between 1500 and 1000 BC Celtic people established states in France. Other settlers followed; by *c.* 600 BC there was a Greek settlement at Massilia (Marseilles).

**Roman conquest: 58–48 BC** In 58 BC Julius Caesar arrived in the territory known to the Romans as Gaul, and within ten years he had conquered the native kingdoms. For the first time, Gaul achieved a rough form of unity. The Romans created towns, built roads, and constructed theatres, aqueducts and temples. Latin replaced Celtic as the language of the people. In the 2nd century AD Christianity made its first appearance in Gaul, and by the 3rd century it was spreading widely.

**Arrival of the Franks** From about the 3rd century, the first Germanic invaders began to arrive in France in search of new lands. The Romans could not spare the manpower to resist them effectively, and by 476 the Roman Empire in the West had ceased to exist. Among the invaders, it was finally the Franks – from whom the name 'France' comes – who triumphed. A French state emerged which stretched from the Mediterranean to the North Sea, and from the Alps to the Atlantic. Clovis,

211,228 sq. miles
52,646,200 people
Capital: Paris

*Wine being transported by boat, shown in a Gallo-Roman carving. Wine was just as important to the Gauls as it is to the French today*

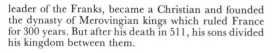

leader of the Franks, became a Christian and founded the dynasty of Merovingian kings which ruled France for 300 years. But after his death in 511, his sons divided his kingdom between them.

**Charlemagne: 768–814** While the Merovingian kings ruled a divided country, the Arabs extended the power of Islam over the Mediterranean. By 725 their armies had moved far up the Rhône, but in 732, a Frankish chieftain, Charles Martel, defeated them between Poitiers and Tours. His grandson, Charles, known as Charlemagne (Charles the Great), became king of France in 768. His kingdom extended beyond the frontiers of what is now France and on Christmas Day 800, the pope crowned him Holy Roman Emperor.

Charlemagne sent officials throughout his lands to make his rule more effective. He also encouraged feudalism in an attempt to cement society by a man-to-man bond; this was a move away from the older Roman concept of state authority. On Charlemagne's death in 814 his empire split up. The Treaty of Verdun in 843 separated France from the remainder of Charlemagne's empire. New invaders, the Vikings, or Norsemen, appeared, and by the early 10th century they had established themselves in the Duchy of Normandy. But the memory of Charlemagne's greatness persisted, and with it the influence of the Christian learning he had encouraged. Unity was restored when Hugh Capet was elected King of France by an assembly of nobles in 987.

*A 9th-century ivory carving depicts the baptism of Clovis, King of the Franks, into the Christian faith by St Remi*

**Capetian France: 987–1328** The Capetian kings built up their kingdom from small beginnings. Many lords owned more land than the Capetians, and the title of king conferred neither power nor revenue on its holder.

The Capetians, however, were well connected and they made good marriages. They had the prestige of being successors to Clovis and Charlemagne, and they had the support of the Church. The Capetians' family domain was a region on the middle Seine, including Paris, which was the heart of a prosperous area. Through the efforts of several able and patient rulers, the Capetians gradually achieved supremacy.

*Louis IX leaves with the blessing of God for a Crusade against the infidels. The king was eventually canonised for his piety*

**Expansionist policies** From 1180 to 1223, Philip II (Augustus) took up the struggle against the English kings, Henry II, Richard I and John, who also ruled much of France. By war and intrigue Philip extended his authority over Normandy, Maine, Anjou, Touraine and Poitou. His grandson, Louis IX (1226–70), who succeeded to the throne when only 11, grew up to win battles both against the English and also against his own rebellious aristocracy. He negotiated treaties with France's neighbours, and his role as a Crusader earned him a great reputation for piety; he was canonised as St Louis in 1297.

By the time Louis IX died, while taking part in a crusade to Tunis, the French monarchy held undisputed power in the kingdom. New institutions, such as the Parlements, dealing with legal matters, had been set up. Feudalism was declining. France was a rich and populous country, and French had become the language of educated people throughout Europe. Louis's successors pursued his policies of strengthening France's government at home and expanding its boundaries.

**The Hundred Years' War** The Capetian line died out in 1328 and Philip of Valois founded a new dynasty. From 1337 to 1453 the so-called Hundred Years' War was fought between France and England. Edward III, King of England, claimed the French throne through his descent from Philip IV and invaded France in alliance with France's neighbours in Flanders. The French were overwhelmingly defeated at Crécy (1346), at Poitiers (1356) and at Agincourt (1415). In 1420 Henry V, King of England, was acknowledged by the reigning French king as heir to the French throne. But Henry died in 1422. Inspired by Joan of Arc, the French soon rallied, and by 1453, England had lost all its French territory, except for Calais and the Channel Islands.

During the wars, power had become concentrated in the hands of princes rather than in the hands of the king. The country was torn apart as great lords fought each other, and in the countryside there were many peasant uprisings or 'jacqueries'. Determined to change this, Charles VII and his successor Louis XI succeeded in winning control of Burgundy, Provence, Artois and Picardy. Under Louis, trade and industry thrived.

**Reformation France** Three themes dominated the history of 16th-century France: the drive to maintain and strengthen the unity of the kingdom; the need for the monarchy to demonstrate its power; and the ferment of ideas caused by the Reformation. Charles VIII (1483–98) led an army into Italy, where he hoped to find wealth as well as renown. Under Francis I (1515–47) the Italian wars expanded into a struggle for European supremacy against Charles V, Holy Roman Emperor and the head of the Hapsburg family, who ruled Spain, central Europe and much of Italy.

New religious ideas made headway in France when Lefevre d'Etaples published his translation of the Bible into French in 1523. But John Calvin was forced to flee from Paris, and Francis I persecuted the Protestants.

In spite of the magnificence and vitality of Francis's reign, the French monarchy remained unstable. As prices rose and as royal expenditure increased, the king sold offices to increase revenue, and the families who bought them increased their power, while the Parlements claimed the right to challenge the king's authority.

*Joan of Arc, a humble peasant girl, inspired French resistance to English ambitions in the closing stages of the Hundred Years' War. Her claim that she was guided by God led to her execution by the English for heresy in 1431*

*A detail from the* Très Riches Heures *of the* Duc de Berry *presents a tranquil picture of country life in 15th-century France*

**Civil wars** Henry II (1547–59) was killed in a joust and was succeeded by his son Francis II (1559–60), aged 15 and in such bad health that he died a year after ascending the throne. For more than 30 years France suffered from civil wars, in which the French nobility struggled for power. The two main factions were led by the Guises and the Bourbons. The rivalry between the two families was intensified by the religious issue, since the head of the Bourbon family, the Duc de Bourbon, and his younger brother the Prince de Condé, were Protestants, while the heads of the Guise family were the leaders of the French Catholics. In 1572, in the St Bartholomew's Day massacre, the Guises slaughtered the Protestants of Paris; persecution soon spread throughout France.

The crisis was intensified when Henry III (1574–86) was assassinated, and Henry of Navarre, a Bourbon and a Protestant, became the legitimate heir. Only his

A revolutionary cartoon. The two privileged classes – nobility and clergy – are alarmed at the prospect of the common man casting off his chains and fetters

## FRANCE *continued*

Protestantism stood between Henry and the throne. Eventually, believing that 'Paris was worth a mass', he renounced that faith and became a Catholic. He defeated the Guises and their Spanish allies, entering Paris in 1594. But he gave liberty of conscience to his Protestant subjects in the Edict of Nantes (1598). By determination in battle, as well as by diplomacy and bribery, Henry succeeded in uniting Frenchmen. He surrounded himself with able and devoted ministers, including the Duc de Sully, whose main objective was to strengthen the effectiveness of royal government.

**Rule of the Cardinals** Henry IV's assassination in 1610 seemed likely to usher in a further period of rebellion, since his son Louis XIII (1610–43) was only 9 years old and Marie de Medici, the unpopular Italian-born Queen Mother, became regent. In 1614 an Estates-General, representing the three 'orders' of the nation – nobles, clergy and commons – presented an impressive list of grievances to the young king.

In 1617 Louis XIII exiled his mother, but they were soon reconciled, and in 1624 she introduced Cardinal Richelieu on to the Council of State as chief minister. From this time the alliance between Louis XIII and Richelieu, however strained it became, was strong enough to resist ambitious nobles. Forces which opposed royal authority were broken. However, Louis XIII died in 1643, shortly after Richelieu, leaving his throne to his son, who was aged only 4. A long period of unrest followed. The regent, Anne of Austria, and her chief adviser, Cardinal Mazarin, had to face revolts known as the 'Frondes'. In these, members of the Royal Family itself, the Parlements which were anxious to maintain their privileges, and the Paris mob, as well as the Spaniards, all took part. At one stage, the Royal Family even had to flee Paris – teaching the young king an unforgettable lesson about the realities of power.

*On St Bartholomew's Day 1572, thousands of French Protestants were massacred. This incident was part of the religious wars between Catholic and Protestant which tore France asunder in the late 16th century*

**Louis XIV (1643–1715)** When Cardinal Mazarin died in 1661, Louis XIV took over power himself. He emerged as the greatest monarch in Europe, becoming known as Le Roi Soleil (the Sun King) because of the splendour of his court. Through long wars and adroit diplomacy he sought to increase France's wealth and territory, sharing his power with no one. Even an important minister such as Colbert, who sought to bring order into France's finances and industries, had little influence over policy.

Louis XIV's reign brought fame to France also through the achievements of thinkers such as Pascal, and through the plays of Corneille, Racine and Molière. But Louis had his failures. The repeal of the Edict of Nantes in 1685 forced many Protestants to flee from France. His attempt to unite the kingdoms of France and Spain was defeated by the other countries of Europe. By the time of his death, the Sun King's long wars had caused widespread distress and discontent throughout his kingdom.

*Louis XIV at a masque, dressed as the 'Sun King' – a title given him because of the magnificence of his court*

**Decline of the monarchy** The 18th century demonstrated the contradictions underlying the despotic rule of the French kings. Royal authority had been reinforced, but it had not been made more efficient. Both under Louis XV and Louis XVI there were efforts to introduce reforms. But none of these measures was successful. They needed a time of peace in which to work, but France fought many wars in Europe and Canada – from which it gained little.

The vast expense of these wars, together with a general rise in prices, meant that the government had to increase its revenue. But it could only do this by taxing the people it had previously exempted from taxation. Thinkers such as Voltaire responded to this crisis by questioning all the assumptions of existing society and criticising its institutions. Other philosophers – Rousseau pre-eminent among them – put forward new ideas of man's role, rights and obligations in society.

**Outbreak of revolution** By 1789 the French government was close to bankruptcy. To meet the crisis the Estates-General was called together for the first time since 1614. This highlighted the role of the Third Estate – those who belonged to neither of the two privileged orders of nobility and clergy. Louis XVI had already shown himself to be weak and indecisive. He thought that he was calling the Estates together to vote him money; the Third Estate saw the meeting as a chance to air its grievances, and press for reforms.

In the spring and summer of 1789 riots flared up in many parts of France. A popular government was established in Paris, and on July 14, 1789 the Bastille fortress was attacked. Riots broke out in provincial cities, largely due to the high price of bread, and in the countryside there was peasant agitation against the feudal privileges of the landlords.

The Third Estate eventually voted itself into a National Assembly. It abolished many aspects of feudalism, sought to remedy the finances by nationalising and selling Church property, and established a constitution which divided France into départements (provinces). But power was kept in the hands of the wealthy: leading revolutionaries, such as Mirabeau, sought to share power between the king and the wealthy citizens.

**Growth of republicanism** The moderate members of the Assembly wanted to establish a constitutional monarchy on the English pattern. But there were many difficulties. Catholics opposed the nationalisation of Church property and many of the nobility emigrated. Finally the Royal Family attempted to escape from France, realising that their position was impossible, but they were captured at Varennes, near Verdun.

More extreme men, the Girondins – so called because their leaders came from the Gironde – now took over power. They believed that success in war would strengthen the Revolution but, also fearing foreign intervention, they determined to strike first. In April 1792 France declared war on Austria, which had already

*Fanatical women demonstrators, spurred on by bread shortages and hatred of the king, marched on Versailles in 1789. They forced Louis XVI and his family to return with them to Paris*

*A new development in warfare. In 1870 balloons were used in the siege of Paris to spot German artillery, and to carry mail out of the beleaguered city*

threatened intervention to protect the French queen, Marie Antoinette, a Hapsburg by birth.

Joined by Prussia, Austria invaded France, sweeping the French armies aside. In the face of defeat, revolutionary and patriotic feelings were united. Louis was imprisoned and the monarchy abolished.

**Reign of terror** After a brief recovery, the military situation again became grave. The Girondins' position in the government was threatened by the rival Jacobin party, led by Robespierre and Danton. (Their name came from their club-house, where Jacobin monks used to live.) The king and queen were tried and executed; many of the remaining aristocrats were guillotined in the so-called 'reign of terror'.

Finally the Jacobins threw out the Girondins – many of whom were later executed – and established an emergency government, working through two committees, the Committee of Public Safety and the Committee of General Security. The whole of France was put on a war footing. Measures were introduced to control prices and stop speculation. The regime tried to unite France by sharing land among the peasants.

**Directory established: 1795** As the war crisis diminished, the surviving moderates took advantage of a reaction against Jacobin terror. Robespierre was executed in July 1794, and in 1795 five 'Directors' of the state were appointed in an attempt to steer a course between extreme republicanism and a restoration of the monarchy. The members of the Directory, chief among whom was Sieyès, sought to distract the French by pursuing a spectacular foreign policy. Napoleon Bonaparte, a young general from Corsica, won fame by his campaigns against Austria in Italy (1796–7).

*A republican banner proclaims French unity in defence of revolutionary ideals*

**Consulate and empire** Bonaparte overthrew the Directory in 1799 and established an authoritarian regime, appointing himself the first of three 'consuls'. In 1802 he became First Consul for life and in 1804 took the title of Emperor of the French. Napoleon set up a centralised administration, establishing a code of laws – known as the Code Napoléon – which confirmed the changes of the Revolution.

But Napoleon's position, although strong, was never completely secure. He could not establish peace, and his wars, though they covered him and his soldiers with glory, brought about his eventual downfall. Defeat forced him to abdicate in 1814. Though he returned to France in the following year, the annihilation of the remnants of his armies at Waterloo forced him to give up power for a second and final time.

*Napoleon, watched by the pope, haughtily crowns himself France's emperor*

**Restoration to Republic** After 1815, Louis XVI's brother, Louis XVIII, was restored to the throne. Louis recognised that France could not return to the system which had existed before the Revolution; he established a parliamentary regime, in which, however, only a small number of people had the vote. But even this concession was too much for his brother, Charles X, who came to the throne in 1824 determined to restore royal authority. Liberals rose against him in the revolution of 1830.

The Orleans branch of the Bourbon family took over the throne, but Louis-Philippe (1830–48) never succeeded in gaining the support of the entire nation. Industrialisation created many problems with which his government failed to cope. The result was an upheaval in 1848, when a socialist republic was established.

Louis Napoleon, Napoleon's nephew, who appealed to the conservative feelings of the peasants and the bourgeoisie, was elected president of the Republic in 1849. Shortly afterwards, assured of the support of the army, he staged a coup d'état; he proclaimed himself emperor, and ruled as Napoleon III from 1852 to 1870.

Though a dictatorial ruler, Napoleon III boasted that, through his system of plebiscites, he had the support of the French people. At home, prosperity increased dramatically. This new wealth was symbolised by Haussmann's reconstruction of Paris, which swept away much of the old city and replaced it with elegant buildings and spacious boulevards. Napoleon also tried to impress the French with an adventurous foreign policy – against Russia in the Crimean War and against Austria in Italy. He was at first successful; but it was his conduct of foreign affairs which was to bring him down. In 1870, provoked by Bismarck, he declared war on Prussia. France's defeat in 1871 brought the 'Second Empire' to an end.

**Third Republic** In September 1870 the Third Republic was proclaimed in Paris. The first task of its leaders was to make peace with the Germans. Surrender led to a rising by the working-class of Paris. This rising – known as the Commune – was ruthlessly crushed by French troops, with the loss of 20,000 lives.

France retained the centralised administration that had been established by the Revolution and Napoleon. To re-assert France's status as a great power, successive Republican governments took an active part in the scramble for colonies. A colonial empire, they thought, would show the importance of France in the world. Paris, though no longer the political centre of Europe, was still the administrative and economic heart of France; and, despite the claims of Berlin, Vienna and London, many regarded it also as the artistic and cultural centre of Europe.

The country's population, however, no longer grew as rapidly as that of other countries. At the beginning of the 19th century it was 28 million, by 1876 about 37 million, but by 1911 only 39 million. Only Ireland had a slower growth rate. The progress of French industrialisation was also slow, especially when compared with that of Britain, and France's feared rival on the European continent – imperial Germany.

*The Eiffel Tower, named after its designer, Gustave Eiffel, was built for the Paris Exhibition of 1889. The success of this trade fair was a mark of France's recovery after defeat in the Franco-Prussian War of 1870–1*

**The Great War: 1914–18** In its search for allies against Germany, France had allied itself to Russia in the 1890's. In 1914, on the outbreak of war between Germany and Russia, the Germans also invaded France. In the first months of the war they occupied about one-tenth of French territory. The worst battles of the war, such as Verdun, were fought on French soil. France's leaders, in particular Georges Clemenceau, were determined to fight on until victory was achieved. By the time the Allies had won in 1918 France had lost 1,325,000 dead – 10 per cent of its able-bodied male population.

**Post-war France: 1919–39** A seriously weakened country emerged from the war. The immediate devastations could be repaired. But France's lost generation could not be replaced. The fact that the war and the costs of reconstruction had been largely financed by loans created serious economic difficulties; the realisation that France had survived the war thanks to its allies (Britain, Russia and the USA) meant that France could no longer stand on its own as a great power – though the French were slow to realise this.

All these difficulties were too much for the political system by which governments were dependent upon the elected assembly. Weak governments followed one another in rapid succession. In 1936 a 'popular front' of Socialists, Communists and Radicals took power. But this, too, proved short-lived and ineffective; its only result was to alienate many Frenchmen – an outlook which persisted after the outbreak of war in 1939.

**Second World War: 1939–45** Disaster overtook France when, after Britain and France had declared war against Nazi Germany in 1939, the French army was completely broken by the Germans in May 1940. An armistice divided France into occupied and unoccupied zones. In the unoccupied zone, in the south, the Republic was abolished and a new authoritarian French state was established under Marshal Pétain – hero of the First World War battle at Verdun – with its capital at Vichy. But soon resistance movements were organised against the Germans. These joined up with General de Gaulle, who had refused to accept the armistice terms and established a 'Free French' government in London.

*A French girl suffers the penalty for collaboration with the Nazis after the liberation of France in 1944*

*De Gaulle leads a victory parade through the Arc de Triomphe in 1944. An obscure French general at the start of the war, he became the undisputed leader of France after the Liberation*

## FRANCE *continued*

After the Allied invasion of Europe in 1944 and the liberation of French territory, de Gaulle formed a provisional government.

**The Fourth Republic** After the war there was controversy about the responsibility for France's defeat, about collaboration with the Germans, and about the revolutionary demands of some factions of the resistance movement. General de Gaulle resigned in 1946 and campaigned for the establishment of strong government. The Fourth Republic quickly showed the same political weaknesses as its predecessor and governments were short-lived and ineffective. The Communist Party, which had been prominent in the resistance movement, appeared as the strongest single party, but it was systematically excluded from power. No one seemed able to check the rate of monetary inflation, which created many social problems.

Above all the Fourth Republic was dogged by colonial troubles. From 1947 the French were fighting to retain their empire in Indo-China. In 1954 the premier, Pierre Mendès-France, ended the war by a French withdrawal after defeat at Dien Bien Phu. In the same year rebellion started against the French in Algeria.

**Return to power of de Gaulle** In May 1958 there was a rising in Algeria of French settlers, who feared that the government would abandon them. They were supported by the army, which flouted the authority of the government in Paris. Rebel paratroops landed in Corsica, and there appeared to be the danger of an armed clash between Frenchmen. De Gaulle, emerging from his retirement, persuaded the Assembly to give him special powers. He established an authoritarian form of government which limited the powers of the Assembly, and he himself became president. In 1962 he revised the constitution so that the president had to be elected by universal suffrage. It was also in 1962 that, after much uncertainty, the French accepted the independence of Algeria and started to withdraw. This angered many Frenchmen. De Gaulle had been brought to power to settle Algeria; he did it in a way many of his supporters had not expected – by withdrawing.

For the first time in many years France was not at war. De Gaulle profited from this fact to assert France's international position. In 1957 France had joined the Common Market – and de Gaulle attempted to make France its dominant force. France also developed nuclear weapons.

The French population rose from nearly 40·5 million in 1946 to 50 million in 1969. The Fourth Republic had instituted planning for investment and for economic development, and by 1958 this was beginning to yield results. Industrial production increased rapidly and France entered a period of dynamic prosperity.

**After de Gaulle** By 1968, the conservatism of the Gaullist regime had alienated many of the young. In the 'événements' (events) of that year, students demonstrated on the streets in favour of widespread reforms in the centralised educational system. Workers, too, launched a vast movement of strikes. Though General de Gaulle succeeded in re-establishing his authority, his prestige had been severely shaken. He decided to revise the traditional system of centralisation. But when he consulted the electorate by his favoured method of referendum, in April 1969, his proposals were rejected. He immediately resigned, and died in November 1970.

However, the Gaullist party continued to hold power and a former political associate of General de Gaulle, Georges Pompidou, was elected president of the Republic. There was increasing industrialisation, and a greater integration of France into the destinies of other European countries. The death of Pompidou in 1974 brought an election in which the Gaullists lost control of the government for the first time in 16 years. Valéry Giscard d'Estaing, a conservative who had been Pompidou's minister of finance, won election as president.

*Film-maker, poet and playwright, Jean Cocteau was a leading figure in French intellectual life for more than 40 years*

*A student poster of 1968 calls for solidarity between university and factory. But the workers showed little interest in the idea*

# Gabon

The people of Gabon, an African republic which was once part of French Equatorial Africa, have an average income twice as high as that of the rest of French-speaking Africa. They owe their comparatively high standard of living to the exploitation of the country's rich mineral resources, especially manganese, which is used in the production of high-quality steel.

**Gabon and colonisation** Over the centuries, the belts of grassland running through Gabon have provided a corridor for the movement of peoples from West Africa to many parts of the continent south of the Equator. Some Bantu-speaking migrants halted here and settled in the country. Later, the Fang, a fierce and reputedly cannibalistic tribe, entered Gabon from the interior of Cameroun. They exchanged ivory for firearms and other goods with the European merchants who had set up trading posts on the coast.

The Portuguese first settled this coast around 1470. British, Dutch, French and Spanish followed, many of them engaged in the slave trade. In 1849, however, the French established Libreville as a colony for freed slaves on the model of the British settlement at Freetown, Sierra Leone. France formally annexed Gabon in 1885, and it became one of four colonies included in the Federation of French Equatorial Africa in 1910. During the 1890's and the first decade of this century Gabon was harshly exploited by French business companies. But with the federation in 1910, the worst abuses came to an end. The French began to develop the colony's economic resources, especially its mahogany forests.

**Independent Gabon** The Federation of French Equatorial Africa broke up in the last years of the colonial era, and Gabon was granted independence in 1960. President Mba, and later President Bongo (who took office in 1967) relied to some extent on the presence of a small force of French troops (who put down an anti-government coup in 1964). The government's conservative, pro-French policies attracted considerable foreign investment, both from private sources and in the form of French and World Bank aid. Gabon's economy made rapid advances with the exploitation of its manganese, iron, oil and uranium resources.

103,346 sq. miles
591,900 people
Capital: Libreville

*Albert Schweitzer (1875–1965), seen at the famous missionary hospital at Lambaréné, Gabon, which he founded*

# Gambia

The state of Gambia is a strip of land along the banks of the River Gambia, one of West Africa's major waterways. It is the smallest state in the continent. A poor country, Gambia depends mainly on ground-nuts. Its people are mostly Muslim Negroes; the Mandingo, or Mande, form the largest linguistic and cultural group.

**Gambia and the Europeans** Gambia has had a long and close relationship with Europeans. It was first visited by the Portuguese in 1444–5, during the voyage of Diniz Dias, and controlled by them until the late 16th century. English merchants, in search of slaves, established a fort on James Island near the mouth of the River Gambia in 1618. In 1763, after the Seven Years' War with France, England took control of all the French possessions in the area, known as Senegambia, but these were returned to France in 1783. From 1821 to 1843, and from 1866 to 1888, Gambia was governed from Freetown in Sierra Leone. Between these two periods it was a separate Crown Colony, ruled from London, and it returned to this status in 1888.

**Independent republic** Gambia became independent in 1965, with Sir Dawda Jawara as the first prime minister. Gambia's minute size is an obstacle to national development, and there have been moves to federate the country with surrounding French-speaking Senegal – moves so far resisted by most Gambians. Gambia became a republic within the British Commonwealth in April 1970, after a national referendum.

4361 sq. miles
399,100 people
Capital: Banjul

*Sir Dawda Jawara – elected first president of Gambia in 1970 – with his wife while on a state visit to West Germany*

Since 1949, Germany has been divided into two states – West Germany (Federal Republic of Germany) and East Germany (German Democratic Republic). But only in June 1973 did they formally agree to recognise each other's sovereignty

# Germany, East

East Germany, as the German Democratic Republic is commonly called, extends between the Federal Republic of Germany to the west and the land now forming part of Poland to the east of the Oder and Neisse rivers. The Free City of West Berlin, which has close links with the Federal Republic, lies in the heart of East Germany, but is not controlled by it.

East Germany's strategic position, combined with its economic power, has given the country a crucial role in East-West relations in Europe. For many years East Germany's Communist leaders tried to obstruct any move towards an East-West understanding, but in the early 1970's their attitude towards the West became more flexible. East Germany now has extensive trade dealings with West Germany, and its political relations with Bonn have recently improved.

East Germany, with its capital in Pankow (part of East Berlin), officially describes itself as a workers' and peasants' state and sees itself as the heir to a tradition of German socialism going back to Karl Marx.

Many places famous in German history are within East Germany. They include Leipzig, the birthplace of Richard Wagner and the home of J. S. Bach from 1723 until his death; Potsdam, the centre of Prussian militarism; and Weimar, which for many years was the main centre of German culture, attracting such figures as the writers Goethe and Schiller. For the history of Germany and its people until 1945, see GERMANY, WEST (p. 390).

## Spartacists and Communists: 1918–45
The German Communist Party was founded at the time of the 'November Revolution' which overthrew the German Empire in 1918. Its basis was the Spartacus League, a revolutionary pacifist movement, led by Rosa Luxemburg and Karl Liebknecht, who were murdered by right-wing extremists in January 1919. The Communist Party's later leaders were of lower calibre.

Towards the end of the 1920's, the party's chief spokesman was Ernst Thalmann, an obedient follower of Russian policy. He was arrested by Hitler's Nazis in 1933 and murdered, and the party was banned. Other leading Communists took refuge from the Nazis in the USSR but, between 1933 and 1939, many of them were victims of Stalin's purges. The most important survivor, Walter Ulbricht, had been a member of the party's Central Committee before 1933; in May 1945 the Russians flew him back to Berlin to rebuild the German Communist Party.

41,776 sq. miles
17,200,000 people
Capital: East Berlin

Johann Sebastian Bach (1685–1750), one of the world's greatest musical geniuses, was born at Eisenach in what is now East Germany

The 'November Revolution' in Berlin, which hastened the downfall of the German Empire and of the Kaiser, also saw the founding of the German Communist Party

**Foundation of the republic: 1949** The Russians gave full-scale support to the Communist Party in their occupation zone of Germany, but the Communists alone could not whip up enough popular support to form a government. In April 1946 the Russians forced the Social Democratic Party to unite with the Communist Party to form the Socialist Unity Party. It was led by Walter Ulbricht, the party's First Secretary, and the former Social Democrat, Otto Grotewohl. In 1949, when Germany's western zones became the Federal Republic, the east took the title of German Democratic Republic, the veteran Communist Wilhelm Pieck becoming its first president; Grotewohl became prime minister, with Ulbricht as his deputy. Although other political parties existed on paper, it at once became a one-party dictatorship.

**East Germany's economic progress** The territory of East Germany contained some industrial areas – in particular the textile and engineering towns of Saxony – but it was poor in coal and other natural resources. Matters were aggravated by Soviet demands for war-damage reparations. Soviet troops seized machinery and transported it back to the USSR.

Despite these handicaps, East Germany developed its industry until it became second only to the USSR, in terms of industrial production, among the nations of the Eastern bloc. Its government nationalised all heavy industry and distributed agricultural land to the peasants, who then were organised into collective farms.

**The Berlin Wall** The Soviet attempt to drive the Western powers out of West Berlin by blockade during 1948 and 1949 was beaten by a massive Western air-lift of coal, fuel and food, and the city continued to be a troublesome enclave in the heart of East Germany. It was possible for East Germans to cross the border freely from East to West Berlin, and almost 2 million of East Germany's original population of 18 million took this escape route between 1949 and 1961.

This was a grave loss to East Germany. Many of those who fled were doctors, technicians and teachers. Ulbricht's only answer was to seal off West Berlin by building a wall between the East and West sectors in August 1961. It was reinforced by barbed-wire obstacles, and guarded by 'vopos', or armed police.

**Political repression** As a westerly outpost of the Soviet bloc, East Germany became obsessed by security – especially when confronted with West German demands for reunification. The country's government became known as one of the most repressive of any Communist state. Ulbricht drove many of his rivals and opponents from power – particularly in a major purge in 1958. A mass revolt in several East German cities in June 1953 was brutally crushed. Any questioning of the regime by intellectuals was severely punished.

**Fears of encirclement** When the process of understanding between the Western powers and the Soviet Union began to develop in the 1960's, East Germany was alarmed. Ulbricht felt his position was threatened – and that his power would be limited by the prospect of better relations between Russia and West Germany.

The Berlin Wall became a symbol of an oppressive regime. It was built by the East German Communists to prevent dissidents escaping to the West

Bertolt Brecht (1898–1956), German Marxist playwright and poet, lived in East Berlin from 1948. His theatre company, the Berliner Ensemble, strongly influenced contemporary drama

A self-portrait by
Albrecht Dürer
(1471–1528).
Dürer became the
leading figure of the
German Renaissance
school of painting

## GERMANY, EAST continued

**Negotiations with Bonn** With West Germany's more flexible approach to the East under Chancellor Willy Brandt, East Germany was forced, partly by Soviet pressure, to respond more favourably. The East German prime minister, Willi Stoph, had two meetings with Chancellor Brandt early in 1970, from which a general understanding between the two German states developed. In 1971 Ulbricht was replaced by the more moderate Erich Honecker. This paved the way for an East-West agreement on Berlin later that year.

East and West Germany ratified a treaty in 1973 establishing diplomatic relations for the first time since World War II. Admission of both Germanies to the United Nations swiftly followed. East Germany thereafter won diplomatic recognition from most Western nations, enabling the nation to acquire a wider market for its industrial products.

Erich Honecker
succeeded Ulbricht in
1971; his more flex-
ible outlook led to
improved relations
between the two
German states

# Germany, West

West Germany, as the Federal Republic of Germany is usually called, is the richest and most populous state in western Europe. Established after the Second World War, the republic occupies only about half Germany's pre-war territory; half the remainder forms the German Democratic Republic (East Germany).

Dramatic changes in its boundaries and political structure have been a feature of Germany's history throughout the centuries. Until the time of the French Revolution, Germany consisted of some 600 sovereign states. Unification into a single nation-state did not take place until 1871, when the Prussian statesman Bismarck created the German Empire by 'blood and iron'. German unity lasted only 74 years – from 1871 to 1945.

After 1871, Germany rapidly developed its military and economic strength, emerging as the most formidable country in Europe. The disturbance of the European balance of power which resulted was one of the basic causes of this century's two world wars.

The contribution of Germans to European culture has been immense, with figures such as Bach, Beethoven and Wagner in music, Kant, Nietzsche, Hegel and Marx in philosophy, Goethe and Thomas Mann in literature, and Albert Einstein in science. Einstein was among those German Jews who managed to escape persecution by emigrating, during Germany's darkest and most tragic phase – the era of Nazi tyranny.

**Early history** Germany has been a rich field for the study of European pre-history. Remains of early man have been discovered at Neanderthal, Heidelberg and Steinheim. The first German tribes to be recorded in history were the Teutons and the Cimbri, who were defeated at the hands of the Roman general Marius in 102 BC. Rome, however, failed to conquer Germany despite efforts by Augustus. After the defeat of Varus in AD 9 by the German chieftain Herman, the Romans concentrated on holding the Rhine and Danube against the Germanic tribes.

The Teutons and Cimbri, together with the Alemanni, Burgundii, Franks, Lombards, Ostrogoths and Visigoths, settled in the territory between the Rhine estuary and the River Elbe. After the fall of Rome, the area was the scene of much fighting between these tribes until the Frankish king, Charlemagne, in an attempt to re-establish the Roman Empire, extended his rule over most of Germany, as well as France. Charlemagne was crowned Holy Roman

95,938 sq. miles
63,000,000 people
(including W. Berlin)
Capital: Bonn

One of Charlemagne's
conquering soldiers.
This 9th-century stone
carving of a Frankish
warrior is now in the
Rhine Museum, Bonn

Henry IV (1056–
1106), the Holy
Roman Emperor
(left, wearing crown)
fighting his rebellious
son Henry, who
eventually deposed and
imprisoned him

Emperor in 800. His son took over the empire after his death in 814, but in 843 it was divided. Rivalry among the German feudal princes made the empire a loose, ineffective federation without much central authority.

The empire was strengthened, however, under the imperial dynasty of the Hohenstaufen, which subdued many of the larger duchies. In 1180 Frederick I dismembered Saxony, the last remaining great duchy. At the end of the reign of his grandson, Frederick II, Holy Roman Emperor from 1220 to 1250, the great days of the empire were over. The authority of the emperors was constantly challenged by the papacy and by powerful local rulers, so that by the 15th century Germany had broken down into total disunity.

**Luther and the Reformation: 1517–1648** A German monk, Martin Luther, appalled by the corruption of the Roman Catholic Church, launched the Protestant Reformation in 1517 by defying the authority of the pope. Before this, Germany, like the rest of Europe, had been Roman Catholic in religion. But soon parts of the country turned Protestant. Luther's views were adopted by several German princes, especially as he supported their claims to supreme power.

Germany's religious divisions led to savage fighting between alliances of rival princes, as well as with the Holy Roman Emperor, Charles V, until a compromise was reached at Augsburg in 1555. The treaty signed there gave each ruler the right to determine the religious faith of his subjects. But the compromise proved to be only temporary. In the 17th century a further period of religious strife amongst the states – the Thirty Years' War – ravaged all Germany. Its effects held back Germany's political development for generations. Some 10 million Germans are believed to have died in the course of the war, which was ended by the Treaty of Westphalia in 1648. Germany was divided into a patchwork of petty kingdoms, whose sovereignty was established at the expense of the Holy Roman Empire.

**Rise of Prussia** The treaty strengthened the position of Frederick William (1620–88), a member of the Hohenzollern family which ruled Brandenburg. Frederick William had already greatly expanded his territories during the Thirty Years' War. Known as the 'Great Elector', he created a centralised administration and reorganised the army and state finances. Under his rule, Berlin became the capital of Brandenburg-Prussia. Prussia's increasing importance was marked when Frederick William's son, Frederick I, took the title of 'King in Prussia' in 1701.

Frederick II of Prussia, known as 'the Great', further increased the size and prestige of the country. At his death in 1786, Prussia, with a population of $5\frac{1}{2}$ million, was one of the major states of Europe. Frederick achieved this expansion by a mixture of war and guile. He developed the powerful army he had inherited from his father, Frederick William I (1688–1740) and used it in a way that astonished the world in the War of the Austrian Succession (1740–8) and in the Seven Years' War (1756–63). Such was his success that Austria was forced into an alliance with its hereditary enemy, France, in an attempt to check him.

**Lull before the storm: 1786–1848** Under Frederick's successors, Prussian influence declined. The kingdom was eclipsed during Napoleon's occupation of Germany.

After the humiliating defeat of its army at Jena in 1806 at the hands of Napoleon, Prussia built up a new army under men such as Scharnhorst, while its statesmen preached the doctrine of German nationalism. After Napoleon's defeat at Waterloo – in which the Prussian army under Blücher played a vital part – Prussia was in a position to make demands at the Vienna peace conference of 1815. The Prussians gained a hold on the Rhine, acquiring territories around Cologne, so that Prussia now straddled the whole of Germany. This, together with the creation of a Zollverein (customs union) with a number of smaller German states in 1834, provided a basis for further expansion.

The papacy in Rome
is depicted in
grotesque allegorical
form in this woodcut
by the 16th-century
German Protestant
artist Cranach

Frederick the Great
of Prussia (1712–
86), a brilliant
administrator, raised
his country to a
dominant position
amongst the
European powers

The German drama-
tist, poet, novelist and
scientist Goethe
(1749–1832) won
immense fame in his
lifetime for the scale
and variety of his
achievements

*Beethoven (1770–1827), a German composer of Flemish descent, was one of the profoundest innovators in the history of European music*

**Revolution and unity** The tensions which had developed in German society since the Napoleonic occupation finally exploded in 1848, as part of a revolutionary movement which swept Europe. A growing feeling of nationalism had developed among German intellectuals, and they now demanded that Germany should be united. This move was opposed by Hapsburg Austria, which feared the power of a united Germany. The intellectuals also sought a more liberal form of government than the absolute monarchies which still ruled most of Germany. The start of an industrial revolution, too, led to social discontent, especially among the class of factory workers which had emerged in the weaving towns of Saxony and Silesia and in the engineering towns of the Ruhr.

In March 1849, the intellectuals came together in an assembly at St Paul's Church in Frankfurt and drafted a constitution for a united and democratic Germany, offering the crown to the King of Prussia. This constitution was never applied. After initial hesitation, Frederick William IV declared that he would not 'pick up a crown from the gutter', and sent his troops to crush the Frankfurt Assembly and the revolutionary workers and students who supported it.

But the desire for national unity remained strong. The example of Italian unification, achieved in the 1860's, led to a renewed upsurge of nationalism in Germany. This was exploited by Prince Otto von Bismarck, a Prussian Junker (nobleman) with a long diplomatic training, who became prime minister of Prussia in 1862. Asserting that 'blood and iron' would unite Germany where the talkers of 1848 had failed, Bismarck placed Prussia at the head of the patriotic movement by taking the lead in a war against Denmark in 1864 to bring Schleswig-Holstein under German control.

In 1866 the rivalry between Prussia and Austria for the leadership of Germany led to war. The Prussian army, with its superior weapons and leadership, won an easy victory in seven weeks. In the following year, Bismarck created a new political structure, the North German Confederation, which incorporated many of the north German states under Prussian leadership.

Bismarck believed that one further war against France would unite the north and south of Germany. In 1870, he provoked Napoleon III into declaring war and in March 1871 the victorious King of Prussia was crowned Kaiser (Emperor) of a united Germany.

**Industrial progress: 1871–90** Germany's unification provided a basis for rapid economic advance. Between 1870 and 1880 industrial production increased by 43 per cent and by a further 64 per cent between 1880 and 1890. Firms such as Krupps and Siemens were quick to seize on new inventions and processes.

Bismarck remained Chancellor of the Reich until 1890, when he was dismissed by the impetuous Kaiser Wilhelm II. Though in the 1880's he introduced social insurance policies which were widely admired and copied abroad, Bismarck distrusted political parties and parliamentary government. The German parliament was democratically elected but the constitution ensured that real power remained with the emperor.

**Prelude to war: 1890–1914** Bismarck had been careful not to antagonise other powers once he had achieved German unity, and he established links with Russia and Austria in the so-called Dreikaiserbund ('League of the Three Emperors'). But the foreign policy of his successors was more risky. To a large extent this policy was now decided by Wilhelm II, for none of the chancellors of Germany from 1890 to 1914 – Caprivi, Hohenlohe, Bülow and Bethmann-Hollweg – managed to control the impulsive nature of their imperial master. The Kaiser encouraged Admiral Tirpitz to build a large navy, which Britain saw as a challenge to its position as the world's leading naval power, while on land the threat of the German army brought France and Russia into alliance. From 1900 onwards, Europe came to the brink of war several times, as in the Balkan crises of 1908 and 1912–13. War finally broke out in 1914.

*Prince Otto von Bismarck (1815–98), known as 'the Iron Chancellor', forged a united Germany by his ruthless methods*

*The ambitious policies of the Kaiser, Wilhelm II, finally brought Germany into conflict with other European powers*

**World war: 1914–18** The First World War originated in a conflict between Serbia and Austria-Hungary – but it was not positively desired by any of the powers involved. It broke out through a series of miscalculations, of which the most serious were probably those made by Germany. The German General Staff ordered a full mobilisation of the army on the assumption that Russia was planning to attack Germany as well as Austria-Hungary. The German government also thought that Britain would stay neutral – even though the German plan for advancing into France required a 'short cut' through Belgium, whose neutrality was protected by a British guarantee.

At first the war went well for Germany. The armies advancing into France almost reached Paris before being checked at the Battle of the Marne. On the Eastern Front, the Germans inflicted a series of crushing defeats on Russia, starting at Tannenberg. On the Western Front the fighting soon settled down into the slow agony of trench warfare, in which the Germans remained largely on the defensive against Allied attacks. Major battles resulted in enormous casualties, and achieved little result. By 1917, however, Germany was slowly being strangled by the British naval blockade. The entry of America into the war brought a last-ditch German offensive in March 1918, the object of which was to win the war before American troops could arrive in strength on the Western Front. Despite initial success, the Germans were in full retreat by summer.

The German General Staff realised the war was lost and called on the government to make peace. Revolt broke out in the fleet and spread to Berlin; the Kaiser was forced to abdicate. Two million Germans had died in battle. Bewildered German opinion sought scapegoats for defeat: these were found in socialists, pacifists and Jews, who were alleged to have undermined Germany by a 'stab in the back'. This belief was to play a fatal role in weakening the post-war Weimar Republic.

**Weimar Republic: 1919–33** A republican constitution was adopted in 1919 by a National Assembly which met at Weimar, 150 miles from Berlin, then still in the hands of revolutionaries. The new democratic regime suffered under many burdens, made worse by militant opposition from right-wing and left-wing extremists. The Treaty of Versailles imposed harsh terms on Germany which was forced to give back Alsace-Lorraine and the Saar to France, surrender its colonies, and pay vast sums of money to the Allies as reparations for war damage. In 1923, when Germany failed to make its reparation payments, the French army occupied the industrial Ruhr. Chaos followed; this reduced the already gravely inflated German currency to complete worthlessness.

Germany's position improved under Gustav Stresemann, who became chancellor in 1923 and subsequently served as foreign minister until his death in 1929. He stabilised the currency and made a series of agreements with the Western powers which brought Germany economic relief, political stability and membership of the League of Nations. But this stability depended on world prosperity, which collapsed in the great slump of 1929–33. As a result, Germany's economy broke down, and nearly 6 million people became unemployed.

In these circumstances many Germans turned to Adolf Hitler's National Socialist or Nazi Party. It became the largest party in the Reichstag (parliament), with 37 per cent of the votes. After much negotiation and intrigue Hitler became chancellor in 1933.

*In 1923, a 1 billion mark banknote would just buy a packet of cigarettes. Ten years earlier, it was worth the equivalent of £50,000 million*

*A cartoon shows Hitler 'crawling out of' the Treaty of Versailles. The Nazi leader based many of his territorial demands on the treaty's 'injustices' to Germany*

*The first major Nazi Party rally was held at Nuremberg in 1933. A martial atmosphere was theatrically engineered to create a mood of mass hysteria*

'Behind the enemy
powers: the Jew' –
this Nazi propaganda
poster represented
Jewry as the force
that spurred on the
Allied war effort

## GERMANY, WEST *continued*

**Third Reich and appeasement: 1933–9** Hitler had set out his beliefs in *Mein Kampf* ('My Struggle'), which he wrote in 1924. He called for the creation of a totalitarian dictatorship, which meant the abolition of all independent political parties, state control of the press and churches, and the elimination of the Jews as a racially impure element from the state. Once in power, he began to carry out these policies systematically.

Hitler was determined to free Germany from the 'shackles of Versailles'. He walked out of the League of Nations and began a large-scale programme of rearmament. In 1936 he re-occupied the Rhineland. In 1938 he brought about the *Anschluss* (union) with Austria, as the first step in his plan to bring all German-speaking people under Nazi rule. Later that year, the German-speaking parts of Czechoslovakia, the Sudetenland, were brought into the Reich. In the hope of 'appeasing' Hitler, Britain and France accepted these acts – particularly in the Munich agreement of 1938, by which Germany gained the Sudetenland. But in 1939, when Hitler attacked Poland, Britain and France foresaw a Europe dominated by him, and so declared war.

**Second World War: 1939–45** As in 1914, Germany scored quick successes at the start of the war. Its generals had developed the technique of blitzkrieg (lightning war). Poland was crushed in a matter of days, and in early 1940 Germany's armies swept through Norway and Denmark, the Low Countries and France. But Hitler's Luftwaffe was defeated in the Battle of Britain and a planned invasion had to be abandoned.

By the summer of 1941 Hitler controlled the whole of western Europe, and the attack on Russia which he launched in June nearly brought him victory there too. Only in the winter of 1942–3, when defeat at Stalingrad in Russia followed defeat at El Alamein in North Africa, did the tide of war turn against Germany.

The Western Allies' advance towards Germany through Italy (1943) and France (1944) converged with the Red Army's move westwards. In May 1945 Hitler committed suicide amid the ruins of a regime which had caused millions of deaths – including 6 million Jews murdered in concentration camps – and had brought untold destruction to Europe.

**Rebuilding from the ruins: 1945–8** Germany's collapse in 1945 was total. Its surviving leaders were tried by an international court at Nuremberg for their crimes against humanity. Bombing had destroyed many of Germany's cities and industries; this destruction was made even worse by the savage house-to-house fighting in the last weeks of the war. Over 10 million refugees fled westwards from Russian-occupied areas.

Each of the four Allies carried out its own policies in its occupation zone. Among the Western Allies, France sought reparations for the damage done during the German occupation, while Britain and America soon found it impossible to cope with the burden of supporting the German population, and began to allow increases in Germany's industrial output.

**Berlin blockade: 1948–9** Allied support for the economic reconstruction of Western Germany included payment of American funds under the Marshall Plan from 1948 onwards. Co-operation with the Russians broke down soon after the war, when the former allies were unable to agree on the future of Germany. In particular, they quarrelled about the four-power government of Berlin. When the Western powers sponsored a currency reform in their main zones, as well as in West Berlin, the Russians imposed a tight blockade on the city. This was beaten by a massive air-lift operated by the Western powers. By May 1949, when the blockade was lifted, solidarity between the Allies and West German political leaders had been greatly strengthened. The result was the setting-up of the Federal Republic of Germany, uniting all the Western occupation zones, with its capital in Bonn.

*Adolf Hitler seen
with his Fascist ally,
Mussolini, during a
visit to Munich by the
Italian dictator*

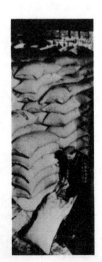

*Reserve stocks, such as this sugar, are
held by West Berlin in case it is ever
again blockaded by East Germany*

**'Economic miracle'** In August 1949, Germany held free elections, the first since 1932. The Christian Democratic Party, led by Konrad Adenauer, won a small majority. Adenauer was to remain Federal Chancellor until 1963. His government, with Ludwig Erhard as economics minister, concentrated on economic rebuilding and development. Within a few years, partly with American help and also because it incurred no defence expenditure until 1955, West Germany became one of the world's most prosperous countries.

Adenauer worked to tie West Germany as closely as possible to the other Western powers. In 1950, he collaborated with the French statesman Robert Schuman in setting up the European Coal and Steel Community. This organisation paved the way for the Rome treaty of 1957 which established the Common Market. In 1955 West Germany joined NATO.

**Berlin Wall** The confidence of Adenauer's government was severely tested by a series of Soviet threats against West Berlin from 1958 onwards. In August 1961 the Soviet and East German authorities took the drastic step of building a concrete wall between the two sectors of the city. The need for this was officially explained by arguing that West Berlin was a centre for sabotage and spying against East Germany – but the true reason was that the 'open frontier' between East and West Berlin had been used as an escape route by 2 million East Germans, who since 1949 had decided that they preferred to live in West Germany.

**Adenauer's successors** After Adenauer's resignation in 1963, Ludwig Erhard, the chief architect of Germany's 'economic miracle', became chancellor. By 1966 economic progress was slowing down. Output and employment were falling and the chancellor's cabinet colleagues, the small but influential Free Democratic Party, lost confidence in him. At the end of the year he was forced to resign. A new cabinet was formed; it consisted of a coalition of the Christian Democrats with their long-standing left-wing opponents, the Social Democrats (SPD).

With the formation of this coalition, under Chancellor Kurt-George Kiesinger (a Christian Democrat), Social Democrats gained experience of government at a national level for the first time. Their leader, Willy Brandt, who became vice-chancellor and foreign minister, had been a popular and successful mayor of West Berlin during the period 1957–66.

**Brandt forms government: 1969** The Christian Democrats were still the largest single party after the 1969 elections. But their former coalition partners, the Free Democrats, now joined the Social Democrats to form a new left-centre coalition. Brandt became chancellor, the first socialist to hold this post since 1930.

He planned to introduce far-reaching reforms. But on the domestic front, change was difficult to bring about. The two ruling parties found it hard to reconcile their ideas on such matters as the extension of workers' control of industry and reform of the tax system. Dramatic developments took place in foreign policy, however, especially in relations with the eastern bloc.

The attempt to reach an understanding with the East, a policy vigorously pursued by Brandt, was not completely new. Under Erhard, trading relations with eastern Europe had been strengthened, and Brandt himself, as foreign minister, had established diplomatic relations with Romania and Yugoslavia.

The more active Ostpolitik (eastern policy) of Brandt after 1969 led to the signing of treaties with the USSR and Poland in the summer of 1970. These were ratified in 1972. Even more significantly, negotiations began with East Germany. Brandt and the East German leader, Willi Stoph, met early in 1970. Though West Germany continued to insist that full diplomatic recognition of East Germany was out of the question, the development of official contacts between the two states helped to make possible a four-power agreement guaranteeing the stability of West Berlin in 1971.

*Konrad Adenauer,
West Germany's first
post-war chancellor,
led his shattered
country into an era of
economic expansion*

*Ludwig Erhard, the
architect of West
Germany's 'economic
miracle' under
Adenauer, became
chancellor in 1963*

*The Ostpolitik followed by Chancellor Willy Brandt (left) led to a treaty of friendship with the USSR. Signing with Brandt is Russian premier Kosygin*

Brandt's Ostpolitik reached a culmination in 1973 when the parliaments of East and West Germany ratified a treaty recognizing their common border and establishing diplomatic relations for the first time. Both were then admitted to the United Nations.

**New leadership: 1974** The dramatic arrest in 1974 of one of Brandt's top aides as a Communist East German spy brought Brandt's resignation, which accepted full responsibility for 'negligence' in having employed the spy. Brandt designated as his successor Helmut Schmidt, who had been minister of finance. The Bundestag then elected Schmidt as the nation's fifth postwar chancellor. Schmidt indicated that, with Brandt's Ostpolitik having been brought to a successful conclusion, West Germany would now turn its attention toward achieving greater unity with its Western allies.

# Ghana

When the British colony of the Gold Coast gained its independence in 1957, its new rulers renamed it Ghana, after the great African empire which had flourished a thousand years earlier in the western Sudan – although actual historical links between the two Ghanas are tenuous. Modern Ghana was the first Black African state to emerge from European colonial rule, and under its flamboyant, dynamic leader, Kwame Nkrumah, it became the pacemaker for other African countries seeking independence. Ghana lost much of its influence in 1966, however, when Nkrumah was overthrown in a coup and the country came near to economic ruin.

Ghana is the world's leading exporter of cocoa, and gold is its main mineral export. Most of the population is divided between two language groups: the Mossi-Grussi speakers in the northern bushlands, and the Kwa speakers in the rain-forest regions of the south.

**Early Ghana** The ancestors of the present-day Ghanaians were invaders from the north, who intermingled with a people present in the region since early Stone Age times. Several kingdoms arose in the 14th century, notably Ga and Ewe in the south-east, Dagomba and Mamprussi in the north, and the Akan states in the forest area and the coastal plains.

*Günter Grass – novelist, dramatist and poet – typified liberalism's revival in postwar Germany*

92,100 sq. miles
9,679,400 people
Capital: Accra

*A British emissary parleys with an Ashanti chief in his village during the Ashanti War of 1873–4. Britain finally annexed Ashanti in 1901*

**European intrusion: 1471–1874** Portuguese explorers reached Ghana's coast in 1471. They traded various goods for the country's ivory and gold; hence the European name for the country, the Gold Coast. By the 17th century the Portuguese had been joined by Dutch, Danish, English, Swedish and other European merchants, and the gold and ivory trade had given way to a trade in slaves to satisfy the huge demands for labour by the plantation-owners of the New World. The Europeans remained on the coast in forts, called 'factories', and the slaves were brought to them by African traders.

It became of great political importance to control the routes down which slaves were taken to the coast, and struggles developed amongst the states of the interior. By the 18th century, Ashanti, an Akan state, had established its supremacy. When the Ashanti people turned southwards in the 19th century and tried to

conquer the coastal peoples, they came into conflict with Europeans – British, Danes and Dutch.

During the first three decades of the 1800's the Europeans outlawed the slave trade and turned to other forms of trading. As the century progressed the British became the dominant power on the Gold Coast, and found themselves increasingly drawn into its affairs. In 1874, after a long series of minor wars, a British military force invaded Ashanti and destroyed Kumasi, the capital; in the same year the coastal region was formally constituted the British Gold Coast colony, after being a protected region for many years.

**British rule: 1874–1947** Further expeditions were sent by the British against Ashanti, which was annexed as a colony in 1901. Britain had already declared the Northern Territories a protectorate in 1898 to forestall expansion by the French from the north. After the First World War the western area of neighbouring Togoland, formerly a German colony, became a British mandate under the League of Nations, and was administered from the Gold Coast. Thus, in the 83 years of their rule, the British created the framework of modern Ghana.

Economically, the country advanced rapidly. The cocoa plant was introduced from Brazil, and by the 1920's the Gold Coast was producing more than half the world's supply of cocoa. Dependence on a single crop had its drawbacks, but it did produce wealth which, in turn, had important social and political consequences. Newly well-to-do and educated Africans – farmers, chiefs, lawyers and merchants – began to seek a voice in the colony's government. In 1947 the United Gold Coast Convention (UGCC) was established to work towards eventual independence for the colony.

*Naturalistic designs, such as this equestrian warrior, were used by the famous goldsmiths of Ashanti for their goldweights cast in brass*

**Nkrumah and independence: 1947–57** The UGCC's gradual approach did not suit the young politician Kwame Nkrumah, who returned from studying in England and America in 1947 to become the Convention's general secretary. Two years later he founded the Convention People's Party (CPP), which demanded immediate independence. African participation in the 1951 Legislative Assembly elections proved a triumph for the CPP and the African majority. Nkrumah, who was under detention at the time for his part in the campaign of 'positive action', was promptly released by the Governor, Sir Charles Arden-Clarke, and invited to form a government. In 1957, the Gold Coast colony, taking the name of Ghana, achieved full independence.

Nkrumah aimed at the rapid economic development of Ghana, through such schemes as the huge Volta River project; he also worked for the independence of all the African colonies, which he hoped to unite into a single African state. The ineffectual unions with Guinea (1958) and Mali (1960) were to have been the first stages in achieving a united Africa, with Nkrumah himself as leader. But his grandiose plans led the country into crippling overseas debts while, politically, he alienated himself from his supporters by his dictatorial rule. By the end of 1963, Ghana was a one-party state in which preventive detention was widely used to suppress opposition, while Nkrumah became increasingly involved in pro-Communist policies.

*Kwame Nkrumah (1909–72) was a leading advocate of pan-African unity. His dictatorial rule alienated the people of Ghana and led finally to his downfall*

**Ghana since Nkrumah** In 1966, while Nkrumah was on a visit to Peking, the army under General Ankrah seized power in an almost bloodless coup. Nkrumah went into exile in Guinea, where he died in 1972. In 1969, the National Liberation Council transferred power, after elections, to a civilian government led by Dr K. A. Busia, exiled during the Nkrumah regime.

But neither of these governments could solve Ghana's economic problems – its dependence on cocoa exports at a time of falling world prices, and the burden of foreign debt inherited from Nkrumah. In 1972, while Busia was in London, the army again took power. The great expectations which accompanied Ghana's independence have yet to be realised.

**GREAT BRITAIN,** *see United Kingdom*

# Greece

Geography has been especially important in shaping the history and character of the Greek people. High mountains, dividing one valley from the next, and scattered islands have made for regional jealousy and political disunity, and a poor soil and lack of mineral resources have always driven the country's surplus population to seek a living abroad. In ancient times the Greeks planted colonies all over the Mediterranean. In modern times they have emigrated to the United States and other countries. With barren mountains behind them and the sea in front, the Greek has always tended to look outwards to a wider world.

Classical Greek civilization spread far beyond the boundaries of present-day Greece. There were Greek cities in Spain and on the eastern shores of the Black Sea. But these cities never constituted a Greek 'empire' like the Roman Empire. They had no political unity, only the bond of a common language and culture. All Hellenes, as the Greeks called themselves, agreed on their own superiority to outsiders, the 'barbarians', but they agreed on little else and were continually at war with each other.

Greece became a single political unit as late as 1830, when the nucleus of the modern Greek nation – its territory since enlarged by successive boundary changes – became an independent kingdom. Following a coup in 1967, a so-called 'colonels' government' was established, which put Greece under martial law. The young king, Constantine, withdrew into self-imposed exile in Rome, and Greece was later declared a republic. In 1974, the army handed over power to a civilian government under the premiership of Constantine Karamanlis.

**Early civilization: 3000–1400 BC** The earliest civilization in the region of modern Greece was the non-Greek Minoan culture of the island of Crete, which developed c. 2500 BC. Fertilised by Egyptian and other oriental influences, and producing an elegant and lively art, it entered its great period c. 2000, when the famous palace of Knossos was built. Crete became the centre of a maritime empire, which collapsed c. 1400, probably as the result of a catastrophic volcanic eruption. The island then came under the control of Mycenaean Greeks from the mainland.

**Mycenae: 1600–1100 BC** The first Greek-speaking peoples entered Greece from the north c. 1900 BC and spread rapidly over the peninsula. A new civilization evolved, influenced by the Minoans of Crete and centred on Mycenae. With the collapse of Crete in 1400, Mycenae became the dominant power of the region.

This was the 'heroic age' of Greece, celebrated in Homer's epic poem, the *Iliad*. It was from Mycenae that the legendary Agamemnon led the Greeks – known to Homer as Achaeans – to the Trojan War. The massive remains of Mycenaean hill fortresses and rock tombs are eloquent evidence of this people's warlike society, contrasting strongly with the exuberant and sophisticated culture of the Minoan palaces. In about 1100 BC, Mycenaean power collapsed, and much of Greece came under the domination of a fresh wave of northern Greek-speaking invaders, the Dorians.

**Age of colonisation: 750–550 BC** The influx of peoples from the north added to the chronic problem of overpopulation and led to a great era of overseas expansion. Greek colonists founded independent city-states all round the Mediterranean and the Black Sea, wherever a

*Greek vases of c. 1000 BC were decorated with simple yet striking patterns. This style, forerunner of a more elaborate type of decoration, is called 'protogeometric'*

natural harbour could be found. Marseilles, Nice, Naples, Syracuse, Trebizond, Varna and other famous ports all began life as Greek settlements.

These new states were ruled in different ways. Some fell under the sway of self-made dictator kings or 'tyrants'. Other states were controlled by cliques of leading families or 'oligarchies'. Still more were governed by a 'democracy' made up of all free males. Yet in all three types of city, almost half the population were slaves, and political conflict kept many states in a constant ferment of coups and counter-revolutions.

**Persian invaders: 490–479 BC** With the rise of the Persian Empire, the Greek Ionian colonies fringing the coasts of Asia Minor turned to their homeland for support. To teach the Greeks a lesson, the Persian king, Darius, sent an army against them in 490. Athens, which had emerged as the leading democratic state, defeated the Persian forces at Marathon.

The next Persian king, Xerxes, came in person with an immense army in 480. A tiny force from Dorian Sparta, a city-state renowned for its military prowess, tried vainly but heroically to block his path in the Pass of Thermopylae. The main Greek forces, however, won a crushing naval victory at Salamis and then a land battle at Plataea (479), after which the invaders withdrew.

**Pericles and Athens** The qualities which the Athenians displayed in the Persian wars had won them the acknowledged leadership of Greece. Their culture reached its zenith under the great democratic statesman, Pericles, who was supreme for 30 years. But Athenian dominance stirred Corinth and numerous other states to combine against Athens under the leadership of Sparta in the Peloponnesian War (431–404 BC). The Athenians had naval superiority, but the Spartans were irresistible on land, and thus no decisive battle seemed possible. It was a war of raids and blockades. Athens was also swept by a terrible plague.

Even so, Athenian art and culture still flourished. Aristophanes wrote his comedies and the youthful Plato heard the teachings of Socrates. But in 404 Athens was forced to make peace with Sparta, whose victory destroyed Athenian dominance for ever.

**Macedonian supremacy** The Greek city-states were ill-equipped to survive in an era of expanding greater powers. Petty squabbles between them opened the way to conquest by Philip of Macedon (382–336 BC). The Athenian statesman Demosthenes preached in vain for a united front against Philip's aggressions. Using their improved fighting formation, the Macedonian phalanx, Philip's spearmen won a victory at Chaeronea in 338 which made him master of Greece. But soon afterwards he was assassinated, and his dream of conquest in Asia was left to his son, Alexander, to realise.

With the military machine he had inherited from his father, Alexander embarked on the invasion of the Persian Empire. In little more than a decade he swept in triumph through the east – from Egypt, where he founded the city of Alexandria in 332, to the threshold of India. With conquest went the spread of Hellenic culture. Alexander died of fever at the age of 33, and his conquests were shared out among his generals, who made separate kingdoms for themselves.

**Rome and Byzantium: 168 BC–AD 1453** After their surrender to Philip, the Greeks were destined to remain a subject people for more than 2000 years. Macedonian dominance was broken by Roman legions at Pydna in 168 BC and Greece itself became a Roman province in 146 BC. Its people were admired and often slavishly imitated by the Romans for their cultural eminence, yet at the same time they were despised as effeminate and immoral. But all in all they made an immense contribution to Roman civilization.

When the Roman Empire was divided in AD 330, Greece fell into the eastern, or Byzantine, half, and so continued, with no separate history or identity, until the fall of Constantinople to the Turks in 1453.

*Under the rule of Pericles (460–429 BC), Athens enjoyed a golden age. The Parthenon was built, and Aeschylus, Sophocles and Euripides wrote their great tragic dramas about man's fate*

*The oratory of Demosthenes powerfully influenced Athenians from 351 BC onwards. But he failed in his main purpose, to persuade his fellow citizens to unite against Macedon*

*Alexander the Great carved out a world empire by the time of his death at 33*

*A Mycenaean soldier, depicted on a vase of c. 1200 BC. He wears a crested helmet, and carries a shield and spear. Attached to the spear is a bag of food*

**Turkish domination** Byzantine control of Greece was often only nominal. The Fourth Crusade, which never reached the Holy Land but sacked Constantinople in 1204, led to the dismemberment of the Greek peninsula into a number of feudal domains.

The Turks appeared in Greece as early as 1387, and for the best part of four centuries Greece stagnated as a province of the Ottoman Empire.

*Two civilizations mingle in this 18th-century view of the Acropolis at Athens: that of ancient Greece – symbolised by the ruins of the Parthenon – and Islam, represented by a Turkish mosque built inside it*

**War of independence: 1821–7** From 1814 onwards a growing nationalist movement developed against the Turks, and revolt broke out in an armed rising on April 22, 1821. The Turks answered with savage repression.

The achievement of Greek independence would have been indefinitely delayed but for the active intervention of Britain, France and Russia. Their combined fleets, under the British Admiral Codrington, destroyed the Turkish and Egyptian fleets at Navarino on October 20, 1827, and by 1832 Greece was fully independent.

*The Greek struggle for independence ended with the defeat of the Turkish and Egyptian fleets at Navarino in 1827*

**Changing frontiers: 1830–1923** Even after independence, the Greeks persisted in their ancient tradition of disunity. Their first president, Capo D'Istrias, tried to make himself dictator. But he was soon assassinated.

The great powers decided to make Greece a monarchy. Prince Otto of Bavaria was made king in 1833 but after he had attempted to suppress the constitution, he was deposed in 1862. The Crown was then offered to Prince George of Denmark, who reigned as George I until his assassination in 1913.

During this period, the Greeks were constantly striving to enlarge their frontiers, conscious that many of their fellow-countrymen were still subjects of the Turkish Empire. They fought a disastrous war against the Turks in 1897, but a more successful one in 1913, when they wrested Crete from the sultan.

In the First World War, the Greeks were neutral at first, but eventually joined the Allies against Turkey. They gained Thrace at the peace conference, but remained dissatisfied and in 1921 launched their own war against Turkey. The Greek armies were completely defeated by the forces of Kemal Ataturk and Greece had to sue for peace. Nearly 1,500,000 Greeks from Asia Minor were compulsorily resettled in Greece.

*Lord Byron in Greek national costume. In 1823 the English poet volunteered to fight for the Greeks in their struggle for independence. He died at Missolonghi the following year*

**Dictatorship and German occupation: 1923–44** Greek politics continued to be as volatile as ever. A republic was proclaimed in 1924, but in 1935 the monarchy was restored by an overwhelming popular vote. Parliamentary democracy produced no stability. General Metaxas, who became premier in 1936, established a fascist-style dictatorship.

In 1940 the Italian dictator Mussolini launched a surprise attack on Greece. But his forces were only saved from defeat by the intervention of Italy's ally, Germany, whose forces overran and occupied Greece until 1944, when British troops liberated the country.

**Recent history** Liberation, however, did not bring peace. Civil war broke out in 1946 between the Communist-led guerrilla groups who had been fighting the Germans, and the monarchist government. Victory for the government did not come until 1950.

In 1967 parliamentary democracy was once more suspended when a coup brought a military junta – 'the colonels' government' – to power. Repression, censorship and the wholesale arrest of political opponents followed. The young king Constantine XIII attempted a counter-coup, failed, and went into exile. In 1973, the monarchy was abolished and a republic established with George Papadopoulos as president. But he was deposed by a new military junta within months.

A confrontation of Greece and Turkey triggered by overthrow of the Cyprus government, resulted in the collapse of the new junta in 1974. The new premier, Constantine Karamanlis, promised a quick return to democracy and the restoration of civil rights.

*Constantine XIII, King of Greece, and his wife. He retired into a self-imposed exile in 1967.*

# Grenada

An island nation that lies only about 100 miles off the coast of the South American country of Venezuela, Grenada won independence in 1974 after a century and a half as a British colony. Tourism, farming, and fishing provide the main sources of income. The source of most of the world's nutmeg, Grenada honors the spice by depicting a nutmeg on its national flag. Most of the people are descendants of African slaves brought to the island to work plantations.

Britain and France fought over the island for many years until Britain gained undisputed control in 1815. The island achieved self-government in 1967 as part of the British West Indies Associated States. Grenada was granted full independence within the British Commonwealth in 1974.

133 sq. miles
96,400 people
Capital: St George's

# Guatemala

The most populous and second largest of the six mainland Central American republics, Guatemala is a country of dramatic beauty. In the north, the jungle around Lake Peten is dotted with the ruins of the civilization of the Maya Indians. The descendants of the Maya, who still live mainly in the Peten area, make up 55 per cent of Guatemala's inhabitants, and form the largest group of Indian people in Central America.

**Early history** Long before Europeans arrived in Guatemala, the area was the centre of the Maya Indian civilization, which flourished for over 1000 years. But the Maya were overthrown c. 1523 by a Spanish force sent by Hernando Cortez and led by Pedro de Alvarado. The Spanish came in search of gold; though they found little or none, the area was soon supplying them with sugar, cocoa, indigo and other products.

In 1821 Guatemala threw off Spanish rule, first joining Mexico and then a union of the other Central American countries. In 1839, however, it became fully independent when the union was dissolved.

**War and dictatorships** Rafael Carrera, a Catholic conservative, was elected president in 1851, and in 1854 became president for life – the country's first dictator. Carrera used his army to suppress the liberals. In 1871 his successor, General Cerna, was overthrown and in 1873 the liberal Justos Barrios became president. A militant advocate of Central American unity, Barrios tried to impose union on neighbouring El Salvador by force in 1885. But he was killed in battle and Guatemala quickly made peace. However, tension between it and other Central American countries continued.

A series of military dictators held power until 1944, when a left-wing revolution brought Juan Jose Arevalo to power. In 1954 Carlos Castillo Armas overthrew the left with US support, but he was assassinated in 1957. In 1963 the armed forces took power. Three years later civilian rule was restored. Violence by right and left-wing terrorists was brought under control by conservative coalition governments in the early 1970's.

42,042 sq. miles
5,861,000 people
Capital:
Guatemala City

*The Maya decorated their stone temples with flamboyant sculptures such as this carving of an owl-idol*

GUINEA      HOLLAND
GUINEA BISSAU HONDURAS
GUYANA     HUNGARY
HAITI

*Sugar-cane under cultivation. The region of Demerara in Guyana gave its name to Demerara sugar*

# Guinea

After gaining independence in 1958, the West African republic of Guinea embarked on a bold programme of socialism under the leadership of Sékou Touré. Touré's militant radicalism led to internal unrest.

**Pre-colonial era** The two main peoples of Guinea are the Fulani, who arrived there in the 10th century AD, and the Mandingo, who followed three centuries later. European influence began with the Portuguese in the 1400's; during the following centuries they competed with Britain and France for the region's trade.

**Guinea under Sékou Touré** In 1898, Guinea was made a French colony, although it was not until 1911 that the whole of its present area came under French rule. African opposition persisted.

In 1958, General de Gaulle gave France's African colonies the choice of self-government within the French Community or outright independence, without French aid. Guinea alone voted for immediate independence. The French abruptly withdrew, and President Touré, an avowed Marxist, turned to the USSR and China for aid. Guinea remained, however, politically non-aligned, and has since received considerable aid from the West.

Under Touré, Guinea continued to play a radical part in African politics. In 1970, an attempted invasion by Guinean expatriates, aimed at overthrowing the regime, was defeated.

94,925 sq. miles
4,821,000 people
Capital: Conakry

# Guinea Bissau

The first of Portugal's African colonies to win independence, Guinea Bissau is one of the poorest countries of Africa. Hot, humid, and swampy, Guinea Bissau has a coastline indented by the mouths of many rivers. The people eke out a living by primitive farming, mainly growing rice, peanuts, and millet. Cattle herds are constantly decimated by disease carried by deadly tsetse flies.

The area, which became known as Portuguese Guinea, was a center for the Portuguese slave trade for hundreds of years. Nationalists began guerrilla warfare against the Portuguese colonial government in 1959. The rebels, supported by adjacent independent black nations, won control of three-fourths of the land by 1973, and declared independence for Guinea Bissau. Portugal recognized the new nation's independence in 1974 after a military coup had overthrown the Lisbon government.

13,948 sq. miles
578,000 people
Capital: Bissau

# Guyana

For four years before it gained independence from Britain in 1966, Guyana was torn by political rivalry between its two dominant groups – Negroes and Asian Indians. Their hostility dates back to the 19th century when Indian indentured labourers were brought in by the sugar-plantation owners to replace Negro slaves. Today, Asian Indians form almost 50 per cent of the population, and Negroes about 35 per cent.

**Before and after independence** The north-eastern coast of South America – where Guyana lies – was sighted by Columbus in 1498, but largely ignored by the Spanish and Portuguese. English explorers were attracted by legends of El Dorado, a fabulous city of gold, but the Dutch were the first to colonise the region. In the mid-17th century they set up sugar plantations and brought in slaves from the West Indies.

Dutch rule lasted until the Napoleonic wars, when Britain captured the colonies. By the peace settlement of 1814 some of the colonies were returned to the Dutch, but the others remained under Britain, and were united to form British Guiana in 1831.

The abolition of slavery in 1834 and a fall in the price of sugar severely affected the new country's

83,000 sq. miles
788,000 people
Capital: Georgetown

prosperity. Despite a partial recovery in the mid-19th century, its sugar-based economy remained unstable into the 20th century. Sugar remained the economic mainstay until the discovery of bauxite, the chief source of aluminium, in the 1950's.

The colony was given internal self-government in 1961. But independence was delayed until 1966 by the outbreak of violent clashes in 1962 between the two main political parties – the People's National Congress, supported by the Negroes, and the People's Progressive Party, under its Marxist leader Cheddi Jagan, supported by the Indians. The Negroes finally triumphed, after combining with other non-Indian groups. The country took the name of Guyana in 1966; it became a republic in 1970.

# Haiti

Inspired by the liberal ideas of the French Revolution, the slaves of Haiti rose against their French masters in the 1790's to form the world's first Negro republic. At one time Haiti dominated the whole of the island of Hispaniola, but today it occupies only the western third; the rest forms the Dominican Republic.

Haiti is the only Latin American republic with French as its official language, though most of its people speak Creole, a native dialect. It is the poorest and most backward state in the Western Hemisphere.

**First New World settlement** The island on which Haiti lies was discovered by Columbus in 1492. He called it Espanola, but this name was soon corrupted to Hispaniola. There the Spanish established their first settlement in the New World. By 1533 they had wiped out the native Arawak Indians, and soon began to bring in Negro slaves to take their place.

Gradually the Spanish colonised the eastern side of Hispaniola – which they called Santo Domingo – but the west became a notorious pirate base. In the early 17th century both the British and French tried to set up their own settlements in the western part. The French were successful and, by the Treaty of Ryswick in 1697, Spain recognised French sovereignty over the area corresponding to the Haiti of today.

French settlers imported vast numbers of African slaves to work the sugar plantations, and the colony became the richest sugar-producing area in the world.

**Negro rebellion** Influenced by the French Revolution, Haiti's Negroes rose against the French settlers in the north in 1791, while the half-caste mulattoes rebelled in the south. News of the rebellion was at first welcomed by the republican French government, as many of the settlers were royalists. But the wholesale massacre of the white population forced them to send troops to crush the revolt in 1792.

The Negro leader was Toussaint L'Ouverture, a self-educated freed slave. He joined the French to fight the British, who attempted to invade the island in 1793; in 1798 he agreed to govern for the French, and went on to occupy the Spanish colony of Santo Domingo in the eastern part of the island as well. In 1801 he set up his own state and abolished slavery.

In reply, Napoleon sent another expedition to recapture the colony and restore slavery. L'Ouverture was captured by treachery and died in prison in France. But the revolt continued. In 1803 the French were again driven out and the new Negro leader, Jean-Jacques Dessalines, proclaimed the independence of Haiti, taking the title of Emperor Jacques I. He ruled as a despot until his assassination in 1806.

**Division, reunification and division** Haiti was now divided into two states – a moderate mulatto regime under Alexander Pétion, and a tyrannical Negro regime under Henri Christophe (Henri I). After Christophe's suicide in 1820, the two states were reunited under the man Pétion chose as his successor, Jean Pierre Boyer, who went on to annex Santo Domingo in 1822.

10,714 sq. miles
5,273,100 people
Capital:
Port-au-Prince

*Toussaint L'Ouverture in ceremonial dress. He led the Negroes of Haiti in their fight for independence from France*

Tegucigalpa

*A voodoo priestess. Even today the mysteries of voodoo have a powerful hold on Haiti's people*

When Boyer was driven from power in 1843, Santo Domingo revolted and became the Dominican Republic. Haiti was torn by dissent and anarchy. A line of Negro 'emperors' – the last was overthrown in 1859 – attempted to seize power and reunify the island.

For the rest of the 19th century Negroes and mulattoes fought for power in Haiti. The Negroes were deeply influenced by their African traditions, including adherence to the tribal religion of voodoo. (Voodoo worshippers believe that the spirits of the dead can be evoked, by magical means, to bless or curse the living.) The middle-class mulattoes clung to the traditions left behind by the French. A succession of presidents from these two rival groups brought the country into complete confusion, and it was burdened with ever-increasing foreign debts.

**Dictatorship** In 1905 the United States took control of Haiti's customs receipts and in 1915 sent troops to occupy the republic. Despite the Americans' efforts to reform the administration, other South American countries eventually persuaded them to withdraw in 1934. Haiti fell under the rule of dictators. The most infamous, Dr François Duvalier – 'Papa Doc' – was 'elected' president in 1957; in 1964 he became president for life. The army brought him to power, but he soon turned against his military supporters. Increasing discontent with his regime led him to set up a police state, which used voodoo and a private army, the Tonton Macoute (Creole for 'bogeyman') as the basis of its power. Many of his opponents were murdered. On Duvalier's death in 1971, his 19-year-old son, Jean-Claude, assumed power.

*François Duvalier ('Papa Doc') ruled Haiti as dictator from 1957 to 1971. His brutal methods turned the country into a police state*

**HOLLAND,** *see Netherlands*

# Honduras

The lure of silver brought Spanish settlers to Honduras in the 1500's. Silver is still mined, but since the 19th century the country has been dependent on the cultivation of bananas – the classic example of a 'banana republic'. This industry, which is mainly owned by US companies, provides 80 per cent of the country's exports.

**Spanish rule and independence** The territory was a centre of the Indian Maya civilization before AD 800. But by the 16th century the Maya had declined and the Spanish found conquest easy. It was soon established that Honduras was rich in gold and silver.

Honduras broke away from Spain in 1821, but it was annexed by Mexico and then joined a Central American federation before becoming fully independent in 1838. Because of its strategic position it became a pawn in the struggle for control of Central America during the rest of the 19th century. Its neighbours, Guatemala and Nicaragua, frequently interfered in its internal affairs.

**US intervention** In 1903 US troops were sent to Honduras to end a war with Nicaragua. They landed again several times between 1912 and 1925 to protect the vast American-owned banana plantations. But political instability persisted; the country's longest period of comparatively stable rule in modern times was between 1933 and 1948 when a Conservative general, Tiburcio Carías Andino, was dictator.

In 1954 banana workers successfully struck for higher wages. A bloodless revolution took place in 1956, after which a new democratic constitution was drawn up and Ramón Villeda Morales, a Liberal leader, was elected president. He was overthrown by a military junta in 1963. The junta's leader, Oswaldo López Arellano, became president in 1965; in 1971 he was succeeded by Ramón Ernesto Cruz, but he regained power in 1972.

**Football war** Relations with neighbouring El Salvador became strained in 1969, when thousands of Salvadoran immigrants were expelled by Honduras. Incidents at a football match sparked off a 15-day war between the two countries; the conflict was settled by the Organisation of American States.

*Belize  Caribbean Sea / Guat. / HONDURAS / Tegucigalpa / El Salvador / Nicaragua*

43,277 sq. miles
2,870,000 people
Capital:
Tegucigalpa

*Honduras's banana industry provides the bulk of the country's export revenue*

*Hungary · Guinea Bissau · Haiti · Guinea · Honduras · Guyana*

# Hungary

Before the First World War, Hungary was the partner of Austria in ruling the vast Austro-Hungarian Empire, which stretched across the greater part of central Europe. Its land-owning Magyar aristocracy, ruling with as firm a grip over the country's non-Hungarian peoples as over their own peasants, made it one of the most reactionary states in Europe. Today Hungary has shrunk in size and is without any subject races: but its Communist rulers have no less strong a hold on the country's life than had the Magyar aristocrats.

Although often under foreign rule, Hungary's people have always maintained a fierce sense of national pride. In 1956 they rose against the Communist system imposed on them after the Second World War; Soviet might crushed all resistance. Since the revolt, Hungary's Communist leaders have followed a cautious policy of reform, mainly in the economic field.

**Before the Magyars** The Middle Danube plain, on which Hungary lies, was settled by Stone Age hunters and herders more than 80,000 years ago. The plain was later occupied by Celts and Slavs, and in the 1st century BC much of the west became part of the Roman province of Pannonia. Roman rule lasted until *c.* AD 200, when the province was overrun by nomadic warriors from the east – Goths, Huns and Turkic Avars.

**Magyar colonisation:** *c.* **800** Unlike most of their neighbours, the Hungarians of today are not of Slav descent. Their ancestors were the Magyars, nomadic horsemen who crossed the Urals from Russia in the 9th century, under their semi-legendary leader, Arpad. They defeated the tribes of the Hungarian plains and set up a kingdom which lasted until the 14th century.

One of the greatest of these Magyar rulers was St Stephen (*c.* 975–1038). He introduced Christianity into Hungary and centralised the country's government, reducing the powers of the Magyar chieftains. Under his rule and that of his successors, Hungary became a powerful state, dominating much of central Europe and the northern Balkans. St Stephen lives on in the national tradition – his crown was used for many centuries at the coronation of the kings in Budapest.

With the death of Alexander III in 1301, the Arpad line died out. During the next two centuries, Hungary had only one native-born ruler, Matthias Corvinus, elected king in 1458. After his death, the country was threatened by the westward advance of the Ottoman Turks. In 1526, Louis II, the last king of an independent Hungary, was killed in the Battle of Mohacs, and the Turks went on to lay waste to much of the country.

**Hapsburgs take power: 1526–1711** The Hapsburg rulers of Austria now fought the Turks for control of Hungary. The struggle between them lasted on and off until 1699, when, by the Peace of Karlowitz, all but a small part of Hungary came under Hapsburg rule.

An attempt by Leopold of Austria to end the privileges of the Hungarian land-owning nobility caused them to revolt under the leadership of Alexander Karolyi in 1704. Agreement between the two sides was eventually reached in the Peace of Szatmar in 1711. By this agreement, the Hungarians promised to remain loyal to the Hapsburgs; in return the Hapsburgs accepted the Hungarian landowners' right to rule themselves.

**Growing independence from Vienna: 1711–1867** The agreement was several times put to the test, as in 1741, when Maria Theresa appealed to the Hungarians to help her against Prussia. They responded to her call – only after she had reaffirmed the terms of the treaty.

In the 1840's the Hungarian nationalist leader, Lajos Kossuth, demanded greater Hungarian independence and in 1848 he led a revolution to secure it. But Russia sent an army to help Austria to crush the revolt, and Bach, the Hapsburgs' chief minister, brought Hungary firmly under Vienna's control with the help of Austrian civil servants known as the 'Bach Hussars'.

*Czechoslovakia / Aus. / Budapest / HUNGARY / Yugoslavia / Romania*

35,919 sq. miles
10,507,000 people
Capital: Budapest

*Arpad, the semi-legendary leader of the Magyars, settled his people in Hungary in the 9th century and founded a kingdom*

*Hungary's patron saint, St Stephen, introduced Christianity into the country*

## HUNGARY *continued*

But after Austria was weakened by its defeat at the hands of Prussia in 1866, Emperor Franz Josef was forced to make far-reaching concessions to Hungary. The Ausgleich (compromise) of 1867 established the Austro-Hungarian dual monarchy, with an emperor common to both Austria and Hungary. Hungary itself became an equal partner in the running of the empire.

**Magyar ascendancy: 1867–1918** Noted for their arrogance and conservatism, the Magyars' main concern was to resist all change within the empire. Hungarian politicians, such as Andrassy in the 1870's and Apponyi at the turn of the century, occupied leading positions in the imperial government. They and their successors consistently tried to keep down the other nationalities of the empire, particularly the Slavs, whom they regarded as racially inferior. At this time, Hungary's population included many non-Magyar peoples, such as Czechs, Slovaks and Serbs, who were mainly settled in the three border provinces of Croatia, Slavonia and Transylvania.

**Independent Hungary: 1918–45** After the collapse of the Hapsburg monarchy at the end of the First World War, a Hungarian republic was proclaimed under the leadership of Count Mihaly Karolyi, a descendant of Alexander Karolyi. But he soon resigned, and Communist insurgents under Bela Kun took power. Kun embarked on a violent campaign against the established order, but after five months his government was brought down by Romanian intervention.

Leading 'counter-revolutionaries' formed a government under Admiral Horthy, the commander of the Austro-Hungarian navy in the First World War, who took the title of regent. Under his regency, Hungary was dominated by a succession of right-wing governments, some of whose leaders, such as Bethlen and Gömbös, were open admirers of Hitler and Mussolini.

Peace with the Allies had been made by the Treaty of Trianon in 1920. Hungary was forced to cede large areas of its territory to Romania and the newly independent nations of Czechoslovakia and Yugoslavia. The recovery of these 'lost territories' became the cardinal aim of Hungarian foreign policy between the wars, and led the government to ally itself with Hitler and Mussolini in the 1930's. Hungary declared war on Russia in 1941, and its troops fought alongside the Germans on the Eastern front.

**Communist take-over: 1947** With Nazi Germany facing defeat, Soviet troops occupied Hungary in the winter of 1944–5. But the Hungarian people were strongly anti-Communist, and in the elections of November 1945 only a few Communist candidates were successful. However, in 1947, having secured key posts in the government, the Communists took over power, with Russian backing. Many non-Communist leaders were arrested, and there were a number of executions.

A new Soviet-type constitution was proclaimed in 1948. It made Hungary a one-party state, which was ruled on Stalinist lines, with full resort to police terror, by Matyas Rakosi until 1953. Rakosi presided over a series of show-trials and purges, in which his chief Communist rival, Laszlo Rajk, was executed.

**Revolt and repression** After Stalin's death in 1953, Rakosi still held power as party secretary, but was replaced as prime minister by Imre Nagy, who began a more liberal policy. Many political prisoners were released. In July 1956, Rakosi was removed from his post under popular pressure, and in October a large-scale anti-Communist rising broke out in Budapest.

Influenced by public demonstrations, a new government under Nagy promised to introduce a neutralist foreign policy and a multi-party democratic regime. In response, Soviet tanks and troops invaded Hungary, setting up a pro-Russian government under Janos Kadar. Nagy proclaimed Hungary's neutrality and

*Cavalry wielding sabres disperse a mob outside Budapest's opera house during the 1848 revolt*

*Lajos Kossuth led the 1848 rebellion against Hapsburg rule. It was crushed by the Russians*

*Fascism gained influence in Hungary under the regency of Admiral Horthy*

*A propaganda poster of 1945, claiming that 'the Hungarian Communist Party is the foundation for reconstruction'*

appealed to the free world to intervene. But Soviet forces crushed the revolt, after bloody street-fighting in Budapest; many Hungarians still remember the courage of men who attempted to fight tanks with their bare hands. Thousands of refugees fled across the Austrian border. Nagy was arrested and deported to Romania, where he was executed in 1958.

**Cautious economic reforms** After the catastrophe of 1956, the Kadar government decided that reforms could only be introduced slowly. The reforms of the 1960's were mainly concentrated on economic policy, which was defined in the 'New Economic Mechanism' in 1968. They brought about a substantial improvement in living standards, and there was also a limited degree of political toleration. But the Kadar government was also careful not to alienate the Soviet Union by showing any public disagreement with Soviet policy.

*A devastated street in Budapest during the ill-fated rising of October 1956*

# Iceland

Active volcanoes and hot springs are found next to glaciers and icefields over much of this island in the North Atlantic. Its hardy people are of Norse descent; their language is still largely that of the Icelandic narrative sagas written down in medieval times.

**Settlement, union and invasion** Iceland was uninhabited until a group of Norwegians, led by an outlaw, Ingolfur Arnarson, settled there in AD 874. Gradually Norse communities spread across the island, and in 930 the Althing – the world's first parliament, which survives to this day – was established. After Christianity arrived c. 1000, Iceland became a stable state. In 1262 the Althing voted for Iceland to join Norway, and with the union of Norway and Denmark in 1380, under the Danish crown, Iceland became a Danish possession.

The island was given limited home rule in 1874, thanks to the efforts of the Icelandic patriot Jon Sigurdsson, and independence in 1918. The monarchy was the only link to survive; Denmark's kings retained the additional title of King of Iceland. The Althing broke this tie after Germany invaded Denmark in 1940, and in 1944 the island, which had been occupied by Allied troops, became a republic.

**Iceland today** After 1944 Iceland entered an era of stability. It became a founder-member of NATO in 1949; it had no armed forces and a 1957 treaty made the United States responsible for defence.

Iceland's dependence on fishing grounds led to a dispute with Britain from 1958 onwards, after the republic extended its territorial waters from 4 to 12 miles. Britain accepted the 12-mile limit in 1961, but the quarrel – which became known as the 'cod war' – broke out again in 1971 when Iceland proposed an extension to 50 miles. In 1972 and 1973 there were several clashes between Icelandic gunboats and British trawlers, while negotiations between the two countries dragged on.

39,772 sq. miles
214,100 people
Capital: Reykjavik

*A 1000-year-old bronze statuette found in Iceland. It probably depicts the Norse god Thor*

*Fishing trawlers near the port of Reykjavik. Iceland's prosperity depends largely on its fishing industry*

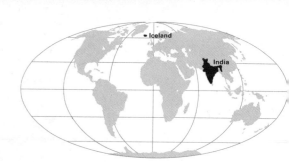

# India

The republic of India is the second most populous country in the world; only China has more people. The total population continues to grow rapidly at the rate of 13 million a year. India is also the world's largest democracy: over 270 million of its citizens voted in the 1971 elections. About 14 major languages and hundreds of dialects are spoken in India. Nearly 85 per cent of the population are Hindu in religion.

The country today is smaller than in the days of British rule. When Britain granted independence to the peoples of its Indian empire in 1947, power was transferred to two successor states and the country was partitioned between them. The predominantly Muslim areas took the name of Pakistan, while the Hindu-dominated remainder kept the name of India.

Indian society is a sometimes uneasy mixture of East and West – the natural consequence of a meeting between a civilization which in many basic ways has changed little in 2000 years, and the ideas and beliefs of foreign conquerors. Though vast new industries are being developed, life in many parts of India still moves at the leisurely pace of the ox cart.

**Aryan invasions** From *c.* 2000 BC onwards, invaders known as Aryans descended upon India through the mountain passes of the north-west, establishing themselves in the Punjab and on the plains of the Ganges. The Aryans destroyed a sophisticated civilization already existing in the Indus valley; but they introduced to India the forerunner of many of its present languages, and also a sacred Hindu work, the *Rig-veda*, which is revered as the fountainhead from which all later Indian philosophy and religion developed.

The Aryans were divided into three social classes; warriors, priests and common people. On settling in India, they added a fourth class, the conquered. From this simple division between conqueror and conquered, between light-skinned Aryan and dark-skinned non-Aryan, India's immensely complicated social system of caste developed amongst its peoples.

**Foundation of the Maurya Empire** Invasion again struck India from the north-west in 327 BC when Alexander the Great marched through the Khyber Pass, bent on conquering the sub-continent. His armies were eventually driven out by the founder of the Maurya Empire, Chandragupta (*c.* 322–298 BC).

The greatest Maurya ruler was Ashoka (273–232 BC). He encouraged the spread of Buddhism and brought the whole of India, except for its southern tip, under his rule. On his death, however, the empire fell apart.

In the north-west, kingdoms rose and fell as invader followed invader. Among the most important of these kingdoms was that of the Kushans, who traded with Rome, as did the spice-producing states of south India.

1,178,995 sq. miles
587,503,700 people
Capital: New Delhi

*The emperor Ashoka erected columns in India to mark his devotion to the Buddhist faith. They were crowned by animal figures such as these*

*A war-horse trampling on a fallen enemy. This 13th-century temple carving is from Kanarak*

**Golden age of the Guptas** In the 4th century AD, a new dynasty, that of the Guptas (named after the Maurya emperor, Chandragupta), spread over northern India. This dynasty held power for more than a century. It nurtured a revival of the Hindu religion and a golden age in Hindu art and literature, which carried on after the collapse of the Guptas under the attacks of Hun invaders in the latter half of the 5th century.

There was a further revival of Hindu power and culture under Harsha of Kanauj (606–47). During this period, central India was dominated by the Chalukya dynasty and the south by the Pallavas of Kanchi – but constant warfare led to division and sub-division of their empires. After the death of Harsha, kingdoms rose and fell in the north, and the whole continent fell into a state of anarchy which was exploited by Muslim invaders from central Asia.

**Muslim conquest** Though Sind had been conquered by the Muslims in the 8th century, the first major Islamic invasions were those of Mahmud of Ghazni between 1001 and 1026, again through the passes of the north-west frontier. These invasions were primarily looting expeditions, and it was not until the capture of Delhi by Muhammad of Ghur in 1192 that the way was open for Muslim conquest. Under successive rulers, the sultanate of Delhi spread across northern and central India, reducing existing rulers to the position of vassals.

In the extreme south, however, the new Hindu empire of Vijayanagar threatened the stability of the sultanate. In 1398, an invasion by the Tatar ruler Tamerlane in the north broke its power.

**Empire of the Mughals** In 1526, Babur, a direct descendant of Tamerlane, defeated the reigning sultan of Delhi and founded the Mughal dynasty (Mughal is a form of the name Mongol). Babur's conquests were expanded and consolidated by his grandson, Akbar (1556–1605). The Mughal Empire, which was Muslim in religion, reached its greatest extent under Aurangzeb (1658–1707), when it covered most of India.

Under both the sultanate and the Mughal Empire considerable changes took place in northern and central India. New modes of thought and styles of art and architecture were introduced, and many Hindus were converted to Islam. Mughal architecture reached a peak of achievement under the emperor Shah Jahan (1628–58), who established Delhi as the Mughal capital. At Agra he erected the Taj Mahal, one of the world's loveliest buildings, as a memorial to his favourite wife.

**First Europeans** The Portuguese were the first Europeans to establish themselves in India. An expedition commanded by Vasco da Gama landed in western India in 1498, and by the mid-16th century the Portuguese had a firm foothold. Their main base was Goa.

Portuguese conquest was confined to small areas on the coast; its purpose was to secure the trade in spices and other luxuries for the European market.

The great profits made from the spice trade, as well as stories of the immense wealth of the Mughal emperors, attracted other Europeans. The first to break the Portuguese monopoly were the Dutch, closely followed by the British. London merchants founded the British East India Company in 1600. The company established a trading post at Surat in 1612, following it with others at Madras (1639), Bombay (1661) and Calcutta (1690). The French arrived in India in 1668.

By the mid-18th century the French and the British were contending for dominion in India. Mughal strength was collapsing in the face of both Hindu rebellion and a power struggle between Mughal provincial governors; the French and British supported the rival leaders as a front for their own ambitions. Direct conflict between the two European powers was confined to the south and to the sea approaches to India. The struggle between them lasted from 1746 to 1763. The British were to triumph through superior sea-power and the more aggressive spirit of their merchants; they also had the advantage of a more stable political system.

*The Red Fort at Agra was built by the great Mughal emperor Akbar during the 16th century*

*Emperor Shah Jahan (1628–58) created the Taj Mahal as a monument to his favourite wife*

*Young 'public school' Englishmen sent to rule the Raj led privileged lives. Indians in time learnt to admire their white rulers – also to resent them*

## INDIA *continued*

**Conquests of Clive** The true foundation of British dominion came with the victory of Robert Clive at Plassey in 1757, when he and his 3000 men defeated the Nawab of Bengal, whose army of 50,000 was supported by a small contingent of French artillerymen. The conflict between the Nawab and the British had begun with a British refusal to dismantle their fortifications at Calcutta. In June 1756, the Nawab seized the town and captured a number of European men, women and children. More than 100 of the prisoners were confined overnight in a small airless room – the notorious 'Black Hole of Calcutta' – and many died of suffocation.

Clive's victory led to British control of Bengal, and this position was consolidated by Warren Hastings, who succeeded him as governor. By 1805 the British had extended their rule in both the north and south of India. Delhi was captured in 1803, and the Mughal ruler became a British puppet. This process continued until all the states were brought under British control, though some were left with a large measure of autonomy under their traditional rulers.

*This near-lifesize model of a tiger mauling a European was once the 'toy' of Tippoo Sultan, the 'Tiger of Mysore'*

*The conquests of Robert Clive (1725–74) laid the foundations of British supremacy in India*

**Indian Mutiny: 1857** Until 1858, the government of India was controlled not by the British Crown but by the East India Company – though from 1773 onwards the activities of the company itself were under the supervision of a British cabinet minister.

In 1857 the soldiers of the East India Company's Bengal army – Hindus, mostly, and Muslims – rebelled. They feared that their British officers were deliberately undermining their religion and trying to make them all Christians. Their suspicions seemed to be confirmed when the British issued them with bullets rumoured to be coated with cow and pig grease; the cow is a sacred animal to Hindus and the pig unclean to Muslims.

The mutineers were joined by others, amongst whom were descendants of the former ruling princes whose states had been annexed and landlords whose property had been taken over. These people feared that the British threatened the foundations of Indian society by their social and economic reforms.

At first the mutineers were successful. They occupied Delhi and laid siege to Cawnpore and Lucknow. Taken by surprise, the British in India faced annihilation. But the arrival of reinforcements enabled them to crush the mutiny 14 months after it had broken out. Bloody reprisals were taken against the mutineers.

After the mutiny, the British government assumed direct responsibility for the government of India, the East India Company was abolished, and the governor-general was given the title of Viceroy. The traditional leaders of the Indian people, the princes and landlords, were conciliated. Social reforms which might have offended the religious beliefs of the masses were either abandoned or carried through in watered-down form.

One of the chief casualties of the mutiny was mutual trust between Indians and Britons. Ignoring the loyalty that the Indian middle class had shown, the British were more reluctant than ever to allow Indians into the higher ranks of the civil service.

*The British East India Company set up its trading post at Bombay during the reign of Charles II*

*The East India Company recruited many Indian soldiers – known as sepoys – into its forces*

*British troops at the siege of Cawnpore during the Indian Mutiny failed to hold the city. It took 14 months for the revolt to be crushed*

**Railways link the Raj** The British Raj (as British rule came to be called, after a Hindu word meaning 'to rule') now concentrated on the material progress of India. Railway construction, which had begun in 1853, was stepped up after 1869. By the end of the century the system was virtually complete, with nearly 35,000 miles of track – the largest railway system in Asia. New canals, too, were built, particularly in the Punjab and Sind, as part of a full-scale campaign against famine. British imperialism reached the apogee of its expression with the proclamation and crowning of Queen Victoria as Empress of India in the year 1877.

**Indian National Congress: 1885–1905** The frustration of the Indian middle classes led to the formation of the Indian National Congress in 1885 by university-educated Indians. Its aim was a moderate one – a fuller share in the running of the country. Some minor concessions were made, but the slowness with which even these were granted led to a split in Congress itself. Two rival groups emerged: the Moderates believed in pressing their case constitutionally, while the Extremists argued that by appealing to India's past they could arouse a revolutionary fervour in the masses.

The division of the unwieldy province of Bengal in 1905 by the ruling Viceroy, Lord Curzon, led to violent unrest. The British responded with concessions. In 1909, as part of the reforms introduced by John Morley, Secretary of State for India, the Legislative Council of the Viceroy, Lord Minto, was expanded to include 25 elected Indian members. Bengal was re-united in 1911. But the Moderates had lost their dominant position in Congress, which now started to build up a mass following and to become more militant.

**Coming of the Mahatma** The outbreak of the First World War in 1914 produced a resurgence of loyalty. Over 500,000 Indians served in the Indian Army. But as the war dragged on, nationalist activity revived. The British conceded a measure of representative government through elected provincial officials by the Government of India Act of 1919. But before this act came into force, circumstances in India had changed.

A new leader, Mahatma Gandhi (1869–1948), had taken over the direction of Congress. Gandhi urged his followers to embark on a series of hartals (general strikes) and these soon led to violence in the Punjab, especially in Amritsar. In April 1919 British troops opened fire without warning on a mass street-meeting in the city: 379 Indians were killed and over 1200 wounded. As a result, Gandhi changed his aims and now declared that India must throw off British rule completely.

**Road to freedom: 1920–47** Under the control of the Mahatma, Congress became a mass party, basing its support on the Hindu majority. Gandhi's method of Satyagraha (non-violent non-co-operation), used against the British, led to further bloodshed, particularly between Hindus and Muslims. His partner in the leadership was Pandit Jawaharal Nehru (1889–1964), a Westernised Brahmin (a member of the highest, priestly caste of the Hindus), who gave Congress the image of a forward-looking, liberal-democratic party, with a socialist bias.

Under the pressure of mass civil disobedience, the British granted responsible parliamentary governments to the provinces of British India. But in October 1939, the Congress ministers resigned in protest at the unilateral declaration of war on Germany by the Viceroy. In 1942 a civil disobedience campaign escalated into open armed rebellion after the arrest of the principal Congress leaders.

In 1945 the British Labour Government's efforts to transfer power to a united India failed when the Muslim League – formed in 1906 to protect the interests of the Muslim minority in predominantly Hindu India – insisted on partition. Violence and anarchy grew, and in August 1947 the last Viceroy, Lord Mountbatten, finally handed over power to the two separate new states of the sub-continent, India and Pakistan.

*Disraeli seeks the favour of Queen Victoria by creating her Empress of India – an irreverent view of imperial majesty*

*Mahatma Gandhi, India's spiritual leader, persuaded the British to grant far-reaching reforms by his policy of mass civil disobedience*

*Homelessness, poverty and malnutrition make Calcutta one of the world's problem cities*

**First years of independence** Partition brought immediate bloodshed; in the Punjab alone, at least 600,000 were killed. Millions of Hindus were trapped in a hostile Muslim Pakistan, while the same fate overtook Muslims in India. Some 14 million people are believed to have migrated between India and Pakistan.

The two new countries quarrelled over Kashmir, which, like the other princely states, had been given the option of joining either country. Its Maharajah, a Hindu, ruled over a Muslim majority, and after a Muslim uprising the Maharajah decided that his state should join India. But Pakistan claimed that Kashmir rightfully belonged to it, and war broke out between India and Pakistan. After renewed conflict over Kashmir, both sides agreed in 1966, at Tashkent in the USSR, to withdraw their troops behind a cease-fire line. Pakistan was left in control of the area north-west of this line, but India maintained its claim to the whole of the state.

India was also shaken by the assassination of Mahatma Gandhi by a Hindu extremist in January 1948. In the first elections held under universal suffrage in 1951, Congress gained an overwhelming majority.

**Age of Nehru: 1947–64** The first prime minister of independent India in 1947 was Pandit Nehru, whom Gandhi had declared his political heir-apparent. Nehru declared that his principal aim was to modernise India, and especially to modify the caste system. New heavy industries were set up under state ownership. But as a result, agriculture was neglected, making India dependent for its food supplies on massive imports of grain.

When India became a republic in 1950 Nehru insisted that it remain a member of the British Commonwealth. Nehru's policy of 'non-alignment' with the super-powers of East and West went unchallenged as long as it brought advantages to India. But in the autumn of 1962 his long-standing refusal to negotiate with the Chinese over the north-east frontier led to an armed clash between India and China. The humiliating retreat of Indian forces before the Chinese brought the whole policy of non-alignment into question.

Despite the considerable social changes under Nehru, the last years of his life saw dissatisfaction at the failure of Congress to achieve major social and economic reforms.

**Split in Congress** Nehru was succeeded by Lal Bahadur Shastri. His period of office was short: it was dominated by a short war with Pakistan in September 1965, and ended by his death in January 1966. Soviet mediation in India's war with Pakistan increased the USSR's influence in India. In 1971, the two countries signed a formal defensive alliance.

Shastri was succeeded by Mrs Indira Gandhi, Nehru's daughter. Her appointment was intended to revive the flagging image of Congress; but in the 1967 elections the party, though keeping its majority in the central parliament, lost heavily in the states. Continuous friction between Mrs Gandhi and the other leading figures of her party ended in a split in 1969. Because she lacked an adequate parliamentary majority, Mrs Gandhi called a general election in 1971. Her overwhelming victory gave Congress an absolute majority in the central parliament and the control of many states. The size of the vote was a sign of protest against the anarchy which had long reigned in Indian political life and had been intensified after the split in Congress.

**War with Pakistan** By the winter of 1971, however, India had again become embroiled in war with Pakistan. Indian forces entered East Pakistan to help the oppressed Hindus, 6 million of whom had already fled into India. After overcoming Pakistani resistance, India supported the people of East Pakistan in setting up a new independent state of Bangladesh.

This short war brought Mrs Gandhi grave problems. The Indian economy was already suffering from the influx of vast numbers of refugees from East Pakistan before war broke out, and actual fighting strained it further. Many refugees were still on Indian soil in 1974.

*Pandit Nehru was independent India's first prime minister from 1947 until his death in 1964*

*A poster in a family planning campaign. India's high birth-rate is a main obstacle to raising the standard of life of its people*

*Mrs Indira Gandhi, Nehru's daughter, became India's prime minister in 1966*

# Indonesia

The republic of Indonesia, formerly the Dutch East Indies, was created in 1949. It consists of a vast cluster of islands stretching in a 3000 mile arc along the Equator from west of the Malay peninsula to New Guinea. It includes the islands of Java, Sumatra, Bali, the greater part of Borneo (Kalimantan), and Celebes (Sulawesi), as well as some 3000 smaller islands.

Indonesia is inhabited by a great variety of racial groups, 300 in all, speaking 250 languages. The Muslim religion, practised by 90 per cent of the people, is a great unifying factor.

The islands are rich and fertile and have been famous since earliest times for their spices, which first attracted Europeans to the area. Java, the main island, contains more than half Indonesia's population.

735,268 sq. miles
135,682,000 people
Capital: Djakarta

**Early times** The islands of Indonesia were colonised by waves of Stone Age peoples from the mainland of south-east Asia between 2500 and 1000 BC. From AD 200 the island kingdoms derived their civilization from India, through contacts with traders and Hindu and Buddhist monks. The remains of many Hindu and Buddhist buildings are to be found in Java today, the most impressive being the temple at Borobudur. The 7th to 13th centuries saw the heyday of the powerful Srivijaya Empire, based on seafaring. Buddhist in culture, it was centred on southern Sumatra and controlled part of Malaya and western Java. The later Hindu empire of Majapahit ruled a large part of present-day Indonesia from 1293 to 1513.

**Islam established** The Islamic faith was first brought to Sumatra by Arab traders in the 13th century, and by the end of the 16th century it had displaced Hinduism and Buddhism as the dominant religion throughout Indonesia (except in the island of Bali, where Hinduism survives to the present day). The Hindu Majapahit kingdom broke up into numerous small and weak Muslim states which were to prove no match for European penetration during the 16th century.

**Coming of the Dutch: 1595** The East Indies had for centuries supplied Europe with spices, the Moluccas being especially noted as spice islands. The construction of new ocean-going vessels from the 15th century enabled the Europeans to trade direct with the Indies via the Cape of Good Hope, ousting the Arab traders. First on the scene were the Portuguese, who captured the vital port of Malacca on the Malay peninsula in 1511. They were followed in 1595 by the Dutch, who established themselves in western Java.

A period of intense rivalry between the Dutch and British East India companies, lasting from 1610 to 1623, ended in victory for the Dutch. The colony of Batavia (present-day Djakarta) was founded in 1619, and the Portuguese were expelled from Malacca and the Moluccas. The Dutch East India Company consolidated their hold over the islands during the 17th and 18th centuries; by 1798, when their interests were taken over by the Dutch government, they controlled much of present-day Indonesia. During the Napoleonic Wars Java fell briefly into the hands of the British and was ruled from 1811 to 1816 by Stamford Raffles, founder of Singapore. In 1824 the British and Dutch agreed on the boundaries between their spheres of influence.

*The 9th-century Buddhist temple at Borobudur in Java, whose intricately carved stones illustrate episodes in the life of Buddha*

*Nutmeg, allspice, cloves and cinnamon were among the valuable spices that attracted Europeans to the East Indies*

*The governor of Batavia and his wife stand watching Dutch East India Company ships, anchored near Java's old capital*

401

*Puppet shows in Java date from earliest times. This traditional Javanese shadow-puppet is in the British Museum*

*The palace of Darius I in Persepolis, one of several cities founded by him as imperial capitals. From them the shahanshah ('King of kings') controlled his empire, communicating with his satraps or local governors by a vast road network*

## INDONESIA *continued*

**Dutch expansion: 19th century** The decline of the spice trade during the 18th century forced the Dutch to exploit the other natural resources of the islands, a move that brought them into conflict with the remaining semi-independent native rulers. A revolt led by Prince Diponegoro lasted for five years before being finally crushed in 1830. In the same year the notorious 'culture system' was introduced in Java by the Dutch. Peasants were required by law to devote part of their land to cash crops, such as coffee, tobacco and cotton, which were sold at a profit in Europe by Dutch firms.

The Dutch middle classes grew rich, but this period of economic exploitation left a legacy of bitterness that was to be exploited by later generations of Indonesian nationalists. Meanwhile, the Dutch completed their territorial conquests, although the Acheh sultanate in northern Sumatra was not finally subdued until 1904.

**Growth of nationalism: 1900–42** New forms of opposition arose in the 20th century, deriving in part from more sophisticated political ideas brought back from Europe by returning students. The Dutch made little or no attempt to come to terms with these stirrings of nationalism. Two Islamic nationalist groups, Budi Otomo and Sarekat Islam, were founded in the first decade of the century, but were challenged after 1919 by the newly formed Indonesian Communist Party.

Communist revolts in western Java and Sumatra in 1926 were quickly put down. From then on, until 1942, the independence movement was led by non-Communists. The Indonesian Nationalist Party was founded by Ahmed Sukarno and Mohammad Hatta in 1927. Dutch policy continued to be repressive, Sukarno spending all but two years between 1929 and 1942 in jail or in island exile, along with other nationalist leaders.

**Problems of independence: 1945–58** Sukarno co-operated with the Japanese during their occupation of Indonesia from 1942 to 1945, and at the end of the war proclaimed his country's independence. The returning Dutch were faced with virtual reconquest of the Dutch East Indies. In 1949 they gave up and granted the islands independence, with Sukarno as president.

Unity, political and territorial, remained a problem. Uprisings in Sumatra and Celebes against Javanese centralism in 1956–8 were suppressed with difficulty. Even more damaging was the economic decline resulting from an over-ambitious foreign policy that called for large military forces, and an expensive building programme to support Sukarno's pretensions as leader of the newly independent countries of Africa and Asia. The country suffered from inflation and a slump in food production; corruption was rampant.

**Guided democracy: 1957–65** Parliamentary democracy, introduced in 1945, was abolished by Sukarno in 1957 and replaced by an authoritarian system known as 'guided democracy'. It created a new balance of power between the politically conscious army and a revived Communist Party. During the same period, Sukarno claimed to maintain a neutralist foreign policy, though he was strongly opposed to the creation of Malaysia in 1963 – terming it Britain's 'neo-colonial creation'. In October 1965, however, the balance of forces was upset by a savage but abortive Communist coup which led to the overthrow of Sukarno and to a cruel massacre of supposed Communists in which the number killed has been variously estimated as from 50,000 to 400,000.

**The new order** The army, which had defeated the Communist coup, now became the dominant political force under the tight control of General Suharto. The 'confrontation' policy with Malaysia was abandoned, the Communist Party outlawed, and economic links with the West re-established. Suharto became president in 1968. Elections held in 1971 gave the army-backed government coalition a landslide victory, and Suharto was re-elected president in 1973.

*Ahmed Sukarno (1902–70), flamboyant first president of the republic of Indonesia, was deposed after an army coup of 1965*

# Iran

Ancient Iran was the home of history's first major empire, founded by Cyrus the Great in the 6th century BC. At its peak, it extended from India to the Aegean Sea, and south into Arabia and Egypt. The empire was centred on the province of Parsa – hence the name Persia, by which Iran became known to the world.

Since the days of Cyrus, the country has always managed to retain its basic Iranian, or Persian, identity, in spite of conquests by invaders such as Greeks, Arabs, Turks and Mongols, and intense pressure from European powers in modern times. Iranians are proud of the length and continuity of their historical tradition, and today's monarchy, although established only in 1926, sees itself as the true heir of the original Iranian dynasty.

Revenues from oil, which was discovered in vast quantities in 1908, have enabled Iran's rulers to carry out far-reaching social and economic reforms.

636,359 sq. miles
32,544,700 people
Capital: Tehran

**Rise of Iran** Some of the earliest known prehistoric settlements have been discovered in Iran. Farming and organised village communities developed there as early as 6000 BC. Recent excavations at Sharh-i-Sokhla, beside the Helmand river in south-east Iran, show that there was a flourishing city and trading centre there by 3000 BC. The Iranians of today are mainly descended from the Aryan tribes of Medes and Persians who settled in the region *c.* 1000 BC. In 559 BC, Cyrus, King of the Persians, rose against his Medean overlord and overran Assyria, Asia Minor and Babylon. By 546 BC, Cyrus had welded his conquests into the Achaemenid Empire, which encompassed most of the known world under Darius I (521–486 BC).

**War with Greece and Rome** The Greeks alone withstood the power of the Achaemenid kings. Darius himself was defeated at Marathon, while his son Xerxes I was crushed by the Greeks in the naval battle at Salamis and on land at Plataea. The weakened empire was overthrown by Alexander the Great in 336 BC.

After Alexander's death in 323 BC, his empire crumbled. One of his generals, Seleucus, gained control of Persia and founded the Seleucid dynasty. Their power was eclipsed by the rise of the Parthians, who in turn were challenged by Rome – an indecisive confrontation that lasted for some 300 years. An internal revolt by Ardashir in AD 226 finally brought the Parthians down, and a native dynasty – the Sasanids – was established. Under it Iran reached new heights of grandeur.

**Muslim conquest** In 637 Sasanid power was finally broken by Muslim Arabs, who remained nominal rulers of Iran for five centuries. The Arabs never established their own system of government; they relied on Persian officials to run Iran for them. By the 9th and 10th centuries local Persian chieftains ruled in the provinces. When the Seljuk Turks seized power in the 11th century they, too, used Persians to govern.

The Seljuks were unable to resist the Mongol hordes of Genghis Khan in the 13th century. The invaders, hungry nomads from central Asia, overran the country. The power of the Mongols was usurped by the Tatar chieftain Timur the Lame (Tamerlane), the greatest of Asiatic conquerors. His descendants ruled Iran from 1405 until native Iranian rule was restored in 1499.

The new Safavid dynasty reached its peak under Shah Abbas the Great (1587–1629), who built a great mosque and palace at Isfahan. After his death, Iran declined, until the emergence of Nadir Shah in the 1730's. Nadir invaded India in 1739, captured Delhi, and took the fabulous Peacock Throne back to Iran.

*Darius I on his throne – a bas-relief from the king's treasury in Persepolis*

*An effigy of Chosroes I, a 6th-century AD Sasanid king, engraved on rock crystal*

*Victims of the Mongols are boiled alive. Two-thirds of Iran's population died when the Mongols ravaged the country in the 13th century*

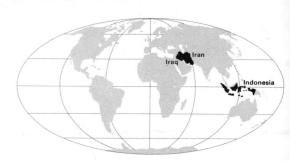

**Pawn of the powers** From the early 19th century onwards, Iran's borders shrank steadily under pressure from European powers. Under Fath Ali Shah (1797–1834), Iran lost the Caucasus to Russia. During the rest of the 19th century, Russia increased its hold.

Russia's influence in Iran alarmed Britain, which feared that it would spread to India. In 1907, however, Russia and Britain agreed to divide Iran into two 'spheres of influence'. The British zone was to be the south, and Russia's the north. Oil was discovered in the south the following year by a British oil company. The new oilfields were rapidly brought under development.

**Revolution, reform and crises** In the early 1900's, Iran's educated class became increasingly alienated from the shah. They criticised his extravagant way of life, and his inability to stand up to pressure from Britain and Russia. Internal unrest came to a head in 1921, when an army officer, Reza Khan, overthrew the government. In 1926 he was crowned shah. Reza was an ardent reformer. He abolished many outworn customs and encouraged industrialisation; German technicians came to Iran to help him. But in 1941, the shah's friendly relations with Nazi Germany led to British and Russian occupation of Iran. Reza was forced to abdicate in favour of his son, Muhammad Reza Shah Pahlevi.

Iran faced a crisis in 1945, when Russia refused to remove its troops from the north-west. Iran took the dispute to the United Nations, and Russia eventually agreed to withdraw. But in 1951 the country was plunged into renewed crisis. The prime minister, Muhammad Mossadegh, nationalised the Anglo-Iranian Oil Company. Britain retaliated by organising an international boycott of Iran's oil exports. This brought the country close to collapse. After coup and counter-coup in 1953, Mossadegh was overthrown. In 1954 the shah came to an agreement with the oil companies.

After the settlement of the dispute, the shah re-established close ties with the West. The United States pumped economic and military aid into Iran. At the same time, Iran's relations with the USSR improved.

**'White revolution': 1961** The shah, in 1961, launched a bold programme of reform, known as the 'white revolution', financed by increasing oil revenues. It called for the end of serfdom, the break-up of vast estates, modernisation of the armed forces, and the development of education. The shah's plan was opposed by traditionalists, who thought some of its aims contrary to Muslim law, and by liberals, who said the reforms did not place sufficient emphasis on democracy.

# Iraq

This Arab country was the home of one of the world's earliest civilizations, that of Sumer. Mesopotamia, between the Tigris and Euphrates rivers, later saw the rise of Assyria and Babylon. Centuries after, the land fell under Arab rule and rose to greatness when Baghdad became the centre of Islamic civilization.

The history of modern Iraq has been dominated by two factors – the wealth of its oil-fields and the turbulence of its politics. The country's oil and its key strategic position in the Middle East have made it a source of rivalry between the West and the USSR.

**Dawn of history: 6000–1170 BC** Sumer, the southern part of ancient Mesopotamia, was a cradle of human civilization. By *c.* 6000 BC, small communities in Sumer had adopted a settled way of life, based on agriculture. From them evolved city-states, such as Ur, Kish, Lagash and Uruk. By 3200 BC each of these had developed its own organised religion and government. Sumer was conquered *c.* 2300 BC by the Semitic people of Akkad, who occupied the north of Mesopotamia. Their king, Sargon, created an empire over the whole of Mesopotamia. After his death the empire broke up, but in 1792 BC, with the emergence of Hammurabi, King of Babylon, Mesopotamia was again united.

*Fath Ali Shah (right) whose war-torn reign (1797–1834) marked a decline in the power of Persia*

*Iran faced economic crisis after Mossadegh nationalised its oil industry*

*In 1961 the shah, using his country's oil revenues, launched a programme of land, social and educational reform*

167,924 sq. miles
10,716,300 people
Capital: Baghdad

**New powers: 1170 BC–AD 638** Around 1170 BC, Babylon and other city-states of Mesopotamia became provinces of the Assyrian Empire, whose lands lay in the Upper Tigris River. Assyrian power reached its height under Assurbanipal (669–627 BC). But increasing inroads made by Egyptians, Medes and Babylonians brought this empire down. In 612 BC, Nebuchadnezzar, the Babylonian king, established the New Babylonian or Chaldean Empire – famed for its luxury and splendour. This, in turn, fell to Cyrus the Great, the Persian king; then to the Greeks under Alexander the Great; and finally to the Parthians.

**Arab and Turkish rule** The area fell to the Arabs in AD 638 and Iraq became a Muslim country. Baghdad succeeded Damascus as capital of the Islamic empire in 762. This brilliant centre of art and learning was sacked by the Mongols in 1258 and again in 1401. Finally, in 1534, the country was conquered by Ottoman Turks and stayed under them for almost 400 years.

**Iraqi nationalism: 1914–45** After the outbreak of the First World War, Britain invaded Turkish possessions in the Middle East, and occupied southern Iraq by 1915. The following year, a British attempt to take Baghdad failed but the city eventually fell in 1917.

British troops put down a nationalist rising in 1920, and the League of Nations made Iraq a mandated territory under the rule of Britain. An Arab prince, Faisal, was placed on the throne. Oil was discovered in Iraq in 1927. After the country was given independence in 1932, it maintained close links with Britain – a policy resented by many Iraqi nationalists. In the Second World War, the nationalist leader Rashid Ali al Gailani seized power. Britain intervened to overthrow him.

**Political turmoil** Iraq joined the Arab League in 1945 and took part in the unsuccessful military campaign against Israel in 1948. Under its pro-Western premier, Nuries-Said, Iraq, though still opposed to Israel, led traditionalist Arab states in their opposition to the socialist policies of Nasser's Egypt from 1954 onwards. Iraq severed diplomatic relations with the USSR, and joined with Britain, Turkey, Iran and Pakistan in the Baghdad Pact defence treaty in 1955.

After Egypt and Syria had formed the United Arab Republic in 1958, Iraq and Jordan formed their own Arab union. But later that year, General Abdul Karim Kassem led a military coup in Baghdad. The king, Faisal II, and Nuries-Said were killed, and Kassem proclaimed a republic. Iraq withdrew from the Baghdad Pact and re-established relations with the USSR.

But, at the same time, Kassem followed a strictly neutral foreign policy, putting down a pro-Communist rising in 1959. In his diplomacy he caused tension by challenging Egypt for Arab leadership. To add to his difficulties, a bloody war broke out with the Kurds, a non-Arab minority settled in north-eastern Iraq. The pro-Egyptian Abdul Salam Arif overthrew Kassem and had him executed in 1963. In the same year Arif ousted the Baathists, the Arab socialist party which had brought him to power.

Arif was killed in a plane crash in 1966 and was succeeded by his brother, Abdul Rahman Arif. He in turn was ousted in 1968. Iraq's new government, under President Ahmed Hassan al-Bakr, was dominated by the Baathist Party, and dedicated to Arab unity and the destruction of Israel. In 1970 the Kurds were recognised as a separate nationality and given a degree of self-rule.

The influence of the USSR greatly increased in 1972, when Iraq signed a friendship pact. Russia was given a major share in future development of Iraq's vast oil-fields – following this, Iraq nationalised the Western-owned Iraq Petroleum Company. In 1973, the Iraqis gave aid to Egypt and Syria in their war with Israel. Warfare between Kurds and Iraqis raged in 1974.

*The Kurds – a non-Arab minority in north-east Iraq – were given a degree of autonomy in 1970*

*General Kassem challenged Egypt for Arab leadership, but he was overthrown and executed by the Baathists in 1963*

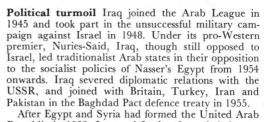

*Oil, piped from inland fields to the coast, gives Iraq its prosperity*

*A Sumerian ruler – Gudea, governor of Lagash, a Sumerian city-state. The statuette dates from c. 2100 BC*

William of Orange surveys his troops at the Battle of the Boyne in 1690. His victory over James II secured him the British crown and confirmed the Protestant ascendancy in Ireland

# Ireland, Republic of

The people of Ireland have had a turbulent and often tragic history. Since medieval times the country as a whole, including what is now Northern Ireland (also known as Ulster), has only been unified under Britain. Many Irishmen fought to overthrow British rule for centuries, and the struggle reached its climax in 1922, when the island was divided – the Catholic south became independent, while the Protestant-dominated north remained part of the United Kingdom. This division is still a source of some bitterness, but for most people in the republic the unity of Ireland has become a long-term ideal, to be attained by peaceful means.

The artistic achievements of Ireland throughout the ages are renowned. Celtic crosses and ruins of ancient monasteries recall the brilliant Irish culture of the early Christian era. In more recent times, the works of Irish writers such as Shaw, Wilde, Yeats, Joyce and Beckett have enriched world literature.

**First Irishmen** Ireland's earliest settlers probably arrived there *c.* 6000 BC from Europe. Slowly a Gaelic society emerged, in which tribes of Celts, Picts and Erainn were predominant. About AD 150, Conn, the ruler of Connacht, formed a large kingdom, but neither he nor his successors managed to unify Ireland.

Until the 5th century, the Irish were pagans. In 432, however, St Patrick, a native of Britain who had previously escaped from slavery in Ireland, returned to teach Christianity there. Many monasteries were founded, and it was from Ireland that missionaries set out to convert northern Britain during the Dark Ages.

**Vikings and Normans** In the 8th century, Viking invaders began to establish bases on the east coast of Ireland. The Irish were slow to meet this threat, but in 1014 they united under an Irish king, Brian Boru, and defeated the Vikings at Clontarf. This unity was short-lived, however, and in 1168 the first Norman invaders arrived in Ireland. They went there in response to an appeal by Dermot MacMurrough, King of Leinster, who promised to share his conquests with them. But they staked out their own claims to Irish soil, and the pope declared Henry II overlord of Ireland.

The land under Norman control soon diminished, as its rulers began to intermarry with the Irish and to adopt their way of life. By the end of the Middle Ages, the English held only a small area round Dublin. This was known as the 'pale', while the Irish 'beyond the pale' continued to rule themselves.

**Protestant ascendancy** Direct English rule of Ireland began with the Tudors, who were determined to establish Protestantism there in place of Roman Catholicism, and was continued by the Stuarts and Cromwell. Irish lands were confiscated and given to pro-British sympathisers or to 'planted' Protestants, such as the Scots whom James I settled in Ulster. The Irish bitterly resented British rule, and rose in desperate rebellion on more than one occasion. In 1688, however, they revolted in support of an English king, the Roman Catholic James II, when he was forced from the throne by William of Orange. But James and his Irish allies were defeated at the Battle of the Boyne.

Despite the granting of an independent parliament to Ireland in 1782, at the insistence of the Protestant leader Henry Grattan, Irish discontent was not

27,135 sq. miles
3,015,800 people
Capital: Dublin

St Patrick (c. 373–463) was inspired by a vision to return to Ireland and convert it to Christianity

The production of the superbly illuminated Book of Kells c. AD 800 marked the peak of Celtic culture in Ireland

appeased. In 1798 Wolfe Tone and his United Irishmen rose against British rule. As a direct result of Tone's rebellion – which was brutally suppressed – Britain and Ireland were united in 1800. The Irish parliament was abolished, though Irish MP's were given seats at Westminster. Even so, it was not until 1829 that Irish Catholics were granted the vote.

**Potato famine** During the 18th and early 19th centuries, the population grew rapidly. It reached 8,500,000 by the 1840's – almost three times the present level. Some 4 million people lived almost entirely on potatoes, which were cheap and easy to grow.

In 1845 and 1846, Ireland's potato crops were hit by blight, and the country's population faced starvation. The British government repealed the Corn Laws, so allowing foreign corn to be imported, and a programme of public works was started to give the Irish employment. But so many came forward that the scheme was abandoned. By 1851 a million had died, while 1,600,000 more had emigrated to the United States.

**Demand for Home Rule** After the potato famine, discontent in Ireland again rose to fever pitch. Eventually the British Liberal leader Gladstone recognised the need for reform in Ireland. Laws were passed to guarantee the Irish fair rents, to protect tenant-farmers from eviction, and give them the right to sell their land.

But such reforms no longer satisfied the Irish. They demanded Home Rule and banded together under Charles Parnell to achieve it. However, Gladstone's two attempts to grant Home Rule failed, and it was not until 1914 that it became law. But Protestant Ulster refused to accept it and prepared for civil war under the leadership of Edward Carson. 'Ulster will fight and Ulster will be right' was the province's rallying cry.

**Easter rising: 1916** Although Home Rule was suspended on the outbreak of the First World War, Ireland rallied behind Britain in 1914. But, as the war dragged on, all the old antagonisms came to the surface. In April 1916 a rebellion, led by Patrick Pearse and James Connolly, broke out in Dublin. Its aim was to secure immediate Irish independence. After several days of bitter fighting, the General Post Office, which the rebels had made their headquarters, was captured. But British reprisals made the Irish all the more determined to shake off British rule.

**Free State and republic** This determination was mirrored in the General Election of 1918 in which the Irish party Sinn Fein ('Ourselves Alone') won an overwhelming majority. In all parts of the country – with the exception of Ulster – there were risings against British rule. In 1921 the British Prime Minister, Lloyd George, realised that Ireland could no longer be subjugated, and signed a treaty with the Sinn Fein to bring about Irish independence. This was granted to the south as the Irish Free State in 1922. The six northern counties, which were largely Protestant, remained in the United Kingdom as Northern Ireland.

After independence, Sinn Fein split into two hostile groups – conservatives, such as Michael Collins, who believed that the terms won from the British were the

A victim of the potato famine of the 1840's is carried off for burial, while his starving compatriots look on. By the time the famine was over a million Irishmen had perished

In 1649, an Irish rebellion against British rule was brutally crushed at Drogheda (left) by Oliver Cromwell whose troops massacred the town's inhabitants

James Connolly (1870–1916) was the chief architect of the Easter Rising. Wounded in the fighting, he was captured by the British, tried, and executed for treason

best Ireland could expect; and republicans, who refused to accept the partition of Ireland. A bloody civil war followed, in which Collins was assassinated; the republican leader, Eamon De Valera, boycotted the Dail (the Irish parliament) until 1927. In that year he returned and in 1932 was elected president. Under De Valera, the Irish Free State broke its remaining links with Britain. In 1937 it was re-named Eire, and in 1949 it became the Republic of Ireland.

Demands for the re-unification of Ireland persisted into the 1950's and, with the outbreak of violence in the north between Catholics and Protestants in 1969, the Irish Republic became deeply involved. The Republic's premier, Jack Lynch, urged moderation and opposed the extremists, who demanded that he give direct aid to the Catholics in the north.

But as the conflict in the north worsened, it became harder for Lynch to maintain his moderate line. After 13 people were killed in the so-called 'Bloody Sunday' shootings in Londonderry in January 1971, the British embassy in Dublin was burnt to the ground. Lynch welcomed the introduction of 'direct rule' by Britain shortly afterwards, and at the same time, with popular backing, took tougher measures against the illegal IRA (Irish Republican Army), which was largely responsible for the campaign of violence in the north.

Under Lynch, too, Ireland joined the Common Market. But in 1973 he was defeated in a General Election, and replaced by a coalition government headed by Liam Cosgrave. Lynch was defeated, however, not over his handling of the situation in the north, but because of his economic policies.

# Israel

With the proclamation of the State of Israel in 1948, an ancient Jewish dream became a reality. For almost 2000 years after they were displaced by the Romans from their homeland, the dream of a return to the 'Promised Land' of Palestine never ceased to burn in the minds of the Jewish people. The dream was sustained by their religion, which spoke of a Messiah who would lead them back from exile, and intensified by cruel persecution.

Not all Jews suffered during the long centuries of the Diaspora (dispersion). Some groups merged successfully into the life of their adoptive countries, becoming leaders of commerce and industry, and making contributions to thought, science and the arts which were out of all proportion to their numbers. But for most Jews of the Diaspora, living precariously in ghettos, persecution was a more usual fate.

Since independence, Israel has been in constant conflict with its encircling Arab neighbours, who deny that the Israelis have any right to the soil of Palestine; four times the dispute has erupted into war. By the end of the six-day war of 1967 the Israelis had gained over 25,000 square miles of territory, stretching across the Sinai Peninsula to the banks of the Suez Canal, and including the West Bank of the River Jordan and Syria's Golan Heights. War broke out again in 1973, when Egypt and Syria attacked the Israelis in a bid to win back their lost territory.

**Children of Israel** The first Jews to reach Canaan (present-day Israel) were wandering migrants who, under the leadership of Abraham, moved there from northern Mesopotamia. They later settled in Egypt, where they were victims of persecution until *c.* 1200 BC when another leader, Moses, led them out of bondage.

Their long and arduous journey back to Canaan took the Hebrews 40 years. But, throughout their trials, they were fortified by their religious faith. They were unique in their belief in one god, Jehovah, who would lead his chosen people to their 'Promised Land'. The basic principles of their faith were laid down in the Ten Commandments which, according to the Bible, were given to Moses by God on Mount Sinai.

After their return to Canaan, the Hebrews preserved their ancient tribal structure until they were united

*c.* 1025 BC by a warrior-king, Saul, to meet the challenge of the Philistines, a seafaring race who were pressing in from the north. Saul defeated the Philistines in several battles, and his successor, David, went on to complete his work, establishing a Hebrew kingdom with its capital at Jerusalem *c.* 1005 BC.

The rule of David's son, Solomon, saw Jewish power reach its height. But after Solomon's death in 928 BC, his kingdom divided into two states, Israel and Judah, the latter ruled by the House of David, with its capital at Jerusalem. The two kingdoms quarrelled and their disputes opened the way to foreign invasion.

**Conquest and dispersion** Israel was the first of the two Jewish states to fall to an outside power, when it was conquered by Assyria in 722 BC. After Assyria's fall, Judah was conquered by Babylon. This 'Babylonian captivity' lasted for 50 years. When the Persians under Cyrus the Great destroyed Babylon in 539 BC, the Jews were allowed to return to their homeland and rebuild Solomon's Temple in Jerusalem; but they did not regain full independence.

Persia was conquered by Alexander the Great in 332 BC, and after his death two Greek dynasties battled for the division of his conquests. The Ptolemies controlled Israel until 200 BC, when they were driven out by the Seleucid ruler, Antiochus III. A Jewish revolt in 141 BC, led by Judas Maccabeus, ousted the Greeks. The Maccabee dynasty held power for 70 years before it was overthrown by the Romans.

Rome ruled Israel through a series of puppet kings. Under one of these kings, Herod Antipas, Jesus Christ embarked on his mission. The Jews could never reconcile themselves to Roman rule and in AD 66 revolt broke out, fomented by a group called the Zealots. Rome's reaction was harsh and brutal. Jerusalem fell to the Roman legions in AD 70 and the city's temple was again destroyed. The remnants of the rebel forces held out at Massada until AD 73, when they took their own lives rather than fall into Roman hands.

The Jewish spirit was not yet crushed. The Jews rose again in AD 132–5. Rome's reaction was even more severe. Many Jews were forcibly deported and their lands laid waste. Thus began the great Diaspora of the Jews. Millions of them settled in what were to become Christian countries of Europe – in lands such as Russia, Poland, Germany, Spain and England.

In many places the Jews were resented, for most Christians held them responsible for the death of Christ. They were confined to ghettos and forbidden to own land or to practise a trade. Many of them could only earn a living by lending money, a practice which further alienated them from Christians who, in medieval times, were forbidden to do so. Pogroms (persecutions) were commonplace.

For nearly 1900 years Palestine, as the Romans had renamed Israel, was ruled and fought over by foreigners. Romans, Byzantines, Sasanid Persians, Arabs, Crusaders and Turks all controlled it at various times. The few Jews who remained there were a subject people.

**Birth of Zionism** In the 19th century, the Zionist movement was founded by the Hungarian Jew Theodor Herzl to press for the restoration of Palestine to the Jews. This movement grew rapidly, and increasing numbers of European Jews began to emigrate to Palestine.

*Another leader of the Rising, Eamon De Valera – seen here on a republican banner – went on to become president of an independent Ireland*

*A Dublin-born expatriate in Paris, Samuel Beckett won fame with his play* Waiting for Godot. *His writings are a wry Irish comment on life, a blend of absurdity and anguish*

*7992 sq. miles
3,292,400 people
Capital: Jerusalem*

*A coin struck by Bar-Kochba, leader of the ill-fated Jewish revolt of AD 135, depicts Herod's Temple in Jerusalem*

*Jerusalem: from a mosaic map of the Holy Land in a 6th-century Christian church in Jordan*

*The menorah, a seven-branched candlestick, is a hallowed symbol of Judaism. This carving is on the Arch of Titus in Rome*

*Under Pharaoh Ramesses II, the Jews suffered severe persecution. They were led out of Egypt by Moses c. 1200 BC*

*This frontispiece to the Old Testament Book of Numbers comes from a Hebrew manuscript of the 13th century AD*

## ISRAEL *continued*

Financial aid came from American Zionists, as well as from Jewish philanthropists in Britain, such as Sir Moses Montefiore and Baron Edmond de Rothschild.

Towards the end of the First World War, Palestine, which since 1516 had been ruled by Turkey, was conquered by Britain. Anxious for Jewish support, the British foreign secretary, Arthur Balfour, pledged British support for the Zionists in making Palestine a national home for the Jewish people.

But this pledge contradicted one given to the Arabs, who thought that Palestine was to become an independent Arab state after the war. When the war ended, the British, in fact, continued to rule Palestine under a League of Nations mandate.

Increasing Jewish immigration under the pressure of Nazi persecution in the 1930's alarmed the Arabs, who began to attack Jewish areas. The British then proposed to divide the country between the two groups. The Jews were prepared to discuss this plan, but the Arabs demanded full independence.

**Foundation of modern Israel** After the Second World War, Britain decided to admit only 2000 Jewish immigrants a month. This decision alienated world opinion, which remembered the 6 million Jews that the Nazis had slaughtered in concentration camps. In Palestine itself, groups of Palestinian Jews – notably the Irgun Zvai Leumi and the 'Stern Gang' – began a terrorist campaign against British troops.

In 1947 the UN proposed that Palestine should be divided into Jewish and Arab states, with Jerusalem as a neutral zone. This plan was rejected by the Arabs but accepted by the Jews who, on May 14, 1948, proclaimed the independent state of Israel. Chaim Weizmann was its first president, and David Ben-Gurion its first prime minister. On the same day, the new state was attacked by Egypt, Jordan, Syria, Iraq and Lebanon. Israel emerged victorious from months of bitter fighting.

**Years of conflict and crisis** In spite of their defeat in 1948, the Arabs declared that they would never recognise Israel's right to exist. In 1956, Israel was again confronted by a hostile Arab military alliance, whose professed aim was the destruction of Israel. Israeli troops struck at Egypt. At the same time an Anglo-French invasion force was sent to safeguard the Suez Canal, which Egypt had just nationalised. United Nations' pressure forced Israel to give up most of its conquests. But the Israelis secured access to the Red Sea through the port of Eilat on the Gulf of Aqaba.

It was the Egyptian blockade of Eilat which again led to war in 1967. Israel struck at Egypt, Syria and Jordan on June 5; six days later, its forces, under General Moshe Dayan, had captured the Gaza Strip, the Sinai Peninsula, the west bank of the Jordan and the Golan Heights. The battle-torn Egyptian army now faced the victorious Israelis along the bank of the Suez Canal.

On October 6, 1973 the fourth Arab-Israeli war began. Massive Egyptian and Syrian armies attacked Israel along the defence lines it had established after the 1967 war; within days the Israelis counter-attacked, and when an inconclusive ceasefire was agreed later in October their forces were on the whole in an even stronger position. But the war proved the costliest and potentially the most dangerous of the four that Israel had fought in the generation since it was founded.

*Theodor Herzl, a Hungarian Jew, founded the Zionist movement in 1897*

*The Shield of David, the universal emblem of Judaism, forms part of the flag of the State of Israel*

*David Ben-Gurion became first prime minister of independent Israel in 1948*

*Leaders of an embattled nation: Mrs Golda Meir, prime minister in 1969–74, with defence minister, Moshe Dayan*

# Italy

The people of the Italian peninsula achieved nationhood only in the 1860's. Before that time, Italy could be dismissed, in the words of the Austrian statesman, Metternich, as a 'geographical expression'.

The strongly regional character of the country has always made for disunity, as well as giving Italian life and history their great richness and variety. It was in central Italy, on the banks of the Tiber, that the seeds of Roman imperial greatness were sown. The hills of Tuscany, to the north, saw the flowering of medieval culture, notably in the poetic thought of Dante; these same hills cradled the Italian Renaissance, which was marked by the many-sided achievements of such artists as Leonardo da Vinci and Michelangelo. Further north still, from Piedmont, came the leaders who created a united Italy during the second half of the 19th century.

Since the decline of Rome, the Italians have never been an aggressive, militaristic people and the attempt by their dictator, Mussolini, to make them one in the 1920's and 1930's was a dismal failure, leading to utter defeat in the Second World War. After the war, Italian creativity quickly reasserted itself. The lasting influence of this gifted nation has been in the fields of art and culture, in scientific discovery and commerce – and not least in their cultivation of the arts of living.

116,303 sq. miles
55,386,300 people
Capital: Rome

*The detail in this carving of an urn lid, made in about 510 BC, shows the skill achieved by Etruscan craftsmen*

*An Etruscan sculpture showing a farmer at the plough. The civilization of the Etruscans dominated central Italy before Rome's foundation*

**Foundation of Rome: *c.* 753 BC** About 3000 years ago, the mountainous Italian peninsula was thickly forested and dotted with tribal settlements, whose people were of a primitive Bronze Age culture. Cities emerged with the arrival of more civilized colonists.

The Greeks established ports in Sicily and the south of Italy as far north as Naples. In central Italy there flourished the civilization of the Etruscans, a people of uncertain origins who were greatly skilled in architecture and engineering. Rome began as an insignificant settlement of one of the native Latin tribes, on a low hill overlooking a crossing-point on the River Tiber. Its petty kings were Etruscans.

**Rome unites Italy: 509–220 BC** The Romans drove out the last of their Etruscan kings, Tarquinius Superbus, in 509 BC. In place of the monarchy they set up a republic, though this was split by class conflict between patricians (aristocrats) and plebeians (commoners). Nevertheless, because of their vitality and the effectiveness of their army, based on the disciplined fighting machine of the legion, the Romans gradually imposed a unified government on the entire peninsula.

*Romulus and Remus, the legendary founders of Rome, were said to have been suckled and tended by a she-wolf*

Republican Rome met its most serious challenge when the Carthaginian general, Hannibal, invaded Italy in 218 BC. Elephants were his army's shock weapon

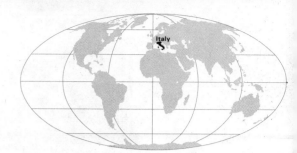

**Carthaginian challenge: 264–146 BC** Rome's expansion brought it into conflict with the mighty North African merchant empire of Carthage. Between 264 and 146 BC the two powers fought three wars; these became known as the Punic wars from *Poeni*, the Latin name for the Phoenicians, who founded Carthage. At times, the Romans came close to complete defeat. Hannibal, Carthage's most able general, crossed the Pyrenees and the Alps with his elephants and invaded Italy in 218 BC, but he was recalled to defend Carthage in 203 BC. The following year the Carthaginians met complete defeat at Zama; and finally, in 146 BC, their capital was destroyed by the Roman general Scipio Africanus.

Loading a grain ship. Rome came to depend on many overseas provinces of its empire for supplies of food

**From republic to empire** Masters of Italy and the Mediterranean, the Romans proceeded to expand their power, until their boundaries extended to the English Channel, the Rhine and the Danube. In the east, they ruled Egypt, Syria and much of Asia Minor.

The old republican methods of administration could not cope with so vast an empire. Rival military leaders, among them Pompey and Julius Caesar, struggled for mastery. Finally, after a prolonged power struggle with Mark Antony, Julius Caesar's adopted heir Octavian emerged as the all-powerful Emperor Augustus, architect of a new and efficient imperial administration.

**Italy under the Roman Empire: 31 BC–AD 476** For four centuries, Italy enjoyed a mainly peaceful and well-ordered existence as the centre of an authoritarian empire controlling most of the known world. The country had fine roads, aqueducts and just laws. These and other material benefits far outweighed the ill effects of occasional scandals at the imperial court – notably during the reigns of Caligula and Nero.

The Roman Empire eventually became dependent on its overseas provinces for food and even for troops to defend its long frontiers. It was weakened in the 3rd century by a prolonged financial crisis, due to the inflation of the imperial currency. Just over a century later, Christian Rome's distant frontiers crumbled under the pressure of nomadic barbarian tribes and the Italians could no longer protect themselves. The country fragmented under the blows of barbarian invaders.

Rome itself was captured by the Visigoths in AD 410, and in 476 the last nominal emperor, a boy named Romulus Augustulus, was contemptuously pensioned off by a barbarian general, Odoacer, who proclaimed himself King of Italy.

**Barbarians and Byzantines: 476–800** There was, however, no true 'kingdom of Italy', for the peninsula was fast assuming the fragmented political character it was to retain until the mid-19th century. Odoacer was soon overthrown by Theodoric, King of the Ostrogoths.

Vespasian, emperor from AD 69 to 79, restored stability to the empire after the disastrous reign of the tyrant Nero

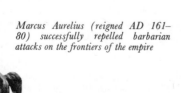

Marcus Aurelius (reigned AD 161–80) successfully repelled barbarian attacks on the frontiers of the empire

This kingdom was shattered in 568 when the country was invaded by another barbarian tribe, the Lombards.

Meanwhile Byzantium, the eastern half of the Roman Empire with its capital at Constantinople, temporarily liberated much of Italy from the barbarians. The Byzantines held Sicily, Rome, Ravenna, Naples and other scattered areas, between which stretched the great northern kingdom of the Lombards, based on Pavia, and the independent Lombard-ruled duchies of Spoleto and Benevento. In this dark age of anarchy, a group of Italians founded Venice as a refuge among lagoons. Others retired to fortified hill-top towns.

In Rome, the citizens, lacking a leader, turned to their bishop, Pope Gregory the Great, and so gave the papacy its status as a political power. Later popes appealed to Pepin, King of the Franks, and his successor, Charlemagne, to march into Italy and subdue the Lombards. On Christmas Day 800, in the Church of St Peter in Rome, Pope Leo III crowned Charlemagne Holy Roman Emperor, in succession to the Caesars.

**Continuing strife** Leo's action could not restore the peace and unity which the Italians had enjoyed under the old Roman Empire. Charlemagne returned to Germany, and neither his officials nor his descendants were able to control Italy, which was plunged into disunity and disorder. Numerous invasions took place, and in 917 Sicily fell to the Saracens, an Arab race, who founded a brilliant culture based on Palermo.

About the time the Normans were conquering England, an adventurous band of their countrymen, led by Robert Guiscard, established themselves in southern Italy and went on to invade Sicily. By 1091 they had completed their conquest, creating a kingdom in which Christians and Muslims lived in harmony.

**Rise of the communes: c. 1000** The inhabitants of central and northern Italy found that they had to depend on themselves for their own defence. Their official overlord, the Holy Roman Emperor, was far away in Germany and his delegates were ineffective. Each town fortified itself, raised its own militia, and chose a popular local leader as podestà (mayor); these men sometimes set up hereditary dukedoms. Venice, a true republic, elected its first dux or doge as early as 697, but the first city to be called a commune or city-state was Milan in the 11th century, when such foundations became widespread. These city-states, nominally subject to the emperor, were in practice independent.

**Pope versus emperor** The Holy Roman Emperor was elected by a group of German princes. But successive popes asserted that the emperor's authority ultimately derived from the Church of Rome. Their claim was hotly disputed and controversy between pope and emperor flared intermittently for centuries. At intervals, an emperor would bring an army across the Alpine passes to assert his position in Italy. One such emperor, Frederick I, known as Barbarossa ('Redbeard'), mercilessly destroyed Milan in 1162. But he was defeated by a league of communes at Legnano in 1176, after which he had to submit to the pope.

Individual cities often changed sides in this long struggle between pope and emperor. The rival factions adopted the German dynastic names of Guelphs, used by the papalists, and Ghibellines, used by the imperialists. In Italy, these names eventually became convenient labels in the party strife of the cities, long after the rivalry between pope and emperor had been resolved.

**Frederick II: 1194–1250** One emperor, Frederick of Hohenstaufen, was more than an occasional visitor to Italy. He inherited the kingdom of Sicily at the age of four, grew up in Palermo, was elected emperor as a young man and, when not in Germany or on a Crusade, spent his time in the south of Italy. There, besides building some remarkable castles which still survive today, he did much for the commercial prosperity of the region. A man of formidable energy and intellect, he was nicknamed Stupor Mundi, the 'wonder of the world'.

Honorius became ruler of the western empire after the Roman Empire was divided in AD 395. Under his ineffective leadership, the west declined

Gregory I, pope from AD 590 to 604, successfully asserted the supremacy of Rome over other branches of the Catholic Church

The influence of medieval Byzantine architecture is seen in St Mark's Cathedral, Venice, rebuilt at a time when the city had important trading links with the East

*Pope Innocent III approves the foundation of the Franciscan Order of friars. Inspired by the teachings of St Francis of Assisi, the Franciscans brought the Gospel to ordinary people*

## ITALY *continued*

**Patchwork history: 1250–1494** Throughout the Middle Ages, Italy was split into many different states, large and small. The papacy was the only force for unity, but the political influence of the popes fluctuated. Their election was often the result of intrigue and intimidation by foreign rulers.

After the election of the Frenchman Clement V in 1305, a succession of French popes kept their court at Avignon for 70 years. Pope Gregory XI attempted to return to Rome, which by then had become almost a ghost town, but a further controversy shortly after his death in 1378 led to the 'Great Schism'. For the next 40 years the Catholic Church had two rival popes, one in Avignon and one in Rome, each supported by a bloc of foreign powers. Only after 1417 was the division healed. The papacy was re-established in Rome and the city became once more a main centre of Italian life.

**Trading cities** During the 14th century the cities of northern and central Italy gained steadily in power. Florence, famous for its cloth, was also a pioneer of international banking. Milan manufactured silk, woollens and armour, and dominated the Alpine passes which led to the markets of north-western Europe. Venice, with its empire of islands in the eastern Mediterranean, controlled the maritime trade between Asia and Europe.

On the basis of their economic strength, these three Italian cities built up a financial and military supremacy, hiring mercenary armies under freelance commanders called condottieri. Other cities became their satellites. Florence was paramount in Tuscany, while Milan and Venice fought to control the northern plain.

Some cities fell under the sway of despotic families, known as the signorie. The Viscontis ruled Milan and were succeeded by the Sforzas. Though Florence preserved the form of a republic, for generations it was governed by the culture-loving banking family of the Medici. Only in Venice did a ruling body of a few hundred wealthy citizens keep strictly to their legal constitution. Elsewhere, most cities had a chequered history of assassinations and coups.

*The poet Dante of Florence was the supreme creative genius of medieval Christendom*

*Florentine wool-traders. Under the rule of the Medici, Florence reached a peak of prosperity*

**Southern struggles** Naples and Sicily in the south remained feudal and backward. Two queens, Joanna I and Joanna II, led scandalous lives, and were dominated by court favourites. Despite various marriages, both of them failed to provide legitimate heirs.

After Joanna II's death in 1435, the south was torn by bloody dynastic struggles between the rival claimants to the throne, whom Joanna had adopted and then disinherited at various times. The issue was finally settled in 1442 by the triumph of Alfonso of Aragon, known as 'the Magnanimous'. But this did not end the chronic poverty of the south.

In 1454 a temporary stability was achieved by an alliance between the five major powers in Italy – Alfonso of Aragon, Pope Nicholas V, Francesco Sforza of Milan, Doge Foscari of Venice, and Cosimo de' Medici of Florence. This alliance, known as the Italian League, was designed to maintain the Italian balance of power as it then existed. By this date, too, the artistic and literary movement of the Italian Renaissance was at its height and spreading out to influence other countries.

*Ludovico Sforza ruled Milan from 1494 to 1499. He was an astute diplomat, and a patron of such artists as Leonardo da Vinci*

**French and Spanish invaders: 1494–1559** Though the Italian states maintained an uneasy balance among themselves, they could not merge their interests and find national unity. This left them a prey to the ambitions of foreign powers.

In 1494 Charles VIII of France invaded Italy, supposedly in support of his claim to the crown of Naples, but in reality because the country was rich and weak. The mercenaries had developed warfare into a kind of chess game, with little blood spilt, but the ruthless fighting methods of the French exposed the military weakness of Italy's disunited states. Machiavelli, the Florentine writer and statesman, appealed in vain for a national resistance based on a citizens' militia, like the one he had organised in Florence.

For the next 65 years, the political framework of Renaissance Italy was shattered by the clash of rival foreign armies. France's attack on Italy soon turned into a struggle with the Holy Roman Emperor for European supremacy. In 1527 Rome was sacked by imperial troops. Italian liberties finally died when the Treaty of Cateau-Cambrésis of 1559 established Hapsburg Spain as the dominant power in Italy.

**Three centuries of servitude: 1559–1871** The 18th-century wars of the Spanish and the Austrian successions changed little but the flags under which the Italians lived. By the time of Napoleon, the Austrians had replaced the Spanish in the north – where the ancient Venetian republic still survived, though it had lost its overseas empire to the Turks. The south was no longer a Spanish province, but a Neapolitan kingdom, ruled by a junior branch of the Spanish Bourbon dynasty, while the border state of Piedmont was united with the island of Sardinia under the ancient House of Savoy.

Napoleon conquered Italy, and tried to impose order on the country, introducing many of the reforms in law and administration that the Revolution had brought to France. But after his fall in 1815 Italy was returned, still disunited, to its reactionary rulers.

Throughout these three centuries, Italy, though lacking a separate political identity, continued to enjoy much of its old reputation as a centre of European culture. Its art, architecture and music were renowned. No English gentleman's education was considered complete unless he made the 'Grand Tour' to Italy and returned with crates of statues and paintings.

*In his Il Principe ('The Prince'), Machiavelli argued that a ruler must be ruthless in order to achieve success*

*Joachim Murat was made King of Naples by his brother-in-law, Napoleon, in 1808. He later betrayed Napoleon to save his throne, but was executed after trying to help him in 1815*

**Triumph of the Risorgimento** The Napoleonic episode, though a failure, had awoken Italian patriotism from its age-old sleep. The Risorgimento ('revival') was led by three strongly contrasted men: Mazzini, an intellectual idealist and founder of the 'Young Italy' movement in 1831, Cavour, an eminently practical politician, and Garibaldi, a daring soldier.

Revolutions in 1848 and 1849 failed to expel the Austrians from Italy. Mazzini and Garibaldi then turned to Cavour, now prime minister of Piedmont, who realised that Italian unity could not be achieved without outside intervention. To bring this about he made an alliance with Napoleon III of France. In 1859 Napoleon sent his army against the Austrians in Italy. After their decisive defeats at Magenta and Solferino, the Austrians agreed to withdraw from Lombardy. In the meantime, Garibaldi, with 1000 volunteers, had conquered Sicily and Naples – the 'Kingdom of the Two Sicilies', ruled by the reactionary Francis II.

*A romantic 18th-century view of the forum at Rome. Such ruins were part of the 'Grand Tour', which English gentlemen undertook as part of their education*

*The Papal States, ruled by the pope, are seen as preventing the union of Italy in this 19th-century nationalist cartoon*

The Italian leader Garibaldi caricatured as a lion nuzzling the 'boot' of Italy

Ethiopians surrender to Italian troops in 1936. Mussolini's ruthless conquest of territory in Africa was part of his attempt to bring back the glory of imperial Rome

Nearly all of Italy, with the exception of Venice and the Papal States, was now united under Piedmontese rule. In 1866, Venice became Italian after the Austrians were again defeated – this time with the aid of Prussia. In 1870 Prussia's attack on France forced Napoleon to withdraw his troops from the Papal States which they had occupied to protect the pope since 1849. This withdrawal gave the Italians their chance to occupy Rome, which in 1871 became the capital of united Italy.

**Uncertain unity: 1871–1915** The new nation, though 'united' in theory, was in practice painfully divided. The north and south of the country had not been under the same government since the days of the Roman Empire: there was a gulf between them – in ways of thought, levels of education and standards of living.

Even in the more developed north, past centuries of rivalry between one region and its neighbour made co-operation difficult. Men thought of themselves as Florentines and Venetians first, and only secondly as Italians. After the heroic period of the Risorgimento the next generation of Italian politicians faced the daunting task of creating a parliamentary system in a country with no living tradition of political responsibility, and of entering the industrial era with few natural resources and a largely illiterate population.

**Italy in the First World War** Italy made a Triple Alliance with Germany and Austria in 1882. But after the outbreak of the First World War, Italy stayed neutral until May 1915, when it denounced the Alliance and entered the war on the side of France, Russia and Britain – largely as the result of Allied promises of vast territorial gains at the end of the war.

Italy's main effort was concentrated on its mountainous north-eastern frontier with Austria. The Italian troops were ill-equipped and in 1917 suffered a disastrous defeat at Caporetto. But they recovered, and a year later they had their revenge by routing the Austrians at the Battle of Vittorio Veneto. Austria surrendered immediately after the battle, one week before Germany also capitulated.

The title-page of Notturno, written by Gabriele D'Annunzio. A flamboyant figure, D'Annunzio won a reputation for daring as a soldier in the First World War

Mussolini (left) under arrest after a pro-war rally in 1915. He became the leader of the Fascist Party which took power in 1922

**Mussolini and Fascism: 1919–45** Russia's 1917 Revolution had strong repercussions in Italy, as in other countries, during the confused months after the war, when disillusioned troops were returning home to face poverty and unemployment. In this atmosphere of unrest, a renegade Socialist, Benito Mussolini, launched his anti-Communist movement, the Fascist Party, which took its name from the ancient Roman emblem of the fasces – a tightly bound bundle of rods with an axe in the middle, symbolising authority and unity.

With its uniform of black shirts and its slogan, 'no discussion, only obedience', the Fascist Party came to power. Mussolini ordered his followers to march on Rome in 1922; the king gave way before this show of force and called on Mussolini to form a government.

Mussolini gradually transformed Italy into a dictatorship, basing his policies on the idea of the 'corporative state'. Under his rule, the Fascists attempted to control every major aspect of Italian life. He took the title of 'Il Duce' (the leader) and suppressed parliament, retaining the monarchy as a figure-head.

The Duce had grandiose ambitions of reviving the glories of ancient Rome and making the Italians once again a conquering, militaristic people. These ambitions, strengthened by the memory of the humiliating defeat the Italians had suffered at Adowa in Ethiopia in 1896, led him to attack and conquer Ethiopia in 1935–6.

**Italy in the Second World War** Despite being linked with Nazi Germany and Japan in an alliance known as the Axis, Italy again remained neutral in 1939. Only in 1940, after the British evacuation at Dunkirk, and when the fall of France was imminent, did Mussolini enter the war. He was sure that Hitler would win and was afraid that the war would end without Italy sharing in the spoils. His decision dismayed countless Italians, who regarded Britain as their traditional friend.

Mussolini's troops fought mainly in North Africa, where, even with the stiffening of the German Afrika Korps, they were resoundingly defeated in 1942. The Allies captured Sicily in 1943. More and more Italians now saw that Mussolini had led them into disaster. The king, Victor Emmanuel III, had Mussolini arrested and a new Italian government was set up which negotiated an armistice with the Allies. In October 1943 Italy declared war on Germany.

But most of the country was still held by strong German forces. Mussolini had been rescued from his imprisonment by German paratroops and set up as a Nazi puppet-ruler in northern Italy. The last phase of the Mediterranean war involved a slow, dogged advance by the Allies up the Italian peninsula, aided by a widespread partisan movement behind the German lines. Italy suffered terribly, both in human casualties and in the devastation of town and countryside. In the final days of the war, Mussolini was captured by partisans and shot near Como on April 28, 1945.

Land reform was a main task of Italy's first postwar leader, Alcide De Gasperi (left). Here he is seen handing over land deeds to a peasant from southern Italy

**Postwar Italy** In 1945, Italy returned to its parliamentary system, but since the king was considered to have been too deeply involved with the Fascists, a republic was set up after a referendum. The president was chosen by the Senate and Chamber of Deputies. Real power was wielded by the prime minister and his cabinet, backed by a majority in parliament.

The Christian Democrats formed the strongest single party, followed by the Socialist and Communist parties, and some smaller splinter groups. But even the Christian Democrats found it impossible, in later elections, to win an overall majority. Their leader, De Gasperi, headed eight coalition governments up to 1953. His Christian Democrat successors, however, found it difficult to steer a middle course towards social justice, between reaction and revolution.

In recent years, a succession of weak Italian governments has led to much unrest. Parties of the extreme right and left have been strengthened by the apparent failure of the democratic system to solve Italy's most pressing problems – the poverty of the south, regional jealousy, unemployment and the Mafia and similar forms of corruption. From 1969 to 1972 the dynamic economic growth of Italy – a founder member of the Common Market – was hampered by crippling strikes. The slow pace of social reform led to riots by workers, students and civil servants. As a result, more power was given to the regions to implement social legislation.

The elegant Pirelli building in Milan is a symbol of the dramatic growth of Italian prosperity since the Second World War

# Ivory Coast

Since gaining independence in 1960 under Felix Houphouët-Boigny, this former French colony has become one of the most prosperous new African states. Houphouët-Boigny, a firm conservative, aroused opposition in Black Africa because of his policy of 'dialogue' with white-dominated South Africa.

**Early history and French rule** Before the arrival of the Europeans, the Ivory Coast was never dominated by any one state or racial group, although the Mandingo peoples, the Mossi and Dagomba, and the Ashanti all penetrated it to some extent. During the 'scramble for Africa' at the end of the 19th century, France annexed first the coastal regions and later the interior of the Ivory Coast. For much of the colonial period it was a 'poor relation'. Modernisation of the port of Abidjan during the 1950's, however, led to a greater exploitation of agricultural and mineral resources.

**Since independence** Under Houphouët-Boigny, the country has maintained close ties with France. The 1960's saw the establishment of authoritarian rule, and an economic boom, mainly in agriculture. In 1960 Houphouët-Boigny expressed his willingness to open a 'dialogue' with South Africa, stating his belief that its apartheid system was more likely to be changed through peaceful means than by force. This approach was strongly opposed by many African leaders.

124,503 sq. miles
4,745,900 people
Capital: Abidjan

# Jamaica

In the 17th century Jamaica became a haven for buccaneers, and was the original home of rum, a by-product of its sugar industry. There are two Jamaicas today: the tropical tourist paradise, and the country of shanty-towns. Despite a prosperous mining industry – Jamaica is the world's largest producer of bauxite, an aluminium ore – 25 per cent of Jamaicans are jobless.

4232 sq. miles
1,977,800 people
Capital: Kingston

**Pirate base** When Columbus discovered Jamaica in 1494 the island was inhabited by Arawak Indians. Spaniards set up sugar-cane plantations and used the Arawaks as labour; but the Indians were soon worked to death and Negro slaves had to be imported from Africa.

British forces occupied Jamaica in 1665, and it became a British possession in 1670. Pirates used it as a base for raids on treasure ships and settlements on the Spanish Main – the north-east coast of South America. Britain officially opposed the raids, but did little to stop them. One buccaneer, Sir Henry Morgan, even became lieutenant-governor of Jamaica.

**Slaves and sugar** The island reached its greatest prosperity in the mid-18th century, when it was the biggest slave-market in the Western Hemisphere. Churchmen and liberal politicians in Britain pressed for the abolition of slavery, and it was ended in Jamaica in 1838. Many planters went bankrupt for lack of labour. Jamaica's economy was also hit when Britain, in the 1850's, stopped allowing colonial sugar to be imported at a low rate of duty. The Negroes suffered severely in the economic depression that followed.

In 1866 Jamaica became a Crown Colony, after which able governors introduced reforms. Dependence on sugar was lessened by the cultivation of bananas.

*A Negro cutting sugar cane. Introduced by the Spaniards, sugar brought great wealth to Jamaica's planters*

**Modern Jamaica** The country was badly affected in the 1930's by the world depression, and by an outbreak of banana blight. Many Negroes emigrated: after the Second World War, the bulk of Jamaica's emigrants settled in Britain. Jamaica was granted internal self-government in 1953 with Norman Manley as chief minister. After a brief attempt to federate with other British Caribbean possessions, it achieved independence in 1962 with Alexander Bustamante as chief minister. He was succeeded by Hugh Shearer in 1967: in 1972 Shearer was replaced by Norman Manley's son, Michael.

*A slave-auction poster of 1829. In the mid-18th century, there were about 3 million slaves in Jamaica*

# Japan

The islands which make up Japan, or Nippon as it is officially known, occupy only a tiny area on the fringe of Asia. Yet the country is the third most powerful industrial nation in the world; it has been predicted that by the turn of this century Japan will outstrip even the United States in economic strength.

143,689 sq. miles
108,152,900 people
Capital: Tokyo

Japan's astonishing rise to the status of economic 'super-power' has been accomplished only in the last hundred years. Before Japan burst on to the world stage, most Europeans regarded it as an exotic and picturesque land of snow-capped mountains, kimono-clad geisha girls and the quaint ritual of the tea ceremony – a style of life epitomised in the Gilbert and Sullivan comic opera, *The Mikado*. Little was known outside the country of the stern traditions of the Japanese samurai, a warrior caste whose uncompromising loyalty to authority was fully utilised by Japan's rulers in the late 19th century, when the country embarked on a programme of modernisation and imperial conquest.

Today the Japanese people – 80 per cent of whom live in towns and cities – enjoy an increasingly high standard of living, achieved by a combination of intense effort and sophisticated technology. They are governed within a democratic system which preserves, as a symbol of national unity, the oldest monarchy in the world.

**Real and mythical origins** The ancestors of the Japanese had probably arrived from mainland Asia by c. AD 100; there may also have been some migration from the islands of south-east Asia in the same period. These immigrants found a Caucasian race, the Ainu, inhabiting Honshu, the main island. The Ainu were gradually subjugated by the first Japanese – and only a small community of them survive today in Hokkaido, the northern island.

According to a Japanese myth, however, the first Japanese were descended from the gods, and the islands of Japan were themselves divinely created. The myth has it that the sun goddess commanded her grandson to descend from Heaven to rule Japan; his great-grandson fought his way to the centre of the country (south of modern Kyoto) and in 660 BC established a capital, founding the Japanese Empire.

**Impact of Korea and China** In the 4th century AD the Japanese seem to have conquered a region at the tip of southern Korea, which they held for some 200 years. From or through Korea, new skills and customs were gradually adopted in Japan – two examples being rice cultivation and the Chinese method of writing.

Communities of Koreans settled in Japan – most of them artisans, scribes and weavers, who were able to instruct the Japanese in a variety of artistic and practical techniques. Records show that by the 9th century more than one-third of Japan's nobility was of Korean or Chinese descent.

**Introduction of Buddhism: c. AD 550** From the middle of the 6th century, Buddhism, introduced from China through Korea, made much headway in Japan,

*A clay figure of a girl holding a cup, from 5th-century Japan. Such figures were used to decorate tombs*

*A goddess of the Shinto religion, which is native to Japan*

The 11th-century Phoenix Hall, at a temple in Uji, shelters an ornate wooden statue of Buddha

where it won the support of the imperial family. Buddhism supplemented the existing Japanese religion, associated with sun worship and known as Shinto ('The Way of the Gods'). The emperors, traditionally the most exalted practitioners of Shinto, became patrons of Buddhism as well. But neither the theology of Buddhism nor the ethics of Confucianism (another religion imported from China) supplanted Shinto. The old beliefs co-existed with the new.

In 710 a new capital was built at Nara on the contemporary T'ang Chinese model, marking the heyday of early Buddhism in Japan. Great care and vast expense were lavished on the building of temples and monasteries, and fine examples of 8th-century Buddhist architecture still survive there.

**Loss of imperial power: 794–1185** A larger capital, Heian-kyo, also built on the Chinese pattern, was founded in 794. It was later to be called Kyoto. The Heian period lasted for almost four centuries; it is notable for two developments – the speedy growth of a distinctive Japanese culture amongst the aristocrats and the loss of effective political power by the emperors.

Heian civilization reached its height in poems, novels (notably the *Tale of Genji*, by Murasaki Shikibu, a lady of the court), paintings and architecture. In such activities the imperial court played a leading part, setting standards for the whole of Japan. But real power passed from the throne to the Fujiwara family of court nobles. Later, in the 11th century, the Fujiwara themselves lost power to a samurai family, the Taira, who were in turn exterminated in civil war by their rivals, the Minamoto, who were also samurai.

An incident from the 12th-century clan wars. The young Emperor Nijo, disguised as a lady, escapes in a carriage with the ex-emperor, Go-Shirakawa

**Samurai domination: 1185–1336** Yoritomo, the leader of the Minamoto, became virtual ruler of Japan after he finally defeated the Taira in 1185. He established a new system of government, known as the Bakufu (camp office) at Kamakura, near the site of modern Tokyo, and far from the existing imperial capital. Henceforth, the samurai, the fighting man, dominated Japanese society, although the imperial family and the court nobles at Kyoto were treated with outward deference. Yoritomo secured official recognition of his position by getting the emperor to grant him the title of shogun, the abbreviation of a Japanese term meaning 'barbarian-suppressing generalissimo'.

Yoritomo's successors in the Kamakura shogunate lacked his ability, and effective power passed to the warrior household of Hojo. In 1274 and 1281 the Hojo led Japan in successful resistance to attempted invasion by the Mongols. They were helped by storms which wrought havoc on the Mongol fleets, the great typhoon of 1281 being known to the Japanese as a Kamikaze (divine wind). The name was used in the Second World War for the Japanese suicide pilots who flew their bomb-laden planes into enemy ships. The Kamakura

Yoritomo became Japan's first shogun, or military dictator, in the year 1185

A wood engraving of a samurai warrior by the artist Hokusai (1760–1849)

period saw the consolidation of warrior society, the growth of a Japanese form of Buddhism, known as Zen, the fine art of the swordsmith and the practice of seppuku (suicide by disembowelment).

**Ashikaga period: 1336–1573** The emperor, Go-Daigo, forced into exile by the Kamakura government, contrived to rally support from a number of important warriors and led them against the Hojo. The struggle against Kamakura was successful, the city being taken by storm in 1333. The Hojo family and their close followers all committed seppuku. But Go-Daigo was unable to enjoy the fruits of this victory for long. One of his main supporters, Ashikaga Takauji, turned against him, made another member of the imperial family emperor, and persuaded the latter to appoint him shogun. Takauji established his government in the Muromachi district of Kyoto.

The age of the Ashikaga shogunate was rich in the arts and economically productive. But politically it was chaotic, being marked by a series of civil wars between various warrior barons. In spite of this, internal and external trade increased, promoting the use of money instead of rice as a means of payment. Such arts as painting, ceramics, drama and the tea ceremony flourished in this stormy, confused era.

**Coming of the Portuguese** From 1543 onwards, Portuguese traders began to arrive in Japan, soon followed by Catholic missionaries. The Portuguese were well received at first, and introduced the Japanese to firearms as well as to Christianity. Oda Nobunaga, a warrior-lord fighting to gain supremacy, befriended the missionaries, and their prospects seemed good.

Nobunaga put an end to the Ashikaga shogunate in 1573 and seemed on the brink of becoming the unchallenged warlord of Japan when he was murdered in 1582. One of his chief retainers, Toyotomi Hideyoshi, completed Nobunaga's task by subduing all rivals and opponents. Having united all Japan under his authority, in the name of the sacred emperor at Kyoto, Hideyoshi launched an invasion of Korea, a costly adventure, which was abandoned after his death in 1598.

**Isolation under Tokugawa rule** The most powerful figure in Japan was now Tokugawa Ieyasu, who defeated his rivals in 1600. Taking up the office of shogun, Ieyasu made Yedo (modern Tokyo) his headquarters. He built a fortress there, the grounds of which form the setting of the 20th-century imperial palace.

Aware of the Spanish conquest of the Philippines, and fearful that his barons would be stirred up by foreign intrigue, Ieyasu looked on the Portuguese missionaries with suspicion. His son, the second Tokugawa shogun, actively suppressed Christianity, while under the third shogun all Portuguese were expelled and the country was 'closed' to the outside world. Japanese themselves were forbidden to travel abroad. The only concession was to the Dutch and Chinese, who were permitted to use Nagasaki for trading, though on a restricted scale.

Great care was taken by the Tokugawa shogunate to maintain its authority. All barons were compelled to spend part of every year in attendance at the castle in Yedo. Society was divided into four classes – warriors, farmers, artisans and merchants. Officially merchants were the least exalted of the four.

Yet merchants in Yedo and Osaka flourished, enjoying great wealth and becoming patrons of the arts. Two cultures now existed side by side, the culture of the samurai – austere, Confucian and pervaded by Zen – and the culture of the townsmen, pleasure-seeking and marked by a love of colour and display. It was for the townsmen above all – the merchants and successful artisans – that Japan's wood-block artists devised their incomparable prints. The work of these artists is known in Japanese as *ukiyo-e*, 'pictures of the floating world', or 'passing scene'. Subjects ranged from low life in Yedo to popular actors and beauty spots. Masters such as Utamaro, Hiroshige and Hokusai influenced many Western artists of the late 19th century.

East looks at West. A Japanese portrayal of a Dutch trader at Nagasaki

The geisha – a female entertainer skilled in singing, dancing and conversation – has long held a respected place in Japanese society

411

'The Great Wave' by Hokusai is a block print from his famous series of views of Mount Fuji

## JAPAN continued

**Coming of the 'barbarians'** Until the mid-19th century attempts by foreigners to 'open' Japan up for trade were firmly rejected. But in 1853 and 1854 Commodore Perry's American naval squadron forced the Yedo government to open certain ports to foreign commerce. The British, Russians, French and others all followed Perry's lead and by the 1860's foreign diplomats and traders had settled on Japanese soil.

The samurai class in particular resented such intrusion, but it was divided over the best course to be adopted. Some urged the forced expulsion of the 'barbarians'. Others argued that the foreign powers were too strong to be resisted in this way; Japan would have to learn from them and then would be able to deal with them on equal terms.

America's first consul in Japan, Townsend Harris, being received by the shogun in 1857. This meeting led to a trade treaty

**Meiji Restoration: 1868** The concessions made to foreigners greatly weakened the prestige of the Tokugawa shogunate, and there was a corresponding revival of interest in the ancient monarchy in Kyoto. In 1868 a coalition of barons from south-west Japan, acting in the emperor's name, overthrew the shogunate. The emperor, a youth still in his teens, moved his capital to Yedo, which was renamed Tokyo. He took the name Meiji (enlightened rule) as the title of his reign. The overthrow of the shogunate was said to have 'restored' ruling powers to the emperor – hence the term 'Meiji Restoration'.

The new government began hastily to modernise Japan. Feudal customs were abolished. Foreign nations – especially Britain, the United States, Germany and France – were taken as models in various fields. Progress was rapid and enthusiastic, despite bitter resistance from some samurai diehards, who fought against the modernisers and the official abolition of the samurai class in 1876. Yet it was the samurai themselves who came to dominate the new world of business and bureaucracy, exchanging the sword for the abacus and the walking-stick. The samurai tradition of loyalty and patriotism served Japan well in the full-scale modernisation called for by the nation's rulers.

Emperor Meiji at the beginning of his successful reign, which saw his country become a world power

**Constitution granted: 1889** The Meiji rulers were slow to distinguish legitimate opposition from seditious revolt. Eventually, however, they gave way to the demand for an elected national parliament. In 1889 the emperor granted a constitution, giving legislative powers to a two-chamber Diet (parliament). In many respects this constitution resembled the authoritarian system prepared by Bismarck for Imperial Germany. Considerable areas of power lay outside the Diet's control. Cabinet ministers were responsible only to the emperor. After 1895 the service ministers were always generals and admirals, and the cabinet had no direct control over the army and navy general staffs.

The first railway in Japan ran from Tokyo to Yokohama. The 18 miles took about 53 minutes

**Japanese victory shakes the world** Rivalry between China and Japan in Korea led to war with China in 1894, in which the Japanese were overwhelmingly successful. The Chinese were forced to cede Formosa and the Pescadores to Japan, together with Port Arthur in south Manchuria, and to recognise the independence of Korea. But pressure from Russia, Germany and France compelled Japan to give up the claim to Port Arthur, which became a Russian base in 1898.

Now recognised as a leading power, Japan entered into alliance with Britain in 1902. In 1904, a long-standing dispute with Russia over Korea boiled over into war. The fighting qualities of its conscript forces, imbued with the samurai tradition, gave Japan victory – a result which astonished the world.

On land were fought some of history's greatest battles, in terms of duration and the numbers of troops involved. Three-quarters of a million Russian and Japanese soldiers contested the Battle of Mukden from February 23, 1905, to March 16. At sea the Japanese navy, largely built in Britain, and with most of its officers British-trained, imposed a crushing defeat on the Russians. Forty Russian warships, under Admiral Rozhdestvensky, left the Baltic in October, 1904, and headed for Vladivostok on the Sea of Japan. While passing through the North Sea they fired on British trawlers in the belief that they had met a force of Japanese torpedo boats. On May 27, 1905, the tsar's

A war that marked the rise of a new power. Japan's fleet shells Russian-held Port Arthur in the year 1904

ships appeared in the Tsushima straits between Japan and Korea, where Admiral Togo engaged them. Only two Russian ships escaped being sunk or captured in the two-day battle. The Japanese lost three torpedo boats.

But the war was draining Japan of money and manpower, and Tokyo asked America's President Theodore Roosevelt to mediate with St Petersburg. By the Treaty of Portsmouth, New Hampshire, signed in September 1905, Russia was forced to give up Port Arthur and cede Southern Sakhalin. Japan also gained control of Korea, which was formally annexed in 1910.

Population growth – from 35 million in 1873 to 46 million in 1910 – accompanied Japan's continued industrial expansion. Emperor Meiji's death in 1912 marked the end of a 45 year reign in which Japan had been transformed into a major world power.

**Taisho Japan: 1912–26** During the next reign – Taisho ('great righteousness') – industry and commerce boomed. In the First World War – which Japan entered as Britain's ally – Japanese exports met demands in Asian and African markets that Britain and Germany could not meet. But a set-back followed with the collapse of the war boom and the disastrous Tokyo-Yokohama earthquake of 1923.

Emperor Taisho's reign was marked by industrial progress, social unrest and a disastrous earthquake

At the end of the war Japan acquired German islands in the Pacific and a seat on the Council of the League of Nations. But various foreign adventures proved unprofitable. Troops were withdrawn from Siberia, where they had intervened against the Bolsheviks. The Anglo-Japanese alliance, formerly a cornerstone of Japan's foreign policy, was not renewed after 1921.

Agreements signed at the Washington Conference (1921–2) appeared to give Japan security at the price of agreed naval disarmament. Japanese imperialism and nationalism also seemed to be in retreat in the face of social unrest and the extension of the franchise to all males over the age of 21.

Village industry in
Japan – a girl
working at a wooden-
built silk loom

A kamikaze – Japan-
ese suicide pilot –
crashes on to a US
aircraft carrier

**Crisis and conquest** Emperor Taisho died in 1926. The new reign – Showa ('radiant peace') – soon witnessed a financial crisis, due to bank failures. This was followed in 1930 by the calamitous results of the great world slump. The American market for Japanese silk collapsed, bringing ruin to the country's farming areas, where silk production played a vital role.

Economic disaster coincided with growing tension between Japan and China. A new nationalist spirit in China, inspired by the success of Chiang Kai-shek's revolutionary party, the Kuomintang, seemed to threaten Japan's political and economic position in south Manchuria. In September 1931, without orders from Tokyo, Japanese troops attacked the Chinese, taking Mukden and other cities. The Japanese government was obliged to accept their actions.

World condemnation, expressed by the Americans and the League of Nations, only hardened Japanese patriotic sentiment. In 1933 Japan completed the occupation of all Manchuria, withdrew from the League of Nations, and recognised the so-called independent state of Manchukuo, under the last emperor of China.

**Terrorism and war: 1932–8** Nationalist hysteria drove revolutionary unrest into support for a Japanese brand of fascism – anti-capitalist scorn for 'Big Business' and Diet politicians, combined with the exaltation of the emperor as 'god-like' and of the imperial army as his only reliable instrument. Extreme nationalist terrorists murdered the moderate Premier Inukai and other public men in 1932. Further assassinations occurred in 1936, when part of the Tokyo garrison, led by a group of young officers, attempted a coup d'état, aimed at establishing military rule.

The successful suppression of this revolt only strengthened the army's political influence, which became unchallengeable after a skirmish near Peking in 1937 led to full-scale undeclared war with China. Within 18 months, Japanese forces had occupied the Yangtse Valley as far as Wuhan, captured Canton and won control of nearly all the main cities of China. But Chinese resistance did not collapse, even though the invaders were able to establish pro-Japanese puppet regimes in north and central China.

**The Second World War** Japan's action in China gravely damaged British and American interests there and shocked public opinion in Britain and America. In Japan, no criticism against the action was tolerated. Moderate statesmen and intellectuals lost further ground to militarists when Hitler overran the Low Countries and France in 1940. Soon afterwards Japan signed a military alliance with Germany and Italy.

Pressure on Vichy France secured bases for Japan, first in northern Indo-China – from which the Burma Road, carrying vital supplies to China, could be threatened – and then in the Saigon region. Washington reacted with a virtual trade embargo against Japan, and Britain and the Netherlands followed suit. Japan faced economic strangulation, especially since it depended totally on imported oil. Japanese-American talks failed to break the deadlock, and Japan struck without warning. Its planes bombed Pearl Harbour, Hawaii, Hong Kong and Singapore, in December 1941, while its troops landed in Malaya. Within six months, the Japanese had conquered an area from the Indian-Burmese border to the highlands of New Guinea.

The tide of war began to turn in June 1942, when the Japanese were defeated at the Battle of Midway. This regained for the Americans the initiative in the Pacific. Ebb-tide for Japan came in 1944, with defeat at Imphal-Kohima on the Burmese frontier and the Americans' return under MacArthur to the Philippines. Devastating air-raids on Japanese cities and crippling losses at sea had brought utter defeat within sight by August 1945, when atomic bombs were dropped on Hiroshima and Nagasaki and the Russians joined Japan's enemies.

The Japanese surrender was ordered by the emperor himself, for his voice alone had the authority to make his troops accept the futility of further resistance.

Emperor Hirohito,
who came to the
throne in 1926,
presided over the
most tumultuous era
in Japan's history

**Foreign occupation: 1945–52** Formal surrender took place on an American battleship in Tokyo Bay in September 1945. Under General MacArthur, the Americans supervised far-reaching political, economic and social changes in Japan – and this process was greatly helped by the generally co-operative attitude of the Japanese government and people.

The Meiji constitution was replaced by an extremely democratic system, largely the work of MacArthur's staff. The emperor officially renounced any claim to reverence as a deity or semi-deity. The new constitution made him a symbol of national unity, sovereignty being vested in the Japanese people.

In the Tokyo Trial, seven Japanese leaders, including the former prime ministers Tojo and Hirota, were sentenced to death, while in a series of minor trials 5000 naval and military personnel were found guilty of cruelty to prisoners of war. A 'purge', directed by the Occupation authorities, kept many hundreds of political, business and educational leaders at least temporarily out of employment. A most important measure was the Land Reform, which revitalised the countryside, turning tenant-farmers into owner-occupiers – and thus creating a stable conservative force unsympathetic to political extremism of any kind.

By 1950 the major work of reform was over and reconstruction had begun. This was accelerated by the industrial boom which followed the outbreak of the Korean War in 1950. From this time, too, can be dated the modest origins (a police reserve force) of the nation's post-war rearmament programme.

**Peace and prosperity** Ratification of the San Francisco peace treaty ended the Occupation in April 1952. A pact made the United States responsible for protecting Japan. Under American pressure, rearmament proceeded steadily, in seeming conflict with the new, pacifist constitution.

Japan's main energies were devoted not to rearmament or diplomacy, but to greater industrial production and expanding trade. By the 1960's, Japanese living standards were well above pre-war levels. The Tokyo Olympics of 1964, opened by the emperor, symbolised the recovery of national confidence and prosperity after the 1945 collapse. Even greater economic advancement was heralded by the success of Expo 71 at Osaka – as well as by the emergence of the yen as one of the world's strongest currencies. Japan's increasing dominance of world trade caused concern among its competitors, and relations with America were shaken by President Nixon's moves to curb imports from Japan. In May 1972 Premier Eisaku Sato negotiated for the return to Japanese control of Okinawa, which had been administered by America since 1945.

**Japan's new role** In July 1972 Sato retired, and the governing Liberal Democratic Party chose 54-year-old Kakuei Tanaka as his successor. Under Tanaka's leadership the Liberal Democrats were returned to power in parliamentary elections in December 1972. Tanaka, the youngest Japanese prime minister since the war, was born in a poor village in north-west Japan: at 15 his formal schooling ended and he went to Tokyo with a few yen in his pocket, becoming a wealthy building contractor before entering politics.

As prime minister Tanaka visited China in 1972 on a mission of reconciliation, ending 35 years of hostility between the two nations. He also made friendly overtures to the USSR for the signing of a peace treaty, and for the use of Japanese technology and capital in exploiting the vast natural resources of Siberia.

Emperor Hirohito's
officials sign the in-
strument of surrender
on an American
battleship in 1945

Japanese manufac-
tures such as this
motor-cycle have
captured many world
markets in the post-
war period

Sinews of modern
Japanese industry.
A worker inspects
molten steel as it
pours out of a furnace

# Jordan

The kingdom of Jordan lies in a region steeped in history. When the state was founded in the 1920's, it took within its boundaries some of the most famous places of biblical tradition, including Bethlehem, Jericho, Jerusalem and the River Jordan.

Since 1948, Jordan has been in the front line of the Arab world's confrontation with Israel; as a consequence it lost its territory on the west bank of the River Jordan to the victorious Israeli armies in the six-day war in 1967. The strain produced by military defeat, and by the mass influx of Palestinian refugees into Jordan, threatened the position of the country's ruler, King Hussein, noted for his moderation in Arab affairs.

37,741 sq. miles
2,634,400 people
Capital: Amman

**Biblical origins and Arab conquest** In biblical times the land which later became Jordan was divided; the area to the west of the River Jordan, including Jerusalem, was part of Palestine, while the area to the east included the kingdoms of Ammon, Edom and Moab. The powerful Nabataean Empire, established *c.* 300 BC with its capital at Petra, formed part of present-day Jordan, but conquest by Rome in AD 106 brought the power of the Nabataeans to an end.

Muslim Arabs conquered the country in the 7th century, and after a brief period of Crusader rule during the 12th century Jordan became part of the empire of the Mameluke rulers of Egypt. The Mamelukes were replaced in the 16th century by the Ottoman Turks, whose rule lasted for 400 years, until their empire collapsed at the end of the First World War.

**British mandate** During the First World War, Arab guerrillas helped British troops to liberate Palestine from Turkish rule. The Arab leader, Prince Faisal, was advised by Colonel T. E. Lawrence – 'Lawrence of Arabia'. In return for their aid, Britain promised the Arabs an independent kingdom after the war, but also promised the Jews a national home in Palestine.

In 1920, the League of Nations gave Britain a mandate over Palestine. Britain, to fulfil its promise to the Arabs, created the emirate of Transjordan from part of this territory and placed Faisal's brother, Abdullah ibn Hussein, on the throne. The emir's loyalty in the Second World War prompted Britain to recognise him in 1946 as king of an independent Transjordan.

*The Treasury at Petra, a city cut from the rocks, which was once the capital of the powerful Nabataean Empire. It lay undiscovered by the Western world until 1812*

**Independent Jordan** Britain was now faced with the consequences of the conflicting promises it had made to the Arabs and to the Jews. In 1948, when Britain gave up the Palestine mandate, Transjordan sided with the other states of the Arab League – Egypt, Syria, Iraq and Lebanon – to attack the new state of Israel. The Arab armies were routed; United Nations mediation ended the war in 1949. In the same year, Transjordan was re-named the Hashemite Kingdom of Jordan.

During the Arab-Israeli war, some 500,000 Arab refugees fled from Israel into Jordan. This mass exodus increased the country's population by one-third and created a lasting economic problem.

Abdullah was assassinated by an extreme Arab nationalist in 1951. His son, Talal, became king, but a year later he was deposed because of mental illness. Talal's 18-year-old son, Hussein, succeeded him.

Jordan suffered great economic and political difficulties during the 1950's. Arab nationalists criticised the regime for its close links with Britain. To placate them, Hussein dismissed the British commander of the Arab Legion, General Sir John Glubb ('Glubb Pasha'), in 1956. After the Anglo-French landings at Suez later the same year, he broke off all ties with Britain.

*Abdullah ibn Hussein (1882–1951), who was emir of the new Transjordan in 1921 and king in 1946*

*A Jordanian Royal Armoured Corps tank crew under training. King Hussein relied on the loyalty of his well-equipped army to break the power of the Arab guerrillas operating from bases in Jordan*

**Struggle to survive** After Israel diverted part of the River Jordan in 1964 for an irrigation scheme, Egypt and Syria demanded an all-out attack on Israel and denounced Hussein's more cautious policies. On May 30, 1967 Hussein finally signed a military pact with Egypt; immediately Israel made a lightning attack, and a week later, at the end of the so-called six-day war, they had captured the entire west bank of the Jordan.

Serious friction now developed between the Jordanian government and the Palestinian refugees, who comprised more than half Jordan's total population. Terrorist attacks against Israel were launched from inside Jordan's borders by Palestinian guerrillas. Though Hussein tried to avoid a direct confrontation with the guerrillas, his acceptance of an Arab-Israeli cease-fire in August 1970 completely alienated his regime from the terrorists.

When Palestinian commandos hijacked several airliners to Jordan in September 1970 to publicise their cause, Hussein was faced with a direct challenge to his authority. He ordered his troops to attack the guerrilla bases and a bloody civil war erupted, which was halted only when Arab leaders arranged a truce. However, renewed violence broke out in January 1971.

Hussein now resumed his efforts to come to an understanding with Israel, especially over the future of the west bank. Relations with other Arab states deteriorated further, and in July 1971 Hussein's policies were condemned at an Arab summit meeting in Tripoli. In November, the Jordanian prime minister, Wasfi Tell, was assassinated by Palestinians in Cairo.

In the fourth Arab-Israeli war, which began in October 1973, Jordan avoided direct confrontation with Israel, itself reluctant to open up a third front in the war. But Hussein gave some military help to the Syrians.

*Smoke rises over Amman in September 1970, after savage street fighting between King Hussein's Jordanian troops and Palestinian guerrillas*

*King Hussein's pro-Western views and his policy of moderation towards Israel were bitterly opposed by many Arabs*

# Kenya

Emerging from one of the severest conflicts of the modern colonial era – the 'Mau Mau' rebellion of the 1950's – Kenya won its independence in 1963 and soon established itself as one of the most stable of Africa's new states. Its president, Jomo Kenyatta, once imprisoned by the British as the instigator of the rebellion, became respected as a wise elder statesman even by many of the settlers and politicians who had formerly been his bitterest opponents.

Kenya's population is among the most diverse in Africa. The Africans, who make up 95 per cent of the total, are divided among some 50 racial groups, many of them Bantu-speaking; non-Bantu groups include the Masai and Somali. There are also important Asian, European and Arab minorities.

The country has a fine tropical coastline and, in the south-west, a highland area which is one of the most fertile in Africa. But nearly two-thirds of the country, in the north and east, is arid bush and semi-desert.

224,959 sq. miles
12,815,600 people
Capital: Nairobi

**Kenya before the Europeans** East Africa was the home of some of man's earliest-known ancestors. In southern Kenya, and just across the frontier at Olduvai Gorge in Tanzania, remains have been found which are some 2 million years old. About a thousand years ago Bantu-speaking migrants – ancestors of the Kikuyu and other present-day tribes – entered Kenya from the south up the coastal belt. Five hundred years later, other peoples, including the nomadic Masai, entered Kenya from the north. Some time later, the Luo entered western Kenya; while within the last 100 years increasing numbers of Galla and Somali have migrated into Kenya from the north-east.

From medieval times the coast of Kenya was visited by traders from Europe, Asia and Arabia in search of slaves and ivory. The Arabs settled in the coastal area, which fell under the control of the sultans of Zanzibar from 1740 onwards. Today's coastal population, the Swahili, are a racial blend of Arabs and Bantu Negroes. Their language, Swahili (a Bantu tongue with Arabic admixtures), has become the national language of Kenya.

*The nomadic Masai are renowned for their courage. Young warriors, armed only with a spear and shield, have to kill a lion to prove their manhood*

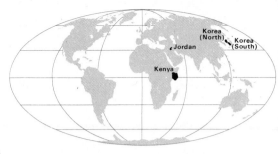

**Early years of British rule: 1895–1920** During the struggle for African possessions by the European powers at the end of the 19th century, Britain and Germany agreed that Kenya should fall within the British sphere of influence. The British established a protectorate in 1895 and built a railway across the territory with the aim of linking the neighbouring protectorate of Uganda with the coast at Mombasa. Immigration from the United Kingdom was encouraged. By 1914 there were several thousand British farmers in the fertile south-western region, the 'White Highlands', producing crops such as coffee, and employing cheap African labour on land formerly used by Kikuyu and Masai. The Indians who had been brought in to build the railway stayed on to operate it and to play an increasingly important role in commerce.

**Settler dominance: 1920–52** In 1920, Kenya became a Crown Colony. Its history between the wars was dominated by three conflicting factors: the settlers' demand for self-government of the kind achieved by the white Rhodesians in 1923; the desire of the Indians for political and social equality with the Europeans; and a growing clamour by the Africans, particularly the Kikuyu, for protection from the exploitation of their land and labour by the settlers. In 1922, rioting followed the arrest of Harry Thuku, leader of the Young Kikuyu Association; in 1928, Jomo Kenyatta, secretary of the Kikuyu Central Association, began campaigning for political and economic reforms.

**'Mau Mau' revolt: 1952–9** After the Second World War, many ex-servicemen arrived from England to swell the ranks of the settlers. This, together with increased government activity in African areas, helped to spread discontent among the Kikuyu; a militant secret society known as 'Mau Mau' was formed. Oath-taking rituals bound the members of Mau Mau to use terrorism to drive out the whites and to command allegiance among the Kikuyu. Sporadic violence flared up into revolt after the declaration of a state of emergency in 1952.

Kenyatta, who had returned to Kenya in 1946 after 15 years' absence in Britain to lead the Kenya African Union (successor to the Kikuyu Central Association), was convicted of organising the rebellion and imprisoned. The hard core of the Mau Mau fighters took to the forests. By 1955, the back of the revolt had been broken at a cost to Britain of several hundred casualties and over £20 million, and to the Kikuyu of 12,000 killed and wounded. With restoration of order, the British began to prepare the colony for self-government.

**Independent Kenya** The transfer of power was protracted, the Kikuyu refusing to co-operate with the British as long as Kenyatta was in prison. When political activity was resumed, two rival parties emerged: the Kenya African National Union (KANU), supported by Kikuyu and Luo; and the Kenya African Democratic Union (KADU), supported by the smaller tribes, suspicious of Kikuyu and Luo dominance. In 1961, Kenyatta was released and became KANU's president. When the country eventually became independent in 1963, it was under a compromise constitution which provided for a degree of regional self-government. But KANU, which won the elections in 1963, was determined to do away with regionalism. The constitution was changed, KANU swallowed KADU, and Kenyatta became president of the new one-party republic.

Kenya has scant mineral resources. Agriculture is still the main occupation. But the relative political stability established under Kenyatta encouraged foreign firms to invest in the country. Tourism, based on the country's fine game parks, has now overtaken coffee as the main source of foreign revenue. In 1968, the government pressed forward with its policy of turning over land and businesses to Africans. Chief sufferers from this were the Asians; those who had kept British citizenship were ordered to close their stores and businesses.

**KHMER REPUBLIC,** *see Cambodia*

*Jomo Kenyatta, once jailed as the leader of the 'Mau Mau' rebellion, became independent Kenya's first president*

*Long-distance runners such as Kip Keino brought Kenya to the forefront at world athletic meetings*

# Korea, North

The Democratic People's Republic of Korea controls the peninsula north of the line drawn in 1945 and confirmed by the armistice of 1953 – roughly the 38th parallel of latitude. Like the Republic of Korea to the south, North Korea's Communist regime claims to be the only legitimate government of Korea.

(For Korean history before 1945, see Korea, South.)

**Foundation of North Korea: 1945–8** From 1910 until the end of the Second World War, the whole of Korea was under Japanese rule. After Soviet Russia declared war on Japan in 1945, its troops moved into the north, while shortly afterwards the Americans occupied the south. The 38th parallel was chosen to divide the two zones until the country's future could be decided.

In the north, the Soviet occupying forces bolstered the power of local Communists, whose leaders now returned from exile in China and Russia. Chief among them was Kim Il-sung who, in 1948, became the leader of the Democratic People's Republic of Korea, after attempts to reunify the country had failed.

**War with the south: 1950–3** In June 1950, the North Koreans invaded the south in an effort to reunite Korea by force. The South Koreans appealed to the United Nations for aid, which was speedily granted. By the end of the year, UN forces had invaded North Korea and were approaching the Manchurian border of China.

Some 200,000 Chinese 'volunteers' were then sent to the aid of the North Koreans. They drove the UN forces back into the south, only to be beaten back again to the 38th parallel. The war eventually bogged down into stalemate. An armistice was signed at Panmunjom, just north of the border between the countries, in July 1953.

**Since 1953** Under Kim Il-sung's rigidly authoritarian rule, North Korea made steady economic progress. In 1961 a Seven Year Plan was launched. The main emphasis was placed on the development of heavy industry and the exploitation of North Korea's considerable mineral wealth. But the country still depends on China and Russia for economic aid.

Though North Korea and South Korea remain firmly opposed to each other in ideology, the two sides jointly stated in July 1972, to the world's surprise, that they had agreed to begin steps towards ultimate reunification.

46,540 sq. miles
15,514,500 people
Capital: Pyongyang

*A propaganda poster used in Communist China at the time of the Korean War, calling on people to 'volunteer' for service in North Korea*

# Korea, South

For almost 3000 years, the history of the Korean people has been closely interwoven with that of the Chinese. Korea's other neighbour, Japan, also helped to shape its destiny. In the 19th century Japan forced Korea out of a self-imposed isolation and, after annexing the country in 1910, gave it the basis of a modern industrial economy. Following Japan's defeat in 1945, Korea was divided along the 38th parallel; the north looked to China and Russia for support, while the south fell under American influence. In 1950 the north attacked the south in an unsuccessful attempt to reunify Korea.

**Early history** Korea's recorded history begins *c.* 1100 BC, when a Chinese colony was founded at Pyongyang. Chinese influence remained until *c.* 100 BC when three warring native kingdoms – Silla, Koguryo and Paekche – rose to power. By the 7th century AD, the south-eastern kingdom of Silla had conquered its rivals. In 935, a rebel general, Wanggon, overpowered Silla and established his own kingdom of Koryo – from which the name Korea is derived. During the 13th century, the Mongols conquered the land. In 1364 they were defeated by Korean troops under General Yi Sung-kei, who established his own dynasty in 1392.

**Prosperity, invasion and isolation: 1392–1910** For two centuries the Koreans progressed, in spite of internal political strife and Japanese piracy. Finally, in

38,022 sq. miles
34,070,200 people
Capital: Seoul

*During the Yi dynasty, Korean arts and sciences flourished, though this picture of Korean dancers still shows Chinese influence*

KUWAIT    LIBERIA
LAOS      LIBYA
LEBANON
LESOTHO

## KOREA, SOUTH *continued*

1637, Korea fell to the Manchus of China. Under their influence, the country was isolated from the non-Chinese world and became known as 'The Hermit Kingdom'. This situation lasted until 1876, when Japan forced Korea to open its ports to outside trade. A war eventually broke out between China and Japan over Korea; it was fought mainly on Korean soil. Following China's defeat in 1895, Russia tried to acquire Korean territory. Japan crushed this threat in 1905, and in 1910 formally annexed Korea.

**Fight for independence** The Koreans never accepted Japanese domination, though the industrialisation it brought was of lasting benefit to the country. In 1919 a government-in-exile was formed in Shanghai under Syngman Rhee, while from 1935 onwards, Communist-led guerrillas harassed the Japanese from bases in the north Korean hills. At the end of the Second World War, Russian troops entered the north and American forces took control of the south, with Korea divided between them at the 38th parallel.

**War in a divided land** Two conferences, to bring about the union of the Communist-backed north and the American-supported south led by Syngman Rhee, both failed. In 1948, South and North Korea were established as separate states, with Syngman Rhee as president of South Korea – officially called the Republic of Korea.

Determined to unify Korea under Communist rule, North Korean forces invaded South Korea in June 1950. The United Nations came to the aid of the South, and 16 member nations sent troops. Communist China entered the conflict on the side of North Korea in 1951. A cease-fire was agreed in July 1953, and Korea remained divided at roughly the 38th parallel. In 1972, the two sides began talks on eventual reunification.

**Syngman Rhee and after** President Rhee served throughout the 1950's. In 1960, however, charges of election-rigging forced him to resign. Fresh elections were held; in 1961 a new democratic government was ousted in a military coup. Its leader, General Park Chung Hee, announced that military government would last until 1967. This led to a wave of violent protest. In response, Park announced presidential elections for 1963 in which he would be a civilian candidate. In that year, and after the elections of 1967 and 1971, he held on to the presidency, despite accusations of election-rigging. Since 1971, Park has ruled with increasingly authoritarian control.

*Syngman Rhee, leader of the Korean exiles in Shanghai in 1919, was the first president of the South Korean republic*

*The flood of refugees from the North after the Korean War intensified the economic problems faced by the South as it strove to repair the ravages of war*

## Kuwait

One-eighth of the world's oil reserves are believed to be under the sands of Kuwait, one of the smallest yet most prosperous countries in the Middle East. Already the tiny desert state is the third-largest producer of oil in the Middle East after Saudi Arabia and Iran.

Portuguese sailors and traders, following the explorer Vasco da Gama in the 15th century, were the first Europeans to set up an outpost in Kuwait. But the area's earliest settlers were nomadic Arabs, who arrived there about 300 years later and founded the town of Kuwait, which became a centre for Persian Gulf trade.

In 1899, at the request of the emir, Britain made Kuwait a semi-protectorate, to ward off a threat from the Ottoman Turks. Newly independent Saudi Arabia invaded Kuwait in 1919, but the invasion was repelled. Saudi Arabia then imposed a land blockade on the country, which lasted for 20 years. Britain finally helped the two sides to make peace in 1942.

With the discovery of oil in 1934 by an Anglo-American company, and its exploitation after 1945, Kuwait prospered greatly. Neighbouring Iraq revived an ancient claim to Kuwait in 1952, but this was rejected by Britain. In June 1961, Kuwait became a fully independent nation.

6,880 sq. miles
1,100,000 people
Capital: Kuwait

Kuwait and other Arab states have made increasing use of their oil as a political weapon. At the time of the 1973 Arab-Israeli war they drastically reduced oil exports, to influence world opinion against Israel.

## Laos

The fortunes of this landlocked kingdom have long been linked to those of its more powerful neighbours, Cambodia, Thailand, Burma and, recently, Vietnam.

The United Nations lists Laos among the world's 20 poorest countries. Most of the people depend for their existence on rice. Roads are bad and there are no railways; the main highway is the River Mekong.

**Origins** Laos was probably first settled during the 12th century by Thai tribes from south China. For a time the region was under Cambodian domination. The earliest important Laotian state was Lan Xang, founded in 1353. In the 17th century Lan Xang enjoyed a period of peace and prosperity, and controlled parts of Vietnam and Cambodia, southern Burma and northern Thailand. But after 1694 it was split by an internal power struggle, and by 1707 three separate kingdoms had emerged, centred on Luang Prabang, Vientiane and, in the far south, Champassak.

**French control** From the end of the 18th century Laos came under the domination of the neighbouring kingdom of Thailand, but this control was challenged after 1880 by the French. In 1893, Laos became part of French Indo-China – although the Luang Prabang monarchy survived.

The Japanese occupied Laos during the Second World War, but in 1946 the French returned. In 1949, Laos was granted self-government within the French Union. In 1953, the Pathet Lao, a left-wing nationalist movement formed in North Vietnam by Prince Souphanouvong with the backing of the North Vietnamese Communists (the Viet Minh), invaded northern Laos. The civil war which followed was ended in 1954 as the result of an international conference at Geneva. In the same year, the country became fully independent.

**Independence and civil war** A coalition government formed by Prince Souphanouvong and the neutralist Prince Souvanna Phouma broke down in 1959, and fighting flared up again between the Pathet Lao and government troops. A three-way struggle for power developed between Souvanna Phouma, Souphanou-vong's Pathet Lao and a right-wing party under Prince Boun Oum. During this civil war, the Pathet Lao gained control of half the country. In 1962, the reconvened Geneva Conference agreed on the neutrality of Laos, and the three factions formed a coalition.

In 1963, the Pathet Lao withdrew from the government and for the rest of the decade government forces, with United States backing, fought the Pathet Lao and North Vietnamese. The Vietnamese Communists used the Ho Chi Minh Trail through the eastern half of Laos and in 1970 took the Laos province of Xieng Khouang. Meanwhile, the United States carried out frequent bombing missions against Communist forces in Laos. In 1973 the two sides reached a ceasefire agreement and in 1974 established a coalition government.

91,428 sq. miles
3,256,700 people
Capital: Vientiane

*Riverside villagers catch fish in nets in the River Mekong, which is the main highway of Laos*

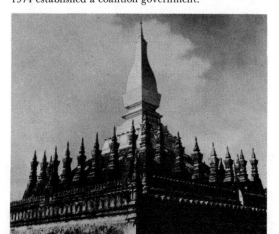

*Built in the 16th century, the sacred shrine of That Luang in Vientiane contains a bone which is supposed to be from the chest of Buddha*

A 13th-century Crusader castle in the modern Lebanese town of Saida – once the site of the ancient Phoenician trading port of Sidon

# Lebanon

The republic of Lebanon is unusual among Arab nations of the Middle East in that its population is half Christian and half Muslim. This division is recognised in the constitution, by which the president is Christian and the prime minister Muslim. Lebanon is traditionally a great centre of trade. Its people are lively and sophisticated, and have the highest literacy rate in the Arab world.

4015 sq. miles
3,130,300 people
Capital: Beirut

**Early history** The eastern shore of the Mediterranean, along which Lebanon lies, was the home of the Phoenician sea-trading empire. Persia, Assyria, Babylon, Egypt, and Greece under Alexander the Great fought in turn for this wealthy area. In 64 BC the country came under Roman rule, during which the Maronite sect of Christians was established. When Islam spread in the 7th century, Lebanon remained largely Christian.

When the Middle East came under the Ottoman Turks in the 16th century, Lebanon was governed with a light touch and the ruling families were allowed considerable freedom. This delicate Christian-Muslim balance was upset in the mid-19th century when an ancient Muslim sect, the Druses, launched a series of massacres against the Maronites. The Maronites appealed for aid, and Britain and France forced the Turks to set up a pro-Christian government.

**Modern Lebanon** In 1920, France was given control of Lebanon by the League of Nations. At the start of the Second World War, the Vichy French administered Lebanon. Allied forces invaded in 1941, and an independent republic was declared in 1945.

Lebanon played a small part in the Arab-Israeli wars of 1948 and 1956, but none in June 1967. Due to Muslim opposition to the country's pro-Western policy, a revolt broke out in 1958, which was quelled by American troops called in by the Christian president Camille Chamoun. In 1968 and 1969 popular demonstrations in favour of guerrilla war against Israel brought down three governments. Although the country allowed Arab guerrillas to operate against Israel from within its borders, Israeli reprisals in the 1970's led to renewed efforts to crush terrorist activities.

# Lesotho

The mountain kingdom of the Basotho nation had its beginnings in the 1820's. It grew out of the remnants of tribes that had taken refuge in the mountains of the Drakensberg from attacks by Zulu and Matabele armies. The new nation feared annexation by the Boers and appealed to Britain for protection. The area became the High Commission Territory of Basutoland in 1868.

In 1966 the country gained independence as Lesotho, with Chief Lebua Jonathan as prime minister. The new state weathered a constitutional crisis in its early years – the king tried to increase his power, was exiled, but was later allowed to return. Chief Jonathan established friendly relations with South Africa, on which Lesotho remained economically dependent. But in 1972 relations became strained, following speeches in which he criticised South Africa's racial policy of apartheid.

11,721 sq. miles
998,000 people
Capital: Maseru

# Liberia

Africa's oldest republic began life in 1847. The American Colonisation Society, a philanthropic institution formed in 1816 to settle freed American slaves in Africa, established its first colony in Liberia in 1822 near the site of present-day Monrovia (named after the then American President, James Monroe). Other settlements of freed American slaves followed, and in 1841 the first Negro governor was appointed. Liberia was declared an independent republic in 1847, with a constitution modelled on that of the United States.

American financial aid kept the republic going until 1926, when the Firestone Rubber Company acquired a

43,000 sq. miles
1,832,000 people
Capital: Monrovia

100 year concession over a million acres of land and began to develop a huge rubber plantation. The inter-war years were an uncertain period for Liberia, with the economy over-dependent upon a single product and on private American capital. In the 1950's Liberia became less dependent on rubber, when its enormous reserves of iron ore began to be exploited.

Politically, the country is controlled by the Americo-Liberian elite, the Negroes of American origin, who make up only 5 per cent of the total population. Their party, the True Whigs, has remained in power since the 1870's. In spite of moves by William Tubman, president from 1943 until his death in 1971, to give the majority a more direct say in affairs, democracy in Liberia remains largely nominal. Tubman was succeeded as president in 1971 by William Tolbert Jr.

Low fees and lack of government control have attracted one-fifth of the world's merchant shipping to register under Liberia's 'flag of convenience'

# Libya

As a province of the Roman Empire, Libya exported fruit and corn to Italy from fertile irrigated coastlands. Today, after 1500 years of poverty and obscurity, Libya is once more rich, from oil discovered deep in its Saharan hinterland. The Libyans' average income is as great as that of the Italians, their one-time masters during the colonial period. Libya is a vast, sparsely populated country, divided into three main regions, Tripolitania, Cyrenaica and Fezzan. Most of the country is desert, an extension of the Sahara.

**First settlers** In ancient times, Cyrenaica was colonised by the Greeks, and parts of Tripolitania by the Phoenicians. Later, the coastal lands of the two regions were united under Roman control. Impressive remains from this period have been excavated, notably those at Leptis Magna, east of Tripoli. Libya remained an outpost of the Byzantine Empire until the Arab invasions of the 7th century AD.

Large-scale Arab settlement did not take place until the 11th century, when Islamic religion and culture were established. During the first 1000 years of Muslim rule Libya was split in two; Tripolitania was ruled from neighbouring Tunisia, while Cyrenaica was largely an extension of Egypt. There was little organised government and, outside the coastal cities, the Bedouin tribes were largely independent.

**Ottoman rule: 1551–1911** In the 16th century the Libyan coastal towns became part of the expanding empire of the Ottoman Turks. The Ottoman sultan in Istanbul was represented in Tripoli and Benghazi by governors. These local rulers had great freedom until direct rule was re-imposed in 1835. The Ottomans, however, were never able to exert control over the Senussi, a Muslim religious brotherhood that sprang to power in 1843 and grew rich from its connections with the caravan trade. The Turks were forced to accept the authority of the Senussi over the Bedouin tribes.

**Italian rule: 1911–43** After the war of 1911–12 between Turkey and Italy, Italy annexed Tripolitania and Cyrenaica but, like the Ottomans, had great difficulty in subduing the Senussi. It was not until 1931, with the capture and execution of the Senussi commander, Sidi Umar al-Mukhtar, that the Italians were able to occupy the whole of Libya. In the 1930's, thousands of Italian peasants were settled in Tripolitania and Cyrenaica, but the outbreak of the Second World War put an end to further development. During the war, Libya became a battleground when the British fought to halt the German and Italian armies advancing into Egypt to take the Suez Canal. Finally, in 1943, the British Eighth Army drove the Germans and Italians out of Libya.

679,358 sq. miles
2,241,500 people
Co-capitals:
Tripoli and Benghazi

A stone carving of the Three Graces from the Great Theatre in the ruined Roman city of Sabratha, west of Tripoli in Libya

Mussolini, the Italian Fascist dictator, inspects a new coast road near Tobruk during the Italian occupation of Libya

417

## LIBYA continued

**The kingdom of Libya: 1951–69** After the war, Anglo-French military government continued for a number of years (the French had conquered the Fezzan, in the south). Finally, after a United Nations vote in 1949, the country became an independent kingdom in 1951 under Idris I, leader of the Senussi. In return for aid, Britain and the US were allowed to maintain military and air bases. In 1959 the discovery of oil in vast quantities transformed Libya's economy.

**Libyan Arab Republic** In 1969 a group of young Libyan army officers, led by Colonel Muammar el Qadhafi, overthrew King Idris and proclaimed a republic. Within months, Qadhafi closed down the British and American bases, and began protracted and bitter negotiations with the oil companies for higher royalties and greater control over their operations. The negotiations led to an agreement in April 1971, which increased oil revenue by almost 50 per cent. But in 1973–74 Qadhafi took over complete control of the oil companies. Qadhafi used Libya's new wealth to increase its military strength and to improve social welfare services.

*Colonel Qadhafi (left) of Lybia with President Sadat of Egypt. The idea of a 'merger' faded when the two leaders quarrelled*

# Liechtenstein

Set high in the Alps between Austria and Switzerland, the tiny principality of Liechtenstein is a romantic land of wooded mountains and narrow valleys. Its prosperity is based on tourism and manufacturing, but much of its revenue comes from the sale of postage-stamps.

Originally, the area of Liechtenstein was made up of the barony of Schellenberg and the county of Vaduz. Johann Adam von Liechtenstein bought the barony in 1699 and the county in 1712; the Holy Roman Emperor joined the two in 1719 to form the principality.

The state remained part of the Holy Roman Empire until the empire's abolition by Napoleon in 1806. From 1815 to 1866 it was a member of the German Confederation; when this broke up the country developed close ties with Austria, which lasted until 1918. Since 1924 Liechtenstein has participated in a customs union with Switzerland, which also looks after its defence and foreign affairs. Many international companies have their headquarters there because of low taxation.

61 sq. miles
23,000 people
Capital: Vaduz

# Luxembourg

Rich deposits of iron ore give the Grand Duchy of Luxembourg an importance out of proportion to its size. Almost half the country's people work in the steel industry, which is one of the most up-to-date in Europe. It produces more than 6 million tons of steel a year.

Luxembourg's history goes back over 1000 years. In 963 a German princeling, Sigrid, acquired the castle of Luxembourg and the area became part of the Holy Roman Empire. Its ruler, Henry IV, was elected Holy Roman Emperor in 1308. The country became a grand duchy in 1354. In 1443 it was sold to the dukes of Burgundy, from whom the Hapsburgs inherited it. When the Hapsburg lands were divided a century later, Spain took over Luxembourg. In 1713 Austria was given the territory by the Treaty of Utrecht.

Napoleon annexed Luxembourg, but the 1815 Congress of Vienna gave it to the kingdom of the Netherlands. In the 1830's Belgium broke away from Holland and annexed much of Luxembourg; the rest was declared an independent, neutral state in 1867. Rulers of Holland held the title of Grand Duke of Luxembourg as well as their own until 1890, when Wilhelmina came to the Dutch throne. The title then passed to the German Nassau family, as the duchy's laws did not permit a woman to rule. The law was changed in 1912. Grand Duke Jean succeeded in 1964. The European Coal and Steel Community made Luxembourg its base in 1952, and the country is a founder-member of the Common Market.

998 sq. miles
350,000 people
Capital:
Luxembourg

# Malagasy Republic

The island of Madagascar which, together with a few small neighbouring islands, forms the Malagasy Republic, was settled by Indonesians who migrated in double-hulled canoes 2000 years ago. Later arrivals from Africa and Arabia mingled with the original stock.

The first Europeans to visit the island were Portuguese traders at the end of the 15th century. In the 17th and 18th centuries, Madagascar was a haunt of pirates, including the notorious Englishman, Captain Kidd. Native Malagasy chiefs created kingdoms, and then in 1896 Madagascar became a French colony, achieving independence in 1960.

The country is the world's largest producer of graphite – used in lead pencils and atomic reactors. Philibert Tsiranana, president since independence, maintained stable rule until a left-wing rebellion in April 1971. In 1972, after massive demonstrations, he handed over power to the army and later resigned.

226,657 sq. miles
7,264,300 people
Capital: Tananani

# Malawi

This Black African state, which achieved its independence in 1964, was formerly the British colony of Nyasaland. It is a long strip of mountainous country, beautiful but largely barren, to the west and south of Lake Nyasa. More than half the country's wage-earners work abroad, mainly in the mines of South Africa and Rhodesia. In the late 1960's Malawi's leader, President Hastings Banda, established cordial relations with these white-ruled countries. His policy towards them was widely criticised in Black Africa as a 'sell-out'; he defended it as realistic.

**Pre-colonial era** In the 15th century native peoples moved southwards to settle in the central and southern parts of the country (the 'Empire of Malawi'). They traded in ivory, gold and slaves with the Portuguese and the Yao tribes. During the early 19th century, Yao warriors and Arab traders raided the Malawi tribes for slaves. Later, Ngoni warriors entered from the south and rapidly dominated northern and western Malawi.

**British rule** The great Scottish missionary David Livingstone, crossing Malawi in 1856, was appalled by the ruthless exploitation of its people by the Arabs. He appealed to the British public to 'heal the open sore of the world'. By 1875, Scottish missionaries and traders were established in the region. In 1891, the British created a protectorate – known, after 1893, as the British Central Africa Protectorate.

In 1904, the territory became a British Crown Colony, and in 1907 was re-named Nyasaland. In 1915, John Chilembwe, a fervent Christian, led an uprising against conscription, which was put down. Nyasaland made little social or economic progress between the wars.

The country was joined in 1953 with Northern and Southern Rhodesia to form the Central African Federation. In 1958, the Nyasaland African National Congress, which had criticised the 'white-dominated' federation, recalled Hastings Banda from abroad, where he had been a doctor for over 20 years. A year later, after an uprising, Banda was arrested and the Congress banned. The nationalist movement grew, and Banda was freed in 1960. Britain dissolved the federation and in 1964 Nyasaland achieved independence as Malawi.

**Independence** Dr Banda became prime minister and then president for life in 1970. He survived much internal unrest and strengthened his autocratic rule, proclaiming a one-party state. Most Black African leaders condemned his links with South Africa and Rhodesia. Banda, in turn, suspected Tanzania and Zambia of backing Malawi political exiles.

45,747 sq. miles
4,732,300 people
Capital: Zomba

*The 19th-century Scottish missionary David Livingstone was determined to right the wrongs which he saw were being done to tribal peoples in Malawi*

*President Banda (left) on a tour of a farm in Malawi*

# Malaysia

Almost half the world's natural rubber comes from Malaya, the dominant partner in the Federation of Malaysia. Malaya's rubber plantations were founded by the British in the 19th century. With the growth of the rubber and tin industries, many Chinese immigrants arrived; their descendants form almost 40 per cent of Malaysia's population, and their rivalry with the Malays is a source of tension. Sabah (formerly British North Borneo) and Sarawak, which make up the rest of Malaysia, are less developed.

127,316 sq. miles
11,507,300 people
Capital: Kuala
Lumpur

**Early history** The ancestors of the Malays arrived *c.* 2000 BC from Yunnan, in southern China. Two thousand years later Indian traders and monks spread throughout south-east Asia, bringing with them two new faiths, Buddhism and Hinduism. The Buddhist empire of Srivijaya, based on Sumatra, conquered much of western Malaya. It prospered on tolls from the ships using the narrow Straits of Malacca between Sumatra and Malaya. The empire lasted from the 8th to the 13th century. The 15th century saw the rise of Malacca, whose rulers became converts to Islam. Other Muslim states grew up, notably Johore, Perak and Kedah.

**European rule** In 1511 Malacca fell to the Portuguese, who used it as a base for their spice trade with the Moluccas and the Far East. The Dutch wrested Malacca from them in 1641, and the Dutch in turn were ousted by the British after the Napoleonic wars. The three British bases of Singapore – founded in 1819 by Stamford Raffles on a mangrove swamp – Penang and Malacca were united in 1826 as the Straits Settlements. In 1867 the British Colonial Office took over control from the East India Company.

To begin with, the British confined their interest in Malaya to trade. Disorder in the sultanates of the interior led Britain in 1874 to establish control over Perak and Selangor, by appointing British Residents (colonial rulers). By 1914 British mastery of the peninsula was complete.

*Henry Wickham in 1911, with one of the rubber trees grown in Malaya from the seeds he smuggled out of Brazil to Kew*

**Sarawak and the Brooke family** In 1841 a young British officer, James Brooke, was made rajah of Sarawak in northern Borneo for quelling a rebellion against the Sultan of Brunei. For over 100 years the 'White Rajahs', as the Brookes were known, ruled Sarawak. They gained territory at the expense of Brunei and suppressed piracy. In 1945 the Brookes handed over their domain to the Colonial Office.

**British North Borneo** A London merchant, Alfred Dent, in partnership with an Austrian, Baron Overbeck, set up the British North Borneo Company with a grant of land from the Sultan of Brunei and a Royal Charter from Gladstone in 1881. Money ran short and the difficult jungle terrain forced the company into stagnation. Borneo remained economically and socially backward until 1945 when it became a British colony.

**Tin and rubber** Malaysia today is the world's leading producer of tin and rubber. Tin production was developed on a large scale by Chinese immigrants early in the 19th century. The rubber industry began in 1877 with 22 seedlings sent from Kew; they had been grown from seeds smuggled out of Brazil by the British explorer Sir Henry Wickham. Rubber boomed in the early 1900's with the demand for car tyres.

*This poster, printed in Chinese, was circulated by the British authorities in Malaysia during the 1948–60 emergency. It offered Communist rebels safe conduct and money if they gave up their weapons*

**Communism and the emergency: 1948–60** Malaya and Borneo fell to the Japanese during the Second World War. Malaya's Chinese-led Communist guerrillas were not slow to learn the lesson that Asians could defeat a Western power, and after Japan's defeat in 1945 they turned against British troops and planters. A state of emergency, declared in 1948, lasted until 1960, when the Communists were defeated. Fortified villages, which cut off the guerrillas from their source of supply, were a major factor in the victory.

**Independence** In 1948, Malaya was formed into a loose federation, in which the sultanates were left with considerable powers. Singapore was excluded because of Malay fears that its million Chinese would dominate the federation; together with the Borneo territories, it remained a Crown Colony. The Malayan Federation became independent in 1957.

Singapore, Sarawak and Sabah (British North Borneo) were united with Malaya in the Federation of Malaysia in 1963. Brunei did not join, remaining a British dependency. Tension between the Chinese of Singapore and the Malays led to Singapore breaking away in 1965. At the same time, President Sukarno of Indonesia condemned the new country as a 'neo-colonialist' creation, and Britain had to defend the Borneo territories from Indonesian guerrilla infiltration. The crisis ended in 1966, when Sukarno was deposed.

Race riots between Malays and Chinese broke out in Kuala Lumpur in 1969, and the constitution was suspended. In 1970 Premier Tunku Abdul Rahman retired and was succeeded by the Deputy Premier, Tun Abdul Razak, who restored parliamentary rule in 1971.

# Maldive Islands

Fishing and coconut growing are the chief industries on the Maldives, a cluster of coral islands south-west of Ceylon. The population is almost entirely Muslim. Their conversion dates from 1173, around which time the islands were frequently visited by Arab traders. In 1796 Britain took over Ceylon from the Dutch, along with the Maldives, which were under Ceylon's protection. Ceylon became independent in 1948, but the British did not give the Maldives freedom until 1965, when a republic was proclaimed. The Maldives have granted Britain a lease on the Gan air base until 1986.

115 sq. miles
116,000 people
Capital: Male

# Mali

In the Middle Ages the vast and barren region of present-day Mali was the home of the Ghana, Mali (or Manding) and Songhai empires. Timbuktu flourished on the trans-Saharan trade in gold and slaves. Timbuktu became a centre of Muslim learning and culture; but by the time the French arrived in 1898 it was in ruins. They ruled the territory as the French Sudan until 1960, when a socialist, Modibo Keita, became Mali's first president. A military coup in 1968 brought in a conservative president, Moussa Traoré. In 1974, a severe drought in the southern Sahara took an uncounted toll of human life and the cattle on which the peasants relied.

478,767 sq. miles
5,473,800 people
Capital: Bamako

# Malta

Since ancient times, Malta's strategic position commanding the Mediterranean sea lanes has attracted foreign powers. The Phoenicians colonised the island before 1000 BC. Later it was ruled by Greeks, Carthaginians, Romans, Byzantines and Arabs. The Normans seized it in 1090, and in 1530 Emperor Charles V gave it to the Knights Hospitallers of St John of Jerusalem, or Knights of Malta. They beat off Turkish attacks but succumbed to Napoleon in 1798. With British help the Maltese ousted the French in 1800 and remained under British rule until given independence in 1964. The George Cross was bestowed upon the island because of its people's courage during the Axis air onslaught in the Second World War.

122 sq. miles
324,000 people
Capital: Valletta

**Mintoff era** The run-down of British bases spelt crisis for the economy. In 1971 Prime Minister Dom Mintoff refused to renew Britain's lease on its remaining bases unless more money was paid. Finally in 1972, Britain agreed to pay Malta £5¼ million a year and other NATO powers a further £8¼ million.

*A Knight of Malta at prayer. He is wearing the Cross of St John of Jerusalem. This order of knights defended the Holy Land and later ruled Malta*

MAURITANIA    MONGOLIA
MAURITIUS    MOROCCO
MEXICO
MONACO

# Mauritania

For centuries Mauritania has been a stronghold of the Islamic faith. Its marabouts (holy men) are famous for their interpretations of the Koran. Mauritania lies mainly in the Sahara. Its people – Arabs and Berbers – are largely nomadic. It is one of Africa's poorest countries, but the exploitation of iron and copper has begun to transform its economy.

Mauritania was the centre from which the Berbers sprang to carve out the Almoravid Empire in the 11th century AD; two centuries later they were conquered by Arabs. France took over the area in 1903.

The country became independent in 1960. For much of its first decade it was at loggerheads with neighbouring Morocco, over the latter's claim to parts of Mauritania's territory, including the north with its immensely rich iron-ore deposits. In 1969 the two countries agreed to share these resources. Mauritania remained stable politically under the leadership of President Mokhtar Ould Daddah, in spite of riots in 1966 by the Negro minority, sparked off by a decision to make Arabic the official second language, after French.

397,956 sq. miles
1,281,000 people
Capital: Nouakchott

# Mauritius

The island of Mauritius – the home of the dodo until it became extinct in the late 17th century – lies in the Indian Ocean, more than 500 miles to the east of Madagascar. Mauritius was probably visited by Arabs, Malays and Portuguese, but the first settlers were the Dutch in 1589. They named the island after their ruler, Prince Maurice of Nassau.

A small Dutch settlement, established in 1638, was abandoned in 1710 as unprofitable. The French started to colonise the island in 1715, but it was taken by the British in 1810 and formally ceded to Britain in 1814. In 1968 it became independent, with an Indian, Sir Seewoosagur Ramgoolam, as prime minister. Since then the country has been troubled by political strife.

The island's economy depends almost entirely on sugar, which accounts for more than 90 per cent of its exports. Tea and molasses are also exported and tourism is increasing in importance. The sugar industry was started in the 18th century by the French, who helped to shape many other features of the island's way of life – customs, law, language and religion. The creoles of Mauritius – people of mixed African and European descent – speak a French dialect, and are mainly Roman Catholic. They are outnumbered almost two to one by Indians, descendants of labourers brought from India in the 19th century to work on the sugar plantations, after slavery was abolished in 1834.

789 sq. miles
896,500 people
Capital: Port Louis

*The flightless dodo of Mauritius became extinct in the 1600's*

# Mexico

Although Mexico lost half its territory to the United States in the mid-19th century, it remains a large country (after Brazil and Argentina, the third largest in Latin America). Its wide range of soil and climate, making possible a varied agriculture, and its extensive mineral resources, have freed Mexico from the economic curse of many Latin American countries – excessive dependence on a single export product. But the country shares with the rest of Latin America an explosive population growth which presses heavily on resources; the estimated population for 1980 is 72 million.

The Spanish conquest of Mexico after 1521 created a dual society of Indians, mainly poor peasants and labourers, and an upper class of creoles (whites born in Mexico); whose wealth was based on landowning and silver mining. This society, whose basic institution was the hacienda, or great estate, was drastically modified, but not completely destroyed, by the Revolution of 1910. Under the powerful political class which emerged out of the chaos of revolution – the so-called 'revolutionary family' – Mexico achieved stability and remarkable economic growth. Over the years, many attempts at

761,605 sq. miles
55,867,000 people
Capital: Mexico City

*A stone mask from the ruined city of Teotihuacan in central Mexico, heart of an Indian civilization c. 1500 years ago*

*Mounted Spanish conquistadores battle with the Aztecs, in this contemporary picture of Spain's conquest of Mexico. Under their leader, Cortez, the Spanish soon crushed the Aztec Empire*

radical reform of Mexican society have been made. But the country's social advance, though striking, has failed to reduce the gap between rich and poor.

**300 years of Spanish rule** For more than 1500 years before the arrival of the Spanish conquistadores (conquerors) in the early 16th century, Mexico was the home of highly organised Indian 'empires'. Those of the Aztecs and the Maya were the most powerful.

The disunity of the Indian peoples and their military weakness allowed a handful of Spaniards to destroy them in the years after 1521. Diseases brought by the Europeans caused a drastic fall in the population of the Indians, and the conquerors exploited the remaining population, as workers in the silver mines or as agricultural labourers on the large haciendas created out of the destruction of the Indians' communal farming system. The Church as a corporation emerged as the largest single landowner in the country. The importance of Mexico to Spain and Europe lay in its silver mines, which by the 18th century made it the world's major producer of the metal. Spain's commercial monopoly and the exclusion of creoles from any share in political power created strong resentment, and by the end of the 18th century there was a growing demand for independence.

**Independence: 1823** The Spanish imposed a rigid control over their lucrative Mexican colony, and it achieved independent nationhood later than the other major countries of Latin America. A rebellion led by a Catholic priest, Hidalgo y Castilla, in 1810, was a failure. Liberal guerrillas fought on against Spain until, with the support of conservative creoles, they succeeded in establishing the country's independence. A republic was proclaimed in 1823.

For the first 50 years of independence, Mexico was torn by violent dispute – between liberals and conservatives; between supporters of the Church and its opponents; and between those who wanted government centralised and those who sought a federal system. Soldier-politicians exploited the chaotic state of Mexican politics for their own ends. The most notorious of these, General Antonio López de Santa Anna, dominated the 1830's and 1840's. His rule survived Mexico's crushing defeat by the United States in the Mexican War of 1846–8. The immediate cause of the war was the annexation of Texas by the American government in 1845. (Texas, settled by Americans during the 1820's, had risen against Mexican control and established its independence in 1836.) Mexico lost more than half its territory – present-day California, Arizona, New Mexico and Texas, and parts of Utah and Colorado.

In 1855, Santa Anna was overthrown and a new government set up under the liberal leader, Benito Juarez. Church property was confiscated and a liberal constitution proclaimed in 1857. In 1858 the conflict between liberals and conservatives erupted into civil war. Though the conservatives were defeated, France came to their aid and installed Maximilian of Austria as emperor. He was defeated and shot in 1867.

*A peasant woman dictates a letter to a scribe. Such scenes are common in Mexico even today, despite government attempts to combat illiteracy*

*General Santa Anna, with two of his subordinates. Santa Anna commanded the Mexican army against Texas in 1836, after the territory broke away from Mexico*

**Dictatorial rule: 1876–1910** In 1876, General Porfirio Diaz seized power. He brought order to the country during his paternalistic dictatorship. In the 1890's, more and more Indian land was absorbed by the great estates. The Indians became increasingly subject to the landowners, to whom they were tied by their debts. Strikes among miners and railwaymen were brutally repressed. By 1910 the Mexican economy was dominated by United States and British investment.

**Revolution: 1910–17** The Revolution of 1910, which overthrew Diaz, was sparked off by a liberal landowner, Francisco Madero, a sincere believer in political democracy as the solution to social problems. He was soon in conflict with the peasant revolutionary Emiliano Zapata, who demanded an immediate distribution of land to the peasants. Madero was deposed by the right-wing General Victoriano Huerta and, in 1913, assassinated. A period of bloody conflict followed, first between Huerta and the revolutionary leaders Zapata, Pancho Villa and Venustiano Carranza, and then, when Huerta resigned in 1914, among the revolutionaries themselves.

In 1917, a constitution embodying the aims of the Revolution was framed under the victor, Carranza. The constitution provided for the separation of Church and state; all mineral resources were declared national property; and land was to be restored to the Indians.

**Interwar period: 1920–40** Revolutionary Mexico was dominated by two problems – the creation of a stable government, and the redistribution of the great estates among the Indian peasantry. Under President Calles (1924–9), land reform took second place to political consolidation, which included a violent attack upon the Church – foreign priests were deported, church schools closed and, when the clergy retaliated by going on strike, the churches were taken over by 'citizens' committees'. The liberal president, Lazaro Cárdenas (1934–40), centralised political power in a governing party – which later became the now dominant Institutional Revolutionary Party (PRI). His reforms included the redistribution of some 45 million acres of land.

**Modern Mexico** After 1940, Mexico combined a large measure of political stability with economic growth. In recent years – in spite of violent outbursts of student unrest – the ruling party, the PRI, has maintained its hold. The country's industrial growth has been the most rapid in Latin America. Industrial development drew many workers to the cities, but even so, it was not able to absorb all the surplus rural population. As a result, half Mexico's people still live in great poverty. Mexico has long been dependent upon the United States as the major importer of Mexican products and chief foreign investor, a fact resented by many Mexicans. Luis Echeverría Alvarez, elected president in 1970, indicated during a world tour in 1973 that he was making a determined effort to lessen this dependence.

# Monaco

The principality of Monaco is the world's second smallest state, after the Vatican. Since 1297 it has been ruled by members of the Grimaldi family. The opening of the famous casino at Monte Carlo in 1863 launched Monaco on its career as a Mediterranean resort. Only 2500 of Monaco's people are native Monégasques, with the status of citizens. The rest are foreign residents, mainly from France. Many of the country's workers are daily commuters from Italy and France.

**Past and present** Monaco was probably first settled in historic times by the Phoenicians. The Genoese built a castle there in 1215, and in 1297 control passed into the hands of the Grimaldi family, also from Genoa. Between the 16th and 19th centuries the country was at various times a protectorate of Spain, France and Sardinia. In

*The ill-starred Maximilian was installed as Mexican emperor by Napoleon III of France. But after French troops left the country Maximilian was executed*

*Porfirio Diaz, strong man of Mexico for over 30 years, brought his country much prosperity. But this benefited only a few and he was overthrown by the Revolution of 1910*

*The revolutionary leader Emiliano Zapata inspired the oppressed Indian peasants of Mexico with his promises of land and liberty. He was assassinated by a rival in 1919*

France     Italy
MONACO
• Monaco
Mediterranean Sea

0·58 sq. miles
24,000 people
Capital: Monaco

1861 it became fully independent, though by a treaty of 1918 Monaco would again become a French protectorate if the male Grimaldi line were to die out. In 1949 Prince Rainier III, a member of the Grimaldi family, became chief of state. He married the American actress Grace Kelly in 1956 and a son was born in 1958.

Monaco has a customs union with France. The use of Monaco as a 'tax haven' by Frenchmen led to a dispute with France in the early 1960's. This was resolved in 1963 by an agreement under which French citizens who had lived in Monaco for less than five years were liable to French income tax. At the same time, the government taxed the profits of foreign companies with their headquarters in the country.

# Mongolia

The Mongolian People's Republic occupies a huge plateau, between 3000 and 4000 ft high, with rugged mountains in the west and the Gobi Desert in the south. The harshness of its climate and terrain is matched by the hardiness of its people, who for centuries have followed a nomadic, pastoral way of life. Mongolia was the first country outside Russia to establish a Soviet-style People's Republic, in 1924.

In the 13th century, Genghis Khan's Mongol horsemen swept westwards across Asia to establish a great empire. In time, the empire split up. The northern part came under Russian domination, while the southern part was taken over by China in the early 17th century. Only the area of the present state – then called Outer Mongolia – remained independent. But it was conquered by China in the 18th century.

With the outbreak of revolution in China in 1911, Outer Mongolia broke away and came under the protection of tsarist Russia. Links with Russia continued after the Bolshevik Revolution of 1917, and in 1946 China finally recognised Mongolia's independence. The ruling Mongolian People's Revolutionary Party today maintains close ties with the USSR.

604,247 sq. miles
1,393,800 people
Capital: Ulan Bator

# Morocco

French rule in Morocco from 1912 until 1956 transformed the country from a backward state, with ill-defined frontiers, into a leading North African nation. During the early Middle Ages Morocco knew greatness as the centre of a prosperous Muslim empire.

**Arabs and Europeans** Phoenician immigrants settled in the area of present-day Morocco in 1100 BC. Their settlements later became part of the Carthaginian Empire, which lasted until Rome conquered it in 146 BC.

With the fall of the Roman Empire in the 5th century AD, Morocco was invaded and conquered by Berbers moving from the west. But, 200 years later, the Berbers in turn fell to the onslaught of Islam and the Arabs. Between 1064 and 1269 two great dynasties, the Almoravids and the Almohades, established a Muslim empire, based on Morocco, which spread over much of North Africa and Spain. The early 16th century saw the Spanish and Portuguese in control of Moroccan ports – Ceuta and Melilla, together with Itric, remain Spanish to this day – but the Portuguese defeat at the battle of Alcazarquivir in 1578, when King Sebastian of Portugal was killed, preserved Moroccan independence.

In 1912, part of northern Morocco came under the control of Spain, while the rest became a French protectorate. The city of Tangier became an international port.

European rule was contested by the leader of the Riff tribes, Abd-el-Krim Khattabi, who led an uprising from 1921 to 1926. After his defeat, Abd-el-Krim was deported, but guerrilla resistance lasted until 1944.

**Independence** The sultan, Sidi Muhammad, was deposed by the French in 1953 for demanding independence. In 1955, however, France restored the sultan; the following year Morocco became independent.

171,834 sq. miles
16,166,000 people
Capital: Rabat

## MOROCCO *continued*

Sidi Muhammad took the title of King Muhammad V; in 1961 he was succeeded by his son, Hassan II. New constitutions in 1970 and 1972 established parliamentary democracy, but Hassan kept considerable powers. Discontent with the monarchy led to abortive coups by army and air-force officers in 1971 and 1972, causing Hassan to suspend all political democracy.

# Mozambique

Although Mozambique supplies many of the cashew nuts eaten at cocktail parties around the world, its people know little of such luxurious living. Most of the people of this East African nation are poor black tribesmen who barely raise enough food for their families to live. This tropical country has many mineral resources, including iron and coal, but development of a mining industry has been hampered by poor transportation facilities.

The Portuguese explorer Vasco da Gama was the first European to visit Mozambique, stopping there on his famous first voyage to India in 1498. Portuguese settlers soon established trading posts and the region became a center for the slave trade. Black nationalists began waging guerrilla warfare in 1964, opposed by some 70,000 Portuguese troops. Following the overthrow of Portugal's dictatorial government in a military coup in 1974, Mozambique won independence, but in the face of active opposition from white locally-born Portuguese

302,328 sq. miles
8,970,000 people
Capital:
Lourenço Marques

# Nauru

The island of Nauru, in the south-western Pacific, is the world's smallest republic. It enjoys a high level of prosperity, due to the rich phosphate deposits which cover most of its area. The deposits, estimated at 60 million tons, are worked by British interests. Royalties are paid to the Nauruan landowners, and also to a community fund to make provision for the people of the island when the stocks are exhausted – this is expected to be by the end of the century. Nauru was discovered in 1798 by a British naval captain, John Fearn. In 1888, the island was annexed by Germany, and in 1914 occupied by Australia. After the First World War, the League of Nations made it a mandate of Britain, New Zealand and Australia, and in 1947 it became a United Nations trustee territory, administered mainly by Australia. In 1968, Nauru was given its independence.

8·25 sq. miles
8000 people
Capital: Vaboe

# Nepal

This kingdom in the Himalayas has the world's highest peak, Mount Everest (29,028 ft). Its tribal peoples include the Sherpas, famous as climbers, and the Gurkhas, whose fighting qualities have given them a unique place in military history.

Modern Nepal dates from 1768, when the small hill-state of Gurkha expanded over the whole area from Bhutan to Kashmir. In 1847 the Shah dynasty was reduced to figureheads by the aristocratic Ranas. In 1951 the Ranas, too, were ousted and a democratic constitution introduced. However, King Mahendra re-imposed direct rule in 1960, banning political parties. His son Birendra succeeded him on his death in 1972. Nepal's foreign policy has been dominated by its geographical position between its two giant neighbours, India and China.

54,362 sq. miles
11,910,700 people
Capital:
Kathmandu

*Gurkha soldiers on parade in Nepal. The Gurkhas, noted for their iron courage, have fought in many British campaigns*

# Netherlands

Much of the Netherlands is the creation of man. For hundreds of years the Dutch have worked to reclaim vast stretches of their land from the sea, driven on by the problems of an ever-expanding population.

The history of the Netherlands as a unified state began in the 16th century, when its people threw off the yoke of Catholic Spain. In the following century the Dutch experienced the most brilliant phase in their history. Dutch sailors and explorers circled the globe, laying the foundations of a great trading empire which was to last into the 20th century. The prosperous life of Dutch merchants of the time is mirrored in the paintings of such artists as Rembrandt and Vermeer.

**Early peoples** The ancestors of the modern Dutch were two Germanic tribes, the Batavians and the Frisians, who migrated to the Rhine delta *c.* 14 BC. The Romans enrolled the Batavians as auxiliaries, but *c.* AD 50 they built a line of forts along the southern bank of the Rhine to mark the boundary of their empire. To the north was a no-man's land and the settlements of the Frisians.

In AD 406 barbarian tribes swept across the Rhine frontier and overwhelmed the Roman Empire. The Netherlands fell to the Franks, and in due time it formed part of a new empire built by the Frankish ruler, Charlemagne (*c.* 768–814). Charlemagne had close connections with the region and sometimes kept his court at Nijmegen on the River Waal. When his empire broke up after his death, part of the Netherlands fell to the Duchy of Lower Lorraine – until that, too, split into smaller feudal states, ruled by barons.

**Feudal period: 922–1384** One of the most powerful of these feudal states was that ruled by the 'Count of Holland', who controlled much of what is now the Netherlands. The position of the barons was soon challenged by the fast-growing strength of the cities, such as Haarlem, whose merchants, as they prospered, were asserting their independence and paying only lip-service to their traditional masters.

**Burgundy and Spain: 1384–1568** In 1384, Philip the Bold, ruler of the French dukedom of Burgundy, began the process by which the whole of the Netherlands gradually came under Burgundian control. The expansion of Burgundy was achieved by means of money, marriage and threats disguised as diplomatic pressure. The court of Burgundy was culturally brilliant, and its rulers dreamed of creating a great middle kingdom between the French and the Germans.

This dream was ended in 1477, when Charles the Bold, the last Duke of Burgundy, was killed in battle. The Low Countries, which at this time included Belgium, were to pay dearly for being involved in the dynastic scheming of the House of Burgundy. For its fortunes became entangled with those of the even more powerful and ambitious House of the Hapsburgs.

In the early 16th century, the young Charles V became heir to all the various Hapsburg dominions. These included Austria and Spain as well as the Netherlands, which, with the election of Charles as Holy Roman Emperor in 1519, became part of a massive European empire. As long as Charles ruled, the Dutch

15,772 sq. miles
13,674,700 people
Capital: Amsterdam
(seat of government
The Hague)

*In the 1600's, the cultivation of tulips became a boom industry in the Netherlands. It gave rise to 'tulipomania'– frenzied speculation in tulip bulbs*

*The Dutch scholar and writer Erasmus (1466–1536) prepared the way for the Protestant Reformation by his attacks on corruption in the Catholic Church*

*William the Silent led the Dutch in their fight for freedom against Spain. He was assassinated by a Spanish agent in 1584*

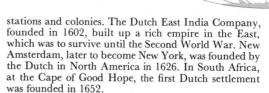

were shielded from the effects of their link with Spain, for he had been born and brought up in the Netherlands and always had understanding and sympathy for his homeland. But in 1555, worn out by the crushing weight of his responsibilities, he handed control of his Netherlands domains to his son, Philip.

The Netherlands, a prosperous land with a tradition of tolerance, was a fertile ground for the spread of Protestantism. Charles was devout enough, and regarded the new faith as heresy; but he was not prepared, apart from one brief attempt, to subject his beloved Netherlanders to the cruelties of the Inquisition. Philip, a fervent Catholic who never went near the Netherlands after a short visit early in his reign, had no such scruples, and his attempts to crush Protestantism stirred the Dutch to revolt against him in 1568.

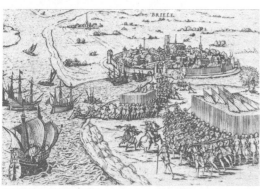

*The Battle of Brill (1572), in which the Dutch defeated the Spanish, was a turning point in the Netherlands' struggle for independence*

**80 Years' War** The struggle which followed became known as the 80 Years' War. The Dutch cause was headed by Philip's own former lieutenant, William the Silent, Prince of Orange. In 1579 the seven northern provinces formed the Union of Utrecht; two years later, they proclaimed their independence as the Republic of the United Netherlands.

Savage fighting continued between the two sides for many decades. The Spanish, for the first years of the war under the Duke of Alva, held their ground in the south (roughly modern Belgium), and launched attack after attack on the north. The worst hour for the Dutch came with the assassination of William the Silent by a Spanish agent in 1584; but his two sons carried on the struggle. A truce between the two sides was signed in 1609, but only in 1648, by the peace of Westphalia, did Spain formally recognise Dutch independence.

**Golden age:** *c.* **1600–1713** The 17th century was an age of glory for the young republic, which seemed to burst with energy and originality in all directions. It led the world in art – this was the era of Rembrandt, Vermeer, de Hooch, Hobbema and many other painters. In science, industry, architecture, horticulture, navigation and countless other fields, the Dutch made contributions of immense importance to European civilization.

In economic and financial matters the Dutch were pre-eminent. Amsterdam had the world's first stock-exchange as far back as 1602. The Bank of Amsterdam was set up in 1609, long before the Bank of England. State lotteries and the concept of 'excise' duties were similarly first introduced in the Netherlands.

**Empire and naval power** Over the same period, the Dutch reached the height of their success as a European power. Their ships and seamen rivalled those of England, another power whose prosperity depended on ever-expanding trade; they soon established trading

*A self-portrait by the Dutch artist Rembrandt (1606–69), one of the world's greatest painters. Rembrandt's masterly use of light and dark led to his nickname of the 'king of shadows'*

*Dutch ships under the audacious Admiral de Ruyter decisively defeated an English fleet moored in the Medway in 1667*

stations and colonies. The Dutch East India Company, founded in 1602, built up a rich empire in the East, which was to survive until the Second World War. New Amsterdam, later to become New York, was founded by the Dutch in North America in 1626. In South Africa, at the Cape of Good Hope, the first Dutch settlement was founded in 1652.

The year 1652 also saw the first of a succession of naval wars with England. Further naval wars – in the first of which the Dutch lost New Amsterdam – were fought between 1664 and 1676, when Charles II of England allied himself with the anti-Dutch policies of his French cousin, Louis XIV. In 1667 the Dutch admiral, de Ruyter, humiliated England by burning its fleet at anchor in the Medway. But the 'Glorious Revolution' of 1688 brought William of Orange, the Stadtholder, or political head, of the Netherlands, to the English throne as joint sovereign with his wife Mary, daughter of the exiled James II. British and Dutch armies fought side by side against the French. But this co-operation ended with the Treaty of Utrecht in 1713.

From the early 18th century, Dutch power began to ebb. The Netherlands became a republic of bankers, minding their own business, and monopolising all political power. Towards the end of the century, these powerful merchants were challenged by a liberal-minded group, known as the 'patriots', who demanded an end to their monopoly of political power. The struggle between the two groups was unresolved when the French Revolution began to spread through Europe.

**Napoleon and the Netherlands: 1795–1815** William V of Orange fled to Britain as Revolutionary France's armies invaded his country, which was renamed the Batavian Republic by the French. (The Batavians of Roman times were the ancestors of the modern Dutch.) In 1806 Napoleon made this republic the kingdom of Holland, giving the throne to his brother, Louis Bonaparte, who vacated it in 1810, when the country was made part of the French Empire.

After Napoleon's fall in 1815, the southern provinces were united with the north into one kingdom of the Netherlands under the House of Orange to act as a buffer state against France. (Since the 80 Years' War, the southern provinces had been separated from the Netherlands.) But this union lasted only until 1830, when the southern provinces revolted and, as Belgium, secured their separate independence.

**Neutrality: 1830–1940** The Dutch enjoyed a peaceful existence over the next 100 years. In 1848, a year in which Europe was shaken by revolutions, they peacefully secured a more liberal political constitution. In 1840, King William had abdicated in favour of his son, establishing a precedent which was followed in 1948 when the aged Queen Wilhelmina gave up the throne to her daughter, Juliana. The neutral status of the Netherlands made its seat of government, The Hague, acceptable to all the great powers of the world as the seat of the Permanent Court of International Justice.

**Second World War** Dutch neutrality, respected in the First World War, was an early victim of Hitler's ambition to master Europe. On May 10, 1940, the Nazi blitzkrieg (lightning war) struck, and in five days, though the Dutch put up a heroic resistance, the Netherlands was blasted into submission. One of its greatest cities, Rotterdam, was pounded into rubble, and others severely damaged. Queen and Cabinet escaped to London, where – thanks to the Dutch population overseas – they were able to muster considerable forces to help the Allied cause.

Japan's entry into the war in December 1941 came as a second staggering blow. The Dutch territories in Indonesia were speedily overwhelmed by Japanese forces. At home in the Netherlands, the people, though at first wooed by the Nazis, suffered great hardship and developed a determined underground resistance movement. The liberation of the country began in September 1944. Hotly contested battles, such as that

*William of Orange became ruler of both England and the Netherlands, as a result of the 'Glorious Revolution' of 1688*

*The ordered existence of a Dutch bourgeois family is captured by the 17th-century artist Pieter de Hooch*

*From exile in London, Queen Wilhelmina inspired her country's resistance to Nazi invaders in the Second World War*

A 19th-century view
of a whale hunt in
New Zealand waters.
Whale-hunters were
among the first Euro-
peans to be drawn to
New Zealand

## NETHERLANDS *continued*

at Arnhem, were fought between the advancing Allies and the German armies, which were still holding out on Dutch soil when Germany surrendered in May 1945.

**Recent history** After the war, the Netherlands faced immense problems. Its industry had been destroyed. Its efforts to recapture Indonesia from the Indonesian nationalists were in vain; it had lost for ever a tropical empire rich in raw materials.

In coping with these and other difficulties, such as the disastrous floods of 1953, the Netherlands was in the main remarkably successful. Its economy started to expand vigorously and in March 1957 it became a founder-member of the Common Market. Its large natural gas fields provide cheap energy that has spurred industrial development.

*A cable car tips debris into the sea during the construction of a new dyke, part of a land-reclaiming operation in the Netherlands*

# New Zealand

Two large islands in a remote corner of the south Pacific form the independent Commonwealth country of New Zealand. It is a land of spectacular beauty, with active volcanoes, hot springs, massive snow-capped peaks and glaciers. Both sections of New Zealand's population were originally immigrants – the Maoris came from Polynesia more than 600 years ago, the whites from Britain, mainly in the last century. The two groups live in harmony, making New Zealand one of the world's most peaceful societies. The prosperity of its people is largely based upon agriculture and manufacturing.

**First inhabitants** By at least the mid-14th century New Zealand was inhabited by people from East Polynesia, the ancestors of today's Maoris. These people sailed across 1000 miles of ocean in their double-hulled canoes. The Maoris appear to have succeeded an earlier group, also from Polynesia, who are known as 'moa hunters', from the bones of the moa – a flightless bird, now extinct – found in their graves. By the 18th century, the Maoris were a settled society.

**European explorers** The first European to reach New Zealand was the Dutch explorer, Tasman, in 1642. The country was rediscovered by Captain James Cook in 1769. In the course of his historic Pacific voyage, Cook sailed round both the North and the South Islands, drew accurate charts and established contact with the Maoris. European traders and whalers followed. Most of the Maoris at first welcomed the new arrivals, and some traded their goods for muskets with which they attacked their ancient tribal enemies.

**Annexation by Britain: 1840** During the 1830's British humanitarians demanded that New Zealand be annexed to save the Maoris from extinction in their tribal wars, and from exploitation by European traders. At a gathering of Maori chiefs on the North Island in 1840, the British envoy, William Hobson, signed the Treaty of Waitangi, by which the Maoris recognised Queen Victoria as sovereign, in return for protection and a guarantee that they would keep their land.

NEW ZEALAND
**Wellington**
*Pacific
Ocean*

103,736 sq. miles
2,992,700 people
Capital: Wellington

*A Maori beauty. Intermarriage between Maoris and whites is an accepted feature of New Zealand society*

*The Dutch explorer Tasman was the first European to reach New Zealand. He discovered the islands in 1642*

The New Zealand Company, founded by Edward Gibbon Wakefield, bought land and sent British settlers out to farm it. But the terms of the treaty were soon broken as settlers took over Maori land. A Maori revolt in the mid-1840's was crushed. Despite efforts by the governor, Sir George Grey, to give the Maoris greater protection, abuses continued. To resist further claims on their land, some of the tribes united in 1858 under an elected 'king' in the so-called 'King Movement'. In 1860, desperation drove the Maoris to revolt again. Attempts to make peace with the Maoris failed, and fighting dragged on intermittently for ten years.

**Self-government and prosperity** In 1852 Britain granted New Zealand a constitution, with a legislative council to assist the governor and an elected parliament. 'Responsible government' followed in 1856. Maori affairs, however, remained in the governor's hands.

The Maori wars of the 1860's checked economic growth in the North Island, where most of the Maoris lived, but in the South Island, sheep and cattle farming – introduced by the first British settlers – expanded steadily. The discovery of gold in the South Island in 1861 also made the colony richer. From 1870 onwards the economy expanded rapidly as a result of the bold financial policies of Julius Vogel, the country's finance minister. The development of refrigerated cargo ships opened up the huge British market to New Zealand's butter, meat and cheese, and the export of these became the backbone of the nation's economy.

**Social progress in the 1890's** A depression in the early 1890's led to the emergence of a progressive Liberal Party under John Ballance and Richard Seddon. Seddon's government introduced much advanced social legislation: women were given the vote, an arbitration court was set up to settle labour disputes, and in 1898 New Zealand became the first country in the world to introduce non-contributory old-age pensions.

**First World War and after** During the First World War, New Zealand sent 100,000 men – over 9 per cent of the population – to fight at Britain's side in Europe and the Middle East. Their exploits at Gallipoli, as part of the Australian and New Zealand Army Corps (ANZAC), earned them widespread respect.

New Zealand suffered severely from the world slump at the end of the 1920's. The depression that followed helped the rise of the Labour Party, founded in 1916. Labour won support from all classes, by pledging itself to a programme of social welfare and cheap loans to farmers and businessmen. In 1935 Labour formed its first government under Michael Savage. In 1938 a free state health scheme was introduced.

**Pacific power** Between the wars, ties of kinship and affection continued firm with Britain. Partly because of these, New Zealand refused to ratify the 1931 Statute of Westminster, which granted independence to the old 'white' dominions (although it finally did so in 1947). In 1939, New Zealanders again fought alongside British troops – in Greece, Crete, North Africa and Italy.

After the war, New Zealand began to reconsider its position as a European outpost in the Pacific. The country began to forge closer links with Australia, the United States and the nations of Asia and the Pacific. Britain's military withdrawal from south-east Asia and its membership of the Common Market helped to accelerate this process. New Zealand's goods no longer had 'imperial preference' on the British market. However, the country's dependence on Britain was recognised by the Common Market, and special arrangements were made so that New Zealand would have time to find and develop other markets for its produce.

*The swirling shapes and grotesque figures of Maori art reflect its Polynesian origin*

*Sir Keith Holyoake (above) led the National Party government as prime minister from 1960 to 1972. Labour's leader Norman Kirk became prime minister in December 1972*

*New Zealand and Welsh forwards clash at Cardiff Arms Park during the 1972–3 visit of the All Blacks, New Zealand's famous rugby team*

*The city of Léon, founded in 1524 by Fernandez de Cordoba, was Nicaragua's capital until 1855*

# Nicaragua

The largest of the Central American republics, Nicaragua is also the least densely populated. The country is poor and backward, and for much of its history has been in the grip of dictatorship or torn by civil strife. It has a special importance in American affairs because of its position across the route from the north to the trans-oceanic Panama Canal.

**Spanish rule and civil war** Columbus claimed the area for Spain in 1502, and in 1524 Fernandez de Cordoba founded the settlements of Granada and Léon. In common with the rest of Spain's Central American colonies, Nicaragua won independence in 1821. A century of civil conflict and foreign intervention followed. In 1856 an American adventurer, William Walker, with 600 followers – the so-called 'American phalanx' – seized power and installed himself as president. But the following year he was overthrown. The United States government saw Nicaragua as a potential site for a canal linking the Pacific with the Caribbean, but Nicaraguan opposition led them, in the end, to choose Panama. US marines were stationed in the country in 1912 in support of pro-American governments, and remained there for much of the next two decades, finally departing in 1933.

**Rule by the Somoza family** In 1936 Anastasio Somoza, with army backing, took over power and ruled as dictator until his assassination in 1956. He was succeeded by his son, Luis. In 1963 René Schick was elected president as 'front man' for the Somozas, but soon emerged as an independent figure. After his death in office in 1966, the Somoza stranglehold on the country was restored when, in 1967, Luis Somoza's brother, Anastasio Somoza, became president, and restored all the trappings of dictatorship. He was succeeded by a triumvirate in 1972, but maintained his hold on the country and was re-elected president in 1974.

Disaster struck Nicaragua in December 1972, when most of the capital, Managua, was destroyed by an earthquake which killed some 10,000 people.

# Niger

Much of Niger's huge land area is inhabited by nomadic peoples such as the desert Tuaregs. The Sahara covers most of the country, leaving only 2 per cent of the land fit for cultivation by its settled Negro peoples, who are often at bitter odds with the nomadic groups. The discovery of rich uranium deposits in the remote Air Massif during the late 1960's held out the hope of a more prosperous future for Niger.

**Early period** Throughout its history, Niger has known wars, migrations and invasions. For a thousand years it formed part of the ancient civilizations of the Sudan. By the 15th century, a Muslim Tuareg sultanate based upon Agades had grown up, whilst Hausa Negroes entered the south of the country from their homelands in northern Nigeria. Conflict between Muslims and Negroes led to continued unrest. A Hausa kingdom, Gobir, repulsed the Tuaregs in the 18th century, but was swallowed up, after a holy war, by the Muslim sultanate of Sokoto early in the 19th century. The first European travellers to visit the region during this period reported a state of chronic warfare.

**Progress to independence** At the end of the 19th century Niger was occupied by the French – although their control of the region was not complete until after the First World War. In 1921, Niger became a French colony and part of the French West African Federation.

Independence was granted in 1960, and Hamani Diori became the country's first president. In 1974 army chief of staff Lt. Col. Seyni Kountche overthrew Diori, charging him with corruption in dealing with the nation's long drought.

50,193 sq. miles
2,028,500 people
Capital: Managua

*Nicaragua has been ruled since 1936 by members of the Somoza family*

489,189 sq. miles
4,469,300 people
Capital: Niamey

*Muslim and Black Africa meet in Niger. This 16th-century Agades mosque was built by Muslim Tuareg sultans*

# Nigeria

More than 100 different peoples, each with their own language or dialect, make up Nigeria's population, the largest of any African state. The three main groups are the Hausa-Fulani in the north, the Yoruba in the west, and the Ibo in the east. Many Ibos and Yorubas are Christians, while most of the Hausa-Fulani are Muslims.

Although gathered together by the colonial rule of Britain, the three peoples maintained their traditional identities and rivalries. Each, on independence, might have formed a nation on its own. The attempt by one of them, the Ibos, to do this, led to the tragedy of a bloody civil war in which the Ibo state, Biafra, went down to defeat and Nigeria, as a federation, survived.

**The Muslim north** For over 1000 years, from the 8th to the 19th centuries, much of north-eastern Nigeria formed part of the empire of Kanem-Bornu. It was here that Islam made its first appearance in Nigeria, at least as far back as the 11th century. Between Kanem-Bornu and the powerful empires of Songhai and Mali, lay seven Hausa city-states, including Kano, Zaria, Gobir and Katsina. By the 15th century they had become flourishing commercial centres, and by the 18th century their ruling classes had become Muslim. Early in the 19th century, the whole of Hausaland was overrun during a jihad (holy war) launched by the Fulanis under a 'holy man', Uthman dan Fodio. The Fulanis were a nomadic, cattle-rearing people who had begun entering the area from the west in the 16th century. The sultanate of Sokoto was established; from it, Islam penetrated south into the forest areas of Yorubaland.

**The forest states and the Ibo** The Yoruba people, who settled the tropical rain-forests west of the Niger, built up the powerful kingdoms of Benin and Oyo from about the 14th century. Artists of both Benin and the Oyo capital of Ife developed a tradition of magnificent bronze sculpture. By the 19th century, the Oyo empire was disintegrating. During the time of the rise and fall of the Yoruba states, the Ibos to the east of the Niger remained organised in small-scale village communities.

**Europeans and the slave trade** Late in the 15th century the Portuguese, soon to be followed by the Dutch, French and English, established themselves on the coast of Nigeria as slave traders. Many Ibo and Yoruba were taken as slaves, and sold to European slavers by powerful chiefs. In 1807, the British outlawed the trade, forcing the African and European merchants to turn to other commodities, notably palm oil.

**Spread of British control** The flag followed trade. In 1848, a British consul was appointed to look after the interests of British traders in Benin and Biafra. In 1861 Lagos was annexed as a British colony and in 1885 the entire Nigerian coast became the Oil Rivers Protectorate (after 1893, the Niger Coast Protectorate). And in Yorubaland, Christian missionary influence was growing fast. Even so, it was 20 years before the whole of Yorubaland and Iboland came under effective British control. In 1886, the Royal Niger Company was formed by Sir George Goldie to explore and trade with the interior. As the company expanded northwards, it clashed with the Sokoto empire. Company forces under Captain (later Sir) Frederick Lugard concluded treaties or waged campaigns against the Muslim emirates.

**Nigeria under the British** In 1899 the British government took over the administration of northern Nigeria from the Royal Niger Company, and Lugard became governor of the new protectorate of Northern

356,669 sq. miles
79,758,969 people
Capital: Lagos

*A 2000-year-old terracotta head from the Nok culture of northern Nigeria*

*This head of a queen-mother of Benin shows the superb skill achieved by the region's bronze-casters*

*Traditional iron-working: a village foundry in Nigeria in the early years of the 20th century*

## NIGERIA *continued*

Nigeria. Slowly, British Nigeria took shape. In 1906, Lagos was combined with the Protectorate of Southern Nigeria (the Niger Coast). In 1914, Northern and Southern Nigeria were joined up and became the Colony and Protectorate of Nigeria under Lugard.

**Regional differences** Although formally united as a British colony, the three main regions of Nigeria remained very different. The Muslim north was a rigid and conservative society: Christian missions were not permitted and there was little Western education. In the east, the enterprising Ibo left their crowded homeland to work in government and commerce in the north and west – where their presence was often resented. The British built roads and railways, introduced new techniques in agriculture, and built up health education and administrative services.

**Independence** Nigerian nationalism, mainly Ibo-inspired, grew up after the First World War. After years of negotiations, Nigeria became independent in 1960. The constitution of the new state was a federal one, which allowed a large degree of self-government to each of the country's three regions (later, with the creation of the Mid-Western Region from part of the Western Region, four). The old tensions between the regions, however, were not dispelled by independence. The northerners, who dominated the country politically, feared and distrusted the southerners; and the southerners, in their turn, considered the Muslim Hausa-Fulani to be reactionaries who were holding up the progress of Nigeria. Ibo and Yoruba distrusted each other. The powder-keg exploded in January, 1966, when a group of young Ibo army officers overthrew the federal government. Many political leaders, including the Prime Minister, Sir Tafawa Balewa, were murdered. Leadership passed to General Ironsi, an Ibo, but July 1966 saw a second military coup in which Ironsi was killed. The new leader, General Gowon, a Christian northerner, was unable to prevent the massacre of Ibos in the north: an estimated 10,000–30,000 were killed and a further million fled the region.

**Civil war and after** Gowon's plans to abolish the regions and substitute 12 states, none of which would be powerful enough to dominate the federation, were resisted by Colonel Ojukwu, an Ibo and the military governor of the oil-rich Eastern Region. In June 1967, Ojukwu declared the secession of the east as the independent state of Biafra. A violent civil war broke out. Ibo resistance, strengthened in the later stages of the war by their fear that surrender would mean their annihilation as a people, continued until January 1970, when Ojukwu fled to asylum in the Ivory Coast.

Following Biafra's collapse, a massive programme of famine relief was organised by many countries. It is not known how many people died in the war, but the toll was probably over a million. After the war – one of the most tragic events in the history of modern Africa – the 12-state constitution was imposed. Economic and political reconstruction continued under Gowon – aided by a boom in oil production that placed Nigeria eighth among the world's oil-producing countries. Biafra was reinstated as the Central Eastern state.

*Frederick Lugard helped to create British Nigeria, and became its first governor in 1914*

*General Gowon became Nigeria's head of state in July 1966*

*Biafrans (left), in Nigeria's tragic civil war of 1967–70, resisted desperately from fear of annihilation as a people*

# Norway

Norwegians have traditionally looked to the sea for their livelihood and inspiration. A thousand years ago, the Vikings of Norway burst on to the northern oceans in a bold quest for land, gold and adventure. Their skill in sailing and ship-building, and also their courage and cruelty, became legendary throughout Europe. Therefore it was fitting that new wealth came from the sea to Norway in the mid-1970's with the discovery and development of huge off-shore oil fields.

**Vikings in Norway** Some 2000 years ago, Germanic tribes moved north into the Scandinavian lands, including Norway, from the European mainland. They soon overcame the hunters and fishermen who already lived there, and formed themselves into small kingdoms, ruled by powerful jarls (earls). These people, the Vikings, were a pagan warrior race, who displayed remarkable enterprise and daring. In their longships, they ventured to many lands, from Russia to North America. Between AD 750 and 1000 they pillaged and plundered the coasts of Britain and France, striking terror into the hearts of Christian men and women.

In 872, the ruler of eastern Norway, Harold Fairhair, conquered the other kingdoms and set up the first Norwegian monarchy. Christianity reached the country under Olaf I (995–1000) and spread over the whole of Norway under his successor, Olaf II. In 1028, Olaf II was deposed in a Danish-inspired revolt, and Norway was torn by civil war. This was finally ended by the accession of a strong king, Sverre, to the throne. He and his successors, Haakon IV (1217–63) and Magnus VI (1263–80), known as the 'Law Mender', brought order to the country. Its culture and economy flourished and the first cities, notably Bergen, were built.

**Rule by Denmark and Sweden** With the death of Haakon V in 1319, the male line of the Norwegian monarchy died out and Norway was united with Sweden. The country was now weakened by plague – in which half its population died – and threatened by the stranglehold the German Hanseatic League developed over its trade. In 1397, Norway and Sweden came under Danish rule. Sweden soon broke away, but Norway remained a Danish province for more than 400 years.

The union with Denmark, cemented by mutual hostility towards Sweden, lasted until the end of the 18th century. In the Napoleonic Wars, however, Denmark's alliance with Napoleon damaged Norwegian trade, which was largely carried on with Britain. At the end of the wars, Norway tried to become independent. But this was not yet to be – the victorious allies had already decided to give the country to Sweden.

**Independent Norway** Sweden promised to give Norway considerable autonomy and the country was allowed its own parliament. But, by the end of the 19th century, Sweden's political dominance and a clash of economic interests led to a revival of hostility between the two nations. In 1905, Norway's parliament declared

125,181 sq. miles
4,000,000 people
Capital: Oslo

*A Viking warrior (right) disposes of an enemy in this medieval carving. The Viking sagas, written mainly in prose, record many such war-like deeds*

*Perspective map of Bergen in 1740, in Bergen University Museum. The city is Norway's most important commercial port as well as being a major fishing centre*

*An early 18th-century Norwegian cork sculpture of a navigator*

*Henrik Ibsen (1828–1906), Norwegian poet and dramatist, outraged conventional opinion in his day with his candid plays about social problems*

the union at an end and Charles of Denmark was elected the country's ruler, taking the title of Haakon VII.

Norway was neutral in the First World War, and sought to remain so in the Second. But in April 1940, German troops invaded the country. A puppet government was set up under Vidkun Quisling, whose name became a universal byword for treachery. Many Norwegians fought in the underground, and the country's shipping fleet joined the allies. The Germans held the country until the end of the war in 1945.

After the war, American aid speeded Norway's economic recovery. The country's Labour Party, continuously in power from 1945 to 1965, sponsored much progressive social legislation. Norway became a member of NATO in 1949, though it refused to allow military bases to be set up in the country for fear of Russian reprisals – Norway is the only NATO country which has a common frontier with the Soviet Union. The country was a founder-member of EFTA (European Free Trade Association) in 1959; in 1972, following a government decision to enter the Common Market, a referendum was held, which resulted in a majority vote against membership.

*Svolvaer, in the Lofoten Islands, a typical Norwegian fjord town whose livelihood is the fishing industry*

# Oman

The sultanate of Oman – known as Muscat and Oman until 1970 – covers the south-eastern corner of the Arabian peninsula. Oman's dates, grown on its fertile coastal plain, are famous for their quality. Much of the country's interior is barren.

The people of Oman were converted to Islam in the 7th century by Saudi Arabian traders. Their first contact with Europeans was with the Portuguese, who conquered the country in the 16th century, and used it as a base from which to control trade in the Persian Gulf. The Portuguese were driven out in the mid-17th century, and in 1741 the present al-bu-Said dynasty came to power.

Since 1891, when the ruling sultan signed an agreement with Britain, Oman has been under strong British influence. Britain intervened on several occasions over the years to help put down revolts. A major upheaval occurred in 1959, when the Imam of Oman, a religious leader, sought independence for the people of the interior. He was forced into exile in Saudi Arabia.

Qabus bin Said came to power as sultan in 1970, after overthrowing his father Said bin Taimur, who had ruled the country since 1932. The new sultan changed the country's name to Oman and announced plans for economic and social reforms. By establishing friendly relations with Saudi Arabia, he neutralised what little support was left for the Imam.

The sultan was faced with a revolt backed by neighbouring Southern Yemen in the large south-western province of Dhofar. His forces pacified large areas of the province, but over 50 per cent of the country's oil revenues had to be diverted from reform programmes into the defence budget.

82,030 sq. miles
740,900 people
Capital: Muscat

*Qabus bin Said overthrew his father, Said bin Taimur, in a palace revolution and became Sultan of Oman in 1970*

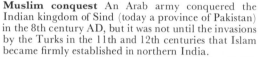

# Pakistan

Following Britain's withdrawal in 1947, the Indian subcontinent was partitioned into two states: Pakistan, predominantly Muslim, and India, mainly Hindu. Pakistan itself was divided into eastern and western 'wings', separated by more than a thousand miles of Indian territory. The new state lasted in this form for only 25 years. The east broke away in 1971, and in 1972 became the independent republic of Bangladesh.

The drive for a separate Muslim state in India started in the 1930's, when the poet Muhammad Iqbal and others urged the creation of a Muslim 'homeland' in the north-western region. In ancient times, this area was a natural corridor for invaders from Central Asia. It was from the north-west that the first Muslim conquerors came. Their successors, the Mughals or Moguls, eventually dominated the whole of India until the British conquest in the 18th century.

310,403 sq. miles
64,900,000 people
Capital: Islamai

**Muslim conquest** An Arab army conquered the Indian kingdom of Sind (today a province of Pakistan) in the 8th century AD, but it was not until the invasions by the Turks in the 11th and 12th centuries that Islam became firmly established in northern India.

The power of the Muslim sultanate, centred on Delhi, soon spread throughout northern India, and by 1320 it had reached the far south. But in 1398 the Tatar conqueror Tamerlane sacked Delhi, and the sultanate broke up into a number of small Muslim kingdoms.

In 1526 a new Muslim conqueror appeared on the Indian scene. Babur, a descendant of Tamerlane and Genghis Khan, defeated the reigning sultan, Ibrahim Lodi, at the battle of Panipat and set himself on the throne. Because of his ancestry, his dynasty took the name Mughal (Mongol).

Internal revolt in the early 18th century so weakened the empire that it fell – first to Hindu warriors, the Marathas, and then to the British. With British expansion in India, Mughal power came to an end.

For a time, the British used Muslim officials in their administration, but by the beginning of the 19th century Muslims were being replaced by young men fresh from Britain. As the British introduced their own Western system of justice, the Muslim legal system was abandoned. In 1835 English replaced Persian as the official language of government.

*Under Aurangzeb (1658–1707) the Mughal Empire reached its peak*

**Muslim rebirth and growth of separatism** After the failure of the Indian Mutiny (1857–9), the position of Indian Muslims became much worse. Though the mutiny had been started by Hindus, the British believed that it had been a Muslim attempt to restore the Mughal Empire, and made it clear that Muslims would not be trusted in positions of responsibility in future. The Muslim response was to strengthen their faith, as a symbol of solidarity.

After the great upsurge of Hindu nationalism created by resentment at the partition of Bengal by the British in 1905, it was decided to grant all Indians the right to some share in government. But the fear of Hindu domination alarmed the Muslims, and they demanded safeguards in the form of separate Muslim constituencies. These demands were accepted, and a political party known as the Muslim League was founded in 1906.

In 1930, Muhammad Iqbal (1873–1938), a leading poet, suggested that a separate Muslim 'homeland' should be created in north-west India. In 1933 Chaudhuri Rahmat Ali coined the name 'Pakistan' for this homeland – an Urdu word meaning 'land of the pure'.

**Creation of Pakistan** Muhammad Ali Jinnah (1876–1948) began his political life as a member of the Indian National Congress. At first he was a believer in Hindu-Muslim unity, though he insisted on proper safeguards for the Muslim minority. He broke with Congress, however, disagreeing with Gandhi's policy of non-cooperation with the British. In 1935, after the announcement that parliaments were to be set up in all the provinces of British India, he led the Muslim League in

*Warriors of the Orakzai, a Pathan tribe of the North-west Frontier region*

427

## PAKISTAN *continued*

its election battle. The League's showing was only modest, and the victorious Congress Party rejected an offer of co-operation by Jinnah. As a result, Jinnah proclaimed his goal to be the creation of Pakistan.

Throughout the negotiations with the British over the transfer of power in India, Jinnah maintained his stand. In June 1947 the British government agreed to his demands and handed over power to two new states – India and Pakistan. The two-part Pakistan the Muslims won was divided by over 1000 miles of Indian territory, and by linguistic and racial differences.

The division of British India meant that millions of both Hindus and Muslims were left in the 'wrong' country. At least 600,000 people died in clashes between the Hindus and Muslims, while 14 million more were uprooted from their homes, to stream over the borders as refugees.

From partition onwards, India and Pakistan disputed the fate of Kashmir, which lay on the border between them. It had a predominantly Muslim population, but its Hindu ruler chose to join India. Late in 1947 an undeclared war was fought there between the Indian and Pakistani armies. It was only temporarily settled by the division of Kashmir along a cease-fire line.

**Politics and war: 1947–65** Until his death in September 1948, Jinnah was undisputed dictator of Pakistan. After the assassination of his chosen successor, Liaquat Ali Khan, in 1951, rival politicians struggled for power. East Pakistan became convinced that the western-based central government was discriminating against it, and political chaos followed.

In September 1954 the government declared a state of emergency and dissolved the National Assembly. After two years of deliberation, a new constitution was adopted making Pakistan an Islamic republic. General Iskandar Mirza became its first president.

Constitutional change, however, made no difference to the anarchy of Pakistan's political and economic life. In October 1958 Mirza abolished political parties and declared martial law. Three weeks later Mirza himself was overthrown by the army, and his place was taken by General Ayub Khan. A new constitution was introduced, and Ayub, ending martial law, became president. Pakistan, however, remained dominated by its army. Though Pakistan's relations with India gradually improved, the question of Kashmir was a running sore. War finally broke out between Pakistan and India in September 1965. It was short and inconclusive; by the Tashkent Agreement both sides pledged themselves to return to the positions they had held before the war.

**East Pakistan breaks away** Strikes, riots, assassinations, and demands for democratic elections led to the fall of Ayub Khan in 1969. He was replaced by General Yahya Khan. Yahya announced that general elections would be held in 1970 and a new constitution introduced by January 1971.

In the east, the result of the elections was an overwhelming majority for Sheikh Mujibur Rahman and his Awami League. Mujibur had made it clear that his party wanted an end to East Pakistan's political status as a 'poor relation', when, in fact, it produced much of the country's revenue. His victory opened up the prospect of great changes in the central government which, since independence, had been dominated by the western half of Pakistan. Politicians in the west, such as Zulfikar Ali Bhutto, urged Yahya to stop Sheikh Mujibur from taking office.

After talks between Yahya and Mujibur failed, units of the army – predominantly West Pakistan-manned – were sent to the east to impose martial law. The crisis worsened during the summer of 1971, and East Pakistan proclaimed itself an independent republic under the name of Bangladesh. West Pakistani troops went to more and more extreme lengths to crush the secessionists. India, unable any longer to bear the burden of feeding 6 million Pakistani refugees who had found sanctuary,

*Muhammad Ali Jinnah, whose efforts led to the formation of Pakistan in 1947*

*Under Ayub Khan's presidency, the army dominated the politics of Pakistan*

finally intervened. After a fortnight of bitter fighting the Pakistani army in the east surrendered. In the west, Yahya was replaced by Bhutto as president.

After a new parliamentary constitution was adopted in 1973, Bhutto gave up the presidency to head the new government as prime minister. His socialist government took over the nation's basic industries. Agreements were signed in 1974 with Bangladesh and India repatriating war prisoners and refugees.

# Panama

Panama's position gives it a special importance – it lies between the Caribbean and the Pacific, on the isthmus linking Central and South America. The Panama Canal, completed in 1914, bisects the country; the Canal Zone, extending 5 miles on both sides of the waterway, is controlled by the United States.

The first European to sight the coast of Panama was Rodrigo de Bastidas, in 1501, and the region was annexed a year later by Christopher Columbus in the name of Spain. In 1513, the explorer Vasco Nunez de Balboa made a historic journey across the isthmus to become the first white man to set eyes on the eastern shores of the Pacific. With the break-up of Spain's American empire in the early 19th century, Panama became a province of newly independent Colombia.

**Making the canal** In 1879 the first serious attempt to cut a canal through the isthmus was made by Ferdinand de Lesseps, creator of the Suez Canal. It ended in disaster – more than 25,000 workmen died, mainly from malaria and yellow fever. The United States government took up the project. In 1903, an uprising in Panama, encouraged by the United States because of Colombia's opposition to the canal scheme, led to Panamanian independence. The new republic gave the United States permission to build and control the canal. Work was begun in 1907, after three years' preparation, and the canal was opened in 1914.

Panamanian politics have often been turbulent. President José Remon was assassinated in 1955. President Arnolfo Arias was deposed in 1968 by a military coup under General Omar Torrijos, whose government demanded the return of the Canal Zone and control of the canal from the United States.

29,208 sq. miles
1,615,000 people
Capital: Panama

# Papua New Guinea

The newest independent nation of the South Pacific, Papua New Guinea covers the eastern half of the huge tropical island of New Guinea. The western half of the island is a province of Indonesia. Much of the mountainous, heavily forested island remains unexplored, so it is not known what wealth of natural resources remain to be discovered, but copper and gold are now mined for export.

Most of the people of the nation live in tribes, fishing and growing food crops for their own use. Some are headhunters and cannibals.

The first European to discover New Guinea was the Portuguese governor of the Molucca Islands, Jorge de Meneses, in 1526. No attempt to colonize the island was made until the 1800's. The Netherlands claimed western New Guinea in 1828. Queensland, Australia, staked its claim on southeastern New Guinea in 1883, and Germany made northeastern New Guinea part of its empire in 1884.

Australia made southeastern New Guinea the Territory of Papua in 1906. After Germany's defeat in World War I, the League of Nations gave Australia control of the former German colony. Australia consolidated eastern New Guinea in a single administration called Papua New Guinea in 1949. Steps toward self-government began in 1964 with election of the first house of assembly. Australia granted complete self-government in 1973. Independence followed a year later with Michael Somare as chief minister.

178,260 sq. miles
2,664,000 people
Capital:
Port Moresby

## Paraguay

A dictator's dream of national glory led Paraguay into the most destructive war in South American history – the 'War of the Triple Alliance' against Argentina, Uruguay and Brazil in the 1860's. Paraguay fought another devastating war in the 1930's with Bolivia. The damage it suffered in both wars is the main reason why Paraguay is such a poor and backward country.

**Early history** Spanish conquistadores came to land-locked Paraguay in 1524. They intermarried with the docile Guaraní Indians, and founded Asunción, the country's present-day capital, in 1537. During the 16th and 17th centuries, Jesuit missionaries were the dominant influence in the country.

Revolt against Spain broke out in 1721, when José de Antequera led the comuneros (citizens) of Asunción in a move to secure their freedom from the autocratic rule of the Spanish viceroy in far-away Peru. The revolt lasted for a decade before it was finally suppressed and de Antequera was executed. In 1811, however, as Spanish rule crumbled throughout South America, Paraguay won independence in a bloodless revolution.

**Rule of the dictators** No sooner had freedom been won from Spain than it was lost, when José Gaspar Francia declared himself dictator in 1814. He met with no resistance and ruled until 1840, when he was succeeded by Carlos Antonio López. In 1862 Francisco Solano López took over from his father.

In 1865 López plunged his country into war with Brazil, Argentina and Uruguay. But, when the war ended in 1870, Paraguay lay in ruins. The terrible price paid in men and materials lay at the root of Paraguay's economic problems for years to come. In 1932 a dispute with Bolivia over the ownership of the Chaco region led to a three-year war. This time, Paraguay emerged victorious, but at the cost of 40,000 men.

Paraguay's succession of short-lived governments was ended by Higinio Morínigo, who made himself dictator in 1940. Under his rule, Paraguay began to recover from the Chaco War, but he was ousted in 1948. After further instability, General Alfredo Stroessner seized power in 1954. His regime became noted for its ruthless suppression of all opposition and the fierce hostility it aroused in the Roman Catholic Church.

## Peru

The lure of gold and silver drew Spanish adventurers to Peru in the 16th century. They found there an Inca Empire rich in treasure which they brutally plundered. Mineral wealth made Peru a centre-piece of Spain's empire in America: and it was the last South American country to gain independence.

More than half of all Peruvians are Indians, many of them descended from the Incas. For centuries, the Indians were slaves, working in the mines of the Andes for European masters. Mining still plays an important part in Peru's economy, and under the lofty peaks of the Andes lie vast resources of many valuable metals, including copper, silver and iron ore.

**Rise and fall of the Incas** About 20,000 years after the first nomadic Indian settlers arrived in the area of present-day Peru, the Incas founded a kingdom with its capital at Cuzco *c.* 1200. At its height, the empire had 12 million subjects. Its religion was based on sun-worship, and its ruler, the Sapa Inca, was revered as a god. His word was law throughout the empire.

The first white man to land in Peru was the Spanish conquistador, Francisco Pizarro, who in 1530 led 180 soldiers south from Panama. Pizarro captured the Inca

*The colonial splendour of the presidential palace in Asunción contrasts vividly with a peasant's simple bullock cart*

157,047 sq. miles
2,305,000 people
Capital: Asunción

*Francisco Solano López (1827–70) led Paraguay into a war in which he himself was killed*

496,225 sq. miles
15,359,200 people
Capital: Lima

emperor, Atahuallpa, and eliminated the entire leadership of the Inca Empire – some 4000 strong. Leaderless, the Incas were easily conquered. Atahuallpa was murdered, and his capital, Cuzco, taken.

Peru rapidly became the most important Spanish territory in the New World. Lima, the country's present capital, was established in 1535 as the seat of government for Spain's possessions in South America, except Venezuela. The Incas were forced into slavery to work the gold and silver mines of the Andes.

**Republican Peru** The country was the last of Spain's South American colonies to gain independence; it was freed in 1826 by a force of Argentinians and Bolivians under José de San Martin and Simon Bolívar. In 1864, Spain, which had never recognised Peru's independence, seized the Chinca islands, rich in *guano* fertiliser – Peru's main source of wealth at that time. Joined by its neighbours, Chile, Ecuador and Bolivia, Peru declared war on Spain. Peace was not made until 1879, when Spain formally recognised Peru's independence.

During this period, however, the allies had fallen out because they feared Chile's territorial and economic ambitions. Peru was eventually attacked by Chile, which seized Peru's nitrate-producing provinces, Tacna, Arica and Tarapaca. The dispute was not settled until 1929, when Chile gave Tacna back to Peru.

**Recovery and struggle** As a result of these wars, Peru's finances were ruined. But recovery soon began, first under Andres Caceres, elected president in 1886, and then under Augusto Leguia, president from 1908 to 1912. He seized power again in 1919 and ruled as dictator until 1930. Little economic progress was made or political stability achieved during the next few decades. A mounting economic crisis in 1968 finally provoked a left-wing military coup which put General Velasco Alvarado in power. Though a programme of reform was set up, the government had to face strikes and riots caused by dissident left-wing groups.

*Francisco Pizarro (c. 1471–1541) invaded and subdued the Inca Empire with a force of only 180 men*

*General Velasco Alvarado, whose left-wing military regime took control in Peru in 1968*

*The majestic ruins of the fortress of Sacsahuaman in Cuzco, which took 30,000 workmen 70 years to build, are a potent reminder of Inca imperial greatness*

## Philippines

Three-and-a-half centuries of foreign rule – first by Spain, and then by the United States – superimposed a Western-style culture on the Muslim way of life in this outcrop of islands. Spain gave the Philippines its main religion, Roman Catholicism. American influence shows in the country's bustling skyscraper cities, such as Manila, and in the use of English as the main language.

The Republic of the Philippines was established in 1946. It consists of some 7000 islands, many of them uninhabited. Almost half the land area is covered in rich forest, whose timber is a valuable export.

**First Filipinos** The first inhabitants of the Philippines were immigrants of Malayan origin. They were a primitive people, with no knowledge of agriculture, who lived by hunting and fruit-gathering. From *c.* 3000 BC onwards, the Malays were joined by a more advanced race from Indonesia. Gradually the two peoples merged, building up a tribal system known as the *barangay*.

In the 13th century AD, the Filipinos were converted to Islam, which reached them through missionaries who travelled to the islands from the Muslim empires of

115,830 sq. miles
41,435,100 people
Capital: Quezon

*Ferdinand Magellan, the first European to land in the Philippines, was killed in a tribal skirmish by Chief Lapulupa*

## PHILIPPINES *continued*

Indonesia. Islamic influence continued unchallenged for 300 years, until the arrival of the first Europeans – Spanish explorers – in the 16th century.

**Foreign rule** In 1521 the explorer Ferdinand Magellan landed in the Philippines during his attempt to sail round the world – only to be killed by a Filipino chieftain, Chief Lapulupa, in a tribal skirmish. It was not until 1564 that another explorer, Miguel López de Legaspi, arrived and with his troops formally claimed the islands for his master, Philip II of Spain.

De Legaspi's main purpose was to bring Christianity to the islanders. Within 20 years he had established Spanish control over all the inhabited areas, with the exception of the Muslim areas of Mindanao and Sulu.

Spanish rule lasted until the end of the 19th century, when it was challenged by a growing nationalist movement, inspired by the Filipino writer and patriot, José Rizal. An unsuccessful revolt against Spain broke out in 1896. Rizal was executed, but the rebellion continued under the leadership of Emilio Aguinaldo.

Rebel guerrillas fought Spanish regulars until 1898. In that year, war broke out between the United States and Spain, the immediate cause being American indignation over the oppressive Spanish rule of Cuba. As part of America's strategy, Admiral Dewey destroyed a Spanish fleet in Manila Bay, and American troops landed in the Philippines. Within months Spain surrendered and, under a treaty, ceded the islands to the United States for 20 million dollars.

The Filipinos had believed that the United States would give them independence, but they now saw the prospect of self-government removed to the distant future. Fighting soon broke out; it lasted for two years before Filipino resistance was finally suppressed. But in 1935 the United States gave the islands internal self-government, and promised that they would become completely independent in ten years' time.

**Japanese invasion** In December 1941 Japan launched a surprise attack on the Philippines. Within a month Japanese troops had occupied Manila, where they set up a puppet government. After fierce battles at Bataan and Corregidor, American and Filipino troops were forced to surrender in May 1942. In October 1944 American forces, under General MacArthur, returned to the country, completing its liberation by July 1945.

**Independence** The Philippines became an independent republic in July 1946. It survived a rebellion by Communist guerrillas, the Hukbalahaps (People's Liberation Army), popularly known as 'Huks'. The country also made slow but steady progress in developing its economy. This was aided by large-scale American investment.

Under President Ferdinand Marcos, re-elected to a second term of office in 1969, discontent again grew. Students allied with workers in mass anti-government demonstrations over the issues of political corruption, poverty and continuing American influence. In the provinces, Huk guerrilla activity flared up again. There was also conflict between government forces and Muslim insurgents. Marcos placed the country under martial law, and in 1973 announced a new constitution which enabled him to rule with unlimited powers for an indefinite period.

*Miguel López de Legaspi, conqueror of Philippines for Spain, brought Christianity to the islands*

*Ramon Magsaysay was president of the Philippines from 1953 to 1957. He worked with the USA to build up Filipino prosperity*

*Mount Taal erupts. Volcanoes are a prominent feature in the tropical landscape of the Philippines*

# Poland

Under the great Jagiellon dynasty in the 16th century, Poland was the heart of an empire stretching across Europe from the Baltic to the Black Sea. But for much of their modern history the Poles have been a nation without a country. From 1795 to 1918 the Polish state vanished entirely from the map of Europe, victim of a series of 'partitions' carried out by its powerful and acquisitive neighbours. The Poles recovered their independence after the First World War, only to see their land dismembered again a generation later.

Through all these upheavals the Poles have never lost their tradition of intense patriotism, which dates back 1000 years. An important factor in maintaining Polish unity has been the strength of the Roman Catholic Church, and even in the Communist Poland of today, religion flourishes with an obstinate vitality.

**Emergence of a nation** The Polish nation was formed in the 10th century AD from a group of Slav tribes occupying the plains through which the River Vistula winds to the Baltic Sea. The dominant tribe were the Polians, who gave the new nation its name and its first ruler – Mieszko I (962–92), founder of the Piast dynasty.

Under Mieszko, the Poles were converted to Christianity from 966 onwards. Fearing invasion by pagan German tribes, Mieszko accepted the overlordship of the Holy Roman Emperor, so establishing a link between Poland and Western Christendom.

Mieszko's son, Boleslaw I (992–1025), known as 'the Brave' waged war in the west, against the Holy Roman Emperor, Henry II, while in the east he pushed his boundaries as far as Kiev. Boleslaw demonstrated his independence of the pope as well as of the emperor by personally appointing the first archbishop to Gniezno in 1000. The cathedral there was to be the scene of all Polish coronations for the next 300 years.

Just over a century after Boleslaw's death, the powerful state which he had created broke up, when Boleslaw III (1085–1138) divided his domains among his sons on his death. Split into many small states, Poland was unable to resist the challenge of new and powerful foreign enemies. The country was swept by Tatar invasion in 1241, while in the west a new threat to the Poles arose – a German military order called the Teutonic Knights, with its base in Prussia. But the power of the Knights was eventually destroyed in 1410.

To improve its prosperity, each small state encouraged immigration from the more advanced West. Many immigrants were Jews, victims of Christian persecution in Germany and other countries. Poland soon had the largest Jewish community in Europe.

**Revival of Poland** Wladislaw the Short (1320–33) reunited the fragmented kingdom and began the revival of Poland, a task continued by his son, Casimir the Great (1333–70). Casimir's long reign gave Poland 37 years of peace and prosperity. Cultured and intellectual, he founded the University of Cracow in 1364, next to Prague the oldest university in eastern Europe. He also gave more freedom to the Jews, and improved the lot of the peasants, punishing those among his nobles who oppressed them.

On Casimir's death, his kingdom passed to his nephew, Louis I of Hungary. But on Louis's death in 1382, Poland became closely associated with the powerful state of Lithuania to the east. Louis's younger daughter, Jadwiga, married Ladislaw Jagiello, Grand Duke of Lithuania. The Jagiellon dynasty which they founded ruled Poland for the next 200 years.

120,725 sq. miles
33,541,300 people
Capital: Warsaw

*The enlightened policies of Casimir the Great (1333–70) improved the welfare of Poland's people*

Poland

## Jagiellon dynasty

Under the Jagiellons, Poland became one of the most powerful states in Europe. By the mid-16th century its territories stretched from the Baltic to the Black Sea. Cracow, the Jagiellon capital, was a flourishing commercial centre, occupying a key position on the trade routes to Muscovy and Asia. In this 'golden age', the arts and sciences flourished. It was at the University of Cracow that the Polish astronomer, Copernicus, the founder of modern astronomy, and the first man to establish that the sun is the centre of the solar system, began his studies in 1491.

Jagiellon Poland had two weaknesses. The Jagiellons kept the old warrior nobility in check, but they failed to deprive it of power, as other European sovereigns managed to do. Moreover, they ruled a multi-national state, which included within its borders Prussians, Lithuanians, Ukrainians and Russians, and in which the Poles formed a minority.

One Jagiellon ruler, Sigismund Augustus (1548–72), attempted to transform the Polish state into an empire. He promoted unity among his divided peoples by establishing a strong central administration. By the Union of Lublin in 1569, he merged Poland and Lithuania into one state. But in 1572 he died without an heir, and the Polish nobles reasserted their old-established right to elect a new ruler. After this, no Polish ruler was in a position to consolidate the empire, and Poland began to decline as a great power.

*Poland enjoyed a cultural golden age during the reign of Sigismund Augustus (1548–72). He left no heir, and with his death the country's Jagiellon dynasty came to an end*

## Rule by elected kings

As the nobles were too jealous of one another to elect one of their own number as king, it now became customary for foreigners to be brought in to rule Poland. The first to be elected was a Frenchman, Henry of Valois. He was followed by a Hungarian, Stephen Bathory, and then by three rulers from the Swedish Vasa dynasty. Many of these foreign monarchs dragged the country into war to satisfy their own non-Polish ambitions. At first, Poland was successful; in 1610, under the Swedish king, Sigismund III, its troops even occupied Moscow. But by the mid-17th century, the country had been exhausted by war and by the squabbles of its nobility. The Diet (parliament) had been reduced to impotence by the introduction of the *liberum veto*. This meant that a single deputy could put a halt to any legislation. Poland's last great military success was in 1683 when, under John Sobieski, its armies lifted the Turkish siege of Vienna. This decisive victory ended the Islamic menace to Europe.

Powerful enemies – Russia to the east and Sweden to the north – had also emerged to threaten Polish territory. Gradually, Poland lost many of its possessions, and by the early 18th century the country had become the helpless battleground for foreign armies.

*John Sobieski, King of Poland from 1674 to 1696, strikes a heroic pose in this print. His armies ended the Turkish menace to Europe by raising the siege of Vienna in 1683*

## Partition of Poland

Having defeated Sweden in war for mastery of the Baltic, Russia became Poland's main enemy in the 18th century. But Russia was not the only power to have grown in ambition while Poland declined. Frederick the Great of Prussia and Maria Theresa of Austria also had designs on their neighbour. The three powers descended like vultures on Poland in 1772 and stripped it of a quarter of its territory.

Too late, the disunited Poles sank their differences. Conspiracies against the foreign oppressors gave way to desperate armed resistance after Prussia and Russia again partitioned the country in 1793. Tadeus

*In this Russian view of the Polish rising of 1863, peasants capture Polish rebels. The brutal suppression of the revolt shocked liberal opinion*

Kosciuszko, who had fought for the American colonists in the War of Independence, led his countrymen against the Russians and Prussians. He was defeated near Warsaw and taken prisoner. Two years later, the last king of Poland, the cultured but ineffectual Stanislaw Poniatowski, resigned his crown, and his country vanished from the map of Europe, swallowed up entirely in a third partition between Russia, Prussia and Austria. The Poles' humiliation was complete.

## Poland in bondage

For a century and a quarter, the Polish nation lived only in the hearts and minds of its people. For a few brief years during the Napoleonic Wars, the Poles looked like regaining some freedom. When Napoleon attacked Russia in 1812, he courted the Poles by creating the Grand Duchy of Warsaw, and Polish lancers fought in his armies. But in 1815, the Congress of Vienna again divided Poland between the three powers of Russia, Prussia and Austria. The tsar's portion, known as 'Congress Poland', was given its own constitution, but it had no real independence.

Late in 1830 a military revolt in Warsaw expelled the grand duke who acted as Russian viceroy. The revolt developed into a national crusade against Russia. The Poles mustered an army of 80,000 men, with guns and cavalry, but they were soon defeated. So was an insurrection of ill-armed peasants in 1863. The repression undertaken by the Russians to crush the revolt, and their reprisals after it, shocked the conscience of western Europe. Reaction was especially strong in France, for long the headquarters of Polish nationalists exiled from their country. Emperor Napoleon III appealed to the tsar to moderate his policies, but to no avail. After this, the country was absorbed into Russia, and the classes capable of giving a patriotic lead – priests, aristocrats and intellectuals – were closely watched by the all-powerful secret police.

Prussia, too, attacked Polish patriotism by restricting the use of the Polish language, and by encouraging thousands of Germans to settle in its Polish territories. Austria, whose share of Poland was Galicia, showed more consideration for Polish feelings.

The outbreak of the First World War in 1914 brought a ray of hope to the Poles, for the ill-equipped armies of the tsar were unable to hold their Polish territory. Almost exactly a year after the outbreak of war, the Germans marched into Warsaw. To win Polish co-operation they promised Poland independence.

The Poles responded with little enthusiasm to German promises. They saw no likelihood of being allowed to reunite with their oppressed fellow-countrymen in Prussia. They regarded the Germans as hereditary enemies hardly less hateful than the Russians. An attempt to recruit a Polish army to fight for the Kaiser met with little success.

The Poles looked with more hope to the allies, especially to the United States, where tireless propaganda for their cause was conducted by the world-famous Polish pianist, Paderewski. Their hopes were answered when President Wilson pledged the allies to create a 'united, independent and autonomous Poland'. In November 1918, when Germany surrendered, the Poles disarmed the German garrison in Warsaw and proclaimed an independent republic.

## Poland reborn: 1918–23

The new state faced many problems, especially over the question of frontiers. The country's western boundaries were settled at Versailles, where the international prestige of Paderewski guaranteed respect for the government of which he was briefly both prime minister and foreign minister.

Eastwards, however, where the new Russian Communist regime was struggling to establish itself, boundaries were drawn with the bayonet rather than the pen. The Poles found their military leader in Joseph Pilsudski (1863–1935), a Socialist with an impressive record of patriotism. In 1920 he led his forces deep into the Ukraine and captured Kiev. Though he and his forces were driven back by the Russians, he decisively defeated the Red Army at the gates of Warsaw. Poland

*Frédéric Chopin, Poland's greatest composer, was a fervent nationalist. His 'Revolutionary Etude' epitomised Poland's longing for independence*

*Pianist turned politician, Ignace Jan Paderewski became head of the Polish government in 1919*

Marshal Pilsudski
became virtual
dictator of Poland
after a coup in 1926

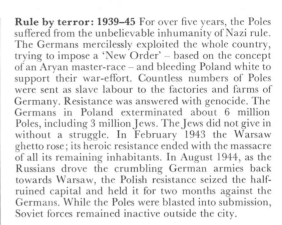

German troops search
a Polish Jew outside
the Warsaw ghetto. In
1943 the Jews of the
ghetto rose against
their Nazi conquerors
but, after a bitter
struggle, the rising
was mercilessly crushed

## POLAND *continued*

also had to settle boundary disputes with Lithuania and a plebiscite was held in Upper Silesia to fix the boundary with Germany. Not until 1923 was the last frontier settled. The new Poland's only access to the sea was by the so-called 'Polish corridor'. This link with the Baltic cut through German territory, dividing East Prussia from the rest of Germany, and thus contained the seeds of future disaster for the country.

**Pilsudski's Poland** Inexperienced in self-government, the liberated Poles found it hard to create a strong democratic system. In addition, there were considerable economic problems. Marshal Pilsudski seized power in a military coup in 1926, resigned it in 1928, seized it again in 1930 and remained master of Poland until his death in 1935. He was succeeded by Marshal Smigly-Rydz, who headed a government dominated by a clique of army officers and landowners.

Long accustomed to being an oppressed minority under foreign rule, the Poles now found themselves coping with the situation in reverse, for in becoming united they had acquired millions of non-Polish citizens – notably the Germans settled in the Polish corridor. Charges of injustice, and notably of anti-Semitism, were frequently levelled against the Poles.

Pilsudski had aligned himself with France, forming part of an alliance designed to deal with any German resurgence. But after Hitler came to power in 1933, Poland's rulers turned towards the Nazis as they sympathised with much of Hitler's ideology. It was only after Hitler's march into Prague early in 1939 that the Polish government saw its danger and accepted guarantees of assistance from Britain and France in the event of German attack.

**Invasion and partition: 1939** On September 1, 1939, using the Polish corridor and the German claim to Danzig, which had been under League of Nations control, as pretexts, Hitler launched the blitzkrieg on Poland which began the Second World War. Without warning, 2000 German aircraft bombed Warsaw and the Polish airfields. Most of the Polish air-force was destroyed on the ground. Both in numbers and weapons, the invading Germans were vastly superior to the Poles, who still relied on horse-drawn transport. The Poles pitched their cavalry against the German panzers, but the German tide was irresistible.

After 17 days another blow struck Poland. Just before the outbreak of war, Hitler and Stalin had agreed a non-aggression treaty – the Nazi-Soviet Pact. Its secret clauses divided Poland between the two powers in yet another partition, and the Red Army swept almost unopposed across Poland's eastern frontier to occupy its share of territory. On September 17, the Polish government fled to safety in Romania. The last defenders of Warsaw were obliterated by bombardment, and very soon Poland lay divided under the heel of its German and Russian conquerors. When the Nazi blitzkrieg struck the Soviet Union in June 1941, the Germans quickly overran the rest of Poland.

German troops are
overtaken by Russian
armour, in this 1939
photograph. As part
of the Nazi-Soviet
pact of that year the
two countries agreed
to divide Poland be-
tween them

**Rule by terror: 1939–45** For over five years, the Poles suffered from the unbelievable inhumanity of Nazi rule. The Germans mercilessly exploited the whole country, trying to impose a 'New Order' – based on the concept of an Aryan master-race – and bleeding Poland white to support their war-effort. Countless numbers of Poles were sent as slave labour to the factories and farms of Germany. Resistance was answered with genocide. The Germans in Poland exterminated about 6 million Poles, including 3 million Jews. The Jews did not give in without a struggle. In February 1943 the Warsaw ghetto rose; its heroic resistance ended with the massacre of all its remaining inhabitants. In August 1944, as the Russians drove the crumbling German armies back towards Warsaw, the Polish resistance seized the half-ruined capital and held it for two months against the Germans. While the Poles were blasted into submission, Soviet forces remained inactive outside the city.

**Fighters in exile** Meanwhile, the legal Polish government continued the war in exile. Smigly-Rydz was dismissed; his place was taken by General Sikorski, who was killed in a plane crash in 1943. Many Poles had escaped abroad, the merchant navy had fled to friendly ports, and the country's gold reserves had been saved. Based in London, the Polish government-in-exile raised naval, military and air forces, which played a leading part in many of the vital battles of the war. Their most famous achievement was the defeat of the Germans at Monte Cassino in Italy. But in July 1944, the exiled government faced a rival, for in that month a Soviet-backed regime was set up at Lublin.

A Polish soldier in a
scene from Kanal –
one of the films which
brought post-war
Polish cinema inter-
national recognition

**Communist Poland** The Red Army occupied Poland in 1944, and when the victorious allies staked out their spheres of influence in 1945, the Soviet leaders ensured that the Poles came within the Russian orbit. 'Free elections' were held in 1947, but it was soon plain to the thousands of exiles returning from the West that there was only a chilly welcome for them in a Poland dominated by the Kremlin. Many of them chose to make their homes in Britain and America.

Since the Second World War, the history of Poland has followed roughly the same course as that of the other eastern European countries subservient to the Russians. There have been purges, persecutions and brief 'thaws'. The career of the Communist Party secretary, Wladyslaw Gomulka, the outstanding figure of post-war Poland, has been typical. He was expelled from the party in 1949 and imprisoned in 1951. In 1956 popular demand forced his reinstatement after bloody riots at Poznan, and he was again dismissed after renewed rioting in the country's Baltic ports in 1970.

Gomulka's successor, Edward Gierek, rapidly introduced new policies designed to change the face of Polish Communism. A drive was launched to increase the standard of living; more consumer goods were produced and private enterprise in farming was encouraged. Gierek ordered that party officials should act in consultation with the workers. In foreign affairs, Poland played its part in easing tension between East and West. In 1972, after Chancellor Brandt of West Germany had visited Poland, a treaty of reconciliation was signed between the two powers.

Edward Gierek re-
placed Wladyslaw
Gomulka as Com-
munist Poland's leader
in 1970. He initiated
policies designed to
win the confidence of
Poland's workers

# Portugal

Cut off by Spain from direct contact with the rest of Europe, the Portuguese have for centuries looked outwards to lands overseas. Portuguese sailors founded a world empire in the 15th century, staking their country's claim to lands as far apart as Africa, Brazil, and India.

The colony of Brazil was lost in 1822 and that in India in 1961, but Portugal hung on to its large territories in Africa long after Britain, France, and other European powers had bowed to the anticolonial winds of change of the 20th century. Portuguese determination to remain a colonial power, in the face of world-wide criticism, was a legacy of the authoritarian regime of Dr Antonio Salazar, who ruled Portugal from 1932 until 1968. Salazar maintained that Portugal's overseas possessions were not colonies, but integral parts of Portugal itself.

35,553 sq. miles
9,056,000 people
Capital: Lisbon

**Early history** The original people of the Iberian peninsula – which is made up of Portugal and Spain – were subdued by the Carthaginians in the 6th century BC. The Carthaginians in turn were defeated in 206 BC by the Romans, who divided the peninsula into three provinces. The westernmost province, Lusitania, corresponded roughly to modern Portugal.

As the Roman Empire broke up in the 5th century AD, the peninsula was overrun by Visigoths and other northern barbarians. Three centuries later Visigoth rule ended, when the country fell to the Moorish rulers of the Islamic Empire in North Africa.

**Portugal achieves independence: 1143** By the 12th century, the tide of Islam was retreating as the Moors were driven south in a Christian reconquest by Alfonso VI of Castile and other Spanish rulers, with the help of volunteers from other parts of Christendom. One of the volunteers, Henry of Burgundy, served Alfonso so well that in 1095 he was rewarded with the hand of the king's illegitimate daughter, Teresa, and the 'county' of Portugal (the northern third of the present state).

But years of conflict followed between Henry and the king. Eventually Henry's son, Afonso Henriques, threw off the yoke of Castile and in 1143 was recognised by Castile as king of an independent Portugal. Afonso was a formidable warrior, known to the Moors as 'the Terrible'. He extended his domains as far south as the River Tagus, and made Lisbon his capital.

The main task of Portugal's early kings was to hold their northern borders against their Christian neighbours, and at the same time push their southern frontier ever deeper into Moorish territory. Sancho II penetrated into the Algarve; his brother Afonso III (1248–79) completed its conquest and thus established the boundaries of Portugal as they are today.

**Diniz – 'Friend of Troubadours'** One of the most outstanding of Portugal's medieval kings was Diniz (1279–1325). A poet himself, his patronage of literature and learning won him the title of 'Friend of Troubadours'. He founded a university at Lisbon in 1290, and in 1307 had it moved to its present home at Coimbra.

His interests were practical too. His concern for agriculture won him the additional nickname of Rei Lavrador, the 'Farmer King'. He encouraged foreign trade by making a commercial treaty with England, and laid the foundations of Portugal's future greatness by establishing a navy – for which he imported a Genoese admiral from Italy, Emmanuele di Pezagna.

Despite being a man of peace, Diniz had to face several wars during his reign. In 1297 a treaty with Castile confirmed Portugal's right to the Algarve. In Diniz's last years, his son rebelled against him and was only persuaded to submit by his mother, Isabella.

**Friendship with England** The impetus generated by Diniz in his long reign was not maintained by his successors. For the next 60 years, they were frequently involved in disputes and wars, chiefly with Castile and with the Moors, who still held southern Spain. Friend-

ship with England continued. In 1381 Richard II of England sent a powerful force to Lisbon to support Ferdinand of Portugal's claim to the vacant throne of Castile. Ferdinand, however, deserted his English allies by making a separate peace, and the English revenged themselves by ravaging the neighbourhood of Lisbon. This episode did not long disrupt the tradition of Anglo-Portuguese friendship. In May 1386, the Treaty of Windsor marked the formal alliance of Portugal and England; it committed the two powers to the defence of each other's interest and territories 'wherever they may be'. The treaty was cemented in 1387 by the marriage of John I of Portugal to Philippa of Lancaster, daughter of the powerful English noble, John of Gaunt.

**Age of discovery** The son born of this marriage, Prince Henry the Navigator (1394–1460), initiated the most splendid era of Portuguese history. Henry was patron and inspirer of Portugal's first voyages of exploration. Though Henry himself never sailed further than Ceuta on the Strait of Gibraltar, he drew into his service experienced navigators and ingenious theorists, closing his door to no one – Christian, Jew or Arab – who had anything useful to contribute.

The Portuguese captured Ceuta, on the North African mainland, in 1415, and their seaward expansion began in earnest in the 1440's. Driven on by a thirst for knowledge and the riches to be won in trade, Henry's captains discovered Madeira (1419), the Azores (1431), Senegal in 1446, and the Cape Verde Islands in 1455. In 1446 the first Negro slaves were brought to Lisbon.

**Builders of an empire** These voyages did not cease with Henry's death; there was the lure of trading profits to be made in exploration. Bartholomew Diaz rounded the southernmost tip of Africa in 1488; Vasco da Gama reached India in 1498. Within a few years, the Portuguese had staked out a world-wide empire. This empire was recognised by the pope, who, by the treaty of Tordesillas in 1494, divided the world outside Europe between Portugal and Spain along a circle west of the Cape Verde islands. Afonso de Albuquerque (1435–1515) took Goa in 1510, and then Malabar, Ceylon and Malacca. As governor of the Portuguese Indies he proved a capable ruler. Other territories were won in Africa and South America, the most important of which was Brazil.

This 'golden age' of Portugal was achieved under Manuel I (1495–1521). Nicknamed 'the Fortunate', he was more grandly styled 'Lord of the conquest, navigation and commerce of India, Ethiopia, Arabia and Persia'. But Portugal's decline began when, to please his parents-in-law, Ferdinand and Isabella of Spain, Manuel expelled the Jews, on whom much of Portugal's economic prosperity depended.

**Independence lost and regained** Manuel had always been master in his own kingdom, but his son, John III, fell increasingly under the influence of his religious advisers. He admitted the Inquisition to Portugal in 1536 to seek out and try the country's heretics. The Jesuits followed four years later. When John died, leaving the throne to his three-year-old grandson, Sebastian, the Jesuits ran the country as regents. Matters

*Henry the Navigator (1394–1460) launched Portugal upon an age of discovery which was to give the country a world-wide empire*

*Bartholomew Diaz sets sail for Africa in 1487. His voyage opened up the sea route to India*

*Luis de Camoens, sailor and poet, celebrated the achievements of Portuguese explorers in his epic poem Os Lusiadas ('The Lusiads'), published in 1572*

## PORTUGAL *continued*

did not improve when Sebastian came of age. He embarked on an ill-advised 'crusade' into Morocco, which ended with his death and the annihilation of his army by the Moors at Alcazarquivir in 1578. The only legitimate heir to the throne was Sebastian's elderly great-uncle, Prince Henry, who was also a cardinal and Inquisitor-General. He became King of Portugal, but died within 18 months.

There were several claimants to the vacant throne but, after a year of conflict, Philip II of Spain, the nephew of John III, was installed by force of arms and the backing of the Jesuits. For the next 60 years Portugal remained subservient to Spanish interests. It was dragged into Spain's European wars and lost overseas territories to the English and the Dutch.

In 1640, the Portuguese took advantage of Spanish weakness. A bloodless coup restored independence, and the native Duke of Braganza was placed on the country's throne as John IV. But Spain did not release Portugal without a struggle. Intermittent war between the two countries lasted for 28 years, until Spain formally recognised Portuguese independence in 1668.

*John IV came to power when a bloodless coup overthrew Spanish rule in Portugal in 1640*

*Portuguese vineyard workers celebrate the end of a harvest. Port wine has long been one of the country's leading exports*

**Gold mines and port wine** Though the glories of the Portuguese Empire were much diminished, one possession – Brazil – now became of vital importance. In 1693 gold and diamond fields were found there. This discovery brought a vast flow of revenue to the Braganzas, which enabled them to dispense with the Cortes (parliament). It met for the last time in 1697 and was not called together again for more than a century.

There was another significant economic development in 1703, when a commercial treaty, named after its British negotiator, John Methuen, was signed with Britain. It provided that Britain would admit port wine and madeira on specially advantageous terms, while the Portuguese in turn would buy British wool.

**Rise of Pombal** Supported by their regular gold shipments from Brazil, the Braganza kings enjoyed the powers of absolute monarchs until the mid-18th century. One far-sighted statesman, the Marquis de Pombal, saw the danger of Portugal's reliance on one source of revenue from the other side of the Atlantic. From 1755 until King Joseph's death in 1777, he was the effective ruler of Portugal. He dominated the country as his statue on the Avenue of Liberty still dominates the Lisbon he rebuilt after a devastating earthquake in 1755. Pombal's swift rise, however, made him many enemies, particularly among the Jesuits and the Portuguese aristocracy.

*The city of Lisbon was almost completely destroyed by an earthquake in 1755. Its rebuilding was largely the achievement of the Marquis de Pombal, chief minister to King Joseph*

**Reform and reaction** Lisbon is all that visibly survives of Pombal's achievements. The rest – the reforms in finance, education and the armed forces, efficient administration and the encouragement of new industries – were brought to an end when Pombal was dismissed by Joseph's successor, the unbalanced Maria I. Once more the Church party was supreme.

When the Napoleonic wars broke out, Portugal's dependence on the sea kept the country on the side of Britain. France and Spain eventually agreed to partition Portugal and, in November 1807, the French general Junot occupied Lisbon. The Portuguese court fled to Brazil and Junot declared that the House of Braganza had forfeited the throne. British troops were sent to Portugal, and Portuguese regiments fought alongside the Duke of Wellington's troops until in 1811 the French were finally driven out. The Portuguese then served with the British in Spain.

*Virtual dictator of Portugal for 22 years, Pombal sought to change the country with his reforms*

*The lines of Torres Vedras were impregnable defences which held up French conquest of Portugal*

**Brazilian connection** After Napoleon's downfall in 1815, the royal fugitives, fearful of the growth of liberalism in Portugal, did not hasten home from Brazil, and discontent in Portugal increased, with criticism of the absentee monarchy and of growing British influence. In 1820 revolution broke out and in the following year John VI hurried home, leaving his son, Pedro, to govern Brazil. In 1822 John accepted the new liberal constitution demanded by the Cortes.

In the same year, revolution also broke out in Brazil. The Portuguese garrison in Rio de Janeiro was overcome, and Pedro was proclaimed Brazil's constitutional emperor. Pedro resigned his claims on the Portuguese throne to his daughter, Maria. When she was overthrown by her brother Miguel, in 1831, Pedro returned to Portugal, and restored her to the Portuguese throne.

**Monarchy to republic** Portugal shared in the general radical ferment which convulsed Europe in the 19th century. Maria reigned until 1853, and four more Braganza sovereigns followed her – Pedro V, Luis I, Carlos I and Manuel II. Strikes, peasant risings and army mutinies ushered in the 20th century. Republican feeling gained ground. Carlos I and the crown prince were assassinated by anarchists in 1908, and Manuel II was forced to abdicate and leave the country in 1910, when a republic was proclaimed.

*Carlos I was unable to halt the growing Republican movement in Portugal. He was murdered by an anarchist group in 1908*

**Republican regime** The monarchy's overthrow brought none of the benefits hoped for by the idealists who had led the revolution of 1910. Portuguese politics continued to be stormy. There were frequent changes of government, spells of veiled dictatorship, an attempt at a royalist counter-revolution, and an equally unsuccessful 'Red' rising, as well as various coups. In 1916 Portugal was drawn into the First World War against Germany, fighting mainly in East Africa, but also on the Western Front. During and after the war, the country was rocked by political instability. There were nine different governments in 1920 alone.

A further decade of chaos and impending bankruptcy made any strong leader welcome, whatever his politics. In 1926, General Carmona seized power. Two years later, he appointed Dr Salazar, an economics professor at Coimbra, as his finance minister. Salazar balanced the budget, and became premier in 1932.

*Dr Salazar was Portugal's leader from 1932 until 1968. His autocratic rule brought stability, but little progress*

## Salazar's New State

Salazar's recipe for Portuguese stability – the Estado Novo (New State) – was accepted in 1933 after a plebiscite. Despite its Fascist flavour – like Mussolini, Salazar introduced a corporative chamber, whose members were drawn from trades and professions – the Estado Novo avoided the crude brutalities of Hitler and Mussolini. His rule gave Portugal a badly needed period of stability and solvency.

Salazar kept Portugal neutral in the Second World War, and afterwards joined Western alliances such as NATO. In the post-war era, Portugal's main efforts were devoted to preserving what remained of its colonial empire, but Goa was lost to India in 1961.

Salazar suffered a stroke in 1968, but lived on until 1970, unaware that he had been replaced by a former minister, Marcello Caetano. But though Portugal's 'strong man' was dead, his Estado Novo continued.

*An Angolan guerrilla. Portugal's hold on its African empire was challenged by nationalist rebellion*

## The End of Empire

Although western Europe's poorest country, Portugal had spent almost half its national budget fighting nationalist guerrilla movements in its African territories for more than a dozen years. In February 1974, the deputy army chief of staff, Gen. António de Spinola, a hero of the African wars, published a book denouncing the continuation of the fighting. On April 25, 1974, Spinola led the army in overthrowing Caetano's government. Spinola organised a government coalition of right and left, restored civil rights, and promised free elections. He also started negotiations with African nationalist groups which led to independence for Guinea Bissau, and a promise of independence soon for Angola. In Mozambique, the Mozambique Liberation Front (FRELIMO) formed a provisional government in 1974, which was to lead to full independence in 1975.

## Five centuries of empire

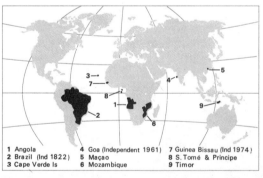

1 Angola
2 Brazil (Ind 1822)
3 Cape Verde Is
4 Goa (Independent 1961)
5 Maçao
6 Mozambique
7 Guinea Bissau (Ind 1974)
8 S. Tomé & Principe
9 Timor

*Portugal's overseas empire was the first to be created by a European power and the last to give in to demands for independence*

During the first two decades following the Second World War, most European countries gave independence to their colonial empires. Portugal, however, did not follow this trend. In 1951 its colonies became the *Provincias Ultramarinas*, provinces of Portugal, officially equal in status with the mother country. The African provinces of Angola and Mozambique were the most important to Portugal. The others include Portuguese Guinea, which became independent in 1974 as Guinea Bissau, and Maçao and Portuguese Timor in the Far East. Goa fell to India in 1961.

Angola has been under Portuguese rule since the late 15th century, except for a brief period of Dutch occupation from 1640 to 1648. From 1575 until 1836 the territory was the main source of slaves for Brazil. In recent years, Angola's exports of products as varied as coffee, diamonds, petroleum, iron ore and sisal formed the main source of Portugal's foreign exchange.

In 1961 an African nationalist revolt broke out in Angola against Portuguese rule. The Angolan guerrillas are divided into three main movements: the National Front for the Liberation of Angola (FNLA), the Angola People's Liberation Movement (MPLA), and the National Union for the Total Independence of Angola (UNITA).

Mozambique has belonged to the Portuguese since the 16th century. In 1965 another African nationalist revolt broke out there, led by the Mozambique Liberation Front (FRELIMO). Opposition crystallised round the building of the Cabora Bassa dam on the River Zambezi which, when completed, will be the biggest of its kind in Africa. The Portuguese claimed that it would bring prosperity to all the peoples of southern Africa, but the nationalists feared that the dam would help to consolidate European rule.

# Qatar

One of the most progressive of the oil states of the Persian Gulf, Qatar has devoted a large part of the revenues it has gained from oil to creating an impressive system of social welfare – including free education and a free health service. This was largely the work of Sheikh Khalifa, who served as prime minister for ten years under the rule of his cousin, Sheikh Ahmad, before overthrowing him in a bloodless coup in 1972.

The sheikhdom became a British-protected state under a treaty of 1916, which gave Britain responsibility for its defence and foreign relations. The country achieved importance in the 1930's with the discovery of oil in commercial quantities.

When Britain, in 1968, announced its intention to withdraw from the Gulf in 1971, Qatar began negotiations with the other British-protected Gulf states – Bahrain and the Trucial Coast states – to try to set up an independent federation. Qatar, like Bahrain, did not join the federation that was formed – the United Arab Emirates – opting instead for independence.

8500 sq. miles
93,700 people
Capital: Doha

# Rhodesia

Legally, Rhodesia is a British colony in the eyes of the world. Yet the rebel white regime which declared Rhodesia independent in 1965 continues in power, and it has weathered the world's official disapproval comparatively unscathed. After being won for the British Empire in the 19th century by Cecil Rhodes, after whom it was named, the country attracted a steady stream of British immigrants, who grew tobacco and maize and reared livestock on its wide tablelands. The great majority of Rhodesians are Africans; they outnumber the ruling white minority by about 20 to 1.

150,820 sq. miles
6,062,000 people
Capital: Salisbury

## Monomatapa and Zimbabwe

By AD 1000 a number of strong Bantu-speaking states were established in the region; the most important was Monomatapa, which controlled the gold and ivory trade with the Arabs of the east coast. From the late 15th century Monomatapa declined into a puppet state of the Portuguese. By the 17th century its former centre, Zimbabwe, had become the capital of the Rozvi Empire. The impressive ruins of Zimbabwe date mainly from this period. In the 1840's a Zulu clan, the Matabele (or Ndebele), part of the great northwards thrust of Zulu warriors from Natal, settled in western Rhodesia – Mashonaland – and conquered the Shona people living there.

## Rhodes and the British South Africa Company

In 1888 the Cape Colony politician and diamond millionaire Cecil Rhodes obtained a mineral concession from the Matabele chief Lobengula, and set up the British South Africa Company. In 1890 Rhodes sent a pioneer force of 200 settlers and 500 police, ostensibly in search of minerals, but really to colonise the Shona country. The settlers clashed with the fierce warriors, defeating them in a war in 1893. In 1896 both the Matabele and the Shona rose against the whites in a formidable rebellion. British troops were sent to the aid of the settlers, but it was not until 1897 that Rhodes himself met the Matabele chiefs and made peace.

## The 1923 constitution

In 1895 the British South Africa Company's territories were given the name Rhodesia, after Cecil Rhodes. After 1911 the areas

*Lobengula led his people, the Matabele, in a vain struggle against European settlers in Rhodesia in the 1890's*

*A 19th-century engraving of the ruins of Zimbabwe, the centre of the powerful empire of Monomatapa in medieval times, and of the Rozvi kingdom in the 17th century*

ROMANIA SAUDI ARABIA
RUSSIA SENEGAL
RWANDA SIAM
SAN MARINO

*Ferdinand I – seen with his wife Marie – brought Romania into the war on the Allied side in 1916*

## RHODESIA *continued*

north and south of the Zambezi were administered separately, as Northern and Southern Rhodesia. In 1923 Southern Rhodesia became a self-governing British colony, following a referendum among the settlers in which they were asked to choose between self-government and becoming part of the Union of South Africa. After the Second World War, Southern Rhodesia's thriving agriculture – based on tobacco, maize and livestock – and its growing industries, attracted many more immigrants from Britain.

**Central African Federation: 1953–63** Southern Rhodesia joined the Central African Federation, established by Britain in 1953, with Northern Rhodesia (now Zambia) and Nyasaland (now Malawi) as the other members. African nationalists, however, saw the Federation, under its prime minister, Sir Roy Welensky, as a device to keep the whites in power, and in 1963 the British yielded to their pressure and dissolved the Federation. Southern Rhodesia once more became a British colony, though the prefix 'Southern' was dropped.

**UDI and after** The right-wing Rhodesian Front government pressed for independence under a constitution which effectively kept political power in the hands of the settlers. When the British refused to grant independence on these terms, the Rhodesians took matters into their own hands: on November 11, 1965, the government of Ian Smith rebelled and issued its Unilateral Declaration of Independence (UDI).

Economic sanctions were imposed by the United Nations but failed to bring down the illegal regime. Discussions in 1966 and 1968 between Britain and the Smith government were fruitless, and in 1970 Rhodesia declared itself a republic. The following year, Britain made fresh approaches, and the terms agreed with the Smith regime were put before the African population in 1972 by a British Commission of Inquiry, headed by Lord Pearce. The result was 4 to 1 against acceptance of the terms, and the agreement was not put into effect.

Rhodesia remained largely isolated from the international community, its existence as a sovereign state not officially recognised by other countries. At home, the Smith regime moved in the direction of South African apartheid policies. Outlawed African nationalist organisations sent guerrillas into Rhodesia from neighbouring Zambia, and this led, early in 1974, to the doubling of draft calls for men to fight in the army.

*Joshua Nkomo, African nationalist leader, whose party, ZAPU, was outlawed in 1961*

*Ian Smith, the prime minister under whose leadership Rhodesia declared itself independent in 1965*

# Romania

The Communist state of Romania is a member of the Soviet bloc, but has won a reputation for going its own way against Russian wishes in making trading and diplomatic arrangements with the West. Its defiance of the USSR went as far as condemnation of Russian intervention in Czechoslovakia in 1968.

A spirit of independence has long sustained the people of this much-invaded country. Unlike the peoples of other Balkan countries, the Romanians are not true Slavs. They claim to trace their descent directly back to the Romans who colonised their land; their language is Latinised, and the very name Romania means 'the Roman land'.

**Roman settlement: AD 106–271** The area corresponding to present-day Romania had a flourishing Bronze Age civilization, which was destroyed by Scythian invaders from southern Russia *c.* 800 BC. The Scythians in turn were overrun by the Celtic Dacians, who migrated to Romania in the 3rd century BC. The Romans, under Trajan, conquered the area in AD 106, and it became one of the most prosperous parts of their empire. After the Roman withdrawal in 271, the country became the prey of barbarian invaders. The Romanised population preserved some of the Roman culture, much of which was adopted by the invaders.

91,699 sq. miles
21,153,000 people
Capital: Bucharest

**Conquest by Ottoman Turks** By the 13th century, two Christian principalities, Moldavia and Wallachia, had come into being. Though both were nominally independent, Wallachia was controlled by Hungarian Magyars, who had already annexed Transylvania, while Moldavia was a Polish satellite. Both states were subject to the Ottoman Turks by the 1500's.

**Struggle for independence: 1856–78** Centuries of Turkish oppression ended when, at the Congress of Paris held in 1856 to end the Crimean War, the leading European powers guaranteed the Romanians' right to elect their own rulers. In 1861, Moldavia and Wallachia were united to form Romania, under the reforming prince Alexander Cuza. At the Congress of Berlin in 1878, Turkey was compelled to recognise Romania's complete independence.

**First World War and after** Romania entered the First World War on the side of the Allies in 1916 – but was quickly defeated. Re-entering the war in 1918, it was rewarded at the peace conference by the restoration of Transylvania from Austro-Hungary and the acquisition of Bessarabia from Russia. Following the war, the Romanian government tried to carry out land and social reforms, but these attempts were defeated by the aristocracy. This failure, combined with the world-wide economic depression of the 1930's, drove Romanians in increasing numbers to either Communism or Fascism.

**War on the side of Germany: 1941–4** Romania's king, Carol II, tried to keep his country neutral in the Second World War, but his prestige was ruined by successful territorial claims made against Romania by Hungary and Bulgaria – with German support – and Russia's re-occupation of the provinces of Bessarabia and North Bukovina in 1940. Later that year, Marshal Antonescu, the leader of the Romanian Fascist Party – the 'Iron Guard' – overthrew the king. In 1941, Romania joined in the German attack on Russia. But when the Eastern Front collapsed in 1944, Carol's successor, Michael, arrested Antonescu and declared war on Germany. Russian troops occupied the country.

*Carol II ruled as royal dictator from 1938 until his overthrow in 1940*

**Defiance of the USSR** Since 1945, Romania has been under strict Communist control. In 1947, Michael was forced to abdicate and the country became a republic. Romania remained an obedient Soviet satellite until 1962, when the Romanians refused to give up their industrial programme, despite Russian demands that Romania should resume its designated role as agricultural 'reservoir' for the Soviet bloc. In 1971, President Ceausescu stated that there should be no interference in the internal affairs of any national Communist Party. He had already condemned Russian intervention in Czechoslovakia, and refused to join the USSR in attacking Chinese policy, retaining friendly ties with China despite the Chinese-Soviet rift. Romania recognised West Germany without consulting Moscow, and the USSR launched a violent press campaign against President Ceausescu for his part in helping to arrange President Nixon's visit to China.

Despite its independent attitude towards the USSR, Romania still practises a rigid form of Communism at home, calling its policy 'Socialism with a national face'.

*Richard Nixon's visit to President Ceausescu of Romania (right) in 1969 was the first time a US president had visited a Communist-ruled state*

*'Miss Pogany' by the Romanian sculptor Brancusi, a pioneer of 20th-century art*

# Rwanda

This is a poor, backward country, where primitive villages sprawl among mountains of spectacular beauty. Rwanda, the most densely populated country in Africa south of the Sahara, was formerly part of Ruanda-Urundi, a UN trust territory administered by Belgium. It separated from Urundi (now Burundi) and became independent in 1962, with the southern Bahutu leader Grégoire Kayibanda as president.

Rwanda's history, like that of Burundi, is a story of bitter conflict between its two main peoples – the Batutsi, a giant-sized aristocratic race with an average height of almost 7 ft, and the Bahutu, who make up four-fifths of the population. For 500 years the Bahutu were ruled and oppressed by the Batutsi minority, who entered the country in the 15th century, probably from Ethiopia. In 1959, while still under Belgian rule, Rwanda erupted into a savage civil war; thousands of Batutsi fled the country. The Bahutu, with Belgian backing, became Rwanda's new rulers when independence was granted in 1962. Fresh massacres of Batutsi occurred in 1963 and 1973. In 1973 General Habyalimana, a northern Bahutu, ousted Kayibanda.

10,169 sq. miles
4,170,000 people
Capital: Kigali

# San Marino

This landlocked state, officially called the 'Most Serene Republic of San Marino', nestles on a spur of the Apennines overlooking the Adriatic. It is the smallest republic in Europe and one of the oldest in the world; San Marino kept its independence for centuries because it was too small to be a threat to anybody and too poor to be worth conquering.

According to legend, the first inhabitants of San Marino were led there by a Christian stonemason called Marinus or Marino, who was fleeing from religious persecution in his native Dalmatia in the 4th century AD. Marinus gave his name to the state, which was recognised as independent in 1631.

In 1862, San Marino and Italy formed a customs union, and in 1879 they signed a treaty of mutual friendship which has been in force ever since. The republic hires its police and judges from Italy. Twelve years of Communist rule ended in 1957 with the formation of a coalition government. In international affairs San Marino has traditionally remained non-aligned.

24 sq. miles
18,400 people
Capital: San Marino

# Saudi Arabia

One man, Ibn Saud, the leader of the Saudi tribe, was largely responsible for the creation of Saudi Arabia. He fought a prolonged war from 1902 to 1925 to bring the scattered tribes of Arabia under his rule. But the importance of this land to the Muslim world goes back 1400 years. It was at Mecca in 570 that the prophet Muhammad was born; today there are about 350 million followers of Islam throughout the world.

The discovery in 1935 of vast oilfields under its barren deserts transformed the country's economy. Today, Saudi Arabia, with about a fourth of the known oil reserves, is the world's third largest oil producer.

830,000 sq. miles
8,627,700 people
Capital: Riyadh

**Foundation of Islam: c AD 600** Though organised communities existed in the far south of Arabia as early as 1000 BC, the area's importance began with the rise to power of the prophet Muhammad (570–632). After converting the nomadic Bedouin tribes to Islam, he formed a Muslim confederacy, with Medina as its capital. By the mid-8th century an Islamic empire stretched from the borders of India to Spain. But this empire had insecure foundations. Rivalry among its rulers and the formation of many sects in Islam itself led to its decline. By the mid-13th century Arabia had split up into many small sheikhdoms.

**Founding of the Saudi nation** Much of Arabia had come under Turkish rule by the 16th century. This lasted until 1902 when the leader of the Saudi tribe, Abd al-Aziz Ibn Saud, embarked on a prolonged struggle to free the peninsula from the Turks. After Turkey entered the First World War against Britain in 1914, the British gave arms and aid to the Arabs. Colonel T. E. Lawrence ('Lawrence of Arabia'), helped the tribes in an audacious guerrilla campaign against the Turkish forces. After the war, Ibn Saud fought his rivals to unify Arabia under Saudi rule. In 1927 Britain recognised Arabia's independence, and in 1932 it became the kingdom of Saudi Arabia.

**Oil discovered** The development of the huge oilfields discovered in 1935 changed Saudi Arabia into one of the world's richest nations. Under Ibn Saud and his successor, Saud, it remained a conservative power.

Saud was replaced by his brother, Faisal, in 1964. Faisal started to share the country's new-found wealth with its people, building schools and hospitals.

During the Arab-Israeli war of 1973, Saudi Arabia took the lead among Arab oil-producing states in using 'oil diplomacy' to further the Arab cause by embargoing oil shipments to nations supporting Israel. In 1974 Saudi Arabia took over 60 per cent control of foreign-owned oil companies.

*King Faisal replaced his brother Saud after his enforced abdication in 1964. Faisal used the country's oil revenues to build schools and hospitals*

# Senegal

The area of Senegal saw the foundation of France's first African colony, Fort St Louis, set up at the mouth of the Senegal River in the 1650's. It was in Senegal, too, in the early 1900's, that the French first adopted the policy known as *assimilation*, which aimed at fully absorbing colonial society into that of France. Close contact with French culture has made Senegal one of the most sophisticated of Black African countries.

75,750 sq. miles
4,318,600 people
Capital: Dakar

**Growth to independence** In medieval times, much of Senegal was part of the powerful African empires of Ghana and Mali. Portuguese explorers reached Senegal's coast in the mid-15th century and began to trade with the tribes of the interior. In the 1650's the French set up the settlements of Fort St Louis and Goree Island, which became notorious as slave-trading centres. But conquest of the interior did not begin until the energetic General Faidherbe was made French governor by Napoleon III in 1854. Senegal became part of French West Africa in 1895; the city of Dakar grew in importance as an administrative centre for the eight territories of the region.

**Independent Senegal** After the failure of an attempt to create a self-governing federation of French West Africa in the late 1950's, Senegal joined with the French Soudan in 1959 to form the Mali Federation. This broke up in the following year, and Senegal declared itself an independent republic.

The poet Léopold Senghor became the country's first president. He helped to give a sense of identity to the emergent Black African nations by his writings on *négritude*, a concept emphasising the distinctive character of African culture. Poor in natural resources and over-dependent upon a single crop, groundnuts, Senegal suffered in the 1970s from Africa's long sub-Saharan drought.

*Senegal's economy is based on groundnuts. The nuts and oil from them account for about 80 per cent of the country's exports*

**SIAM,** *see Thailand*

*Mecca, the birthplace of Muhammad, is the most sacred city of Islam. Every believer is expected to visit the city at least once*

# Sierra Leone

The anti-slavery movement that grew into a world crusade in the early 19th century is symbolised by the name of Sierra Leone's capital, Freetown, which was founded by British abolitionists in 1787 as a settlement for slaves liberated from their owners.

Before then, Sierra Leone, like other parts of West Africa, was notorious as a slave-trading area. Portuguese explorers first discovered the country in 1462. The British took over Freetown as a naval base in 1808. Helped by British teachers and missionaries, repatriated slaves, or 'Creoles', became the colony's first clerks, solicitors, teachers, doctors and politicians – and a source of resentment to Sierra Leone's native people, because of their privileged status.

Britain gradually extended its rule into the interior of the country, which it completely controlled by 1896. Nationalism and constitutional reforms developed rapidly over the next 50 years, and by the 1950's political power had shifted from the Creole minority into the hands of the African tribal peoples.

Agitation by the tribes led to independence in 1961. In 1967 army officers staged a coup and installed a military government, after a disputed election in which Siaka Stevens narrowly defeated the former prime minister, Sir Albert Margai. Sierra Leone returned to constitutional rule in 1968 when Stevens formed a civilian cabinet. Before the country became a republic in 1971, Stevens called in troops from neighbouring Guinea to support his regime, after an attempted coup by the leaders of the army ended in failure. Stevens became president and signed a treaty of mutual defence with Guinea, which sent troops into his country.

27,699 sq. miles
2,726,800 people
Capital: Freetown

# Singapore

When the British empire-builder Sir Stamford Raffles visited Singapore in the early 19th century, he found the island virtually uninhabited, and covered in jungle. Under his inspiration and the guidance of his successors, Singapore, lying at a junction of the trade routes of the Far East, prospered. Today it is still one of the area's most important trading centres.

**Growth of Singapore** The earliest known colonists of Singapore were Sumatrans, who landed there in the 11th century AD. They called the island *Singa pura* (lion city), which became corrupted to Singapore. Later, Javanese, Siamese and Chinese merchants settled there, founding a small trading state, which flourished briefly in the early 14th century. But the island was soon conquered by nearby Malacca and, with this conquest, its early prosperity came to an end.

Modern Singapore was founded in 1819 by Sir Stamford Raffles, at the time governor of Sumatra for the East India Company. His intention was to create a 'free emporium' – a port open to traders of all nations – and so to capture control of Far Eastern trade from the Dutch, who had built up a powerful trading empire. Singapore became part of the British Straits Settlements in 1826, and (apart from a period of Japanese occupation) remained under British rule until 1963.

Singapore's trade expanded rapidly, and the population grew – from 10,000 in 1823 to 560,000 by 1931. Much of the increase was due to immigration from China, and today three-quarters of Singapore's population are Chinese by origin. Before the Second World War, Singapore was an important British naval base. Fixed defences were constructed at enormous expense, but they never saw action. When the colony fell to Japan in 1942, it did so from a landward attack; the island's forts had been designed solely to prevent seaborne invasion. More than 70,000 British and Commonwealth troops were forced to surrender. The British finally returned after Japan's surrender in 1945.

Aided by Britain, the country from 1945 to 1959 enjoyed steady progress towards self-government. In 1963 Singapore joined with Malaya, Sarawak and

225 sq. miles
2,239,100 people
Capital: Singapore

*Sir Stamford Raffles (1781–1826) founded Singapore largely to offset Dutch influence in the East*

Sabah to form the Federation of Malaysia. Tension grew between Singapore's Chinese-dominated government and the Malayan leaders of the federation. Singapore's prime minister, Lee Kuan Yew, led it out of the federation to complete independence in 1965.

After 1965 Lee Kuan Yew's regime became steadily more authoritarian. In 1971 Lee claimed that Communists were stirring up conflict between the country's Chinese and Malays. He restricted freedom of the Press, and some journalists were arrested. In 1972, Lee's party, the People's Action Party, repeated its victory of 1965 by winning all the seats in a general election.

*Lee Kuan Yew, on becoming leader of independent Singapore, made the country's economic progress his main concern*

*The Tanjong Pagan docks of Singapore. Under British rule the port became a hub of Eastern trade*

# Somalia

Officially the Somali Democratic Republic, this union of the two former colonies of British and Italian Somaliland is one of the few African states whose people have a common origin, language and culture. Somalis are Muslims and have the reputation of being a proud, fierce, warrior people. Much of the country is arid, and most Somalis live a nomadic existence.

**Early history** The Somalis emerged as a distinct people hundreds of years ago, in the southern part of the country. They gradually spread over the whole of the Horn of Africa. Arab settlers on the coast introduced Islam to the Somalis in medieval times.

**European era** After the opening of the Suez Canal in 1869, the Somali coast was occupied by European powers; France seized Djibouti, Britain took the area of Zeila and Berbera, and Italy occupied the whole of the Indian Ocean side of the Horn of Africa. Ethiopia occupied the Ogaden region of the Somali hinterland. British rule was fiercely contested from 1899 to 1920 by a Somali leader, Sheikh Mohammed bin Abdulla Hassan, nicknamed the 'Mad Mullah' by the British, who regarded him as a fanatic. He led frequent raids against British forces until, in 1920, his stronghold was destroyed by RAF bombers. He died in exile.

**Independence** Italy lost Somalia in the Second World War, but was given it as a UN mandate in 1950. When independence came in 1960, Somalia was joined by British Somaliland. The new state was poor and had to cope with the difficulty of unifying two different systems of administration, Italian and British. A 'Greater Somalia' movement, which aimed to include all Somalis living outside the country's borders, led to friction with the French in French Somaliland, Ethiopia, and Kenya – whose northern region was largely inhabited by Somalis. After seven years of virtual war, the 'Greater Somali' concept was abandoned. In 1969, a coup established General Muhammad Siyad Barreh in power. In 1971 an anti-government plot was foiled.

246,201 sq. miles
3,066,200 people
Capital: Mogadishu

*A gathering of Somali dervishes. Inspired by Islam, they fought to free their country from British rule from 1899 to 1920*

# South Africa

The Republic of South Africa is the most advanced and prosperous country on the African continent. Mining is the basis of its wealth; it is one of the leading gold, diamond and platinum producers in the world.

About 17 million people out of the republic's total population of 24 million are Bantu-speaking Africans, made up of various groups, such as the Zulu and Xhosa. Another 4 million are of European descent. Some 2 million more are Coloureds – people of mixed race, most of whom are in the western Cape Province. The country's 600,000 Asians, descendants of labourers imported from India in the 1860's, live mainly in Natal.

South Africa's whites control the economic life of the country, and only they have the right to vote. Three-fifths of the white population are Afrikaans-speaking; they are descendants of the Dutch families who settled in the Cape during the 17th century and of later French and German immigrants. The rest of the white community are English-speaking, mainly of British descent. Africans provide the main labour force. They have a much lower standard of living than the whites, and have no say in the central government of the country. But in the Bantustans – areas set aside as African 'homelands' – Africans have received some measure of autonomy.

South Africa's policy of apartheid (literally, 'apartness') aims ultimately to separate the country's racial groups in every sphere of life. Its implementation, which falls mainly on the non-whites, has aroused widespread international criticism.

*471,445 sq. miles*
*24,210,000 people*
*Capitals: Cape*
*Town (legislative),*
*Pretoria*
*(administrative)*

*The vivid Bushman cave-paintings discovered in southern Africa are among the finest examples of prehistoric art*

**Early men in southern Africa** Evidence of pre-historic habitation dating back at least 2 million years has been found in southern Africa. The aboriginal peoples first encountered by the Europeans who landed at the Cape in the late 15th century were of two types: the Bushmen (San) and the Hottentots (Khoikhoi). Both peoples were living in a late Stone Age culture. The Bushmen were scattered over much of the sub-continent, and were hunters and gatherers; the Hottentots herded sheep and cattle, and lived mainly along the western and south-eastern coastal regions.

Much later, as they moved across from the western Cape, the Europeans encountered Bantu-speaking Africans, whose ancestors had entered the country from the north by about AD 1000. In the course of time, various groups of Africans emerged – the Xhosa and Zulu in the south-east, the Sotho and Tswana in the central region, the Venda further north, and the Herero and Ovambo peoples in south-west Africa.

**European settlement** The Portuguese explorer Bartholomew Diaz was the first European to land in South Africa. His ship came ashore at Mossel Bay in 1488. Diaz was followed by other Portuguese explorers, notably Vasco da Gama. But it was only in the mid-17th century that European settlement began. In 1652, the

Dutch East India Company sent an expedition, led by a ship's surgeon, Jan van Riebeeck, to set up a base at the Cape to supply the company's ships with fresh meat, vegetables and water. In 1657, some former servants of the company won permission to strike out for themselves as farmers. They moved into Hottentot land, provoking the first serious clash between whites and non-whites in South Africa.

The company's determination to preserve its monopoly of trade angered the farmers. Their resentment reached its height at the turn of the 17th century, when the company's governor, Willem van der Stel, and other of its officials, embarked on large-scale farming on their own account. Regarding this as unfair competition, the settlers appealed to the company in Holland and van der Stel was recalled. But many of the settlers, who had become known as Boers (the word means 'farmers'), remained discontented with company rule and began to move further into the interior of South Africa.

Conflicts over land, cattle and labour broke out between Boers and Xhosa in the closing decades of the 18th century. The Boers on the eastern frontier complained that the authorities at the Cape did not protect them. But Dutch rule was drawing to a close. Britain occupied the Cape in 1795. Dutch rule was briefly restored in 1803, but in 1806 the British returned to govern the Cape as a colony until 1910.

While the British were establishing themselves at the Cape, a power struggle was in progress in the interior of South Africa, which was so far almost completely untouched by European influence. In the fertile country north of the Tugela River, there arose a highly organised and land-hungry military state, that of the Zulu nation, led first by Dingiswayo and then consolidated by Shaka. The iron discipline of Shaka's impis, or regiments, made them invincible in close combat with the short stabbing assegai (spear). As the Zulus thrust outwards, entire peoples fled before them, in the time known as the Difaqane ('forced migrations').

**The Great Trek** After the Napoleonic Wars, Britain kept the Cape because of its strategic importance on the route to India. Some 5000 British settlers were sent to the colony in 1820. The Boers, who had now started to call themselves Afrikaners, resented British interference with their traditional way of life. By about 1837 more than 4000 Afrikaners had packed their belongings on to ox wagons and trekked north of the Orange River. The Voortrekkers (pioneers, literally 'travellers on in front') were led by Louis Trigardt, Andries Potgieter, Gert Maritz, Piet Uys and Piet Retief. The Great Trek, as this migration is called, was a watershed in South African history. Boer communities were now scattered over much of the interior. They were a sturdily individual people, with a fierce desire to live their own lives, free from official rule.

The main body of Afrikaners made for Natal. In 1838 an advance party under Retief was murdered by Zulus under Dingane, who were fearful of white encroachment. Almost a year later the massacre was avenged when 470 Boers defeated a 12,000-strong Zulu army at Blood River. Some 3000 Zulus died.

The Boers were now close to establishing control of Natal. Britain, unwilling to let a white 'foreign' power establish itself on the coast of South Africa, annexed Natal in 1843. But it recognised the independence of the inland Boer republics: the Transvaal (South African Republic) in 1852, and the Orange Free State (which had been annexed by Britain as the Orange River Colony only six years earlier) in 1854.

*A 19th-century view of shipping in Table Bay. Because of its use as a supply station, Cape Town became known as the 'tavern of the seas'*

*The Hottentot people were first encountered by Dutch settlers in the 17th century. The word Hottentot was probably coined in imitation of their 'clucking' speech*

*Afrikaner Voortrekkers on the move. They travelled into the interior to escape British rule*

439

## SOUTH AFRICA *continued*

**British expansion** In 1868 Basutoland (now Lesotho) was annexed by Britain, while during the 1870's and 1880's the Cape government annexed most of the independent African kingdoms in the Transkei, between the Cape and Natal.

In the 1870's Britain tried to federate the various parts of South Africa. This was an ill-fated scheme which led to the annexation of the Transvaal against the wishes of its Afrikaners in 1877, and to war with the Zulus in 1879, when Britain tried to curb their power. The British finally crushed the Zulus, but only after their army suffered at Isandhlwana its worst defeat since the Crimean War. Of the 950-strong British army, only 55 men escaped, while the 20,000 Zulus suffered 2000 casualties. In 1881 the Transvaal Boers defeated British forces at Majuba and won back their independence.

**Diamonds and gold** However intense the desire of the Boers to be left alone, their wish was not to be granted. The discovery of diamond-fields near Kimberley in 1868, and gold on the Witwatersrand in the Transvaal in 1886, brought thousands of immigrants, many of them British, pouring into these areas.

The beginning of South Africa's industrial revolution worsened relations between British and Boers. The conflict between them was personified by the clash between Paul Kruger, the strong-willed president of the South African Republic (the Transvaal) and the equally determined British financier, Cecil Rhodes.

The thrusting industrial economy which sprang up on the gold-fields of the Transvaal was soon on a collision course with the traditionalist, puritanical Boers who controlled the republic. The Boers feared the growing strength of the uitlanders (foreigners) working the mines, and denied them an effective say in government. In 1895, Rhodes's lieutenant, Dr Jameson, invaded the Transvaal, with a body of British South Africa Company police, to support a planned uitlander rising. But the uitlanders failed to rise; Jameson was defeated and Rhodes was implicated.

**Anglo-Boer War: 1899–1902** Kruger had won the first round, but the next was more serious. Alfred Milner, the British High Commissioner, was determined on a showdown with the Boers. The immediate cause of the war which followed was the continued refusal of Kruger's government to grant full political rights to the uitlanders. War broke out in October 1899. At first, the Boers scored impressive successes, but later the British gained the upper hand. Boer commandos fought a guerrilla campaign against the British until, realising their struggle was hopeless, they made peace at Vereeniging in May 1902. The two Boer republics became British colonies. In 1910, however, all four colonies – as the provinces of the Cape of Good Hope, Natal, the Transvaal and the Orange Free State – came together to form the Union of South Africa.

**Age of the generals** With peace, many Afrikaners who had played a distinguished part in the struggle against the British were willing to 'bury the hatchet' and work for a united South Africa. From the outset, unity among the Afrikaner and British sections meant a common acceptance of 'white supremacy'. General

*The royal kraal (settlement) of the Zulu chief Cetewayo (c. 1836–84). The military might of the Zulu nation was finally destroyed by the British*

*A caricature of Cecil Rhodes, who was inspired by a vision of a British African empire stretching from the Cape to Cairo*

Louis Botha, a former Boer leader, was the first Union prime minister, with General Jan Christiaan Smuts, a fellow-Afrikaner, as his right-hand man.

But not all Afrikaners were reconciled to the compromise of Union. In 1912 General Hertzog left the government to form the National Party, which, with its declared policy of 'South Africa first', steadily grew in strength. The 1920's saw a struggle for power between moderate Afrikaners, led by Smuts, and the more extreme Nationalists under Hertzog. Smuts held power from 1919 to 1924, when Hertzog replaced him. Hertzog and his fellow Nationalists refused to make any concessions to the growing force of African nationalism, represented by the African National Congress (ANC), which had been founded in 1912. The government's basic policy was segregation of whites and non-whites, laid down in its 'civilized labour' policy.

South Africa was badly hit by the world depression of the 1930's. In 1932 it abandoned the gold standard, and in the following year Hertzog and Smuts came together in a coalition government. Their followers took the name of the United Party. Dr Daniel Malan broke away from it to form a new National Party in 1934. The Smuts-Hertzog alliance did not survive the outbreak of the Second World War in 1939. Hertzog opposed war, but he was defeated in a dramatic debate in the Union parliament and replaced as prime minister by Smuts, who declared war on Germany. After the war, the National Party came to power in 1948 with Dr Malan as the new prime minister.

**Nationalist rule** Dr Malan held power until 1954, when he was succeeded by Johannes Strijdom. Strijdom was in turn replaced by Dr Hendrik Verwoerd in 1958. Verwoerd ruled the country until his assassination in 1966, when Balthazar Johannes Vorster took over as prime minister.

The Nationalists introduced the controversial policy of racial separation known as apartheid. The core of apartheid is the establishment of Bantustans ('homelands') for Africans. The government plans to make the Bantustans self-ruling political units under the 'umbrella' of white South Africa. About 13 per cent of the country's land is set aside for such areas, but more than half the African population still live outside them, mainly in the cities such as Johannesburg, where they provide an essential labour force. The movement of Africans is rigidly controlled by the so-called Pass Law system, by which every African must carry his 'reference book' or 'pass' with him at all times and needs a permit before he can travel from one district to another.

South-west Africa, or Namibia as it has been called by the United Nations since 1968, has become a centre of international controversy, as both South Africa and the United Nations claim that they should control it. Though the International Court of Justice upheld the United Nations case in 1971, South Africa rejected the ruling and still governs the country. During 1973, there was widespread industrial and political unrest. In 1974, there were trials and detentions as well as public floggings of political activists.

In 1960, protest abroad against apartheid reached a height after South African police fired to disperse an African demonstration against the Pass Laws at Sharpeville, and 69 Africans were killed. In the following year, South Africa became a republic and decided to leave the Commonwealth.

During the 1950's and 1960's, the government initiated a massive programme of legislation to clamp down on what it regarded as subversive activity. By the early 1970's the state had virtually unlimited power over most spheres of South African life.

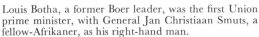

*A Boer soldier. Using guerrilla tactics, such men inflicted shattering defeats on the British*

*General Smuts, South Africa's wartime leader. His distinguished role in world affairs greatly enhanced his country's international standing*

*B. J. Vorster (centre) became Prime Minister of South Africa after the assassination of Hendrik Verwoerd. In 1974 his National Party further strengthened its position*

*The British met with reverses in the early days of the Anglo-Boer War. Besieged Mafeking printed its own banknotes*

# Spain

The year 1492 marked the emergence of Spain as a nation. It was the year when the last Moorish stronghold, Granada, was reconquered, ending seven centuries of Muslim presence – and the year, too, when Christopher Columbus discovered the New World and claimed it for the Spanish crown. Spain soon became the most powerful country in Europe and the possessor of a vast empire in the Americas.

Spain's imperial greatness lasted only for a century. The riches of Spanish America were squandered in a fruitless pursuit by the country's Hapsburg monarchs of their dream of supremacy in Europe, and rapid and catastrophic decline followed. In face of this decline, Spain's rulers retreated into rigid orthodoxy in politics and religion, an outlook which came to be bitterly challenged by those who saw in liberal reforms Spain's only hope of recovering its greatness. This conflict dominates modern Spanish history. It emerged in the struggle between liberalism and Catholic conservatism in the 19th century, and in the Civil War of 1936–9.

194,883 sq. miles
35,273,000 people
Capital: Madrid

Spain's Stone Age people developed a superbly expressive art, as this 10,000-year-old cave-painting at Altamira shows

**Early peoples** Men of Stone Age culture, who lived by hunting and food-gathering, occupied parts of the Iberian peninsula (present-day Spain and Portugal) at least as far back as 13,000 BC. They developed a remarkable pictorial art, seen at its best in the cave-paintings of Altamira in north-west Spain. A later people, who came to be known as the Iberians, entered Spain from Africa, probably *c.* 3000 BC. They mingled with Celtic tribes from the north during the 4th century to form the so-called Celtiberian culture.

Between *c.* 1100 BC and *c.* 509 BC, the peninsula was invaded by Phoenicians, Greeks and Carthaginians. These invaders were mainly interested in the country's rich resources of minerals, such as silver, iron and copper, and they left no lasting influence of their civilizations behind them.

**Romans and Visigoths: 202 BC-AD 711** After expelling the Carthaginians from the peninsula in the Second Punic War (218–202 BC), the Romans set about subduing the fiercely independent Iberian tribes. The Romans made Spain a single political unit, linking its regions together by 12,000 miles of roads, including the *Via Augusta*, which stretched from Cadiz to the Pyrenees. The peninsula became known as Hispania; its inhabitants, the Hispano-Romans, shared the cultural heritage of Rome. This included a common language, Latin, out of which Spanish later developed. Romanised Spain, part of the flourishing urban civiliza-

In AD 98 the Spanish-born Trajan became the first non-Roman to rule over the Roman Empire

tion of the western Mediterranean, contributed many illustrious names to the history of Rome, including the emperors Trajan, Hadrian, Marcus Aurelius and Theodosius the Great, and the writers Seneca, Lucan and Martial. Later, Spain, together with the rest of the empire, adopted Christianity.

The Visigoths, one of the Germanic tribes who invaded the Roman Empire, conquered most of the peninsula in AD 475. They were unable to establish stable political rule, or to assimilate the subject Hispano-Romans, although in time they adopted Christianity from them. Squabbles for leadership among the Visigoths, combined with the apathy of the people, laid the country open to Arab conquest in the 700's.

**Moors in Spain** The expansion of the militant new faith of Islam had a profound impact on Spanish history. In 711 and 712 Arab and Berber armies crossed the Strait of Gibraltar from Africa. Within eight years the invaders had conquered the entire peninsula, except for the mountainous regions of the north, which survived as Christian kingdoms. For the next six centuries, Spain remained divided between Christians and Moors – as the Muslim invaders came to be known (from the Mauri, a Berber people).

The power of the Moors was centred on the city of Cordoba, in the fertile region of Al Andalus (present-day Andalusia). It reached its height under the caliph Abd el-Rahman (912–61). Islamic culture in Spain – symbolised by the great mosque which still stands in Cordoba – was at first markedly superior to that of the small Christian kingdoms centred in the north: Asturias, Leon, Castile, Navarre and Aragon.

**The Christian Reconquest** With the break-up of the Caliphate of Cordoba after 1002 into a score of petty kingdoms, the power of the Moors began to decline. Slowly they were pushed south by Christian forces, until by the end of the 13th century only Granada was under Moorish control. But the Reconquest was not a continuous process; it was interrupted by long periods of peace with the Moors, as well as by wars between the Christian kingdoms themselves. (The legendary hero of this early phase of the Reconquest was 'El Cid' – Rodrigo Diaz de Vivar – even though he allied himself with the Muslims for a time.) As a result of these conflicts, Castile absorbed Leon, and Catalonia became part of the kingdom of Aragon.

The Reconquest, under Castilian leadership, became a religious crusade in the 13th century. Strict Catholic orthodoxy and an obsession with racial purity became the hallmarks of a new Spanish nationalism, leading in

A view of the Roman aqueduct at Segovia. Rome's rule brought Spain much prosperity

Rodrigo Diaz de Vivar, known as 'El Cid' ('The Lord'), became a legendary hero of Christian Spain through his exploits against the Moorish invaders in the 11th century

441

## SPAIN *continued*

1478 to the foundation of the Spanish Inquisition – a court, entirely controlled by the Spanish kings, whose purpose was to root out heresy – followed by the expulsion of the Jews from Spain in 1492.

**Emergence of a nation** In 1479, the two most powerful kingdoms of Spain were united, with the marriage of Ferdinand of Aragon to Isabella of Castile. The union of the 'Catholic Monarchs', as they were called, gave Spain the basis of its nationhood. The power of the nobility was curbed. The Moors were driven from Granada, their last stronghold on the peninsula, in 1492 – and, in the same year, the Italian Christopher Columbus, sailing under the Spanish flag, discovered the New World. The foundations of Spanish power in Europe and the Americas were laid.

**Coming of the Hapsburgs: 1516** The years of the Hapsburg dynasty saw the rise and decline of Spain as a great power. In 1516 Charles I, Ferdinand's grandson, came to the throne. He was the first of the Hapsburg line in Spain. Charles was later elected Holy Roman Emperor, taking the title of Charles V. Born in the Low Countries, he came to Spain as a foreigner and, as ruler of the empire, his interests remained mainly in Germany. The rich rewards, in silver and gold, of the Spanish conquests of Mexico (1521) and Peru (1533) went to pay for Charles's wars in pursuit of his European ambitions, and the suppression of heresy in his German possessions. Charles ended his reign bankrupt, and the riches of the Americas flowed into the hands of his numerous European creditors.

**Philip II: 1556–98** Under Charles's son, Philip II, Spain became the greatest power in Europe. With the annexation of Portugal in 1580, the entire Iberian peninsula came under Spanish rule. But the overstraining of Spanish resources continued. Gold and silver from the New World brought inflation, which struck at the roots of the economy. Philip saw Spain as the sole defender of Catholicism in Europe. He fought against the Protestant Netherlands and England, as well as supporting Catholic nobles in France in their struggle to control the throne. In 1581, after years of bitter conflict, the northern provinces of the Netherlands broke free of Spanish rule to form the Dutch Republic. This, together with the defeat of the Spanish Armada by the English in 1588, marked the beginning of the decline of Spain as the dominant European power.

**17th-century Spain** Under Philip's weak successors, Spain sank deeper into decline. Prolonged wars with Spain's chief rival France, now the leading nation in Europe, bled the country white. To worsen the position, the rigid centralising policies of the Conde Duque de Olivares, Philip IV's chief minister from 1621 to 1643, led to the loss of Portugal and a revolt in Catalonia.

By 1700 the pattern of traditional Spain had become fixed: unyielding Catholic orthodoxy, the vision of world empire without the means to sustain it, and a fierce pride in aristocratic values. Spanish literature of the 'golden age' (*c*. 1530–1680) reflects this outlook – notably in Cervantes's novel *Don Quixote*, with its hero's futile pursuit of an unattainable ideal, and in Calderon's numerous dramas, where honour is held up as the most important of the aristocratic virtues.

**Bourbon rule: 1700–1808** Charles II, last of the Spanish Hapsburgs, died in 1700 without leaving an heir. The succession was disputed by two rival claimants – a French-backed Bourbon prince, Philip of Anjou, grandson of Louis XIV, and an Austrian Hapsburg, the Archduke Charles. The Austrian claimant was supported by England, Austria and the Netherlands, all fearful of French ambitions. After a decade of war – the so-called War of the Spanish Succession – Philip was recognised as King of Spain. But the Peace of Utrecht (1713), which ended the war, stripped Spain of most of

*A contemporary view of Columbus's voyage to the New World. Spanish explorers followed him to create a vast Spanish-American empire*

*Cervantes's hero, Don Quixote, with his servant, Sancho Panza. In his novel Don Quixote and other works, the Spanish author satirised his countrymen's obsession with honour and chivalry*

*A lady of the Spanish court, painted by Francisco Goya, painter to the Bourbons of Spain. Goya brought a new humanity to the stylised art of his day*

its European possessions, including the Spanish Netherlands and its territories in Italy. Gibraltar was ceded to Britain. Nevertheless, the 18th century saw a remarkable Spanish recovery. Under the Bourbons, the running of the country was entrusted to an able civil service, which was aided by French advisers. The ministers of Charles III (1759–88), influenced by the ideas of the European enlightenment, encouraged industry, built roads and improved the administration of Spain's American empire. But these reforms were fiercely opposed by Spain's conservatives, the Church and the aristocracy.

**War of Independence: 1808–14** Napoleon marched into Spain in 1808 and made his brother, Joseph Bonaparte, the country's king. Ferdinand VII, the Bourbon king, was held captive in France. Resentment at French rule soon erupted into a national uprising; local committees, known as juntas, organised resistance against the invading French armies. The Spanish made an alliance with Britain, and in the name of Ferdinand VII set up a Cortes (Parliament).

Under the command of Sir Arthur Wellesley (later to become Duke of Wellington), British and Spanish troops, with the aid of Spanish guerrilla bands, drove Joseph and the French from Spain in the so-called Peninsular War. Before the French were forced to withdraw in 1814, the Cortes proclaimed a liberal constitution, which severely curtailed the powers of the crown.

**Liberals versus conservatives: 1814–74** On his return to the Spanish throne in 1814, Ferdinand refused to accept the constitution and reigned as an absolute monarch. Opposition to his regime came from the liberals, whose strength lay in the towns and the army. In 1820 the liberals rose, and restored the constitution. Ferdinand's despotic rule had also alienated Spain's American colonies, which gradually broke away to become independent. On the death of Ferdinand in 1833, the liberals wanted the monarchy to go to his three-year-old daughter, Isabella, while the conservatives gave their backing to Ferdinand's brother, Don Carlos, a devout Catholic of reactionary outlook. The movement that supported Don Carlos and his heirs became known as Carlism; its influence disrupted Spain for the next 50 years.

In 1833, civil war broke out between the Carlists and the liberals. The war had the effect of bringing the army on to the stage of Spanish politics and making the pronunciamiento (military rebellion) a regular method of political change. Isabella's supporters won, but the rest of her reign, from 1839 to 1868, was marked by a confused struggle between the forces of constitutional government and despotism, often with generals as party leaders. In 1854 Isabella attempted to rule without parties, but she was at once confronted by a revolution – though it failed.

In 1868 another revolution dethroned Isabella and forced her into exile in France. A republic – the First Republic – was established in 1873, but a year later it collapsed in anarchy, and yet another revolution brought Isabella's son, Alfonso, to the throne. The instability and disorder of the First Republic discredited democratic institutions for a generation.

*In this scene from his* The Disasters of War, *Goya showed the brutal aspect of the French occupation of Spain in the Peninsular War*

*In pursuit of his claim to the throne, Don Carlos plunged the Spanish people into civil war in the 1830's*

## Last Bourbons: 1874–1931
Under Alfonso XII (1874–85), it became customary for liberals and conservatives to hold office in turn. But this apparently democratic system was marked by extensive corruption and bargaining behind the scenes. It remained in force almost 50 years. The period was also one of economic growth – in banking, textiles, and iron and steel.

Attempts by the Spanish government to put down a nationalist rising in Cuba led in 1898 to war with the United States, which supported the Cuban nationalists. After only a few months, Spain was forced to make peace and give up almost the whole of its remaining empire – Cuba, Puerto Rico and the Philippines.

The first two decades of the 20th century, under Alfonso XIII (1886–1931), were years of acute unrest in Spain. The strains of a war to maintain Spanish rule in Morocco led to discontent in the army, while at home, Catalonia, a region with its own separate culture and a now prosperous industrial economy, pressed for a measure of self-government. After the First World War, in which Spain remained neutral, this pressure turned to violence. From 1919 to 1923 there were bitter clashes in Catalonia's chief city, Barcelona, between employers and a trade union, the CNT (Confederacion Nacional del Trabajo). The union was run by anarchists and syndicalists, who held that the state was always an instrument of oppression, and should be destroyed. Spain's anarchist movement was the strongest in Europe.

## Primo de Rivera's dictatorship: 1923–30
Meanwhile Alfonso and the army were becoming increasingly hostile to politicians, who seemed incapable of providing stable government. In September 1923, Miguel Primo de Rivera, Captain-General of Catalonia, set up a dictatorship, which received Alfonso's backing. He enjoyed considerable popular support in his early years, and was helped by the prosperity resulting from the high world prices for Spanish exports. But in 1929, with the fall of the peseta, Spanish prosperity crumbled, and Rivera was forced to resign in the following year.

## Second Republic: 1931–6
The municipal elections of 1931, the first to be freely held for eight years, resulted in victory for the republican parties in the large cities. Alfonso left Spain and a republic was declared.

The republic was first led by a moderate liberal regime, but it met increasing opposition from extremists on both the left and right, and eventually fell to a 'Popular Front' (made up of Republicans, Socialists and Communists) in 1936. At the same time, however, plans for a military coup were being laid. A few months later, General Francisco Franco, sent into semi-exile on the Canary Islands by the Republican government, took command of Spanish forces in Morocco, and led them in an invasion of Spain.

## Spanish Civil War: 1936–9
Spain quickly split into two armed camps – the army's supporters came to be known as Nationalists, while the government's supporters were called Loyalists. General Franco soon emerged as unchallenged leader of the Nationalists.

In the opening days of the war the Nationalists, hoping to bring their rising to a quick and successful conclusion, tried to take Madrid and Barcelona. But in this they failed, meeting determined resistance

*The Spanish statesman Antonio Cánovas del Castillo was assassinated by anarchists in 1897. Spain had the largest anarchist movement in Europe*

*In his* Guernica *the Spanish artist Pablo Picasso protested against the German air-raid on the Basque town in 1937*

organised by the trade unions. In 1937, however, they overran the northern industrial areas and split Loyalist territory in two. The bitterly fought Battle of the Ebro (July to November 1938) finally exhausted the Loyalist armies, which were now largely under Communist control. Nationalist troops entered Madrid at the end of March 1939, and on April 1 the war ended. Some 750,000 people had lost their lives in the war.

The Nationalists owed their success to their greater political unity, and superior military training; they were also more adequately supplied with arms and personnel by Germany and Italy than the Loyalists were by the USSR. The civil war made Spain to some extent a battleground for two rival international ideologies – Fascism and Communism. Left-wing volunteers fought on the Loyalists' side in the so-called 'International Brigades' organised by the world Communist movement. Many of these volunteers came from countries which officially supported a policy of 'non-intervention' in the civil war.

## Franco's early years: 1939–55
The new Spanish state under Franco was harshly authoritarian. It was based upon the support of the Falange – the Spanish Fascist party – the army, and the Catholic Church.

During the Second World War, Spain remained neutral. Allied victory, however, left the country an outcast among European nations, and it was not until 1955 that Spain was admitted to the United Nations.

## Prosperity and challenge
The early years of the regime had been years of economic hardship, but by the 1960's economic development quickened.

Since 1964 a major goal of Spanish foreign policy has been the recovery of Gibraltar, held by Britain since 1704; but in 1967 the colony's population voted overwhelmingly to remain British.

Franco's authority continued to come mainly from the army. But by the late 1960's, the dominant group in Spain's government were Catholic 'technocrats', advocates of rapid economic growth, guided by state planning. Opposition to the regime came from workers discontented with the government-controlled trades unions, young socially conscious priests, university students, and extreme Basque nationalists. In 1972, Franco appointed Don Juan Carlos, grandson of Alfonso XIII, eventually to succeed him as chief of state. Franco's right-hand man, Admiral Carrero Blanco, was made prime minister in June 1973. But six months later Blanco was assassinated. He was succeeded as premier by Carlos Arias Navarro. When Franco became seriously ill in 1974 he appointed Prince Juan Carlos as acting chief of state. Demonstrations in Spain triggered by the overthrow of the dictatorship in neighbouring Portugal in 1974 were suppressed with many arrests by the police.

*Francisco Franco led the Nationalists in the Spanish Civil War. After victory in 1939 he became Spain's chief of state*

*The 'cellist Pablo Casals exiled himself from Spain in protest against Franco's authoritarian regime*

## SRI LANKA *see Ceylon*

# Sudan

Outside the fertile Nile valley, most of this huge country – Africa's largest – is sparsely populated bush and desert. The northern two-thirds of the country is Arab and Muslim, while the remainder belongs to Black Africa in race and religion. After independence in 1956, this division led to bitter and prolonged conflict.

**Early history** Some 3000 years ago, Egypt established outposts in the Sudan, from which grew the kingdom of Kush. In AD 350, Kush was overthrown by the Ethiopian kingdom of Axum. During the 6th century, Christian missionaries from Egypt set up states in the area. These kingdoms lived peaceably with Muslim-Arab Egypt for over 600 years. By the late 13th century Arabs from the north had taken over Christian Nubia and settled in the Sudan, where they introduced Islam. Further south, a people called the Funj conquered Christian Alwa, which had dominated central Sudan.

967,494 sq. miles
17,476,500 people
Capital: Khartoum

Picasso: Guernica, 1937

SWAZILAND
SWEDEN
SWITZERLAND
SYRIA

## SUDAN *continued*

**Egyptian and British rule** In 1820 troops of the Ottoman Viceroy of Egypt, Muhammad Ali, overwhelmed the Funj and established Turko-Egyptian rule throughout most of the northern Sudan. The southern Sudan was conquered during the reign of the Khedive Ismail (1863–79) with the help of the Englishmen Samuel Baker and Charles Gordon, both of whom later served as governors.

The Sudanese resented the corruption and harshness of Turko-Egyptian rule, and under the leadership of the religious fanatic Muhammad Ahmed, the Mahdi or 'saviour', they revolted. The Mahdi's followers took Khartoum and killed its defender, General Gordon. By 1885 they had driven out the Egyptians. Gordon's death aroused a storm of protest in Britain, and many people demanded vengeance. In 1896, Anglo-Egyptian forces – under Sir Herbert Kitchener, later Earl Kitchener of Khartoum – invaded the Sudan. The Mahdist state was crushed, after a battle at Omdurman in 1898 – in which the young Winston Churchill fought.

Britain and Egypt governed the Sudan jointly. Both before and after the Second World War Egypt tried to regain full control, but when the British departed in 1956 they left a Sudan independent of Egypt.

**Since independence** Instability was marked in Sudan's early years of independence. A military coup by General Nemery in 1969 brought firm government. From the early 1960's, the Khartoum government was challenged by Negro rebels in the south, attempting to break away from the Arab north. Nemery's government ended the bitter conflict – in which thousands were killed – when a peace agreement was signed in 1972.

*Turko-Egyptian rule in Sudan, already corrupt, was made worse by unchecked Arab slave raiding on the Negro provinces*

*General Gordon, suppressor of Sudan's slave trade, made an epic ten-month stand against the Mahdi in Khartoum. He was killed in 1884, with a relief force only two days from the town*

# Swaziland

The small African kingdom of Swaziland has long been closely tied to its powerful neighbour, the white-ruled Republic of South Africa, whose mining and business interests play a major role in the country's economy.

Originally settled by Sotho-speaking peoples, Swaziland was overrun in the early 19th century by Nguni-speaking peoples from the south. Their chief, Sobhuza I, having conquered the Sotho, set up a kingdom modelled upon that of the Zulus. The Swazi welcomed the British and Boers as allies against the Zulus, but under the weak chief Mbandzeni huge areas of land were signed away to the whites in the 1880's. Following the Anglo-Boer War of 1899–1902, Swaziland became a British protectorate. With Bechuanaland and Basutoland, it remained under the control of the British High Commissioner to South Africa when the Union became self-governing in 1910. Sobhuza II, who became Paramount Chief four years before the British established their protectorate, survived to lead Swaziland to independence in 1968.

6705 sq. miles
446,000 people
Capital: Mbabane

# Sweden

Neutrality is the keystone of Sweden's relations with the world. The country has kept out of wars since 1814, and during this long period of peace, the Swedes have built up the highest standard of living in Europe, based on their country's rich forests and its mineral resources.

The Swedish way of life has been called 'the middle way', because it combines both state and private enterprise. The country has an advanced system of social welfare, but in recent years this has been questioned by many Swedes as tending to make life too uniform and predictable.

**Foundation of Sweden** The first known settlers of the north of Sweden were the Lapps, but it was Svear tribesmen, later migrants from mainland Europe, who gave the country its name. Soon after their arrival, the Svears entered into a long period of conflict with the Gothars, settled further to the south. But the two tribes

173,666 sq. miles
8,301,000 people
Capital: Stockholm

*Eric IX, King of Sweden (1150–60), with a bishop. A zealous Christian, he became Sweden's patron saint*

united in the 6th century AD to form the first Swedish state. This nation, along with the other Scandinavian peoples, launched the Viking raids that terrorised western Europe. Under Eric IX it was fully converted to Christianity in the 12th century.

The early Swedish rulers were weakened by feuds with a powerful aristocracy, and with the country's merchants, who formed a trading alliance with a commercial union, the German Hanseatic League. Sweden, its power divided between these factions, became an easy prey to Danish ambitions, and in 1397 a treaty united Sweden and Norway under Danish sovereignty.

**Revolt and independence** Sweden gained little from the Danish union, and many Swedes fiercely resented it. In 1523 a national rising under Gustavus Vasa drove the Danes from the country. Vasa was elected king, founding the Vasa dynasty which was to rule Sweden until 1751 and establish it as a modern state.

Under Vasa, an effective central government was imposed on the country. He broke the power of the Roman Catholic Church, and made Lutheranism the state religion; he also curbed the nobles, stamped out peasant unrest, and ended Sweden's economic dependence on the Hanseatic League.

**Baltic struggle** For the next 200 years, Sweden fought with Denmark, Poland and Russia to win territory which would give the Swedes access to the Atlantic, and make their country mistress of the Baltic. At first the Swedes were successful. Under Gustavus Adolphus (1611–32), the greatest military commander of the age, Sweden gained new territory around the Baltic. His small but disciplined army fought on the Protestant side in the religious conflict known as the Thirty Years' War (1618–48), and its exploits became famed throughout Europe. Gustavus's policies were continued by his successor, Queen Christina, who allied herself with France. In 1654, Christina abdicated in favour of her cousin Charles Gustavus, and became a Catholic. With Charles's death in 1660, she tried to regain the throne, but she was forced to leave the country.

Charles XI (1660–97) took advantage of the monarchy's enhanced prestige to crush the nobility and set up a complete autocracy. Charles XII (1697–1718), however, drained the country's resources in the Great Northern War (1700–21). He invaded Russia in 1708, but the Swedish army was totally destroyed by Peter the Great at Poltava in the following year. Dominance in the Baltic passed to Russia when Sweden was finally forced to give up all its Baltic conquests in 1721.

Defeat by Russia ended Sweden's role as a great European power. In 1723 the monarchy was stripped of its absolutist powers by the nobility, and for the rest of the 18th century Sweden was ruled by aristocratic factions, closely linked with other countries. These factions were known as the 'Hats' (pro-French) and the 'Caps' (pro-Russian). Gustavus III tried to re-establish royal despotism, but nobles murdered him in 1792.

**New dynasty founded** In the early 19th century Sweden fought unsuccessfully against Napoleon. In addition, it lost Finland to Russia in 1809. Napoleon's brilliant general, Jean Baptiste Jules Bernadotte, although he fought against the Swedes, so impressed them that he was elected heir-apparent to the childless Charles XIII in 1810. At the same time, the Swedish Riksdag (parliament) adopted a new democratic constitution, still in force today.

Under Bernadotte, the last war in Swedish history was fought when, in 1814, Norway tried to resist union with Sweden. The two countries remained united until 1905, when the union was peacefully dissolved. In 1818 Bernadotte was at last crowned, as Charles XIV.

*Under Gustavus Vasa (1523–60), known as the 'Lion of the North', Sweden became the strongest of the Baltic states*

*Gustavus III (1771–92) was assassinated by nobles when he tried to re-establish absolute rule by the monarchy in Sweden*

**Modern Sweden** The history of 19th-century Sweden was dominated by industrial development and socialist ideas in government – though universal suffrage was not introduced until 1909. Much social legislation was pioneered – Sweden was the first country in Europe to establish a welfare state. The country's policy of neutrality was maintained in both world wars. From 1939 to 1945 Sweden was almost completely cut off from the West. Surrounded by German-occupied territory, the Swedes considered themselves unable to refuse supplies of iron ore to the Nazi war machine.

After 1945 Sweden kept up its economic progress, and continued its tradition of liberal socialism, under the premiership of Tage Erlander. Leading Swedes made their mark on international affairs. Chief among them were Count Folke Bernadotte, who was UN mediator in Palestine – he was assassinated by Jewish extremists in 1948 – and Dag Hammarskjold, Secretary-General of the UN from 1953 until his death in a plane crash in 1961. Hammarskjold was posthumously awarded the Nobel Peace Prize. This prize, together with others in the fields of science and literature, was created by another Swede, Alfred Nobel (1837–96).

Sweden's Social Democratic party has held power since 1932 (with the exception of a few months in 1936). The prime minister, Olof Palme, succeeded Tage Erlander in 1969.

King Carl XVI Gustaf, who succeeded to the throne in 1973, was reduced to a figurehead by a new constitution in 1974.

*August Strindberg (1849–1912), Sweden's greatest dramatist. In powerful plays such as* The Father *he explored the darker recesses of the human mind*

# Switzerland

Scenically the most celebrated country in Europe, Switzerland has built up an exceptionally high standard of living, in which tourism has played a large part.

The Swiss have achieved unity in the face of marked cultural differences from region to region, and even though there is no common language: French, German, Italian and Romansch are equal in status. The country's tradition of neutrality has greatly encouraged the growth of banking – the Swiss currency, known as the 'Holy Franc', is one of the world's strongest.

15,941 sq. miles
6,554,100 people
Capital: Bern

**Early history** The first settlers in Switzerland were Celtic tribes, who were conquered by Caesar's legions in 58 BC. Roman control lasted for 400 years until the legions were withdrawn in AD 401 and Germanic tribes from the east overran the country. French missionaries converted them to Christianity in the 6th century. In 768 Switzerland became part of Charlemagne's domains. After his death most of the country became a province of the Holy Roman Empire.

**Hapsburg rule and Swiss revolt** At first the emperors allowed the Swiss cantons (local communities) considerable freedom. In the 12th and 13th centuries, however, the Hapsburgs won control of the empire. Their rule was harsh, and in 1291 three cantons – Uri, Schwyz and Unterwalden – pledged themselves by a treaty known as the Perpetual Edict to end Hapsburg

*According to legend, William Tell, a Swiss patriot, was forced to shoot an apple from his son's head, as punishment for disobeying a Hapsburg official. The legend seems to have no factual basis*

rule. By 1315 they had won a precarious freedom and they were later joined in their struggle by Lucerne, Zurich and Bern. Finally, in 1499, after a century of conflict with the Hapsburgs, the Swiss won their independence by the Treaty of Basle. Their troops, regarded as Europe's best, were often hired as mercenaries.

The country's newly won freedom was almost immediately threatened by the religious disputes of the Reformation. Political differences between the cantons were further aggravated by quarrels between Protestants and Catholics. Two of the leading Protestant theologians, Calvin and Zwingli, lived in Switzerland, and they and their supporters were bitterly opposed by the Catholic cantons. In spite of these troubles, the country managed to preserve its independence and neutrality.

**Prosperity: 1648–1815** A century of Swiss independence was formally recognised by the major European powers with the Treaty of Westphalia in 1648. The country's mountainous isolation and the reputation of the Swiss soldier helped preserve this status, while trade through the Alpine passes brought prosperity. During this peaceful period, a loose confederation of cantons developed, though there was still no effective central government. Prosperous cities sprang up, in which power was usually in the hands of the merchant class – a fact that belied the country's reputation as a model of democracy.

Following the French Revolution in 1789, the Swiss gave secret help to restore the Bourbon monarchy. In 1798, French armies invaded Switzerland and a puppet state was set up. After Napoleon's defeat in 1815, the old system was restored and the European powers guaranteed Swiss neutrality.

**Struggle for unity** Many Swiss, influenced by the ideas of the French Revolution, were not content with the return to the old 18th-century constitution. They wanted also to establish an effective central government. These reformers, mainly Protestants, were opposed by the conservative Catholic cantons, who formed an alliance known as the Sonderbund. In a brief civil war in 1847 the Sonderbund was defeated, and in the following year a new constitution was drawn up.

This constitution set up a central federal government, elected on a basis of 'one man, one vote'. The cantons were allowed to keep some of their powers, and issues which divided the nation were to be decided by national plebiscites. (But the conservative Swiss did not allow women to vote until 1971.)

**Modern Switzerland** Due largely to their policy of avoiding conflict with other nations, the Swiss have enjoyed almost unbroken prosperity. They managed to preserve their neutrality in both world wars. After the First World War, the country became the headquarters of the League of Nations, but in 1945 the Swiss refused to join the United Nations on the grounds that membership would compromise their neutrality. Yet Switzerland is the headquarters of several UN agencies – as well as being the home of the International Red Cross, founded by a Swiss, Jean Henri Dunant, in 1864.

*John Calvin (1509–64), a leader of the Reformation, set up a government in Geneva which was based on strict religious teaching*

# Syria

Syria's age of greatness was in the 7th and 8th centuries, when it was the centre of a vast Arab empire. But for much of its long history Syria itself has been under foreign domination. Since independence in 1946 the country has been involved in the Arab conflict with Israel, and has been shaken by a series of internal coups.

**Invasion and conquest** In ancient times Syria was invaded and settled by many races. Alexander the Great introduced Greek civilization, and in 64 BC Syria became a Roman province. Roman and then Byzantine rule lasted until the 7th century AD, when the area fell to the fanatical Arab warriors of Islam who established the 200 year rule of the Omayyad caliphs.

71,498 sq. miles
7,111,000 people
Capital: Damascus

TAIWAN    TONGA
TANZANIA    TRINIDAD AND TOBAGO
THAILAND
TOGO

The 1¾ million-year-old skull of Homo habilis (third from left) discovered in Tanzania by Dr Louis Leakey, strengthened the belief that Africa may have been the cradle of mankind

## SYRIA *continued*

With Damascus as their base, the Omayyads held sway until 750, when the rival Abbasid family overthrew them and set up a new caliphate in Baghdad. Syria then fell in turn to the Seljuk Turks, Crusaders and Egyptian Mamelukes until the Ottoman Turks finally took over the country in the year 1516.

**Promises and revolts** Syria remained a part of the Ottoman Empire until the end of the First World War. During the war, Britain had promised Syrian Arab nationalists their freedom from Turkey if the Allies won. But, under the secret Sykes-Picot agreement, the British government had also pledged the country as a French sphere of influence.

In 1920 the French drove out the nationalists and the League of Nations gave France a mandate over Syria. In 1925 Damascus rose in revolt and the French had to bombard the city into submission. The Syrians were promised independence in 1936, but only in 1946 was full independence finally achieved.

**Independence and after** From 1946 the country suffered a succession of military and political coups. Between 1958 and 1961 it was part of the United Arab Republic under Egypt's President Nasser. Syrian forces took part in the Arab-Israeli wars of 1948, 1956, 1967 and 1973. Syria lost the strategically valuable Golan Heights to Israel in 1967, and won them back at the start of the 1973 war. But the heights were later re-taken by the Israelis.

Syrian politics have been dominated since 1963 by the ideology of the Baath Party, which advocates Socialist revolution throughout the Arab world. In 1966 Nureddin al-Atassi seized power; he himself was ousted in 1970, and Hafez al-Assad became president in 1971.

A member of a Syrian border patrol. Syria spends a large part of the national budget on its armed forces

## Taiwan

The island of Taiwan (Formosa) provided a refuge in 1949 for Chiang Kai-shek's Nationalist government when it was driven out of mainland China by the Communists under Mao Tse-tung. The Taiwan regime claimed to be the legal government of China, as the 'Republic of China', while Communist China demanded that Taiwan should come under its control.

The first Chinese emigrated to Taiwan at the time of the T'ang dynasty (618–906). The Portuguese were the first Europeans to reach the island, naming it Formosa ('beautiful'). The Dutch later set up outposts there, but were driven out in 1662. The Manchus conquered the island in 1683 and made it into a province of China. After the Chinese-Japanese war of 1894–5, Taiwan was ceded to Japan, which modernised the economy and built roads and railways. But the Japanese made no effort to colonise the island, using it mainly as a source of food for Japan itself.

Japan surrendered Taiwan to China in 1945. Four years later, defeated in China's civil war by the Communist forces of Mao Tse-tung, President Chiang Kai-shek's Nationalist government and its remaining followers – about 2 million – fled to Taiwan. United States support allowed Taiwan to keep its 'great power' status in the United Nations. Over the years it became one of the most prosperous countries in Asia. In 1971, however, after the USA had decided to back Communist China's admission to the UN, Taiwan was expelled and Communist China seated in its place.

13,887 sq. miles
15,652,300 people
Capital: Taipei

Chiang Kai-shek emerged as leader of the Chinese Nationalists in the 1920's

Kites carry propaganda slogans from mainland China to Nationalists living on the offshore islands of Quemoy and Matsu

## Tanzania

The United Republic of Tanzania was born in 1964 from the union of the large East African mainland state of Tanganyika and the tiny island republic of Zanzibar, 25 miles off its coast. But Zanzibar proved a troublesome partner, and unity was only nominal. Under the virtual dictatorship of Sheikh Abeid Karume, the island pursued a violent and largely independent course until Karume was killed by assassins in 1972. By contrast, mainland Tanzania, under the leadership of Julius Nyerere, acquired a reputation as one of the most stable and progressive of the new African countries.

**Early inhabitants** Nearly 2 million years ago, Olduvai Gorge in northern Tanganyika was the home of *Homo habilis*, one of the earliest-known of man-like creatures and a forerunner of *Homo sapiens sapiens*. In comparatively recent times – probably in the medieval period – ancestors of today's Bantu-speaking African population settled the fertile highland regions surrounding Tanganyika's arid central plateau. The coastal region, including the fertile islands of Zanzibar and Pemba, was colonised in the 8th century from southern Arabia and the Persian Gulf. The resulting mixed Arab-Bantu culture and language is known as Swahili. Today, Swahili is Tanzania's national language.

**Arabs and Europeans** The Portuguese, securing bases on their trade route to the Indies, established control of the Swahili coastal region during the 16th and 17th centuries, but were ousted in their turn during the 18th century by a fresh Arab invasion from Oman. By 1840, Zanzibar was ruled by the Sultan of Oman, who also controlled the trade in ivory and slaves from the interior of Tanganyika. Most of the great European explorers of East Africa – such as Burton, Speke and Stanley – based themselves on the thriving state of Zanzibar, and followed the caravan routes into the interior.

**Tanganyika: colony and mandate** In 1883–4, Germany annexed part of the coastal regions and, in 1890, the whole of Tanganyika. Zanzibar, however, became a British protectorate. In 1905–6, many of the peoples of southern Tanganyika rose against German rule. In the First World War, the country became a battleground between German and Allied forces. Following Germany's defeat, Tanganyika was ruled by Britain, first as a League of Nations mandate and then – after 1945 – as a United Nations trust territory.

**Independence** Although the poorest of Britain's East African territories, Tanganyika was the first to achieve independence: this was gained in 1961, under the leadership of Julius Nyerere, a former school teacher. Zanzibar became independent in December, 1963. The following year, after a bitter revolution, in which the African majority of the population overthrew the Arab sultan, Zanzibar joined with Tanganyika to form the new state of Tanzania. Under its first president, Nyerere, Tanzania became a one-party state. The Arusha declaration of 1967 formally committed Tanzania to socialism and to a policy of self-reliance which would free her from dependence on outside aid, whether from East or West. The cornerstone of this programme of 'African Socialism' was rural development through farming co-operatives – the so-called *ujamaa* villages.

Sheikh Abeid Karume, who had emerged as ruler of Zanzibar after the overthrow of the sultanate in 1964, became Tanzania's first vice-president. Until his assassination in 1972, the island was largely isolated from mainland Tanzania, turning to Communist countries such as China and East Germany for economic aid.

Relations between Tanzania and its neighbour, Uganda, dramatically deteriorated in September 1972, when, after Ugandan exiles in Tanzania had launched an unsuccessful invasion, Ugandan aircraft bombed Bukoba in reprisal. Tanzanian troops were moved to the border, but a peace plan, negotiated by the Somali Democratic Republic, was soon accepted by both sides.

364,900 sq. miles
14,725,300 people
Capital:
Dar es Salaam

During the 19th century Zanzibar's Arab rulers established the plantations that now supply most of the world's cloves

Julius Nyerere, a former schoolteacher, became Tanzania's first president in 1964

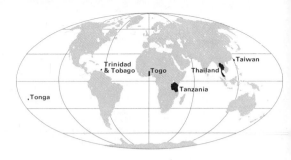

# Thailand

The kingdom of Thailand (formerly Siam) was the only country of south-east Asia to avoid conquest by the European powers in the 19th century. This was due in part to the stability of Thai society, strengthened by a policy of modernisation under popular monarchs. The policy was initiated by King Mongkut, who in the 1850's brought a Welsh governess, Anna Leonowens, to Bangkok to educate his children. (Her story was to become famous through the book *Anna and the King of Siam*.) Thailand produces over a million tons of rice a year; it is known as the 'rice bowl of Asia'.

**Early history** From the 11th to the 13th centuries the first Thai migrants moved from their settlements in southern China to the area of the Menam basin. The first Thai state in the Menam lowlands was Sukhothai, established in the 13th century. By 1438, however, it had been conquered by another Thai state, with its capital at Ayuthya. From 1548 to 1592 Ayuthya faced a succession of attacks by the Burmese. The 17th century was a golden age of peace and prosperity for Ayuthya, but a further war with Burma from 1760 to 1767 ended with the total destruction of the city. Thai unity was quickly restored, and in 1782 the present ruling Chakkri dynasty was founded, with its capital at Bangkok. Thailand expanded to conquer Chieng-Mai from the Burmese and Vientiane (Laos), as well as to dominate part of Cambodia and the northern Malay states.

**European challenge** From the middle of the 19th century Thailand came under pressure from the European powers. The Thais were forced to accept a series of commercial agreements; they lost Cambodia and Laos to the French and four Malay states to the British. But Anglo-French rivalry saved the rest of the country from attack, and Thailand, helped by its internal stability, managed to survive within its traditional borders. The Chakkri kings Mongkut (1851–68) and Chulalongkorn (1868–1910) gradually modernised Thai society.

**Revolution: 1932** In 1932, a group of young army officers and officials seized power and forced the monarchy to accept a constitution. The civilian leader Pridi Phanomyong was later ousted by the army. General Pibun Songkram became virtual dictator, but in 1944 he was replaced by Pridi.

**Civilians and generals** Pridi's attempts to introduce parliamentary democracy failed, and in 1947 Pibun returned. Strongly opposed to the spread of Communism, he allied Thailand with the United States, which saw the conservative Thai regime as a dependable ally in south-east Asia. These policies were continued by General Sarit, who overthrew Pibun in 1957, and by Marshal Thanom Kittikachorn, who succeeded Sarit in 1963. In 1968 a new constitution was introduced and Thailand held its first elections for ten years. In 1971, the constitution was abolished by Thanom and a group of army officers. Effective power in Thailand lay with the army, working with the king, Bhumibol Adulyadej. But in 1973 the regime collapsed, after its failure to put down a student revolt. The monarchy, however, survived the crisis.

*Buddhism is one of the strongest forces in Thai national life. This mythical figure guards the Temple of the Emerald Buddha in Bangkok*

Burma / Laos
THAILAND
Bangkok
Cambodia (Khmer)
Gulf of Siam / Vietnam (South)
Malaysia

198,455 sq. miles
38,275,100 people
Capital: Bangkok

*King Chulalongkorn, the 'Beloved Monarch', made sweeping reforms of Thai laws and customs during his reign (1868–1910)*

*Temples in the ruined city of Ayuthya, which compared, in the 17th century, with London in size and wealth. Buddhists gain merit in the after-life by building new temples rather than repairing old ones*

# Togo

Until 1914, the territory of this small West African republic formed the eastern part of the German colony of Togoland. In spite of the development of rich phosphate deposits since the 1960's, Togo remains one of the poorest countries of West Africa.

Before the colonial era Togoland was divided into a number of small tribal states, often at the mercy of their powerful neighbours, Ashanti and Dahomey. German missionaries became active among the Ewe peoples of the south during the 1840's, and in 1885 Togoland became a German colony. In 1914, it was occupied by British and French forces.

In 1922, the League of Nations divided Togoland between Britain and France as a mandated territory. French Togoland, the eastern and more developed part, included the railways and the port of Lomé. It became independent in 1960 as the Republic of Togo.

The new state found political stability hard to achieve. The Ewe peoples campaigned for reunification of the two Togos (British Togoland had been incorporated in Ghana). Togo's first president, Sylvanus Olympio, was assassinated in 1963, and his successor, his brother-in-law Nicholas Grunitzky, was ousted in 1967 in a military coup led by General Gmassingbe Eyadema.

Upper Volta
Dahomey
Ghana
TOGO
Lake Volta
Lomé

21,623 sq. miles
2,177,500 people
Capital: Lomé

# Tonga

Some 150 coral islands – only 36 of which are inhabited – make up the kingdom of Tonga in the south-east Pacific. They are known as the 'Friendly Islands'.

Tongans are descended from migrant Polynesians, who voyaged to reach the islands thousands of years ago, probably from Samoa. The islanders' system of land sharing is unique: all male Tongans are entitled to a free grant of $8\frac{1}{4}$ acres of land, known as an *api*, when they reach the age of 16.

**Hereditary kings** Tonga's ruling dynasty was founded *c*. AD 950. In the 15th century, the reigning king transferred much of his authority to his brother, and by the time the Dutch reached the islands in the 17th century, a system of dual kingship had become established. Captain James Cook was the first Briton to visit Tonga, which he christened the 'Friendly Islands', unaware that the natives were hatching plots against his life – he left before they had the chance to carry them out. British missionaries arrived in 1797, but were driven out of the islands by a devastating civil war.

George Tupou (reigned 1845–93) ended the war and Christianised his people. In 1900, Tonga was made a British protectorate; during Queen Salote's reign (1918–67), it became one of the most loyal members of the Commonwealth. In June 1970, Tonga was made an independent state within the Commonwealth.

Papua New Guinea / Western Samoa
Fiji
Australia / TONGA
New Zealand

270 sq. miles
99,800 people
Capital: Nuku'alofa

# Trinidad and Tobago

Asphalt (from the Pitch Lake on Trinidad) and oil form the basis of Trinidad and Tobago's wealth today – although, like the rest of Britain's former Caribbean possessions, the islands' economy was originally built on the sugar its vast plantations produced.

Columbus discovered the two islands in 1498. The Spanish established cocoa and sugar plantations, worked largely by slave labour imported from Africa. In 1797, Trinidad was captured by a British expedition, and it became a Crown colony in 1802.

After Trinidad's slaves were freed in 1833, more than 150,000 Indians were brought in to replace them on the plantations. Oil was discovered in 1909. Tobago – British since 1814 – was joined with Trinidad in 1889. The islands became independent in 1962, under the leadership of Dr Eric Williams. In 1970 an abortive 'Black Power' rebellion against Williams's government led to a period of martial law.

Caribbean Sea / Tobago
Port-of-Spain
TRINIDAD AND TOBAGO
Venezuela

1980 sq. miles
999,300 people
Capital: Port-of-Spain

*The Mosque of Sultan Ahmet, the Blue Mosque, is one of Istanbul's most splendid buildings*

# Tunisia

With the neighbouring Arab states of Algeria and Morocco, Tunisia forms the region known as the Maghreb (Arabic for west). In recent years, there have been moves to unite the Maghreb. After Tunisia gained independence from France in 1956, it prospered under the rule of Habib Bourguiba to become one of the most stable states of the Arab world. For centuries its chief source of wealth has been agriculture, but today industry and tourism are increasingly important.

63,378 sq. miles
5,311,000 people
Capital: Tunis

**Early period** Light-skinned Berber tribesmen occupied Tunisia at least 3500 years ago. The next settlers were Phoenicians from Palestine, who arrived on the coast in the 12th century BC and built the city of Carthage, in the area of present-day Tunis. By the 5th century it had become the capital of a thriving maritime empire. In the 3rd century BC, however, the Carthaginians came into conflict with the Romans.

Rivalry with Rome led to the three Punic Wars – so called from the Latin *Poeni*, meaning Phoenician. In the Second Punic War, Carthage came close to defeating Rome, when its greatest general, Hannibal, invaded Italy. But Rome rallied and, in the third war, completely defeated Carthage (146 BC). The city was destroyed and the rest of Tunisia was added to the Roman Empire. The country became one of Rome's main suppliers of wheat. As the power of Rome declined, so Tunisia again became open to invasion. Berbers from the interior threatened the province, while Vandals from Spain arrived in Tunisia in AD 439. The Byzantine emperor, Justinian, restored order in 533.

**Under Islam** Arab armies sweeping through North Africa captured Tunisia in 697. Under Arab rule, Tunisia and parts of what later became Algeria were called Ifriqiya (Africa). Many Berbers were converted to Islam, and a brilliant Muslim culture flourished. In the 11th century Ifriqiya was devastated by Bedouin tribes from the east.

From the 12th to the 16th centuries, the country was ruled by Berber dynasties. From the 15th century onwards, Tunisia and neighbouring Algeria joined in the struggle between Christianity and Islam. Khair al-Din (Barbarossa) and other naval chiefs fought Spanish fleets. By 1574 Ifriqiya had become a loosely controlled part of the Ottoman Empire. In the 18th century the sultanate of Tunisia was established.

**European intervention** In 1881 the French made Tunisia a protectorate. From 1907 onwards, nationalist opposition grew. In 1934 the Neo-Destour (New Constitution Party) was founded by a young lawyer, Habib Bourguiba. After the Second World War the French tried to suppress the nationalists by force, but in 1956 they yielded to the Tunisians' demands and Tunisia became a republic.

*Habib Bourguiba was the main architect of Tunisia's independence*

**Independent Tunisia** The French held on to their naval base at Bizerta, but in 1961 the Tunisians ordered them to leave and fighting broke out. Tunisia lost 1200 men before the French agreed to withdraw.

In recent years Tunisia has known steady progress. Its first president, Habib Bourguiba, won respect for his vigorous rule, moderation and far-sightedness.

# Turkey

The history of Turkey as a nation dates back to the 15th century, when the Ottoman Turks conquered Constantinople (present-day Istanbul) and created the great Ottoman Empire on the ruins of Byzantium. After the First World War a reborn Turkey emerged out of the collapse of the Ottoman Empire. Its leader, Kemal Ataturk, dragged Turkish society out of its centuries-old rut and made Turkey a modern state. He overthrew many cherished Turkish traditions, and ended Islam's status as the official religion. 

301,382 sq. miles
38,886,500 people
Capital: Ankara

**Colonisation of Anatolia: c. 6000 BC** The Anatolian plateau, which forms the heart of Turkey, was settled c. 6000 BC by peoples from the east, who established primitive farming communities.

Hittite invaders from central Asia, who knew how to use iron, swept through the Anatolian peninsula c. 1800 BC. Their empire lasted for nearly six centuries. Revolts, combined with attacks by Greek migrants, led to its collapse c. 1220 BC.

**Greek settlement: c. 600 BC** After the fall of the Hittites, two new kingdoms, Phrygia and Lydia, were founded by Indo-Europeans. Civilization reached an advanced stage in Lydia. In the 7th century BC the Lydians minted the first known coinage.

At about this time, Greek settlements were founded along the Anatolian coast, but by 550 BC many of these had fallen under Lydian control. Lydia itself was conquered by the Persians c. 546 BC, and the Greek settlements came under Persian rule. Persian dominance lasted until Persia itself was overthrown by Alexander the Great 200 years later. After his death, Macedonian immigrants established control in much of Anatolia and Greek civilization gradually spread over the entire area. The Romans began to make inroads into Anatolia in 133 BC, but it was not until 67 BC that the region was brought fully under their rule.

**Byzantine Empire** When the Roman Empire was divided by the Emperor Diocletian in the 3rd century AD, Byzantium, a Greek city, became the capital of the eastern empire. In AD 330, the Christian emperor, Constantine, moved his capital there from Rome, rebuilding the city and renaming it Constantinople. The Byzantine Empire, as the eastern empire became known, outlasted the Roman Empire in the west, surviving until 1453. Its 'golden age' was in the 6th century AD when, under Justinian, it spread westwards to Spain, northwards to the Danube and along the coast of North Africa.

From the 10th century onwards, the empire gradually contracted under attack from Turkic-speaking tribes – first the Seljuks and then the Ottomans. By the early 14th century, the once-mighty Byzantine Empire had shrunk to Constantinople and the area immediately surrounding it. The city was finally captured by the Ottomans in 1453 under the leadership of Mehmet II. The last emperor, Constantine XI, was killed in battle.

*Under Suleiman I (1520–66), known as 'The Magnificent', the Ottoman Empire reached its zenith*

**Expansion and decline** Ottoman expansion continued apace after the fall of Constantinople. Its highest point was reached under Suleiman I, known as 'The Magnificent' (1520–66). The Turks controlled Asia Minor, the Arabian peninsula, Egypt, North Africa and the Balkans; their armies threatened Vienna. The tide began to turn when Spanish and Venetian fleets won the Battle of Lepanto (1571). During the 17th and 18th centuries, Turkey was attacked by both Austria and Russia. The country fell into decay under a long line of incompetent sultans.

The army, too, was giving trouble, especially the elite fighting corps, the Janissaries. Originally its members had been Christian captives who were converted to Islam and then bound by an oath of loyalty to the sultan. But in time, the Janissaries became corrupt as well; they controlled the sultan rather than served him.

**War of Greek independence** In 1821, Greece – part of the Ottoman Empire since 1460 – rose against the Turks, who suppressed the revolt with great cruelty. In 1826 Britain and Russia agreed to co-operate in securing

*Heroism in the Crimean War. Turkish troops under Omar Pasha advance across the River Ingour*

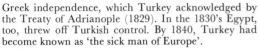

Greek independence, which Turkey acknowledged by the Treaty of Adrianople (1829). In the 1830's Egypt, too, threw off Turkish control. By 1840, Turkey had become known as 'the sick man of Europe'.

**Crimean War: 1854–6** As part of its aggressive policy towards Turkey, Russia claimed the right to 'protect' Christian subjects of the sultan. In 1853 Russian troops occupied Turkish territory on the Black Sea, and the sultan declared war. Public opinion in Britain regarded the idea of the Russians capturing Constantinople as disastrous. France, too, wanted to keep the Russian navy out of the Mediterranean. Britain and France went to the sultan's aid (1854) and, after an inconclusive campaign in the Crimea, peace was agreed in 1856.

**'Peace with honour': 1878** Europe was horrified when in 1875 and 1876 the Turks brutally crushed revolts in Herzegovina, Bosnia and Bulgaria. Russia stepped in, and an independent Bulgaria stretching from the Black Sea to the Aegean was created. Britain supported Turkey. A Congress at Berlin in 1878 settled the issue: the Turks lost some territory – a smaller Bulgaria was formed – but their remaining empire was guaranteed. The British prime minister, Disraeli, claimed that this settlement had brought 'peace with honour', but Turkey had, in effect, lost more prestige.

**Reform and revolution** Reformers, led by Midhat Pasha, forced Sultan Abdul Hamid II to introduce a democratic constitution in 1876. But Abdul Hamid soon re-established despotic power.

In the 1890's, the Committee of Union and Progress was set up by youthful reformers who became known as the 'Young Turks'; among them was Mustafa Kemal, who later became the nation's president. In 1908, troops revolted and the sultan had to restore the constitution of 1876. His attempt to organise a counter-revolution failed; he abdicated and the Young Turks took over.

The regime was soon threatened by the Balkan powers, who defeated Turkey in wars in 1912 and 1913. As a result, it looked to Germany for support. German officers were sent to train the army, and in 1914 Turkey signed a secret alliance with Germany against Russia.

**First World War: 1914–18** Turkey allied itself with Germany in the First World War. Allied forces landed at Gallipoli in 1915 – a costly attempt at invasion that ended in failure.

Elsewhere, however, Turkey met little but defeat, losing the last remnants of its vast empire. British armies commanded by General Allenby – aided by Arab guerrillas under T. E. Lawrence ('Lawrence of Arabia') – drove the Turks out of Palestine and Syria.

In 1920, the last sultan, Mehmet VI, accepted the Treaty of Sèvres, which reduced Turkey to the level of a minor power. Much territory was given to Greece. This provoked a nationalist uprising; the sultan was deposed and the Greeks were driven out. Allied occupation forces were eventually withdrawn.

**Ataturk's rule** The leader of the nationalist revolt, Mustafa Kemal, a soldier who had distinguished himself at Gallipoli, became first president in 1923. As dictator, he embarked on a policy of Westernisation. His people were forced to give up wearing the fez, and to take surnames. Kemal chose the name Ataturk (father of the Turks). The capital was moved from Constantinople (now Istanbul) to Ankara in 1923.

After Ataturk's death in 1938, his appointed successors held power until 1950. Turkey was neutral in the Second World War up to 1945, when it declared war on Germany. After the war Russia pressed claims to Turkish territory. America and Britain gave arms and financial aid to Turkey and it joined NATO in 1951.

**Turkey today** In 1950 the Democratic party, under Adnan Menderes, won power in free elections. The ten years of his rule were marked by corruption and repression. He was overthrown by the army in 1960,

*The sultan's way with his subject races: Turks slaughtering Armenians in 1896*

*Sultan Abdul Hamid in 1908, at the time of his overthrow by — the Young Turks*

*The man who created modern Turkey: Mustafa Kemal in soldier's uniform in 1922, during his struggle for power*

tried and executed. Unrest dominated the 1960's: civilian rule was restored, but in 1971 the army again dismissed the government. In the following year, the country returned to civilian rule with army sanction, but left-wing terrorism led to a period of martial law, often applied with extreme harshness. After elections in 1974, a new coalition government was formed by Bülent Ecevit. He promised to restore democratic freedom and speed economic development.

In recent years, Turkey's foreign policy has been dominated by the question of Cyprus. After a Greek-led overthrow of the Cyprus government in 1974, Turkish troops invaded Cyprus to set up an autonomous Turkish Cypriot state.

# Uganda

The early history of this beautiful African country by the shores of Lake Victoria was dominated by conflicts between Bantu warrior kingdoms. The strongest of these, Buganda, was until recently a 'state within a state'. Since gaining independence from Britain in 1962, Uganda has suffered from much unrest, culminating in the rise to power of the military dictator Idi Amin in 1971. Amin's expulsion of Asian citizens from the country in 1972 and mounting evidence of a reign of terror and killing involving thousands of Africans aroused world criticism.

**Kingdoms and missionaries** The rise of the Bantu kingdoms dates from the 13th century. The largest kingdom was Bunyoro, but by the 1700's Buganda had become the most powerful. Arabs and Swahilis from the East African coast began to arrive at this time, lured by the trade in slaves and ivory.

In the 19th century, explorers such as the Englishman, Speke – who discovered that Lake Victoria was a principal source of the Nile – and the American journalist Stanley visited Buganda. Mutesa I, Kabaka (king) of Buganda, which was at war with Bunyoro and threatened by Egyptian expansion, appealed to Christian missionaries for support, the first of whom arrived in 1877. In 1894 Britain established a protectorate over Buganda, and later the whole of Uganda. Exports of cotton and coffee were encouraged, and this gave the country economic stability. Relations between Britain and Buganda were often strained: in 1953 Mutesa II (known as 'King Freddie') was exiled for not co-operating in plans for independence.

**Independent Uganda** In 1962 a federal constitution gave Uganda its freedom, leaving Buganda with considerable control over its own affairs. Milton Obote became prime minister in 1963, with Mutesa, now returned, as president. In 1966, Obote set himself up as president and Mutesa fled to London, where he died in 1969.

Obote's rule grew oppressive, and the army under Amin, a Kakwa northerner from the West Nile district and a Muslim, took over. In 1972 he announced that he had been inspired by a dream to expel all Asians with British passports and to hand over all Asian businesses to black Ugandans. Indian traders and craftsmen had been in the country for generations. Most commercial firms were in Asian hands, and half of the industrial sector; Asians formed the backbone of the professions. By 1973, 40,000 had left, of whom 27,000 came to Britain. Amin's 'Africanisation' policy was closely watched by African states with large Asian populations. In 1972 there were border clashes and an abortive invasion by pro-Obote exiles from Tanzania. There were numerous reports of large-scale killings in the country.

91,134 sq. miles
10,970,000 people
Capital: Kampala

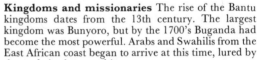

*Christian missionaries have long been established in Uganda*

*As part of their tribal traditions, the Bunyoro of Uganda re-enact the coronation of their ruler on each anniversary of his accession*

*Idi Amin (centre), later to become Uganda's president, directs army exercises. Watching him is Obote (with stick), whom Amin overthrew*

The USSR, or Soviet Union – the heir of the Russian Empire which was built up by the tsars – comprises 15 so-called republics. By far the largest is the Russian Soviet Federal Socialist Republic

# Union of Soviet Socialist Republics

The USSR is the largest country in the world, covering nearly one-sixth of the earth's land surface. Except for the United States, with which it shares the rank of 'super-power', no other country today has comparable economic and military strength.

8,649,489 sq. miles
253,268,300 people
Capital: Moscow

Russia's totalitarian system of government, established after the Bolshevik Revolution of 1917, is directed by a small body of men drawn from the ranks of the Communist Party, the only political party permitted in the country. The Soviet rulers also control the destinies of some 100 million people in the 'satellite' countries of eastern and central Europe – Czechoslovakia, Poland, Hungary and others – which were engulfed by Soviet expansion during and after the Second World War.

Expansion, ruthless though interrupted, is a major theme of Russian history. It received its main impetus from the ambition of autocratic rulers such as Peter the Great and Catherine the Great. With expansion came tyranny; Peter's obsessive desire to 'catch up with the West' in the 17th and 18th centuries imposed a burden on his subjects which foreshadowed the brutal oppression suffered under Joseph Stalin in the 20th century.

Russia's long frontiers made it vulnerable to invasion from every direction. The country's rulers countered the menace by militarising the whole of society and by concentrating all power in their own hands. The Revolution of 1917 did indeed change Russia, but the rigid system which the Communist élite has developed to rule the Soviet Union is in essence very similar to the tsarist autocracy which created the Russian Empire.

Scythian warriors, pictured on this comb, were among the first settlers of the vast Russian steppes

**Earliest inhabitants:** The first people in what is now Russia were Stone-Age Neanderthal men who moved into the southern grassland steppes 80,000 years ago. They were succeeded by modern men *c.* 35,000 BC, but the peopling of Russia was a slow process, lasting thousands of years. Dominant among the many tribes who roamed the steppes were the Scythians, nomadic horse warriors who arrived *c.* 500 BC, and the Sarmatians who followed and replaced the Scythians two centuries later.

By AD 400 a wave of Eastern Slavs from the area covered by present-day Romania had begun farming the land between the Rivers Dnieper and Dniester, and by the 8th century they had spread over a large territory, forming tribal regions that developed into principalities such as Kiev.

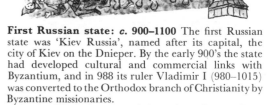

A medieval Russian chronicle shows the Christian warriors of ancient Kiev fighting pagan invaders

**First Russian state: *c.* 900–1100** The first Russian state was 'Kiev Russia', named after its capital, the city of Kiev on the Dnieper. By the early 900's the state had developed cultural and commercial links with Byzantium, and in 988 its ruler Vladimir I (980–1015) was converted to the Orthodox branch of Christianity by Byzantine missionaries.

As the Kiev state expanded northwards, non-Slavs came under its rule. The power of its central government weakened and by *c.* 1100 the state had developed into a loose union of principalities.

**Democracy in Novgorod: *c.* 1100** One of Kiev's northern principalities was the city of Novgorod, near the Baltic Sea. In the 12th century Novgorod grew into an important trading centre. Its merchants flourished, and borrowed ideas and institutions from the German cities with which they traded. Novgorod was unique among early Russian states in having some form of democracy; the well-to-do were allowed to elect their own representatives.

**Mongol invasion: *c.* 1250** The development of Kiev Russia was cut short in the mid-13th century by an invasion of Mongols from the east, led by the heirs of Genghis Khan. The Mongol conquest was followed by the setting up of the 'Golden Horde', a Moslem state whose inhabitants were Tatars. The Golden Horde allowed the Orthodox Church freedom to manage its own affairs, and also protected the Russian princes, provided they paid tribute.

**The rise of Moscow: 1300–1500** Rivalry developed between the princes of the different Russian territories. The Church supported the princes of Muscovy, or Moscow. This city was founded in 1147 near the head-

Alexander Nevsky (1236–63), prince of Novgorod, defended Russia's frontiers against invasion. He became a national folk-hero

Moscow, founded in 1147, was Russia's capital up to the time of Peter the Great, who made St Petersburg his capital. Moscow regained its status in 1918

waters of the Dvina, Dnieper and Volga rivers, a useful site for trade. Moscow's princes built up their power on the basis of the Byzantine doctrine of autocracy, combined with the ruthless methods of Tatar government. Under Muscovite rule, the democratic institutions of Novgorod were suppressed.

By the end of the 15th century the ruling prince of Moscow, Ivan III, known as 'the Great' (1462–1505), felt strong enough to reject the authority of the Khans (rulers) of the Golden Horde, which had already broken up into smaller units.

Ivan III saw himself as the heir to Byzantium's traditions and confirmed his belief by marrying the niece of the last Byzantine emperor. The religious advisers of Ivan's successors assured them that Moscow was the heir to Constantinople, the Third Rome, and 'a fourth there shall not be'.

### Ivan the Terrible, the first tsar: 1533–84
Ivan III's grandson, Ivan IV – known as 'the Terrible' – also believed in Moscow's imperial destiny. He took the title of tsar (derived from the Latin *caesar*). Ivan's appetite for power and territory was insatiable, leading him to excesses of cruelty. By 1555 he had crushed the Khanates of Kazan and Astrakhan and brought the whole Volga valley under his rule.

Ivan strengthened the central government of the state and created a ruthless security police force, to which he transferred large parts of his realm. The territory which the security police occupied, the *Oprichnina*, formed a state within the state.

### Nobles and serfs
Ivan also created a nobility to carry out his policies. They kept their rank as long as they served him faithfully. There were still some ancient and very rich aristocratic families – the 'boyars' – but these too were brought more and more under the tsar's control. The boyars did not demand legal institutions to guarantee their status, such as western European nobilities enjoyed; the idea of law, with its clearly defined rights and duties, was alien to the Russian mind, and long remained so. Power and responsibility belonged to the tsar alone.

In return for their obedience to the tsar, the nobility were given land and were entitled to the services of the peasants who lived on it. During the 16th and 17th centuries, the situation of the peasants became even less enviable as their few liberties were restricted. Serfdom was fully established in Russia by a law of 1649; by then it had virtually disappeared from most of western Europe.

### 'Time of Troubles': 1605–13
In 1598 a boyar named Boris Godunov, who had been a favourite of Ivan the Terrible, seized the throne. After Boris's death in 1605 various pretenders fought for power, with foreign support. During part of this period, known as the 'Time of Troubles', Moscow was occupied by Polish troops, and Swedish armies invaded the north. The country was ravaged by peasant rebellions, which were ruthlessly suppressed.

### Peter the Great looks to Europe
The history of the modern Russian state begins with the reign of Peter I, known as 'the Great' (1682–1725). Peter believed that to become a great power Russia had to copy modern European methods of warfare and government. He set himself to reform the country with ruthless energy. Young Russians were sent to the West to learn military and naval techniques, ship-building and industrial skills, as Peter himself had done. Foreigners were imported to reorganise the government service, and European methods of education and science were introduced. Peter rebuilt the fleet and created a new army.

Peter's main successes were military. He won important victories over Sweden, Turkey and Persia. At Poltava in 1709, he defeated Charles XII of Sweden, one of the greatest commanders of the age. Russia annexed a large part of the Baltic coast, and a new capital, named St Petersburg (now Leningrad), was

*Ivan the Terrible was the first Russian ruler to call himself tsar*

*The ambitious Boris Godunov was believed to have murdered the rightful tsar when he succeeded to the throne in 1598*

*Peter the Great saw beards as a sign of Russian backwardness and ordered their removal. He himself cut the beards of some of his nobles*

built on the Gulf of Finland. The city became known as 'Russia's window on to Europe', while Peter himself took the title of Emperor of Russia.

### 'Westernisation' and expansion
Catherine the Great (1762–96) came to the throne after the murder of her husband, Peter III. She embraced Peter the Great's work of modernisation, and advances were made in provincial administration and education, with the energetic adoption of Western methods.

The Russian army created by Peter the Great had become one of the most formidable in Europe. During Catherine's reign vast new territories were added to the empire by annexation and conquest. Three partitions of Poland, the last completed in 1795, brought millions of Ukrainians, Byelorussians, Lithuanians and Poles under Russian rule. The annexation of Kurland, with its mixed Latvian and German population, increased Russia's Baltic coastline. In the south, Russia expanded to the shores of the Black Sea and took the Crimean peninsula from the Ottoman Empire. Further gains were made in the Caucasus and in the steppes lying between Siberia and Turkestan.

During the 18th century, the social and political ideas of the European Enlightenment began to reach Russia. At first these ideas were encouraged by Catherine the Great herself, who entertained such men as the French philosopher Diderot at her court. But at the end of her reign, disturbed by accounts of the violence of the French Revolution, she began to persecute those who held liberal ideas.

### Pugachev's rebellion: 1773–5
Under Catherine, industry progressed, especially in the Urals. The country became a major producer of iron ore. But agriculture remained stagnant, and the poverty of the serfs grew worse. In 1773–5 a large-scale rebellion broke out in the Urals and Volga regions, led by Emilian Pugachev, who claimed to be Peter III. (Peter had in fact been murdered in 1762.) Pugachev's followers consisted mainly of Cossacks, the expert horsemen who had been settled in the eastern and southern border areas. Pugachev was himself a Cossack. The rebels also included Muslim tribesmen and runaway Russian serfs. Catherine crushed the rebellion, and Pugachev was publicly executed in Moscow.

### Plans to reform the empire: 1801–12
Catherine's grandson, Alexander I, planned to reform the empire. While retaining a centralised state he wanted to ensure that it worked efficiently and that as its absolute ruler he would be a benefactor of the people. His plans, including a scheme for modernising education, were frustrated by war with France.

### Napoleon invades: 1812
Napoleon led 675,000 men into Russia in a bid to crush his last major rival on the European continent. At the Battle of Borodino, outside Moscow, both sides had heavy losses. The Russians retreated and the French entered Moscow. But the tsar rejected offers of peace, and Napoleon, fearing his army's food supplies would not outlast the Russian winter, decided to retreat into Poland.

Illness and hunger, due largely to the Russian 'scorched-earth' policy of destroying their own crops and animals as they retreated, harassment by Cossacks and guerrilla bands and, worst of all, the extreme cold of the Russian winter, reduced the French army to a fighting force of only 30,000 men. The Russian armies invaded Prussia in 1813 and played a leading part in the defeat of Napoleon at the Battle of Leipzig.

*Catherine's policies are attacked in a British cartoon showing her being tempted by the Devil's offer of Warsaw and Constantinople*

*Alexander I's career began with liberal reform but ended in harsh repression*

*A fire ravaged Moscow in 1812, shortly after the entry of the French. The fire was probably accidental. Napoleon, however, saw it as a sign of Russian determination to make any sacrifice rather than surrender to him*

## USSR *continued*

**Triumph of conservatism: 1815** Russia's victories over Napoleon – the prelude to his final downfall in 1815 – strengthened the hands of the extreme conservatives, who argued that a regime which had so gloriously crushed the great Napoleon was clearly the best that could be desired. Floods of patriotic rhetoric extolled the glories of Russia's past and justified existing conditions, including serfdom. Alexander's dreams of reform were abandoned.

Some Russians of liberal outlook passionately wished to change the regime, but they could neither grasp the apparatus of power nor break it, and they could not communicate their ideas to the serfs who might have chiefly benefited. A group of brave and enlightened military conspirators tried to stage a revolution in December 1825, when Alexander I died and there was uncertainty about his successor. The revolt was quickly crushed. These 'Decembrists', as they were known, came to be regarded as the first martyrs of the Russian revolutionary cause.

**Growth of tsarist bureaucracy** Nicholas I (1825–1855), who succeeded Alexander, was served by an impressive host of policemen and civil servants. They were strong enough to force the small but increasing number of liberal-thinking Russians into silence. Although the government machine compelled obedience, it was not efficient. Excessive numbers of poorly paid officials, charged with the execution of complicated, unjust and contradictory laws, inevitably became both inefficient and corrupt.

Under Nicholas, autocracy was upheld without the least concession to current liberal thought. The tsar felt called upon to defend monarchical government even outside Russia's boundaries. In 1848, Russian forces suppressed revolution in Romania, and in 1849 they helped the Hapsburg rulers of Austria crush the Hungarians. These actions gained Nicholas the label of 'gendarme of Europe'.

**War in the Crimea: 1854–6** Soon Nicholas became involved in war in the Crimea, which was largely brought about by British and French determination to check Russian designs on Turkey. Russian soldiers fought hard, especially in defence of Sebastopol; yet the war ended in Russia's defeat. The campaign revealed the inefficiency of the army's commanders, the weakness of its supply services and communications, and the inability of Russia's economy to support a major war.

*Russia's first revolutionary martyrs were executed for their part in the Decembrist conspiracy (December 1825), the earliest attempt to overthrow tsarist rule*

*The institution of serfdom was long preserved in Russia. A 19th-century cartoon shows landlords gambling – using serfs as stakes*

*British and French fears of the Russian 'bear' and its designs on Turkey led to the Crimean War*

**Alexander II, the 'Tsar Liberator'** Nicholas I's successor, Alexander II, came to the throne in 1855. Like Alexander I, he was determined to reform, modernise and strengthen Russia. Alexander, and some enlightened officials and landowners who advised him, believed that reform should be the work of a benevolent sovereign, operating through a strong bureaucracy, though discounting public opinion and private initiative. Despite this reformist outlook, they too were faithful to the mainstream of Russian political tradition and to the ideas of Alexander I.

By the Edict of Emancipation, passed in 1861, serfdom was abolished in Russia. The peasants were enabled to buy land, paying annuities to the government, which in turn compensated the landowners. In practice, the landlords' control of the serfs was replaced by that of government officials. The emancipated peasants of Russia were still far from achieving free and equal citizenship.

In 1864 a modern judicial system was set up, and citizens in the provinces were allowed to take part in local government. The tsar refused, however, to institute any central parliament.

**Assassination of Alexander II: 1881** Alexander's government had tried to make valuable reforms, but these did not satisfy the political extremists. Young educated Russians were appalled by the gulf between their own Europeanised culture and the squalor and ignorance in which the Russian peasants lived; between the material progress of the West and the backwardness of Russia; and between the comparatively enlightened administration of European countries and the corruption, brutality and unpredictability of Russian government. They could see no remedy but revolution. Small conspiratorial groups were formed, and attempts were made, with some success, to organise workers in the growing industrial cities. In 1881 a revolutionary group, called the 'People's Will', killed the tsar. His successor, the reactionary Alexander III (1881–94), was an autocrat of the most conservative type. All plans for reform were shelved, and there were to be no more political concessions.

Education suffered in particular. Though Russia could now afford to pay for a system of efficient primary schools, very little money was spent on this. It was not government policy to allow children from the lower social classes to rise to the higher levels of education. Thus the dangerous cultural gap between the élite and the huge mass of Russia's peasant population – which had done so much to drive the young intellectuals into revolution – was deliberately maintained.

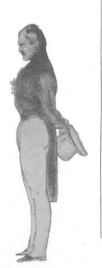

*Leo Tolstoy (1828–1910), in his novels* War and Peace *and* Anna Karenina, *posed basic questions about life's meaning, as well as painting a vivid portrait of Russian society in the 19th century*

*The reforming tsar Alexander II was killed by an extremist's bomb as he travelled through St Petersburg, his capital. Seven previous attempts had been made on his life*

*Nicholas I admitted that serfdom was both unjust and inefficient. But he feared that to end it would undermine the regime*

**Industrial revolution reaches Russia** Under the despotic rule of Alexander III and that of his successor, Nicholas II (1894–1917), Russia went through the decisive early stages of an industrial revolution. The statesman most responsible for this progress was Count Sergei Witte, Minister of Finance from 1893 to 1903. With the help of large foreign investments, especially by France, mining and metallurgy advanced rapidly, and oil and electrical industries were established. The French government also made huge loans.

The price of industrial expansion was paid by the peasants, whose taxes were spent, not on improving agriculture, but on industry and the army. Government neglect of agriculture, and the problem of over-population, were the main causes of growing peasant poverty. In many parts of Russia the large estates in the hands of nobles, many of them absentee landlords, caused great bitterness and led politically minded peasants to demand that the landlords be dispossessed.

**National oppression: c. 1890** Russia was a multi-national empire: less than half of its population were Russians. In the 1890's, the Russian government embarked on a new policy, which became known as 'Russification'. It was not now enough that all subjects should obey the tsar: they were ordered to consider themselves part of the Russian nation, and to adopt the Russian language and the Orthodox religion. This policy made enemies of peoples who until then had been loyal to the regime – for example, the Finns, Armenians, Baltic Germans and Tatars.

Special forms of oppression were reserved for the Jews in tsarist Russia. They endured many legal forms of discrimination, and also had to face frequent mob attacks (pogroms) on their lives and property. These outrages, carried out by gangs of poor townspeople, were tolerated by the police and sometimes deliberately started by them; there were often fatalities.

**Russo-Japanese war: 1904–5** A policy of territorial and economic expansion in the Far East brought Russia into conflict with Japan. To the surprise of the world, tiny Japan defeated the Russian army in Manchuria and annihilated the tsar's fleet in the Tsushima Straits. Humiliation in war brought political unrest in Russia to boiling point.

*Sergei Witte, the ablest of Nicholas II's ministers, created the conditions for the rapid growth of Russian industry*

**Revolution of 1905** While still trying to stave off defeat by Japan, Russia was shaken by large-scale revolt at home, the so-called Revolution of 1905. It was sparked off by the events of 'Bloody Sunday' on January 22, when demonstrators marching to petition the tsar in the Winter Palace in St Petersburg were shot down by troops.

By the end of the month nearly half a million workers were on strike; in some cities there was street fighting, peasants rose against their landlords in provinces all over Russia, and workers in St Petersburg armament factories set up the first Soviets (workers' councils). Units of the armed forces revolted; mutiny occurred on

*Tsarist troops confront St Petersburg workers on their way to petition the tsar on January 22, 1905. The clash, in which the troops opened fire, sparked off revolution in Russia*

the *Potemkin*, a battleship of the Black Sea fleet. In October a national railway strike brought the regime to the verge of collapse, and the tsar, Nicholas II, was compelled to introduce a constitution.

**Parliamentary experiment: 1905–7** The constitution established a Duma (parliament); but though it was elected on a broad franchise, it had little real power. The first two Dumas proposed sweeping reforms, but they were rejected by the tsar, whose only answer was to dissolve the Duma. In 1907 the newly appointed prime minister, Peter Stolypin, reduced the franchise by decree. Subsequent Dumas had conservative majorities, but even they were antagonised by the authoritarian behaviour of ministers and officials. After 1907 the imperial government, under Stolypin, made efforts to reform Russia, notably in education and agriculture. Industry also advanced rapidly. But after the assassination of Stolypin in 1911, the tsarist regime reverted to its former reactionary character. Waves of strikes once more swept the country.

*The Russian ballerina Anna Pavlova (1885–1931). The beauty and emotional power of Pavlova's art won her a legendary reputation in her lifetime*

**Russia in the First World War: 1914–17** Russia entered the First World War in 1914. Its armies suffered appalling casualties and shattering defeats. A majority in the Duma became hostile to the government, largely because even the best conservative ministers were replaced by inferior politicians – due, it was widely claimed, to the malevolent influence of a Georgian monk called Rasputin on the pliable tsar and tsarina. Poor administration caused the disruption of agriculture, war industries and transport. Early in 1917 food shortages became acute in the capital.

*Many Russian soldiers, demoralised by disaster at the front and reports of chaos at home, gave themselves up to the Germans in 1917*

**'February Revolution': 1917** In 1917, strikes and demonstrations against the government escalated as workers in the capital took to the streets. Mutinies occurred in the army units stationed in Petrograd (formerly St Petersburg, later Leningrad). The troops joined forces with the demonstrators, and the imperial regime ceased to function. Nicholas II, Russia's last tsar, abdicated at the insistence of the Duma, and a newly formed provisional government proclaimed Russia a republic.

These events – which took place in March but are known as 'the February Revolution', owing to a difference of 13 days between the calendars then in use in Russia and the rest of Europe – initiated the great Russian Revolution, which lasted more than three years. The Revolution fell into three main stages: the struggle of the moderates to hold power, the Bolshevik 'October Revolution', and the long period of civil war which followed.

*Nicholas II withdrew into family life rather than face Russia's many problems. His secret execution in 1918 marked the end of the 300-year-old Romanov dynasty*

*Rasputin, a dissolute peasant-monk, established a sinister influence over the weak Tsar Nicholas II and his family*

## USSR *continued*

**Moderates lose power** In the first eight months after the February Revolution, the moderate socialist politicians of the Duma, led by a lawyer, Alexander Kerensky, struggled to establish themselves in power. Their failure to do so was due to the rapid breakdown of the machinery of government, the appeal to the masses by the extreme left and the hostility of conservatives and army commanders. The moderates' fate was sealed at last by their failure to beat the Germans or to extract Russia from the war. Morale in the army collapsed, and the extremists won influence among the soldiers.

**'October Revolution': 1917** On November 7, the extreme left-wing socialist group known as the Bolsheviks, who later took the name of Communists, seized power. Their supreme leader was Vladimir Ilyich Lenin, a great theorist and practitioner of revolution, who had built up his party ever since 1903 – partly in Russia and partly abroad – according to his own ideas of revolutionary organisation and tactics. The Bolshevik Revolution – known as the 'October Revolution' – was almost bloodless. The so-called 'storming' of the Winter Palace, the seat of the moderate socialist government under Kerensky, encountered virtually no resistance. The Bolsheviks' military action was planned and led by Leon Trotsky, a former opponent of Lenin who had now become his closest comrade-in-arms.

The Bolsheviks soon established a monopoly of political power. They forcibly suppressed the Constituent Assembly elected in November 1917, in which they held only a quarter of the seats. In March 1918 they made a peace settlement with the German government under the Treaty of Brest-Litovsk.

**Civil war: 1918–20** In the summer of 1918 civil war broke out. Bolshevik forces, led by Trotsky, were opposed at various times by democrats, military dictators and by nationalist movements among the non-Russian peoples. From the beginning of 1919 the anti-Communists or White Russians received large supplies of war material, as well as military advice, from the Allied powers of the West. The war brought massive bloodshed, destruction and starvation. Both sides tortured and executed opponents and robbed peasants of their crops. The end of 1920 saw a Communist victory, but Russia was exhausted.

**Establishment of the USSR: 1920–2** After the Revolution, the new rulers of Russia set up a rigid system of government which has lasted until the present day. The regime was supposed to be based on the Soviets (workers' councils). But in practice power was concentrated first in the hands of the Central Committee of the Communist Party and then in those of the Politburo, which decided all major policy questions, and the Secretariat, which was responsible for appointments within the party. The new government promised freedom to the non-Russian nationalities, such as the Ukrainians and Tatars. But despite the establishment of a federation of 'republics' – the Union of Soviet Socialist Republics – Moscow still kept absolute control.

*The theories of Karl Marx (1818–83), a German-Jewish philosopher, gave the Russian Bolsheviks their essential inspiration. Marx called on the working classes to unite against capitalism. In his major work* Das Kapital *he attempted a scientific analysis of how capitalist economies work*

*A caricature of Leon Trotsky, leader and organiser of the Bolsheviks' army, who became Commissar of War after the Revolution. He was feared as a rival by Stalin, who forced him to leave Russia in 1929*

*A patriotic poster of 1920 depicts the Russian worker as a ploughman, ripping up an old world littered with money-bags and crowns*

*A tsarist passport photograph of the young Lenin. After years of exile he returned to Russia in 1917 to lead the Bolsheviks into power*

**Recovery from the effects of war** The Communist programme called for total nationalisation of all Russia's resources. But the losses and disruption resulting from the long years of war forced Lenin to formulate what became known as the New Economic Policy (NEP). Private ownership of land was tolerated, to appease the peasants who had acquired the former landowners' estates during the revolutionary period. Small businesses were also allowed to operate in industry and trade.

**Stalin wins struggle for power: 1924–7** Lenin was rendered helpless by a stroke in 1922, and after his death in 1924 a struggle for the succession developed. Within three years this was won by the party secretary, Joseph Stalin, a Georgian, who defeated his rivals Trotsky, Zinoviev and Kamenev.

Stalin's victory was due to his control over the appointments of party officials, and also to his pursuit of moderate economic policies and his appeal to Russian national pride. He maintained that the Russian workers and peasants could, by their own efforts, 'build socialism in one country'. His rivals, such as Trotsky, argued that the Revolution's success could only be maintained if it spread throughout the world, or at least to such advanced industrial countries as Britain, Germany and the United States. Its failure to do so weakened the position of Trotsky and his supporters. (Trotsky, exiled in 1929, was murdered in Mexico in 1940, reputedly by a Stalinist agent.)

**Drive for industrialisation: 1928–37** Once firmly in control, Stalin changed his moderate economic policy. He was convinced that Russia would be in great danger until it became a full-scale industrial power, and he determined to achieve this at any cost. The result was the forced 'collectivisation' of agriculture and a drive for intensive industrialisation in the first two Five-Year Plans (1928–37).

The effect of collectivisation was not so much to make farming more efficient – in fact, there was little gain in output – as to ensure that a much larger share of the crops was taken by the state, at very low prices. The peasants paid the bill for industrialisation.

Forced collectivisation caused immense upheaval, leading to the starvation of millions of peasants and the destruction of more than half of Russia's livestock. Of the peasants who survived the process many millions were herded into the new industrial and mining centres and construction sites.

Mass suffering produced discontent, which took political form in agitation against the regime, especially among the non-Russian peoples. Stalin's response was to give the security police almost unlimited power, and to pursue 'Russification' no less ruthlessly than the tsars had done. Millions were deported to forced labour camps; vast factories and farms were established in remote parts of the country, under the direction of the security police.

**Purge of the party: 1936–9** By the mid-1930's Stalin's attention had turned to the removal of real or possible enemies inside the Communist Party. In the 'Great Purge' of 1936–9, the existing leadership of the party, the central ministries, industry and the armed forces was swept away. The purges started as an attack on the surviving followers of Stalin's former rivals, but the number of arrests got out of control as police officials competed with each other in unmasking 'enemies of the people'. Every level of society was hit. Especially sensational were the 'show trials' of leading figures, and the execution of army commanders in 1937. About half the officer corps, from the rank of major upwards, were arrested. Stalin called a halt to the purges in 1939.

**Second World War: 1941–5** The Russians believed that if the victors and vanquished of 1918 were reconciled, the Soviet Union would be in danger of attack from a united capitalist world. Thus they supported Germany against the West in the 1920's and the West

*Vladimir Tatlin's design, in the 'constructivist' style, for a monument to the world Communist movement. Experimental art forms such as constructivism lost official favour in the late 1920's*

*Stalin, idealised in a propaganda poster, is seen against a background of industrial progress. Born Djugashvili, he adopted the name Stalin (meaning 'man of steel') as a young revolutionary*

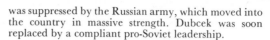

Eisenstein's patriotic film Alexander Nevsky, made in 1938, depicted the 13th-century Russian struggle against Teutonic invaders

against Germany from 1935 to 1939. They turned to Germany once more from 1939 to 1941. In 1941, however, the Russians found themselves faced with the full might of the German war machine.

Hitler's invasion in 1941 was the first major test of Soviet Russia's strength. At first the Germans achieved great success, but with the heroic Russian defence of Stalingrad (now Volgograd) in the winter of 1942–3, the tide turned. By 1945, the Soviet Union's armies had advanced from the depths of Russia to control more than half of Europe.

**'Cult of Personality': 1945–53** Just as the defeat of Napoleon in 1815 had strengthened tsarist conservatism, so the victory of 1945 increased the prestige of Stalin and his regime. In the following years a totalitarian autocracy prevailed in Russia; Stalin was glorified by a 'cult of personality', which accorded him a god-like status. Party, army, bureaucracy and security police were tools in his hands, and he manipulated each according to his whim.

The alliance between the Soviet Union, Britain and the United States broke down at this time and gave place to the 'Cold War'. The determination of Russia to impose its political system on eastern Europe, by force if necessary, alarmed Western opinion. Deadlock was reached over the future of Germany. In 1948, the Soviet Army tried to blockade Berlin, but the West kept the city supplied by an air-lift. In 1952 the North Atlantic Treaty Organisation (NATO) was set up: the United States was committed to defend western Europe against a Soviet attack.

A May Day parade in Moscow's historic Red Square, with part of the Kremlin (right) and St Basil's Cathedral in the background. The parade is held annually to commemorate the 1917 Revolution

**'Thaw' after Stalin** When Stalin died in March 1953, his successors, distrusting each other, established what they called 'collective leadership'. The feared and hated chief of the MVD (security police), Lavrenti Beria, Stalin's closest confidant, was arrested and executed. After his death the powers of the security police were curtailed; many political prisoners were released, and the Russian people received more and better consumer goods. By 1957 one man, Nikita Khrushchev, had emerged as the leader of the Soviet Union. He avoided the excesses of Stalin's 'personality cult'. He himself denounced this cult, the police terror and 'show trials', in a historic speech in 1956.

Khrushchev made enemies among the leadership of the party; in particular he offended the leaders of the armed forces by cutting the defence budget to pay for more consumer goods. In 1964 he was voted out of power by the party's Central Committee. He was succeeded by Leonid Brezhnev as Party First Secretary and Alexei Kosygin as Prime Minister. The new leadership continued Khrushchev's policy of trying to achieve 'peaceful co-existence' with the West, but at the same time the country's armed forces were strengthened.

**Rebellious satellites** After Stalin's death, Russia's control of its satellites in eastern Europe was somewhat relaxed. This led to outbursts of national feeling, culminating in the Hungarian Revolution of October 1956. The Soviet rulers suppressed the revolt by armed invasion. In 1968, a new crisis occurred in Czechoslovakia, where the Czech leader, Alexander Dubcek, led a movement to reform the political system. This too

Nikita Khrushchev argued the need for peaceful co-existence between East and West

was suppressed by the Russian army, which moved into the country in massive strength. Dubcek was soon replaced by a compliant pro-Soviet leadership.

**Cuba missile crisis: 1962** While maintaining a stranglehold over half of Europe, the Soviet rulers did their best, from the death of Stalin onwards, to exploit anti-European and anti-American feeling in Asia, Africa and Latin America. Fidel Castro's Cuba became a centre of Soviet influence. Khrushchev's attempt to set up a nuclear missile base there in 1962 brought the world to the brink of nuclear war. He was forced to withdraw the missiles after a confrontation with President Kennedy.

**Quarrel with Communist China** In the Far East, the victory of the Chinese Communists in the civil war in 1949 seemed likely to strengthen Soviet power in the world. But during the 1960's animosity developed between the two countries. In 1969, their armed forces clashed along the frontier on the River Amur. The Chinese accused the Russians of betraying the principles of Marxist-Leninism; the Russians replied by bitterly accusing China of copying all the worst features of Stalinism, especially the 'personality cult'.

**A super-power shares world dominance** At the beginning of the 1970's Soviet Russia was a super-power, with the full panoply of nuclear arms and intercontinental missiles, but it faced two formidable rivals – the United States, a still more powerful super-power, and China, potentially a third. The advance of post-war Soviet technology had already been highlighted by the launching of the world's first artificial space satellite – Sputnik I – in 1959 and the first manned space ship in 1961.

**Détente and dissent** By the end of the 1960's, the Soviet Union and the United States were showing increasing willingness to co-operate in space exploration, trade and other fields, and over such issues as disarmament. The visit to Moscow in May 1972 of President Nixon set the seal on this improved relationship between the two countries. In Europe, a Soviet-West German treaty renounced the use of force and recognised existing European frontiers.

But while pursuing a more flexible policy in international affairs, the Soviet government under Leonid Brezhnev sought to maintain its absolute control over the lives of the Russian people. In the early 1970's a campaign was launched to suppress dissent among writers, scientists and intellectuals. Minority groups seeking to assert their rights, notably the Jews, were subjected to harassment and even persecution.

The Russian writer Alexander Solzhenitsyn was deported by the Soviet authorities for his critical portrayals of the regime

In 1961, the Russian cosmonaut Yuri Gagarin became the first man to be launched into space

# United Arab Emirates

Seven Arab sheikhdoms on the Persian Gulf, formerly the Trucial States, make up this federation. The largest is Abu Dhabi, whose oil wealth, first exploited in the early 1960's, makes it one of the richest countries in the world, in terms of income per head of its tiny population. The other states are Dubai, also rich in oil, Ras al Khaimah, Umm al Quwain, Sharjah, Ajman and Fujairah. In 1853, the Perpetual Maritime Truce, arranged and supervised by Britain, ended the piracy for which the Gulf was notorious. Under later treaties, Britain assumed responsibility for defence and foreign relations, while leaving the sheikhs as absolute rulers in their domains. When the British withdrew from the Gulf in 1971, the Trucial States banded together to form the United Arab Emirates (UAE).

The occupation by Iran of the tiny Tumb islands at the mouth of the Gulf two days before the UAE became independent led to the loss of four lives; a month later, in January 1972, the ruler of Sharjah was shot dead in a coup that failed. However, the revenues from the two oil-rich states of Abu Dhabi and Dubai, together with a strong defence force, provide a basis for stability.

32,278 sq. miles
215,300 people
Main town:
Abu Dhabi

# United Kingdom of Great Britain and Northern Ireland

The history of the United Kingdom as a single political unit occupies little more than one-and-three-quarter centuries. England and Wales, united in 1536, were not formally joined with Scotland into one kingdom until 1707, and it was only in 1800 that the United Kingdom of Great Britain and Ireland was formed. During the 19th century the country enjoyed unrivalled power, prestige and influence as the centre of the largest empire the world had ever known. The British were admired or envied by other nations for their social stability and the strength of their liberal political institutions, as well as for their prosperity.

The United Kingdom won its dominant position thanks to its early start in the Industrial Revolution during the later decades of the 18th century, allied with existing trading and financial strength. But other powers, notably the United States and Germany, caught up economically by the beginning of the 20th century, and Britain's supremacy was lost.

Britain's unity has not always been maintained easily. In the 1740's, England resorted to force to put down a Scottish rebellion. After the First World War, force was used again to keep control of Ireland, but the attempt failed, and Southern Ireland became independent in 1922. At the end of the 1960's civil strife between Roman Catholics and Protestants broke out in Northern Ireland, and by 1973 the British Army was engaged in a full-scale operation to keep the peace in the province.

97,500 sq. miles
56,235,500 people
Capital: London

*Stonehenge, built between 1900 and 1300 BC, may have been both a temple and observatory where priests plotted the seasons from stars*

**Prehistoric migrations** Early migrants moving into Britain simply walked across from the Continent about 40,000 years ago. But Stone Age man could travel between Europe and Britain even after the sea separated them about 9000 years ago. The English Channel was easily forded, and the coasts of southern England seldom defended. The Irish Sea and the Scottish and Welsh mountains were more formidable barriers to migrants.

Many early migrations were peaceful, but by the 3rd century BC ferocious Celtic warlords of the Iron Age were sweeping in from France, driving the earlier inhabitants of Britain north and west. The Celts carved out kingdoms which straddled the Channel.

**The coming of Rome: 55 BC–AD 43** Julius Caesar invaded Britain in 55 BC and again the following year, but troubles in Gaul (France) forced him to withdraw. In AD 43, however, the Emperor Claudius launched another Roman invasion, aiming to acquire a land known to be a rich source of metals, wheat, cattle and slaves, and to put down British leaders who had adopted a bold anti-Roman policy, supporting rebels in Gaul. The attacking legions gradually subdued the native tribal kingdoms. A network of roads and forts took Roman rule to the borders of Scotland and west to Wales and Cornwall. But the conquest of Ireland was never attempted by the Romans, while that of Scotland was a failure. Hadrian's Wall, which the Romans built across what is now the north of England, soon became an outpost for defending the province rather than a base from which to rule Scotland. Since the Scottish and Pictish tribes would not submit, the Romans frequently laid waste the land and deported groups of the people.

By the end of the 4th century, with Rome itself under attack by barbarians, the Romans withdrew their legions from Britain, and the Picts and Scots poured across the abandoned Hadrian's Wall to ravage the lands lying to the south. A little later, a fierce three-cornered struggle developed between the Romanised Britons in the south, Pictish invaders from Scotland, and sea-borne Angles, Saxons and Jutes invading from northern Germany and Denmark. The romantic legend of King Arthur dates from this period.

*A Briton carved this portrait head in the fashion of his Roman masters, but added native patterns to the hair, ear and eyes*

*Roman Britain was dotted with well-designed villas, like the one at Lullingstone, Kent, where this piece of mosaic floor was found*

**The Anglo-Saxon kingdoms: 7th–9th centuries** By the end of the 7th century, seven powerful Anglo-Saxon kingdoms covered the central and eastern regions of England. These were Kent, Sussex, Essex, Wessex, East Anglia, Mercia and Northumbria. Mercia became dominant under the rule of Wulfhere (658–75) and its supremacy lasted until the beginning of the 9th century.

Originally pagan, the Anglo-Saxons were gradually Christianised. The Christianity of Britain under the Romans had not been particularly ardent. Far more vigorous was the Church founded by St Patrick in Ireland and carried by St Columba to Scotland. Irish Christianity was more than a century old when St Augustine arrived in 597 to convert the Anglo-Saxons to the Church of Rome. Irish and Roman monks met at Whitby in 663 at a conference called by King Oswy of Northumbria. The Synod of Whitby established the supremacy of the Roman monks, with the result that England was drawn into the mainstream of Christian Europe.

**Danish and Norman conquests** Alfred the Great and his successors defended England against Danish invaders in the 9th century with temporary success, but by 1016 England had become part of the Scandinavian empire of Canute, a Danish king. By 1066, however, because of a lack of direct heirs, the English throne was being contested by four rivals who claimed royal descent: the Saxon nobleman, Harold; his brother, Tostig; Harold III of Norway; and Duke William of Normandy. Harold defeated his own brother and the Norwegian king, but fell to William at the Battle of Hastings. Having escaped direct rule from Scandinavians, England now belonged to the Scandinavian settlers of northern France – the Normans, Christianised Norsemen who had colonised parts of Europe.

**Dividing the spoils: 1066–1154** William's followers in his conquest had to be rewarded. The Norman knights and barons, like the Saxon nobility they replaced, were given the land not only because they had helped to win it, but because they alone could help to hold it. The peasants on the land were bound to them to provide a labour force in time of peace and foot soldiers in war. The Normans introduced the name 'feudalism' for this system, but the structure itself was several centuries old.

Kings, however, were determined to keep as much power as possible in their own hands. In 1086, William ordered a survey of the kingdom's economic resources. The book which recorded the results was nicknamed the Domesday Book, because the thoroughness of the survey made people think of the Last Day of Judgment, or 'Domesday'. The survey made possible direct taxation by the king, rather than levies through the feudal lords. William's son, Henry I, continued trying to centralise law and administration, but his death was followed by civil war – for the crown, promised to his daughter, Matilda, was contested and temporarily gained by his nephew Stephen. Matilda's son, Henry II, however, restored order and did much to ensure that the king's law should be obeyed throughout the land instead of leaving local justice in the hands of nobles.

**Power of the barons** By the 13th century, extortions of money by the monarchs, especially by King John, had caused widespread resentment. Eventually the nobility forced King John at Runnymede in 1215 to seal the document known as Magna Carta, the Great Charter. Although the charter mainly confirmed the nobles' own privileges, the lords were able to pose with some success as the defenders of 'the whole community of the realm'. For many commoners were now finding the king's hand heavier than that of the feudal lords, despite the fact that they traditionally looked to the supreme authority of the king for protection against the excesses of nobles.

**Kings and churchmen** While William had been strengthening his grip on England, Pope Gregory VII had been seeking to dominate the rulers of Christendom. He considered that the authority of God upon earth, as represented in the Church, should overrule the power of kings. Most English churchmen nevertheless came to terms with the monarchy, but Henry II appointed an archbishop, Thomas Becket, who denied that the Crown had any power over the clergy. After his murder in 1170 by some of the king's over-enthusiastic followers, Becket became a celebrated martyr. Yet the Church soon returned to its former tasks, laying down the rudiments of a civil service and the roots of an educational system. Religious fervour was left to others; it was King Richard the Lionheart who went off crusading to the Holy Land to free it from the infidel, while his bishops bought government offices from him and ruled for their profit the land he neglected.

**Struggle with the French: 1337–1453** Through marriage and inheritance, Henry II's realm had covered half of France. Though he invaded Ireland and claimed to be overlord of both Scotland and Wales, his real concern was to extend his French dominions. But after his death many of these were lost and the French turned the tables by using the struggle between John and his rebellious nobles as an excuse for an unsuccessful invasion of England.

The result was an intense hatred between the English and the French, which finally grew into the Hundred Years' War, begun by Edward III. This long struggle was originally waged to prevent French interference in Scotland and protect the wool trade with Flanders, but soon became an attempt to reconquer French lands. Despite English victories at Crécy (1346), Poitiers (1356) and Agincourt (1415), the attempt failed; by 1453 the English were left with nothing but the port of Calais.

**Growth of national identity** Rivalry with the French helped to give the English more of a sense of their own identity. English was gradually emerging as the national language, ousting the Latin of the clergy and the bastard French of the court.

The sense of liberty, the belief in the inborn independence of the English character which was to sustain Englishmen for many centuries, also dates from this period. It found expression in the growth of parliament, which by the 15th century had become an established part of the English scene, being called to vote taxes in time of war. Many feudal lords were themselves destroying feudalism, preferring to receive money rents from their tenants rather than feudal service, so that England was becoming a land of tenant farmers and hired labourers, rather than serfs. The terrible plague, known as the Black Death, which first appeared in 1348, and killed one-third to half of the 5 million people of England, hastened the process of change. So did the Peasants' Revolt in 1381, in which militant serfs led by Wat Tyler confronted Richard II with their demands. But they were crushed.

**Nobles in open conflict: 1455–85** The image of the sturdy English yeoman, tilling his fields in peace and bending his longbow against the French, became a cherished part of national legend in later times.

Yet the armies that fought France were not mainly composed of such yeomen. Feudal lords who had exchanged their dues for cash used it to pay professional soldiers who were often formed into private armies in England. In these unstable conditions, worsened by recriminations and financial strain resulting from defeat in France, rivalry broke out between the two noble families who claimed the throne – the house of York (whose badge was a white rose) and that of Lancaster (red rose). The ensuing struggle became known as the Wars of the Roses, which lasted off and on for 30 years.

*Shipwrecked and made the prisoner of William of Normandy, Harold was forced to swear support for William's claim to the English throne. The scene appears in the Bayeux Tapestry, woven to celebrate the Norman conquest*

*Knights murder Thomas Becket in Canterbury Cathedral. King Henry II later denied that he had ordered the killing*

*The Knight of Chaucer's Canterbury Tales rides as a pilgrim to Becket's shrine. Chaucer (1340–1400) helped to establish English as the national language*

*Richard the Lionheart (left) is seen in a late medieval manuscript, fighting against the Muslim leader Saladin*

*Wat Tyler, leader of the Peasants' Revolt, was killed by the mayor of London in 1381 at a meeting between rebels and Richard II*

The Globe Theatre, London, was a centre of Elizabethan drama. The London theatres drew weekly audiences of 15,000 by the 1590's

## UNITED KINGDOM *continued*

**Tudor stability: 1485–1547** The Battle of Bosworth in 1485 was later recognised as the end of the Wars of the Roses. Henry Tudor, the Lancastrian victor, was proclaimed Henry VII, and married Elizabeth of York. Soon it was clear that the age of conflict was giving way to an age of consolidation.

But memories of civil strife were still fresh, and Henry's successor, Henry VIII, fearing that a female successor would weaken the Tudor dynasty, was determined to produce a male heir. Since his Spanish queen, Catherine of Aragon, seemed unable to give him a son, he decided to annul his marriage. Cardinal Wolsey failed to persuade the pope to do this, so Henry turned against him. Taking the advice of a new chief minister, Thomas Cromwell, Henry broke with Rome altogether, setting up a new Church with himself at its head. The monasteries were abolished and their lands and wealth seized by the Crown. Later, these lands were sold, creating a powerful class with a stake in the Protestant succession.

**Years of danger: 1547–58** Henry VIII died in 1547. His only son Edward VI (by Jane Seymour) succeeded, aged nine, and England was governed by men whose rivalry led to a revival of baronial feuding. These men were extreme Protestants; instead of keeping the English Church aloof as Henry VIII had done, they made it part of the Protestant Reformation which had divided Europe. England also came to be regarded as a potential prize by the two great Catholic rivals of Europe, France and Spain.

When he died aged 16 in 1553, Edward VI was succeeded by his Catholic sister Mary Tudor, Henry VIII's daughter by Catherine of Aragon. Mary married Philip II of Spain, giving Spain an apparent advantage in its conflict with France. But Mary lost support through her religious persecutions – 300 Protestants were burnt in the reign. She died childless in 1558. France now tried to control England by using the only child of James V of Scotland: Mary Stuart (Mary, Queen of Scots), Queen of France by marriage, was put forward as Catholic Queen of England. But because of her husband's death she returned to Scotland, only to find that her Protestant subjects were hostile. Eventually, she sought refuge in England but was made prisoner and later executed on grounds of being implicated in plots to murder Elizabeth I.

*The Ark Royal was the flagship of Lord Howard of Effingham, commander of the British fleet which defeated Spain's armada in 1588. Less than half the Spanish fleet managed to return home safely*

**Age of Elizabeth: 1558–1603** Elizabeth I, daughter of Henry VIII by Anne Boleyn, effectively guarded the English throne against both French and Spanish designs. She played the two powers off against each other and, when she had brought her country to a position of strength, she risked open war with Spain.

Elizabeth's diplomatic balancing act was mirrored by a similar one at home in the field of religion. Avoiding both the passionate Protestantism of Edward VI's reign and the Roman Catholicism to which Mary had tried to reconvert the country, Elizabeth established a compromise Church of England owing allegiance neither to Rome nor to the extreme Protestantism of the Lutheran

*Abbots in procession to parliament in a 16th-century drawing. But monastic power was soon to disappear under the rule of Henry VIII*

*Mary I (1516–58), the first English queen to rule in her own right, was a devout Catholic. In her zeal to restore England to 'the old religion', she sanctioned the burning of Protestants – hence her nickname, 'Bloody Mary'*

and Calvinist Churches of Europe. The main function of this Church was to buttress the authority of the Crown: and with its help Elizabeth imposed an unprecedented measure of control upon the country. Her justices of the peace regulated prices, wages and hours of work. Her bishops and parish priests exercised similar discipline in church affairs, repressing those – they became known as Puritans – who refused to accept their authority. The achievements of Shakespeare and his contemporaries such as Christopher Marlowe and Ben Jonson made this the most glorious age in English literature. The cultural upsurge of Elizabethan England, marked by a great extension of education and scholarship, bore witness to the widening of horizons, geographical as well as intellectual, which had begun in the Renaissance in Europe during the previous century. And the Elizabethan seamen, by trade and raiding, secured for England her share of the profits which the new geographical horizons brought with them.

**Social and economic upheaval** These horizons also brought loss, for the opening up of the New World led to inflation and economic disruption in the old. The immense quantities of gold and silver pouring in from the recently discovered Americas reduced the value of money. Men who still believed that God had ordained that there should be a just price for everything were horrified to see prices soaring. Merchants blamed labourers for wanting higher wages; labourers blamed landlords for raising rents; landlords blamed merchants for putting up prices. The government tried to halt the rise, but lacked the techniques to do so.

The government did, however, provide its servants with an investment which kept pace with inflation; those who had bought offices (official posts) under the Crown found that their value rose steadily, as did the fees and other perquisites they brought in. This invited resentment. People aggrieved or impoverished by the economic situation became convinced that the whole process was the work of corrupt and self-seeking courtiers. Thus, social tensions became political ones and paved the way for civil war.

**Parliament and king** In 1603 Elizabeth was succeeded by James Stuart, King of Scotland. He was thwarted in his plan to unite the two countries into one, but he and his son, Charles I, tried nevertheless to achieve some degree of uniformity in the two kingdoms. Both kings were, however, opposed to parliaments, and Charles succeeded in doing without one for 11 years of his reign. But when Charles tried to impose English Church organisation upon the Scots in 1638 they revolted and invaded England.

The king was forced to call a parliament which demanded the redress of its own grievances as the price for its co-operation in driving out the Scottish invaders. It turned out to be a high price. For two years Charles yielded to parliament, giving up in the process not only corrupt courtiers but also wise counsellors and some of the powers of the Crown. The king's principal counsellor, the Earl of Strafford, was even tried by parliament and executed, Charles being virtually forced to sign the death warrant.

*Elizabeth I's coffin is carried in her funeral procession. Conflict between Crown and parliament had been staved off by her diplomacy and skill, but grew worse after her death in 1603*

*Guy Fawkes and his fellow-conspirators of the Gunpowder Plot were executed for attempting to blow up parliament in 1605*

Parliament refused to pay for Charles to send troops to Ireland to put down a rebellion there in 1642, and the crisis that followed led to war. The king rallied his forces at Nottingham on August 22.

**Civil war and Cromwell: 1642–58** A country squire and member of parliament, Oliver Cromwell, emerged as a gifted military organiser on the Parliamentarian side, and after early indecisive fighting his well-trained forces crushed the Royalists at Marston Moor in 1644 and more decisively at Naseby in 1645. The king surrendered at Oxford in 1646, but conspired to play the Parliamentarian army off against parliament and both of them off against the Scots. His plotting brought about calls for his trial and he was beheaded for high treason in 1649. Military rule was eventually established under Cromwell, who dissolved parliament and became Lord Protector – virtually dictator – but at the same time refused the Crown. Cromwell ruled personally through administrative major-generals.

Cromwell's regime, propped up solely by his own strength, collapsed after his death in 1658. Many army leaders believed that a restoration of the monarchy was the only alternative to chaos. Charles's son came to the throne in 1660 as Charles II. James II, brother of Charles II, became king in 1685.

*A great five-day fire
destroyed much of
London, including the
old St Paul's (left)
in 1666. Christopher
Wren later built the
new cathedral which
exists today*

**Restoration to revolution: 1660–88** The reigns of Charles II and James II were dominated by the religious hatred and power politics of western Europe. James, a Catholic, was seen by many as an instrument of the increasing power of the Catholic Louis XIV of France. There were deep suspicions that the restored Stuarts sought to weaken parliament. William of Orange, ruler of the Dutch and defender of European Protestantism against the French, was a possible alternative monarch; he was Charles II's nephew and had married James II's Anglican daughter, Mary. But a move by the Whigs under Shaftesbury to 'exclude' James from the succession to the throne failed.

In 1688, however, a group of English lords sought William's help against James's Catholic policies. James fled and parliament gave the Crown to William and Mary, who promised to respect the rights of parliament. The outbreak of war with France made William and Mary financially dependent on parliament, and thus ensured that the promise was kept.

**War in Europe: 1701–14** England and Holland, fearing the political and commercial power of France, came together with Austria against France and Spain when war broke out over a quarrel about the succession to the Spanish throne. The situation was aggravated by the support Louis XIV gave to the exiled Stuarts. The English Duke of Marlborough gained fame for his military victories such as Blenheim (1704). The necessities of war, too, produced the Bank of England and the credit facilities which made possible the country's later economic and maritime expansion.

**Whigs and Tories** Two political groups had developed by the 18th century: the Whigs – traditionally anxious to limit royal power; and the Tories – traditionally Stuart supporters and Anglicans.

The Whigs threw themselves energetically behind the principles of the 'Glorious Revolution' of 1688, and supported continental involvement, but the Tories

*This emblem was used
by the early Bank of
England. Founded in
1694, the bank be-
came popularly known
as 'The Old Lady of
Threadneedle Street'*

saw little need for the Calvinist Dutchman or for the wars he brought with him. During the reign of Anne (1702–14), the Tories were slightly happier, for she was a Stuart and Anglican; but when she died childless and the throne passed to the German Lutheran elector of Hanover, the loyalty of the Tories was severely strained. Many Tories became secret Jacobites – supporters of James II and his successors.

Some people had hoped that party divisions would wither away, but the king's ministers needed a following in parliament and those who wished to oust them often formed a united unofficial opposition in parliament. Party politics had come to stay, even though the parties had by no means rigid membership, and were divided mainly over the scramble for office. The first Hanoverians, George I (who spoke only a few words of English) and George II, relied a great deal on their ministers, and Robert Walpole, principal minister from 1721 to 1742 (and often called first prime minister) was able to use the king's patronage to sell offices and thus ensure a loyal following in parliament.

Two short-lived and unsuccessful rebellions, in 1715 and 1745, attempted to restore the Stuarts to the English throne. The Old Pretender, James, son of James II, arrived in Scotland in 1715 only to see his mission fail. His son, the Young Pretender, Bonnie Prince Charlie, led another Scottish rising in 1745 but was defeated at Culloden the following year.

**Growth of empire: 17th and 18th centuries** Conflict with France over trade broke out in the mid-18th century. Under the leadership of William Pitt the Elder (later the Earl of Chatham), Britain used its sea power and army in combined operations such as the capture of Quebec (1759) and gained possessions at the expense of the French in India. As a result, a British Empire had been acquired by the 1760's. Originating from trading posts and colonies developed in the 17th century, the empire now controlled much of India and North America, as well as possessing sugar islands in the Caribbean and slaving stations in Africa.

But the British did not yet have either the resources or the desire to govern their possessions overseas. They merely wanted to exploit them for the purpose of trade. Consequently, there were violent quarrels over the problem of ruling India, as well as a complete break-away by the American colonies in 1783.

**The Industrial Revolution** Western Europe in the 18th century was becoming increasingly industrialised. In Britain, the creation of the Bank of England had made credit easier to obtain and use than in many continental states. The comparative lack of internal customs barriers – such as those which criss-crossed many other countries – also made Britain, with its abundant coal and iron, into an early 'common market' where producers found easily accessible consumers. The commercially opportunist climate provided ready backers for inventors like James Watt and George Stephenson. With these advantages, Britain gained a substantial though temporary lead over the rest of the world in industrialisation. Communications expanded rapidly, first canals, then railways.

**Growth of parties** Politics in Britain were changing, too, as the 18th century ended. Under George I and George II, the Whigs had a monopoly of political power. Tories were still labelled Jacobites – and regarded as little better than traitors. When George III came to the throne in 1760 a dramatic change took place. George believed that his father and grandfather had been tricked by the Whigs into giving up many of their

## UNITED KINGDOM *continued*

rightful prerogatives. Determined to recover these, George gathered a party of 'King's friends', led first by his Scottish favourite, the Earl of Bute, to his support. Toryism became respectable and eventually the two-party system was born.

**Wars with France: 1793–1815** Britain's eventual success in the Napoleonic Wars was another contribution to national pride. Yet the wars went badly at first, with the failure of an expedition to capture French possessions in the Caribbean and the bungling of an attempt to gain a foothold on the European continent via the Netherlands. Alliances of other European nations against France were crushed, despite vast cash subsidies handed out to its allies by Britain.

The British navy, under successful leaders such as Nelson and Collingwood, gained control of the seas and gave the death blow to the combined French and Spanish fleets at Trafalgar (1805). In 1808 a small British army established a continental bridgehead in Spain. Napoleon failed in his attempt to impose a trade embargo upon Britain and to invade Russia. He was finally crushed by Wellington at Waterloo in 1815.

*The Duke of Wellington caricatured as commander of the army. The cartoonist stresses the boots worn by the Duke, which were subsequently named after him*

*A contemporary print records the Battle of Trafalgar in 1805. It shows how Nelson's tactics split the enemy fleet and (inset) his death at the moment of victory*

**Radicalism and repression** But there was a darker side to the picture. The beginning of the 19th century saw increasing poverty. Agricultural change and the enclosure of open land created landless and redundant workers who drifted into towns. The wars themselves strained resources and made prices unstable.

Fear of revolution led William Pitt the Younger, principal minister in the darkest days of the wars, to introduce repressive measures. Radical leaders were tried for treason, trades unions outlawed, and Habeas Corpus suspended. Later, in 1815, restrictions on corn imports were tightened to keep home prices high and prevent an agricultural depression. Hardest hit by the Corn Laws were the new industrial working classes, who were most affected by the rise in bread prices.

Agitation mounted, taking the form of the smashing of machines and other isolated actions. Theft was widespread despite stern penalties that included death or transportation. One harsh reaction was the 'Peterloo massacre' at St Peter's Fields, Manchester, in 1819, when cavalry charged a reform rally.

**A new society** A capitalist economy, dedicated to the ever-increasing production of goods and services, was being born, and it needed more sophisticated techniques of government. During the reign of George III (1760–1820) those techniques began to be evolved. Government became a task for the trained professional rather than an investment for the ambitious amateur. The process continued under George IV and William IV, especially after the 1832 Reform Bill had brought men with new wealth into politics alongside the men with old titles. As the electorate widened and the parties became concerned with programmes rather than patronage they changed their names: Liberals and Conservatives replaced Whigs and Tories. Under their leader William Gladstone, four times prime minister between 1868 and 1894, the Liberals became con-

*Four of the six 'martyr' workmen of Tolpuddle, Dorset, who formed a trades-union branch in 1834 despite anti-union laws. Sentenced to seven years' transportation to Australia, they were brought back after an outcry*

vinced that reforming legislation was all that was needed to make people contented and virtuous. The Conservatives under Benjamin Disraeli, Premier twice between 1868 and 1880, were also concerned with reform, as well as desiring an even bigger empire. Their 1867 Reform Bill doubled the electorate. Gladstone's Reform Bill of 1884 added another 2 million voters.

**The monumental years** During the reign of Queen Victoria (1837–1901), the growing success of industrial capitalism bred a confidence that verged on complacency. The Great Exhibition of 1851 showed how Britain had become the workshop of the world.

Knowing it could out-produce any other country, Britain dropped its protective policies and took up free trade, introduced by a Conservative, Robert Peel, who abolished the protective Corn Laws to relieve famine in Ireland in 1846. Britain could flood the markets of the world with her goods; and even if other countries tried to keep them out, there were always the markets provided by the ever-expanding empire. But the price paid was a new inflexibility in foreign policy. Colonies in which millions of pounds worth of railways had been built were not to be abandoned in the same carefree manner as that in which the 18th century had exchanged plantations and trading stations.

Britannia seemed really to rule the waves. Britain's navy was kept at an immense strength, and British merchant ships carried the bulk of the world's goods. The confidence of these years is reflected in the monumental Victorian architecture still dominating parts of London, such as the Royal Albert Hall.

*The opening of the Stockton to Darlington railway in 1825 marked the beginning of the world's first train service for freight and passengers*

*The novelist Charles Dickens exposed much of the injustice and complacency of Victorian society*

**Edwardian twilight: 1901–14** Doubts crept in during the reign of Victoria's successor Edward VII. The imperialist policy of the Conservatives produced a quarrel in which Dutch settlers in South Africa were defeated in the Anglo-Boer War (1899–1902). Free trade could not hold the empire together now that other countries were challenging Britain's industrial supremacy, and the Conservative Party was torn by an agonising debate, initiated by Joseph Chamberlain, over the need to return to a policy of protection.

The Liberal Party's confident continuation of Gladstone's work also ran into trouble. Lloyd George's plan for higher taxes on the rich brought such uncompromising resistance from the aristocracy that the crisis resulted in the House of Lords being stripped of its power of vetoing laws in 1911. The poor turned increasingly to militant trade unionism. Equally militant were the impassioned suffragettes who demanded votes for women. Most militant of all were the Irish, who were bitterly divided over the Home Rule which the Liberals wanted to grant them: the Protestant Northern Irish feared Catholic dominance from the south if the whole of Ireland became independent.

**War and depression** Under George V these troubles came to a head. In the summer of 1914, with industrial strife in Britain still unresolved and Ireland on the point of civil war, war broke out with Germany. The German invasion of neutral Belgium led to Britain entering the European war.

At first there was exhilaration; but after four years of murderous warfare, victory was accompanied by bitterness and disillusionment. After the promise of a

*Disraeli (left) and Gladstone, two dominant statesmen of the 19th century, were political enemies, yet both worked for social and political reforms*

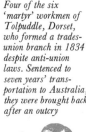 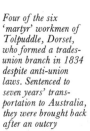

*Suffragettes march for their rights in Edwardian England. All women over 21 were finally given the vote in 1928*

'land fit for heroes', the industrial decline of the 1920's caused massive unemployment and lower wages. Alarmed by the Bolshevik Revolution in Russia in 1917, the British government saw the General Strike which broke out in 1926 over miners' pay disputes as an attempt to spread revolution to Britain. But, after only a week, the strike collapsed, though the miners prolonged their own struggle.

Britain was becoming more democratic. With the electorate widened further (all men over 21 and all women over 30 who were ratepayers or the wives of ratepayers received the vote in 1918) the Labour Party caught up with the two older parties and in 1924 it formed its first government. But Britain's economic problems grew until 1929, when the Wall Street crash in the United States set off a world-wide depression. Recovery was slow and before it was completed Europe was moving once again towards world war.

**Second World War: 1939–45** Through the Statute of Westminster (1931) part of the empire had become the British Commonwealth of Nations, with official independence for its larger dominions such as Canada, Australia and South Africa. Territorially, the British Empire was still large, but much of its former power had vanished beyond recall.

Yet it was in these years of declining imperial power that the British experienced what Winston Churchill described as the Commonwealth's 'finest hour'. After trying unsuccessfully to appease Hitler's Germany, Britain entered the Second World War in a far less confident state of mind than in 1914. With the British Army quickly driven from France and Nazi invasion expected, imperial matters for a while seemed remote, and Britain returned to its earlier role as a small nation involved in European conflict. Its air force defeated a massive German air attack and the immediate Nazi threat receded. At the same time, defeats suffered by Germany's ally, Italy, temporarily ended the threat to the Suez Canal. Britain's imperial lifeline. With the entry of Russia and the United States into the war in 1941, Britain acquired new and powerful allies, but a new enemy in Japan. The tide turned against Hitler at the end of 1942; the following year Italy surrendered, and in 1944 France was liberated. Germany finally surrendered in May 1945. Japan surrendered in August of the same year.

**TO-DAY-UNEMPLOYED**

*A Labour Party poster illustrates unemployment, which caused great bitterness between the wars*

*The vigorous leadership of Winston Churchill saw Britain through its darkest hour in 1940, the year he came to power*

**Post-war Britain** Political opinion in Britain during the Second World War had moved to the Left, and in the 1945 election the Labour Party under Clement Attlee was swept into power. A programme of nationalisation of industries and provision of social security began. When the Conservatives returned to power in 1951 there was some denationalisation, but the welfare-state reforms were continued.

After the defeat of Germany and Japan, Britain attempted to continue playing a world role, during the twilight of its empire. British troops saw action in the Far East, Africa and the Mediterranean in the post-war years while former imperial possessions went through the birth-pangs of independence. The largest country to be granted independence in this period was India, in 1947. British troops fought in the Korean War and a large army was maintained in West Germany. In 1956 the nationalisation of the Suez Canal led to intervention in Egypt by Britain and France, but their troops were withdrawn after an international outcry.

The problems which confronted Britain in the 1960's and 1970's, under both Conservative and Labour governments, reflected old and enduring themes in British history. Governments struggled to ease inflation while people blamed each other for wanting higher wages or higher prices. A British army went once again to a strife-torn Ireland. In 1973 Britain entered the European Common Market and became, once more, part of a system bridging the English Channel. In 1974, inflation and a worsening balance of payments problem was partly off-set by the development of Britain's huge off-shore oil resources.

RATION BOOK

*Rationing, introduced by Britain in the First World War, reappeared in the Second, and was not fully abolished until the mid-1950's*

*British armoured cars move into the Roman Catholic area of Londonderry. Troops were sent to Northern Ireland in 1968 to combat terrorism. In the 1970's violence spread to England.*

# Remnants of empire

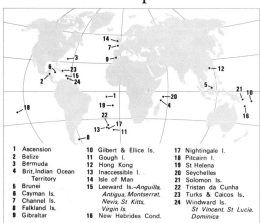

*Today, Britain still controls many territories scattered throughout the world*

| 1 | Ascension | 10 | Gilbert & Ellice Is. | 17 | Nightingale I. |
|---|---|---|---|---|---|
| 2 | Belize | 11 | Gough I. | 18 | Pitcairn I. |
| 3 | Bermuda | 12 | Hong Kong | 19 | St Helena |
| 4 | Brit. Indian Ocean Territory | 13 | Inaccessible I. | 20 | Solomon Is. |
| 5 | Brunei | 14 | Isle of Man | 21 | Solomon Is. |
| 6 | Cayman Is. | 15 | Leeward Is.–Anguilla, Antigua, Montserrat, Nevis, St Kitts, Virgin Is. | 22 | Tristan da Cunha |
| 7 | Channel Is. | | | 23 | Turks & Caicos Is. |
| 8 | Falkland Is. | | | 24 | Windward Is. St Vincent, St Lucia, Dominica |
| 9 | Gibraltar | 16 | New Hebrides Cond. | | |

The British Empire in its heyday was often described as one on which 'the sun never sets': not only an empire which stretched right round the globe, but one which would last for ever. Even today, the phrase is still partly true. The remaining fragments of the empire are so widely scattered that throughout 24 hours there is still always daylight somewhere on some tiny piece of British-dependent territory. And although the British Empire has proved to be no more durable than other great empires of the past, Britain still has large-scale military and financial commitments to its remaining dependencies, as well as

maintaining close trading links, strengthened by programmes of economic aid, with those given independence.

In Europe, Britain has three dependencies: the Channel Islands, off the French coast, gained at the time of the Norman conquest (1066); the Isle of Man in the Irish Sea; and the Rock of Gibraltar, a tiny peninsula extending from the Spanish mainland, and gained by Britain during the War of the Spanish Succession against Spain and France (1701–13).

In the Americas, several chains of islands, many of which were once the haunt of pirates, are British dependencies. Among them are the Falkland Islands in the South Atlantic, long claimed by Argentina, and, in the Leewards, in the Caribbean, the little island of Anguilla. Anguilla was 'invaded' by Britain in 1969 when it declared itself independent and tried to break away from two associated islands, St Kitts and Nevis.

Off the western coast of Africa, the best-known British dependencies are St Helena, where Napoleon was exiled after his defeat at Waterloo in 1815 until his death in 1821 and, 1,500 miles to the south-west, the remote island of Tristan da Cunha. It was evacuated after a volcanic eruption in 1961, but its people returned in 1963. On the other side of Africa lie the British Indian Ocean Territory and the Seychelles. The Seychelles have recently sprung to prominence as the site of a major new international airport.

The principal British dependency in Asia and the Pacific is Hong Kong, acquired from China in 1842, and developed into a great port and trading centre. Kowloon and Stonecutters Island were added to the colony in 1860, and in 1898 a piece of the Chinese mainland, the New Territories, was leased from China for 99 years. Since the Communist takeover in China in 1949, relations between the mainland and the colony have sometimes been tense. Among other British dependencies in the Pacific is Pitcairn — a mountainous island whose inhabitants are mostly descended from mutineers from the British ship *Bounty,* who settled there in 1790. Further south still, Britain possesses some 200 square miles of Antarctic territory.

# United States of America

Two centuries ago, the United States was a tiny republic on the Atlantic seaboard. Today it stretches 3000 miles from the Atlantic to the Pacific; one state, Alaska, borders on the Arctic Ocean; and another, Hawaii, is in the mid-Pacific. The United States is the richest and one of the two most powerful states on earth. Its spectacular growth was made possible by the energy, courage and ambition of its varied peoples.

The ancestors of today's Americans sought the religious and political freedom and economic opportunity denied them in their homelands. In the 18th century America's original 13 colonies rebelled against British rule, and during the 19th and early 20th centuries the young republic opened its doors freely to immigrants from Europe. (Asian newcomers were accepted at first though barred after the end of the 19th century.) Altogether, some 42 million immigrants shared in a gigantic mass migration to utilise the opportunities and the challenge of a new world.

In recent years, many Americans – young people prominent among them – have begun to question how far the American dream of freedom and dignity for all men has been able to survive when contrasted with the vast problems of the modern world. The USA's open, democratic society has always thrown up reformers and critics, in a kind of self-correcting process. Today, the critics point to the scars on American life – racial bitterness, slums and unemployment, crime and corruption, and pollution. But one issue that had deeply divided the nation – US involvement in the Vietnam war – was resolved in 1973, when, after lengthy negotiations, a cease-fire agreement was signed.

**America's first immigrants: c. 30,000 BC** As far as is known, the continent's first inhabitants were immigrants from north-east Asia, who came over the Bering Strait land-bridge (now covered by water) in a series of migrations probably 30,000 years ago when an Ice Age lowered the level of the seas. These people, hunters and food gatherers, were the ancestors of America's

3,615,122 sq. miles
212,031,000 people
Capital:
Washington, DC

*An American Indian made this wood-carving of a deer's head in the 15th century. It was probably used by the tribe as a magical device to ensure good hunting*

*A typical Indian village in Virginia, as depicted by the 16th-century English artist John White*

Indians. By *c.* AD 1500 there were about a million Indians in North America. They were a dispersed and divided race. Each tribal group had its own language; about 500 were spoken in all. The Indians' way of life varied and their economic and cultural distinctions made it rare for any leader to unite even a few tribes; the Indians' divisions made it relatively easy for the invading white man to defeat them.

**European discovery** The first Europeans to make contact with North America were Norsemen, who crossed the Atlantic in longboats in the early 11th century. Under a leader named Leif Ericson, some landed in an area which he called Vinland, or Wineland, possibly because of the wild grapes growing there. Its exact location is unknown, but it may have been as far south as Cape Cod, in Massachusetts. Ericson and his men stayed there only for a few winters.

The continent's rediscovery began with the epic voyage in 1492 of the Italian-born navigator Christopher Columbus, and a wave of exploration followed. The vast quantities of gold found in Mexico and Peru inspired some Spaniards to venture northwards from the West Indies, hoping for similar good fortune. In 1513, Don Juan Ponce de León reached Florida; in 1541 Hernando de Soto discovered a great river which was later to be called the Mississippi; in 1541 Francisco Coronado discovered part of the Colorado River and reached as far north as present-day Kansas. But Spain found no gold north of Mexico.

A Spanish settlement was founded at St Augustine, in Florida, in 1565, the oldest white settlement to survive in what is today the United States. By then, Spain's New World empire extended from Argentina to California, but only 150,000 Spanish inhabitants were scattered over this vast region.

**Rivals to Spain** In 1493 the pope decreed that the world outside Europe should be divided between Portugal and Spain. The Americas, except for Portuguese-owned Brazil, were 'given' to the Spanish king. England quickly became the first power to dispute this monopoly when John Cabot claimed Newfoundland in 1497. France also refused to recognise the pope's decree. In 1524 Giovanni da Verrazano, a Florentine serving the French, explored the Atlantic coast. In 1535 Jacques Cartier penetrated the St Lawrence valley.

The English were as interested as the Spanish in exploiting the New World for reasons of strategy and the profit in gold or furs. But from the start the English also wanted colonies in which to settle some of their people. The first settlement to survive was founded by a British trading company at Jamestown, Virginia in 1607.

In 1620, a group of English religious non-conformists, known later to Americans as the 'Pilgrim Fathers', decided to escape harassment by the government of

*Amerigo Vespucci, an Italian explorer and geographer, whose name was given to the American continent*

*Turkeys, native to America, were introduced into Europe by returning colonists*

*A Red Indian princess, Pocahontas, was presented at James I's court by John Rolfe, the English settler she had married*

Virginia's colonists prospered through the cultivation of tobacco, building great houses on their plantations. Such wealth made them the aristocracy of the New World

James I. They sailed from Plymouth, aiming for a landfall north of the extensive territories held by the Virginia Company, which had founded Jamestown. They arrived in November on the cold and forbidding coast of Massachusetts. In the cabin of their vessel, the *Mayflower*, the Pilgrims made a compact with disgruntled non-Pilgrim passengers who had been kept unaware of their plans. The compact called for the formation of a self-ruling community, thus planting the idea of government by consent early in the history of England's New World colonies.

Both the Virginia and Massachusetts 'plantations', as they were called, suffered grim early years. But gradually, hardships were overcome. Following the foundation of the colony of Massachusetts Bay in 1629, waves of settlers arrived. New colonies were soon established. Two of these (New York and New Jersey) were taken from the Dutch in 1664, and by 1733 a group of stable agricultural and commercial English communities stretched along the Atlantic coast from New Hampshire to Georgia.

**The tobacco lords: 17th and 18th centuries** The southern colonies quickly found profitable crops in tobacco and, to a lesser extent, rice and indigo. It was the practice to give generous grants of land to Englishmen who would migrate to Virginia with workers or 'servants', and this encouraged the formation of large plantations, which were particularly suited to tobacco culture. Almost from the start, Negro slaves were imported from Africa in large numbers to work on the farms and plantations of the South.

In Virginia, Maryland and North Carolina, a small, white aristocracy developed. It consisted of a few families who owned much of the land and dominated the government of the colonies. A similar aristocracy grew up in the steamy South Carolina country.

These settlements along the river-mouths, where large plantations and many slaves were common, became the 'Old South' of legend. But there was another South – the wooded country that ran from Maryland, through the great valley of Virginia, into the Carolina foothills and on into the pine forests of Georgia. This area was settled by a medley of nationalities, moving south from Pennsylvania. Land-holdings there were apt to be smaller, and slaves fewer in number.

Tobacco was first brought to Europe from America in the mid-16th century. It was then believed to have healing qualities

**New England and the middle colonies** The poor soil of Massachusetts was unsuited to large-scale agriculture. For the most part, small farms were worked by families of free men, attracted by the economic prospects of farming and fishing. The chance of religious freedom was also a powerful attraction – though this varied with the colony and the era. Rhode Island and Pennsylvania, for example, were relatively tolerant, as was Maryland, founded by a Catholic family. But in Massachusetts the Congregationalist Church – a Puritan body – was officially established and dissent was discouraged.

Between New England and the South lay the 'middle colonies' — New York, New Jersey, Pennsylvania and Delaware. The first two began as 'New Netherland', the Dutch name for their colony. The capital of New Netherland was New Amsterdam, on Manhattan Island, 'bought' from the Indians in 1626 for about 24

Many religious nonconformists left Britain for the freedom the New World offered them

dollars' worth of goods. When the English conquered New Netherland, they named both city and province after the Duke of York (later James II). William Penn, the Quaker, made his colony of Pennsylvania – granted to him by Charles II in 1681 – into a refuge for nonconformists. These four colonies were prosperous, attracted many immigrants, and provided meat and grain for themselves and for the West Indies.

**Stirrings of revolt** The French also had settlements in North America. But with the Treaty of Paris in 1763, following Britain's victory in the Seven Years' War, French power disappeared from Canada. Victory soon exposed the growing tensions between the British home government and the colonists. Long before 1763, colonial law-making assemblies had come into being. They saw themselves as local parliaments, and attempts by London to extend its control were resented and resisted. The British government thought of the colonies only as providers of raw materials, and insisted on monopolising American markets for Britain's own manufacturers. In addition, the colonists' trade with other countries was forbidden or heavily taxed. Only the fact that these laws were lightly enforced before 1763 had prevented earlier trouble.

British territory in North America had more than doubled as a result of the Treaty of Paris. British politicians feared trouble with their new Catholic French subjects, as well as a possible renewal of the French threat. They wanted to build a new defence system, and considered it both fair and essential that the colonists should help to pay for it.

**'No taxation without representation'** Attempts to raise money and tighten imperial administration widened the rift between Britain and the colonies. In 1764 a Sugar Act placed stiff duties on imported foreign molasses and other goods – and gave teeth to the collection machinery. Then, in 1765, another revenue-raising measure, the Stamp Act, was introduced. This ordered that revenue stamps had to be fixed to all printed documents circulated in the colonies – newspapers and legal papers included. The money raised would be used in 'defending, protecting and securing' the colonies, but the Act aroused the resentment of the most powerful and articulate groups among the colonists: merchants, lawyers, clergymen and journalists.

The colonists argued that they had no seats in the British parliament, and invoked the principles of English resistance to Charles I in their slogan 'No taxation without representation'. Leaders of Massachusetts called representatives from other colonies to a meeting in New York in October 1765. They responded to the Act with a trade boycott on goods from Britain.

The British government yielded to pressure by repealing the Act in 1766. But parliament and the ministers maintained that they had a right to tax the colonies, and refused to recognise the claims of colonial assemblies. In 1767, Charles Townshend, the Chancellor of the Exchequer, introduced new taxes on tea, lead and glass. Again an organised protest followed and again the British government backed down. All the acts were repealed in 1770 – except for the tax on tea.

**The Boston Tea Party: 1773** To help the financially hard-pressed East India Company, the British government, under Lord North, gave it a monopoly on the sale of tea in America. By now the incensed Americans saw the tax on tea as a symbol of all their grievances. Moreover, the grant of a monopoly to a British company was

The works of the scientist, writer and statesman Benjamin Franklin (1706–90) did much to win respect for the new American nation. His name became synonymous with the national ideals of self-reliance and common sense

A mock revenue stamp expresses American bitterness at the Stamp Act, imposed on the colonies by the British government in 1765

In December 1773, colonists disguised as Indians raided tea ships in Boston harbour and threw their cargoes overboard. This protest against the tea tax became known as the 'Boston Tea Party'

463

*A contemporary drawing sums up the 'spirit of 1776' – the year that the Americans made their Declaration of Independence from Britain*

## USA *continued*

seen as a dangerous precedent and a threat to the future of every American merchant. The crisis came when three tea ships arrived at the port of Boston. The Governor of Massachusetts, Thomas Hutchinson, insisted, against all advice, that the tea must be landed. On December 16, 1773, a group of Boston patriots, thinly disguised as Indians, boarded the ships at their wharves and threw the entire consignment overboard.

**The 'Intolerable Acts': 1774** The British government now determined to show firmness. In the spring of 1774 it passed what Americans called the 'Intolerable Acts'. The port of Boston was to be closed until the tea was paid for; Massachusetts' powers of self-rule were sharply limited; and troops were to occupy Boston and be quartered on the populace.

In America this firmness was seen as tyranny. On September 5, 1774, a Continental Congress of 55 delegates from 12 of the 13 colonies met in Philadelphia. The delegates unsuccessfully petitioned George III to remove the 'Intolerable Acts'. Incidents multiplied, and finally open fighting broke out near Boston on April 19, 1775, between British regulars and colonial militiamen. In June 1775 the Continental Congress authorised the raising of a Continental Army and a Virginia landowner, George Washington, a skilled veteran of the French and Indian Wars, was given command. By the beginning of 1776 open warfare was widespread.

*A medal struck in 1792 shows George Washington parleying with an Indian chief. Washington tried to secure just treatment for the Indians from his fellow countrymen*

**War of Independence: 1775–81** As hopes of conciliation faded, a majority of the Continental Congress delegates brought themselves to vote for formal separation from Britain. A Declaration of Independence was officially adopted on July 4, 1776. The immediate aftermath of the Declaration was not encouraging. A British force under General William Howe seized New York and then drove Washington's forces back across New Jersey. By the spring of 1777, it seemed as if one major blow would end the rebellion. But in attempting to deliver it, the British suffered a severe setback. General John Burgoyne led an army south from Canada to cut New England off from New York, but was surrounded at Saratoga and forced to surrender in October 1777. As a result of the victory – and skilful diplomacy by Benjamin Franklin in Paris – France recognised the colonies' independence in February 1778, and sent troops and a fleet to their aid.

The alliance boosted the morale of the hard-pressed Americans. Washington's army had wintered during 1777–8 at Valley Forge, Pennsylvania, where harsh conditions sapped its strength and reduced it to 8000 men. But loyalty and hope kept this frozen half-starved remnant of an army in the field and, in the end, time worked for the American cause. In 1780, Redcoat forces under Lord Cornwallis mounted a campaign in the south. They moved to the coast at Yorktown to receive supplies, but these were cut off by a French fleet. In October 1781 Cornwallis was forced to surrender. By now France, Spain and Holland were at war with Britain. The House of Commons voted for peace with the colonies and, in 1783, Britain recognised the independence of the United States of America.

*Thomas Jefferson, as both architect and statesman, found inspiration in the harmonious art of ancient Greece. The drawing shows Jefferson's design for his own house at Monticello*

**Planning a nation** The colonies, now states, were still far from being fully united. A government set up in 1781 under the Articles of Confederation had little real authority, because each state retained almost total sovereignty in all affairs, foreign and domestic, and the central government had no power to raise taxes. This system soon became unworkable, and 55 delegates from all the states except Rhode Island met at Philadelphia in 1787 to devise a new form of government. After a long summer of debate, the delegates agreed on a Constitution. The new Federal government was to have exclusive power in the conduct of war, diplomacy and commerce, and its own armed forces, revenues and courts. But the states retained all powers not expressly granted to the central government.

*One of the drafters of the Declaration of Independence, John Adams succeeded Washington as US president in 1797*

Within that government itself, power was carefully divided and separated. Executive power – the power to administer and enforce the laws – was vested in the president. The law-making body, Congress, was to consist of two houses. In the upper, the Senate, each state, regardless of size, would have two members. In the lower, the House of Representatives, a state's delegation would vary in size with its population. Thus a compromise was reached between the claims of large and small states. The House was the more popular branch; its members, elected for two years, were chosen directly by qualified voters. The senators served a six-year term and were chosen by the state legislatures. (Popular election of senators did not come until the passing of the 17th Amendment in 1913.)

The Constitution contained provisions for its own formal amendment (26 have been added to date) but also soon showed a capacity to adapt through unwritten changes. As an example, the president was to be chosen, not by direct popular vote, but by members of an Electoral College. Almost from the very first election, however, candidates for that body ran under the name of a candidate for whom they were honour-bound to vote, so that in effect there was a direct choice for voters. Similarly, a Supreme Court was set up to interpret the Constitution. But as early as 1801 it began to refuse to apply laws of both the state legislatures and Congress if it found them contrary to the Constitution. This added an additional check to the powers of Congress and the president, which were already balanced against each other. The president was given a veto over laws passed in Congress, but they could be re-passed over his veto by a two-thirds vote in each house. He was responsible for foreign policy and was commander-in-chief of the armed forces. But senatorial consent was necessary for treaties and certain presidential appointments and Congress alone had the power to raise money.

*War broke out between America and Britain in 1812. The British captured and burnt Washington in 1814, but were defeated at the Battle of New Orleans*

**Growth of parties** Within five years two parties had emerged. One, led by Thomas Jefferson, was more or less the ancestor of the modern Democratic Party. In its early years, it voiced primarily the views of the farmers and the advocates of states' rights. The Federalist Party, led by Alexander Hamilton, called for a strong central government, and encouragement to the industrial, financial and commercial classes. Some of its basic ideas re-emerged in the Whig Party and finally, in 1854, in the Republican Party.



*James Monroe's most important achievement was his proclamation of the Monroe Doctrine, designed to prevent European interference in American affairs*

**Monroe Doctrine: 1823** For 20 years the new republic tried to remain aloof from world affairs. But in 1812 war broke out between Britain and the USA. The basic causes were British interference with American shipping during the Napoleonic wars, and continued conflict over control of the Indians and the fur trade in the Great Lakes region which formed the boundary between Canada and the USA. The Americans briefly invaded Canada; the British captured and burnt Washington in 1814; but the war ended in a stalemate.

Shortly afterwards, Britain and the USA found themselves on the same side in a world quarrel. Between 1815 and 1822 Spain had lost most of its New World colonies by nationalist revolutions. She planned to recapture them with the aid of France. Britain proposed a joint Anglo-American effort to prevent this. President Monroe, however, chose to act unilaterally. In 1823 he

*Abraham Lincoln and his fourth son, Thomas, nicknamed 'Tad'. Both met tragic ends – the father was assassinated and 'Tad' died of typhoid fever at the age of 18*

proclaimed that the USA would not allow future colonisation in the Western Hemisphere by any European power. The Monroe Doctrine, as his statement was later called, became the cornerstone of US foreign policy, and applied not only to Russia, Spain, France and other powers, but to Britain itself.

*Slaves hoe fields for their Southern masters. By 1860 slavery had divided the nation into two opposing political camps*

**Early expansion** Soon after its formation, the new nation started to push west and south to the territory between the Appalachians and the Mississippi River. Ohio became a state in 1803, Indiana in 1816 and Illinois in 1818. To the south, Mississippi achieved statehood in 1817 and Alabama in 1819. Meanwhile, in 1803, President Jefferson bought the Louisiana territory from Napoleon for 15 million dollars. This doubled the area of the republic and pushed its western boundary to the Rockies. Louisiana and Missouri, part of this territory, also became states in 1812 and 1821.

In the states of the old north-west (Ohio, Indiana, Illinois and, later, Michigan and Wisconsin) slavery was forbidden by the terms of the North-west Ordinance of 1787. This region attracted many small farmers and immigrants. The states of the old south-west, however, depended heavily on cotton production. Thus by the 1820's a line of demarcation between North and South was appearing. It was a line between a free area, and one dominated by slave-worked plantations.

**Slavery threatens unity** In 1790 Negro slaves numbered just under 700,000. By 1860 there were 4 million, almost all living in the South, and producing a cotton crop which by then was the nation's major export. Slavery no longer existed anywhere north of Maryland after 1804. Further importation of slaves was barred after 1808 and a humanitarian movement for the nationwide abolition of slavery began to grow. This emotionally charged issue produced acute tension between the 'slave' and 'non-slave' states.

The first major crisis over slavery resulted in the Missouri Compromise of 1820–1. Congress, during President Monroe's administration, permitted Missouri to enter the Union as a slave state, but brought in Maine as a non-slave state, thus maintaining balance between the two sides in Congress. This process of admitting states more or less in pairs was continued, but further tension came as a result of the Mexican War of 1846–8. The war broke out when Texas, an American-settled province of Mexico, which had broken away from Mexico nine years earlier, was annexed as a state by the USA in 1845. Mexico refused to accept this, and war followed. The clash between the two nations was short but bitter. In 1847, US troops occupied Mexico City and peace was finally made the following year. Mexico was forced to sell California and New Mexico (both provinces included most of the modern south-

*Settlers like these, travelling thousands of miles in their covered wagons, opened up the American West*

west) to the United States for 15 million dollars. But Southerners felt that they had not fought in the war to have these conquests declared non-slave, and began to talk of secession from the Union.

Another compromise was achieved in 1850. But then, in 1854, the Kansas-Nebraska Act was passed, which repealed the Missouri Compromise and left the slavery question in those territories to the vote of the actual settlers. This alleged betrayal inflamed anti-slavery passions anew. Opponents of the Act from both the Democratic ranks and the fatally split Whig Party formed the Republican Party. The abolitionists' rage was increased by the Dred Scott decision of 1857, in which the Supreme Court denied the right of Congress to ban slavery in any of the territories of the USA.

In this turbulent atmosphere the election of 1860 was held. Abraham Lincoln of Illinois, the Republican candidate, was elected as a result of the split of the Democrats into northern and southern wings. This election convinced major Southern leaders that the Union would soon have a majority of voters ready to destroy slavery by Constitutional amendment or other means. South Carolina seceded, and was joined by six other states to form the Confederate States of America in February 1861; Mississippi's Jefferson Davis was chosen as president. Four other states were to join the Confederacy later. War broke out almost immediately.

*Robert E. Lee commanded Confederate (Southern) forces in the Civil War. He was the war's outstanding general, and won the admiration of both North and South*

**Civil war: 1861–5** The first two years of the war were marked by a succession of Confederate victories. In 1862 General George McClellan led a vast Northern army to attack Richmond, the Confederacy's capital, but he was forced to withdraw. At Fredericksburg and Chancellorsville, Northern attacks were beaten off.

Confederate strategy was to fight a defensive war, in the hope that the North would recognise that victory was impossible and would agree to a compromise peace. But this strategy was not adhered to. There were Confederate offensives northwards. In 1863, General Robert E. Lee's army advanced into Pennsylvania, but was forced to retreat after the Battle of Gettysburg, a defeat regarded as the turning-point of the war. The Confederacy had overstretched its resources, and the enormous industrial strength and manpower of the North now made their full impact. The Confederates had few arms factories, and could not import munitions because of the Northern blockade of their ports.

In the West, meanwhile, Northern forces under General Ulysses S. Grant captured Vicksburg in July 1863, giving them complete control of the Mississippi. In the autumn of that year they drove the Confederate army out of Tennessee. In 1864, Grant was transferred to the East and took overall command. While he besieged Richmond, General William T. Sherman, on his march to the sea, scythed through Georgia and cut the Confederacy in two. The Civil War ended when General Lee surrendered his forces at Appomattox Courthouse, Virginia, in April 1865.

**Aftermath of war** Though the North began the war simply to restore the Union, the result of its victory was the end of slavery in the United States. But the price for this was the economic disruption of the South for generations, and a tortured legacy of bitterness. At the very moment of victory, Lincoln was assassinated by a Southern sympathiser, an actor named John Wilkes Booth. This deed set the mood for later developments.

Political power fell into the hands of a Republican faction known as 'Radicals' who wanted to punish the slaveholders guilty of rebellion and remake the South in the Northern image. Employing military occupation, the Radicals forced the South to accept new state governments that were controlled by 'carpetbaggers' – Northern newcomers – in alliance with those Southerners who would collaborate with them, and by freed slaves.

These state governments were often arbitrary, corrupt and deserving of disrepute. But on the other hand, all of them undertook important social steps such as building schools, and giving Negroes and poor whites their first opportunity to share in democratic rule. Gradually

*Ulysses S. Grant became commander-in-chief of the Union armies in the Civil War in 1864. His ruthless military policy brought about the South's defeat*

In the 1920's Henry Ford used new mass-production methods to make his Model T automobile the cheapest on the market

## USA *continued*

white Democratic Southerners regained control, as Northerners lost interest in the South. When the last troops were withdrawn in 1877, Radical Republican rule ended. Southerners remained bitter, however, and determined to enforce white control. By various enactments known as Jim Crow laws – Jim Crow being a derogatory term for Negro – they nullified civil and voting rights conferred on the blacks by amendments to the Constitution, and imposed segregation on them. Such laws reached their peak between 1890 and 1910, and survived until the 1950's. In 1954 the Supreme Court declared the segregation of races in the public schools to be unconstitutional, and in succeeding years struck at other aspects of segregation in the South.

The railroad comes to the West. Such progress meant the end of the buffalo – and suffering for the Indians, whose lives depended on it

**Growth and change: c. 1870** The North's victory in the Civil War was largely due to its speedy industrial development in the mid-19th century. Industrial progress was mirrored in technology and agriculture, and the continent at last was spanned by railroads. The Indians, victims of progress, were driven from their last strongholds, the Great Plains, on to reservations. The buffalo herds, which had sustained the plains Indians, were almost exterminated. Farmers poured westwards and, with the aid of such inventions as the McCormick reaper, converted the land into the world's granary. Cattle, pigs, corn and wheat were produced in lavish abundance. Forests were levelled to provide timber and make way for farms and cities. Mountains yielded gold, silver, iron, copper and other indispensable industrial resources. Underground reservoirs of oil were tapped.

The process of industrialisation was assisted by a growing labour force. The national population almost trebled, from 31 million in 1860 to almost 92 million in 1910. This dramatic increase was aided by the rising tide of immigration from many of the major countries of Europe. Six times between 1905 and 1914 annual immigration topped 1 million. Most of these new arrivals settled in the cities, helping to transform the country from a predominantly agricultural society into an urban one.

The Apache chief Geronimo (c. 1829–1909) led his people in a long but hopeless struggle against the white man

**War with Spain: 1898** As the USA became an industrial nation, increasingly concerned with exports and foreign investments, an imperialist mood developed. It was assisted by other factors: the scramble by European powers to acquire colonies in Asia and Africa; aggressive Christianity eager to civilise the 'heathen', and the popular Darwinian belief that the 'advanced' and 'fittest' races must rule in order to guarantee progress. These feelings underlay an American desire to free Cuba from what was seen as Spanish tyranny. The popular press – especially the New York newspapers of Joseph Pulitzer and William Randolph Hearst – lashed these emotions into a demand for war on Spain, which was declared in 1898 and quickly won. Afterwards, the US insisted on its right to intervene in Cuban affairs and to establish a naval base there. Through the collapse of Spain's empire, the United States also won its first colonies – Puerto Rico, Guam and the Philippines. In 1898 the United States annexed the Hawaiian Islands, which had been taken over from the Hawaiian kings by a revolutionary junta of American settlers. Thus, the USA became a full-fledged Pacific power by 1900.

**Roosevelt's presidency: 1901–9** The imperial mood was reflected in the young Theodore Roosevelt, a hero of the Spanish-American War, who was elected vice-president under President William McKinley in 1900. When McKinley was assassinated in 1901, Roosevelt succeeded him. Roosevelt built up the navy, making the USA a leading naval power. He encouraged a revolt in Colombia which made it possible for the United States to build the Panama Canal.

On the domestic front, Roosevelt willingly fell heir to a growing movement to curb the irresponsible powers of the railroads and the 'trusts', or major industrial monopolies. This movement had already created a Federal railroad-control body, the Interstate Commerce Commission, in 1887, and the Sherman Anti-Trust Act of 1890. Roosevelt sponsored legislation increasing the ICC's power. However, neither he nor his successors significantly slowed the tendency towards concentration of industrial ownership.

Theodore Roosevelt won fame through his exploits in the Cuban War of 1898. He and his 'rough-riders' typified the imperial outlook of the age

**Woodrow Wilson: 1913–21** The Democrat Woodrow Wilson took office in 1913 as a result of a split in the Republican Party between Roosevelt and William Howard Taft, president from 1909 to 1913. Wilson continued the war on the trusts, reduced the tariff, sponsored government loans for farmers and protection of certain classes of labourers, and promoted a Federal Reserve System which reduced the power of private banks to control interest rates, and therefore the pace of business activity. But the outbreak of the First World War in 1914 forced him to turn increasingly to foreign affairs, despite America's tradition of isolationism.

The USA remained neutral until 1917. But many influences drew the nation towards Britain and France. The Allied governments borrowed heavily in the United States; American factories became major suppliers of the Allied war machine; the journalistic and political élite of the country was generally pro-British. Germany's embarkation on unrestricted submarine warfare in 1917 was the final straw. In April Wilson called for a declaration of war and by its end, in 1918, 2 million US troops were serving in France.

Wilson now tried to carry idealism into the peace-making process. He proposed Fourteen Points for a treaty, calling for the reduction of tariffs, armaments, colonialism, secret diplomacy and other alleged war-breeding factors. He also successfully urged the creation of a League of Nations. But the Paris Peace Conference failed to implement his other principles, and Congress refused to allow the United States to join the League. In 1920 the Republican, Warren G. Harding, who promised a swift return to pre-war 'normalcy', was overwhelmingly elected to the presidency.

**Boom and slump** Reaction against the First World War led in the 1920's to a partial return to isolationism and, among some intellectuals, to a mood of escapism. Under three Republican presidents, Warren G. Harding, Calvin Coolidge and Herbert Hoover, there was an era of booming but hollow prosperity. Much of its tone was created by national prohibition – a ban on the manufacture and sale of intoxicating liquors introduced in 1919. Many Americans resented the law, and patronised illegal suppliers known as bootleggers, and drinking places called speakeasies. Such support encouraged crime, and gang warfare spread. Eventually, public disgust with prohibition led to its repeal in 1933.

The prosperity of the 1920's was mirrored in a feverish stock-market boom and an orgy of speculation. But there were deep flaws in this prosperity. Agriculture was depressed. New consumer goods were being bought on credit, which was often shaky. Certain old-established industries, like coal and textiles, suffered from declining markets, ageing machinery and unemployment. High tariffs caused other nations to retaliate by

The sinking of the Lusitania by a German submarine in 1915 caused the loss of 128 American lives. It was a crucial factor in turning American opinion against Germany. But America remained neutral until 1917

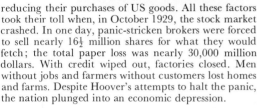

reducing their purchases of US goods. All these factors took their toll when, in October 1929, the stock market crashed. In one day, panic-stricken brokers were forced to sell nearly 16½ million shares for what they would fetch; the total paper loss was nearly 30,000 million dollars. With credit wiped out, factories closed. Men without jobs and farmers without customers lost homes and farms. Despite Hoover's attempts to halt the panic, the nation plunged into an economic depression.

**The 'New Deal'** By 1932, some 15 million Americans were out of work. The Democratic candidate, Franklin D. Roosevelt (a distant cousin of Theodore Roosevelt) swept to power and inaugurated what became known as the 'New Deal'. This was a programme in two parts. In the short term it fought the depression by such measures as public works, price supports to farmers and loans to business corporations. But there were also long-term developments. A Tennessee Valley Authority (TVA) was set up to provide flood control and cheap electric power for part of the rural South. In an attempt to cope with the problems of an industrial society, Congress enacted a vast legislative programme of urgent reforms.

There was debate about the effectiveness of such measures in promoting recovery. But this debate remained unresolved because the threat of war in Europe during the late 1930's stimulated industry through increased armament orders, especially from Britain.

**Second World War** Roosevelt never concealed his dislike of Nazism and Fascism. But during the 1930's, he was hampered in efforts to resist aggression by strong isolationist sentiment. After the defeat of France, however, public opinion changed enough to support the sale of 'surplus' armaments to beleaguered Britain. In January 1941 Roosevelt, just elected to an unprecedented third term in office, introduced 'Lend-Lease' legislation permitting war material to be sent directly, without payment, to the British. After the invasion of Russia by Germany in June 1941, the Soviet Union also received Lend-Lease supplies. American attention was mainly focused on the Pacific. Japan, deep in an invasion of China since 1937, had occupied French Indo-China in 1941. The United States struck back with a virtual economic blockade and demanded a Japanese withdrawal as the price for ending it. While negotiations were in progress, the Japanese made a surprise attack on Pearl Harbour on December 7, 1941. The following day, Congress declared war on Japan, whose allies, Germany and Italy, in turn declared war on the USA.

The USA soon became the main arsenal for the Allies. The Second Front in Europe, which opened in June 1944, was led by an American general, Dwight D. Eisenhower. The Pacific war against Japan was largely an American campaign. It ended with the atomic bombing of Hiroshima and Nagasaki in August 1945.

Now the leading world power, the USA determined not to retreat into isolation as it had done after 1918. It played a leading role in the formation of the United Nations, which it joined as a founder member.

**Cold War** American aid helped a devastated Europe to recover from the aftermath of war. In 1947, the Marshall Plan was introduced to help speed Europe's economic recovery. The same year, President Harry S. Truman established the Truman Doctrine, which committed the USA to oppose Communist expansion. Wartime co-operation between the Soviet Union and the USA was replaced with an armaments race and a Cold War of threats and counter-threats. The USA played a leading part in establishing NATO (the North Atlantic Treaty Organisation) in 1949 – an alliance of non-Communist nations of Europe to resist Soviet penetration.

The USA also committed itself to the containment of Communist expansion in Asia. This turned out to be more difficult. Despite American support for the Nationalist Chinese government of Chiang Kai-Shek, it was defeated in a civil war by Mao Tse-tung's Communist armies in 1949, and forced into exile on Formosa. The next year, Communist North Korea attacked the

American-supported regime of South Korea. With UN authorisation, the United States sent troops to resist. A three-year war ended in stalemate, with the frontiers more or less as they were at the start.

In 1954 the United States sponsored the South-east Asia Treaty Organisation (SEATO). But the complexities of America's Asian policy were tragically revealed in Vietnam, temporarily divided in 1954 when the French abandoned Indo-China. In 1960 US 'advisers' were sent to aid anti-Communist South Vietnam against the Viet Cong guerrillas, Communist-controlled and aided by North Vietnam. By 1968 US forces had swollen to more than half a million men.

**The Eisenhower era** Early in the 1950's American domestic politics were conditioned by the fears and frustrations of the Cold War. Senator Joseph McCarthy was prominent in a witch-hunt from 1952 to 1954, in which many leading citizens were attacked, often irresponsibly, as Communists or Communist 'fellow travellers'. However, the election of the popular general, Dwight D. Eisenhower, as president in 1952 and 1956 had a unifying effect. The decade was one of prosperity, spurred by major advances in technology.

Like the prosperity of the 1920's that of the fifties had its hidden flaws. Many groups – the aged, the unskilled, minorities – were excluded from it. Some Americans also thought that too much of the national product went into armaments and costly consumer goods, and not enough into education and urban renewal; that natural resources were being wasted; and that the preservation of the environment was being ignored.

**America today** With the election of the Democrat John F. Kennedy to the presidency in 1960, a new mood swept through the USA. Kennedy reflected this mood in his inaugural speech, when he called for a renewal of pride and patriotism in a drive for a New Frontier, with special emphasis on black equality. But he was soon confronted with an international crisis, when the Soviet leader, Nikita Khrushchev, moved missiles into Cuba. Kennedy imposed a blockade of the island and won the battle of nerves, and the missiles were withdrawn. Kennedy was assassinated in November 1963. An ugly development had entered American public life. Other prominent men to fall to the bullets of assassins were the Negro leader, Martin Luther King, shot in Memphis in 1968, and John Kennedy's younger brother, Robert, killed at an election meeting the same year.

John Kennedy's successor, Lyndon Johnson, tried to carry on his domestic policies, but found himself bogged down by the escalating US commitment in Vietnam, which divided the nation. In America's cities, Negro unrest mounted. In 1968, Johnson decided not to run for re-election; the Democratic choice, Hubert Humphrey, was defeated by the Republican Richard Nixon, who was re-elected in 1972.

Abroad, Nixon – with his adviser Dr Henry Kissinger – dramatically improved America's relations with the USSR and China, making historic visits to both countries. The *détente* was perhaps the key factor in the achievement of a ceasefire in Vietnam in 1973. Later in the year, however, the president faced a grave domestic crisis in the 'Watergate affair', in which senior members of his staff were convicted for being involved in a plot to cover up malpractices by Nixon supporters during the 1972 presidential election campaign. The crisis deepened with each new revelation in the Senate's Watergate hearings, and public concern intensified as Nixon's own role in the affair was exposed bit-by-bit. The resignation of Vice-President Spiro Agnew in October 1973, following tax-evasion and bribery charges against him, further undermined the standing of the administration. Rather than face certain impeachment and removal from office by Congress, Nixon resigned on August 9, 1974. He was succeeded by the first non-elected president, Gerald Rudolph Ford, who had been appointed to fill the vice-presidential vacancy. He chose as his vice-president Nelson Rockefeller, four time Governor of New York state.

UPPER VOLTA      VIETNAM, NORTH
URUGUAY      VIETNAM, SOUTH
VATICAN CITY
VENEZUELA

*St Peter's, the heart of the Vatican, is the largest Christian church. Designed partly by Michelangelo, it is one of the chief glories of Renaissance architecture*

# Upper Volta

This small republic, a landlocked and comparatively densely populated country, was part of French West Africa. Every year, thousands of its inhabitants, unable to find work in their own country, cross the border into Ghana and the Ivory Coast to find seasonal work in their neighbours' cocoa and coffee harvests.

105,869 sq. miles
5,844,200 people
Capital:
Ouagadougou

**Early history** The plateau lands which are now Upper Volta were dominated for centuries by the Mossi, who are still the country's main national group. Mossi states raided the rich trading cities on the Niger river during the 14th and 15th centuries. Later, they established the Dagomba state in what is now Ghana. The Mossi-Dagomba states survived intact until the 19th century, when French explorers reached the area. In 1896 the country was annexed by France.

**Independence** Upper Volta became independent in 1960. Under President Yamageo, the country faced a period of economic crisis and austerity, which produced widespread discontent. Demonstrations by students and trades unionists led to the army seizing power in 1966, when General Sangoulé Lamizana became head of state. All political parties were suspended and the National Assembly was dissolved. In 1974 Lamizana suspended the constitution and assumed all power for himself.

# Uruguay

By the early 1900's Uruguay, the smallest republic in South America, had emerged from a long period of civil disorder to become a model of political and economic stability. But in the 1950's Uruguay's stability was shaken by acute inflation. Harsh measures, taken to deal with the inflationary situation, produced much social unrest, which in turn led to more repression.

68,536 sq. miles
3,027,400 people
Capital:
Montevideo

**Colonisation: 1515–1828** The first Spanish settlers in 1515 found the country inhabited by Charrua Indians, who resisted conquest, but were killed off or absorbed. Uruguay was controlled by Portugal during the 1600's, and became part of the Spanish Empire in the 18th century. In 1820 it was forcibly annexed to Brazil. A movement led by Juan Antonio Lavalleja declared independence in 1825, and the new country's republican constitution was adopted in 1830.

**Civil and international wars: 1830–1903** The country was soon plunged into civil war between power-seeking factions calling themselves Colorados (reds) and Blancos (whites). Uruguay joined Brazil and Argentina to fight Paraguay in the War of the Triple Alliance (1865–70), South America's longest and bloodiest war.

**Progress and inflation** The enlightened ideas of Jose Batlle y Ordoñez, who became president in 1903, made Uruguay the first welfare state in South America. But the economic crisis that came with the world depression of the 1930's brought political instability, and Gabriel Terra suspended the constitution. Uruguay's economy declined sharply after 1955, when a fall in meat and wool prices led to grave inflation. In a climate of unrest, Jorge Pachecho Areco, elected president in 1968, governed under repressive emergency powers.

*Death of a Tupamaro rebel. The Tupamaros, anti-government 'urban guerrillas', won notoriety for their spectacular acts of terrorism*

**Guerrilla opposition** The government was opposed by a ruthless guerrilla group, the Tupamaros – a name derived from an 18th-century Indian rebel, Tupac Amaru. In January 1971 the British ambassador, Geoffrey Jackson, was kidnapped by them and held hostage for eight months. Under a state of emergency introduced by President Bordaberry in 1972, action by the army effectively halted the Tupamaros. Inflation continued unchecked, and the armed forces exerted increasing influence on the government. In mid-1973 Bordaberry suspended Uruguay's parliament, establishing a system of rule by presidential decree.

# Vatican City

Situated within Rome on the west bank of the Tiber river, the Vatican City is the headquarters of the Roman Catholic Church and the official residence of the pope. It is the world's smallest state, and depends on the protection of Italy. Yet its influence is immense, extending throughout the world to 590 million adherents of the Roman Catholic faith who look to the pope for guidance in moral and spiritual matters.

0·17 sq. miles
1000 people

The territory of the Vatican is all that remains of a papal domain which once included large areas of central Italy. This domain was greatly reduced in size during the unification of Italy in the 19th century. After the first king of united Italy, Victor Emmanuel, seized Rome in 1870, the popes refused to accept loss of temporal power and remained inside the Vatican (a papal residence since the 5th century), calling themselves 'prisoners'. But in 1929 the Italian dictator Mussolini negotiated the Lateran Treaty which recognised the Vatican's independence.

# Venezuela

Oil has made this one of the most prosperous Latin American countries. Venezuela is the world's third largest exporter of oil after Saudi Arabia and Iran, deriving three-quarters of its revenue from this source. But experts calculate that the country's oil reserves will be exhausted by the end of the 1980's and Venezuelans have therefore begun to develop new industries.

352,143 sq. miles
11,852,700 people
Capital: Caracas

**Rule by Spain** Christopher Columbus discovered what is now Venezuela in 1498. It was part of Spain's South American empire from 1521 until the early 19th century. In 1811 a wealthy landowner, Francisco Miranda, led a bid for independence. After Miranda's capture, the Venezuelan-born revolutionary Simon Bolívar organised an armed insurrection against the Spanish. Venezuela became fully independent in 1830.

**Dictators and oil** Venezuela suffered more than any other South American country in the struggle for independence. Its economy was ruined and almost a quarter of its population were killed. For the whole of the 19th century, the country was ruled by a series of corrupt dictators.

In 1908 Juan Vicente Gomez seized power. His position was strengthened by the discovery of oil in vast quantities in 1918. Oil revenues enabled Gomez to pay all Venezuela's foreign debts and also to modernise the army and secret police.

After Gomez's death in 1935 the army's leaders continued to hold power. They were overthrown in 1945 by a group of liberal-minded junior officers, who installed a civilian government.

*Juan Vicente Gomez, an early 20th-century Venezuelan dictator, won popularity through his stand against the foreign oil companies*

**Fragile democracy** The country's new civilian leaders, Romulo Betancourt and Romulo Gallegos, tried to modernise Venezuela and turn it into a welfare state. But their policies antagonised the rich, who overthrew them in 1948. By 1950 power had passed into the hands of Marcos Perez Jimenez. He won US support through his firm anti-Communist measures, but corruption flourished under his regime. Jiminez was overthrown in 1958.

In 1968 Rafael Caldera Rodriguez became the first opposition candidate ever to win power democratically. He attempted to conciliate the Left and reduce the power of Communist guerrillas. Carlos Andrés Pérez of Betancourt's Democratic Action Party won the 1973 presidential election and was inaugurated in 1974.

*Oil derricks symbolise Venezuela's prosperity. Three-quarters of the country's revenue comes from oil*

# Vietnam, North

An armistice agreement in 1954 led to the formation of North and South Vietnam. These states were created out of a country which had been struggling on and off for nearly a century against French rule. Division and foreign conquest are nothing new to a region which has been a united and independent country only once in its history – from 1802 until its conquest by the French in the late 19th century.

The Communist rulers who have held power in the Democratic Republic of Vietnam (North Vietnam) since 1954 have made the reunification of Vietnam under Communism their goal. This led them to support a Communist uprising against the South Vietnamese regime in the 1960's, and eventually to play a major role in the Vietnam war – one of the most destructive in history.

**Chinese rule** The northern part of Vietnam was originally occupied by Indonesian peoples, with a Bronze Age civilization. The Chinese invaded *c.* 100 BC, and brought northern Vietnam under control by AD 42. It remained a province of the Chinese Empire until the fall of the T'ang dynasty in 906, and became fully independent in 938. The Chinese reoccupied the country in 1407, but were driven out in 1427.

**Conquest and division** The Vietnamese expanded south at the end of the 15th century, conquering the kingdom of Champa in central Vietnam. During the following century, northern Vietnam was divided by civil war and only reunited in 1592 under the rule of the Trinh family, which lasted for 200 years. But during this period the Vietnamese lost control of central Vietnam and a long war was fought between the two regions. In 1802, the whole of Vietnam was unified for the first time by the Nguyen dynasty, with its capital at Hué. The French, concerned about the persecution of Catholic missionaries, invaded the south in 1859, and in 1885 established a protectorate over the rest of the country.

**Struggle for independence** From the start, the Vietnamese stubbornly resisted French rule. In the early 1900's a revolutionary movement arose, which looked to China for its model. But revolts in 1930–1, in which Communists and nationalists took part, were suppressed by the French. The opportunity for effective revolution came in the Second World War when the leading revolutionary movement, the Viet Minh, led by Communist Ho Chi Minh, won the support of the Allies by fighting against the Japanese. With liberation in 1945, Ho proclaimed Vietnamese independence.

**War with France: 1946–54** France sent troops to re-assert its control of Vietnam in 1946. They rapidly established themselves in the south, but fought unsuccessfully for nearly eight years to recover control of northern and central Vietnam. This struggle reached a climax in 1954, culminating in the shattering defeat of besieged French forces at Dien Bien Phu. An international conference, held at Geneva in the same year, negotiated an armistice.

**Partition and renewal of war** The Geneva agreement gave the Viet Minh control of the northern half of Vietnam, and they set up a government at Hanoi. Ho Chi Minh's government instituted a programme of social revolution and land reform. Several hundred thousand small land-owners fled to the south.

From the early 1960's, the North Vietnamese sent arms and troops in support of a Communist uprising in the south, hoping to bring about the overthrow of the South Vietnamese government. By 1965 North Vietnam was involved in full-scale war with US troops sent to support South Vietnam. US planes bombed the north. In 1968 peace talks opened in Paris but the conflict dragged on for another four years before terms were finally agreed in January 1973. With the official ending of hostilities, the US withdrew its troops from Vietnam, but fighting continued.

61,293 sq. miles
23,187,500 people
Capital: Hanoi

*Chinese influence is seen in the dress of a 19th-century Vietnam 'mandarin' – a title borrowed from China*

*Ho Chi Minh was the leader of Communist North Vietnam from partition in 1954 until his death in 1969. He strove to establish a unified Vietnam*

# Vietnam, South

The Republic of Vietnam (South Vietnam) was set up after an armistice agreement made at Geneva in 1954, which divided Vietnam into northern and southern zones along the 17th parallel. The whole of Vietnam was formerly part of French Indo-China, conquered by the French between 1859 and 1885.

From the early 1960's until 1973, when a cease-fire agreement was reached, South Vietnam was torn by a violent conflict between South Vietnamese government forces, backed by the United States, and a Communist guerrilla movement, the Viet Cong, linked with armies from North Vietnam. The Communist forces were given material aid by China and the USSR.

67,108 sq. miles
20,314,600 people
Capital: Saigon

*In war, it is inevitably the innocent who suffer – like these South Vietnamese children, fleeing in terror from a napalm bomb attack. By a tragic irony, the attack was a mistake – it was accidentally launched by South Vietnamese forces*

The struggle developed into a major war, causing immense destruction and loss of life. The ruthless conduct of the war on both sides, and the hardship it brought to the civilian population, aroused tense and often bitter controversy throughout the world.

**Vietnamese conquest: 1500–1760** Advancing into the country from the north, the Vietnamese did not enter the territory of what is now South Vietnam until the late 15th century. They conquered the kingdom of Champa but the extreme southern part of the country remained in Cambodian hands until *c.* 1760. By that time, however, the Vietnamese kingdom had split into two parts. A struggle for power in Hanoi (today the capital of North Vietnam) in 1660 led the Nguyen family and their followers to retreat to Hué (today in South Vietnam) where they ruled over a separate kingdom until 1775. By 1802 the Nguyens had succeeded in conquering the rest of the country.

**French invasion: 1859–67** French interest in Vietnam arose out of a desire to protect persecuted Catholic missionaries. By 1867 the French had conquered the south, which became the colony of French Cochin-China. The rest of Vietnam was conquered after 1882, but became a protectorate rather than a colony. The French exercised more direct rule and greater cultural influence in the south than in the north.

**Independence and war** The Japanese occupied Vietnam in 1941. After Japan surrendered, a nationalist movement under Communist leadership, the Viet Minh, set up an independent government. By 1946, the French had largely regained control of the south. But they were unsuccessful in crushing the Viet Minh, who retreated to the north. In 1954, an international conference at Geneva negotiated peace terms, and divided Vietnam into two zones. The anti-Communist governments of the South, under Ngo Dinh Diem, looked increasingly to the USA for support, especially after the Communist Viet Cong guerrillas became active in the country after 1960. But his oppressive regime was attacked by Buddhist leaders and army generals, and in 1963 he was arrested and murdered in a military coup.

In 1965 United States forces were committed to the fighting to save the South Vietnamese regime from collapse. There were over half a million American troops in South Vietnam by 1968, when negotiations

*General Nguyen Van Thieu became president of South Vietnam in 1967. He pledged himself to preserve South Vietnamese independence*

## VIETNAM, SOUTH *continued*

| FOR THE GOVERNMENT OF THE UNITED STATES OF AMERICA: | FOR THE GOVERNMENT OF THE DEMOCRATIC REPUBLIC OF VIET-NAM: |
| --- | --- |
| William P. Rogers<br>Secretary of State | Nguyen Duy Trinh<br>Minister for Foreign Affairs |

between the contending sides opened in Paris. The war, marked by increasing military intervention from the Communist north, dragged on for another four years, however, before a cease-fire was agreed in January 1973. American troops withdrew, having saved the South Vietnamese regime, although Communist forces were left in position. It was hoped that the two parts of the country would become reunited by peaceful negotiation. However, the loss of 230,000 American and South Vietnamese troops and an untold number of civilian dead, did not bring an end to fighting between North and South in this war-shattered land.

*The world hoped that the peace agreement signed in Paris on January 27, 1973 would at last end the fighting in Vietnam. Fighting was soon resumed, however, though without U.S. involvement*

# Western Samoa

A chain of islands in the Pacific, half-way between Honolulu and Sydney, forms the state of Western Samoa. The islands' tropical beauty attracted the writer Robert Louis Stevenson (1850–94), who settled there from 1890 until his death.

The Samoan islands, though sighted by the Dutch in 1722, were still largely unexplored by Europeans when English missionaries landed there in 1830. They found a bloody civil war in progress between the islands' Polynesian tribes. In 1889 a local chief, Malieto Laupepa, was recognised as king. After a short time fighting broke out again and continued until after his death. This ended when Germany, the USA and Britain agreed in 1900 to a division of the islands between the USA and Germany. The USA still controls some of the islands.

After Germany's defeat in the First World War, New Zealand took over responsibility for Western Samoa. With independence in 1962 the islands became the world's first Polynesian state.

1097 sq. miles
153,200 people
Capital: Apia

# Yemen, Northern

In ancient times, Yemen was an important link in the trade route from the Mediterranean to the East. The biblical kingdom of Sheba lay within its boundaries. Yemen was converted to Islam in the 7th century AD, and in 885 the Rassid dynasty started a period of rule which was to last in Northern Yemen until 1962.

For centuries the Muslim Imams (rulers) of Yemen kept their country in strict isolation from the outside world, despite Egyptian and then Turkish control of the coast. In 1839, however, the south came under British influence with the capture of Aden. Only after the Second World War did the remainder of Yemen begin to pursue a more outward-looking policy. It became a partner in the United Arab Republic from 1958 to 1961.

**Civil war: 1962–9** But change brought internal disturbance, and in 1962 the last Imam was overthrown by an Egyptian-supported army coup. The country became the Yemen Arab Republic. Civil war followed; Egyptian troops were sent to support the revolutionaries, while Saudi Arabia aided the exiled Imam. In 1969 royalist resistance collapsed.

Tension developed between the country and its southern neighbour, the People's Democratic Republic of Yemen (Southern Yemen) in the late 1960's.

A military coup led by Col. Ibrahim al-Hamidi overthrew the government in 1974.

75,290 sq. miles
6,391,000 people
Capital: San'a

*Amir el Hassan, leader of the royalist armies in the Yemen civil war, surveys the battlefront during the fighting*

# Yemen, Southern

For over a century the port of Aden was the base from which the British controlled the Persian Gulf and access to the eastern exit of the Suez Canal. Since 1968, Aden and its hinterland have been independent, first as Southern Yemen, and now as the People's Democratic Republic of Yemen. The country is still often called Southern Yemen. After a period of tension between Southern Yemen and its northern neighbour, the Yemen Arab Republic (also known as Northern Yemen), the two countries have moved closer together.

**Before and after independence** The history of Southern Yemen is identical with that of the north (see Yemen, Northern) up until the year 1839, when the British captured the port of Aden from the Arabs. The importance of the region began after the opening of the Suez Canal 30 years later. To protect Aden from overland attack, the British government negotiated treaties with the sheikhs of the south.

In 1959 the British established the Federation of South Arabia in which Aden and 17 sheikhdoms joined. Following a revolt by the National Liberation Front (NLF) in 1963, Britain announced independence for the Federation by 1968. In January 1968, fierce fighting broke out between two rival Arab organisations, with the British caught in between. The conflict ended with the victory of the NLF, which took over the government when Britain's troops withdrew in November 1968.

111,075 sq. miles
1,611,800 people
Capital: Aden and Madinet al-Shaab

*Patrolling a road in crisis-torn Aden. Fierce clashes occurred between British troops and Arab nationalists at the time of Aden's transition to independence in the 1960's*

NLF leaders used drastic methods to hold power. The regime moved more and more to the left. In 1969, President Qahtan al-Shaabi resigned, to be replaced by a self-proclaimed Marxist-Leninist government headed by a three-man presidential council.

Increasingly strained relations with the neighbouring Yemen Arab Republic in the north led to fighting between the two countries during 1972. Peace was negotiated at the end of the year, and an agreement was signed providing for eventual unification. Southern Yemen's conflict with its eastern neighbour, Oman, continued. Oman accused the Southern Yemeni government of aiding a revolt in its southern province of Dhofar.

# Yugoslavia

The people of this rugged, mountainous country achieved nationhood after the First World War, when Serbia, Montenegro, Croatia, Slovenia, Bosnia-Herzegovina and Macedonia were united to form the new kingdom of Yugoslavia – the 'land of the South Slavs'. After the Second World War, Yugoslavia became a Communist republic within the Soviet bloc, dominated by the war-time resistance leader, Marshal Tito. But his determination to uphold Yugoslavia's national identity led him to break with Stalin.

**Slav invasion: 7th century AD** The territory which makes up present-day Yugoslavia was once part of the Roman Empire. After the Romans withdrew, its people kept up Roman traditions and came under the influence of Byzantium. In the 7th century AD they were driven into the mountains by Slav invaders from the east.

98,766 sq. miles
21,172,700 people
Capital: Belgrade

*Stephen Dushan, one of medieval Europe's greatest conquerors, made Serbia into a rich and powerful nation*

**Rise and fall of Serbia: 900–1459** By the 14th century the Slav state of Serbia had become the predominant Balkan power, after conquering Macedonia and parts of Greece. Its greatest ruler, Stephen Dushan, planned to attack the Byzantine Empire, but he died on his march to Constantinople in 1355. Serbia later disintegrated under attack by the Ottoman Turks, who finally conquered the country in 1459.

**Foreign rule and independence: after 1459** From the mid-15th to the mid-19th centuries most of modern Yugoslavia was part of the Ottoman Empire. In 1878 the Congress of Berlin gave Serbia and Montenegro their freedom. But Turkey kept its hold on Macedonia, while Austria-Hungary, which already ruled Slovenia and much of Croatia, annexed Bosnia-Herzegovina in 1908. Serbia, however, expanded as a result of the Balkan Wars against Turkey (1912–13).

*Gavrilo Princip is led away (right) after killing the Archduke Franz Ferdinand. His act sparked off the First World War*

**Establishment of Yugoslavia: 1918** In June 1914, Gavrilo Princip, who belonged to a Serbian nationalist society known as the 'Black Hand', assassinated the Archduke Franz Ferdinand, heir to the Austro-Hungarian throne, at Sarajevo. Austria-Hungary declared war on Serbia; Russia, Germany and the other great European powers were drawn in, and the First World War had begun. The surrender of Germany, Austria and Turkey in 1918 was followed by the creation of Yugoslavia under the rule of Peter I of Serbia.

**Disunity leads to dictatorship** The newly united Slavs soon quarrelled among themselves. Rivalry between the Croats and the Serbs for political supremacy led Alexander I to set up a royal dictatorship in 1929. Alexander was assassinated in 1934.

In the 1930's the disunited country came increasingly under the influence of the Axis powers, Germany and Italy. Finally the Regent Paul joined the Axis in 1941, but he was overthrown by a popular uprising. Germany immediately invaded the country.

*Prince Paul, Regent of Yugoslavia, was invited to Berlin as a guest of Hitler*

**From resistance to republic: 1941–5** Resistance movements sprang up to fight the Germans. But many Croats supported the occupying forces, while some supporters of the Royalist General Mihajlovic fought against Tito's Communist partisans. By 1944 Tito had emerged as victor against Mihajlovic (who was later executed) and in 1945 he assumed the leadership of the liberated country and abolished the monarchy.

**Yugoslavia since 1945** Soviet leaders expected Tito's Yugoslavia to be an obedient puppet state. But in 1948 Tito refused to toe the Stalinist line and Yugoslavia was expelled from the Soviet bloc. After Stalin's death in 1953, the new Soviet leaders re-established friendly relations. Tito still resisted any attempt to make him follow the Kremlin's dictates, accepting aid from both East and West to bring prosperity to his people.

In 1970 Tito declared his intention of liberalising the government, and in 1971 he established a 22-man collective presidency to rule the country after his death. But this 'liberalisation' led to pressure from the Croats to be given more independence, culminating in widespread rioting and the resignation of Croatian party leaders.

*Josip Broz adopted the name of Tito while a partisan leader in the Second World War. In 1945 he became Yugoslavia's ruler*

# Zaïre

This African country, once the Belgian Congo, was plunged into chaos and bloodshed immediately after gaining its independence in 1960 as the Democratic Republic of the Congo. Some observers believed that this disaster was mainly caused by the failure of the Belgians to equip the Africans for self-government; others blamed it on political power struggles and communal rivalry among the Africans. By 1971, under Mobutu Sese Seko, the country had achieved stability, and that year its name was changed to Zaïre.

905,568 sq. miles
25,429,700 people
Capital: Kinshasa

**Early kingdoms** Zaïre is inhabited by Bantu-speaking African people, and also by pygmies in the eastern equatorial forests. Some of these peoples formèd powerful, centralised states at least as early as the 15th century. The kingdom of Kongo, in the south of the estuary of the Zaïre (formerly Congo) River, had close ties with Portugal in the 15th century, but was largely destroyed by the transatlantic slave trade.

*The explorer H. M. Stanley arriving by boat at a gathering of African chiefs. Stanley was the first white man to explore the entire length of the Congo River*

**The Congo under Leopold** The Anglo-American explorer H. M. Stanley travelled down the Congo River in 1877, and in the following year Leopold II of Belgium formed an association to exploit the resources of the vast river basin. The 'Congo Free State' was recognised by the Congress of Berlin in 1885. It was in effect a private empire of Leopold. But the brutal methods used by Leopold's agents to obtain such products as wild rubber and ivory became an international scandal, and in 1908 Leopold was forced to cede the territory to Belgium.

**The Congo under the Belgians** Belgian rule over the Congo lasted 52 years. Communications were improved and primary school education was provided for many. In the rich province of Katanga, the huge *Union Minière* company established one of the world's largest copper-mining industries. The Second World War, and the post-war boom, greatly boosted the economy, but when the Belgian Government unexpectedly decided to grant independence to the colony in 1960 there were few Congolese sufficiently well trained and experienced to rule the new African state. The Congo lacked the efficient bureaucracies which had been set up in most British and French colonies; political organisation was weak and regionally based.

*Congolese chained and under guard in 1907, when the Congo was a private colony of the Belgian King Leopold II. Such treatment caused a world outcry*

**Zaïre since independence** At independence, when the country was named the Democratic Republic of the Congo, Joseph Kasavubu was elected president, and Patrice Lumumba prime minister. But, within days, troops of the Congolese Army mutinied against their white officers, and the whole state was in danger of disintegrating. Moise Tshombe declared the secession of Katanga, with the connivance of *Union Minière*, Belgium and the white government of the Federation of Rhodesia and Nyasaland. Revolts broke out in other provinces. A United Nations force was sent to the Congo. Lumumba tried to bring in Russian support, while Tshombe employed white mercenary soldiers. In 1961 Lumumba was murdered, probably at the instigation of Tshombe.

## ZAÏRE *continued*

By 1963 Katanga was reunited with the Congo, but only at the price of admitting Tshombe and his followers to the central government. In 1965 the army seized power, led by Col. Joseph Mobutu (later changed to Mobutu Sese Seko), and Tshombe went into exile, only to be kidnapped in 1969 and taken to Algeria, where he died in prison. Meanwhile, with United States aid and a considerable force, President Mobutu's government maintained stability and revived the economy. Revolts by European mercenaries in 1966 and 1967 in the eastern provinces were put down, and *Union Minière* was brought under nominal government control. The first stage of the huge Inga hydro-electric project was opened in 1972. In the same year the government launched its campaign of 'authenticity', aimed at strengthening national identity; all European place and personal names in Zaïre were ordered abolished.

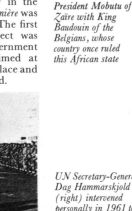

*President Mobutu of Zaïre with King Baudouin of the Belgians, whose country once ruled this African state*

*UN Secretary-General Dag Hammarskjold (right) intervened personally in 1961 to halt fighting in the Congo. But he was killed in an air crash before he could accomplish his mission*

# Zambia

The name Zambia comes from the River Zambezi, which separates this Black African republic – once the British protectorate of Northern Rhodesia – from its white-dominated neighbour, Rhodesia, formerly Southern Rhodesia. Zambia's vast copper reserves make it potentially one of the richest countries in Africa; it is the world's second-largest copper producer after the USA. Since Rhodesia's Unilateral Declaration of Independence (UDI) in 1965, tension has grown between the two countries. Zambians have condemned the policies of Rhodesia's white minority regime towards its African people, while the Rhodesian government has accused the Zambians of allowing African guerrillas to infiltrate across the border.

290,585 sq. miles
4,657,800 people
Capital: Lusaka

**Before the Europeans** Zambia's first inhabitants were a Stone Age people akin to the Bushmen of South Africa. They were absorbed by waves of Bantu-speaking peoples who entered the region between the 1st and the 15th centuries. During the 18th and early 19th centuries, the Zambian tribes became the prey of Portuguese and Arab slave-traders. The existence of the slave trade brought the region to the attention of European missionaries and explorers in the mid-19th century.

*A 19th-century artist's attempt at a bird's-eye view of the Victoria Falls. On the far side of the Zambezi lies present-day Zambia*

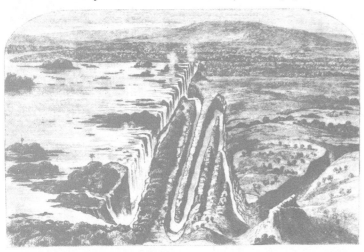

**European explorers** The Scots missionary-explorer David Livingstone travelled up the Zambezi in 1851 and discovered the Victoria Falls in 1855. European traders followed. Between 1891 and 1894 British troops under Sir Harry Johnston stamped out the Arab slave trade and established British control over the eastern part of the country. The territory was administered by the British South Africa Company of Cecil Rhodes (1853–1902), who saw it as a link in an imperial route from the Cape to Cairo. The Company's territories were named Rhodesia after him in 1895. From 1911, the areas north and south of the Zambezi were administered separately as Northern and Southern Rhodesia. When the Company's charter expired in 1923, Southern Rhodesia (present-day Rhodesia) opted to become a self-governing colony; Northern Rhodesia became a British protectorate in the following year.

**Road to independence** Between the two world wars the territory's wealth increased with the development of its rich northern copper belt. European companies poured in millions of pounds of capital, while the copperbelt's white miners and engineers were among the highest paid in the world. The white population, however, remained small by comparison with Southern Rhodesia's relatively large settler population. In 1953, the two territories were merged with Nyasaland (now Malawi) to form the Central African Federation.

The new state, however, was not a success. From the start, the move was bitterly opposed by Northern Rhodesian nationalists, under Kenneth Kaunda, who worked to destroy it. They saw it as a means of diverting the territory's mineral wealth to sustain a white-dominated society. In 1963, the Federation was dissolved and Northern Rhodesia, under the name of Zambia, became independent in the following year.

*The Scots missionary and explorer David Livingstone (1813–73) exposed the evils of slavery in the Zambezi region*

*The mines of Zambia's rich northern copper belt are the world's second-largest source of copper*

**Tension with Rhodesia** The European mining companies collaborated in schemes for the Africanisation of responsible jobs on the copper belt, but Rhodesia's unilateral declaration of independence in 1965 created tension between Zambia's black and white communities. President Kaunda firmly opposed the white regime on his doorstep – despite Zambia's dependence on Rhodesia for power and for road and rail communications with the east coast ports. This led to a gradual worsening of relations between the two countries. Early in 1973, Rhodesia closed the border across the Zambezi in reprisal for the use, it was claimed, of Zambian territory as a base for African guerrilla fighters operating in Rhodesia. Meanwhile, with Chinese financial and technical aid, a new railway was under construction from Zambia to the port of Dar es Salaam in Tanzania.

**One-party rule** The banning of the opposition United Progressive Party and the imprisonment of its leader, Simon Kapwepwe, a former vice-president, set the scene for the establishment of a one-party state in December 1972. (Kapwepwe was released in 1973.) New legislation was enacted which allowed no political party or organisation to exist other than the ruling United National Independence Party (UNIP).

*Kenneth Kaunda, who became Zambia's leader on independence, proclaimed his belief in a policy of 'Humanism'*

# Index

Page numbers in **bold** type refer to a chapter or gazetteer entry devoted to a subject.
Other text references are indicated by page numbers in roman type. Figures in *italics* refer to
illustrations, which are often accompanied by mention in the text on the same page. The panels
provide quick reference to some of the major themes occurring throughout the book.

---

| BUILDINGS OF THE WORLD | |
|---|---|
| | |

Henry III, King of France 385
Henry IV, Holy Roman
  Emperor 218, *390*, 418
Henry IV, King of France
  (Henry of Navarre) 240, 368
Henry V, Holy Roman
  Emperor *390*
Henry V, King of England 385
Henry VII, King of England
  233, 458
Henry VIII, King of England
  216, 233, 236, 278, 313,
  348, 349, 458
  armour of *346*
Heraclius 125, 274
Herakleiopis 66
Heraklion 89
Hercules 95
Herero 437
Herman *390*
Hermes 95, *97*
Hermitage Museum, Leningrad
  134
Hermon, Mt, Israel 27
Herod Antipas 86
Herodotus 58, 79, 82, 271,
  305, 333
Herod the Great 86
Hero of Alexandria 102, 271, *311*
Hertz, Heinrich 319
Hertzog, General James 440
Herzl, Theodor 405, *406*
Heyerdahl, Thor 340
Hezekiah 56, 84
Hiero *311*
hieroglyphic writing
  Cretan 91
  Egyptian *62*, *65*, 70
Hillary, Sir Edmund 343
Himalayas 159, 163, 343, 375
Hinduism 158–67, *288–9*, 399,
  *400–1*, 427
  Buddhism and 274
  Burma and 275, 366
  Cambodia and 367
  Ceylon and 271, 276, 370
  Islam and 277, 279, 281, 428
  Java and 277
  sculpture and 275
  Sumatra and 275
Hipparchus *297*, 333
Hippocrates 102, 271, 323, 326
Hippodrome, Constantinople
  *122*, 124, 126
Hirohito, Emperor *413*
Hiroshima 281, 352, 413, 467
Hispania 441
Hispaniola 233, *380*, 396
Hissarlik 92
Hitler, Adolf 262–3, 281, 321,
  352, *391*, *392*, 413, 432
  Austria and 361
  Britain and 461
  Czechoslovakia and 379
  Netherlands and 423
  Russia and 455
Hittites 85–86, 266, 269, 270,
  448
  armour and weapons of
  *311*, 344
  Assyrians and 55
  Egypt and 68, 70
  iron-working by 44
Hobart, Australia *358*
Hogarth, William *247*, 280
Hohenzollern dynasty 237
Hokkaido 181, 410
Hokusai, Katushika *411*, *412*
Holbein, Hans 233, 278
Holland (*see also* Netherlands)
  **422–4**
  Africa and 211, 279
  arms and warfare *348*, 360,
  459
  East India Company 335,
  338, 371, 438, 439
  England and 245, 348
  explorers from 358
  New World colonies 279, 338,
  396, 463
  pirates 234
  Portugal and 279
  prehistory 31, 43
  Reformation and 236, 278
  Renaissance and 233
  scientists in 299
  South Africa and 279, 281,
  439
  Spain and 237, 244, 348,
  278, 279
'Holland, Count of' 422
Hollywood 265
Holmes, Oliver Wendell 328
Holy Land, the
  Crusades 155, 220, 276, 334,
  346, 457

Holyoake, Sir Keith *424*
Holy Roman Empire 217–18,
  240, 274–5, 360, 362, 385,
  390, 407, 408, 418, 430, 442,
  445
Homer 88, 90, 91, 92, 93, 96, 97,
  98, 101, 119, 270, 333, 394
*Homo erectus* 13, 16, 17–18,
  *17*, *19*
*Homo habilis* 16, 17, *446*
*Homo sapiens* 13, 16, 18, 24
*Homo sapiens sapiens* 11, 18,
  19–20, *19*, 21
Honduras 191, 272, 275, 382,
  **397**
Honecker, Erich *390*
Hong Kong 242, 373, 374, 413,
  461
Hoover, Herbert 466–7
Hopkins, Frederick Gowland
  331
Horace 105, 114, 272
Horatius 112
Horthy, Admiral *398*
Horus 63, 64, 66, 71
Horyuji temple *181*
Hosea 285
Hottentots *439*
Houphouët-Boigny, Felix 410
Hoxha, Enver *356*
Hoyle, Fred 300–1
Hsiung-nu (*see also* Huns) 172,
  372
Hsu Wei *173*
Hudson, Henry 234, 338, 368
Hudson, R 234
Hudson's Bay Company 338,
  *368*, *369*
Hugo, Victor 256
Huguenots 236, 240, 243
Hui-tsung *373*
Huitzilopochtli 189, 194, 196
Hulagu Khan 78
Humanism 291–2
Humay *79*
Humbaba 54
Hume, David *293*
Hume, Hamilton 340–1, 358
Humphrey, Hubert 467
Hungary **397–8**
  Austria and 261, 360–1
  prehistory 31, 32, 40, 310
  Huns 139, 142, 158, 163–4,
  172, 274
  Austria and 360
  Byzantium and 125, 347
  China and 372
  Hungary and 397
  India and 273
Hunter, John 326, 327
Hunter, William 326, 327
Hunt, Sir John (*now* Lord
  Hunt) 343
Husack, Gustave 379
Hus, Jan 226, 235, 277, *378*
Hussein, King of Jordan *414*
Hussians 269
Huxley, Thomas 299
Hven, Denmark 297
Hvirring, Denmark *42*
Hwang Ho *see* Yellow River
Hyderabad 333
Hyksos 66, 268, 269, 344, 381

I

Iberian peninsula *see* Spain
Ibn Battuta 157, 209, 334, 277
Ibn Butlan 152
Ibn Khaldun 157, 277
Ibo 425, 426
Ibsen, Henrik *427*
Icarus *320*
Ice Age
  animal life in 22, 26, 27
  prehistoric man in 13, 16, 19,
  20
  sea level in 21, 462
Iceland *398*
  Norsemen in 145, 147, 274,
  332, 368
  icons 123, 125, *130–1*, *132*
Ictinus 99
Idrisi 276
Ieiatsu 181, 186
Ieyasu, Tokugawa 186
Ife *211*, 277, 425
Il Gesu Church, Rome 236

*Ilium* (*see also* Troy) 92
Illauntannig, Isle of 144
Illinois 465
Illyria 112
Imhotep 63, 66
'Immortals' *73*
Incas **198–203**
  conquistadores and 234, 279,
  337, 363, 429
  in Ecuador 380
  *quipu* 306
India **158–67**, **399–401**
  Alexander the Great and 103,
  271, 333, 345, 394
  armies of ancient 345
  Babylon and 58
  Buddhism 272
  Christianity 290
  foreign travellers to 174, 176,
  234, 333, 335, 373
  France and 252, 254
  Hinduism 271, 277, 288
  Independence 264, 427, 428,
  461
  Islam and 151, 157, 208, 274,
  276, 287
  Jainism 289
  medicine in 322–3, *330*
  Mughal Empire 279, 287–8
  Persia and 74, 78
  Portugal and 177, 278, 279,
  334, 335, 337, 433, 435
  prehistory 12, 19, 21, 30,
  42, 266
  sciences and 155, 295, 301,
  307
Indiana 465
Indian Mutiny 280, 400, 427
Indian Ocean 208, 234, 275,
  277, 333, 335
Indians, American
  counting by 306
  in Central and S. America
  362, 357, 364, 371, 396,
  420, 421
  in N. America 294, 340, 341,
  368, 369, 462, 463, 464, 466
Indo-China 367, 388, 413, 467
Indo-Europeans 288
Indonesia **401–2**, 418, 419, 429
Indus, R 150, 158, *160*, 333
Industrial Revolution
  Britain and 456, 459
  Europe and 257, 279, 459
  France and 255
  Germany and 391
  Russia and 453
  South Africa and 440
  technical advances 314–15,
  351
Ingres, Jean 254, *255*
Innocent III, Pope 218, 224,
  291, *408*
Inquisition, the 236, 291, 298,
  442
Iona, Isle of 144, 217
Ionia 96, 103, 270, 271, 307,
  345, 394, 395
Iqbal, Muhammad 427
Iran (Persia) 74, 79, **402–3**, 416
  prehistory 29, 31, 36, 38,
  266, *310*
Iraq 150, 152, **403**, 406, 416
Ireland, Northern 404, 456, *461*
Ireland, Republic of **404–5**
  Celtic civilization 47, 143,
  271, 274, 275
  Christianity in 143–4, 273, 456
  Corn Laws and 460
  culture *143*, 144
  Home Rule 460
  independence 456
  prehistory 35, 36, 40, 42, *45*
Irkutsk, Siberia 18
Iron Age **44–47**, 266, *362*, *425*,
  448, 456
Isabella of Castile 155, 233,
  278, 336, 433
Isaiah 86
Isandhlwana, Battle of 440
Ise, Japan 183
Isfahan *76*, 78, 79, 279
Ishtar Gate, Babylon *59*
Isis 69, 71, 118, 272
Islam 77, **148–57**, 274, 287–8,
  *287*, 290
  armies 347
  astronomers 295
  Battle of Tours 217, 218
  Byzantine Empire and 125,
  126, 127, 347
  calendar *308*, 309
  Christianity and 278, 286
  commerce 209, 210, 275
  Crusades and 220, 221, 222,
  223, 276

Golden Horde 450
  Hinduism and 164–6, 167,
  277, 279, 281
  invasions of India 158, 159,
  164
  Judaism and 285, 286, *294*
  Moorish Empire 217, 278,
  356, 371, 381, 420, 421,
  438, 441
  script and language 305
Isle of Man 145, 461
Ismail, Khedive 444
Isma'il I, Shah of Persia 78, 279
Israel 86, 270, 281, **405–6**
  Arabs and 355, 445, 446
  Egypt and 381, 382
  Natufians 27
Israelites (*see also* Hebrews)
  68, 81, 84, 86
Issus, Battle of 76, 103
Istanbul (*see also* Byzantium
  *and* Constantinople) *122*, 156
Italy **406–9**
  barbarians and 123, 139, 273,
  347
  Byzantium and 123, 125,
  126, 277
  Crusades 220, 222, 223
  culture 143, 145, 224, 242, 256
  Inquisition in 298
  Joseph II and 244
  prehistory 31, 32, 33, 35, 39,
  40, 45
  Renaissance 228, 230, 278
  warfare 218, 255, 346
Ithaca 92
Itza 193–4, 277
Ivan III, the Great 127, 128,
  132, 278, 451
Ivan IV, the Terrible 133, 134,
  137, 278, *451*
Ivan V 133
Ivory Coast *410*

J

Jacob 85
Jacobites 459
Jagan, Cheddi 396
Jainism 271, 284, *289*
Jamaica 336, **410**
Jamestown, Virginia 462–3
James I of England and VI of
  Scotland 404, 458, 462
James II, King of England 243,
  245, 248, 404, 423, 459, 463
James V, King of Scotland 458
Jansen, Johannes *and* Zacharius
  325, 327
Janszoon, William 339, 358
Janus 47, 309
Japan **180–7**, **410–13**
  Ainus 21
  China and 178, 179, 275, 281,
  374, 375, 467
  early explorers and 336, 337
  Kublai Khan and 277, 373
  porcelain in 177
  Second World War and 281,
  352, 375, 461
  writing in 304
Jarrow 142
Java *401*, 402
  Islam and 157
  Janszoon in 339
  prehistory 16, 18, 21
  shadow puppets *163*, *402*
Jawara, Sir Dawda *388*
Jefferson, Thomas *251*, 280, 341,
  *464*, 465
Jehovah 84
Jena, Battle of 256, 350, 390
Jenne 208
Jenner, Edward 326, 327
Jeremiah 86
Jericho *29*, 31, 414
Jerusalem 86–87, *405*
  Assyrians and 56, 84
  Crusades and 155, 220–2, 275
  Dome of the Rock 151
  Marco Polo and 333
  Nebuchadnezzar and 58, 270
  Temple of Solomon 74, 83,
  86, 270, 285, 405
Jesuits 236, 433, 434
  China and 170, 177, 374
  Descartes and 292
  India and *291*

Jesus Christ *86–87*, 120, 212–13,
  272, 285, 286–7, 405
  Anglo-Saxons and 142, 144
  Byzantium and 121, *123*
  Crusades and 221
  Franciscans and 225
  Islam and 148
  medieval Europe and 215,
  218, 219, 291

Jews (*see also* Hebrews) **80–87**,
  286–7, 405
  Crusaders and 221
  Nazis and 262, 281, 290,
  391–2, *392*, 406, 432
  Nebuchadnezzar and 58
  Persians and 74
  Poland and 430
  Prussia and 243
  Russia and 453, 455
  Sabbath 309
  Spain and 442
  Turks and 155
Jinnah, Mohammed Ali 427–8,
  *428*
Joan of Arc 385
Job 285
Jodrell Bank, Cheshire *301*
Johannesburg, South Africa
  440
John, King of England 218,
  385, 457
John of Gaunt *220*, 433
John I, Emperor of Byzantium
  125
John VI, King of Portugal 364,
  434
Johnson, Dr Samuel 293, *459*
Johnson, Lyndon B. 467
Jolliet, Louis 341
Jonathan, Chief Lebua 417
Jones, Inigo 245, 246
Jonson, Ben 235
Jordan 29, 31, *414*
Joseph 85
Joseph II of Austria 244, 360
Joshua 85
Joyce, James 281, 404
Juan Carlos, Don 443
Judaea (*see also* Judah) 86, 87,
  104, 105, 112
Judah (*see also* Judaea) 84,
  *84–85*, 86, 285, 405
Judaism 78, 81, 84–87, 207,
  285–7, *285*, 287, *405*, 406
Judas Iscariot *86*, *87*
Juliana, Queen of the
  Netherlands 423
Julius II, Pope 232
Jundashapur 79
Jupiter, Temple of *110*
Jurched, the 176, 178, 373
Justinian I, 102, *121*, 123–5,
  *125*, 347, 448
  Legal Code of 119, 124, 127
Jutes 140, 142, 456
Jutland, Battle of 351, *352*

K

'K2', mountain 343
Kaaba, the *148*, 150, 151
Kabul 356
Kadar, Janos 398

# Z

# X

# Y

# WHERE TO SEE THE WORKS OF MAN

The source of many of the illustrations in this book, as indicated in the following list, is also in many cases the historical site, museum or art gallery where the object depicted may be seen. Names of photographers appear in brackets. The details are arranged according to chapter and page number (**bold** figures), reading from top left to bottom right on each page.

### Part 1 Countdown to civilization

**The world before man 8** Eruption of Surtsey, 1967 (Hjalmar R. Bardarson)

**The Stone Age 14** Lake Rudolf, Kenya (Douglas Botting) **22** Venus of Willendorf, Naturhistorisches Museum, Vienna (Holle Verlag); female idol from Dolni Vestonice, Moravian Museum, Brno (Holle Verlag); Venus of Laussel, Musée d'Aquitaine, Bordeaux **23** Wounded bison, from Lascaux (Peter Bellew); engraved pebble from Le Colombière, courtesy Professor Movius, Peabody Museum, Harvard University; Lady of Brassempouy, Musée des Antiquities Nationales, Paris **24** 'Sorcerer', from Les Trois Frères, Ariege, drawing after Henri Breuil **25** Cow, from Lascaux (Colorphoto Hinz, Basel); carved mammoth from Bruniquel, British Museum; reindeer carving from Lortet, Musée des Antiquities Nationales, Paris; pierced staff with carved heath cock, from Le Mas d'Azil, Musée des Antiquities Nationales, Paris (Holle Verlag); engraved horse from Lascaux (Archives Photographiques) **27** Sandstone sculpture from Lepenski Vir (Dr Dragoslav Srejovic)

**The first farmers 28** Tower at Jericho (Georg Gerster from Magnum) **30** Painting of a dead man's face from Catal Hüyük (Mrs M. A. Mellaart) **31** Necklace of beads from Catal Hüyük (Mrs M. A. Mellaart); plaster relief of leopards from Catal Hüyük (Mrs M. A. Mellaart); reconstruction of the Temple of the Bull God, drawing by Grace Huxtable, courtesy Prof. James Mellaart **33** Pottery figure from Cernavoda (Institute of Archaeology, Bucharest, Romania); funnel beaker, National Museum, Copenhagen; model of a neolithic house from Strelice, Moravian Museum, Brno (Thames and Hudson); female idol in form of a jar, from Vidra, Romania, National Museum of Antiquities, Bucharest (Holle Verlag) **34** West Kennett barrow (Michael Holford) **35** Minajdra Temple, Malta (C. M. Dixon); dolmen at Kilclooney, County Donegal (The Green Studio, Dublin)

**The metal age 37** Solar wagon of Trundholm, National Museum, Copenhagen (Lennart Larsen) **38** Bronze Age swords and processional axe, National Museum, Copenhagen **39** Chieftain, Sardinia, National Museum, Copenhagen; gold collar from County Clare, National Museum, Dublin; gold earrings from England, Ashmolean Museum, Oxford; Hove amber cup (E. Meacher); solar disc from Moordorf, Lower Saxony (Holle Verlag); Rillaton Gold Cup (Edwin Smith) **40** Avebury (Penny Tweedie) **41** Stonehenge (Picturepoint) **42** Bronze razor, National Museum, Copenhagen; female acrobat, National Museum, Copenhagen; lurer from Maltbaed, National Museum, Copenhagen **43** Votive wagen, Landesmuseum, Joanneum, Graz, Austria (Ernst Matthaus Furbock) **44** Maiden Castle (Penny Tweedie) **45** Head of a man, from Msecke-Zehrovice, National Museum, Prague (Holle Verlag); Desborough Mirror, British Museum; model boat, National Museum of Ireland; gold neck-ring, National Museum of Ireland; wine flagon from Mozelle, British Museum **46** Tollund Man, National Museum, Copenhagen **47** Deity holding stags, and Cernunnos as 'Lord of the Animals', from the Gundestrup Cauldron, National Museum, Copenhagen

### Part 2 The great civilizations

**Mesopotamia 51** Sumerian votive figures, Iraq Museum, Baghdad (Georg Gerster from Rapho) **52-53** Detail from Standard of Ur, British Museum **53** Gilgamesh relief from Khorsabad, Louvre (Hirmer Fotoarchiv, Munich) **54** Goat in the Thicket, from Ur, British Museum; gold helmet from Ur, Iraq Museum, Baghdad (Hirmer Fotoarchiv, Munich); gaming board from Ur, British Museum **55** Bull's head lyre from Ur, University Museum, Philadelphia (Frank Scherschell, Life © 1972, Time Inc.); crushed skull from Ur, Iraq Museum, Baghdad (Hirmer Fotoarchiv, Munich); necklace from Ur, Iraq Museum, Baghdad (Hirmer Fotoarchiv, Munich) **56** Head of Hammurabi, Louvre (Holle Verlag, Baden-Baden); detail from the Law Code of Hammurabi, Louvre (Cliché des Musées Nationaux) **56-57** Assurnasirpal shooting lions, British Museum **57** Fresco from Til Barsip, Aleppo Museum (Hirmer Fotoarchiv, Munich) **58** Detail of Assyrian archers, British Museum **59** Ishtar Gate from Babylon, Staatliche Museum, Berlin (Erich Lessing from Magnum)

**Egypt 60** The Great Sphinx, and Pyramid of Cheops, Giza (Michael Holford) **62** Palette of Narmer, Egyptian Museum, Cairo (Jean Vertut) **63** King Mycerinus, Egyptian Museum, Cairo (Roger Wood) **64** Wooden model of oxen, British Museum (Michael Holford); wall-painting from Tomb of Menna at Thebes: winnowing grain and bearers carrying basket of grain (Michael Holford) **65** Model of cattle inspection from tomb of Meketre, Egyptian Museum, Cairo (Erich Lessing from Magnum); seated scribe, Louvre (Cliché des Musées Nationaux) **66** Wooden stele with Re-Harakhte, Louvre (Giraudon); Shu creates the World, papyrus, Egyptian Museum, Cairo (John G. Ross) **67** Temple of Amun, Karnak (William MacQuitty) **68** Nefertiti, Staatliche Museum, Berlin (Hirmer Fotoarchiv, Munich); Akhenaton, Egyptian Museum, Cairo (John G. Ross) **69** Head of Ramesses II, Egyptian Museum, Cairo (Dingwall Photo from John Hillelson Collection); mourners from tomb of Ramose at Thebes (Hassia, Paris); Book of the Dead, British Museum; model of funerary boat from Thebes, British Museum (Michael Holford) **70** Gold mask of Tutankhamun, Egyptian Museum, Cairo (William MacQuitty) **71** Tutankhamun harpooning game, Egyptian Museum, Cairo (Roger Wood); painted casket showing Tutankhamun battling Asians, Egyptian Museum, Cairo (F. L. Kenett © George Rainbird Ltd, 1963); drinking cup, Egyptian Museum, Cairo (F. L. Kenett © George Rainbird Ltd, 1963); gold throne, Egyptian Museum, Cairo (Roger Wood); gold pectoral, Egyptian Museum, Cairo (F. L. Kenett © George Rainbird Ltd, 1963)

**Persia 73** Frieze of archers from Susa, Louvre (William MacQuitty) **74** Head of a Persian king, Louvre (Erich Lessing from Magnum) **74-75** Silver plate showing royal hunt, Teheran Museum (William MacQuitty) **75** Prehistoric beaker, Teheran Museum (William MacQuitty); gold rhyton, Teheran Museum (William MacQuitty); gold chariot, British Museum **76** Shah's mosque at Isfahan (William MacQuitty) **77** Ardabil carpet (detail), Victoria and Albert Museum (Crown Copyright) **78** Page from a Persian Bestiary of Ibn Bakhtishu, 1295, courtesy Pierpont Morgan Library, New York **79** Golestan poems from *Shah-nama* of Firdausi (William MacQuitty); tooled leather book binding embossed with gold, Gulistan Library, Teheran (William MacQuitty); battle scene from the *Shah-nama* of Firdausi (William MacQuitty); Humay at Castle of Humayun, from the *Khamsa* of Khwaju Kirmani, 1396, British Museum (William MacQuitty)

**Phoenicians and Hebrews 80** Jebel Mousa, Sinai (Erich Lessing from Magnum) **81** Semitic nomads, wall-painting from the Tomb of Shnum Hotep at Beni-Hassan (Erich Lessing from Magnum) **82** Lion in a lily grove, Phoenician ivory from Nimrud, British Museum (Eileen Tweedy, photo Thames and Hudson); lioness attacking Negro boy, Phoenician ivory from Nimrud, British Museum (Michael Holford) **83** Canaanite, on glazed tile, courtesy the Oriental Institute, University of Chicago; Phoenician sailors transporting cedars of Lebanon, stone relief from the Palace of Sargon II, Louvre (Erich Lessing from Magnum) **84** 'Woman at the window', Phoenician ivory from Nimrud, British Museum (Michael Holford); bronze god Baal, Louvre (Holle Verlag); floor mosaic depicting tabernacle, from synagogue near Tiberias (Erich Lessing from Magnum) **85** Deportation of the inhabitants of Lagash, relief from Nineveh, Louvre (Erich Lessing from Magnum) **86** Bronze pyx with silver coins, Israel Museum, Jerusalem (Erich Lessing from Magnum); floor mosaic depicting loaves and fishes, from Tabgha, Galilee (Rene Burri from Magnum) **87** Crucifixion, on ivory box, British Museum

**Minoans and Mycenaeans 88** Death mask of a Mycenaean king, National Museum, Athens (Erich Lessing from Magnum) **90** Gold pendant from Mallia, Heraklion Museum, Crete (D. Harissiadis from Rainbird); octopus vase, Heraklion Museum, Crete (Hamlyn) **90-91** Fresco of acrobats and bull, Heraklion Museum, Crete (D. Harissiadis from Rainbird) **91** Faience goddess, Heraklion Museum, Crete (D. Harissiadis from Rainbird) **92-93** The Lion Gate and Citadel of Mycenae (Alex Liberman from Peter Schub) **93** Bronze dagger from Mycenaean grave, National Museum, Athens (Emile Sarafis)

**Greece 94** Bronze head of Athena, National Museum, Athens (Roloff Beny) **96** Laconian cup showing King Arcesilas II, Bibliothèque Nationale (Hirmer Fotoarchiv, Munich); Attic vase with merchant ships, British Museum **97** Bronze figure of Zeus or Poseidon, National Museum, Athens (R. Descharnes); detail from vase painting showing Theseus killing the Minotaur, British Museum (Hamlyn); detail from cup showing Achilles tending Patroclus, Staatsbibliothek, Berlin; 5th century BC pyx showing the Judgment of Paris, Metropolitan Museum of Art, Rogers Fund, 1907 **98** Maenad with leopard, on Attic cup, Staatliche Antikensammlungen, Munich (Colorphoto Hinz, Basel) **99** Theatre at Epidaurus (R. Descharnes); Greek wine cooler depicting Alcaeus and Sappho, Antikensammlungen, Munich (Caecilia Moessner); bronze tragic mask, National Museum, Athens (D. Harissiadis) **100** Draped warrior, 5th century BC, Wadsworth Atheneum, Hartford, Connecticut, the J. P. Morgan Collection; Spartan girl, British Museum (John Webb) **100-1** Panathenaic Prize amphora depicting footrace, *c.* 530 BC, Metropolitan Museum of Art, Rogers Fund, 1912 **101** Terracotta plate from Rhodes showing Hector and Menelaus, British Museum; discus thrower, detail from 5th-century amphora, Museo Nazionale, Naples (Emmett Bright); Panathenaic amphora showing Athena, Metropolitan Museum of Art, Fletcher Fund, 1956 **102** Vase painting of Greek hetaira, Louvre (Rapho); detail from a Greek kylix showing a boy fishing, courtesy Museum of Fine Arts, Boston, H. L. Pierce Fund **103** Onyx cameo of Alexander the Great and Roxane, Kunsthistorisches Museum, Vienna **104-5** Erectheum, Athens (Ray Manley from Shostal Associates)

**Etruscans 106** Chimera, 4th century BC, Museo Archeologico, Florence (Alinari) **107** Two wrestlers, tomb fresco at Tarquinia, *c.* 530 BC (Scala) **108** Etruscan lancer, Museo Civico, Perugia (Dimitri Kessel, Life © 1972, Time Inc.); gold tablet, Museo di Villa Giulia, Rome (Emmett Bright) **109** Couple reclining, Museo di Villa Giulia, Rome (Emmett Bright); canopic jar, Museo Archeologico, Florence (Scala); clay model hut, Museo di Villa Giulia, Rome (Scala); bronze replica of sheep's liver, 3rd century BC, Piacenza City Museum (Scala)

**Rome 110** Forum reconstruction, based on drawing by Alan Sorrell from *Imperial Rome* (Lutterworth Press) **111** Soldiers of the Praetorian Guard, Louvre **113** Roman army crossing a bridge, detail from the column of Marcus Aurelius, Rome (Josephine Powell); standard of the Praetorian Guard, 2nd century AD, Museo della Civilitá Romana, Rome (Hachette-Lubtchansky); Roman bireme (Alinari) **114** Bronze statuettes of mirmillo and retiarius, Bibliothéque Nationale (Helene Adant from Arthaud) **115** Amphitheatre, Nîmes (YAN); hunt mosaic, Musée Archeologique d'Hippone, Algeria (Pierre Belzeaux from Rapho) **116** Virgil reading from *Aeneid*, Bardo Museum, Tunis (Roger Wood); cameo of Augustus, British Museum (C. M. Dixon) **117** Bronze Lares, Bibliothèque Nationale; 'Victory' from Leptis Magna, Archaeological Museum, Tripoli (Roger Wood); fresco of Diana from Stabiae, Museo Nazionale, Naples (Josephine Powell) **118** Pont du Gard, Nimes (Mike Newton) **119** 'Frozen body' from Pompeii (Josephine Powell); fresco from a villa at Boscoreale, Metropolitan Museum of Art, Rogers Fund, 1903; lady playing a cithara, detail of fresco from Boscoreale, Metropolitan Museum of Art, Rogers Fund, 1903

**Byzantium 120** Christ Pantocrator, Daphni, AD 1100 (C. M. Dixon) **122** Map of Constantinople by Matrakçi Nasuh, 1534–5, Library of Istanbul University (Sonia Halliday) **123** Reliquary, 10th century, Monopoli Cathedral (Mercurio); reliquary cover, *c.* 960, Limburg an der Lahn, Domschatz (Hirmer Fotoarchiv, Munich); reliquary Cross, 9th century AD, Victoria and Albert Museum (Hirmer Fotoarchiv, Munich); St Simon Stylites, miniature from Menologion of Emperor Basil II, *c.* AD 985, Vatican Library (Emmett Bright) **124** Empress Theodora, mosaic in San Vitale, Ravenna (Scala) **125** Emperor Justinian and his retinue, mosaic in San Vitale, Ravenna (Scala) **126** 'Greek Fire', Stylitzes Codex, *c.* AD 1300, Biblioteca Nacional, Madrid **127** Mehmet II, by Sinan Bey, 15th century, Topkapi Museum, Istanbul (Sonia Halliday); Siege of Constantinople, from *Voyage d'Outremer* of Bertrandon de la Brocquiere, Bibliothèque Nationale

**Russia 128** St Vladimir, 17th-century book illustration, State Historical Museum, Moscow (Novosti) **129** Church of the Transfiguration at Kizhi (Arnaud de Rosnay from Peter Schub) **130** Easter procession, from *Voyages* by Adam Olearius, 1719 edition (British Museum); icon of St George and the Dragon (Novosti) **131** Battle between Novgorod and Suzdal residents, Tretyakov Gallery, Moscow (Novosti); head of an Archangel, State Russian Museum, Leningrad (UNESCO, Paris ©); Boris and Gleb, 1340 (Novosti) **132** Virgin of Vladimir, Tretyakov Gallery, Moscow (Novosti) **133** Peter the Great by Rastrelli, Russian Museum, Leningrad (Novosti); gold cup, Armoury Palace, Kremlin (Novosti) **134** Peasant playing a balalaika, by Fabergé, courtesy Messrs. Wartski (John Webb); Easter egg by Fabergé, courtesy Messrs. Wartski (John Webb) **135** Palace of Peter the Great at Peterhof (Jerry Cooke); procession of boyars, woodcut by Michael Peterle, 1576, Victoria and Albert Museum (Michael Holford) **136** Nijinsky and Karsavina, and Anna Pavlova (Radio Times Hulton Picture Library); costume design for *Le Buffon Russe* by Leon Bakst, Victoria and Albert Museum © by S.P.A.D.E.M. Paris 1972 (Michael Holford) **137** Painted box lid from Palekh (Novosti)

**Saxons, Vikings and Celts 138** Detail, helmet depicting King Agilulf, Museo Nationale del Bargello, Florence (Ann Munchow) **139** Bronze ornament from Lombard chief's shield, Berne Historisches Museum **140** Objects from Sutton Hoo Treasure, British Museum **140-1** Egil the Archer, carved relief on whalebone box, British Museum **142** The Venerable Bede, from Ms in Engelberg Abbey, Switzerland (Snark International) **143** Tara Brooch, National Museum of Ireland, Dublin (Holle Verlag); Alfred Jewel, Ashmolean Museum; Ardagh Chalice, National Museum of Ireland, Dublin (Holle Verlag); eagle fibulae, Walters Art Gallery, Baltimore; King Recceswinth's crown, Museo Arqueologico Nacional, Madrid **144** Cross at Monasterboice (Edwin Smith) **145** Lion of St Mark from Eternach Gospels, Bibliothèque Nationale; initial letter from St. Matthew in the *Lindisfarne Gospels*, *c.* AD 698, British Museum; St. John the Evangelist from *Book of Kells*, courtesy Trinity College, Dublin (The Green Studio, Dublin) **146** Viking ship stone relief, 8th century, Statens Historiska Museum, Stockholm **147** Objects from 'grave ship' at Oseberg, southern Norway, Universitetets Oldsaksamling, Oslo

**Islam 149** Muhammad replaces the Black Stone, from Jami at-Tawarikh by Rashid ad-Din, Edinburgh University Library (BPC Picture Library) **150** Standard-bearers of the Caliph, from *Maqamat* of Al-Hariri, Baghdad, 1237, Bibliothèque Nationale **151** Stoning of Muhammad, from 16th-century Turkish Ms, Spencer Collection, New York Public Library, Astor, Lennox and Tilden Foundations; opening chapter of a 14th–15th-century Koran, British Museum; leaf from 9th-century Koran, Metropolitan Museum of Art, Rogers Fund, 1937 **152** Traders loading a camel, from *Maqamat* of Al-Hariri, Baghdad, 1237, Bibliothèque Nationale; mosque lamp, Victoria and Albert Museum (Emmett Bright) **153** Musicians, detail of ewer, Blacas Collection, courtesy British Museum (Michael Holford); labourers cultivating plants, from the *Book of Antidotes*, Bibliothèque Nationale; detail from astrological treatise by Abu Maasher, Bibliothèque Nationale (BPC Picture Library) **154** Window at Alhambra, Granada (Emmett Bright); fragment of silk cope from Saint Sernin, Toulouse, Musée de Cluny, Paris **155** Court of the Lions, Alhambra, Granada (Emmett Bright) **156** Leaf from the *Book of Conquests* of Suleiman the Magnificent, Topkapi Museum, Istanbul (Sonia Halliday) **157** Suleiman's Mosque, Istanbul (Emmett Bright)

**India 159** Kandariya Mahadeo Temple, Khajuraho (Roloff Beny) **160** 'Priest King' bust from Mohenjo Daro, National Museum of Pakistan, Karachi (Josephine Powell); toy cart (Larry Burrows, Life © 1972 Time Inc.) **161** Buddha preaching, Archaeology Museum, Sarnath (Copyright Bury Peerless) **162** Detail of wall-painting, Ajanta Caves (Colorphoto Hinz, Basel) **163** Angkor Wat, Cambodia (Rapho); Javanese 19th-century shadow puppet, British Museum; face of Lokeshvara from Angkor Thom (Douglas Dickens) **164** Brahma kneeling before Krishna, National Museum, New Delhi (Raghubur Singh from Magnum); Parvati, Victoria and Albert Museum (C. M. Dixon); Vishnu, National Museum, New Delhi (Colorphoto Hinz, Basel) **165** Shiva as Lord of the Dance, 10th century, Victoria and Albert Museum (C. M. Dixon); columns from Temple at Sriringam, India (Roloff Beny) **166** Radha and Krishna, Victoria and Albert Museum (C. M. Dixon) **167** Taj Mahal, Agra (William MacQuitty)

**China 169** Jade screen, K'ang Hsi, 1622–1722, Seattle Art Museum, Eugene Fuller Memorial Collection **170** Emperor Wu (Snark); model house, Han Dynasty, Nelson Gallery, Atkins Museum, Kansas City, Missouri **171** Tomb figure of Prince Liu Sheng, 2nd century BC, from Mancheng, Hopei (Marc Riboud from Magnum); bronze of Sakyamuni and Prabhutaratna, AD 518, Musée Guimet, Paris (Michael Holford) **172** Court party, National Palace Museum, Taipei, Taiwan **173** Detail of scroll by Hsu Wei, courtesy of the Smithsonian Institution, Freer Gallery of Art, Washington, D.C.; portrait of a calligrapher, ink and colours on silk, Museum of Fine Arts, Boston; porcelain brush, Percival David Foundation of Chinese Art, London; Fu Hsi, National Palace Museum, Taipei, Taiwan; T'ang glazed pottery tomb model, British Museum **174** Sung celadon bowl, Gift of Russell Tyson, courtesy of the Art Institute of Chicago; vase in Mei-ping form, British Museum; stoneware jar, 13th century, Munsterberg Collection, New Paltz, New York (Raphael Warshaw) **175** Mongol groom and horse by Chao Yung, courtesy of the Smithsonian Institution, Freer Gallery of Art, Washington, D.C. **176** Detail of scroll, *Street Scenes in Times of Peace*, *c.* 1300, Kate S. Buckingham fund, courtesy of the Art Institute of Chicago **177** Courtesan and lover, courtesy of the Smithsonian Institution, Freer Gallery of Art, Washington, D.C.; view of Kinsai (modern Hangchow), courtesy of the Smithsonian Institution, Freer Gallery of Art, Washington, D.C.; Kublai Khan, National Palace Museum, Taipei, Taiwan **178** Ming dynasty family group, Metropolitan Museum of Art, Anonymous Gift, 1942 **179** Ming dragon vase, Musée Guimet (Cliché des Musées Nationaux); *famille verte* plate, Ashmolean Museum, Oxford; Emperor Kuang Wu, National Gallery of Canada, Ottawa

**Japan 180** Death of Buddha, painting on silk, Kongobuji, Koyasan (Bradley Smith) **182** Illustration to *The Tale of Genji*, Goto Art Museum, Tokyo (Sakamoto) **183** Shukongojin, painted terracotta from Nara (Sakamoto); scroll showing exile of Michizane, Kitano Temmangu, Kyoto (Bradley Smith) **184** Shiraishi Rokuro leading soldiers into battle, Imperial Household Collection, Kyoto (Bradley Smith) **185** Detail from *Nine Stages in the Putting on of Armour*, colour print by Go-un Sadahide, 1853, Victoria and Albert Museum; Akita armour, suit assembled in 1741, Victoria and Albert Museum (Michael Holford); swordsmith, Okura Shukokan Museum, Tokyo (Bradley Smith) **186** *Preparing tea*, print by Koryusai, Tokyo National Museum; 16th-century scroll painting of floral arrangement, British Museum (Michael Holford); Shino tea bowl, courtesy of the Fogg Art Museum, Harvard University, Gift of the Peabody Museum, Harvard University **187** Saijohi Gardens, Kyoto (Brian Brake from Rapho); Nō mask (Bradley Smith); portrait of female impersonator, woodblock print by Toshusai Sharaku, Museum of Fine Arts, Boston (Bradley Smith)

**Maya and Aztecs 188** Pyramid of the Soothsayer, Uxmal (Robert Freson from Peter Schub) **190** Jadeite head, fragment of a statue from Tenango del Valle, Mexico, 6th–1st century BC, National Museum of Anthropology, Mexico City (Lee Boltin); Olmec jade carving in form of a human figure, British Museum; helmeted head, Park of the Museum at La Venta, Tobasco State (Constantino Reyes-Valerio from Hamlyn) **191** Page from Dresden Codex, reproduced from Humboldt's *Nouvelle Espagne Atlas*, Paris, 1810, Collection Sachsische Landesbibliothek (Thames and Hudson) **192** Seated dignitary, American Museum of Natural History, New York **193** Door carving showing woman sacrificing, *c.* 700, British Museum; Chama vase, University Museum, Philadelphia **194** Feather shield, Museum für Volkerkunde, Vienna; skull with inlaid decoration, British Museum; breast ornament, British Museum **195** Mixtec ornament,

Regional Museum of Archaeology, Oaxaca (Constantino Reyes-Valerio from Hamlyn) **196** Xolotl, Landesmuseum, Wurttemberg (Holle Verlag, Baden-Baden) **197** Chichén Itzá (Alex Oliver); Xipe Totec, Volkerkundemuseum, Basle); sacrifice to sun god, from Codex Magliabechiano, Biblioteca Nazionale, Florence; sacrificial knife, British Museum

**Incas** **198** Silver alpaca and llama, American Museum of Natural History, New York **199** Machu Picchu (Georg Gerster from Magnum) **200** Moche warrior, British Museum (Hamlyn) **201** Clay pot of jaguar and human figure, and Nazca pot, University Museum of Archaeology and Ethnography, Cambridge; Chimu bowl, Volkerkunde Museum, Munich (Michael Holford); Paracas textile (Michael Holford) **202** Gold pouch, and funerary mask, Collection Senor Mujica Gallo, Lima (Michael Holford); water carrier (J. C. Spahni); incense burner (Lee Boltin) **203** Ceremonial knife, National Museum of Archaeology, Lima (Lee Boltin)

**Africa** **204** Benin bronze plaque, British Museum (Michael Holford) **206** Views of St George's Church, Lalibela, Ethiopia (Georg Gerster from Rapho); three elephants and cattle gathering, copies after fresco at Tassili n'Ajjer, Collection Henri Lhote, Musée de l'Homme, Paris (Erich Lessing) **207** Christ's entry into Jerusalem (Georg Gerster from Rapho) **208** Mosque at Jenne (Werner Forman) **209** Trader on a camel, from *Maqamat* of Al-Hariri, Baghdad 1237, Bibliothèque Nationale **210** Benin ivory mask, and ivory and brass leopard, British Museum **211** Bronze head from Ife, British Museum

**Western Civilization** **212** Reredos of the Crucifixion, Dorchester Abbey, Oxfordshire (Michael Holford)

**The Middle Ages** **214** Fresco of the Dominican Order, Santa Maria Novella, Florence (Scala) **215** Reconstruction of Cluny Abbey, based on drawing from *Cluny les Eglises et la Maison du Chef d'Ordre* by R. J. Connant (Medieval Academy of America) **216** Reliquary bust of Charlemagne, Domschatz, Aachen (R. W. Schlegelmilch from Thames and Hudson) **217** Trees of Good and Evil from *Liber Floridus*, Centrale Bibliotheek, Ghent (A. Dierick); the writing of the Rule, from *Life of St Benedict*, Biblioteca Apostolica Vaticana; Cistercian monk reaping, initial from St Gregory's *Moralia in Job*, early 12th century, Bibliotheque de Dijon; cellarer tasting wine, from a health manual by Aldebrandius of Siena, French, 13th century, Trustees of the British Museum **218** Section from the Bayeux Tapestry, Musée de la Tapisserie, Bayeux (Michael Holford) **219** September, from the *Très Riches Heures du Duc de Berry* by Pol de Limbourg, Musée Condé, Chantilly (Giraudon) **220** Banquet, from *Chronique d'Angleterre*, Flemish, late 15th century, British Museum; tournament from 15th-century Ms, British Museum; medieval knight, from *Address by the town of Prato to Robert of Anjou*, Italian, 1335–40, British Museum **221** Richard Coeur de Lion, from *Passages Faiz Oultre Mer*, 1490, Bibliothèque Nationale **222** Charlemagne Window, Chartres Cathedral (Telarci–Giraudon) **223** *Dream of the Magi*, by Gislebertus (Lauros–Giraudon from Mansell); Nave of La Madeleine, Vezelay, courtesy of Burkhard-Verlag Ernst Heyer, Essen, Germany; nave of Notre Dame, Chartres (Robert Freson from Peter Schub) **224** Detail of tapestry *Lady with the Unicorn*, 15th century, Cluny Museum, Paris (Giraudon); tomb of Eleanor of Aquitaine, Fontevrault Abbey (H. Pierrehumbert from *Selection du Reader's Digest*, Paris) **224–5** *Good Government in the City*, by Ambrogio Lorenzetti, Palazzo Pubblico, Siena (Scala) **225** St Francis banishing demons over Arezzo, S. Francesco, Assisi (Alinari) **226** Two illustrations from *Livre des Proprietez des Choses*, British Museum **227** Edward I's Parliament, from the Wriothesley Ms, Royal Library, Windsor Castle, reproduced by gracious permission of Her Majesty the Queen

**Renaissance and Reformation** **228** Lunette, Palazzo Pitti by Giuseto Utens, Museo Mediceo, Florence (Scala) **229** Adoration of the Magi, detail of fresco by Benozzo Gozzoli, Medici Palace, Florence (Scala) **230** Dome of Florence Cathedral by Brunelleschi (Scala) **231** Morzocco, copy after Donatello, Piazza della Signoria, Florence (Scala); Isabella d'Este, by Leonardo da Vinci and pupils, Louvre (Giraudon); Cesare Borgia, Palazzo Venezia, Rome (Scala); execution of Savonarola, Museo di San Marco, Florence (Scala); Giuliano de Medici by Botticelli, Accademia Carrara, Bergamo (Scala); Doge Loredano, by Giovanni Bellini, courtesy the National Gallery, London; Francesco Sforza, by Bonifacio Bembo, Brera, Milan (Scala); sketch of a tank by Leonardo da Vinci, Trustees of the British Museum **232** Madonna of the Chancellor Rolin, by Jan Van Eyck, *c.* 1433–4, Louvre (Musées Nationaux); *The School of Athens*, by Raphael Stanza, Vatican (Scala); Gattamelata, by Donatello, Padua (Alinari from Hamlyn) **233** Rondanini *Pièta* by Michelangelo, Castello Sforzesco, Milan (Scala); *The Moneychanger and his Wife*, by Quentin Massys, Louvre (Musées Nationaux) **234** Interior of an Art Gallery, 17th century, Flemish school, reproduced by courtesy of the Trustees, The National Gallery, London **235** Shakespeare's First Folio, 1623, British Museum; Armada Portrait of Elizabeth I by George Gower, the Woburn Abbey Collection, by kind permission of his Grace, the Duke of Bedford **236** Erasmus, by Hans Holbein the Younger, Louvre (Musées Nationaux) **237** Presumed wedding portrait of Martin Luther, by Lucas Cranach the Elder, Kunstmuseum, Basle (Colorphoto Hinz, Basel); Service in the Lyons Temple, 1564, Bibliotheque Publique et Universitaire, Geneva (Jean Arlaud); title page of Thomas Cranmer's *Book of Common Prayer*, 1549 (Thames and Hudson)

**Age of Kings** **238** Detail, *Le Roi Visitant le Manufacture des Gobelins*, tapestry designed by Charles le Brun, Musée de Versailles (Musées Nationaux) **239** St Paul's Cathedral, design by Sir Christopher Wren, All Souls College, Oxford **240** Portrait of Louis XIV by Pierre Mignard, *c.* 1658, Galleria Sabauda, Turin (Scala) **241** Painting of Versailles by Pierre Patal, 1668, Versailles Museum (Musées Nationaux); Louis XV as a small child, Musée Carnavalet, Paris (Giraudon); Marquise de Pompadour by François Boucher, reproduced by permission of the Trustees of the Wallace Collection, London (John R. Freeman); *Lecture chez Mme Geoffrin*, by Charles Lemonnier, Musée des Beaux Arts, Rouen (Giraudon) **242** Sta. Maria della Salute by Antonio Canaletto, Staatliche Museen Preussischer Kulturbesitz, Gemäldegalerie, Berlin (West) **243** Harlequin, Meissenware model by Kandler, German National Museum, Nuremberg; Gilles by Antoine Watteau, Louvre (Telarci-Giraudon); Mozart playing at the Princess de Conti's tea party by Michel Barthelemy Ollivier, Louvre (Scala); Messie violin, Ashmolean Museum, Oxford; oboe made by Johann Floth, Dresden, Yale University Collection of Musical Instruments; interior of Teatro Regio in Turin, by Pietro Domenico Olivero, Museo Civico, Turin (Scala) **244** *The Letter*, by Jan Vermeer, Rijksmuseum, Amsterdam **245** *The Syndics of the Cloth Drapers' Guild* by Rembrandt, Rijksmuseum, Amsterdam **246** Robert Bakewell's 'Two Pounder', by J. Digby Curtis, 1790, University of Oxford, Institute of Agricultural Economics (B. J. Harris); Henlow Enclosure, from map by John Goodman Maxwell, 1798, Bedfordshire County Council; *The Reapers*, by George Stubbs, The National Trust, Bearsted Collection, Upton House, Banbury; *Mr and Mrs Robert Andrews*, by Thomas Gainsborough, reproduced by courtesy of the Trustees, The National Gallery, London **247** *Beer Street and Gin Lane*, by Hogarth (Mansell Collection)

**The Age of Revolution** **248** Voltaire, bust by Houdon, Victoria and Albert Museum (Michael Holford) **249** *Volunteers leaving for the frontier*, by Pierre-Etienne Le Sueur, Collection of M. Bidault de l'Isle, Musée Carnavalet, Paris (Giraudon) **250** *Britons Behold*, print by Nathaniel Hurd, 1762, American Antiquarian Society **251** *Attack on Bunker Hill*, National Gallery of Art, Washington, D.C., Gift of Edgar William and Bernice Chrysler Garbisch; *The Declaration of Independence*, by John Trumbull, Yale University Art Gallery; George Washington at Princeton, by Charles Willson Peale, Pennsylvania Academy of Fine Arts; Voltaire, Rousseau and Franklin on French snuffbox, Metropolitan Museum of Art, Gift of William H. Huntington, 1823; Thomas Jefferson by Rembrandt Peale, United States Information Service, London **252** Fall of the Bastille, Musée de Versailles (Giraudon); Jacques Brissot, Musée Carnavalet, Paris (Giraudon); Mme Roland, Musée de Versailles (Musées Nationaux); Robespierre, lithograph by Bourdon and Kellwauer (Mansell Collection); Danton, engraving by Bonneville (Mansell Collection) **253** Execution of Louis XIV, Musée Carnavalet, Paris (Giraudon); A sans-culotte, anonymous print, Bibliothèque Nationale; *Marat Assassinated*, by Jacques-Louis David, Musées Royaux des Beaux-Arts, Brussels (Scala) **254** *The Third of May* by Goya, Prado, Madrid (MAS, Barcelona) **255** Napoleon as Emperor, by Ingres, Musée de l'Armée (Lauros–Giraudon); study at Malmaison (Lauros–Giraudon); plate from the Egyptian service, reproduced by permission of His Grace the Duke of Wellington (Michael Holford); The Crowning of Napoleon in Notre Dame by Jacques-Louis David, Musée de Versailles (Musées Nationaux) **256** *Rain, Steam and Speed*, by J. M. W. Turner, reproduced by Courtesy of the Trustees, The National Gallery, London **257** *A Pit Head*, British School, *c.* 1800, Walker Art Gallery, Liverpool; the Krupp Gun, exhibited in Paris, 1867 (Ullstein, Berlin); Textile of the Crystal Palace, Victoria and Albert Museum (Michael Holford)

**Making of the modern world** **258** Manhattan (Howard Sochurek/John Hillelson) **259** Apollo 15 astronaut James B. Irwin (AP) **260** Dog Leap Stairs slum, Newcastle (Radio Times Hulton Picture Library) **261** *Body Presses and Assembly of Chassis*, detail of fresco by Diego Rivera, Detroit Institute of Arts, Gift of Edsel B. Ford **262** War Graves, Verdun (Christopher Barker); Nuremburg Rally (Ullstein); bombed houses in Berlin (Ullstein) **263** *The Bathers* by Georges Seurat, by permission of the Trustees of the National Gallery, London **264** Factory chimneys (Pictor) **265** Franklin D. Roosevelt (UPI); Charlie Chaplin, courtesy of John Kobal; Coco-Cola poster, courtesy of Coca-Cola Ltd ('Coca-Cola' and 'Coke' are registered Trade Marks which identify the same product of the Coca-Cola Co.); television set, courtesy of Rank Bush Murphy Ltd; the assassination of J. F. Kennedy (UPI); record cover (EMI)

**Part 3 Man and his world**

**The quest for truth** **284** Chinese ritual vessel, Musée Cernuschi, Paris (Michael Holford); votive stele with Ba'al (Michael Holford); Apollo as Sun God, Roman mosaic (C. M. Dixon); Melanesian chalk figures from New Ireland, Horniman Museum, London (Michael Holford) **285** Limestone relief of Akhenaton and Nefertiti from El-Amarna, Egyptian Museum, Cairo (photograph courtesy of the Metropolitan Museum of Art, New York); mural showing Socrates, from Ephesus (Sonia Halliday); Isis and Osiris, from the *Book of the Dead*, British Museum (C. M. Dixon); goblet from Jewish catacombs in Rome, Israel Museum, Jerusalem; Qumran text, fragments of Exodus, Israel Museum, Jerusalem; Moses, from Jewish Prayer Book, Staats und Universitatsbibliothek, Hamburg (Ralph Kleinhempel from Aldus Books Ltd); Scroll of Esther, Jewish Museum, London **286** Christians, Jews and Muslims in the bosom of Abraham, from *Bible de Souvigny*, Bibliothèque, Moulins (Giraudon); Crowning of Ardeshir II, rock-cut relief from Taq-i-Bustan, Iran (Copyright Bury Peerless); Adoration of the Magi, from the *Très Belles Heures du Duc de Berry*, *c.* 1380, Bibliothèque Nationale, Paris; Pentecost from Codex Monacensis, Bayerische Staatsbibliothek, Munich **287** Virgin and Child, mosaic from Cyprus (Sonia Halliday); plan of the Kaaba, tile, Topkapi Museum, Istanbul (Sonia Halliday); The Deposition, ivory, English School, *c.* 1150, Victoria and Albert Museum; Muhammad at Uhud, Turkish miniature, by Siyar-i-Nebevi, Topkapi Museum, Istanbul (Sonia Halliday); bronze cross, Kunsthistorisches Museum, Vienna; Birth of Muhammad, detail from Turkish miniature by Siyar-i-Nebevi, Topkapi Museum, Istanbul (Sonia Halliday); Muhammad with Ali, Persian miniature, Tabriz 1307, Edinburgh University Library; Title page of a Koran, Egypt 1304, British Museum **288** The Potala of Lhasa, Musée Guimet, Paris (Michael Holford); steatite seal from Mohenjo Daro, National Museum, New Delhi (Hamlyn); Vishnu, and Siva, Musée Guimet, Paris (Michael Holford); Shore Temple at Mamallapuram (Holle Verlag) **289** Ms illustrating Kalaka, Gujurat School, Musée Guimet (Michael Holford); portrait on silk of Confucius, Collection of the National Palace Museum, Taipei, Taiwan; Taoist plate showing Fu, Lu and Shou, Victoria and Albert Museum (C. M. Dixon); Siva, Parvati and children, Victoria and Albert Museum (C. M. Dixon); Buddha and school friends, Gandhara, Victoria and Albert Museum (C. M. Dixon); Sanskrit roll illustrating Vishnu, British Museum (Thames and Hudson); The Conception of Buddha, Gandhara style, British Museum (C. M. Dixon); The Death of Buddha, Thai bronze, Museum für Völkerkunde, Munich (Pictor Ltd); Temple of Wat Phra Keo, Bangkok (Pictor Ltd) **290** Thomas Aquinas, by Francesco Traini, Church of St Catherine, Pisa (Alinari); Crusader Knight, French School, Museo Nazionale, Florence (Giraudon–Alinari); The Bodhisattva Avalokitesvara, Victoria and Albert Museum (Michael Holford); itinerant preacher in India, lithograph (Eileen Tweedy) **291** Mosque of Okba at Kairouan (Michael Holford); portrait of Calvin, Musée Historique de la Reformation, Geneva; Jesuits at the Court of Akbar, from Abul Fazl's *Akbar-Nama* by Nan Singh, 1602–6, Chester Beatty Library, Dublin; Tibetan tanka The Western Paradise of Amitabha, Victoria and Albert Museum (Michael Holford); detail of Paradise from *The Last Judgment*, by Fra Angelico, San Marco, Florence (Scala from Pictor Ltd); right side of triptych *The Garden of Earthly Delights* by Heironymus Bosch, Prado (Michael Holford); Buddhist Hell Scene, Japanese scroll painting, Horniman Museum, London (Michael Holford) **292** David Hume, by William Walker (Mansell Collection); René Descartes, ascribed to Pierre Mignard, courtesy of The Trustees of the National Gallery, London; Spinoza, Herzog-August Bibliotheque, Wolfenbutte, Germany; Rousseau, engraving by Robert Hart (Mansell Collection); John Locke, detail of painting after Kneller, National Portrait Gallery, London **293** Sören Kierkegaard, drawing by his cousin Christian, *c.* 1840 (Royal Danish Embassy, London); Immanuel Kant, detail of painting by J. W. Becker, 1768, and George Hegel, lithograph by L. Sebbers, 1828 (Archiv für Kunst und Geschichte, Berlin); Bertrand Russell, 1945 (E. K. Hutton from Radio Times Hulton Picture Library); John Stuart Mill, detail from painting by G. F. Watts, National Portrait Gallery, London; Friedrich Nietzsche (Archiv für Kunst und Geschichte, Berlin); Karl Marx, *c.* 1880 (Radio Times Hulton Picture Library)

**Secrets of the universe** **294** God the Architect of the Universe, Osterreichische Nationalbibliothek; Creation of Adam (Scala); Polynesian creation myth (C. M. Dixon); Aboriginal bark painting (Axel Poignant); Adam and Eve, Pierpont Morgan Library; scene from the *Book of the Dead* (Michael Holford) **295** Navajo sand-painting (Freelance Photographers Guild); Yoruba creation myth, British Museum; astronomers from a Persian Ms (Emmett Bright); The ark (Mansell Collection); The Four Elements, New York Academy of Medicine; Ptolemy's Universe, British Museum **296** Mythical beast (Radio Times Hulton Picture Library); Roger Bacon (Mary Evans Picture Library); alchemists at work (Radio Times Hulton Picture Library) **297** Da Vinci calculations, courtesy of the Earl of Leicester; Brahe's Star Castle and Great Quadrant, and Copernicus (Mansell Collection); Frontispiece of Kepler's Tabulae (Ronan Picture Library/Royal Astronomical Society); Galileo (Mansell Collection); woodcut of Galileo's drawings of the moon, and facsimile of Newton's telescope, Science Museum, London (Crown Copyright) **298** 18th-century chemist's workshop, Deutches Museum, Munich; *Ex Ovum Omnia*, title page of Harvey's De Generatione Animalium, British Museum; Lamb of Tartary (Thames and Hudson); Newton's 'jet' engine (Ronan Picture Library) **299** *The Beagle*, Charles Darwin, anti-Darwin Punch cartoon, and Mendel (Mansell Collection) **300** Crab nebula, courtesy of the Hale Observatories; Hilac accelerator (Barnaby's Picture Library); Albert Einstein (Fox Photos); Rutherford's first atom-splitting apparatus (Radio Times Hulton Picture Library); John Dalton, Science Museum, London (Crown Copyright) **301** Niels Bohr (Radio Times Hulton Picture Library); orange grove (John Shelton); Mt Palomar telescope (Barnaby's Picture Library); Jodrell Bank (Fox Photos); Arecibo Observatory, courtesy of Cornell University, Operator of the Observatory for the National Science Foundation

**Writing and counting** **302** Detail from Tomb of Thethi, Assurbanipal, and Mesopotamian cylinder seal, British Museum **303** Phaistos Disc, British Museum (Eric Symes); Rosetta Stone, British Museum; Maya inscription (Michael Holford); Jean François Champollion, Musée du Louvre, Paris **304** Miniature from the Canterbury Psalter, by permission of the Master and Fellows of Trinity College, Cambridge; schoolboy from ancient Greek vase, Staatsbibliothek, West Berlin; page from a Koran, British Museum; pedestal of a statue to Caius Antonius, British Museum; page from the Codex Dresdenus (Ferdinand Anton) **305** Part of the Frank's Casket, British Museum; page of 15th-century Russian Cyrillic script (Erich Lessing, Magnum); page from the Gutenburg Bible, Bodleian Library; illuminated 'C', by permission of the Dean and Chapter, Durham Cathedral; illuminated 'R', Bibliothèque Municipale, Dijon **306** Quipu, Musée de l'Homme, Paris; Chinese abacus, Science Museum, London (Crown Copyright) **307** Egyptian land surveyors, and Pythagoras's theorem, British Museum; **308** Scholars and astronomers, Bibliothèque de l'Arsenal, Paris; Babylonian calendar tablet, British Museum; Aztec calendar stone (Hamlyn Group); Arabic scroll calendar (Streeter Collection, Yale Medical Library) **309** 'February' from the *Très Riches Heures du Duc de Berry*, Musée Condé, Chantilly; sand glasses, Science Museum, London (Crown Copyright); portable sundial, by permission of the Dean and Chapter of Canterbury Cathedral; Flemish sundial, The Metropolitan Museum of Art, Harris Brisbane Dick Fund, 1957

**Inventions** **310** Irrigation machine, Tomb of Api, Metropolitan Museum, New York; winged figure from Luristan, British Museum (Michael Holford); clay beaker, British Museum **311** Transport of Egyptian colossus (Mansell Collection); Roman water pump, British Museum; Archimedean screw (Mansell Collection); Royal Standard of Ur, British Museum; Hittite chariot, Ankara Museum (Mansell Collection); Hero's steam turbine (Mary Evans Picture Library) **312** Perpetual-motion machine (Mansell Collection); peasants with ox-plough, Luttrell Psalter, British Museum; portrait of Gutenberg (Mansell Collection); medieval horizontal loom, courtesy of the Master and Fellows of Trinity College, Cambridge; William Caxton, and illustration from *The Fox and the Grapes* (Mansell Collection) **313** Wells Cathedral clock (Weidenfeld and Nicolson); trip hammer (Ronan Picture Library); man with spectacles, and Japanese paper-making (Mansell Collection); early barometers, E. P. Goldschmidt and Co. Ltd (Ronan Picture Library); paper-making at Maidstone (Mary Evans Picture Library) **314** Richard Trevithick's railway track, Euston Square (Mansell Collection); Newcomen's steam engine (Mary Evans Picture Library); blacksmith, British Museum; blast furnace (Ronan Picture Library); iron foundry, 1802 (Mansell Collection) **315** The *Rocket*, Hargreaves's 'spinning jenny', the *Charlotte Dundas*, blast furnace, I. K. Brunel, and Royal Albert Bridge (Radio Times Hulton Picture Library); Iron Bridge, Coalbrookdale (Mansell Collection); Sir Henry Bessemer (Popperfoto); The *Great Eastern* (Radio Times Hulton Picture Library) **316** Early Swan carbon filament lamp, Science Museum (Crown Copyright); Faraday electro-magnetic relics, and portrait of Faraday (Radio Times Hulton Picture Library); Thomas Edison (Popperfoto) **317** Singer sewing machine (Radio Times Hulton Picture Library); instrument gallery of Central Telegraph Office (Mary Evans Picture Library); Edison's electric lamp, and Remington typewriter (Mansell Collection); Edison's phonograph (Radio Times Hulton Picture Library); Bell telephone, Bell Telephone Laboratories; flowing oil well, British Petroleum Co. Ltd **318** London traffic, National Motor Museum; Gottlieb Daimler (Popperfoto); Otto gas engine (Mary Evans Picture Library) **319** Early diesel engine, Science Museum (Crown Copyright) (Mansell Collection); Marconi (Mansell Collection); Baird (Radio Times Hulton Picture Library); Model T Ford, National Motor Museum; daguerreotype (Radio Times Hulton Picture Library); Lumière camera (Mansell Collection); *Blue Flame* rocket car (UPI); Louis Daguerre, and Kodak No. 1 Camera, Kodak Museum **320** Otto Lilienthal, Montgolfier balloon, Frank Whittle, and Icarus (Radio Times Hulton Picture Library); Wright Bros. (Popperfoto); da Vinci design (Mansell Collection) **321** Saturn 1 rocket (USIS); Hovercraft (British Hovercraft Corporation); Pascal-type adding machine (Ronan Picture Library); Sputnik (Novosti Press Agency); Charles Babbage (Radio Times Hulton Picture Library); Babbage engine, Science Museum (Crown Copyright); micro-integrated circuit, International Computers Ltd

**Man under the microscope** **322** 'Bone Man', 13th-century Ms illustration, Bodleian Library; prehistoric skull, and Egyptian polio victim, by permission of the Wellcome Trustees **323** Galen (Mary Evans Picture Library); acupuncture chart, by permission of the Wellcome Trustees; body with signs of the Zodiac, Royal Astronomical Society (Ronan Picture Library); mandrake gathering, and Avicenna, by permission of the Wellcome Trustees; foetal position, Bodleian Library **324** da Vinci diagram, by gracious permission of Her Majesty the Queen; medieval hospital, Biblioteca Medicea Laurenziana (Guido Sansoni); leper and cripple (Mary Evans Picture Library); plague victims at Tournai, Royal Library, Brussels **325** Skeleton from Vesalius Ms, and plague doctor, by permission of the Wellcome Trustees; rat flea (Natural

Science Photos); amputation of a leg, and blood circulation diagram, by permission of the Wellcome Trustees; two da Vinci diagrams, by gracious permission of Her Majesty the Queen **326** Anatomy lecture, by permission of the Royal College of Physicians of London; Thomas Sydenham, by permission of the Wellcome Trustees; Gillray cartoon, British Museum **327** Apothecary's shop, by permission of the Wellcome Trustees; Edward Jenner (Mary Evans Picture Library); cowpox pustules, quack doctor, early thermometers, Culpeper microscope, ophthalmoscope, stethoscope, and portrait of Morgagni, all by permission of the Wellcome Trustees; X-ray of Rontgen's wife's hand, Deutches Museen, Munich; X-ray tube, Science Museum London (Crown Copyright) **328** Florence Nightingale, by permission of the Wellcome Trustees; Louis Pasteur, Institut Pasteur; *The Madhouse*, by William Hogarth, by permission of the Trustees of Sir John Soane's Museum; William Norris, by permission of the Wellcome Trustees **329** Jean-Martin Charcot (Culver Pictures); Sigmund Freud, Mrs L. Freud (Mansell Collection); Pierre and Marie Curie, by permission of the Wellcome Trustees; Eno Advertisement (Snark); an operation in 1870 (Bettman Archive); carbolic spray, by permission of the Wellcome Trustees **330** Cancer cell (Observer/Transworld); penicillin culture, D. Lawson, Beecham Research Laboratories; artificial hand, and plastic surgery, by permission of the Wellcome Trustees **331** Iron lung, artificial heart, and pacemaker (Observer/Transworld); pills (Michael Newton); liver operation, and ultrasonic illustration of foetus (Observer/Transworld)

**Exploring the world 332** Vikings, Pierpont Morgan Library; Egyptian ship, courtesy of the Oriental Institute, University of Chicago; Phoenician war galley (Radio Times Hulton Picture Library) **333** Alexander the Great, Private Collection, Cambridge Mass.; Icelandic map, Royal Library, Copenhagen; part of the Catalan Atlas, Bibliothèque Nationale, Paris; Marco Polo, Das Puch des Edeln Ritters un Landtfarrers, Nuremburg 1477, Columbia University Libraries; Marco Polo leaving Venice, Bodleian Library, Oxford **334** Portuguese ships, Pierpont Morgan Library; astrolabe (William MacQuitty), nocturnal, British Museum; 16th-century mariner's compass, National Maritime Museum, London **335** Henry the Navigator, Portuguese Tourist Office; Vasco da Gama, Bibliothèque Nationale, Paris; Harrison's Chronometer, National Maritime Museum, London; Cook's quadrant (Hamlyn Group); sextant, Peabody Museum, Salem (M. W. Sexton); Portuguese lateen-rigged ship (Mary Evans Picture Library); *Great Harry* galleon, Pepys Library, Magdalene College Cambridge; nao, Victoria and Albert Museum, London **336** Map of Peru, Bibliothèque du Ministère des Armées (Giraudon); portrait of Columbus, Biblioteca Central da Marinha, Lisbon; Spanish priest baptising an Indian, Bibliothèque Nationale, Paris; Montezuma and Cortez at Tenochtitlan, American History Division, New York Public Library, Astor, Lenox and Tilden Foundations **337** Magellan's *Victoria*, Rare Book Division, New York Public Library, Astor, Lenox and Tilden Foundations; Magellan's route, Bibliothèque Nationale, Paris; Sir Francis Drake, National Portrait Gallery, London; Hernando Cortez, Collection of the Duque Del Infantado, Seville (Archivo Mas); map of Mexico, Huntington Library, San Marino, California; Atahualpa, by permission of His Grace the Duke of Wellington **338** HMS *Resolution*, Mitchell Library, Sydney; red honeysuckle (Michael Holford); Martin Frobisher, Bodleian Library, Oxford **339** Captain Cook, Dixson Galleries, Sydney; eskimos attacking English sailors, British Museum; Easter Island statue (Michael Holford); sketch of a native craft by Abel Tasman, British Museum; map of New Zealand, British Museum (Hamlyn Picture Library); Maori war canoe, and Maori chief, Anderson, *The Travels of Captain Cook* **340** Stanley hauling canoes (Mansell Collection); Lewis and Clark, St Memin, Lewis and Clark Collection of the Corcoran Gallery of Art; buffalo, Glenbow Foundation, Calgary; Comanche village, by courtesy of the National Collection of Fine Arts, Smithsonian Institution; Indian dance, *Costumo Antico e Moderno*, British Museum; pineapple, British Museum **341** 'Dr Livingstone, I presume' (Mansell Collection); Stanley on the march (Mary Evans Picture Library); portrait of Livingstone, National Portrait Gallery, London; mining at Comstock, Bancroft Library, University of California; the *Ma Robert*, Royal Geographical Society **342** Space walk (NASA); Andrée balloon (UPI); Ross and the Eskimos, courtesy of the Mariners' Museum, Newport News, Virginia; the *Terra Nova* (Popperfoto); Roald Amundsen (Norwegian Photo Service) **343** Scott at the pole (Popperfoto); Eskimo woman, British Museum; Hillary and Tensing, Mount Everest Foundation; Earth rise on the moon (NASA); Mount Everest (Camera Press)

**Man the warrior 344** Relief from palace of Tiglath-Pileser (Michael Holford); Sumerian soldiers, from the Standard of Ur, British Museum; Egyptian bronze axe, British Museum (Edwin Robert Laffont); German two-handed sword, French halberd *c.* 1400–50, and German rapier *c.* 1610 (Wallace Collection) **345** Greek chariot, detail from Greek vase-painting, 8th century BC (André Held); Hannibal (Mary Evans Picture Library); Greek phalanx (Radio Times Hulton Picture Library); Roman testudo, from *Roman*

*Imperial Army* by Graham Webster, published by A. & C. Black; bust of Pompey (Mansell Collection); Caesar, Archiv für Kunst und Geschichte **346** Battle of Sluys, Bibliothèque Nationale; assault chariot, from Ms dedicated to Sigismondo Pandolfo Malatesta (1417–68), British Museum (Editions Robert Laffont); Visigoth foot soldier, from Ms in the British Museum; Crusader knight, Bodleian Library; armour for man and horse, Tower of London, British Crown Copyright, reproduced with the permission of Her Majesty's Stationery Office **347** Charlemagne and Pepin, Biblioteca Capitolare, Modena; Mongol horseman, Musée Guimet (Musées Nationaux); crossbow, Germanisches Nationalmuseum, Nuremburg; longbowmen from the Luttrell Psalter, British Museum; medieval Spanish warriors, Pierpont Morgan Library; siege of Ribodane, British Museum **348** Siege of Nieuport, British Museum; Spanish armada off Weymouth, from a chart by Augustine Rythek (Mansell Collection); Battle of Lepanto, National Maritime Museum; the *Peter*, from the Anthony Roll, Magdalen College, Oxford (Edward Leigh); Dutch galleon of 1629 (Mary Evans Picture Library); the *Victory* painted by Monamy Swaine in 1792, National Maritime Museum **349** Sapping operation from Vauban's *Traité des Siege*, Bibliothèque Nationale; Gustavus Adolphus, British Museum; Duke of Marlborough at the Battle of Blenheim (Mary Evans Picture Library); engraving from *Exercices d'Armes* by J. de Gheyn, 1607, British Museum; Wheel-lock pistol, Metropolitan Museum of Art, New York; Flemish matchlock and long-barrelled musket, British Crown Copyright, reproduced with the permission of Her Majesty's Stationery Office; flintlock musket, Kungliga Livrustkammeren, Stockholm; Baker rifle, Wallis and Wallis, Arms and Armour Auctioneers, Lewes, Sussex **350** Battle of Gettysburg, BPC/New York Public Library; Battle of Bennington (Radio Times Hulton Picture Library); Napoleon by David, Musée de Versailles (Giraudon); Wellington at Waterloo (John Freeman) **351** Frederick the Great's infantry, Anne S. K. Browne Military Collection, Providence, Rhode Island; Boer War (Radio Times Hulton Picture Library); Dreyse needle gun, Bildarchiv der Osterreichischen Nationalbibliothek; Colt rifle (Weidenfeld and Nicolson); Battle of Hampton Roads, National Maritime Museum; Maxim gun (Weidenfeld and Nicolson); Mitrailleuse gun (Mansell Collection); US Civil War recruitment poster, BPC/Confederate High Command; HMS *Dreadnought*, Imperial War Museum **352** Kitchener recruiting poster, Imperial War Museum; Atlas missile (Camera Press/G-S); Battle of Jutland, troops in trench, gas attack, U-boat, tank, Messerschmitt 109, Hurricane, Lancaster, Boeing B29, and V2 rocket, all Imperial War Museum (Camera Press); A-bomb explosion (Camera Press/American Stock Photos)

**Part 4 The nations of the world 353–472**

Photographs and other material used as illustrations in this section of the book were supplied by: Archives Nationales; Arts Council of Great Britain; Associated Press; Australian News and Information Service; Christopher Barker; Belgrade Military Museum; Bettman Archive; Bibliotheca del Risorgimento, Rome; Bibliotheca Riccardiana, Florence; Bibliothèque Nationale; Bildarchiv der Ost National Bibliothek, Vienna; Bodleian Library, Oxford; Bodley Head; British Museum; Bulloz; Bundesarchiv; Camera Press; Canadian High Commission; Canadian Pacific; Central Press; Colorsport; Communist Party of Great Britain; Conway Picture Library; Culver Pictures; Denver Public Library; Department of the Environment; Douglas Dickins; C. M. Dixon; Mary Evans Picture Library; J. R. Freeman; Fogg Art Museum, Harvard University; Ford Motor Company; Fox Photos; Gabinetto Fotographico Nazionale; Giraudon; Gloucester City Museum and Art Gallery; Su Gooders; Madame T. Hassia; André Held; Hermitage, Leningrad; John Hillelson Agency; History Today; Michael Holford; Holle Verlag; Honda; Hudson's Bay Company; Imperial War Museum; India Office Library; Institut Belge d'Information, Brussels; Keystone Press Agency; David King; Kunsthistorisches Museum, Vienna; Louvre; Magnum; The Mansell Collection; Metropolitan Museum of Art, New York; Mitchell Library, Sydney; Motif Editions; City of Montreal; Moravian Museum, Brno; Moro, Rome; Musée Calvert, Avignon; Musée de Picardie, Amiens; Museum of the American Indian, New York; Museum of Fine Arts, Boston; National Archaeological Museum, Athens; National Film Archive; National Galleries of Scotland; National Gallery; National Maritime Museum, Bergen; Nationalmuseet, Copenhagen; National Museum of Ireland; National Museum, Tokyo; National Portrait Gallery; New York Public Library; Novosti Press Agency; Bury Peerless; Philadelphia University Museum; Pirelli Ltd; Pix Incorporated; Popperfoto Ltd; Josephine Powell; Press Association; Public Archives of Canada; Radio Times Hulton Picture Library; George Rainbird Ltd; Rheinisches Landesmuseum; Christopher Ridley; H. Roger-Viollet; Royal Netherlands Embassy; Royal Norwegian Embassy; Bradley Smith; Smithsonian Institution; National Portrait Gallery; Snark International; Lord and Lady Snow; Sport and General; Statens Historiska Museum, Sweden; Tanjug Press Agency; Thames and Hudson; Tiroler Landesmuseum, Innsbruck; Ullstein; United Press International; University Library, Bergen; US Information Service; US

Signal Corps; Vatican Library; Verlag Fritz Molden; Victoria and Albert Museum; Warburg Institute; John Webb; Weidenfeld & Nicolson; Alfredo Zennaro

**End-papers** Tassili rock painting (Jean-Dominique Lajoux); *The Professor's Dream* by C. R. Cockerell, Royal Academy of Arts

# ACKNOWLEDGMENTS

The publishers also acknowledge their indebtedness to the following books and journals which were consulted for reference:

*The Acropolis* by R. J. Hopper (Weidenfeld & Nicolson); *Africa Handbook* edited by Colin Legum (Penguin); *African Mythology* by G. Parrinder (Hamlyn); *The Age of Augustus* by Donald Earl (Elek); *The Age of the Dinosaurs* by Bjorn Kurten (Weidenfeld & Nicolson); *The Age of the Rococo* by Michael Schwarz (Pall Mall Press); *The Alphabet* by David Diringer (Hutchinson); *The American Heritage Histories of the Civil War, the Great West, and the Indians*; *The Ancient Civilization of Rome* by G. Picard (Barrie Cresset); *Ancient Civilizations* (Barrie and Jenkins); *Ancient Europe: a Survey* by Stuart Piggott (Edinburgh University Press); *Ancient Mexico* by Ignacio Bernal (Thames and Hudson); *Ancient Peoples and Places* edited by Glyn Daniel (Thames and Hudson); *The Anglo-Saxons* by D. M. Wilson (Thames and Hudson); *The Archaeology of Early Man* by J. M. Coles and E. S. Higgs (Faber & Faber); *Arms and Armour of Old Japan* (Her Majesty's Stationery Office); *Art of Ancient Egypt* by K. Michaelowski (Thames and Hudson); *Art of the Byzantine Era* by David Talbot Rice (Thames and Hudson); *The Art of Warfare in Biblical Lands* by Yigael Yadin (International Publishing); *Art Treasures in Russia* by D. and T. Talbot Rice (Hamlyn); *Arts of Ancient Mexico* by Jacques Soustelle (Thames and Hudson); *The Arts of Egypt* by I. Woldering (Thames and Hudson); *Arts of Mankind* (Thames and Hudson); *Asia Handbook* edited by Guy Wint (Penguin); *Astronomy* by Patrick Moore (Oldbourne); *Aztecs of Mexico* by G. C. Vaillant (Penguin); *The Bible* by Erich Lessing (Macmillan); *The Bog People* by P. V. Glob (Paladin); *A Book of World Religions* by E. G. Parrinder (Hulton Educational); *The Carnac Alignments* by A. Thom and A. S. Thom (Journal for the History of Astronomy); Cassell-Caravel books; *Castles from the Air* by W. Douglas Simpson (Country Life); *Castles in England and Wales* by W. Douglas Simpson (Batsford); *The Cell* (Life Science Library); *Celtic Mythology* by P. MacCana (Hamlyn); *Chinese Architecture and Town Planning* by Andrew Boyd (Tiranti); *The Christian Faith in Art* by Eric Newton and William Neil (Hodder & Stoughton); *Civilisation* by Kenneth Clark (John Murray/ BBC); *The Civilization of Rome* by Pierre Grimal (Allen & Unwin); *Civilizations of the Indus Valley* by Mortimer Wheeler (Thames and Hudson); *The Columbia Encyclopedia* (Columbia University Press); *The Concise Encyclopedia of Living Faiths* (Hutchinson); *A Concise History of France* by Douglas Johnson (Thames and Hudson); *A Concise History of Russian Art* by T. Talbot Rice (Thames and Hudson); *Crusader Castles* by R. Fedden and J. Thomson (Murray); *Dawn of the Gods* by Jacquetta Hawkes (Chatto & Windus); *The Dawn of the West* by E. A. Delahay (Thames and Hudson); *Dictionary of Archaeology* by E. Bray and D. Trump (Allen Lane); *A Dictionary of Egyptian Civilization* by Georges Posener (Methuen); *Divine Kingship in Africa* by William Fagg (British Museum); *Early Christian and Byzantine Architecture* by W. MacDonald (Studio Vista); *Early Man* by F. Clark Howell (Life Nature Library); *The Economist*; *Egypt in Colour* by Roger Wood and M. S. Drower (Thames and Hudson); *An Encyclopedia of World History* by William L. Langer (Harrap); *Epic of Man* edited by Courtlandt Canby (Time-Life International); *The Etruscans* by Raymond Bloch (Barrie & Jenkins); *Everyday Life in Bible Lands* (National Geographic Society); *The Evolution of Man* by D. Pilbeam (Thames and Hudson); *Evolution* (Life Nature Library); *Excavations at Ur* by Sir Leonard Woolley (Benn); *The First Civilizations* by Glyn Daniel (Thames and Hudson); *Foundations of Chinese Art* by W. Willett (Thames and Hudson); *Framework for Dating Fossil Man* by Kenneth Oakley (Weidenfeld & Nicolson); *Geography of World Affairs* by J. P. Cole (Penguin); *Germany, 1870–1970* edited by Roger Morgan (Macdonald); *The Golden History of Art* by G. Pischel (Hamlyn); *Gothic Cathedral* by Wim Swaan (Elek); *The Grandeur that was Rome* by J. C. Stobart (Sidgwick & Jackson); *Great Ages of Man* (Time-Life International); *Great Civilizations* (Thames and Hudson); *The Great Moghuls* by B. Gascoigne (Cape); *Greece and Rome* (National Geographic Society); *Greek Art* by John Boardman (Thames and Hudson); *The Greeks Overseas* by John Boardman (Penguin); *The Hamlyn History of the World in Colour* (Hamlyn); *A History of Architecture on the Comparative Method* by Sir Banister Fletcher (Athlone Press); *A History of Far Eastern Art* by Sherman E. Lee (Thames and Hudson); *A History of Latin America* by George Pendle; *The History of Man* by Carleton S. Coon (Penguin); *A History of Modern Japan* by Richard Storry (Penguin); *A History of New Zealand* by Keith Sinclair (Penguin); *History of South-East Asia* by D. G. E. Hall (Macmillan); *A History of the Jewish*

*People* by James Parkes (Life/Collins); *A History of Weaponry* by Courtlandt Canby (Leisure Arts Ltd); The Horizon Books of Ancient Greece, Ancient Rome, China and the Arts of China, the Elizabethan World, and the Middle Ages; *The Ice Age* by Bjorn Kurten (Hart Davis); *Illustrated World History* edited by E. Wright and K. M. Stampp (McGraw Hill); *India* by Roloff Beny and Aubrey Menen (Thames and Hudson); *Japanese Temples* by J. E. Kidder (Thames and Hudson); *Keesing's Contemporary Archives* (Keesing's Publications Ltd); *Landmarks of the World's Art* (Hamlyn); *Larousse Encyclopedias of Ancient and Medieval History, Byzantine and Medieval Art, Prehistoric and Ancient Art*, and *Renaissance and Baroque Art* (Hamlyn); *Library of the Early Civilizations, Library of Early Medieval Civilizations, Library of Medieval Civilizations, Library of European Civilizations* (Thames and Hudson); *Life Before Man* by Z. Spinar and Z. Burian (Thames and Hudson); *Life in Ancient Lands* (Evans); *Living History* by Alan Sorrell (Batsford); *Lost Worlds* by Leonard Cottrell (Penguin); *Man the Toolmaker* by Kenneth Oakley (British Museum); *Mathematics* (Life Science Library); *The Maya* by Michael D. Coe (Penguin); *The Medieval Castle* by Philip Warner (Arthur Barker); *The Medieval Establishment* by Geoffrey Hindley (Wayland); *The Middle East and North Africa 1972–3* (Europa); *The Neolithic Revolution* by Sonia Cole (British Museum); *New Cambridge Modern History* (Cambridge University Press); *The New States of West Africa* by Ken Post (Penguin); *The Old Stone Age* by François Bordes (Weidenfeld & Nicolson); *Olduvai Gorge* by L. S. B. Leakey (Cambridge University Press); *Out of the Ancient World* by Victor Skipp (Penguin); *Panorama of World Art* (Abrams); *The Pelican History of Art* (Penguin); *The Pelican History of Greece* by A. R. Burn (Penguin); *The Penguin Atlas of Ancient History, The Penguin Atlas of Medieval History, The Penguin Encyclopedia of Places* (Penguin); *Persia, the Immortal Kingdom* by Sanghri and Ghirshman (Transorient); *Persian Architecture* by A. Upham Pope (Thames and Hudson); *A Pictorial History of Inventions* (Weidenfeld & Nicolson); *Picture History of Archaeology* by C. W. Ceram (Thames and Hudson); *Pompeii and Herculaneum* by Marcel Brion (Elek); *Pre-Columbian Architecture* by D. Robertson (Hamlyn); *Prehistoric Art in Europe* by N. K. Sanders (Pelican); *Prehistoric Europe* by Grahame Clark (Methuen); *Prehistoric Europe* by Philip van Doren Stern (Allen and Unwin); *Prehistoric Man* by Anthony Harvey (Hamlyn); *Prehistoric Societies* by Grahame Clark and Stuart Piggott (Penguin); *Prehistory: an Introduction* by Derek Roe (Macmillan); *The Pyramids of Egypt* by I. E. S. Edwards (Penguin); *Races of Man* by Sonia Cole (British Museum); *The Roman Forum* by Michael Grant (Weidenfeld & Nicolson); *Roman Empire* by Graham Webster (Black); *Romanesque Architecture in France* (Heinemann); *The Romans* (Brockhampton Press); *Rome: the Story of an Empire* by J. P. V. D. Balsdon (Weidenfeld & Nicolson); *The Russian Empire* by Hugh Seton-Watson (Oxford University Press); *Santa Sophia* by W. R. Lethaby and H. Swanson (Macmillan); *Science in History* by J. D. Bernal (Penguin); *The Science of Life* by G. Rattray Taylor (Thames and Hudson); *A Short History of Africa* by Roland Oliver and J. D. Fage (Penguin); *Shorter Atlas of Western Civilization* by F. van der Meer and G. Lemmens (Nelson); *Spain, 1808–1939* by Raymond Carr (Oxford University Press); *The Statesman's Year Book, 1972–1973* (Macmillan); *The Stone Age Hunters* by Grahame Clark (Thames and Hudson); *Stonehenge* by R. J. C. Atkinson (Hamish Hamilton); *Stonehenge Decoded* by Gerald S. Hawkins (Fontana); *A Study of History* by Arnold Toynbee (Oxford University Press); *The Sutton Hoo Ship Burial* (British Museum); *Time* (Life Science Library); *The Times History of our Times* edited by M. Cunliffe (The Times); *Treasures of the British Museum* edited by Sir Frank Francis (Thames and Hudson); *Treasures of the British Museum* (Collins); *Tutankhamun* by C. Desroches Noblecourt (Michael Joseph); *The Universe* (Life Nature Library); *Vanished Civilizations* edited by Edward Bacon (Thames and Hudson); *The Viking* (C. A. Watts and Co.); *Webster's New Geographical Dictionary* (G. and C. Merriam); *West Kennett Long Barrow: Excavations 1955–56* by Stuart Piggott (Her Majesty's Stationery Office); *What Happened in History* by Gordon Childe (Penguin); *World of Art Library* (Thames and Hudson); *The World of the Egyptians* by Jacques Champollion (Minerva); *World Prehistory: a New Outline* by Grahame Clark (Cambridge University Press)

Many consultants and artists, as well as those named on p. 4, helped in the preparation of this book. The publishers wish to thank them all, particularly:

Ronald L. Carter BSc(Econ), FRGS, Brian Coulson, Michael H. Day MB, BS, PhD, Peter Gillman, Van Haggerty, Susan Hibbert, Keith Lye BA, FRGS, Richard Orr, J. d'A. Waechter PhD(Camb), FSA, Edward Wade, Bernard A. Weisberger PhD, Phili Whitting, Ann Winterbotham, D. J. Wiseman OBE, DLitt, FBA, FSA

Paper, Printing and Binding by: Bowater Pape Sales Ltd; Brown, Knight & Truscott Ltd, Tonbridge; City Engraving Co. (Hull) Ltd; Commercial Process Co. Ltd, London; F. A. Churchill & Partners Ltd, Southampton; East Lancashire Paper Co. Ltd, Radcliffe; Jarrold & Sons Ltd, Norwich; Litra Machine Plates Ltd, Edenbridge; Redbridge Book Cloth Co. Ltd, Bolton; Schwitter Ltd, Zuric

Published by The Reader's Digest Association Limited, 25 Berkeley Square, London W1X 6AB

The Reader's Digest Association, Inc., Pleasantville, New York

The Reader's Digest Association (Canada) Limited, 215 Redfern Avenue, Montreal

The Reader's Digest Association South Africa (Pty) Limited, Nedbank Centre, Strand Street, Cape Town

The Reader's Digest Association Pty. Limited, 26-32 Waterloo Street, Surry Hills, Sydney